THE OXFORD HANDBOOK OF

THE HISTORY

OF ETHICS

Philosophical ethics consists in the human endeavour to answer rationally the fundamental question of how we should live. *The Oxford Handbook of the History of Ethics* explores the history of philosophical ethics in the western tradition from Homer until the present day. It provides a broad overview of the views of many of the main thinkers, schools, and periods, and includes in addition essays on topics such as autonomy and impartiality. The authors are international leaders in their field, and use their expertise and specialist knowledge to illuminate the relevance of their work to discussions in contemporary ethics. The essays are specially written for this volume, and in each case introduce the reader to the main lines of interpretation and criticism that have arisen in the professional history of philosophy over the past two or three decades.

D1604944

THE OXFORD HANDBOOK OF

THE HISTORY
OF ETHICS

Edited by
ROGER CRISP

OXFORD
UNIVERSITY PRESS

OXFORD
UNIVERSITY PRESS

Great Clarendon Street, Oxford, OX2 6DP,
United Kingdom

Oxford University Press is a department of the University of Oxford.
It furthers the University's objective of excellence in research, scholarship,
and education by publishing worldwide. Oxford is a registered trade mark of
Oxford University Press in the UK and in certain other countries

First published 2013
First published in paperback 2015

Published in the United States of America by Oxford University Press
198 Madison Avenue, New York, NY 10016, United States of America

British Library Cataloguing in Publication Data
Data available

Library of Congress Cataloging in Publication Data
Data available

ISBN 978-0-19-954597-1 (Hbk.)
ISBN 978-0-19-874440-5 (Pbk.)

PREFACE

The very notion of the history of ethics can be understood in at least two ways, both relevant to this volume. First, and most obviously, it refers to past human thought and writing on how we should live. Second, it is the name for that sub-discipline in professional philosophy concerned with elucidating and criticizing that history. Taken as a whole, the chapters in this book aim to provide a broad, though not comprehensive, account of the history of western ethical thought from Homer until the present day, as well as to introduce the main lines of argument in professional history of philosophy from the last few decades on the topics at hand. That professional history, however, has been uneven. Significantly more attention has been paid to Aristotle than to Aquinas, say, or to Kant than to Rousseau. Nor has any balance between the two senses of history been prescribed for any particular contributor. Some have preferred to concentrate more on past thought than on its recent interpretation, others less. The same freedom has been extended to the authors of chapters which focus on themes, such as autonomy or relativism, rather than on individual thinkers or schools.

Knowledge of past ethical thinking may be worth having in itself. But even if it is, that knowledge is valuable also as a resource for answering the fundamental questions of ethics themselves. So authors have been encouraged to bring out ways in which the lines of argument they address may be relevant to contemporary philosophical ethics.

I wish to thank all contributors for providing such outstanding chapters, and for their perseverance. I am grateful in particular to earlier contributors for their patience; Peter Momtchiloff at Oxford University Press deserves thanks for this reason also, and for having the idea for the volume in the first place. For invaluable assistance during the final stages of publication, I am indebted to Tobias Beer, Daniel Bourner, and Christopher Malone.

The first complete typescript I received was from Annette Baier. Sadly she died just two months before the book was published.

R.S.C.

Contents

LIST OF CONTRIBUTORS

Maria Rosa Antognazza is Professor of Philosophy at King's College London. Her research interests lie in early modern philosophy and in the philosophy of religion. She is the author of *Leibniz on the Trinity and the Incarnation: Reason and Revelation in the Seventeenth Century* (Yale, 2007), and of *Leibniz: An Intellectual Biography* (Cambridge University Press, 2009; winner of the 2010 Pfizer Prize for best scholarly book in the history of science). She has edited texts by H. Grotius, G. W. Leibniz, and J. H. Alsted, and has published numerous contributions on seventeenth- and eighteenth-century philosophy.

Annette Baier was a graduate of the universities of Otago and Oxford. She taught briefly at the universities of Aberdeen, Auckland, and Sydney before moving to Pittsburgh, Pennsylvania, where she taught at Carnegie Mellon University, then at the University of Pittsburgh, from 1973 till her retirement in 1996. She then lived in Dunedin, and was an associate at the University of Otago. She gave the Tanner Lectures, at Princeton, in 1991, speaking about trust. She was the first woman to give the Carus Lectures, in New York in 1995, speaking on the commons of the mind. She wrote four books about Hume (three in retirement) and published three collections of essays, two of them on ethics and one on the philosophy of mind. She had a long, happy marriage to Kurt Baier. She had a daughter, Sarah, and four grandchildren, Jack, Tom, Emily, and Alice. She died in 2012.

Christopher Bertram is Professor of Social and Political Philosophy at the University of Bristol and author of *Rousseau and The Social Contract* (Routledge, 2004). He has published on Rousseau and on topics in political philosophy including social contract theory, justice, and global ethics. He is currently working on justice, territory, and migration. He is a former president of the Rousseau Association.

Richard Bett is Professor of Philosophy and Classics at Johns Hopkins University. His scholarly work has focused particularly on the ancient sceptics. He is the author of *Pyrrho, his Antecedents and his Legacy* (Oxford, 2000), and has translated Sextus Empiricus' *Against the Ethicists* (Oxford, 1997), with Introduction and Commentary, and *Against the Logicians* (Cambridge, 2005) and *Against the Physicists* (Cambridge, 2012), both with Introduction and Notes. He is the editor of *The Cambridge Companion to Ancient Scepticism* (Cambridge, 2010). He has also published articles on Plato, Socrates, the Sophists, the Stoics, and Nietzsche.

John Christman is Professor of Philosophy, Political Science, and Women's Studies at Penn State University. He is the author of *The Politics of Persons: Individual Autonomy* *and Socio-Historical Selves* (Cambridge University Press, 2009), *Social and Political Philosophy: A Contemporary Introduction* (Routledge, 2002), and *The Myth of Property: Toward an Egalitarian Theory of Ownership* (Oxford University Press, 1993). He is also co-editor, with Joel Anderson, of *Autonomy and the Challenges to Liberalism: New Essays* (Cambridge University Press, 2005), the co-editor with Thomas Christiano of *Debates in Political Philosophy* (Wiley-Blackwell, 2009), and the editor of *The Inner Citadel: Essays on Individual Autonomy* (Oxford University Press, 1989).

John Cottingham is Professor Emeritus of Philosophy at the University of Reading, Professorial Research Fellow at Heythrop College, University of London, and an Honorary Fellow of St John's College, Oxford. His publications include *Philosophy and the Good life: Reason and the Passions in Greek, Cartesian and Psychoanalytic Ethics* (1998), *The Spiritual Dimension* (2005), *Cartesian Reflections* (2008), and *Why Believe?* (2009). He was from 1993-2012 Editor of RATIO, the international journal of analytic philosophy.

Roger Crisp is Uehiro Fellow and Tutor in Philosophy, St Anne's College, Oxford, and Professor of Moral Philosophy at the University of Oxford. He is author of *Mill on Utilitarianism* (Routledge, 1997) and *Reasons and the Good* (Clarendon Press, 2006), and has translated Aristotle's *Nicomachean Ethics* for Cambridge University Press.

John Deigh teaches moral, political, and legal philosophy at the University of Texas at Austin. He is the author of *The Sources of Moral Agency: Essays in Moral Psychology and Freudian Theory* (1996), *Emotions, Values, and the Law* (2008), and *An Introduction to Ethics* (2010). He was the editor of *Ethics* from 1997 to 2008.

Julia Driver is a Professor of Philosophy at Washington University in St. Louis. She received her PhD in Philosophy from The Johns Hopkins University. Her main areas of research are normative ethics, moral psychology, and metaethics. She has published articles in journals such as the *Journal of Philosophy, Philosophy & Phenomenological Research, Nous, Philosophical Studies, Utilitas, Ethics,* and the *Australasian Journal of Philosophy*. She has written three books: the latest, on *Consequentialism*, was published in 2012 in Routledge's New Problems in Philosophy series.

Miranda Fricker is Professor of Philosophy at the University of Sheffield London. She is the author of *Epistemic Injustice: Power and the Ethics of Knowing* (Oxford University Press, 2007); co-editor of *The Cambridge Companion to Feminism in Philosophy* with Jennifer Hornsby (2000); and co-author of *Reading Ethics*, written with Sam Guttenplan, a book of commentaries on selected readings in moral philosophy (Wiley-Blackwell, 2009). Her main areas of interest are ethics, social epistemology, virtue epistemology, and those areas of feminist philosophy that focus on issues of power, social identity, and epistemic authority.

Aaron Garrett is Associate Professor of Philosophy at Boston University. He works primarily in the history of early modern philosophy, specializing in the history of moral philosophy, Spinoza, and the Scottish Enlightenment.

Lloyd P. Gerson is Professor of Philosophy in the University of Toronto. He is the editor of the recent *Cambridge History of Philosophy in Late Antiquity*. He is the author of many books in ancient philosophy including *Ancient Epistemology*, *Aristotle and Other Platonists*, *Knowing Persons: A Study in Plato*, *Plotinus* (Arguments of the Philosophers), and *God and Greek Philosophy*. He has also translated works of Aristotle (with H.G. Apostle), the Hellenistic philosophers (with Brad Inwood), and Neoplatonists (with John Dillon). He is currently leading a team in producing a new complete translation of the *Enneads* of Plotinus.

Raymond Geuss teaches in the Faculty of Philosophy at Cambridge University and is the author of *Outside Ethics* (Princeton University Press, 2005), *Philosophy and Real Politics* (Princeton University Press, 2008), and *Politics and the Imagination* (Princeton University Press, 2010).

Christopher Gill is Professor of Ancient Thought at the University of Exeter. His work is centred on psychology and ethics in Greek and Roman thought, especially ideas about personality and self. A current focus is on Stoic philosophy and its significance in the contemporary philosophical context. He is the author of *Personality in Greek Epic, Tragedy, and Philosophy: The Self in Dialogue* (1996), *The Structured Self in Hellenistic and Roman Thought* (2006), and *Naturalistic Psychology in Galen and Stoicism* (2010). He has edited a number of volumes of essays, including *The Person and the Human Mind: Issues in Ancient and Modern Philosophy* (1996) and *Virtue, Norms, and Objectivity: Issues in Ancient and Modern Ethics* (2005) (all these books published by Oxford University Press).

Paula Gottlieb is Professor of Philosophy and Affiliate Professor of Classics at the University of Wisconsin-Madison. Her work on Aristotle's ethics includes an analysis of books 1 and 2 of Aristotle's *Nicomachean Ethics*, with commentary, for Project Archelogos on the web (2001), 'The Practical Syllogism', an essay in *The Blackwell Guide to Aristotle's Nicomachean Ethics*, ed. Richard Kraut (2006), and *The Virtue of Aristotle's Ethics* (Cambridge University Press, 2009).

Otfried Höffe is director of the Research Centre for Political Philosophy (Forschungsstelle Politische Philosophie) at the University of Tübingen, Germany. He has held chairs at philosophy departments at the University of Duisburg, Germany (1976–1978), the University of Freiburg, Switzerland (1978–1992), and the University of Tübingen, Germany (1992–2011). He is fellow of the Heidelberger Akademie der Wissenschaften, fellow and senator of the German National Academy: Akademie der Naturforscher Leopoldina, and sole international fellow of the Teheran Academy for Philosophy and Sagacity. His areas of research include moral and political philosophy, philosophy of law, and epistemology. He has published numerous books and essays, which have been translated into more than twenty languages. Among them are *Political Justice: Foundations for a Critical Philosophy of Law and the State* (1987, 1995), *Democracy in an Age of Globalization* (1999, 2007), *Can Virtue Make Us Happy? The Art of Living and*

Morality (2007, 2010), as well as *Aristotle* (1996, 2003) and *Kant's Critique of Pure Reason: The Foundation of Modern Philosophy* (2003, 2009).

Brad Hooker has published articles on egoism, the Golden Rule, self-sacrifice, impartiality, utilitarianism, and contractualism. His book *Ideal Code, Real World: A Rule-Consequentialist Theory of Morality* was published by Oxford University Press in 2000. He has taught at the University of Reading since 1993.

T. H. Irwin is Professor of Ancient Philosophy in the University of Oxford and a Fellow of Keble College. From 1975 to 2006 he taught at Cornell University. He is the author of: *Plato's Gorgias* (translation and notes) (Clarendon Plato Series, Oxford University Press, 1979); *Aristotle's Nicomachean Ethics* (translation and notes) (Hackett Publishing Co., 2nd edn, 1999); *Aristotle's First Principles* (Oxford University Press, 1988); *Classical Thought* (Oxford University Press, 1989); *Plato's Ethics* (Oxford University Press, 1995); *The Development of Ethics*, 3 vols. (Oxford University Press, 2007–2009).

Dale Jamieson is Professor of Environmental Studies and Philosophy, and Affiliated Professor of Law at New York University. He is the author of *Ethics and the Environment* (Cambridge University Press, 2008), and *Morality's Progress* (Oxford University Press, 2002).

Richard Kraut is Charles E. and Emma H. Morrison Professor of the Humanities at Northwestern University. He is the author of *Against Absolute Goodness* (2011), *What is Good and Why* (2007), and several studies of the moral and political philosophies of Plato and Aristotle.

Colleen McCluskey is Associate Professor in the Department of Philosophy at Saint Louis University. She received her PhD from the University of Iowa. She is a co-author of a book (with Rebecca Konyndyk De Young and Christina Van Dyke), *Aquinas's Ethics: Metaphysical Foundations, Moral Theory, and Theological Context* (2009), as well as other writings in medieval philosophy and feminism.

David McNaughton is currently Professor of Philosophy at Florida State University, having previously been at Keele University. He is the author of *Moral Vision* (Blackwell, 1988), which has been continuously in print since its publication, and (with Eve Garrard) *Forgiveness* (Acumen Publishing, 2010). He has also written articles, many with Piers Rawling or with Eve Garrard, on a range of topics in ethics, ethical theory, and metaethics. At present, he is editing a new edition of Butler's *Sermons* for Oxford University Press.

W. J. Mander is a Fellow and Tutor in Philosophy at Harris Manchester College, Oxford. His books include *British Idealism, a History* (2011) and *An Introduction to Bradley's Metaphysics* (1994).

Adrienne M. Martin is Assistant Professor of Philosophy at the University of Pennsylvania, where she has taught since 2006. She works in moral philosophy and moral psychology, with particular interest in the nature of moral agency and deliberation.

Susan Sauvé Meyer is Professor and Chair of Philosophy at the University of Pennsylvania, where she has taught since 1994. A historian of Greek and Roman philosophy, she has special interest in the ethical tradition. Her publications include *Aristotle on Moral Responsibility* (1993) and *Ancient Ethics* (2008).

Phillip Mitsis is A. S. Onassis Professor of Hellenic Culture and Civilization at New York University and Academic Director of the American Institute of Verdi Studies. He has published papers on Greek epic and tragedy, and on the history of ancient and early modern philosophy. His writings on Epicurus include *The Pleasures of Invulnerability: Epicurus' Ethical Theory* (1988).

James Otteson is the Thomas W. Smith Presidential Chair in Business Ethics at Wake Forest University. He has written extensively on Adam Smith, on the Scottish Enlightenment, and on the nature and implications of liberalism that developed in Britain in the eighteenth century. His books include *Adam Smith's Marketplace of Life* (Cambridge University Press, 2002), *Actual Ethics* (Cambridge University Press, 2006), and *The End of Socialism* (Cambridge University Press, 2014).

Derk Pereboom is Professor of Philosophy at Cornell University. He is the author of *Living without Free Will* (Cambridge University Press, 2001); *Consciousness and the Prospects of Physicalism* (Oxford University Press, 2011); co-author (together with Robert Kane, John Martin Fischer, and Manuel Vargas) of *Four Views on Free Will* (Wiley-Blackwell, 2007); and he has published articles in free will, philosophy of mind, history of modern philosophy, and philosophy of religion.

Terry Pinkard is Professor of Philosophy at Georgetown University and *Ehrenprofessor* at Tübingen University (Germany). His publications include: *Hegel's Phenomenology: The Sociality of Reason* (1994), *Hegel: An Intellectual Biography* (2000), *German Philosophy 1760–1860: The Legacy of Idealism* (2002), and *Hegel's Naturalism* (2012).

Andrews Reath is Professor of Philosophy at the University of California, Riverside. He has written widely on Kant's and Kantian moral philosophy. He is the author of *Agency and Autonomy in Kant's Moral Theory* (Oxford University Press, 2006) and has co-edited (with Jens Timmermann) *Kant's 'Critique of Practical Reason': A Critical Guide* (Cambridge University Press, 2010) and (with Barbara Herman and Christine M. Korsgaard) *Reclaiming the History of Ethics: Essays for John Rawls* (Cambridge University Press, 1997).

Bart Schultz is Senior Lecturer in Humanities (Philosophy) and Director of the Humanities Division's Civic Knowledge Project at the University of Chicago, where he has taught since 1987. His books include *Essays on Henry Sidgwick* (Cambridge University Press, 1992), *Henry Sidgwick: Eye of the Universe* (Cambridge University Press, 2004, Winner of the American Philosophical Society's Jacques Barzun Prize in Cultural History), and, with Georgios Varouxakis, *Utilitarianism and Empire* (Lexington Books, 2005). With Placido Bucolo and Roger Crisp, he is part of the scientific committee that has produced the University of Catania World Congresses on Henry Sidgwick, and he has also published numerous essays and reviews, including 'Obama's Political Philosophy: Pragmatism, Politics, and the University of Chicago', *Philosophy of the Social Sciences* 39 (2) 2009.

Robert Shaver is Professor of Philosophy at the University of Manitoba. He is the author of *Rational Egoism* (Cambridge University Press, 1999) and, more recently, papers on utilitarianism, Sidgwick, Moore, Ross, Scanlon, Korsgaard, ethical non-naturalism, and experimental philosophy.

Nancy Sherman is a distinguished University Professor and Professor of Philosophy at Georgetown University. She is a faculty affiliate of Georgetown's Kennedy Institute and also teaches at Georgetown University Law Center. In 1997–1999, she served as the inaugural holder of the Distinguished Chair in Ethics at the United States Naval Academy. During 1982–1989 she taught at Yale University. She is the author of *The Untold War: Inside the Hearts, Minds, and Souls of our Soldiers* (W.W. Norton 2010); *Stoic Warriors: The Ancient Philosophy Behind the Military Mind* (Oxford University Press, 2005); *Making A Necessity of Virtue: Aristotle and Kant on Virtue* (Cambridge University Press, 1997); *The Fabric of Character: Aristotle's Theory of Virtue* (Oxford University Press, 1989). She is also the editor of *Critical Essays on the Classics: Aristotle's Ethics* (Rowman and Littlefield, 1999).

Daniel Star is Assistant Professor of Philosophy at Boston University. His research interests lie in ethics and epistemology. He is working on book projects, and has published papers in *Analysis, Boston University Law Review, Ethics, Hypatia, Journal of Moral Philosophy, Jurisprudence, Oxford Studies in Normative Ethics, Oxford Studies in Metaethics*, and *Ratio*.

Philip Stratton-Lake is Professor of Philosophy at Reading University. He is the author of *Kant, Duty, and Moral Worth* (Routledge, 2000), and editor of *Ethical Intuitionism: Re-evaluations* (Clarendon, 2002), the new edition of W. D. Ross' *The Right and the Good* (Clarendon, 2002), and *On What We Owe to each Other* (Blackwell, 2004).

John Tasioulas is Quain Professor of Jurisprudence at University College London. He works in moral, legal, and political philosophy and in recent years his research has focused on human rights, punishment, and the philosophy of international law. He is the co-editor of *The Philosophy of International Law* (Oxford University Press, 2010).

Henry R. West is Emeritus Professor of Philosophy at Macalester College, USA. His recent work on J. S. Mill includes *An Introduction to Mill's Utilitarian Ethics* (Cambridge University Press, 2004), the editing of *The Blackwell Guide to Mill's Utilitarianism* (Wiley-Blackwell, 2006), and *Mill's* Utilitarianism: *A Reader's Guide* (Continuum, 2007). He is also author of encyclopedia articles on Mill and on Utilitarianism.

Nicholas White has taught at the University of Michigan at Ann Arbor (1968–1995), the University of California at Irvine (2000–2006), and the University of Utah (1995–2000, 2006–2012). He has published on Plato, Aristotle, and the Stoics, and on topics in contemporary philosophy.

Thomas Williams is Professor of Catholic Studies and Professor of Philosophy at the University of South Florida. He is the editor of *The Cambridge Companion to Duns Scotus*, co-editor of *Philosophy in the Middle Ages*, 3rd edn., and co-author of *Anselm* (Great Medieval Thinkers). His work focuses on ethics, moral psychology, and philosophical theology from Augustine through Ockham.

CHAPTER 1

···

HOMERIC ETHICS

···

ROGER CRISP

THE Homeric poems are among the earliest surviving works of western literature. The *Iliad* concerns itself with various episodes towards the end of the Trojan War, beginning with a quarrel in the Greek camp between the godlike Achilleus and King Agamemnon. After the death of his companion, Patroklos, Achilleus re-enters battle, killing the Trojan hero, Hektor, and dishonouring his corpse in front of his father, King Priam. The *Odyssey* tells the story of the long journey home after the war of another Greek hero, Odysseus, who, after various adventures with the Cyclops, the Sirens, and others, returns to his palace to punish the suitors who have been hounding his wife Penelope for many years. Who composed these poems, where, and when remain matters of debate, though their written versions are frequently dated to the eighth or seventh centuries BCE.

The other chapters in this *Handbook* mostly concern philosophers, their views, and their works. So why begin with a chapter on a couple of poems? One reason is the central importance of the poems in the history of philosophy, and hence of philosophical ethics. Xenophanes, a very early Greek philosopher who died at the beginning of the fifth century BCE, justified his own engagement with the poems by suggesting that 'from the beginning, everyone has learnt according to Homer' (B10; cited in Irwin 1989: 6). The poems were an educational staple and recited in public, and many Greeks—including not only the early philosophers but Plato, Aristotle, and other later thinkers—drew inspiration from them, either developing the implications of the Homeric world view or, more commonly, reacting against it. Indeed, as Bernard Williams, one of the most important moral philosophers of the twentieth century, points out, in a central work on ancient Greek literature and philosophy which will come to occupy us much throughout this chapter, the ancient Greeks are among our cultural ancestors and to learn about them is part of our own self-understanding (Williams 2008: 3).[1]

The poems raise deep problems of interpretation. The most immediate difficulties arise in translating certain words which appear to have no immediate correlate in English,

---

[1] For excellent introductions to Williams' thoughts in this area, see Long 2007; 2008.

some of them central to the meaning of the text, such as *aidōs* (usually translated as 'shame' or 'respect') (see especially Cairns 1993: ch. 1) or *aretē* (which is used to refer to several different types of excellence, most often that exemplified on the battlefield) (Yamagata 1994: 185). Further questions then arise about many basic aspects of the Homeric picture, including morality. Thinking about these questions, in the light of reading the poems and their interpreters, itself raises issues about the nature of morality itself, the human self and agency, responsibility, shame and other moral emotions, and the nature of the virtues in general, and of particular virtues such as courage and compassion.

It is vital, then, in seeking to answer the questions raised in philosophical ethics not to restrict one's reading to works traditionally categorized as 'philosophical'. Ethics is best understood as the attempt to answer Socrates' question: 'how should one live?' (Plato 1903: 500c3). As Williams (1985: 19) puts it, this question is equivalent to 'how has one most reason to live?', and it would of course be absurd to think that reflection on and insight into those reasons is available only in philosophical works. There is in Homer a view of the nature of human beings and their place in the world, and their reasons for living and acting in that world. But exactly what that view is has been a matter of much discussion over the centuries.

In recent years, the debate has become especially polarized.[2] In the early to mid-twentieth century, Bruno Snell and other classical scholars proposed a developmental view which has come to be known as 'progressivism', according to which the Homeric understanding of the human mind, and consequently morality, is in certain important ways 'primitive'.[3] There was disagreement about exactly when development took place after Homer, but it was generally agreed that the modern position on such issues was superior. The debate about progressivism led to the adoption of various positions, some more antagonistic to progressivism than others, on the nature of virtue in the poems, the role of shame in Homeric morality, and justice (especially the justice of Zeus, by far the most powerful of the gods). In this chapter, I shall say something about each of these positions and debates, the second section concentrating in particular on shame and guilt, on which Williams had especially interesting and suggestive things to say. I shall conclude with a section on virtue, including a sub-section on pity, a highly salient emotion and virtue in Homer which appears not to have received the attention in the literature it might have.

One final *caveat*. I am inclined to think that even if there is a single, detailed, correct interpretation of Homer, we may never know what it is. Rather, there are available a number of reasonable ways of understanding the individual concepts, the sentences in which they are embedded, and the poems as a whole. One question to ask, then, is whether you believe a particular interpretation to be less reasonable than another, indeed perhaps so much less reasonable that it counts as unreasonable.

---

[2] I shall restrict my discussion to works available in English. References to works in other languages are easy to obtain through these English works (see the notes in e.g. Gaskin 1990; Cairns 1993; Williams 2008).

[3] Progressivist interpretations were also offered of other texts. See e.g. Beresford 2009, on Simonides.

1.1 PROGRESSIVISM

1.1.1 The Self and Practical Reasoning

The very title of Snell's *The Discovery of the Mind* (1953) encapsulates progressivism. According to Snell's 'lexical method' (Gaskin 1990: 3; Williams 2006: 66), if a culture lacks the word for something, then we should assume that it does not recognize that thing as an independent item. He claims first (Snell 1953: 5–8) that Homer has no word for 'living body', *sōma* referring only to a corpse (cf. Clarke 1999). Rather Homer uses plurals to refer to bodily components, speaking of 'limbs' (*guia*), or of a weapon's piercing the *skin* of a warrior. Since early Greek art depicts human beings as a collection of separate limbs, we can conclude that these Greeks did not see the body as a unit. The same is true, Snell claims, of the intellect or soul (Snell 1953: 8–19). For Homer, the *psuchē* is a life-giving force which leaves someone when they die. We also find the *thumos*, which is a motivating and emotive force, while *noos* is the site for ideas and mental images.[4] But these are 'separate organs', each with its own special function. Indeed, Homer's conception of these intellectual capacities themselves depends on an analogy with physical organs: 'The belief in the existence of universal, uniform human mind is a rationalist prejudice'. This has the further implication that there is no room in Homer for genuine reflection, the 'dialogue of the soul with itself', since its elements are independent of one another.

Snell was a great classicist, and his view was influential. Another great classicist, E. R. Dodds (1951: 16–17), having referred to Snell, goes on to claim that there is in Homer no word for the 'living personality'. The Homeric *thumos* is not the self; rather, it *instructs* the individual to eat or to slay an enemy. What we see in Homer is the 'objectification' of emotional drives as 'not-self'.

But the progressivist influence was not to last.[5] Richard Gaskin (1990: 2–5) suggests that Snell is assuming too rich and too modern a conception of self. If we see the self as merely what organizes and makes coherent the different mental activities of a person, then clearly Homeric characters have selves. Gaskin goes on to claim that there is nothing more to a self than that which is referred to using a personal pronoun or proper noun.[6] This claim runs into the problem that we can refer in this way to individuals whose personalities vary radically over short periods of time, and have fallen into disarray. But the organizational conception of the self stands independently of this linguistic claim. With that notion in mind, Gaskin points out that *noos* and *thumos* can both be

---

[4] For a more recent discussion of Homeric psychology, focusing on the *phrēnes* and related notions such as *prapides*, see Sullivan 1988.

[5] Though it did not disappear entirely. See e.g. Taylor (1989: 117–18), discussed in Williams (2008: 176 n. 9).

[6] See Sharples (1983: 4). Sharples provides an interesting account of the psychic divisions in Homer according to which they represent different stages of decision-making.

seen as proxy-terms for 'the self', and this indeed allows for the possibility of a self in dialogue with itself. Consider for example a well-known passage in the *Iliad* in which Odysseus considers retreat:

> And troubled, he spoke then to his own great-hearted spirit:
> 'Ah me, what will become of me? It will be a great evil
> if I run, fearing their multitude, yet deadlier if I am caught
> alone; and Kronos' son drove to flight the rest of the Danaans.
> Yet still, why does the heart within me debate on these things?
> Since I know that it is the cowards who walk out of the fighting,
> but if one is to win honour in battle, he must by all means
> stand his ground strongly, whether he be struck or strike down another. (xi.403–10)[7]

The debate in Odysseus' *thumos* just is a debate within himself.[8]

Williams (2008: 21–8) develops this line of argument, arguing that Snell was resting too much on the (according to Williams, correct) thesis that there is no dualistic distinction between soul and body in Homer. So stated, however, this thesis about Homer is debatable (see Gaskin 1990: 2 n. 6). If the soul is a life-force that accompanies an individual when alive and then departs at death, that may be interpreted as a form of dualism. But Williams may well be right that Snell was seeking a richer account of the soul, and when he found that neither *thumos* nor *noos* could fill that role, then he saw it as occupied by several parts.

Long (2007: 166; see Gill 1996: 31–2) suggests that what Snell was really after was not 'the mind', but Hegelian *Geist*, or self-consciousness, and he failed clearly to distinguish the two. According to Long, since there is no self-consciousness—'explicit recognition of the "mind" as the unitary locus of action, practical and theoretical thought, and consciousness'—in Homer, Snell had a good point to make about the contrast between the Homeric and the modern conception of the self, but he fumbled it. As in the case of Williams on dualism, however, we might want to question the view that there is no self-consciousness in Homer. Consider again Odysseus' soliloquy above. How could Odysseus ask why he is making a decision if he is unaware of the fact that he is making a decision (although, of course, he does not explicitly *state* any such awareness)?

Williams himself advocates a form of *regressivism* concerning the Homeric view of the self (and indeed other matters, as we shall see) (Williams 2008: 42–6). He finds lacking in Homer the view, which emerged in the Platonic theory of the tripartite soul in the *Republic*, that mental functions are to be defined in ethically significant terms. According to that theory, Williams claims, reason's essence lies in its *controlling* the desires, with a view to the good, and in general that kind of ethicized psychology is something we would be better off without.

---

[7] All translations are by Lattimore. Gaskin himself translates line 407 as 'But why has my *thumos* spoken to me thus?'. As is customary, I shall refer to books of the *Iliad* using roman numerals and to those of the *Odyssey* using arabic.

[8] Note also the common use of the verb *mermērizein*, 'to ponder', with an individual person as its subject; e.g. *Il.* v. 671; *Od.* 17.235.

But if all there is to a psychology's being ethicized in this sense is that reason be able to control desire with an eye on the good, it is not clear that this notion is absent in Homer (Irwin 1994: 53; Long 2007: 167–8). Consider again the passage on Odysseus' decision to stand fast in battle. Williams may claim that there is more to a psychology's being ethicized than this, perhaps making reference to the notion that ethics involves other-regardingness (Williams 1985: 12). But such other-regardingness can quite plausibly be said to be absent from the Platonic account. Further, there are better and worse ways of thinking in Homer, and characters are often praised or criticized in the light of the norms that govern these ways of thinking. So, in this sense, Homer does have an ethicized psychology. In general, indeed, we shall find that regressivist claims about Homer tend to be no more plausible than progressivist ones, which may well help to explain the continuing popularity of the poems in the modern world.[9]

1.1.2 Agency: Will, Intention, and Responsibility

Unsurprisingly, given his pluralistic conception of the Homeric self, Snell believes that there is no room in Homer for self-control or indeed the will more generally (1953: 19–22). He ask us to consider a passage at *Il.* xvi.492–529 in which the Trojan Sarpedon asks his friend Glaukos for assistance. Glaukos is himself wounded and prays to Apollo to relieve his pain and restore his strength, which the god does. We might prefer to imagine that Glaukos is 'pulling himself together', but of course for Snell that would require the kind of self he finds lacking in Homer. And this explains, according to Snell, why Homer has to appeal to theological machinery rather than an act of will. Indeed, Snell claims, whenever a hero 'decides', it is through the intervention of a god. Just as there is no personal reflection, so there is no personal decision.

We have already seen in the case of Odysseus a personal decision without any intervention by a god, and there are many others (Williams 2008: 29). Further, as Williams points out (2008: 30–1), when the gods do intervene, they often do so by giving the agent genuine reasons for action (see Gaskin 1990: 5–9). At *Iliad* i.207–18, for example, Athene asks Achilleus to obey a command from her and Hera not to kill Agamemnon, and he decides to do so on the ground that the gods will be more likely to listen to him in future.[10] When an agent is making a decision, he is asking in general what reasons he has, not 'Which course of action is it that some god is going to make me do?'. This is particularly clear, of course, in the case of the gods themselves. We can also ask exactly what Homer is meant to be lacking through having no word for 'the will' (Williams 2008: 34–40).

[9] Williams (2008: 18) says that the fact that we, now, can respond to the tragedies is nearly sufficient to show that we have more in common with the original audience than progressivism allows. But a similar claim applies, *mutatis mutandis*, to Homer and regressivism. As we shall see, this is in part because modern morality is not as dominated by Kantian ideas as Williams implies; but it is also because some of those allegedly 'Kantian' ideas, including that of obligation, are there in Homer.

[10] For a case in which such reasons are ignored, see Aigisthos' failure to heed the warning from Hermes at *Od.* 1.37–43.

Homeric heroes clearly can make decisions, as we saw with Odysseus: Homer 'has the idea of wondering what to do, coming to a conclusion, and doing a particular thing because one has come to that conclusion; and that is what a decision is' (Williams 2008: 36). As for Snell's use of the Sarpedon episode, we should note that Apollo offers Sarpedon medical help: 'If Snell really thought that those services would be replaced in the modern world by an effort of will, I am glad he was not in charge of a hospital' (Williams 2008: 37). In fact, there are passages describing self-restraint, such as that at *Od.* 20.17–24, in which Odysseus is tempted to kill those maid-servants who have consorted with the suitors but prevents himself from doing so by reminding himself of the terrible things he has had to endure in the past. With all this in place, as Williams asks, 'Who could ask for anything more?' (Williams 2008: 40).

Another progressivist, Arthur Adkins, argues that intentions do not matter in Homer, since success in battle is so important to the survival of the community (1960: 35; see 1972: 12; 1996: 699; also Dodds 1951: 3; MacIntyre 1981: 115).[11] This, however, can be a difference only in degree between modern and Homeric morality. For intention certainly can matter in the Homeric world. Consider, for example, the successful plea by the bard Phemios to Odysseus not to kill him along with the suitors (Gagarin 1987: 296–7; see Cairns 1993: 74–6):

> it was against my will, and with no desire on my part,
> that I served the suitors here in your house and sang at their feasting. (22.351–2)

The presence of the notion of acting intentionally in Homer allows for the ascription of a fairly comprehensive theory of responsibility to the poet (Williams 2008: ch. 3). In his so-called 'apology', Agamemnon claims that, though he is prepared to compensate Achilleus, he is not to blame (*aitios*) for the quarrel between him and Achilleus:

> but Zeus is, and Destiny and Erinys the mist-walking
> who in assembly caught my heart in the savage delusion
> on that day I myself stripped from him the prize of Achilleus.
> Yet what could I do? It is the god who accomplishes all things. (*Il.* xix.87–90)

This passage can be compared to that at *Od.* 22.154–6 in which Telemachos takes the blame for mistakenly (i.e. unintentionally) leaving open a door which gives access to armour to the suitors. Williams goes on:

> Just from these two Homeric incidents, then, we have four ideas: that in virtue of what he did, someone has brought about a bad state of affairs; that he did or did not intend that state of affairs; that he was or was not in a normal state of mind when he brought it about; and that it was his business, if anyone's, to make up for it. We might label these four elements cause, intention, state, and response. These are the basic elements of any conception of responsibility. (Williams 2008: 55; see Williams 2006: 67–8)

---

[11] Long (2007: 162) claims that Adkins' book is 'less grounded on progressivist premises than Williams implies'. By this, he seems to mean that Adkins does not *begin* from a progressivist claim. Long accepts on the following page that Adkins does believe that moral thought has 'advanced' since the early Greeks.

1.1.3 Competitive and Cooperative Virtues

The thesis for which Adkins became best known is that Homeric morality is dominated by 'competitive' values or excellences, in particular that of courage, at the expense of the 'quieter' or 'cooperative' values, such as fairness (Adkins 1960: 6–7, ch. 3, 70; 1972: 12–14; 1996: 697, 699). This thesis chimes with his playing down of the significance of intention. If what matters is results, then getting results—winning the 'competition'—will be more important than the criterion of fairness relevant to the cooperative values. Homeric heroes could not rely on any 'state' to defend them and their *oikoi* (their 'houses', understood to include their family and other dependants).[12] Their *oikoi* depended on them for survival, so success, especially in battle, was crucial. The most powerful word of commendation for a Homeric character is *agathos* (usually translated as 'good'), and the *agathos* is the man who can defend his *oikos* in times of war and peace. Since such defence will require expensive armour, an *agathos* will be rich; and he will also be of high birth. Failure in such enterprises is *aischron* (disgraceful), and success brings *timē* (honour). Honour is not just a matter of the attitudes of others; it also involves material goods, such as booty in war, or compensation for wrongs (so when Athene is trying to persuade Achilleus not to kill Agamemnon in the passage we discussed above, she also mentions that he will receive a great deal of compensation if he waits).

This is not to say, Adkins claims, that cooperative values were entirely absent. But they were entirely secondary. So an *agathos* could behave as Agamemnon does to Achilleus, or the suitors to Odysseus, without any loss to his moral reputation or virtue (*aretē*). Irwin (1989: 9–10) suggests that Achilleus loses none of his heroic virtue by being selfishly indifferent to the lives and well-being of others, and remains the 'best of the Achaeans'. But if he had failed in battle, and been sold into slavery, he would have lost half his virtue.[13]

Though to my knowledge no one has tried to invert Adkins' thesis by suggesting that cooperative values are prior in Homer, many have expressed doubts about it. Finkelberg (1998: 14–18) helpfully points out that the very notion of Homeric *timē* suggests that the term 'competitive' is out of place. Much honour is merely a matter of status, and not some good in a zero-sum competition. Finkelberg provides an excellent illustration of this: the spear-throwing 'competition' held by Achilleus at the tomb of Patroklos (*Il.* xxiii.884–97), in which Agamemnon is awarded first prize before any spears are thrown.[14]

There is also a concern that *agathoi* can be criticized for moral failures in addition to 'competitive' failures on the battlefield (Dover 1983: 37). So consider Agamemnon's words to Achilleus at *Il.* i. 131–2:

> Not that way, good fighter [*agathos*] though you be, godlike Achilleus,
> strive to cheat, for you will not deceive, you will not persuade me.

---

[12] But the importance of the *polis* in understanding the archaic world should not be forgotten. See e.g. Scully 1990.

[13] Irwin probably has *Od.* 17.322–3 in mind here.

[14] Postlethwaite 1995 suggests that, since Agamemnon hits no one with a spear in the poem, the awarding of the prize is done in jest, to assert Achilleus' superiority over Agamemnon.

In his discussion of the passage, Adkins appears to imply that, as an *agathos*, Achilleus has a right to deceive. But is it not more plausible to think that Agamemnon is seeking to evoke some kind of sympathetic indignation from the Greek assembly?[15] The word *agathos* can be used to refer merely to a member of the superior, ruling class (compare the English 'gentleman') (Long 1970: 126; Yamagata 1994: 188).

The competitive/cooperative distinction has also been said to break down in two further ways (Long 1970: 123–30).[16] First, the kind of competition Adkins has in mind often *requires* cooperation with others. In such work, 'the so-called quieter virtues are essential, above all loyalty, without which not even a gang of thieves, let alone an army, can hope to operate successfully' (Lloyd-Jones 1983: 15). Second, honour is involved, quite independently of attempts to gain prowess in battle, in cases involving fairness and other cooperative values or virtues. Consider, for example, *Il.* xvii.149–51, in which Glaukos, having upbraided Hektor for abandoning Sarpedon's corpse, continues:

> How then, o hard-hearted, shall you save a worse man in all your
> company, when you have abandoned Sarpedon, your guest-friend…?

Hektor's failure to rescue Sarpedon's body may be seen as a failure in the competitive arena. But Glaukos is also criticizing Hektor for a failure in his obligations of guest-friendship. Or consider the criticism of the suitors at *Od.* 1.227–9 for their insolent swaggering and scandalously disgraceful behaviour.[17]

Though the *Odyssey*—with its stress on the obligations of 'guest-friendship'—is traditionally seen as a more 'moral' tale (Rutherford 1986: 145), it is the *Iliad* on which most commentators have focused when explicating heroic morality. And since the poem itself concerns a war, it appears to have been too easy for these commentators to have forgotten that heroes have a life beyond war.[18] In peacetime, heroes are—of course—not expected to behave within their *oikoi* as they would on the battlefield. Nor is it at all plausible to interpret Homer as implying anything other than that it would be the most horrific barbarism to fan the flames of war in the hope of winning martial glory.[19] It may be that on the battlefield the competitive virtues, concerned with military honour, are prior. But this is only what one would expect: consider the virtues that are most often attributed to soldiers in contemporary military dispatches. In peacetime, the community will value not only stability through defence, but also the positive good of harmony,

[15] Consider also Menelaos' accusation of cheating against Antilochos, in which he appeals to the authority of the assembly (*Il.* xxiii.570–85).

[16] For a response, see Adkins 1971.

[17] See also e.g. Cairns' (1993: 69–70) claim that Nestor's speech at *Il.* xv.661–6 shows that *aidōs* 'involves living up to standards of bravery and manhood *and having regard for other people*' (my italics) and Gill's (1996: 148–54) discussion of Achilleus' great speech, which Gill sees as 'based on what he sees (understandably) as essential principles of co-operative nobility in his society, rather than on some private and self-related ethic' (1996: 152).

[18] An exception is Yamagata (1994: 188).

[19] An 'anti-war' interpretation of the *Iliad* is often based on the contrast between war and peace on the shield of Achilleus described in *Il.* xviii; see Taplin 1980. For caution here, see Scully 2003.

and this is maintained by an *agathos* in his capacity as king: 'He is expected to entertain his visitors generously, to talk politely, to care for his wife, and to have an understanding, placable mind' (Yamagata 1994: 122).[20]

1.2 Shame and Guilt

The distinction between so-called 'shame-cultures' and 'guilt-cultures' was popularized by the American anthropologist Ruth Benedict, in her book on Japanese culture *The Chrysanthemum and the Sword* (1946: especially 222–4). A guilt-culture, according to Benedict, is one in which individuals are taught and expected to feel guilt at violating moral standards. In a shame-culture, however, there will be a greater expectation of shame at the violation of such standards. Relief from guilt can be found through confession and atonement, whereas in a shame-culture a violator will remain untroubled as long as any violations remain hidden from others.

Given the importance of honour and reputation for Homeric heroes, it is not surprising that Homeric society was soon identified as a shame-culture (Dodds 1951: 17–18; see also e.g. Adkins 1960: 48–9). According to Dodds, the *aidōs* that motivates a Homeric hero is 'fear of public opinion'. So Hektor, after his parents have begged him not to go out to fight Achilleus, says that he feels shame before the Trojans, that some inferior to him might say, 'Hektor believed in his own strength and ruined his people' (*Il.* xxii.105–7). What really matters is not losing face (see Scodel 2008).

Shame is importantly related to Homeric *aidōs*, but the two concepts do not entirely overlap (Cairns 1993: 14–26). *Aidōs* is seen as a virtue of 'respect', valued for maintaining correctness of behaviour in social practices bound up with honour and obligation. It involves an awareness of the limits of one's own 'measure' or lot (*moira*), which allows one to avoid transgressing those limits and bringing upon one the anger and disapproval (*nemesis*) of others (Yamagata 1994: 149, 174). Shame, however, or the capacity to feel it, is clearly an important component of *aidōs*.

What is shame, how does it contrast with guilt, and what is the Homeric conception of it? We might begin by understanding shame as involving fear of exposure to the blame or ridicule of others. That certainly seems to be at least an important aspect of shame, and many commentators, in addition to Dodds, have seen this as the whole of Homer's view of the matter (e.g. MacIntyre 1966: 8; Long 1970: 136). Yamagata goes so far as to say: 'In principle, if nobody sees you to say it is unseemly, it does not matter what you do' (1994: 237).

But as Williams points out (2008: ch. 4; endnote 1), we should not understand Homeric shame as the mere fear of being seen, as if Achilleus, had he been able to get away with it, might have stolen the treasure he had been offered as compensation. Benedict, indeed, had allowed that a shame-culture can operate partly with the idea of a

[20] Of course, it will also be expected that the king will periodically lead his retainers in search of material enhancement at the expense of others.

'fantasy of an audience' or, as Williams puts it, an 'imagined observer'.[21] Further, as Williams goes on to point out, the observation should be understood, at least in certain cases, as observation by someone *with a certain view*. The mere opprobrium of others does not matter in itself. Shame involves sharing the attitudes of others, as we saw in the case of Hektor. He would not be concerned about what an inferior said of him did he not think what they were saying to be true.

Williams draws further helpful contrasts between shame and guilt.[22] He notes the interesting suggestion that guilt is based in hearing (the voice of judgement), shame in sight and being seen. In the experience of shame, my being seems diminished, and I wish to disappear. But with guilt I am inclined to think that, if I disappear, it will come with me. Williams also claims that what arouses guilt 'is an act or omission of a sort that typically elicits from other people anger, resentment, or indignation', picking up also the point we saw in Benedict connecting guilt with reparation.[23] This might seem less plausible. Consider for example so-called 'survivor guilt'. Surviving some disaster in which others have died might, at a stretch, be called an act, it could be claimed, but it is not, or at least need not be, one that usually arouses anger from others. But the guilt does not arise from mere survival, I suggest. Rather it comes from a sense that one has benefited unfairly; and benefiting unfairly *is* something that characteristically elicits moral indignation from others. Finally, Williams claims that the 'internalized figure' for guilt is that of a *victim* or an *enforcer*, whose attitude is one of anger—*at* which, rather than *of* which, the subject is afraid. Anger need not be part of shame, the root of which lies in a *loss of power*.

There is a lot more work to be done on the distinction between shame and guilt, but already it should be clear that the difference between a shame-culture and a guilt-culture is likely to be one of degree rather than in kind.[24] And it is worth asking oneself, in light of the distinction, just *how* great a degree of difference there is between Homeric and modern society (see Cairns 1993: 44–5). Unless one is already convinced that Homer lacks the concept of guilt, it is hard not to read Achilleus' words to his mother on the death of Patroklos as an expression of guilt as well as shame (see Lloyd-Jones 1983: 21; Edwards 1991, *ad loc.*):[25]

> I must die soon, then; since I was not to stand by my companion
> when he was killed. (*Il.* xviii.98–9)

Or consider Helen's words of self-loathing and self-recrimination to Hektor:

> Brother
> by marriage to me, who am a nasty bitch evil-intriguing,

---

[21] Lear (2004) argues plausibly that this brings Williams close to offering a psychoanalytic account.

[22] He refers to Morris (1976), Taylor (1985), and Wollheim (1984). See also Cairns (1993: especially 'Introduction', ch. 1). For his earlier thoughts on shame and ancient ethics, see Williams (1981: 241–53).

[23] Here Williams refers to Rawls (1971: sects. 67, 70–5) and Gibbard (1990: ch. 7).

[24] See Dodds (1951: 43), Lloyd-Jones (1983: 25–6). Hooker (1987) goes so far as to say that the Homeric world is not really a shame-culture at all, since what motivates the heroes is primarily a desire for glory and *aidōs* is a matter mainly of respect or religious awe rather than of shame. For a powerful critique of any sharp form of the distinction, see Cairns (1993: 27 –47).

[25] Arieti (1985) goes too far, perhaps, in claiming that Achilleus rejects shame-culture entirely and discovers the sense of guilt. For a more balanced view of Achilleus as an exception, see Griffin (1986: 50–6).

> how I wish that on that day when my mother first bore me
> the foul whirlwind of the storm had caught me away and swept me
> to the mountain, or into the wash of the sea deep-thundering
> where the waves would have swept me away before all these things had
>   happened.(*Il.* vi.344–8)

We should beware, then, of unconsciously applying something like Snell's lexical principle. Just because there is no word in Homer that can systematically be translated as 'guilt' does not mean that Homeric characters cannot feel guilty. Dover's view is worth serious consideration: 'the difference between "guilt-cultures" and "shame-cultures" ... [is] ... a difference more in the way people talk than in the way they feel' (Dover 1974: 220 n. 3).[26]

Williams (2008: 91–5) agrees that Homeric *aidōs* covers both shame and guilt, but argues that we should not conclude that Homeric society is not after all a shame-culture. This is because '[w]hat people's ethical emotions are depends significantly on what they take them to be'. Williams is not, in the end, denying that Homeric heroes feel guilt; rather, 'they did not make of those reactions the special thing that they became when they are separately recognised as guilt'. Guilt is closely tied to the idea of morality, whereas shame is broader. If we (mistakenly, according to Williams) take the moral/ non-moral distinction to be deep and important, then we may learn from studying a culture in which no such assumption is made.

One particular advantage here, Williams suggests, is that we may better understand the links between guilt and shame themselves. We can feel both guilt and shame for the same action, but *what I have done* points in two directions: towards what has happened to others (the focus of guilt), and towards what I am (the focus of shame). This suggestion of Williams, however, is problematic. Many actions for which people feel guilty do not point in the direction of others, since they are entirely self-regarding (as any good Catholic will tell you). Further, though perhaps I cannot easily feel guilt for what I am, I can feel guilt for allowing myself to have *become* what I am. Finally, confronted by the person I have let down in such a cowardly way and their suffering (Williams' example), will I not feel shame? We have no reason, then, to agree with Williams' conclusion that shame and not guilt enables us to understand our ethical identity.

---

[26] The passage is cited in the most detailed study of *aidos* to date by Cairns (1993: 46 n. 109). Cairns himself says: 'In the end, one must ask oneself how much difference there is between a society which possesses two conceptual clusters, shame (the more extensive) and guilt (which often overlaps with one form of shame), and one which has one main concept resembling shame more than guilt, but not excluding elements of the latter, and which is capable of adumbrating other aspects of guilt in various different ways. In my view Greek and English, in this respect at least, differ more in style and tone than in the psychological facts to which their concepts refer.' He suggests the abandonment of the distinction in favour of more detailed attempts at noting the differences and similarities between ancient Greek and modern constructions of experience (1993: 47). Note here Dover's surely correct view that '[t]he determinants of the moral values of an individual or a society are remarkably heterogeneous' (1983: 46). Very few modern individuals are 'shameless'; we are concerned with respect and reputation. The degree of this concern varies greatly, but it is worth remembering that honour codes remain dominant in some cultures and in sub-cultures within any modern culture, broadly construed.

Again we see Williams' regressivism emerging at this point:

> The conceptions of modern morality...insist at once on the primacy of guilt, its sig-
> nificance in turning us towards victims, and its rational restriction to the voluntary.
> It is under considerable strain in insisting on all these things at once.

We have already seen that guilt is often not other-regarding. Williams' claim that modern morality prioritizes guilt appears to be based mainly on the fact that we have a word for it and the Greeks did not. But this is dangerously close to applying a weakened version of the lexical principle. Further, as Williams notes (2008: 52), Homer has a word for being causally responsible for something and liable to make reparation for it, that is, being to blame: *aitios*. Once that is in place, and characters speak as we saw Achilleus and Helen speak above, the Dover/Cairns position, on the concept of guilt at least, looks attractive.

A potentially damaging tension in Williams' claims about morality begins to appear here. On the one hand, he doubts any claim by moral philosophers that we—that is, we moderns—really, in our lives, put great weight on the moral/non-moral distinction. On the other, he wishes to claim that our having a word for 'guilt' implies that that feeling, with its special relation to morality, is being given undue recognition. Is it modern culture which is at fault, or a Kantian form of philosophical anthropology or ethics which over-emphasizes guilt and morality? The former claim, as we have seen, seems doubtful. If we are at fault, then so is Homeric society. The latter claim is significantly more plausible and suggestive. But it needs finessing. The rational restriction of guilt to the voluntary is itself something that makes sense in a Homeric context (consider again the plea of the bard Phemios). So the question is whether that is justifiable, and whether we should not allow that we can rationally blame individuals for involuntary actions. I have no doubt that we often *do* experience the feeling of blame for such actions: part of the guilt we feel in cases of what Williams calls 'agent-regret' involves blaming ourselves for something we did invol-untarily, and there is surely an other-regarding analogue to that ('patient-regret', for exam-ple, or 'participant-regret' as might be felt by a mother towards the driver of the car which has—as she is well aware, quite by accident—killed her daughter). Further, I can see a broadly utilitarian case for seeking to extend the scope of such 'strict ethical liability'. But the utilitarian case depends on seeing morality as a social phenomenon, to be put to use to advance the human good. From within the perspective of morality itself, strict ethical lia-bility seems interestingly analogous to the punishment of the innocent Williams elsewhere objects to utilitarianism for being so ready to countenance (Williams 1973: 98–9).

1.3 MORALITY AND VIRTUE

1.3.1 Duty in Homer

The moral/non-moral distinction also features in Williams' discussion (2008: 40–2) of the progressivist conception of the will, and the issue again arises as to whether he is claiming a difference between archaic and modern culture, or between archaic culture and a modern philosophical conception of modern culture or ethics:

> I suggest that the strangeness, to some people, of the Homeric notions of action lies ultimately just in this, that they did *not* revolve round a distinction between moral and nonmoral motivations. What people miss, I suspect, is a 'will' that...serves in the interest of only one kind of motive, the motives of morality. Duty in some abstract modern sense is largely unknown to the Greeks, in particular to archaic Greeks.

Who are the 'people' to whom Williams refers here? It is tempting to think he is speaking of Kantian philosophers and classicists, and indeed it is Adkins' infamous claim that 'we are all Kantians now' (1960: 2) that Williams cites in a footnote. But a little later he says:

> If the Greeks disagreed with us about duty, this should not—one might suppose— make us think that therefore in the Greek picture of things people did not decide or did not decide for themselves.

The reference to 'us' suggests he is now speaking of modern culture rather than Kantian scholars. It is very plausible to claim that Homeric morality is not full-bloodedly Kantian;[27] but of course it is equally plausible to make the same claim about modern morality. As Long comments on Adkins:

> The notion that modern western man's moral values may be properly distinguished from those of an ancient Greek by reference to Kantian ethics is a highly debatable proposition.

But it is far less plausible to claim that the ancient Greek conception of duty was radically different from ours. The idea of a binding moral code, the transgression of which makes appropriate feelings of guilt, blame by self and others, indignation, resentment, atonement, forgiveness, and so on, is clearly present in Homer. Consider, for example, Sarpedon's words to Glaukos. Having noted the material honours which the two of them have received at home in Lykia, Sarpedon goes on:

> Therefore it is our duty in the forefront of the Lykians
> to take our stand. (*Il.* xii.315–16)

The Greek word Lattimore here translated by 'it is our duty' is *chrē*, a very common word in Homer.[28] If, as I suspect, Williams wishes to persuade us that modern culture has taken a backward step by incorporating into itself a notion of duty absent from early

---

[27] As MacIntyre (1966: 7) points out, for example, Homer does not respect the 'ought implies can' principle. Moral predicates are applied to actions in cases where the agent could not have acted otherwise.

[28] See the definition in Autenrieth's Homeric dictionary (1891: *s.v.*): 'impers., there is need, w. acc. of person and gen. of thing, Od. 1.124; then, one must, ought, should, w. acc. and inf. (either or both), *oude ti se chrē*, "it behooves thee not," Od. 19.500, etc.'; also Cunliffe (1963: *s.v.*): 'one needs must...it befits, it is fitting or proper, it behoves, one ought'. See also Meier-Brügger (2010: *s.v.*). For useful discussion, see Goodell (1914: especially 94). I make the case against G. E. M. Anscombe's similar attempt to drive a wedge between ancient and modern morality in Crisp (2004). See also Long (1970: 124 n. 10; 2007: 174).

Greek culture, his argument appears no more plausible than those of the progressivists. Indeed, on this interpretation of Williams, there is some agreement between him and the progressivists. Both he and they believe that modernity is Kantian; the difference is on whether we should see this as a good or bad thing.

1.3.2 The Gods

A modern reader, imbued by classical theism with a conception of God as all-good, might expect to find the Homeric gods to be perfect beings, with a deep concern for justice and morality in general.[29] Any such expectation will soon disappear (Allan 2006: 26). The gods appear, like the heroes, to be deeply concerned with their own honour; they take strong likings to and dislike of certain human beings, often capriciously; and they do things which are at least morally questionable. Even Zeus, the father of the gods and more powerful than the rest of them put together, and the source of *dikē* ('justice' and/or 'order') can be subject to moral criticism from within the text.[30] Athene cares greatly for the Argives, and criticizes Zeus for being so hard on them after she herself helped Zeus' son Herakles. She speaks of his 'heart of evil' and calls him 'forever wicked' for his ingratitude (*Il*. viii.360–3).[31]

The gods are not entirely unconcerned with justice, however. Offences against parents are punished by the gods (see e.g. *Il*. ix.456–7), and we are once told that Zeus is angered by the passing of crooked decrees (*Il*. xvi.385–8).[32] Further, an important function of Homeric kings is to protect customary justice—the *themistes*. These kings hold their position by divine dispensation (*Il*. i.238–9; ix.98–9), so, as Lloyd-Jones (1983: 6–7) says, 'it would be strange if [Zeus] had not, as they had, the function of protecting justice'. Abstaining from injustice to one another is part of the honour mortals owe to Zeus and he may punish an offender, or indeed his descendants (Adkins 1960: 65–6; Lloyd-Jones 1983: 161). Adkins (1960: 62) claims: 'Though right triumphs in the main plots of both *Iliad* and *Odyssey*, it does not do so *because* it is right.' Indeed one way to understand Zeus' anger about the crooked decrees is entirely in terms of resentment at impiety constituted by a lack of respect for divine honour: the assemblies 'care nothing for what the gods think'.

From the moral point of view, however, Zeus is in a different category from the other gods. He is the *source* of *dikē*—that is, the source of both natural order and justice. The very beginning of the *Iliad* tells that the result of the Trojan War is a matter of his will. It seems to me indeterminate in the poem whether Zeus wills this because it is right, or

---

[29] Interestingly, this appears to have been the view of at least some Homeric characters themselves. See e.g. *Od*. 14.83–4; 17.485–7.

[30] For the view that there is no concept of justice in Greek epic, see Havelock (1978: 192).

[31] Yamagata (1994: 192) points out that we have here another example of someone who is clearly 'good' (*agathos*) (*Il*. xv.185) not behaving as an *agathos* should.

[32] See Dodds (1951: 32). Dodds himself thinks the book xvi passage may have entered the poem late.

whether we are meant to see it as right because he so wills it.[33] Indeed, because the result does satisfy a rather basic principle of natural justice, the Trojans having started the quarrel, there is a strong case for the former position (cf. *Od.* 20.394).

Zeus stands in a problematic relation to 'the fates' (*moirai*) (Irwin 1989: 16–17). One's own *moira* is one's 'lot' or 'portion', and if one is a hero in battle one may end up with Zeus' weighing one's fate against that of one's opponent to see who should die. Each fate appears to have a weight independent of Zeus' will, though he does deliberate about whether to save his son Sarpedon from his fate (*Il.* xvi.433–61; see also xxii.174–6). Zeus' discussion with Hera here suggests that he *could* change fate (at *Od.* 4.237, Helen says that Zeus can do *anything*).[34] Hera motivates him not to do so by pointing out how resentful the other gods, who would like to save their favourites, will be; indeed Zeus never opposes the fates. The relations between the gods, natural order, and moral principles are, ultimately, left unclear in Homer, and doubtless this was one reason for these questions' becoming a major issue for the early Greek philosophers who followed.

1.3.3 Virtue and Social Role

Human virtue or excellence is clearly very closely related to social role in Homer. The heroes are expected to exemplify martial prowess and courage on the battlefield and protectiveness of their dependents, for example, while women should be beautiful, good at weaving, faithful, and chaste (Adkins 1960: 36–7). This leads MacIntyre to *identify* Homeric morality with the heroic social structure: 'Morality as something distinct does not yet exist…Evaluative questions *are* questions of social fact' (1981: 116; see 1966: 6–7). MacIntyre need not be understood here to be equating moral and descriptive social concepts. Rather, his thought is that Homeric characters, when they are considering what to do, will always ask what it would be best, most fitting, or the duty of someone of their social status to do. The Homeric evaluative vocabulary, MacIntyre claims, does not allow the characters to view their own culture 'as if from the outside'.

It is true enough that we do not find Achilleus, Odysseus, or Hektor asking questions about the moral status of their culture.[35] But it is going too far to claim that they do not even have the vocabulary to do so. All that is required is the notion of one thing's being better than another, and they clearly have that. It is true that they may be utterly committed to heroic values, or at least to their unavoidability, and so disinclined to question them. But they have the conceptual apparatus to do so. Further, by not depicting external

---

[33] The problem here is analogous to that of the so-called '*Euthyphro* dilemma' (Plato 1995: 10a–11b).

[34] Lloyd-Jones (1983: 5) suggests that Hera is in fact reminding Zeus that he cannot save his son because one's *moira* is, ultimately, identical with the will of Zeus. But at xvi.443, she clearly seems to think he could do it. Nor is there any suggestion that Zeus is considering whether to change his mind, and so change fate.

[35] Though even this is not clear. See e.g. Achilleus' response to Odysseus at *Il.* ix.318–27. Indeed the characters in the poems do question a great deal about their world—the point of the war, the wisdom of the gods, and so on.

cultural reflection, Homer's poems are no more parochial or dogmatic, in this respect, than the majority of other works of literature.

Nor should we think that all virtues are *tied* to social roles, so that only the male heroes, for example, can be courageous. Penelope is surely intended to be seen as a woman of courage (see e.g. *Od.* 16.37). And courage is explicitly attributed to a woman at *Od.* 6.140. Athene breathes it into Nausikaa so she can face the naked, salt-encrusted Odysseus who has been washed up on the shore. Of course, there are some excellences or virtues no hero would ever be expected to possess, such as being good at weaving. But the list of potentially universally virtuous qualities in the poems, in addition to courage, is long and includes fidelity;[36] gratitude;[37] justice;[38] honesty;[39] industriousness;[40] patience;[41] pride;[42] resourcefulness;[43] thoughtfulness;[44] and wisdom.[45] It is illuminating to compare this far from exhaustive list (along with the Homeric virtue of justice already mentioned in this chapter) with the also open-ended list of 'prima facie' duties Sir David Ross arrived at in the late 1920s after deep reflection upon the common-sense morality of his day: fidelity; reparation; gratitude; justice; beneficence; self-improvement; non-maleficence (1930: 21–2). Reparation we know already to be a central aspect of respect for honour. 'Self-improvement' in virtue we might take to be part of what is expected of many recipients of moral advice in the poems. But what of beneficence and non-maleficence?

1.3.4 Pity and Compassion

Much of the secondary literature on Homer of the last half-century or so might leave a reader unfamiliar with the poems themselves with a picture of an ethic that encourages ruthless, self-seeking pursuit of honour, with no concern for others. In fact, the poems again and again refer to the feeling of appropriate pity or compassion (*eleos*) for others as a virtue (see Konstan 2001: index *s.v.* 'Homer'). And pity also appears to be a universal virtue in Homer. Zeus is said by Nestor to care for and pity Agamemnon (*Il.* ii.27). Individual gods often feel pity. So Hephaistos rescues Idaios from death in battle out of pity for his father Dares (*Il.* v.23–4), and Apollo pities Hektor when Achilleus is dishonouring his body (*Il.* xxiv.19).

It is true that pity is often connected with loyalty (Lloyd-Jones 1971: 20). So it is pity for dead twin warriors that prompts Menelaos to face down their killer, Aineias (*Il.* v.561; see xvii.346). And it is Achilleus' sense of pity for the Greeks as a whole on which Odysseus relies in asking him to return to the fighting (*Il.* ix.249–50; see Gagarin 1987: 301). The thought is that a hero's honour depends on his properly defending his dependants, and

---

[36] e.g. *Il.* ii.286; iv. 157; v.715; *Od.* 11.439. [37] e.g. *Il.* xiv.235; xvii.147; xxiii.647; *Od.* 4.695.
[38] e.g. *Il.* vi.62; xxiv.40; *Od.* 2.231; 6.120. [39] e.g *Il.* iv.404; v. 831; ix.312–13; *Od.* 11.363–6.
[40] e.g. *Il.* x.121, 157–9; *Od.* 6.25. [41] e.g. *Il.* i.586; xviii.246–7.
[42] e.g. *Il.* ii.654; v.625; xii.45; *Od.* 11.269. [43] e.g. *Il.* x.148; *Od.* 22.1.
[44] e.g. *Il.* v.403; x.350; xiii.254; *Od.* 1.7, 34, 230.
[45] e.g. *Il.* xiii.631–2; xv.239; *Od.* 7.168. On loyalty, see the following section.

on his feeling proper concern for them. What we have here is the idea of a 'community of honour' (Cairns 1993: 70).

Pity indeed is generally implicit in personal relationships. So, when Hektor is proposing to enter battle, his wife Andromache asks Hektor to pity her and their son (*Il.* vi.407–8), and indeed he does pity her (vi.494). Pity is also appropriate for suppliants (*Il.* xxiv.158), and for those who are weak, such as the very young and the very old (*Il.* xxii.419–20, 494; xxiv.516). It might be thought that the kind of universal concern for humanity which characterizes Christian-influenced conceptions of compassion and benevolence is lacking from the Homeric world. This would be a mistake, however. Diomedes is said to be 'a friend to all humanity', because he opens his doors to everyone (*Il.* vi.14–15). And Menelaos' description of Patroklos as someone 'gentle', who 'understood how to be kindly toward all men' (*Il.* xvii.671), is consistent with a conception of a general principle of benevolence which can of course be overridden by the requirements of military virtue.[46]

It has often been suggested, however, that in the Homeric world pity and concern for others must always be secondary to the concern for honour.[47] There is no case of a hero's sacrificing honour for the sake of the well-being of others. So Hektor, for example, despite being moved by the pleas of his wife on behalf of herself and their son, cannot bear the thought of the shame he would have to bear were he to refrain from battle (*Il.* vi.441–3). But again it is not clear that this conception of morality is so different from our own. Though we might expect modern soldiers to be concerned for their families when they go off to fight, reluctance to engage or desertion for that reason would usually be met with criticism. Pity and compassion, in other words, are themselves bounded by other virtues.[48] And it is not as if Hektor is not riven internally by the thought of what will become of his family. As Jasper Griffin puts it: 'These terrible events produce glory, but we are not dealing with heroes for whom that is an adequate reward' (1980: 102; see Yamagata 1994: 182). Finally, one may even see the *kudos* (*Il.* xxiv.110) that Achilleus wins through his pity towards Priam as greater than anything he achieves on the battlefield (Yamagata 1994: 183).

As we have seen, recent decades have seen a great deal of fascinating and suggestive scholarly work on the ethics of the Homeric poems. According to the progressivists (Snell, Adkins, et al.), the conceptions of the self, agency, and morality we find in Homer can be seen, from our own more advanced position, to be unsatisfyingly primitive; while according to the regressivist interpretation championed in particular by Williams, modern morality (either as a cultural phenomenon, or as a philosophical conception) has much to learn from the archaic culture depicted in the poems. Both of these positions, however, may be seen as the result of reading the poems in the light of general theoretical presuppositions. There is much to be said for the more nuanced view found in the work of, for example, Dover and Cairns that the differences between archaic and modern

---

[46] See the reference to the boundaries of the virtues in the following paragraph.
[47] In addition to the progressivist position of Adkins, see also e.g. Irwin (1989: 10–11).
[48] See Foot 1985, who makes this argument about benevolence in particular.

morality are of degree rather than in kind, and that this explains the remarkable freshness and humanity modern readers find in Homer. One thing we can be sure of is that there is still much work to be done on plotting those differences, and much more to learn from Homer about the archaic past, and about our selves and our moralities.[49]

BIBLIOGRAPHY

Adkins, A. W. H. 1960. *Merit and Responsibility*. Oxford: Clarendon Press.

—— 1971. 'Homeric Values and Homeric Society', *Journal of Hellenic Studies* 91: 1–14.

—— 1972. *Moral Values and Political Behaviour in Ancient Greece*. New York: Norton.

—— 1996. 'Homeric Ethics', in I. Morris and B. Powell (ed.), *A New Companion to Homer*. Leiden: Brill, 694–713.

Allan, W. 2006. 'Divine Justice and Cosmic Order in Early Greek Epic', *Journal of Hellenic Studies* 126: 1–35.

Arieti, J. A. 1985. 'Achilleus' Guilt', *Classical Journal* 80: 193–205.

Autenrieth, G. 1891. *A Homeric Dictionary for Schools and Colleges*. New York: Harper and Brothers.

Benedict, R. 1946. *The Chrysanthemum and the Sword: Patterns of Japanese Culture*. Boston: Houghton Mifflin.

Beresford, A. 2009. 'Erasing Simonides', *Apeiron* 42: 185–220.

Cairns, D. 1993. *Aidōs: The Psychology and Ethics of Honour and Shame in Ancient Greek Literature*. Oxford: Clarendon Press.

Clarke, M. 1999. *Flesh and Spirit in the Songs of Homer*. Oxford: Clarendon Press.

Crisp, R. 2004. 'Does Modern Moral Philosophy Rest on a Mistake?', in A. O'Hear (ed.), *Modern Moral Philosophy*. Cambridge: Cambridge University Press, 75–93.

Cunliffe, R. J. 1963. *A Lexicon of the Homeric Dialect*. Norman: University of Oklahoma Press, 2nd edn.

Dodds, E. R. 1951. *The Greeks and the Irrational*. Berkeley: University of California Press.

Dover, K. 1974. *Greek Popular Morality in the Time of Plato and Aristotle*. Oxford: Basil Blackwell.

—— 1983. 'The Portrayal of Moral Evaluation in Greek Poetry', *Journal of Hellenic Studies* 103, 35–48.

Edwards, M. 1991. *The Iliad: A Commentary*, books 17–20. Cambridge: Cambridge University Press.

Finkelberg, M. 1998. '*Time* and *arête* in Homer', *Classical Quarterly* 48: 14–28.

Foot, P. 1985. 'Utilitarianism and the Virtues', *Mind* 94: 196–209.

Gagarin, M. 1987. 'Morality in Homer', *Classical Philology* 82: 285–306.

Gaskin, R. 1990. 'Do Homeric Heroes Make Real Decisions?', *Classical Quarterly* 40: 1–15.

Gibbard, A. 1990. *Wise Choices, Apt Feelings*. Cambridge, MA: Harvard University Press.

Gill, C. 1996. *Personality in Greek Epic, Tragedy, and Philosophy: The Self in Dialogue*. Oxford: Clarendon Press.

Goodell, T.D. 1914. 'ΧΡΗ and ΔΕΙ', *Classical Quarterly* 8, 91–102.

[49] For comments and/or helpful discussion of an earlier draft, I am grateful to Charles Griswold, Adrian Kelly, Nalin Ranasinghe, Stephen Scully, and Jacob Zwaan. This chapter was completed during my tenure of the Findlay Visiting Professorship in the Department of Philosophy, Boston University. I would like to thank the department for its intellectual, social, and practical support.

Griffin, J. 1980. *Homer on Life and Death*. Oxford: Clarendon Press.

—— 1986. 'Homeric Words and Speakers', *Journal of Hellenic Studies* 106: 36–57.

Havelock, E. A. 1978. *The Greek Concept of Justice: From its Shadow in Homer to its Substance in Plato*. Cambridge, MA: Harvard University Press.

Homer 1951. *The Iliad*, trans. R. Lattimore. Chicago: University of Chicago Press.

—— 1967. *The Odyssey*, trans. R. Lattimore. New York: Harper & Row.

Hooker, J. T. 1987. 'Homeric Society: A Shame-Culture?', *Greece & Rome* 34: 121–5.

Irwin, T. H. 1989. *Classical Thought*. Oxford: Oxford University Press.

—— 1994. 'Critical Notice of Bernard Williams, *Shame and Necessity*', *Arion* 27: 45–76.

Konstan, D. 2001. *Pity Transformed*. London: Duckworth.

Lear, J. 2004. 'Psychoanalysis and the Idea of a Moral Psychology: Memorial to Bernard Williams' Philosophy', *Inquiry* 47: 515–22.

Lloyd-Jones, H. 1983. *The Justice of Zeus*. Berkeley: University of California Press, 2nd edn. (1st edn. 1971).

Long, A. A. 1970. 'Morals and Values in Homer', *Journal of Hellenic Studies* 90: 121–39.

—— 2007. 'Williams on Greek Literature and Philosophy', in A. Thomas (ed.), *Bernard Williams*. Cambridge: Cambridge University Press, 155–81.

—— 2008. 'Foreword' to Williams 2008, xiii–xxi.

MacIntyre, A. 1966. *A Short History of Ethics*. New York: Macmillan.

—— 1981. *After Virtue*, London, Duckworth.

Meier-Brügger, M. 2010. *Lexikon des Frühgriechischen Epos*, fasc. 25. Göttingen: Vandenhoeck & Ruprecht.

Morris, H. 1976. 'Guilt and Shame', in *On Guilt and Innocence*. Berkeley: University of California Press, 59–63.

Plato 1903. *Gorgias*, in *Platonis Opera*, ed. J. Burnet. Oxford: Clarendon Press.

—— 1995. *Euthyphro*, in *Platonis Opera*, ed. E. Duke et al. Oxford: Clarendon Press.

Postlethwaite, N. 1995. 'Agamemnon Best of Spearmen', *Phoenix* 49: 95–103.

Rawls, J. 1971. *A Theory of Justice*. Cambridge, MA: Harvard University Press.

Ross, W. D. 1930. *The Right and the Good*. Oxford: Clarendon Press.

Rutherford, R. 1986. 'The Philosophy of the *Odyssey*', *Journal of Hellenic Studies* 106: 145–62.

Scodel, R. 2008. *Epic Facework*. Swansea: Classical Press of Wales.

Scully, S. 1990. *Homer and the Sacred City*. Ithaca: Cornell University Press.

—— 2003. 'Reading the Shield of Achilleus: Terror, Anger, Delight', *Harvard Studies in Classical Philology* 101: 29–47.

Sharples, R. 1983. '"But Why Has My Spirit Spoken with Me Thus?": Homeric Decision-Making', *Greece and Rome* 30: 1–7.

Snell, B. 1953. *The Discovery of the Mind*, trans. T.G. Rosenmeyer (trans. of 2nd edn., orig. pub. 1948).

Sullivan, S. D. 1988. *Psychological Activity in Homer: A Study of Phrēn*. Ottawa: McGill-Queen's Press.

Taplin, O. 1980. 'The Shield of Achilleus within the *Iliad*', *Greece & Rome* 27: 1–21.

Taylor, C. 1989. *Sources of the Self*. Cambridge, MA: Harvard University Press.

Taylor, G. 1985. *Pride, Shame, and Guilt*. Oxford: Clarendon Press.

Williams, B. 1973. 'A Critique of Utilitarianism', in J. Smart and B. Williams, *Utilitarianism: For and Against*. Cambridge: Cambridge University Press, 77–150.

—— 1981. 'Philosophy', in M. Finley (ed.), *The Legacy of Greece*, 202–55.

—— 1985. *Ethics and the Limits of Philosophy*. London: Fontana.

Williams, B. 2006. 'Understanding Homer: Literature, History and Ideal Anthropology', repr. in *The Sense of the Past: Essays in the History of Philosophy*. Princeton: Princeton University Press, 60–8.

—— 2008. *Shame and Necessity*. Berkeley: University of California Press, 2nd edn. (1st edn. 1993).

Wollheim, R. 1984. *The Thread of Life*. Cambridge, MA: Harvard University Press.

Yamagata, N. 1994. *Homeric Morality*. Leiden: Brill.

CHAPTER 2

....

PLATO'S ETHICS

....

NICHOLAS WHITE

2.1

....

IN what are evidently Plato's *earlier works*,[1] he recounts conversations conducted by a character called 'Socrates'. Besides the *Republic* these are Plato's most popular works. What this character says provides a starting point for considering Plato's thinking about ethics and his way of engaging in it.

The distinctive nature of the earlier works is best conveyed by giving the main questions that they pose, which I'll call the *earlier questions*, and the terms that they say are necessary for answering them. The questions are: the *question of identity*:

(*a*) Which traits are virtues (*aretai*), and what are the general definitions of each of them?

the *question of unity*:

(*b*) Are the virtues all 'one'?

the *question of teachability*:

(*c*) Can virtue, or the virtues, be taught, and are they forms of knowledge, especially, knowledge of the good?

the *question of choice*:

(*d*) If one knows or believes that a thing is good, will one necessarily choose or do or seek it?

---

[1] Here I assume a certain widely accepted but nevertheless somewhat conjectural chronology for Plato's works. Most importantly, I suppose that the works listed below as 'earlier works' were written before the *Phaedo*, *Symposium*, and *Republic*, which were written before the *Philebus* and *Laws*, which were both written late.

the *question of well-being*:

    (*e*) Does being virtuous, and especially just, bring one well-being?

and the *question of hedonism*:

    (*f*) What is the relation between pleasure and happiness?

The terms that the earlier works seek to define are: courage (*Laches*), moderation (*Charmides*), friendship (*philia*, *Lysis*), beauty (*Hippias Major*), piety (*Euthyphro*), virtue (*Meno*), and justice (*Republic*, Book I). The *Euthydemus* pursues questions about the value of 'philosophy'. Then the *Gorgias* and *Republic* I (near or at the end of this group, §2.4) ask whether moderation and justice are indeed virtues.

Many scholars suppose that on this basis, plus some evidence from Plato's *Apology* and *Crito* and other authors, views can be ascribed to the historical Socrates.[2] These include affirmative answers to (*b*)–(*e*), and the theses that one must never act unjustly, that no one willingly does what's wrong, and that it's worthwhile to examine ethical questions, especially about oneself.

However, we have substantial reason to think that Socrates was the kind of philosopher who wouldn't espouse many positive views, being so good at exposing the weaknesses of others' views. Plato pictures him this way in the *Meno*, comparing him to a sting-ray that benumbs itself as well as others (80c–d).[3] Likewise there's no reason to think that his beliefs about ethics fitted into a systematic framework, though some scholars, assuming that he must have had one in mind, try to reconstruct a picture of it.[4]

We ought to admit, however, that we have very little secure information on Socrates' views. The evidence is conflicting. Even within Plato's early works definite answers to (*a*)–(*f*) aren't given, only conflicting arguments. Moreover even a complete set of answers to these questions wouldn't add up to a full position on or framework for ethics. Ascribing such a position to Socrates is simply guesswork.

2.2

But Plato's earlier works exert a philosophical fascination that doesn't allow them simply to be put aside. Their allure arises from the fact that they pose and discuss difficult philosophical *questions*, and show how difficult important ethical terms are to define, even when their use is familiar. Indeed, it's the very fact that the questions are *not* answered in the earlier works, and that all of the answers and definitions suggested encounter objections, that makes the works so interesting. Philosophically this interest

---

[2] The best introduction to the evidence is still Field 1948; for prominent examples of attempts to reconstruct views of Socrates see Vlastos 1991.
[3] See White 2006.   [4] Recently, e.g. Vlastos 1991 and 1994.

lies in the meta-questions that they raise about how such questions are to be addressed, and whether they can be answered at all.[5]

Why aren't the ethical questions answered in the earlier works? The obstacles arise mainly from inconsistencies that constantly appear in the uncritical responses by interlocutors in the earlier works. Inconsistencies also appear repeatedly between the suggested definitions of virtues, etc., and the particular judgements that are made involving those terms.[6] The reader ends up just as benumbed as the Socratic self-benumbing sting-ray: certain that one somehow means something definite, but unable to say what it is.

Are we perhaps to suppose, though, that Plato or his character 'Socrates' has answers to the questions and the right definitions up their sleeves, and that the reader is supposed to guess them?

Not an appealing proposal, for the same reason that the earlier works don't provide a coherent picture of supposed views of Socrates. The works present disputes over the questions, with no conclusive arguments for particular resolutions. We'd have to suppose that Plato wants us to ascribe particular views to him even though he doesn't support them against counterarguments.

For instance, one might wish to construe the end of the *Euthyphro* as hinting at an account of piety as a kind of justice viewed under a religious aspect.[7] But then questions necessarily arise: how is the definition actually to be formulated? And will the formulation be immune to the kinds of difficulty that undermined the definitions already offered? This interpretative strategy of relying on such hints seems highly unattractive, given Plato's evident conviction that judgements often fall prey to unforeseen difficulties and so must be articulated and defended by argument. The proposed definition of piety might be felt to be on the right track, but as Plato repeatedly makes clear, such a feeling falls far short of actually establishing a reliable definition.

2.3

No, the earlier works' *point* is to raise the questions, and issues about definitions, and to show them stumping people, including 'Socrates'. Doing philosophy means realizing how ubiquitous such problems are, and squaring up to them without thinking that hints and suggestions are solutions.

In Plato's *classical works*, on the other hand—which present the thinking now classically associated with him (especially the *Phaedo*, *Republic*, and *Symposium*)—we see what looks more like a definite ethical position. This material, especially the *Republic*, constitutes

---

[5] For further development of related themes, see Matthews 1999.

[6] Vlastos 1991 worried that this procedure takes judgements illegitimately for granted, but the worry is unsupported (see White 2008).

[7] E.g. Woodruff 2005.

Plato's ethics, i.e. norms and values for individuals, along with his political philosophy. (The two aren't separable, though here the emphasis will be mainly on the former.)

One's picture of Plato's ethics can be focused—partially—by thinking of it as reacting to questions (a)–(f) in the earlier works. Thus one regards *Republic* IV as responding to (a) by telling us what wisdom, courage, moderation, and justice are, and giving affirmative answers to (b) and (e) and a qualified affirmative answer to (c)–(d). Question (f) is postponed to the later *Philebus* (§2.20). Reading the *Republic* with this orientation can be helpful.

However, the *Republic* doesn't react to the earlier questions by straightforwardly *answering* them. Indeed, it to some extent sidesteps all of them. Book IV gives accounts of four virtues: (wisdom, 428a–429a, 442c; courage, 429a–430c, 442c; moderation, 430c–432a, 442c; justice 432b–434c, 442d–443e), but it does this without explaining how to tell which traits are virtues, and without answering the *Meno*'s question what a virtue is (71a–b). Moreover the *Meno*'s demand for *general* definitions of the virtues (72b–d) is tacitly dropped. In *Republic* IV we encounter only *some* applications of the four virtues: to polities (*poleis*, cities, city states) and to personalities (*psychai*, souls), with a derivative account of justice as applied to actions (443e).

The *Republic*'s answers to (b)–(d) are partial and inexplicit. The accounts of the four virtues link them closely to each other, and to judgements by reason (*logos*). However, it's neither clearly nor explicitly said whether they're identical (interpreters diverge on this). Question (c) is sidestepped with particular deftness. A fully knowledgeable judgement about what's best to do is throughout assumed to bring about conforming action, as does the teaching of virtue; but each of these is effective only with the help of elaborate stage-setting. The answer to (f) is postponed to the *Philebus*, as noted. Only (e) seems to receive a hearty 'Yes', though that's not quite as clear-cut as it might seem (§§2.11–2.13).

<h2 style="text-align:center">2.4</h2>

Philosophically the *Republic*'s message concerning the earlier questions is that rather than being directly answered, they have to be *recast*, and addressed otherwise than they are in the earlier works. The earlier works opened up no avenue towards saying anything helpful about them. Likewise those works made no headway in defining virtues or other concepts. By reconsidering how to deal with these matters, the classical works aim to make progress, especially the *Republic*, though they don't claim to settle every issue (cf. §2.5).

Two of the latest of the earlier works, the *Gorgias* and *Republic* I, display signs of deep trouble,[8] which seems to force Plato into the more systematic thinking of the classical works. The *Charmides* assumed that moderation is a virtue, and the *Laches* and

---

[8] As Shorey says (1930: x), it's an 'easy but idle and unverifiable conjecture' that Book I was originally separate from the rest of the *Republic*. I myself think that Book I was written to go with the later books, but was designed to reproduce a conversation like those in the earlier works, as an illustration of the deficiencies of their approach to defining, which the rest of the *Republic* then abandons, thus reaching more positive results (§2.5).

Euthyphro dealt with traits, namely courage and piety, that were considered virtues uncontroversially. The *Gorgias* and *Republic* I, on the other hand, show sharp disagreement about moderation and justice. The character Socrates wants to assume that they're virtues, but two of his interlocutors, Callicles and Thrasymachus, insist that they're not, and deny that they're beneficial to their possessors.

Both of the latter two works thus exhibit disagreement over how to think about ethical questions, which is centred on disagreement over which traits are virtues. Callicles is for satisfying desires as they happen to occur, the stronger the better, and rejects moderation as limiting one's good. Thrasymachus rejects justice, holding that one shouldn't cooperate with others but instead should simply be out for oneself. The policies of Callicles and Thrasymachus both challenge customary conceptions of virtue.

Both of these policies, however, are argued in the two works to be not merely objectionable but incoherent. Against Callicles it's urged that if one doesn't coordinate one's satisfactions, they will almost certainly conflict (e.g. *Gorg.* 494c–e). Thrasymachus' policy of rejecting justice leads him, roughly, to condemn cooperation. He's then confronted with the danger of incoherence, that rejecting cooperation completely means abjuring cooperation from others even though it will sometimes be needed for success (350c–352c).

Neither Callicles nor Thrasymachus, though, accepts the objections to his policy (*Gorg.* 510a, 522e; *Rep.* 350e, 358b)—a clear symptom of a limitation on the investigations in the earlier works, traceable to an inability to find unanimity about which traits are *virtues*, which is in turn traceable to an inability to determine which traits are *beneficial*. A different approach seems called for, one that will reveal what benefit amounts to.

Both arguments speak for coherence in deliberative thought. A hallmark of Plato's classical works is—in contrast to the unconnectedness of the earlier ones—a push towards systematicity and organization, primarily of evaluative judgements.

Lurking behind the dispute over whether moderation and justice are virtues is the concept that Plato in the *Republic* will say is the central concept for ethics (and indeed for all knowledge): *goodness* (534b–c). In the earlier works it was assumed that if a trait is a virtue, then it must have only good effects and no bad ones (e.g. *Lach.* 193d). At the root of Callicles' and Thrasymachus' denial that moderation and justice are virtues is a denial that they benefit their possessor. In *Republic* I, Thrasymachus calls justice 'high-minded foolishness', because he says it's 'another's good' (343c). Moreover a virtue (*aretê*) is by definition a feature that makes a thing or person that has it good. To settle question (*a*), the question of identity, Plato has committed himself to clarifying the notion of goodness. Settling (*f*), the question of hedonism, requires the same thing.

2.5

After the unsuccessful effort in *Republic* I to establish a definition of justice, Plato embarks in Books IIff. on a renewed attempt. However, he recasts the earlier works' search for definitions. The definitions of justice and three other virtues that he accepts in

Book IV are of an entirely different type, and lead him into a different approach to ethical questions from the one in the earlier works.[9] He pursues this approach consistently to the end of the main argument of the *Republic* at 580b–c, for a version of the thesis that justice benefits its possessor (§§2.10–2.14).

From the comparative systematicity of the *Republic*'s approach, one shouldn't infer that it claims to settle all of the major questions that it addresses or provokes. Though it makes far more direct assertions than the earlier works, it places heavy emphasis on large open questions, which its major theses require but which it doesn't answer (see especially §§2.9 and 2.19). One should read the work, like the earlier ones, mainly with an eye to its discussion of questions rather than to its promulgation of doctrine.

In the earlier works, candidate definitions mainly try to give necessary and sufficient conditions for applying their definiendum term to both persons and especially actions: action A has virtue *V* if and only if it's thus-and-so. The candidate is then hostage to interlocutors' objections. These objections often involve counterexamples (actions that are agreed to have *V* but aren't thus-and-so, or vice versa), or, as noted, cases in which the action designated by the definiens can have bad effects. Against these objections the candidate definitions are extremely vulnerable.

The accounts of the virtues that Plato accepts in *Republic* IV work differently. Instead of definitions by necessary and sufficient conditions, these accounts say what it is, or would be, for something to exemplify the concept *paradigmatically*, or ideally or perfectly. Plato's description of the paradigmatic polity ('city state', or city or state, *polis* or *politeia*), and in parallel the completely just personality or character ('soul', *psychê*), sets the stage for these accounts. No more of the standard refutations of the earlier works or Book I are entertained. Plato treats this strategy as giving new life to the use of definitions for attacking problems.

This *Paradeigmatist* general strategy, as it can be called, holds that the explanation of a term consists in a specification of the conditions for its ideal application, not of general necessary and sufficient conditions for its application.[10] Hence ethics is in the business of determining, for each ethical term, which ideals are associated with it. This is sometimes difficult, since especially in ethics (unlike geometry, perhaps), the claim that a particular ideal corresponds properly to the notion expressed by a term will be controversial (§2.9).

---

[9] In my opinion it's unimportant, as well as philosophically uninteresting, to press the question whether Plato actually *changed his mind* or not. He could equally well have intentionally written the earlier works to prepare the way for his classical works, by using the earlier ones to show how their approach failed to produce results.

[10] It's of course also Plato's view that the condition is ideally satisfied by a non-perceptible *entity*, a 'Form' (*eidos*). That Metaphysical or Ontological Paradeigmatism, however, is much less important here than the parallel Conceptual Paradeigmatism: that understanding the term consists in grasping its associated ideal condition.

2.6

Following this Paradeigmatist strategy for constructing these new definitions, Plato hopes to use them to gain what the earlier works had also sought. Those works demanded that definitions provide guidance in two areas. One was guidance for determining the *applications* of terms. Thus a definition of piety or moderation was expected to tell us which actions or types of actions are pious or moderate (e.g. *Euthpr.* 6e, *Chrm.* 176a–c). The other was guidance about *causal* judgements, in a broad sense of 'causal'. For instance, a definition of virtue or courage was to be helpful in determining what 'makes' someone virtuous or courageous (*Lach.* 190d; cf. *Phdo.* 100b–101b); and through a definition of justice we'd learn whether justice 'brings' happiness (*Rep.* 354b–c). Plato expects his account of justice and the other virtues in *Republic* IV to give guidance on both topics. Its main role is to explain the contribution of justice to happiness, as I'll explain (§§2.10–2.14).

The *Republic* also expects its account of justice to show how to determine which polities are just and to what extent. From Book II onward, though, we don't get an attempt to find the kind of necessary and sufficient conditions for being just that the earlier works hoped in vain to provide. Instead the paradigm of a fully just polity is something like what's nowadays called a 'model'. Then, in *Republic* VIII–IX, Plato describes deviations from the model, which are less just the further they depart from it (timocracy, 545c–548d, oligarchy, 550c–552e, democracy, 555b–558c, and tyranny, 564b–569c). In parallel, after each political description we also hear of personalities that diverge from complete justice. These deviations can be thought of as deficient approximations of the ideal (cf. *Phdo.* 75b–d).

Such definitions are only oblique responses to the searches for definitions in the earlier works. This account of justice simply doesn't speak to the wish, expressed clearly in those works, for a yes-or-no answer as to whether something is just. (Precisely because they tried to supply such detailed information about applications of terms, they were exposed to counterexamples.) Rather, Plato here gives us accounts allowing degrees of justice. Such informativeness as they have depends on our capacity to make use of the idea of an approximation to the paradigm. Philosophers differ about how useful this idea can be (Aristotle took a dim view of both it and Plato's other explanations; see *Metaphysics* XIII.4–5).

Similar questions arise concerning the informativeness of Plato's account of justice in application to actions. An action should be called just, he says, in so far as it produces or strengthens a just condition in the doer's personality (443e).[11] The idea is illustrated by

[11] Since it's normal in modern times to believe that the value of an action depends partly or even wholly on the value of the intention from which it issues or on the character of the doer, it's easy to suppose that Plato must believe that the justice or virtue of an action is constituted by its *issuing from* a just or virtuous condition of soul. That's mistaken. He never says such a thing, and *Rep.* 443e has it exactly the other way around. Aristotle is the first to introduce something like the modern idea, when he maintained that we judge a person by his choices or decisions (*proaireseis*; see *Nicomachean Ethics* II.5, III.2–5). (Another way in which one can confuse Plato's thinking with modern views is by assuming, also without any good grounds, that he employed a notion of 'agency'. He didn't.)

Plato's extensive description of the education of the philosopher-rulers of the ideal polity in Books V–VII. This education is designed to cause those with the requisite aptitude to have just personalities, and bring them to the philosophical understanding needed for ruling well.

2.7

This account of just action incorporates causal notions of 'producing' and 'strengthening' justice in the personality. This is only one of several ways in which the *Republic* makes use of causation in treating the virtues.[12]

Start with Plato's explanation of justice in application to polities and personalities. He identifies it as a harmony or balance or absence of conflict among the functional components of each of these things (433a–c, 443d). In a personality these are reason, spirit, and appetites; in the polity they are philosopher-rulers, auxiliaries (military and police), and artisans or producers. Each of their components has a natural function or task, which it performs without interference when and only when, as Plato puts it, 'justice' prevails in the whole structure of the personality.

The effect of justice within the personality and the polity is then sketched through this model. A paradigm person or polity is assumed to have components that behave according to certain dynamic patterns. That makes the whole person or polity do certain things and not others. When Books VIII–IX portray the graded deviations from the paradigms (e.g. oligarchy and the oligarchic personality), the descriptions of the deviations are derived from the paradigm, i.e. by describing how their components fail to perform their paradigmatic functions.

Plato's *main argument*[13]—that justice, as harmony, is beneficial to polity or personality—then proceeds, ending finally at 580b–c. The leading idea of the argument is that if each functioning component performs its task and doesn't interfere with the others, the structure will best deal with its needs. A *balance or harmony* of appropriate satisfactions for the components will result. One balance—of motivations—produces another—of satisfactions.

---

[12] It's no accident, I believe, that one of the earliest of Plato's classical works, the *Phaedo*, explores the notion of a 'cause' (*aition* or *aitia*, *Phdo.* 97ff.). This is a very broad notion (different from typically modern notions of causation), under which being fire can make something hot, and being three can make something odd (104a–c). The *Phaedo* sets up the notion of causation that the *Republic* employs, and treats causal connections, like other notions, as explicable through paradigms.

[13] It ends at Book IX, 580b–c (cf. Kraut 1992a: 332–3). Two supporting arguments follow (580c–583a and 583b–586e), but at the end of this first argument it's declared that they should 'hire a herald' to announce that the completely just person is the happiest, and the completely unjust person is the unhappiest. So this argument is supposed to stand on its own without the other two. A further argument is given in Book X (see §2.14).

In this main argument, it's of course tacitly assumed that happiness is constituted by this balance of satisfactions that the harmony of the personality produces.[14] No argument is given for this assumption, but the main argument can't hold up without it.[15]

Likewise the main argument depends on assuming that Plato's paradigms of polity and individual do indeed manifest justice in the correct sense of the term. (He plainly believes that there is such a 'correct' sense, which expresses the ideal that gives the term its content; and he rejects the idea that it must closely match the everyday use of the word.) Plato makes this assumption in passing (433d), though he nowhere argues for it. This is a case of the deep general problem for his paradeigmatist strategy: how to defend the claim, in the case of each term, that it really expresses the particular ideal that he associates with it.

2.8

The main argument is based on the ideal paradigms.[16] That is, it's presumed that the polity or personality will behave in accordance with the ideal specifications of justice. If it does, one's told, then it will possess well-being. This conclusion is applied to the personality most explicitly, but the same point is clearly intended to hold for the polity too.

Plato appears to guarantee that a fully just person is better off than a fully unjust person regardless of circumstances. That makes it seem that besides the balanced or unbalanced condition of a person's soul, nothing else plays a role in his or her well-being. It therefore might seem mysterious that Plato should indicate, as he does (580d–587c), that bodily pleasures and pains and other states of affairs actually possess some—though very small—value or disvalue. For if happiness is fixed by the degree of harmony of one's soul, then how can these other things play any part?

The answer isn't far to seek. Pleasures (pains) of whatever kind can be (dis)valuable as long as they don't disrupt psychic balance. A balanced soul that gains bodily pleasure on a particular occasion can be better off than a soul that doesn't, so long as the former's pleasure doesn't, for example, distract the soul into attaching more value to the pleasure than the pleasure actually has, and so lead it to misestimate values in the future. An especially well-balanced soul will be resistant to such disruptions, though Plato can't

---

[14] For discussion of psychic balance, see especially Vlastos 1971a and Cooper 1977.

[15] The argument that's strongly suggested is that disharmony in the soul engenders frustration of motivations because of their conflict with each other (e.g. 559d–561e, 439a–442b). It's not clear, however, exactly how superiority of psychic condition is measured, e.g. whether it's somehow the quantity of satisfaction obtained, or whether the orderly distribution of satisfactions is taken to be valuable in its own right (see White 1979: 54–60).

[16] If we said that the paradigm is 'idealized' we'd be wrong, since that would suggest that it's derived from observations of particular cities, whereas Plato thinks it's cognitively accessible to us through intellection, not perception, and that through it we recognize features of particular polities.

offer a *guarantee* of full success, given the unpredictability and uncontrollability of events in the world that the soul inhabits.

Because of Plato's use of ideal paradigms, the argument that justice brings about happiness must deal in a complicated way with the events that might occur in empirically observable situations. For with a model like Plato's, malfunctions—deviations from the paradigm—are always possible and inevitably occur (546a). So his claim that justice leads to happiness can't mean that as facts are, a polity or personality conforming to his specifications will inevitably continue to be happy in the future, no matter what circumstances may arise.

On the other side, Plato doesn't believe *merely* that his polity, or a just personality, can simply *hope* to be happy as long as potentially disruptive forces luckily are absent. For that structure is in addition designed precisely to *resist* forces, internal and external (422a–d, 461e–462e), that are liable to disrupt it. After all, the *point* of having a polity in the first place is to fulfil people's *needs* (369b–d), which requires coping with their surroundings by avoiding both want and excessive plenty; and the point of dividing tasks among the polity's components is to fulfil those needs effectively but not too abundantly (e.g. 369e–370e, 420b–421c; cf. 571d–e).

Equally, a harmonious personality is one that can act to forestall harmful external conditions to some extent, and to move to counteract them when they arise. These potentially harmful conditions include both pains *and* pleasures. The soul can take attitudes towards both that will tend to diminish their harm to itself.

This point is illustrated by Plato's story of the virtuous man whose son dies (603e–604d). With effort, the man can adopt a measured attitude towards his loss—i.e. recognize the true values involved in the situation, and see what will improve it and what won't. The same point is illustrated by what Plato says about the training of children to take part in fighting (466e–468a). A measured attitude towards pleasures, too, plays the same role in preserving psychic harmony—something that the tyrannical soul fails to do (571b–572a).

On Plato's view, then, the happiness of a soul at a given time must be mainly a function of its psychic balance. However, it's apparently also affected to a small extent by various circumstances including pleasures and pains, through the minor value that they have at that time; and these things also play a role, in conjunction with the soul's capacity to remain harmonious in the face of them, in affecting the future condition of the soul. Though Plato doesn't lay out these complications (and others) systematically, his discussion makes them fairly plain. I'll return to them (§§2.13–2.14).

2.9

Republic VII emphasizes that a systematic grasp of the concept of goodness is central to Plato's scheme. At the end of the philosopher-rulers' education, they'll learn a definition of the good, which distinguishes it from everything else (534b–c). They'll then use it as a 'paradigm' (*paradeigma*) for governing their polity (540a–b). Plato also says that without such a definition, one won't know 'any other good', and that if one apprehends an 'image' of it, that will only be 'opinion' and not 'knowledge' (534c; cf. 505a–b).

Plato hereby acknowledges the need for an account of goodness in order to identify the virtues, so as to show that they make whatever or whoever possesses them good, and to vindicate the thesis that they have only good consequences.[17] But he doesn't provide a definition of goodness, or claim to have one. He plainly alludes to a link to notions like harmony and unity (see e.g. 427e with 462a–b), but that doesn't supply a definition and he doesn't give one or even discuss candidates.

The need to explain goodness is as strong in the *Republic* as it was in the earlier works. Plato's identification of the virtues in Book IV relies essentially on the claim that his polity is 'completely good' (427e). One can see what he has in mind: the unity and stability of the polity are presumed to be important. But he doesn't discuss how this thinking is to be justified.

Moreover his main argument that justice brings happiness depends on the view, for which he never argues, that the harmony of satisfactions that's claimed to arise from justice is indeed happiness and is good. Here again we have the problem of identifying an ideal to be associated with a given term (cf. §2.5). The impression that he has unfinished business is confirmed by the continuation of the discussion in the *Philebus* (§2.20).

Another need to explain goodness, or something closely related, arises from Plato's Paradeigmatist claim to be able to use ideals to explain the concepts of justice, of a polity (422e–423c), and others (e.g. beauty in the *Symposium*). The statement that his polity is 'perfectly good' (427e) is what backs up the employment of it as a paradigm. But that raises the question why one should take *that* polity as the paradigm representing the notion of justice, or indeed as an ideal worth pursuing at all.

Critics protest that Plato's polity doesn't exhibit what we or the Athenians 'ordinarily' mean by 'justice', and some critics deny that his polity should be called just.[18] This is simply an instance of a more general problem that Plato faces, of assigning to a term a putative ideal and showing, convincingly, that *that* ideal is what represents the term's content.[19]

---

[17] For closely related issues, see Irwin 1995: 35–6, 37–8. For discussion of what's arguably a kind of duality in Plato's conception of goodness see Santas 1985.

[18] See Sachs 1963, with Santas 2001, especially pp. 104 and (on a similar but additional problem) 150 with 165.

[19] It's likely enough that Plato intends to attack this difficulty through an understanding of the good. If each term is to be understood through a corresponding ideal (as seems to be indicated by Plato's view that each term corresponds to an ideal 'Form', in the cognition of which the understanding of the term consists), the understanding of any term would require the understanding of the notion of an 'ideal'; and there's some reason to believe that Plato's notion of goodness is, or includes, a notion of ideality (Hare 1965). However, it's not at all clear how this idea is to be articulated and implemented—which is the import of one of Aristotle's main criticisms of Plato's views on goodness (*Nicomachean Ethics*, I.6, 1096a18–b5).

2.10

Shelving this problem for the remainder of this essay, I'll now consider the main thesis of the *Republic*: Plato's 'praise of justice' (358d, 580b). Of all the issues in the *Republic*, this one still possesses the greatest philosophical interest. Acting justly is something like doing what's right, and being just is something like being 'righteous' (though without that word's biblical flavour).[20] But what exactly does Plato's praise of justice amount to?

Modern readers may well come to the *Republic* with expectations about what his praise *should* say. These expectations are provoked partly by his remarks in earlier works on question (*e*). For instance if one takes *Euthd.* 278e–282d to say that virtue guarantees happiness, one might expect a demonstration of this in the *Republic*. But then one has to ask just what form the guarantee takes.

Some modern ethics encourages readers to expect something as strong as an assurance that each just action will itself guarantee a corresponding increase in happiness, or that each increase in justice in a soul (whatever that might mean) will do likewise.[21]

One also has to ask why any guarantee of happiness should be asked for. Is it supposed that Plato took one's happiness to be the only possible motivation for being just, or could think of no other way of encouraging justice? Or could he conceive of some other consideration that would speak for being just, such as the thought that justice is choiceworthy in itself, perhaps even at some sacrifice of some amount of happiness?

I'll postpone the question why a guarantee should be asked for (§2.15), and for the next while discuss whether a guarantee is indeed offered, and if so, what form it takes (§2.11–2.14).

2.11

First it should be remarked that in view of Plato's aforementioned belief in the irregularity and unpredictability of events in the physical world, it would be surprising for him to *guarantee* that regardless of circumstances, each particular just action or increase in justice in a personality *must necessarily* bring an increase in happiness.

Having observed this fact, one might then notice that, indeed, Plato's 'praise of justice' isn't *stated* as a guarantee either that the just man will be happy *no matter what*, or that every 'conventionally' just act increases one's happiness, or even that every increment of justice in a soul does so. He could support these things only by excluding any influence on happiness of contingencies, and he doesn't do that (§2.8). Nor does he

---

[20] I avoid 'moral(ity)', not because it's entirely wrong, but because recent philosophy has given it confusing connotations.

[21] On the question whether such a guarantee is consistent with modern conceptions of morality, see especially Prichard 1968.

issue this guarantee for his ideal polity: on the contrary, he says that it can't sustain its justice forever, precisely because the world is inescapably subject to contingency (546a–b, 547a–b).

In fact, Plato's explicit thesis seems carefully circumscribed: that the *completely just* life or person is happier than the *completely unjust* one (361a, 472b–d, 580b–c). This is his stated position.

But can this really be all that he wishes to assert? First, it seems to leave a wide opening for an unjust person to be by chance happier than a just person, and so to lose its power to persuade the unjust to try to be just. Second, a comparison of the two extreme points alone—complete justice and complete injustice—might appear to allow that the best strategy for maximum happiness might be to be less than completely just without being completely unjust. Would Plato want to admit that possibility?

The desire to interpret Plato's argument as closing all such contingent loopholes has led many interpreters to try to read the *Republic* as offering a more airtight 'conceptual' guarantee that would eliminate all contingencies. This interpretation has been normal.

Recently the most widely used strategy for reading Plato in this way is to contend that his notion of happiness '*includes*' virtue (and so justice) as a 'part', which is both essential to it and so dominant in it that the more virtuous are bound to be happier than the less so.[22] The thought is that virtue's being a part of happiness will somehow conclusively ensure that the only way to be happy is to be fully virtuous (and so fully just).

Though this interpretation is in some ways attractive, it encounters two serious obstacles. One is that Plato doesn't use this language of 'parts' or anything that seems equivalent to it. That seems weighty.[23]

The other obstacle is that no matter how essential and dominant a part of happiness virtue (including justice) may be, nevertheless if virtue has *other* parts, they may compete with virtue as a source of or path to happiness. And as long as that's so, then a person might be reasonably motivated to go for them instead of complete virtue. For even if any degree of happiness must contain *some* virtue, the possibility is left open that one might be best advised to cultivate it less than completely, so as to devote oneself more to the other parts. So the advantage that was supposed to attach to this interpretation, of delivering an airtight guarantee that justice always brings more happiness than injustice, seems not to be realized.

---

[22] See especially Irwin 1995: ch. 15, and 2007: especially pp. 98–9. An even more daring variant of this strategy is to claim that according to Plato, happiness and justice are actually *identical* (Mabbot 1971). This claim, however, doesn't seem to be supported by the text and has found little favour recently.

[23] Irwin 2007: 98–9 seems to infer that Plato must be following this strategy from the fact that he claims that virtue brings about happiness but seems not to think that this 'bringing about' is causal. This inference looks invalid, however, since there are bringings-about that are neither causal nor mereological. So the absence of part-whole talk in this context ought to make us doubt that Plato means such a thing. By contrast, Aristotle *does* sometimes think in terms of 'parts' of happiness, and says so (*Rhet.* 1360b6–11).

2.12

I'll accordingly revisit the interpretation that says that Plato is comparing complete justice with complete injustice, and saying only that the former brings more happiness than the latter. Recall that this leaves a large loophole open: that the best course might be somewhere in between. But putting that loophole aside for the moment (until §§2.13–2.14), I should remark that there's a reason why Plato might wish to focus on the comparison of these two extreme states.

To see this, we should remark on a substantial difference between Plato's concerns and more recent approaches to ethics. He directs his praise of justice against a particular type of view, represented by Callicles and Thrasymachus. Both of them advocate a specific sort of *policy*, namely, one *of injustice*; their admirers are likewise inclined.[24] Such people are willing or even eager to contravene ordinary ethical norms. They believe that gaining the benefits of some injustice requires yet more injustice so as to escape detection and punishment, and so they conclude that the best strategy is injustice undiluted.

Most recent defenders of justice, however, face different opponents. These people *don't see any reason* to be just. Their motivations may be of various types, or themselves multifarious. But such people don't *affirmatively aim* to go *against* ethical norms, or adopt that policy.

Accordingly the modern defender of justice typically tries to *supply* a motivation to conform to justice, perhaps by commending a blanket ethical motivation to counteract whichever miscellaneous possible motivations drive the opponents just mentioned. What the modern champion of justice is up against isn't a policy, but rather a *non*-policy, or *lack* of a policy of justice, or else a multifarious class of aims that diverge from ethical standards.

For Plato to meet *his* opponents, however, he needs merely to oppose their specific policy of going against justice or anything equivalent. Hence he undertakes to argue that the policy of justice is better than that. It would be superfluous for him to try to demonstrate that aiming to be just is beneficial compared to any policy whatsoever, or no matter what.

Therefore Plato's main argument is directed *against* a *policy*. He does also have reasons against having no policy at all. They're contained in his replies to Callicles in the *Gorgias* and his treatment of the democratic personality in *Republic* VIII. People with no policy are claimed to be doomed to frustration, because without a policy one will have chaotic and conflicting aims (574e–575a, 585e–586b). But the same disadvantage, Plato maintains (575e–576b, 588e–589a), afflicts the policy of complete injustice.

---

[24] For overview and discussion of some positions that Plato confronts on this front and his reactions to them, see e.g. Santas 2001: ch. 3 (though he argues for a different overall interpretation from mine).

2.13

Nevertheless the price to be paid for adopting this interpretation might seem too high. Couldn't it work out by chance that one is happiest if one's somewhere between complete justice and complete injustice? Or, even worse, couldn't it *happen* that being completely unjust is best? The same old problem recurs. Once other factors are allowed to affect one's happiness besides the harmony of the personality that's identified with justice, the possibility looms that the course of maximal justice won't be the happiest.

We seem to have no way open except to return to external circumstances, so as to see how Plato could offer the strongest guarantee that despite their influence, the more just will be better off than the less just. So I'll take up again where I left off discussing the influence of circumstances on happiness (§2.8).

Complete injustice, as the portrait of the tyrant in Book IX shows, is a *complete* lack of capacity to deal well with the world. By definition that *entails* a lack of capacity both to act so as to find good circumstances, and to deal with them and adopt an attitude enabling one to bear them. That's why the tyrant is pictured as being so exaggeratedly miserable. Indeed, *any* degree of such capacity in a personality is bound to be better.

One can then see why Plato would then contend that, as a corollary, the more just have quite generally much better chances of coming off well in any circumstances than the less just. It's not that the more just are luckier than the less just. It's that the more just, having the most fully balanced motivations and aims, are *eo ipso* the better able to cope with circumstances without losing their balance.

This idea is illustrated, as noted, by the descending graded series of personalities described in Books VIII–IX (§2.8). Here Plato can only claim that the chances are better, not (as in the comparison with the completely unjust) that the results must necessarily be so. But that doesn't seem to go against what he can expect to maintain. It would, as I've said, be impossible on his terms to claim to be certain that a capacity to deal with contingencies can *never* be thwarted by the world. The case of the good man whose son dies is again a case in point (603e–604d).

2.14

I've described Plato's main argument up to *Republic* 580b–c. It may seem surprising that that main argument includes consideration of external circumstances (§2.8 and §2.13). For he states that the benefits that he'll treat in that argument include only things that justice brings directly 'of itself within the soul' (357b with 358b). Moreover it's thought that *only* in Book X, after 612a, does he introduce other effects of justice in cooperation with external circumstances. If that's so, then seemingly the main argument shouldn't deal with these at all. But that seems wrong.

First a misunderstanding needs to be cleared away. Misinterpretation is encouraged by Plato's aforementioned phrase 'of itself within the soul', along with an anachronistic assumption that he's talking in some quasi-Cartesian mode about processes entirely 'within the mind'. Thus one falls prey to the anachronistic thought that the main argument urges only the avoidance of purely 'subjective' motivational inconsistencies.

That interpretation can't be right. That issue seems to be settled by the ubiquitous references in the main argument, as noted, to the advantages of structural harmony *in dealing with what are obviously circumstances in the world* around the polity and the individual. The main argument would make no sense if these circumstances weren't actually present and accounted for. Indeed, the polity and the person couldn't exist without them.[25] Moreover as I've already indicated (§2.8), the *Republic* II–VII is full of references to the way in which the harmony of motivations within polity and personality are there to cope with physical circumstances, such as other hostile polities (373d–374d, 414b).

When Plato proposes to deal with what justice does within the soul, it's not external, non-subjective factors *in general* that he excludes from the main argument (366e, 367b), and reintroduces after 612a. He excludes those external influences that are produced by *reputation*, i.e. people's belief that one is just. These are the 'wages' (*misthoi*) and rewards the come from what people believe about one's character (612a–b). One doesn't *get* wages when the boss doesn't believe that one's done the job.

One reason for not counting *these particular* external factors in the main argument is evident. The unjust person can feign justice, thus reaping the benefits that come from being believed to be just (612a–b). Another reason for Plato to exclude these wages is that his opponents are pictured as *agreeing* that a reputation for justice is unambiguously beneficial. *They* believe, moreover, that that's the *only* reason why people behave justly (360b–d, 362e–363e).

Thus, even though Plato defers to Book X the discussion of the effects of reputation, and so keeps the main argument of Books II–IX from including them,[26] he isn't thereby stripping the main argument of all consideration of circumstances. On the contrary, these considerations (aside, officially, from reputations) are an indispensable part of that argument.[27]

---

[25] If one adheres to a purely metaphysical conception of the polity, then it's a non-perceptible 'Form'. But that shouldn't force us to say that Plato's describing a non-perceptible entity. The polity contains *people*, and even very just ones need to do things like *eating food* (369b–d, for example).

[26] Reputation can't even be entirely kept out of the main argument, since a philosopher-ruler must be believed by at least some fellow citizens to be just (428e–429a, 431c). In any case, 612a–613e isn't an *argument* at all; it simply accepts the judgement of the interlocutors (612d–e with 362e–363e).

[27] Most interpreters believe that the discussion of the afterlife in 614b–621d is a crudely vulgar and irrelevant appeal to external factors as a motivation to be just. I think that it has a serious philosophical purpose, of asserting that the long-term reward of living justly for a given period must simply be to *continue* to live justly subsequently—which would fit with the claim that what's genuinely valuable about a just condition of soul is: that condition itself. For notice that in Plato's 'Myth of Er', the next life that a soul gets is partly a function of the luck of being near the door (620c), but partly also (i) of how good a life it led before and (ii) of its own *choice* of what kind of life to lead next. The moral, I think, is that the reward of virtue is at best (the opportunity of) choosing a continuation of virtue. But being in a position to *collect* on this reward is contingent (see White 1989).

2.15

The exact conclusion of Plato's main argument bears on his views about his philosopher-rulers' reason to undertake the task of governing in the ideal polity at all. This is a crucial and complex issue for the history of ethics.

In *Republic* VII it's asserted that such people would be better off philosophizing than governing, and that they know it (519d–521b). He has said in Book I that a well-governed city requires a ruler who prefers not to rule (346b–347e). Plato recurs to that statement when he asserts that although philosophizing would make his rulers better off, they'll choose governing anyway because it's just (520a–e), and also because it's good *simpliciter* even though it's not the best life *for them* (541a–b; cf. 466a–c,). Nevertheless they're happier than all others.

This thought surprises readers who expect all ancient ethics to be 'eudaimonist' in a strict sense that would preclude ever reasonably choosing a course that one knew would make one less happy than one would be otherwise.[28] This kind of eudaimonism claims that all rational aims must contribute to or are components of one's happiness, so that no consideration lying outside one's own happiness could compete with it. Many ancient philosophers are indeed eudaimonist in this sense, including Aristotle.[29]

Plato, however, recognizes the existence of one consideration that can lead a philosopher-ruler to act, rationally, against his or her own maximum well-being. Just as he recognizes a notion of goodness *simpliciter*, which isn't a notion of goodness *for* oneself or *for* anyone in particular. This notion appears in the *Timaeus* too. There the 'demiurge' shaping the kosmos aims to make it simply good (30a), not good for himself, or indeed *for* anybody.

2.16

The idea of a reasonable motivation that doesn't regard one's own happiness also appears in Plato. The *Apology* makes Socrates say (28b),

> You're wrong if you think that a man who's any good should take account of life or death; in his actions he should look only to this, whether what he does is right or wrong, and whether he's acting like a good or bad man.

---

[28] For a typical and influential expression of the eudaimonist interpretation see Vlastos 1991: 203 (it goes back to Sidgwick and through him no doubt to Kant; for a brief history of the interpretation see White 2002: ch. 2). For reasons against thinking that the rulers govern the city out of a concern for their own happiness—because otherwise the city would collapse and they'd be worse off, or for some other self-regarding or eudaimonist consideration—see White 1979 with 2002: ch. 5, and 2006: 368–71. For reasons on the other, eudaimonist side, see e.g. Irwin 1995: ch. 15; Irwin 2007: ch. 5; Reeve 1988: 202–8, 311; and Kraut 1992b: 227–331. For readings closer to the former, see Cooper 1977 and Annas 1981: ch. 13.

[29] Aristotle, however, acknowledges the existence of conflicts *within* happiness; see White 2002: ch. 6.

The *Crito*, after making Socrates hold that 'the good life, the beautiful life, and the just life are the same' (48b), has him add that 'the only valid consideration is whether we should be acting rightly', and that (48c–d)

> [i]f it seems that we'll be acting justly, then we have no need whatever to take into consideration whether we'll have to die if we stay here and keep quiet, or *suffer in another way*, rather than do wrong.

Some interpreters assume that in Plato *all* considerations, including right and wrong, must fall under one's happiness.[30] These passages don't say that. Nor can one find a statement of this eudaimonist assumption in these works, though it's often assumed (wrongly, in my opinion) always to be tacitly in the background.[31]

Thus there's a tendency to suppose that when Plato makes Socrates advise people to do things by arguing that they'll gain happiness thereby (e.g. *Charm.* 175d–176a and *Euthd.* 278c–282b), or says that 'we all wish to be happy' (*Euthd.* 282a), he *must* be presupposing a 'eudaimonist' stance, or is presuming that there are no other consideration that could convince them other than a contribution to their own happiness. However, arguments that you should do something because it will make you happy, or statements that we all wish to be happy, aren't evidence that one takes as reasonable considerations *only* contributions to your happiness.[32]

There's also good reason to say that the milieu within which Plato wrote recognized the force of considerations that are distinct from one's well-being. When in *Republic* II Glaucon takes up Thrasymachus' challenge to Socrates, he makes clear his belief that just actions are to be done even though they come at a cost in well-being, and doesn't agree with Thrasymachus' willingness to bring the issue down to one's own benefit. Thrasymachus had urged that many are unjust only because they don't think they can get away with not being so (343d–344c). But he'd also tried to unmask the 'high-minded simplicity' of those who ascribe value to justice itself (348c–d), who are fooled by the fine label, 'just', which those in power place on laws that actually are for their benefit alone (338d–e). If all agreed that one's motivated only to do what contributes to one's happiness, the label couldn't fool anyone.[33]

It's no surprise, accordingly, when Plato claims in Book VII that philosopher-rulers will govern the polity even though that's not conducive to their own maximum happiness. They do it despite that, because it's just and good *simpliciter*.

[30] See e.g. the claim in Vlastos 1991: 203, that Socrates tacitly takes for granted the 'eudaimonist axiom', though Vlastos offers no text in which such an axiom is expressed, and indeed says that throughout virtually all Greek ethics it's taken for granted without being explicitly stated.

[31] Again, the *locus classicus* is Vlastos 1991: 203.

[32] Contrast Aristotle's statement at *Rhet.* 1360b9–11:

> For all advice to do things or not to do them is concerned with happiness and the things that make for or against it; whatever creates or increases happiness or some part of it we ought to do, and whatever destroys or hampers it, or gives rise to its contrary, we ought not to do.

That's a real eudaimonist's assertion of eudaimonism.

[33] For disussion see White 2002: 166–73.

2.17

Nevertheless in this area Plato's outlook *is* different from modern and recent ones. Since well before Kant it's been contended that it's rational to conform to moral obligation and justice quite apart from *any* connection with one's own happiness and possibly in conflict with it. It's also a familiar idea that one's happiness is the *wrong kind of consideration* to support one's choice to do what one morally ought to do, and that a moral obligation is somehow sullied if it's undertaken for the sake of happiness.

These lines of thought don't appear in Greek ethics, including Plato. All Greek thinkers regard it as entirely *reasonable*, and not in any way ignoble or otherwise objectionable, to strive for one's own happiness. They recognize no affirmative value attached to self-sacrifice per se (even though a friend's well-being can be sought for the friend's sake[34]).

Furthermore, although Plato and other Greek philosophers associate 'reason' (*logos*) with universality in science and the best kind of cognition, this idea doesn't translate into the view, as in Kant and others, that rationality in ethics dictates a regard for all people that doesn't give oneself a privileged position.

In addition, philosophizing in Plato's time accords no importance in ethics to benevolence or a sense of *attachment* to other people, or an associated general warmth or 'sympathy' towards them. This isn't to say that warmth is lacking. It just doesn't have the role we expect in ethical theorizing.

Thus even though Plato sometimes speaks of friendship (*philia*) among citizens (449c, 461a–465d), no overt role in the dynamics holding the polity together is assigned to benevolence or warmth, not to mention the fact that the breaking up of biological families that the *Republic* recommends (457c–471c) works against the attachments that we think of as strongest.

Moreover Plato never mentions any such thing as universal benevolence or universal human friendship. The *Republic* recommends that practices in warfare be changed so as to treat all other Greeks as enemies in the same city were then treated, and non-Greeks as Greeks were (470b–e). But no issues of universal benevolence are raised.

2.18

So when Plato comes to assert that his philosopher-rulers should govern the city despite that's being a less than optimal life, the reasons they can have for doing so are quite different from what a modern writer might give. They don't spring from benevolence towards fellow citizens, or a sense of the value of self-sacrifice, or the concept of rationality or humanity that underpins some modern conceptions of morality.

---

[34] As in Aristotle, *Ethics* VIII.2.

Instead, the rulers' reasons for governing are built squarely on Plato's scheme of functional roles for the components of the polity. For the city to fulfil its function of providing for the needs of citizens (369b–d), it has to have guardians and rulers (373d–374e, 412a–c). For these to fulfil their function of preserving the city, their motivation can't be to govern the city for the sake of anything but its preservation (374e). So their function-fulfilling motivation can't be to govern the city for the sake of their own maximum happiness.

Rather than merely saying that they'll govern the city for its good and not for the sake of their own maximum good, Plato says that there *must* be something *else* that would be better for them to do. Philosophy is invoked in part precisely to be that something else.[35] For philosophy includes an understanding of justice, so it provides the rulers with the realization that, despite what the best life for them would be, they *should* rule, because it's more important for them to do that than seek their own maximum good (though they're still, for all that, much better off than anyone else, 521a). By this ingenious argument, Plato provides his philosopher-rulers with their non-self-benefiting motivation to govern.

This philosophical role for a non-self-regarding consideration in favour of governing is thus firmly planted in Plato's special scheme of the paradigmatic polity and its paradigmatic rulers, with their special functional role in the polity's harmonious structure. It has its main *raison d'être* there, and so doesn't transplant easily to other ethical views. It also doesn't apply to people besides the philosopher-rulers. They're the only ones who need this non-self-regarding motivation to perform their function. Hence it's unsurprising that it doesn't bear fruit in philosophical Greek ethics outside Plato (except, in a complex way, in Stoic ethics[36]). Still, *Republic* 519d–521b makes fully explicit what's also clear enough in the other passages mentioned (and shouldn't anyway be in doubt for any philosophical reasons), that there was no obstacle in the way of Plato's conceiving of such a consideration.

2.19

Plato's classical works, I've said, are like his earlier ones in being best regarded as often exploring questions rather than as always propounding doctrine. The *Republic* leaves several gaps when it applies the notion of goodness without offering an account of it (§2.9). Another gap—question (*f*) on the relation of pleasure to happiness—shows up in Plato's use of the notion of pleasure from the *Protagoras* and *Gorgias* through the *Republic*.

---

[35] It doesn't seem to me that any of the eudaimonist interpretations of Plato (such as Irwin 1995 and Kraut 1992a) has produced any way of taking account of this aspect of Plato's argument concerning the function of ruling, nor does it seem possible for such interpretations to do so.

[36] See White 2002: 311–25.

On pleasure Plato presents a moving target. The *Protagoras* says that most people think it's the good. Then the *Gorgias* denies that it is. Neither work attends to what's said in the other. The *Republic* at one point denies that pleasure is the good (505c–e). Then, however, in the middle of arguing that justice brings 'happiness', he switches without warning to using the term 'pleasure' instead, as if it made no difference. Moreover (cf. §2.8), he quite noticeably refrains from asserting that bodily pleasures have no value at all, contenting himself with the assertion that the value of most pleasures is very low (580c–583a and 583b–586e).

It's at any rate inadvisable to regard the *Republic* as propounding an entirely clear-cut or dogmatic view (either implied by his words or in his mind but coyly screened from us) about either the value of pleasure or the terms in which it's to be evaluated. Its ambiguous role in the main argument—the wavering in Book IX about its relation to happiness, and the absence of an actual specification of the good and its exact relation to pleasure—obviously leaves Plato with urgent unfinished business.

2.20

No surprise, then, that the *Philebus*, a late work, goes back and treats pleasure extensively. It denies that pleasure is the good. However, it asserts unambiguously that when pleasure is combined properly with knowledge, it's a *component* of the good (62e–64a, or the human good, 11d, 64c—strikingly and oddly, Plato doesn't keep these clearly distinct). This is clearly a response of sorts to the *Republic*'s unclarity, and certainly moves in the direction of saying expressly that pleasure can't be denied a role in the good life. But the *Philebus* is very unclear about exactly what that role is. Once again, there's no point guessing at a clear-cut doctrine; Plato's working on the issue.

It's also no surprise that the *Laws*, probably Plato's last work, says more about pleasure than about any other psychological issue. (Its main topic is a detailed code of laws for a polity; its relation to the political structure in the *Republic* is uncertain.)

Like the *Philebus*, the *Laws* in this aspect receives insufficient attention from philosophical readers. Its leading idea seems to me probably this: to distinguish between saying that pleasure is *good* and saying that it's essential to *motivating human beings* to aim at what's good. Plato implies that one can recognize something's goodness without enjoying it or the thought of it, though enjoyment is essential to motivation. Hence Plato insists that a polity should teach people to enjoy only what's good.

At 732e–733d he says (cf. 782d–e, 663a),

> Human nature involves above all pleasures, pains, and desires... [We should praise the life that...] excels in providing what we all seek: a predominance of pleasure over pain throughout our lives. ... we should think of all human lives as bound up in these two feelings [sc., pleasure and pain],

and at 782d–e, 'all human actions are motivated by a set of three needs and desires', which are listed as the desires for 'food' and 'drink' and 'the imperious lust to procreate'. Some readers take these statements to be reassertions of a blanket hedonism.

However, he next says (783a),

> These three unhealthy instincts must be canalized away from what men call supreme pleasure, and towards the supreme good, . . . by the three powerful influences of fear, law and correct argument.

He also says that people must be taught that the life of justice is the most pleasant (662c–e).

These passages seem to broach a way of dealing with the importance of pleasure without asserting that it's as such good (cf. *Prot.* 354a, 358a). Determining what's advisable doesn't *consist in* determining what's most pleasant (667a–668b, 792c–e), and certainly not most *intensely* pleasant (734c). Rather, the governing evaluations consist in determining what's *good* (783a) so that pleasures and pains and desires can be 'canalized' towards those things.[37]

This isn't by any means a full response to the questions that the earlier works opened, and that the *Republic* had pursued without settling them. But it demonstrates Plato's style of enquiry, and also shows that near the end of his life he was, happily, still thinking.

Bibliography

Annas, J. 1981. *An Introduction to Plato's Republic.* Oxford: Clarendon Press.
Bambrough, R. (ed.) 1965. *New Essays on Plato and Aristotle.* New York: Humanities Press.
Cooper, J. M. 1977. 'The Psychology of Justice in Plato', *American Philosophical Quarterly* 14: 151–7.
Hare, R. M. 1965. 'Plato and the Mathematicians', in Bambrough (ed.), 21–38.
Irwin, T. 1995. *Plato's Ethics.* Oxford: Oxford University Press.
—— 2007. *The Development of Ethics*, vol. 1. Oxford: Oxford University Press.
Kraut, R. 1992a. 'The Defense of Justice in Plato's Republic', in Kraut (ed.) 1992b, 311–37.
—— (ed.) 1992b. *Cambridge Companion to Plato.* Cambridge: Cambridge University.
Mabbott, J. D. 1971. 'Is Plato's Republic Utilitarian?', in Vlastos (ed.) 1971b, 57–65 (a revised version of a paper of the same title, *Mind* 46 (1937), 468–474).
Matthews, G. B. 1999. *Socratic Perplexity and the Nature of Philosophy.* Oxford: Oxford University Press.
Prichard, H. A. 1968. 'Duty and Interest', in *Moral Obligation and Duty and Interest.* Oxford: Oxford University Press, 201–238. (Reprint of an Inaugural Lecture, Oxford University Press, 1928.)
Reeve, C. D. C. 1988. *Philosopher Kings.* Princeton: Princeton University Press.
Sachs, D. 1963. 'A Fallacy in Plato's Republic', *Philosophical Review* 72: 141–58.

---

[37] The value beauty (*kalon*, also sometimes translatable by 'noble' and 'fine') is treated in the *Symposium* (especially 209–12). Plato never makes clear how this value is related to goodness, though he usually seems to hold that goodness is the only scale of value that there is, or that really matters: see e.g. White 1979: 176–7, 194.

Santas, G. 1985. 'Two Theories of Good in Plato's Republic', *Archiv für Geschichte der Philosophie* 67: 223–45.

—— 2001. *Goodness and Justice*. Oxford: Blackwell.

Shorey, P. 1930 and 1935. *Plato, The Republic*, vols. I and II. Cambridge, MA: Harvard University Press.

Vlastos, G. 1971a. 'Justice and Happiness in the Republic', in Vlastos (ed.) 1971b, 66–95.

—— (ed.) 1971b. *Plato*, Vol. 2. Garden City: Anchor.

—— 1991. *Socrates: Ironist and Moral Philosopher*. Ithaca: Cornell University Press.

White, N. 1979. *Companion to Plato's Republic*. Indianapolis: Hackett.

—— 1989. 'Happiness and External Contingencies in Republic X', in W. Starr and R. Taylor (ed.), *Moral Philosophy: Contemporary and Historical Essays: Essays in Memory of Joan Kung*. Milwaukee: Marquette University Press, 1–21.

—— 2002. *Individual and Conflict in Greek Ethics*. Oxford: Clarendon Press.

—— 2006. 'Plato's Concept of Goodness', in Hugh H. Benson (ed.), *Blackwell Companion to Plato*. Oxford: Wiley-Blackwell, 356–72.

—— 2008. 'Definition and Elenchus', *Philosophical Inquiry* 30 (Essays in Honor of Gerasimos Santas), 1–19.

Williams, B. 2006. *The Sense of the Past*. Princeton: Princeton University Press.

Woodruff, P. 2005. 'Plato's Shorter Ethical Works', *Stanford Encyclopedia of Philosophy*, <http://plato.stanford.edu/entries/plato-ethics-shorter>.

ADDITIONAL WORKS

A voluminous literature has grown up around the interpretation of Plato's ethics. Even just a representative sampling is impossible here. The problem is exacerbated by the absence of any line in Plato's work between his ethics and other parts of his philosophy. The present chapter focuses on the ethical issues that I believe to be most important and most interestingly discussed in English recently. The above Bibliography reflects that choice of issues. The following list presents additional works, some of them collections of articles, that the reader might profitably consult.

Blackburn, S. 2007. *Plato's Republic: A Biography*. New York: Grove Press.

Cross, R. C. and Woozley, A. D. 1964. *Plato's Republic: A Philosophical Commentary*. New York: St. Martin's Press.

Ferrari, G. R. F. (ed.) 2007. *Cambridge Companion to Plato's Republic*. Cambridge: Cambridge University Press.

Field, G. C. 1948. *Plato and his Contemporaries*, 2nd edn. London: Methuen.

Fine, Gail (ed.) 1999. *Plato*, 2 vols. Oxford: Oxford University Press.

Heinaman, Robert (ed.) 2003. *Plato and Aristotle's Ethics*. London: Ashgate.

Kraut, R. (ed.) 1992. *Cambridge Companion to Plato*. Cambridge: Cambridge University Press.

Murphy, N. R. 1951. *The Interpretation of Plato's Republic*. Oxford: Oxford University Press.

Santas (ed.) 2006. *The Blackwell Guide to Plato's Republic*. Oxford: Blackwell.

Schofield, M. 2006. *Plato Political Philosophy*. Oxford: Oxford University Press.

Shorey, P. 1903. *The Unity of Plato's Thought*. Chicago: University of Chicago Press.

Vlastos, G. (ed.) 1971b. *Plato*, Vol. 2. Garden City: Anchor.

Wiggins, D. 2006. 'Glaucon's and Adeimantus' Interrogation of Socrates', *Ethics*. Cambridge, MA: Harvard University Press, 9–29.

CHAPTER 3

....

ARISTOTLE'S ETHICS

....

PAULA GOTTLIEB

ARISTOTLE (384–322 BCE) was born in Stagira in north-east Greece, an ideal coastal spot for a city, according to his own description in the *Politics* (*Pol.* VII 5). Aristotle's father was doctor to King Amyntas of Macedon. In his ethical works, Aristotle shows great respect for medicine. When Aristotle was eighteen, he left Macedon to study with Plato in Athens. On Plato's death in 348 BCE, he moved to the court of Hermeias in north-west Asia Minor, and then to Lesbos. During those years Aristotle did much of his copious research on biology that is reflected in over a quarter of his extant work. In 343–342 BCE Amyntas' son King Philip chose Aristotle to tutor his teenage son, the future Alexander the Great. When Plato's successor at the academy died, Aristotle returned to Athens, founding his own school, the Lyceum. On the death of Alexander in 323 BCE, anti-Macedonian feeling flared in Athens, and Aristotle, charged with impiety, left for Chalcis in Euboea where he spent the rest of his life.[1]

Aristotle was a prolific author, composing seminal works on logic, metaphysics, psychology, biology, ethics, politics, aesthetics, and rhetoric. The *Nicomachean Ethics* (*EN*), named after his son Nicomachus, is Aristotle's pre-eminent work in ethics. It has three books in common with the *Eudemian Ethics* (*EE*). Books IV, V, and VI of the *Eudemian Ethics*, generally agreed to belong originally to the *Eudemian Ethics*, are the same as books V, VI, and VII of the *Nicomachean Ethics*. For a while during the nineteenth century the *Eudemian Ethics* was not treated as authentic, but the tide has changed.[2]

The *Nicomachean Ethics* is usually treated as the later, more philosophically mature work and continues to receive the lion's share of translations, commentaries, books, and articles.[3] In the late 1970s, Anthony Kenny sparked renewed controversy, using stylometric methods

---

[1] For a fuller discussion, see, e.g. Anagnostopulos 2009. The main historical sources are to be found in Düring 1957. Diogenes Laertius (third century CE) provides colourful details.

[2] But see Pakuluk 1995: 241–4.

[3] Thornton Lockwood's bibliography of work on the *Nicomachean Ethics* alone from just 1880 to 2004 runs to 116 pages (Lockwood 2005), and his recent, draft bibliography on that text for the next several years shows the same trajectory. Since 1980, there have been several translations with introductions and/or

of analysis to argue that the *Eudemian Ethics* is the later work.[4] Kenny has since recanted,[5] but there is burgeoning interest in the *Eudemian Ethics* as an important treatise in its own right.[6]

Two books survive from a further work, the *Magna Moralia*. Its origin is unknown, but it is perhaps the published notes of a student who attended a course of Aristotle's lectures before the *Eudemian* and *Nicomachean Ethics*. Alternatively, it may be the work of a later writer.[7] The *Protrepticus*, which Aristotle wrote at Plato's Academy, survives in fragmentary form.[8] How much Aristotle is indebted to Plato is controversial.[9]

Aristotle's *Politics* also dovetails with the issues in his ethical works, especially the discussions of happiness in *Politics* VII and VIII. Although Aristotle's *Politics* logically follows the *Nicomachean Ethics*, it was probably written between the *Eudemian* and *Nicomachean Ethics*.[10]

The extant manuscripts of Aristotle's ethical works date from no earlier than the tenth century CE, descendants of Andronicus' editions of the first century BCE. Since these works were probably compiled from Aristotle's lecture notes, the texts are terse and often cryptic. Different interpretations abound, depending on how Aristotle's densely formulated ideas are expanded, and which are considered to be the most significant. Not surprisingly, then, the ethical works of 'The Philosopher', as Thomas Aquinas referred to Aristotle, have appealed to philosophers of many different religious backgrounds and persuasions down through the ages.

In the nineteenth century, J. S. Mill praised Aristotle for his 'judicious utilitarianism',[11] more recent commentators on Aristotle's ethics have argued for a rapprochement between Aristotle and Kant,[12] and modern virtue ethicists have often been inspired by Aristotle.[13] Even Rawls invokes an 'Aristotelian principle' in his theory of justice.[14] Aristotle's ethical work has been compared profitably with Indian philosophy[15] and Chinese philosophy.[16]

commentaries on the whole *Nicomachean Ethics*, e.g. Irwin 1985, 1999; Natali 1999; Crisp 2000; Sachs 2001; Broadie and Rowe 2002. Ross' influential translation was most recently revised with a new introduction by Lesley Brown in 2009, and the original version (Ross 1923) is now on the web. By contrast, there was no Oxford Classical Text of the *Eudemian Ethics* until 1991, and the most recent major translation and commentary is Woods' Clarendon series volume on books I, II, and VIII (Woods 1992 [1982]).

   [4] Kenny 1978.
   [5] Kenny 1992.
   [6] Three complete translations are in the offing, one by Anthony Kenny with introduction and notes, now published, by Oxford University Press, 2011, another with introduction and notes by Inwood and Woolf, the third by Jost.
   [7] See the debate between Cooper 1999: 195–211 (1973) and Rowe 1975.
   [8] On its status as Aristotle's first ethical treatise see Bobonich 2006: 18–23.
   [9] On Aristotle's philosophical development in general see Jaeger 1923 and the contributors to Wians 1996. See Gerson 2004 and 2006 for a Platonic reading of the *Nicomachean Ethics*.
   [10] Kraut 2002: 17–19.
   [11] Mill, *On Liberty*, 150.
   [12] e.g. Sherman 1997 and most of the contributors to Engstrom and Whiting 1996.
   [13] e.g. Anscombe 1958; Foot 1978 and 2001; Hursthouse 1999. On Aristotle and contemporary ethics, see, e.g. Gardiner 2005; Gill 2005; and Chappell 2006.
   [14] See the discussion of pleasure below. On the central position of Aristotelian naturalism in the development of ethics from ancient times to Rawls, see Irwin 2007–2009.
   [15] Clark 1975.   [16] Sim 2007; Yu 2007.

The following addresses the main issues in the *Nicomachean Ethics*, with room for only the occasional nod to Aristotle's other work in ethics.[17] No doubt in all Aristotle's ethical works there are gems waiting to be discovered and fruitful new lines of enquiry to be pursued, even after over two thousand years of study.

3.1 HAPPINESS

Aristotle's *Nicomachean Ethics* begins (and ends) with the highest good, which he argues is the ultimate goal of human endeavour and the subject of the present enquiry which is 'a sort of politics'. According to Aristotle, this is what people call happiness (*eudaimonia*). According to Aristotle, happiness is objective.[18] It is an activity, not a state of 'feeling good', although the good human being will live a happy and enjoyable life. As Aristotle explains, different things may be good for different people, but that does not mean that there is no fact of the matter about what is good for whom. Each individual is not the measure of all things, as Protagoras thought. It is the good human being who is the measure of what is good and pleasant.

In his *Nicomachean Ethics*, Aristotle approaches the topic of happiness from various angles. Following his method of examining current beliefs and beliefs that have something to be said for them (*EN* I 4),[19] Aristotle considers different views of happiness drawn from the lives that people lead—a life centred on physical gratification, a life of political acclaim, a life of contemplation, and a life of making money.

However, Aristotle begins, more abstractly, by presenting a hierarchy of human goals, activities, and choices, with the topmost goal the aim of politics (*EN* I 1–2).[20] Aristotle later describes a hierarchy of goods, those that are choiceworthy only for the sake of something else, for example, wealth or flutes, and again those that are choiceworthy for their own sake *and* for the sake of something else, for example honour, pleasure, understanding, and virtue, and finally one good, happiness, that is choiceworthy for its own sake and never for the sake of anything else (*EN* I 7). In each case, Aristotle argues, the good at the pinnacle of the hierarchy is identical with happiness. Happiness suffices for a full and worthwhile life, not for an isolated individual, but for one with family, friends, and fellow citizens.[21]

Whether happiness is an exclusive goal, consisting in only one activity, or whether it is an inclusive goal, including some or all of the types of goods below it in the hierarchy,

---

[17] But see the table at the end of this chapter.

[18] Some therefore think that 'flourishing' is a better translation of '*eudaimonia*' than 'happiness', but that makes the issue of whether happiness is subjective or objective merely a verbal dispute (e.g. Cooper 1975: 89–90).

[19] On method, see especially Kraut 2006a.

[20] See Richardson Lear 2006 and Meyer 2008: 51–5.

[21] On self-sufficiency, see Heinaman 1988; Lawrence 1997; Cooper 2004: 270–308; and Schofield 2006: 311–13.

continues to be a matter of controversy.[22] Aristotle's second hierarchy has proved equally puzzling. Kantians have been baffled by the suggestion that something can be chosen both for its own sake and for the sake of something else, while Millians have argued that it is possible for some things to be chosen *as parts* of happiness.[23]

Aristotle also tackles Plato's Form of the Good (*EN* I 6), pointing out problems arising from the connection between the Form of the Good and Plato's mathematical theory[24] and arguing that there is no universal good because what it is for something to be good depends on the kind of thing it is. For example, what it is to be a good time (the right opportunity) is different from what it is to be a good quality (virtue), because what it is to be a time is different from what it is to be a quality. In any case, Aristotle argues, a universal good would be useless for action. According to Aristotle, contemporary artisans do not look for it, and the doctor is not interested in the universal health (or good), but in the health of *this* human being.[25]

Aristotle does concede that different goods may all be related to one focus, or be good by analogy.[26] Aristotle himself relates various goods to *happiness* and draws analogies between medicine and ethics.[27] Aristotle's discussion shows that the good must be something practical, within our ken and power, and he later emphasizes the practical nature of ethical reasoning, and its relation to particulars. Mathematical rigour, he argues, is inappropriate for ethics. Ethical claims, though not arbitrary or merely conventional are 'for the most part'.[28] The idea that what it is for something to be good depends on the kind of thing it is, is important for Aristotle's function argument to which I now turn.[29]

In very brief outline, the *Nicomachean* function (*ergon*) argument runs as follows (*EN* I 7 1097b25–1098a17): If something has a function, for example, a flautist or an artisan, what is good for it or what it is for it to do well, depends on that function. Human beings have a function. As befits a biologist, Aristotle argues that since the human function is

---

[22] W. F. R. Hardie 1965 uses the term 'dominant' instead of 'exclusive' and is the first to draw the distinction between 'dominant' and 'inclusive' ends. He and Ackrill 1974 argue that Aristotle is inconsistent in *EN* I and X. Others argue that Aristotle is consistent. Kenny 1978, Kraut 1989, and Reeve 1992 take the exclusive view. Gauthier and Jolif 1958, Ackrill 1974, Irwin e.g. 1985a, Devereux 1981, Keyt 1983, Whiting 1986, Cooper 1999: 212–36 (1987), and Roche 1988 take the inclusive view. Others, for example, White 1988, Broadie 1991: 29, and Lawrence 1997 argue that happiness is the *focus* of the best life, but differ on what the focus contains. White 1988 argues that the focus is simply contemplation. Lawrence 1997: 73 argues that the focus has more than one component. Kraut 1989 and Curzer 1991 think that the happy life aims at contemplation but includes ethical activity too. On combining elements of the two views, see Crisp 1994 . For more on the inclusive view, Irwin 2007: 122–33. On the exclusive view, see Richardson Lear 2004. See too the final section of this chapter.

[23] The classic papers are Prichard 1935 and Ackrill 1997: 179–200.

[24] On Plato's mathematics see e.g. Burnyeat 1984 especially 239–40 and *Metaphysics* XIV 1–5 with Annas 1976 especially 214–16. Aristotle's criticisms are made at greater length in *EE* I 8.

[25] Ackrill 1997: 201–11. For arguments pro and con Aristotle's view, see Shields 1999 especially 208–15; Santas 2001: 194–223; and Yount 1998.

[26] For recent discussion of the varieties and connections between different goods, see Wiggins 2009.

[27] On medical analogies, see especially Jaeger 1957; Lloyd 1968; and Hankinson 1988.

[28] On claims 'for the most part', see especially Reeve 1992 and Anagnostopoulos 1994.

[29] See e.g. Wilkes 1978; Korsgaard 2008: 151–73 and 129–50; Santas 2001: 236–50; and Barney 2008.

what is distinctive of human beings, by a process of elimination it must involve a certain complexity of thought that non-human animals and plants lack, i.e. activity (*en-erg-eia*, exercise of the *ergon*) of the psyche in accordance with or not without reason. The function of an F and of an excellent F are the same in kind. So the human *good* (happiness) will be activity of the psyche in accordance with or not without reason done *well*, i.e. in accordance with virtue,[30] or, if there is more than one virtue, in accordance with the best and most complete/final virtue, and not just for a short time.

The argument depends implicitly on Aristotle's division of the human psyche into three main parts, (1) the rational part (to be subdivided later), (2) the appetitive part (which is susceptible to reason and is often treated as part of the rational part) comprising feelings, appetites, and sense-perception, and (3) the nutritive part, containing capacities for nutrition, growth, and reproduction (*EN* I 13, VI 1). At this stage it is unclear whether the human function involves exercising (1) or (2) or both. The exact type of reasoning or thinking involved in exercising the human function, and the virtues Aristotle has in mind, still need to be spelled out.

Nothing in this argument has remained unchallenged. Alexander of Aphrodisias was the first to complain about an equivocation between faring well and acting virtuously. Why suppose that being a virtuous human being is something that is good *for* a human being, any more than, for example, being a good knife is good *for* a knife?[31] Why think that humans have a function as do carpenters and eyes,[32] or that what is distinctive of humans should be their function? Suppose humans are the only creatures who can perform somersaults or build warships.

A deeper question concerns how these questions are best answered. Is it by appeal to Aristotelian metaphysics and biology, or by further reflection on the virtues?[33] For example, one response to Alexander is that human beings are natural kinds, not artefacts like knives and forks, and just as being healthy or functioning well physically is good for a human being, so being a good human being—functioning well in general—is good for a human being.[34] A different response is that acting virtuously just is what it is to have a happy life, and that this point can only be appreciated from the virtuous person's own point of view.[35]

Aristotle has been charged with arguing from what the human function *is* to how people *ought* to function, but that is not quite right. He argues that what is good for humans is not merely to exercise their function, but to exercise their function *well*.[36] Indeed, Aristotle's account of a function as something that can be carried out well or

---

[30] Translators often prefer the term 'excellence' to 'virtue' since in English 'virtue' does not apply to a knife or an eye, as it does in Greek. See e.g. Broadie and Rowe 2002.

[31] Cf. Glassen 1957.

[32] See especially Tuozzo 1996.

[33] On the view that Aristotle needs special argument involving metaphysics to anchor his general ethical views to the truth, see Irwin 1980 and 1988 especially 23–4, and, for more recent reflections, Irwin 2007: 234–43.

[34] Whiting 1988, 38.

[35] McDowell 1980, especially 371, 1995, 2009: 23–40, and Broadie 1991: 35 who argues for the further point that we think that reason is our essence because it is our most important characteristic from an ethical point of view (cf. Broadie 2006: 344).

[36] Gómez-Lobo 1989.

badly, as opposed to well or not at all, makes way for his triadic view of virtues and vices. Still, one might think that the result is too mundane. Why function well at human affairs, when one could aspire to a more godly life?

The conclusion of the function argument needs supplementing, because human beings need external goods like friends and wealth in order to thrive. This poses a new puzzle. If happiness depends on external goods, why is it not simply a matter of luck? The reputed sage Solon agrees that happiness is objective, but thinks that it depends entirely on external factors and goods, which is why he thinks it only safe to say that people are happy once they are dead and immune to any further bad luck.[37] Aristotle shows that matters are worse than Solon thinks, on Solon's own view. If happiness depends entirely on external factors, and these factors can affect the agent's happiness whether she knows about them or not, then it will not be safe to say that she is happy even after death.

Aristotle argues that happiness is not entirely a matter of luck, but depends on virtuous activities that are up to the agent. Even if misfortunes and fortunes after death can contribute to a person's happiness, they cannot make a person unhappy who was happy or vice versa, according to Aristotle. Hence Aristotle's account of happiness is vindicated. Virtue is decisive, although external goods are needed for the happy life.[38] While people are praised for their virtue, they are congratulated on their happiness.

However, virtue is not sufficient for happiness, according to Aristotle. The virtuous person who is in dire circumstances will not be happy. Nor will he be miserable, since he will never do anything vicious. This is a controversial claim, going against the beliefs of the Greek tragedians as well as modern views about moral luck and moral dilemmas. Also, even if the good person's virtue allows him to take control in situations of bad luck, one might wonder if Solon is ultimately correct if there is luck involved in the good person's becoming virtuous in the first place.[39] Aristotle returns to these issues later.

3.2 Becoming Good and the Doctrine of the Mean

If happiness is exercising the human function well, i.e. in accordance with *virtue*, the next step is to explain what the virtues are. There are two types of virtue, virtues of character and virtues of thought. Aristotle introduces his virtues of character by reminding his audience that virtue makes a thing carry out its function well. In accord with the practical nature of his enquiry, Aristotle discusses how people become good before saying what virtue of character is.[40] According to Aristotle, virtue is not innate, nor is it

[37] See especially White 1992: 49–108.
[38] On the role of external goods, see Cooper 1999: 173–96, 292–311 and Irwin 1985a. For an argument that Aristotle's view about virtue and external goods is unstable, see Annas 1993: 364–84.
[39] See e.g. Card 1996.
[40] The classic paper on becoming good is Burnyeat 1980. See too, e.g. Sherman 1989 and Vasiliou 1996.

against nature. Since it is not against nature, the point of virtue is not to remedy defects in human nature as Hobbes and others have thought, nor to quash natural desires and emotions. The key to becoming a good person is practice, usually translated 'habitua-tion'. The translation is misleading, since virtue cannot be achieved by mechanical and mindless repetition of behaviour, but involves careful attention and thought.[41] Just as a pianist adjusts her playing as she practises so that it is in tune and musical, and enlarges her repertoire so that she becomes good at playing different types of music, so the learner has to adjust her emotions to different situations, giving careful thought to her actions, and enlarging her experience so as to become good in all areas of life.

Virtue of character, the result of such practice, is not to be identified with an emotion, or the capacity to have an emotion, but with an acquired disposition (*hexis*) to have the appro-priate emotions at the appropriate time, in the appropriate way, for the appropriate reasons and so on, and to act accordingly.[42] For example, the virtue of mildness is a disposition in relation to the emotion of anger. The mild person only gets angry at the appropriate time, in the appropriate way, for the appropriate reasons and so on, and will act accordingly. Each virtue is a mean between two vices, one of deficiency and one of excess.[43] For exam-ple, the virtue of mildness comes between the vices of meekness and irascibility.

The triadic apparatus of virtue and vices has led to criticism that Aristotle is present-ing a doctrine of moderation. For example, Kant argues that Aristotle's view is therefore false[44] and Bernard Williams comments, 'The theory oscillates between an unhelpful analytical model…and a substantively depressing doctrine in favour of moderation. The doctrine of the mean is better forgotten.'[45] However, according to Aristotle, the mild human being will get very angry when the occasion warrants, and not angry at all when it does not.[46] Perhaps the terms 'deficiency' and 'excess' are inapplicable to feelings and actions, since what is important is that the good person's feelings and actions have a cer-tain qualitative rather than quantitative aspect.[47] A different way of understanding the doctrine of the mean is as a doctrine of equilibrium, by analogy with health. The good human being, having a balanced character, will have the correct emotions on the correct occasions and act accordingly.[48] Aristotle also uses a musical analogy, suggesting that the good person's character, like a well-tuned instrument, will sound the correct tones.

Each virtue is 'in a mean relative to us'. Aristotle contrasts 'the mean relative to us' with 'the mean in the object' using an example from dietetics. Consider Milo, champion wrestler at the Olympic games, and consider a beginning athlete. If two pounds of food are too little and ten pounds too much, six pounds, though the mean in the object, the arithmetical mean, are not necessarily appropriate for either Milo or the learner. The trainer needs to

---

[41] See especially Sherman 1989 and Annas 1993: 67–8.   [42] Kosman 1980.
[43] Young 1996 refers to this as 'location', to be distinguished from 'intermediacy', the fact that the virtues aim at what is intermediate.
[44] Kant *DOV* 163.
[45] Williams 1985: 36.
[46] Urmson 1973.
[47] Hursthouse 1980–1981 and 2006 vs. Urmson 1973 and Curzer 1996.
[48] Cf. Kretzmann in discussion. Alexander Grant even translates the word for 'mean' as 'balance' (Grant 1874: 257).

give Milo and the learner whatever amount is appropriate for each. Aristotle does not spell out the ethical analogy here, but he elsewhere explains, for example, why generous people may spend different amounts. A generous person is one whose spending fits her means.

Aristotle's discussion of 'the mean relative to us' is open to interpretation. While the mean relative to us does not depend solely on the agent's point of view, it could be simply relative to us as human beings,[49] or it could be relative to particular human beings with particular abilities, temperaments, and roles.[50] The debate raises intricate questions about which factors are relevant to ethical decision-making and whether Aristotle's own theory entails that men, women, and slaves should be treated differently.

A major objection to Aristotle's doctrine of the mean is that it provides no decision procedure for action. Aristotle certainly has advice to give about hitting the mean (*EN* II 7). But it is precisely Aristotle's point that there is no *mathematical algorithm* to point the way.[51] Are we left, then, with what Bernard Williams claims is merely 'an unhelpful analytical model'?[52] The answer depends upon taking seriously the triadic nature of virtue and vices on Aristotle's account, and noticing the underlying psychological profiles. The vices of excess often go together as do the vices of deficiency. For example, people who underestimate their own worth and abilities will have the vices of cowardice, pusillanimity, inirascibility, and indifference to honour. People who overestimate their own worth and abilities will have the vices of rashness, vanity, irascibility, and excessive interest in honour. According to Aristotle's taxonomy, the self-aggrandizing qualities admired by Plato's Thrasymachus and certain followers of Ayn Rand line up as vices on one side, whereas 'Christian' qualities of meekness, asceticism, and the like line up as vices on the other. Aristotle's virtues do not come at the expense of others or oneself. The Aristotelian good person has self-knowledge. This is a substantive account.[53]

3.3 MORAL RESPONSIBILITY AND MORAL DILEMMAS

Aristotle defines virtue of character as a disposition involving choice (*prohairetikē*) in a mean, the mean relative to us, defined by the reason (*logos*) by which (or in the way in which) the person with practical wisdom (*phronēsis*) would define it (*EN* II 6 1106b36–1107a2). Aristotle has yet to explain what choice or practical wisdom are, although he has already introduced them in his discussions of the virtues of character. Not all voluntary actions are chosen, but all chosen actions are voluntary.

---

[49] Brown 1997.

[50] Leighton 1992 and 1995; Losin 1987; Ackrill 1973: 248. Against the inclusion of temperaments and roles, see Curzer 1996a.

[51] See too Annas 2004, defending virtue ethics on this issue.

[52] Williams 1985: 36.

[53] For more on this interpretation, and on the connections between Aristotle's view here and other aspects of his ethics, see Gottlieb 2009.

Aristotle's discussion of the voluntary has inspired work on philosophy of action, on free will and determinism, and on moral dilemmas.[54]

Aristotle defines the voluntary by contrasting it with its opposite, the involuntary.[55] Praise and blame are due to the voluntary, pity and pardon to the involuntary. Actions are voluntary when they are up to us, and when we know all the particulars of the situation. Actions under duress are voluntary, as are actions due to passion. Not knowing that a type of action is bad does not make it involuntary. There is also a third category, the non-voluntary. Here the agent does not know all the particulars of the situation, but lacks regret when she finds them out.[56] Pity and pardon would hardly be appropriate in such a case, but, perhaps more to the point, the agent's character is not free from blame. Finally, Aristotle discusses 'mixed actions', actions that, considered out of context, would not be ones that anyone would want to perform, but in context, are voluntary, for example, throwing cargo overboard in a storm to save the lives of the crew.[57] As one would expect from a proponent of the doctrine of the mean, the actual context and the particular stakes involved trump other considerations.

The case of the cargo is easily solved, but Aristotle presents another case that is difficult. If a tyrant threatens the lives of family members unless you do something shameful, would it be voluntary to do as he says? Would it be right to do as he says? Aristotle's answer depends on further details, and differs from the either/or analysis of such dilemmas by modern philosophers.[58] As Aristotle argued in *Nicomachean Ethics* I, the good person will never act viciously and so will never be miserable.

We might now wonder whether a person is responsible for his own character. Aristotle's answer is that we are 'in some way co-causes' for our characters. Presumably, this means that whatever our upbringing and circumstances, we are partly responsible for how we turn out. But suppose we are *born* with a sense of what is good that is faulty? Aristotle's reply is that, still, the good and bad would be equally responsible for their characters. This refutes the Socratic view that nobody errs voluntarily, but a modern philosopher might wonder whether people are responsible for their actions at all. Solon's concerns about luck are perhaps more intractable than they seemed.

3.4 VIRTUES OF CHARACTER

Aristotle lists ten virtues of character, five named, five 'nameless', and justice (*EE* II 7 1108a17–31.) He begins with bravery (*andreia*), the disposition that would have been most familiar to his contemporaries and that best fits the etymology of 'virtue' (and the Greek '*aretē*'),

[54] e.g. Charles 1984; Sorabji 1980; Hursthouse 1984, 1999; Nussbaum 1986, especially 418–19; Stocker 1990; Nielsen 2007; Dahl 2008.
[55] See Furley 1967; Heinaman 2009. For a detailed treatment of this topic as it appears in *MM*, *EE*, and *EN*, see Meyer 1993. For a shorter discussion see Meyer 2006.
[56] Austin 1956–1957.
[57] On the controversial nature of mixed actions, see Card 1999.
[58] e.g. Hursthouse 1999: 43–87; Stocker 1990: 51–84.

manliness.[59] Along with magnanimity and justice, it gets pride of place in modern anthologies. In the *Nicomachean Ethics*, though not in the *Eudemian Ethics*, bravery, between recklessness and cowardice, is restricted to the battlefield (*EN* III 7 1115a32–5, *EE* III 1). The brave person has fear and confidence in the right way, at the right time, and so on. Aristotle distinguishes bravery from five other states that mimic bravery but are not. The brave human being acts 'for the sake of the fine',[60] a motive to be distinguished from acting merely for approval, or out of fear of penalties, or merely out of spirit or hopefulness or unawareness of the true nature of the situation, all of which are exemplified by the ersatz states. Given their devotion to the fine, the brave may not make the best soldiers, according to Aristotle. Conversely, those who have been considered the best soldiers may not have been brave.

Next is temperance, a virtue concerned with the pleasures of taste and especially touch. It is a mean between intemperance and insensibility.[61] Asceticism is not a virtue according to Aristotle.

Generosity (between stinginess and wastefulness) and magnificence (between niggardliness and vulgar ostentation) are paired together. Generosity concerns giving *and taking* on a small scale. Magnificence is the nearest virtue to modern philanthropy. It concerns public expenditure, and spending on large private expenditures such as weddings or building a house. Small items, such as a child's toy, can also be the subject of magnificence. Magnificence has an aesthetic side. The spending must be done tastefully.[62]

Magnanimity (or greatness of *psuchē*) is the good human being's 'crowning virtue'. The magnanimous individual has the right attitude to great honours, knows he is worthy of them and puts himself forward for high office. His apparent high-handedness has made him seem insufferably arrogant, and least congenial to modern sensibilities.[63] On closer inspection, he only seems arrogant because he has the correct view of what is important, which others lack, and because others, who lack all the virtues that he has, try to imitate his behaviour. While the pusillanimous person has low self-esteem and the vain person thinks too much of himself, the magnanimous person correctly assesses his own qualities and acts accordingly. He has the self-knowledge necessary to be virtuous.[64]

The next virtue, a nameless virtue concerned with honours on a small scale, between indifference to honour and honour-loving, only occurs in the *Nicomachean Ethics*. It complements the virtue of magnanimity as generosity does magnificence. It provides a niche for the good person who lives in a society where he lacks citizenship, and it also solves a contemporary debate between those who argued that indifference to honour is the virtue and those who thought honour-loving was the virtue. Each side failed to apply the doctrine of the mean and to see that there is a nameless virtue in between. While those

---

[59] For commentary on all of these virtues see Taylor 2006.

[60] For an aesthetic account of the fine, see, e.g. Richardson Lear 2006. For an account of the fine as instead involving concern for a common good, see Irwin 2007, especially 206–10.

[61] See S. White 1992: 159–197; Young 1988a.

[62] Cf. Wingo 1998.

[63] e.g. Taylor 2006: xx–xxi.

[64] For more, see Cooper 1989: 312–77; Curzer 1990; White 1992: 247–71; Annas 1993: 115–20; Pakaluk 2004; Crisp 2006.

on the extremes may claim the intermediate ground even when the mean is named, the phenomenon is clearer in the nameless case.

As a nameless virtue, between meekness and irascibility, mildness comes next in line in the *Nicomachean Ethics*, although in the *Eudemian Ethics* and *Magna Moralia* it is listed with courage and temperance instead (*EE* III 3, *MM* 1 22). As with the other 'nameless' virtues, Aristotle uses existing names, even if these do not apply exactly to the dispositions he wishes to point out. The term 'mildness' points more to the deficiency. Similarly, the term 'truthfulness' does not quite capture the point that the truthful person is discriminatingly truthful about, and in expressing, his own abilities when speaking, as opposed to the boastful or self-deprecating person. Being witty, between boorishness and buffoonery, is not simply a matter of delivery, but of knowing how to make and to appreciate jokes at the expense of those who deserve them. Friendliness, as distinguished from friendship (although the same term is used in the Greek), between quarrelsomeness and obsequiousness, does not require any special feeling of fondness for the people we meet. Also, it is not the part of the friendly person to be unfailingly pleasant; sometimes it is appropriate to cause pain. According to Aristotle, the friendly person will take a different attitude to familiar companions and strangers. Presumably, the point is not that the friendly person should be less pleasant to those he knows less well, but that different actions are appropriate to be pleasant to each.

In the *Eudemian Ethics*, consistently with the *Magna Moralia*, Aristotle argues that truthfulness, wit, and friendliness do not count as proper virtues because they do not involve choice.[65] It seems that Aristotle thinks of them as mere matters of temperament here, although later he sees that they require as much thought and discrimination as their named counterparts. Aristotle's *Nicomachean* account is also at odds with Kant's view that the social virtues are not virtues. One of Kant's complaints is that these virtues demand no self-control, but that is true of all the Aristotelian virtues of character, bravery included.[66] The good Aristotelian human being enjoys acting virtuously; his thinking and feelings are in sync.

Justice has a whole book to itself, common to both *Nicomachean* and *Eudemian Ethics* (*EN* V=*EE* IV).[67] Aristotle first distinguishes general justice, which is the whole of virtue of character 'as it relates to another' and particular justice. General justice covers everything that is legal in a good society; it need not imply that there are laws for everything. There are three types of particular justice, distributive justice, rectificatory justice, and justice in exchange. Distributive justice refers to the fair distribution of honours and wealth in society. The paradigm case of rectificatory justice is where an injured party receives damages in a law-court. Justice in exchange depends on proportionate reciprocity.[68] Aristotle demarcates the sphere of particular justice by pointing out a particular motive associated with particular *injustice*, the pleasure of making a profit, greed.[69]

---

[65] On these virtues, see Sorabji 1973–1974: 210–11; Fortenbaugh 1968; Engberg-Pedersen 1983: 86–93.

[66] Kant *LE* 236–7, *LE* 218. On the distinction between bravery/courage and self-control, see Young 2009: 445–7.

[67] See Jackson 1879; Williams 1980; Young 2006, 2009a; Curzer 1995.

[68] See Scaltsas 1995; Judson 1997. Also, Meikle 1995.

[69] On whether Aristotle succeeds in demarcating the sphere in this way, see e.g. Williams 1980; Young 1988.

Notoriously, Aristotelian particular justice is not a mean in the same way as are the other virtues. It concerns an intermediate position between two states of affairs, having too much for oneself while others have too little and having too little oneself while others have too much. In addition, it is impossible to do injustice to oneself according to Aristotle. Suicide, he argues, is an injustice *against the polis*. Given these views, and the thesis that while different political systems may have different laws, true or natural justice will be enshrined in the laws of the best political system, why then is justice not a virtue of institutions rather than of people? First, according to Aristotle, the correct laws will reflect the practical wisdom of the good person, so the good person's thinking is logically prior to the laws. Second, due to the universal nature of the laws, there will be situations where applying the laws strictly is unjust. In order to make just decisions, the good person needs to have equity, a disposition that is just, but superior to a certain way of being just (*EN* V 10, VI 11). In paying attention to the particulars of the situation, to the spirit rather than to the letter of the law, and by using sympathetic judgement, the equitable person is the embodiment of a person whose character is in a mean.[70]

3.5 PRACTICAL WISDOM AND VIRTUES OF THOUGHT

Aristotle begins Book VI of the *Nicomachean Ethics* (*EE* V) with a promise to clarify the nature of practical wisdom as it appears in the definition of virtue of character and the doctrine of the mean. He finds out what practical wisdom is by contrasting it with skill (*technē*) and other virtues of thought. Skills aim at products, whereas practical wisdom has action as the goal. Wisdom, comprising one type of understanding (*nous*) and knowledge (*epistēmē*), concerns necessary truths as opposed to the contingencies that are important to practical wisdom. What is known by wisdom can be represented by axioms (the subject matter of understanding), and deductive argument (the purview of knowledge), as in Euclidean geometry. Such a method is unsuitable for practical wisdom which cannot be represented as a deductive science and which concerns items that can be picked out by indexicals. Unlike comprehension (*sunesis*), a virtue of thought that merely concerns judging the words of others, practical wisdom is prescriptive. Practical wisdom concerns living well in general. In short, it is 'a state grasping the truth, involving reason, and concerned with action about human goods' (*EN* VI 5 1140b20–21).

Aristotle also explains that there are several types of practical wisdom relating to politics. Taking part in the polis will require deliberation, to make the right choices, comprehension, to follow speeches in the assembly or law-courts, and consideration (*gnōmē*) to judge fairly and equitably, a virtue that appeared in the Athenian jurors' oath.[71]

---

[70] On equity see Sherman 1989: 13–55; Nussbaum 1993: 92–7; Brunschwig 1996: 135–41.
[71] See Gifford 1995.

Comprehension is also the virtue needed to understand treatises on political systems (*EN* X 9 1181a17–19), and perhaps to understand Aristotle's *Nicomachean Ethics*. *Nous* is also mentioned as a type of understanding involved in practical reason.

At the beginning of the book, Aristotle says that the definition of virtue of character which mentions the person of practical wisdom is as unhelpful as saying that what is medical is what the doctor orders. The concluding chapter shows that this complaint misses the point. It is not possible to be more specific without gaining practical wisdom for oneself. The argument is as follows: It is not possible to have one virtue of character fully without having all the rest because they require and are required by practical wisdom. While the learner may act merely in *accordance with* the correct reason (*kata...logon*), following instructions, the fully virtuous person's disposition will *involve* the correct reason (*meta...logou*), thought and feelings being integrated. In this respect, becoming healthy and becoming good are disanalogous. One can become healthy simply by consulting the doctor and without learning medicine, but one cannot become good merely by consulting the local guru. Reading the *Nicomachean Ethics* is not sufficient. But is it necessary? It is a difficult question what exactly the good person has to know, and whether too much reflection impedes activity, like the fabled centipede who could no longer walk when she thought about how she did it.

The above is not the only possible interpretation of *Nicomachean Ethics* VI. In a second introduction, Aristotle divides the rational part of the soul into two further parts, one for theoretical and one for practical reasoning. On a different reading of the text, Aristotle's main aim is to prepare the reader to understand the superiority of wisdom (*sophia*) and its exercise (contemplation [*theōria*]) over practical wisdom, as presented in the puzzles at the end of the book (*EN* VI 12 1143b35–37 cf. 13 1145a6–12).[72]

3.6 PRACTICAL REASONING, CHOICE, AND *AKRASIA*

Aristotelian virtue of character involves choice, choice involves deliberation, and it is the mark of the person with practical wisdom to deliberate well. Chosen actions are all voluntary, as explained before. Aristotle defines choice as understanding combined with desire (*orektikos nous*) or desire combined with thought (*orexis dianoētikē*) (*EN* VI 2 1139a23, 1139b4, 5), showing the importance of each. Choice is deliberative desire, the result of deliberating about what to do in a particular situation, with a set goal in mind. For example, the doctor does not deliberate about whether to cure. That is because if she lacked the goal of curing she would not be a doctor. Similarly, the good person does not deliberate about whether to act virtuously, but will deliberate about what to do in order to achieve that goal in a particular situation. Aristotle describes deliberation in terms reminiscent of the doctrine of the mean, as 'correctness in accordance with what is

---

[72] See e.g. Burger 2008: 109–30, 207.

beneficial, about the right thing, in the right way and at the right time' (*EN* VI = *EE* V 9 1142b27). Deliberation itself is no mechanical process.[73]

In the case of the doctor, correct deliberation requires being a doctor and using some general knowledge. The doctor also needs to be able to perceive what needs to be done now for this particular patient. Having practical wisdom is analogous, but instead of having a skill, the agent has to be a certain kind of person, one who has the virtues, and must have the emotions and perception to pinpoint, for example, when someone is in need and when generosity is called for. Formulating this more precisely, we have the following practical syllogism.[74] The conclusion is the action, or the specification of an action, if the action is impeded:

> Universal Premise: Generous people help friends in need.
> Particular Premise: I'm a generous person. This is my friend in need. Now is the time to help, and so on.
> Conclusion: Help her.

It is because the agent is a generous person that the universal premise is applicable. That is why the first part of the particular premise is important. It explains why he acts as he does. It is possible to explain the point of being generous by reference to the agent's happiness, but it is implausible to think that the agent's happiness is a lodestone with reference to which the agent consciously makes all decisions.[75] The good person will only have the thoughts 'This is my friend in need. Now is the time to help' in mind when he acts. The indexicals are important for the syllogism to be *practical*.

Given the above formulation, how does the person with practical wisdom go wrong? According to Aristotle, someone with practical wisdom gets all stages in thinking and action correct.[76] Akratics lack practical wisdom. They are people who act voluntarily against their own better judgement. Socrates thought that there are no such people because knowledge cannot be dragged about like a slave.

Aristotle's explains that he will proceed by 'setting out the phenomena', then go through the puzzles, and then solve the puzzles, keeping as many as possible of the reputable beliefs (*endoxa*).[77] After describing a series of difficulties, Aristotle draws various distinctions to show a Socratic that he is wrong about the strength of knowledge. First, one can indeed have knowledge and not use it. Second, a person may have the appropriate universal premise but lack the relevant particular premise. Aristotle also shows that it is possible to combine the first two mistakes; one can go wrong by having, but not exercising, the particular premise. He then expands the first category to include those who are asleep or mad or drunk, and also those affected by strong emotions or sexual desires.

---

[73] See Wiggins 1975–1976; Tuozzo 1991; McDowell 2009, 41–58; Segvic 2009.

[74] The syllogism is speculative and controversial. See e.g. Anscombe 1957, 1965; Kenny 1973, 1979; Cooper 1975: 1–88; Charles 1984; Dahl 1984; Reeve 2006; Price 2008.

[75] Broadie 1991: 198–202 against 'the grand end view'.

[76] But see Bäck 2009.

[77] On Aristotle's philosophical method, see Kraut 2006a; Owen and Nussbaum 1986; 240–63; Barnes 1980; Irwin 1988; Cooper 2009.

Finally Aristotle explains that these people, like learners and actors, can recite the work of Empedocles without knowing what they are saying.

Aristotle's explanation of akrasia makes use of these distinctions, but his account is especially cryptic. It is therefore very controversial what his solution is, how many syllogisms, if any, are involved, and how far he agrees with Socrates after all.[78] The idea seems to be that the akratic has the universal premise, for example, 'Temperate people should avoid sweets' (at the appropriate time, in the appropriate way, and so on), but part of the minor premise 'This is sweet' is dragged off by appetite, on the grounds that all sweets are pleasant, and the akratic eats the sweet. If the akratic person formulates the correct conclusion that he should abstain from eating, he only says it as a learner or actor might. His understanding is 'kata logon' and not 'meta logou', to use Aristotle's earlier phrases.

3.7 PLEASURE

There are two discussions of pleasure, one in the second half of the common book *Nicomachean Ethics* VII = *Eudemian Ethics* VI, following the discussion of *akrasia*, and one in the first half of *Nicomachean Ethics* X.[79] Aristotle explains that pleasure is important to the political philosopher because virtues and vice concern pleasure and pain, and because most people think that happiness involves pleasure. Pleasure and pain are also important for moral education. In general, we get better at activities and judge them more accurately the more we enjoy them, and the more we enjoy them the better we get (*EN* X 1175a30–1175b1). Rawls develops Aristotle's insight into his 'Aristotelian Principle': 'Other things being equal, human beings enjoy the exercise of their realized capacities (their innate or trained abilities) and this enjoyment increases the more the capacity is realized, or the greater its complexity.'[80]

Earlier philosophers and medical writers thought that pleasure and pain were disturbances towards and away from the natural state (presumably, a state of physical equilibrium). Pain, for example, hunger, was a process leading away from the natural state, and pleasure, for example refilling one's stomach, was a process leading back to the natural state of being replete. This view of pleasure as a process towards a superior end led some to think that pleasure is not good at all. Aristotle disputes this account, arguing that it puts too much emphasis on eating as a pleasure, that some pleasures, for example the pleasure of doing mathematics or seeing, do not depend on prior pain, and that the body should not be the subject of pleasure. Pleasure is not remedial. We can enjoy activities even when we are in our natural state. Pleasure is not a process towards a superior natural state because it is not a process at all.

[78] See e.g. Natali 2009; Charles 2009; Price 2006; Bobonich and Destrée 2007; Pickavé and Whiting 2008; Gottlieb 2008: 207–11; Moss 2009; Dahl 2009; Pakaluk and Pearson 2011.
[79] See especially Urmson 1967; Austin 1968; Annas 1980; Gosling and Taylor 1982; Taylor 2008: 91–106, 107–20, 240–64; Natali 2008.
[80] Rawls 1971: 426.

So much is clear. However, Aristotle's positive account is more difficult to ascertain. In the early book, Aristotle says that pleasure is an unimpeded activity (*energeia*) of the natural state (*EN* VII 12 1153a14–15), but in book X he says that pleasure *completes* the activity as a sort of supervenient end (*EN* X 1174b30-33). In book X, Aristotle says that 'the pleasure is close to the activity, and so little distinguished from it that disputes arise about whether the activity is the same as the pleasure' (1175b1–3), suggesting that the account in book X is correcting the earlier account. It has been argued that in book VII, Aristotle is thinking of pleasure in the sense of 'gaming is one of my pleasures', whereas in book X he has in mind the fact that 'I get pleasure out of gaming'.[81] On the other hand, it has been argued that Aristotle always had the view that pleasure and gaming are distinct but conjoined activities.[82]

There is a second difficulty. While Aristotle's original distinction between processes and activities was meant to distinguish processes to and from the natural state from activities carried out when one is in a natural state, it is not clear that the distinction itself does all the work Aristotle requires. According to Aristotle, processes are incomplete until they reach their goal, whereas the goal of activities is intrinsic to them so that they are complete at any time (e.g. *EN* X 4). The problem is that a sophisticated process theorist might argue that when we see (supposedly an activity) we are also scanning the room (a process), or that when we are thinking (supposedly an activity) we are following a train of thought (a process).[83]

Whatever the solution, in book X Aristotle captures the phenomenology of pleasure well. When one is fully engrossed in an activity and doing it well, the activity is pleasurable.[84] There is no homogenous feeling of pleasure, on Aristotle's account. Different activities are pleasant in different ways. The good person is the judge of what to enjoy.

One scholar deems Aristotle's treatment of pleasure worthy of the Nobel Prize.[85] Although not without difficulties, it is perhaps the most sophisticated account of pleasure in the philosophical literature. It has a final brilliant implication. Happiness, activity of the soul carried out *well*, though not identical with pleasure, will be pleasurable.

3.8 FRIENDSHIP

There are three books on friendship (*philia*) in the corpus, *Nicomachean Ethics* VIII and XI, *Eudemian Ethics* VII, as well as a discussion in the *Magna Moralia*. Both *Eudemian* and *Nicomachean Ethics* address puzzles raised in Plato's *Lysis*, which was

---

[81] Owen 1971–1972.   [82] Irwin 1999: 270–1, 306.
[83] See *Metaph* IX 6 1048b18–35; Penner 1970; Taylor 1965.
[84] See Annas 2008 and Rudebusch 2009: 413–14 on the cross-cultural phenomenon of 'flow'.
[85] Frede 2006.

subtitled 'On Friendship' in ancient times.[86] According to Aristotle, a person cannot be friends with an inanimate object and needs friends in order to be self-sufficient. Aristotelian friendship covers lovers, family bonds, civic ties (which are based on usefulness), and relationships in general. Aristotle distinguishes three types of relationships, those for pleasure, those for usefulness, and those based on virtue of character. Friendship requires reciprocated goodwill, and awareness of that goodwill. Since only good people know what is really good and are able to wish that for their friends for the friends' own sake, the friendship of good people is the best type of friendship. Good people are trustworthy and reliable, and so their friendship endures. Good friends improve one another and share activities. They also gain self-knowledge from one another.[87] Good friends are also useful, because they help out when needed, and pleasant, since they have wit and other congenial Aristotelian virtues of character. Given the time and commitment needed to get to know someone's character, it is not possible to have many good friends.

A good friend, according to Aristotle, is 'another oneself'. Such a friend is not possessive or selfish. He loves his friend as he loves himself, when he loves himself in the correct way. Aristotle describes two types of self-love. The good self-lover gratifies his understanding and competes to do virtuous actions which will leave everyone better off. The bad self-lover goes after as much money, honours, and physical pleasures for himself as possible, harming himself and depriving his neighbours of their due. The good self-lover exhibits the mentality of Aristotle's good person, the bad self-lover exhibits the mentality of many of the excess vices on Aristotle's list. Presumably, there is no mention of the person with the vices of deficiency as it is hard to describe this person as a self-*lover*.

Aristotle's discussion raises various questions. Can bad people be devoted to one another in the same way as good people can?[88] Do good friends only care about their friends' good character or do they care about the very friends themselves?[89] Why does Aristotle think that friendship is not at odds with justice?[90] Is Aristotelian friendship too parochial? Should Aristotle restrict civic friendship to mere mutual advantage?[91]

In each work on friendship, Aristotle argues for a disanalogy between god and humans (*EE* VII 12 1245b18, *EN* VIII 7 1159a6–10, cf. MM II 15), but in the final book of the *Nicomachean Ethics* he appears to take a different tack.[92]

---

[86] See e.g. Annas 1977; Whiting 2006. On friendship in general, see Price 1989; Schollmeier 1994; Badhwar 1993; Stern-Gillet 1995; Pakaluk 1998, 2009; Smith-Pangle 2003.
[87] Cooper 1999: 336–55; Veltman 2004; Biss 2011; Osborne 2009.
[88] Cooper 1999: 312–35; Whiting 2006.   [89] Vlastos 1973; Whiting 1991.
[90] Curzer 2007.   [91] Curren 2000.
[92] e.g. Nussbaum 1986: 373–7; Jost 2009.

3.9 Happiness and 'A Sort of Politics' Revisited

At the end of the function argument of *Nicomachean Ethics* I, Aristotle concluded that happiness is exercising the human function *well*, i.e. in accordance with virtue, or, if there is more than one virtue, in accordance with the best and most complete/final virtue, but he had yet to identify the virtues or virtue at issue. By *Nicomachean Ethics* X, he has argued that there are two main virtues of thought, wisdom, the virtue of theoretical reasoning, and practical wisdom, the virtue of practical reasoning. There are also virtues of character which, in accordance with Aristotle's thesis about their unity, require and are required by practical wisdom. The conclusion of the function argument is therefore unclear. If Aristotle is saying that happiness is in accordance with the *most final* virtue, we might conclude that happiness is simply the exercise of theoretical thought, contemplation, in accord with the virtue of wisdom. On the other hand, if Aristotle is claiming that happiness is in accord with the *most complete* virtue, we might conclude that happiness covers a range of activities, involving the exercise of wisdom, practical wisdom, and virtues of character too.

On the face of it, in *Nicomachean Ethics* X, Aristotle is arguing that the best, because most godly, type of happiness is contemplation and the second best type is the exercise of practical wisdom and virtue of character, although even if contemplation is best, human beings, unlike gods, cannot spend all their time contemplating and so need virtue of character and external goods to deal with other aspects of their lives. The discussion is difficult, and many different interpretations have been canvassed.[93] If contemplation turns out to be happiness par excellence, why should the contemplator care about virtues of character?[94]

There is a prior problem. Given Aristotle's doctrine of the mean and his emphasis on the particulars of the situation and the abilities of particular individuals, it is puzzling why he is attempting an abstract ranking of types of happiness at all. On Aristotle's account, happiness for an individual should depend on that particular person's abilities and circumstances. Perhaps Aristotle's ranking is for the legislator rather than for the individual, to ensure that legislators provide education and laws for the citizens for peace no less than for wartime activities, and so that they do not forget to include contemplation for times of leisure,[95] whether or not it is suitable for all.

If so, Aristotle has returned full circle to ethics as a 'sort of politics'. He encourages his readers to consider different types of political arrangements next.[96, 97]

---

[93] See the inclusive/exclusive controversy discussed in the section on happiness.

[94] Kraut 1989 raises issues of egoism, Charles and Scott 1999 argue for structural similarities between virtuous activity and contemplation, and Richardson Lear 2004 argues that virtuous activities mirror contemplation. See too Cooper 2004: 302–8.

[95] On leisure as a neglected Aristotelian theme in modern times, and further comparison between ancient and modern ethics, see Broadie 2006. Garver 2006 highlights the alien, but accessible nature of Aristotle's thought.

[96] See Striker 2006 and Cooper 2010.   [97] Thanks to Roger Crisp for his help.

Table 1. Parallel Passages in the Ethical Works

Nicomachean Ethics (EN)	Eudemian Ethics (EE)	Magna Moralia (MM)
I Happiness	I	I 1–4, II 8
II Mean	II	I 5–9
III Moral Responsibility	II cont.	I 11–16
III 6–12; IV The Ethical Virtues	III	I 20–32
V Justice =	IV	I 33, II 1–2
VI Virtues of Thought =	V	I 34, II 1–3
VII *Akrasia* and Pleasure =	VI	II 4–6 and 7
VIII Friendship	VII Friendship	II 11–17
IX Friendship cont.		
X Pleasure, Happiness, Education, and Introduction to Politics	VIII Good luck, Fine-and-Goodness (The fine-and-good person, unlike the merely good person, cares about virtue for its own sake, and not merely for the sake of external goods), Happiness.	II 9 Fine-and-Goodness

BIBLIOGRAPHY

Ackrill, J. L. 1973. *Aristotle's Ethics*. Translation with notes. New York: Humanities Press.

—— 1974. 'Aristotle on *Eudaimonia*', reprinted in Rorty 1980, 15–33.

—— 1981. *Aristotle the Philosopher*. Oxford: Clarendon Press, especially 135–55.

—— 1997. *Essays on Plato and Aristotle*. Oxford: Oxford University Press.

Anagnostopoulos, G. 1994. *Aristotle on the Goals and Exactness of Ethics*. Berkeley: University of California Press.

—— (ed.) 2009. *A Companion to Aristotle*. Malden, MA: Oxford: Wiley-Blackwell.

Annas, J. 1976. *Aristotle's Metaphysics Books M and N*. Translation, introduction, and commentary. Oxford: Clarendon Press.

—— 1977. 'Plato and Aristotle on Friendship and Altruism', *Mind* 86: 532–54.

—— 1980. 'Aristotle on Pleasure and Goodness', in Rorty 1980, 285–300.

—— 1993. *The Morality of Happiness*. Oxford; New York: Oxford University Press.

—— 2004. 'Being Virtuous and Doing the Right Thing', *Presidential Address to the Pacific Division Meeting of the American Philosophical Association*.

—— 2008. 'The Phenomenology of Virtue', *Phenomenology and the Cognitive Sciences* 7 (1): 21–34.

Anscombe, G. E. M. 1957. *Intention*. Oxford: Blackwell.

—— 1958. 'Modern Moral Philosophy', reprinted in *Collected Philosophical Papers*, vol. 3. Minneapolis: University of Minnesota Press, 1981, 26–42.

—— 1965. 'Thought and Action in Aristotle', in Bambrough 1965, 143–58.

Anton, A. L. 2006. 'Breaking the Habit: Aristotle on Recidivism and How a Thoroughly Vicious Person Might Begin to Improve', *Philosophy in the Contemporary World* 13: 58–66.

Anton, J. P. and Preus, A. (eds), 1983 and 1991. *Essays in Ancient Greek Philosophy*, vols. 2 and 4. Albany: State University of New York Press.

Austin, J. 1968. 'Pleasure and Happiness', *Philosophy* 43: 51–62.

Austin, J. L. 1956–1957. 'A Plea for Excuses', *Proceedings of the Aristotelian Society* 19: 1–30.

Bäck, A. 2009. 'Mistakes of Reason: Practical Reasoning and the Fallacy of Accident', *Phronesis* 54: 101–35.

Badhwar, N. 1993. 'The Nature and Significance of Friendship', in N. Badhwar (ed.), *Friendship: A Philosophical Reader*. Cornell University Press, 1–36.

Bambrough, R. (ed.), 1965. *New Essays on Plato and Aristotle*. London: Routledge and Kegan Paul; New York: Humanities Press.

Barnes, J. 1980. 'Aristotle and the Methods of Ethics', *Revue Internationale de Philosophie* 37: 490–511.

——1984. *The Complete Works of Aristotle: The Revised Oxford Translation*. Princeton: Princeton University Press, vols. 1 and 2.

——Schofield, M., and Sorabji, R. (eds), 1977. *Articles on Aristotle: Ethics and Politics*, vol. 2. London: Duckworth.

Barney, R. 2008. 'Aristotle's Argument for a Human Function', *Oxford Studies in Ancient Philosophy* 34: 293–322.

Biss, M. 2011. 'Aristotle on Friendship and Self-Knowledge: The Friend beyond the Mirror', *History of Philosophy Quarterly* 28 (2): 125–40.

Bobonich, C. 2006. 'Aristotle's Ethical Treatises', in Kraut 2006 (ed.), 12–29.

——and Destrée, P. 2007. *Akrasia in Greek Philosophy*. Leiden: Brill.

Bosley, R., Shiner, R. A., and Sisson, J. D. (eds). 1995. *Aristotle, Virtue and the Mean. Apeiron* 25 (4).

Bostock, D. 2000. *Aristotle's Ethics*. Oxford: Oxford University Press.

Boudouris, K. J. (ed.) 1995. *Aristotelian Political Philosophy*, vols. 1 and 2. Athens: Ionia.

Broadie, S. 1991. *Ethics with Aristotle*. New York: Oxford University Press.

——2003. 'Aristotelian Piety', *Phronesis* 48 (1): 54–70.

——2006. 'Aristotle and Contemporary Ethics', in Kraut 2006 (ed.), 342–61.

——and Rowe, C. (eds). 2002. *Aristotle's Nicomachean Ethics*. Translation and Commentary. Oxford: Oxford University Press.

Brown, L. 1997. 'What is 'the mean relative to us' in Aristotle's Ethics?', *Phronesis* 42 (1): 77–93.

Brunschwig, J. 1996. 'Rule and Exception: On the Aristotelian Theory of Equity', in Frede and Striker 1996, 115–56.

Burger, R. 2008. *Aristotle's Dialogue with Socrates*. Chicago: University of Chicago.

Burnet, J. 1900. (ed.) with introduction and notes. *The Ethics of Aristotle*. London: Methuen.

Burnyeat, M. F. 1980. 'Aristotle on Learning to be Good', in Rorty 1980, 69–92.

——1984. 'Platonism and Mathematics. A Prelude to Discussion', in *Mathematics and Metaphysics in Aristotle (Mathematik und Metaphysik bei Aristoteles)*. Akten des 10. Symposium Aristotelicum Sigriswil, 6–12 September 1984, ed. Andreas Graeser. Bern; Stuttgart: Haupt, 1987, 213–40.

Card, C. 1996. *The Unnatural Lottery: Character and Moral Luck*. Philadelphia: Temple University Press.

——1999. 'Groping Through Gray Zones', in Card (ed.), *On Feminist Ethics and Politics*. Kansas: University Press of Kansas, 3–26.

Chappell, T. (ed.) 2006. *Values and Virtues: Aristotelianism in Contemporary Ethics* (Mind Association Occasional Series). Oxford: Oxford University Press.

Charles, D. O. M. 1984. *Aristotle's Philosophy of Action*. Ithaca: Cornell University Press.

——1986. 'Aristotle, Ontology and Moral Reasoning', *Oxford Studies in Ancient Philosophy* 4: 119–44.

—— 2009. 'Nicomachean Ethics VII. 3. Varieties of *Akrasia*', in Natali 2009, 41–71.

—— and Scott, D. 1999. 'Aristotle on Well-Being and Contemplation', *Proceedings of the Aristotelian Society, Suppl.* 73: 205–23; 225–42.

Clark, S. R. L. 1975. *Aristotle's Man: Speculations upon Aristotelian Anthropology*. Oxford: Clarendon Press.

Cooper, J. M. 1975. *Reason and Human Good in Aristotle*. Cambridge, MA: Harvard University Press.

—— 1999. *Reason and Emotion: Essays on Ancient Moral Psychology and Ethical Theory*. Princeton: Princeton University Press.

—— 2004. *Knowledge, Nature and the Good: Essays on Ancient Philosophy*. Princeton: Princeton University Press.

—— 2009. 'Nicomachean Ethics VII 1–2', in Natali 2009, 9–40.

—— 2010. 'Political Community and the Highest Good', in Lennox and Bolton 2010, 212–64.

—— 2012. *Pursuits of Wisdom: Six Ways of Life from Socrates to Plotinus*. Princeton: Princeton University Press, especially pp. 70–143.

Cooper, N. 1989. 'Aristotle's Crowning Virtue', *Apeiron* 22: 191–205.

Corcilius, K. 2008. 'Two Jobs for Aristotle's Practical Syllogism?', in Rapp and Brüllman 2008, 163–184.

Crisp, R. 1994. 'Aristotle's Inclusivism', *Oxford Studies in Ancient Philosophy* 12: 111–36.

—— 2000. *Aristotle's Nicomachean Ethics*. Translation and introduction. Cambridge: Cambridge University Press.

—— 2006. 'Aristotle on Greatness of the Soul', in Kraut 2006 (ed.), 158–79.

—— and Slote, M. 1997. *Virtue Ethics*. Oxford: Oxford University Press.

Curren, R. R. 2000. *Aristotle on the Necessity of Public Education*. Lanham; Boulder; New York; Oxford: Rowman and Littlefield.

Curzer, H. J. 1990. 'A Great Philosopher's Not so Great Account of Great Virtue: Aristotle's Treatment of "Greatness of Soul"', *Canadian Journal of Philosophy* 20 (4): 517–38.

—— 1991. 'The Supremely Happy Life in Aristotle's Nicomachean Ethics', *Apeiron* 24 (1): 47–69.

—— 1995. 'Aristotle's Account of the Virtue of Justice', *Apeiron* 28: 207–38.

—— 1996. 'A Defense of Aristotle's Doctrine of the Mean', *Ancient Philosophy* 16: 129–38.

—— 1996a. 'Aristotle's Mean Relative to Us', *American Catholic Philosophical Quarterly* 80: 507–19.

—— 2007. 'Aristotle: Founder of the Ethics of Care', *The Journal of Value Inquiry* 41: 221–43.

—— 2012. *Aristotle and the Virtues*. Oxford: Oxford University Press.

Dahl, N. O. 1984. *Practical Reason, Aristotle, and Weakness of the Will*. Minneapolis: University of Minnesota Press.

—— 2008. A book-length analysis of and commentary on Aristotle's *Nicomachean Ethics Book III* for Project Archelogos on the web at <www.archelogos.com>.

—— 2009. 'Aristotle on Action, Practical Reason, and Weakness of the Will', in Anagnostopoulos 2009, 498–511.

Devereux, D. T. 1981. 'Aristotle on the Essence of Happiness', in D. J. O'Meara (ed.), *Studies in Aristotle*. Washington, DC: Catholic University of America Press, 247–60.

—— 1986. 'Particular and Universal in Aristotle's Conception of Practical Knowledge', *Review of Metaphysics* 39 (3): 483–504.

Diogenes Laertius. 1959. *Lives of Eminent Philosophers*, vol. 1. Tr. R. D. Hicks. Cambridge, MA: Harvard University Press.

Düring, I. 1957. *Aristotle in the Ancient Biological Tradition*. Göteborg: Institute of Classical Studies at the University of Göteborg.

Engberg-Pedersen, T. 1983. *Aristotle's Theory of Moral Insight*. Oxford: Clarendon Press.

Engstrom, S. and Whiting, J. (eds), 1996. *Aristotle, Kant and the Stoics: Rethinking Happiness and Duty*. Cambridge: Cambridge University Press.

Fine, G. 1992. 'Aristotle's Criticisms of Plato', in J. C. Klagge and N. D. Smith (eds), *Methods of Interpreting Plato and his Dialogues*. Oxford Studies in Ancient Philosophy, supplementary volume, 13–41.

Flashar, H. 1965. 'Critique of Plato's Theory of Ideas in Aristotle's Ethics', reprinted in Barnes, Schofield, and Sorabji 1977, vol. 2. 1–16.

Foot, P. 1978. 'Virtues and Vices', in *Virtues and Vices and Other Essays in Moral Philosophy*. Berkeley: University of California Press, 1978, 1–18.

—— 2001. *Natural Goodness*. Oxford: Oxford University Press.

Fortenbaugh, W. W. 1968. 'Aristotle and the Questionable Mean-Dispositions', *Transactions of the American Philological Association* 99: 203–31.

Frede, D. 2006. 'Pleasure and Pain in Aristotle's Ethics', in Kraut 2006 (ed.), 255–75.

—— 2009. 'Nicomachean Ethics VII. 11–12: Pleasure', in Natali 2009, 183–208.

Frede, M. and Striker, G. (eds) 1996. *Rationality in Greek Thought*. Oxford: Oxford University Press.

Furley, D. J. 1967. 'Aristotle on the Voluntary', reprinted in Barnes, Schofield, and Sorabji 1977, 47–60.

Gardiner, S. 2005. *Virtue Ethics, Old and New*. Ithaca, New York: Cornell University Press.

Garver, E. 2006. *Confronting Aristotle's Ethics: Ancient and Modern Morality*. Chicago: Chicago University Press.

Gauthier, R. A. and Jolif, J. Y. 1958. *Aristote: L'Ethique à Nicomaque*. Translation with introduction and commentary. Paris, Louvain: Publications Universitaires, vols. 1 and 2.

Gentzler, J. 1998. *Method in Ancient Philosophy*. Oxford: Oxford University Press.

Gerson, L. 2004. 'Platonism in Aristotle's Ethics', *Oxford Studies in Ancient Philosophy* 27: 217–48.

—— 2006. *Aristotle and other Platonists*. Ithaca, NY: Cornell University Press.

Gifford, M. 1995. 'Nobility of Mind: The Political Dimension of Aristotle's Theory of Intellectual Virtue', in Boudouris 1995, vol. 1, 51–60.

Gill, C. (ed.) 2005. *Virtue, Norms and Objectivity: Issues in Ancient and Modern Ethics*. Oxford: Oxford University Press.

Glassen, P. 1957. 'A Fallacy in Aristotle's Argument about the Good', *Philosophical Quarterly* 7: 319–22.

Gómez-Lobo, A. 1989. 'The Ergon Inference', *Phronesis* 34 (2): 170–84.

Gosling, J. C. B. and Taylor. C. C. W. 1982. *The Greeks on Pleasure*. Oxford: Clarendon Press.

Gottlieb, P. 1991. 'Aristotle and Protagoras: The Good Human Being as the Measure of Goods', *Apeiron* 24 (1): 25–45.

—— 1996. 'Aristotle's Ethical Egoism', *Pacific Philosophical Quarterly* 77 (1): 1–18.

—— 2001. A book-length analysis of and commentary on Aristotle's *Nicomachean Ethics Books I and II* for Project Archelogos on the web at <www.archelogos.com>.

—— 2005. 'Aristotle's *Nicomachean Ethics*', in J. Shand (ed.), *Central Works of Philosophy*, vol 1: Ancient and Medieval Philosophy. Bucks, UK: Acumen Publishing, 46–68.

—— 2006. 'The Practical Syllogism', in Kraut 2006 (ed.), 218–33.

—— 2008. 'The Ethical Syllogism', in Rapp and Brüllman 2008, 197–212.

—— 2009. *The Virtue of Aristotle's Ethics*. Cambridge: Cambridge University Press.

Gourinat, J.-B. 2008. 'Is There Anything Logically Distinctive About Practical Syllogisms?', in Rapp and Brüllman 2008, 133–50.

Grant, A. 1874. *The Ethics of Aristotle*. Illustrated with Essays and Notes. Vol 1. 3rd edn. London: Longmans, Green and co.

Grene, M. 1963. *A Portrait of Aristotle*. Chicago: University of Chicago Press.

Halper, E. 1999. 'The Unity of the Virtues in Aristotle', *Oxford Studies in Ancient Philosophy* 17: 115–43.

Hankinson, R. J. (ed.) 1988. *Method, Medicine and Metaphysics: Studies in the Philosophy of Ancient Science, Apeiron* 21 (2).

Hardie, W. F. R. 1965. 'The Final Good in Aristotle's Ethics', in Moravscik 1967, 297–322.

—— 1980. *Aristotle's Ethical Theory*. 2nd edition. Oxford: Clarendon Press.

Harte, V. and M. Lane (eds) 2013. Politeia *in Greek and Roman Philosophy: A Festschrift for Malcolm Schofield*. Cambridge: Cambridge University Press.

Heinaman, R. 1988. '*Eudaimonia* and Self-Sufficiency in the *Nicomachean Ethics*', *Phronesis* 33 (1): 31–53.

—— 1993. 'Rationality, *Eudaimonia* and *Kakodaimonia* in Aristotle', *Phronesis* 38 (1): 31–56.

—— 1995. *Aristotle and Moral Realism: The Keeling Colloquia 1*. London: University College London Press.

—— 2003. *Plato and Aristotle's Ethics*. London: Ashgate.

—— 2009. 'Voluntary, Involuntary and Choice', in Anagnostopoulos 2009, 483–497.

Hippocrates. 1923. *Ancient Medicine and other works*, vol. 1. Tr. W. H. S. Jones, the Loeb Classical Library, Cambridge, MA: Harvard University Press.

Hursthouse, R. 1980–1981. 'A False Doctrine of the Mean', *Proceedings of the Aristotelian Society* 81: 57–92.

—— 1984. 'Acting and Feeling in Character: Nicomachean Ethics 3.i', *Phronesis* 29.3: 252–66.

—— 1999. *On Virtue Ethics*. Oxford: Oxford University Press.

—— 2006. 'The Central Doctrine of the Mean', in Kraut 2006 (ed.), 96–115.

——, Lawrence, G., and Quinn, W. (eds) 1995. *Virtues and Reasons: Philippa Foot and Moral Theory: Essays in Honour of Philippa Foot*. Oxford: Oxford University Press.

Hutchinson, D. S. 1986. *The Virtues of Aristotle*. London; New York: Routledge and Kegan Paul in association with Methuen.

Inwood, B. and Woolf, R. 2012. *Aristotle's Eudemian Ethics*. Translation, introduction, and notes. Cambridge Texts in the History of Philosophy. Cambridge: Cambridge University Press.

Irwin, T. H. 1980. 'The Metaphysical and Psychological Basis of Aristotle's Ethics', in Rorty 1980, 35–53.

—— 1985. *Aristotle's Nicomachean Ethics*. Translation and notes. Indianapolis: Hackett.

—— 1985a. 'Permanent Happiness: Aristotle and Solon', *Oxford Studies in Ancient Philosophy* 3: 89–124.

—— 1988. *Aristotle's First Principles*. Oxford: Clarendon Press (especially Part 3).

—— 1988a. 'Some Rational Aspects of Incontinence', *The Southern Journal of Philosophy* 27, supplementary volume, 49–88.

—— 1999. *Nicomachean Ethics*. Translation with introduction, notes and glossary. 2nd edn. Indianapolis: Hackett.

—— 2007-2009. *The Development of Ethics: A Historical and Critical Study*. 3 vols. Oxford: Oxford University Press.

Jackson, H. (ed.) 1879. *The Fifth Book of the Nicomachean Ethics of Aristotle*. Cambridge: Cambridge University Press.

Jaeger, W. 1923. *Aristotle: Fundamentals of the History of his Development*. Oxford: Oxford University Press. Reprinted 1962.

—— 1957. 'Aristotle's use of medicine as a model of method in his ethics', *Journal of Hellenic Studies* 77: 54–61.

Joachim, H. H. 1978. *Aristotle: The Nicomachean Ethics*. A commentary ed. D. A. Rees. Oxford: Clarendon Press.

Jost, L. 2009. '*Theōria*, *Theos* and *Therapeia* in Aristotle's Ethical Endings', presented to the *Society of Ancient Greek Philosophy*, December meeting.

Judson, L. 1997. 'Aristotle on Fair Exchange', *Oxford Studies in Ancient Philosophy* 15: 147–75.

Kant, I. Doctrine of Virtue (cited as 'DOV'). In *The Metaphysics of Morals*. Tr. and ed. Mary Gregor with introduction by Roger J. Sullivan. Cambridge: Cambridge University Press, 1996.

—— Lectures on Ethics (cited as 'LE'). Tr. Louis Infield with introduction by Lewis White Beck. Indianapolis: Hackett, 1963.

Kenny, A. 1965–1966. 'Aristotle on Happiness', in Barnes, Schofield, and Sorabji (eds), 1977, 25–32.

—— 1973. 'The Practical Syllogism and Incontinence', in *The Anatomy of the Soul: Historical Essays in the Philosophy of Mind*. Oxford: Blackwell, 1973, 28–50.

—— 1978. *The Aristotelian Ethics: A Study of the Relationship between the Eudemian and the Nicomachean Ethics of Aristotle*. Oxford: Clarendon Press.

—— 1979. *Aristotle's Theory of the Will*. London: Duckworth.

—— 1992. *Aristotle on the Perfect Life*. Oxford: Clarendon Press.

—— 2011. *Aristotle: The Eudemian Ethics*. Translation with an introduction and notes. Oxford: Oxford University Press.

Keyt, D. 1983. 'Intellectualism in Aristotle', in Anton and Preus 1983, 364–87.

—— and Miller, F. (eds) 1991. *A Companion to Aristotle's Politics*. Oxford; Cambridge, MA: Blackwell.

Korsgaard, C. M. 1986. 'Aristotle and Kant on the source of Value', *Ethics* 96: 486–505.

—— 2008. *The constitution of agency: essays on practical reason and moral psychology*. Oxford; New York: Oxford University Press.

Kosman, L. A. 1968. 'Predicating the Good', *Phronesis* 13 (2): 171–4.

—— 1980. 'Being Properly Affected: Virtues and Feelings in Aristotle's Ethics', in Rorty 1980, 103–16.

Kraut, R. 1976. 'Aristotle on Choosing Virtue for Itself', *Archiv für Geschichte der Philosophie* 58: 223–39.

—— 1989. *Aristotle on the Human Good*. Princeton: Princeton University Press.

—— 1997. *Politics, Books VII and VIII*. Oxford: Oxford University Press.

—— 1998. 'Aristotle on Method and Moral Education', in Gentzler 1998, 271–90.

—— 2002. *Aristotle: Political Philosophy*. Oxford; New York: Oxford University Press.

—— 2006a. 'How to Justify Ethical Propositions: Aristotle's Method', in Kraut (ed.) 2006, 76–95.

—— 2010. 'Aristotle's Ethics', *Stanford Encyclopedia of Philosophy*, <http://plato.stanford.edu/entries/aristotle-ethics>.

—— (ed), 2006. *The Blackwell Guide to Aristotle's* Nicomachean Ethics. Oxford: Blackwell.

—— 2013. 'An Aesthetic Reading of Aristotle's Ethics,' in Harte and Lane (eds), 231–50.

Lännström, A. 2006. *Loving the Fine: Virtue and Happiness in Aristotle's Ethics*. Notre Dame, IN: University of Notre Dame Press.

Lawrence, G. 1993. 'Aristotle and the Ideal Life', *Philosophical Review* 102.1: 1–34.

—— 1997. 'Nonaggregability, Inclusiveness, and the Theory of Focal Value: *Nicomachean Ethics* I. 7. 1097b16–20', *Phronesis* 42 (1): 32–76.

—— 2006. 'Human Good and Human Function', in Kraut 2006 (ed.), 37–75.

Lawrence, G. 2009. 'Is Aristotle's Function Argument Fallacious? Part 1, Groundwork: Initial Clarification of Objections', *Philosophical Inquiry* 31: 191–224.

—— 2009a. 'Human Excellence in Character and Intellect', in Anagnostopoulos 2009, 419–41.

—— 2011. 'Acquiring Character: Becoming Grown-Up', in Pakaluk and Pearson 2011, 233–83.

Lear, G. R. 2004. *Happy Lives and the Highest Good: An Essay on Aristotle's* Nicomachean Ethics. Princeton: Princeton University Press.

—— 2006. 'Aristotle on Moral Virtue and the Fine', in Kraut 2006 (ed.), 116–36.

—— 2009. 'Happiness and the Structure of Ends', in Anagnostopoulos 2009, 387–403.

Leighton, S. 1992. 'Relativizing Moral Excellence in Aristotle', *Apeiron* 25: 49–66.

—— 1995. 'The Mean Relative to Us', in Bosley, Shiner, and Sissons 1995, 67–78.

Lennox, J. and Bolton, R. 2010. *Being, Nature, and Life: Essays in Honor of Allan Gotthelf.* Cambridge: Cambridge University Press.

Lloyd, G. E. R. 1968. 'The role of medical and biological analogies in Aristotle's ethics', *Phronesis* 13 (1): 68–83.

Lockwood, T. 2005. 'A Topical Bibliography of Scholarship on Aristotle's Nicomachean Ethics: 1880 to 2004', *Journal of Philosophical Research* 30: 1–116.

Long, A. A. 1991. 'The Harmonics of Stoic Virtue', in H. Blumenthal and H. Robinson (eds), *Aristotle and the Later Tradition. Oxford Studies in Ancient Philosophy*, supplementary volume, 97–116.

Lorenz, H. 2006. *The Brute Within: Appetitive Desire in Plato and Aristotle.* Oxford: Oxford University Press, especially 187–201.

—— 2009. 'Virtue of Character in Aristotle's Nicomachean Ethics', *Oxford Studies in Ancient Philosophy* 37: 177–252.

Losin, P. 1987. 'Aristotle's Doctrine of the Mean', *History of Philosophy Quarterly* 4 (3): 329–41.

McDowell, J. 1979. 'Virtue and Reason', *Monist* 62: 331–50.

—— 1980. 'The role of Eudaimonia in Aristotle's Ethics', in Rorty 1980, 359–76.

—— 1995. 'Two Sorts of Naturalism', in Hursthouse, Lawrence, and Quinn 1995, 149–79.

—— 2009. *The Engaged Intellect: Philosophical Essays.* Cambridge: Cambridge University Press.

MacIntyre, A. 1981. *After Virtue.* Notre Dame: Notre Dame University Press.

Meikle, S. 1995. *Aristotle's Economic Thought.* Oxford: Oxford University Press. Reprinted, 2002.

Meyer, S. Sauvé. 1993. *Aristotle on Moral Responsiblity: Character and Cause.* New York: Blackwell (to be reissued with a new introduction by Oxford University Press, 2012).

—— 2006. 'Aristotle on the Voluntary', in Kraut 2006 (ed.), 137–57.

—— 2008. *Ancient Ethics: A Critical Introduction.* New York; Oxford: Routledge, 50–94.

Mill, J. S. 1962. *Utilitarianism, On Liberty, Essay on Bentham and selected writings of Jeremy Bentham and John Austin.* Ed. with introduction by Mary Warnock. Glasgow: Collins.

Miller, F. D. 2003. 'Aristotle: Ethics and Politics', in Shields 2003, 184–210.

Miller, J. (ed.) 2011. *Aristotle's Nicomachean Ethics: A Critical Guide.* Cambridge: Cambridge University Press.

Moravscik, J. M. E. (ed.) 1967. *Aristotle: A Collection of Critical Essays.* Garden City, New York: Doubleday.

Morel, P.-M. 2008. 'The Practical Syllogism in Context: *De Motu* 7 and Zoology', in Rapp and Brüllman (eds), 2008, 184–96.

Moss, J. 2009. '*Akrasia* and Perceptual Illusion', *Archiv Für Geschichte der Philosophie* 91 (2): 119–56.

Müller, A. 2008. 'Formal and Material Goodness in Action. Reflections on an Aristotelian Analogy between Cognitive and Practical Teleology', in Rapp and Brüllman 2008, 213–28.

Natali, C. 1999. Aristotele. *Etica Nicomachea*. Introduzione, traduzione e note. Laterza: Roma-Bari.

—— 2001. *The Wisdom of Aristotle*. Translated by Gerald Parks. Albany: State University of New York Press.

—— 2008. A book-length analysis of and commentary on Aristotle's *Nicomachean Ethics* Book X for Project Archelogos on the web at <www.archelogos.com>.

—— (ed.) 2009. *Aristotle's Nicomachean Ethics Book VII: Symposium Aristotelicum*. Oxford: Oxford University Press.

Nielsen, K. 2007. 'Dirtying Aristotle's Hands? Aristotle's Analysis of "Mixed Acts" in the *Nicomachean Ethics* III 1', *Phronesis* 52 (3): 270–300.

Nussbaum, M. C. 1986. *The Fragility of Goodness: Luck and Ethics in Greek Tragedy and Philosophy*. Cambridge: Cambridge University Press.

—— 1993. 'Equity and Mercy', *Philosophy and Public Affairs* 22 (1): 83–125.

O'Meara, D. J. (ed.) 1981. *Studies in Aristotle*. Washington, DC: Catholic University of America Press.

Ober, J. 1998. *Political Dissent in Democratic Athens: intellectual critics of popular virtue*. Princeton: Princeton University Press.

Osborne, C. 2009. 'Selves and Other Selves in Aristotle's EE vii 12', *Ancient Philosophy* 29: 349–71.

Owen, G. E. L. 1971–1972. 'Aristotelian Pleasures', in Barnes, Schofield, and Sorabji 1977, 92–103.

—— 1986a. '*Tithenai ta phainomena*', in G. E. L. Owen and M. Nussbaum 1986, 239–51.

—— and Nussbaum, M. (eds) 1986. *Logic, Science and Dialectic*. Cambridge: Cambridge University Press.

Pakaluk, M. 1995. Review of Anthony Kenny *Aristotle on the Perfect Life*. Ancient Philosophy 15: 233–44.

—— 1998. *Nicomachean Ethics* VIII and IX. Translation and commentary. Oxford: Oxford University Press.

—— 2004. 'The Meaning of Aristotelian Magnanimity', *Oxford Studies in Ancient Philosophy* 26: 241–75.

—— 2005. *Aristotle's Nicomachean Ethics: An Introduction*. Cambridge: Cambridge University Press.

—— 2009. 'Friendship', in Anagnostopoulos 2009, 471–82.

—— and Pearson, G. (ed.) 2011. *Moral Psychology and Human Action in Aristotle*. Oxford: Oxford University Press.

Pears, D. 1980. 'Courage as a Mean', in Rorty 1980, 171–87.

Penner, T. M. I. 1970. 'Verbs and the Identity of Actions: A Philosophical Exercise in the Interpretation of Aristotle', in Wood and Pitcher 1970, 393–460.

Pickavé, M. and Whiting, J. 2008. '*Nicomachean Ethics* 7.3 on Akratic Ignorance', *Oxford Studies in Ancient Philosophy* 34: 323–72.

Prichard, H. A. 1935. 'The meaning of agathon in the Ethics of Aristotle', in Moravscik 1967, 241–60.

Price, A. W. 1989. *Love and Friendship in Plato and Aristotle*. Oxford: Clarendon Press.

—— 1995. *Mental Conflict*. London: Routledge.

Price, A. W. 2006. 'Acrasia and Self-Control', in Kraut (ed.) 2006, 234–54.

—— 2008. 'The Practical Syllogism in Aristotle: A New Interpretation', in Rapp and Brüllman 2008, 151–62.

—— 2011. *Virtue and Reason in Plato and Aristotle*. Oxford: Oxford University Press.

Rackham, H. 1935 (Tr.) *Aristotle: The Athenian Constitution, The Eudemian Ethics and On Virtue and Vices*. The Loeb Classical Library. Cambridge, MA: Harvard University Press, revised 1952, reprinted 1982, vol. 20.

Rapp, C. 2006. 'What use is Aristotle's doctrine of the mean?', in Reiss 2006, 99–126.

—— and Brüllman, Philipp (eds) 2008. *Philosophiegeschichte und Logische Analyse/Logical Analysis and History of Philosophy Focus: The Practical Syllogism/Schwerpunkt: Der praktische Syllogismus.*

Rawls, J. 1971. *A Theory of Justice*. Cambridge, MA: Harvard University Press.

Reis, B. 2006. *The Virtuous Life in Greek Ethics*. Cambridge: Cambridge University Press.

Reeve, C. D. C. 1992. *Practices of Reason*. Oxford: Oxford University Press.

—— 2006. 'Aristotle on the Virtues of Thought', in Kraut 2006 (ed.), 198–217.

Roberts, J. 1989. 'Political Animals in the *Nicomachean Ethics*', *Phronesis* 34 (2): 185–204.

Richardson, H. S. 1994. *Practical Reasoning about Final Ends*. Cambridge, MA: Cambridge University Press.

Roche, T. D. 1988. '*Ergon* and *Eudaimonia* in *Nicomachean Ethics* I: Reconsidering the Intellectualist Interpretation', *Journal of the History of Philosophy* 26: 175–94.

Rorty, A. O. (ed.) 1980. *Essays on Aristotle's Ethics*. Berkeley and Los Angeles: University of California Press.

Ross, W. D. 1923. Translation of Aristotle's *Nicomachean Ethics*, revised with an introduction by Lesley Brown, Oxford: Oxford University Press, 2009. (The original translation is on the web, for example, at the Internet Classics Archive.)

Rowe, C. J. 1971. *The Eudemian and Nicomachean Ethics: A Study in the Development of Aristotle's Thought*. Cambridge: Cambridge Philological Society. Supplement no. 2.

—— 1975. 'A Reply to John Cooper on the *Magna Moralia*', *American Journal of Philology* 96: 160–72.

Rudebusch, G. 2009. 'Pleasure', in Anagnostopoulos 2009, 404–19.

Sachs, J. 2001. *Aristotle's Nicomachean Ethics*. Translation, glossary, and introductory essay. Newbury Port, MA: Focus Publishing, R. Pullins company.

Santas, G. 2001. *Goodness and Justice: Plato, Aristotle, and the Moderns*. Malden, MA: Blackwell.

Scaltas, T. 1995. 'Reciprocal Justice in Aristotle's *Nicomachean Ethics*', *Archiv Für Geschichte der Philosophie* 77: 248–62.

Schofield, M. 2006. 'Aristotle's Political Ethics', in Kraut 2006 (ed.), 305–22.

Schollmeier, P. 1994. *Other Selves: Aristotle on Personal and Political Friendship*. Albany: State University of New York Press.

Segvic, H. 2009. *From Protagoras to Aristotle: Essays in Ancient Moral Philosophy*, ed. Myles Burnyeat with introduction by Charles Brittain. Princeton: Princeton University Press.

Sherman, N. 1989. *The Fabric of Character: Aristotle's Theory of Virtue*. Oxford: Clarendon Press.

—— 1997. *Making a Necessity of Virtue: Aristotle and Kant on Virtue*. Cambridge: Cambridge University Press.

Shields, C. J. 1999. *Order in multiplicity: Homonymy in the philosophy of Aristotle*. Oxford: Oxford University Press.

—— (ed.) 2003. *The Blackwell Guide to Ancient Philosophy*. Oxford: Blackwell.

—— 2007. *Aristotle*. London: Routledge, especially 306–49.

Sim, M. 2007. *Remastering Morals in Aristotle and Confucius*. Cambridge: Cambridge University Press.

Smith-Pangle, L. 2003. *Aristotle and the Philosophy of Friendship*. Cambridge: Cambridge University Press.

Sorabji, R. 1973–1974. 'Aristotle on the Role of Intellect in Virtue', reprinted in Rorty 1980, 201–19.

—— 1980. *Necessity, Cause and Blame: Perspectives in Aristotle's Theory*. Ithaca: Cornell University Press.

Stern-Gillet, S. 1995. *Aristotle's Philosophy of Friendship*. New York: SUNY Press.

Stewart, J. A. 1892. *Notes on the Nicomachean Ethics*. Oxford: Clarendon Press, vols. 1 and 2.

Stocker, M. 1990. *Plural and Conflicting Values*. Oxford: Oxford University Press.

Striker, G. 2006. 'Aristotle's Ethics as Political Science', in Reis 2006, 127–41.

Taylor, C. C. W. 1965. 'States, Activities and Performances', *Proceedings of the Aristotelian Society suppl.* 39: 85–102.

—— 2006. *Aristotle: Nicomachean Ethics Books II–IV*. Translation with an introduction and commentary. Oxford: Clarendon Press.

—— 2008. *Pleasure, Mind, and Soul: Selected Papers in Ancient Philosophy*. Oxford: Clarendon Press.

Thomson, J. A. K. 1976. *Aristotle's Nicomachean Ethics*. Translation with appendices by Hugh Tredennick and introduction and bibliography by Jonathan Barnes. Middlesex, England: Penguin.

Tuozzo, T. M. 1991. 'Aristotelian Deliberation is not of Ends', in Anton and Preus 1991, 193–212.

—— 1996. 'The Function of Human Beings and the Rationality of the Universe: Aristotle and Zeno on Parts and Wholes', *Phoenix* 50, 146–61.

Urmson, J. O. 1967. 'Aristotle on Pleasure', in Moravscik 1967, 323–33.

—— 1973. 'Aristotle's Doctrine of the Mean', reprinted in Rorty 1980, 157–70.

—— 1988. *Aristotle's Ethics*. New York: Basil Blackwell.

Vasiliou, I. 1996. 'The Role of Good Upbringing in Aristotle's Ethics', *Philosophy and Phenomenological Research* 56: 771–97.

Veltman, A. 2004. 'Aristotle and Kant on Self-Disclosure in Friendship', *Journal of Value Inquiry* 38 (2): 225–39.

Vlastos, G. 1973. 'The Individual as Object of Love in Plato', in Vlastos 1973a, 3–42.

—— 1973a. *Platonic Studies*. Princeton: Princeton University Press.

Vranas, P. B. M. 2005. 'Aristotle on the Best Good: Is *Nicomachean Ethics* 1094a18–22 fallacious?', *Phronesis* 50: 116–28.

White, N. P. 1988. 'Good as Goal', *The Southern Journal of Philosophy* 27, supplementary volume, 169–93.

—— 2002. *Individual and Conflict in Greek Ethics*. Oxford: Clarendon Press.

White, S. A. 1992. *Sovereign Virtue: Aristotle on the Relation between Happiness and Prosperity*. Stanford, California: Stanford University Press.

Whiting, J. E. 1986. 'Human Nature and Intellectualism in Aristotle', *Archiv für Geschichte der Philosophie* 68: 70–95.

—— 1988. 'Aristotle's Function Argument: A Defense', *Ancient Philosophy* 8.1: 33–48.

—— 1991. 'Impersonal Friends', *Monist* 74 (1): 3–29.

—— 2006. 'The Nicomachean Account of *Philia*', in Kraut 2006 (ed.), 276–304.

Wians, W. (ed.) 1996. *Aristotle's Philosophical Development*. London: Rowman and Littlefield.

Wiggins, D. 1975–1976. 'Deliberation and Practical Reasoning', in Rorty 1980, 221–40.

—— 2009. 'What Is the Order Among the Varieties of Goodness? A Question Posed by Von Wright; and a Conjecture Made by Aristotle', *Philosophy* 84: 175–200.

Wilkes, K. 1978. 'The Good Man and the Good for Man in Aristotle's Ethics', reprinted in Rorty 1980, 341–58.

Williams, B. A. O. 1980. 'Justice as a Virtue', in Rorty 1980, 189–99.

—— 1985. *Ethics and the Limits of Philosophy*. Cambridge, MA: Harvard University Press.

Wingo, A. H. 1998. 'African Art and the Aesthetics of Hiding and Revealing', *British Journal of Aesthetics* 38 (3): 251–64.

Winter, M. 1997. 'Aristotle, Hōs Epi to Polu Relations, and a Demonstrative Science of Ethics', *Phronesis* 42 (2): 163–89.

Wood, O. P. and Pitcher, G. W. 1970. *Ryle: A Collection of Critical Essays*. New York: Doubleday.

Woods, M. J. 1992. *Aristotle's Eudemian Ethics Books I, II and VIII*. 2nd edn. Oxford: Clarendon Press. (First edn., 1982.)

Young, C. 1988. 'Aristotle on Justice', *Proceedings of the Spindel Conference, Southern Journal of Philosophy* 27, suppl. 233–49.

—— 1988a. 'Aristotle on Temperance', *Philosophical Review* 97: 521–42.

—— 1996. 'The Doctrine of the Mean', *Topoi* 15: 89–99.

—— 2006. 'Aristotle's Justice', in Kraut 2006 (ed.), 179–97.

—— 2009. 'Courage', in Anagnostopoulos 2009, 442–56.

—— 2009a. 'Justice', in Anagnostopoulos 2009, 457–70.

Yount, D. 1998. 'Plato v. Aristotle: Is the Form of the Good Relevant to Ethics?', Ph.D. thesis, University of Wisconsin-Madison.

Yu, J. 2007. *The Ethics of Confucius and Aristotle: Mirrors of Virtue*. New York: Routledge.

CHAPTER 4

··

EPICURUS: FREEDOM, DEATH, AND HEDONISM

··

PHILLIP MITSIS

EPICURUS (341–270 BCE) first gave shape to three powerful and interconnected strains of argument that, at different periods in the subsequent history of ethical thought, have remained at the heart of productive philosophical controversy. So, for instance, his views about the nature of pleasure and its role in ethics, first fully recovered by Gassendi, and then taken over at least in part by a long tradition of thinkers from Locke to Mill, have featured prominently in debates between hedonists and their critics over the past several centuries. By the same token, the Epicureans were arguably the first to formulate an incompatibilist defence of the freedom of choice. This defence was grounded, moreover, in a particular view of rational human agency that has been subsequently adopted not just by incompatibilists, but perhaps more surprisingly (again through the influence of Gassendi and then Locke) by a long tradition of compatibilists as well. Moreover, what Epicurus thought to be his most important ethical discovery—that death is not to be feared because it is merely our annihilation and as such in no way harms us—although being mostly derided or ignored by countless generations of philosophers convinced of their own immortality, has become the one ancient philosophical argument still most capable of capturing the attention of some of our most technically skilled contemporary philosophers, at least if one is to judge by the ever increasing and increasingly sophisticated literature devoted to addressing it.

The Epicureans, like their ancient Stoic counterparts, believed that philosophy needs to be rigorously systematic and that their ethical claims not only depend on the truth of their epistemological, physical, and metaphysical doctrines, but that these, in turn, depend on the truth of their ethical arguments. Unlike the Stoics, however, they do not seem to have been especially committed to a particular order in the exposition of topics, either for reasons of pedagogy or for justification. It will therefore perhaps be helpful to begin with the Epicurean account of freedom of choice, not only because it proved to be enduringly philosophically influential, but also because it allows us to see some of the larger contours of Epicurus'

ethical aims in the context of his materialism. It also can serve as a salient point of departure for gauging the overall plausibility of his general project of 'naturalizing reason', to use
a contemporary slogan Epicurus might well have endorsed.

4.1 FREEDOM, RATIONALITY,
AND THE VOLUNTARY

In 1967 Pamela Huby published an article entitled 'The First Discovery of the Freewill
Problem' in which she argued that the ancient Epicureans should be credited for discovering the 'modern' conception of free will and along with it, the resultant problem
of defending it in the face of determinism. By 'modern', she meant the view that we are
free just in so far as that, at the moment of choice, we are sufficiently unencumbered
by prior determining factors to be able to choose freely between the alternatives of
doing x or not x. As we shall see, it is by no means clear how coherently the Epicureans
themselves could hope to defend such an account of freedom in the context of their
own materialism. But if they could not be credited with offering a completely compelling defence of such a conception of freedom, they at least could be credited with discovering it and making an initial attempt to preserve it against the perceived threat of
determinism. Huby was no doubt correct in claiming that earlier Greek philosophers
had not felt the problems raised by determinism in quite the same way, in part because
most had not been forced by their physical theories to account for human freedom in
a world of blind material motions. True, there had been earlier Greek materialists,
such as Democritus, but he seemed merely to deny the possibility of free choice and
was sceptical in general, moreover, about any evidence derived from the world of phenomenal experience. It was because of Epicurus' twin commitments to atomism and
to the phenomenology of human free choice, Huby argued, that he was induced to
first formulate the problem of free will in a form readily recognizable to modern philosophers. Such had not been the case with Plato and Aristotle, for instance, whose
accounts of human agency were grounded in teleological categories that tend to
bypass the kinds of tensions that Epicurus had discovered looming between our free
voluntary movements and the causally determined movements of matter stretching
back eternally. In a sense, in arguing that the Epicureans discovered the free will problem, Huby was giving voice to a tradition stemming back to early modern discussions.
At the very beginnings of Epicurean scholarship in the seventeenth century, Gassendi
had argued that Epicurus' introduction of indeterminacies or random swerves in the
movements of atoms in order to deflect the threats of determinism and fatalism was
ill-conceived and that it conflicted with the manifest non-arbitrariness of God's providence. But even though rejecting this feature of the Epicurean account, he nevertheless took the Epicureans to be early proponents of what eventually came to be called
an incompatibilist defence of our freedom of choice.

One strong tradition of interpreting Epicurus' account had long affirmed Huby's claim that Epicureans hold a contra-causal account of free will and its supporting scholarship, for the most part, has tried to understand how to construe the relations between our phenomenal experiences of free will and the indeterminacies Epicureans postulated at the atomic level in order to preserve them (Sedley 1983; Englert 1987; Asmis 1990; Fowler 2002). If atomic indeterminacies are completely random, how, for example, are we to understand their effects on human action in a way that does not make our choices themselves appear correspondingly arbitrary and random? Or how can randomness at the atomic level itself be smoothly correlated with deliberate human choices at the phenomenal level in a way that is not merely question begging? In the same year that Huby's article appeared, however, David Furley, in part worried by what he saw as the implausibility of such a project, attempted to close the gap between Epicurus' understanding of freedom of choice and those of his predecessors, especially Aristotle (Furley 1967). He argued that Epicurus' account of voluntary action is better understood in the light of Aristotle's theory of the voluntary and the causal dependence of voluntary actions upon character. He concluded that Epicurus, like Aristotle, was neither interested nor aware of any conception of contra-causal freedom guaranteeing individual instances of free choice. Rather, for the Epicureans, our actions can be sufficiently described as voluntary if they flow causally from our characters. To the extent that Epicureans were worried about the problems of determinism, such worries could be displaced from the mechanisms involved in our individual ongoing choices between alternatives to those that form our characters more generally. As a result, Epicurus, he argued, must have postulated randomness at the atomic level because of a worry that our characters themselves might be determined by prior causal conditions stretching back far beyond our control. While not attributing to the Epicureans an entirely coherent theory—why, for instance, should I be held any more responsible for my character if it has been altered previously by atomic interventions that are themselves purely random?—it at least freed them from the implausibility of trying to correlate each and every instance of deliberate human choice with a corresponding indeterminate atomic event. Moreover, Furley's account lent some indirect luster to Epicureanism as a whole, since by focusing on the mechanisms of character formation Epicureans could now be admitted, albeit somewhat awkwardly because of their hedonism, into the exciting new conversations surrounding virtue ethics at the time. It also seemed to allow scholars to re-embed Epicurus into his putative intellectual milieu more generally, something that recently has been of particular concern to Suzanne Bobzien, who has argued that no ancient Greek philosopher, at least through the period that included the Hellenistic Stoa and Garden, ever conceived of human freedom in terms of choosing between alternatives (Bobzien 1998; 2000). Like Alasdair MacIntyre and others who have seen a deep divide between ancient and modern conceptions of both the will and the self, Bobzien has been keen to show that in fact there was no discovery of the free will problem in this period of antiquity since none of its philosophers, including the Epicureans, held a conception of free will in the required contra-causal sense.

In order to get our initial bearings on this dispute, it might be helpful to turn to a passage from the fourth book of *De rerum natura* (*DRN*) by the Roman Epicurean poet, Lucretius (c.99–55 BCE). Given the lamentable paucity of evidence in the remains of Epicurus' own writings, questions of its interpretation have featured centrally in these two dominant approaches to his theory. Caution is in order, however, since key features of Lucretius' Latin, such as the critically important notion of '*voluntas*' ('will' or 'volition') described here, have no straightforward equivalent in Epicurus' Greek, and in fact may be Lucretius' own philosophical coinage. Nor do the exigencies of his poetic metre and expression always allow us to sort out the exact relation that is supposed to hold between various items in the causal mechanisms he describes. These problems have perhaps exercised proponents of these two interpretations less than they should, but to set the argumentative context, in the midst of giving material explanations of a series of human functions such as thirst, perspiration, sex, etc., Lucretius turns his attention to the material mechanisms of voluntary movements, in this case, walking:

> Now I shall tell you—and mark what I say—how it comes about that we can take steps forward when we want to, by what means it is given to us to move our limbs, and what it is that regularly pushes forward this great bulk of our body. First let me say that the images of walking impinge on our mind and strike it, as I explained earlier. After this, volition (*voluntas*) occurs. For no one embarks on any course of action before the mind first has previewed what it wants to do. And an image exists of whatever it previews. So when the mind stirs itself to want to go forwards, it immediately strikes all the force of the spirit distributed all over the body throughout the limbs and frame: it is easily done, because the spirit is conjoined with it. Then the spirit in turn strikes the body, and thus gradually the whole bulk is pushed on and moves forward. (*DRN* 877–891. Trans. Long and Sedley, 14E; modified)

At first glance, this passage seems to describe a fairly straightforward stimulus/response model of voluntary motion that makes no particular room for choices between alternatives. The mind previews what it wants to do, is struck by the appropriate image, stirs itself to want something, then spurs into movement the spirit or vital force (*vis*) which is understood as being materially dispersed throughout the body. If Lucretius believes that every instance of individual volition is accompanied by a corresponding random atomic swerve, he certainly omits mention of it. Of course, proponents of contra-causal freedom might argue that Lucretius, in keeping with his overall intent in this section of the poem, is merely trying to give a material description of the actual mechanics of volition and is therefore not obliged to give a full account. However, David Furley, followed more recently by Bobzien and O'Keefe 2005, seems to be on somewhat firmer textual grounds in claiming that Lucretius is here presenting an account of voluntary movements whose mechanisms themselves remain fully causal. Images, in this case, of walking, have struck the mind and appear to it as pleasant. The mind sets itself in motion voluntarily in accordance with the image, or perhaps, the mind as it decides to move forward sets in motion *voluntas*. There seems to be nothing in this passage in its own right that is obviously incompatible with the view that such volitions themselves are causally determined by the mind. At the same time, until we know what Epicureans think about the status of the mind itself and its relations both to its prior causal conditions and to the images striking it, it is hardly clear where Epicureans ultimately stand on questions about the nature and locus of human freedom.

Part of the problem is the looseness of Lucretius' expression '(a)fter this, volition occurs'. It is not exactly clear whether volitions are being construed as motions of the mind itself or as a separate class of movement that arises from movements of the mind— or indeed as both, since Lucretius says that the mind stirs itself to want to go forward and it is this that sets the mechanisms of volition in motion. But note that all that is being claimed in this passage is that voluntary motions flow causally from the mind after the mind stirs itself to want to do something by means of previewing images. It would be premature at best, I think, to conclude from this passage that we have anything like a full account of the mind's capacities or of its role in initiating action. Moreover, there seems to be no evidence in this passage, *pace* both Furley and Bobzien, that Epicureans believe our actions can be characterized as free only in so far as they voluntarily flow from our characters or are the outcome of the causal mechanisms that have fixed our characters. Such a conclusion can be arrived at only by shoehorning Lucretius' account of volition into an Aristotelian account of the voluntary, or at least, into one standard interpretation of Aristotle in which an agent's action is held to be voluntary just so long as it is determined by his character. The passage itself, however, makes no mention whatsoever of dispositions, fixed characters, prior causal history, etc., or any of these Aristotelian concerns. It only describes motions originating in the mind. Indeed, it strikes me that this particular feature of the tradition of interpretation inaugurated by Furley and continued by Bobzein is, in many ways, little more than an unsubstantiated Aristotelian fantasy with no real basis in Lucretius' text. Moreover, there are ample reasons external to this passage for thinking that Epicureans do not hold any of these particular Aristotelian tenets. For instance, at *DRN* 3.314 ff, Lucretius argues that no matter the nature of one's inherited make-up, one can still come to live a life worthy of the gods by means of *ratio* or reason alone. This is strictly in keeping with Epicurus' optimistic rationalism about our capacity to respond to reason and rational argument and to transform our lives at any time, no matter our past history or present condition. Our choices and actions are not determined by aspects of our prior character, no matter how deeply ingrained. Be that as it may, what this passage overtly is concerned to describe is a material process through which the body is set in motion by means of *voluntas,* once the mind receives an external image. Such a general picture is surely compatible with any number of views about the relation of the voluntary and our freedom, especially since the Epicureans offer an account of how the mind itself is freely able to select from a welter of images those which move it to action.

When we turn to a much disputed passage on the swerve in book two of *De Rerum Natura*, we find much the same account of the relation of mind and *voluntas* (2.251–93), but with some further important clarifications:

> Moreover, if all motion is always linked, and new motion arises out of old in fixed order, and atoms do not by swerving make some beginning of motion to break the decrees of fate, that cause should not follow cause from infinity, from where does this free volition (*libera voluntas*) exist for animals throughout the world? From

where comes this volition wrested away from the fates, through which we proceed wherever each of us is led by his pleasure, and likewise swerve off our motions at no fixed time or fixed region of space, but wherever the mind (*mens*) itself carries us? For without doubt it is volition that gives these things their beginning for each of us, and it is from volition that motions are spread through the limbs... Thus you may see that the beginning of motion is created from the heart* (*where the mind is located) and proceeds initially from the mind's volition, and from there is spread further through the entire body and limbs... But that the mind should not itself possess an internal necessity in all its behaviour, and be overcome and, as it were, forced to suffer and be acted upon—that is brought about by a tiny swerve of atoms at no fixed region of space or fixed time. (Long and Sedley 20F)

Again, Lucretius here describes how the mind itself makes a beginning to motion that is then passed on through the body by *voluntas* or *voluntate animi*, the volition of the mind. Many scholars have fastened their attention on the phrase 'libera voluntas' and have translated this as 'free will', but it seems clear that in this account, volition is actually free only to the extent that the mind itself is free, since volitions are causally dependent on the movements of the mind. That is, volition is viewed as a material force that conveys the decision of the mind to the limbs materially and is strictly determined by the mind. Conversely, what guarantees the freedom of the mind is the swerve, which brings it about that 'the mind should not itself possess an internal necessity in all of its behaviour'. Exactly how atomic indeterminacies are supposed to underwrite the freedom of the mind is left unexplained, but the passage makes it clear that freedom originates in mental movements that are not wholly determined by prior causal conditions.

In this context, it might be useful to recall a distinction of Locke, who most likely was influenced by this general Epicurean picture of the relation of mind and the voluntary through Gassendi. Locke insists that describing such volitions as instances of 'free will' is actually a loose way of speaking. In a much quoted argument (*An Essay Concerning Human Understanding*, II.21.14), he remarks that 'in an inquiry about freedom, the question is not proper, whether the will be free, but whether a man be free'; and 'it is as significant to ask whether a man's will be free, as to ask whether his sleep be swift or his virtue square; liberty being as little applicable to the will as swiftness of motion to sleep or squareness to virtue'. For Locke, our liberty consists in our reason's capacity to choose between alternative courses of action and then to direct the will to carry out its decision. The voluntary motions of the will depend entirely on the executive function of reason, which itself is the ultimate origin of our freedom. This is why it is misleading to describe them as being free *simpliciter*. Lucretius, I suggest, offers in this passage the origins of such an account of the voluntary and its relation to the mind. Voluntary motions are initiated by the mind and then serve to materially convey its commands to the rest of the body. It is the mind itself, however, that is free in the sense of its capacity for initiating movements that are not determined by prior causal factors.

Lucretius claims, therefore, that what preserves this freedom of the mind from internal necessity are atomic indeterminacies, though he leaves unspecified how this is exactly supposed to work. However, if this overall picture is right, it allows us to draw two initial conclusions. First, the tradition of scholarship that has tried to link the swerve directly to *voluntas* in the sense of a capacity of 'free will' has made a kind of category mistake of the sort noticed by Locke, since as Lucretius claims in this passage, the swerve frees the mind from internal necessity, and presumably our freedom of decision ultimately lies there. Volitions themselves are strictly causally dependent on the mind. To be sure, Lucretius himself calls volitions free and treats them both as movements of the mind and as separate movements caused by the mind. This, no doubt, can lead to confusion, as Locke points out. Yet, at the same time, the Epicureans give an account of voluntary action that ultimately depends on the freedom of the mind and, as we shall see, its ability to choose between alternatives—a function of mind that they ascribe to reason. At the very least, then, Epicureans can hardly be said to inhabit, as claimed by MacIntyre and others, a conceptual space that is radically foreign to early modern philosophers such as Locke, for example, or, indeed, even to many contemporary philosophers. By the same token, Bobzien uses this passage as fodder for her general claim that no Hellenistic philosopher, indeed no one until Alexander, several centuries later, ever thought of freedom of choice as choosing between two alternatives. But, of course, her argument too is misaimed, since showing that *libera voluntas* in this passage is a strictly unidirectional causal process tells us nothing about whether Epicureans think that the freedom of the mind and of our reason are themselves characterized by an ability to choose between two alternatives. In fact, it is just this famous Lockean characteristic of rationality and liberty that is driven home again and again not only in extant Epicurean texts but also, presumably, in such lost Epicurean texts as *On Choice and Avoidance*. What characterizes the rational pursuit of pleasure and the good life for the Epicurean is our rational evaluation of every pleasure and our deciding whether to choose it or not in the light of our happiness (*Letter to Menoeceus* (*Ad Men.*) 127.4–16).

Thus, in a sense, Huby was right to claim that Epicurus discovered the free will problem, to the extent that he thought that our freedom was incompatible with determinism. But he did not necessarily think that our will is free, since, like Locke, he took our volitions to be strictly causally dependent on our reason. By the same token, Furley was right to emphasize the causal nature of volitions for the Epicurean, although this too is only part of the story. To find the ultimate source of our ability to act freely, Epicureans think that we must look not to the causal dispositions of our character, but to reason's ability to rationally evaluate and deliberate between alternatives.

We have evidence that Epicurus argued that in order to give an adequate explanation of this particular feature of reason and of rational deliberation, it must be defended from a kind of mechanical determinism that would preclude the possibility of genuine reasoning and rational argument. Accordingly, he claims that the determinist's conclusions, if they are arrived at through reasoning that is causally necessitated, fail to be based on genuine reasoning. Even if the determinist bases his beliefs on evidence that is good, his assessment of the evidence will itself be causally necessitated and thus the determinist cannot adequately show the requisite sensitivity needed in assessing the merits of particular arguments. In an intriguing stretch of his badly lacunose *On Nature*, Epicurus apparently tries to show that arguments for determinism are self-refuting because of this kind of a failure in their sensitivity to an argument's rational merits (34.26–30 = Long and Sedley 20C). To be sure, his argument as its stands is inadequate on its own, since it addresses only one extreme form of determinism, namely fatalism. Only the fatalist is committed to claiming that we must accept the conclusion of an argument simply because we would have accepted it, no matter what. Determinists can still insist that the truth of propositions certainly influences the processes and outcomes of their reasoning as well as their assessment in appropriately rational ways. In fact, they might readily agree with Epicurus that fatalism precludes rationality, since it fails to show the requisite sensitivity to the merits or truth of particular arguments. If the causes that fix beliefs are appropriately sensitive to the relations that obtain between the processes, conclusions, and assessments of our arguments, however, they can maintain that the rationality of our beliefs is not undermined.

But why, we might ask, is Epicurus so keen to defend the possibility of rational argument and deliberation in the first place? One key reason is that he thinks that the rational evaluation of our desires is our most fundamental source of freedom and of our responsibility for our actions (Mitsis 1988: 132–52). He affirms, moreover, as opposed to Aristotle, a general optimism about the ongoing power of our reason, no matter our present state of character, to take evaluative attitudes towards our desires and 'to examine the good and evil on every occasion of every choice and avoidance' (*Principal Doctrines* (*KD*) 25). In a sense, Epicurus comes to treat reason as a kind of ongoing Archimedean point from which to leverage every aspect of our person and agency, no matter our present state, prior habits, or the nature of our settled beliefs about the good. This raises some difficult questions, of course, about how exactly we are to account for and explain these powers of reason in the light of nature's wider causal laws—questions that take us to the heart of Epicurus' particular form of incompatibilism.

Here, a final contrast to both Gassendi and Locke might again prove useful. Locke's thoughts about the crucial dependence of our liberty on reason were heavily dependent on Gassendi, who in turn had affirmed key features of Epicurus' account of voluntary action in opposition to the faculty psychology of both Descartes and the Scholastics. Like the Epicureans and Gassendi, Locke allows voluntary actions to be embedded in strictly causal sequences of stimulus and response while ascribing liberty, 'the great privilege of finite human beings', to the ability of our reason to scrutinize and examine alternative courses of action and to judge which of them better promotes our happiness. For Epicureans, the freedom of our mind's reason is connected, in ways that have yet to be satisfactorily explained, with uncaused atomic events. Gassendi, on the other hand, while subscribing generally to an Epicurean model of rational agency and freedom, roundly condemns the notion of uncaused events, since he thinks it would undermine arguments for divine providence and the rational causality of nature. That both share the same view about the powers of human reason and its relation to the voluntary, while sharply differing on the question of how reason itself is to be integrated into their wider views of natural causality, raises an intriguing question about the extent to which such shared models of voluntary and rational action are able to generate both libertarian and determinist positions. Epicurus, Gassendi, and subsequently Locke, who follows Gassendi, all attribute to reason the same power of deliberating between alternatives. Of course, it can be rather mysterious trying to figure out how Epicurus thinks that these powers of reason can be underwritten by indeterminacies in the universe, but it is perhaps no less mysterious how Gassendi hopes to base reason's powers of scrutiny and judgement in causal motions differing from those that characterize the movements of other natural objects, including those that are voluntary. Gassendi claims that *libentia*, voluntary movement, is a natural causal movement solely in one direction, whereas *libertas*, liberty, is able to intervene and to change its directions. We thus might well wonder if Gassendi's postulation of a different kind of causal motion grounding *libertas* is, in the end, all that different in terms of its explanatory mysteriousness from Epicurus' postulation of uncaused motions. Interestingly, all three proponents of the freedom of our rationality are reticent about attempts to thoroughly naturalize reason—if by that we mean coupling explanations of the power of reason to freely direct our desires with explanations of other natural physical motions. They are less worried on this score, however, about actions that are merely voluntary—those of animals and children, for instance—since these are more easily viewed as part of an ongoing natural causal sequence governed by mechanisms of stimulus and response. Of course, it is no great secret that the prospect of naturalizing reason has often turned out to be equally problematic for determinists and indeterminists alike, but it is perhaps worth noting that neither the problems confronted nor the solutions proffered should be taken to be radically different in the theories of the ancient Epicureans and early modern heirs such as Gassendi and Locke, who themselves stand at the head of a long modern philosophical tradition. Thus, Huby's claim that Epicureans discovered the problem of free will, even if somewhat askew, helpfully serves to illustrate how paying attention to the origins of a philosophical problem as well as to its subsequent historical outcomes can often cast light on both.

4.2 DEATH

Epicureans offered a series of arguments for the claim that we have no reason to fear death because 'it is nothing to us'. They were not alone among ancient philosophers in trying to defuse such fears, of course. In their own way, Socrates, Plato, and the Stoics all made corresponding attempts, though perhaps not in such grandiloquent and triumphant terms. But it is Epicurus' arguments in particular that have garnered by far the most contemporary attention, largely, no doubt, because of his insistence that death does us absolutely no harm, even though it means our utter extinction or annihilation. However counterintuitive, this central Epicurean claim harbours a series of difficult philosophical challenges (Rosenbaum 1986). Indeed, even though contemporary discussions of Epicurus' arguments have harnessed an increasingly impressive array of logical and metaphysical machinery in order to defend or combat what the ancient Epicureans took to be a rather commonplace set of considerations supporting their arguments, little agreement has emerged about the relative success of any of these efforts (see Warren 2004 for a clear, comprehensive account). At the same time, most contemporary arguments take the form of what the Epicureans themselves would have regarded as a distinctly rearguard action, in the sense that few contemporary ethical theorists have seriously considered, much less taken to heart, Epicurus' broader claim that a proper recognition of our mortality needs to be at the very heart of any systematic ethical theory. True, there may be a growing sense that when we read such fundamental works as, say, Rawls' *A Theory of Justice*, it can be slightly discomfiting to find in it barely a nod to the fact that rational moral agents must confront death and that their attitudes towards this prospect may have a significant impact on their overall prudential and moral deliberations. But it is only very recently that philosophers have started to seriously link their analyses of the metaphysical puzzles generated by Epicurus' claims about death with broader ethical concerns (Parfit 1984), for the most part still focusing on questions about individual welfare and happiness (Feldman 1992). Thus, the verdict remains out on whether this key aspect of Epicurus' ethical project will begin to gain further traction in wider arenas of contemporary ethical argument.

There is a succinct statement of Epicurus' basic claim about death in his *Letter to Menoeceus*:

> Therefore that most frightful of evils, death, is nothing to us, seeing that when we exist, death is not present, and when death is present, we do not exist. Thus it is nothing either to the living or the dead, seeing that the former do not have it, and the latter no longer exist. (*Ad Men.* 125 = Long and Sedley 24 A5)

The Epicureans are materialists and they offer an impressive battery of empirical observations in defence of the view that we are strictly material entities whose matter is dispersed upon death, and along with it the relevant atomic structures upon which both our existence and identities as persons are grounded (cf. *DRN* 3, 1–857). Of course, there are other available views about our post-mortem prospects and the Epicureans cast doubt on many of them. But before looking at some of these responses, it might be helpful to focus, as do most contemporary critics of Epicurus, on the question of annihilation itself. In a short paper in 1970, Thomas Nagel defended the claim that even though, or perhaps just because, we are annihilated at death, we have reason to regard it as being harmful to us. Since it is probably no exaggeration to say that much of the subsequent philosophical work done on this question consists in a series of elaborations of various claims found in a compressed form in Nagel's paper, it remains the best single starting point for addressing the problems raised by Epicurus' views. At the same time, it is important to be aware of the particular ethical context and goals of Epicurus' arguments, since someone might hold, as Hobbes did, for instance, that we not only have ample reason to fear death, but also that such fear actually benefits us since it make us both more inclined to look after our own self-interest and to be more tractable in our dealings with our neighbours. If we did not fear death, he claims, we could not properly cultivate our own best interests. The Epicureans, on the other hand, strongly disagree and the aim of their thanatology is, thus, twofold. They argue that the fear of death is based on a series of conceptual mistakes, hence irrational and unnecessary; but they are also keen to show how the fear of death in its own right has bad systemic effects on our lives. In fact, for Epicureans, it is the greatest obstacle we must overcome if we wish to live a happy life since it infects our lives with anxiety and leads us to engage in self-defeating and self-destructive pursuits. Fortunately for us, it is completely eliminable in their view, since further reflection shows that, strictly speaking, we can never actually experience our death; hence, we can experience nothing good or bad from it. Quite simply, it is nothing to us.

Epicurus' argument raises three important challenges for anyone who maintains that death both harms us and is to be feared (Rosenbaum 1989a). One must show *when* death harms us; *how* it does so; and that it actually harms *us*, in the sense of our being subjects whose existence is located in particular categorical spatio-temporal states. Epicureans assert that we typically make mistakes on all three of these counts because we fail to apprehend the nature of our extinction and continually project ourselves into our deaths as if we were still alive and experiencing a series of continued harms at death's hands. We often do this even while claiming to understand that we will be annihilated at death. The point is made in the following way by Lucretius:

> For if there is going to be unhappiness and suffering, the person must also himself exist at that same time, for the evil to be able to befall him. Since death robs him of this, preventing the existence of the person for the evils to be heaped upon, you can tell that there is nothing for us to fear in death, that he who does not exist cannot be unhappy, and that when immortal death snatches away mortal life it is no different from never having been born. So when you see a man resent the prospect of his body being burned and rotting after death, or being destroyed by fire or by the jaws of wild beasts, you may be sure that his words do not ring true, and that there lurks in his heart some hidden sting, however much he may deny the belief that he will have any sensation in death. For he does not, I think, grant either the substance or ground of what he professes. Instead of completely stripping himself of life, unawares he is making some bit of himself survive. (*DRN* 3.861–78 = Long and Sedley 24 E, trans. modified).

Epicurus often moves easily between the claim that death cannot harm someone who does not exist and the claim that death cannot harm someone who does not perceive it as being painful. The latter claim derives from his hedonism: something that causes us no pain is no harm to us. Since our death is a state without any sensation, it is painless, hence harmless. Before turning to these two claims, however, it is perhaps worth pointing out one further conceptual point that Epicureans like to make. In trying to conceive of our own deaths we find it difficult—Freud would later say impossible—to extract ourselves from the imagined scene of our death. As a consequence, we continually project ourselves into our own and others' deaths in a way that makes us view death 'not as the annihilation of consciousness, but as the consciousness of annihilation'—to quote the nice Epicurean-like jingle of Silverstein 1980. Instead, we should come to understand, they argue, that there is really nothing that we can intelligibly imagine about a state of non-existence.

For the Epicureans, this kind of conceptual error regularly colours one of our most important worries about death, that is, that it deprives us of the *praemia vitae* or the rewards of life:

> No more for you the welcome of a joyful home and a good wife. No more will your children run to snatch the first kiss... 'Unhappy man', they say, 'unhappily robbed by a single hateful day of all those rewards of life'. What they fail to add is this: 'Nor does any yearning for those things remain in you.' If they properly saw this with their mind, and followed it up in their words, they would unshackle themselves of great mental anguish and fear. (*DRN* 3.894–903 = Long and Sedley 24 E)

The notion that death robs us of the goods of life, or even just some further moments of life itself, is one of our most common intuitions, but it is one that quickly runs up against the Epicurean's demands for further clarification. For instance, exactly when does death rob us of life or life's goods? It certainly cannot rob us of anything when we are dead, the Epicurean replies, since we are not there to be robbed. By the same token, to claim that our future death is currently harming us by robbing us of something while we are now alive would seem to assume some form of backwards causation, otherwise how can a posthumous event do us any harm now? From these two considerations, the Epicureans conclude that since death can harm us neither when we are dead nor when we are alive, it never harms us. One might object, of course, that it is possible to locate the harm of death in that very moment of transition between our life and death (cf. Luper 2009). However, it is hard to see how such an objection escapes from difficulties of its own. If I am not alive at that particular moment of transition, how is it that I am being harmed? Or if I am in some sense still alive, worries again arise about backwards causation, since how is it that I am now being harmed by my future state of being dead? It seems open to the Epicurean, that is, to ask for clarification about the nature of the subject meant to be experiencing this transition. If there is a subject persisting through the transition, then there is not yet really a case of death—a case of dying perhaps, but not death. If there is no persisting subject, however, then it is hard to see how something that no longer exists can be said to be undergoing a transition. In Aristotelian terms, we might say that the notion of a moment of transition between life and death needs to be disambiguated between mere alteration and substantial change. Neither of these options by itself, however, conflicts with the Epicurean claim that death harms us neither when we exist nor after we have been annihilated.

In the light of such difficulties in fixing the harm of death in a temporal sequence, many have thought to cash out Nagel's suggestion that the harm of death occurs at no particular fixed time. This claim is part of his larger argument that the harm of death is 'irreducibly relational' and that 'most good and ill fortune has as its subject a person identified by his history and his possibilities, rather than by his categorical state of the moment' (1970: 77). One common way of illustrating this claim is by appealing to judgements about the relative worth of lives based on comparative counterfactual judgements. So, for example, Mozart, Bellini, and Schubert all had intensely creative, but relatively short lives. Wouldn't their lives have been better and the world of music much richer, if they had not been cut off by death so early? Nagel argues that our common intuitions suggest that we can recognize the harm that death caused in each of these cases, even if we cannot exactly place it temporally. It lies precisely in the enormous range of possibilities lost to these extraordinary lives because of their early deaths.

In attempting to give more precision to such intuitions, a large literature relying on possible world semantics has recently arisen (Bradley 2009). We can only speculate how Epicureans might have responded to such arguments (cf. Warren 2004: ch. 2), however, it is fairly clear that they would have been suspicious of comparisons based on modal properties of persons and so-called possible-world counterparts. Given their deeply rooted empiricism, they would insist on conclusions cashed out in categorical states of agents. There is a brief bit of evidence to this effect from Cicero (*Tusculan Disputations* (*Tusc.*) i. 9–11), where it is suggested that Epicureans think that comparisons involving the dead rest on simple mistakes of logic because one cannot coherently predicate properties such as 'happy' or 'miserable' of something that does not exist. The Epicurean holds that the benefits and harms that I experience today and will experience tomorrow can be compared coherently only if it turns out that I am there at both those times as an existing subject so that their effects on me can be gauged. Comparisons between times when I do and do not exist can appear to be of the same form, but they are crucially different and fail to go through because there is no persisting subject to ground both sides of the comparison.

Such considerations are not likely to move possible worlds theorists, of course, but they do point to some importantly different background assumptions. The Epicureans are worried about the practical effect of theories and expect that metaphysical and ethical beliefs will be mutually reinforcing. So, for instance, the Epicurean would register a general worry about how modal accounts of individual identity might affect our ethical beliefs because of their likely indifference to capturing any meaningful sense of our mortality. Grant, for instance, that there are possible worlds in which I may live forever. How should that affect my attitudes towards death? Nagel, for instance, concludes his paper with the claim that 'if there is no limit to the amount of life it would be good to have, it may be that a bad end is in store for us all' (Nagel 1970: 79). For the Epicurean, the idea that we should base our judgements about death in accordance with a theoretical framework that allows for the possibility of our continuing on forever makes two fundamental mistakes. First, it is likely to engender irrational and unsatisfiable yearnings for immortality that will turn out to be the source of troubling anxiety:

> Hence a correct understanding that death is nothing to us makes the mortality of life enjoyable, not by adding infinite time, but by ridding us of the desire for immortality. (*Ad Men.* 124 = Long and Sedley 24 A)

Second, by failing to be bound by the actual natural limits of human desires and lives, such an account conjures up a view of immortality that is itself unnatural and undesirable. An unending life, Epicureans argue, would become unendurable because of its repetitiveness and tediousness. Most people who think they would like to live forever have given little thought to what such a life actually would entail. Engaging in the same tasks again and again for an eternity would, the Epicurean insists, make us like Sisyphus and it would empty our tasks of all interest and meaning. To the objection that, despite the tedium of immortality (cf. Williams 1973), at least we would not need to fear death if we were immortal, the Epicurean claims that everyone would naturally prefer a shorter happy life to one of unending tedium. More important, the notion of an unending life is nothing but an irrational fantasy in the first place. Given our nature and the fact of our annihilation at death, speculations about unending possible lives can only lead us to be fearful of death by engendering desires for something that is neither actual nor desirable. If we want to usefully think about ourselves in terms of modal properties, we might do so not, as it were, horizontally, but vertically, in the sense of realizing in the here and now our potential understanding of both the natural world and ourselves, and as a consequence, learning to lead the happy lives that are at this very instant within our grasp.

One might agree with the Epicurean that counterfactual speculations about what it would be like to live forever are of limited practical use when confronting the prospect of our actual annihilation. Yet, even if one agrees that an unending life is neither possible nor desirable, one might still want just a little extra time, say, either to give one's life the kind of overall shape one expects for it (Striker 1988) or to finish the narrative one would like to tell about oneself (Velleman 2000; Mitsis 2007). If death can interrupt these potential goals of mine, don't I have reason to fear it? Again, the Epicurean thinks that such worries are based on a series of mistaken assumptions.

Let us take first the question of life's duration and the notion that, even if we have rid ourselves of the desire for immortality, we still might reasonably wish for some extra time and, as a consequence, have reason to fear death's arrival. Epicureans offer the following thought experiment to show that we will not harbour such wishes once we rationally comprehend the actual nature of our non-existence instead of irrationally projecting ourselves or possible future selves into our post-mortem annihilation. Their argument depends on what they take to be a commonly held, but irrational, asymmetry in our attitudes towards the two periods of non-existence that encompass our lives. Lucretius offers the following version:

> Look back again to see how the unending expanse of past time, before we are born, has been nothing to us. For Nature holds this forth to us as a mirror image of the time to come after our death. Is there anything terrible there, does anything seem gloomy? Is it not more peaceful than any sleep? (DRN 3.972–77)

We typically live our lives without being bothered by the thought that there was a time in the past when we did not exist. Yet, we seem frightened by the thought of our future non-existence. How can we justify this asymmetry in our attitudes towards these two periods of our non-existence? The Epicurean argues that it is irrational to hold asymmetric attitudes towards two states that are the same; hence there can be no justification. Moreover, once we recognize that they are the same, we can come to revise our attitudes and regard our death with the same indifference with which we typically regard our prevital non-existence. Such recognition will enable us, moreover, to stop projecting ourselves into our future non-existence and to come to understand that we are not really worried by the duration of our lives *per se*. If we were, we might wish that we had been born earlier so that our lives would have been longer, or we might bemoan the lost possibilities of our earlier non-existence. But we do not do either; nor do we appeal to modal properties in cases when we actually understand their true purchase. Thus, if it seems merely irrational to lament the lost possibilities of the time before we were born, it is equally irrational to lament the loss of our possibilities in death, since they are both equivalent states of our non-existence.

The Epicurean argument can be attacked on many fronts since we can question whether the alleged symmetry is in fact strong enough to warrant regarding both periods of our non-existence in the exact same manner (Luper 2009). Our pre-vital non-existence is followed by life, whereas our post mortem non-existence is followed by nothing, so we might appeal to that difference to justify holding an asymmetric attitude. Moreover, it might seem that Lucretius' general strategy of getting us to revise our attitudes could backfire. An alternative way of keeping my attitudes symmetrical is to begin viewing my pre-vital non-existence with the same dread as I view my death. Of course, the Epicurean would argue that such a strategy is mistaken both because it increases anxiety and because it makes mistakes about the nature of our non-existence (Rosenbaum 1989a). But the mere demand for consistency that this argument makes may be insufficient on its own to block its strategy from backfiring.

The Epicureans have a final argument, however, for their claim that we should have no concern for the length of our lives. Although it seems rather obscure at first blush, it relies on central features of their hedonism and attempts to show how a pleasurable life can come to be complete in such a way that its duration does not matter. If I am leading a pleasurable life in the right way, Epicurus' claims, my life cannot be made any better by living longer; thus I need have no anxiety that death might rob me of time I would need for living a completely happy life. Clearly, such a view is strikingly at odds with typical conceptions of hedonism that ascribe value to such features as the varying intensity and duration of pleasures, so it will be helpful to turn to Epicurus' arguments to see what could lead a hedonist to reject such criteria as being crucially valuable characteristics of pleasure.

4.3 PLEASURE

At first glance, Epicurus' hedonism seems to have a familiar ring. He claims that we are all naturally disposed to pursue pleasure from birth and that it serves as the final goal of all our actions. In our most extensive and connected surviving discussion, Cicero's *De Finibus*, the Epicurean interlocutor, Torquatus, gives the following account:

> as soon as every animal is born, it seeks after pleasure and rejoices in it as the greatest good, while it rejects pain as the greatest bad and, as far as possible, avoids it; and it does this while it is not yet corrupted, on the innocent and sound judgement of nature itself. Hence, he says that there is no need to prove or discuss why pleasure is

to be pursued and pain avoided. He thinks that these matters are sensed just like the heat of fire. (*Fin.* 1.30 = Long and Sedley 21 A2)

Unlike their rivals, the Cyrenaics who argue that the true hedonist will just pursue the next pleasure that presents itself without troubling over any overall balance sheet, the Epicureans argue that we need to exercise prudence in our choices to make sure that the things we pursue actually produce pleasure in the long run:

> for this reason we do not choose every pleasure either, but we sometimes pass over many pleasures in cases where their outcome for us is a greater quantity of discomfort;...Every pleasure, then because of its natural affinity, is something good, yet not every pleasure is choiceworthy. (*Ad Men.*129=Long and Sedley 21 B3)

So far, these points about the pursuit of pleasure and its justification are fairly commonplace. Complications arise, however, in Epicurus' account of pleasure itself. We might think that pleasure is to be identified with a certain positive, agreeable feeling and pain with its opposite, and that we might then treat both along a sliding scale divided in the middle by a neutral state that is neither pleasurable nor painful. Epicurus, however, rejects such a view and distinguishes two sorts of pleasure. He argues that there are 'kinetic' as well as 'katastematic' or 'static' pleasures. Kinetic pleasures consist in those positive sensations and feelings that are often taken to be the hallmark of pleasure, whereas katastematic ones are those that arise in an organism when bodily pain or mental distress has been removed. For Epicurus, moreover, it is this latter freedom from pain and distress that is the greatest pleasure.

> The pleasure we pursue is not just that which moves our actual nature with some gratification and *percipitur* (is received, perceived, felt) by the senses in company with a certain delight; we hold that to be the greatest pleasure which *percipitur* (is received, perceived, felt) once all pain has been removed. For when we are freed from pain, we enjoy (*gaudemus*) the actual freedom and absence of all distress; therefore the complete removal of pain has rightly been called a pleasure;...Hence Epicurus did not accept the existence of anything between pleasure and pain. What some people regarded as in between—the complete absence of pain—was not only pleasure but also the greatest pleasure. For anyone who *sentit* (feels, perceives, is aware of) his own condition must either have pleasure or pain. Epicurus, moreover, supposes that complete absence of pain marks the limit of the greatest pleasure, so that thereafter pleasure can be varied and differentiated but not increased and expanded. (*Fin.* 37–8 = Long and Sedley 21 A 6–7; modified)

How Epicureans conceived of the exact relation between these two types of pleasure is much debated (see Purinton 1993; Wolfsdorf 2009), but it seems fairly clear how Epicurus' might have hoped that such a view of hedonism, among other things, could serve to anchor his thanatology. Most of Epicurus' critics both ancient and modern have thought that the project of trying to fit any sort of hedonism into his strong claims about the harmlessness of death is doomed to failure, since no plausible conception of pleasure could possibly emerge from such a project. Indeed, some critics have argued that, given his hedonism, his claims about death must be something of a bluff. This is unlikely, however, given the amount of effort that later Epicureans, such as Philodemus, spent in showing how his views about death and pleasure cohere (cf. *De Morte* XII.26 ff; Warren 2004: ch. 4). It is perhaps suggestive as well in this context that another group of hedonists, the Cyrenaics, also believed that their hedonism freed one from the fear of death. Thus, before dismissing such a project outright, it might be useful to contrast Epicurus' views of pleasure with those of the Cyrenaics to see what kind of case hedonists can make for eliminating our fear of death.

The Epicureans were often called upon to distinguish and defend their own more austere and sober form of hedonism from the seemingly simpler, albeit uncompromising, version of the Cyrenaics (cf. Annas 1993). If we turn to their respective opening moves, we immediately see the nature of the gulf separating them. Both offer so-called 'cradle arguments' (see Brunschwig 1986) that make inferences from the behaviour of infants and animals to our primary natural motivation. The Cyrenaics argue that infants are motivated by an appetite for sensual pleasures and delight (Diogenes Laertius (D.L) 2.88), while the Epicureans, for their part, maintain that at the most basic level infants shun pain (D.L 10.137). Whether we are more convinced by the evidence of a baby squealing with delight upon seeing a toy or of one quieting down for the night after having been given a bottle, their differing assessment of our earliest state displays in capsule form the overall trajectory that their theories take. For the Cyrenaic, life consists in a continual restless movement from one lively unplanned pleasure to another, while the goal for an Epicurean is to maintain a carefully controlled life of undisturbed satisfaction and tranquillity. Thus, from the point of view of the Cyrenaic, the Epicurean pursues the pleasures of a corpse, while for the Epicurean, the Cyrenaic engages in an emotional rollercoaster ride that will leave him inevitably unsatisfied and at the mercy of fortune. Interestingly, both think that their own strategy will make them immune to the fear of death, however, since the Cyrenaic believes that if he cares only for present pleasures in the right way, he will have no concern for the future nor cause for any worry about himself in the future, since he is sceptical about any connections between his present and future selves. Indeed, since he has eliminated all concern for a future self, he need not worry that death might harm *him* or interrupt anything that he cares about in the future. The Epicurean, on the other hand, claims that once one achieves the proper state of mental tranquillity (*ataraxia*) and freedom from bodily pain (*aponia*), one no longer cares about the duration of one's life. At first glance, this may look perilously close to the Cyrenaic and what can only be described as a deeply counterintuitive and peculiar conception of personal identity, but the Epicurean tries to fashion a normative source of personal identity compatible with fearlessness towards to the future. The Epicurean claims that his mental pleasures are temporally extended in the sense that at any moment he can confidently rely on future expectations and also summon up memories of past pleasures. With these techniques of mental pleasure the Epicurean can hold together an extended self without, however, fearing death.

Even though both the Epicureans and Cyrenaics couch their arguments in terms of pleasure and its characteristics, it is clear that both hope to import certain values and attitudes along an axis that starts to stretch purely hedonic criteria in competing directions.

The Cyrenaics think that the radically subjective nature of knowledge and perception makes it the case that pleasure itself is radically subjective. Epicurus, on the other hand, values rational control and individual invulnerability in a way that leads him to demote the lively present pleasures of the Cyrenaics. He does so in ways, moreover, that place him at the head of a long tradition of hedonists who try to build in certain objective normative criteria for 'true' pleasures as opposed to 'false' or 'empty' ones. Of course, disputes typically arise between hedonists and their critics precisely about the extent to which such criteria are actually hedonic or whether they are rooted instead in non-hedonic sources of value. In Epicurus' case, the hedonic nature of these criteria may fall under some suspicion since he seems to embrace as katastematic pleasures states of an agent that are dependent on various favoured beliefs about the world—fearlessness towards death, an understanding of atomism, recognition of divine indifference, etc.—and it might be argued that such beliefs are prior and independent sources of value that an agent's particular pleasures are causally dependent on. In one of his so-called *Key Doctrines*, we find the claim that:

> the limit of pleasure in the mind is produced by rationalizing those very things and their congeners which used to present the mind with its greatest fears. (*KD* 18 = Long and Sedley 21 E 1)

As Aristotle famously argued, to the extent that my pleasures are dependent upon prior beliefs about value, they cannot themselves serve as the kind of independent standard of the good that is claimed for them by the hedonist. At the same time, however, Cicero's report of the Epicurean theory (p. 88 above) suggests that if one is aware of or feels (*sentit*) one's condition—and this presumably includes such attitudinal states as fearlessness towards death—one either experiences pleasure or pain. Though admittedly speculative given our evidence and the ambiguity of Cicero's phrasing, one distinction that Epicurus' account may be pointing to is one that is often hard won for contemporary hedonists and arguably non-existent in other ancient accounts of pleasure: that there is something about the way that holding a particular belief feels. Holding the right belief feels pleasurable. It is not just that the Epicurean maintains various cognitive attitudes to the world that cause pleasure, but that such attitudes themselves are united and justified by a particular sort of pleasurable feel. Of course, the Cyrenaics would find such pleasurable attitudinal states too far removed from the 'hot' affective bodily ones that they favour. But to the extent that there are katastematic mental states that are pleasurable, one possible way of understanding them is to view them as occurrent attitudinal states that are themselves pleasurable, or as Cicero writes, that we enjoy or take pleasure in (gaudemus, above p. 88). That is, such states are not just purely cognitive, but have a particular feel that makes them pleasurable to hold.

Indeed, the Epicurean thinks that such katastematic states are so pleasurable that everything else that people value in life pales before them. That is why they deny that reaching particular stages in life, performing a wide range of Aristotelian-approved activities, or telling and completing an elaborate narrative about how one has lived are important for the achievement of such a state of katastematic pleasure and happiness. Moreover, one can reach such a condition of complete happiness and pleasure at any time. Epicurus' follower, Pythocles, apparently did so as a young man and one can do so just as well when one is old. That is why Epicurus rejects the saying of Solon that one must look to the end to judge one's life (*S. V.* 76). Solon's judgement is based on the wrong sort of criteria, since one at any time can achieve complete happiness immediately upon reaching a state of Epicurean *ataraxia*.

Epicurus' claim that achieving a particular sort of psychic and physical condition is sufficient itself for happiness clearly cuts across many common intuitions. But we might object that even so, such a condition is still not immune from being harmed by death. Why wouldn't an Epicurean want to continue in such a supremely pleasurable state and, hence, be compelled to harbour some sort of disturbing negative attitude towards a potential interruption by death? The Epicurean answer is, as we have seen (above p. 88), the stipulation that once one has achieved the limit of pleasure, it cannot be increased or expanded by duration. Moreover, one can only maintain such a state if one remains unperturbed by worries about its continuance. To fear its loss is already to have lost it.

The idea that one would want or be able to live such a life focused on achieving a particular state of feeling that is rooted in knowledge of a particular set of objective truths may at first glance seem to have little in common with the great majority of Epicurus' hedonist successors. That is, until one remembers, say, how Locke claims that God has made sure that we will all enjoy the eternal post-mortem pleasures awaiting us. If we weigh up properly the paltriness of present pleasures against those that await us in eternity, we can come to see their objective superiority. No mortal could rationally prefer earthly pleasures and no mortal would fail to find eternal ones pleasant in the right way, since 'could we suppose their relishes as different there as they are here, yet the manna in heaven will suit every one's palate' (*Essay* II.21.67).

If the Epicurean would find Locke's account of eternal post-mortem pleasures a bit mysterious, then it may perhaps be fitting to close this discussion of the more obscure reaches of Epicurus' secular pleasures not with more argument, but, as often happens in ancient arguments when one reaches in impasse, with an exemplum—in this case, Philodemus' description of the Epicurean wise man.

> The one who understands, having grasped that he is capable of achieving everything sufficient for the good life, immediately and for the rest of his life walks about already ready for burial, and enjoys the single day as if it were eternity. (Philodemus, *De Morte* XXXVIII.14–19 Kuiper)

BIBLIOGRAPHY

Annas, J. 1993. *The Morality of Happiness*. Oxford: Oxford University Press.

Asmis, E. 1990. 'Free Action and the Swerve', review article of Walter G. Englert's *Epicurus on the Swerve and Voluntary Action*', *Oxford Studies in Ancient Philosophy* 8: 269–85.

Bobzien, S. 1998. *Determinism and Freedom in Stoic Philosophy*. Oxford: Oxford University Press.

Bobzien, S. 2000. 'Did Epicurus Discover the Free-Will Problem?', *Oxford Studies in Ancient Philosophy* 19: 287–337.

Bradley, B. 2009. *Well Being and Death*. Oxford: Oxford University Press.

Brunschwig, J. 1986. 'The Cradle Argument in Epicureanism and Stoicism', in G. Striker and M. Schofield (eds.), *The Norms of Nature: Studies in Hellenistic Ethics*. Cambridge/Paris: Cambridge University Press, 113–44.

Englert, W. G. 1987. *Epicurus on the Swerve and Voluntary Action*. Atlanta, Georgia: Scholars Press.

Fowler, D. 2002. *Lucretius on Atomic Motion. A Commentary on De rerum natura book two, lines 1–332*, ed. P. Fowler. Oxford: Oxford University Press.

Feldman, F. 1992. *Confrontations with the Reaper*. New York: Oxford University Press.

Furley, D. J. 1967. *Two Studies in the Greek Atomists*. Princeton: Princeton University Press

Huby, P. 1967. 'The First Discovery of the Freewill Problem', *Philosophy* 42: 353–62.

Long, A. A. and Sedley, D. N. 1987. *The Hellenistic Philosophers*, 2 vols. Cambridge: Cambridge University Press.

Luper, S. 2009. *The Philosophy of Death*. Cambridge: Cambridge University Press.

Mitsis, P. 1988. *The Pleasures of Invulnerability: Epicurus' Ethical Theory*. Ithaca: Cornell University Press.

—— 2007. 'Life as Play, Life as a Play: Montaigne and the Epicureans', in S. J. Heyworth and P. Fowler (eds), *Classical Constructions: Papers in Memory of Don Fowler, Classicist and Epicurean*. Oxford: Oxford University Press, 18–38.

Nagel, T. 1970. 'Death', *Nous* 4 (1): 73–80.

Nussbaum, M. 1994. *The Therapy of Desire: Theory and Practice in Hellenistic Ethics*. Princeton: Princeton University Press.

O'Keefe, T. 2005. *Epicurus on Freedom*. Cambridge: Cambridge University Press.

Parfit, D. 1984. *Reasons and Persons*. Oxford: Oxford University Press.

Purinton, J. S. 1993. 'Epicurus on the *Telos*', *Phronesis* 38: 281–320.

Rosenbaum, S. E. 1986. 'How to be Dead and not Care: A Defense of Epicurus', *American Philosophical Quarterly* 23: 217–25.

—— 1989a. 'Epicurus and Annihilation', *Philosophical Quarterly* 39: 81–90.

——1989b. 'The Symmetry Argument: Lucretius Against the Fear of Death', *Philosophy and Phenomenological Research* 50: 353–73.

—— 1990. 'Epicurus and the Complete Life', *Monist* 73: 21–41.

Sedley, D. N. 1983. 'Epicurus' refutation of Determinism', in ΣΥΖΗΤΗΣΙΣ *Studi sull'epicureismo greco e latino offerto a Marcello Gigante*. Naples: Biblioteca della Parola del Passato, 11–51.

Silverstein, H. 1980. 'The Evil of Death', *Journal of Philosophy* 77: 401–24.

Striker, G. 1988. 'Commentary on Mitsis', *Proceedings of the Boston Area Colloquium in Ancient Philosophy* 4: 323–30.

Velleman, J. D. 2000. 'Well-being and Time', in his *The Possibility of Practical Reasoning*. Oxford: Oxford University Press.

Warren, J. 2004. *Facing Death: Epicurus and his Critics*. Oxford: Oxford University Press.

Williams, B. 1973. 'The Makropoulos Case: Reflections on the Tedium of Immortality', in his *Problems of the Self*. Cambridge: Cambridge University Press, 82–100.

Wolfsdorf, D. 2009. 'Epicurus on *Euphrosyne* and *Energeia*', *Apeiron* 42: 221–57.

CHAPTER 5

CYNICISM AND STOICISM

CHRISTOPHER GILL

STOIC ethical theory was widely seen as one of the most important in Greco-Roman antiquity, and is, increasingly, regarded as one that modern thinkers should take seriously as a contributor to current debates. Cynicism was more marginal to mainstream ancient ethical thinking, and there is a question how far it counts as a theory at all. However, it was a significant influence on Stoic ideas, and also encapsulated—in a highly radical and provocative form—themes and attitudes that recur in other ancient theories. Both approaches adopt in a strong form the prevalent ancient view that ethics is, or should be, founded on 'nature', in some sense, and not on social convention. Both approaches also express another common ancient belief that espousing an ethical theory or position carries with it the adoption of a specific form of life. Both Cynic and Stoic ideas on ethics were well known from their emergence in the fourth or third century BC till the second century AD and beyond. However, while Cynicism presented its ideas in a highly simplified, popularizing form, Stoicism evolved a very sophisticated and systematic ethical theory, combining strong claims with powerful argumentation.

5.1 CYNICISM

Like most other philosophical movements, Cynicism traced its origins to a single pioneering individual, Diogenes of Sinope (c. 412/403–c. 324/321 BC), the most colourful and outrageous of all such founders of philosophical movements. There is extensive evidence about Diogenes' life; although the factual status of these reports is unclear, they played a crucial role in perpetuating the ideals of the movement.[1] When accused,

---

[1] For a resumé of the ancient sources for Cynicism, see Moles 2000: 415–16 and Desmond 2008: 262–3; for a survey of scholarship see Moles 2000: 415 n. 1 and Desmond 2008: 263–73.

along with his father (who was responsible for coinage in his city), of 'defacing the currency' at some point after 362 BC, he spent the rest of his life in exile, much of it in Athens, the intellectual centre of ancient Greece. The way of life he took up in exile became fundamental for the Cynic movement. This involved the rejection of everything associated with human civilization and culture, including normal clothing, cooked food and houses, marriage and family life, as well as more elaborate features such as athletic competitions, literature, and complex philosophical theories. He lived in the open air, with no shoes and wearing only a simple, single garment (worn doubled in winter), carrying a bag for scraps of food and a staff for protection. He lived by gathering food from the countryside, or begging or stealing food; he drank only water. He performed all natural functions in public including eating (not normally done in public in Greece) and defecating; he satisfied his sexual needs by masturbation, also done in public. His only shelter was a wine-jar (*pithos*). His way of life was that associated with animals, such as dogs, and was called 'dog-like' (*kunikos*), giving the movement its name.[2]

Diogenes not only lived this kind of life but vigorously commended it to others (in principle, everyone), and combined this with intense, virulent denunciation of the civilized life. Among the many targets of his attacks are those who held or pursued political power, wealth, and luxury, and those who spent resources and effort in gaining sexual, or other types of sensual, pleasures. His messages were communicated in blunt, forceful speeches or comments. For instance, when asked by Alexander the Great if he wanted anything, he told the king to get out of the sun which Alexander was blocking by his presence.[3] Diogenes' way of life and message were promoted by numerous reports of such anecdotes, and by followers and imitators, both in his own lifetime and throughout later Classical antiquity. Surprisingly, given Diogenes' lifestyle, there are also reports of a number of his writings; and later Cynics, or Cynic sympathizers, wrote extensively, using a variety of literary forms (including a distinctive mix of serious and comic styles), despite the Cynic devaluation of literature and philosophical writings. Among those following him, we can distinguish 'hard' Cynics, who adopted in full Diogenes' lifestyle, from 'soft' Cynics, such as Dio Chrysostom, who combined key Cynic themes with more conventional approaches. We can also distinguish 'practising' Cynics, who adopted the distinctive way of life, from those, such as Lucian, who adopted Cynic attitudes and motifs for literary purposes.[4]

The core Cynic doctrines, if we can call them that, articulate the principles embodied in Diogenes' way of life. The central theme is that of following nature, understood as leading a life of extreme primitiveness or self-chosen bestiality. A linked assumption

[2] See Moles 1997a, Desmond 2008: 19–24.
[3] Cicero, *Tusculans* 5.92, Diogenes Laertius (D.L.) 6.38. All names of authors and titles not found in the Bibliography are ancient (Greek and Roman) authors or works available in many editions and translations. The numbers cited refer to standard book or page divisions of those works, also found in all editions or translations.
[4] See Moles 1997b, Desmond 2008: ch. 1.

is that nature, in the form of the cultivated or wild environment, is capable of satisfying our needs (assumed to be very simple ones) for food and protection.[5] A second assumption is that human beings are naturally capable of leading this kind of life, or at least of undergoing the rigorous training (*askēsis*) required to make this possible.[6] A correlated principle is the wholesale rejection of anything associated with human culture, civilization, or convention, a principle sometimes characterized as 'defacing the currency', in a reference to the event that brought about Diogenes' life-changing exile.[7] The main assumption made here is that culture involves the perversion or obscuring of what human nature actually needs. A graphic image for these two principles lies in the contrast between Diogenes, meeting all his needs without effort in the open air, and a rich man, hidden behind thick walls, living off specialist foodstuffs brought at great cost from all over the world and titillating his sexual appetite with slaves of both genders.

Can we, with any intellectual plausibility, chart links between such a starkly simplified 'philosophy' and other ancient ethical theories? In fact, our evidence, especially the early third-century AD philosophical handbook of Diogenes Laertius, invites us to draw such connections.[8] We can also see indications of the influence of earlier philosophical figures or movements, notably Socrates (Diogenes was allegedly described by Plato as 'Socrates gone mad').[9] We are told, for instance, that Diogenes held virtue to be the 'end' or goal of life (*telos*); 'virtue' here must signify the quality of character needed to live the life according to nature, as understood in Cynicism.[10] The Cynic life was also presented as the supreme expression of 'self-sufficiency' (*autarkeia*), a standard ancient requirement for happiness or the good life.[11] We also hear that pain or hard work (*ponos*) and training (*askēsis*) are good things. This stress on indifference to pain evokes Socrates or his follower Antisthenes (sometimes presented as founder or predecessor of Cynicism), although 'hard work' is also presented in Cynicism as the best way of securing pleasure.[12]

One of the most striking features of Cynic thought is its cosmopolitanism. This is also an idea that was, it would seem, supported by a set of formal arguments in one of Diogenes' key works, his *Republic* or *Constitution* (*politeia*). There, Diogenes claimed that 'the only correct constitution is the one in the universe (*kosmos*)'. He also defended this claim with the following syllogism:

---

[5] See Desmond 2008: ch. 3, especially 150–61.

[6] On Cynic *askēsis*, see D.L. 6.70–1, also Goulet-Cazé 1986: 17–92, Desmond 2008: 101–2, 153–9, 219–21.

[7] See D.L. 6.20, 71: also Desmond 2008: 125 (more broadly, ch. 2).

[8] D.L. 6 (on Cynics, especially Diogenes).

[9] D.L. 6.54; Socratic elements include the simple, outdoor life, the role of being a 'gadfly' of Athens (cf. Plato *Apology* 30e–31a), the presentation of virtue as the goal of life, and the close linkage between ethical stance and way of life; see Desmond 2008: 15–16.

[10] D.L. 6.70, 104.

[11] D.L. 6.104: for self-sufficiency as a criterion of happiness, see e.g. Aristotle, *Nicomachean Ethics* (*NE*) 10.7, 117a27–b1, b16–24. On Cynic self-sufficiency, see Desmond 2008: 121–2, 172–8.

[12] D.L. 6.71, Dio Chrysostom 3.83–5; see Desmond 2008: 158–9 and 16–18 (on Antisthenes).

All things belong to the gods.
The gods are friends of the wise.
The possessions of friends are held in common.
Therefore all things belong to the wise.[13]

What positive content can we give to these claims, given Diogenes' radical rejection of standard views about political communities and about what constitutes wisdom? In part, the claims are simply an expression of this rejection. Normal ideas of what counts as a state or constitution are repudiated in favour of the puzzling assertion that the universe as a whole provides the context of citizenship. This assertion, in turn, rests on the belief that the universe, in the form of wild or cultivated nature, offers the resources and scope for the Cynic way of life, and does so without reference to political boundaries. The syllogism cited argues that the gods (as guardians of the natural world) make this state of affairs possible, and thus enable the 'wise' (that is, those who follow the Cynic way of life) to enjoy this possession, which is, in this sense, a 'world-community'. Clearly, there is no aspiration to extend legal or political rights, in the normal sense, beyond state boundaries to all humanity. A related syllogism, cited in the same context, undermines the idea that a proper form of communal life depends on laws by linking laws with what is civilized or 'urbane' (*asteios*), assumed to be something that is contrary to nature and therefore bad. An implied idea is that a world-community of the type Diogenes sees as valid could be created, if everyone followed his lead; and the self-publicizing Cynic style can be seen as designed to promote the growth of a community of this type. In this sense, Diogenes' cosmopolitanism can be taken as implying a coherent set of ideas, though these differ radically from conventional thought and are only partly similar to later Stoic ideas about cosmopolitanism.[14]

Cynic ideas and attitudes, though generally regarded as extreme, even repulsive, exercised a continuing and diverse appeal throughout the Hellenistic and Roman Imperial eras, especially in semi-popular thought and literature. Within ancient philosophy, more narrowly understood, Cynicism prefigures much that is typical of Epicurean ethics (though Epicureans are notably cool in their attitude towards Cynics). Points of resemblance include the claim that the core ethical principles are simple and intelligible by all, praise of a simple ('natural') life coupled with rejection of much that is linked with civilization, and the idea that nature can provide all that humans really need.[15] However, Cynic influence on Stoicism is yet more obvious and is sometimes fully acknowledged. We are told that Crates, a direct follower of Diogenes, was one of the teachers of Zeno, the founder of Stoicism, and Cynicism seems to lie behind the ideas of Aristo, another early Stoic. The Cynic idea that 'following nature'

---

[13]   D.L. 6.72; translation and lay-out here follow Moles 2000: 424.

[14]   See further Moles 2000: 423–32, also 1995. The ideal of 'Cynic kingship' developed by some later Cynics (on which see Höistad 1948) does not seem to reflect Diogenes' own thinking; see Moles 2000: 432.

[15]   On relevant features of Epicureanism, see Long and Sedley 1987 (=LS) 21 A(2), B (4), G(1), H (1, 4), I–J (LS refs are normally to sections and paragraphs). On the negative response to Cynicism of the Epicurean Philodemus, see Moles 2000: 416.

is the primary ethical principle was taken as fundamental for Stoicism (though very differently understood). Stoicism also took over, and transformed, the radically innovative Cynic idea of cosmopolitanism. Two works on political theory (both called the *Republic*) by Zeno and a later head of the school, Chrysippus, have been widely taken to express a Cynic-style rejection of conventional ideas about citizenship and sexual morality, though this interpretation has also been challenged.[16] Among the Stoics of the Roman Imperial period, Seneca and Epictetus both present the Cynic way of life as one whose validity Stoics can recognize, and the emperor Marcus Aurelius sometimes uses Cynic-style images in his Stoic-inspired meditations. In these and other ways, Cynic themes exercised a recurrent influence on Stoicism, despite the very substantial differences between the two movements.[17]

Beyond Classical antiquity, Cynicism has continued to have a wide reception, exerted either by its stark, simplistic moral messages or its distinctive serio-comic literary expressions. The influence of Cynic ideas has been traced in early Christian thought (perhaps even that of Christ himself, though this is more controversial), as well as in Renaissance and Enlightenment writings.[18] Among more modern thinkers, Nietzsche (1844–1900) adopted Cynic motifs in thought and, still more, in his itinerant style of life and provocative, unsettling mode of writing. He seems to have found in the Cynics precursors for his own radical challenges to standard ethical (and religious) ideas, and the correlated ideal of being 'free, *very* free spirits'. His project of 'revaluation of values' (perhaps echoing the Cynic 'defacing the currency') and assertion of a purely personal power of will that rests on a rejection of all established creeds and systems has a consciously Cynic character, though the stance is reconceived in more modern terms.[19] More recently, Peter Sloterdijk has adopted a form of Cynicism which identifies it with a post-modernist disillusionment with the 'grand narratives' of philosophy and religion that have sustained Western thought. L. E. Navia is both a contemporary scholar of Cynicism and someone who advocates a Cynic-style rejection of the modern conspicuous consumption and materialism that he sees as undermining both social life and the natural environment.[20]

For those living at the end of the start of the second decade of the twenty-first century, the damage done by uncontrolled acquisitiveness (in the name of advanced civilization) to the natural environment, and even to the financial system that is the vehicle of this acquisitiveness, is all too obvious. But is a revived Cynicism the most effective response we can make? Despite its potent images and admirable linkage between principles and way of life, the massive simplifications built into the theory make it a fragile basis for constructing a strong modern ethical theory and lifestyle. Just to note one

[16] See LS 67 A–G; also Schofield 1991: ch. 1, Vander Waerdt 1994, Vogt 2008: 154–60.
[17] On Cynic influence on Stoicism, see Moles 2000: 432–3, Desmond 2008: 210–11 (also 50–1, 58–60). On Cynic-Stoic ideas in Dio Chrysostom, see Gill 2000: 603–7.
[18] See Desmond 2008: 211–29.
[19] See Desmond 2008: 229–34.
[20] See Desmond 2008: 235–6; also Navia 1996.

problem: the idea that 'following nature' has to entail the rejection of *all* forms of human culture, including family life, cooking, and house-construction, is quite under-argued. There are also fundamental difficulties in a mode of ethical thought that denies the validity of sustained reflection and constructive argument. For these and other reasons, I think that, if we are drawn towards certain Cynic themes, including the ideas of following nature and cosmopolitanism, we will gain more from examining the Stoic transformation of these motifs than from reviving Cynicism in modern dress, like the thinkers just noted.

5.2 STOICISM

Cynicism, as noted already, had significant influence on Stoicism, in its origins and subsequently. Stoicism, like Cynicism (indeed, much more so) was widely influential in antiquity from its formation in the early third century BC until late antiquity, as well as having a substantial reception after antiquity. However, in other respects, the two movements are very different. Stoicism was an organized philosophical school, with a formal leader or 'head' (for much of its history) and a highly systematic body of teachings, grouped under the three general headings of logic, ethics, and physics. Founded around 300 BC by Zeno (*c*.334–*c*.262), Stoic theory was further developed by a series of powerful thinkers, the most important of which was Chrysippus (280/76–208/4). His many writings, now largely lost, did much to give Stoic philosophy its systematic character, which is reflected in the later summaries and reports on which we depend for our knowledge of Stoic doctrines. Stoic ethical theory was especially influential, shaping the dominant themes and tendencies in philosophical debate between the third century BC and the second century AD.[21] It also generated much teaching and writing on ethics approached from a practical standpoint, by (among others) Cicero, Seneca, Epictetus, and Marcus Aurelius, which further enlarges our understanding of the theory. These writings in turn helped especially to perpetuate interest in Stoic ethical ideas among Platonic and Christian thinkers in late antiquity and the Middle Ages as well as among 'Neo-Stoics' in the post-Renaissance thought-world.[22]

In contemporary ethical theory, Stoicism has taken on additional interest with the revival of virtue ethics and eudaimonism (theory centred on happiness). Stoicism offers an alternative to Aristotle, who has been the main Classical source of inspiration for those evolving modern versions of virtue ethics. A striking feature of Stoic ethical theory lies

[21] The most important accounts of Stoic ethics are those of Cicero, *On Ends* 3, Arius Didymus, preserved by Stobaeus, and Diogenes Laertius 7. For an overview of Stoic ethical theory, see Inwood and Donini 1999; for Stoic ethics viewed within ancient philosophical debate, see Annas 1993.

[22] On the history of the Stoic school, see Sedley 2003 and Gill 2003; on Stoic practical ethics see Sellars 2007; on the reception of Stoicism, especially in the early modern period, see Irwin 2003 and Long 2003, Miller and Inwood 2003.

in its combination of radical moral rigour or aspiration and a strongly naturalistic outlook. The distinctive Stoic claims about value, centred on the idea that virtue is both necessary and sufficient for happiness, are integrated with rich accounts of human psychology, and of individual and social development. They are also combined with a sophisticated analysis of the relationship between ethics and the study of nature, which they call 'physics'. This combination of ethical rigour and naturalism marks a contrast with what have been, until recently, the dominant modern versions of ethical theory, namely (Kantian-style) deontology and (especially Utilitarian) consequentialism. There is a partial contrast too with much modern virtue ethics, which has not tended to stress the linkage between virtue and human psychology or the place of humanity in the natural universe. However, these features of Stoicism strike a chord with some strands in contemporary thought. The interface of ethics and the scientific study of psychology, and the borderline between ethics and science more generally, especially bioethics, is a zone of intense interest at the present time. In this context, the ambitious mix of moral aspiration and naturalism we find in Stoicism offers something not present in quite the same way in Platonic or Aristotelian ethics. Of course, there are real questions about whether we moderns can take seriously the kind of combination of ideas found in Stoic theory. But, in the first instance, we need to make out what this combination consists in, which is the main focus of the following account.[23]

It is characteristic of ancient ethics, at least after Aristotle, to assume that happiness (*eudaimonia*) is the overall goal (*telos*) of a human life, though different theories offer different accounts of what constitutes happiness. The Stoics adopted what was seen as the 'hard' position on this question, namely that virtue is both necessary and sufficient for happiness. This position was also expressed as the idea that virtue is the only good, or that, of the three types of good normally recognized in ancient thought, only psychological goods (virtues) were *really* good, and not goods of the body (health or beauty) or external goods (material possessions or social relations).[24] In Books 4–5 of his work *On Ends* (or *Goals*), Cicero presents an extended debate between this view and an important competing position, that of Antiochus (*c*.130–*c*. 68 BC), which constituted an independent synthesis of Platonic, Aristotelian, and Stoic approaches. For Antiochus, virtue is, far and away, the most important contributor to happiness; but goods of the body and external goods also have some intrinsic value. Hence, although for Antiochus too virtue is both necessary and sufficient for the happy life, the other types of good contribute to making a life that is *most* happy.[25] In Cicero's version of the debate, both positions

---

[23] On ancient and modern versions of virtue ethics and eudaimonism, see Gill 2005: 1–7, also Annas 1993: 439–55, on ancient and modern ethics. On Stoicism correlated with Aristotle and Kant, see Engstrom and Whiting 1996; on Stoicism (or Stoic-style thinking) in connection with the interface of ethics, the philosophy of mind, and psychology, see Nussbaum 2001, especially chs. 1–2; for advocacy of Stoic ethics as a position we moderns can embrace, see Becker 1998.

[24] For evidence, see Long and Sedley (1987) (=LS) 60, 63.

[25] See Cicero, *On Ends* 4.2, 14–15, 19–23, 5.67–75, 77–95. Antiochus' position seems to represent a more systematic version of Aristotle's, as set out in *NE* 1.7–10, which attaches value both to virtue and external goods but does not work out fully the relationship between them (see further Annas 1993: 364–84).

make substantive points in defence of their view and against the opposing one. From Antiochus' standpoint, the Stoic position is, on the one hand, extreme and unrealistic in denying that bodily or external goods have *any* real goodness and, on the other, inconsistent in allowing that, even so, such things are not without any value (a point explained shortly). For the Stoics, Antiochus is inconsistent in seeing virtue as the supreme contributor to happiness, indeed, as necessary and sufficient for happiness, and yet still insisting that the other categories have intrinsic goodness. The competing merits of the two types of position have been analysed closely by modern scholars as well as in ancient sources; and the whole debate can be seen as instructive for modern theorists of virtue ethics and eudaimonism.[26]

The Stoic position is sometimes understood as an elaboration of an argument in Plato's *Euthydemus*, which is taken by some scholars to represent the characteristic position of the historical Socrates. The salient claim is that virtue is the only thing that benefits human beings *consistently and invariably*, whereas other things do so only intermittently and are, indeed, potentially harmful unless combined with virtue. It is suggested that reflection on this argument produced the core (orthodox) Stoic thesis on value. This is that, although virtue is the only good (the only thing that benefits consistently), the other so-called goods are naturally 'preferred' or 'preferable', even though, in comparison with the goodness of virtue, they are 'matters of indifference' (*adiaphora*). Although often attacked by ancient critics, such as Antiochus, this Stoic theory represents a coherent and defensible account of value.[27]

A related aspect of the theory (which also has Socratic or Platonic roots) is that the virtues constitute a unified or at least inter-entailing set or system. The virtues are not the only component of happiness, for the Stoics; this also includes features such as psychological beauty or harmony and a 'good flow of life', as well as certain characteristic affective states (the 'good emotions', *eupatheiai*). But these further features of happiness depend on the prior existence of virtue; hence, as it is sometimes put, happiness (and these further features) 'supervene' when virtue has completely shaped the personality of the agent.[28] The Stoic theory also rests on a further implicit thesis. The notion of good is characteristically conceived in Stoicism in terms of wholeness and structure (as well as benefit). It is partly for this reason that the Stoics conceive the universe as a whole as being good, indeed as the paradigm of goodness. Both virtue and happiness are conceived as aspects of goodness. Virtue is seen as having goodness partly because it confers

---

[26] See e.g. Irwin 1986, Annas 1993: 419–25, 431–5.

[27] See Plato, *Euthydemus* 281d2–e5, 291b–292d and LS 63–4. On the Stoic theory, see Striker 1996: 298–315; on the relationship between Plato's Socrates and the Stoic theory, see Annas 1994, Long 1996: ch. 1, McCabe 2002. Aristo (active mid-3rd century BC), an early Stoic subsequently seen as unorthodox, did not accept the validity of the idea of 'preferred indifferents' (LS 58 F–G, I).

[28] See LS 61 (on the virtues); and, on the unity or inter-entailment of virtues, Cooper 1998. On the features that depend on virtue, see Stobaeus 2.62.15–63.5 (section 5b4), translated in Inwood and Gerson 1997: 205, Diogenes Laertius 7.90–1, 94–6, LS 60 J–M. For the idea that happiness 'supervenes' on virtue, see LS 59 I (also 63 F), and preceding references in this note.

wholeness and structure on the agent's personality in a way that the other so-called 'goods' (the Stoic preferred indifferents) do not. The virtues, understood as a cohesive and inclusive set of dispositional states, both give the personality this wholeness and structure and provide the basis for the other components of happiness, such as psychological harmony and good affective responses such as 'joy'.[29] These further aspects of the Stoic theory involve additional claims and assumptions which can, of course, be challenged. But they bring out the links between the Stoic theory of value and other ancient (or modern) accounts of the relationship between virtue and happiness and indicate some of the supporting arguments for a position which can otherwise seem extreme or even arbitrary.

As suggested earlier, Stoic ethical theory is notable in combining a morally rigorous position on value with a strongly naturalistic outlook.[30] The Stoic theory of value is closely interlocked with accounts of ethical development (both individual and social), of human psychology, and of the place of humanity in the natural universe. In broad terms, the underlying claim is that Stoic ethical ideals, regarding virtue and happiness, for instance, are fully compatible with—and are indeed supported by—the best possible understanding of human psychology and development, and of the natural universe.

A central feature of the Stoic naturalistic outlook, and one crucial for their theory of value, is their account of ethical development. It is characteristic of ancient ethical theory, from Plato onwards, to give a prominent place to ideas about development; and the Stoic pattern is perhaps especially inspired by that of Plato's *Republic*, in which (as in Stoic thought) development is subdivided into psychological, or individual, and social strands.[31] However, there is an important difference between Stoic thinking about ethical development and that of Plato and Aristotle. For Plato and Aristotle, and for a number of later ancient thinkers such as Plutarch, effective ethical development depends on a combination on the right kind of inborn nature (*phusis*), habituation (*ethos*) in the right kind of family and community, and an education that gives scope for the proper exercise of reason (*logos*). The Stoics hold, by contrast, that 'all human beings have the starting-points of virtue'.[32] They believe that human beings are all constitutively capable of developing, in principle, to ethical perfection (or 'wisdom'), regardless of their social context.

At first sight, this seems to be another rather extreme or arbitrary claim; but it is supported by two other important Stoic theses. One is that all human beings are fundamentally capable of forming 'preconceptions' (*prolēpseis*) of key ethical notions such as 'good', and, in principle again, of reaching a correct understanding of these notions.[33] Another claim, explained more fully later, is that human motivation functions in a

[29] On Stoic 'good', see LS 60; see further M. Frede 1999, Gill 2006: 150–7.

[30] On different forms of naturalism in ancient ethics, see Annas 1993: 135–41, and, in Hellenistic ethics, Schofield and Striker 1986; on Stoicism and Epicureanism as competing versions of naturalism, see Gill 2006: 14–29.

[31] For different interpretations of the educational programme (combining psychological and communal or political strands) in Plato's *Republic* 2–4, 6–7, see Gill 1996: 260–87.

[32] LS 61 L (ascribed to Cleanthes) (= Stobaeus 2.65.8), my translation, cf. LS 61 K.

[33] See LS 60 B–F, 39 D(8); also Jackson–McCabe 2004, Inwood 2005: 271–310, Gill 2006: 132–3, 180–1.

unified or holistic way, rather than being subdivided into rational and irrational strands, as supposed by Plato and Aristotle. Hence, for the Stoics, changes in belief or understanding inform the whole personality. There is no need or scope for separate habituation of emotions or desires, as envisaged by Plato and Aristotle. Thus, in Stoic thought, there is no equivalent for the idea put forward by Aristotle that, at a certain point in one's life, change in ethical character is no longer possible because of the presence of ingrained, non-rational, dispositions.[34]

In Stoic theory, ethical development is seen as consisting in two, distinct but coordinate, strands, individual and social; both are characterized as forms of *oikeiōsis* ('familiarization' or 'appropriation'). As regards the individual side of the process, there are two main claims. One is that human beings, and other animals, are naturally attracted towards things that benefit their constitution (their make-up as natural kinds), rather than towards pleasure, as the Epicureans maintained.[35] 'Preferred' indifferents, in the scheme of value outlined earlier, consist in things that enable us to maintain our constitution, towards which we are instinctively attracted, such as health or material possessions.[36] The second claim relates only to ethical development in adult human beings, who are seen as being constitutively rational. If ethical development proceeds as it should, adult humans will, increasingly, select in a rational way the preferred indifferents towards which they were formerly drawn instinctively. The culmination of this process is described, in an especially important account, as one in which the agent comes to see virtue (or 'the regularity and harmony of conduct') as the only thing that is really good and desirable in itself. In this, culminating, stage one realizes that what matters, ultimately, is not just securing preferred indifferents but doing so in a virtuous way. The presentation of virtue as 'regularity and harmony' reflects the idea outlined earlier that goodness (and virtue as an expression of goodness) is characterized by wholeness, order, and structure.[37] Although the process outlined is an ideal one—and one that is, in fact, hardly ever achieved in full, as the Stoics allow—it is, none the less, conceived as a natural one, and one that represents the only proper expression of the nature of human beings as rational animals and thus the only proper target for human aspiration.

This analysis of (individual) ethical development raises a number of quite difficult interpretative and philosophical questions. One of these is how to understand exactly what is meant by selecting preferred indifferents in a virtuous way, and how this differs

[34] See Aristotle, *NE* 3.5, especially 1114a–21. For this contrast between Platonic-Aristotelian and Stoic patterns of thinking about development, see Gill 2006: 132–45. By 'Platonic-Aristotelian' is meant shared or overlapping themes in Plato, *Republic* and *Laws* and Aristotle's ethical treatises, especially *NE* 2.1, 10.9, which are adopted by later thinkers such as Plutarch and Galen (Gill 2006: 414–15, 420–1; Gill 2010a: 246–80). On the Stoic holistic approach to human psychology, see below.
[35] See LS 57 A–C, contrast 21 A(2). See also Brunschwig 1986.
[36] See LS 58.
[37] LS 59 D (=Cicero, *On Ends* 3.17, 20–2), especially (4–5); see also text to n. 29 above. See further Inwood 1985: 182–215, Annas 1993: 159–79, Striker 1996: 281–97, Gill 2006: 145–66 (with full references to previous scholarship).

from simply selecting preferred indifferents. It could mean that one chooses, consciously and deliberately, to act virtuously or to do the right thing for its own sake. However, Tad Brennan has recently suggested that a virtuous choice, in Stoic theory, should not be seen as one in which there is a conscious preference for the virtuous rather than the advantageous act. The explicit content of such deliberation will be, rather, obtaining things that are advantageous to oneself in a way that does not contravene other people's rights and which takes into account the needs of the larger community. Even so, objectively considered, such a choice should be seen as wholly virtuous.[38]

Brennan's account draws on at least some of the evidence for ethical decision-making in Stoicism, especially in Cicero's *On Duties*, which is based on an earlier Stoic treatise *On Appropriate Actions*. In Aristotle's case too, it has been argued that when a virtuous choice is defined as one that the agent does 'for its own sake' or 'for the sake of the fine', this does not mean she chooses the act under this description. The agent may simply think, 'This is the thing to do now', although from an authoritative third-personal standpoint (that of the person of practical wisdom, or *phronimos*), the choice might be correctly described as a virtuous one.[39] In Stoic terms, the virtuous agent might think, 'this is the appropriate (or 'fitting', *kathēkon*) thing to do now'. On the other hand, Stoic ethics, like most ancient ethical theories, is strongly aspirational in approach. Stoic ethical writings present at length ideals of character or state of mind, and patterns of life for people to adopt and make part of their own thinking. In Cicero's *On Duties 1*, the analysis of the virtues seems designed precisely for this purpose; and this account is linked with the theory of the four *personae* (roles), the explicit aim of which is to guide the agent's (deliberate) choice of life. This analysis is supplemented, in Cicero and elsewhere, by exemplary descriptions of actions and saying, sometimes attached to specific figures including Socrates and Diogenes the Cynic.[40] This dimension of Stoicism suggests that its adherents are meant to think of their actions as part of a conscious programme of aiming towards the life of virtue, which is also, of course, the happy life. The accounts of ethical development, both individual and social, can also be seen as depictions of a quest or journey that Stoics are encouraged to make fundamental to their lives. This is very much how teachers or writers of practical ethics, such as Seneca, Epictetus, or Marcus Aurelius invite one to think about the shaping of one's life.[41]

Perhaps one can reconcile these two approaches, to some extent at least. In Cicero's *On Duties*, the account of the virtues (along with other features) can be seen as designed to inform our understanding of the kind of actions that should present themselves as 'appropriate' ones to perform in specific situations. Such actions can still be chosen on the basis of the kinds of consideration stressed by Brennan. But these considerations, as

[38] Brennan 2005: chs 11–13, especially 210–11, 220–6.
[39] See e.g. Aristotle, *NE* 2.4, especially 1105a28–33, 3.7, especially 1115b11–13; see also Price 2005: 260–1, 272–8, especially 276.
[40] On the virtues, see Cicero, *On Duties* 1.18–99, linked with the theory of the four personae in 110–28; on Regulus as an exemplary figure, see 3.99–115. On the theory of the four *personae*, see Gill 1988; on exemplary figures in Epictetus, see Gill 2000: 610–11.
[41] See further Sellars 2007, Gill 2006: 380–91, 2007: 179–84.

well as providing criteria for what is 'appropriate', can also be seen as providing what Chrysippus calls 'the material (*hulē*) of virtue'.[42] In other words, virtuous actions may be chosen by the agent under two (compatible) descriptions, as being beneficial to oneself and the larger community, and as the expression of a broader, life-long, quest to realize the virtuous (and happy) life. On this view, discriminating between actions which are merely advantageous to oneself (preferred indifferents) and those which can also serve to express the quest towards virtue may reasonably form part of an agent's conscious deliberations, as is strongly suggested by Book 3 of Cicero's *On Duties*.[43]

Stoic theory offers a separate account of the social side of ethical development. A key claim is that the motivation to benefit others is a primary and universal one in all human beings, and indeed all animals. This parallels the claim noted earlier, that all animals, including humans, are motivated to benefit themselves by maintaining their constitution. In this side of the theory too, there is an ideal programme of development, which is relevant only for adult humans conceived as rational animals. One aspect of this programme is reaching the point of recognizing that all human beings as such (and not only those with whom we are directly linked) are, in principle, objects of concern and people we would wish to benefit. This aspect is sometimes expressed in terms of the ideal of the 'brotherhood of humankind' or 'cosmopolitanism'. Another aspect is full engagement in family, communal, and political life, conducted with a view to benefiting other people in that way.[44] These aspects might seem to be pulling in opposite directions; and they are, indeed, sometimes seen as belonging to different phases or strands of Stoic thought and linked with responses to Cynic or to more conventional social ideals. However, they can also be understood as coordinate aspects of a single process. The underlying thought may be that the full development of human rationality, combined with our basic desire to benefit others, leads to a recognition that we can and should benefit others both through the normal process of social engagement and through our relationships with other human beings (other rational animals) whom we encounter. There is no reason, that is to say, why our other-benefiting concern should be limited to those in our own family or community any more than there is any reason in principle why we should not engage actively in family and communal life as a means of expressing this concern.[45]

It seems reasonable to assume that the individual and social aspects of ethical development need to be integrated with each other for either strand to be carried to a conclusion. Although we do not have surviving theoretical treatments of this relationship, we can reconstruct some of the main lines, in part from writings on practical ethics. Thus, for instance, getting a grasp of what kinds of action count as 'appropriate' (a process crucial

---

[42] LS 59 A.

[43] See Cicero, *On Duties* 3.7–19; see also Inwood 1999: 112–13, 120–7.

[44] See LS 57, especially F (= Cicero, *On Ends* 3.62–8).

[45] See LS 67; also, stressing discontinuity in Stoic thought, Schofield 1991, and, stressing continuity, Annas 1993: 302–11, Vander Waerdt 1994, Vogt 2008: chs 1–2; also Gill 2000: 599–600. See also text to n. 16 above. See also Reydams-Schils 2002, 2005, underlining the importance of family and communal life in Stoic thought.

for individual development) depends in part on engaging in the kind of family or communal, or more broadly human, relationships that enable us to express the primary motive to benefit others. Without such engagement, our grasp of what the virtues are (and how this might inform our sense of what is 'appropriate') is necessarily incomplete. Correspondingly, if we fail to apply to our social relationships our growing understanding of the contrast in value between virtue and (preferred) indifferents, those relationships will go badly wrong. Our behaviour towards other people will express an over-valuation of preferred indifferents such as health or wealth (our own or that of other people), rather than expressing the aspiration to use such indifferents as a vehicle for acting virtuously.[46]

Stoic thinking on development shows how their theory of value is combined with a naturalistic outlook, at least in showing how this theory is combined with an account of what counts as 'natural' human development. 'Naturalism' of a rather stronger kind is expressed in the two remaining aspects of their thought considered here, their thinking on human psychology and on the relationship between ethics and the natural universe.[47]

In psychology, the key relevant point, noted earlier, is that (adult) human motivation is seen as functioning in a unified or holistic way, rather than being subdivided between rational and non-rational strands, as in Platonic and Aristotelian thought. Hence, in the process of development, changes in belief (for instance, about values or proper forms of relationship) necessarily bring about changes in desire or emotion without any need for separate training of non-rational parts of the personality. This has sometimes been seen, both in antiquity and subsequently, as an implausible or unrealistic claim. Those criticizing Stoic theory from this standpoint often presuppose the validity of the competing (Platonic or Aristotelian) view that psychology consists of separate 'parts', that is, independent sources of motivation. Hence, the Stoics are thought to claim that human emotions and desires derive from a (purely) rational or intellectual part of the personality.[48] In fact, the Stoic thesis is that human motives, which they call 'impulses' (*hormai*), constitute unified or holistic expressions of the psychological state of the person at any one time, in a way that cuts across the distinction made in other accounts between beliefs or reasoning and emotions or desires.[49] This is combined, in the part of their theory that falls under 'physics' (study of nature) with the belief that there is a single, unified, directing psychological organ (the *hēgemonikon*), which they locate in the heart, rather than separate psychophysical centres for rational and non-rational functions.[50] In contemporary thought too, human emotions or desires are sometimes analysed as being 'cognitive' or 'belief-based'

---

[46] See further Gill 2000: 607–11, 613–14, 2004: 119–24.

[47] Both these aspects, especially the latter, involve the combination of the perspectives of ethics and physics.

[48] For this kind of criticism, in antiquity, by Plutarch and Galen, see Gill 2006: 219–29, 244–66 (also Gill 2010a: 189–213); the validity of this criticism is presupposed by Sorabji 2000: 29–54.

[49] See Brennan 2003: 265–79, Gill 2006: 246–8; Graver 2007: 21–34.

[50] LS 53 G–H. See also Long 1999: 562–72, Gill 2010a: 87–103.

in a way that is comparable to the Stoic view. Also, some recent brain research, notably by Antonio Damasio, has stressed the extent to which psychological functions operate in a more unified, or at least interconnected, way than has often been presupposed.[51] Hence, in the current intellectual context, the Stoic unified approach to psychology may strike us as pioneering rather than outlandish.

The links between Stoic thinking about psychology and ethics come out especially clearly in their analysis of emotions. Emotions (*pathē*), which for them constitute a function of adult human beings, express the rationality that is constitutive of adult humans, while also involving correlated affective and psychophysical reactions. More precisely, they express the belief that 'it is appropriate to react' in a given way, for instance, with anger or grief, to a certain state of affairs, a belief that is taken necessarily to bring about anger or grief, which are 'impulses' with characteristic affective features. Most emotions (apart from the 'good emotions', *eupatheiai*, characteristic of the wise person) are seen as defective responses. They express misguided judgements about value; in particular, they express the belief that a preferred indifferent, such as wealth or health, is good (in the strong, Stoic sense) or that a 'dispreferred' indifferent, such as poverty or ill health, is bad in the same sense.[52] Defective emotions also have correlated affective features; typically, they entail intense (subjectively felt) psychophysical responses and have an 'overwhelming' impact on the overall motivational state of the person involved. Hence, for instance, pleasure is defined in this way: 'an elevation of the psyche [personality] which is disobedient to reason [i.e. ethically misguided], and its cause is a fresh believing that some bad thing is present at which it is appropriate to be elevated'.[53] The 'overwhelming' effect of such emotions is conveyed by comparing the state of those involved to people running rather than walking and thus not having the control over their movements that they would have when walking.[54] Thus, the Stoic account of emotions combines certainly widely recognized features of emotions, such as their character as intense 'feelings', with a unified psychological analysis which is interlocked with their ideas about value notions.

The Stoic theory of emotions raises at least two substantive questions for modern thinkers. One, already noted, is whether this kind of account is psychologically credible. A second question is whether we find morally acceptable a theory that presents most human emotions as being misguided and forms of psychological sickness. This question can be coupled with that raised by the theory of individual and social development outlined earlier. According to this theory, the health and welfare of those we love (as well as our own) is something that is only 'preferable', and not intrinsically good. The account of emotions presupposes this valuation. Hence, the theory challenges the standard view that, for instance, grief at the death of a loved person is an appropriate, indeed virtuous,

---

[51] The Stoic approach to emotions and that of Damasio 1994 are linked by Nussbaum 2001: 115–19 (which adopts a 'Neo-Stoic', cognitivist account of emotions), and Gill 2010a: 333–50. On modern cognitivist theories of emotions, see Goldie 2010: 26–32, 304–6.

[52] See LS 65 B, D, E; also Brennan 2003: 269–74, Graver 2007: 35–60.

[53] Stobaeus 2.90.16–18, translation based on Graver 2007: 42; see also Inwood and Gerson 1997: 218.

[54] LS 65 J; also A; see also Graver 2007: 61–83, Gill 2010b: 151–2.

reaction. Arguably, this aspect of the theory marks a point at which Stoic thinking diverges too far from normal ethical intuitions to be acceptable.[55]

However, it is not obvious that we have to reach this negative conclusion. As regards the Stoic theory of emotion, the core point is that our emotions do and should form part of our overall pattern of ethical thinking and responses. The Stoic wise person is not, as is often supposed, wholly emotion-free; rather, her 'good emotions' (*eupatheiai*) reflect the outcome of the interconnected programmes of individual and social development.[56] As regards our relations to other people, including loved individuals, benefiting such people (though not them alone) forms an integral part of development towards virtue and wisdom. Benefiting includes seeking what is naturally 'preferable' for them, including their health. However, the Stoic ideal is not limited to this objective. Its overall aims are those of benefiting oneself and others in a way that reflects one's developing understanding of the difference between (merely) selecting indifferents and doing so as an expression of the aspiration towards virtue. The Stoic viewpoint also urges us to accept, and to make integral to our structure of beliefs and emotions, facts which we would naturally prefer not to exist, including our own death and that of those we love (and all other human beings).[57] This is a rather complex, indeed profound, ethical programme; but it is one which may present itself to modern thinkers as valid and illuminating, as it did to people in antiquity.

The other aspect of Stoic naturalism considered here is the belief that ethical principles are, in some sense, consistent with the natural universe as a whole, or (put differently) that ethics is compatible with, and reinforced, by physics. Quite what this means is rather difficult to say and has been much debated in recent scholarship. A rather standard view is that the natural universe embodies principles, in particular those of structure and order or providential care, which represent normative ideals for human beings. It is for this reason that the Stoics sometimes present the study of physics, or certain aspects of this, notably, theology, as in some sense foundational for ethics.[58] On the other hand, some scholars, including Julia Annas, have stressed the extent to which Stoic ethics, and also Stoic physics and logic, are, for the most part, presented as independent bodies of knowledge, with their own internal coherence and completeness. Core aspects of Stoic ethical theory, such as their account of value or ethical development, are presented as inherently credible and not needing the support of a foundational account of the natural universe. Annas also points out, in a recent treatment, that, when Stoics discuss explicitly the relationship between the three main branches of knowledge, this is typically analysed as one of reciprocation and mutual support, rather than one in which one branch (physics) is foundational for another (ethics).[59]

---

[55] For this criticism of the Stoic theory, see Sorabji 2000: 173, Nussbaum 2001: 12.

[56] On 'good emotions', see LS 65 F, and Graver 2007: 51–5; the linkage between the theories of emotion and development are stressed by Gill 2006: 257–8, Graver 2007: 149–63, Gill 2010b: 150–4.

[57] For a related line of thought, see Graver 2007: 173–90.

[58] See LS 60 A and (on divine order and providential care) LS 54; see further Striker 1996: 228–31, M. Frede 1999, White 2002: 312–17.

[59] See LS 26 A–E; also Annas 1993: 159–66, 2007 (for the latter view, cf. Gill 2004: 111–16, 2006: 161–6, 197–200).

The latter point may offer a way of reconciling these emphases in recent scholarship. The case of theology may be an instructive one in this connection. Theology in Stoicism is seen, perhaps surprisingly to modern eyes, as a subdivision of physics, and, in fact, as the culminating subject in the study of nature.[60] However, it is clear that at least some aspects of the study of theology are also strongly informed by Stoic thinking on ethics and also logic (a branch of knowledge which is very broadly conceived in Stoicism). In particular, the account in theology of the topics of divine order and providential care is best understood as derived from a fusion of ideas, drawn equally from ethics, logic, and physics.[61] However these ideas (those of divine order and providential care) are ones which are usually seen as based on Stoic physics but able to play a crucial, even foundational, role in Stoic ethics. This line of thought may seem to involve a kind of circularity or infinite regress in Stoic thought: ideas based on a combination of ethics and physics are used to provide a framework for ethics, which in turn rests on ideas based on a combination of ethics and physics.[62] But the circularity, if it is one, is not necessarily a problematic one—provided we do not suppose that theology (or physics) is used to provide what one might call an 'Archimedean', that is, wholly external, foundation for ethics.[63] For the most part, the three branches of knowledge in Stoicism are, indeed, as Annas has argued, largely complete and independent.[64] However, there are certain important themes and principles, including those of order and providential care, which are common at least to ethics and physics. The significance that these ideas have in each of these areas is deepened and enhanced by the significance they have in the other area (or areas, if Stoic logic is brought into the picture). This seems both an inherently credible position and one that is compatible with most of our evidence, even if more work is needed to explore all the implications.[65]

This discussion also offers material for a question broached earlier and touched on subsequently: how far we moderns can take seriously the kind of combination of moral rigour or aspiration and naturalism we find in Stoicism. Both aspects of this combination (the ethical rigour and the naturalism) raise questions for us. But I focus here on the combination of these features found in Stoicism. The attempt to correlate ethics and the study of nature has a special interest for contemporary thought since it is one that is crucial for one of the most active areas of modern intellectual enquiry, that of bioethics. Particularly relevant for the comparison with Stoicism are modern attempts to derive principles from science (especially those relating to genetics or evolution) that are also

[60] LS 46 and 26 C.

[61] The ideas drawn from ethics include 'good'. For some indications of this fusion, see LS 54 B–D, F, H–K. On the fusion involved (including the logical dimension), see Graeser 1972 and Long 1996: 134–55.

[62] Plutarch highlights this kind of circularity in his critical discussion of this topic in *Moralia* 1035 D–F.

[63] For the idea of an 'Archimedean' (external) foundation for ethics, which he regards as a mistaken one, see Williams 1985: 28–9.

[64] Annas 1993: 162–6, 2007: 58–65.

[65] I propose to develop the view outlined in this paragraph elsewhere; on the idea of order as central in Stoic ethics, see text to nn. 29 and 37 above. On Stoic thought about divine providence, see D. Frede 2002.

relevant for ethics.[66] The reverse process, applying ethical principles to practical dilemmas posed by modern scientific developments, especially in genetics or bio-science more generally, is less relevant. The Stoic position, as outlined here, can be seen as embodying a methodology that can be applied more generally. The project is not one of trying to find for ethics foundational principles (in Stoicism, those of order and providential care) drawn from physics. Rather, it is one of treating each area (science and ethics, in modern terms) as independently coherent and complete. But it is also a matter of using concepts and methods developed in any one area to deepen and enhance analogous ones in another area. Put differently, it is a matter of establishing a kind of dialogue between the best available understanding of ethics and of science, each of these being treated as, potentially at least, mutually informing and reciprocal, rather than foundational for any other area.[67] Although this bare outline of the Stoic position, obviously, needs further exploration, it may be enough to show that the Stoic combination of ethics and naturalism has an unexpected relevance for one of the most important and intense modern debates. [68]

BIBLIOGRAPHY

Annas, J. 1993. *The Morality of Happiness*. Oxford: Oxford University Press.

—— 1994. 'Virtue as the Use of Other Goods', in T. H. Irwin and M. C. Nussbaum (eds), *Virtue, Love, and Form: Essays in Memory of Gregory Vlastos* (Edmonton, Alberta = *Apeiron* 36.3–4): 53–66.

—— 2007. 'Ethics in Stoic Philosophy', *Phronesis* 52: 58–87.

Becker, L. 1998. *A New Stoicism*. Princeton: Princeton University Press.

Brennan, T. 2003. 'Stoic Moral Psychology', in B. Inwood (ed.), *The Cambridge Companion to the Stoics*. Cambridge: Cambridge University Press, 257–94.

—— 2005. *The Stoic Life: Emotions, Duties, and Fate*. Oxford: Oxford University Press.

Brunschwig, J. 1986. 'The Cradle Argument in Epicureanism and Stoicism', in M. Schofield and G. Striker (eds), *Norms of Nature: Studies in Hellenistic Ethics* Cambridge: Cambridge University Press, 114–44.

Cooper, J. M. 1998. 'The Unity of Virtue', *Social Philosophy and Policy* 15: 233–74.

Damasio, A. 1994. *Descartes' Error: Emotion, Reason and the Human Brain*. London: Vintage Books.

Dawkins, R. 1976. *The Selfish Gene*. Oxford: Oxford University Press.

Desmond, W. 2008. *Cynics*. Stocksfield: Acumen.

Engstrom, S. and Whiting, J. (eds) 1996. *Aristotle, Kant, and the Stoics: Rethinking Happiness and Duty*. Cambridge: Cambridge University Press.

Frede, D. 2002. 'Theodicy and Providential Care in Stoicism', in D. Frede and A. Laks (eds), *Traditions of Theology: Studies in Hellenistic Theology*. Leiden: Brill, 85–119.

---

[66] A celebrated, and controversial, example is Dawkins 1976.

[67] On methodological issues in bioethics, see Steinbock 2007: part 1.

[68] I am grateful for the helpful comments of Julia Annas and Brad Inwood on an earlier draft of this chapter.

Frede, M. 1999. 'On the Stoic Conception of the Good', in K. Ieradiakonou (ed.), *Topics in Stoic Philosophy*. Oxford: Oxford University Press, 71–94.

Gill, C. 1988. 'Personhood and Personality: The Four-*Personae* Theory in Cicero, *De Officiis* 1', *Oxford Studies in Ancient Philosophy* 6: 169–99.

——1996. *Personality in Greek Epic, Tragedy, and Philosophy: The Self in Dialogue*. Oxford: Oxford University Press.

——2000. 'Stoic Writers of the Imperial Period', in M. Schofield and C. Rowe (eds), *The Cambridge History of Greek and Roman Political Thought* Cambridge: Cambridge University Press, 597–615.

—— 2003. 'The School in the Roman Imperial Period', in B. Inwood (ed.), *The Cambridge Companion to the Stoics*. Cambridge: Cambridge University Press, 33–58.

—— 2004. 'The Stoic Theory of Ethical Development: In What Sense is Nature a Norm?', in J. Szaif and M. Lutz-Bachmann (eds), *Was ist das für den Menschen Gute: Menschliche Natur und Güterlehre: What is Good for a Human Being: Human Nature and Values*. Berlin: De Gruyter, 101–25.

——2006. *The Structured Self in Hellenistic and Roman Thought*. Oxford: Oxford University Press.

——2007. 'Marcus Aurelius', in R. Sorabji and R. W. Sharples (eds), *Greek and Roman Philosophy 100 BC–200 AD*, vol. 1. London: Institute of Classical Studies, 175–87.

—— 2010a. *Naturalistic Psychology in Galen and Stoicism*. Oxford: Oxford University Press.

—— 2010b. 'Stoicism and Epicureanism', in P. Goldie (ed.), *The Oxford Handbook of the Philosophy of Emotion*. Oxford: Oxford University Press, 143–65.

——(ed.) 2005. *Virtue, Norms, and Objectivity: Issues in Ancient and Modern Ethics*. Oxford: Oxford University Press.

Goldie, P. (ed.) 2010. *The Oxford Handbook of the Philosophy of Emotion*. Oxford: Oxford University Press.

Goulet-Cazé, M. O. 1986. *L'Ascèse cynique: Un commentaire de Diogène Laërce VI 70–71*. Paris: Vrin.

Graeser, A. 1972. 'Zirkel oder Deduktion? Zur Begründung der stoischen Ethik', *Kant Studien* 63: 213–24.

Graver, M. 2007. *Stoicism and Emotion*. Chicago: Chicago University Press.

Höistad, R. 1948. *Cynic Hero and Cynic King: Studies in the Cynic Conception of Man*. Uppsala: C. W. K. Gleerup.

Inwood, B. 1985. *Ethics and Human Action in Early Stoicism*. Oxford: Oxford University Press.

——1999. 'Rules and Reasoning in Stoic Ethics', in K. Ieradiakonou (ed.), *Topics in Stoic Philosophy*. Oxford: Oxford University Press, 95–127.

—— 2005. *Reading Seneca: Stoic Philosophy at Rome*. Oxford: Oxford University Press.

—— and Donini, P. 1999. 'Stoic Ethics', in K. A. Algra, J. Barnes, J. Mansfeld, and M. Schofield (eds), *The Cambridge History of Hellenistic Philosophy*. Cambridge: Cambridge University Press, 675–738.

—— and Gerson, L. 1997. *Hellenistic Philosophy: Introductory Readings*. Indianapolis: Hackett.

Irwin, T. H. 1986. 'Stoic and Aristotelian Conceptions of Happiness', in M. Schofield and G. Striker (eds), *The Norms of Nature: Studies in Hellenistic Ethics*. Cambridge: Cambridge University Press, 205–44.

—— 2003. 'Stoic Naturalism and its Critics', in B. Inwood (ed.), *The Cambridge Companion to the Stoics*. Cambridge: Cambridge University Press, 345–64.

Jackson-McCabe, M. 2004. 'The Stoic Theory of Implanted Preconceptions', *Phronesis* 49: 323–47.

Long, A. A. 1996. *Stoic Studies*. Cambridge: Cambridge University Press.

—— 1999. 'Stoic Psychology', in K. A. Algra, J. Barnes, J. Mansfeld, and M. Schofield (eds), *The Cambridge History of Hellenistic Philosophy*. Cambridge: Cambridge University Press, 560–84.

—— 2003. 'Stoicism in the Philosophical Tradition', in B. Inwood (ed.), *The Cambridge Companion to the Stoics*. Cambridge: Cambridge University Press, 365–92.

—— and Sedley, D. N. 1987. *The Hellenistic Philosophers*. Cambridge: Cambridge University Press.

McCabe, M. M. 2002. 'Indifference Readings: Plato and the Stoa on Socratic Ethics', in T. P. Wiseman (ed.), *Classics in Progress: Essays on Ancient Greece and Rome*. Oxford: Oxford University Press, 363–98.

Miller, J. and Inwood, B. (eds) 2003. *Hellenistic and Early Modern Philosophy*. Cambridge: Cambridge University Press.

Moles, J. L. 1995. 'The Cynics and Politics', in A. Laks and M. Schofield (eds), *Justice and Generosity: Studies in Hellenistic Social and Political Philosophy*. Cambridge: Cambridge University Press, 129–58.

—— 1997a. 'Cynics and Cynicism', in D. Zeyl (ed., *Encyclopedia of Classical Philosophy*. Westport, CT: Greenwood Press, 160–2.

—— 1997b. 'Diogenes', in D. Zeyl (ed.), *Encyclopedia of Classical Philosophy*. Westport, CT: Greenwood Press, 194–6.

—— 2000. 'The Cynics', in M. Schofield and C. Rowe (eds), *The Cambridge History of Greek and Roman Political Thought*. Cambridge: Cambridge University Press, 415–34.

Navia, L. E. 1996. *Classical Cynicism: A Critical Study*. Westport, CT: Greenwood Press.

Nussbaum, M. C. 2001. *Upheavals of Thought: The Intelligence of Emotions*. Cambridge: Cambridge University Press.

Price, A. W. 2005. 'Aristotelian Virtue and Practical Judgement', in C. Gill (ed.), *Virtue, Norms, and Objectivity: Issues in Ancient and Modern Ethics*. Oxford: Oxford University Press, 257–78.

Reydams-Schils, G. 2002. 'Human Bonding and *Oikeiōsis*', *Oxford Studies in Ancient Philosophy* 22: 221–51.

—— 2005. *The Roman Stoics: Self, Responsibility, and Affection*. Chicago: Chicago University Press.

Schofield, M. 1991. *The Stoic Idea of the City*. Cambridge: Cambridge University Press.

—— and Striker, G. (eds) 1986. *Norms of Nature: Studies in Hellenistic Ethics*. Cambridge: Cambridge University Press.

Sedley, D. N. 2003. 'The School, from Zeno to Arius Didymus', in B. Inwood (ed.), *The Cambridge Companion to the Stoics*. Cambridge: Cambridge University Press, 7–32.

Sellars, J. 2007. 'Stoic Practical Philosophy in the Imperial Period', in R. Sorabji and R. W. Sharples (eds), *Greek and Roman Philosophy 100 BC–200 AD*, vol. 1. London: Institute of Classical Studies, 115–40.

Sorabji, R. 2000. *Emotion and Peace of Mind: From Stoic Agitation to Christian Temptation*. Oxford: Oxford University Press.

Steinbock, B. (ed.) 2007. *The Oxford Handbook of Bioethics*. Oxford: Oxford University Press.

Striker, G. 1996. *Essays on Hellenistic Epistemology and Ethics*. Cambridge: Cambridge University Press.

Vander Waerdt, P. A. 1994. 'Socrates and Stoic Natural Law', in Vander Waerdt (ed.), *The Socratic Movement*. Ithaca: Cornell University Press, 272–308.

Vogt, K. 2008. *Law, Reason, and the Cosmic City: Political Philosophy in the Early Stoa*. Oxford: Oxford University Press.

White, N. P. 2002. *Individual and Conflict in Greek Ethics*. Oxford: Oxford University Press.

Williams, B. 1985. *Ethics and the Limits of Philosophy*. London: Fontana.

CHAPTER 6

....

ANCIENT SCEPTICISM

....

RICHARD BETT

6.1

....

THE term 'scepticism' has meant a number of different things in the history of Western philosophy. In recent times J. L. Mackie referred to the thesis that *there are no objective values* as a species of moral scepticism.[1] For this he was taken to task by, among others, Bernard Williams, who maintained that 'Scepticism is basically concerned with doubt, and not necessarily with (the denial of) knowledge.'[2] But this seems to go wrong in two ways. First, Mackie's use of the term did not appear to have as its focus an issue about knowledge or its absence; his moral scepticism was, as he said, an ontological thesis, and the reason for calling it a form of scepticism appeared to be, roughly, that it was (as he saw it) a *rejection* of an important and widely shared everyday belief about the status of ethics. (The arguments for the thesis were in part epistemological in character, but the thesis itself was not.) And second, given the variety of usage in the term historically, it is hard to see that there is anything wrong with this.[3] Still, it is true that, in modern philosophy, the term 'scepticism' has more commonly been used in epistemology than in ethics, referring to positions according to which the possibility of knowledge—concerning the existence of the external world, for example, or of other minds—is denied or put in doubt. Of course, there is also a place where epistemology and ethics intersect, and hence there can also be sceptical theses about the epistemology of moral beliefs.[4]

---

[1] Mackie 1977: ch. 1.

[2] Williams 1985, at 204.

[3] The *OED* gives as one (albeit loose) sense of 'sceptic' 'an unbeliever in Christianity, an infidel'. If denial of the existence of the Christian God can count as a form of scepticism, why not also denial of the existence of objective values?

[4] This is the particular focus of Sinnott-Armstrong 2006. But note also the many non-epistemological varieties of moral scepticism that he introduces in a preliminary classification (ch. 1.3); again, scepticism at least in the area of ethics is not always about either doubt or the denial of knowledge.

One thing these observations bring out is that scepticism as it is now understood in philosophy is a piecemeal affair; one can be interested in or inclined towards scepticism on one topic without this interest or inclination being extended to other topics. Scepticism nowadays is, as Julia Annas has put it, 'local' as opposed to generalized or global.[5] In ancient Greek philosophy, however, it was not like this; instead, scepticism was an outlook that extended over all subject matters—one could not pick and choose what one was going to be sceptical about. Hence there was no such thing as scepticism purely about ethics; scepticism about ethics went along with scepticism about lots of other things, and the route to scepticism was essentially the same regardless of topic.

It can also be said, however, that in the ancient context there is an ethical aspect to scepticism as a whole. For ancient scepticism was not something merely to be studied or discussed (as scepticism in contemporary philosophy, whether of an epistemological or a moral variety, often seems to be); it was also something to be put into practice. In this respect scepticism is no different from any other ancient philosophy. Pierre Hadot in particular has emphasized the ancient conception of 'philosophy as a way of life', by contrast with more abstract, theoretical conceptions of the subject that in his view have largely (though not entirely) superseded it, for a variety of reasons, since the middle ages.[6] And as Hadot is well aware, the Greek sceptics were no exception to this general tendency in ancient thought.

A philosophy, in this period, is not *just* a way of life; according to the usual picture, at least, there need to be doctrines underpinning the way of life, and arguments supporting those doctrines. This is why Diogenes Laertius records a disagreement about whether Cynicism, a movement with a highly distinctive lifestyle, but minimalist in its doctrines and even more so in its use of argument,[7] should be considered a philosophy at all, as opposed to a (mere) way of life (*enstasin biou*, 6.103). And that is why the Pyrrhonist sceptic Sextus Empiricus has to give a highly nuanced answer to the question whether scepticism is a *hairesis*—literally 'choice', but used of philosophical schools (*PH* 1.16–17); the answer is 'no' if a *hairesis* involves accepting definite beliefs, but 'yes' if it simply involves going along, at least provisionally, with an account (*logos*) that shows how a certain way of life is possible. However, as this passage nicely illustrates, a certain way of life is at any rate a crucial component of the story; a set of arguments and conclusions, or an 'account', that had *no* consequences for one's life would simply not count as a philosophy.

Ancient Greek scepticism, then, is a comprehensive outlook. It discusses ethical topics, but many other topics besides; and the ways in which it treats ethical topics are fundamentally no different from the ways it treats any other topic. And since the discussion of all

---

[5] Annas 1986/1998. This essay remains an extremely valuable point of entry into many of the issues with which my contribution deals.

[6] See especially Hadot 1995. For some reservations about Hadot's thesis—which do not, however, affect the picture I am about to sketch—see Cooper 2007.

[7] Or at any rate, arguments in the usual sense. But some of the Cynics' *performances*—such as Diogenes' display of a plucked chicken, in response to Plato's definition of human being as a featherless biped (DL 6.40)—can be considered arguments of a kind. See Sluiter 2005.

these topics is supposed to have a practical effect on one's life, one may speak of ancient scepticism quite generally as in a sense ethical, regardless of the topics under discussion at any given time. All of this is in sharp contrast with how we now tend to see scepticism, ethics, and the intersection between them.

Nonetheless, it is in their discussions of ethical topics specifically that the ancient sceptics are most likely to be relevant to contemporary concerns in ethics (including the kinds of scepticism in ethics that I mentioned at the outset). So my survey of the ancient Greek sceptics, while giving some sense of their general orientation, will focus especially on this side of the subject. I will devote the most attention to Sextus Empiricus; as the only Greek sceptic whose writings have survived in bulk, but perhaps for other reasons as well, he is far more philosophically accessible than any of the others. Still, it will be worthwhile to begin with a look at the other important sceptical figures (all of whom preceded him), both for their intrinsic interest and to set the context for Sextus' work.

6.2

The hallmark of ancient Greek scepticism, most generally, is suspension of judgement; one withdraws from definite claims concerning how things really are. The differences among the sceptics have to do largely with how, precisely, this suspension of judgement is conceived, and what consequences, if any, are supposed to result from it. There are two traditions of ancient Greek thought that are now standardly recognized as sceptical: the Pyrrhonists, stemming in some loose sense from Pyrrho of Elis, and, for a certain extended period of its existence, the Academy founded by Plato. The Pyrrhonists were the ones who actually called themselves *skeptikoi*, 'enquirers'. But from antiquity onwards, the Academics in question have generally been seen as having enough in common with them to warrant the label.

The thought of Pyrrho himself (c.360–270 BC) is, to put it mildly, difficult to pin down. Only one short text survives that purports to provide a general picture of Pyrrho's philosophical attitudes, and this is very far from first-hand; it is a summary by the Peripatetic Aristocles (late 1st century BC or early 1st century AC) of an account by Timon, Pyrrho's most assiduous disciple, itself surviving only as a quotation in the work of Eusebius, the fourth-century bishop of Caesarea (*Praeparatio evangelica* 14.18.1–5). The passage speaks of *ataraxia*, freedom from worry, as the outcome, according to Pyrrho, of reflection about the nature of things and about the attitude one should take towards them. Scholarly opinion is sharply divided as to whether Pyrrho's answer to the question 'What is the nature of things?' is 'their nature is unknowable' or 'their nature is indeterminate'—in other words, whether their true qualities are beyond our cognitive reach or whether, in reality, they have *no* definite qualities.[8] But either way, the result is

---

[8] For a brief exploration of these two options, see Bett 2010. The first option is advocated in Stopper 1983 and Brennan 1998, the second in Long and Sedley 1987: section 1, and Bett 2000: ch. 1.

that one should avoid saying or thinking anything about them that would attribute to them any definite qualities. And it is this refraining from definite views or assertions that is said to yield *ataraxia*. Whatever the precise relation between Pyrrho and the later thinkers that called themselves Pyrrhonists—and this too is a matter of much dispute—it is this connection between a withdrawal from definite claims and the attainment of *ataraxia* that is the obvious common thread between them; more on this later.

Why ceasing to hold such definite opinions should yield *ataraxia* is not explained in the passage from Aristocles. But a passage in Diogenes Laertius' life of Pyrrho suggests that prominent among the definite claims that one ceases to make, if one follows the recommended program, are ethical or evaluative ones. 'He said that nothing was either fine (*kalon*) or foul (*aischron*), just or unjust; and similarly in all cases nothing is the case in reality, but humans do everything by convention and habit; for each things is no more this than that' (9.61). Our actions, then, are not based on a response to real qualities inherent in the nature of things, and, especially, not on a response to real *values*, such as fineness or justice, inherent in the nature of things (either because these qualities do not exist or because they are inaccessible to us). Now, if one ceases to hold any opinions to the effect that things really have value (or disvalue), it is natural to assume that one will care a great deal less about what happens than one would if one did hold such opinions. And this may be why the practical outcome of adopting this attitude will be *ataraxia*: one is tranquil because one has much less of a stake in any particular course of events than one used to.[9] As we shall see, Sextus explains the sceptic's attainment of *ataraxia* in similar terms, and this may be another point of contact between Pyrrho and the later Pyrrhonist tradition. Certainly a large part of the evidence we have about Pyrrho, from Diogenes Laertius and elsewhere, consists of anecdotes that illustrate his extraordinary lack of concern about what he did and what happened to him. These stories are, of course, not necessarily to be taken as reliable reports; but they do show that Pyrrho's image, at least, was of someone who really did not see genuine differences of value among different objects or courses of action—an attitude referred to in some sources as *adiaphoria*, 'indifference'.

Cicero, indeed, seems to regard Pyrrho as entirely an ethical thinker, with this message of blanket 'indifference' as his central tenet. But Cicero also ascribes to Pyrrho—along with the extremist Stoic Aristo of Chios—two crucial exceptions: virtue is not indifferent but good, and vice is not indifferent but bad. There is good reason to think that Cicero is mistaken about this latter point.[10] None of the other evidence on Pyrrho suggests such an orientation towards virtue and vice (and the Diogenes passage emphasizing his evaluative neutrality points against it). But we know from elsewhere that Aristo did believe in the special status of virtue and vice, while also holding that everything *else* was indifferent. Cicero's knowledge of Pyrrho seems to derive from a source in which a taxonomy of ethical positions was offered, and in which Pyrrho and Aristo were

---

[9] For further exploration of this possibility, see Bett 2000: ch. 2.3; or, more briefly, Bett 2010: section 5.
[10] For further detail on this, see Bett 2000: ch. 2.6.

treated together; he has no inkling of Pyrrho as a sceptical thinker, and virtually no sense of Pyrrho as an individual. Concerning the indifference of everything other than virtue and vice, Pyrrho and Aristo can indeed be placed together; Cicero (or perhaps his source) seems to have made the unwarranted inference that they agreed as well about the special status of virtue and vice. However, in his emphasis on the ethical or practical dimension of Pyrrho's thought as primary, Cicero does seem to be on target. We are told that Pyrrho travelled in Alexander's expedition to India and encountered 'naked wise men' (*gumnosophistai*, DL 9.61), and it is suggested that this was actually the source of his philosophy. This east–west connection is fascinating to speculate about; and clearly there is some similarity between Pyrrho's 'indifference' and the quietist aspect of much ancient Indian thought. But speculation on the topic is really all that is possible.

Pyrrho seems to have attracted a considerable following in his own lifetime, but his immediate influence appears to have been short-lived; although Timon's writings certainly celebrated him, he himself wrote nothing, and it may be that his lived practical demeanour was the main thing that attracted people to him. In any case, scepticism next makes its appearance in the Academy. Diogenes Laertius tells us that Arcesilaus of Pitane (316/5–241/0 BC), the fifth head of the Academy after Plato himself, was the first to 'suspend his assertions because of the oppositions of arguments' (DL 4.28). In the same place Diogenes says that Arcesilaus was the first to disrupt the type of discussion (*logos*) initiated in the Academy by Plato and 'make it more argumentative by means of question and answer'. It may well be true that Arcesilaus changed what had been standard practice since Plato; but of course, as was noticed in antiquity, the description given here of Arcesilaus does answer to aspects of the portrait of Socrates in a number of Plato's dialogues. In any case, the exercise of inducing suspension of judgement by generating equally powerful opposing arguments—either from one's own argumentative resources or by juxtaposing the competing arguments of others, or both—became the centre of Academic practice for close to two centuries, the other leading figure in this movement being Carneades of Cyrene (214–129/8 BC).

Like Pyrrho, both Arcesilaus and Carneades wrote nothing, and this is one reason why a secure reconstruction of their thought is very difficult. Our main evidence about them comes from Sextus and Cicero, but both of these have an axe to grind; Sextus wants to make their approach look as different as possible from his own Pyrrhonist scepticism, and Cicero is a party to debates about the true nature of the Academy—debates that indeed led to its collapse as a single institution—in which the correct understanding of the earlier sceptical Academics, especially Carneades, was a central issue. One particularly difficult question is whether we should understand the Academics as aiming for, or claiming to attain, suspension of judgement in their own persons, or whether their sceptical argumentation is purely critical or dialectical in character, directed against the proponents of positive philosophical doctrines and designed to show that, on their own showing, *they* should be sceptics. That many of the Academics' arguments are targeted at others, especially the Stoics, is undeniable. On the other hand, this is not incompatible with their having themselves been sceptics. And Arcesilaus is reported by both Sextus and Cicero as enthusiastically *recommending* suspension of judgement, not just claiming to have forced others into it (*PH* 1.232–233, *Acad.* 2.76–77), while Carneades is reported to have accomplished a Herculean task in ridding our minds of that 'wild and savage monster', assent (this being the opposite of suspension of judgement—*Acad.* 2.108). This latter report, though, comes from Carneades' associate Clitomachus, and does not purport to reproduce Carneades' own words; it is hard to find anywhere in the evidence a direct indication of Carneades' own attitude to suspension of judgement, and Clitomachus' florid language may be his own embellishment.[11]

One thing that is clear is that the Academics have nothing to say about *ataraxia* as the supposed outcome of suspension of judgement. But they nonetheless take an interest in the question what it would be like to live while suspending judgement (whether this is for their own benefit, or for the opponents whom they take themselves to have forced into this position). Arcesilaus is credited with the puzzling remark that one is still left with the option of deciding and acting on the basis of 'the reasonable' (Sextus, *M* 7.158), while Carneades offers a much more elaborate account of various levels of 'persuasive impressions' (*M* 7.166–189). But while the latter, at least, looks like a relatively detailed picture of how practical reasoning might be feasible in the absence of any commitment to definite truths, it operates at a purely formal level; there is no suggestion in the surviving evidence as to *what* decisions might seem 'persuasive' to a sceptic at any given time. But then, perhaps there is nothing informative to say about this; the answer may simply depend on whatever factors had shaped the sceptic's particular mindset up to that point.

We do have evidence of arguments from Carneades about several ethical or ethically relevant topics—justice, the *telos* (that is, the end or goal of life), freedom and determinism (or its opposite), divination, and the existence of the gods.[12] Again, these arguments tell us nothing about Carneades' own views on the topics in question; the aim is not to convince the audience of any particular position, but to induce suspension of judgement on the topic. The arguments are frequently negative in character; for example, Carneades argues that divination is a fiction and that the gods do not exist. The point, however, is not to get us to accept these conclusions, but rather to undermine the positive beliefs of non-sceptics on these subjects, leaving us holding no definite position either way. Sometimes Carneades himself argues on both sides of the case; while on a visit to Rome as an ambassador, he shocked the Romans by arguing first in favour of justice and then against it. And sometimes he devises a whole taxonomy of dogmatic positions, including positions of his own invention; here the goal seems to be to show how they undermine one another. His 'division' of views on the *telos* (Cicero, *De finibus* 5.16–20) is perhaps

---

[11] John Cooper has recently argued against a purely dialectical reading of Arcesilaus; see Cooper 2004. But Cooper does not suggest the same about Carneades. The most recent substantial article on Carneades does not even attempt to resolve the issue in his case, calling it 'completely unclear'; see Obdrzalek 2006 (quoted phrase on p. 243). For more on the issue, see Brittain 2005 (Arcesilaus) and Allen 2004 (Carneades).

[12] e.g. Lactantius *Divinae institutiones* 5.14.3–5=LS 68M (justice), Cicero *De finibus* 5.16–20 (the *telos*), Cicero *De fato* 20–33 (free will), Cicero *De divinatione* 2.9–10 (divination), Sextus *M* 9.139–141, 182–184 (the gods).

the most famous example of this,[13] but his engagement with both the Epicureans and the Stoics on how our actions can be free (Cicero, *De fato* 23–33) seems to be another. His arguments on the latter subject are highly suggestive and acute; among other things, he asserts (against the Epicureans) that randomness is no more favourable to freedom than determinism is, and (against both the Stoics and the Epicureans) that accepting the principle of bivalence does not mean accepting that everything is fated. The position he advances, relying on the insight—derived perhaps from the basic experience of agency—that 'something is in our power' (31), looks like a serious alternative to its Stoic and Epicurean rivals, and seems to anticipate some modern views on the subject. But, to repeat, a serious alternative, subverting assent away from the other views on offer, is *all* it is attempting to be—not a replacement for, or improvement on, those views.

We do not hear of Arcesilaus specifically discussing ethical topics. But there is no reason not to think that he did so; the subjects about which he was prepared to argue are said to have been quite unrestricted (e.g. Cicero, *De finibus* 5.10). On the other hand, there is no reason to think that this would have allowed us any more of a glimpse into his own practical attitudes than Carneades' engagement with ethics allows us with respect to his. And there is no reason in his case any more than in that of Carneades to think that ethical topics were approached in any different spirit from other topics.

In sharp contrast to this, we are told that the later Academic Philo of Larissa devised his own ethical system (Stob. 2.39, 20–41, 25). But this too is in keeping with Philo's approach more generally; unlike the earlier Academics, he often appears to put forward positions of his own, albeit explicitly tentative and revisable ones. The system appears to have contained many of the components of standard dogmatic ethical theory: a specification of the *telos*, a delineation of what things are genuinely good and bad, and so on. The details are difficult to reconstruct, although an excellent attempt is made by Charles Brittain in his book on Philo.[14] But although Brittain has a point in calling Philo (in the book's subtitle) 'the last of the Academic sceptics', it is clear that his scepticism—if that is what we should call it[15]—is of a highly mitigated kind, and his willingness to develop a positive ethical position is a striking symptom of this. Indeed, it was precisely *not qua* proponent of a sceptical outlook that he had concrete things to say about how to act—even if the mitigated variety of scepticism that he adopted was consistent with his saying these things.

The Academy ceased to exist as an organized school after the period of Philo. But Philo's mitigated scepticism, and the wholesale abandonment of scepticism by his Academic rival Antiochus, seems to have led to a reaction. At some point in the early first

[13] On Carneades' 'division', its possible purposes in Carneades' own hands, and the uses made of it by later authors, see Annas 2007.

[14] Brittain 2001: ch. 6.

[15] Brittain reconstructs three distinct, and progressively less sceptical, Philonian positions. In Brittain 2001 he seems to be willing to call even the last position (with which he is inclined to associate Philo's ethical thought, 276–77) scepticism; explicit statements on the question are rare, but see 165–66. However, in the Introduction to Brittain 2006, Philo's last position is characterized as no longer sceptical (xiv, xxx–xxxi). The issues are too complex for us to engage with here; but they do not affect the central claims in this paragraph.

century BC Aenesidemus of Cnossos, apparently for a time himself a member of the Academy, started a new movement of thought, claiming inspiration from Pyrrho and self-consciously directed against what he considered the watered-down scepticism of the Academy—especially the Academy of his own day. The evidence for these various points comes from a summary of Aenesidemus' work *Pyrrhonist Discourses* (*Purrôneioi Logoi*) by Photius, the ninth-century patriarch of Constantinople (*Bibliotheca* 169b18–171a4). Unfortunately the summary is very brief, and the work itself is lost; Photius gives us a page or two on the first book, which appears to have explained the Pyrrhonist outlook in general terms, followed by thumbnail sketches, just a sentence or two for each, of the remaining seven books, which addressed more specific topics. One thing suggested by the general summary is that Aenesidemus took from Pyrrho the idea that a sceptical attitude results in *ataraxia,* or something closely resembling it; the non-Pyrrhonist is described as being in the grip of 'continuous torments' (*Bibliotheca* 169b24), whereas the Pyrrhonist is said to be happy in his withdrawal from claims to know things (*Bibliotheca* 169b26–9). The last three of the specific books were devoted to topics in ethics. Book 6 was about the good and the bad and related topics, and Photius says that Aenesidemus 'closed these things off from our apprehension and knowledge' (*Bibliotheca* 170b25–6); he also says that this was done by means of 'the same tomfoolery' (*Bibliotheca* 170b24–5) as was employed in connection with other topics (Photius is far from an admirer), and the sketch of Aenesidemus' procedure in other cases seems to confirm that it was essentially the same whatever the subject matter. Book 7 was about the virtues; in this case Photius simply says that Aenesidemus claimed to undermine the pretensions of those who took themselves to have achieved a solid theory on the subject (*Bibliotheca* 170b27–30).

So far—except for the payoff in terms of *ataraxia,* which is a distinctively Pyrrhonist move—the picture, while not developed in any detail in Photius' summary, seems consistent with the strategy of inducing suspension of judgement that we have seen with Arcesilaus and Carneades. But Photius' report on the eighth and final book, about the *telos,* points in a different direction; here Aenesidemus' approach consisted of 'allowing neither that happiness nor pleasure nor practical wisdom, nor anything else that one of the philosophical schools would believe in, is a *telos,* but saying that the *telos* they all celebrate simply does not exist' (*Bibliotheca* 170b31–5). The assertion that *there is no such thing* as a *telos* sounds rather different from suspension of judgement, at least as we have considered it so far. However, this too is something Photius attributes to Aenesidemus in other cases; the summary also includes the claims that there is no such thing as a sign and no such thing as a cause (*Bibliotheca* 170b12–14, 18–19). In addition, Aenesidemus' general method, as explained in the first book, seems to have included a willingness to make relativized assertions of the form 'X is F at some times but not at others' or 'X is F for one person but not for another'; these are contrasted with what Photius (perhaps reproducing Aenesidemus' language) calls 'unambiguous' assertions (*Bibliotheca* 169b40, 170a29), which he attributes to the Academics of his day and treats as a key instance of their failure to maintain a sceptical outlook. As with the negative existential claims, the question arises how assertions of relativities can be considered consistent with suspension of judgement.

The answers to these questions will be easiest to address in the context of Sextus' work. As we shall see, Sextus (sometimes, at least) makes precisely the same kinds of assertions about the good and the bad; but in his case we have the advantage of extended original texts to work with. As for the remainder of the Pyrrhonist tradition besides Aenesidemus and Sextus (who appears to have lived in the second century AD), we know very little more than the names of a few leading practitioners, and nothing of particular relevance to ethics. From now on, then, I concentrate on what is by far the richest of those records, the surviving works of Sextus Empiricus.

6.3

In what is probably the most important sentence from his best-known work *Outlines of Pyrrhonism (PH)*, Sextus says 'The sceptical ability is one of placing in opposition things that appear and are thought in any way at all, an ability from which, because of the equal strength in the objects and arguments that stand in opposition, we come first to suspension of judgement, and then after that to freedom from worry' (*PH* 1.8). Again, as with Pyrrho and Aenesidemus, we have *ataraxia* as the result of a withdrawal from definite claims. And again, as with Arcesilaus and Carneades, we have suspension of judgement produced by means of oppositions. The items opposed are not only arguments, but also include 'things that appear'; this need not refer only to sensory impressions, but may also refer to any way in which things strike us pre-reflectively and non-philosophically. And the phrase 'in any way at all' indicates that these common-sense 'appearances' may be juxtaposed either with other, conflicting common-sense appearances or with countervailing philosophical arguments; Sextus' writings give us plenty of examples of both. What is, if not new, at least more explicit in Sextus' statement than in our evidence from earlier sceptics is that suspension of judgement is the result of the 'equal strength' of the items opposed; and the same may be said of the claim that scepticism is an 'ability'. Both points indicate the Pyrrhonist's lack of theoretical commitment. 'Equal strength' is a psychological notion. It is not that one comes to the conclusion that suspension of judgement is *rationally required*. Rather, one simply *finds oneself* equally drawn to—or perhaps, equally repelled by—the two or more alternatives presented; and so, since one cannot help but see these alternatives as mutually exclusive (this too being viewed as simply a fact about one's psychological make-up, not anything with a grounding in logical theory), one cannot help but withdraw from definite commitment to either (or any) of them. And scepticism is characterized as an 'ability' rather than a theory or doctrine; the sceptic is not someone who holds certain views, but someone who engages rather successfully in a certain type of activity—the activity of generating oppositions. This latter point also underscores the practical character of Pyrrhonism. It is not just that there is a practical consequence, *ataraxia*. Scepticism itself consists of *doing* something on an ongoing basis (as Sextus' own works illustrate at length); it is not a conclusion, and it is not achieved once and for all. Rather, suspension of judgement is maintained by a constant flow of opposing arguments and impressions, and the sceptic's way of life centres around ensuring the continuation of that flow.

This raises an obvious question, one that non-sceptics in antiquity did not hesitate to press: how is such a life even possible? There has to be more to life than *just* generating oppositions. Living also requires such mundane things as food, shelter, and interaction with those around one; and these things require one to act in certain ways, and also to choose between alternatives, which seems on the face of it incompatible with suspension of judgement. Sextus would reply that one is not, in fact, required to make *choices*, if by that is meant decisions concerning the superior rational basis for one course of action over others. The sceptic does indeed act, and does indeed in a sense opt for some courses of action over others; but this 'opting', again, is not a matter of what he judges as the best or the most rational course of action, but simply of which course of action he in fact, because of the particular repertoire of dispositions that has developed in him, happens to be drawn to. As Sextus puts it, the sceptic follows the *appearances* (*PH* 1.22), without taking any stand on whether things actually are as they appear. *That* things appear to one a certain way is not itself up for dispute (and is not what one suspends judgement about); but whether they are really that way is another issue altogether. And how things do appear to one, he says, is due to various factors, some of which we might call natural and some cultural (*PH* 1.23–4). On the natural side, it is just a brute fact that we are built in such a way as to have certain types of sense-perceptions and certain types of thoughts; under the latter heading would come the tendency, mentioned in the previous paragraph, to see some propositions as incompatible with others. It is also a brute fact that we experience hunger, thirst, pain (etc.), and that these feelings spur us to eat, drink, and take evasive action (etc.). On the cultural side, each of us is raised in a certain society, and this society reinforces certain patterns of behaviour and suppresses others. The sceptic, then, will conform to the laws and customs of his society—not because he thinks this is the right thing to do, but simply because he was raised that way (the 'because' here being purely causal or explanatory, not justificatory). And the sceptic will make a living by developing (and passing on to his successors) certain kinds of expertise; virtually the only thing we know about Sextus is that he was a doctor, and this is an obvious example.

A modern medical student would find this last point incredible. Learning to be a doctor, the student would object, is not just a matter of learning how to perform surgeries, administer drugs, and so on; it also involves an understanding of how the body works and hence of *why* these procedures can be expected to help the patient. But this is precisely what Sextus is denying, and he was not alone. The Empiric school of medicine claimed to practice medicine simply by learning and exercising a set of routines (routines developed historically through the *experience* of what succeeds in given circumstances—hence the name), without holding any theory about the underlying workings of the body that would justify those routines. We are told (e.g. DL 9.116) that Sextus was an Empiric, as his name (or title) would suggest,[16] and he was not the only Pyrrhonist of whom this was true; given the common features just mentioned, this is

---

[16] In one puzzling chapter (*PH* 1.236–41) Sextus addresses the question whether medical Empiricism is the same as scepticism, and answers 'no: another medical school, Methodism, is closer'. But it is at least possible to read this as expressing opposition to one form of Empiricism, rather than to any thought or practice that might deserve the label.

not surprising.[17] Learning to be a doctor, then, is like learning to ride a bicycle; it is know-how, with no propositional knowledge supporting it. And this is of a piece with Sextus' conception of the sceptic's life as a whole. One acts in given ways in given circumstances because one has a whole set of dispositions, both natural and culturally induced, that incline one in those directions in those circumstances. In no case does one act in a certain way because one thinks one *ought* to act that way, or that this is the *best* way to act—whether the 'ought' is moral, prudential, or of any other kind; one acts that way because one's dispositions push one in that direction—end of story. In the moral case, at least, non-sceptics clearly found this unacceptable. Sextus at one point considers an objection: what if a tyrant forces you to commit some atrocious act, or you will be tortured and killed (*M* 11.163—166)? The point of the objection, as Sextus makes quite clear, is that such a choice is impossible without making a principled (and hence non-sceptical) decision about what things are really important.[18] And Sextus' answer is simply 'no, it isn't'; the sceptic will act as his complex of dispositions inclines him to act, and no issue of principle need enter the picture. We shall return to this example; but for now the point is that the sceptic's practice, as Sextus portrays it, is in this respect quite consistent across the board.

That practice, as we have seen, includes no commitment to certain things being genuinely good or bad. Now, given the centrality of the concepts good and bad in ancient Greek ethics generally, it is not surprising that they figure among the topics that Sextus explicitly addresses. What is surprising, however, is the way this subject is treated in at least one of the works that address it. One would expect Sextus to produce a series of opposing arguments and impressions designed to lead us to suspension of judgement about whether anything is in reality good or bad, or about what things, if any, are in reality good or bad. This is indeed what happens in the portion of *Outlines of Pyrrhonism* that deals with ethics (*PH* 3.235). But in *Against the Ethicists*, which covers much of the same ground at somewhat greater length, Sextus instead argues for the conclusion that *nothing* is in reality (or 'by nature') either good or bad (*M* 11.78, 89, 95). Of course, a sceptic can argue for anything he likes, so long as this is balanced by something of 'equal strength' on the other side. But Sextus offers no such balancing considerations, nor does he expect us to bring them to bear from our own pre-existing ethical consciousness or from our knowledge of opposing, non-sceptical positions. For he several times makes clear that the sceptic's goal of *ataraxia* is to be attained not by suspending judgement about the topic, but by coming to *accept* the conclusion of his arguments. We will attain *ataraxia*, he says, 'when reason has established that none of these things is by nature good or bad' (*M* 11.130); that there is nothing good or bad by nature is also referred to as the sceptic's 'teaching' (*M* 11.140). But while the sceptic, according to this picture, is willing to deny the existence of anything good or bad by nature, he is also willing to call

---

[17] On connections between the Pyrrhonists and the Empiricists, see Allen 2010.

[18] The point is not that the sceptic will not do the *right* thing (by the objector's lights)—although this may well be true, and I return to this point below. The point is that *whatever* the sceptic does, this must be the result of a principled decision, and hence the sceptic will be convicted of inconsistency.

things good or bad (or at least, 'to be chosen' and 'to be avoided', which apparently amount to the same thing) in a relative or qualified way—that is, at certain times (but not others) or in relation to certain persons (but not others) (M 11.114, 118). These relativized assertions are, then, compatible with, indeed part and parcel of, the denial of things being good or bad by nature.

This is the closest we get among the ancient sceptics to modern moral scepticism à la Mackie. 'By nature good and bad' functions as a rough equivalent to Mackie's 'objective values'; and one of Mackie's arguments for the thesis turns on considerations of relativity. I return briefly to Mackie below. For now, though, I want to return to the oddity of this argument in the context of Sextus' other writings; it is by no means what one would expect from Sextus' central description of what scepticism is, with which I began this section. Instead, it looks like an instance of the same pattern of thought as we observed in passing at the end of the previous section in connection with Aenesidemus; there too there were negative existential claims coupled with a willingness to make relativized assertions. But here we get a little more detail about how this is supposed to work.

The key point is a particular conception of what it is for something to be a certain way by nature, or in reality. For anything to be good or bad by nature, Sextus says, its goodness or badness would have to be 'common to all' (M 11.69–71), not—as turns out to be the case, according to the argument that follows—restricted only to some people. The reason for believing that there are, as Sextus puts it, only 'private goods' (M 11.78) is simply that people have different conceptions of the good; apparently, then, if something does not strike a person as good, it *is not* good for that person—the idea of someone's being *mistaken* about what is in fact good does not seem to enter the picture. Subsequent discussion (M 11.114, 118) makes clear that the relativity is not only to persons, but to circumstances. Thus, for something to be by nature good, its goodness would have to be apparent to everyone and applicable in all circumstances; to say that nothing is by nature good is simply to say that nothing meets that standard. And if this is the standard, then of course relativized assertions are not even in the running for being about the nature of things; for universal applicability is precisely what they avoid.

Yet Sextus does say in *Against the Ethicists* that the sceptic suspends judgement. How is this possible if these assertions are permitted? Though Sextus never explicitly says so, the answer must be that suspension of judgement means something different here from what it means in his official statement of what scepticism is. Rather than a withdrawal from any definite claims about how things are, it must here consist in a withdrawal from any attempt at a *positive* specification of the characteristics things possess by nature— that is, invariably. To deny that anything is by nature good or bad is not by itself to offer any such positive specification; for 'not by nature (that is, invariably) good' does not imply 'by nature (that is, invariably) not good' or 'by nature (that is, invariably)' anything else. This form of Pyrrhonism, apparently derived from Aenesidemus, is not the same as Sextus' usual and official variety; but it is nonetheless understandable as a form of scepticism, in the ancient sense of the term. It does, however, have in common with Mackie's moral scepticism a focus on the question what things *would* have to be like in order for there to be things good or bad by nature (or in Mackie's case, objective values), leading to the conclusion that nothing can be like that; this is the function of Mackie's 'argument from queerness'. But the argument from queerness is clearly very different from Sextus' line of thinking. For Sextus, it is not that the idea of things being invariably a certain way is inherently peculiar; it is just that, as it happens, nothing measures up to that standard, at least as regards goodness and badness. Where Sextus and Mackie have more in common, as suggested earlier, is in the notion of relativity as counting against things being a certain way in reality. But again, the approaches differ considerably in the details. For Mackie, relativity—understood as the fact of differences in moral codes—is a phenomenon best *explained* by the hypothesis that there are no objective values. For Sextus, relativity—understood the same way—appears to *entail* the conclusion that nothing is by nature good or bad, given the very strong conditions for being by nature a certain way.

Against the Ethicists is the most explicit and unadulterated instance of this style of argument in Sextus; but there are other examples, both in ethics and in other fields. As noted earlier, the parallel treatment of good and bad in *Outlines of Pyrrhonism* proceeds as one would normally expect Sextus to proceed. But it is interesting that there are traces in this discussion, too, of the approach apparently inspired by Aenesidemus. Although Sextus does here suspend judgement about the existence of anything by nature good or bad, he also includes a shortened version of the very same argument as appears in the *Against the Ethicists* (PH 3.179–182), which he then somewhat unconvincingly tries to convert from an argument for nothing's being by nature good (which it what it is) into a set of considerations leading to suspension of judgement about that question (PH 3.182). It looks as if his goal is to adapt this inherited material to suit his own official, post-Aenesidemus variety of Pyrrhonism, but he has not been entirely successful.

What both approaches have in common is that one is freed from beliefs to the effect that things are by nature good or bad. And this, according to Sextus in both works, is where the distinctive payoff of scepticism is to be found. As we have seen, Sextus claims that *ataraxia* is the result of suspension of judgement. He also says that *ataraxia* (at least as regards matters of opinion—that is, the things on which sceptical argument can make a difference) is the sceptic's *telos* (PH 1.25). It may seem surprising that Sextus would even mention a *telos*—especially since, as we saw, Aenesidemus had argued that there was no such thing. But Sextus makes very clear that he does not think of his *telos* in a dogmatic fashion, as something that all human beings should, or by nature do, aim towards (which was presumably what Aenesidemus attacked). Instead, it is simply a description of what he and his fellow sceptics *in fact* aim towards. There is no element of prescription, and there is a clear signal that this is merely a provisional, not necessarily a fixed, aim on their part; Sextus says that this is the sceptic's aim 'up to now', which is a standard device he uses to avoid seeming to claim anything universally.

How exactly is the sceptic's procedure supposed to yield *ataraxia*? Although Sextus' general characterization of scepticism makes *ataraxia* out to be the result of suspension of judgement in general, it is striking that whenever he specifically addresses this question—as he does in several places—it is always freedom from beliefs about good and bad that takes centre stage (PH 1.25–30, 3.235–238, M 11.110–167). The general idea is that these beliefs bring the believer immense turmoil. One is constantly attempting to get or keep the good things and to get rid of or keep away from the bad things; and since one thinks these things are good or bad *by nature*, one thinks it is really important to succeed in these endeavours. The only way to be free from this obsessive mindset is to abandon the beliefs themselves; that way, the stakes become a great deal lower, and one can stop worrying. Sextus does allow that the sceptic feels pain, hunger, etc.; these are things over which we have no control, and here the goal is said to be not *ataraxia*, but moderate (as opposed to excessive) feeling (*PH* 1.25). But even here the sceptic is better off than other people, because the sceptic does not have the additional belief that what he is experiencing is really a bad thing (*PH* 1.30).

This idea of the sceptic as *better off* than other people is perhaps one of the elements most surprising to those familiar with scepticism only in its modern guise (whether in ethics or epistemology or both). I mentioned at the outset the much clearer practical orientation of the ancient sceptic. But even aside from that contrast, scepticism nowadays—in fact, at least since Descartes—has typically been seen as a threat to be contended with, rather than a welcome source of relief. The goal is usually to show that, contrary to appearances, we do not need to *worry* about scepticism (because it is incoherent, or true but harmless, or whatever); scepticism is rarely seen as something to be embraced. And even if it is, this is to be understood at a rarefied intellectual level; again, the notion of *practical* advantages from scepticism is, from a contemporary perspective, absolutely alien.[19]

It must be admitted that the considerations Sextus uses to show that the sceptic is better off are less than compelling. The notion that belief that things are in reality good or bad is a source of disturbance, and freedom from such belief a source of calm, seems to be plausible in some cases, but not in others; often, on the contrary, firm moral beliefs are themselves a comfort in difficult situations, whereas the lack of a clear moral compass causes anxiety. The precise mix of these factors would surely also vary from person to person. Sextus' blanket assertion that believers in things by nature good and bad are afflicted by constant worry, and that sceptics are simply free from all of that, seems excessively one-sided—and also excessively dogmatic.

Other questions can be raised about the practical attitude Sextus describes. I mentioned his response to the tyrant example: when faced with an appalling choice, the sceptic will simply do whatever his upbringing has disposed him to do, without having any convictions either way about the rightness or wrongness of his action. One might wonder, first, whether this is really possible; could anyone in such a crisis be expected to remain as detached from his own reactions as Sextus says the sceptic is? No doubt automatic responses shaped by habit can and do govern much of our lives; but a case

---

[19] Walter Sinnott-Armstrong 2006 espouses what he calls 'moderate moral Pyrrhonism' and calls it 'attractive' (2006: 131). But he is talking about (as we would now put it) purely philosophical attractiveness; there is no suggestion of anything like *ataraxia* as the outcome. Note also Myles Burnyeat's comment on the 'insulation' of Mackie's scepticism from first-order ethical issues in Burnyeat and Frede 1997: 112.

like this does seem to force a conscious and deliberate choice, in which one identifies with certain values and rejects others, and in which one is invested as a *self*, not merely as a bundle of dispositions the unfolding of which one observes as if from afar. In other words, the objection to which Sextus is responding seems to have a lot more intuitive appeal than he allows. Second, supposing such detachment is after all possible, it seems very implausible that which way the sceptic reacts to the tyrant's demand is really, as he presents it, an open question; if habitual dispositions are what determines the sceptic's response, it is overwhelmingly more likely that he will take the easier course—that is, submit to the tyrant's demand rather than stand up to him. Nor is it open to Sextus to suggest that which decision *counts* as easier is itself relative to one's societally induced dispositions. Thwarting the tyrant, in this example, will result in torture, and Sextus concedes that the sceptic is affected by pain, regardless of what dispositions his society has inculcated in him. In such situations it is difficult to imagine that these dispositions— absent the extra motivational force that they would have if (contrary to the sceptical outlook) they took the form of definite moral commitments—would prove stronger than the sceptic's natural inclinations to avoid hardship.

Quite apart from the fraught circumstances of the tyrant's challenge, the more general conformism of the sceptic, as Sextus portrays him, is another unattractive feature. It is not that Sextus wholly identifies with the ordinary person in moral matters (as he claims to do in some other contexts). For he is quite explicit—and in this he is surely right—that the ordinary person believes in things that are by nature good and bad (*PH* 1.30); in this respect the ordinary person and the non-sceptical philosopher are in the same boat. But the sceptic does *do* the same kinds of things as the ordinary conventional member of his society does, and this is no accident. Challenging the status quo would require one to have some dispositions at odds with the prevailing norms; but, as we saw, Sextus cites the prevailing norms of one's society as precisely one of the central influences on the character of the sceptic's dispositions. Besides, even if we depart from the letter of Sextus' account, and allow that other factors (such as very unconventional parents) might compete with those prevailing norms in shaping the sceptic's dispositions,[20] it is still unlikely that the sceptic will step far outside the status quo if (as will surely often be the case) that would be difficult or unpopular. This is because, again, the attitude that the sceptic has towards his own dispositions is peculiarly passive and unengaged; and this makes them far more liable to be overridden by the natural inclinations towards safety, absence of pain, etc. than they would be if they were convictions about which he cared deeply.

A fully-fledged self, genuinely moral motivations, autonomy in anything like the sense we normally understand it—these things all go together in our conception of a robust and responsible human agency.[21] And, although he does not speak of these

---

[20] The possibilities here were no doubt more limited in Sextus' time than they would be in ours, given the much more homogeneous nature of ancient society. But Sextus' picture of the factors influencing the sceptic's dispositions is perhaps still excessively limited.

[21] I have discussed the sceptic's pared-down self in Bett 2008.

things directly (but rather of beliefs concerning the good and the bad by nature), it is fundamentally these things from which Sextus is delighted that the sceptic is free.[22] He is no doubt right that the passive, stand-offish attitude he describes would relieve one of a great many concerns (although, as noted earlier, the matter may not be as clear-cut as he suggests). But the question is whether this is worth what one would have to give up in order to achieve it. If *ataraxia*, tranquillity, is what one values above all else, then the answer may be yes. But most of us care a good deal about some other things as well. And this is no doubt one reason why scepticism was never a very widespread movement in the ancient world.

BIBLIOGRAPHY

Allen, J. 2004. 'Carneades', in *Stanford Encyclopedia of Philosophy*, <http://plato.stanford.edu/entries/carneades>.

—— 2010. 'Pyrrhonism and Medicine', in Richard Bett (ed.), *The Cambridge Companion to Ancient Scepticism*. Cambridge: Cambridge University Press, 232–48.

Annas, J. 1986/1998. 'Doing without objective values: ancient and modern strategies', in Malcolm Schofield and Gisela Striker (eds), *The Norms of Nature: Studies in Hellenistic Ethics*. Cambridge: Cambridge University Press, 3–29. Revised version in Stephen Everson (ed.), *Companions to Ancient Thought 4: Ethics*. Cambridge: Cambridge University Press, 193–220.

—— 2007. 'Carneades' Classification of Ethical Theories', in Anna Maria Ioppolo and David Sedley (eds), *Pyrrhonists, Patricians, Platonizers: Hellenistic Philosophy in the Period 155–86 BC*. Naples: Bibliopolis, 187–223.

Bett, R. 2000. *Pyrrho, his Antecedents and his Legacy*. Oxford: Oxford University Press.

—— 2008. 'What Kind of Self Can a Greek Sceptic Have?', in Pauliina Remes and Juha Sihvola (eds), *Ancient Philosophy of the Self*. Springer: New Synthese Historical Library, 64, 139–54.

—— 2010. 'Pyrrho', in *Stanford Encyclopedia of Philosophy*, <http://plato.stanford.edu/entries/pyrrho>.

Brennan, T. 1998. 'Pyrrho on the Criterion', *Ancient Philosophy* 18, 417–34.

Brittain, C. 2001. *Philo of Larissa: The Last of the Academic Sceptics*. Oxford: Oxford University Press.

—— 2005. 'Arcesilaus', in *Stanford Encyclopedia of Philosophy*, <http://plato.stanford.edu/entries/arcesilaus>.

—— 2006. *Cicero, On Academic Scepticism*, Translated, with Introduction and Notes. Indianapolis: Hackett.

Burnyeat, M. and Frede, M. (eds) 1997. *The Original Sceptics: A Controversy* Indianapolis: Hackett.

---

[22] Consider an existentialist, who would be on Sextus' side in doing without objective values, but who nonetheless places a great deal of value on personal commitment. From Sextus' perspective this would be no improvement. He connects deep commitments with a belief in things by nature good and bad, and in the ancient context this is understandable. But if we imagine these two elements apart from one another, as we now can, it becomes clear that deep commitments are what he is at bottom trying to get away from.

Cooper, J. 2004. 'Arcesilaus: Socratic and Skeptic', reprinted in John M. Cooper, *Knowledge, Nature, and the Good: Essays on Ancient Philosophy*. Princeton: Princeton University Press, 81–103.

—— 2007. 'Socrates and Philosophy as a Way of Life', in Dominic Scott (ed.), *Maieusis: Essays on Ancient Philosophy in Honour of Myles Burnyeat*. Oxford: Oxford University Press, 20–43.

Hadot, P. 1995. *Philosophy as a Way of Life*, edited with an introduction by Arnold I. Davidson. Oxford/Malden, MA: Blackwell.

Long, A. and Sedley, D. 1987. *The Hellenistic Philosophers*. Cambridge: Cambridge University Press.

Mackie, J. L. 1977. *Ethics: Inventing Right and Wrong*. Harmondsworth: Penguin.

Obdrzalek, S. 2006. 'Living in Doubt: Carneades' *Pithanon* Reconsidered', *Oxford Studies in Ancient Philosophy* 31, 243–79.

Sinnott-Armstrong, W. 2006. *Moral Skepticisms*. New York: Oxford University Press.

Sluiter, I. 2005. 'Communicating Cynicism: Diogenes' gangsta rap', in Dorothea Frede and Brad Inwood (eds), *Language and Learning: Philosophy of Language in the Hellenistic Age*. Cambridge: Cambridge University Press, 139–63.

Stopper, M. R. 1983. 'Schizzi Pirroniani', *Phronesis* 28, 265–97.

Williams, B. 1985. 'Ethics and the Fabric of the World', in Ted Honderich (ed.), *Morality and Objectivity: A Tribute to J. L. Mackie*. London: Routledge, 203–14.

CHAPTER 7

....

PLATONIC ETHICS IN LATER ANTIQUITY

....

LLOYD P. GERSON

I intend to make three related points with my somewhat tendentious title. First, I am referring to the ethical thought of Platonists as distinct from the ethical thought of Plato himself. Second, I mean to indicate that Platonists themselves did not suppose that this distinction amounted to a difference. Third, I am suggesting that Platonic ethics is more or less a unity; that is, we shall not find substantial differences among *soi-disants* Platonists in what they have to say about human happiness and virtue. I shall not here argue for these claims, though if they are true, an exposition of Platonic ethics might be expected to be gratifyingly concise: 'assimilate yourself to god; all the rest is an explanation of this'.[1] Much of the explanation that was in fact provided for this famous exhortation amounts to its metaphysical context. I can only provide some of this in the course of this chapter, and then only as it directly bears on the ethical claims being made by Platonists. My primary focus will be on Plotinus, both because later Platonists follow him in his exposition of the Platonic position and because it is for him that we have the largest amount of material extant pertaining to our subject. By way of a supplement, I shall have something to say about how Plotinus' pupil, Porphyry, and later Platonists systematized Plotinus' account of virtue.

7.1

....

It is well to begin with the point, obviously central to the Platonists, that Plato makes the first metaphysical principle of all the Idea of the Good.[2] Whatever else we wish to make of this claim, it does not seem unreasonable to insist that Plato thereby means to indicate the

---

[1] The famous text in Plato's *Theaetetus* 176A–B did indeed serve to encapsulate the Platonic view on ethics. But like the Talmudic sage Rabbi Hillel, who, when asked to express the essence of the Torah, said, 'What is hateful to you, do not do to your fellow: this is the whole Law; the rest is the explanation; go and learn', so for the Platonists, quite a bit of explanation is called for.

[2] See *Republic* 509B6–10; cf. 505A3; 508E1–4; 533C8–D1. For Aristotle's testimony that the Good is identical with the 'One' see *Metaphysics* 13.4.1091b13–14; cf. 1.9. 990b17–22 and *Eudemian Ethics*

relevance of metaphysics to ethics.[3] If, as was universally maintained in ancient philosophy, all humans desire the good for themselves, then the claim that the first principle of all is the Idea of the Good is one with numerous, undoubtedly disputable, consequences. First, if there *is* an Idea of the Good, then it is of course possible that x is good for me, though x is bad for you. It is, however, not possible that if x is good for me, then it is bad for you that x is good for me, just as it is not possible that if $2+2=4$ is true for me, then it is possible that it is false for you. The objectivity of the Idea of the Good guarantees that my good is never achievable at your expense: if x is good for me, then it is just an instantiation of the Good that makes this so, and this is just as much the case for you as for me, which means that it cannot be not-good or bad for you that x is good for me. It is difficult to exaggerate this consequence of positing an Idea of the Good, particularly in the light of the confrontations Plato creates between Socrates and all those interlocutors whose entire lives are more or less dedicated to the proposition that one's own good is *always* achieved at the expense of others.

The second major consequence drawn from the positing of an Idea of the Good is that 'achieving' it can never be reduced to or identified with attaining a finite good. The textual basis for this is clearly the 'higher mysteries' of love in Plato's *Symposium* (210A–212B) where, on the basis of an identification of the love of the beautiful with the desire for good, an 'ascent' or progression of the right order is described in which the lover passes from love of one beautiful body upward to all beautiful bodies, to beautiful souls, then to beautiful practices and laws, then to beautiful areas of knowledge and then, finally, to beauty 'by itself'. It is only when the lover has reached this goal that he is able to give birth not to images of virtue but to true virtue, since he is only then in touch with true beauty. Leaving aside for the moment the difficult question of the exact relation between good and beautiful in this passage, we can say initially that if they are in fact identified, one apprised of the higher mysteries will never be satisfied with a particular good anymore than he will be satisfied with a particular beautiful object.

The Platonic way of representing the relation between the Idea of the Good and particular goods is, as the above passage suggests, analogous to the relation between true virtue and its images. If this analogy holds, it is clear why the philosopher will prefer the Good to particular goods. But when we come to ask why a particular good—say, pleasure or honour—is analogous to a mere image of the Good, the answer is not so clear at all. Briefly, the Platonic answer is this. The Idea of the Good, as Plato says, is the ultimate cause of the being of everything else. As such, it is distinct from any finite nature or essence or 'whatness', just in the way that 'one' (for Platonists and non-Platonists of antiquity alike) is not a number, but the principle of number. So, the goodness of anything will not be owing to its being the kind of thing it is, but rather owing to its participating in the Good. If, then, you

---

1.8.1218a24–8. It is worth emphasizing that Platonists took the Aristotelian testimony pretty much at face value, though they frequently disputed the conclusions that Aristotle drew from that testimony.

[3] It is presumably this claim that Aristotle is contesting when he separates theoretical from practical science and when in his *Nicomachean Ethics* (1.6) he complains that the knowledge of the Idea of the Good does not seem to be useful for knowing what the good is in any particular circumstance. As we shall see below, Platonists have an interesting reply to this complaint.

want what is good for yourself, you want the goodness of the object of your desire, not that object itself, whether that be pleasure or honour or anything else. To want honour or pleasure 'for their own sakes' can only mean to want them *because* they are good or *despite* their not being good. The former confirms the Platonic point; the latter is impossible if one wants only one's own good. To insist that one's own good might 'conflict' with the Good is perforce to reject the objectivity of the Idea of the Good.

It might be objected that the goodness of pleasure is constituted by the pleasure itself and it is *that* that is desired, not the Good in which, it may be granted, it participates. The Platonist will reply that there is not one possible instance of pleasure that is not in certain circumstances anything but good for oneself. Though the pleasure can indeed be isolated from these circumstances, its goodness cannot. To admit that the pleasure that one seeks is sought on the condition that it is good is to admit at once that the goodness is *not* constitutive of the pleasure, but something distinct from that.

In the light of such an argument, it is not unreasonable to query the grounds for making the first principle of all the Idea of the Good. After all, one could, like Aristotle, agree that there must be a first principle of all without conceding that this is to be identified with the Idea of the Good. At this point, the Platonic interpretation of the very specific claim by Plato about the Idea of the Good is especially powerful and little noticed in the contemporary literature. As Plotinus argues, since the Good is not any specific nature, the limit of achievement of that Good for most things most of the time consists in the fulfilment of its nature. This is true for human beings as well, but since humans are rational creatures, the fulfilment of our natures consists in identifying ourselves with our intellects, and realizing the intellect's full achievement which is knowledge of all that is intelligible. I shall return to the crucial point about identification below. How is this achievement supposed to be equivalent to attaining the Good? Plotinus maintains that the Good is virtually all that is knowable, just as white light is virtually all the colours in the spectrum or a mathematical function is virtually all its domain and range. Since our good consists in fulfilling our nature, and since our nature is to know all that is knowable, and since the first principle of all is virtually all that is knowable, it is correct to identify that principle with the Good.[4] If this is so, then knowing all that is knowable is not quite the having of something good in the way that having pleasure or honour is having something good, that is, having a simulacrum of the real thing. For there is nothing between the having of the good of intellect and the Good itself. Stated otherwise, the highest good we can have is that of the intellect, even while we recognize that this attainment is not equivalent to identification with the Good itself.[5]

There are many other direct and indirect consequences of the positing of an Idea of the Good to which Platonists attended. If we add to these the consequences of the

[4] Plato at *Republic* 509B5 specifically says that the Good is that which makes all knowable things knowable. And in so far as we are really or ultimately intellects, it follows that the good of an intellect is doing what intellects do, that is, knowing all that is knowable. I mean to stress here how closely Plotinus is following Plato's argument.

[5] I leave out of account the so-called mystical union with the Good or the One that Plotinus' pupil Porphyry reports Plotinus to have experienced four times in his life. Whatever this amounts to, it plays no part in his ethics in the sense that it is never proposed as a goal or result of virtue or as constitutive of happiness. The adventitiousness of the experience suffices to indicate that.

identification of the Idea of the Good with the One, as per Aristotle's testimony, we shall have the elements necessary for a reconstruction of what much later came to be given the pejorative label 'Neoplatonism'. Here, we shall focus exclusively on ethics. First, I shall deal with Plotinus' account of human happiness, and then with his account of virtue, along with Porphyry's adumbrations of this.

7.2

Plotinus' *Ennead* 1.4, titled by Porphyry *On Happiness*, is, according to Porphyry, a late work (46th out of 54 in his relative chronological ordering), probably written near the end of Plotinus' life. It has a straightforward structure: a criticism of Aristotelian, Epicurean, and Stoics accounts of happiness, and then an exposition of the Platonic position. The above metaphysical superstructure is evident throughout. Plotinus assumes that a defensible account of human happiness will amount to an application of general metaphysical principles. If happiness is the good for human beings, then that good must be understood as an expression or image of the primary or Absolute Good.[6] It is proximity to the Absolute Good or One that provides the index of a thing's goodness, including the goodness of a human being.[7] More specifically, a human life can be 'graded' according to whether it is approaching or retreating from the Good. Hence, the terminus of our identification with the Good as human beings is our identification with our intellects. In identifying the human being ideally with his intellect, Plotinus is in general following the Stoics as well as Plato and Aristotle. It is a slightly more complicated matter to explain how, despite this, Plotinus wishes at the same time to side with Plato against his illustrious successors.[8]

Aristotle, in the first book of his *Nicomachean Ethics* claims that the human end is happiness (*eudaimonia*) and that happiness is virtuous activity. Perhaps the central problem

---

[6] See *Enneads* 1.4.3.28–33: 'So its [the human being's] good will not be something brought in from outside, nor will the basis of its goodness come from somewhere else and bring it into a good state; for what could be added to the perfect life to make it into the best life? If anyone says, "the Absolute Good", that is our own way of talking, but at present we are not looking for the cause, but for the immanent element.' See *Philebus* 60B10–C4 which is perhaps the text indicating why Plotinus refers to 'our own [i.e. Platonic] way of talking'.

[7] See *Enneads* 4.3.6.27–34: 'For we must understand that souls were called "second" and "third" according to whether they are nearer to or farther from [the intelligible world]; just as among us too not all souls have the same relationship to the realities there, but some men may unify themselves, others nearly reach this point in their striving, and others attain it in a lesser degree, in so far as they act by powers which are not the same, but some by the first, others by that which comes after it, others by the third, though all of them have all.'

[8] Cf. *Republic* 443E1 and 554D9–10 where Plato describes the virtuous person as 'becoming one out of many' which Plotinus interprets as a sort of self-unification. Cf. *Enneads* 1.2.6.3–7, 17–28 where Plotinus specifically mentions the state of one who has 'become one' and who in this state practises embodied virtue. So, too, 6.9.3.20–3.

with these claims is revealed in the standard English translation of the Greek term *eudaimonia*. As we are frequently told by scholars, Aristotle is not talking about a subjective state when he claims that *eudaimonia* is the human end. The achievement or failure to achieve happiness is quite independent of any feeling of happiness. This is evident from the fact that Aristotle acknowledges that a life in pursuit of pleasure is one view about *eudaimonia*, but only one among several.[9] On the other hand, Aristotle does later in the work argue that the life of virtuous activity is in fact the most pleasant life, but only for the person who is actually virtuous.[10] Such a claim, it goes without saying, will have no persuasive force for someone who is not otherwise attracted to virtuous living. If the virtuous life is subjectively 'happy' only for the virtuous person, it might well be the case for all we know that the life of someone otherwise disposed has as much or more subjective happiness. Why, after all, should one want the happiness of a kind of life other than his own?

Aristotle implicitly acknowledges the distinction between objective and subjective happiness when he insists that happiness is not 'blessedness' (*makaria*). The latter is primarily a characteristic of the gods.[11] The gods are blessed because they are immortal. Their immortality makes them impervious to the misfortunes that threaten human life. A god may become irritated, but he or she is sure to get over it in short order. A god is perpetually subjectively happy, or practically so. Human beings are, so long as they live, faced with the possibility of tragedy. So, though a human being may be happy in Aristotle's sense, he cannot thereby be counted blessed. A happy man will indeed possess a prophylactic against disaster, because he can draw on his inner virtuous resources to get him through trouble. But he will not be blessed if he should meet with the fortunes of Priam.[12] If he is happy and if he manages to avoid personal tragedy right up to the end, then we will call him 'blessed', that is, blessed only in the secondary qualified way that befits a mortal. Moreover, the blessed state of the gods is precisely what makes virtue irrelevant for them. The fact that it is relevant, indeed, essential, for us, on Aristotle's account, underscores the gap between happiness and blessedness.[13]

Aristotle's principal response to the problem of the gap between what we might call an objective and a subjective account of happiness is to say in addition to the fact that the virtuous life is the most pleasurable for the virtuous, that a virtuous life is maximally impervious to misfortune.[14] But the fact that a virtuous person will bear life's tragedies with equanimity and a certain 'nobility', as Aristotle puts it, hardly amounts to an unanswerable recommendation. Better, one might respond, to avoid avoidable misfortunes in the first place, including those that arise from the exigencies of virtuous living. Ancient ethics after Aristotle is strongly characterized by its focus on this problem.[15]

---

[9] *Nicomachean Ethics* 1.3.   [10] *Nicomachean Ethics* 1.9.1099a11–21.
[11] Cf. Homer, *Odyssey* 10.299.   [12] *Nicomachean Ethics* 1.10.1101a6–8; cf. 1.9.1099b2.
[13] Aristotle's only extant poem, *Hymn to Hermeias*, expatiates on the arduousness of virtue.
[14] *Nicomachean Ethics* 1.11.1100b22–33.
[15] Antiochus of Ascalon, *apud* Cicero, *De finibus* 5.68, 81, defends the Aristotelian distinction in the course of his rejection of the Stoic *identification* of happiness (*vita beata*) and blessedness (*vita beatissima*). Antiochus identifies the latter as depending on 'external' goods, the possession of which would put us on a par with the gods who have these automatically, so to speak.

Epicurus and the Old Stoa employ a similar strategy, that is, they attempt to show that in fact happiness and blessedness are identical. Epicurus straightforwardly treats 'happy' as synonymous with 'blessed'.[16] So, there is no possibility that one should be happy and 'unhappy' or wretched at the same time. He does this by claiming, in effect, that 'happy' and 'blessed' are two different names for one state, that of an 'absence of disturbance' (*ataraxia*).[17] Against the obvious objection that this cannot be so because the divine nature is blessed owing to its immortality, Epicurus famously argues that 'death is nothing to us'.[18] If the gods are blessed just because they need not fear death, then if we, too, need not fear death, we can be blessed as well. Epicurus does not, however, maintain that virtue is irrelevant to the blessed state of satisfaction: 'we choose virtues, too, for the sake of pleasure and not for their own sake'.[19] Epicurus refuses to consider the life of virtue and the life of pleasure as alternatives, the commensuration of which makes any sense at all. He refuses to countenance the possibility that one could rationally conceive of happiness and blessedness as real alternative goals, opting for the former in the hopes that only in this way will he come as close as possible to the latter.

In the case of the Old Stoa, as with Epicurus, the identification of happiness and blessedness is made by identifying them both with 'absence of disturbance'.[20] But, unlike Epicurus, for the Stoics, since happiness (and therefore blessedness) is constituted of virtue, virtue is chosen for its own sake.[21] And so like Epicurus, there is no possibility for rational opposition between virtue and happiness, if happiness is taken subjectively. The sense in which the Stoics make this claim is best seen in their view that things normally indicated as constituting subjective happiness—health, pleasure, beauty—are in fact 'indifferents' (*adiaphora*).[22] It is possible to be happy without these.[23] By contrast, one cannot be happy if one is not virtuous.[24]

In the face of such an extreme view, one might suppose that the Stoics have merely redefined 'happiness' to exclude or trivialize the subjective altogether. If this is so, then their position is hardly compelling. Surely, what the Stoics need is an argument designed to show that objective Stoic happiness—the virtuous life—is the life that anyone would choose if we were fairly apprised of the contents, so to speak, of that life, from the inside. If, however, being apprised of the contents of the virtuous life from the inside requires that one be virtuous, then the sought for Stoic argument would only show, in effect, that virtuous people prefer being virtuous. To insist, as the Stoics do, that all non-virtuous

[16] Diogenes Laertius, *Lives and Opinions of the Philosophers* (D. L.), 10.128; cf. 122.
[17] D. L., 10.78; cf.Cicero, *de natura Deorum* 1.53.
[18] D. L, 10.124–6.
[19] D. L., 10.138; cf. 140 = *Principal Doctrines* 5.
[20] Cf. Seneca, *Epistles* 92.3: *securitas et perpetua tranquilitas*.
[21] D. L., 7.89 = *Stoicorum Veterum Fragmenta* (*SVF*) 3.39.
[22] D. L., 7.101–3. On the distinction between preferred and dispreferred indifferents. Also,Stobaeus, *Eclogues* 2.7d, p.79, 18ff Wachsmuth-Hense = *SVF* 3.133, 140.
[23] D. L., 7.104 = *SVF* 3.104.
[24] Plutarch, *de Stoicorum repugnantiis* 1042A = *SVF* 3.55; cf. *SVF* 3.585, where the Stoics are reputed to have insisted, presumably, against Aristotle or other Peripatetetics, that it is indeed possible to be happy inside the notorious bull of Phalaris.

people are mad is not likely to count as a telling point against those who are satisfied to live the putative madness of the dissolute life. How, then, does one convince the 'mad' non-Stoic that he is indeed mad?

The Stoic approach is to hearken back to Socrates.[25] Their insistence on the sufficiency of virtue for happiness is equivalent to the Socratic absolutist prohibition of wrongdoing.[26] According to Socrates, wrongdoing inevitably and necessarily harms the soul of a person. Why, though, should one prefer the health of one's soul at all costs, in particular, at the cost of harm to one's body? The Socratic response in brief is that the soul is identical with the self, and the neglect of soul care is equivalent to self demolition. Wrongdoing is presumably the antithesis of soul care. A wrongdoer can no more hope to benefit from his wrongdoing than one can hope to preside over one's own funeral. Why exactly wrongdoing should lead to self destruction is nowhere explicitly explained in Plato's dialogues. However, Plato's remarks on personhood, especially in *Republic* and *Timaeus*, do indicate the direction of an answer, and it is this direction that the Stoics and Plotinus will eventually follow.

The Socratic identification of the soul with the self is sophisticated by Plato's tripartition of the soul and his subsequent designation of the rational part as the true self, the 'human being within the human being'.[27] It is somewhat misleading to speak of the rational part if this suggests that reason or rationality is not involved in the operation of the other two parts of the soul, the appetitive and the spirited. Thus, the embodied person who acts to satisfy an appetite is not acting independent of his reason, for reason is deployed both in conceptualizing the object of desire and in calculations made on how to achieve it. The identification of the person with the rational part of the soul is the identification of the person with the subject of embodied human action, all of which is rational in the above sense. But reason, and hence, the self or subject, is present both as the subject of a desire and as the subject that endorses or fails to endorse the desire that it has itself.[28] The rational subject is essentially self-reflexive in this way. So, to address questions about the satisfaction or happiness of the self and self destruction, one must consider how rationality thus construed is exercised and how it is destroyed.

Crucially, Plato argues for a disembodied rational self, identified with the immortal part of the soul.[29] This disembodied self evidently desires nothing that requires a body; it has no bodily appetites, for example. Yet, it is no doubt continuous with the embodied self. If it were not, post-mortem rewards and punishments would be meaningless, to say nothing of reincarnation. So, we must suppose that the embodied person is a sort of image of its disembodied exemplar. I would argue that this is so in exactly the way that instances of Plato's Forms are images of these Forms, but that is not the central point here.[30] That point is that if I make a commitment to pursuing what 'I' really

---

[25] The Socrates of the dialogues, who in my view is not distinguishable from the author of the dialogues, Plato.

[26] See *Crito* 49B8: 'One must never do wrong'; cf. 49A6–7, *Apology* 29B6–7; *Gorgias* 469B12, 508E, etc.

[27] *Alcibiades* I 130E8–9; *Republic* 589A7–B1.

[28] Failing to endorse it is the prerequisite for incontinence or *akrasia*.

[29] *Timaeus* 90C.

[30] See my *Knowing Persons* (Oxford: Oxford University Press, 2003), chs 3 and 6.

want—objective or subjective happiness—then I must be in a position to identify that 'I'. And the identification in a Platonic context is not so straightforward, since I can identify it either as the embodied 'I' or the disembodied 'I', the former being merely an image of the latter.

The ambiguity imported into ethical calculation by the distinction between an ideal and its image is not uniquely Platonic in origin. Consider, as the Stoics do, for instance, the person who has to choose between present satisfaction and future well-being. The choice between what the present 'I' wants and what the present 'I' thinks the future 'I' will want is exactly analogous to the choice between what the subject qua image wants and what the subject qua image thinks the ideal subject wants. This is so even if in the former case the future 'I' is bound to become a present 'I' with another future 'I' to consider. Now just as a claim about what 'I' want now might be challenged (whether by oneself or by another) by a comparison with what 'I' will want in the future, so the choices of the subject qua image might be challenged by a comparison with the ideal self. The point of course is that the challenger does not have to say things like, 'you ought to want something different for yourself' but rather either 'you will want something different for yourself' or, more radically in the case of the ideal self, 'you do want something different for yourself'. A youth does not have to be convinced that he does not now want what he wants; he only (!) needs to be convinced that when he grows up he will want something else and that his present pursuits will make that impossible or at least unlikely. The argument for privileging the future person over the present is in part that one is likely to spend a much longer time as an adult than as a youth. How much stronger would this argument be if the two poles of comparison were a mortal embodied self and an immortal disembodied self?

The Stoic exhortation to 'live in agreement with nature' is the basis for their interpretation of the Socratic-Platonic account of the self.[31] In one sense, a human being cannot fail to live in agreement with nature. That is the sense in which he is an embodied subject of rational activity. But in another sense, a human being can and typically does fail to live in agreement with nature, when living in agreement is taken to be an ideal. For the Stoics, the ideal is not a disembodied one; nevertheless, it is an ideal wherein the subject is identified with the rule of reason or with Zeus himself.[32] It is to be emphasized that the Stoics thus import normativity into the fabric of nature. The ideal is as natural as an endowment. And the Platonic identification of the endowment with a counterfeit or image is no less censorious than is the Stoic description as mad of anyone who lives a life according to the endowment and not according to the ideal.

It may be worth noting as we proceed to Plotinus that the Socratic-Platonic-Stoic view is not at all rejected by Aristotle himself. In his remarks concerning the best life at the end of his *Nicomachean Ethics*, he says,

> Such a life would be above that of a human being, for a human being will live in this manner not in so far as he is a human being, but in so far as he has something divine

---

[31] D. L., 7.87 = *SVF* 3.4; Stobaeus, *Eclogues* 2.7, 6a, p.76, 3 Wachsmuth-Hense = *SVF* 1.55.2.
[32] D. L., 7.88 = *SVF* 1.162.

in him; and the activity of this divine part of the soul is as much superior to that of the other kind of virtue as that divine part is superior to the composite soul of a human being. So, since the intellect is divine relative to a human being, the life according to this intellect, too, will be divine relative to human life. Thus we should not follow the recommendation of thinkers who say that those who are human beings should think only of human things and that mortals should think only of mortal things, but we should try as far as possible to partake of immortality and to make every effort to live according to the best part of the soul in us; for even if this part be of small measure, it surpasses all the others by far in power and worth. It would seem, too, that each man is this part, if indeed this is the dominant part and is better than the other parts; so it would be strange if a human being did not choose the life proper to himself but that proper to another. And what was stated earlier is appropriate here also: that which is by nature proper to each thing is the best and most pleasant for that thing. So for a human being, too, the life according to his intellect is the best and most pleasant, if indeed a human being in the highest sense is his intellect. Hence, this life, too, is the happiest.[33]

This remarkable passage, so frequently discounted in the literature, explicitly acknowledges first that 'a human being in the highest sense is his intellect'. So, the life according to the intellect (whatever that means) is the happiest life for a human being. But this life is 'above that of a human being'; it is a divine life compared with a human one. The divine life is the ideal. It is that life which is unqualifiedly blessed. It is that life which is most pleasant, but only for one who acknowledges that it is his own ideal life. One who prefers satisfaction to virtue or blessedness to happiness as construed by Aristotle is not completely wrong because he is implicitly acknowledging the distinction between the divine ideal and the human endowment. And in this acknowledgment is the starting point for a substantive dispute over the nature of that ideal as opposed to a mere conflict of incommensurable subjective valuations.

7.3

Plotinus identifies 'happiness' with 'blessedness', not, like the Epicureans and Stoics because both terms express or are equivalent to 'absence of disturbance', but because both terms are equivalent to 'identification with intellect', that is, with intellectual activity.[34]

It is obvious from what has been said elsewhere that a human being has a perfect life by having not only a soul capable of sense-perception but also one capable of reasoning and true intellection. But is he different from this when he has it? No, he is not entirely a human being if he does not have this, whether in potency or in actuality (happiness being the actuality, we maintain). But shall we say that he who

---

[33] *Nicomachean Ethics* 10.7.1177b26–1178a8. Cf. 9.4.1166a22–3, 9.8.1168b31–3. Cf. *Protrepticus* B62, 85–6 Ross.

[34] See *Enneads* 1.4.4 with 1.6.7.33 and 5.1.4.14–19.

has this kind of perfect life has this as a part of himself? Is it not the case rather than other human beings have it as a part by having it potentially, whereas the happy human being who is this life in actuality and has transformed himself in becoming identical with it, is this. The other things are then just what he wears, which one could not call a part of him since he wears them without wanting to. It would be a part of him if it were joined to him according to an act of will. What then is the good for him? He himself is the good for himself which he has.[35]

The transformation to which this passage refers is from the use of intellect to the identification with it, roughly in the way that, say, one identifies with a 'cause' or with the plight of another person.[36] With this identification, one detaches from embodied desires such that they seem (almost) to be those of another. This detachment is the psychological manifestation of the ontological distinction between goods and the Good. All in fact desire the Good, but those who have not transformed themselves in the way that Plotinus indicates, mistake particular goods for that one true object of desire.[37] The desire for the Good is, for an intellect, satisfied in the cognitive identification with all that is intelligible, all that the Good is virtually. This is what the 'undescended' intellect of each of us is eternally achieving.[38] So, the identification we are able to achieve with our own intellects while embodied is limited. Contrary to Epicurus and the Old Stoa, and in line with Plato, Plotinus rejects the idea of a 'heaven on earth'. Accordingly, perfect happiness for an embodied human being is a relative notion.

Plotinus considers the perfectly reasonable objection that a life of detachment from embodied desires amounts to a life bereft of the satisfaction that is subjective happiness.

If some people were to say that a human being in this state is not even alive, we shall insist that he is alive, but that his happiness, like his life, escapes them. If they are not persuaded, we will ask them to begin with the living human being or the excellent person (*spoudaios*), and thus to ask if he is happy, and not having diminished his life, to seek to discover if he is living well, and, without removing his humanity, to seek to discover human happiness, and while conceding that the excellent person turns inward, not to seek for his happiness in external activities nor in general to seek the object of his will in externals. For if one were to say that externals were willed and that the excellent person willed these, in this way one would be denying that happiness exists.[39]

The central point of this passage is that the critic, before dismissing the present account of happiness as inhuman, must look at the actual life of the excellent person (*spoudaios*). In the interstice between disembodiment and a life of embodied desire, his happiness is to be found.

---

[35] *Enneads* 1.4.4.6–19.

[36] Cf. the Old Testament story of Ruth and Naomi (Ruth 1: 16–17): Ruth declares to her mother-in-law Naomi, 'Your people will be my people; your God will be my God.'

[37] Plotinus tends to use one word for desire for the Good (*ephesis*) and another for desires for particular goods (*orexis*). Cf. *Enneads* 1.6.7.3; 6.7.21.1–6; 6.7.27.24–7.

[38] See *Enneads* 1.1.2.25–30; 4.7.13, 4.8.8; 6.7.5.26–9.   [39] *Enneads* 1.4.11.1–12.

The principal characteristic of the life of the excellent person is that he is 'self-sufficient' (*autarkēs*).[40] The excellent person is happy because he is self-sufficient or perhaps his excellence consists in his self-sufficiency. We recall that Aristotle makes self-sufficiency a hallmark of happiness. But we also saw that for Aristotle this self-sufficiency falls short of blessedness. Plotinus, identifying happiness with blessedness, alters the meaning of 'self-sufficient' in order to identify it with the interior life of the excellent person. This interiority or self-sufficiency is the obverse of attachment to the objects of first order embodied desires. Interiority is happiness because the longing for the Good for one who is ideally an intellect is satisfied by cognitive identification with all that is intelligible. If this is not unqualifiedly possible for the embodied human being, it does at least seem possible that one should have a second-order desire that amounts to a profound indifference to the satisfaction of first-order desires. Whether one takes this indifference to be a symptom of depression or of a morbid asceticism or whether it is evidence of true self-discovery no doubt depends entirely on one's assessment of the metaphysics adduced to justify it. Understanding that the Good for an intellect is contemplation of all that the One is means that the will is oriented to one thing only, whatever transient desires may arise.[41] The 'weight' that one gives to these desires depends entirely on one's metaphysics, even if that consists in the position that metaphysics is irrelevant to ethics.

7.4

Plotinus' account of virtue in *Ennead* 1.2 should be viewed in the light of all the above. Although this treatise is relatively early (number 19 in Porphyry's ordering), it considers virtue in so far as it contributes to identification with one's intellect and, therefore, achievement of the Good. It is in fact an extended commentary on *Theaetetus* 176A–B, the passage cited at the beginning as an emblem of Platonic ethics. Thus, virtue is necessary for the assimilation to god. The basis for the assimilation is the metaphysical hierarchy with the Idea of the Good at the top and the human being somewhere in the middle, struggling to appropriate once again his or her ideal self. The process of appropriation is the assimilation itself. The completion of the process perforce amounts to the transcending of virtue, or at least to the transcending of embodied virtue.

Plotinus naturally presents his account of virtue as simply that of Plato. Despite his disagreements with Aristotle regarding the nature of happiness, he is evidently content to employ a considerable amount of material from the *Nicomachean Ethics* as a

---

[40] See *Enneads* 1.4.4.23–5; 1.4.5.23–4.

[41] In *Ennead* 1.3., 'On Dialectic', Plotinus argues that the practice of dialectic as described by Plato is essential to moral improvement. He frequently describes this practice as a sort of purification. It is essential because, though all desire the Good, one must first know what that is. The goal of dialectic is to know what the Good is virtually, that is, the intelligible world. In knowing that, one longs for it, and interiority is a state of willing the achievement of that longing. The language of purification is applied here especially to desire which is transmuted into the resultant purified longing for the Good.

means to articulate the Platonic position. In particular, he employs Aristotle's distinction between moral and intellectual virtue as an expression of a hierarchical ordering of virtue that he finds in Plato. The superiority of the intellectual to the moral reflects the ideal identification of the person with the intellect, as Aristotle himself acknowledges. Thus, the transcending of embodied virtue amounts to the transcending of embodied intellection, that is, practical thinking.

In *Phaedo*, we find a reference to 'popular or political virtues'.[42] These are the 'ordinary virtues' that human beings practise by custom and habit and 'without philosophy and intellect'. As the parallel *Republic* passages make clear, this sort of virtue is concerned with 'externals', that is, with behaviour. By contrast, the virtue that is 'a sort of purification' is the justice, temperance, and courage of a philosopher.[43]

With this background, Plotinus' treatise begins with a reflection on the *Theaetetus* passage. He asks how the practice of virtue can make us like the divine and intelligible reality since there is no virtue there. The divine has no need of virtue because it is perfect.[44] In particular, it has no need of the popular or political virtues, which Plotinus identifies as achievements of an embodied tripartite soul.[45] All true virtues are understood as advancements or contributions towards the identification of the person with the activity of a disembodied intellect.[46]

Plotinus asks if the popular or political virtues are real virtues. And his answer is an insistence that whatever serves to make us godlike is a virtue.[47]

> These virtues do truly organize our lives and make us better by giving limit to and giving measure to our appetites and in general to all our feelings. And they eliminate false beliefs, by what is generally better and by limiting the unmeasured and unlimited.[48]

These virtues, as they are described by Plato in the fourth book of *Republic*, are aspects of an embodied life under the aegis of reason. The practice of these virtues contributes to our godlikeness because they nudge us towards identification with our intellects. They do this because acting as reason dictates means at least sometimes acting against our appetites or emotions, those parts of our embodied lives which we falsely believe identify us.

---

[42] *Phaedo* 82A10–B3. Cf. 69B6–7, where this sort of virtue is called an 'illusory façade', fit for slaves. Cf. *Protagoras* 323A7, B2; 324A1 where Protagoras uses the term 'political virtue' in the same way without of course the pejorative Platonic overtones. Cf. *Republic* 365C3–4 and 500D8 with 518D3–519A6 where the 'popular' virtues are identified as the 'so-called virtues of the soul' and especially 619C7–D1 for participation in virtue by 'habit' 'without philosophy'. At 430C3, courage is characterized as 'political'. At 443C10–D1, characterizing justice, Plato contrasts 'external' behaviour with 'internal' virtue, which is concerned with what is 'truly oneself and one's own'.

[43] See *Phaedo* 67C5, 69B8–C3.

[44] *Enneads* 1.2. 3. 31.

[45] *Enneads* 1.2.1; 1.1.10.11–13.

[46] See *Enneads* 1.1.10.11–14, where Plotinus distinguishes the virtues that result from 'habit' as belonging to the 'composite' whereas the intellectual virtues belong to the true person.

[47] *Enneads* 1.2.1.23–6.

[48] *Enneads* 1.2.2.13–18. These virtues are here understood according to a general account of *Philebus* 23Bff., especially 26B–C, in which the imposition by the Demiurge of form on the sensible world is taken to be the imposition of limit on the unlimited. Plotinus simply assumes this metaphysical framework for his account of virtue.

Since every person acts on behalf of his own good as he perceives that, continual acting under the aegis of reason and over the blandishments of appetite and emotion contributes to a self-identification with the former. We become habituated to believing that what reason determines is good is our good. This is the principal true belief that virtue substitutes for those false beliefs the substance of which is that one's good is to be identified with the satisfaction of an appetite or the discharge of an emotion.

What, then, of the 'higher' virtue that is a 'purification'? In contrast to the popular and political virtues which consist essentially in behaviour, these virtues constitute a 'disposition' of the soul. According to this disposition, the soul 'thinks and is in this way free of affections'. Plotinus, no more than Plato, is endorsing or even contemplating the extirpation of anything that is natural to the embodied state. It is a confusion to see in this a recommendation of a kind of pathological asceticism. It is something else. It is more a psychological distancing of oneself from one's embodied state than it is self-mortification.

Plotinus goes on to argue that the person purified by virtue will have transcended incontinence or weakness of the will.[49] This means that the person has no or few desires that are 'unchosen', meaning not that he never desires food or sleep or sex or other pleasures, but that he never acts on them except under the aegis of reason. And that is because, as a virtuous person, he has identified with his rational self and never supposes that his own good is other than a rational one. We should notice here in particular how Plotinus uses incontinence to make the conceptual distinction between the two types of virtue. The popular and political virtues in *Republic* are developed on the basis of a theoretical argument explaining how incontinence is possible. The incontinent person, like the pathetic Leontius, has an appetite he knows is bad but cannot control. A continent person is one who has the bad appetite, but can control it. Someone practising continence would be practising the 'lower' virtue. But the truly virtuous person has been purified of bad desires. He does not have them in the first place. Or at least ideally so. Plotinus seems to recognize degrees of purification and an ideal purified state which is, nevertheless, not unqualifiedly ideal since it is still embodied.[50]

The distinction between the two types of virtue parallels exactly the distinction between the virtuous person envisioned at the end of book four of *Republic* and the philosopher or 'aristocratic human being' envisioned at the end of book nine. Platonists recognized that the virtues described in book four are capable of being present in a man,

[49] *Enneads* 1.2.5.17–21.

[50] *Enneads* 1.2.4.1–7. One might argue that in *Republic* 4, Plato holds that the presence of ethical virtue rules out continence, not just incontinence. But this is not I believe so clear. If the 'appetitive part of the soul' (*to epithumētikon*) does its job and obeys the 'rational part of the soul' (*to logistikon*), this does not necessarily mean that there are present no appetites whose satisfaction (like that of Leontius) would constitute a vicious act. It just means that they are not 'strong' enough to prevail. I am inclined to believe that if we take seriously the distinction between popular or political virtue on the one hand and the true virtue of the philosopher on the other, we shall be obliged to recognize that only the latter transcends continence. That is, only the latter is authentically virtuous. The distinction between continence and virtue is, of course, thematized by Aristotle.

as Plato later says, 'without participating in philosophy'.[51] In the case of every virtue of the purified person, there is an activity 'in the direction of' intellect.[52] The person in each case affirms his identity with reason much as someone might be said to identify with a cause or the fate of another. Such a person is profoundly different, for example, from the wise person as described in book four.[53] The latter's wisdom consists entirely in knowing what is 'beneficial' for each part of the soul and for the whole soul together. This prudential wisdom is available to one who knows that he ought to obey the dictates of the philosopher even though he himself has no philosophy in him.[54] It is only he who pursues philosophy 'in a sound manner' who is destined for happiness.[55]

In the last chapter of the treatise, Plotinus asks two questions: (1) do the virtues entail each other and (2) do the higher and lower virtues entail each other? The answer to the first question is that since in the intelligible world all the Forms are mutually implicated or virtually identical, so here below possession of one virtue entails possession of all. More convincingly, Plotinus argues that since there is a single process of purification, when that process is completed, all the virtues are present.[56] This is the 'principal part of the life of the excellent person'.[57]

The answer to the second question would seem to be equally straightforward, but though the person in possession of the higher virtues is said to have the lower 'in potency', it is not so clear that he will practise these in the way that the one in possession *only* of these practises them.[58] Plotinus is here worried about how one who has been purified of attachments to embodied life can be said to possess the virtues which consist in giving 'limit and measure' to desires. He seems to think that practising the lower virtues implies an 'impure' attachment to embodied life, in other words, to a political life.

> But when he [the one who is purified] attains to higher principles and different measures he will act according to these. For example, he will not locate self-control in that measure [i.e. of the lower virtues], but completely separating himself as much as possible, he will completely not live the life of the good human being as political virtues conceive of it, but leaving this behind, he will choose another life, the life of the gods. For assimilation is in the direction of these, not in the direction of good men. The latter type of assimilation is a case of making one image like another, both of which are derived from another. Assimilation to the other [the life of the gods] is in the direction of the paradigm.[59]

---

[51] See *Republic* 619C6–D1.   [52] *Enneads* 1.2.6.23–7.   [53] See *Republic* 442C5–8.
[54] See *Republic* 445C10–D1 where the philosopher is described as a lover of truth and where, by implication, his wisdom consists in attaining that truth.
[55] See *Republic* 619D8–E1.
[56] *Republic* 1.2.7.8–10.
[57] See 1.4.16, where Plotinus compares the *spoudaios* with the ideal of political life, the *epieikēs anthrōpos*. See Alexandrine Schniewind, *L'éthique du sage chez Plotin. Le paradigm du spoudaios*, Paris: Vrin (2003) on the *spoudaios* in Plotinus. The *spoudaios* is one who has attained the heights of embodied virtue. Such an attainment is, nevertheless, short of the disembodied ideal.
[58] *Republic* 1.2.7.10–12. Cf. 1.3.6.17ff where he suggests that the lower and higher virtue can grow at the same time.
[59] *Republic* 1.2.7.21–30.

As many scholars have pointed out, this claim implies neither world-renouncing asceticism nor Nietzschean transcendence of value any more than Socrates' claim that philosophy is preparation for dying is an endorsement of suicide.[60] There is nothing inconsistent in choosing not to live a political life and yet practising political virtue in so far as this is required. That is the key. Practising this virtue as required is opposed to making it the central focus of one's life.[61] As Plotinus elsewhere says, one does not wish for the drowning of a child in order that one can practise virtue and save him. To have missed such an 'opportunity' is not to suffer a diminution of virtue.

Porphyry in his *Sentences Leading to the Intelligible World* 32, offers an influential expansion or precision of the Plotinian scheme.[62]

> It has been shown then that there are four kinds (*genē*) of virtue: (1) those of intellect, which are paradigmatic and coincide with its essence; (2) those of the soul already in relation to intellect and imbued (*plēroumenēs*) with it; (3) those of the human soul that is being purified (*kathairoumenēs*) and has been purified of the body and of arational passions; (4) those of the human soul that manage the human being, putting limits to and moderating the passions (*metriopatheian*) by means of imposing measures (*metra*) on the arational.[63]

As Porphyry has already explained, at each of these levels, the four virtues of temperance, courage, wisdom, and justice can be found in a distinct form. That is, the virtues

---

[60] See, for example, J. Bussanich, 'The Invulnerability of Goodness. The Ethical and Psychological Theory of Plotinus', *Proceedings of the Boston Area Colloquium on Ancient Philosophy* 6, edited by J. J. Cleary, University Press of America: Lanham, Md. (1990), 151–84; J. M. Dillon, 'An Ethic for the Late Antique Sage', *The Cambridge Companion to Plotinus*, edited by L. Gerson, Cambridge University Press: Cambridge (1996), 315–35; A. Smith, 'The Significance of Practical Ethics for Plotinus', *Traditions of Platonism. Essays in Honour of John Dillon*, edited by J. J. Cleary, Aldershott: Brookfield, USA (1999), 227–36.

[61] See *Enneads* 6.8.6.14–18 where Plotinus expresses the core world–renouncing idea. One may compare in this regard the point of Martin Luther's provocative remark: 'Christianity has nothing to do with virtue'.

[62] See I. Hadot, *Le problème du néoplatonisme alexandrien : Hiéroclès et Simplicius*. Paris: Études Augustiniennes (1978), 152–8; J. M. Dillon, 'Plotinus, Philo, and Origin on the Grades of Virtue', *Platonismus und Christentum. Festschrift für Heinrich Dörrie*, edited by Horst–Deiter Blum and Friedholm Mann, Munster: Aschendorf (1983), 92–105; C. Wildberg, 'Pros to telos: Neuplatonische Ethik zwischen Religion und Metaphysik', *Metaphysik und Religion. Zur Signatur des spätantiken Denkens*, edited by T. Kobusch and M. Erler, München/Leipzig: K.G. Saur (2002), 261–78; M Lurje, 'Die Vita Pythagorica als Manifest der neuplatonischen Paideia. Jamblich', ΠΕΡΙ ΤΟΥ ΠΥΘΑΓΟΡΕΙΟΥ ΒΙΟΥ, edited by M. von Albrecht, J. M. Dillon, M. George, M. Lurje, and D. du Toi, Darmstadt: Wissenschaftliche Buchgesellschaft (2002), 221–54, especially 242–48, on the Porphyrean gradations of virtue and its development in later Platonism.

[63] Porphyry, *Sentences Leading to the Intelligible World* 32.71–78. Olympiodorus, evidently relying on Iamblichus, *Commentary on Plato's Phaedo* 8.2–3, expands the Porphyrean list of four levels of virtue to five: (1) 'natural' (*phusikai*), resulting from temperament; (2) 'moral' (*ēthikai*), owing to habit; (3) 'civic' or 'political' (*politikai*), concerned with the tripartite soul and the moderation of the passions; (4) 'purificatory' (*kathartikai*); and (5) 'contemplative' (*theōrētikai*). The same list is given in Damascius' *Lectures on Phaedo* I, 138–144. Both give the 'paradigmatic' referring to the virtues of the gods as a sixth category, alluding to Plotinus, *Enneads* 1.2.7.2–6. See Westerink (1976), v.1, 18, on Proclus' relation to Olympiodorus and Damascius. See also Eustratius' Christianized version of the grades of virtues and the ascent to union with God, *Commentary on Aristotle's Nicomachean Ethics* 4. 25–38.

at level (2) are an image of those at (1), and so on. The lower are images of the higher in the Platonic sense that the ontologically derived or posterior is an image of the ontologically prior. According to Porphyry's description of these levels, (4) is equivalent to the political and popular virtue as understood by Plotinus in *Phaedo*; (1) and (2) comprise a division of Plotinus' theoretical virtue into its practice by intellect and by the soul.[64] I would suggest that this is in fact a division of theoretical activity as practised intuitively and discursively, though I cannot develop this interpretation now. Porphyry here seems to be relying on the distinction Plotinus makes elsewhere between using intellect and being identified with it.[65] In addition, in (3) Porphyry erects a distinct form of virtue constituted by the purification process of *Phaedo*. These are the virtues of the soul that is being 'elevated' (*aphistamenēs*) to the intellectual realm.[66] At this level, wisdom consists in refusing to 'share the opinions of the body' (*sundoxazein*), and in acting according to intellect; temperance in refusing to 'feel what the body feels' (*homopathein*); courage in having no fear of separation from the body; and justice in the unimpeded rule of reason.[67]

The virtue of refusing to share the opinions of the body should put us in mind of *Phaedo* where Socrates in the affinity argument warns his interlocutors of the perils of embodiment: by sharing opinions and pleasures with the body the soul is forced to become of like character and nurture with it.[68] We should not suppose that the possibility of 'sharing the body's opinions' indicates that the body is being represented by Plato as the sort of thing capable of having opinions. Rather, one is being exhorted to refuse to share the opinions possessed by oneself in so far as one is the subject of bodily states, namely, opinions that the satisfaction of bodily desires constitutes one's good.[69] One is being exhorted to renounce those opinions. Similarly, refusing to feel what the body feels amounts to refusing to make one's bodily feelings the principle of one's actions. Courage is the refusal to believe that one's good is eliminated by the death of the human being. The unimpeded rule of reason is just the establishment of reason as the sole principle of action. This establishment is identical with the identification of oneself as ideally a rational agent or subject.

The cathartic virtues serve to indicate the continuity of the practices of ethical and intellectual virtue. That is why, as Porphyry insists, the possession of the higher *necessitates* the possession of the lower.[70] I take Porphyry here to be making the important claim that there is a linear progression in moral development leading ultimately towards

[64] On the equivalence of the political and ethical virtues see Hierocles of Alexandria, *Commentary on the Carmen Aureum* Proem 3.9–10 (Koehler).

[65] Cf. *Enneads* 5.3.3.44; 5.3.4.1.

[66] *Sentences Leading to the Intelligible World* 32.18–19. Cf. Iamblichus, *Life of Pythagoras* 122.10–123.4. Iamblichus insisted that 'theurgic' virtues were above the philosophical and necessary for union with God. See *On the Egyptian Mysteries* II 11; Olympiodorus, *Commentary on Plato's Phaedo* 114.20–2; Marinus, *Life of Proclus* 26.

[67] Marinus, *Life of Proclus*, 23–9.

[68] *Phaedo* 83D7–8.

[69] See L. Gerson, *Knowing Persons*, cc. 2–3 on the incoherence of treating the bodily appetites as originating in a *homunculus* within the soul.

[70] See *Sentences Leading to the Intelligible World* 32, 78–9: 'And he who has the greater necessarily has the lesser, though not vice versa.'

identification with the divine. Life is a continuum in which one is either approaching or receding from the ideal state. One who has ascended to the practice of the cathartic virtues will necessarily manifest the behaviour of one who possesses the 'popular and political virtues' as well. But one who merely practises the latter has not thereby achieved what a person is ideally capable of, that is, identification with his intellect. This necessary linear progression also, I believe, explains why Porphyry tends to disdain the 'theurgical virtues' of Iamblichus, that is, the devotion to religious rites that might enable one to omit one or more of the hard won stages on the way to the divine.

What Porphyry has here done is in effect recognized that the practices of the philosopher are distinct from the achievement of the philosopher as a contemplator. He recognizes philosophy as part of a virtuous way of life other than yet, importantly, inferior to, the virtuous state consisting of the contemplation of eternal truth. A moral preparation or purification of the soul is a necessary prelude to intellectual activity.[71] In other words, one does not prepare for the virtues of the intellect merely by practising moderation of the passions.

In my opinion, the fundamental truth contained in the Platonic interpretation of Plato's ethics is the refusal to foist upon Plato a facile view of human personhood. Platonists never for a moment supposed that Plato thought that what was good or virtuous for the human being, the anthrōpos, was identical with what was good or virtuous for the person. For persons have a destiny that transcends humanity.[72] The 'popular and political' virtues pertain to the human being. But the philosopher and the philosopher alone recognizes that persons are souls, not human beings. More particularly, they are rational souls or minds and their ideal activity is thought. As Plotinus might put it, the ability to identify and pursue human virtue is itself proof that human virtue is insufficient to fulfil one capable of such recognition. Thus, ethical virtue or 'relational [read: 'interpersonal'] activity' (schetikē energeia) as Proclus aptly puts it, is inferior to theoretical virtue which, at its highest, constitutes identification with the divine.[73]

The Platonic interpretation of Plato's ethics does not so much contradict those modern interpretations of Plato's ethics that more or less focus on the so-called Socratic paradoxes as it does supersede them in its comprehensiveness. That interpretation supposes that 'assimilation to god' is equivalent to 'achieving the good' and that 'achieving the good' for us consists in cognitive identity with the intelligible world, which is what the Idea of the Good is virtually. The role of 'ordinary' virtue in this achievement is to foster the rediscovery of our true identities as intellects. At least for Platonists, if in fact we were not really or ideally intellects, then Plato's central ethical claims would be at best question-begging and at worst, sadly, false.

---

[71] Sentences Leading to the Intelligible World, 51–5.

[72] There is a particularly vivid description of this in Hierocles of Alexandria's Commentary on the Carmen Aureum 84, 16–20 (Koehler): 'For the rational soul, being midway between intellect and the irrational [part of the soul], can only associate without disturbance with the intellect that is before it when it is purified of its attachment to the things that come after it thereby grasping them in a purified manner.'

[73] See Commentary on Plato's Republic 1.208.27. The life of relational activity is contrasted with the life 'in itself' (kath' auto) (209.4).

Bibliography

Bussanich, J. 1990. 'The Invulnerability of Goodness. The Ethical and Psychological Theory of Plotinus', *Proceedings of the Boston Area Colloquium on Ancient Philosophy* 6, ed. J. J. Cleary. Lanham, MD: University Press of America, 151–84.

Dillon, J. M. 1983. 'Plotinus, Philo, and Origin on the Grades of Virtue', in H.-D. Blum and F. Mann (eds), *Platonismus und Christentum. Festschrift für Heinrich Dörrie.* Munster: Aschendorf, 92–105.

——1996. 'An Ethic for the Late Antique Sage', in L. P. Gerson (ed.), *The Cambridge Companion to Plotinus.* Cambridge: Cambridge University Press, 315–35.

Gerson, L. P. 2003. *Knowing Persons.* Oxford: Oxford University Press

Hadot, I. 1978. *Le problème du néoplatonisme alexandrien: Hiéroclès et Simplicius.* Paris: Études Augustiniennes, 152–8.

Lurje, M. 2002. 'Die Vita Pythagorica als Manifest der neuplatonischen Paideia. Jamblich', in M. von Albrecht, J. M. Dillon, M. George, M. Lurje, and D. du Toi (eds), PERI TOU PUQAGOREIOU BIOU. Darmstadt: Wissenschaftliche Buchgesellschaft, 221–54.

Schniewind, A. 2003. *L'éthique du sage chez Plotin. Le paradigm du spoudaios.* Paris: Vrin.

Smith, A. 1999. 'The Significance of Practical Ethics for Plotinus', in J. J. Cleary (ed.), *Traditions of Platonism. Essays in Honour of John Dillon.* Brookfield, USA: Aldershott, 227–36.

Wildberg, C. 2002. 'Pros to telos: Neuplatonische Ethik zwischen Religion und Metaphysik', in T. Kobusch and M. Erler (eds), *Metaphysik und Religion. Zur Signatur des spätantiken Denkens.* München/Leipzig: K.G. Saur, 261–78.

CHAPTER 8

....

THOMISM

....

COLLEEN McCLUSKEY

THOMISM is a philosophical movement that takes for its foundation the writings of
Thomas Aquinas.[1] Thomas Aquinas is arguably one of the most recognized intellectual
figures from the European Middle Ages. That he did not fall into obscurity as did so many
other medieval thinkers is due in large part to the impressive tradition of commentary by
philosophers and theologians who find his work fruitful for their own endeavours.

In this chapter, I discuss first the historical context within which Thomism originated
and some of the general issues that arise in Thomistic discussions. I go on to discuss the
two main approaches to Thomistic ethics, namely eudaimonism and natural law. I end
the chapter by considering an application of Thomistic ideas to a current discussion of
justice and practical rationality, that of Alasdair MacIntyre.

8.1

....

Thomas Aquinas was born in what is now Italy around 1224. He was educated at the
monastery at Monte Cassino and at the University of Naples, where he joined the then
recently established Order of Preachers, commonly known as the Dominicans. He
studied at the Dominican House of Studies in Cologne, Germany under the guidance
of Albert the Great and at the Faculty of Theology at the University of Paris. He taught
both at Paris and in Italy and died while travelling to Lyon for an ecclesiastical council
in 1274.[2]

Aquinas is perhaps most famous for his mature work, *Summa theologiae* (part three
of which was completed by one of Aquinas' disciples after his death, using writings from
his *Sentences* commentary), but he composed an astonishing number of other texts,

---

[1] For a brief and concise history of Thomism, see Haldane 1999. A longer, more detailed history can
be found in McCool 1994.

[2] Summaries of Aquinas' life are abundant, but the standard biography continues to be that of Torell 1996.

including the four-volume *Summa contra gentiles*, a multi-volume commentary on Peter Lombard's *Sententia* (a standard theological text of the time), commentaries on the works of Aristotle (including one on *Nicomachean Ethics*), commentaries on the Scriptures, and a number of smaller treatises on various subjects, some of which were written for specific individuals (including one on kingship written for the ruler of Cyprus). We also have records of his public disputations on such topics as the virtues, truth, and evil.

Although today Aquinas is often celebrated as one of the most original and profound thinkers to have ever engaged in philosophy, it is good to keep in mind that he has also been regarded as one of the most controversial. In 1277, Etienne Tempier, the bishop of Paris, published a list of 217 theses, which he condemned as heretical. Although no individual theorist was named in the condemnations, the list included positions attributed to Aquinas. In the same year, Robert Kilwardby, the bishop of Canterbury, issued his own condemnation, and the pope sustained Tempier's declaration. In 1279, William de la Mare, a member of the Franciscan order, published a response to Aquinas' *Summa theologiae*, the so-called *Correctorium fratris Thomae*, which in 1282 was adopted by the general chapter as required reading for all Franciscans who were studying Aquinas' work. Of course, such criticism was not left unchallenged by Aquinas' supporters. Albert the Great and other Dominicans challenged the Paris and Oxford condemnations. William of Macclesfield and John of Paris each responded to de la Mare's treatise with treatises of their own (cf. Haldane 1999: 159–60). Scholars in the subsequent centuries continued to study Aquinas' work and to defend his ideas. The most well-known Thomists prior to the modern Thomistic revival of the late nineteenth and twentieth centuries include Jean Gerson (1363–1429), John Capreolus (1380–1444), Thomas de Vio Cajetan (1469–1534), Francisco Suárez (1548–1617), and John of Poinsot (John of St. Thomas, 1589–1644).

Although Aquinas' texts continued to be discussed, particularly by Dominicans, by the seventeenth and eighteenth centuries, study of all the medieval masters, including Aquinas, had largely fallen out of favour.[3] One of the major exceptions (besides the Dominicans) was the Society of Jesus (the Jesuits), which emphasized Aquinas' work in its theology programmes. The plan of studies for Jesuit centres of education (which included primary and secondary education as well as colleges and universities), the *Ratio studiorum*, was first put into use in 1599 and was in force until well into the nineteenth century.[4] It stipulated the study of a significant number of Thomistic texts for the degree in theology, in areas such as the nature of theology, the existence and nature of God, knowledge of God, the ultimate end for human beings, free will, morality, sin, grace, faith and charity, the Incarnation, and the sacraments.[5] Theology was the highest level of study in the Jesuit colleges of the time, and since most students would not have gone on to study theology, most would not have read these texts. Nevertheless, the

[3] Cf. Boyle 1987: 13–14 and McCool 1994: 16–21. For a list of Thomistic scholars, broken down by century and by affiliation with religious order, see Kennedy 1987.

[4] Cf. Pavur 2005: vii. The document was revised and reissued several times, the final time in 1832, but by that date, Jesuit schools were no longer required to follow its specifications.

[5] See Appendix 2 in Pavur 2005: 220–5 for a list of the relevant questions from *Summa theologiae*.

emphasis on Aquinas' intellectual positions within Jesuit theological studies helped to keep the study of his philosophy alive.

In the late nineteenth century, Pope Leo XIII published an encyclical, *Aeterni Patris*, which promoted the study of Aquinas in Catholic higher education, triggering a major revival of interest in his writings, still in effect today.[6] Leo's main concern was with a world that he believed increasingly regarded religion as irrelevant to the acquisition of knowledge, glorifying the efforts of human reason independently of faith in the face of the ascendancy of science (Brezik 1981: 173–5). Leo viewed Aquinas as a sophisticated thinker who respected both revealed religious doctrines and the achievements of human reason, integrating both within his world view (Brezik 1981: 187–8). Leo argued that Aquinas' writings and methodology should be the basis for not only a Christian philosophy, but for all acquisition of knowledge, including that of science (Brezik 1981: 193–4).

One important result of the encyclical was the establishment of an organization to produce critical editions of Aquinas' texts. Named after the Pope, the Leonine Commission continues to produce such editions. But Leo's exhortation on behalf of Aquinas' philosophy gave rise to a number of vexing questions. Was he issuing a call to return to Scholastic method? Was he advocating the defence of Thomistic positions, and if so, how was that to be accomplished? After all, the world was a much different place in the late nineteenth century than it had been in Aquinas' time. Aquinas took himself to be a theologian; what implications would this have for those working in other areas, such as philosophy or natural science? Furthermore, except for pockets of intellectual communities concentrated mainly in Europe, few scholars of the time possessed the expertise required to implement Leo's vision. Thus, the immediate reaction to the encyclical was one of bewilderment.[7] Leo's rather open-ended call to a return to things Thomistic gave rise in the twentieth century to a debate over the proper approach to Aquinas' texts. This debate in turn gave rise to a diverse philosophical movement.

8.2

Within twentieth-century Thomism, there have been two major general approaches.[8] One approach, which Brian Shanley calls the conservative approach (conservative in the sense of conservation), sees its primary task as, in Shanley's words, 'exegesis, commentary, and defense against external criticism' (Shanley 2002: 1–2). The other camp takes as its primary task not only exegesis and associated activities, but also dialogue with the major philosophical issues and movements of the current day.[9] Some important proponents of

[6] For the text of the encyclical, I have used Brezik 1981: 173–97.
[7] Cf. Weisheipl 1981: 25–7.
[8] For a general survey of twentieth-century Thomism, see Shanley 2002, 1–20.
[9] See Shanley 2002: 1–4. Vernon Bourke calls the first approach the historical-textual approach. He does not provide a ready label for the second approach but describes it as a kind of engagement with current philosophical ideas. Cf. Bourke 1981: 169–71.

the first approach include Marie-Dominique Chenu, O. P. and Etienne Gilson. Included in the other camp are Jacques Maritain, Bernard Lonergan, and the so-called Analytic Thomists.

Traditionally those who have worked on Aquinas' ideas have accepted some form of theism and in particular (although not exclusively) Catholicism. In the second half of the twentieth century, interest in Aquinas spread to larger circles, that is, to historians of philosophy who have no commitment to theism or who do not take themselves to be philosophizing within the Catholic intellectual tradition. In particular, interest in Aquinas has arisen among those philosophers who specialize in the medieval period and who have been trained in the so-called analytic tradition. Although it has become increasingly difficult to delineate among different philosophical approaches, the analytic approach is roughly the legacy of early twentieth-century British philosophers such as Bertrand Russell and G. E. Moore. Notoriously difficult to describe, this philosophical approach is often thought to involve the careful analysis of concepts, arguments, and ideas, often incorporating the principles of formal logic. At its heart are the twin aims of clarification and evaluation. Analytical Thomism has been characterized as the application of 'the methods and ideas of twentieth-century philosophy—of the sort dominant within the English-speaking world—in connection with the broad framework of ideas introduced and developed by Aquinas' (Haldane 1997: 486).[10]

A great deal of credit for the increase of interest in Aquinas among analytic philosophers (who have often been accused of lacking interest in the history of philosophy) must go to Norman Kretzmann. Through his published work, Kretzmann demonstrated to an often sceptical analytic audience the valuable resources that Aquinas (and other scholars from the European medieval period) brings to bear on the important philosophical issues of our own time.[11]

8.3

The interpretation of Aquinas' moral theory is controversial in part because of the nature of his texts. Aquinas thought of himself primarily as a theologian and did not separate what we would call philosophical issues from theological ones. Thus, all interpreters of

---

[10] Of course, this approach has its critics; cf. Theron 1997: 611–18, although it is not entirely clear to me that Theron fully understands what Analytical Thomism takes itself to be doing. Theron interprets the analytic project as a synthesis between Aquinas' philosophical systems and particular analytical theories, e.g. those of Frege. In my view, Analytical Thomism is, first and foremost, the attempt to understand Aquinas' views using the methodological approach of analytic philosophy. Any additional application of Aquinas' ideas is a further project. I suspect that fundamentally the dispute between Theron and Analytical Thomism is really a dispute over whether one should be a Thomist in the first sense or the second sense. See also Shanley 1999: 125–37.

[11] A brief discussion of Kretzmann's achievements and a list of his publications on Aquinas can be found in MacDonald and Stump 1999: 9–11; 277–9.

his ethics recognize and agree that there is much in Aquinas that we would call philo-sophical and that his philosophical ideas exist embedded within a theological context. This raises the following question: to what extent are the theological elements of Aquinas' thought inherently bound to his moral theory? In other words, is Aquinas' theory irrevo-cably theological in nature or can a wholly philosophical account of ethics be extracted (so to speak) from his writings? Those who argue that one can recognize a wholly philo-sophical theory of ethics in Aquinas include Ralph McInerny, John Finnis, and Anthony Liska (McInerny 1982, Finnis 1980, Liska 1996). Those who deny this possibility include David Gallagher, Denis Bradley, Mark D. Jordan, Servais Pinckaers, and Alasdair MacIntyre (Gallagher 1998, Bradley 1997, Jordan 1999, Pinckaers 1995, MacIntyre 1988).[12]

In order to address this issue, one must first clarify what exactly is meant by these terms, philosophy and theology. Traditionally the distinction has been taken to refer to the roles of reason and divine revelation within a given theorist's work. Traditionally philosophy has been taken to be rooted in what can be known by human intellectual efforts and observation alone, while theology has been understood to take as its basis what has been revealed by a divine being.[13] This of course does not rule out the use of cognitive capacities in doing theology; it is merely to state that one does not rely solely on whatever information one can obtain from the use of such capacities. This distinc-tion also does not rule out the examination of theological subjects as a domain within philosophy; thus, philosophy of religion or philosophical theology, as it is sometimes called, is a recognized sub-discipline within philosophy. This traditional understanding of the distinction between philosophy and theology has been challenged in recent years, but Thomists by and large grant that it represents Aquinas' understanding, and so I will proceed on the basis of it in my remarks here.[14]

Although David Gallagher distinguishes between what he calls Aquinas' natural ethic, by which he seems to mean a philosophical ethic, and his supernatural ethic, he argues that any *philosophical* account of ethics developed on the basis of Aquinas' texts would necessarily be incomplete; it would not be a 'systematic whole' in his words (Gallagher 1998: 1024). This is because, as we will discuss later, Aquinas argued that the ultimate end of human life (which is the goal of ethics) is supernatural in nature, i.e. union with God through what Aquinas calls the beatific vision, which is possible only in the next life, not in this world. Gallagher argues that although one can reach the conclu-sion that human beings are meant to love God on the basis of reason alone, one cannot comprehend the nature of humanity's ultimate supernatural end without revelation. Thus, a purely philosophical ethic would be a deficient interpretation of Aquinas' views.

Denis J. M. Bradley agrees with Gallagher. He argues that philosophy is able to estab-lish that human natural inclinations cannot be satisfied by anything in this world, but

---

[12] There is a controversy over which camp should claim Jacque Maritain. David Gallagher argues that he belongs to the negative camp, yet Denis Bradley argues for the opposing view; cf. Gallagher 1998: 1024 n. 1 and Bradley 1997: 495–506. Ralph McInerny agrees with Gallagher; cf. McInerny 1993: 17, 40–1.

[13] Cf. McInerny 1993: 42.

[14] For an implicit challenge to the traditional distinction, see Plantinga (1984).

not that God will in fact enable human beings to receive the beatific vision. That God will do so is known to human beings only through divine revelation (Bradley 1997: 526–8). But once philosophers incorporate divine revelation into their arguments, they are no longer doing philosophy. They could concede that human beings might never find ultimate fulfilment, but to do so would be to acknowledge that, for all anyone knows, an important human inclination might be futile. Such an admission, however, violates Aquinas' commitment to teleology. Since teleology by definition holds that beings are moved towards particular ends on the basis of their natures, Aquinas must argue that human desires be directed towards ends that at least in principle can be fulfilled. Thus, Aquinas cannot accept the view that human beings could have an unfulfillable desire (Bradley 1997: 528–9). For Bradley, a wholly philosophical moral system is not possible on Thomistic principles.

Although Ralph McInerny acknowledges that a commitment to theism makes a difference in how one lives one's life, still he argues for a distinction between moral philosophy and moral theology. On McInerny's view, philosophical ethics for Aquinas is not rooted essentially in a foundation of faith, although a commitment to faith grounds and benefits such a moral system (McInerny 1993: 48; 52–3). He argues that Aquinas arrives at the basic outlines of his ethical theory (including the commitment to the beatific vision as humanity's ultimate end) on the basis of argumentation alone without the benefit of revelation (McInerny 1993: 23–34). The purpose of ethics is to provide guidance on how to live a good human life, and on Aquinas' view, a purely philosophical ethics is able to do just that (McInerny 1993: 44–8; 51–3).

Now that we have looked at Aquinas' general approach to ethics (i.e. whether it is essentially theological), we shall now consider the structure of Aquinas' account. That is, what kind of an ethical theory does Aquinas hold?

8.4

All Thomists recognize that Aquinas' account of ethics involves both eudaimonism and natural law as elements. A eudaimonistic account of ethics holds that there is a particular form of life that human beings are meant to live because of the kind of being that they are. If they pursue such a life, they flourish; if they do not, they suffer. Virtues play a role in this account in so far as they move human beings towards good actions, that is, those actions that bring about human flourishing. Thus, they enable human beings to live good lives.[15] Vices have the opposite effect in so far as they move human beings towards action that detract from human flourishing. Although these issues occupy much of the (very large) second part of *Summa theologiae*, there is another (considerably smaller)

---

[15] This description implies that the virtues are merely a means to a good end, which eudaimonists would deny. The virtues (or their exercise) are also constitutive of the good life and thus are valuable for the kind of thing that they are. On this point, see McKinnon 1989: 326.

section of the same text for which Aquinas' ethical theory is also famous, that is, his discussion of the so-called natural law.

Aquinas defines law in general as something rational that is directed to the common good promulgated by those individuals (or individual) responsible for the good of the community (*ST* I–II.90.4).[16] Aquinas defines the natural law as human participation in God's governance of creation, whose governance is specified in what he calls the eternal law (*ST* I–II.91.2). Although, as we shall see in more detail later, the exact character of the natural law is disputed, the natural law provides guidance for living a meaningful life.

The question then is how do these two elements function in Aquinas' account? Some commentators argue for a eudaimonistic account and then describe the role of natural law within this system. Others emphasize Aquinas' account of natural law and then examine the contribution of the virtues from this perspective. We shall consider each of these positions in turn.

I shall begin with the eudaimonia interpretation, and I shall take Ralph McInerny as my representative of this view. McInerny argues that on Aquinas' view, morality is concerned with the evaluation of action (McInerny 1982: 1). Actions, for Aquinas, are never performed except for the sake of an end, and then only for the sake of an ultimate end (McInerny 1982: 2; 12–34). All human beings perform the actions they do for the sake of something they regard as good (i.e. for the sake of a particular end) because all human action is willed and the will is (in Eleonore Stump's words) 'a hunger for the good'.[17] Something's being good is a necessary condition for choice, for the will does not choose anything not regarded as a good, but it is not a sufficient condition. That is to say that the will does not choose something simply because it is good. Thus, the moral life is structured around what human beings want above all (their ultimate end), which on Aquinas' account is happiness. Aquinas grants that there is no consensus on what in fact will make human beings happy, but he argues strenuously that one cannot make sense of human life without acknowledging the fact that human beings pursue happiness above all else (Cf. McInerny 1982: 26–31).

Aquinas of course has a specific view on what in fact will make human beings happy. For him it is a direct relationship with God through the vision of the divine essence (McInerny 1982: 31). This relationship with God is fully accessible only in the next life. The morally good life is oriented around the pursuit of this end.[18] Human beings have this particular end because of the kind of beings they are, that is, beings who possess intellect and will, which enable them to enjoy a relationship with God. Possessing cognitive capacities enable human beings to identify the good that they ought to pursue; possessing the will enables them to be moved in accordance with that good (McInerny 1982: 69–72).

---

[16] I have used the Marietti edition of *Summa theologiae* which is based upon the Leonine edition. References to Aquinas' text follow the standard practice of indicating part, question, article, and if applicable, objection and/or reply.

[17] For a discussion of the will as a hunger for the good, see Stump 1997: 577–83. See also McInerny 1982: 69–73.

[18] Aquinas' account is complicated by his commitment to the position that human beings obtain this end only in virtue of divine assistance. Cf. McInerny 1982: 67–8; 118–20.

Moral appraisal of actions is necessary because while something's being good is a necessary condition for choice, it is not a sufficient condition. Thus, human beings are free to choose among goods. They cannot will misery for its own sake, for to do so is to will an evil simply because it is evil, which violates the nature of the will as a capacity or inclination towards the good. Human beings, however, are free to choose lesser goods over greater goods and to pursue things that will in fact not contribute to their happiness as long as there is some aspect of the good in that thing, at least in a particular respect (McInerny 1982: 66–9). Thus, Aquinas holds that human beings bring about what is in fact evil because there is something that appears good to them about that evil. There can be a gap between what in fact is good and brings about one's happiness and what one believes is good and will make one happy (McInerny 1982: 77–8).

What determines the good for human beings is their nature. That is to say that our being structured as we are determines what is conducive to our flourishing. Morally good actions are constitutive of human flourishing in the long run; morally bad actions diminish flourishing. Virtues are habits acquired by making good choices and performing good actions, which in turn help us to continue in these good activities, while vices are the result of choices to perform bad actions that in turn move us to continue performing bad actions. Thus, over time, virtues enable human beings to work effectively towards their end while vices act to detract from achieving the end (McInerny 1982: 91–4; 96–9).

A major objection to a eudaimonistic account is that such an account cannot be action-guiding.[19] According to this objection, eudaimonism cannot tell us what to do or how to resolve moral disputes, for it says that what we ought to do is what the virtuous person would do. Such a claim has no real content. The critic continues, only appeal to moral principles or general moral rules can adjudicate such questions under a particular set of circumstances. I will not comment on this dispute or discuss how virtue theorists address it but simply note that for Thomists, Aquinas' theory of natural law provides a way to respond to this concern.

8.5

Aquinas' discussion of law in general and the natural law in particular has generated a long tradition of commentary. Among the most prominent are Germain Grisez, John Finnis, Anthony Liska, Mark Murphy, Jean Porter, Martin Rhonheimer, Wolfgang Kluxen, Russell Hittinger, and Ralph McInerny, just to name a few.[20] For this chapter, I have chosen Pamela Hall's interpretation of natural law and its place in Aquinas' ethics,

---

[19] See for example, Louden 1984: 227–36 and Schneewind 1990: 42–63. Both are reprinted in Crisp and Slote 1997.

[20] A list of some of their most notable writings can be found in the bibliography at the end of this chapter.

which I will contrast with that of McInerny. No doubt some will be startled to find that I have favoured her account over more well-known accounts, but in my view, Hall provides an interpretation that is worth considering and that differs distinctively from the more standard lines developed by others.[21]

Aquinas says that the natural law is that by which human beings participate in divine Providence. For Hall, this claim does not make the natural law into a set of moral principles, although such a set can be derived from it (Hall 1994: 23; 41–3). On Aquinas' account, the creator has a plan in virtue of which the universe is governed. For most created beings, participation in this plan follows a deterministic path, governed by what we would call the laws of nature. Because human beings possess cognitive capacities, by which they are able to comprehend the natural (created) order, and volitional capacities, in virtue of which they are able to choose and determine their own actions, human beings have the capacity to understand (at least in principle) God's plan. Following God's plan makes one's flourishing more likely, but human beings also have the freedom (in virtue of the divinely provided intellect and will) to accept or reject God's will.[22]

Despite Aquinas' characterization of law as something promulgated by one who is responsible for the care of a community, a characterization that implies a set of statutes or decrees, Hall argues that the natural law does not have the literal nature of a rule or principle as that notion is typically understand. On her interpretation, the natural law for Aquinas is rooted in human nature, and in particular, in the character of human inclinations (Hall 1994: 28). Natural law directs us to our ultimate end, an end determined for us by our nature as rational beings with particular inclinations. In so far as human beings are inclined by nature towards their good, they naturally come to understand that good is to be pursued and evil avoided. Thus, a connection exists between natural law as a kind of inclination and the subsequent understanding of what that entails, which provides a set of criteria for human behaviour. This knowledge of how human beings ought to behave in order to pursue the ultimate end rightly constitutes the principles of the natural law, the most basic of which holds that good is to be pursued and evil avoided (Hall 1994: 29–30). This of course looks like a simple tautology. Given that a perception of goodness is a necessary condition for choice and action, human beings cannot help but fulfil this principle.

But to think of this fundamental principle as a simple tautology misses the point, for it assumes that the natural law stipulates particular statutes to be obeyed. Hall argues that this general principle functions in practical reasoning much like fundamental principles

---

[21] Grisez and Finnis are probably the most well-known of the natural law theorists, but Hall, among others, argues that their account deviates significantly from Aquinas', a deviation which they intend; cf. Hall 1994: 16–19; McInerny 1980: 9–10. For a useful summary of their account, see Grisez, Boyle, and Finnis 1987: 99–151. For a useful summary and critique of Hall, McInerny, and Benedict Ashley, as well as a summary and defence of Grisez and Finnis, see May 2004: 113–56.

[22] God wills that all human beings achieve happiness, but in so far as it is also part of God's plan that human beings act freely, human rejection of God does not constitute a violation of divine providence on Aquinas' account.

of logic function for speculative reasoning. Just as our basic patterns of thought presuppose such fundamental principles as the laws of non-contradiction and identity and would make no sense without them, so too for our basic patterns of practical reasoning. Human action, for Aquinas, is not intelligible apart from the assumption that the agent is pursuing something she at least perceives to be good, which presupposition is expressed in the first principle of the natural law. Thus, the natural law is not a statute to be obeyed but rather has the character of a basic rule of thought that guides practical reasoning and underlies our behaviour.[23] This principle provides a starting point (as Hall calls it) for living an ethical life. Built into our very nature is at least some rudimentary direction from which moral reflection can commence (Hall 1994: 31). Much more of course is required; moral reasoning can go very badly. In fact, Hall argues that on Aquinas' account, comprehending the natural law in its greater detail requires both time and a great deal of intellective reflection. It requires the possession of virtue, especially prudence. It is a community effort and in the end also requires divine guidance (Hall 1994: 30–1; 35–44; 94–106).

Natural law is grounded in human inclinations, what Hall calls 'the primary constituents of the natural law.'[24] These inclinations, together with our basic understanding of the good, direct our deliberation about what to do. Although the specific content and judgements about what we should do are importantly influenced by our experiences and the communities in which we live, on the very general level the natural law is universal for all of humanity. Hall takes this idea to underlie Aquinas' claim that the natural law, in its most fundamental form, is apparent to all human beings and cannot be eliminated from the human heart (Hall 1994: 31). These inclinations include the basic drive for survival and preservation of life, reproduction and care of offspring, and the intellectual desire to search for meaning and truth (for Aquinas, a search for God) as well as the desire for life lived in community (Hall 1994: 32). These inclinations map onto the various human goods towards which we are naturally attracted and the realization of which constitute human flourishing. The individual precepts of the natural law specify particular activities that promote the acquisition of these goods and prohibit those activities that detract from or prevent their realization in human life.

The natural law is not simply a matter of following inclinations. If it were, human beings would function in the same way as non-rational animals. Human beings have cognitive capacities that enable them to reflect upon the nature and function of those inclinations and their roles in promoting flourishing. They can recognize the conditions under which particular goods should be pursued and when their pursuit should be postponed for the sake of other goods. Human beings also have the ability to direct their actions, either in accordance with what in fact brings about flourishing or what violates that flourishing (although actions that violate flourishing must seem good to the agent

---

[23] Hall 1994: 29–30. Hall discusses these ideas in terms of Aquinas' notion of *synderesis*. I have chosen not to adopt this language in the hopes of promoting a more intuitive and less technical understanding, but the interested reader should consult pages 28–32.

[24] Hall 1994: 31. Not surprisingly, Hall's view that the natural law fundamentally is constituted by inclinations has been challenged; cf. May 2004: 119–20.

in some respect). Furthermore, what particular precepts are in effect in any particular community is a function of both the circumstances under which that community operates and their basic understanding of human flourishing (about which of course they could be mistaken). Thus, specific precepts vary from community to community, but all precepts are derived from and are a reflection of the fundamental principle that the good is to be pursued and evil avoided.

For Hall, Aquinas' description of the natural law as the human participation in the eternal law is instantiated in two respects: first, in terms of being directed to (inclined towards) particular goods suited to the kind of nature we have; and secondly, in terms of our cognitive capacities, which allow us to recognize particular things as good and allow us to choose the means by which we pursue those goods (Hall 1994: 37). Thus, while the natural law can be expressed as propositions, it is ultimately grounded in something both objective and non-propositional, which is not reducible to what is propositional. On Hall's account, this is advantageous to Aquinas for several reasons. First, it does not reduce Aquinas' account to an intuitionist account (Hall 1994: 37). We come to understand the moral law through our upbringing and our community, on the basis of reflection and experience (Hall 1994: 94–5). Furthermore, Aquinas' system admits of flexibility in so far as its primary purpose is to realize human flourishing and what will in fact bring flourishing about varies with historical and environmental circumstances (Hall 1994: 106).

In so far as it is a fundamental part of God's plan (expressed in the eternal law) that human beings flourish, the natural law, since it specifies what it is for beings such as us to flourish, is an expression of the eternal law. In so far as human societies explicitly codify laws meant to promote human flourishing, human law is an expression of the natural law. And finally in so far as human beings have an imperfect understanding of what in fact promotes flourishing, their understanding of the natural law must be guided by divine law revealed by God in the Scriptures (cf. Hall 1994: 36–44).

Hall uses Aquinas' account of natural law as the framework for his moral theory, moving from there to discuss the role of the virtues in moral deliberation, especially the virtue of prudence. Prudence is a virtue of practical reasoning that ensures correct judgement about what to do, that is, how to achieve one's goals or ends (Hall 1994: 39). In so far as the natural law is tailored to human ends and directs human beings to those ends, prudence works in concert with the natural law. Indeed, Hall argues that for Aquinas, the natural law sets the content and direction for prudence. It sets the ends towards which prudence operates (Hall 1994: 39). Prudence aids practical reason in determining the conduct appropriate for achieving human ends. Thus, it specifies human conduct. Not only does it aid an agent in determining the means appropriate to achieve her ends, it in fact helps to specify particular principles of the natural law (Hall 1994, 40). Acting rightly in accordance with the natural law requires understanding of the particular situation and knowledge of what rules apply in that situation. Prudence enables the agent to engage successfully in such instances of practical reasoning.

Hall does not discuss in any detail how the other virtues fit into this natural law schema, but on Aquinas' account, prudence is not able to fulfil its function without the aid of the other virtues, so at least in so far as they enable the functioning of prudence, all of the virtues contribute to the ethical enterprise.[25] A eudaimonist interpreter of Aquinas would insist that the virtues are much more central to the ethical life than this rather thin instrumental role would indicate, and in my view, this is the weakest part of Hall's treatment, given Aquinas' emphasis and detailed discussion of the virtues in *Summa theologiae*, but at the very least, Hall recognizes that the virtues have a relevant role to play within a natural law interpretation of Aquinas.

I will now contrast Hall's conception of the natural law and the role of virtue with that of McInerny. McInerny defines the natural law as 'the view that there are true directives of human action, which arise from the very structure of human agency and which anyone can easily formulate for himself' (McInerny 1982: 40). McInerny defines the natural law as precepts that direct human beings towards those actions that help to achieve the highest good (McInerny 1982: 46). The natural law provides Aquinas with a source of moral dictates that adjudicate among good and bad human actions. The natural law in this sense is a system of what McInerny terms 'non-gainsayable principles whose application to the circumstances of action is what is going on in moral decision' (McInerny 1982: 38).

Thus, McInerny asserts what Hall denies, that is, the idea that the natural law is constituted by a set of (albeit very general) moral principles. Nevertheless, he agrees with Hall that the individual precepts of the natural law are rooted in the basic inclinations of human nature that we saw in Hall's discussion (McInerny 1982: 44–5). In so far as human beings possess these inclinations, there are both appropriate and inappropriate ways of satisfying them. Given that human beings, unlike other animals, possess intellective capacities, the actions appropriate to human nature involve those capacities in particular respects. In other words, although, for example, the satisfaction of hunger involves a basic inclination that human beings share with other animals, humans make judgements as to how, when, and where to satisfy this fundamental need (McInerny 1982: 45–6). Consideration of what is good at a particular time includes not just the satisfaction of basic physical urges, but also how those physical needs fit into the overall picture of what promotes an agent's flourishing. The precepts of the natural law govern these kinds of choices.

The natural law then specifies the ways that basic human goods constitutive of flourishing can be realized (McInerny 1982: 45–6). As we saw earlier, the first principle of the natural law is very general and in fact descriptive of the basic human orientation (cf. McInerny 1982: 42). Subsequent precepts specify how this precept is to be instantiated; they prohibit that which violates the human good and prescribe that which comprises and advances the human good (McInerny 1982: 46–7; 56–9). Because the natural law is tied to human nature in this way, a human being who follows the precepts of the natural law

---

[25] Hall acknowledges this aspect of Aquinas' theory, although she does little more than mention it; cf. Hall 1994: 39. For Aquinas' discussion of the relationships among the virtues, see *ST* I–II.58 and *ST* I–II.65.

will be more likely to lead a flourishing life and achieve the ultimate end.[26] Thus, for McInerny, there is no fundamental conflict between Aquinas' eudaimonism and the natural law; the two parts work in concert with one another (McInerny 1982: 35). But for McInerny, unlike Hall, Aquinas is fundamentally a eudaimonist, who incorporates an account of natural law into his ethical theory (McInerny 1982: 40–1). And this element of Aquinas' ethics is fundamentally expressed in the form of principles or precepts by which human beings direct themselves to their proper ends (McInerny 1982: 41). They are, as McInerny puts it, 'dictates of reason' (McInerny 1982: 46).

As we saw earlier, McInerny defines the natural law in terms of 'true directives of human action, which ... *anyone can easily formulate for himself*' (McInerny 1982: 40, my emphasis). In so far as the natural law is tied to and specifies the ways in which the human good is brought to fruition, human beings are capable of recognizing the ways in which their behaviour and choices promote or fail to promote the human good, and thus able to recognize the precepts of the natural law (McInerny 1982: 47–8). The measure of morality, as McInerny puts it, is human nature. Those actions that perfect that nature are good, those actions that do not are bad. Thus, there are standards for human conduct that are independent of human desires or judgements that are nevertheless tied to human nature, which provide the ground for and guidance to the moral law (McInerny 1982: 54). The fundamental precepts of the natural law are built into practical reasoning and therefore cannot be avoided.

On the other hand, in his discussion of the doctrine of the Fall and the necessity of grace, McInerny acknowledges that for Aquinas, outside of a faith context, it can in fact be difficult to recognize or judge correctly the right action to take (cf. McInerny 1982: 120–2). Nevertheless, although he would agree that human beings make mistakes in moral reasoning and that there is such a thing as moral controversy, he is remarkably optimistic about the human ability to understand what morality requires of us, especially with religious guidance.[27] Hall would agree with McInerny that human nature provides the foundation for the natural law, but she seems not to share his optimism over coming to understand the natural law.[28] For Hall, comprehension of the natural law takes place in a historical context as a result of both collective and individual experiences. Although human beings strive after perfection and flourishing as a result of their nature, they come to understand what in fact instantiates and promotes those states only over time and within a particular lived historical context. They can in fact make mistakes about what constitutes human flourishing, mistakes that can persist over centuries. Hall takes this to be Aquinas' implied position from his discussion of the ancient Germans who come to realize that stealing is wrong only after generations of experience and changes

---

[26] Aquinas acknowledges that human beings encounter hardships that adversely impact human lives and make it more difficult to flourish, so following the precepts of the natural law cannot be a sufficient condition for flourishing; cf. *ST* I–II.5.3. Furthermore, Aquinas is committed to the position that human beings are not capable of achieving the ultimate end on their own merits; they are utterly dependent upon God's mercy and grace; cf. *ST* I–II.109.

[27] See especially McInerny 1982: 118.   [28] On this issue, see also Hittinger 1997.

in their material environment.[29] Thus, human beings come to recognize the structure of the natural law progressively over time within a particular social context of life lived in a particular community with a particular history through reflection upon both individual and collective experiences, as Hall puts it, 'reflection upon our own and our predecessors' desires, choices, mistakes, and successes' (Hall 1994: 94). On her reading, it takes time and hard intellectual work to come to understand what the natural law requires of human behaviour.

McInerny would not necessarily disagree with Hall on these issues, for he recognizes that agents operate within a particular social-historical context (McInerny 1982: 121–2). But what is interesting about Hall's discussion is the way in which she sees in Aquinas a constitutive role for social and individual experience in comprehending the natural law. McInerny tends to emphasize the cognitive/reflective aspect. For Hall, one discovers and learns about the natural law in one's ordinary experience, and such experience is context-dependent. McInerny implies that our understanding of the natural law is independent of our social context in so far as all human beings, regardless of their social contexts, come to recognize what the natural law requires of them in virtue of possessing basic cognitive capacities. Thus, for him, understanding the natural law is in some sense timeless. The social environment is merely the occasion upon which we comprehend the natural law, whereas for Hall, the particular social environment in which we are located importantly affects our understanding of human flourishing and the means for its realization.[30]

8.6

As we saw in section 8.2, many Thomists not only present interpretations of Aquinas' theories; they also use those theories to provide insights into larger issues. Some of the most prominent projects of this sort have been those undertaken by Alasdair MacIntyre. Although his focus is not solely on Aquinas, Aquinas' ideas have often formed a significant part of his writings, especially in *After Virtue* and *Whose Justice? Which Rationality?*, two of his most famous works. Because he states in the preface of the latter book (a sequel to the former), that he revised his understanding of Aquinas' ethics in writing this book, I shall focus on his treatment of Aquinas in *Whose Justice? Which Rationality?*

MacIntyre argues that *pace* the Enlightenment view, there are no independent, ahistorical moral principles. All ethical systems (or systems of justice, which is MacIntyre's major concern) develop within a particular historical/social context and cannot be

---

[29] Aquinas mentions this case in *ST* I–II.94.5; the case comes from Julius Caesar's *Commentarii de Bello Gallico*. For Hall's discussion of the Germans, see Hall 1994: 95–106.

[30] Both acknowledge the role of guidance from such external sources as divine revelation and the Church; cf. Hall 1994: 45–64 and 65–92 and McInerny 1982: 114–22. Both maintain that the moral law constitutes a set of objective moral standards; cf. McInerny 1982: 51–9; 118 and Hall 1994: 97.

understood apart from recognition of that context. Furthermore, each set of principles is grounded in a particular understanding of practical reasoning and cannot be made intelligible apart from recognizing that particular account of rationality. In adjudicating moral disputes, one must first come to comprehend individual systems of justice and their underlying concepts of rationality in order to evaluate their solutions. MacIntyre holds that we must examine the various concepts of justice and rationality that operate within our own social milieu if we are to have any hope of resolving deeply entrenched ethical questions. MacIntyre's project in this book is to clarify the various accounts of justice and rationality that have helped to shape our own discussions.

He examines four traditions in particular, acknowledging that there are many more that have had a hand in influencing our thought. The four he considers are: the Aristotelian system that culminates from the Homeric-Platonic tradition; the Thomistic synthesis of Aristotle and Augustine; the Scottish Enlightenment, rooted in Augustinian Calvinism and Renaissance Aristotelianism; and finally modern liberalism.[31] Each of these traditions generates an account of justice that is comprehensible only from a particular conception of rationality that developed within a particular cultural context. Furthermore, these accounts of justice are incompatible with one another. I shall now look at his interpretation of Aquinas' moral system and the conception of practical rationality that provides its foundation.

MacIntyre argues that although Aquinas was influenced by other thinkers, his system is primarily a synthesis of Aristotelian and Augustinian ideas. Aquinas' achievement is all the more remarkable in so far as he was able to adapt two incompatible systems into a single coherent theory. He was able to do so only in so far he possessed the empathy and insight necessary to understand both perspectives on their own terms (MacIntyre 1988, 168). He recognized the resources and strengths that each brings to the table in resolving philosophical and theological problems, enabling him to reformulate basic ideas from each, integrating them into a single framework. Thus, Aquinas developed an account of rationality and justice that moves beyond the basic premises of either system.

On MacIntyre's view, morality for Aquinas is rooted in the capacity for right judgement on the basis of fundamental principles. The development of this capacity requires the possession of the virtues, which are acquired through a sound moral education (MacIntyre 1988: 176–7). This much Aquinas adopts from Aristotle. But MacIntyre argues that Aquinas faces a potential conflict between this part of his ethical theory and his other commitments, in particular his commitment to the view (which comes from his religious tradition) that human beings naturally possess sufficient knowledge of the moral law such that they can be held responsible for their actions, regardless of their education (MacIntyre 1988: 177).

MacIntyre resolves this potential conflict by noting that on Aquinas' view, in so far as human beings have the natural capacity to reflect upon their own good, they are led to

---

[31] Cf. MacIntyre 1988: 10, where he introduces the four traditions. Some of the traditions that MacIntyre decides to leave unexamined include Judaic traditions, Prussian systems, Islamic influences, and those systems of China and India.

seek out the company of others in friendship (MacIntyre 1988: 177). In coming to recognize the requirements for being a good friend on the basis of one's social relationships, human beings satisfy the basic precepts of the natural law and acquire on their own a kind of moral education. In the course of these social interactions, they perform actions in accordance with what the natural law dictates, and over time they acquire the requisite virtues, even if they lack formal moral instruction (MacIntyre 1988: 181). Thus, on Aquinas' view, the natural human inclination to seek one's own good and determine how to achieve that good moves the agent towards the kinds of experiences on the basis of which one both becomes acquainted with the fundamental moral principles that make up the natural law and acquires the virtues. Thus, moral education, whether formal or experiential, is, to use MacIntyre's word, 'inescapable'.[32]

Another departure from Aristotle has to do with Aquinas' characterization of the ultimate end as a state that is beyond our experiences in this life and his commitment to the idea that human beings cannot follow the moral law perfectly without the help of God's grace; both ideas Aquinas inherits from Augustine (MacIntyre 1988: 181; 192). Aristotle held that happiness, the ultimate end of human life, was a function of life lived virtuously in the here and now. As we have seen, Aquinas holds that the ultimate end is union with God in the next life, although how we live in this life is importantly connected to that further goal.

MacIntyre is not unique in pointing out the ways in which Aquinas' account both borrows from and departs from Aristotle's account, but because of the nature of his overall project, MacIntyre emphasizes the particular elements of Aristotle and Augustine that ground Aquinas' accounts of practical rationality and ethics. The overall framework, MacIntyre argues, comes from Augustine's theology: the character of the ultimate end; the theological virtues, which are necessary for proper function of the natural (i.e. cardinal) virtues in so far as they orient the agent towards the proper end, i.e. God (MacIntyre 1988: 205); the need for grace. Aquinas' theory of action, however, comes largely from Aristotle: the idea of an ultimate end itself; the ordering of goods around this ultimate end; the process of deliberation over means to achieve those goods; and the basic theory of practical reasoning that leads to correct judgement about action. But even here one finds Augustine's influence; MacIntyre argues that Aquinas adopts his notion of the will, which plays an important role in his account of choice, from Augustine (MacIntyre 1988: 189–90). And as we have seen, although Aquinas adopts Aristotle's teleological notion of the good life structured around an ultimate end, he disagrees with Aristotle over the specification of that end, following Augustine in holding that human beings cannot be truly happy until they are granted union with God in the next life. Thus, Aristotle's account, on Aquinas' view, is incomplete, in so far as it restricts the happy, flourishing life to the here and now, and

---

[32] MacIntyre 1988: 180. Of course there is no guarantee that human beings will become virtuous as a result of their experiences. They can always choose not to become good friends or act virtuously. But MacIntyre holds that regardless of the kind of one's ultimate character, whether virtuous or vicious, one cannot escape the lessons of life regarding the nature and acquisition of virtue.

defective, in so far as it fails to acknowledge fallen human nature, another theological element gotten from Augustine (MacIntyre 1988: 192–3; 205).

The virtue of justice itself has both a theological and philosophical dimension. What ultimately grounds justice is God. MacIntyre argues that Aquinas substitutes God for a Platonic Form; God is the personification and exemplification of justice (MacIntyre 1988: 198). Although Aquinas also includes Augustine's definition of justice in his discussion in *Summa theologiae*, ultimately he structures his discussion in terms of Aristotle's idea that justice involves giving to another what is due to him (MacIntyre 1988: 199). But although justice in the main has to do with ordering relationships among human beings, even here is a theological dimension not found in Aristotle, in so far as human beings have particular obligations to God. Thus, religion, which specifies what is owed to God, becomes a virtue that is part of justice on Aquinas' account (MacIntyre 1988: 201).

MacIntyre argues that the various concepts of practical rationality and justice that he examines are both different from and incompatible with each other (cf. MacIntyre 1988: 199–203). For MacIntyre, one must always keep in mind that theories are developed within a particular social or cultural context and cannot be understood independently of that context. Aquinas developed his ideas within a social environment in which both religious and secular elements structured daily life. This is in contrast with other theories that were developed under quite different social conditions. Nevertheless, MacIntyre maintains that traditions can develop and flourish under conditions very different than the ones in which the theory was originally formulated (MacIntyre 1988: 392). This is because theories bring with them resources that may be applicable to issues that arise in other social contexts. The extent to which any given theory possesses such resources depends upon the theory itself and the particular issue involved. MacIntyre argues that some accounts are more adept at this than others. But one will come to understand this only in so far as one comprehends the various accounts on their own terms, coming to see which problems they can address adequately and what kinds of problems they face. One evaluates traditions on the basis of their own terms as well as from one's own particular contextual standpoint. MacIntyre argues that the only hope we have of resolving issues of justice is to identify various accounts and examine the resources each brings for that particular issue. At the end of the book, he suggests that the Aristotelian tradition as transformed by Aquinas is better able to address problems of justice more adequately than other traditions (MacIntyre 1988: 402–3).

Thus what we find in MacIntyre's discussion is, first of all, an explication of Aquinas' moral theory, but secondly, an argument that under certain conditions, this theory could serve as a resource in addressing current moral questions. Like those who engage primarily in exegetical study (the conservative approach in Shanley's terms), MacIntyre pays close attention to the structure and content of Aquinas' writings (although he admits to be giving a decidedly nonstandard interpretation of Aquinas' views in a number of ways—cf. MacIntrye 1988: 187–8) as well as the particular cultural context in which Aquinas is working. But MacIntyre also uses Aquinas' ideas to dialogue with important philosophical issues of our time, ultimately falling into Shanley's second camp.

Although MacIntyre's ideas have been influential, they have also been controversial. Robert George, for example, argues that a tension exists between MacIntyre's claim that there are no universal time-transcendent moral principles and Aquinas' own commitment to timeless universal principles that hold across cultures (George 1989: 599–600). He also argues that MacIntyre's position cannot avoid relativism, which, if true, is another conclusion that Aquinas would not want to accept.[33]

The philosophical literature on Aquinas' ethics is immense, and I do not pretend to have surveyed it adequately. What I hope to have done is to provide a useful summary of some of the major issues and positions within the Thomistic tradition.[34]

BIBLIOGRAPHY

Aertsen, J. A. and Speer, A. (eds) 1998. *Miscellanea Mediaevalia: Was ist Philosophie im Mittelalter?* Berlin: Walter de Gruyter.

Aquinas, T. 1882. *Opera Omnia*, ed. Leonine Commission. Rome: Vatican Polyglot Press.

——1911, 1920, 1981. *Summa theologiae*, trans. Fathers of the English Dominican Province. Allen, TX: Christian Classics.

——1952. *Summa theologiae*, ed. Petri Caramello. Turin: Marietti Editori, Ltd.

Bourke, V. J. 1981. 'The New Center and the Intellectualism of St. Thomas', in Brezik (ed.) 1981, 169–71.

Boyle, L. E. 1987. 'A Remembrance of Pope Leo XIII: the Encyclical Aeterni Patris', in Brezik (ed.) 1981, 7–22.

Bradley, D. J. M. 1997. *Aquinas on the Twofold Human Good*. Washington, DC: Catholic University of America Press.

Brezik, V. B., C.S.B. (ed.) 1981. *One Hundred Years of Thomism: Aeterni Patris and Afterwards*. Houston: Center for Thomistic Studies.

Crisp, R. and Slote, M. (eds) 1997. *Virtue Ethics*. Oxford: Oxford University Press.

Cromartie, M. (ed.) 1997. A Preserving Grace: Protestants, Catholics, and Natural Law. Grand Rapids, MI: William B. Eerdmans Publishing Company.

Finnis, J. 1980. *Natural Law and Natural Rights*. Oxford: Clarendon Press.

Gallagher, D. 1998. 'The Role of God in the Philosophical Ethics of Thomas Aquinas', in Aertsen and Speer (eds) 1998, 1024–33.

George, R. P. 1989. 'Moral Paricularism, Thomism, and Traditions', *Review of Metaphysics* 43: 593–605.

Goyette, J., Latkovic, M. S., and Meyers, R. S. (eds) 2004. *St. Thomas Aquinas and the Natural Law Traditions: Contemporary Perspectives*. Washington, DC: Catholic University of America Press.

Grisez, G., Boyle, J., and Finnis, J. 1987. 'Practical Principles, Moral Truth, and Ultimate Ends', *American Journal of Jurisprudence* 32: 99–152.

---

[33] George 1989: 599. MacIntyre of course recognizes the threat of relativism and labours long and hard to address it; George argues that those attempts fail. For an examination of MacIntyre's work, see Horton and Mendus 1994.

[34] I am especially grateful to my graduate research assistant, Beth Rath, for her assistance on this project.

Haldane, J. 1997. 'Analytical Thomism: a Prefatory Note', *The Monist* 80: 485–6.

——1999. 'Thomism and the Future of Catholic Philosophy', *New Blackfriars* 80: 158–71.

Hall, P. 1994. *Narrative and the Natural Law: an Interpretation of Thomistic Ethics.* Notre Dame, IN: University of Notre Dame Press.

Hittinger, R. 1987. *A Critique of the New Natural Law.* Notre Dame: University of Notre Dame Press.

——1997. 'Natural Law and Catholic Moral Theology', in Cromartie (ed.) 1997, 1–30.

Horton, J. and Mendus, S. (eds) 1994. *After MacIntyre: Critical Perspectives on the Work of Alasdair MacIntyre.* Notre Dame, IN: University of Notre Dame Press.

Jordan, M. D. 1999. 'Ideals of *Scientia moralis* and the Invention of the *Summa theologiae*', in MacDonald and Stump (eds) 1999, 79–97.

Kennedy, L. A., C.S.B. (ed.) 1987. *A Catelogue of Thomists: 1270–1900.* Houston: Center for Thomistic Studies.

Kluxen, W. 1980. *Philosophische Ethik bei Thomas von Aquin.* Hamburg: Meiner.

Liska, A. J. 1996. *Aquinas's Theory of Natural Law.* Oxford: Clarendon Press.

Louden, R. B. 1984. 'On Some Vices of Virtue Ethics', *American Philosophical Quarterly* 21: 227–36. Reprinted in Crisp and Slote (eds) 1997, 201–16.

McCool, G. 1994. *The Neo-Thomists.* Milwaukee: Marquette University Press.

MacDonald, S. and Stump, E. (eds) 1999. *Aquinas's Moral Theory: Essays in Honor of Norman Kretzmann.* Ithaca: Cornell University Press.

McInerny, R. 1980. 'The Principles of Natural Law', *American Journal of Jurisprudence* 25: 1–15.

——1982, 1997. *Ethica Thomistica.* Washington, DC: The Catholic University of America Press.

——1993. *The Question of Christian Ethics.* Washington, DC: The Catholic University of America Press.

MacIntyre, A. 1988. *Whose Justice? Which Rationality?* Notre Dame, IN: University of Notre Dame Press.

McKinnon, C. 1989. 'Ways of Wrongdoing: A Theory of the Vices', *Journal of Value Inquiry* 23: 319–35.

May, W. E. 2004. 'Contemporary Perspectives on Thomistic Natural Law', in Goyette, Latkovic, and Meyers (eds) 2004, 113–56.

Murphy, M. 2001. *Natural Law and Practical Rationality.* Cambridge: Cambridge University Press.

Pavur, C. S. J. (ed.) 2005. *The Ratio Studiorum: the Official Plan for Jesuit Education.* St. Louis: The Institute of Jesuit Sources.

Plantinga, A. 1984. 'Advice to Christian Philosophers', *Faith and Philosophy* 1: 253–71.

Pinckaers, S., O.P. 1995. *The Sources of Christian Ethics*, trans. Sr. Mary Thomas Noble, O.P. Washington, DC: The Catholic University of America Press.

Porter, J. 2005. *Nature as Reason: a Thomistic Theory of the Natural Law.* Grand Rapids, MI: William B. Eerdmans Publishing Company.

Rhomheimer, M. 2000. *Natural Law and Practical Reason: a Thomist View of Moral Autonomy*, trans. Gerald Malsbary. New York: Fordham University Press.

Schneewind, J. B. 1990. 'The Misfortunes of Virtue', *Ethics* 101: 42–63. Reprinted in Crisp and Slote (eds) 1997, 178–200.

Shanley, B. J. 1999. 'Analytic Thomism', *The Thomist* 63: 125–37.

——2002. *The Thomist Tradition.* Dordrecht: Kluwer Academic Publishers.

Stump, E. 1997. 'Aquinas's Account of Freedom: Intellect and Will', *Monist* 80: 576–97.

Theron, S. 1997. 'The Resistance of Thomism to Analytical and Other Patronage', *The Monist* 80: 611–18.

Torrell, J. P., O.P. 1996. *Saint Thomas Aquinas*, Vol. 1, *The Person and His Work*, trans. Robert Royal. Washington, DC: The Catholic University of America Press.

Weisheipl, J. A., O.P. 1981. 'Commentary', in Brezik (ed.) 1981, 25–7.

CHAPTER 9

....

THE FRANCISCANS

....

THOMAS WILLIAMS

It is somewhat misleading to think of the Franciscans as forming a 'school' in ethics, since there was a fair bit of diversity among Franciscans. Nonetheless, one can identify certain characteristic tendencies of Franciscan moral thought, and certain 'celebrity' Franciscans whose views in ethics and moral psychology are particularly noteworthy. I shall first offer an overview of the general character of Franciscan moral thought in the late thirteenth and early fourteenth centuries and then turn to a more detailed examination of the thought of John Duns Scotus (1265/66–1308) and William Ockham (c.1288–1347) on three central matters of debate: the nature of the virtues, the relationship between intellect and will, and the relationship between moral requirements and the divine will.

9.1 GENERAL CHARACTERISTICS OF FRANCISCAN MORAL THOUGHT

Myths of philosophical historiography take a lot of killing, and despite a half-century of criticism, Etienne Gilson's picture of a three-way battle among reactionary Augustinians, radical Aristotelians, and synthesizing Thomists has endured. Gilson regarded almost all Franciscan thought as Augustinian, and Augustinianism was said to be marked by (among other things) a general hostility to Aristotle. But when we turn to the major Franciscan authors of this period, we find that they are not in general hostile to Aristotle. We could come a lot closer to the truth by saying that they are hostile to *Aquinas*.

As Bonnie Kent notes, 'In the late 1260s Franciscan theologians at Paris were far more worried about the radical Aristotelians' teachings than the teachings of Thomas Aquinas. They acted together with Aquinas in trying to bring the arts masters to heel' (Kent 1995: 45). We find only sporadic criticism of Aquinas before 1270. Around 1270 the criticisms became more common, but the real turning point came with the publication of William de la

Mare's *Correctorium fratris Thomae* in 1277. The *Correctorium* offered rebuttals or 'corrections' to 117 passages in Aquinas, and in 1282 the Franciscan order officially endorsed the work and forbade Franciscans to read the *Summa theologiae* without William's corrections. At this point 'there emerges in the Franciscan Order a general opposition to the philosophy and influence of Aquinas' (Kent 1995: 45).

Opposition to Aquinas did not, in general, mean opposition to Aristotle. Instead, it meant opposition to the claims of Aquinas and the Thomists that they were the legitimate Aristotelians. Walter of Bruges, a student of Bonaventure[1] who was regent master at Paris from 1267 to 1269, was frequently critical of Aquinas, but he cited Aristotle frequently in his disputed questions concerning virtue and the will and would rarely acknowledge any conflict between Aristotle and Augustine or other Christian authorities. In the *Correctorium* William de la Mare continued this pattern, frequently citing Aristotle *against* Aquinas and in support of the Condemnation of 1277: 'Where he can find passages in Aristotle to use against Thomas' opinions, he uses them; where he cannot, he cites Christian writings and ignores Aristotle. Virtually never is Aristotle admitted to be solely on the side of Thomism' (Kent 1995: 82).

The most noteworthy exception to this pattern was Peter John Olivi (1248–1298). Olivi was hostile to pagan ethics in general—all the pagans, he insists, were idol-worshipers: wrong about God, wrong about happiness, and wrong about virtue—but Aristotle, as the leading pagan authority of the day, was the target of his greatest scorn. And Aquinas, for Olivi, was much of a muchness with the hated Aristotle.

With the exception of Olivi, then, the Franciscans did not reject Aristotle or Aristotelianism (in some sense) in ethics; they rejected Thomas Aquinas' version of Aristotelianism. In particular, they regarded Aquinas as unsound when it came to the will, its freedom, and its relationship to the intellect. The most characteristic feature of Franciscan thought, in other words, is its *voluntarism*. But 'voluntarism' has a variety of possible meanings. For the sake of clarity, I shall distinguish three types of voluntarism: (1) psychological voluntarism, (2) ethical voluntarism, and (3) theological voluntarism.[2] Psychological voluntarism is more an approach than a thesis or set of theses: it involves a general emphasis on the volitional aspects of human nature, a tendency to focus on the will (or on the affective aspects of human nature more generally). Ethical voluntarism adds the claims that the will is superior to the intellect, that happiness consists chiefly in an act of will, that human freedom derives from the will rather than from reason, that the will can act against the dictates of reason, and that the will (rather than the intellect) commands the other powers of both body and soul. Theological voluntarism is the view that the divine will establishes the moral law, and that God is not bound or constrained

---

[1] It is difficult to pin down Bonaventure's attitude towards Aristotle as an authority in ethics in particular, in part because of contentious textual issues concerning Bonaventure's treatment of the *Ethics* in his *Hexaemeron*. See Kent 1995: 46–58, for an even-handed account of the difficulties.

[2] These names for the different positions are my own stipulations for the purposes of this chapter, though I take (1) and (2) from Bourke 1970, 1: 138, 147. My characterization of the three kinds of voluntarism is indebted to Kent 1995: ch. 3, though I characterize what I call 'theological voluntarism' much more narrowly than her third sense of voluntarism in order to limit the discussion to ethics.

in his moral legislation by any truths known pre-volitionally by his intellect. We find psychological voluntarism in the earliest Franciscan masters, ethical voluntarism beginning with Bonaventure's successors (such as Walter of Bruges and William de la Mare), and theological voluntarism—possibly—in John Duns Scotus and William Ockham. In the next section of this chapter I consider what Scotus and Ockham have to say about virtue. This discussion bears on Franciscan voluntarism in so far as both thinkers accept the view, defended at least as early as Bonaventure, that all virtues properly so called are in the will. In section 9.3 I turn to ethical voluntarism as it appears in Scotus's and Ockham's accounts of the relationship between will and intellect and the nature of human freedom. In the section 9.4 I examine the debate over whether to attribute theological voluntarism to Scotus or Ockham or both.

9.2 VIRTUE

It is characteristic of Franciscan ethics to locate all virtues of character in the will, and Scotus agrees with his Franciscan brethren on this point. Properly speaking, he says, a virtue is a disposition that inclines whatever possesses it to choose rightly; since it is the will that chooses, it is the will that possesses virtues. It generates such virtues in itself by repeatedly making right choices (choices consonant with right reason). If the will in turn repeatedly commands the sensitive appetite rightly, a disposition that inclines the sensitive appetite to experience pleasure in being moved in this way by the will can be 'left behind' in the sensitive appetite. 'This disposition that is left behind' in the sensitive appetite, Scotus says, 'is not properly speaking a virtue because it is not a disposition for choosing or a disposition that inclines to choices; nonetheless, one can grant that it is a virtue in some sense, since it does incline to what accords with right reason' (*Ord.* 3, d. 33. q. un., n. 45, X: 163).

The possession of a virtue is neither necessary nor sufficient for right action, according to Scotus. One can develop a virtue—a disposition to perform morally right acts —only by performing morally right acts; so if one cannot perform morally right acts without possessing a virtue, one can never perform morally right acts. So much, then, for the necessity of virtue for right action. Scotus' understanding of the will's freedom (about which I will have much more to say in section 9.3) rules out the claim that the possession of a virtue is sufficient for right action. I can have the virtue of honesty, for example, but still choose to tell a lie when an occasion for lying presents itself to me. I will be inclined, and perhaps very strongly inclined, not to tell a lie;[3] and if I do tell the truth, I will do so with ease and pleasure because I possess the appropriate virtue. Even so, Scotus insists, I must retain the power to act contrary to my habit; otherwise, my will would be acting as a purely natural power and would therefore be an inappropriate target of moral praise

---

[3] Or perhaps not even that: Scotus is open to the idea that a habit has no active causal power, though he prefers an account that 'attributes more to the habit'. See *Ord.* I, d. 17, pars 1, qq. 1–2, nn. 32–54 and 69–70, V: 152–160, 170–171, and Kent 2003: 362–3.

or blame. Even the divinely infused habit of charity does not undermine freedom. Examining the dictum that 'charity is to the will what a rider is to his horse',[4] Scotus comments that the analogy works only if we think of the horse as free and the rider as 'directing the horse in the mode of nature to a fixed destination'. Then 'the horse in virtue of its freedom could throw its rider, or else move itself toward something else, contrary to the rider's direction toward the destination' (*Ord.* 1, d. 17, pars 1, qq. 1–2, n. 155, V: 213).

Scotus denies that the moral virtues are necessarily connected. The virtues are partial perfections, he argues; otherwise a single moral virtue would be all we needed. So it is no more surprising that someone could be perfect in the domain of temperance but not in the domain of fortitude than it is that someone could have keen eyesight or an acute sense of touch but be unable to hear. Just as someone who sees well but cannot hear is no less perfect in his vision, though he is less perfect in his sensing, someone who is temperate but lacks fortitude is no less perfect in his temperance, though he is less perfect morally (*Ord.* 3, d. 36, q. un., n. 33, X: 233–234). For that matter, one can be perfect in one area within the domain of temperance but not another: 'Someone can be unqualifiedly temperate regarding sex, willing not to have sex with anyone other than his wife or willing not to have sex at all, and intemperate regarding food, willing to eat what he should not or willing not to eat what he should' (*Ord.* 3, d. 34, q. un., n. 56, X: 204).[5] And corresponding to these micro-virtues are micro-prudences: 'Just as someone can have morally good affections [*moraliter bene esse affectus*] regarding some possible actions and morally bad affections regarding others, so too in [reason's] dictating, one can be habituated to dictate rightly concerning these things but not those' (*Ord.* 3, d. 36, q. un., n. 96, X: 259). As Bonnie Kent aptly puts it, 'The specialized prudences can indeed combine to form a harmonious "macroprudence". Such macroprudence must nonetheless be considered an aggregate, says Scotus, not the indivisible organic unity that Aristotle and his uncritical followers claim' (Kent 2003: 371).

Ockham agrees with Scotus that virtue exists only in the will[6] and that the virtues are not necessarily connected.[7] Perhaps the most characteristic feature of Ockham's

---

[4] Scotus took this to be a saying of Augustine, but in fact it comes from the pseudo-Augustinian *Hypognosticon* III c. 11 n. 20.

[5] 'willing not to have sex with anyone other than his wife or willing not to have sex at all' translates *nolens uti nisi sua vel simpliciter nolens uti*. To the word *sua* the critical edition attaches the following note: 'rectius: suis.—Verbum 'utor' in tardiore latinitate construebatur etiam cum accusativo'. But if *sua* is an accusative, what is the neuter plural noun that would complete the phrase? What are these 'things of his own' to which the sexually temperate person restricts himself? I can make no sense of this suggestion, and it seems quite clear that *sua* is ablative, just as we should expect after *utor*, and we are to supply *uxore*.

[6] Oddly, Rega Wood (1997: 256) cites this as a point of *disagreement* between Scotus and Ockham. It appears that she misreads a claim Scotus makes in *Quodlibet* 18, n. 16, about *actual* justice (the rectitude of a particular act) as a claim about the *habit* of justice. There is, as far as I am aware, unanimity among Scotus scholars that Scotus regarded the will as the seat of virtue. See, among others, Wolter 1986: 75–8, and Kent 1995: 238–45.

[7] He does, however, argue that under certain circumstances, 'higher degrees of virtue are incompatible with vice and do incline us to other virtues' (Wood 1997: 34). Ockham's views on this question are too complex to take up here. For the text and translation, see Wood 1997: 90–141; for commentary, see Wood 1997: 219–51.

discussion of the virtues, however, is a point in which he differs strikingly from Scotus. In Scotus, every bit as much as in Aristotle or Aquinas, the language of virtue and vice concerns *habits* or *dispositions*. In Ockham, by contrast, the language of virtue and vice is frequently used to talk about particular *actions*. For example, when Ockham lists the five grades or degrees of virtue in *On the Connection of the Virtues*, he illustrates them exclusively by talking about particular acts of will and particular intentions. And when he asks whether the theological virtues are compatible with vice, he distinguishes between 'habitual vice'—and what could habitual vice be other than what previous thinkers would have called simply 'vice'?—and 'actual vice,' which appears to mean 'immoral action' (not even *vicious* action properly so called, which is immoral action that expresses an immoral disposition, but simply immoral action).[8] This is not to say that Ockham gives no attention at all to the ways in which acts of a particular character tend to generate a disposition to perform more acts of that sort (or to destroy a disposition to perform acts of a contrary sort); but his focus is clearly on individual acts. Habits are of secondary interest at best, as we should expect, given the view (which he shares with Scotus) that the will is always free to act against any habit, however strong. Ockham's focus on the moral evaluation of particular acts, accompanied by his revision to the traditional Aristotelian vocabulary concerning virtue(s) and vice(s), aligns him with the approach that is commonly said to be characteristic of modern moral philosophy, of which Ockham is, in this respect at least, the earliest important representative.

9.3 INTELLECT AND WILL

As I noted earlier, the cluster of views that I have called 'ethical voluntarism'—which includes the claims that the will is superior to the intellect, that happiness consists chiefly in an act of will, that human freedom derives from the will rather than from reason, that the will can act against the dictates of reason, and that the will (rather than the intellect) commands the other powers of both body and soul—come to be characteristic of Franciscan moral thinking in the 1270s with Bonaventure's successors.[9] The development of ethical voluntarism is associated with the shift from *liberum arbitrium* to *libertas voluntatis* in the 1270s and particularly after the Condemnation of 1277. The early Franciscan masters, such as Alexander of Hales, John of La Rochelle, and Bonaventure, all talk in terms of *liberum arbitrium*[10] and see it as involving intellect and will working

---

[8] *De connexione virtutum* 2.116–192 and 3.425–444, in Wood 1997: 80–5 and 116–19. The translation somewhat obscures the focus on acts rather than habits by consistently translating *deformitas* in Article 3 as 'deformity of character'; Ockham is actually much less interested in character in this text than one would gather from the English translation.

[9] William de la Mare defended all these claims in the *Correctorium*, and 'later Franciscans tended to adopt, albeit with varying degrees of conviction, the same positions as William' (Kent 1995: 96).

[10] Any translation will be misleading, but 'free decision' is probably the least misleading in this context.

together in some way. John of La Rochelle and Bonaventure do at least make the claim, characteristic of later ethical voluntarism, that freedom is formally in the will and that the will is essentially active; but we do not yet see in them the idea that the will has the ability to 'go rogue' and act against the intellect's judgement. In Bonaventure's student, Walter of Bruges, however, we do find such a view, under the new banner of *libertas voluntatis*, freedom of the will. Not only does the will's freedom not derive from reason, as Aquinas had argued, but the will is free to act against reason. William de la Mare argued in a similar vein in the *Correctorium*.

By the time John Duns Scotus came to address the question of the relationship between will and intellect, this claim about the will's ability to act against the intellect's judgement had become more or less the party line among the Franciscans, and Scotus is of one mind with his predecessors on this point. There was, however, a closely connected question that still elicited a range of opinions among Franciscans: what exactly is the intellect's causal role in the will's act? Does the intellect move the will *per modum finis* (in the manner of a final cause), or is it a partial efficient cause of the will's act, or merely a *sine qua non* condition? On this question Scotus' views underwent some development.[11] In his earliest engagement with the issue, the Oxford *Lectura*, Book 2, d. 25, Scotus attempts to steer a middle position between, on the one hand, the intellectualism of Thomas Aquinas and Godfrey of Fontaines, and, on the other hand, the voluntarism of Henry of Ghent. He understands Aquinas and Godfrey as having held that the object is the sole efficient cause of volition: Aquinas meaning the object as it exists in the intellect and Godfrey the object as it exists in the imagination. Scotus argues against both the general view that the object is the sole cause of volition and against the particular versions of that thesis defended by Aquinas and Godfrey. He then turns to the view of Henry of Ghent, who held that the will is the sole efficient cause of its own action and the cognized object is only a *sine qua non* condition. Scotus deploys several arguments against Henry's view, drawing some of them from Godfrey. Scotus then sets out his own middle view, according to which the will and the object together make up the total efficient cause of the act of will. The will and intellect concur in the way that male and female concur in the production of offspring (according to the biology that he accepts): neither depends on the other for its causal power, but both are required for the production of the effect: one as 'the more principal and perfect agent' and the other as a less perfect agent. The will is the more principal agent because it is responsible for the freedom and contingency of the volition, but the intellect is nonetheless required. As Scotus realizes, it might seem that this position is not so different from Henry's view that the intellect is merely a *sine qua non* condition. But Scotus argues that if the intellect is merely a *sine qua non* condition, *liberum arbitrium* does not include both intellect and will, and so it is blind. One must therefore ascribe some efficient-causal role to the intellect in producing the act of willing.

---

[11] I have considered this development, as well as other matters relevant to Scotus' views on intellect and will, at much greater length in Williams 2010.

In the later *Reportatio* of Scotus' lectures in Paris, however, Scotus adopts Henry's view that the will is the total cause of its act and the intellect's presentation of an object merely a *sine qua non* condition. The *Reportatio* largely recapitulates the arguments from the *Lectura* against the position of Aquinas and Godfrey, but it does not present Henry of Ghent's position and argue against it, as the *Lectura* had—after all, now Scotus is adopting that very position as his own. Though some recent scholarship has sought external, institutional reasons to explain Scotus' change of mind,[12] there are straightforwardly philosophical explanations for the development. Scotus structures his *Lectura* discussion in such a way that his view will be the moderate alternative that is left after the two views at either end of the spectrum—one attributing all causality to the intellect, the other attributing all causality to the will—are rejected. We already see in the *Lectura* discussion that Scotus has his suspicions that his *via media* is going to collapse into Henry's view, and it requires no great effort of philosophical imagination to suppose that as he reflected on his position, he found that it did in fact so collapse. His *Lectura* argument against Henry's position—that without some causal role for the intellect, *liberum arbitrium* would be blind—is already an odd one for Scotus to make, since the shift in philosophical discussion from talking about *liberum arbitrium* to talking about the freedom of the will was already well underway. Scotus does not ordinarily talk in terms of *liberum arbitrium*, and he may well have come to realize that his invocation of it was not only philosophically retrograde but question-begging, since the requirement that there be some causal role for the intellect is built into the notion of *liberum arbitrium*. Furthermore, even in the *Lectura* it is not clear what the efficient-causal role of the intellect could come to. Unlike in the case of the production of offspring, in which the mother does exercise a non-derived efficient-causal role, though a subordinate one, the intellect's causal contribution seems to be determined entirely by the will. It's not that the intellect does not exercise a non-derived causality in *presenting* the object; the intellect does not derive its power to cognize potential objects of will from the will. But it *is* up to the will whether the intellect's presentation of an object results in an act of will: the intellect's presentation of an object is an efficient-causal dead end if the will does not will the object presented. This line of thought very quickly leads to the *Reportatio* position that the intellect's presentation of the object is merely a *sine qua non* condition for an act of will whose total efficient cause is the will itself.

Though the *Lectura* and the *Reportatio* differ about the causal role of the intellect in volition, Scotus is always consistent in holding that the will's freedom in no way derives from the intellect or from the will's association with the intellect; the will is free in its own right. This feature of Scotus' account of the will raises the question of what Scotus means by calling the will a 'rational power', especially given that the will is free to act *against* reason (which is to say, against the intellect's judgement about what is to be done). The question is a live one in current scholarship, since some interpreters rely heavily on Scotus' claim that the will is a rational power in seeking to mitigate the arbitrariness or

---

[12] See Dumont 2001: 776–7.

caprice that seems to characterize volition according to ethical voluntarism, and even in attempting to rebut the arguments of interpreters who find theological voluntarism in Scotus.[13]

The *locus classicus* for Scotus' understanding of the rationality of the will is his *Questions on the Metaphysics*, Book IX, q. 15, where Scotus asks whether Aristotle's distinction between rational powers, which are powers for opposites, and irrational powers, which are for only one of a pair of opposites, was drawn correctly (*bene assignata*). He answer that it was and goes on to explain, first, how it ought to be understood and, second, what its cause is. By a 'power for opposites', Scotus clarifies, we mean a power for opposite *actions*, not merely for opposite *effects* or *products*. The sun can soften wax and harden mud, but that is not the kind of 'opposite' Scotus has in mind. At issue is a power that is sufficient for eliciting both an act and its negation (as would be the case if the sun had the power either to soften wax or not soften it) or for eliciting opposite acts (as would be the case if the sun had the power either to soften wax or to harden it). Though Aristotle tried to account for the difference between rational and irrational powers in another way, the fundamental distinction between the two is in how these powers elicit their acts. There are only two possible ways of eliciting acts:

> Either a power is by its very nature (*ex se*) determined to acting in such a way that, as far as it is up to that power, it cannot not act when it is not impeded by something extrinsic to it; or else it is not by its very nature determined, but can do this act or the opposite act and can also act or not act. The first power is commonly called 'nature' and the second is called 'will'. (*In Metaph.* 9, q. 15, n. 22)

The division into nature and will is the most basic division of active powers. And what is the cause of this division? Scotus says that there is no cause: it is a brute fact that will is a power for opposites and nature is not. Just as that which is hot heats, and there is no further explanation for why it heats, so too there is no further explanation for why it heats *determinately*; nor is there any further explanation for the fact that a will does not will determinately.

One would expect, given general Aristotelian metaphysical principles, that what is in itself indeterminate would require some extrinsic cause to determine it. Scotus argues, however, that this is not so. There are two kinds of indeterminacy:

> There is a certain indeterminacy of insufficiency, in other words, an indeterminacy of potentiality and deficient actuality, as matter that does not have a form is indeterminate with respect to doing the action of that form; and there is another indeterminacy of superabundant sufficiency, which derives from an unlimitedness of actuality, whether altogether or in some particular respect. (*In Metaph.* 9, q. 15, n. 31)

---

[13] Scotus' doctrine of the rationality of the will is a particularly important theme in the work of Mary Beth Ingham. Of most relevance to our present purposes is Ingham 2001. I reply to Ingham's arguments about the will as rational power, in so far as they concern theological voluntarism, in section III of Williams 2004. That paper was to have been published in *Medieval Philosophy and Theology* (as had the paper to which it is a reply); because that journal has gone into what appears to be permanent limbo, I have made the paper available online.

Something that is indeterminate in the first way does not act unless it is determined to some form by something else, but something that is indeterminate in the second way can determine itself. If there were no such thing as the indetermination of superabundant sufficiency, Scotus argues, it would be impossible for God to act, since God is 'supremely undetermined to any action whatsoever' (*In Metaph.* 9, q. 15, n. 32).

So in calling the will a 'rational power', Scotus means neither more nor less than this: the will is a power for opposite actions, which is, in and of itself (that is, not in virtue of its relationship to the intellect or any other power of the soul), indeterminate but self-determining through its 'superabundant sufficiency'. It is clear, then, that by calling the will a rational power Scotus is not somehow tying the will more closely to reason and thereby mitigating the apparent arbitrariness or caprice of its action. On the contrary, it is (paradoxically enough) precisely because it is a rational power *in Scotus' sense* that the will can act against the judgements of reason.

Ockham carries on the general spirit of Scotus' ethical voluntarism, though he differs from Scotus on certain particular issues. On the question of the intellect's contribution to volition, he is closer to Scotus' position in the *Lectura*, since he holds that an agent's intellectual cognitions are ordinarily partial efficient causes of the will's acts. He agrees with Scotus that the intellect's judgement never determines the will, since such determination would undermine the agent's responsibility: in the technical language of Scholasticism, the act would not be 'imputable' to the agent. He also agrees with Scotus that no innate inclination or acquired habit in the will—not even a virtue—causally determines the will's actions.

Despite these points of agreement, Ockham's view of the will's neutrality is much more radical than Scotus'. For Scotus, human beings can will only what they take to be good and will-against[14] only what they take to be bad. Presented with complete happiness—an object in which there is good and no evil—we can refrain from willing it, but we cannot will-against it. Ockham contends that we can will or will-against anything we can conceive. We can will evil as such—evil 'under the aspect of evil'—and we can will-against happiness. As Marilyn Adams explains, 'Liberty of indifference implies we could have such love for evil-in-general, or such hatred for goodness-in-general, right reason, or God, as to adopt these as our reason and have them as efficient partial causes of our efficaciously willing something else' (Adams 1999: 261). Though such conclusions might seem extreme, Ockham believes that neither moral imputability nor the evident implications of our own experience can be accounted for in any other way. If any deliverance of reason, any natural inclination, or any acquired habit determines the will's action, that action is not in the agent's power; and what is not in our power cannot be imputed to us for praise or blame, merit or demerit. And experience makes it plain that

---

[14] 'Will-against' is my translation of *nolle*; some translators prefer 'nill'. Not to will something (*non velle*) is to refrain from willing it, to have no act of will concerning it; to will-against or nill something (*nolle*) is to have an act of will with respect to that thing, where the act is one of refusal, repudiation, or rejection.

we frequently act against our best judgement, not merely in forgetfulness or haste, but deliberately and with our eyes wide open. Any moral psychology that makes of such 'incontinence' or weakness of will a *theoretical* problem is obviously misguided, Ockham holds; incontinence is not a theoretical difficulty but a *moral* problem.[15] Furthermore, we cannot account for sins of *commission*, as opposed to sins of *omission*, unless we are able to say that the will can knowingly choose evil as such.

9.4 DIVINE-COMMAND ETHICS

The most contentious question in recent scholarship on Scotus and Ockham is whether either or both of them were divine-command theorists of some sort. If one goes back far enough, one finds a widespread consensus that both Scotus and Ockham held that moral rightness and wrongness depend largely or entirely on the divine will, which is not in turn constrained by any judgement of the divine intellect. Beginning in the 1970s, Allan Wolter overturned this consensus about Scotus, arguing that a divine-command interpretation could not be sustained in light of Scotus' emphasis on the divine rationality, the 'orderliness' of God's love, and the connection between human nature and moral norms. Wolter's reading became the dominant interpretation of Scotus' ethics.[16] From the mid-1980s through the late 1990s, a similar movement took place in Ockham scholarship, thanks to influential contributions by Marilyn McCord Adams and Peter King, among others.[17] Notwithstanding more recent efforts to rehabilitate a divine-command interpretation of either thinker—by me, in the case of Scotus, and by Thomas M. Osborne, Jr., in the case of Ockham[18]—it seems fair to say that the consensus of current scholarship remains strongly opposed to the voluntaristic readings of Scotus and Ockham that were dominant forty years ago.

The case for reading Scotus as a kind of divine-command theorist can be seen most clearly by considering his treatment of the moral law in *Ordinatio* III, d. 37, q. un., where he asks whether all the commandments of the Decalogue belong to the natural law. His answer is that the natural law in the strict sense includes only 'practical principles known in virtue of their terms or conclusions that necessarily follow from

---

[15] This point is brought out very ably in Perkams 2006.

[16] Indeed, it is not much of an exaggeration to say that Wolter's work is single-handedly responsible for what is now the received view of Scotus' ethics, though he did take some inspiration from Frederick Copleston's (1950) treatment of Scotus. For an accessible overview of Wolter's reading, see his introduction to Wolter 1986.

[17] Marilyn McCord Adams' reading of Ockham was first worked out in Adams 1986 and 1987 and achieved its widest influence through the appearance of Adams 1999. For Peter King's account, see King 1999. Thomas S. Osborne, Jr. (2005: 19 n. 4) writes that both Adams' and King's interpretations 'have either their remote or proximate source' in Freppert 1988.

[18] See in particular Williams 1998 and 2000 and Osborne 2005.

them' (*Ord.* 3, d. 37, q. un., n. 16, 10: 279). Only the commandments of the 'first table', those that have to do directly with God, meet this criterion:

> Indeed, if we understand the first two commandments as purely negative—the first as 'You shall not have other gods' and the second as 'You shall not take up the name of your God wantonly,' that is, 'You shall not do irreverence to God'—they belong to the law of nature strictly speaking, because this follows necessarily: 'If God exists, he alone is to be loved as God.' And it likewise follows that nothing else is to be worshiped as God and that no irreverence is to be done to him. (*Ord.* 3, d. 37, q. un. n. 20, X: 280–281)

But the other commandments do not belong to the natural law in this strict sense, since 'the goodness in the things that those precepts command is not necessary for the goodness of the ultimate end, and the badness of the things they prohibit does not necessarily turn one aside from the ultimate end' (*Ord.* 3, d. 37, q. un., n. 18, X: 280). Those commandments, the precepts of the 'second table', belong to the natural law only in a looser sense: they do not follow necessarily from the necessary and self-evident practical principles, but they are 'highly consonant' (*valde consonans*) with them.

There is no debate about the status of the necessary precepts. Scotus could hardly be clearer that God cannot will contradictions, and the denial of any of the self-evident first principles is a contradiction. So even God cannot bring it about that God is not to be loved, or that God may licitly be treated with irreverence.[19] The debate, then, is about how to understand the contingent precepts. The revisionist view draws on what Scotus has to say about the relation of contingent truths in general to the divine will and the divine intellect. Consider these representative passages, the first taken from the discussion of divine justice, the second and third from discussions of contingency:

> The [divine] intellect apprehends a possible action before the [divine] will wills it, but it does not apprehend determinately that this particular action is to be done, where 'apprehend' means 'dictate.' Rather, it offers this action to the divine will as neutral, and if the will determines through its volition that it is to be done, then as a consequence of this volition the intellect apprehends as true [the proposition that] it is to be done. (*Ord.* 4, d. 46, q. 1, n. 10, translated from the Latin text in Wolter 1986: 250)

> In terms of a distinction between instants of nature: in the first, [the divine intellect] apprehends every possible operation—those that are principles of

[19] Notice that Scotus' preferred formulation of moral precepts is as indicative sentences using the gerundive, represented in English by sentences of the form 'φ is [not] to be done', rather than as imperatives. Accordingly, Scotus' moral precepts are propositions, which are either true or false, rather than commands, which do not have truth values. Thus, where Ockham will later ask whether God can command someone to hate him—and whether, if God does so, it is then good or obligatory for that person to hate God—Scotus asks whether God can bring it about that 'God is to be hated' is true. Scotus' question, unlike Ockham's, has a clear answer: 'God is to be hated' is necessarily false, independently of the divine will.

possible operations, just like particular possible operations. And in the second, it offers all these to the will, which from among all of them—both practical principles and particular possible operations—accepts [only] some. (*Ord.* 1, d. 38, q. un., n. 10, VI: 307)

Hence, when the divine intellect, before an act of the will, apprehends the proposition '*x* is to be done', it apprehends it as neutral, just as when I apprehend the proposition 'There is an even number of stars'; but once *x* is produced in being by an act of the divine will, then *x* is apprehended by the divine intellect as a true object. (*Lect.* 1, d. 39, qq. 1–5, n. 44, XVII: 493)

Thus, the truth of contingent practical precepts is dependent on the divine will; and Scotus tells us that we are not to look for any reason why the divine will chooses one of a pair of contradictories rather than the other:

And if you ask why the divine will is determined to one of a pair of contradictories rather than to the other, I must reply that 'It is characteristic of the untutored to look for causes and proof for everything.'... There is no cause why the will willed, except that the will is the will, just as there is no cause why heat heats, except that heat is heat. There is no prior cause. (*Ord.* 1, d. 8, q. 2, n. 299, IV: 324–325)[20]

Relying on such passages, the revisionist interpretation holds that Scotus is a divine-command theorist when it comes to the contingent part of the moral law, in the following sense: the truth of those precepts depends wholly on the divine will, and there is no reason external to the divine will that explains God's willing as he does with respect to those contingent precepts.

The dominant view does not deny that the precepts of the second table are contingent and therefore dependent in some way on God's will, but it employs various strategies to eliminate any sense of arbitrariness or caprice in God's act of moral legislation. The appeals most commonly made are to divine *justice* and divine *rationality*. According to Wolter, Scotus holds that God's *justice* causes him to 'give to natures such perfections as are due or becoming to them' (Wolter 1990: 158). It is not that God owes anything to creatures, but that he 'owes it to himself' to make his creation naturally good.[21] The appeal to divine *rationality* takes two forms. Some arguments focus on passages in which Scotus speaks of God as willing in a 'most orderly' or 'most rational' way (*ordinatissime, rationabilissime*).[22] Others rely on Scotus' doctrine that the will is a rational power (Ingham 2001).

Most of the debate over Scotus-interpretation since the 1990s took place when little of the crucial material in Scotus' *Ordinatio* relevant to ethics had been critically edited.

---

[20] The context of this passage is worth noting. Scotus is arguing that God alone is immutable and necessary. All other things are contingent because God causes them freely. Thus, the statement about the divine will as the immediate cause of the existence of contingent things is meant to have the widest possible application.

[21] Ingham 2001: 199–200, makes a similar appeal to divine justice. I argue at length against this reading of divine justice in Williams 2000: 171–89.

[22] See in particular Bonansea 1983: 190–1; Wolter 1986: 9, 17, 19–20, 55, 57. For the revisionist take on such passages, see Williams 2000: 189–202.

During that period some proponents of the received view attempted to argue that the revisionist case relied improperly on non-critical editions or poorly chosen manuscripts, but as I have shown elsewhere, the practice of the revisionist interpretation was actually better than the precept of the received view (Williams 2004: n. 4). Readers should be aware that complaints about the use of inauthentic texts of Scotus were made very selectively; it frequently happened that a scholar was criticized for using a text that another scholar approved by the critic—or even the critic him- or herself—was allowed to use without a word of reproach. That said, now that the critical edition of the *Ordinatio* is nearly complete, the time is certainly right for a full-scale treatment of Scotus' ethics and moral psychology.[23]

For whatever reason, it is not Scotus but Ockham in whom historians have tended to see a decisive break with the naturalism and eudaimonism of earlier Scholastic moral theories, and the beginning of the rule-based and act-focused approach to ethics that would come to dominate modern moral philosophy. Armand Maurer, for example, wrote that Ockham 'severs the bond between metaphysics and ethics' that we find in earlier scholastics, who 'looked upon goodness as a property of being'. Instead, Maurer writes, Ockham 'bases morality not upon the perfection of human nature (whose reality he denies), nor upon the teleological relation between man and God, but upon man's obligation to follow the laws freely laid down for him by God' (Maurer 1962: 285–6).[24]

Marilyn McCord Adams acknowledges Ockham's departures from earlier scholastic thought, particularly regarding natural teleology; but she contends that Ockham's critics 'drastically overstate the consequences for ethics' (Adams 1999: 246). Despite Ockham's rejection of natural teleology, she argues, Ockham continues to uphold an ethics of right reason, not a purely authoritarian ethics: 'Ockham accepts an Aristotelian model of rational self-government in which considerations of natural excellence undergird right reasons that are normative for action' (Adams 1999: 265).[25] But considerations of natural excellence extend beyond human natural excellence to include God's natural excellence; and when reason properly grasps God's excellence, it correctly infers that God ought to be loved above all else, and loved for his own sake. Given that God does issue certain commands, right reason also concludes that these 'divine commands are a secondary ethical norm' (Adams 1999: 266). Since Ockham, much like Scotus, holds that

---

[23] Kent 2007: 191, rightly emphasizes the important role in this dispute of Scotus' claim that 'everything other than God is good because it is willed by God and not vice versa'. In light of the fact that the text in question does not even appear in the critical edition of the *Ordinatio*, and the parallel text in the *Lectura* reads quite differently, that whole strand of the discussion now appears quaintly misguided.

[24] For similar interpretations, see Pinckaers 1995: 516–39, and Bourke 1970: 104–7, 122–3.

[25] If I am reading Adams correctly on this point, the criticism in Osborne 2005—namely that right reason is not a source of moral obligation but merely the correct discernment of an obligation whose source is external to reason—is not well taken. For Adams here takes natural excellence, both human and divine, to be the source of the moral obligations that right reason discerns. Osborne does seem to acknowledge as much at one point, noting that 'Adams seems to argue that dictates of right reason are based on considerations of natural goodness' (Osborne 2005: 7). Later, we shall examine Osborne's argument that natural goodness does not play the role in Ockham's thought that Adams envisions for it.

God's will is completely unconstrained in his moral legislation, it is theoretically possible for God to issue commands that conflict with what right reason dictates. Fortunately, however, 'God actually commands rational creatures to follow the dictates of right reason and in fact rewards adherence to right reason and sacramental participation with eternal life' (Adams 1999: 266). So although these two independent criteria for morally right action, divine commands and right reason, could in principle come into conflict, they are (contingently, and as a consequence of God's wholly unconstrained choice) in fact compatible. This compatibility is sufficient to preserve the coherence and intelligibility of the moral life.

Peter King likewise emphasizes the role of right reason in Ockham's ethics. Ockham, he notes, recognized both positive and non-positive moral knowledge. 'Nonpositive morality consists of principles that are either known per se or derived from experience' (King 1999: 228), and among these principles are such precepts as 'Murder is wrong' and 'Theft is wrong.' Positive morality consists of divine commands; it can be known if God tells us what he has commanded. Following God's commands is morally obligatory because the act of loving God above all else and for his own sake is necessarily and intrinsically virtuous, and 'to love God above all else is this: to love whatever God wants to be loved' (*Quodlibet* III.14, quoted in King 1999: 237).

Though King says that loving God for his own sake is '*the* act of the will that is intrinsically virtuous' (King 1999: 232, emphasis mine) he cannot really mean that loving God above all else is the *only* necessarily and intrinsically virtuous act. For Ockham is unambiguous in holding that an unbeliever who (say) tells the truth because right reason dictates that the truth should be told acts virtuously. If only an act of loving God is intrinsically virtuous, the unbeliever's truth-telling is not intrinsically virtuous; and since an extrinsically virtuous act derives its value from an intrinsically virtuous act, the unbeliever's act could not be extrinsically virtuous either. Presumably, then, Ockham as King reads him also holds that willing to act according to right reason is also intrinsically virtuous.[26]

Both Adams and King, in their different ways, read Ockham as holding that at least some moral norms have their source in something other than divine commands. Thomas M. Osborne, Jr., has recently objected that no such source can be found in Ockham. Contrary to Adams, natural goodness (what she calls 'natural excellence') cannot be a source of moral norms: 'When discussing the nature of moral obligation Ockham does not mention natural goodness but instead he focuses on the will of God' (Osborne 2005: 8). Even acts such as adultery and theft, which God has in fact prohibited, would be virtuous

---

[26] Osborne takes King as claiming outright that loving God is the only intrinsically virtuous act for Ockham and complains that King thereby 'makes Ockham's theory absurd and contradictory' (Osborne 2005: 6). But apart from King's use of the definite article in the passage I quoted, there is no suggestion that he actually interprets Ockham in that way, and the passage from *Quodlibet* III.14 that King cites to make his point about the love of God says only that loving God is *an* intrinsically virtuous act, not that it is the only one. So my reading of King (on which the definite article is simply an infelicitous choice) seems to me to be more charitable.

in some other world in which God's commands are different. We would no longer *call* them 'adultery' or 'theft', because those words 'signify these acts not absolutely, but through the connotation of their being prohibited' (Osborne 2005: 8; cf. King 1999: 239). But the label for the acts is beside the point: what matters is that all the considerations about natural goodness could be exactly the same in the alternative possible world as they are in the actual world, and yet the act that is virtuous in the alternative possible world is vicious in the actual world. This shows quite clearly, Osborne argues, that natural goodness is not a source of moral norms in the way Adams envisions.[27]

Against King, Osborne argues that the obligation to obey God does not derive from the obligation to love God. Instead, the converse is true: in *Reportatio* 2, q. 15, Ockham expressly claims that the duty to love God derives from God's command that one love him, and he 'lists the hatred of God along with adultery and theft as an act whose moral value depends on a divine command' (Osborne 2005: 12). And the passage from *Quodlibet* III.14 to which King appeals in arguing that loving God is necessarily intrinsically virtuous contains an important qualification. Ockham wrote:

> I state that the act that is necessarily virtuous *in the way described above* is an act of will, because the act in which God is loved above all else and for his own sake is an act of this kind; for this act is virtuous in such a way that it cannot be vicious, and this act cannot be caused by a created will without being virtuous—because on the one hand everyone, no matter where or when, is obligated to love God above all else, and consequently this act cannot be vicious; and, on the other hand, because this act is the first of all good acts. (*Quod.* III.14.60–67, 255–256)

'In the way described above', Osborne argues, refers back to the qualification *stante divino praecepto*: 'provided that the divine precept remains what it is'. Even here, then, Ockham makes the moral worth of loving God contingent upon God's commands.

9.5 FUTURE DIRECTIONS FOR RESEARCH

The debate over theological voluntarism in Scotus and Ockham is likely to continue. As I noted earlier, the critical editions of Scotus' works have only now reached the point at which a much-needed full-scale reassessment of Scotus' ethics is possible; and the divine-command interpretation of Ockham has only recently been revived. Moreover, in both thinkers the issue of theological voluntarism is bound up with so many other matters of philosophical dispute—the relation of the divine will to the divine intellect, God's justice and rationality, the nature of divine omnipotence, the status of *possibilia*, and a range of metaethical questions—that any adequate treatment of the topic requires

[27] Alternatively, Osborne suggests (2005: 10), it might be the case that the natural goodness of the acts would be different in the two different worlds precisely because of the difference in God's commands. Either way, natural goodness turns out not to be a source of norms independent of God's commands.

a good deal of further work. But there is also need for work on topics and authors who have hardly been treated at all. Franciscan authors after Ockham have been largely neglected (and indeed fourteenth-century philosophy in general remains strikingly understudied). And there is much for philosophically minded historians of ethics to do in evaluating the claims of some historians of thought, particularly within theology, that some kind of decisive 'rupture' occurred with Scotus or Ockham. Such narratives of a dramatic intellectual shift—such as the story of wide-ranging intellectual disruption that theologians associated with Radical Orthodoxy trace to Duns Scotus—cannot be properly assessed apart from a sober, textually responsible, and philosophically informed examination of Scotus' and Ockham's ethical views and of the place of those views within the totality of their philosophical and theological work.

BIBLIOGRAPHY

Adams, M. McCord. 1986. 'The structure of Ockham's moral theory', *Franciscan Studies* 46: 1–35.
—— 1987. 'William Ockham: voluntarist or naturalist?', in J. F. Wippel (ed.), *Studies in Medieval Philosophy*. Washington, DC: The Catholic University of America Press, 219–47.
—— 1999. 'Ockham on will, nature, and morality', in Spade (ed.) 1999, 245–72.
Bonansea, B. M. 1983. *Man and His Approach to God in John Duns Scotus*. Lanham, MD: University Press of America.
Bourke, V. 1970. *History of Ethics*. 2 vols. Garden City, NY: Doubleday.
Copleston, F. 1950. *A History of Philosophy*, vol. 2. Westminster, MD: Newman Press.
Dumont, S. D. 2001. 'Did Scotus change his mind on the will?', in J. A. Aertsen, K. Emery, Jr., and A. Speer (eds), *After the Condemnation of 1277: Philosophy and Theology at the University of Paris in the Last Quarter of the Thirteenth Century*. Berlin: Walter de Gruyter, 719–94.
Duns Scotus, J. 1950. *Opera omnia*. Vatican City: Vatican Polyglot Press. (References to the *Lectura* and *Ordinatio* are indicated by '*Lect.*' and '*Ord.*', respectively, followed by the standard internal divisions and then the volume and page number of the edition.)
—— 1997. *Quaestiones super libros Metaphysicorum Aristotelis, Libri VI–IX*. Vol. 4 of *Philosophical Writings of Blessed John Duns Scotus*. Saint Bonaventure, NY: Franciscan Institute Publications. (References are indicated by '*In Metaph.*' followed by the standard internal divisions and then the page number of the edition.)
Freppert, L. 1988. *The Basis of Morality According to William Ockham*. Chicago: Franciscan Herald Press.
Ingham, M. B. 2001. 'Letting Scotus speak for himself', *Medieval Philosophy and Theology* 10: 173–216.
Kent, B. D. 1995. *Virtues of the Will: The Transformation of Ethics in the Late Thirteenth Century*. Washington, DC: The Catholic University of America Press.
—— 2003. 'Rethinking moral dispositions: Scotus on the virtues', in Williams (ed.) 2003, 352–76.
—— 2007. 'Evil in later medieval philosophy', *Journal of the History of Philosophy*. 45: 177–205.
King, P. 1999. 'Ockham's ethical theory', in Spade (ed.) 1999, 227–44.
Maurer, A. 1962. *Medieval Philosophy*. New York: Random House.

Ockham, W. 1980. *Quodlibeta septem*. Vol. 9 of *Opera theologica*. Saint Bonaventure, NY: Franciscan Institute Publications. (References are indicated by 'Quod.' followed by the standard internal divisions and then the page number of the edition.)

Osborne, T. M., Jr. 2005. 'Ockham as a divine-command theorist', *Religious Studies* 41: 1–22.

Perkams, M. 2006. 'Ockhams Theorie der Unbestimmtheit des Willens als Auseinandersetzung mit dem Problem der Willenswäche', in T. Hoffmann, J. Müller, and M. Perkams (eds), *Das Problem der Willenschwäche in der Mittelalterlichen Philosophie*. Recherches de Théologie et Philosophie médiévales, Biblioteca 8. Leuven: Peeters, 307–29.

Pinckaers, S. 1995. *The Sources of Christian Ethics*, trans. M. Thomas Noble. Washington, DC: The Catholic University of America Press.

Spade, P. V. (ed.) 1999. *The Cambridge Companion to Ockham*. Cambridge: Cambridge University Press.

Williams, T. 1998. 'The unmitigated Scotus', *Archiv für Geschichte der Philosophie* 80: 162–81.

—— 2000. 'A most methodical lover? On Scotus's arbitrary Creator', *Journal of the History of Philosophy* 38: 169–202.

—— 2004. 'The divine nature and Scotus's libertarianism: a reply to Mary Beth Ingham', <http://shell.cas.usf.edu/~thomasw/The Divine Nature and Scotus's Libertarianism.pdf>.

—— 2010. 'Duns Scotus', in C. Sandis and T. O'Connor (eds), *A Companion to the Philosophy of Action*. Oxford: Wiley-Blackwell, 466–72.

—— (ed.) 2003. *The Cambridge Companion to Duns Scotus*. Cambridge: Cambridge University Press.

Wolter, A. B. 1986. *Duns Scotus on the Will and Morality*. Washington, DC: The Catholic University of America Press.

—— 1990. 'Native freedom of the will as a key to the ethics of Scotus', in Marilyn McCord Adams (ed.), *The Philosophical Theology of John Duns Scotus*. Ithaca, NY: Cornell University Press, 148–62.

Wood, R. 1997. *Ockham on the Virtues*. West Lafayette, IN: Purdue University Press.

CHAPTER 10

....

LATER CHRISTIAN ETHICS

....

T. H. IRWIN

10.1 MORALITY AS SOURCE AND PRODUCT OF CHRISTIANITY

....

It would be unwise to try to distinguish an area of 'Christian ethics' apart from moral philosophy as a whole. As we will see in later sections, different Christian moralists take different positions according to their different philosophical views, not necessarily because of specifically Christian convictions that might distinguish them either from non-Christian philosophers or from other Christians. But while 'Christian ethics' does not pick out a distinctive school of moral philosophy, or some sort of Christian alternative to moral philosophy, it marks out some large and worthwhile topics in moral philosophy, from the metaphysics and epistemology of morality to questions of method in practical ethics. The complex relations between Christian faith and doctrine, on the one hand, and moral practice and theory, on the other hand, have provided sources for reflexion and debate among moral philosophers and moral theologians in the modern period no less than in earlier times.

The rather specific moral precepts of the Scriptures and of early Christian pastoral writings make relatively precise moral demands. Mediaeval Scholasticism elaborates these demands into a moral system. In this respect, Christianity provides input into morality. Equally, however, Christian doctrines of the nature of God, human nature, sin, grace, salvation, and the Incarnation, all rest on ethical assumptions that might be supported or contested on the basis of philosophical views on goodness, justice, virtue, freedom, and responsibility. In this respect, morality provides input into Christianity.

Three different approaches may be distinguished: (1) Some Christian moralists argue that Christian morality is not only consistent with moral philosophy, understood as the product of correct reason unaided by divine revelation, but actually brings out the best in it. This is a point in favour of Christianity, judged from a philosophical point of view.[1] (2) Some argue that Christianity presents a moral outlook that conflicts fundamentally with rational morality. Christian believers must replace rational morality systems with a quite different moral system resting on the authority of revelation and divine commands. To unbelievers the Christian system is bound to be foolishness, and Christians are wasting their time if they try to refute unbelievers on their own ground.[2] (3) Some argue that Christianity neither fulfils nor rejects ordinary rational morality, because it is not really a moral system at all.[3] It shows that we cannot satisfy God with our moral goodness, but we can achieve salvation without moral virtue. Christianity tells us about our relations with God, not about how to get on with other people.

An account of Christianity and morality that did not present these three elements would be incomplete and misleading, but accounts may intelligibly differ in the degree of importance they assign to one or another of them. Speaking very roughly and generally, we may say that mediaeval Scholasticism, despite important philosophical and theological disagreements, tends to favour the first view, which is fully developed by Aquinas. An equally rough generalization might attribute something more like the second or third view to some moral theologians of the Reformation era. In the 17th and 18th centuries we can trace some of the disputes between these different views, and some of their impact on moral philosophy.

This essay takes the period of the Reformation (from the early 16th century) as its rough starting point and the death of St Alphonsus Liguori (in 1787) as its rough terminus, but, since sharp chronological divisions are rarely useful in the history of ethics, it also strays beyond these limits in the exploration of some of the central themes.

The questions that are surveyed below certainly do not include everything that might reasonably be discussed under the head of Christian ethics. Some have been chosen because they are central questions in modern moral philosophy; others have been chosen to illustrate the range of questions on which a Christian outlook has something to say. Even on these questions I have not discussed all the relevant sources. I have mostly, though not entirely, drawn on the British moralists, but not only on those that are best known to the modern student.[4]

---

[1] See Origen, *Contra Celsum*, vi 15–16.

[2] See 1 Corinthians 1:23; Justin, *Apology*, 1.13.

[3] One might draw this conclusion from the Lutheran contrast between 'civil righteousness' and 'spiritual righteousness'. See Augsburg Confession §18, in P. Schaff, *The Creeds of Christendom*, 6th edn. 3 vols. (New York: Harper & Row, 1931), iii.

[4] I have said more about the questions discussed in this essay, and given fuller references to sources, in Irwin, *Development of Ethics* (3 vols., Oxford University Press, 2007–2009), mostly in vol. 2.

10.2 MORALITY AND DIVINE COMMANDS:
VOLUNTARISM

The Reformation encouraged the first-hand study of Scripture without the overlay of Scholastic doctrine. Luther sometimes suggests that this doctrine leads us astray from a true understanding of Scripture. That is why he says 'I believe that I owe this duty to the Lord of crying out against philosophy and turning men to Holy Scripture'.[5] He charges that the Scholastics have replaced the genuine Church with a 'Thomist or Aristotelian Church'.[6]

In particular, Luther's study of St Paul persuades him that some Scholastic views about God and morality conflict with the Christian revelation. According to Aquinas, morality consists in the provisions of natural law, and hence is determined by facts about human nature that do not result from any divine legislation. Luther objects that, if this account of morality were correct, God would be determined by facts independent of his will to do what he does. This conclusion is intolerable because we know that God is not required to act as he does. God's treatment of us is not owed to us in justice, as a response to our merits, but is an expression of his mercy and grace. God does not love something because it is an appropriate object of love; on the contrary, 'the love of God living in a human being loves sinners, evil people, fools, and weaklings in order to make them just, good, wise and strong.... For sinners are beautiful (pulchri) because they are loved, not loved because they are beautiful.'[7]

A similar doctrine of the sovereignty of God might be taken to underlie Calvin's view that 'whatever God wills must be accounted just from the very fact that he wills it'.[8] It is by no means clear, however, that Calvin accepts the voluntarist claim that rightness is wholly dependent on the will of God. Indeed, he rejects any conception of the power of God that separates it from God's justice; and so he takes himself to reject the Scholastic division between the absolute and ordered power of God.[9] It is clearer that some later Calvinists affirmed voluntarism. They are among the 'divers modern theologers' whom Cudworth attacks for their view 'that there is nothing absolutely, intrinsically and naturally good and evil, just and unjust, antecedently to any positive command or prohibition of God; but that the arbitrary will and pleasure of God...is the first and only rule and measure thereof'.[10]

---

[5] Luther on Romans 8:19, in *Lectures on Romans*, tr. W. Pauck (London: SCM Press, 1961), 236.

[6] Luther, *Babylonian Captivity*, in *Selections*, ed. J. Dillenberger (Garden City, NY: Doubleday, 1961) 265f.

[7] Luther, *Heidelberg Disputation* §28, in *Luther's Works*, ed. J. Pelikan and H. T. Lehmann. 56 vols. (St Louis: Concordia, 1955–1976), xxxi.

[8] J. Calvin, *Institutes of the Christian Religion*, ed. F. L. Battles, tr. J. T. McNeill. 2 vols. London: SCM, 1960, iii 23.2.

[9] Calvin, *Institutes of the Christian Religion*. i 17.2.

[10] Cudworth, *Eternal and Immutable Morality*, ed. S. Hutton (Cambridge: Cambridge University Press, 1996), i 1.5.

Theological voluntarism also appeals to many English moral philosophers, because it seems to offer satisfying answers to questions that other theories cannot answer. They reject both the rationalist conception of morality (represented by Samuel Clarke) and the sentimentalist conception (represented by Hutcheson)[11] on the ground that neither conception can say what constitutes moral duty and obligation without reference to divine commands. The voluntarist critique of these other conceptions can be illustrated from two representative writers, John Clarke and William Paley. According to John Clarke, obligation 'signifies the necessity a person lies under, to comply with some law, or suffer the penalty denounced against the violation of it'.[12] Paley agrees; in his view, an air of mystery seems to hang over moral philosophy until we grasp the essential facts about obligation.[13] We dispel the air of mystery once we recognize that 'a man is said to be obliged when he is urged by a violent motive resulting from the command of another'.[14] As Paley explains, the commander is God, and the violent (i.e. forceful) motive results from the sanctions of reward and punishment. These sanctions are attached to utilitarian rules.

John Clarke, Paley, and other voluntarists rely on two claims: (1) We are under an obligation to act morally if and only if we have a reason and a motive that is sufficient for us to follow morality. (2) But we have a good reason and sufficient motive to follow morality if and only if it is the product of divine commands supported by sanctions that involve post-mortem rewards and punishments. If the first claim is correct, we cannot be satisfied with the rationalist answer that moral principles are accessible to rational enquiry and insight, or with the sentimentalist answer that they express our benevolent sentiments. Morality might have these features even if we had no good reason and sufficient motive to follow moral principles; hence these features cannot be all there is to morality. To give us both the good reason and the sufficient motive, we need a divine command with a sanction. Morality, therefore, requires a divine imperative law supported by a sanction.

These claims about obligation do not imply that we cannot recognize the content of morality without reference to God. Many English voluntarists accept a utilitarian account of the content of morality. But they argue that our basic reason for following morality is not the fact that it promotes the general happiness. We would have no obligation, and no sufficient motive, to promote the general happiness, unless we recognized that God commands the promotion of the general happiness. An obligation requires a

[11] On rationalism and sentimentalism, see chs. 15 and 17, this *Handbook*.

[12] J. Clarke, *Foundation of Morality in Theory and Practice* (York, 1726), 9.

[13] 'When I first turned my thoughts to moral speculations, an air of mystery seemed to hang over the whole subject; which arose, I believe, from hence, – that I supposed, with many authors whom I had read, that to be obliged to do a thing, was very different from being induced only to do it; and that the obligation to practise virtue, to do what is right, just, etc., was quite another thing, and of another kind, than the obligation which a soldier is under to obey his officer, a servant his master; or any of the civil and ordinary obligations of human life.' (Paley, *Principles of Moral and Political Philosophy*, ed. D. L. Le Mahieu. Indianapolis: Liberty Fund, ii 3)

[14] Paley, *Principles of Moral and Political Philosophy*, ii 2 = R 848.

sufficient motive, and hence—given an egoist account of motives—requires divine commands supported by sanctions that appeal to one's self-interest.

This clear answer to the main questions of moral theory made Paley's work influential in education. For over fifty years his book was prescribed for study in Cambridge.[15] Apart from his immediate influence, his position is also relevant to later utilitarianism. Bentham and his successors retain Paley's utilitarianism. But they do not clearly answer the questions about obligation and motivation that Paley answers with his voluntarism. Why, one might ask, are we obliged to promote the general happiness, and why should we care about it? Some of Bentham's remarks suggest that he accepts Paley's egoist answer; but he does not do much to show that my own happiness and the general happiness converge. Both Mill and Sidgwick clearly reject Bentham's egoist answer; but it is less clear that they offer good substitutes for it. Theological voluntarism raises questions that its opponents cannot afford to ignore.

The influence of theological voluntarism is not confined to English and Scottish moral philosophy. It has also affected modern Roman Catholic teaching on the necessity of divine commands for moral obligation. Writers in the Scholastic tradition in the 17th and 18th centuries draw a distinction that agrees both with Pufendorf and with the English voluntarists, between fundamental and formal morality. Fundamental morality consists of facts about what is good and bad for human beings because of their nature. But only formal morality includes obligation, which requires divine legislation. Since complete morality requires obligation, only formal morality is complete morality. Without divine commands things would be intrinsically good and bad, but nothing would be morally good or bad, or morally right or wrong.[16] This aspect of theological voluntarism receives papal approval from Popes Pius IX (1864), Leo XIII,[17] and Pius XII.[18] Voluntarist assumptions about law and obligation underlie the assertion that if the existence of God is denied, the principle of all rightness (honestas) also collapses.

A voluntarist account of obligation can be used to argue from the presumed existence of moral obligation to the existence of God as legislator, or from the presumed non-existence of God to the non-existence of moral obligation. From the voluntarist point of view, moralists who believe in moral obligation but do not take it to require a divine legislator are confused and inconsistent. This is the basis of Anscombe's objections to modern moral philosophy.[19] She takes morality to require a concept of 'ought' and obligation

[15] See William Whewell, *Lectures on the History of Moral Philosophy in England* (London: Parker, 1852), 165; D. L. Le Mahieu, *The Mind of William Paley* (Lincoln: University of Nebraska Press, 1976), 155–62.

[16] The division between fundamental and formal morality is explained in *Dictionnaire de Théologie Catholique*, A. Vacant et al., eds (15 vols. Paris: Letouzey et Ané, 1903–1946), xv.2, col. 3317.

[17] Leo XIII, *Libertas Praestantissimum*, in H. Denziger and A. Schönmetzer, *Enchiridion Symbolorum* (36th edn. Freiburg: Herder, 1976), §3247.

[18] Pius XII, *Summi Pontificatus*, in Denziger §3781. See J. Mahoney, *The Making of Moral Theology* (Oxford: Oxford University Press, 1987), 82.

[19] G. E. M. Anscombe, 'Modern moral philosophy', in her *Collected Philosophical Papers*, vol. 3 (Minneapolis, University of Minnesota Press, 1981), 26–42. (From *Philosophy* 33 (1958), 1–19.)

that implies legislation. According to her version of Roman theological voluntarism, those who do not believe in divine legislation should confine themselves to 'fundamental' and incomplete morality without 'ought' and obligation.

10.3 AGAINST VOLUNTARISM

The tenacity of these elements of voluntarism in Christian reflexions on morality provokes equally tenacious opposition. The position opposed to voluntarism might be called 'naturalism', in so far as it maintains that right and wrong are fixed by the nature of human beings and other creatures, apart from divine legislation. Hence it maintains a doctrine of 'intrinsic morality' that makes right and wrong intrinsic to actions, and not the product of legislative will.

In 16th-century England the more rigorous Reformers emphasize divine legislation, for metaphysical, moral, and ecclesiological reasons. In their view, the correct principles of morality, political and social order, and church government all depend on divine legislation, revealed primarily in the Scriptures. Christians, therefore, need to study the Scriptures to see whether God requires a specific moral outlook; to see whether God enjoins monarchy or some other form of government; and to see whether the required form of church government is episcopal, presbyterian, or congregational.

Against these claims for divine legislation, Hooker argues that in all these areas right and wrong do not depend on legislation. Morality and the natural law are not products of God's legislative will.[20] They are law only in an 'enlarged' sense; they do not depend on any command or act of imposition, but they constitute a rule and norm.[21] The principles of morality are accessible to reason, and we should not try to rest them primarily on divine legislation. They express the divine will in so far as the divine will follows divine wisdom, which grasps the right rational order. But they are not products of divine legislation. We can learn about them by reason, but not by direct revelation of the divine legislative will. Nor should we try to determine the right form of government, civil or ecclesiastical, by demanding Scriptural evidence of divine legislation. While rational reflexion shows us that the basic principles of morality are universal, it does not show that the more specific principles are equally applicable to all circumstances. Nor should we expect authoritative divine legislation on civil and ecclesiastical government; we ought to settle these questions by rational reflexion on the requirements of morality and the specific circumstances of this or that situation. Hooker does not claim, therefore, that monarchy is the divinely required system of civil government, or that episcopacy is the divinely required system of ecclesiastical polity; he argues that each of them is best in the circumstances.

---

[20] Hooker, *Of the Laws of Ecclesiastical Polity*, in J. Keble (ed.), *The Works of Richard Hooker*. 7th edn. 3 vols. (Oxford: Oxford University Press, 1888), i 2.5, p. 203.

[21] Hooker, *Laws* i 3.1.

Hooker's view of natural law and morality is largely followed by Robert Sanderson, the leading moral theologian of the mid 17th century in England. The same naturalist influence persists in the Scholastic and Platonic outlook of Nathanael Culverwell, Benjamin Whichcote, and Ralph Cudworth. The objections that this outlook aroused among the more rigid Calvinists in 17th-century Cambridge is illustrated by an exchange of letters between Anthony Tuckney and Whichcote.[22] Tuckney expresses his disquiet at Whichcote's alleged preference for the study of Scholastic philosophy over the Scriptures. In Tuckney's view, the naturalist outlook gives too much weight to reason and too little to divine legislation. In particular it presumes to limit God's freedom by independent standards of goodness.

Cudworth rejects this attempt to connect naturalism about morality with the rejection of orthodox Christianity. He replies that the voluntarist position is both philosophically unsound and theologically dangerous. Contrary to voluntarism, morality does not depend on divine legislation to make actions morally right or wrong. To see why this is so, we need only ask why it is right to obey divine laws. If God commands us to obey them, why does that command have moral force? It seems that it must be right to obey the legislator.[23] And so some obligation must be prior to any command that is capable of imposing an obligation. A purely legislative theory of right and wrong undermines itself.

Though Shaftesbury does not imitate Cudworth's presentation of morality within an elaborate Platonist metaphysics, he supports Cudworth's rejection of a purely legislative view of moral properties.[24] In Shaftesbury's view, voluntarism has infiltrated orthodox divinity[25] because it purports to defend absolute divine sovereignty against a moral outlook that would limit divine freedom.[26] Tuckney's objections to Whichcote illustrate the voluntarist view that Shaftesbury has in mind. These voluntarist theologians are 'nominal' moralists, as opposed to moral 'realists',[27] because they do not believe that moral properties belong to things by their own nature. Voluntarists believe that if they take a servile attitude to God, separate from any belief in divine moral attributes, they honour God. But we honour God appropriately, according to Shaftesbury, only if we recognize God's inherent goodness.[28] Since voluntarists make moral goodness depend on divine legislation, their view is no better than Hobbes' view that morality is the product of legislation or convention.[29]

[22] These letters are printed in B. Whichcote, *Moral and Religious Aphorisms*, eds J. Jeffery and S. Salter (London, 1753), Appendix.

[23] Cudworth, *Eternal and Immutable Morality*, i 2.3 = R122.

[24] Shaftesbury, *Characteristics of Men, Manners, Opinions, Times*, ed. L. E. Klein (Cambridge: Cambridge University Press, 1999), 42, 157.

[25] Shaftesbury, *Characteristics*, ed. Klein, 57.

[26] Shaftesbury, *Characteristics*, ed. Klein, 262.

[27] 'For 'tis notorious that the chief opposers of atheism write upon contrary principles to one another, so as in a manner to confute themselves. Some of them hold zealously for virtue, and are realists in the point. Others, one may say, are only nominal moralists, by making virtue nothing in itself, a creature of will only or a mere name of fashion.' (*Characteristics* 262)

[28] Shaftesbury, *Characteristics*, 46.   [29] *Characteristics*, 175.

Shaftesbury adds an argument to Cudworth's case against voluntarism. He relies on his belief in a moral sense, a natural sense of right and wrong that belongs to us apart from any religious beliefs. Voluntarists cannot give the appropriate weight to our moral sense; for they have to maintain that it only contingently identifies what is morally right. Since, according to the voluntarist, rightness consists in conformity to the will of God, the qualities we intuitively recognize as right are right only in so far as they conform to the will of God. If we accept this analysis of our moral sense, we agree that it would be right to abandon our moral sense, and to lie, cheat, and deceive if those actions turned out to conform to the will of God.[30]

Shaftesbury's conception of a moral sense is developed, and in important ways altered, by Hutcheson. For the purposes of his argument against theological voluntarism, the relevant point is his belief that our moral sense gives us reliable access to objective moral properties, not dependent on or constituted by our sentiments or beliefs; that is why he takes his belief in a moral sense to be an aspect of his moral realism. He maintains that unless we rely in this way on our moral sense, we have no sufficient reason to predicate moral goodness of God. That is why he takes voluntarism to be misguided.

10.4 FUNDAMENTAL MORALITY AS GENUINE MORALITY

These English moralists illustrate the opposition to theological voluntarism among both Roman and Protestant moralists. As Leibniz remarks, Luther's antagonism towards Aristotle and Scholasticism was not typical of later Lutheran moralists.[31] Indeed Leibniz claims that in his time Lutheran theologians all reject voluntarism, and most Roman and Reformed (Calvinist) theologians reject it, on both Scriptural and philosophical grounds. Even if Leibniz, who opposes voluntarism, exaggerates its unpopularity, some of Pufendorf's remarks suggest that it faced vigorous opposition among contemporary moral theologians. He accuses his Lutheran opponents of misguided respect for the Jesuit Suarez.[32]

We have seen, on the other side, that Scholastics did not all accept naturalism, and that in fact a voluntarist position similar to Pufendorf's gained ground among modern Roman moralists. But it also provoked a naturalist reply. The dispute among Roman Catholic writers is usefully surveyed by W. G. Ward (in 1860). Ward argues that Roman Catholics are permitted to believe in 'independent morality' (i.e. morality that is independent of divine

---

[30] *Characteristics*, 181.

[31] Leibniz, *Theodicy*, tr. E. M. Huggard (London: Routledge, 1951), Preliminary Discourse §12.

[32] Pufendorf, *Eris Scandica*, in *Gesammelte Werke*, ed. W. Schmidt-Biggemann. 5 vols. (Berlin: Akademie-Verlag, 1996–), v 209. 19–30.

commands), and that a cogent case for it can be made.[33] He argues that the Church has recognized that action against rational nature is wrong in its own right, apart from any divine command.[34] Such action is described as 'moral' or 'philosophical' sin. In that case, independent morality is possible; it consists in right action, which is in accord with rational nature, and wrong action, which is contrary to it. According to the voluntarist, philosophical sin is not really sin, but only 'fundamental sin', which corresponds to fundamental morality (falling short of formal morality). According to the voluntarist, fundamental sin is intrinsically bad, because it is inappropriate to rational nature. Hence it deserves to be prohibited, but it is not really wrong (inhonestum) without a divine prohibition. In Ward's view, this account of fundamental sin leaves the voluntarist without a good reason to claim that intrinsically bad actions deserve prohibition. If naturally bad actions deserve prohibition precisely because they are intrinsically bad, must it not be intrinsically wrong to permit them?

These arguments about fundamental and formal sin have no precise parallels in the disputes among English moralists that we have discussed. But Ward's argument against voluntarism relies on the basic objections raised by Cudworth and Shaftesbury. He argues, as they do, that voluntarism is superficially attractive for a Christian moralist, but ultimately dangerous. It is superficially attractive because it seems to assign the right place to divine sovereignty, by making divine commands indispensable for genuine morality. But it is ultimately dangerous, because it casts doubt on the moral attributes of God. According to the naturalist, the moral principles underlying Christian doctrine ought to determine the possible moral implications of Christianity.

10.5 PAGAN VIRTUE

If we believe that the Christian faith prescribes distinctive principles of morality, we may infer that unbelievers have no prospect of following true moral principles or of acquiring genuine moral virtues. This attitude to unbelievers results in the debate about 'pagan virtue', the type and degree of moral virtue that is open to a non-Christian. One's answer to these questions both reflects and determines one's view about the extent to which Christian morality improves virtues that are in principle available to anyone, and the extent to which it rejects and replaces the deceptive appearances of virtue that unbelievers achieve.

---

[33] W. G. Ward, *On Nature and Grace* (London: Burns and Lambert, 1860), 429–90.

[34] Ward cites (450) the definition by Pope Alexander VIII: 'A philosophical or moral sin is an action unfitting to rational nature and to correct reason. A theological and mortal sin, however, is a free transgression of a divine law' (Denziger §2291). Contrast H. Davis, *Moral and Pastoral Theology*. 5th edn. 4 vols. (London: Sheed and Ward, 1946), i 208.

According to St Paul, Christians should be directed towards God not only in their actions, but also in their aims and motives, so that they act for the glory of God and not for the reasons that move non-Christians (Colossians 3:17). One might infer that pagans who lack this distinctive sort of motive cannot acquire genuine virtue. Though they might perform the right actions, they cannot do them for the right reasons, and so their pagan virtue is not virtue. In this spirit Augustine argues that we are moved either by the love of God or by self-seeking appetite,[35] and that since the love of self is the basis of vice, we cannot form true virtue without the love of God.[36] In the same spirit Luther maintains that all the alleged virtues of pagans rest on self-love, and are therefore vices and not virtues. To allow that pagans can have virtues, in his view, is to deny the necessity of divine grace, and to allow justification by works.[37] A similarly rigorous attitude to pagan virtue gained support among Roman Catholics, though not from authoritative sources. Michael Baius attacked pagan claims to virtue in *De Virtutibus Impiorum*, condemned in 1567.[38] His Augustinian argument was revived by the Jansenists, who were condemned in 1690.[39]

Ecclesiastical authorities maintained a less rigorous position. The Council of Trent rejects the view that all the actions of pagans, whatever their reason or motive, are really sins and deserve the hatred of God.[40] The English Articles say that the works of unbelievers have the 'nature' or 'character' of sin.[41] The Westminster Confession takes a similar view, that the works of unbelievers are sinful in so far as they lack the appropriate motive.[42] Neither of these judgements agrees with Luther and Baius.

John Maxwell examines pagan virtue from a moderate point of view. While he agrees that the actions of pagans are sinful,[43] he maintains nonetheless that they have real virtues, in so far as they value moral goodness for its own sake.[44] A defence of Christianity, in his view, does not require us to ridicule all reasons or motives for morality that are accessible to those who do not know the specific rewards and punishments offered by Christianity. Maxwell argues that such ridicule erodes the necessary moral basis for appreciation of Christian claims about God.

---

[35] 'aut cupiditate aut caritate' (Augustine, *De Trinitate*, ix 13).

[36] 'In the earthly city the love of self prevails (praecessit), but in the heavenly city the love of God prevails' (Augustine, *De Civitate Dei* xiv 13). Augustine is sometimes alleged to have described the virtues of the pagans as no more than 'glittering sins' (*splendida peccata*); see Pierre Bayle, *Historical and Critical Dictionary: Selections*, tr. R. H. Popkin (Indianapolis: Bobbs-Merrill, 1965), 401 (Clarification I).

[37] Luther, *Heb.* 1:9, in *Works*, xxix, 119.

[38] On Baius, see Denziger §1925; C. E. Trinkaus, *In Our Image and Likeness* (Chicago: University of Chicago Press, 1970), 74.

[39] On Jansenism, see R. A. Knox, *Enthusiasm* (Oxford: Oxford University Press, 1950), chs 9–12; N. J. Abercrombie, *The Origins of Jansenism* (Oxford: Oxford University Press, 1936), 87–92, 125–58.

[40] Trent: Denziger §1557.

[41] English Articles, §13, in Schaff, *Creeds*, iii.

[42] Westminster Confession, 16.7, in Schaff, *Creeds*, iii.

[43] John Maxwell, in Richard Cumberland, *A Treatise of the Laws of Nature*, tr. J. Maxwell (London, 1727; reprint. ed. J. Parkin, Indianapolis: Liberty Fund, 2005), cxxxvi.

[44] Maxwell, 193–4, 197.

10.6 WHAT DOES CHRISTIAN MORALITY ADD TO MORALITY?

Christian moralists who recognize morality without Christianity have to face a further question: If Christianity is not the foundation of morality, but simply endorses morality, why do we need Christianity as well as morality? Samuel Clarke, John Balguy, and their opponents discuss this question. In Balguy's view, basic moral principles are accessible to reason, and a rational agent who grasps these principles will also be moved to act on them. God, therefore, being a rational agent, knows basic moral principles and acts on them. Being wise and just, God also wants us to act on them; hence God enjoins action on the principles that commend themselves to natural reason. Balguy needs to explain why he does not make Christianity superfluous to morality.

Balguy defends Clarke both against Christians who impugn his Christianity and against Deists who criticize him for failure to embrace Deism. While Deists recognize some sort of divine origin of the world, they see no basis for the personal God of Christian belief, and still less for the Trinity, the Incarnation, and the other distinctive elements of Christianity.[45] They argue that if Clarke puts Christian morality on a secure rational basis, he makes Christianity morally unnecessary, and so ought to be a Deist.

Balguy defends Clarke's view that principles of right hold independently of the will of human beings and of the divine will. We discover them apart from revelation, and our confidence in them increases our confidence in revelation.[46] If we reject natural reason as a source of moral obligation, we cannot explain how religion could oblige our consciences.[47] Balguy comments that if Hobbes thought God's power by itself implied right, 'he must, I think, have laboured under the greatest confusion of ideas that ever befell any understanding'.[48]

But though the basic principles of morality are contained in the natural law and are knowable through natural reason, revelation is still needed to make moral principles more widely known. Human beings have a defective grasp of the truths contained in natural law, because of their proclivity to various vices. Even if the natural law is clear in itself, it may still be obscure to people who are negligent or inattentive or distracted. We can therefore see why God reveals to us principles that we could grasp without revelation, but are unlikely to grasp firmly and clearly.

Moreover, God not only reveals these principles to us, but also makes us aware of the divine command that we observe them, and of the sanctions that support the command.

---

[45] John Balguy, 'Second Letter to a Deist', in *A Collection of Tracts Moral and Theological* (London, 1734), 271–343. This is a reply Matthew Tindal's *Christianity as Old as the Creation* (London, 1731).

[46] See Balguy, *Tracts*, xxix; 370 f.

[47] 'But if the obligations of reason are disowned, and looked upon as mere philosophical fancies, and abstract shadows, I see not, for my part, how any religion can be valid.' (Balguy, *Tracts* 400)

[48] Balguy, *Tracts*, 391.

These sanctions appeal to self-interest.[49] They offer us a further reason for morality, but they do not replace our previous reasons; they simply strengthen our commitment to morality.[50] Deists give no reason for believing that the motives produced by divine sanctions are superfluous or irrelevant to morality, or that they undermine non-religious moral motives.

Maxwell defends a view similar to Balguy's in so far as he takes divine rewards and punishments to be important, but not the only appropriate basis, for morality. Maxwell attacks the Stoics for their view that death is unimportant,[51] and, more generally, for their doctrine of indifferents. If we correct the Stoic position, and allow preferred indifferents to be goods,[52] we are right to see imperfections in our happiness in this life and to hope for complete happiness in an afterlife.[53] Similarly, Clarke argues that belief in the afterlife is morally necessary, because God's approval of virtue and disapproval of vice is not completely manifested in this life. He agrees with the Stoics that 'virtue is truly worthy to be chosen, even merely for its own sake, without any respect to any recompense or reward', but he rejects the rest of the Stoic position.[54] Even if we have a sufficient motive to follow morality without reference to future rewards, we need the appeal to future rewards to support morality by removing objections to it. This is why, according to Clarke, pagan moral precepts are both maintained and perfected in Christian moral teaching and religious practice.[55]

10.7 Moral and Positive Obligations

Should a Christian be satisfied by Clarke's and Balguy's defence of rational morality as a foundation for Christian morality? Some have argued that their defence misses a vital fact, because the Christian revelation imposes demands that do not simply go beyond rational morality, but are basically opposed to it. This objection to rational defences of Christianity is most forcefully presented by Kierkegaard. In Kierkegaard's view, Christianity requires a 'teleological suspension of the ethical'.[56] If he is right, any attempt to contain the Christian life within the bounds of rational morality misses its main point.

---

[49] See Balguy, *Tracts* 9.   [50] See Balguy, *Tracts* 7f.
[51] Maxwell, translation of Cumberland, 73.
[52] This modification would result in a position close to the one defended by Antiochus and presented in Cicero, *De Finibus* v.
[53] Maxwell, 75–6.
[54] Samuel Clarke, *A Discourse concerning the Obligations of Natural Religion*, Proposition 4, in *The Works of Samuel Clarke*, ed. B. Hoadly. 4 vols. (London, 1738), ii 646. See also 629–30.
[55] Clarke, *Discourse*, Proposition 10, 13, in *Works* ii, 675, 680.
[56] S. Kierkegaard, *Fear and Trembling*, tr. H. V. Hong and E. H. Hong (Princeton: Princeton University Press, 1983), 54–67. See also *The Works of Love*, tr. H. V. Hong and E. H. Hong (Princeton: Princeton University Press, 1995).

A version—less extreme than Kierkegaard's—of this Christian criticism of the ethical is presented by some critics of the rational defence offered by Clarke and Balguy.

According to Daniel Waterland's critique of Clarke, Christianity includes 'positive' duties (in the sense of 'positive' in 'positive law' as opposed to natural law). These duties are directly imposed by God, and they are not necessarily constrained by the demands of morality; hence they may sometimes take precedence over moral duties.[57] Since the moral principles that belong to natural law are also expressions of divine commands, they do not necessarily take precedence over positive divine commands.[58] On the contrary, Abraham's willingness to sacrifice Isaac and Mary's willingness to become a mother without being married show that it is sometimes obligatory to obey positive commands rather than moral principles. Obedience to God comes first, and this is the proper basis for observance of the moral law. To deny the primary status of divinely imposed positive duties is to reject Scripture, tradition, and orthodox Christianity.[59]

Some of Waterland's opponents are Deists, who agreed with his view that naturalism about the basis of morality conflicts with any distinctive moral role for Christian doctrine. Butler, however, is an orthodox Christian who accepts naturalism about morality, and yet refuses to draw the conclusion that both Waterland and the Deists accept. Butler's Analogy (published in 1736)[60] defends naturalism, but rejects Deism. In Butler's view, Christianity is both a 'republication of natural religion' including natural morality, and a 'revelation of a particular dispensation of Providence' that enjoins new duties.[61] The Christian revelation introduces both new moral relations apart from commands[62] and new positive duties based on commands that produce moral obligations.[63] None the less, if a positive duty were to conflict with a moral duty (i.e. a duty arising from natural morality without any command), the moral duty would take precedence. We have a positive duty when we do not see the reason for the action we are commanded to do; we have a moral duty when we see the reason for the action. In case of conflict, we ought to do what we see a reason to do rather than what we see no reason to do.[64]

Butler's argument against Waterland rests on the familiar naturalist argument that the right understanding of the moral force of divine commands requires the recognition of moral principles apart from divine commands. If we do not recognize such principles, we cannot explain why we are morally obliged to observe the positive duties enjoined by

---

[57] D. Waterland, Works, ed. W. van Mildert. 6 vols. (Oxford: Oxford University Press, 1856), iv 45.

[58] Waterland, iv 57, 61.

[59] Waterland, Works iv 46, 48.

[60] Full title: The Analogy of Religion, Natural and Revealed to the Constitution and Course of Nature, in The Works of Bishop Butler, ed. J. H. Bernard, 2 vols. (London: Macmillan, 1900), vol. 1.

[61] Butler, Analogy ii 1, 4, 14.

[62] Analogy ii 1.16.

[63] 'Moral precepts are precepts, the reasons of which we see: positive precepts are precepts, the reasons of which we do not see. Moral duties arise out of the nature of the case itself, prior to external command. Positive duties do not arise out of the nature of the case, but from external command; nor would they be duties at all, were it not for such command, received from him whose creatures and subjects we are.' (Analogy ii 1.21)

[64] Analogy ii 1.24.

divine commands. But if we recognize them, we can see why divine revelation is a source of moral duties and motives that go beyond those that are accessible to natural moral understanding.

10.8 DIVINE LOVE AND DIVINE JUSTICE

If we agree that that the moral authority of divine commands depends on the moral attributes of God, what are these attributes? We can find Biblical grounds for ascribing anger, justice, and mercy to God. But above all Christian doctrine speaks of a God of love, and Christian moral reflexion gives love towards God and towards one's neighbour a primary place among moral virtues and principles. Divine love is not a reward for human merits, but the source of all human merit, such as it is. What account of God's moral character can we plausibly construct on this basis?

Hutcheson answers that God is essentially and exclusively benevolent. Divine love necessarily consists in the aim of maximizing the total quantity of good in the universe. Hence God is a utilitarian. The ideal human agent comes as close as possible to God's disinterested concern for maximizing the good.[65] Thomas Bayes agrees with Hutcheson on this point; he argues that all other moral properties we might reasonably ascribe to God are to be analysed into this concern for the total good.[66]

Other Christian moralists disagree with Hutcheson and Bayes about the ultimate moral character of God. Balguy argues for divine rectitude, and Henry Grove for divine wisdom; both of them deny that these properties allow a utilitarian analysis.[67] According to one defender of this conception of the divine attributes, God is perfectly good or benevolent, in so far as God 'promotes the happiness of others so far as it is fit to be promoted'.[68] The reference to fitness implies that other moral principles limit the pursuit of happiness. Similarly, Butler argues that just as benevolence is not the whole of morality, it is not the whole of God's moral character either.[69]

According to the critics of Hutcheson and Bayes, the Christian belief in divine love does not support the reduction of the moral outlook to utilitarian concern for maximizing happiness. In their view, the morally appropriate love of individual persons is formed and guided by principles of justice, fairness, generosity, mercy, and so on, that are not simply derived from a supreme principle of maximizing happiness.

---

[65] Hutcheson on divine benevolence: see W. R. Scott, *Francis Hutcheson* (Cambridge: Cambridge University Press, 1900), 20f; 83f; J. Rae, *Life of Adam Smith* (New York: Kelly, 1965 [originally published 1895]), 12f.

[66] T. Bayes, *Divine Benevolence* (London, 1731).

[67] Balguy, *Divine Rectitude*, reprinted in *Tracts*; Grove, *Wisdom the First Spring of Action in the Deity*. 2nd edn. (London, 1742).

[68] Philip Doddridge, *A Course of Lectures on the Principal Subjects in Pneumatology, Ethics, and Divinity*, ed. S. Clarke (2nd edn. London, 1776), 111.

[69] Butler, *Analogy* i 6.12n.

10.9 Disinterested Love of God

Though the love of God for human beings is not a response to human love for God, it invites and demands a response of love for God. What sort of attitude is this, and how is it related to morality?

If we accept the Augustinian division between self-love and the love of God, so that we take the two alternatives to be mutually exclusive, we will infer, as Luther infers, that the appropriate love of God must be entirely selfless. This demand for selflessness is accepted, and pursued to extremes, by the French Quietists. In their view, Christians are required to love God entirely without reference to thoughts of their own salvation.[70] To the extent that love for God is combined with self-love, to that extent it is unacceptable. Mixed motives are to be rejected: the selfless motive must not be combined with a self-directed motive, even if the selfless motive is sufficient by itself to move us to the right action.[71]

Quietism was fiercely opposed by Bossuet in his controversy with Fénelon, and condemned by ecclesiastical authority.[72] But it exerted some influence in England, on (among others) the early Methodists, and stimulated a debate about the role of disinterested motivation. The Christian moralists who combine voluntarism with egoism assert that disinterested moral approval is neither possible nor desirable.[73] They denounce Quietists as 'enthusiasts' (i.e. fanatics) who revive the error of the Stoics. In so far as the Stoic outlook insists on the supreme value of moral virtue for its own sake, it underestimates self-interest, and so it ignores the importance of the afterlife and of divine rewards and punishments.

Shaftesbury opposes this reaction against Quietism.[74] In his view, the Quietists are right to treat God as a proper object of disinterested love. If we do not regard God in this way, our attitude to God is the servile fear that undermines morality. The prospect of rewards and punishments, in this life or the next life, should not be the sole or primary motive for virtue.[75]

---

[70] On Quietism in 18th-century England see E. Duffy, 'Wesley and the Counter-Reformation', in J. Garnett and C. Matthew (eds), *Revival and Religion since 1700* (London: Hambledon, 1993), 1–19.

[71] A similar demand for purity is sometimes ascribed to Kant, on the assumption that he thinks that we act from duty only if no other motive supports the moral motive in moving us to action. I believe this interpretation of Kant's view is mistaken. Kant's position is discussed further by R. G. Henson, 'What Kant might have said: moral worth and the overdetermination of dutiful action', *Philosophical Review* 88 (1979), 39–54; B. Herman, 'On the value of acting from the motive of duty', in *The Practice of Moral Judgment* (Cambridge, MA: Harvard University Press, 1993), 1–22. (From *Philosophical Review* 90 (1981), 359–82.)

[72] Bossuet's eudaemonism is rather severely examined by Ward, *Nature and Grace*, ch. 3.

[73] See Berkeley *Alciphron* 3.14, in *Works*, eds A. A. Luce and T. E. Jessup. 9 vols. (London: Nelson, 1948–64), iii 136.

[74] Shaftesbury, *Characteristics*, 268.   [75] *Characteristics*, 189f.

Butler agrees with Shaftesbury's defence of a disinterested outlook on morality and of the disinterested love of God. Without the disinterested love of God, religion is nothing more than self-interested calculation.[76] But Butler also asserts the moral appropriateness of self-love and the harmony of self-love and conscience. Just as the disinterested outlook of conscience both can and should coexist with self-love, disinterested love towards God can and should coexist with self-love that refers to God. A sound moral outlook includes disinterested love, directed both to one's neighbour and to God. We avoid the irrational extremes of enthusiasm, therefore, if we ground love for God in awareness of God's moral perfection, as understood by reference to independent standards of moral perfection.[77] We recognize the moral perfection of God in so far as we grasp that God 'cannot' approve anything except what is right 'in itself'. According to Butler, if we hold the correct naturalist view of morality, and the correct view about self-love and disinterested concern for morality, we have the basis for appropriately disinterested love of God as a morally perfect being.

10.10 CASUISTRY

Since Christians believe that Christianity is relevant to morality, they have the task of explaining how it is relevant, and what it requires in specific situations. Since they condemn some actions as wrong and sinful, they need to decide which actions are sinful. In so far as the institutional Church claims to offer guidance and to impose discipline, it needs to guide individuals, and not to leave them to make up their own minds without moral and pastoral direction. These demands on individuals, pastors, and teachers, have produced complex and sophisticated discussions of 'cases of conscience'. The casuistical methods designed to offer advice and direction in these cases are useful outside the pastoral and directive institutions of the Church.

We would not need casuistical advice if we were intuitionists or sentimentalists who believe that the right course of action is always clear in a particular case to someone who has absorbed the right moral principles, or undergone the right moral education, or formed the appropriate sentiments. We could give unqualified advice to such a person,

---

[76] 'Everybody knows,...that there is such a thing as having so great horror of one extreme as to run insensibly and of course into the contrary; and that a doctrine's having been a shelter for enthusiasm, or made to serve the purposes of superstition, is no proof of the falsity of it:...It may be sufficient to have mentioned this in general, without taking notice of the particular extravagances which have been vented under the pretence or endeavour of explaining the love of God; or how manifestly we are got into the contrary extreme, under the notion of a reasonable religion; so very reasonable as to have nothing to do with the heart and affections, if these words signify anything but the faculty by which we discern speculative truth.' (Butler, *Sermons* xiii 1)

[77] 'suppose that they had a real view of that "righteousness, which is an everlasting righteousness"; of the conformity of the Divine will to the law of truth, in which the moral attributes of God consist; of that goodness in the sovereign Mind, which gave birth to the universe' (Butler, *Sermons* xiv 14).

to do what seems right in the particular situation. Nor would we need casuistry if we were act utilitarians who believe that the right action is always discoverable by fully-informed reflexion on maximum utility in a particular case. According to this view, it might be difficult to discover what to do, but the difficulty would result from lack of empirical information, not from any unavoidable moral perplexity. If we accept neither of these views about the character of right action, we need to face the possibility that a good moral case can be made for two or more incompatible courses of action.

The Christian moral outlook that is based on natural law readily leaves room for reflexion on particular cases. The precepts of natural law include rather general principles that prohibit murder and lying, but we need further reflexion to tell us what counts as murder or lying in a particular case. Most Christian moralists agree that self-defence and just war do not count as murder, and that a false statement made in ignorance of the truth does not count as lying. But other cases are more difficult. Some have argued that equivocation, ambiguity, and mental reservation are not cases of lying, because those who speak ambiguously or with mental reservation say what they believe, though their audience does not take them to say what they in fact say. Though these are misleading ways of speaking, they are not wrong because they are lies. They are still normally wrong, but they may sometimes be justified. If the questioner is not entitled to ask the questions, and if I would be open to blame if I gave an unequivocal answer, I ought to give an equivocal and misleading answer.[78] If, for instance, a dangerous armed intruder asks me where his intended victim is, I ought to say 'I don't know'. What I mean is 'I don't know anything that I am obliged to tell you about this'. If the intruder supposes that I mean 'I don't know anything at all', his mistake does not result from any wrongdoing of mine.[79]

Scholastic moralists discuss such question when they consider the scope of the different virtues (as Aquinas does in the Secunda Secundae). Protestant moralists follow their example. In 17th-century England Protestant casuists continue the discussion pursued by Roman Catholic writers, and often use the Roman books on casuistical questions.[80] After the 17th century, casuistry is less popular in England, perhaps partly because of the growing influence of intuitionism and utilitarianism (as described above). The elaboration of casuistical systems and arguments in the 18th century and later has been characteristic of Roman Catholic moral and pastoral theology.[81]

One central debate about casuistical method concerns the resolution of practical doubt. The Church teaches that we are obliged to resolve doubts if we are to act without

---

[78] See Francisco Suarez, *De iuramenti praeceptis* iii 9–10, in *Opera Omnia*, ed. C. Berton, 28 vols. (Paris: Vivès, 1866), xiv 695–9; P. Zagorin, *Ways of Lying* (Cambridge, MA: Harvard University Press, 1990), 182–4.

[79] On mental reservation and its critics see K. E. Kirk, *Conscience and its Problems* (London: Longmans, 1927), 205–6.

[80] An informative survey of casuistry in 17th-century England is Keith Thomas, 'Cases of conscience in seventeenth-century England', in J. Morrill, P. Slack, and D. Woolf (eds), *Public Duty and Private Conscience in Seventeenth-Century England* (Oxford: Oxford University Press, 1991), 29–56.

[81] A good general discussion of casuistry is Kirk, *Conscience*. A historical treatment is offered by A. R. Jonsen and S. E. Toulmin, *The Abuse of Casuistry* (Berkeley: University of California Press, 1988).

sin, and so moralists look for ways to resolve doubts sufficiently for practical purposes. Suppose, then, that we are in doubt about whether we are allowed to equivocate in a particular case, and something can be said on each side of the question. Casuists say that in such a case we have a 'probable' (probabilis, i.e. 'approvable') argument for each side. In this context 'probable' should not be confused with the modern sense of 'probable'; it is crucial for the debate that a case can be probable (in the casuistical sense) even if an argument on the other side is much more probable.[82]

How, then, are we to resolve our doubt about what to do? Different casuistical systems offer different answers. Probabilism answers that if I want to do x, and a probable case can be made to show that a putative law forbidding x either does not exist or does not apply to this situation, I am free to do x. Since this defence of the permissibility of x only has to be probable, I am still free to do x even if I agree that a more probable case can be made to show that the law in question exists and applies to my situation. Probabiliorists take Probabilism to be too lax in its permissions, and so require a more probable case in favour of freedom than in favour of the prohibition. Those who take Probabilism to be too lax and Probabiliorism to be too demanding maintain Equiprobablism, and so require the case for freedom to be at least as probable as the case for prohibition.[83]

These systems are not meant to apply to every sort of case. In particular, they do not apply if my proposed action involves some danger to another person. If, for instance, I am at shooting practice, and it is more probable that a shot will hit a passer-by, the fact that it is merely probable that I will miss the passer-by does not make it permissible to shoot. Nor would it be permissible to shoot if it were simply more probable that I would miss. In such a case I am required to take the safest course of action—the one that will minimize danger to my neighbour, consistently with my legitimate interests.[84]

Setting aside these cases where the safest course of action is mandatory, should we prefer Probabilism or one of its rivals? The case for Probabilism depends on the assumption that we are asking whether we are required to follow a putative law in a particular case. It is generally acknowledged that an uncertain law does not bind. If, however, a probable case can be made to show that there is no law or that it does not apply here, that is enough to make the law uncertain, and therefore non-binding.

Critics of Probabilism reply that a merely probable case to show that the putative law does not apply is not enough to make the law genuinely doubtful. If the probable case for freedom is far less probable than the case for the law, surely we ought not to act as though the law were doubtful. If we think the case for freedom should be at least equal to the

[82] On probable opinions and probability see Ian Hacking, *The Emergence of Probability* (Cambridge: Cambridge University Press, 1975), 20–5.

[83] J A. McHugh and C. J. Callan, *Moral Theology* (New York: Wagner, 1929), Part 1, Question 4, discuss the different casuistical systems. Defences of Probabilism can be found in T. Slater, *A Manual of Moral Theology*, 5th edn. (London: Burns, Oates, and Washbourne, 1925), 37–42; Davis, *Moral and Pastoral Theology* i, 64–115.

[84] These cases are discussed by Alphonsus Liguori, *Theologia moralis*, ed. L Gaudé (Graz: Akademische Druck- und Verlagsanstalt, 1954), i 43–52.

case for the law if we are to justify our acting as though we are free, we are Equiprobablists. If we insist that the law is not doubtful unless we have a more probable case for freedom, we are Probabiliorists.

In defence of the Probabilist approach to these cases, we may consider the parallel with the presumption of innocence in the criminal law. Since being found guilty of a criminal offence is a serious matter, we set the standards of proof rather high. Juries are not permitted to convict a defendant unless they find that guilt is proved beyond a reasonable doubt. To express this standard in casuistical terms, we might say that they cannot convict as long as a probable case for innocence can be made; even if this is less probable than the case for guilt, it is probable enough to create a reasonable doubt. In the civil law we set a lower standard; the plaintiff wins if the case is supported by a preponderance of evidence even if it is not proved beyond a reasonable doubt. Here we take a Probabiliorist view.

These examples of Probabilist and Probabiliorist reasoning may suggest that each method fits different sorts of cases. If it is vital for children who have a certain disease to receive vaccination that is harmless to those who do not have the disease, a merely probable ground for believing that a child has the disease may be thought sufficient to warrant vaccination, and a merely probable ground for believing that a child has not got the disease may be thought an insufficient reason not to vaccinate. If, on the other hand, vaccination is likely to be fatal to those who do not already have the disease, a merely probable ground for believing that a child has the disease is insufficient to warrant vaccination, if the opposing view is more probable.

On this basis we can see how Probabilism and Probabiliorism might also be appropriate for different kinds of moral considerations. Suppose that we recognize a more probable case for the conclusion that we ought to give 50 per cent of our income to charity. The hardship resulting from the imposition of this rule as a requirement would be severe; and so we might refuse to impose it if a probable case can be made for the conclusion that we are not required to do this. But if the hardship resulting from the imposition of a requirement would be very slight, we might be more willing to impose it on Probabiliorist grounds. One might try to justify discrimination between more and less demanding 'Good Samaritan' laws prescribing mutual aid on this basis.

The severity of the hardship resulting from the imposition of a requirement helps to explain the popularity of Probabilism among Roman Catholic moralists. If we are concerned with moral requirements whose violation constitutes mortal sin, it is reasonable to insist on a high standard of proof, and to hold that the appropriate standard has not been met as long as a probable case can be made against a given requirement.

Such a defence of Probabilism, however, has to be qualified not only by the limits on Probabilistic reasoning mentioned above (when various dangers are involved, and the safer course of action is required), but also by the further caution that Probabilism is not meant to give moral advice. It is intended to answer a specific question: Am I committing a sin by violating a moral requirement if I do what I would prefer to do? If a probable case can be made for what I would prefer to do, it is permissible, according to the Probabilist, for me to do it. But it does not follow that it is advisable to do it. It may be far better to do the action for which I see a more probable case.

Probabilism is plausible, therefore, only in conjunction with a division between strictly obligatory actions and supererogatory actions. This division is firmly grounded in Scholastic moral theology, and remains central in modern Roman Catholic systems, including those that accept Probabilism. If some actions are supererogatory, though not obligatory, we may be advised to do them, without being required. Not all Christian moral theologians, however, have accepted the division between the required and the supererogatory. Since the possibility of supererogatory works depends on the possibility of doing more than is required, the (especially) Lutheran view that what we can do is always far less than is required seems to exclude the possibility of doing more than required. The suggestion that we could acquire extra merit by going beyond what is required is especially unwelcome to the forms of Protestant Christianity that take all claims of merit to be inappropriate to Christian morality.[85]

These objections to supererogation may not be decisive. Even if we reject the quasi-commercial idea of accumulating merit automatically by each action that goes beyond what is strictly required, we still have reason to distinguish actions that are impermissible from those that are simply not the best that could be done. If we describe impermissible actions as simply suboptimal, we seem to underestimate their seriousness, so that our attitude is too demanding. If we describe suboptimal actions as impermissible, we seem to impose unreasonable burdens. In so far as Probabilism tries to make moral demands that are both exacting and realistic, it deserves careful attention.

BIBLIOGRAPHY

Abercrombie, N. J. 1936. *The Origins of Jansenism*. Oxford: Oxford University Press.

Alphonsus Liguori 1954. *Theologia moralis*, ed. L Gaudé. Graz: Akademische Druck- und Verlagsanstalt.

Anscombe, G. E. M. 1981. 'Modern moral philosophy', in her *Collected Philosophical Papers*, vol. 3. Minneapolis: University of Minnesota Press, 26–42. (From *Philosophy* 33 (1958), 1–19).

Augustine, 1924. *De Civitate Dei*. ed. J. E. C. Welldon. 2 vols. London: SPCK.

—— *De Trinitate*. Various editions.

Balguy, J. 1734. *A Collection of Tracts Moral and Theological*. London.

Bayes, T. 1731. *Divine Benevolence*. London.

Bayle, P. 1965. *Historical and Critical Dictionary: Selections*, tr. R. H. Popkin. Indianapolis: Bobbs-Merrill.

Berkeley, G. 1948–1964. *Works*, ed. A. A. Luce and T. E. Jessup. 9 vols. London: Nelson.

Butler, J. 1900. *The Works of Bishop Butler*, ed. J. H. Bernard. 2 vols. London: Macmillan.

Calvin, J. 1960. *Institutes of the Christian Religion*, ed. F. L. Battles, tr. J. T. McNeill. 2 vols. London: SCM.

Cicero, *De Finibus*. Various editions.

Clarke, J. 1726. *Foundation of Morality in Theory and Practice*. York.

---

[85] See Augsburg Confession §32; English Articles, no. 14, on works of supererogation. Contrast Davis, *Moral and Pastoral Theology*, i 84.

Clarke, S. 1738. *The Works of Samuel Clarke*, ed. B. Hoadly. 4 vols. London. Reprinted Bristol: Thoemmes, 2002.

Cudworth, R. 1996. *A Treatise concerning Eternal and Immutable Morality, with a Treatise of Freewill*, ed. S. Hutton. Cambridge: Cambridge University Press.

Cumberland, R. 1672. *De Legibus Naturae*. London.

—— 1727. *A Treatise of the Laws of Nature*, tr. J. Maxwell. London. (Reprinted, ed. J. Parkin, Indianapolis: Liberty Fund, 2005.)

Davis, H. 1946. *Moral and Pastoral Theology, 5th edn.* 4 vols. London: Sheed and Ward.

Denziger, H. and Schönmetzer, A. (eds) 1976. *Enchiridion Symbolorum.* 36th edn. Freiburg: Herder.

Dictionnaire de Théologie Catholique. 1903–1946. A. Vacant et al., eds 15 vols. Paris: Letouzey et Ané.

Doddridge, P. 1776. *A Course of Lectures on the Principal Subjects in Pneumatology, Ethics, and Divinity*, 2nd edn., ed. S. Clarke. London: Buckland (1st edn., 1763).

Duffy, E. 1993. 'Wesley and the Counter-Reformation', in J. Garnett and C. Matthew (eds), *Revival and Religion since 1700*. London: Hambledon, 1–19.

Grove, H. 1742. *Wisdom the First Spring of Action in the Deity*. 2nd edn. London.

Hacking, I. 1975. *The Emergence of Probability*. Cambridge: Cambridge University Press.

Henson, R. G. 1979. 'What Kant might have said: moral worth and the overdetermination of dutiful action', *Philosophical Review* 88: 39–54.

Herman, B. 1981. 'On the value of acting from the motive of duty', in *The Practice of Moral Judgment* (Cambridge, MA: Harvard University Press), 1–22. From *Philosophical Review* 90 (1981), 359–82.

Hooker, R. 1888. *Of the Laws of Ecclesiastical Polity*, in *The Works of Richard Hooker*. 7th edn. ed. J. Keble. 3 vols. Oxford: Oxford University Press.

Irwin, T. H. 2007–2009. *Development of Ethics*, 3 vols. Oxford: Oxford University Press.

Jonsen, A. R. and Toulmin, S. E. 1988. *The Abuse of Casuistry: a history of moral reasoning.* Chicago: University of Chicago Press.

Justin Martyr 1857. *First Apology*, in J.-P. Migne (ed.), *Patrologia Graeca*, vol. VI. Paris.

Kierkegaard, S. 1983. *Fear and Trembling; Repetition*, trs. H. V. Hong and E. H. Hong. Princeton: Princeton University Press.

—— 1995. *The Works of Love*, trs. H. V. Hong and E. H. Hong. Princeton: Princeton University Press.

Kirk, K. E. 1927. *Conscience and its Problems*. London: Longmans.

Knox, R. A. 1950. *Enthusiasm*. Oxford: Oxford University Press.

Le Mahieu, D. L. 1976. *The Mind of William Paley*. Lincoln: University of Nebraska Press.

Leibniz, G. W. 1951. *Theodicy*, tr. E. M. Huggard. London: Routledge and Kegan Paul.

Luther, M. 1955–1976. *Luther's Works*, ed. J. Pelikan and H. T. Lehmann. 56 vols. St Louis: Concordia.

——1961a. *Lectures on Romans*, tr. W. Pauck. London: SCM Press.

—— 1961b. *Selections*, ed. J. Dillenberger. Garden City: Doubleday.

McHugh, J. H. and Callan, C. J. 1929. *Moral Theology: a Complete Course*, 2 vols. New York: Wagner.

Mahoney, J. 1987. *The Making of Moral Theology*. Oxford: Oxford University Press.

Origen 1967. *Contra Celsum*, ed. M. Bonnet. 5 vols. Paris: Cerf.

Paley, W. 2002. *Principles of Moral and Political Philosophy*, ed. D. L. Le Mahieu. Indianapolis: Liberty Fund.

Pufendorf, S. 1996. *Eris Scandica*, in *Gesammelte Werke*, ed. W. Schmidt-Biggemann. 5 vols. Berlin: Akademie-Verlag, vol. v, 209. 19–30.

Rae, J. 1965. *Life of Adam Smith*. Reprinted with introduction by J. Viner. New York: Kelly. (First published 1895).

Schaff, P. 1931. *The Creeds of Christendom*, 6th edn. 3 vols. New York: Harper & Row.

Scott, W. R. 1900. *Francis Hutcheson*. Cambridge: Cambridge University Press.

Shaftesbury, Earl of 1999. *Characteristics of Men, Manners, Opinions, Times*, ed. L. E. Klein. Cambridge: Cambridge University Press.

Slater, T. 1925. *A Manual of Moral Theology*, 5th edn. London: Burns, Oates, and Washbourne.

Suarez, F. 1866. *Opera Omnia*, ed. C. Berton. 28 vols. Paris: Vivès.

Thirty-Nine Articles, in P. Schaff (ed.), *The Creeds of Christendom*, 6th edn. 3 vols. New York: Harper & Row, volume iii.

Thomas, K. V. 1991. 'Cases of conscience in seventeenth-century England', in J. Morrill, P. Slack, and D. Woolf (eds), *Public Duty and Private Conscience in Seventeenth-Century England*. Oxford: Oxford University Press, 29–56.

Tindal, M. 1731. *Christianity as Old as the Creation. or, the Gospel, a Republication of the Religion of Nature*. London.

Trinkaus, C. E. 1970. *In Our Image and Likeness: humanity and divinity in Italian humanist thought*. Chicago: University of Chicago Press.

Ward, W. G. 1860. *On Nature and Grace*. London: Burns and Lambert.

Waterland, D. 1856. *Works*, ed. W. van Mildert. 6 vols. Oxford: Oxford University Press.

Whewell, W. 1852. *Lectures on the History of Moral Philosophy in England*. London: Parker.

Whichcote, B. 1753. *Moral and Religious Aphorisms*, eds. J. Jeffery and S. Salter. London.

Zagorin, P. 1990. *Ways of Lying*. Cambridge, MA: Harvard University Press.

CHAPTER 11

NATURE, LAW, AND NATURAL LAW

T. H. IRWIN

11.1 WHY A LAW OF NATURE?

THE first known use of the phrase 'law of nature' occurs in Plato's *Gorgias*, in the mouth of Callicles, who rejects the 'convention' or 'law' (*nomos*) of ordinary social morality by appeal to a distinct law that is derived from nature. He treats natural law as a source of action-guiding principles independent of the rules and practices of particular societies, and grounded in facts about human nature.

Later defenders of natural law do not share Callicles' desire to avoid the normal demands of other-regarding morality. On the contrary, they try to show that these demands have a firm basis in nature. But they share Callicles' ambition of finding a basis for morality outside rules and practices that rely on the decisions or conventions of a particular society.

Hence natural law theories claim: (1) Some moral principles do not rest simply on human agreements. (2) They have an objective basis in facts about human nature. (3) These facts about human nature are (or underlie) a law for human actions.[1]

These claims raise some elementary questions about theories of natural law: (1) What are the relevant natural facts? (2) How do they provide a basis for morality? (3) What makes them a natural law, and how does law provide a source of morality?

Since different people accept the three claims, but give different answers to the three questions, natural law theories display considerable variety.

---

[1] On 'are' v. 'underlie' see section 11.11 below.

11.2 Theories of Natural Law[2]

Outlines of a conception of natural law are present in Plato's *Laws*, and in Aristotle's *Ethics*.[3] A doctrine of natural law is clearly formulated by the Stoics.[4] Philo combines the Stoic and Platonist views with his interpretation of some elements of the Mosaic Law as a statement of the requirements of natural law.[5]

These sources probably underlie St Paul's recognition of a universal natural law that reveals the basic principles of morality. The Gentiles are capable of grasping the moral law, because they are 'law to themselves' without the guidance of the Mosaic Law.

> For whenever Gentiles, those who have not law, by nature do the things belonging to the law, these, not having law, are law to themselves, <since> they show the work of the law written in their hearts, their conscience co-witnessing, and their reasonings among one another accusing or else excusing. (*Romans*. 2:14–15)

St Paul's formulation, accepted by John Chrysostom, Lactantius, Augustine, and other Christian Fathers, fixes a doctrine of natural law firmly in Christian moral theology and philosophy.

Among the mediaeval Scholastics, Aquinas, Scotus, and Ockham examine the connexion between the natural aspects of natural law, and the legal aspects that consist in divine commands such as those summarized in the Decalogue. Later Scholastics (including Vasquez, Hooker, and Suarez) and their 17th-century successors (including Grotius, Hobbes, Pufendorf, Barbeyrac, Leibniz, Locke, and Cumberland) pursue this debate about the natural and the legal elements in natural law.

Butler's *Sermons* offer a compact statement of a naturalist doctrine. The first three sermons set out his account of human nature. He alludes to Classical, Biblical, and Scholastic sources to describe the connexion between morality and nature:

> That the ancient moralists had some inward feeling or other, which they chose to express in this manner, that man is born to virtue, that it consists following nature, and that vice is more contrary to this nature than tortures or death, their works in our hands are instances. (*Sermons*, Preface 13)

> The apostle asserts that the Gentiles *do by* NATURE *the things contained in the law*.... He intends to express, more than that by which they *did not*, that by which they *did* the works of the law; namely, *by nature*.... [T]here is a superior principle

---

[2] Further details, and fuller reference and quotations, may be found in Irwin 2007–2009, especially chs. 21, 26, 30–3, 41–4, 51, 53, 72, 94. Crowe 1977 offers a historical account of views on natural law. The main text in Aquinas is *Summa Theologiae* (*ST*) 1–2 q90–7. Some relevant passages in Scotus are collected in Wolter 1986. Some passages from modern authors are collected in Schneewind 2003.

[3] I have discussed the *Laws* in Irwin 2010. Aquinas connects natural law with Aristotle's views on natural justice, at *Commentary on EN* §1018.

[4] See Lactantius, *Divinae Institutiones,* vi 8.6–9 = Cicero. *De Re Publica.* iii 27; Cicero, *De Legibus* i 23.

[5] Philo, *Abraham* 275–6.

of reflexion or conscience in every man, which distinguishes between the internal principles of his heart, as well as his external actions; which passes judgment upon himself and them; pronounces determinately some actions to be in themselves just, right, good; others to be in themselves evil, wrong unjust…It is by this faculty, natural to man, that he is a moral agent, that he is a law to himself. (*Sermons* ii 8–9)

Butler maintains that nature and natural law are a basis for morality. His view has been both attacked and defended. In contemporary moral theory, some version of naturalism is defended, on the one hand, by the Roman Catholic Church, and, on the other hand, by non-theological philosophers such as Philippa Foot.[6]

This bare chronological outline shows that the discussion of natural law is a major theme of ancient, mediaeval, and modern moral philosophy. In fact, this discussion should warn us not to draw sharp lines between ancient, mediaeval, and modern views, if we want to mark philosophically significant differences.

Some critics, however, have claimed that Grotius' treatment of natural law marks a distinctively modern point of view, beginning in the 17th century.[7] Claims about discontinuity, originality, and modernity betray inattention to the Scholastic sources of the modern disputes.

In the rest of this chapter, therefore, I neglect chronological order, in order to discuss some of the main questions thematically. Since the best statement of a particular position is sometimes found in one of its later defenders, I will use, for instance, Pufendorf and Butler to clarify some of the questions that arise in earlier discussions.

11.3 NATURE AND LAW

In my historical outline I have not separated naturalism—the appeal to nature and natural facts—from a doctrine of natural law. Should we separate them? Might we not believe that appeals to nature are morally relevant, but deny that these appeals introduce natural law? I suggested above that an appeal to nature is one thing, and an appeal to law is another. Perhaps my failure to distinguish questions about naturalism from questions about natural law has led me to exaggerate the breadth or the continuity of the debate about natural law.

A sound distinction between naturalism and natural law theory requires some understanding of law in this context. But questions about the relevant type of law, or the relevant sense of 'law', are among the disputed questions about natural law. I will explain this point later, but for the moment I will speak indifferently of naturalism (appeal to natural facts) and natural law theory (appeal to natural laws).

The various theories of natural law all take facts about nature, and specifically about human nature, to be morally important. As Suarez puts it, rational nature is the

[6] See Foot 2001.   [7] See Schneewind 1997; Tuck 1987; Haakonssen 1996, 1998.

foundation of objective right and wrong in human moral actions.[8] Facts about human nature provide a basis from which we can derive correct moral conclusions. These conclusions do not simply state our preferences; they are objectively correct in so far as they are derived from the appropriate objective facts.

This statement of the moral significance of a doctrine of natural law may persuade some readers that this doctrine does not deserve further consideration. Some critics maintain that no facts of this sort could do what the doctrine of natural law requires them to do. We may suppose that no facts whatever could provide the right sort of basis for moral conclusions, or that no natural facts could provide it.

And so the common core of different views about natural law may already appear to be so implausible that it is not worth trying to decide between the different views. It is useful, therefore, to ask how implausible the core really is.

11.4 METAETHICAL OBJECTIONS

Natural law theory appears to commit the metaethical error that Moore calls the 'naturalistic fallacy'. If an appeal to nature identifies moral properties such as goodness, rightness, and obligation, with natural facts, it seems not to give an acceptable account of such properties, since one can significantly ask whether acting in accord with one's nature is good.

This anti-naturalist argument claims:[9] (1) The meaning of moral terms is not given by definitions that mention natural properties, such as being in accordance with human nature. (2) Meanings correspond to properties. (3) Therefore, moral properties cannot be identical to natural properties.

We may reasonably question the first premiss of this argument. Moore's main reason for claiming that naturalism commits a fallacy is his Open Question Argument. But since this argument rests on unreasonable conditions for definitions, it does not expose any fallacy in naturalistic definitions. Even if Moore had a clear account of what natural properties or naturalistic definitions are, he would not have shown that they raise any special difficulties.

But even if we accept some version of Moore's argument against naturalism, it does not affect the main naturalist contentions. If one claims, as Butler does, that what is right is what accords with nature, this need not be a claim about meanings or concepts. It may be a claim about properties. When Aristotle claims that happiness or virtue depend on living in accord with nature, he does not claim that the concepts or meanings of 'good', 'happiness', 'virtue', and so on are to be identified with the concepts of function, agreement with nature, and so on. He claims that the relevant terms refer to natural properties.

---

[8] Suarez, *De Legibus* ii 5.6.

[9] The relation between Aristotle's claims and Moore's arguments is complex. It depends on, e.g., (i) Moore's conception of a natural property; (ii) whether Aristotelian claims about nature involve only the properties that Moore counts as 'natural' (or those he counts as 'metaphysical'; see his comments on Stoic claims about nature, *Principa Ethica* §67).

11.5 AN AGGREGATIVE CONCEPTION
OF NATURE: MILL AND HOBBES

Even if naturalism commits no conceptual error, we might still doubt whether it could give sufficient reason for moral conclusions.

This doubt is reasonable if claims about human nature tell us what everyone, or almost everyone, is like and what everyone does.[10] Mill's essay 'Nature' is a clear statement of this doubt. Mill assumes that human nature is simply the aggregate of traits and characteristics that human beings share apart from those they acquire socially.[11] Attempts to justify actions or states of affairs by appeals to nature and to natural law rest on the untenable assumption that what is generally true of people, apart from training or education or society, is what they ought to do. If, then, Mill's purely aggregative conception of human nature is the only possible one, he is right to suppose that appeals to human nature do not supply a good guide to what is right.

Despite these criticisms, however, the aggregative conception of nature may contribute to the explanation and justification of morality. According to Hobbes the science of the laws of nature is 'the true and only moral philosophy', which is 'nothing but the science of what is good, and evil, in the conversation and society of mankind'.[12] To discover the laws of nature, we begin with an aggregative conception of human nature as a collection of desires without a system. Nothing about one desire makes it inherently better or more reasonable than another, and practical reason does not endorse any desires in their own right. The only use for practical reason is instrumental, because it can find the means to satisfy our predominant desire.

Our predominant desire is to preserve ourselves and to secure the way of our future desire. Practical reason, therefore, can find the means to self-preservation, and the laws of nature are exactly these means. Hence a law of nature is 'a precept, or general rule, found out by reason, by which a man is forbidden to do that which is destructive of his life or taketh away the means of preserving the same'.[13] Reason prescribes means to ends that, in the circumstances Hobbes describes, everyone will want more than they want any other ends.

Human beings without morality are in the state of nature. In these circumstances reason does not prescribe the observance of moral rules or practices, because an individual can see that it is in his interest to follow them. To this extent morality cannot be justified by direct appeal to human nature. Nevertheless an understanding of human nature helps to explain and to justify morality. In the state of nature, we compete for scarce resources, without any moral restraint, but we also recognize that we would all be better off if we

---

[10] Moore discusses naturalism, so understood, in *Principa Ethica* ch. 2. He discusses a metaphysical conception of nature in ch. 4.

[11] 'Those parts of our mental and moral constitution which are supposed to be innate, in contradistinction to those which are acquired' (Mill, 'Nature' 399).

[12] *Leviathan*, 15.40.   [13] *Leviathan*, 14.3.

could rely on the security that we would gain if could rely on each other to keep promises, tell the truth, guarantee security from assault, and so on. When self-interested reason recognizes all these things, 'reason prescribes peace to be good'.[14] The precept of reason is the empirical proposition that peace promotes the satisfaction of our predominant desires.

We might object that this empirical proposition is not a precept of reason because it is not a genuine precept at all; it does not assert that we ought to seek peace, that we have a reason to seek peace, or that we have a duty or obligation to seek peace. Hobbes answers that natural laws, as he understands them, impose obligations. As Hobbes conceives obligation, it consists in the removal of freedom. Physical obligation obliges us to stay where we are if we are bound hand and foot. In non-physical obligation 'liberty is taken away...by hope or fear', rather than by physical restraint.[15] If we believe that peace best promotes our self-preservation, we want peace above all, so that we are no longer free not to seek peace, and we are 'bound' to seek peace. This binding creates our obligation to seek peace. Our predominant desire is the motive that is the obligation.

In this way, then, the laws of nature oblige us. When we see that observance of them[16] promotes our interest, hope and anticipation of future good to ourselves dominates every other motive, and so compels us to act. This compulsion is obligation, which removes our freedom to violate the laws of nature.[17] Ignorance of the content and implications of the laws of nature explain why some people violate them.[18] But once we understand the benefits of peace, we can find ways to secure our general agreement to follow the principles of morality, and to remove the circumstances that make people believe that they will be better off if they violate morality. Recognition of the benefits of peace moves us to make a 'covenant', or social contract, to set up a sovereign; the sanctions available to the sovereign remove the remaining incentives to violate the terms of the covenant.[19] Our obligation to abide by moral principles results partly from the motives that are attached to peace and partly from the motives that result from fear of punishment for violation.

This is what Hobbes means by saying that the laws of nature and the virtues connected with them oblige us, and are laws, in the court of conscience,[20] because the fulfilment of the natural law is 'all we are obliged to by rational nature'.[21] The laws of nature do not oblige any agents who do not seek to preserve themselves and to secure the way of their future desire. They do not tell us to preserve ourselves; they only tell us what we need to

---

[14] Hobbes, *De Cive* 3.31.   [15] *De Cive* 15.7.

[16] In the state of nature the laws of nature bind only 'in foro interno': 'that is to say, to a desire they should take place: but in foro externo; that is, to the putting them into act, not always' (*Leviathan* 15.36).

[17] *De Cive* 3.26.

[18] *De Cive* 2.1n4: 'the whole breach of the laws of nature consists in the false reasoning, or rather folly of those men who see not those duties they are necessarily to perform towards others in order to their own conservation.'

[19] Questions about Hobbes' account of the basis of the social contract are discussed by Hampton 1986; Gauthier 1990.

[20] *De Civ.* 3.29. Conscience; cf. *De Cive* 12.2.   [21] *De Civ.* 3.30.

do if we want to preserve ourselves. They create obligations by being empirical propositions about means to self-preservation. If they were not propositions about self-preservation, we could not explain how reason could prescribe them, or how they could oblige everyone who understands what they say.

11.6 NATURE AND MORALITY: HOBBES

Why should we suppose that counsels of self-preservation give us the content of morality? Hobbes' answer relies on two main claims: (1) The principles of morality prescribe means to the preservation of peace. (2) The supreme counsel of self-preservation tells us to seek peace and preserve it. To support his first claim, Hobbes offers a consequentialist account of the basic principles of morality to show that they are rules and practices that preserve stability, security, and mutual trust among members of a society. To support his second claim, he argues that self-preservation requires the preservation of a stable society that averts the dangers of a war of all against all.

Hobbes describes the laws of nature as different ways of treating other people fairly and with respect. They prohibit arrogance and they prescribe truthfulness, the keeping of promises, living in harmony with one's neighbours, and so on. Sometimes they require us to act against our advantage. But since they preserve peace, reason instructs us to observe them in our own interest.[22]

This derivation of morality from human nature explains why Hobbes believes that he is the first to have discovered that the study of the laws of nature reveals the essential character of the virtues. In his view, previous moral philosophers, even those who believed in natural law, have not recognized that the moral virtues are 'the means of peaceable, sociable, and comfortable living'. Even though they have identified particular virtues and moral principles, they have not understood what they have in common. They have assumed that moral principles create obligation, but they have not explained why. Hobbes answers these questions by arguing that the virtues are essentially laws of nature, as he conceives them, and that therefore we have a predominant motive, hence an obligation, to observe them in the appropriate circumstances.

If Hobbes' argument is cogent, he has shown that an appeal to human nature can do what Mill says it cannot do; for he has argued that we can both explain and justify the principles of morality by reference to the dominant motives in human nature. How cogent is his argument?

We may raise questions at different stages: (1) We may doubt whether morality consists entirely of principles that preserve the peace of society. If a given society can be preserved only by wrongdoing, morality and the peace of society may conflict. (2) We may doubt whether self-preservation always requires us to do what promotes the preservation of a society. Though Hobbes is right to emphasize the connexion between

---

[22] This indirect egoist aspect of Hobbes' views is explored by Kavka 1986.

peace and self-preservation, we might decide that he exaggerates the coincidence between them. (3) We may doubt whether the desire for self-preservation is as dominant as Hobbes supposes. On the one hand, we seem to be capable of acting irrationally against our self-preservation. On the other hand, we may believe we are capable of acting rationally against self-preservation for moral reasons. (4) We may question Hobbes' attempt to reduce practical reason and obligation to empirical propositions that promote the satisfaction of our predominant desire.

These doubts about Hobbes' main claims are all well founded, but they do not require us to reject his views entirely. For even if he is mistaken, he may grasp part of the truth about human nature, and may capture some of the aspects of morality that make it a relatively stable institution for human beings who are sometimes moved by some degree of prudence. But our doubts about the questionable elements in his conception of human nature and its relation to morality may encourage us to ask whether something more can be made of an appeal to nature.

11.7 A HOLISTIC CONCEPTION OF NATURE

Mill and Hobbes assume that facts about the natural traits and characteristics of human beings are all the facts about human nature. According to Butler's Aristotelian conception of nature, this purely aggregative conception is wrong, because facts about human nature as a system are distinct from facts about what human beings naturally do. To speak of a thing's nature and of what is in accord with its nature is to select among its natural tendencies, since they may not all accord with the nature of the whole. Hence Aristotle connects a thing's nature with its function, its essence, and with the kind that it belongs to.[23] The essence of a natural organism is the whole goal-directed system in which different parts, processes, and activities have functions that maintain the whole. States and processes that are in accord with something's nature as a whole are suitable for the whole system.

This holistic and teleological conception of a nature implies that not everything natural accords with a thing's nature. We have natural tendencies that need to be restrained because they do not accord with our nature as a whole; if we fall ill, or eat or drink too much, or tire too easily, or exert ourselves too much at the wrong times, we behave in accord with natural tendencies, but we act against our nature as a whole. We assume that our nature constitutes a system, in so far as the different parts of it are explained functionally. They work as they do because of their role in maintaining the system. To this extent a natural system is similar to a machine, but it differs from a machine in so far as it tends to maintain itself.[24]

---

[23] Annas 1993: ch. 4 discusses Aristotle's appeal to nature, and its development in later Peripatetics.
[24] Cummins 1975 discusses some of the relevant questions about functional and teleological explanation.

Holistic judgements about something's nature explain some familiar judgements about welfare.[25] There used to be an advertisement for stout that said 'Guinness is good for you'. It was withdrawn after a complaint that it made an unsubstantiated claim. The complaint was reasonable, because it took the claim about the benefits of stout to rely on a holistic judgement. The claim that stout is good for us does not simply mean that all or most of us will like stout, or that drinking it will strengthen some natural tendencies (e.g. by making us thirsty when we think of stout); both of these claims might be true even if stout were bad for us. It means that drinking stout will strengthen some natural tendencies and weaken others, in ways that will strengthen the natural system as a whole. To show that stout is good for us, therefore, we presuppose some judgements about our nature as a whole. These judgements do not simply record what happens to us without intervention. On the contrary, medical interventions, such as transfusions of blood or transplantations of organs, may interfere with the ordinary course of nature and may conflict with strong natural tendencies, but they may still be in accord with nature, according to the holist conception.

These holistic judgements about nature show that Mill's objection to naturalism rests on a misunderstanding. If we believe that illness is bad for us and health is good for us, we do not think of ourselves as we would be if our natural tendencies were left without any human intervention; we think of the proper working of the system that constitutes our human nature. Though further enquiry may be needed to understand these judgements completely, the naturalist may fairly observe that we treat them as familiar and indispensable.

11.8 NATURE AND THE PRECEPTS OF NATURAL LAW

If, then, holistic judgements about nature are sometimes legitimate, how often are they legitimate and how much can they prove? Since naturalism offers an account of the basis of morality and the moral virtues, it has to go beyond the simple holistic judgements we have considered. Naturalism claims that human nature gives us the right account of the human good and of the virtues that make someone a good human being. What, then, do we have to understand about human nature in order to reach the correct conclusions about the good and about the virtues?

Aquinas claims that 'according to the order of natural inclinations is the order of precepts of the law of nature'.[26] He explains this general claim by connecting different provisions of the natural law with different natural inclinations. (1) The inclination that supports precepts about self-preservation rests on the nature we share with all other natural substances. (2) The inclination that supports precepts about the satisfaction and

---

[25] On 'medical goodness' see Von Wright 1963: 50–62.   [26] 1–2 q94 a2.

control of bodily appetites rests on the nature we share with other animals. (3) The inclination that supports precepts about social life rests on our nature as rational animals.[27]

These claims about different inclinations and the appropriate precepts depend on a holistic conception of nature. Aquinas does not mean that because we want to stay alive we need precepts about self-preservation; a precept corresponding to every desire would result in morally questionable precepts. He means that as goal-directed systems that can aim at our good, we need to stay alive and to preserve ourselves. Similarly, the second set of precepts, those applying to the nature we share with other animals, coordinate our natural desires so that the excessive satisfaction of one of them does not prevent the satisfaction of the others.

These appeals to nature help us to understand Aquinas' claims about the rational aspects of human nature and the naturally social character of human beings.[28] He believes that the human good essentially requires the exercise of practical reason in the direction of one's life. We need it to discover the appropriate precepts for the regulation of the desires we share with other animals, but this instrumental function of practical reason does not exhaust the contribution of practical reason to our good. We recognize the non-instrumental good of practical reason, in so far as we value self-direction by our own practical reason, apart from its instrumental effectiveness.

Aquinas believes that the good of a human being as a rational agent requires social life. Grotius affirms this naturalist view in so far as he finds the basis of natural law in 'necessary appropriateness or inappropriateness to rational and social nature'.[29] Rationality requires sociality because a rational agent recognizes other rational agents as potential collaborators in rational deliberation and action. Someone who aims at the exercise of practical reason in his life cannot reasonably confine it to himself; he needs to improve his rational agency in cooperation with the rational agency of others.

11.9 Nature and the Human Good

If we can understand appeals to nature through Aquinas' division of precepts, can we derive anything useful from them? A few examples may suggest how they support some defensible moral claims.

---

[27] q94 a2; a4; q95 a4.

[28] q95 a4. 'Thirdly, a human being has a tendency towards a good in accordance with the nature of reason, which is proper to him. Thus he has a natural tendency towards grasping the truth about God, and towards living in society. And on this ground the things that refer to this sort of tendency belong to the natural law; for instance, to avoid ignorance, not to offend those he ought to interact with, and other things of this sort that refer to this.' (q94 a2).

[29] *De iure belli et pacis*, i 1.12.1. Grotius adds in §7: 'But a human being of mature age knows to treat like cases alike, and has a dominant desire for society, and is the only animal who has language, as a special means to fulfil this desire. Hence it is reasonable to suppose that he also has a capacity for knowing and acting in accordance with general precepts; the things that turn out to be appropriate for him do not belong to all animals, but are suitable for human nature.'

Naturalism appeals to nature in two ways: (1) Nature provides the basis for claims about the good for, or the good of, or the welfare of, a person. (2) It also provides the basis for claims about the goodness, excellence, or perfection of a person. According to an Aristotelian view, the virtues that perfect a person's nature also achieve the good of a person with this nature.[30]

The first naturalist claim rejects a subjectivist view of a person's good. According to a subjectivist view, a person's good is his pleasure, or the satisfaction of his desires, or the satisfaction of his rational desires. But such a view faces the objection that we can enjoy and want what is bad for us.[31] Naturalism argues that this subjective conception of welfare leaves out an essential element. What is good for a tree, a dog, or a human being depends on the different natures and characteristics of these organisms, and a person's desires are correct only if they match what is good for the kind of thing a person is.

Is this naturalist conception of welfare clear enough to inform our choices? The Aristotelian claim that a human being is essentially a rational agent may seem too general to be useful. But sometimes it seems to make a difference. A subjective view of welfare is unhelpful whenever our actions will alter the character of our own desires or of other people's. If we form someone's desires so that they are easiest to satisfy (if we want to minimize the number or unsatisfied desires) or result in the greatest pleasure, we do not seem to have done our best to promote their welfare. If children growing into adults, or adults modifying their desires, never acquire anything beyond childish desires, they are missing something that would make them better off.[32] What they are missing depends on what they are capable of, and what they are capable of reflects their nature.

That is why we promote the welfare of children and of the adults they will become by helping them to develop their abilities, and not by simply assuring the satisfaction of their desires. The development of one's abilities does not necessarily increase one's pleasure or the satisfaction of one's desires. It may indeed have the opposite effect; for the more one tries to achieve, the greater the opportunity for frustration and dissatisfaction. None the less, we achieve the good for ourselves only in so far as we achieve the good for the kind of thing we are. Our nature gives us the law, in so far as it is the basis for a true conception of our good.

Some implications of this naturalist conception of welfare are set out by Mill in *On Liberty*. We have seen that he criticizes appeals to nature, on the assumption that the aggregative conception of nature is correct. But elsewhere he implicitly recognizes that a

---

[30] Here I present naturalism as a specific version of eudaemonism. But one might also be a naturalist without being a eudaemonist, as Butler is.

[31] See, e.g., Brandt 1979; Velleman 1988. Attempts to modify a subjectivist theory to meet this obvious objection appeal to hypothetical wants (what we would want in idealized circumstances; what the idealized agent would want. Such modifications seem to face a dilemma: (a) Perhaps the hypothetical wants are defined non-circularly, without any reference to the desires of agents who know what is good for them. In that case, they still face plausible counterexamples of people who want what is clearly bad for them. (b) They avoid these counterexamples only by introducing some unreduced reference to the agent's good.

[32] See Aristotle, *EN* 1174a1.

holistic conception is tenable, and that therefore some aspects of naturalism are defensible. For he appeals to the human good 'in the largest sense, grounded on the permanent interests of man as a progressive being'.[33] He understands this good as 'human development in its richest diversity'.[34] When Mill argues for freedom of thought and for experimentation in ways of living, he assumes that the human good consists in the development and realization of distinctively human capacities. Hence he appeals to nature to support his social and political arguments, since his account of the human good includes naturalist and perfectionist elements.[35] To make his position consistent, he ought to abandon his general attack on naturalism, since he acknowledges that some appeals to nature are legitimate and morally important.

We can strengthen the case for naturalism by noticing a similar appeal to nature in a theorist who officially maintains, as Mill does, a subjective conception of the good. Though Rawls takes a person's good to be the satisfaction of rational desire, he also endorses an 'Aristotelian Principle', which says that 'other things equal, human beings enjoy the exercise of their realized capacities'. The realization of capacities is subordinate to Rawls' subjective account of the good. If some people do not enjoy the exercise of their realized capacities, it is not good for them. If they prefer to count blades of grass, their good consists in the satisfaction of that preference.[36]

Though Rawls' position is more consistent than Mill's, it is less plausible. According to Mill, we would harm people by training them to be content to count blades of grass, even if that is what they would prefer after they had been trained. According to Rawls, we would do them no harm if we trained them to form this preference. This implication is difficult to accept; if A had formed B's preferences in this way, A would hardly have attended to B's welfare. If Mill is right against Rawls, we should abandon Mill's opposition to naturalism.

11.10 NATURAL SOCIALITY AND MORALITY

These arguments about nature and welfare indicate the contribution of naturalism to the understanding of the good. What, then, does it contribute to the understanding of morality? How plausible is it to claim that basic moral principles are requirements of natural law?

When Butler claims that morality is natural, he intends to contrast his position with Hobbes' view. According to Hobbes' purely aggregative view of human nature, morality is not natural, and, contrary to Aristotle, a human being is not naturally a political animal.[37] Society does not come naturally to human beings, both because they compete for scarce goods and because they struggle for superiority.[38] Human nature gives us a sufficient reason and motive, in the circumstances of the state of nature, for establishing

---

[33] Mill, *On Liberty*, 1.11.   [34] Mill quotes from Humboldt.
[35] On naturalism and perfectionism see Hurka 1993. Kitcher 1999 expresses some sceptical doubts.
[36] Rawls 1999: 364, 372–80.   [37] Hobbes on Aristotle; *De Cive* 1.2.   [38] Hobbes, *Leviathan* 17.7–8.

moral practices as a means to the preservation of peace. Morality removes an obstacle to our goals; it does not embody any of our goals. Morality is desirable for me not because of my nature, but because of the unwelcome results of behaviour that tends to disturb peace and security.

Butler rejects Hobbes' view in favour of Hutcheson's view that human nature itself, rather than the specific circumstances of our environment, supports morality.[39] According to Hutcheson, the moral outlook is natural because it is a natural altruistic sentiment, and is not simply a means to secure some end that would appeal to us even if we had no such sentiment. Butler agrees that we have this altruistic sentiment,[40] but he rejects Hutcheson's sentimentalist claim that our moral attitudes consist in a non-rational moral sense.[41] Sentimentalists do not see that human nature is a system and morality is part of the system.[42]

Butler argues, therefore, against both Hobbes and Hutcheson, that morality is essential to the rational guidance of human life in accordance with the nature of human beings as rational agents. He agrees with Grotius' Scholastic view that human beings are naturally social. According to this view, we have no reason to regret the aspects of human life that make cooperative action necessary and beneficial for us. We should welcome rational cooperation for its own sake, because it allows us to guide our lives in accordance with practical reason.

The rational and social character of human nature determines the character of the moral virtues.[43] These virtues perfect virtuous agents as rational and social beings. The virtues do not simply restrain one's own natural tendencies for other people's benefit. They belong to 'human development in its richest diversity' (as Humboldt and Mill put it). Someone is not better off if he can satisfy all his desires without any non-instrumental cooperative relations to other people. He is missing something, just as he would be if he cared only about childish amusements. Cooperative rational agency develops and extends rational agency. In so far as morality encourages and supports cooperative rational agency, it fulfils human nature.

This belief in the natural character of morality opposes not only Hobbesian and sentimentalist views, but also a Kantian view of nature and morality.[44] From a

[39] See Hutcheson's *Inaugural Lecture on the social nature of man.*

[40] Butler, *Sermons*, Preface, 18–21.

[41] Butler, *Sermons*, Preface, 25–6.

[42] 'But it may be said, "What is all this, though true, to the purpose of virtue and religion?. These require, not only that we do good to others when we are led this way, by benevolence or reflection happening to be stronger than other principles, passions, or appetites, but likewise that the whole character be formed upon thought and reflection; that every action be directed by some determinate rule, some other rule than the strength and prevalency of any principle or passion.... it does not appear that there ever was a man who would not have approved an action of humanity rather than of cruelty; interest and passion being quite out of the case. But interest and passion do come in, and are often too strong for and prevail over reflection and conscience.... does not man...act agreeably to his nature, or obey the law of his creation, by following that principle, be it passion or conscience, which for the present happens to be strongest in him?"' (Butler, *Sermons* ii 3)

[43] Rational and social nature; Grotius, *De iure belli et pacis*, i 1.12.1.

[44] This is a one-sided claim about Kant. I do not mean to suggest that his position is wholly opposed to naturalism.

non-naturalist[45] point of view, morality belongs to the area of freedom rather than nature, and so does not reveal any natural facts to us. A naturalist believes that our understanding of nature is incomplete until we have grasped the natural facts that morality reveals. Moral knowledge belongs to knowledge of nature as a whole, because it reveals one aspect of human fulfilment.

11.11 DIFFERENT CONCEPTIONS OF NATURAL LAW

Our discussion of appeals to nature has not distinguished claims about nature from claims about natural law. It is time to see how these claims might be distinguished, and what, if anything, we add by saying that the morally relevant facts are not only natural, but also belong to natural law.

We have suggested that natural facts give reasons for acting one way or another. Some questions readily arise:

1. Do the natural facts themselves give reasons for action, or must something be added to make the natural facts into normative (i.e. reason-giving) facts?
2. Are the natural facts a natural law, or must something be added to them?
3. Are the normative facts a natural law, or are there natural and normative facts that are not natural law?

Different answers to these questions suggest different conceptions of natural law. A reductive naturalist view claims that natural facts constitute both normative facts and natural law, so that nothing needs to be added to them. If we suppose that something needs to be added to them to give us normative facts, we may differ about whether the added element is sufficient for natural law.

Our answers to these questions depend on our view about the character of a law. The most familiar examples of laws are (1) imperative in form; (2) the product of deliberate acts of legislation, by (3) legislators recognized as being authorized to legislate for a particular society or in a particular area.[46] Hence if something lacks an imperative character, or is not the result of any deliberate act, or is the act of someone who is not socially recognized, it is not a law. According to this test, a natural fact cannot be a law, since it meets none of these conditions. This is true from a theistic as well as from a non-theistic view. Many theists believe in God as creator, but they distinguish acts of creation from acts of legislation, and they do not take God's authority to depend on anyone's authorization or recognition.

---

[45] By 'non-naturalist' here I mean simply the rejection of the naturalist view I have ascribed to Butler. I do not have in mind the specific metaethical outlook that accepts Moore's criticism of naturalist definitions of moral concepts. As I explain in §11.4 above, one might accept Moore's metaethical non-naturalism and still accept Butlerian naturalism.

[46] On necessary conditions for law see Hart 1961; Finnis 1980.

If, then, we rely on these familiar examples of laws, there are no natural moral laws. Those who believe in natural moral laws relax one or more of these conditions. They all reject the third condition. Naturalists also reject the first two, whereas voluntarists accept them.[47]

The dispute between naturalists and voluntarists, therefore, results partly from different conceptions of law. We might infer that the dispute is purely verbal, since naturalists who believe in a natural law in their sense of 'law' do not believe in what the voluntarists regard as natural law, in their sense of 'law'.

It would be a mistake, however, to regard the dispute as purely verbal. Different claims about law and nature try to capture different alleged features of the normative character that is derivable from nature and natural facts. We can understand this normative character better if we turn to some defences of naturalist and voluntarist views.

11.12 A DEFENCE OF NATURALISM

Aquinas begins his discussion of the natural law by affirming that a law is a rule[48] that involves commands, moves agents to action, imposes obligation, and requires publication.[49] These features recall the intuitive examples of laws, and may suggest that a law essentially involves legislation and a legislator. If that is so, a natural law requires both natural facts and a legislator who prescribes observance of the relevant items of legislation. Since the legislators who prescribe rules for particular societies do not prescribe moral principles that are independent of the agreements of particular societies, the legislator of the natural law has to be a divine legislator. Hence Aquinas seems to treat morality as the product of legislation by a divine legislator.

This, however, is not Aquinas' position; for he explains the relevant features of law without reference to acts of legislation. The natural law contains rules and action-guiding requirements, but it does not essentially consist in commands that express the will of a legislator. Natural law is present in a rational creature who shares in divine providence by exercising foresight for herself and for others.[50] It consists of principles discovered by

---

[47] Hence Hooker speaks of a narrower and a wider sense of law: 'They who thus are accustomed to speak [sc. those who take laws to require commands] apply the name of Law unto that only rule of working which superior authority imposeth; whereas we somewhat more enlarging the sense thereof term any kind of rule or canon whereby actions are framed, a law.' (Hooker, *Of the Laws of Ecclesiastical Polity* i 3.1)

[48] 'Law is some sort of rule and measure of acts, in accordance with which someone is led towards acting or is restrained from acting; for law (lex) is spoken of from binding (ligare), because it binds (obligat) one to acting.' (Aquinas, *ST* 1–2 q90 a1)

[49] *ST* 1–2 q90 a4. Finnis 1998 discusses Aquinas on natural law.

[50] 'it is obvious that all things share in some way in the eternal law, namely to the extent that from its impression on them they have a tendency towards the acts and ends proper to them. Among other things, however, a rational creature is subject to divine providence in a more excellent way, to the extent

practical reason as a result of deliberation about the human good.[51] Though Aquinas believes in a divine legislator, he does not take divine legislation to be essential to the existence of a natural law.[52] Since he takes natural law to consist essentially in facts about rational nature, he is a reductive naturalist about natural law.

11.13 A Voluntarist Conception of Natural Law

Opponents of Aquinas, and especially Scotus and Ockham, believe that he underestimates the role of the divine legislative will in the constitution of the natural law. Their view is voluntarist, in so far as it takes the provisions of natural law to consist essentially in divine commands that express the will of God.

To see why one might incline towards a voluntarist view of natural law, it is useful to move forward from the mediaeval debates to Pufendorf's critique of naturalism and defence of voluntarism. Pufendorf responds to Grotius' reaffirmation of the naturalist view maintained by Aquinas and defended by Suarez. He argues against the naturalist belief in 'intrinsic morality'—the view that moral rightness and wrongness (honestas and turpitudo) belongs to actions in their own right, apart from anyone's will.

According to Pufendorf, obligations, and therefore moral requirements, require commands that express the will of a legislator. Though actions have natural goodness and badness apart from the legislative will of God, they have no moral goodness or rightness.[53] The natural properties of actions are a source of reasons in their own right, but these reasons refer only to the pleasant (iucundum) and the advantageous (utile, commodum). They do not include moral reasons, which depend on goodness as rightness (the bonum honestum). If an action is right, it deserves to be chosen for its own sake, apart from its pleasure, and apart from any further advantage. No natural property gives us this sort of reason.[54]

Pufendorf assumes that reasons arise from natural properties only in combination with our desires. The fact that an action has certain results gives us a reason only on the assumption that we want these results. If natural properties give us only these conditional

---

that it itself acquires a share in providence, by exercising foresight (providens) for itself and others. Thus it shares in eternal reason, through which it has a natural inclination to the required (debitum) action and end. And in a rational creature this participation in the eternal law is called the natural law.' (1–2 q91 a2)

[51] 1–2 q90 a1.
[52] Schneewind 1997: 20, 287, states the position that I dissent from here.
[53] [The naturalist view to be rejected:] 'that some things in themselves, apart from any imposition, are right (honesta) or wrong, and these constitute the object of natural and everlasting law (ius), whereas those things that are right are wrong because the legislator willed, come under the heading of positive laws (leges)' (Pufendorf, *De iure naturae et gentium*, i 2.6).
[54] 'But this natural goodness and badness of actions in themselves does not at all place them in the area of morals.' (Pufendorf, *De iure naturae et gentium*, i 2.6)

reasons expressed in hypothetical imperatives (as Kant puts it), and moral reasons are not hypothetical, moral properties are not natural.

According to Pufendorf, morality imposes requirements that are independent of inclination and override considerations of pleasure and advantage. They could not do this if they simply arose from natural goodness. The appropriate reaction to my violation of a moral requirement is to recognize that I am open to justified blame or punishment. But if moral requirements depended simply on natural goodness and badness, the only appropriate reaction would be disappointment at my failure to get what I wanted. Since, therefore, moral principles rest on categorical (non-conditional) reasons apart from my pleasure and advantage, there cannot be any intrinsic morality.

Morality is distinctive, according to Pufendorf, because it depends on laws imposed by commands. The relevant commands impose necessity, and thereby override our preferences and inclinations; their requirements are categorical and do not depend on what we want. If we acknowledge that our actions sometimes deserve blame or punishment, we regard them as violations of laws expressed in commands. Only divine legislation imposes requirements with the peculiar stringency of morality. Natural facts cannot impose such requirements without reference to our desires; hence morality cannot be intrinsic. Nor can our desires impose such requirements; for if I impose any requirement on myself I can also release myself from it, but I cannot release myself from moral requirements. Hence only legislation can explain morality.[55]

These arguments support a voluntarist view of natural law. Voluntarists about natural law believe in natural law, not simply in divine law, because they believe that natural facts and our knowledge of them are a necessary foundation for moral reasons. But they believe that morality is not intrinsic. Moral reasons are present only when something external to the natural facts is added to them. This added element is a command expressed in legislation.

11.14 AN OBJECTION TO VOLUNTARISM

If we grant Pufendorf's claim that natural facts alone cannot be the source of moral reasons, should we accept his derivation of moral reasons from divine legislation? Moral reasons are not reducible to reasons of pleasure and advantage, but they represent an action as unconditionally worth choosing in its own right. Do divine commands give this sort of reason?

In Pufendorf's view, if we simply consider natural goodness, apart from any reference to divine commands, we act only on self-interested concerns that refer to pleasure or advantage. How do divine commands change that? If our attitude to natural goods is self-interested, we may also take a self-interested attitude to divine commands, so that we obey God simply to avoid the pain and disadvantage of punishment.

---

[55] This argument is developed at length by Barbeyrac. See Schneewind 1996.

Perhaps this objection misunderstands Pufendorf's conception of divine commands. Perhaps he means that God does not represent divine commands as arbitrary prescriptions supported by threats and promises, but as principles that deserve obedience in their own right. But if this is what Pufendorf means, he does not believe that the mere fact of being divinely commanded introduces moral obligation and moral reasons. He needs to say that divine commands deserve obedience because they command what is morally right.

If Pufendorf understands divine commands in this way, further difficulties arise for him. (1) If we suppose that God commands actions as a result of recognizing their moral rightness, moral rightness must be some property distinct from being commanded by God. God's recognition of moral rightness does not consist in recognition that an action is divinely commanded. How is this distinct property of moral rightness to be understood? (2) If we suppose that God's commands deserve obedience not only because they carry sanctions but also because God has a right to command, what is the basis of this right? If God is a morally legitimate commander, moral legitimacy must be distinct from being commanded; for if it were claimed that a second-order divine command determines the moral legitimacy of God as a commander, a question could be raised about the moral legitimacy of this second-order command. If, then, Pufendorf claims that God is a morally legitimate commander, he needs to recognize moral rightness that does not depend on commands. (3) If we are to respond to the moral requirement to obey divine commands, we must be capable of responding to moral requirements that do not depend on divine commands; for the moral requirement to obey divine commands cannot itself depend on divine commands (for the reasons given above).

These objections to Pufendorf all appeal in different ways to the well-known argument that Socrates presents in Plato's *Euthyphro*, to show that the pious cannot be defined as what the gods love, because the gods love actions only because they are pious.[56] The distinction that Socrates marks (between 'pious because loved' and 'loved because pious') is similar to a distinction that Scholastics mark between actions that are 'bad because prohibited' and those that are 'prohibited because bad'.[57] If we state Pufendorf's view in these terms, he claims that moral rightness and wrongness depends ultimately on actions that are bad because prohibited or good because commanded. According to the three objections above, he is wrong about this, and he should recognize that basic moral principles state what is prohibited because bad or commanded because good.

This argument suggests that if Pufendorf is to attribute the appropriate moral status to divine commands, he has to recognize intrinsic morality after all. If God is to be an authoritative legislator because God has a right to command and because God commands what is morally right, divine commands depend on intrinsic morality. Pufendorf does not see that his claims about divine commands conflict with his rejection of intrinsic morality.

---

[56] On morality and divine commands see Adams 1987.

[57] 'But Adam sinned by doing what was bad only because it was prohibited. Many, however, sin by doing what is bad in both ways, both in its own right and because it is prohibited.' Aquinas, *2Sent* d21 q2 a2 sc1.

11.15 A FURTHER DEFENCE OF VOLUNTARISM

If Pufendorf's position is inconsistent, one way to restore consistency is to accept a naturalist account of natural law. But it is not the only way. One might also try a more strongly voluntarist position. Pufendorf falls into inconsistency because he tries to combine voluntarism about natural law with the claims that God's commands are morally right and that God is a morally legitimate legislator. He would avoid inconsistency if he abandoned these claims about the moral status of divine commands. He might simply claim that divine commands are the foundation of morality, but are neither morally right nor morally wrong in themselves. According to this strongly voluntarist position, the basis for moral principles is non-moral.

This position agrees with some of Hobbes' remarks about divine commands and morality. In Hobbes' view, God is a legitimate legal authority because God has power to compel us to obey, through fear of punishment. This basis for divine authority is non-moral. It invites the objection that Hobbes does not distinguish the orders of a tyrant from the laws of a legitimate authority. Pufendorf agrees with this objection.[58] Had he agreed with Hobbes on this point, his voluntarism would have been consistent.

But though the Hobbesian version of voluntarism is consistent, it is unattractive. Pufendorf relies on the reasonable assumption that moral reasons are distinct from reasons of pleasure and advantage, and he criticizes naturalism on the ground that it cannot account for their distinct character by appeal to natural facts. But the Hobbesian position denies that moral reasons have this distinct character. It seems to be voluntarism, rather than naturalism, that fails to account for it.

If, therefore, voluntarists would be ill advised to accept a Hobbesian version of voluntarism, no version of voluntarism seems to give a satisfactory account of the relation of moral facts to facts about nature. We have some reason to prefer naturalism. Though we may suppose that natural facts leave out something essential to morality, further examination shows that the demand for some imperative and legislative element is both unnecessary and misleading.

11.16 NATURAL MORALITY
WITHOUT NATURAL LAW

The naturalist and voluntarist positions that we have considered do not exhaust the possibilities. Suarez defends a third position.[59] We have seen why a naturalist account of moral reasons is preferable to a voluntarist account. But we need not infer that a

---

[58] *De iure naturae et gentium* i 6.9–17. Pufendorf discusses Hobbes, *De Cive* 15.5.
[59] My account of Suarez on natural law may be contrasted with the views of Finnis 1980; Darwall 1995; Pink 2005.

naturalist account of natural law is also preferable. This distinction between natural moral reasons and natural law is absent from Aquinas; he assumes that a natural rule of right and wrong is a natural law. Suarez rejects this assumption.

He distinguishes an indicative from a prescriptive law.[60] An indicative law points out something that we ought to do or avoid without commanding anything. In this sense a teacher can instruct us about what to do without commanding us. If the natural law were purely indicative, God would be the teacher of it, but would not be commanding us to do anything.

Suarez believes that genuine law is prescriptive,[61] and that natural law is genuine law. Hence natural law cannot be purely indicative, and must be prescriptive. Hence it results from divine commands, not simply from facts about nature itself. Natural law does not consist essentially in intrinsic natural facts apart from any exercise of God's legislative will. Suarez agrees (in anticipation) with Pufendorf about the relation of law to commands. He also agrees with Pufendorf's view that natural law imposes an obligation, and that only commands can impose obligations. If the natural law imposes a genuine obligation, it proceeds from a divine command.[62]

Suarez, however, differs both from Aquinas and from Pufendorf about the relation of morality to natural law. He does not suppose that moral rules and principles are to be identified with provisions of natural law. On the contrary, since he supposes that natural law is prescriptive law, and hence requires divine commands, he infers that morality is prior to natural law. God's command and prohibition presupposes a necessary rightness and wrongness, not only a necessary goodness and badness, in actions themselves.[63] Even without divine commands, the intrinsic rightness and wrongness of certain actions implies that we are required to do and avoid them.[64] Similarly, failure to refrain from actions that are wrong by nature is a sin (peccatum), even if we abstract from any divine prohibition. Sin and blameworthiness (culpa) follow from the fact

---

[60] Suarez, *De legibus*, ii 6.3. Suarez agrees with the naturalists that the natural law is indicative, but he rejects their view that it is purely indicative.

[61] '[Law:] a common precept, just and stable, sufficiently promulgated.' (Suarez, *Leg.* i 12.4)

[62] 'Finally, the obligation of natural law is genuine obligation. Moreover, this obligation of natural law is a good in its own way, existing in the nature of things. Therefore it is necessary that this obligation is from the divine will willing that human beings be required to keep what right reason dictates.' (*Leg.* ii 6.10)

[63] 'This will of God, prohibition or command, is not the whole character of the goodness and badness that is present in the observance or transgression of natural law, but it assumes in the actions themselves some necessary rightness or wrongness, and joins to them a special obligation of divine law.' (*Leg.* ii 6.11)

[64] 'Hence, if we speak strictly about a natural obligation, it certainly cannot be separated from an obligation in conscience. For if it is <an obligation> to avoid something, it arises from the intrinsic wrongness of an action that is therefore to be avoided in conscience. But if it is to do something, it arises from the intrinsic connexion of such an action with the rightness of virtue, which we are also required in conscience to maintain in our actions. Hence in that case the omission of an action that is a duty is bad in itself.' (*Leg.* ii 9.6)

that a voluntary act is contrary to right reason.[65] These moral properties are intrinsic to actions,[66] because they are determined by rational nature.[67]

Suarez, therefore disagrees with Aquinas in so far as he takes natural law to be unnecessary for intrinsic morality. Aquinas supposes that if natural facts make an action right or wrong, natural law makes it right or wrong. Suarez believes that if God commanded nothing, there would be no natural law, but (if everything else in the universe were unchanged) there would still be right and wrong. This disagreement with Aquinas, however, implies agreement with him on the relation of morality to natural facts. Suarez agrees that the relevant natural facts are sufficient for rightness and wrongness and are sources of moral reasons; he simply denies that these facts and reasons are sufficient for natural law. If we regard law as prescriptive law, then we are naturalists about morality if we suppose, as Suarez does, that natural facts are sufficient for morality.

We can now answer our earlier question about the relation of naturalism to belief in natural law. If we regard law as prescriptive, we need to distinguish natural facts from natural law. If we accept Aquinas' broader conception of law, we will take the right sorts of natural facts to be natural law.

If we agree either with Aquinas or with Suarez against voluntarism, we affirm the features of morality that both Aquinas and Suarez take to be natural and that Aquinas takes to belong to natural law. The debates about natural facts and divine legislation support the naturalist view that explains moral requirements as requirements of human nature. This explanation of moral requirements is neither empty, nor metaethically untenable, nor readily refuted by plausible factual or normative argument. On the contrary, it belongs to a sound conception of the objective facts that underlie true moral judgements.

BIBLIOGRAPHY

Adams, R. M. 1987. 'A modified divine command theory of ethical wrongness', in *The Virtue of Faith and Other Essays in Philosophical Theology*. Oxford: Oxford University Press, ch. 7.
Annas, J. 1993. *The Morality of Happiness*. Oxford: Oxford University Press.
Aquinas, T. 1952. *Summa Theologiae*, ed. P. Caramello. 3 vols. Turin: Marietti. Translated in *Summa Theologica, translated by Fathers of the English Dominican Province*. Westminster, MD: Christian Classics, 1981.
—— 1964. Commentary on the *Ethics* = Aquinas, in *Decem Libros Ethicorum Aristotelis ad Nicomachum Expositio*, third edition, ed. R. M. Spiazzi. Turin: Marietti. Tr. C. L. Litzinger. Chicago: Regenry, 1964.
—— 1980. *Scriptum super Sententiis*, in R. Busa (ed.), *Opera Omnia*. Stuttgart-Bad Cannstatt: Frommann-Holzboog.

---

[65] 'In that case, therefore, the bad action would be a sin and a fault morally, but not theologically, or as directed towards God.' (*Leg.* ii 6.18)

[66] *Leg.* ii 16.3.

[67] Because of the facts about human nature, the natural law 'presupposes in its material an intrinsic rightness or badness altogether inseparable from this material' (*Leg.* ii 15.4).

Aristotle. 1894. *Ethica Nicomachea*, ed. I. Bywater. Oxford: Oxford University Press.

Brandt, R. B. 1979. *A Theory of the Good and the Right*. Oxford: Oxford University Press.

Butler, J. 1900. *Fifteen Sermons Preached at the Rolls Chapel*, in J. H. Bernard (ed.), *The Works of Bishop Butler*. 2 vols. London: Macmillan, 1900. Reprinted in Butler, *Fifteen Sermons*, ed. T. A. Roberts. London: SPCK, 1970.

Cicero 2006. *De Legibus* and *De Republica,* ed. J. Powell. Oxford: Oxford University Press. Tr. C. W. Keyes. London: Heinemann, 1928.

Crowe, M. B. 1977. *The Changing Profile of the Natural Law*. The Hague: Nijhoff.

Cummins, R. 1975. 'Functional explanation', *Journal of Philosophy* 72: 741–65.

Darwall, S. L. 1995. *The British Moralists and the Internal 'Ought'*. Cambridge: Cambridge University Press.

Finnis, J. M. 1980. *Natural Law and Natural Rights*. Oxford: Oxford University Press.

—— 1998. *Aquinas: Moral, Political, and Legal Theory*. Oxford: Oxford University Press.

Foot, P. R. 2001. *Natural Goodness*. Oxford: Oxford University Press.

Gauthier, D. P. 1990. *Moral Dealing: Contract, Ethics, and Reason*. Ithaca: Cornell University Press.

Grotius, H. 1853. *De iure belli et pacis*, tr. W. Whewell. 3 vols. Cambridge: Cambridge University Press. Also translated in *On the Law of War and Peace*, tr. F. W. Kelsey, Oxford: Oxford University Press, 1925.

Haakonssen, K. 1996. *Natural Law and Moral Philosophy*. Cambridge: Cambridge University Press.

—— 1998. 'Divine/natural law theories in ethics', in D. E. Garber and M. R. Ayers (eds), *The Cambridge History of Seventeenth-Century Philosophy*. 2 vols. Cambridge: Cambridge University Press, 1317–57.

Hampton, J. 1986. *Hobbes and the Social Contract Tradition*. Cambridge: Cambridge University Press.

Hart, H. L. A. 1961. *The Concept of Law*. Oxford: Oxford University Press.

Hobbes, T. 1983. *De Cive*, ed. H. Warrender. 2 vols. Oxford: Oxford University Press.

—— 1994. *Leviathan*, ed. E. M. Curley. Indianapolis: Hackett.

Hooker, R. 1888. *Of the Laws of Ecclesiastical Polity*, in J. Keble (ed.), *The Works of Richard Hooker*. 7th edn. 3 vols. Oxford: Oxford University Press.

Humboldt, W. 1969. *The Limits of State Action*, ed. J. W. Burrow. Cambridge: Cambridge University Press.

Hurka, T. 1993. *Perfectionism*. Oxford: Oxford University Press.

Hutcheson, F. 1993. *On Human Nature* (= *Reflections on our common systems of morality* and the *Inaugural Lecture on the social nature of man*), ed. T. Mautner. Cambridge: Cambridge University Press.

Irwin, T. H. 2007–2009. *The Development of Ethics*. 3 vols. Oxford: Oxford University Press.

—— 2010. 'Morality as law and morality in the *Laws*', in C. Bobonich (ed.), *Essays on Plato's Laws*. Cambridge: Cambridge University Press.

Kavka, G. S. 1986. *Hobbesian Moral and Political Theory*. Princeton: Princeton University Press.

Kitcher, P. 1999. 'Essence and perfection', *Ethics* 110: 59–83.

Lactantius 1890. *Divinae Institutiones*, ed. S. Brandt. Vienna: Tempsky.

Mill, J. S. 1963–1991a. 'Nature', in J. M. Robson (gen. ed.), *Collected Works*. 33 vols. Toronto: University of Toronto Press, vol. x.

—— 1963–1991b. *On Liberty*, in J. M. Robson (gen. ed.), *Collected Works*. 33 vols. Toronto: University of Toronto Press, vol. xviii.

—— 1963–1991c. *Collected Works*, J. M. Robson (gen. ed.). 33 vols. Toronto: University of Toronto Press.

Moore, G. E. 1903. *Principia Ethica*. Cambridge: Cambridge University Press.

Philo 1929. *Abraham*, in *Works*, tr. F. H. Colson and G. H. Whitaker, vol. 6. London: Heinemann.

Pink, T. 2005. 'Action, will, and law in late Scholasticism', in J. Kraye and R. Saarinen (eds), *Moral Philosophy on the Threshold of Modernity*. Dordrecht: Springer, 91–111.

Plato 1907. *Laws*, ed. J. Burnet, Oxford: Oxford University Press.

Pufendorf, S. 1934. *De iure naturae et gentium*, tr. C. H. Oldfather and W. A. Oldfather. Oxford: Oxford University Press.

Rawls, J. 1999. *A Theory of Justice*. 2nd edn. Cambridge, MA: Harvard University Press.

Schneewind, J. B. 1996. 'Barbeyrac and Leibniz on Pufendorf', in F. Palladini and G. Hartung (eds), *Samuel Pufendorf und die europäische Frühaufklärung*. Berlin: Akademie Verlag, 181–9.

—— 1997. *The Invention of Autonomy*. Cambridge: Cambridge University Press.

—— (ed.) 2003. *Moral Philosophy from Montaigne to Kant*. 2nd edn. Cambridge: Cambridge University Press.

Scotus, Duns. See Wolter.

Suarez, F. 1971–1981. *Tractatus de Legibus ac Deo Legislatore*, ed. L. Perena et al. 8 vols. Madrid: Consejo Superior de Investigaciones Cientificas. Partly translated in *Selections from Three Works*. 2 vols. (vol. i, text; vol. ii, tr. G. L. Williams et al.). Oxford: Oxford University Press, 1944.

Tuck, R. 1987. 'The "modern" theory of natural law', in A. Pagden (ed.), *The Languages of Political Theory in Early-Modern Europe*. Cambridge: Cambridge University Press, 99–122.

Velleman, D. 1988. 'Brandt's definition of "good"', *Philosophical Review* 97: 353–71.

Von Wright, G. H. 1963. *The Varieties of Goodness*. London: Routledge.

Wolter, A. B. (tr.) 1986. *Duns Scotus on the Will and Morality*. Washington: Catholic University of America Press.

CHAPTER 12

SEVENTEENTH-CENTURY MORAL PHILOSOPHY: SELF-HELP, SELF-KNOWLEDGE, AND THE DEVIL'S MOUNTAIN[1]

AARON GARRETT

12.1 INTRODUCTION

IF this *Handbook* is representative of the values and interests of contemporary moral philosophers and historians of moral philosophy, then the Western moral philosophy of the greatest interest and value to us either ended in late antiquity or began in the eighteenth century. This is in particular true of the great difference in the valuing and interest of the works of moral philosophers of the seventeenth century and those of the eighteenth century. There are probably a hundred scholarly articles on Kant's or Hume's ethics for every article on Descartes' or Spinoza's ethics. This also holds of how we teach moral philosophy. Two out of three of the basic kinds of normative ethical theories in the common trichotomy between utilitarianism, Kantian deontology, and virtue ethics have their beginnings in the early eighteenth century. This preference is not just due to unfounded prejudices on the part of scholars and teachers. When compared with Hume's incisive discussions of whether moral distinctions are derived from reason, many of the best-known works by seventeenth-century moral philosophers read like

[1] Thanks to Roger Crisp, John Grey, Knud Haakonssen, Paul Katsafanas, Eugene Marshall, Amelie Rorty, Eric Schliesser, Sanem Soyarslan, Susanne Sreedhar, Justin Steinberg, for reading drafts of the chapter and providing many detailed comments. I have responded to their many points but have been unable to note each individual comment in the text. Readers should be aware that they have saved me from many errors and they have suggested some of the most important ideas in the chapter. Errors remain and these are my own! Many other people have read sections and thanks to them are noted in the text. Thanks to Knud Haakonssen for his guidance and inspiration in writing on this theme: *sine qua non*.

self-help manuals buttressed with psychology, speculative law, and religion. Much that is recognizably philosophy appears not to be moral philosophy but metaphysics, scientific methodology, and the theory of knowledge.

I will argue that this perception is in part accurate in so far as self-help was a (or even *the*) central issue for a lot of early modern moral philosophy and self-help was connected with arguments in areas of philosophy we do not often think of as relevant to moral philosophy (as well as many that we do). A large chunk of early modern ethics (the chunk I will focus on in this chapter) focused on counsels, techniques, justifications, and in some cases foundations for the happiness, care, and cultivation of the self[2] in order to have the best and (normally) happiest life (where best and happiest are understood both in comparison with other sorts of lives as counselled and argued for by other philosophers and best and most happy *simpliciter*).[3] But I will also argue that in the works of some early modern moral philosophers—notably Descartes, Spinoza, La Rochefoucauld, and Shaftesbury—'self-help' involved transforming reader's understanding of themselves[4] in ways quite beyond the scope of 'The Power of Positive Thinking' or 'When Bad things Happen to Good People'.[5] It involved transforming how readers understood what they were fundamentally and by extension transforming how they understood what sort of life they should lead. When so understood early modern moral philosophy is not a strange lull but rather the continuation of many of the themes of ancient and Hellenistic philosophy, accommodated and transformed to respond to the new science and to the great differences between early modern Europe and the ancient world.

Ethics in this sense involved explicit or tacit discussion of the greatest happiness, virtue, the good, etc. Pierre Gassendi's *Ethics* for example is divided into three sections, the first two of which are 'Of Felicity' and 'Of Virtues'. But in tandem with the focus on happiness and a good life, the breadth of what counted as moral philosophy was far greater, and not clearly differentiated from politics,[6] or the cultivation of intellectual virtues and attitudes crucial to discovering what one truly was and serving as guides for practical reason (as well as from politics), or even from metaphysics, the philosophy of mind, and scientific methodology and practice. The third and final section of Gassendi's *Ethics* was 'Of Liberty, Fortune, Fate, and Divination'. The philosophy of mind, metaphysics, and even criticisms of astrology or divination were relevant to or even belonged to moral philosophy in so far as they were relevant to the care of the self, the acquisition of virtue, and above all to answering the question: 'What is the best life?'

Spinoza's *Ethics* is a perfect example of the breadth of early modern moral philosophy, as I will argue in §4. The main point of the work is to help the reader to acquire 'freedom

---

[2] See Foucault 1986. I'm using 'self' in a very general sense reflecting the early modern use.

[3] Life could include the 'afterlife'—or eternity—as well as this mortal coil depending on the philosopher.

[4] Thanks to Amelie Rorty for help with this point.

[5] Although the first would be a good subtitle to Spinoza's *Ethics*, and the second to La Rochefoucauld's *Maxims*!

[6] I will only discuss what we think of as political philosophy in so far as it is connected with what we normally understand as moral philosophy due to constraints of length.

of mind, or blessedness, from which we shall see how much to be preferred the life of the wise man is to the ignorant man' (Shirley 2002, *Ethics* V, 'Preface'). Spinoza directly follows this statement with a criticism of the Stoics and Descartes for arguing that the passions could be controlled by the will—a contest between different schools with different beliefs as to what the content of and way to the best life are. To understand why the life of the wise man is to be preferred, and why Descartes and the Stoics are wrong in arguing for the sort of life that they do, the reader must know quite a lot of metaphysics, mind, and a theory of knowledge (none of which are at first blush obviously relevant to leading the best life). This is true of much metaphysically informed philosophical ethics, from Aristotle to Hegel, but the boundaries between these areas and the way in which different regions of philosophy were connected to ethical norms and ends in the philosophers I will be discussing were often quite distinctive. Spinoza's answers to the perennial questions 'What is the best life?', 'Why is it the best life?', and 'How do I achieve this life?' involve distinctive attitudes towards metaphysics and the role of metaphysics in our self-knowledge and self-fashioning.

Alongside these long-standing questions, early modern moral philosophers gave unity to their enquiries by casting them in terms of the Greek, Latin, and Hellenistic philosophical schools, both the philosophy associated with particular schools and 'eclectic' syntheses of these schools (such as Cicero's version of Academic scepticism). It is difficult to overstate the ubiquity and depth of influence of Cicero, Marcus Aurelius, Epictetus, Lucretius, Sextus Empiricus, and so many others (both directly and indirectly) on early modern moral philosophers from Montaigne and Machiavelli to Hume and Kant. Many of the practical techniques, assumptions, and arguments of modern moral philosophy have their sources in the Hellenistic philosophical schools—not least that logic, metaphysics, theories of mind, theories of knowledge, and other parts of a complete philosophical system might bear on or be part of the best life.

It was also common for early modern philosophers to associate themselves with one or another school and to criticize other philosophers as being members of suspect rival schools—like Spinoza's criticism of Descartes as a Stoic above. When Grotius posed his infamous question in *De Jure Belli ac Pacis* whether self-interest might be the sole source of natural law, he used Carneades the ancient sceptic and antagonist in Cicero's dialogues as the mouthpiece. This allowed Grotius to identify himself with an eclectic mixture of Stoicism and scepticism and to place potentially irreligious sentiments in the mouth of an ancient to provide some distance.[7] When we ask 'Was Descartes a Stoic?', 'Was Hobbes an Epicurean?', or 'Was Shaftesbury a Stoic, and Epicurean, or a Platonist?' we are asking questions their contemporaries asked.[8] These identifications furthermore allowed modern philosophers to place themselves in ongoing debates.

---

[7] See Grotius 2005, 'Preliminary Discourse' §17. On Grotius and Stoicism see Blom and Winkel 2004.

[8] This way of looking at philosophy in general and moral philosophy persisted throughout the eighteenth century (but dwindled in the second half). Cf. Hume's four essays on the philosophical schools: 'The Epicurean', 'The Stoic', 'The Platonist', and 'The Sceptic' in Hume 1987: 138–80.

I am not, though, suggesting an unbroken and continuous philosophical tradition from Socrates to Shaftesbury. As I have already mentioned, many early modern philosophers were extremely (and sometimes overtly) eclectic and their influences are not always straightforward: what looks to us as Stoic in an author could often just as well be Epicurean (i.e. the restriction of one's desires in order to be satisfied and happy) or a mixture of ancient sources, or a modern variant generally influenced by ancient schools without strong commitments to one school. Or they might identify with one or some aspects of a school, or of one figure or branch within a school, while criticizing others. For example Walter Charleton began his collection *Epicurus' Morals* with 'An Apologie for Epicurus' (Charleton 1656: v–vi) where he disassociated himself from the denial of the immortality of the soul, the denial of divine reward and punishment as a motivation to worship, and the approval of suicide.[9]

And, importantly, most modern philosophers were acutely aware that they were not ancients at the same time that they appropriated from the ancient schools. They were drawn to Stoicism, Epicureanism, Platonism, etc., in part due to real affinities, but in part because this differentiated them from the Scholastic philosophers who were still dominant in many institutional contexts, and in no small part because the ancient schools provided a means to discuss moral philosophy independent of potentially conflicting confessional orientations.[10] Unsurprisingly the philosophical combination of ancient school doctrines and modern philosophy, modern lives, modern science, modern politics, modern learning, etc., gave rise to sophisticated, self-conscious, and often ambiguous or even ironic thinking.

To use an image to illustrate this last point: the frontispiece for Shaftesbury's *Characteristics*, which he designed like all of the other illustrations for the work, has the author in a toga resting on volumes of Xenophon and Plato (see image below). On second glance we see that he does not have sandals, his shoes are modern, and he has a shirt under his toga. On third glance we see that what at first appeared to be a toga might instead be a curtain playfully wrapped around him, or it might not. It is clear that Shaftesbury thought about himself and his own philosophy in terms of the ancients and moderns but just what he thought about it is more difficult to pin down.

I will begin with the seventeenth-century moral philosopher whose writings one would be least likely to encounter in the self-help section of a bookshop, Thomas Hobbes. I will engage with those aspects of Hobbes' moral philosophy that posed a challenge for many philosophers of the second half of the seventeenth century who were committed to philosophy as a form of self-help: there were many other challenges in Hobbes' moral philosophy as well as important aspects not viewed as challenging by his contemporaries. Unlike Shaftesbury and some of the other

---

[9] Charleton argues that all of these doctrines are the consequence of properly reasoning about nature without any additional supernatural illumination, and that those who argued against Epicurus were worse since they also lacked supernatural illumination but drew bad inferences. Consequently we should not blame Epicurus for being 'educated in times of no small Pagan darknesse'.

[10] It may be true that Plato sought to provide a philosophical response to Greek religion (among many other things), but it was not a response to early modern religion.

The Right Honorable Anthony Ashley
Cooper Earl of Shaftesbury, Baron Ashley of
Winbourn S.ᵗ Giles, & Lord Cooper of Pawlett.

J. Closterman Pinx.   Sim: Gribelin Sculp.

FIGURE 1 Frontispiece for Shaftesbury's *Characteristics*

philosophers I will discuss, Hobbes placed some of the central elements of classical Epicureanism on a new post-Baconian footing and attempted to explain morals solely by reference to the mechanical interaction of matter in simple bodies, human passions, and states.

To do this Hobbes drew on a new conception of self-knowledge and self-consciously transformed Socrates' adage 'nosce te ipsum' to mean knowing oneself not through *a priori* reflection but rather through a geometrical analysis of shared desires and passions. The analysis of the passions led Hobbes to conclude that men had to deny that morality was found in man's natural state, give up aspiring to the best life, and instead should accept a life of satisfying restricted and accommodated desires. This involved a new sort of transformation: from natural men into civil subjects. The denial of natural sociability, and the denial of the presumption shared by many ancient philosophers that natural was good was combined with a new analysis of the human passions on which the passions were just one more object of a new post-Baconian science. This was held in tandem with the denial of providential explanations and of the attainability of a best, philosophical life. These positions when taken together were Hobbes' complex and powerful challenge to his peers, a challenge that many moral philosophers of the later seventeenth century of vastly different commitments responded.

The next section will focus on Justus Lipsius and Descartes, and their appropriation of ancient and Hellenistic, mainly Stoical, moral philosophy in connection with changing ideas about control of the passions and the happiest and best life. Lipsius wrote before Hobbes, and Descartes formulated the main principles of his moral philosophy before Hobbes published his best-known works. They represent successive attempts to appropriate moral philosophy as self-help and self-transformation within a modern context.

Spinoza was deeply influenced by both Descartes and Hobbes (as were many other Dutch philosophers) and is discussed in the next section. Spinoza, Lipsius, and Descartes all assumed that self-knowledge was the key for a happy life. For both Spinoza and Descartes self-knowledge was, like for Hobbes, understanding oneself in terms of proper efficient, causal, and mechanistic explanations of the world in general and the passions in particular. Unlike for Hobbes this self-understanding was itself therapeutic in a way that allowed Descartes and Spinoza to advocate for techniques and doctrines similar to those of the ancient schools, in particular in the stress on moral philosophy as techniques for attaining felicity through reflection, but which were like Hobbes justified by tacit or explicit reference to the new science. In Spinoza's case we see an attempt to synthesize Hobbes with Descartes and accept some of Hobbes' arguments while responding to the main aspects of the Hobbesian challenge.

In the fifth section I will discuss the maxim or epigram, a literary form with ancient sources that many moralists, including Descartes and Spinoza, used to counsel readers on how to best know and govern themselves. They were also an enormously popular literary form that many writers outside of standard moral philosophy used to present their views about matters moral. Consequently, the content of maxims ranged from fairly commonly held moral beliefs to some of the most surprising and challenging moral views in the seventeenth century. I will focus on the maxims of three writers—the poet Anne Bradstreet, the clergyman and Cambridge Platonist Benjamin Whichcote, and the nobleman La Rochefoucauld. All used maxims to present moral philosophy. La Rochefoucauld, in particular, used the maxim form to powerfully challenge mainstream moral philosophy in a way that paralleled and if anything was even more destructive than Hobbes.

In the sixth section I will turn to a realist tradition in moral philosophy that begins with Whichcote—the Cambridge Platonists. I will argue that this represents a parallel realist (and Platonist tradition), to neo-Stoicism and Epicureanism, and a parallel and powerful response to the Hobbesian challenge. It was a far more influential moral philosophical tradition than most of these others, though, due to its influence on a group of late seventeenth- and early eighteenth-century moral philosophers who had a decisive impact on moral philosophy for the next century.

I will conclude by focusing on the two most important philosophers, who developed themes in Whichcote and the Cambridge Platonists: Lord Shaftesbury and Samuel Clarke. Shaftesbury drew on the Cambridge Platonists to develop a criticism of Hobbes that powerfully influenced the sentimentalist traditions of the eighteenth century.[11] Samuel Clarke presented a different response to Hobbes (and Spinoza), a response that influenced among others Joseph Butler.

12.2 THE CHALLENGE FROM THE DEVIL'S MOUNTAIN

It is no surprise that both late antiquity and the sixteenth and seventeenth centuries had a surfeit of moral philosophy concerned with caring for the self and a happy life since both periods were high watermarks for war, civil strife, and the upending of identities. Thomas Hobbes opened 'Behemoth' with the claim that 'If in time, as in place, there were degrees of high and low, I verily believe that the highest of time would be that which passed between the years of 1640–1660' where 'all kinds of injustice' could be viewed as if 'from the Devil's Mountain' (Hobbes 1990: 1). When one lists the French Wars of Religion, the Fronde, the Franco-Spanish War, the Dutch War of Independence, the English Civil War, the Revocation of the Edict of Nantes, and many other conflicts, massacres, and state actions, one can see why many intellectuals felt themselves dragged down in a whirlpool of violence.[12] It certainly made for fair comparison to the civil strife of the late Roman republic and the late Empire.

---

[11] For the breadth and depth of Shaftesbury's influence see Rivers 2000.

[12] Descartes also uses the metaphor of rebuilding a destroyed city to describe his new science in the *Discourse*. There is disagreement as to whether Descartes was present at the battle of White Mountain, but he was clearly very aware of the war.

In a letter written to the secretary of the Royal Society Henry Oldenburg during the Anglo-Dutch War, Baruch Spinoza succinctly described the philosopher's life among bands of brigands:

> I rejoice that your philosophers are alive, and are mindful of themselves and their republic. I shall expect news of what they have recently done, when the warriors are sated with blood and are resting so as to renew their strength somewhat. (Shirley 2002, Letter 30)

The lives of philosophers and their audiences in the seventeenth century were obviously not always this difficult. But, it is little surprise that many moral philosophers would reflect on and respond to the threat of the outbreak of religious and political conflict.

For many philosophers political conflict and conflict between different Christian confessions and sects were inseparable. All of the armed conflicts listed above had a religious component or were straightforward religious conflicts—Catholics against Jansenists, Reformed Calvinists against Arminians, Church of England against Puritans, Puritans against all sorts of radical religionists, and so on. The permutations seemed nearly endless.

A common response was to make the shared religious and moral commitments of the combatants evident and thus provide the basis for peace. Following Grotius' landmark *De Jure Belli ac Pacis*, Hobbes and natural lawyers who drew on and responded to Grotius and Hobbes such as Pufendorf, Locke, and Leibniz argued for duties (including to God), obligations, and interests that cut across religious confessions and nation states and beyond, to the regulation of domains ungoverned by particular states and legal codes such as wars and oceans. All humans capable of minimal reason could be shown to have fundamental interests in a working state, sometimes in a degree of religious tolerance, and often in a minimal natural religion and to be obligated to a core set of natural laws arising from their interests (Haakonssen 1996; Hunter 2006).

What were these laws and interests? Grotius argued that these laws arose from natural sociability, and the interests were the basic interests in happiness and security shared by all people. A central aspect of Hobbes' challenge[13] was to deny natural sociability and by extension to bring into question the account of interest on which natural sociability led rational beings to discover laws that led naturally to satisfying their interests. Human beings may naturally feel passions of love towards one another but these passions are insufficient to draw them to, to establish, and to preserve a stable society capable of securing physical safety for all of its members.

Hobbes' scepticism about natural sociability was argued for perhaps most famously in the notorious passages from *De Cive* and *Leviathan* comparing the behaviour of humans and ants and bees to human's detriment (Hobbes 1996: II.17; 1998: V.5). Ants and bees are cooperative and sociable in a way that humans clearly aren't. It seems by the standards of nature that humans are more naturally unsociable than any animal. For Hobbes empirical arguments for man's natural unsociability went hand in glove with, in

---

[13] I am not denying the continuity between Hobbes and Grotius. See Tuck 1993.

fact were explained by, his distinctive version of the Epicurean theory of motivation and desire satisfaction. Happiness and security are interests shared by all people. But from the fact that all human beings each desire their own happiness and security it does not follow without further argument that they should desire happiness and security for all. And lacking further argument the prudential course seems to be to attempt to satisfy one's individual desires with little thought to those of others unless they are directly relevant to one's own desires. These desires are directed towards particular objects, events, or persons in absence of education or a state. For Hobbes this account followed from the fact that desires and passions were ultimately explained in terms of a materialist physiognomy that rested on a mechanist, efficient causal explanation compatible with atomism. The satisfaction of particular desires (both the pleasure of attaining the object desired and the pleasure of satisfying the desire) and avoidance of pain was happiness.

So far the theory seemed compatible with classical and early modern Epicureans (the best known of which were Hobbes' friends Gassendi[14] and Charleton) but there was a central difference between Hobbes and the early modern Epicureans. For both Gassendi and Charleton one could gain happiness and security for oneself without worrying too much about happiness and security for all by aiming for the best sort of life, the life of felicity. By purifying oneself through philosophy ('the physic of the mind') and using one's prudential reasoning one could restrict one's desires to the objects and interests that one could consistently satisfy—tranquillity of mind and living in the moment (Charleton 1656: 3–5, 22–3). (For early modern Epicureans this life was also wholly compatible with natural virtues: the aforementioned prudence, justice, friendship, and others. Charleton and Gassendi were both arguing for moral philosophy as a form of self-help leading to attaining the best sort of life (which will be discussed at greater length in the next section).)

For Hobbes, though, there were three problems with this picture. The first problem concerned felicity and drew on an additional aspect of Hobbes' account of desire. The second problem concerned the possibility of an ordinal ranking of pleasures. And the third problem concerned what path prudence dictated. When combined with Hobbes' attempt to explain morals wholly through natural causes compatible with mechanism (i.e. without recourse to providence, or supernatural explanations, or natural teleology) these three problems constituted Hobbes' deep and destructive challenge to ancient self-help theories and the moderns who drew on them.

For Gassendi and Charleton the pleasure of tranquillity of the mind and lack of agitation of the body was felicity and was an attainable goal for philosophers. For Hobbes no sort of 'continual delight' could be attained: 'there is no such thing in this world, or way to it, more than to Utopia: for while we live; we have desires, and desires presupposeth a farther end' (Hobbes 1994: 44 (I.vii.6)).[15] The traditional analysis of felicity was

---

[14] Gassendi seems to have influenced Hobbes' atomism and Hobbes seems to have influenced Gassendi's moral theory, not the least in trying to avoid Hobbesian conclusions from shared Epicurean premises. For the relation of Hobbes and Gassendi (and also for Gassendi's initial formulation of his ethics in response to Descartes) see Sarasohn 1985.

[15] See also Hobbes 1658: XI. 15 and Hobbes 1996: I. xi.

psychologically inaccurate. Human beings could not be fully satisfied since as soon as they had satisfied one desire they became restless and wished to satisfy a new, different, or further desire.

The desire for felicity was self-undermining because it led to further and greater conflict disrupting any happiness. Consequently the belief that one ought to desire felicity was destructive and false. When held by individual agents in absence of a strong state it was a constant threat to bodily security. The desire for beatitude, or felicity in the next world, had the potential to be even more destructive when not mediated by a state church in so far as it potentially led to unbridled fanaticism with no fear of earthly death (or even positive delight in martyrdom). As Hobbes remarked from the Devil's Mountain in *Leviathan*:

> Whence comes it, that in Christendome there has been, almost from the time of the Apostles, such jostling of one another out of their places, both by forraign, and Civill war? such stumbling at every little asperity of their own fortune, and every little eminence of that of other men? and such diversity of ways in running to the same mark, *Felicity*, if it be not Night amongst us, or at least a Mist? wee are therefore yet in the Dark. (Hobbes 1996: IV.44)

Second, that prudence dictated seeking intellectual pleasures and tranquillity over satisfying other desires assumed that a philosopher had access to clear ranking of pleasures, a ranking that in turn dictated what one ought to desire. For Hobbes, the problem was that in absence of a state or other sort of organization there was no accessible and trustworthy ranking of pleasures to determine what a virtuous and rational man or woman ought to desire. There was just what one did desire, the desire to satisfy it, and the pleasure arising from discharging the desire. If one happened to be an Epicurean sage, and happened to prefer to satisfy the desires of an Epicurean sage, so be it. But this could not be a general ranking unless there was a clear means of adjudicating between desires. It goes without saying that not everyone is convinced that they are suited to the life of an Epicurean sage.

This was also a reason that Hobbes held one of his most notorious doctrines, that morality did not pre-exist the advent of stable authority. Good and evil were defined by Hobbes as what we call those objects that we desire or avoid. There were all sorts of passions prior to the establishment of a stable system of rules, some of them benevolent and some of them vicious, but they were not moral in so far as there were no publically propagated and clear laws, duties, and obligations which one could be expected to satisfy or discharge, and there was no clear means to adjudicate disagreements or conflicts. The consequence was that for Hobbes some form of stable authority that could administrate and arbitrate between these desires was a precondition of morality.

The only resolution to this problem was for combatants to see the connection between the restriction of desires for future pleasure and future lack of pain and death, or to be restrained from acting on their desires by a more powerful external force. This led to the third problem, the problem of exactly what prudence dictated. For ancient Epicureans prudence dictated a retreat, moving to the Garden and seeking the friendship of only the like-minded who could help in the search for tranquillity. For Gassendi and Charleton this could be combined with political association, and political association could support seeking tranquillity, but the two were relatively independent. Yet both also stressed the importance of 'indolence' or lack of disturbance of the body in attaining happiness. For Hobbes, both from the perspective of the Devil's Mountain and from that of materialist mechanist science, it was clear that bodily integrity was the necessary condition of any pleasure. If for Epicurus death was nothing to us and therefore the wise man did not fear death, for Hobbes fear of death (and of mutilation) was the master motivation. A world where the many did not fear death was not a world like ours. If it could exist with agents otherwise motivated as we are, it would be frightful.

If all agents can come to recognize that they fear death and that the necessity of securing their bodies in order to continue in motion and to continue to pursue their desires was the *sine qua non*, as opposed to utopian felicity, then they might agree to the establishment of a state or central authority. Philosophical prudence was clearly far too high a bar to ask of ordinary prudential reasoned thought. Consequently for Hobbes 'come to recognize' included everything from reflective endorsement, to acquiescing under direct threat, to promises of the rewards and punishments of religion as dictated by the state, to education, to keeping agents ignorant as to a wide range of possibilities that could be potentially destructive.

Hobbes argued that this picture was the consequence of the application of modern, Bacon-inspired science to moral philosophy. The Delphic maxim 'Know thyself' associated above all with Socrates was reinterpreted as

> He that is to govern a whole Nation must read in himself, not this or that particular man, but a Man-kind, which though it be harder to do, harder than to learn any Language, or Science, yet when I shall have set down my own reading orderly and perspicuously, the pains left another will only to be consider if he also find not the same in himself. For this kind of doctrine admitteth no other demonstration. (Hobbes 1996)

Just as modern geometers had charted new oceans in order to discover new worlds (cf. Hobbes 1998, 'Epistle Dedicatory'), so too modern moral philosophers would chart the passions to know how best to arrange men into new stable orders. In other words one could only properly know oneself through a scientific account of the passions, etc., applied to oneself and others—not through reflection.

In sum, then, Hobbes' challenges to moral philosophies inspired by the schools and their doctrines of self-help were (1) to give up the ideal of felicity in so far as it is self-refuting and at odds with the facts of human psychology, (2) to admit that there is no ordinal ranking of goods and hence no objective adjudication on what constitutes *the* or even *a* good life, and instead (3) to establish a far lower goal dictated by proper prudential reasoning circumscribed by an accurate analysis of human desires and the human propensity to seek power after power. This was justified by a well-founded method consistent with the new science—unlike the Utopian fantasies of the schools.

12.3 MODERN SELF-HELP:
LIPSIUS AND DESCARTES

What could then be said on behalf of self-help? The advocates of self-help shared something important with Hobbes, the belief that transformation of how one understood oneself (and even transformation of what one was) was necessary to have a relatively happy life. For Hobbes in order to end conflict natural men and women had to relinquish many natural desires and restrict their natural right to take on the identity of citizens. For some natural lawyers influenced by and responding to Hobbes, notably Pufendorf and the tradition following from him, this mandated disconnecting of one's civic roles from one's special relationship with God, one's duties to self and one's family and thus hiving off different obligations which might lead to conflict.

Another, sometimes overlapping, response to conflict was to centre moral philosophy on a process of discovering one's core, true (and often *natural*) self and disengage this self from its encumbrances by transforming one's attitude towards oneself, in particular disengaging from identifications of the self with roles which led to conflict and disruption. This discovery of the true self also often involved the acquisition of associated virtues and embraced a degree of elitism (like many ancient and Renaissance philosophers). Those with sufficient intellect and proper calling came together in small groups and circles, often as initiates or elective families clustered around a wise father, where wisdom was discussed and transmitted.[16] The true moral philosophy was a means for the few who were seriously committed to separate themselves from the many. To paraphrase the closing words of Spinoza's *Ethics*, attaining the best sort of life, and in particular acquiring the knowledge of what one truly was in order to attain that life was exceedingly difficult and so it was unsurprising that so few attained it. Even Descartes, who emphasized the accessibility of his teachings to all readers and attempted to present his teachings in forms accessible to the schools, also recognized that few would have a sufficiently strong will to follow through on them.

Like Hobbes, few of the philosophers I will discuss taught in universities. This meant that their philosophical ideas were less often communicated in the academic treatise and commentary form.[17] The Cambridge Platonists, Charleton, Gassendi, Shaftesbury, Spinoza, La Rochefoucauld, Lipsius, and many others developed their ideas in small discussion circles reinforcing elitism. They thought carefully about how best to communicate them and what not to communicate to the general public. Consequently the literary form of philosophy was far more central an issue than for many academic natural lawyers.[18]

---

[16] For example Marie de Gornay referred to herself as Montaigne's adoptive daughter and sought a similar relationship with Lipsius after Montaigne's death. See Gournay 1998: 25 n. 11.

[17] Which is not to say that they didn't write in this form, or that natural lawyers did not also use a wide range of forms.

[18] This was also the case for Hobbes. See Skinner 1996.

As mentioned, the ancient schools provided many of the resources used by these philosophers to respond to conflict. In particular Stoicism, Epicureanism, Scepticism, and Platonism all provided means to discover one's true self behind and beyond particular social and religious commitments and entrapments—that what one was most was not one's religion, rank, or wealth. The opening few sentences of Descartes' *Meditations* (a form used by Marcus Aurelius), where the 'I' divests itself of its social standing and particular entanglements to discover that it is most of all a thinking thing, or Spinoza's *Tractatus de Intellectus Emendatione*, where various worldly goods are rejected in order to pursue the highest goods of the mind, are prime examples of this process. In a different way Montaigne's and La Rochefoucauld's scepticism about our motivations were also attempts to assess what we really were in order then to—at least in Montaigne's case— achieve the best life, the life of self-knowledge.[19] One needed to discover what one was beyond civil, social, religious, and familial commitments in order to answer the question: What is the best sort of life for me? Because many ancient philosophical models were not Christian and yet were highly and widely regarded by the learned, they provided a means to identify what one truly was independent of the specifics of this or that Christian confession (although some allegiance to Christianity was assumed by many philosophers as I will discuss in a moment). They provided intellectual communities beyond particular universities or even eras—for example, the eternal community of Stoic sages.

In *The Invention of Autonomy* J. B. Schneewind drew a contrast between 'modern perfectionists' who held 'ignorance and error resulting from failure to use reason properly are what stand between us and a life of moral virtue' (Schneewind 1998: 169) and 'natural lawyers' who viewed the central moral problem to be providing pragmatic solutions to permanent conflict. I would like to suggest an alteration to Schneewind's taxonomy. First, Schneewind's contrast was epistemic, i.e. between the *a priori* reasons of the modern perfectionist and the pragmatic probable evidence of the natural lawyer. This was in part to show the development of this fault line in the later arguments of Hume, Kant, et al. But although some philosophers like Gassendi and Charleton (who Schneewind has difficulties classifying or does not treat) were opponents of the role of *a priori* necessary reasons in morals (or in general), they were committed to the modern perfectionist position as stated above when reasons are construed to include both probable evidence and necessary *a priori* reasons.[20] I would suggest that this was due to the shared commitment to a modernized Hellenistic school philosophy, even if of opposed schools. Spinoza, Charleton, and Gassendi also all wrote in response to Hobbes, so we might

---

[19] For Montaigne, and perhaps for La Rochefoucauld as well, the search for self-knowledge *was* ethics. Thanks to Justin Steinberg for this point, which I will discuss in the next section.

[20] Schneewind only briefly discusses Gassendi (Schneewind 1998: 263–71) and classifies him with religious thinkers in so far as for Gassendi reason is not sufficient for morality. But although Gassendi was not a rationalist he was strongly committed to the thesis that Schneewind associates with the perfectionists as being necessary for a happy life. It is unlikely that Lipsius and Descartes held that it was sufficient, although Spinoza may have. Schneewind seems to classify Gassendi due to the demands of his master narrative.

reformulate Schneewind's distinction as between two different responses to Hobbes rather than a primarily epistemic distinction—the first stressing the civic good or (at a minimum) civic stability as prior condition to the individual good (along Hobbesian lines), the second stressing individual self-help but modified in order to respond to Hobbes' challenge

That said, the two categories should be thought of more as general orientations or ideal types than anything precise since many of the philosophers whom Schneewind labels as modern perfectionists were responding no less to the potential for permanent conflict than those he labelled as natural lawyers. And many natural lawyers drew extensively on the Hellenistic schools. This is unsurprising since all were interested in a prudentially *secure* life and person, and for all the difference between strictly moral *desiderata* and strictly prudential goods is either unclear, or different from how post-eighteenth-century philosophers tend to make such divisions, or non-existent. This is an issue I will return to in the final section of the chapter. The problem that confronted these philosophers was: given the pervasiveness of conflict, how does one govern, secure, or change oneself in order to have the best and happiest sort of life?

This was, of course, the problem that had confronted Hobbes as well and motivated the critique of felicity—the desire for felicity conflicted with happiness. The response to pervasive violence took a different form though, in the philosophers who drew on ancient schools—a defence of felicity. Techniques of self-governance and self-knowledge helped the reader to learn to identify with their rational part and to control their passions. Knowledge gave rise to virtues that dislodged central stumbling blocks to a happy life. It dislodged incorrectly directed self-interest arising from confusion about what one truly was and sadness arising from allowing oneself to be acted upon by the passions and the external world. I will argue in what follows that this identification of self-help with self-discovery allowed Spinoza to respond to Hobbes' challenge when conjoined with a metaphysical understanding of the new science as part of morality as argued for by Descartes. First, though, I will discuss a central work in the early modern appropriation of Hellenistic moral philosophy written around the time Hobbes was born, the Belgian philosopher Justus Lipsius' widely read dialogue *De Constantia*.[21]

De Constantia addressed an issue that divided Stoics and Epicureans[22] with specific reference to the violence surrounding the Dutch revolt from Spain. 'Does running away from the violence make one happy and lead to a happy life?' Lipsius answered 'No', that violence is perennial, there is no permanent refuge to be found in any garden or political association however remote, and the only permanent refuge is to be found in oneself by a reform of one's attitudes so as not to be disturbed by what is beyond one's external control. Self-reform and the transformation of one's attitudes depended on acquiring the supreme virtue of constancy or strength of mind which Lipsius defined as judging and

---

[21] It went through eighty editions (Schneewind 1998: 170). On Lipsius as the founder of neo-Stoicism see Kraye 1984: 370. Schneewind uses Lipsius to introduce modern perfectionism.

[22] Lucretius had famously suggested that running away from conflict and then looking back at those who are still suffering is pleasing in the opening of Book II of *De Rerum Natura*. The Epicurean garden was a removal as well.

acting from right reason. Constancy followed in turn from the cultivation of patience. As we become more patient we deliberate more rationally and eradicate the effects of negative affects that nurture chauvinism towards country, religion, and customs and opinions as opposed to impatiently giving in to them. Patience gives time to reason, engendering acting from stable reasons that in turn gives rise to attitudes towards external disturbances that make for more permanent happiness.

That 'ignorance and error resulting from failure to use reason properly are what stand between us and a life of moral virtue' is (as Schneewind suggests) a core theme of Lipsius' dialogue—although no clear line is drawn between moral and other virtues. But as I have suggested in the first section, Lipsius' dialogue is also a tutorial in practical techniques for attaining constancy: a work of self-help—the very sort of self-help that Hobbes provided his withering challenge to.[23] Much of De Constantia is devoted to the outline of techniques (many of them from Epictetus and Marcus Aurelius) for transforming the self, which range from meditating on astrology and the destiny of the stars to learning to distinguish rational responses (like mercy) from destructive affects (such as pity) and to winnow reason from the affects. It is hard to remember as historians of philosophy that a philosopher like Lipsius is not just presenting arguments but also techniques for self-reform and governance which he held to be transformative and efficacious.

As the dialogue evolves and Lipsius (qua dialogue participant) recognizes that applying these techniques brings better results than running away from conflict, he also secures a more constant and more generic self. Transforming the self involves discovering what one truly is, one's rational part and capacity for reasoning, as opposed to identifying with or being burdened by what is not truly oneself or beyond one's control: body, negative affects, social station, wealth or poverty, etc. Constancy thus involves identifying with a generic and rational self (and with universal reason) by giving up particular attachments and identities and so hiving off threats to the tranquillity of the self.[24]

Descartes' 'provisional morality' in the Discourse on Method had affinities with Lipsius' De Constantia and commentators have pointed to its Stoical elements.[25] It was written fifty years later against the continuing background of political and religious

[23] For an argument that Lipsius' De Constantia was written as a spiritual exercise primarily for Lipsius himself, see Sellars 2007.

[24] De Constantia has extended illustrations of techniques for becoming tranquil and walling off threats but there is little discussion of the content of the happy life or justification of the premise that an undisturbed life is a happy life. Rather, it is assumed that this is a good and supported by copious references to authorities, particularly Seneca, Epictetus, and Marcus Aurelius. Which is not to say that Lipsius took these authorities as the final word. By stressing the importance of free will (with reference to St Augustine), in arguing that God's will is not subordinated to fate, in tangling with theodicy problems, and not least in trying to harmonize the account with divine punishment (again contra the Epicureans), Lipsius accommodated these Stoic authorities to a few core Christian beliefs (and vice versa) and the result was neo-Stoicism: eclectic, modern, Stoic-inspired techniques for the care of the self tailored to early modern Christianity but devoid of confessional specificity and conflict.

[25] See Rutherford 2004; Shapiro 2008. John Marshall associates Descartes with Philo of Larissa's probabilism but sees Stoical elements at work as well (Marshall 2003).

conflict, but also after the major works of Galileo, Bacon, and the other progenitors of the new science had appeared. The interpretation of Descartes' moral philosophy has sometimes hung on the interpretation of 'provisional' or *par provision*, which has been read either as provisional in the broad sense of uncertain or tentative[26] and awaiting further justification *or* in the sense of offering provisions or advances for seeking the supreme good.[27] When the brief moral philosophy in the *Discourse* is supplemented with the later *Passions of the Soul* and his correspondence with Princess Elisabeth (hence *Correspondence*) and Queen Christina, it seems most likely that Descartes is not stressing the sceptical contingency of morality but rather that a few moral maxims are essential preconditions to one acquiring the supreme good. These maxims are necessarily general, simple, and not wholly theoretically justifiable before said good is acquired.[28]

In other words the maxims are provisional techniques discovered and pragmatically justified by Descartes for self-governance necessary to the acquisition of further goods— most importantly well-justified true ideas—essential to the best life. That Descartes' moral philosophy is to be found in correspondence and methodological introductions as well as in his scientific psychology is indicative of the breadth of what might be considered moral philosophy in the mid-seventeenth century: theoretical arguments and practical techniques centred on justifying and attaining the best (and happiest) life. In a famous passage in the French 'Introduction' to the *Principles of Philosophy* Descartes makes this explicit, suggesting that knowledge is a tree and that perfect moral science depends on the knowledge of the other sciences that make up the branches of the tree. The perfect moral science also is the crown of the other sciences and brings them to their perfection (Adam and Tannery 1996, IXB, 14; Cottingham, et al. 1985, v. 1, 186).[29]

In the earliest and most discussed of the presentations of his moral philosophy, the *Discourse*, Descartes presented 'three or four maxims' (the aforementioned 'provisional moral code' also discussed in the *Correspondence* but formulated differently (Adam and Tannery 1996: IV, 265; Cottingham, et al. 1991: 257–8)). The first maxim counselled submission to the most moderate laws, religion, and moral practices of one's country. Descartes' tacit message was to identify oneself with country and religion *only* in so far as these did not impede the cultivation of reason and burden the will with desires and beliefs beyond its control. Reasoning independent of any particular custom and conventions was intrinsically desirable, but this did not mandate dispensing entirely with customary roles or laws.[30]

The second maxim counselled the familiar constancy or strength of mind, i.e. that one should remain firm and constant in one's reasoning and course of action. Particularly

---

[26] See most recently Naaman-Zauderer 2010: 160–4.

[27] Michele LeDoeuff has argued that 'provisional' or *par provision* should be understood as a judgement awarded 'in advance to a party' as opposed to 'temporary', which jibes well with the second sense (LeDoeuff 1989: 59). Thanks to Lisa Shapiro.

[28] Thanks to Dennis Des Chene.

[29] Descartes also reiterates the importance of provisional moral rules for guiding action in this passage.

[30] Descartes underscored this in the correspondence with Elizabeth when he reformulated the rule as trying 'to employ his mind as well as he can to discover what he should or should not do in all circumstances of life' (Adam and Tannery 1996: IV, 265; Cottingham, et al. 1991: 257–8).

one should follow one's arguments through to the end even when only arguing from probable evidence. Descartes further identified this maxim, and by extension constancy and stability, with virtue. This rule was partly prudentially justified by an argument that inconstancy led to remorse and unhappiness and constancy to tranquillity and happiness—although in this case the tranquillity arising from resoluteness.[31] Constancy was also the virtue exemplifying the principle which gave rise to hyperbolic doubt in the *Essays* and the *Meditations*—following one's arguments through to the end in an exhaustive and systematic manner without a particular final cause in mind.

In the third maxim Descartes suggested that one would be happier if one restricted oneself through reason. One should seek to control only what was within the scope of the free will (mostly one's thoughts and attitudes) since that alone was wholly within our power. By so restricting ourselves we do not risk being made unhappy due to changes beyond our control. Descartes drew the connection between this rule and ancient meditative techniques for attaining happiness: 'I believe that this is the principal secret of those philosophers who have been able in earlier times to escape from the demands of empire and fortune and who, despite pains and poverty, could rival their gods in happiness' (Adam and Tannery 1996: IV, 265; Cottingham, et al. 1991: 257–8). Just as for Lipsius, for Descartes this restriction also presumed a process of self-discovery—in this case discovering that one was above all a rational thinking thing and a free will prior to biographical, social, and religious entanglements (that one was essentially a thinking thing was briskly justified later in the *Discourse* and thoroughly in the *Meditations*).[32]

The three moral maxims[33]—following moderate local customs, cultivating constancy, and only seeking to control what was within one's control—were necessary to the mastery of the passions (Descartes drew an explicit connection between the third rule and the mastery of the passions in the *Correspondence* (Adam and Tannery 1996: IV, 266; Cottingham, et al. 1991: 258)) and attaining a happy life and the supreme good. The maxims did this by helping to clarify, limit, and direct desires: 'since our will tends to pursue only what our intellect represents as good or bad, we need only to judge well in order to act well, that is to say, in order to acquire all the virtues and in general all other goods we can acquire. And when we are certain of this, we cannot fail to be happy' (Adam and Tannery 1996: IV, 266; Cottingham, et al. 1991: 258).

In the *Passions*[34] Descartes promoted the master virtue of 'true generosity'.[35] Virtues were habits that dispose minds to have thoughts—in the case of generosity thoughts

---

[31] Thanks to Justin Steinberg for this point.

[32] Towards the end of the seventeenth century, Poulain de La Barre would draw the consequence from these and similar Cartesian arguments that there were no essential differences in nature or capacity between male and female minds. See De la Barre 1984: 60.

[33] I take it that there are three maxims and a fourth general consideration about the best sort of life in conjunction with adopting the maxims.

[34] On the passions in Descartes, Spinoza, and in the seventeenth century more generally see James 1997 and 1998.

[35] 'True generosity' had affinities to Stoical magnanimity (Descartes explicitly distinguished it from Aristotelian magnanimity) but differed in (among other things) Descartes' stress on the free will.

about one's own worth connected to the passion of generosity (i.e. feeling generous towards others). The virtue of true generosity was a habit of proper appraisal of one's own self-worth. This 'perfect virtue' had two components, both of which centrally involve the free will. First, to possess the virtue is to know 'that nothing truly belongs to him but this freedom to dispose his volitions, and that he ought to be praised or blamed for no other reason than using this freedom well or badly'. Second, this was coupled with 'the firm and constant resolution to use the virtue well—that is never to lack the will or strength of mind to undertake and carry out whatever he judges best'[36] (Cottingham, et al. 1985: v.1, III.153). From true generosity follows the mastery of the passions and other virtues (courtesy, courage). It is also the *sine qua non* of felicity or beatitude—the 'perfect contentment of the mind and inner satisfaction' (Adam and Tannery 1996: IV, 264; Cottingham, et al. 1991: 257). One can be contingently happy without this virtue, but one cannot attain felicity.

In the *Correspondence* Descartes claimed that the 'supreme good—which consists in the exercise of virtue, or, what comes to the same, the possession of all those goods whose acquisition depends on the free will' is independent of the happiness and 'satisfaction of mind which results from that acquisition' (Adam and Tannery 1996: IV, 304; Cottingham, et al. 1991: 268). He then contrasted his view on the supreme good with those of Zeno, and Epicurus (Aristotle was notably deemed irrelevant) whom he claimed could be made consistent with one another and with his own views if properly understood. He agreed with Zeno that the pursuit of virtue, again broadened beyond expressly moral virtues, was the only good we can possess wholly dependent on our wills but he criticized Zeno for his extremism in desiring total detachment from the body (Adam and Tannery 1996: IV, 276; Cottingham, et al. 1991: 61).

He agreed with Epicurus that happiness was pleasure in general while criticizing him for not distinguishing the appropriate object of our desire, the supreme good or virtue, and the happiness that results from it. This was the point that Gassendi and Charleton would reject, following Epicurus in holding the inseparability of pleasure and virtue.[37]

Descartes was not arguing, though, that happiness as a good is independent of what is morally right in a post-Clarkean much the less a post-Kantian sense. The exercise of the virtue of true generosity—proper appraisal of one's own self worth—makes us happy because the proper appraisal of self-worth diminishes disruptive desires for what is outside of us and outside of our control. By knowing our self-worth we are able to concentrate on only those pursuits that benefit us and to control the negative and destructive passions impeding happiness. But true generosity must be pursued independent of the goal of happiness due to the crucial second maxim—not coincidentally the second part of the definition of true generosity. In order to be happy we must seek the *truth* resolutely according to a method unconcerned with results or final causes including our happiness. To seek the truth or to seek to acquire virtues of truth as instruments to happiness would conflict with the acquisition of virtue in so far as they are independent

---

[36] This component was a variant on constancy and on the second maxim discussed above.
[37] See Sarasohn 1996: 61–75.

objects. The life of true generosity is the life of intellectual enquiry according to the principles of the new science. It is the perfection of the sciences and the *best* sort of life. It is also the happiest life, but as following from acquiring the supreme good.

To know oneself is to know what goods one should seek, to know one's most rational part, and also to know one's passions (and one's body). In the *Passions* Descartes argued that we have passions in order to survive in the world—'they are all by nature good' (Cottingham, et al. 1985: v.1, III §211)—but they tend to draw us to erroneously represent states of affairs in ways that limit our ability to correctly judge and act. By reasoning properly we know the proper targets for the passions and we restrict their extending beyond these targets and giving rise to evils. Thus reason manages the passions by clarifying their proper extension and their appropriate objects and by developing techniques to counter the most stubborn of them. This in turn allows reason to seek higher goods.

The theoretical analysis of the passions is itself a practical therapy. Reflecting on the passions loosens their grip and manages them for a happy life.[38] The theoretical analysis involved efficient causal, mechanistic explanations of the physiological bases of the passions, a taxonomy of basic or primitive passions as part of an explanation of how different passions are related to one another, and an account of how the physiological causes impact the mind and the will through the imagination. Passions are distinguished from actions of the will as ways in which our minds were acted upon by our bodies and particularly the physical imagination (Cottingham, et al. 1985: v.1, I §17). Notably for Descartes the mastery of the passions was closely connected to reasoning about them in terms of mechanism and efficient cause.[39]

More generally the type of theoretical reasoning that Descartes advocated and justified in his best-known works was part of moral philosophy broadly construed (as opposed to a prerequisite of or justification for moral philosophy). In the *Correspondence* Descartes illustrated this by offering a conclusion of the *Principles* (the immensity of the universe) alongside a more overtly moral rule—that we should subordinate our interests to the whole within reason—as 'truths most useful to us' (Adam and Tannery 1996: IV, 291–4; Cottingham, et al. 1991: 265–6). The moral rule is action-guiding in an obvious way that the conclusion from the *Principles* is not, but the conclusion helps us to recognize that 'each one of us is really one of the many parts of the universe', which in turn helps us to see that we should subordinate our interests. Reflecting on a fact about the physical world is an important step in controlling our passions, cultivating virtue, and leading a happy life.

In Descartes elements of ancient and Hellenistic moral theory are altered, broadened, and combined in an Eclectic mix to take account of changing conceptions of reason and reasoning. Scientific reasoning and practices and the life dedicated to them are the most efficacious practices and techniques for the mastery of the

---

[38] Minimally in so far as when one understands a passion one can provide an efficacious means or instrument to counter it. More controversially in so far as knowledge of the causes of a passion can dissolve its grip in some cases (but not all).

[39] Descartes' position is far more sophisticated and nuanced than I can present here. See James 1998; Rorty 1984, 1992.

passions, the restriction and satisfaction of the desires, and the cultivation of crucial virtues. The explanations of the passions afforded by the mechanistic philosophy, and the advocacy of 'true generosity' and other virtues derived from these explanations are more secure than previous similar but unjustified beliefs. These explanations are, as noted, also part of ridding ourselves of negative passions and reasoning rightly. They allow us to more effectively discover what we are—minds seeking the supreme good connected to bodies and giving rise to passions which help us to care for it— and to separate ourselves from what we are not (what is beyond the control of our will or what we can only have confused knowledge of). Practical techniques and provisional morality are necessary in a life dedicated to the cultivation of reason—the best life and also the happiest life—in order to seek the highest goods. They allow us in turn to use our reason to make instruments, mental and physical, which make for a happier life.[40]

Consequently when Descartes claims in the *Correspondence* to make the views of Zeno and Epicurus consistent, he should be understood to be arguing that when the moral and metaphysical principles argued for by the ancient schools are properly understood—i.e. when they are understood through Descartes' own philosophy and when Cartesian reasoning is embraced—the conflicts between the ancient schools will either be dissolved or rejected. When what is true in the beliefs of these schools are put on a more certain footing, the techniques of the schools, some drastically transformed, will become more efficacious. This way of understanding the relation between modern philosophy and the ancient schools can be seen in many who came after Descartes: from Spinoza, to Shaftesbury, to Hume.[41]

12.4 MODERN SELF-TRANSFORMATION: SPINOZA

Spinoza's *Ethics* offers an even more radical development of this line.[42] Unlike Hobbes, and like Descartes, Spinoza argued that felicity is attainable by understanding oneself as part of a non-teleological, infinite, efficient causal universe. As it was for the ancient schools, ethics is a process of self-discovery utilizing techniques to identify one's rational part and attain the best life. Spinoza's *Ethics* is an ethics in the Cartesian sense, i.e. an argument for the best and happiest life and techniques (in particular as part of a scientific psychology) for attaining said life that follow from the pursuit of knowledge. This was combined with many Hobbesian elements and a response to Hobbes' challenge where Spinoza argued that Hobbes insufficiently recognized the close connection between morals and metaphysics and so misunderstood the nature of power.

---

[40] This is a central theme in early modern thinkers influenced by Bacon.
[41] For a careful treatment of the Scholastic predecessors and the immediate Cartesian responses see Ariew 2014.
[42] For an excellent introduction to Spinoza's moral philosophy see Garrett 1996.

Hobbes, Descartes, and Spinoza all agreed that mechanistic and efficient causal reasoning associated with modern philosophy and the new science (and about the passions and in general) was crucial to one's happiness but disagreed as to how to construe it and as to what the consequences of accepting it were.

Spinoza had a fundamental disagreement with Descartes (and agreement with Hobbes) concerning what he took as Descartes' unwillingness to follow the truth wherever it might go when it conflicted with intuitive and widely held beliefs. In the corollary to the final proposition to Part II (IIP49C) of the *Ethics*, Spinoza argued for an anti-Cartesian identity of the will and the intellect[43] as an extension of Spinoza's naturalistic metaphysics and philosophy of mind and an anti-teleological and mechanistic world view. This was a crucial divergence given Descartes' stress on restricting what we can control to the free will. In the Scholium appended to the proposition, Spinoza suggested that there were four 'practical advantages' that followed from the doctrine and that the reasoned denial of Descartes' libertarianism had positive consequences for one's life.

First, one recognized that one becomes more virtuous in so far as one better understands God. Since Spinoza equated God with Nature, to understand Nature was to understand God, by which Spinoza understood a wholly non-personal and wholly metaphysical being—an infinite substance with infinite attributes (from which follow infinite and finite modes). In so far as we are a part of Nature, to understand ourselves as following necessarily from God was to understand ourselves as part of an efficient causal process and no different in many respects from the many other modes that follow from God, whether space dust or Holy Roman Emperor.

For Spinoza one had to see that one was a mode in an infinite world, and particularly that one was what Spinoza referred to as a 'conatus': a mode which like all modes seeks to preserve itself. Conatus was Spinoza's metaphysical analogue to (and generalization of) Descartes' principle of inertia in his physics and Hobbes' accounts of the quantification of motion and of natural right.[44] Spinoza defined the closely connected concept 'appetite' as 'the very essence of man, from whose nature there necessarily follow those things that promote his preservation' (Spinoza 1985: EIII9S). Spinoza used 'desire' to designate an appetite plus consciousness of said appetite (implying that we are not conscious of at

---

[43] There is some disagreement as to how to read this identification but see Della Rocca 2003.

[44] Descartes' first law of motion reads [1.] 'Each thing (*unamquamque rem*), insofar as it is simple and undivided, remains, *quantum in se est*, always in the same state, never changing unless as the result of external causes' [my emphasis]. Spinoza's version of this law of motion in the *Principles of Descartes' Philosophy* reads [2.] 'Each thing (*unaquaeque res*), insofar as it is simple and undivided, and it is considered in itself alone (*& in se sola consideratur*), *quantum in se est*, always perseveres in the same state (*in eodem statu perseverat*) [my emphasis].' *Ethics* IIIP6, which is the first to introduce the *conatus* reads: [3.] 'Each thing (*unaquaeque res*), *quantum in se est*, endeavors to persevere in its being (*in suo esse perseverare conatur*). Hobbes defined the *conatus* as the initial quantification of motion that allows motion to be analyzed geometrically: 'to be motion made in less space and time than can be determined by exposition or number; that is, motion made through a point' (Hobbes 1655 I: 205). He defined natural right in *De Cive* as the 'right to use any means and to do any action by which he can preserve himself' (Hobbes 1998: I. 8).

least some of our appetites). Desire was one of three fundamental affects.[45] The other two fundamental affects were joy—becoming more powerful—and sadness—becoming less powerful.

These three fundamental affects provided a general mechanism for explaining many of the passions populating our folk psychology; love is joy in relation to an object, titillation is joy referred to a part of the body, and so forth. It also allowed him to recommend passions as joy-producing and suggest avoiding passions that were sadness-inducing. Spinoza's choice of desire as the fundamental affect, as opposed to appetite, is closely connected with the practical goals of a theory of the passions and his response to Hobbes. The expressly cognitive component in desire—consciousness *of* the appetite—allowed him to suggest mental techniques and cognitive therapy for seeking joy, avoiding sadness, and cultivating the virtues of self-knowledge leading to the most joyous or best sort of life. By changing the consciousness of the appetite one could transform the appetite.

Much like Descartes' *Passions* that inspired it then this was both a descriptive psychology and a means to the best life via the self-knowledge acquired from reflection on and control of the passions. Unlike both Descartes and Hobbes, there is very little discussion of the physical basis of the passions; Spinoza's therapy is almost exclusively cognitive. Even more than Descartes and Hobbes, Spinoza is interested in the passions in so far as recognizing their proper objects is part of the best life.

Unlike Descartes for whom virtues were psychological habits and epistemic attitudes for directing them, and much like Hobbes, for Spinoza virtue was identified with the causal power or force that belonged to the individual (a play on the Latin word for force—*vis, virtus*). 'Virtue' was the essence of a person (or thing) in so far as it acts (Spinoza 1985: IVD8) and an 'act' was any effect that follows from a person (or thing) and is clearly, distinctly, and wholly knowable through that person or thing (Spinoza 1985: IIID2). This made for a very high bar for some process or event to qualify as an action[46] in so far as in order for X to be an action it had to be an internal metaphysical cause—i.e. arising from a thing's essence (as opposed to external causes)—and the effect had to be knowable through the cause. None of this figured in Hobbes' account of human action where an action could be unknown and was just an effect caused by appetite and fear in response to external objects or some sort of stimulus.[47] Hobbes' looser, materialist account of action assumed that the sources of actions were the limits of human physical bodies under particular affective (appetite and fear) and causal (some sort of causal connection to the effect) conditions.

This hints to Spinoza's tacit strategy in dealing with Hobbes' challenge, which was kin to his criticisms of Cartesian voluntarism. Hobbes tried to explain all moral terms in a

---

[45] I will use affect, emotion, and passion interchangeably. There are distinctions between them but they are not relevant to this discussion.

[46] The height of the bar could be lowered by taking action not to instantiate a distinction of kind, i.e. X is an action if it wholly satisfies the definition and not an action if it does not, but satisfiable to a *degree*, i.e. X is an action just to the degree it satisfies the definition.

[47] See Hobbes 1994: 71–3 (Chapter XII). See also Richard Tuck, 'Introduction' in Hobbes 1998: xvii–xxi.

manner consistent with and extending from his materialist base and Spinoza tried to explain all basic moral terms and all physical terms as consistent with and extending from his anti-teleological metaphysics that in turn was consistent with (and backed) the best version of the new science.[48] This led Spinoza to argue that Hobbes' claims could be altered or defanged when it could be shown that Hobbes' materialist explanations were inconsistent with the metaphysics he should have adopted (or needed to adopt to make his morals consistent).

For example, Hobbes' claim that human beings continuously seek 'power after power' was understood by Spinoza as an error arising from thinking about natural right in terms of physical causes and physical bodies. That individual is most powerful which acts the most and which has the most effects. Hobbes assumed that the sufficient conditions for action were: (1) being a physical body or group of physical bodies, (2) initiating motion in other bodies, and (3), for human actions, possessing particular psychological dispositions. This was insufficient to explain how effects had their *source* in this body or group of bodies (as opposed to mere concurrence) and how the putative source was an individual (as opposed to an ever changing flux of bodies). When action is properly defined[49] it becomes clear that many of the things that are commonly viewed as powerful actions— crushing, molesting, and thieving—are not actions at all or more being acted upon than acting. If Hobbes denied this then he would need to provide an explanation of how a body is a source of a particular action. Spinoza's suggestion is that a physical theory without a fairly robust metaphysics is insufficient to do so. Consequently, for Spinoza, to seek power after power turns out to involve knowing more of the world and acting in ways that conduce to individual tranquillity and general happiness. Power and tranquillity are not mutually exclusive, indeed maximal power is maximal tranquillity.

Relatedly, when one defined virtue in terms of internal metaphysical causes arising from the essence of a thing, punishment and reward could no longer be a motivation to virtue since this would entail an external cause outside the essence of the individual and thus not be a virtue. So Hobbes' idea that morality was anchored in a system of rewards and punishments set in place by a legislator and nothing beyond this was a non-starter.

Like Descartes, and like the ancient schools, Spinoza wished to show that his ethics had the greatest practical therapeutic advantages for the care of the self. For example to return to the advantages of Spinoza's philosophy, the second practical advantage of identification of will and intellect is that if helps us 'to expect and endure with patience both faces of fortune': i.e. good and evil. Good and evil were relative to the essence of whatever they were good and evil for: good was 'what we certainly know to be useful to us' (Spinoza 1985: IVD1) and evil was correlatively whatever restricted our mastery of whatever was good. But since things that are good and evil for both our minds and bodies follow from

[48] That it was consistent with the new science was insufficient for Spinoza. The anti-teleological metaphysics gave the ontological and metaphysical prerequisites for any efficacious and consistent natural philosophy. Descartes and others erred when they failed to make their natural enquiries reflect what should have been their metaphysical and ontological commitments. See Letter 27 in Shirley 2002: 175–6.

[49] This involves a theory of composition, identity, and an account of cause—all of which are far beyond the scope of this chapter.

God by necessity, removing our selves from our body or restricting our selves to our free will are not options. When we recognize that the world was not created for us (indeed it was not created at all) by coming to understand ourselves to be finite modes in an infinite causal world we will be better able to 'expect and endure with patience'.

Some later philosophers, notably Julien Offray de La Mettrie[50] and (perhaps) Nietszche,[51] took the combined definitions of virtue and good and evil and the lack of external motivation and punishment and reward to license amoralism, in so far as 'good' was relative to the inner tendencies essential to an individual nature.[52] Spinoza seemed to court this with his famous assertion that 'If men were born free, they would form no concept of good and evil so long as they remained free' (1985: IVP68).[53] But the constraint 'certainly know' in the definition of good and evil restricted the good and bad to what was infallibly known to be good and bad for human beings (not just for this or that human being or for human beings in general) in so far as they shared basic beliefs and powers and were well suited to helping one another.

This was a reason for Spinoza's denial of (2), i.e. that there are no objective rankings available of goods in the state of nature. According to Hobbes a free man in the state of nature has the right to do whatever *seems* necessary to self-preservation[54] because there is no arbitrator or judge to adjudicate between permissible means to preserve one's life. Since preservation is a precondition of happiness, one can't offer any moral codes, recommendations, etc.—i.e. rules, prohibitions, duties, obligations, etc., for attaining happiness—if preservation has not been secured. The state is the most effective means to secure the necessary conditions of happiness. Since stability and preservation are prior conditions of individual happiness, the establishing of duties and obligations concerning happiness assume the existence of a state. Since anything undermining the stability of the state makes happiness impossible, the state can use whatever means necessary to preserve the stability. Finally, since the sovereign is in the state of nature, there is no arbitrator to adjudicate what is the best means for the state to preserve itself.

On Spinoza's account human beings could have certain metaphysical knowledge even if they were at best capable of probable knowledge of the external physical world. This metaphysical knowledge did provide an objective constraint on what was more or less conducive to happiness through an account of the passions and recommendations of how to cultivate the passions. Certain knowledge of what one was—a mode in an infinite efficient causal world—extended to certain knowledge of and constraints on the state and preferences for the type of state.[55] Unlike for Hobbes, for whom we would form no conception of the correlative terms good and evil if born free because of (2), for Spinoza if we were free (and powerful agents in the sense discussed above) we would only have positive affects and be wholly rational and wise.

---

[50] See Ann Thomson 'Introduction' in La Mettrie 1996: xiii.   [51] See Katsafanas (2011).

[52] i.e. A sadist's good would be sadism and no more general welfare could be justified beyond the individual specific goods.

[53] See Kisner 2011: 106–9.

[54] 'vel conducere ad sui conservationem, vel saltem conducere videri' (Hobbes 1642: I.x).

[55] See Garrett 2012.

Spinoza's third 'practical advantage' is that it teaches us both 'not to envy and to help our neighbours from the guidance of reason as occasion and circumstance require' and the fourth 'that citizens should be governed and led . . . not so as to be slaves, but so as to do freely what is best'. These practical advantages were further elucidated in Part IV of the *Ethics* where Spinoza described the life of 'the wise man' and painted the life of felicity. Acting from reason to preserve one's nature is the supreme virtue of fortitude which Spinoza distinguished into two further virtues: *animositas* (tenacity or courage) or acting in order to promote the advantage of the agent and *generositas* (nobility) or acting to promote the advantage of others. For Spinoza there was no possibility of conflict between the two virtues when properly understood since dictates of reason could not lead to contradictory actions. At the same time Spinoza was well aware that very few were capable of the life of the wise man, and that a failing of the ancient Stoics was to hold the bar far too high. Consequently Spinoza was able to give different (although consistent) council both to the few capable of the life of the wise man and those many capable of admiring this life as rational but incapable of attaining the ideal. This allowed Spinoza to distinguish between what is most rational and what is recommended for most of us.[56]

For example, Spinoza asserts in the *Ethics* that 'a free man always acts honestly, not deceptively' (1985: IVP72). He justifies this with the argument that if the free man were to act deceptively then he would act from a dictate of reason. But then deception would be a virtue and all human beings should interact with one another with deceitful intentions. Both the assertion and Spinoza's justification have a strongly proto-Kantian appearance, and they most certainly do draw on the idea of universally coherent dictates of reason. Spinoza's point seems to be, like some formulations of the categorical imperative, that since reason cannot dictate that free men in general should act deceitfully to preserve themselves, it cannot dictate this in particular.

Spinoza's justification rests though on an unKantian argument that for the free man deceitful action does not educe to one's true *advantage*. But since it always seems to be to one's advantage not to be killed, and since one can under some circumstances use deceit in order not to be killed, this seems to be a non-starter. There are two steps to avoiding this apparently repugnant consequence. First it is important to distinguish between what reason dictates that a free man should do in general and what those of us who are not entirely free but wise and are in the throes of our passions should do under particular difficult circumstances.[57] This draws on the distinction between different readerships mentioned above.

Second, an explanation of why the free man acts as he does is in order. According to Hobbes when men are free some of them are violent and destructive. Fear of death dictates prudential action, joining a state. This in turn rules out felicity. According to Spinoza the free man does not act deceitfully, because he would be acting from the external sanction of fear of death ('the free man thinks of nothing less than death') that diminishes his power and makes him sad. Instead the free mans act from positive internal

---

[56] See Garrett 1990.
[57] See Garrett 1990; Della Rocca 1998: 1232; Michael LeBuffe 2007; Kisner 2011: ch. 8.

dictates that preserve his being and augment his power. Spinoza makes clear in Part Five of the *Ethics* that one's rational part is eternal, it can't be killed, and the more one acts from virtue the more one has and is this rational, deathless part. Indeed Spinoza identifies blessedness with the highest kind of knowledge of and love of God, which involves conceiving of oneself as eternal and indestructible (Spinoza 1985: VP34, VP36–7) and which removes the fear of death (VP38).[58] Consequently Spinoza is not arguing that one must act rightly and rationally even if it conflicts with one's interest. He is arguing that acting rationally cannot conflict with the free man's interest properly understood while accepting that since most people are not wholly rational and are fearful of death and dismemberment what educes to their advantage may be different. This depends on identifying with one's rational part, and not making putatively rational judgements on the basis of the frightened and potentially frightening ways that others view themselves.

This is not to say that Spinoza thinks of the life of the free man as a kind of metaphysical removal at odds with the lives of the semi-rational many. His discussion of the free man includes numerous practical moral recommendations: to be grateful to other free men (Spinoza 1985: IVP71), to live in a state (Spinoza 1985: IVP73), to not fear death, to cultivate love, piety, and strength of mind, etc. Rather these should be understood, in combination with the many practical techniques offered by Spinoza, as providing a rational therapy and rules for moral conduct in connection with ideals that men ought to strive towards but which are not always appropriate for the incremental pursuit of the best life.

Spinoza's account had many affinities with his Hellenistic predecessors, and commentators have stressed the affinities with Plato, Aristotle, Epicureans, the Stoics[59] (despite his criticisms of Stoicism), and with Cicero[60] among others. The general focus on the best life, happiness, and practical techniques for self-preservation as well as the particular advantages and techniques suggested have the flavour of the ancient schools. Indeed what Spinoza describes in the conclusion of Part IV of the *Ethics* reads like the description of an idealized Hellenistic school with Epicurean, Stoical, Platonist, and even Sceptical elements, but reducible to no one school. Like Lipsius, the school framework is used to avoid discussion of particular religious doctrines and to respond to violence (this is far more explicit in Spinoza's *Tractatus Theologico-Politicus* and *Tractatus Politicus*). But Spinoza pushes it in an extreme direction where efficient causal reasoning provides an alternative to the ancient schools as a means of avoiding confessional specificity, although leading to irreligious consequences in Spinoza!

Like the ancient schools there is a model of a wise man. But it is no particular founding individual—in keeping with Spinoza's stress on the free man as a rational ideal and ordinary men as always overcome with their passions. For example, the second practical

---

[58] I am here referring to Spinoza's difficult doctrine of the eternity of the mind, i.e. that there is a part of the mind that is eternal and that the more one knows by what Spinoza calls the third kind of knowledge the greater the part that is eternal. This doctrine makes the connection between knowledge and happiness via eternity.

[59] See for a few of many examples De Brabander 2007; Kristeller 1984; James 1993; Pereboom 1994; Gaitens and Lloyd 1999.

[60] See James 2012.

advantage discussed above, 'to expect and endure with patience both faces of fortune', is a particularly useful counsel to ordinary semi-rational men but would be unnecessary for the free man. Like Descartes, Spinoza's affinities with the schools follow from trying to build a moral theory consistent with a non-teleological and anti-providentialist world view—a view that Stoics, Epicureans, and Sceptics shared to different degrees—and showing that the 'practical advantages' of predecessor theories and much more could be captured more reasonably on this basis.

Consequently we see in Descartes and Spinoza more and more general rational foundations and justifications for the discovery and care of the self consistent with scientific knowledge, more and more vague and general appropriations of the schools, and at the same time a great deal of practical moral philosophy focused on psychology and practical techniques for the cultivation and care of the self. The form and substance of the techniques, as well as the goal of a tranquil and happy life, would be recognizable to Marcus Aurelius, Seneca, and Epictetus. But the justifications for these techniques and goals reflected a world after Bacon and Galileo, in particular in how self-knowledge is an extension of what it is to properly know an infinite and efficient causal world. Consequently (as noted above) these theories involve an expansion of what is moral— whatever is theoretically and practically relevant to identifying and attaining the best life and understanding the self—and at the same time a radical transformation of both how one knows the self and what the self that is known is. A central example of this is Spinoza's discussion of techniques for moderating the passions in the first third of Part 5 of the *Ethics*. Here Spinoza argues that the more we refer our sense perceptions or mental images to God the less our minds are occupied by these negative passions (Spinoza 1985: VP14 and VP20 Note).

What we do not see in these thinkers is a separation of what makes an action right as distinct from our welfare or interest. The assumption is that the two will harmonize if fully rational and that happiness will (mostly) follow if the truth is properly pursued for itself. In Spinoza we rather see a distinction between an ideal rational action as the sort of action a free man undertakes and the action we semi-rational men ought to undertake.

12.5 MAXIMS, SELF-GOVERNANCE, AND THE LIMITS OF SELF-KNOWLEDGE

The philosophers I have discussed so far wished to show their readership and their students, friends, and followers a means to self-knowledge, the best life, and happiness. The form in which they expressed themselves was paramount in order to convince readers to apply moral techniques and doctrines to their own lives. The form chosen also often had its own implicit assumptions about the function of moral philosophy. Descartes presented his morals in maxims and they had a central role in Spinoza's techniques for regulating the passions for Spinoza. The maxim or aphorism form is particularly interesting for thinking about the role of form in early modern moral philosophy and its connection to self-help.

Bacon began his brief essay 'On Counsel' by holding the relation implicit in counsel above all others (except the relation between man and God):

> THE greatest trust, between man and man, is the trust of giving counsel. For in other confidences, men commit the parts of life; their lands, their goods, their children, their credit, some particular affair; but to such as they make their counselors, they commit the whole: by how much the more, they are obliged to all faith and integrity. (Vickers 1996: 379)

Bacon went on to note that even God needed counsel. To write moral maxims was to take on the role of personal moral counsellor, a moral analogue to the spiritual aphorisms of the minister or religious leader or the prudential political maxims of the privy counsellor (as seen in Machiavelli's, Guicciardini's, and De La Court's maxims), and to take trust of the whole of someone's life. This was not unique to maxims, but it was particularly evident in maxims, letters (Epictetus' and St Paul's letters to their followers, for example), and sometimes in brief essays.

The writing of moral maxims went well beyond writers who we usually consider philosophers. Take for example:

> Ambitious men are like hops that never rest climbing so long as they have nothing to stay upon, but take away their props, and they are of all the most dejected. (Hensley 1967: 278)

The Puritan poet Anne Bradstreet's maxim—from an unpublished series of maxims grouped as 'Meditations Divine and Moral'—reminded readers that ambitious actions might be seductive and self-affirming when undertaking them, but give rise to dejection when things go wrong. More generally, the maxim was often used to remind a reader of negative consequences of a course of action (dejection), or even more generally a way of life, when in the grip of that course of action. Similarly:

> None Loves *himself* too little. (Whichcote 1703: Aphorism 351)

The Cambridge Platonist (and minister) Benjamin Whichcote (who will be discussed at greater length in the next section) intended to remind the reader of a potential insidious vice which all humans are gripped by. Bradstreet's maxims were generally practical counsels and Whichcote's generally theoretical moral philosophy rendered *in breve*. But both assumed that excessive self-love was bad and destructive and that the moral counsellor was to point to insidious vices and to offer help with counsels to offset them. Both also assumed similar virtues, and assumed that there was no conflict between religious virtues, moral virtues, interest properly understood, and happiness. Human beings were often confused, due to their passions, or original sin, or due to inadequate intellects, and in need of sharp shocks to stop them from acting on destructive desires and passions and to motivate them to act decently.

The purpose of a maxim was not just to convince a reader to undertake certain actions and avoid others while reading the maxim, but to lodge in the reader's memory in order to provide strong governing principles to offset self-destructive tendencies and to aid readers in better guarding themselves against unpredictable and enticing future destructive actions and circumstances. As with Epictetus' *Enchiridion*, Marcus Aurelius' *Meditations*, *Proverbs*, and Jesus' aphorisms, effective modern maxims attractively and pointedly distilled a central teaching so that it would be present to the reader's mind when most needed.

The pleasing manner in which maxims were written, their form, was crucial to their success. Another of Whichcote's maxims reads 'Men are not to be *Taught* with *Clubs*, but with Fescues (i.e. straws or twigs—AG) pointing to the Letters. Letters are not to be knocked into the Head, but offered to the eye' (Whichcote 1703: Aphorism 353). Aphorisms or maxims, like this one, are meant to be fescues in the sense that they allowed moral principles to be offered to the reader in pleasing form. This is an implicit assumption of maxim writing in general: reading maxims is intended to be pleasurable in a way that study of a systematic treatise might not be. In so far as reading maxims is pleasurable, and they can be taken up briefly, it can provide moral governance to those who do not have 'Spirits for very long attention' (Whichcote 1703: ii).

Once seen and retained, maxims provided condensed and easily recalled techniques for 'the great Government, that of our selves' (Whichcote 1703: Aphorism 703), and when recalled under difficult conditions when careful reasoning might be impractical or impossible they motivate the agent to act in accordance with what they might embrace under more rational conditions. Put differently, they provided a technique for detecting the borders or limits of appropriate conduct in murky circumstances, in particular circumstances where one tends to be consistently misled by one's passions and desires, as well as a general means to reorient one's desires and actions. Descartes, as we have seen, formulated his provisional morality as three maxims. Even Spinoza's moral recommendations, derived from highly abstract treatments of metaphysics and mind, were formulated as 'maxims': 'The free man thinks of nothing less than death, and his wisdom is a meditation on life' (1985: IV).

In Whichcote's preface to his posthumously published *Moral and Religious Aphorisms*, he asserts that though maxims could be profitably derived from a moral system, and systems were valuable, the maxims did not need to be connected back to the justifying system in order to be of use:

> I am so far from being an Enemy to Systems, that I confess I have an inveterate prejudice in favor of them; Notwithstanding which I must Acknowledge, that the Doctrine of Morality and Religion may be delivered with special advantage in the form of Aphorisms. (Whichcote 1703: ii)

Descartes and Spinoza both made similar use of maxims, although both likely would have held (as perhaps Whichcote would have as well) that in order to be as effective as possible, the user of the maxims should have previously grasped the systematic arguments from which they derived and which justified the synoptic counsel they offered.

Whichcote continued, 'For proof of this I appeal to the *Excerpta* of Marcus Antoninus; and the Proverbs of Solomon, wherein the most Important Truths of these kinds are represented without any of the Artificial Dependence, and Method, which some Men find hard to Comprehend' (Whichcote 1703: ii).[61] This points out that aphorisms drew on and combined two (or more) traditions—the ancient schools and biblical aphorisms and parable. As noted, for most moral philosophers I am considering the line between moral philosophy and natural religion (and even revealed religion) was flexible or non-existent. At minimum natural or revealed religion was a precondition to natural morality. The continuity between these Hellenistic and Biblical aphoristic traditions and between revealed and natural religion and natural morality allowed Bradstreet and Whichcote to place religious and moral maxims side by side. For Whichcote the aphorisms pointed to a worked out system (which the reader might access through rational reflection independent of social norms), for Bradstreet to an assumed shared morality and natural religion.

This general background, i.e. maxims as a technique of practical philosophy to govern the self under trying circumstances, a touchstone for meditation, and an entryway to more systematic justifications of moral principles, is important for understanding the works of perhaps the most notorious practitioner of the maxim: La Rochefoucauld. His maxims were and are widely read by philosophers and were also read by the nobility, including Queen Christina with whom Descartes had corresponded on the supreme good. What made La Rochefoucauld's maxims so popular and notorious?

La Rochefoucauld belonged to a salon organized by his friend Madame de Sablé that had earlier included Pascal. The members of the salon wrote maxims and read, and criticized one another's work. The few of Madame de Sablé's maxims which survive were pointed attempts to remind a reader that immoral action and deception led to dissatisfaction and that one had to be constantly aware of one's own deceptive nature. Unlike Whichcote's rationalist optimism (which I will discuss at the beginning of the next section) and closer to Bradstreet's Puritanism, many of her maxims had a Jansenist or Augustinean flavour (although De Sablé was critical of Augustineanism as well) and stressed human weakness which could not be overcome through unaided human reason. For example 'we so love all new and unusual things that we even derive a secret pleasure from the saddest and most awful events, both because of their novelty and because of the natural malignity that exists within us'.

Augustineanism was a major current in some of the most important works of moral philosophy of the late seventeenth and early eighteenth century. In some authors it was clearly religiously motivated, as in the hugely influential *Essais de Morale* of the Jansenist Pierre Nicole (a few of which were translated into English by John Locke) and Pascal's *Pensées*. Nicole portrayed human beings as weak and driven by vanity, vice, and interest, self-deceiving, and incapable of intellectual or moral self-perfection. This fit a theology centred on salvation by grace

---

[61] See Gill 1999, 2006 : Part 1; Schneewind 1998: 196–8.

(as it did for Calvinist and Lutheran intellectuals as well) and an Epicurean theory of motivation (although as a consequence of human depravity).[62]

Some works with a libertine flavour also use Augustinean arguments: for example Mandeville's *Fable of the Bees*. For Mandeville human beings are weak and depraved, self-deceiving, and motivated by pleasure, and their personal vices lead to public virtues. Similarly Montaigne's 'On Cannibals' walked a fine line between scepticism and moral relativism or even immoralism. There is little or no hint in Mandeville of salvation by grace or a divine plan.

La Rochefoucauld's *Maxims* falls in between. Like Mandeville's *Fable of the Bees*, there is little or no reference to religion for justification. But like in Madame de Sablé and Nicole there are allusions to traditional Augustinean themes. And unlike in Mandeville there is a strong and often tacit condemnation of human weakness and vice. Consequently La Rochefoucauld has been interpreted as both an Augustinean and a libertine from the time that the *Maxims* first appeared (Moriarty 2006: 228–9) because of the unrelenting and acute descriptions of human self-deception vice and fallibility. In the famous 'Note to the Reader' attached to the first edition (and then withdrawn from subsequent editions) La Rochefoucauld remarked that the *Maxims* contain 'nothing more than a moral digest in keeping with the thought of various church fathers' but as always it is difficult to know how seriously to take the remark.

The most recent major English-language study of the French Moralists has argued that it can't be conclusively decided where La Rochefoucauld falls, or even whether it makes sense to view him in terms of this opposition, due to changes in the different editions of the *Maxims* (Moriarty (2006: 247)). This is amplified by the maxim form itself that did not rely on systematic presentation.[63] In contrast with Whichcote, whose aphorisms were entryways into a carefully worked out system hinted to be elsewhere, or Bradstreet who assumed a familiar moral picture shared by her readers which they needed reminding of, La Rochefoucauld used aphorisms as a way to punch holes in moral presuppositions.

One could say even more strongly that La Rochefoucauld's maxims punch holes in the sort of perfectionism exemplified by (among others) his contemporaries Descartes and Spinoza.[64] The presupposition of Descartes and Spinoza was that self-knowledge and knowledge of the passions led to the best life and happiness. La Rochefoucauld's maxims question whether such self-knowledge is possible due to the force of self-love or *amour propre*. Bradstreet, Whichcote, De Sablé and many others used their maxims to counterbalance or offset *amour propre*, when readers were in its grips, with self-governance in order to protect the self from grave harm. Both Spinoza and Descartes argued that self-knowledge, knowledge of the passions, and knowledge that led to identification with one's rational part transformed desires for satisfaction of interested passions into desire for truth and higher goods and was far more conducive to one's fundamental interests.

---

[62] This combination can also be seen in Pufendorf, Hobbes, and many others who argued that human beings were weak and depraved, motivated by pleasure, and needed laws and superiors to keep them in check.

[63] See James 1998: 1361.

[64] I am not suggesting that he read Spinoza. He may have read Descartes.

Consider three maxims taken from many similar maxims of La Rochefoucauld:

> Self-interest, which is accused of all our crimes, often deserves to be praised for our good deeds (La Rochefoucauld 2007, V: 305)

> Most men's gratitude is merely a secret wish to receive greater favors (La Rochefoucauld 2007, V: 298)

> Moderation cannot claim any merit for fighting ambition and subjugating it; the two things are never found together. Moderation is sluggishness and laziness of the soul, as ambition is its activity and passion. (La Rochefoucauld 2007, V: 293)

In the first maxim self-interest is not just inevitable, or in need of conversion to an intellectual love of higher goods, but often praiseworthy as it is. This can be interpreted in an Augustinean manner: God is capable of drawing virtue even from such depraved creatures as us. Or it can be interpreted as asserting that common selfishness and self-interest is as much the source of praiseworthy actions as blameworthy actions simply because it is the source of almost all of our actions. In the second maxim we see that a virtue, gratitude, often has self-interest as its motive.[65] In the third maxim La Rochefoucauld attacks an assumption of virtue theories—Aristotelian and Christian—that moderation reduces ambition. Moderation and ambition never arise together because they are opposites—one is laziness and the other activity. La Rochefoucauld also suggests elsewhere that kindness is a form of laziness often allied to self-interest. In this and other maxims the activity or passivity of particular human beings is not mostly a consequence of their cultivation of virtues but instead due to the character or temperament they just so happen to have (La Rochefoucauld 2007, V: 189).

For La Rochefoucauld self-knowledge is centrally knowledge that we are deceptive and self-deceiving creatures, bound by our characters. In a famous passage from the 'Note to the Reader' he draws a picture of fathomless selfishness and self-deception:

> Self-love (*amour propre*) is the love of oneself (*amour de soi-même*), and of all things for the sake of oneself. It makes men idolize themselves, and it would make them tyrannize other people, if fortune gave them the means to do so . . . Its convolutions are beyond imagining; its transformations surpass those of any metamorphosis, and its subtleties those of chemistry . . . it is like our eyes, which discover everything and are blind only to themselves. (La Rochefoucauld 2007: 147–9)

The idea that we can control the passions through causal knowledge of them and through introspective self-knowledge is not even tendered—whenever we think that we have managed to control *amour propre* and the connected passions we can discover that *amour propre* was in the driver's seat (Moriarty 2006: 326).

Given the background assumptions of the maxim form described above, and given what appears to be a denial of the capacity for most or all men and women to effectively self-govern through self-knowledge, what do we make of La Rochefoucauld writing these sorts of maxims? First, La Rochefoucauld appeared to write these sorts of maxims

[65] By virtue La Rochefoucauld seems to just mean those qualities that people generally esteem, and vice those qualities they generally deplore. See also La Rochefoucauld (2007, V: 236).

precisely because of people's capacity for self-deception, i.e. he is presenting his readers with difficult truths that can only be tolerated briefly. Since one cannot maintain them for very long as truths about oneself, it is unlikely that these truths will impact one's conduct although they may promote more general reflection. Like Bradstreet and Whichcote, a maxim by La Rochefoucald reminds one of one's true motivations (and the motivations of others) when one doesn't realize one is in difficult circumstances. But unlike them, the goal seems more fleeting self-knowledge than self-transformation for most. There is also great pleasure in reading them, a delight in savage, well-turned, and surprising observations.[66] Both of these uses of the maxims can be found in writers from Augustine to Nietzsche.

La Rochefoucauld greatly influenced La Bruyère, whose celebrated work *Characters* described different character types, and many of the maxims are more descriptions of human motivation and psychology than counsels. But there are a few touchstones of counsel throughout the *Maxims* and *Reflections*. These have to be taken with a grain of salt because of the changes in editions of the works, because of the lack of system in the maxims, and because of La Rochefoucauld's great subtlety in use of terms (which could be interpreted less charitably as a tendency to contradict himself!). Greatness of mind—the ability to penetrate through appearances—combined with consistency and an intellectual wide-range is valuable. It is particularly rare when applied to oneself since deception is the normal human condition, i.e. we all seek to present ourselves in the best possible light (which means as something we are not) in order to satisfy *amour propre*.

This is connected to a central theme in Montaigne that ethics just is the quest to know oneself from a sceptical point of view. La Rochefoucauld criticizes self-knowledge when allied to perfection or the dissolution of the grip of the passions, but he also sometimes qualifiedly extols integrity[67] and sincerity,[68] sometimes in tandem with his praise of greatness of mind. This might be construed as an ethic of integrity in the sense now associated with Bernard Williams,[69] that whatever we are due to historical contingencies and to the contingent nature of our psychology we ought to identify with it since these contingencies are part or all of us and the grounds of whatever sort of life we will have.

La Rochefoucauld's suggestion that the guide to our conduct should be the virtues and qualities appropriate to our social station or situations also hints towards an affinity with integrity: kings 'should imitate Alexander, who wanted to compete only . . . for specifically royal qualities' (La Rochefoucauld 2007: 227).[70] The emphasis on avoiding competing with those outside of one's class fits with La Rochefoucauld as an ideologist of French Court culture.[71] It can be seen as a way of channelling *amour propre* without denying its overwhelming force, its role in motivating virtues (and more generally the connection of vice and virtue in human nature), or denying human deceit. But in addition it can be seen as embracing the contingencies of a particular social station and the contingencies one is born into. In opposition to Descartes, Spinoza, and Lipsius

[66] See De Mourges 1978: 77.   [67] For example, La Rochefoucauld 2007, V: 170.
[68] De Mourges 1978: 64–5.   [69] See particularly Williams 1981.   [70] See also 'Truth', p. 193.
[71] See Clark 1994.

(for whom acquiring deep knowledge of what one most is, is independent of social ties or station and the precondition of the best life) these contingencies are the standard of the best and happiest life. Maxims express them better than long tracts. La Rochefoucauld's maxims were a poison pill deeply antithetical to the tradition described in the previous two sections and at least as destructive as Hobbes' challenge.

12.6 THE CAMBRIDGE PLATONISTS

Whichcote was also influential although he published no books, maxims, or sermons in his lifetime. He was born in 1609, in between Descartes and Spinoza. His influence was mainly oral and was transmitted by his students at Emmanuel College like John Smith, younger friends like Henry More, John Locke, [72] and Ralph Cudworth,[73] and their correspondents, friends, and even children (notably Cudworth's daughter Damaris Cudworth Masham). Whichcote's posthumously published aphorisms and sermons implied an optimistic, rationalist, and anti-Calvinist moral system[74] that was argued for in detail by his more explicitly systematic *confreres* and *consoeurs*.[75] Cudworth, More, and Masham are not interchangeable as philosophers but their moral philosophies are all committed to a cluster of doctrines that we first glimpse in Whichcote's maxims and sermons.

Given that we call these intellectuals 'the Cambridge Platonists', it is also unsurprising that in addition to being associated with Cambridge they, like Lipsius, Gassendi, and others I have discussed, desired to appropriate the ancient schools for a modern age in a way that cut across religious differences—infamously so in the countless Hebrew, Latin, and Greek quotations and references to ancient wisdom in Cudworth's massive *True Intellectual System of the Universe* (1678). Cudworth used the ancient philosophical schools to describe modern atheism and materialism as variants on perennial false positions first argued for by the ancients, and to argue for the superiority of his own True Intellectual System which also drew on ancient wisdom.

Similarly in *A Treatise Concerning Eternal and Immutable Morality*, Cudworth defended a Platonic moral theory against Protagorean objections. This involved lengthy excurses into sense perception and atomism to show that man is not the measure of all things. Here and elsewhere their Platonism, i.e. their commitment to the existence of eternal and immutable entities or norms independent of the human mind, was presented in contradistinction to other ancient and modern schools (particularly Epicureans and Sceptics).[76] Like Lipsius' and Gassendi's variants on the ancient Schools,

---

[72] Locke attended Whichcote's sermons. See Hutton 2004.

[73] Whichcote died in Cudworth's house and Cudworth gave him the sacrament. See Tillotson 1683: 28.

[74] See the excellent discussion of the anti-Calvinism of Whichcote, Cudworth, and More in Gill 2006: 7–29.

[75] See Goldie 2004 and Hutton 2008.

[76] For example see Cudworth's criticisms of Gassendi in addition to the ancient Epicureans in Cudworth 1996: 24.

their positions were complex due to their Christian commitments (more in a moment). For example, Cudworth drew on some aspects of Stoicism in moral philosophy while attacking Stoic determinism.[77]

This points to a further kinship with the philosophers discussed so far. For the Cambridge Platonists moral philosophy was a part of a system that included theology, theories of mind, metaphysics, speculations on physics, etc. The borders between parts of the system were porous and all parts were viewed as components in a happy life. The Platonists also shared, unsurprisingly, a stress on the integration of theoretical moral philosophy and practical advice as a means to self-help in attaining the best life—the moral life. In Henry More's *Enchiridion Ethicum* (1667), the most important Cambridge Platonist writing on ethics published while the main figures were still alive, ethics was defined by More as 'the Art of Living well and happily' (More 1690: 1–2) and felicity as both living well *and* happily. Ethics was divided into three parts—the first primarily concerned with the passions and drawing extensively on Descartes, the second on the virtues, and the third 'concerning Life and good Manners' (More 1690: i–ii) or on practical advice on how to acquire the virtues in order to have the best sort of life (including techniques for controlling the imagination and the passions and even dietetics (More 1690: 235–6)). Consequently, Cambridge Platonism was an unalloyed expression of many of the themes discussed above—a modern philosophical circle patterned on the ancients and placing itself within a tacit map of ancient and modern positions. In this case it was also formed around an exemplary founder in pursuit of self-knowledge for acquiring the best life—i.e. living well and happily.

The Cambridge Platonists' moral philosophy took diverse forms including treatises, letter, dialogues, maxims, sermons, and even poems. Despite this stylistic heterogeneity they shared core systematic commitments, many of which were derived from the founder. Men and women are naturally good and made in God's image (although in need of governance). As noted all human knowledge, including moral knowledge, was or depended on knowledge of immutable, eternal, and natural moral features of the world. This knowledge was necessary for governance and in particular self-governance. Moral duties, obligations, and virtues are not mere consequences of arbitrary acts of a divine will but must be good in and of themselves or partake of something good in and of itself. As Cudworth put it, 'things may as well be made white or black by mere will, without whiteness or blackness…as morally good and evil, just and unjust, honest and dishonest (*debita* and *illicita*), by mere will, without any nature of goodness, justice, honesty,' (Cudworth 1996: 17).[78]

Knowledge of these eternal and immutable features of the world is natural to men and women both (1) in so far as it is accessible by unaided human reason and (2) in so far as possessing and acting on the good is part of their natures. The basic truths of natural religion and morality are self-evident, knowable, and necessary like geometrical axioms and propositions. For example, More listed twenty-four 'Noema' or

---

[77] But see Sellars 2012.

[78] Cudworth viewed this as consistent with Descartes and against Gassendi. See Cudworth 1996: 23–5.

certain and undeniable moral axioms such as 'return good for good, and not evil for good' (More 1690: 25). Each man and woman had access to these axioms and other self-evident truths of morality through an internal moral law or 'candle of the lord', the mark of our being created in God's image that also served as a standard for conduct.

Unfortunately, due to the corruption of society, and due to their own inability to control their passions, men and women often fail to see the divine law in themselves. But it can be recovered through introspective self-knowledge that aids in control of the passions and gives rise to objective and public moral standards. These standards are eternal and so hold independent of arbitrary rulers, civil wars, and contingent social circumstances. The profound anti-Calvinism and anti-Hobbesianism of this picture is quite apparent.[79] If the moral realism could be argued for compellingly, if there were eternal standards of morality that held independent of all conditions, then a much stronger response to the modern Protagoras—Hobbes—could be given. In particular the exhibition of objective moral standards would counter Hobbes' denial of objective rankings of preferences.

This points to an important connection between Cambridge Platonism and the movements discussed in prior sections of this chapter: its central figures took themselves to be responding to Hobbes' challenge (and to Spinoza). The positive characterization of duties or virtues as self-evident and eternal ruled out that they might be arbitrary products of a sovereign's or God's will. Hobbesian, Catholic, and Calvinist submission was arbitrary, or at minimum paternalist, in the sense that no justification was needed for why this duty or obligation was binding beyond that it had been posited by a superior. The superior did not give self-evident reasons for its commands.[80] Consequently, according to the Cambridge Platonists, religious voluntarists, advocates of submission to church hierarchy, and authoritarian atheists[81] all identified the binding character of moral obligation with a non-rational or irrational justification of the particular religious and moral principles held. For Hobbes, the Catholic, or the Calvinist, that duties were willed and propagated by a legitimate authority was sufficient that they obliged. Of course Calvinists, Catholics, and Hobbes argued for why this educed to our interest. But even if it educed to our interest, if the obligation itself was not rational then any sort of obedience might be obligatory if posited by a more powerful will.[82] For the Cambridge Platonists the necessity of moral obligation was derived from the rational, self-evident, and necessary character of these truths themselves. Similarly, that they were these truths

---

[79] For an excellent discussion of Cudworth, More, and Whichcote on the necessity of morals and particularly Cudworth's non-Hobbesian response to the English Civil War, see Gill 2006: 38–57. Gill argues for Cudworth's realism as a response to Hobbes and to the Civil War.

[80] See Passmore 1951: ch. 4.

[81] To be clear, I'm not saying that Hobbes was an atheist. I'm saying the Cambridge Platonists thought of Hobbes as an atheist.

[82] And if an answer was given it was often along the lines of 'God said well the next time you see me coming you'd better run', giving rise to the response 'Where do you want that killing done?'

was due to something rationally evident about them, which ruled out their being supplanted by the arbitrary volition of a superior.[83]

Religious and moral rationalism, the ideal of moral knowledge as certain like geometrical knowledge, the rejection of divine voluntarism, the influence of Descartes, and the stress on general metaphysical commitments pointing towards one true philosophy in response to Hobbes all sounds very similar to Spinoza. But there were fundamental differences that made Spinoza, like Hobbes, a main target of the Cambridge Platonists. First for Spinoza, like Hobbes, good and evil referred to things that aided and abetted the interests and power of agents. For the Cambridge Platonists, as evinced in the quote from Cudworth above, good and evil referred to properties independent of our preservation although they might educe to them, i.e. fitnesses in the world or nature of things. For Cudworth they were objects of the divine Mind, but it was crucial that the goodness, and other properties of the objects, held independent of the mind that perceived them. In this sense Spinoza was on the Hobbesian side of a central divide, albeit for different reasons.

So far I've been discussing the Cambridge Platonists as if they were secular moralists, but they were not. Many of the male members of the movement were ministers and were central figures in the rise of Latitudinarian Anglicanism and a broad church. Moral realism and moral rationalism were intertwined with, indeed part of, a basic commitment to a rational form of Christianity. The force of the rationalism was succinctly stated by Damaris Masham: 'It is as undeniable as the difference between Men's being in, and out of their Wits, that Reason ought to be to Rational Creatures the Guide of their Belief' (Masham 1705: 32). Again this might sound like Spinoza's famous arguments concerning morality and Scripture: only that which stands up to reason is true and rational, and everything else can be discarded as superstition. The tacit presumption of the Cambridge Platonists was nearly the opposite: revealed Scripture was true and rational. It defined the content and worth of core Christian duties and virtues. There was no need for reference to a mechanistic model of reason or to individual self-interest construed as efficient causal power to justify these virtues and duties. The Platonists saw this, unsurprisingly, as tending to atheism and denying providence.[84] God was wholly rational in many causal and rational guises as was his religion expressed through Scripture.

The virtues commanded and described in Scripture, above all by Christ, were presumed to be consistent with Platonic and other ancient virtues in so far as they were all rational and self-evident. Consequently, staking out the boundaries or content of morality was not

---

[83] Richard Cumberland in particular saw this as central to responding to Hobbes' arguments that a sovereign was necessary for political obligation. Cumberland's attempt to use the new science to argue that self-preservation is connected with sociability and his stress on love as the foundation of the duties of natural law are very similar to Samuel Clarke, whom I will discuss in the next section. The moral obligations are grounded in the tendency of certain sociable actions and virtues to promote the common good, the most happiness for the most people. This is much closer to Shaftesbury than Clarke. See Cumberland 2005: V §§9–10 and Parkin 1999. That Cumberland is not treated in this chapter is due to: (1) length and (2) the mostly arbitrary distinction between natural law, political philosophy and moral philosophy.

[84] Put differently, arguments drawing on formal and final causes were appropriate to morals and theology, were as or more capable of *a priori* self-evidence and even mathematical certainty.

a central concern, as it had been for Hobbes. The rough shape of morality is a given, i.e. humility *is* a virtue[85] and the golden rule is self-evident. Because they are Christian virtues they are obligatory; the question is rather how are they rationally obligatory?

Consequently, Cambridge Platonism was as much a theological movement as a philosophical movement and the divisions between moral philosophy and theology for the Cambridge Platonists were fluid (and in some places non-existent). Their commitment to the identity of natural religion and morality might look like secular moral philosophy, but it is not due to basic presuppositions about the connections between revealed religion and the content of natural religion and morality. Like Locke, they wished to exhibit shared Christian rational commitments and through these shared commitments find a way to discuss morals and religion in terms of their shared religious commitments as opposed to arguing like Hobbes and Spinoza for reason on a natural scientific model that was independent of any particular moral and religious commitments.

This is not to suggest that the virtues and duties were just culled from Scripture and antiquity and that was the end of it. More defined virtue as 'an intellectual Power of the Soul, by which it over-rules the animal Impressions of bodily Passions; so as in every Action it easily pursues what is absolutely and simply the best'.[86] The Christian and ancient virtues were assumed consistent with this intellectualist account of virtue and the basic obligation to rational self-understanding.

It is no mean feat to combine a tradition that stresses free choice and the salvation of the ignorant with an intellectualist tradition stressing control of the passions by the intellect and that knowing the good to be necessary means doing the good. If knowledge of morality, and knowledge in general, is knowledge of necessary self-evident truths, aren't the volitions it gives rise to necessary as well?[87] But then how can this be made consistent with moral culpability and responsibility, justified punishment, and the praiseworthiness of virtues, all of which Cudworth thought to be essential to morals? If we deny freedom of the will we are perilously close to Hobbesian necessitarianism or Calvinist predestination.

Cudworth tried to overcome this problem by arguing for the centrality of intellectual self-command to moral action, or what the Stoics referred to as the *hegemonikon*.[88] The *hegemonikon* was a kind of capacity for autonomous agency and self-control in intelligent beings which arose from self-reflection and was intended for self-perfection.[89] This was not the freedom of indifference in choosing two equivalent goods that was criticized by determinists like Spinoza and Hobbes, but a freedom to pull oneself together and perfect oneself in a way that made one more autonomous. A freedom to engage in self help! Through its exercise we know and are bound by the necessity of virtues and duties that educe to our greater moral perfection. Sin and vice also need not be imputed to God in so far as they are the consequence of our abusing this power.[90]

---

[85] See, for example, Whichcote 1702: v. 2, 202–5.   [86] More 1690: 11.

[87] 'A Treatise of Freewill', in Cudworth 1996: 158.

[88] See Darwall 1995 : ch. 5; Schneewind 1998: 213–14.

[89] Cudworth 1996: 185.

[90] Cudworth 1996: 196. I do not mean to suggest that Cudworth argued for a Kantian conception of autonomy, or that his arguments were entirely cogent independent of theological premises. See Darwall 1995: 147–8.

That we are naturally virtuous and capable through reflection of self-perfection and self-help was taken to be a partial refutation of man's basic self-interestedness as argued for by Hobbes, Spinoza, and La Rochefoucauld. Instead, love of others is natural to us *and* conducive to our interest. But finite creatures are not mere occasions for the love of God as the long Augustinean tradition inherited by Malebrancheanism might have it. As Masham pointedly noted against John Norris: 'When I say that I love my Child, or my friend, I find that my Meaning is, that they are things I am delighted in' (Masham 1696: 18).[91] To argue that I love my child solely as an occasion for the love of God is nearly as laboured and sophistical as to argue that I love them solely in order to further my self-interest.[92] That which we love gives rise to sentiments of benevolence and other-directed virtues that are determined both by our passions and the nature of the object loved. When they have a proper object and conform properly to it, 'passions are not only good, but singularly needful to the perfecting of human life' (More 1690: 41).

As Masham and More make clear, Cambridge Platonism was an introspective and intellectualist tradition, but also a moderate and social one.[93] Again as stated by Masham: 'In short, our Natures are so suited to a mediocrity in all things, that we can scarce exceed in any kind with Safety, To be always busy in the Affairs of the World, or always shut up from them, cannot be born: Always Company, or always solitude, are Dangerous: And so are any other Extreams' (Masham 1696: 126).

12.7 LORD SHAFTESBURY AND SAMUEL CLARKE AT THE CUSP OF THE EIGHTEENTH CENTURY

These two sides of Cambridge Platonism, on the one hand Christian moral rationalism and intellectualism stressing moral knowledge as self-evident, mathematically certain and *a priori*, and, on the other hand, a moderate account of moral life drawing on the ancients for the moderns and stressing the important place of self-command and the other-directed and worldly benevolent passions[94] were taken up (and combined) by a number of philosophers at the turn of the eighteenth century. These currents are ideal types, but I have distinguished them to conclude by discussing two extremely influential philosophers influenced by Whichcote (indeed both published volumes of his sermons) each of whom exemplifies one of these currents. I will first discuss Shaftesbury who exemplifies the latter current. Shaftesbury met Masham through his teacher and her close friend John Locke (who was a member of her household). Through Masham Shaftesbury had access to her father's manuscripts.[95] I will then turn to Samuel Clarke

---

[91] On the context of the debate see Broad 2006; Wilson 2004.   [92] See More 1690: 32.

[93] See Passmore 1951: 52–3.

[94] Passmore argues that the moral psychology distinguishes Cudworth from Whichcote. See Passmore 1951: 53. Passmore sees Cudworth's moral psychology as proto-Humean, which seems a bit strong.

[95] See Gill 2006: 77–8.

who exemplifies the former current. Both saw themselves as attacking Hobbes. Shaftesbury was influenced by Spinoza's moral and political philosophy whereas Clarke saw Spinoza as no better (and perhaps worse) than Hobbes.

Shaftesbury's 'Solioquy, or Advice to an Author' (1710) begins with some thoughts about the problem of maxims or counsel. As we have just seen, the advice genre was hugely popular in the seventeenth century. But according to Shaftesbury, by the turn of the eighteenth century the model of moral counsel on which the popularity of the moral maxim was predicated was fading. Readers assumed a new, anti-counsel maxim to be self-evident: 'That, as to what related to private Conduct, *No-one was ever the better for* Advice.'[96] We happily take advice on how to be a better musician or how to be a better mathematician, but we rebel at the thought that someone might give us advice on our private conduct.

Shaftesbury's response in the 'Soliloquy' was to suggest the self-reflective conversation with oneself or soliloquy—modelled on Marcus Aurelius' *Meditations*—as a form of mental examination and medicine or psychic surgery. Through '*Self-dissection*' the soliloquizer becomes 'two distinct Persons. He is Pupil and Preceptor. He teaches and he learns' in an environment where he (or she) can put anything to the test and need not fear public opinion swaying them from the truth. The self-knowledge this dissection gives rise to was described in the dialogue 'The Moralists' as 'To know Ourselves, and what That is, which by improving, we may be sure to advance our Worth, and real Self-Interest.'[97]

Self-knowledge was rare in part because of the sorry consensus at the turn of the eighteenth century that private moral conduct was distinct from public moral performance. Shaftesbury felt that this separation was destructive of both. When virtuous characters were separated from the public good, disaster was in the offing whether through the ascent of Nero or James II. By contrast, in the Roman republic Cicero, Livy, and many other authors argued for the continuity of virtuous private characters—Cincinnatus, Scipio, etc.—and public flourishing. The greatness of the Roman republic in comparison with the reign of William and Mary made for strong evidence for Shaftesbury's thesis. The paucity of public virtue and vigorous public discussion after the Glorious Revolution suggested that self-knowledge was far more likely to be acquired in such times by turning inward (this was a consistent theme in Stoic philosophy as well). The inward turn of Cambridge Platonism was symptomatic of the need for a renewal.

Shaftesbury's criticism of the maxim contained a slap at Hobbes that drew on and extended the Cambridge Platonist's criticisms of Hobbes. For Hobbes and for Calvinists,

---

[96] 'Solilquy, or Advice to an Author' in Cooper 2001: v. 1 97. Shaftesbury's published writings from the 'Inquiry Concerning Virtue' (1699) to the 'Solilquy' were collected, supplemented, and published in the *Characteristicks* in 1711. Shaftesbury died in 1713 and the second edition of the *Characteristicks* with engravings designed by Shaftesbury—including the engraving I discussed in the opening section of this chapter—appeared after his death.

[97] Shaftesbury, 'The Moralists', in Cooper 2001: v. 2, 238.

and indeed for everyone who held a selfish hedonistic theory[98] of moral motivation, including Pufendorf and Shaftesbury's teacher Locke, the satisfaction of one's duties rested on one's selfish desires and avoiding pain: punishment and reward. These motivations could be remote (my final punishment or reward in the afterlife) or proximate (I sign this contract because I fear being killed by you right now).

For Shaftesbury, this performance of a duty spoke:

> no more of *Rectitude, Piety,* or *Sanctity* in a Creature thus reform'd, than there is *Meekness* or *Gentleness* in a Tiger strongly chain'd, or *Innocence* and *Sobriety* in a Monkey under the Discipline of the Whip.[99]

Like Cudworth, an arbitrary punishment or reward was insufficient to make an action or obligation moral. But Shaftesbury objected further that the satisfaction of a duty for reasons of self-interest or other non-praiseworthy motives fails because it draws on the wrong sort of motivation. For an action to be morally approved it must arise from a morally approved character acting on the right kind of benevolent and just sentiments and motives. Appropriate moral motivation was here central to the satisfaction of a moral duty or obligation. When we recognize that an agent is acting on selfish motives our moral approval wanes for the agent and the action.[100]

Shaftesbury also held that virtue and true interest were natural; they arose from the immediate natural benevolent and social passions for family and friends. For the Hobbesian, partial selfish passions were natural and hope and fear were the only reliable motivations to guarantee compliance with obligations via the state of nature. Only once these were restrained was morality possible, and this meant morality was artificial. But the so-called state of nature on which the argument depended was not natural. It was the unnatural reflection of the horror of an age of religious conflict. Furthermore, the very submission to authority that Hobbes and the Calvinists saw as integral to our nature gave rise to dogmatic beliefs which in turn lead to the kind of conflict that Hobbes' testified to from the Devil's Mountain. Hobbes' methodological stress on knowing oneself through reading others ramified his belief that conflict sprang eternal.

To put the point slightly differently, Hobbes confused self-interest with what Shaftesbury called the selfish, partial, and unnatural passions.[101] Hobbes' confusion rested on the analogy between a body continuing in motion with power after power and natural affections and desires to 'power after power'. Against Hobbes, the natural affections are essential to our happiness—'the Natural Affections of Parents to their Children, and of Children to their Parents; of Men to their Native Country; and, indeed, of all Men

---

[98] By selfish hedonistic theory of interest I mean one where the pleasures and pains of others are not taken to be part of, or even opposed to, the agent's interest. Shaftesbury argued for an enlarged hedonism where the pleasures and pains of others are components in the agent's well-being. See Crisp 2006: ch. 4 for a sophisticated contemporary defense of hedonism as an account of well-being.

[99] 'An Inquiry concerning Virtue,' in Cooper 2001: v. 2, 32 (I.iii.3).

[100] See Shaftesbury, 'Inquiry', in Cooper 2001: v. 2, 16–17 (I.ii.3).

[101] See 'Inquiry', II.ii.3 for the distinction between natural public and private affections that lead to the public and private good and unnatural affections (particularly Cooper 2001: v. 2, 50 (II.ii.3)).

in their several Relations to one another.'[102] They are also the affections that give rise to virtuous motives and virtues. Crucially, although these affections are praiseworthy and conducive to (indeed part of) our happiness, they are felt and acted upon with no thought to power or self-preservation. To quote Masham again 'When I say that I love my Child, or my friend, I find that my Meaning is, that they are things I am delighted in', not that I am motivated to love my child as instrumental to self-preservation.

But though feeling and acting upon benevolent affections is rarely motivated by selfish interest, benevolent affections are more conducive to both public and private interest and well-being than the narrowly hedonic selfish passions. First 'to love, and to be kind' is extremely pleasurable and satisfying in and of itself whereas the selfish pleasures as described by Hobbes are uneasy and their satisfaction sufficiently unsatisfying that the agent is moved on to the next pleasure. For Shaftesbury, this was connected to the Platonic idea that the selfish passions make for a disordered soul and the social affections bring the individual soul into harmony.

Furthermore, by attacking Hobbes' account of motivation and showing true prudence to be consistent with virtue, Shaftesbury could reject Hobbes' denial of felicity. The social and benevolent affections 'are the only means which can procure...a certain and solid *Happiness*'.[103] Hobbes failed to see this because of his restriction of motivation to self-interest and his restriction of self-interest to the selfish passions. The distinction between prudential reasoning and morally praiseworthy motivation responded to the third point of Hobbes' challenge—what prudence dictates. To paraphrase Hume, who was deeply influenced by Shaftesbury's argument, what is most useful or prudential is not at odds with what is agreeable and distinctive of natural morality. What is prudential for individuals and societies is to possess virtues and to act on praiseworthy motives. Once Hobbes' theory of motivation is rejected, it becomes apparent that the private good harmonizes with the public good as was the case in the flourishing Roman republic. The other-directed affections and the patriotic affections are mutually reinforcing, and virtuous citizens essential to the public good. As these affections are cultivated, *contra* the maxim that Shaftesbury rejected and *contra* Hobbes, our private and civic selves come into harmony.

Like the Cambridge Platonists, Shaftesbury was a moral realist, i.e. he took the moral obligations, duties, and properties to reflect or depend on eternal and immutable features of the world not reducible to partiality and selfish desires. He was also deeply inspired by Platonism and viewed the soul's order as reflecting the order of the cosmos.[104] This was connected to his moral realism in so far as the soul had access through reflection to a larger system of eternal relations that dictated eternal proportions of beauty and morality. At the same time, he was the main font of eighteenth-century British moral sense theory and sentimentalism.[105] He argued for the analogy between the visual sense,

---

[102] Shaftesbury 'Preface', in Cooper 1698: ix.
[103] 'An Inquiry concerning Virtue', in Cooper 2001: v. 2, 58 (II.ii.1).
[104] 'An Inquiry concerning Virtue', in Cooper 2001: v. 2, 48 (II.i.2).
[105] See the very interesting discussion of these tendencies in Irwin 2008: ch. 45.

the sense of beauty or proportion, and the moral sense, and stressed our immediate non-reflective approval of the benevolent affections.[106] For Shaftesbury there was no conflict between moral realism, the importance of reflection, the moral sense, and the pivotal role of sentiment. They were all components in the acquisition of virtue and happiness and all reflected Shaftesbury's deepest commitment: to the cosmopolitan Stoic idea that moral duties, obligations, and benevolent affections were natural to us and were perfected and progressed through a combination of private reflection and public and free intellectual commerce.[107]

The civic character of Shaftesbury's philosophy separated him from the Cambridge Platonists, although it has affinities with the passage from Masham that concluded the previous section. Shaftesbury was surprisingly successful in his efforts and became one of the main figures to initiate the central elements we associate with the Enlightenment in moral philosophy. His admirers ranged from Toland, to Hutcheson, to Hume, to Diderot, Lessing, and Mendelssohn, and beyond.[108]

At the same time, no figure better united the themes of seventeenth-century moral philosophy as presented in this chapter. In his 'Introduction' to an edition of Shaftesbury's letters, John Toland remarked of the late Earl, 'perhaps no modern ever turn'd the Antients more into sap and blood, as they say, than he. Their Doctrines he understood as well as themselves, and their Virtues he practis'd better' (Toland 1721: vii). Shaftesbury's admirers saw in him the ideal union of urbane aristocratic personality, handsome visage, playful style, and philosophical acuity: the admirable character at the centre of the *Characteristicks*. He was one of the last leaders of a school whose life was a model for his followers who discussed his works in the coffee shops that Shaftesbury advocated for as places of free discussion (the modern *agora*). Like the ancient schools, the many different aspects of Shaftesbury's philosophy converged in a vision of morals as the best and happiest life—a free, often funny, no holds-barred discussion with oneself and others about beauty, morals, and whatever else. Shaftesbury's *Characteristicks* was an attempt to seed the conditions for this discussion.

This may explain part of the reason why it is so difficult for contemporary moral philosophers to recognize Shaftesbury's works as moral philosophy. The *Characteristicks* provided many viewpoints on moral practice through a wide variety of examples, literary forms, and argument styles—from soliloquy to open discussion in a coffee house to dialogue between a few philosophers with very different viewpoints. To loosen the grip of Hobbesian and religious dogmatism on his readership, he had to awaken and inspire the development of more urbane and reflective taste and desires by giving his readers a sample of the pleasures and virtues which he advocated for.

When we read Shaftesbury we see conflicts between his theory of moral sense, his sentimentalism, and his realism. We see a hodgepodge of aesthetics, moral philosophy,

---

[106] 'An Inquiry concerning Virtue', in Cooper 2001: v. 2, I.ii.3.
[107] Shaftesbury's commitments are beautifully stated in a letter to Coste, where he discusses his beloved Horace's shifts from Stoicism to Epicureanism and back again. See Rand 1900: 355–66.
[108] See Rivers 2000 for an extensive discussion of Shaftesbury's influence.

political discussion, and strange miscellany. We also see a mixture of unfamiliar styles for presenting moral philosophy. Shaftesbury saw them united in an ascent towards the good and the beautiful, from sense and sentiment to reflection on the providentially ordered system of nature. He wished his readers to see that cultivated capacities were mutually supporting—in particular the sense of beauty and morality. He also wished to provide different inroads for readers to see that that they do recognize moral standards whether in the world, through reflection in their sentiments, or via an immediate sense, standards that have been covered over by destructive theology and philosophy. These standards point towards a happier, more natural, and better life than the standards they currently recognize. All were part of philosophy or 'the Study of Happiness'.[109]

There was a further difference with the Cambridge Platonists in addition to this stress on public and cosmopolitan cultivation of the affects and the intellect that 'marks a tectonic shift' crucial for the 'development of secular ethics'.[110] Like the Cambridge Platonists, he rejected the new science or mechanism as the basis for morals and like them he had a central place for providence in justifying morals. But unlike them, Shaftesbury was no Christian theologian; indeed his discussions of God and providence seemed to his critics to point towards atheism and Deism.[111] The moral picture that Shaftesbury argued for was, although accepting of teleology and providence, at least as pagan as Christian. This brought him much closer to Spinoza than to the Cambridge Platonists on this question. Morals did not rest on any special connection to Christianity or Christian virtues. In fact, one of the most important themes in Shaftesbury was showing that the natural virtues also were and could be the virtues of our modern age as well as of any other virtuous age: ancient, Christian, or otherwise.

Shaftesbury's response to the Hobbesian challenge was taken by many readers to be decisive. Hobbes was hardly republished in the eighteenth century. But while Shaftesbury was still alive, Mandeville developed many Hobbesian and Calvinist themes in a challenge to Shaftesbury and the argument continued in a new form. Did private virtues really give rise to public virtues? Were they the best basis for a happy life? Or did private vices and luxury make for a happier society without the necessary connection between virtue and happiness? The legacy of Shaftesbury and his proponents and critics can be seen in philosophers ranging from Hutcheson to Hume to Smith to Rousseau to Marx. But notably moral philosophy as a school of counsel, self-help, and cultivation patterned on the ancients and circumventing religious conflict began to fall by the wayside. Towards the end of the eighteenth century, the Scots philosopher Lord Monboddo, who

---

[109] Shaftesbury, 'The Moralists', in Cooper 2001: 244. At the same time, for Shaftesbury philosophy should not be too self-serious or it stilted the affections it wished to cultivate. Hence the playful mix and the advocacy of ridicule which often make it hard to see the argument.

[110] Gill 2006: 117. See Gill more generally for a thesis concerning Shaftesbury's role in the rise of secular morality.

[111] Berkeley's *Alciphron* is a particularly good example of this. It's also a sign of Shaftesbury's enduring influence in the eighteenth century, both because Berkeley, despite his criticisms of Shaftesbury, is so influenced by him, and because he bothered to write a work criticizing Shaftesbury in 1732, nearly twenty years after Shaftesbury's death.

was a great admirer of Shaftesbury, of introspection, and ancient wisdom, and who engaged in ancient regimes of spiritual and physical exercise, was viewed (perhaps rightly) as retrograde and ridiculous.

Samuel Clarke was four years younger than Shaftesbury and published his main works at the same time that Shaftesbury published the essays that would make up the *Characteristicks*. He has often been dismissed; for example Passmore refers to his moral writings as 'rationalist psychology' in its 'crudest form'.[112] And it is generally assumed that Hutcheson's and Hume's decisive criticisms of Clarke annihilated almost anyone taking his arguments for moral rationalism seriously. I would like to suggest that Clarke's way of doing and thinking about moral philosophy was at least as influential as Shaftesbury, albeit in a rather different and in some ways more familiar direction.

Unlike Shaftesbury, and like the Cambridge Platonists, Clarke was a strong advocate of the identity of natural religion and morals. All natural religion was ultimately reducible to three fundamental duties: devotion to God, dedication to promoting the welfare of all men, and temperance and moderation of the passions.[113] Clarke saw these fundamental moral duties as justified via *a priori* argument with further a posteriori support. For example, we can know *a priori* that God created the world and all the goodness in it. God is consequently the standard of goodness and we ought to do good for our fellow-creatures like God does for all creatures. Since God is omnipotent, which can also be known *a priori*, he maximally promotes the good. Consequently we have a duty to maximally promote the welfare of other men.[114] This *a priori* argument unsurprisingly led to duties of equity and the golden rule, strengthening the thesis that natural religion is morality!

Clarke's response to Hobbes and Spinoza developed in connection with his agreements with the Cambridge Platonists' commitment to moral realism and to moral knowledge as involving self-evident and necessary propositions arranged in *a priori* arguments of the sort just described. In his two sets of extremely influential Boyle Lectures—*A Demonstration of the Being and Attributes of God* (1705) and *Discourse concerning the unchangeable obligations of natural religion, and the truth and certainty of the Christian Revelation* (1706)—Clarke tried to show that a consistent proof of God according to rigorous geometrical principles argued not for determinism but for the freedom of God's will. Human freedom in morals was derived from divine freedom, human moral attributes were derived from the necessity of divine attributes, and so on down.

Clarke argued, like Cudworth, that the reasoning of Hobbes and Spinoza was flawed or unwarrantedly restricted and this led to atheistic and materialist conclusions. Unlike Cudworth, he saw this supplanting of Hobbesian and Spinozist moral arguments as parallel to Newton's supplanting of Cartesian theories in natural philosophy (a shift which

---

[112] Passmore 1951: 52.   [113] Clarke 1706: ch. 5.

[114] 'To which end, *universal Love and Benevolence* is as plainly the most direct, certain and effectual means as in Mathematicks the *flowing of a Point* is, to produce a Line' (Clarke 1706: 72).

Clarke had a central role in[115]). The Newtonian world was consistent with a God who freely created it, not with determinism, and this dictated commitments in moral philosophy. Changes in natural philosophy supported a better moral philosophy and showed predecessor accounts to be trading on outmoded analogies that according to Clarke led them to embrace materialism and atheism.

Consequently, again much like the Cambridge Platonists, rational creatures could access eternal moral fitnesses in a rational world created by God through introspection. It was these eternal fitnesses that made the actions good, not the happiness the actions produced. In so far as God was maximally rational, fitnesses were not arbitrary volitions but were good and choiceworthy in themselves and reflected immutable and eternal facts about the world. Similarly, duties to self-preservation were not foundational—as they were for Hobbes and Spinoza—but followed from, and conformed with, what was eternally and immutably fit to do. For example, because God brought us into the world, only he could take us out. To try to take ourselves out before God does is to go against God's rational will.

The metaphysical necessity justifying the duties gave rise, for Clarke, to the necessity of our compliance in order to be moral. This was the crux of moral obligation. For Clarke, moral obligation followed upon rationally understanding a necessary moral duty or obligation that was as self-evident as a mathematical truth.[116] To understand the proposition but not to act in the way in which it dictated was to be as 'guilty of an equal absurdity and inconsistency in Practice' as the denial of a mathematical truth.[117] To possess virtues, such as self-command, was also obligatory but in order to support duties, since a failure of self-command might result in a failure to assent to and act on moral reasons due to an overwhelming passion.

That the metaphysical necessity of a proposition to which one assented dictated that one necessarily ought to act in accordance with it, that the virtues are commanded as supports for the discharge of obligation, and above all that morality concerns duties discovered by reason and is binding on one's actions in the world were all hinted at in the Cambridge Platonists but Clarke drew out the consequences of hints in a rigorous account of the rational source of duties and obligations. This also offered a powerful response to Hobbes' challenge. What morality dictated was obligatory, not recommended but required, for any assenting rational being independent of prudential considerations. Clarke held, like Shaftesbury, that this was also in accordance with happiness, although because of a benevolent deity. Furthermore, felicity was connected with the afterlife. But in Clarke we see a justification of moral duties that can be argued for without any reference to prudence and a fulcrum for a break between the moral life and the good life, the sort of fulcrum denied or rejected by the tradition outlined in the previous sections.

---

[115] Clarke was Newton's amanuensis in his debates with Leibniz, translated the Optics into Latin, and produced and published an edition of Rohault's popular Cartesian *System of Natural Philosophy* with notes that demonstrated the superiority of Newton's approach. The edition was central to the ascendency of Newton's natural philosophy.

[116] Clarke 1706: 63.   [117] Clarke 1706: 63.

Which is not to say that this is wholly cogent in Clarke. It is unclear what fitnesses mean for him and whether it is our reasoning or the reasons in the fitnesses themselves that make the actions obligatory (or indeed whether these are distinct).[118] Hume and Hutcheson criticized the putatively motivating capacity of mathematically self-evident *a priori* moral reasons, and the conception of metaphysical morality in the background. Duties might be obligatory, but without a theory of motivation other than the one offered by Hobbes, what motivates us to act morally? And finally, the very idea that these duties and virtues were immutable features of the world and necessary was parasitic on the shape and force that Scripture gave to morality for Clarke even though morality was natural religion. Clarke himself spent much ink trying to show his arguments consistent with revealed Scripture.

But one shouldn't underestimate the importance of the way in which Clarke thought about what a moral theory was and the questions one should ask of it. For Clarke, a moral theory involves the derivation and justification of eternal duties. These duties are binding independent of whether they educe to a happy life. Techniques for a happy life and the virtues that are part of it are not to be dismissed, but for Clarke they tend to be relevant to morals in so far as they are supporting of or relevant to the discharge of these duties. This is admittedly a tendency in Clarke. There is some self-help and references to Hobbes' Epicureanism (Clarke was an extremely skilled classicist). But the picture of moral philosophy is drastically different from Shaftesbury despite their shared commitments to core doctrines and arguments of the Cambridge Platonists. Philosophy is not the study of happiness, the advocacy for a particular best life, or the development of techniques for attaining this life, but the establishing of clearly and rigorously justified moral duties essential to be a morally fit actor.

The questions which Clarke asked or which his arguments posed for the next generation of moral philosophers were even more influential. What makes an obligation binding? Where does the necessity or ought in our moral duties derive from and what sort of necessity or ought is it? Is what it is fit to do independent of what makes us happy, even if the two might converge providentially? What makes a duty morally authoritative and how do we know it? These questions were often combined with questions from Shaftesbury, some of which involved his responses to Hobbes, and many of which had the flavour of the other authors I have discussed in this chapter. What is the motivation to morally praiseworthy actions? Is private virtue really the best means to public happiness?

These questions began to define the central subject matter of moral philosophy in the works of Butler, Hume, Rousseau, Smith, Kant, and many others. The idea of philosophy as centred on schools led by exemplars advocating techniques for the best life, or as being about lives and techniques at all, began to fade. It was still there in Shaftesbury and in many inspired by him, but it began its slow movement to the periphery of the discipline of moral philosophy.

---

[118] See Korsgaard 1996: 31.

Bibliography

Adam, C. and Tannery, P. 1996. *Oeuvres de Descartes*. Paris: J. Vrin.

Ariew, R. 2014. *Descartes and the First Cartesians*. Oxford: Oxford University Press.

Blom, H. and Winkel, L. C. (eds) 2004. *Grotius and the Stoa*. Assen; Van Gorcum.

Broad, J. 2006. 'A Woman's Influence? John Locke and Damaris Masham on Moral Accountability', *Journal of the History of Ideas* 67 (3): 489–510.

Charleton, W. 1656. *Epicurus' Morals*. London.

Clark, H. 1994. *La Rochefoucauld and the Language of Unmasking in Seventeenth Century France*. Geneva: Droz.

Clarke, S. 1706. *Discourse concerning the unchangeable obligations of natural religion, and the truth and certainty of the Christian Revelation*. London.

—— 1704. *The whole duty of a Christian, plainly represented in three practical essays, on baptism, confirmation, and repentance*. London, 2nd edn.

Cooper, A. (ed.) 1698. *Select Sermons of Dr. Whichcote*, London. [Anthony Ashley Cooper (Lord Shaftesbury)]

—— 2001. *Characteristicks of Men, Manners, Opinions, Times*, Indianapolis: Liberty Fund. [Anthony Ashley Cooper (Lord Shaftesbury)]

Cottingham, J., Murdoch, D., and Stoothoff, R. (trans.) 1985. *The Philosophical Writings of Descartes*. Cambridge: Cambridge University Press, 2 v.

—— Murdoch, D., Stoothoff, R., and Kenny, A. (trans.) 1991. *The Philosophical Writings of Descartes: The Correspondence*. Cambridge: Cambridge University Press.

Crisp, R. 2006. *Reasons and The Good*. Oxford: Oxford University Press.

Cudworth, R. 1996. *A Treatise Concerning Eternal and Immutable Morality with a Treatise of Freewill*. Cambridge: Cambridge University Press.

Cumberland, R. 2005. *A Treatise of the Laws of Nature*. Indianapolis: Liberty Fund Inc.

Darwall, S. 1995. *The British Moralists and the Internal Ought: 1640–1740*. Cambridge: Cambridge University Press.

De Brabander, F. 2007. *Spinoza and the Stoics*. London: Continuum.

De la Barre, P. 1984. *De L'Égalité des Deux Sexes*. Paris: Fayard.

De Mourges, O. 1978. *Two French Moralists: La Rochefoucauld and La Bruyère*. Cambridge: Cambridge University Press.

Della Rocca, M. 1998. 'Determinism and Human Freedom: Spinoza', in D. Garber and M. Ayers (eds), *The Cambridge History of Seventeenth-Century Philosophy*. Cambridge: Cambridge University Press, 1226–36.

—— 2003. 'The Power of an Idea: Spinoza's Critique of Pure Will', *Noûs* 37 (2): 200–31.

Foucault, M. 1986. *The Care of the Self*. New York: Random House.

Gaitens, M. and Lloyd, G. (eds) 1999. *Collective Imaginings: Spinoza, Past and Present*. London: Routledge.

Garrett, A. 2012. 'Knowing the Essence of the State in Spinoza's Tractatus Theologico-Politicus', *European Journal of Philosophy*. 20 (1): 50–73.

Garrett, D. 1990. 'A Free Man Always Acts Honestly, Not Deceptively: Freedom and Good in Spinoza's Ethics', in E. Curley and P.-F. Moreau (eds), *Spinoza: Issues and Directions*. Leiden, E.J. Brill, 221–38.

—— 1996. 'Spinoza's Ethical Theory', in D. Garrett (ed.), *The Cambridge Companion to Spinoza*. Cambridge: Cambridge University Press, 267–314.

Gassendi, P. 1964. *Opera Omnia*. Stuttgart: Friedrich Frommann Verlag.

Gill, M. 1999. 'The Religious Rationalism of Benjamin Whichcote', *Journal of the History of Philosophy* 37 (2): 411–40.

—— 2006. *The British Moralists on Human Nature and the Birth of Secular Ethics*. Cambridge: Cambridge University Press.

Goldie, M. 2004. 'Cambridge Platonists (*act.* 1630s—1680s)', *Oxford Dictionary of National Biography*. Oxford; Oxford University Press.

Gournay, M. 1998. *Preface to the Essays of Michel de Montaigne by his Adoptive Daughter, Marie le Jars de Gournay*, translated with supplementary annotation by R. Hillman and C. Quesnel. *Medieval and Renaissance Texts and Studies*, vol. 193. Tempe, Arizona.

Grotius, H. 2005. *The Rights of War and Peace*. Indianapolis: Liberty Fund Inc.

Haakonssen, K. 1996. *Natural Law and Moral Philosophy*. Cambridge: Cambridge University Press.

Hensley, J. (ed.) 1967. *The Works of Anne Bradstreet*. Cambridge, MA: Harvard University Press.

Hobbes, T. 1642. *Elementa Philosophica De Cive*. Paris.

—— 1655. *Elementorum Philosophiae Sectio Prima de Corpore*. London.

—— 1658. *Elementorum Philosophiae Sectio Secunda de Homine*. London.

—— 1990. *Behemoth: or the Long Parliament*. Chicago: University of Chicago Press.

—— 1994. *Human Nature and De Corpore Politico*. Oxford: Oxford University Press.

—— 1996. *Leviathan*. Cambridge: Cambridge University Press.

—— 1998. *On the Citizen*. Cambridge: Cambridge University Press.

Hume, D. 1987. *Essays Moral and Political*, rev. ed. Indianapolis: Liberty Fund Inc.

Hunter, I. 2006. *Rival Enlightenments: Civil and Metaphysical Philosophy in Early Modern Germany*. Cambridge: Cambridge University Press.

Hutton, S. 2004. 'Whichcote, Benjamin (1609—1683)', *Oxford Dictionary of National Biography*. Oxford: Oxford University Press.

—— 2008. 'The Cambridge Platonists', in Edward N. Zalta (ed.), *The Stanford Encyclopedia of Philosophy*, <http://plato.stanford.edu/archives/fall2008/entries/cambridge-platonists>.

Irwin, T. H. 2008. *The Development of Ethics: From Suarez to Rousseau*. Oxford: Oxford University Press, v. 2.

James, S. 1993. 'Spinoza the Stoic', in T. Sorell (ed.), *The Rise of Modern Philosophy*. Oxford: Oxford University Press, 289–316.

—— 1997. *Passion and Action: The Emotions in Seventeenth-Century Philosophy*. Oxford: Oxford University Press.

—— 1998. 'Reason, The Passions, and the Good Life', in D. Garber and M. Ayers (eds), *The Cambridge History of Seventeenth-Century Philosophy*. Cambridge: Cambridge University Press, 1358–96.

—— 2012. 'When Does Truth Matter? Spinoza on the Relation between Theology and Philosophy', *European Journal of Philosophy* 20 (1): 91–108.

Katsafanas, P. 2011. 'Deriving Ethics from Action: A Nietzschean Version of Constitutivism', in *Philosophy and Phenomenological Research* 83 (November): 620–60.

Kisner, M. 2011. *Spinoza on Human Freedom: Reason, Autonomy, and the Good Life*. Cambridge: Cambridge University Press.

Korsgaard, C. 1996. *The Sources of Normativity*. Cambridge: Cambridge University Press.

Kraye, J. 1984. 'Moral Philosophy', in C. Schmitt and Q. Skinner (eds), *The Cambridge History of Renaissance Philosophy*. Cambridge: Cambridge University Press, 303–86.

Kristeller, P. O. 1984. 'Stoic and Neoplatonic Sources of Spinoza's Ethics', *History of European Ideas* 5 (1): 1–15.

La Mettrie, J. 1996. *Machine Man and other Writings*. Cambridge: Cambridge University Press.

La Rochefoucauld 2007. *Collected Maxims and Other Reflections*. Oxford: Oxford.

LeBuffe, M. 2007. 'Spinoza's Normative Ethics,' *Canadian Journal of Philosophy* 37 (3): 371–92.

LeDoeuff, M. 1989. *The Philosophical Imaginary*. London: Athlone.

Lipsius, J. 1939. *Two Bookes of Constancie*. New Brunswick, NJ: Rutgers University Press.

Lucretius 1922. *De Rerum Natura*, 2nd edn. Oxford: Oxford University Press.

Marshall, J. 2003. 'Descartes's *Morale par Provision*' in B. Williston and A. Gombray (ed.), *Passion and Virtue in Descartes*. New York: Humanity Books, 191–238.

Masham, D. 1696. *A Discourse Concerning the Love of God*. London.

—— 1705. *Occasional Thoughts in Reference to a Vertuous or Christian Life*. London.

More, H. 1690. *An Account of Virtue*, London. [This is the English translation of *Enchiridion Ethicum* (1667)]

Moriarty, M. 2006. *Fallen Nature, Fallen Selves: Early Modern French Thought II*. Oxford: Oxford University Press.

Naaman-Zauderer, N. 2010. *Descartes' Deontological Turn*. Cambridge: Cambridge University Press.

Parkin, J. 1999. *Science, Religion, and Politics in Restoration England: Richard Cumberland's De legibus naturae*. Woodbridge: Boydell & Brewer.

Passmore, J. 1951. *Ralph Cudworth—An Interpretation*. Cambridge: Cambridge University Press.

Pereboom, D. 1994. 'Stoic Psychotherapy in Descartes and Spinoza', *Faith and Philosophy* 11: 592–625.

Rand, B. (ed.) 1900. *The Life, Unpublished Letters and Philosophical Regimen of Anthony, Earl of Shaftesbury*. New York: Macmillan.

Rivers, I. 2000. *Reason, Grace, and Sentiment: A Study of the Language of Religion and Ethics in England: 1660-1780*. Cambridge: Cambridge University Press.

Rorty, A. 1984. 'Formal Traces in Cartesian Functional Explanation', *Canadian Journal of Philosophy* 14 (4): 545–60.

—— 1992. 'Descartes on Thinking with the Body', in J. Cottingham (ed.), *Descartes*. Cambridge: Cambridge University Press, 371–92.

Rutherford, D. 2004. 'On the Happy Life: Descartes vis-à-vis Seneca', in S. Strange and J. Zupko (eds), *Stoicism: Traditions and Transformations*. Cambridge: Cambridge University Press, 188–93.

Sarasohn, L. 1985. 'Pierre Gassendi, Thomas Hobbes and the Mechanical World-View', *Journal of the History of Ideas* 46 (3): 363–79.

—— 1996. *Gassendi's Ethics: Freedom in a Mechanistic Universe*. Ithaca and London: Cornell University Press.

Schneewind, J. B. 1998. *The Invention of Autonomy*. Cambridge: Cambridge University Press.

Sellars, J. 2007. 'Justus Lipsius's De Constantia: A Stoic Spiritual Exercise', *Poetics Today* 28 (3): 339–62.

—— 2012. 'Stoics against Stoics in Cudworth's "A Treatise of Freewill"', *British Journal for the History of Philosophy* 20 (5): 935–952.

Shapiro, L. 2008. 'Descartes' Ethics' in J. Broughton and J. Carriero, (ed.), *Companion to Descartes*. London: Blackwell, 445–64.

Shirley, S. (trans.) and Morgan, M. (ed.) 2002. *Spinoza: The Complete Works*. Indianapolis: Hackett Publishing Company.

Skinner, Q. 1996. *Reason and Rhetoric in the Philosophy of Hobbes*. Cambridge: Cambridge University Press.

Spinoza, B. 1985. *Ethics*, in E. Curley (ed.), *The Collected Works of Spinoza*. Princeton: Princeton University Press.

Tillotson, J. 1683. *A Sermon Preached at the Funeral of the Reverend Benjamin Whichcot, D. D.* London.

Toland, J. (ed.) 1721. *Letters from the Right Honourable the Late Earl of Shaftesbury to Robert Molesworth, Esq.* London.

Tuck, R. 1993. *Philosophy and Government: 1572–1651*. Cambridge: Cambridge University Press.

Vickers, B. (ed.) 1996. *Francis Bacon: A Critical Edition of the Major Works*. Oxford: Oxford University Press.

Whichcote, B. 1702. *Several Discourses*, 2nd edn. London.

—— 1703. *Moral and Religious Aphorisms*. Norwich.

Williams, B. 1981. 'Persons, Character and Morality', in *Moral Luck: Philosophical Papers 1973–1980*. Oxford: Oxford University Press, 1–19.

Wilson, C. 2004. 'Love of God and Love of Creatures: The Masham-Astell Debate', *History of Philosophy Quarterly* 21 (3): 281–98.

CHAPTER 13

....

ROUSSEAU AND ETHICS

....

CHRISTOPHER BERTRAM

13.1 BACKGROUND

....

MODERN ethical theories are principally of two kinds. On one side are the intellectual descendants of David Hume who aim to make ethics continuous in some sense with the human sciences and who locate the source of the moral in the affective: in sentiment, disposition, and sympathy (e.g. Gibbard 1990). Alternatively, followers of Kant conceive of morality as being most basically about what we have good reason to do, and tend to ask questions about which principles could be the object of agreement among suitably situated free and equal agents, which could not be reasonably rejected, and other variations on that theme (a good example would be Scanlon 1998). Anyone who reads Rousseau today will therefore be tempted to situate him against that landscape but in doing so will quickly encounter the problem that he appears to have a foot in both camps. Rousseau's moral psychology is very much about affect, about the natural drives and dispositions that either bring about conflict, resentment, and unhappiness or, perhaps, dispose us to help another person in distress. Sentiment both guides our actions and governs our attitudes towards the actions of others. However, when we look at Rousseau's political philosophy, and particularly at concepts like the general will, we see a clear historical and intellectual connection to the Kantian project, a connection that is reflected clearly in some of Kant's own writings, and most notably in the third formulation of the categorical imperative, where Kant conceives of the moral agent as both legislator and subject in a kingdom of ends.[1] To further complicate this picture of apparent Rousseavian eclecticism, his ideas about moral motivation include eudaimonistic elements, since he believes that an interest in one's own flourishing, properly conceived, should lead a person to favour relations of mutual respect and equality with others, thus making a link to a third tradition of moral discourse, that of virtue ethics.

---

[1] For a recent determinedly Kantian reading of Rousseau, see Mandle 1997. The classic Kantian reading is Cassirer 1954.

The appearance that Rousseau belongs in all of these camps also turns out to be the reality. Strictly speaking, Rousseau's view is that the *content* of morality is a matter of principles that could be the object of agreement for rational creatures, or perhaps would be chosen by some ideally rational agent. This is the case at least for those parts of morality having to do with the right: with justice, rights, duties, and so forth. Unfortunately, though, we are not by nature such ideally rational agents and those features of our psychology that approximate such a nature are the products of a long history of change involving the transformation both of our individual characters and of the species as a whole. This transformative process, though making morality possible, also tends to subvert behaviour that aims at the good of others. This is because the growth of self-consciousness and rationality displaces or mutes the natural dispositions that we have to care for one another. The capacity for reason might make it possible for us to heed the voice of reason, but it also enables us to engage in the self-serving rationalization of actions that are actually guided by pride, vanity, or greed. Philosophers and ethical theorists are not immune from the psychological corruption that other humans are prone to and, according to Rousseau, often play a most deplorable role in rationalizing and justifying the conduct of the powerful (or of their own failure to act). However, though Rousseau often adopts a highly pessimistic attitude to the modern world, he does think of something approximating moral conduct as *possible*, but believes that it needs to be bolstered by the right type of formative processes, whether educational or political in nature.

13.2 ROUSSEAU'S THEORY OF PSYCHOLOGICAL DEVELOPMENT

The essential background to understanding Rousseau's views on morality is his account of human social and psychological development, a theory that has come in for renewed attention in recent years. Rousseau sets this forward in a number of texts, but, most importantly in *Emile* (his treatise on childcare and education) and in the *Discourse on the Origins of the Foundations of Inequality among Men* or *Discourse on Inequality* (his conjectural history of human development). Though the theory differs somewhat from text to text, the essential ideas are as follows. All creatures, and humans are no different in this respect, have a basic drive to survive and to attend to those things they need to do to satisfy their basic needs. This fundamental drive Rousseau calls *amour de soi*. As natural creatures, we need to eat, to keep warm, to escape predators, and so forth, and *amour de soi* impels us to do these things. Alongside this drive is another, which Rousseau sometimes presents as basic but more often as derivative of *amour de soi* via an expansion of our concern for our own well-being into a sympathetic identification with others. This second set of impulses is *pitié* or compassion and it directs us (and maybe some other animals also) to attend to the suffering of others and to act to relieve that suffering if we can do so without endangering ourselves. In addition to these two drives, Rousseau also invokes a third, which comes into existence both in the course of human history and in the individual development of each modern human being. This third drive he calls *amour propre* and is directed towards the care of the self as a social being, as a being among others. Rousseau sometimes presents *amour propre* as a modification of *amour de soi* and sometimes as something quite different from it.

Rousseau's account of historical development in the *Discourse on Inequality* begins with primitive and solitary beings who wander through the forest and occasionally encounter others of their kind. The most primitive individuals have physical and cognitive powers that are proportional to their needs and they do not therefore depend on others for the satisfaction of their *amour de soi*. These beings differ from other non-human creatures in their freedom and perfectibility. Gradually, increasing population density brings these creatures into greater contact with one another, simple modes of cooperation develop, as well as small settled communities. It is at this moment that a revolution takes place in the conception that humans have of themselves and that *amour propre* is born. Sex is key here. Humans start to make comparisons among potential mates and, crucially, come to see themselves for the first time as being the object of comparison by others. This emergence of comparison, of concern with relative standing, and of a sense of being-for-others results in what amounts to almost a rebirth of the human species.

Amour propre, in generating a concern with relative standing in the eyes of others, makes people psychologically dependent on those others in a way in which previous humans were not. To this psychological dependence Rousseau adds material dependence: as humans develop new technologies and a division of labour, their needs expand to match. Soon, they can no longer eat, be clothed, and housed in the manner they deem essential (and indeed the manner that may be essential, since their natural hardiness has atrophied somewhat) without the cooperation of others. Private property develops to protect individual investment in farming and other enterprises. People can no longer get what they want and need without the agreement and help of others. Rousseau believes that this generates new forms of inauthenticity and insincerity as people try to act in ways that they believe will lead those others to act to satisfy their needs. People start to flatter and deceive others and to try to make themselves into the sorts of people those others will find attractive or useful. Paradoxically, this leads to the frustration of what is now the dominant drive, *amour propre*, as the need to receive recognition from others is thwarted by a perception that those others may simply be simulating love, loyalty, or affection for their own instrumental purposes. Modernity for Rousseau is usually a looking-glass world of enraged egos: self-defeatingly demanding recognition but unable to get it, even from those who appear to be doing so. Both Rousseau's educational theory in *Emile* and his political philosophy in the *Social Contract* are attempts to think of ways in which human flourishing might still be possible in a world in which this concern for recognition has become a pervasive and ineliminable feature of human life.

Since *amour propre* plays such a prominent role in the pathologies of modern life according to Rousseau, it is perhaps unsurprising that much commentary has stressed its negative features (see e.g. Charvet 1974). In recent years however, there has been a revaluation of Rousseau's moral psychology which stresses that *amour propre* can also have positive features and which distinguishes between *inflamed amour propre* and the benign desire of the agent to achieve recognition as being of value, as having standing in the eyes of others. In the English-speaking world at least, the breakthrough in this revaluation of Rousseau came particularly with the work of N. J. H. Dent (1988, 2005), who emphasized the ways in which non-inflamed *amour propre* can play a part in the psychological life of the mature adult and of the citizen rather than being simply banished from the good society (see Shklar 1969: 202). After many decades of neglect, during which Rousseau was principally thought of either as a political theorist or as a woolly proto-romantic, Dent provided a compelling reading of Rousseau's psychological thinking based on close attention particularly to the texts of the *Discourse on Inequality*, *Emile* (especially Book 4), and *Of the Social Contract*. Dent showed how Rousseau's thought achieved unity via the related concepts of *amour de soi*, *pitié*, and *amour propre*. Dent's reading has not gone uncontested (see Rosen, 1996: 85 n. 77) but it has largely been adopted by other Anglophone philosophers (see e.g. O'Hagan 1999; Bertram 2004; Rawls 2007; Cohen 2010). Frederick Neuhouser (2008) builds critically on Dent's work to provide a yet more sophisticated interpretation of the key ideas.

13.3 CONCERN FOR SELF AND OTHERS

So what, according to Rousseau, is morality, and why should we be moral? This section explores a number of possible answers to this question, beginning with the most obvious, that of a simple application of *pitié* to support a pure ethics of sympathy. On the surface, the concept of *pitié* looks like the most promising foundation for constructing a Rousseauvian moral theory. This is because *pitié* plays a similar role to morality in many circumstances. It moderates the pursuit of narrow self-interest in favour of a concern with the needs of others, particularly their need to avoid suffering. It moves people to act in various other-regarding ways: perhaps rushing to their assistance or intervening to prevent conflict. It affects our evaluation of other people, of their actions, of events, by causing us to react adversely to cruelty or sympathetically towards pain. In *Emile*, the commonality of suffering and the reaction that we have to it is the basis for our identification with others as fellow members of humanity. Rousseau's writing provides many episodes where sympathy is engaged in this way.

However, despite the fact that *pitié* often moves people to behave in ways that are congruent with morality, it is clear that for Rousseau, action guided by *pitié*, taken on its own, falls short of being genuinely moral action. This is for at least two reasons. First, though *pitié* may contingently be pro-social in its effects, this is not essential to its character. The solitary creatures who inhabit the earliest pages of the *Discourse on Inequality* are not social animals, but they are guided by *pitié* when the occasion presents itself. Second, and much more importantly, *pitié* does not, for Rousseau, qualify as a genuinely moral sentiment because of its purely instinctual nature. For morality properly speaking, it is not just behaviour of a certain kind that is needed but also deliberate choice by a being possessed of self-consciousness. Rousseau makes this clear when he discusses moral responsibility in children in Book 1 of *Emile*:

> Reason alone teaches us to know good and bad. Conscience, which makes us love the former and hate the latter, although independent of reason, cannot therefore be developed without it. Before the age of reason we do good and bad without knowing it, and there is no morality in our actions. (Rousseau 2012: 67)

He makes basically the same point in the 'Geneva manuscript' draft of the *Social Contract*, where he argues that had the original isolates not come together with all the dreadful psychological consequences that ensued

> all our happiness would consist in not knowing our wretchedness; there would be neither kindness in our hearts nor morality in our actions, and we should never have tasted the most delightful feeling of the soul, which is the love of virtue. (Rousseau 2012: 143)

For Rousseau, then, genuinely moral action has both an objective and a subjective side to it. It is not enough that the right behaviour be engaged in—an effect that might be down to instinct in the form of *pitié* alone—but an action must, to count as moral, be undertaken for the right kind of reason.

Acting for reasons is only possible once human beings have moved beyond merely instinctual action and have achieved a sense of themselves as beings among others who exist for others. Unfortunately, the very conditions that make moral action possible also conspire to make it unlikely, and the same capacities that are required for people to act morally can also be put in the service of self-interest, pride, and vanity and in ways that silence the instinctual promptings of *pitié*. Moreover, though Rousseau believes that reason can give us knowledge of moral principles, even when it does so this knowledge alone will be insufficient to motivate us to act on those principles.

We can see this last point in Rousseau's critique of the account of moral knowledge and motivation given by Diderot in an article on 'Natural Right' for the *Encyclopédie* (in Diderot 1992). In that article Diderot identifies morality (or, at least that component of morality having to do with rights and duties) with a 'general will of the human race'. In a fascinating but frustratingly brief discussion, Diderot invokes the idea of a hypothetical assembly of the human race to determine the content of the right. He even goes further than this, canvassing the idea that if animals could reliably communicate their thoughts and feelings to us, they too would have to be admitted to such an assembly. Though such an assembly is hypothetical, Diderot believes that we can divine what it would decide by looking in two places. First, we can examine the institutions and practices of existing societies, since moral principles are bound to have been approximated in their conventions. Second, we can look within and see that 'the general will is in each person a pure expression of the understanding, which, in the silence of the passions calculates what every individual may demand from his fellow-man, and what his fellow-man has a right to demand of him' (Diderot 1992: 20–1).

Rousseau's response to Diderot is, tellingly, not to question his account of the content of morality, but rather to question why a person, in the absence of law and the state, should be moved to action by mere knowledge of moral principles. Since our natural first impulse is to care for ourselves, we require, at the very least, an assurance that others will comply with the principles of right before we have any reason to do so ourselves. In this emphasis on assurance, Rousseau adopts a similar position to Hobbes.

Not only is the capacity for reason and for the discernment of moral principles not sufficient for moral conduct, but it can also be actively harmful when not properly directed since it can assist in the rationalization of self-interested conduct by supplying casuistical arguments reconciling apparent self-interest with morality. Something therefore needs to supplement reason to get moral action going. The obvious candidate would appear to be, once again, *pitié*, but, confusingly, Rousseau sometimes invokes a further faculty which he calls *conscience*. Unfortunately, he never gives a systematic account of *conscience* and we are forced to reconstruct his thinking from various remarks that he makes in places including the *Lettres morales*, the 'Profession of Faith of the Savoyard Vicar' (a text-within-a-text that forms part of *Emile*), and the *Letter to Christophe de Beaumont*. In those texts, *conscience* appears both as a distinct faculty from reason, but also as part of our nature as rational creatures. Although it is a moral faculty, it seems to be much more than that, since it is also implicated in aesthetic appreciation, in our wonder at the natural world, and even in our commitment to truth as a norm of discourse. Often it seems to be a quasi-aesthetic element that is to the fore, as *conscience* appears as a love for the well-orderedness of the world and a corresponding distaste for its disordered states. Nor, as so often with the elements of Rousseau's psychology, is it entirely clear how *conscience* relates to the other drives and passions.

In remarks Rousseau makes in *Emile*, he seems to emphasize the common root of *conscience* and *pitié* and thereby to incorporate *conscience* in his naturalistic account of the passions. There he writes of how 'the first voices of conscience arise out of the first movements of the heart' (Rousseau 1979: 235). In a footnote to the same passage in *Emile* which covers similar ground to the reply to Diderot in the *Geneva Manuscript*, Rousseau writes of how:

> the strength of an expansive soul make me identify myself with my fellow and, and I feel that I am, so to speak, in him, it is in order not to suffer that I do not want him to suffer. I am interested in him for love of myself, and the reason for the precept is in nature itself, which inspires in me the desire of my well-being in whatever place I feel my existence. (Rousseau 1979: 235 n.)

Here the connections seem to be reasonably clear between *amour de soi*, *pitié*, and *conscience*, with sympathetic identification playing a major role. But only a few pages later, in the 'Profession of Faith', a different set of relationships seem to be in place when he writes:

> Conscience is the voice of the soul; the passions are the voice of the body. Is it surprising that these two languages are often contradictory? And then which should be listened to? Too often reason deceives us. We have acquired only too much right to

challenge it. But conscience never deceives, it is man's true guide. It is to the soul what instinct is to the body. (Rousseau 1979: 286)

In this passage, far from being based on the passions, *conscience* seems to have some kind of parallel existence to them in a dualistic account of body and mind in which human beings partake of both an animal and a rational nature. In the *Letter to de Beaumont* Rousseau reinforces this picture:

> Man is not a simple being; he is made up of two elements...self-love is not a simple passion; but has two principles, namely the intelligent being and the sensitive being, whose well-being is not the same. The appetite of the senses tends to that of the body and the love of order to that of the soul. This second love, when developed and made active, is called conscience; but conscience is only developed and only acts from enlightenment. (Hope Mason 1979: 233)

It may not be possible to reconstruct a fully consistent picture of *conscience* from Rousseau's texts then, precisely because of the degree of equivocation there between a naturalistic account of the passions and a rival dualist picture and because of the entanglement between an evolutionary-historical account of the emergence of reason and that same theologically inspired dualism.[2] Rousseau seems to move between an account in which self-consciousness and reason emerge as our second nature as a result of history and socialization and one in which we are, by our nature as humans, somehow suspended between our animal nature and fully rational beings made in God's image and guided by an inherent love of order. The unclear relationship between *pitié* and *conscience* expresses this hesitation.

13.4 THE NATURAL GOODNESS THESIS

One aspect of Rousseau's thought that is liable to confuse the modern reader somewhat is his claim that man is good by nature but is made evil by society. Rousseau often claims that this is the thesis that gives unity to all of his mature works. He recounts in various places that it came to him suddenly, as he was on his way to visit Diderot in prison in Vincennes and read of the essay competition of the Academy of Dijon that would provoke him to write his *Discourse on the Sciences and the Arts*. The confusing aspect here is that Rousseau cannot mean that human beings are *morally* good by nature and yet this is the sense in which the unwary reader will take him. He means instead two things. First, that there was nothing in the nature of the original, wood-wandering humans that disposed them to conflict. Nature had proportioned their powers to their needs so there was little occasion for scarcity or competition to cause difficulties among them and, in

---

[2] For reflections on the contrast between these rival and inconsistent visions in Rousseau, see O'Hagan 1999. Dent 2005: ch. 4 argues that the dualist elements, though present in Rousseau, are an aberration.

any case, lacking the self-consciousness necessary for the reactive attitudes, they could not take offence, bear grudges, or become jealous in the manner that Hobbesian individuals would. Both the expansion of needs and the development of self-awareness are consequences of history and society. The second aspect to the thesis is the more positive but tentative one that, since society in its current configuration is the cause of our unhappiness and predisposition to conflict, alternative social arrangements might improve matters. Rather than thinking of humans as disposed to perennial conflict because of fixed parts of their psychological make-up or because of original sin, Rousseau believes that the right institutions could reform people with more cooperative dispositions.[3]

13.5 RESHAPING THE PSYCHE

Rousseau's work contains two main accounts of how, even in a world in which *amour propre* has become a pervasive feature of human psychology, individuals can still achieve a flourishing and satisfied life. The first of these is his educational theory, as articulated in *Emile*; the second is the political philosophy he advances in the *Social Contract*. In *Emile* he puts forward a programme of education involving the careful management of the passions that aims at delaying the emergence of *amour propre*. The tutor carefully manipulates the pupil's environment rather than issuing the instructions and commands that might lead to conflict between his will and the student's and thereby cause resentment and alienation. When *amour propre* eventually surfaces at puberty, the pupil is able to confront the world with a balanced estimation of his place in it and his relationship to other people and with his native sense of *pitié* intact. His drive for recognition as being of value will be satisfied by the respect of his peers and the love of a woman and he will not crave domination over others.

The *Social Contract* account centres on the notion of the general will.[4] Whilst the characteristic condition of modernity is to subject individuals to the arbitrary will and opinion of others, a situation of toxic mutual dependence that renders everyone unfree, Rousseau believes that harmonious coexistence and freedom are possible in a state governed by a genuine general will which limits freedom in a manner consistent with the equal freedom of others. In a just society governed by the general will, individual psychology will be reshaped over time via a process in which citizens, forced to contemplate general rules that apply to everyone (including themselves), are drawn towards an impartial perspective (at least in relation to their own society).[5] Once they have the habit of thinking in this general and impartial manner, the general will becomes incorporated as a component of their own will and they start to acquire something like a moral

[3] For an insightful account of the natural goodness thesis see Cohen 1997 and 2010.
[4] On the general will see especially Neuhouser 1993. On the *Social Contract* more generally, see Bertram 2004.
[5] Sreenivasan 2000 particularly stresses this impartializing effect of the choice situation faced by the citizens.

sensibility. The citizen of a state governed by a general will continues to have the desire for recognition that is engendered by *amour propre*, but that desire is supposed to be met by the enjoyment of equal citizen status and by the fact that instead of the damaging subjection to the alien will of another that causes resentment and hatred, the individual is subject only to a law that he himself has chosen.[6]

Needless to say there are some acute problems here. The idea of the general will suffers from a serious ambiguity between a democratic notion of what the people have legislated and an ideal that holds independently of their choice, an ambiguity that has informed many later hostile critiques of Rousseau on the grounds of 'totalitarianism'. Rousseau never really satisfactorily addresses issues such as the problem of minorities who did not vote for the law to which they are subject and his ideal of mass participatory sovereignty looks impractical for the modern world. Both *Emile* and the *Social Contract* also rely on the rather implausible device of an individual (the tutor in one story, the legislator in the other) who has somehow escaped the moral and psychological deformations of the modern world and is able to select methods (pedagogical routines or just laws) that reliably shape or reshape the psyches of the individuals subject to them.

13.6 ROUSSEAU AND MORAL THEORISTS

No account of Rousseau's relationship to ethics would be complete without some remarks on his attitude to philosophers and other theorists and thinkers about morality. In the struggle for the recognition of others and the achievement of relative advancement, any capacity might prove useful, and reason is no exception. Those who concern themselves professionally with reason are not immune to these pressures themselves and are also likely to legitimate the self-seeking schemes of the powerful and influential. The Savoyard Vicar condemns the entire profession:

> Where is the philosopher who would not gladly deceive mankind for his own glory? Where is the one who in the secrecy of his heart sets himself any other goal than that of distinguishing himself? (Rousseau 1979: 269)

In the *Discourse on Inequality*, following a passage where Rousseau is concerned to demonstrate that, despite the corruptions of modern society, the reactions of theatregoers to tragedy show that *pitié* still lives as a force in human hearts, he depicts the philosopher as the figure most immune to these natural impulses to pro-social behaviour:

> It is reason that engenders amour propre, and reflection that reinforces it; reason that turns man back upon himself; reason that separates himself from everything that troubles and afflicts him: It is Philosophy that isolates him; by means of Philosophy he secretly says, at the sight of a suffering man, perish if you wish, I am safe.

[6] Whether it is plausible to think that the citizens of a just society would have satisfactorily achieved the recognition that they crave is a matter of sceptical commentary by Frederick Neuhouser (2008: part 3).

Only dangers that threaten the entire society still disturb the Philosopher's tranquil slumber, and rouse him from his bed. (1997: 153)

By contrast, ordinary folk, moved by *pitié*, intervene in street brawls in an immediate horrified reaction to the prospect of bloodletting. In *Emile* he condemns fanaticism only to deplore the amoralism of the atheistic philosopher:

If atheism does not cause the spilling of men's blood, it is less from love of peace than from indifference to the good. Whatever may be going on is of little importance for the allegedly wise man, provided that he can remain at rest in his study. Philosophic indifference resembles the tranquility of the state under despotism. It is the tranquility of death. It is more destructive than war itself. (1979: 333)

The posthumous fragment *Principles of the Right of War* discusses the seductive discourses contained in books on law and morality and then contrasts this with the human reality legitimated by international law and just war theory:

I approach and perceive a scene of murder, ten thousand men butchered, the dead stacked in heaps, the dying trampled underfoot by horses, bearing the image of death and its last agony. So that is the fruit of those pacific institutions. Pity and indignation well up in the depths of my heart. O barbarous Philosopher! come read us your book on a battlefield. (Rousseau 2012: 153)

In this text philosophers have the role of apologists for the established order who provide justifications to support the interests of the wealthy and powerful. Princes and states promise philosophers membership of academies, chairs at prestigious universities, and pensions; the people have nothing comparable to offer. Philosophers provide an account of law and morality that masks the truth about systems of oppression, violence, and exploitation, and natural human reactions to suffering are muted by elaborate moral reasoning. In this vein, Rousseau is the ancestor of post-modern critics like Michel Foucault.

13.7 RESIDUAL ISSUES: MORAL ACTION IN A NON-IDEAL WORLD

Rousseau sets out no systematic moral theory of his own but rather a series of theories about other matters (political, educational, religious) that contain remarks and opinions relevant to ethics. Although Rousseau cared deeply about morality, it is not entirely clear that the political theories that he espoused were compatible with it rather than representing a kind of second best. With inflamed *amour propre* loose in the world, Rousseau believes that we need just institutions to socialize individuals, to provide them with satisfaction for their desire for standing in the eyes of others, and to allow them to remain free whilst subject to the authority they need to coordinate their collective action. However, the consciousness of the patriotic citizen is not moral consciousness in the way in which we standardly understand that idea. To function effectively as a citizen and a comrade, the individual needs a particular attachment to the *patrie* rather than to universal principles of right and justice. One of the reasons Rousseau got into trouble for the *Social Contract* was precisely because he thought that true Christians, with their universalistic morality, would inevitably make lukewarm citizens. The citizen may act in ways that closely track morality, and this may be, generally speaking, the best that imperfect humans can do, but the Rousseauvian citizen does not, in the end, act morally, but in the general interest of the fatherland.

Rousseau's understanding of the relationships between self-interest, knowledge, morality, and human nature is complex. On the one hand, a perfectly enlightened and fully rational individual would, in acting in ways that respect the personhood and dignity of others and which show a due sensitivity to their needs and vulnerabilities, also be acting in ways that further his or her own true interest. This rejection of a sharp conflict between self-interest and morality establishes some continuities between Rousseau's thinking and that of ancient philosophers (with the Plato of the *Protagoras* and *Gorgias* a strong influence). On the other hand, we inevitably fall short of such a perfect standard and our human nature has been shaped in ways that incline us towards selfishness even when this is personally and mutually self-defeating. Creatures such as we are have difficulty acting morally even when we come to know what morality requires. The sceptical individual, whom Rousseau addresses in his critique of Diderot, knows perfectly well the requirements of justice, but sees no reason to comply with them unilaterally. But even given a world of selfishness and inflamed *amour propre*, Rousseau believes that individuals have reason to control their own passions and seek relations of respect and equality with their fellows, as the pupil in *Emile* is brought up to do. To get us to act on those reasons is, however, normally beyond our individual powers. We need to be shaped and trained by highly artificial educational and political schemes if we are to stand a chance of living flourishing lives in a world of mutual dependence. Rousseau himself wavered between the devising of schemes and systems and a despair at the pathologies of modernity such that the best personal choice was withdrawal and isolation (an option that he contemplates at the beginning of *The Reveries of the Solitary Walker*).

Bibliography

Bertram, C. 2004. *Rousseau and The Social Contract*. London: Routledge.

Cassirer, E. 1954. *The Question of Jean-Jacques Rousseau*. Bloomington: Indiana University Press.

Charvet, J. 1974. *The Social Problem in the Philosophy of Rousseau*. Cambridge: Cambridge University Press.

Cohen, J. 1997. 'The natural goodness of humanity', in A. Reath (ed.), *Reclaiming the History of Ethics: Essays for John Rawls*. Cambridge: Cambridge University Press, 102–39.

—— 2010. *Rousseau: A Free Community of Equals*. Oxford: Oxford University Press.

Dent, N. J. H. 1988. *Rousseau: An Introduction to his Psychological, Social and Political Theory*. Oxford: Blackwell.

—— 2005. *Rousseau*. London: Routledge.

Diderot, D. 1992. *Political Writings*, eds J. Hope-Mason and R. Wokler. Cambridge: Cambridge University Press.

Gibbard, A. 1990. *Wise Choices Apt Feelings*. Cambridge MA: Harvard University Press.

Hope-Mason, J. 1979. *The Essential Rousseau*. London: Quartet.

Mandle, J. 1997. 'Rousseauvian constructivism', *Journal of the History of Philosophy* 45: 545–62.

Neuhouser, F. 1993. 'Freedom, dependence and the general will', *Philosophical Review* 102: 363–95.

—— 2008. *Rousseau's Theodicy of Self-Love*. Oxford: Oxford University Press.

O'Hagan, T. 1999. *Rousseau*. London: Routledge.

Rawls, J. 2007. *Lectures on the History of Political Philosophy*. Cambridge, MA: Harvard University Press.

Rosen, M. 1996. *On Voluntary Servitude*. Cambridge, MA: Harvard University Press.

Rousseau, J. J. 1979. *Emile*, ed. A. Bloom. London: Penguin.

—— 1997. *The Discourses and Other Early Political Writings*, ed. V. Gourevitch. Cambridge: Cambridge University Press.

—— 2012. *The Social Contract and Other Political Writings*, ed. C. Bertram, trans. Q. Hoare. London: Penguin.

Scanlon, T. M. 1998. *What We Owe to One Another*. Cambridge MA: Harvard University Press.

Shklar, J. N. 1969. *Men and Citizens: A Study of Rousseau's Social Theory*. Cambridge: Cambridge University Press.

Sreenivasan, G. 2000. 'What is the general will?', *Philosophical Review* 109: 545–81.

CHAPTER 14

··

UTILITARIANISM: BENTHAM
AND RASHDALL

··

ROBERT SHAVER

TODAY, many explain the attractiveness of utilitarianism by noting that, like any consequentialist theory, it permits one to bring about the most good.[1] To an earlier (perhaps less self-absorbed) generation, utilitarianism was attractive in large part because, again like any consequentialist theory, it requires one to bring about the most good.[2] In both cases, the contrast is with deontology, and in both cases, no particular theory of what is good plays any role.

This understanding of the attractiveness of utilitarianism has a history. Utilitarians through Sidgwick, though aware of other possibilities, took pleasure as the only good. The 'ideal utilitarians', Moore and Rashdall, added further goods, but kept the structure found in Mill and Sidgwick: the right act maximizes the production of the good. Before ideal utilitarianism was established, it was unclear whether, when one objected to utilitarianism, one objected to the view that pleasure is the only good or to the view that the right act maximizes the good. Those who rejected utilitarianism, such as Green, seemed to quarrel only with pleasure, and even Kant was sometimes read as a consequentialist who takes the good will as the most important good.[3] With Moore and Rashdall, it became easier to isolate what one found objectionable—thus it became easier, with Prichard, Carritt, and Ross, to clearly formulate deontology, the view that sometimes one is not permitted to bring about the most good, or that the right action can sometimes bring about less good than some alternative action. Once this alternative was established, many saw what deontology rejected in utilitarianism as its strength, and so much of the debate since Prichard began.

---

[1] See, for example, Scheffler 1982: 4.

[2] See, for example, Ewing 1947: 188, 1953: 62, 76, Moore 1965 [1912]: 77, Laird 1926: 21.

[3] For this reading of Kant, see Prichard 2002 [1920s, 1930s]: 153–9, 208, 215, 216 or, more cautiously, Rashdall 1924: i, 130, 301.

The modern understanding of the appeal of utilitarianism does not fit all of the utilitarians. To illustrate the history, I shall concentrate on Bentham and Rashdall.[4] Although I shall argue that a scalar interpretation of Bentham, on which utilitarianism is not a theory of the right or permitted at all, goes too far, it is true that Bentham has lit- tle interest in working out the connection between the right and the good. And for him, the view that pleasure is the only good is central, rather than, as today, something many consequentialists reject. It is with Rashdall and Moore that the modern understanding of the appeal starts. In sections 14.1 and 14.2, I consider the character of Bentham's utili- tarianism. In section 14.3, I consider his argument for utilitarianism. In section 14.4, I consider Rashdall's criticisms of deontologists and hedonistic utilitarians.

14.1

Utilitarians often link goodness and rightness. Mill states the principle of utility as hold- ing that 'actions are right in proportion as they tend to promote happiness, wrong as they tend to produce the reverse of happiness.'[5] Sidgwick writes that '[b]y Utilitarianism is here meant the ethical theory, that the conduct which, under any given circumstances, is objectively right, is that which will produce the greatest amount of happiness on the whole' (1981 [1907]: 411). Rashdall states ideal utilitarianism as the position that 'actions are right or wrong according as they tend to produce for all mankind an ideal end or good' (1924. i: 184). Part of Moore's statement of utilitarianism is that 'if we had to choose between two actions one of which would have intrinsically better total effects than the other, it would always be our duty to choose the former, and wrong to choose the latter' (1965: 28).

Bentham is different. According to his 'explicit and determinate account', the princi- ple of utility is 'that principle which approves or disapproves of every action whatsoever, according to the tendency which it appears to have to augment or diminish the happi- ness of the party whose interest is in question' (1996 [1789, 1823]: 11, 12).[6] Rightness is introduced only later. An action is 'conformable to the principle of utility...when the tendency it has to augment the happiness of the community is greater than any it has to diminish it...Of an action that is conformable to the principle of utility, one may

---

[4] For Bentham as the first consistent utilitarian, in contrast to (for example) Paley and Beccaria, see Schneewind 1977: 125–6, Sidgwick 1896: 239, Hart 1982: 49–52.

[5] Mill 1969 [1863]: 210 (*Utilitarianism*). He does not always mention rightness. In *Utilitarianism*, ch. IV, the proof of utilitarianism seems concerned only with the good. In the *Logic*, the 'ultimate principle of Teleology' is 'the promotion of happiness' (Mill 1974 [1872]: 951).

[6] Similarly, a 'man may be said to be a partisan of the principle of utility, when the approbation or disapprobation he annexes to any action...is determined by, and proportioned to the tendency which he conceives it to have to augment or to diminish the happiness of the community' (1996: 13). The principle is that 'by which approbation is called for, for such measures alone as are contributory to human happiness' (1983c: 296).

always say...that it is one that ought to be done...One may say also, that it is right it should be done... When thus interpreted the words *ought*, and *right* and *wrong*, and others of that stamp, have a meaning: when otherwise, they have none' (1996: 12–13). Talk about rightness seems, for Bentham, optional—one *may* label actions conformable to the principle of utility 'right', but there seems no need to do so, and rightness does not appear in the principle itself. (Elsewhere, Bentham frequently writes of the greatest happiness as the 'end', without 'ought' or 'right'.[7])

This suggests that Bentham may be a scalar utilitarian, making claims only about goodness and badness, showing little interest in rightness. In particular, there is no mapping from claims about goodness to claims about rightness.[8]

This fits Bentham's attitude toward 'ought' and 'right'. As Ross Harrison notes, Bentham often suggests a subjectivist, non-cognitivist, or eliminativist treatment: 'he ought to be so—that is to say, the idea of his being so is pleasing to me' (Bentham 1838–1843, iii: 218); when I say 'it is right that he should have the coat or land', 'nothing more do I express than my satisfaction at the idea of his having this coat or land' (1838–1843, iii: 218); '[w]hen I say the greatest happiness of the whole community ought to be the end or object of pursuit...I express—this and no more: namely that it is my wish, my desire, to see it taken for such' (1989: 230); '[w]ere I to be asked what it is I mean when I call an action a *right* one, I should answer very readily: neither more nor less than, an action I *approve* of' (1977: 53); 'I say, it ought not to be established; that is, I do not approve of its being established' (1838–1843, ii: 495); '[i]f [I say] his own well-being ought to be the sole object of pursuit...what I mean...is that the conduct of him who...takes his own well-being for the object of his pursuit is approved by me...As often as...I say he ought to do so and so...what...I know and acknowledge myself to be doing is neither more nor less than endeavour[ing] to bring to view the state of my own...affections...—this much and nothing more' (1983c: 149; also 1983a [1815]: 202). Sometimes Bentham suggests eliminating 'ought' and 'ought not': 'these words—if for this one purpose the use of them may be allowed—*ought* to be banished from the vocabulary of Ethics' (1983c: 253; also 1977: 496 n.). Harrison, who notes these passages after giving an admirable reconstruction of Bentham's proof of the principle of utility, despairs of them; they ignore that Bentham has a proof and make the principle of utility Bentham's caprice.[9] (Bentham himself asks 'whether, when two men have said, "I like this," and

---

[7] For example, the greatest happiness is the end of the legislator and the Constitutional Code (1838–1843, ii: 8, 192, 537, iii: 33, vi: 6; 1983b [1830]: 18; 1970 [1782]: 31; 1989 [1822]: 232, 235, 270; 1996: 14 n., 32; 1831: 7 (quoted by Postema 2002: xxi, 2006b: 114 n. 8). It is 'the only right and proper and universally desirable end' (1977 [1776]: 446, 1996: 1; also 1983c [1814–1831]: 60, 62).

[8] I first heard the scalar interpretation of Bentham (and utilitarianism) from Bob Bright, who gave it in ch. 5 of Bright 1991. It is also suggested for Bentham in an excellent paper by Howard-Snyder (1994: 128 n. 8). Scalar utilitarianism has been defended recently by Norcross 2006. Sidgwick notes the possibility of ethics understood as 'an inquiry into the nature of the...the Good' as opposed to enquiry into 'rational precepts of Conduct', but rejects limiting oneself to the former on the ground that 'we must still arrive finally, if it is to be practically useful, at some determination of precepts or directive rules of conduct' (1981: 3). For the same point, see Rashdall 1924, i: 5 n.

[9] Harrison 1983: 192–4, 273.

"I don't like it," they can … have any thing more to say?'; it is clear that Bentham thinks he is not in this position (1996: 16).) But 'ought' and 'right' do not appear in the statement of the principle.[10] This suggests that Bentham may hold that, while there are moral facts about what is good or better, there are no moral facts about what one ought to do or what is right; here some versions of subjectivism, non-cognitivism, or eliminativism are appropriate.

One might object that Bentham could be read as having a particular theory of rightness, namely that the right act increases happiness.[11] But this has three drawbacks.

(a) It attributes to Bentham a silly view. On it, if I can increase happiness by 1 unit or a million, it is right to increase it by 1 (and right to increase it by a million). And if I can decrease happiness by 1 or a million, and must do one or the other, it is wrong to decrease it by 1 (and wrong to decrease it by a million).[12]

(b) Bentham often suggests a different view, according to which the right act maximizes happiness. For example, the principle says that 'the greatest happiness of all those whose interest is in question [is] *the standard of right and wrong*' (1996: 11 n.).[13] And sometimes Bentham suggests a more complex view. I have a duty to prevent mischievous actions if I can 'without too great a sacrifice' (1996: 29 n.). Here duty seems a function not only of the happiness produced, but also of the cost to the agent.[14] Bentham is not, then, consistent in holding that the right act (merely) increases happiness. This looseness fits with an attitude that is suspicious of, and not much interested in, rightness.

(c) If what is crucial is that approval is proportioned to the amount of happiness increased, it is unclear why the point at which happiness is increased has special significance. To adapt an example from Alastair Norcross, if a utilitarian could influence either A to produce 1 billion units of happiness rather than 1, or B to produce 1 rather than –1, the utilitarian should influence A.[15] The difference in amount between 1 billion and 1,

[10] An objection is that at one point Bentham seems to suggest the same treatment for 'good' as he gives for 'ought' and 'right': 'By a good thing, he who speaks of it means that by the idea of which a sentiment of approbation … is excited in his mind'. But immediately before this, Bentham writes that '[u]nless some end in view considered in the character of a standard of reference be taken into account, the epithets good and bad will be designative of nothing but the state of human affections in relation to the subject matter to which these qualities are respectively attributed' (1989: 244–5). Bentham's position seems to be that although when I call x 'good' I report my approbation of x, 'good' need not refer to my approbation, provided I provide a 'standard of reference'. In the case of 'right' and 'ought', Bentham half-heartedly suggests various standards (see below), but seems happier opting for the mere-reference-to-my-approbation option. It is perhaps noteworthy that in the case of 'ought', but not in the case of 'good', Bentham often says that there is 'nothing more' than the expression of sentiment.

[11] This theory is also suggested in Bentham 1977: 67 and 1838–1843, x: 70.

[12] Slote, who attributes this theory of rightness to Bentham, then makes the same objections (1985: 49–50).

[13] Sprigge 1999: 179–80 and Postema 2002 note that Bentham has two views of obligation. Postema adds that Bentham 'said surprisingly little … about the precise nature of this function' from goodness to rightness and that '[p]erhaps Bentham thought this was not a matter of great practical importance' (2002: xv).

[14] This is noted by Bright 1991: 229 n. 12.   [15] Norcross 2006: 222.

two 'right' acts, is great; the difference in amount between 1 and -1, a right act and a wrong one, is small; and the principle of utility takes the amount to be of fundamental importance.

One might instead—rightly—object to the scalar interpretation that Bentham often does not suggest it. For example, 'it is the greatest happiness of the greatest number that is the measure of right and wrong' (1977: 393, also 509). '[T]o prove an institution is agreeable to the principle of utility is to prove ... that the people *ought* to like it' (1830: 69, cited by Harrison 1983: 180; also 1977: 497). A 'law *ought not* to be established, because it is not consistent with the general welfare' (1838–1843, ii: 495; also v: 265, 1989: 230). The principle of utility 'holds up to view, as the only sources and tests of right and wrong, human suffering and enjoyment' (1838–1843, vi: 238). It is 'a true standard for whatever is right or wrong', 'a standard of rectitude for actions' (1838–43, x: 79, 70; also 1983c: 304). 'Morals is the doctrine of what ought to be done' (1983c: 318). In the *Principles* itself, Bentham starts by claiming that pain and pleasure 'point out what we ought to do'. They are 'the standard of right and wrong' (1996: 11, 11 n.). (Bentham does note, however, that some of this is 'metaphor and declamation', and goes on to give the 'explicit and determinate account' quoted above (1996: 11).) He asks an opponent of the principle of utility to 'ask himself whether his statement is to be a standard of right and wrong' (1996: 15; also 25, 28 n., 31). Utility gives 'the reason why [an act] ought to have been done' (1996: 33). Thus according to the principle of utility, punishment 'ought only to be admitted in as far as it promises to exclude some greater evil' (1996: 158). 'There is no case in which a private man ought not to direct his own conduct to the production of his own happiness, and of that of his fellow-creatures ... Every act which promises to be beneficial upon the whole to the community (himself included) each individual ought to perform' (1996: 285).

There is a further worry about ascribing the scalar interpretation to Bentham. One motivation for favouring scalar utilitarianism is that it avoids a popular objection to utilitarianism understood in the traditional way—it is too demanding. Since scalar utilitarianism makes no demands, it is not too demanding.[16]

I do not think Bentham would see this as an attraction, and so I do not think Bentham has this motivation for being a scalar utilitarian. The objection most clearly applies to private individuals rather than to those occupying a political office. But (unlike Godwin) Bentham says little about private individuals acting as utilitarians.[17] When he does address private individuals, he sometimes demands only that they pursue their own happiness: 'Private ethics teaches how each man may dispose himself to pursue the course most conducive to his own happiness' (1996: 293; also 1983c: 122–3, 124). In other places, Bentham does ask private individuals to follow the principle of utility—'private ethics' may be characterized as it is because, legislation aside, Bentham thinks the only

---

[16] Norcross 2006: 219, Howard-Snyder 1994: 121.

[17] Consider, for example, Godwin's example of saving Archbishop Fénelon rather than oneself, one's father, mother, or brother (Godwin 1971 [1798, 1801]: 70–1, 325–6).

reliable way to get individuals to maximize the general happiness is to urge them to pursue their own happiness when this coincides with what maximizes the general happiness.[18] And no doubt he is wrong to ask so little of them. But this would show only that, were Bentham rather different, he might feel the force of the objection and then see scalar utilitarianism as a way around it.

I suspect that there are three explanations for the passages which suggest scalar utilitarianism.

First, some of the passages can be explained away by their context. Thus Bentham's subjectivist or expressivist gloss on 'it is right that he should have the coat' is offered as all that a believer in natural rights can mean. Bentham does not offer the gloss when the claim is backed by positive law (1838–1843, iii: 218).

Second, Bentham at one point suggests that his objection to 'ought' is that those who use it do so to avoid giving reasons. After stating that he means by 'ought' only to express his approval, Bentham notes that he does not mean that his ought-claim 'should…be regarded…as constituting of itself a reason why the line of conduct…should be…pursued' (1983c: 149). Making ought-claims is a way to avoid giving 'good reasons': 'the office of moralist requires nothing but the repetition of these expressions…To the question 'but why ought I?'…no answer does he consider it as incumbent on him to give' (1983c: 252, 253). 'Observation, enquiry, reflection—these and all other mental operations are altogether as superfluous as they are laborious' (1983c: 255; also 1977: 54). This objection motivates giving reasons for ought-claims, rather than the scalar utilitarian's rejection of them altogether.

Third, leading up to Bentham, some tending towards utilitarianism write in deontic terms. Gay, like many others, holds that '[o]bligation is the necessity of doing or omitting any action in order to be happy'; God, who aims at the general happiness, makes it the case that I must aim at the general happiness in order to be happy myself.[19] Paley has the same view.[20] Others tending towards utilitarianism do not make obligation central and instead stress virtues, approvals, or ends. It is the latter—Hume, Priestly, Helvétius, Beccaria—who Bentham routinely cites with approval as his predecessors (for example, 1983c: 289–91). He gives an analysis of 'obligation' that, like Gay and Paley, requires painful sanctions (e.g. 1838–1843, viii: 206, 247); but without either God or a natural harmony

---

[18] For this reading, and discussion of the issue, see Harrison 1983: ch. 10, Hart 1996: xciii–xcvi, and especially Dinwiddy 1982. All are replying to David Lyons' provocative interpretation, according to which Bentham has two standards—the general happiness of the community for those in charge of the community, and one's individual happiness for each individual (1973: pt. I). On Dinwiddy's reading, one expects private ethics to be silent when what maximizes my happiness would fail to maximize the general happiness. Dinwiddy notes that Bentham does say that in the section of the *Deontology* on 'extra-regarding prudence' he will show 'so far as the regard for his own general and ultimate interest allows of his pursuing his particular and immediate interest at the expense of theirs, what course of conduct is most conducive to his purpose' (Dinwiddy 1982: 296 n. 37; Bentham 1983c: 124). But Bentham does not seem to give such a case there. The closest is a case in which prudence dictates offending one's superior to win the approval of a third party, but it is not clear that this fails to maximize the general happiness (1983c: 272).

[19] Gay 1969 [1739]: 411–13.   [20] Paley 1969 [1806]: 258–61.

of interests, this could not be extended past legal to moral obligation.[21] Bentham might, then, when careful, resist putting the principle of utility in terms of moral obligation (or duty or rightness) because he lacks any way of assuring that I would be caused pain for failing to aim at bringing about the general happiness—but, when not so careful, he pre-figures the use of deontic terms standard by the time of Sidgwick, in which there is no need to provide this assurance.

14.2

Before moving to Bentham's argument for utilitarianism, I want to consider a different revisionary interpretation of his principle of utility.

The traditional view that Bentham favours maximizing the total amount of pleasure has been challenged.[22] Critics argue that, especially in later writings, Bentham instead favours maximizing the level of happiness that can be equally distributed, with the happiness of some sacrificed only when 'the nature of the case renders the provision of an equal quantity of happiness for every one of them impossible, by its being a matter of necessity to make sacrifice of a portion of the happiness of a few, to the greater happiness of the rest' (Bentham 1831: 7, quoted by Postema 2002: xxi, 2006b: 114 n. 8). But (as Postema notes) without more gloss on 'the nature of the case', this is not clearly different from the traditional view.[23] Say one must die for the rest to live. Presumably I am permit-ted to sacrifice the one. But I could give everyone equal happiness—all could die. If the reason for not letting everyone die is that more happiness is brought about by sacrificing one, then departures from equality are endorsed whenever happiness would be maxi-mized, and the requirement of equal distribution is idle. Bentham himself suggests as much when he writes that 'the greatest happiness of the greatest number is the only right and proper end of government: of all, in so far as the happiness of all can be increased without lessening the happiness of any: of the greatest number, in so far as the happiness of some can not be encreased unless by defalcation made from the happiness of others' (1989: 3). Another way to put the worry is that when Postema writes that Bentham is 'committed not to aggregate net happiness...but rather to the greatest equal happiness' and that '[o]nly when this goal cannot be achieved and some sacrifice is inevitable does the backup principle come into play', it is not clear what counts as making 'the greatest equal happiness' impossible, given that there is *some* (perhaps unattractive) equal distri-bution possible (Postema 1998: 157).

---

[21] For Bentham on moral and (mainly) legal obligation, see Hart 1982: 82–7, 127–47. Bentham does write occasionally of moral obligation, but he means cases in which the painful sanction is carried out by popular opinion rather than the law (e.g. 1983c: 207).

[22] Postema 1998, 2002, 2006a, 2006b, Rosen 1998.

[23] Postema 1998: 158. Postema also admits that there is clear textual evidence for the traditional maximizing view (2006b: 114 n. 9, citing Bentham 1998 [1811–1830]: 206).

One way to avoid this, also offered by the critics, is to note that late Bentham sometimes states the principle of utility in terms of the 'universal interest', which he characterizes as the overlapping interest everyone has in public goods such as security. The critics suggest that aiming at the universal interest is offered not as a means for maximizing happiness, but as the statement of the fundamental goal itself. One result might be that Bentham would not endorse taking away the security of one person when doing so would give many others small enjoyments that summed, in terms of pleasure, to more than the pleasure lost by the victim. (This sort of example motivates a great deal of the current opposition to utilitarianism.) He would, however, endorse taking away the security of one to provide for the security of many.[24]

I do not think there is convincing textual evidence for this reading. Postema cites Bentham's claim that '[t]he more perfect the enjoyment of all these particulars [such as security], the greater the sum of social happiness' (1838–1843, i: 302; Postema 2002: xviii). But it is not clear whether 'social happiness' is constituted by the enjoyment of these public goods, or whether their enjoyment is the means to maximize happiness. Bentham does call them 'subordinate ends' (e.g. 1989: 157, 1998: 291, 1838–1843, i: 302, iii: 211, ix: 63). Elsewhere Postema himself seems to favour the latter reading, noting that Bentham justifies pursuit of the goods as leading to happiness (Postema 1998: 148, citing Bentham 1838–1843, i: 304–7). Postema also notes that Bentham says 'in the instance of each individual such part of the whole mass of his happiness as is not adverse to the happiness of any other individual will be, in so far as depends upon the agency of the government, secured to him:... while all such portions of happiness as he could not be made to enjoy without depriving others of happiness to greater amount will not be given to him' (Postema 2006a: 42, 2006b: 121; Bentham 1989: 135–6). But this privileges overlapping interests only in so far as satisfying non-overlapping interests would deprive others of greater happiness, which is what one expects a traditional maximizer to say.

14.3

Bentham's argument in the *Principles* for the principle of utility is much maligned.[25] He seems to give no positive argument for the principle. His arguments against rivals target asceticism, which is of little interest, and lump all other rivals into the category of 'sympathy and antipathy', according to which actions are approved or disapproved

---

[24] At one point, Postema denies that Bentham would require even this sacrifice (2006b: 131–2; but compare 2002: xxi, 1998: 151, 157). But this does not fit the 'nature of the case' passage quoted above. Nor does it fit the legislator's pledge to maximize the happiness 'of all without exception, in so far as possible: of the greatest number, on every occasion on which the nature of the case renders it impossible by rendering it matter of necessity, to make sacrifice of a portion of the happiness of a few, to the greater happiness of the rest' (1983b: 136; also 1989: 234–5, 1998: 250). Nor does it seem plausible: it would be odd to further overlapping interests by letting everyone perish.

[25] For an example of early criticism, see Mill 1969 [1833]: 5–6 (*Remarks on Bentham's Philosophy*).

'merely because a man finds himself disposed to approve or disapprove of them: holding up that approbation or disapprobation as a sufficient reason for itself, and disclaiming the necessity of looking out for any extrinsic ground' (1996: 25). But Bentham's argument is actually not so bad.

I take the key point to be the claim that a proof of the principle of utility is 'needless'. Most people, most of the time, 'tr[y]' actions according to the principle of utility and 'defe[r]' to it (1996: 13; also 1945: 116). Since Bentham does not go on to give positive grounds for the principle, his point seems to be that positive grounds are unnecessary; 'the use of reasons for a method of proceeding is to satisfy those who without them might be dissatisfied' (1977: 75). Arguments are needed to show, not that pleasure is a good and relevant to rightness, but that it is not. (Bentham does consider one argument, concerning pleasures from evil. He replies that our disapproval is explained by the pain caused by the evil action; we would not disapprove of pleasure taken in an imaginary crime that has no tendency to cause pain (1996: 18; also 1945 [1782]: 115–16).) This is plausible, provided that (a) our agreement cannot be undermined by, for example, being shown to rest (as Bentham often thinks) on coercion by 'sinister interests'; (b) what is taken to be established is that the principle of utility is *one* principle for the approval of actions—there is no agreement that it is the only principle; and (c) the argument is understood as a pragmatic account of when we ask for reasons, rather than a (much more controversial) contextualist account of when our beliefs count as knowledge.

Bentham suggests the burden of proof argument more clearly elsewhere:

> No man will deny but that occasion has place in which the enjoyment and accordingly the pursuit of pleasure...and the endeavour to avoid experiencing pain...are modes and courses of action not exposed to well-grounded reproach. But if this is true in any one case...it rests upon him who says that there is any occasion on which it is not true to produce this same occasion and say why it is that, on that same occasion it is not true—and so in the case of every exception which he would be for cutting out of the general rule. In a word, on the opponent of the greatest happiness principle...lies the burthen of proof. (1983c: 313)

Bentham should not say that, if pleasure is approved of in one case, the burden is on one who disapproves of pleasure, or disapproves of what maximizes pleasure, in another case. If pleasure were approved and disapproved in an equal number of cases, one would need to explain why pleasure is approved, where it is, just as one would need to explain why it is not approved, where it is not. But say that pleasure is almost always approved (as 'general rule' suggests), that nothing else receives such widespread approval, and that in a case where, say, keeping a promise is taken to outrank maximizing pleasure, the loss of pleasure is seen as a real loss. Then it is plausible to think the burden is on Bentham's opponent to justify the loss.[26]

I take the rest of the proof to consist in rejecting additions to pleasure that might justify the loss. Additions might be offered as either further goods or as good-independent

---

[26] I say more to try to defend this strategy in Shaver 2004.

ways of deciding what to do. In moves familiar from later utilitarians, Bentham explains away potential additional goods, and potentially good-independent rules such as that enjoining promise-keeping, as really approved of because of their connection to pleasure (1996: 32, 1977: 444–6).

This reconstruction of Bentham's proof ignores a different argument he offers. When Bentham addresses someone whose approvals are offered as independent of utility, his objection is that they 'consist…in so many contrivances for avoiding the obligation of appealing to any external standard, and for the prevailing upon the reader to accept of the author's sentiment or opinion as a reason and that a sufficient one for itself' (1996: 25–6). The reference to an 'external' or 'extrinsic' standard suggests that facts about pleasure and pain are special in that 'a person addressing himself to the community' can point to them to justify his approvals (1996: 28 n.).[27] Elsewhere Bentham argues for the superiority of the principle of utility over sympathy/antipathy by saying that '[p]ains and pleasures…are the only clear sources of ideas in morals. These ideas may be rendered familiar to all the world. The catechism of reasons is worthless…if it cannot be made the catechism of the people' (1838–1843, i: 163). Making utility the standard makes moral questions turn 'upon the issue of fact: and mankind are directed into the only true track of investigation which can afford instruction or hope of rational argument, the track of experiment and observation' (1838–1843, ii: 495; also vi: 238, 1977: 491–2).

The problem is that the same goes for some rivals of utility. For example, Ross could justify his approval of an action by noting the external, observable fact that the action is an instance of promise-keeping. Whether an act is an instance of promise-keeping is something, like utility and perhaps unlike an appeal to 'reason', that is 'distinct from [our] judgment itself', something 'founded upon matter of fact' (Bentham 1977: 199). As Bentham notes, 'whether a promise is made or no is always a matter of fact' (1970: 79c). Bentham may think his requirement of an external standard is more successful than it is because he directs it against appeals to 'reason' or 'the law of nature' or 'God's will' or 'the moral sense', rather than to properties of actions that are on a par with their properties of pleasure-production. (He might reply that what is not external is the process of weighing, say, a duty of promise-keeping against a duty to maximize happiness. He asks his opponent '[i]f he should be for…adopting his own principle in part, and the principle of utility in part, let him say how far he will adopt it? When he has settled with himself where he will stop, then let him ask himself how he justifies to himself the adopting it so far? and why he will not adopt it any farther?' (1996: 16). But the process of coming up with the weighting that maximizing happiness is the only relevant thing seems no more external.)

So goes Bentham's argument for utilitarianism.[28] Despite its odd patina of ascetics and sympathy/antipathy, most of it consists of moves that are now very familiar, and

---

[27] The best presentation of this argument is in Harrison 1983: 183–90.

[28] Elsewhere he might seem to suggest other arguments. In *Limits*, Bentham asks a question which 'answer[s] the purpose of all argument' for the principle: 'Supposing…that any other than the happiness of the community ought to be the end of legislative policy, what motive has the community to pursue it?' (1945: 116) Since for Bentham communities are not agents of whom psychological theories such as

very inconclusive. Many simply reject Bentham's approval of pleasures from evil; many simply reject the proposed explanations of their anti-utilitarian judgements; many try to work out justifications for departing from utility in some but not all cases. What makes Bentham's argument distinctive is that these moves are put in a context in which nothing positive need be said for pleasure, and the burden of proof lies on the opponent. In this context, inconclusive arguments may suffice.

14.4

Rashdall, as an ideal utilitarian, cannot follow Bentham in making his argument for (ideal) utilitarianism turn on the special status of pleasure. Rashdall proceeds by, first, arguing against Intuitionism, the view that 'we discover what is right or wrong by an immediate judgment or "intuition" which tells us that this or that act is right without any knowledge of its consequences' (1913: 45). In arguments familiar from Sidgwick, Rashdall objects that an appeal to good or bad consequences is needed to explain our judgements, to settle doubts about them or conflicts between them, and to specify exceptions (1913: 52, 56–7, 75, 1924, i: 85–7, 89–90). He takes as a 'more formidable difficulty' the worry that sometimes some consequences are included in the description of the act— 'drunkenness...would not be drunkenness at all' if we excluded that it makes 'a man thick in his speech, unsteady in his gait, erratic in his conduct, incoherent in his thoughts'—and that, if so, we should consider all of the consequences. When we do not, that is because we presuppose that the consequences are so clearly good or bad, not because we can judge the act in abstraction from all of its consequences. 'There is hardly any act now called wrong about which we might not theoretically be compelled to recon-sider our verdict if a sufficiently revolutionary discovery were made as to its ultimate consequences' (1913: 58, 59; 57–9, 75, 1924, i: 87–9, 198).

Rashdall also suggests a different argument against Intuitionism. Sidgwick writes that the axiom that 'as a rational being I am bound to aim at good generally...not merely at a particular part of it' passes his tests for highest certainty (1981: 382). But he does not explicitly use this axiom against deontological claims found in common sense morality. Indeed, he gives the axiom very little attention. It seems intended to attack egoism (1981: 382, 500). In *Principia*, Moore defines 'x is right' as 'x produces at least as much good as any other possible action'. He does use this definition against deontology.[29]

---

psychological egoism could be true, it seems best to interpret 'motive' here as 'justifying reason'. If so, this seems the same sort of argument as in the *Principles*: Bentham asks his opponent to produce an argument for decreasing what all find valuable. For the germ of a different argument, appealing to impartiality, see Harrison 1983: 190–2.

   [29]   Moore 1903: 25, 147–8. He argues for his definition by, in effect, treating any supposedly non-good-based consideration the deontologist might offer as merely introducing a different good. In *Ethics*, where he offers the same claim as self-evident but not analytic, he again targets deontology (Moore 1965: 74–7).

Rashdall, like Moore, objects against the Intuitionist that 'it [is] impossible to regard it as right to bring about what is not really good; and if every act ought to realize some good, the supreme end of all action must surely be to realize the greatest attainable good…That action is right which tends to bring about the good' (1913: 53, 1924, i: 135; also 1924, i: 91, 110 n.).[30] Admitting goods in addition to pleasure casts light on the connection between the right and the good, a connection that was largely implicit in earlier utilitarians.[31]

The second part of Rashdall's argument for ideal utilitarianism concerns what consequences are good and bad. Some of this is again familiar: pleasure is not the only good since we think that some pleasures are higher than others, and some are bad. (Rashdall gives, as examples of bad pleasures, those derived from bullfighting, Roman wild-beast and gladiatorial fights, German students' face-slashing duels, coursing, pigeon-shooting, and drunkenness (1924, i: 98–9).) We do not value mental states just according to the pleasures they contain. We value virtuous character, intellectual and aesthetic goods, and 'various kinds of affection or social emotion'. The value of virtue explains how we can condemn suicide even 'in cases where it is clearly conducive to the happiness of the individual and of all connected with him' (1885: 219; also 1913: 67, 1924, i: 208). The value of affection explains how we can condemn possibly pleasure-maximizing practices such as 'the permission of unlimited freedom of divorce', 'the gratification of the sexual impulse except in a way that is duly subordinated to the higher and more spiritual ends promoted by monogamous and relatively permanent marriage', and (again) occasional drunkenness (1913: 70; 65–70, 1924, i: 189, 197, 200, 202–3). Without goods in addition to pleasure, we could not explain our approval of humility or quite strict (though not exceptionless) veracity (1924, i: 204–7, 192–3).[32]

One difference between Rashdall and Bentham is obvious. Rashdall takes as given many common-sense moral judgements, and posits goods to explain them. As he notes, this allows him to avoid many objections to hedonistic utilitarianism (1913: 65, 1924, i: 72–3). The cost, as the examples show, is that the theory has little critical bite.[33] (He does try to explain away the appeal of Intuitionism, as above. Perhaps he thinks philosophers

[30] I try to clarify Rashdall's views about the definitional connections between 'good', 'right', and 'ought' in Shaver forthcoming.

[31] When Rashdall explains the superiority of ideal utilitarianism to Intuitionism, he also notes that weighing conflicting goods against one another is preferable to weighing duties against one another, since judgements about what is good, unlike judgements about duty, remain true even when outweighed—just the point Ross accommodated with prima facie duties (1924, i: 92, 95–6).

[32] For more on Rashdall's case for ideal utilitarianism, see Skelton 2011.

[33] He seems prey to Bentham: 'One man…says, he has a thing made on purpose to tell him what is right and what is wrong; and that it is called a *moral sense*: and then he goes to work at his ease, and says, such a thing is right, and such a thing is wrong—why? 'because my moral sense tells me it is'…Another man…comes, and says, that as to a moral sense indeed, he cannot find that he has any such thing: that however he has an *understanding*, which will do quite as well…Another man…says that there are certain practices conformable, and others repugnant, to the Fitness of Things; and then he tells you, at his leisure, what practices are conformable and what repugnant: just as he happens to like a practice or dislike it' (1996: 26–7).

reflecting on common-sense judgements stand in need of correction, but the judgements themselves do not.) The move to ideal utilitarianism makes it easier for Rashdall to be so prudish, and, worse, to make claims such as 'the lower Well-Being—it may be ultimately the very existence—of countless Chinamen or negroes must be sacrificed that a higher life may be possible for a much smaller number of white men' (1924, i: 239–40; also 241).[34] If Rashdall could not invoke 'higher' goods than pleasure, it would be very difficult to make these judgements. Bentham explains many common-sense moral judgements, as resting on pleasure-production, but is willing to reject judgements that lack this explanation. He defends equality for women, homosexuality, representative government, and humane treatment of animals—though also, more controversially, infanticide and torture in some cases.[35]

Rashdall sees the problem. He notes that he finds incest, drunkenness, and cannibalism (where the corpse is dead already, rather than killed to be eaten) 'intrinsically degrading' (1924, i: 158, 203, 212). This is what shows these things to be bad, despite perhaps maximizing pleasure. But he notes that he has a similar reaction to eating rat's flesh, and that 'a strictly educated Scotchman' probably 'experiences no less horror…at the thought of Sunday music' (1924, i: 212, 213; also 1914: 152–3). To distinguish between true judgements of value and 'pathological affection[s]', he proposes that for the former, the repugnance 'persists after a due consideration of all the consequences of yielding to it'. In the case of coursing and bull-fighting, the repugnance persists even when we grant that they maximize pleasure. In the case of Sunday music, the repugnance does not persist after one 'learns the history of the traditions about Sabbath-observance' (1924, i: 212–13; also ii: 404). Similarly, retributivists confuse 'a mere emotion or feeling' with 'a judgment of the Practical Reason' (1924, i: 305).

The Scotchman's repugnance would disappear, or at least be granted no authority, once he sees that it rests on false beliefs. But the retributivist judgement, like many of Rashdall's own judgements, does not seem based on beliefs. It 'arises naturally and spontaneously' (1924, i: 304). Rashdall suggests that when we see the origins of the judgement in an 'instinct of vengeance', we similarly grant it no authority (1924, i: 291). Reflection on the origins of a judgement can show that our mere making of the judgement does not justify us, since (for example) the judgements may have 'outlived their justification'; this reflection 'leave[s] the question to be decided on its own merits', by 'different reasons' (1924, ii: 411, 407).[36] This is plausible but, for Rashdall, dangerous. For there may not *be* different reasons for some of his anti-hedonist judgements (such as those concerning drinking),

[34] Rashdall also gives, as an example of permissible punishment of innocents, a case in which 'a savage village that has sheltered a murderer is burnt by a European man-of-war' (1924, i: 290). Less clearly objectionable is his defence of inequality as needed to produce higher goods (1924, i: 263–4 n., 265 n. 1, 272, 276–7, 280).

[35] For brief discussion and references, see Dinwiddy 1989: 79–84, 110–112; for animals see Bentham 1996: 282–3b.

[36] Compare the critical approaches to intuitions in Unger 1996, Singer 2005, Greene 2008, and Huemer 2008.

and one might view many of them as, like retributivism, overgeneralizations from cases in which some instances of the behaviour are good or bad on hedonist grounds.

Rashdall does not see a different (potential) problem. The ideal utilitarian strategy of justifying common-sense judgements by invoking a range of goods cannot account for the deontologist's judgement that, say, I ought not to tell one lie to prevent five other people from telling (equally significant) lies. If lying is bad, I should act to minimize it, and so should lie. These 'paradox' cases are not given as the definitive way to distinguish ideal utilitarianism from deontology until the 1970s, although Broad gives a close variant.[37] Rashdall, however, writes that there 'are cases in which a lie has to be told in the interests of Truth itself… [A] statement literally untrue must be made that a higher truth may be taught' (1924, i: 194). He quotes Höffding with approval: 'The duty of speaking the truth amounts to this, the duty of promoting the supremacy of the truth:… the end may, however, often be interfered with by speaking the truth' (1924, i: 194–5 n.). (One instance he has in mind is that allowing clergymen to say false things increases religious truth in the long run by fostering liberty of interpretation within one church, keeping smart people in the church, and not alienating those in the congregation who might otherwise reject the church (Rashdall 1897).) Rashdall has no interest in justifying veracity when lying would lead to more true belief and, like Moore, finds the notion of an agent-relative good or reason, that might underlie the judgement that I ought not to lie, incomprehensible (1913: 63 n. 2, 1924, i: 79 n., 1914: 162–3, 1916: 117–19, Matheson 1928: 179). Given the much-discussed worry that the deontologist's judgement is paradoxical, this disinterest might be a good thing.

Rashdall also has difficulty with a different judgement. Say we think it is right to make a fair distribution, even when doing so leads those concerned to have fewer of the usual goods of pleasure, virtue, knowledge, etc. One might explain the rightness by viewing the distribution as itself good. Rashdall objects that something 'which cannot be regarded as the good of any one of the persons affected nor of all of them collectively' cannot be good (1924, i: 266). He solves the problem by taking the will to distribute fairly to be, as a virtue, good. But if the fair distribution is not itself good, it is unclear why the will to bring it about is good. This is an especially pressing problem for Rashdall, since he suggests that the value of virtue lies in 'the intrinsic worth of promoting what has worth', and that unless the consequences willed by the good will are good, 'the will cannot be good either. Charity is no doubt better than the eating of food by hungry persons, but unless that eating be good, there is no reason for applying the word… "good" to the charitable act' (1924, i: 59, ii: 42; also i: 137). Rashdall might be better off developing his suggestion that choosing more of the usual goods by being too unfair shows a will that lacks 'sympathy and mercy toward individuals', 'kindness and goodwill for individuals' (1924, i: 267, 268). The relevant virtue would be the will to prevent 'extreme hardships' (1924, i: 267).[38]

---

[37] Nozick 1974: 30–2; Broad 1930: 210–11.

[38] For more on Rashdall on justice, see Raphael 2003: 150–9.

Rashdall's most distinctive argument for goods other than pleasure, however, does not merely elicit intuitions about cases. He tries to show that Sidgwick's hedonism involves a 'psychological contradiction' (1913: 64, 1924, i: 58). Its 'inner logic' leads to a good in addition to pleasure (1913: 65). Say that what maximizes the general happiness would require me to sacrifice some of my happiness.

> Sidgwick contends that the reason for my doing so is that it seems intrinsically unreasonable...that a smaller amount of good should be promoted rather than a larger...[B]ut [Sidgwick holds] there is nothing good...in the act itself, in the state of mind from which it results...Morality is...no good at all to the agent.

Rashdall then objects that the person making the sacrifice has

> an impossible state of mind, or...one so rare that it might fairly be described as pathological. If a man really cares about being reasonable, is it conceivable that he should at the bottom of his heart believe it a matter of no importance at all whether he is reasonable or not—that he should think it an advantage indeed to somebody else, but a matter of no importance and (if it involves him in painful consequences) a dead loss to himself? If he really did regard Morality or character...as a completely valueless asset, would he any longer care whether his conduct was reasonable or not? (1913: 63–4; also 1924, i: 57–9, 69–71, 1885: 216–22)[39]

Rashdall concludes that Sidgwick must concede that a character that aims at maximizing happiness is itself good.

On the most obvious reading, Rashdall's point is that I would lack motivation to make the sacrifice unless I believed that the character of one who makes the sacrifice is intrinsically good.[40] Since Rashdall admits the possibility of altruism, he could not back this up by claiming that one always needs to see some net good for oneself to be motivated.[41] He could, however, say that the motive Sidgwick counts on—the desire to do what is rational—is 'not a very strong one' and 'has been enormously exaggerated', so *it could*

---

[39] Rashdall does sometimes claim that he has shown 'that it is impossible logically to establish the duty of preferring the general pleasure to our own without recognizing the intrinsic value of such a preference'. The argument shows the 'impossibility' of constructing 'a logically coherent system of Ethics without the assumption that the reasonableness of an act is a sufficient ground for its being done' (1924, i: 100, 101). Rashdall should stick with the more modest claim that the state of mind Sidgwick needs is very rare.

[40] This is clearer in the statement of the argument in *Theory*: 'for me to act on this rational principle there must be a...motive...Destroy that conviction [that character is intrinsically good], and I have no motive for trying to cultivate the love of rational action...[T]he desire to escape...contradiction...is not by itself a very powerful motive of conduct when it is pronounced to have no intrinsic value' (1924, i: 57–8).

[41] For altruism, see, for example, 1924, i: 23, 28–9, 1913: 19–20. Rashdall does, however, put the argument as follows: 'The whole force of the subjective hold which the precept "be reasonable" has exercised over me...has lain in its inseparable connexion with another conviction—that...to act in accordance with the reasonable was a good to me, *a greater good* than I could obtain by pursuing the pleasure which you tell me is the only true good' (1924, i: 57–8, my emphasis). He implies that the motivation problem is solved only by giving 'the good will the highest place in [the] scale of goods' (1924, i: 79 n.).

not motivate without help from thinking that the character is good (1924, i: 57, 1914: 114; also 1924, i: 58). Thus Rashdall sometimes claims that Sidgwick's position is self-defeating: 'The acceptance of rationalistic Hedonism kills and eradicates all those impulses upon which it has to depend for the practical fulfilment of its own precepts, by pronouncing that they have no true worth or value' (1924, i: 58; also 59).

Sidgwick might ask why Rashdall takes the desire to do what is rational to be so weak. Even if it is true, as Rashdall claims, that those who sacrifice usually believe that virtue is intrinsically valuable, it does not follow that the belief is necessary (1913: 64–5, 1924, i: 57–9).[42] Many have noted the prevalence and motivational force of the related desire to justify one's conduct to others. And elsewhere Rashdall holds, with Sidgwick, that 'the recognition that something is our duty supplies us with ... a sufficient motive for doing it' (1924, i: 104; also 105, 106, 121, 140–1, 1914: 140).[43] Perhaps Rashdall's view is that while this desire can win out on its own to motivate, it usually cannot. But what Rashdall thinks is in addition needed to motivate is not belief that a certain character is good, but rather the belief that 'our own happiness ... other people's happiness ... knowledge ... the contemplation of beauty' are good, so this does not help him (1914: 114; also 1924, i: 121, 140).

Sidgwick might also ask why ascribing instrumental value to character would not suffice. Rashdall asks 'if a man really cares about being reasonable, is it conceivable that he should at the bottom of his heart believe it a matter of no importance at all whether he is reasonable or not?' or that character is for the hedonist 'completely valueless', of 'no true worth'. But being reasonable, having a certain character, promoting the larger rather than the smaller amount of good—these have importance and value, though only instrumentally. The same goes for Rashdall's charge that it 'is in vain that you tell me that concentration upon my private happiness is selfish and irrational, for you tell me also that selfishness and irrationality are not bad in themselves' (1924, i: 58; also 59, 1885: 217). Rashdall gives Sidgwick's position the air of paradox by omitting or devaluing instrumental value.[44]

Sidgwick might also note that, even if one must believe that one's character has intrinsic value, there seems at best the same sort of benign paradox as in the paradox of hedonism. In the moment of pursuit, I must believe that some end other than pleasure is intrinsically valuable in order to maximize pleasure; at the moment of sacrifice, I must believe that a sacrificing character is intrinsically good in order to make the sacrifice. In neither case does it follow that my belief is true, or that in a cool hour I must believe it to be true.

Finally, Sidgwick might complain that there is something unattractive about Rashdall's view. When I sacrifice, I am (say) motivated to prevent the greater unhappiness of someone else. This, we think, is what should motivate me—not a desire to have a

[42] At one point Rashdall claims that the 'idea of value' is 'de facto found inseparable' with the 'idea of the intrinsic worth of promoting what has worth' (1924, i: 59; also 70–1).

[43] Rashdall writes that for the 'ideal man ... respect for duty as such will tend to pass into a sense of the relative value of the goods which he loves' (1924, i: 128). It is unclear why the good of maximising the general happiness could not be what he loves.

[44] This also mars Rashdall's argument that virtue is superior to pleasure (1924, i: 72).

certain character. If I must, in order to make the sacrifice, be thinking about the virtue of my character, this takes away from my virtue. Rashdall seems to agree: the virtuous man 'will labour for the good of his family because he cares about it as much or more than he does for his own good' or 'relieves suffering because "he cannot bear" to see another man in pain' (1924, i: 126, 121). 'Every rational act ought...to be directed toward the realization of some good other than the good will, however true it may be that the good will possesses a higher value than anything else in the world' (1914: 114–15).

One might value virtue and lessen the unattractiveness by taking virtue to be a less important good than the prevention of greater unhappiness. Perhaps needing to think that the further good of virtue would be brought about is not so unattractive if the primary good is preventing the unhappiness. But Rashdall cannot say this, since he takes virtue to be the most important good (as in the charity example given earlier). Perhaps Rashdall could instead reply that his argument does not require aiming at one's virtue, but only thinking that it has value, or at least that it is not bad for one. My aim is to prevent the unhappiness of others; I must have the thought that my character is good, but when my character is not my aim, perhaps this is not so unattractive.[45]

At times, Rashdall gives a different gloss on the argument. The problem for Sidgwick is that 'I cannot from my own point of view condemn myself when I pursue what, as you say, Reason itself tells me is my own true good, and decline ... to trouble myself about an end which is not my good' (1924, i: 57). '[W]hat the irrational man secures to himself by selfishness is intrinsically better than what the good man gets by obeying the voice of Reason' (1924, i: 69). A person's 'approval of himself when he does right and disapproval when he does wrong are quite inexplicable upon the assumption that bad conduct is merely conduct which is irrational from the point of view of Society though wholly rational from his own private point of view' (1924, i: 107). If sacrifice is reasonable only in the sense that it '"may reasonably be desired by the larger whole", the reasonableness of the individual's desiring it and sacrificing other inclinations to it is not made out' (1885: 219).

These are not points about motivation.[46] They make sense if Rashdall holds that it is a necessary condition on rational action that it be good for me.[47] But there is no other evidence that Rashdall imposes this condition, nor argument for it. Nor is it clear how he could impose this condition, given that he endorses Moore's argument that egoism is contradictory: if my well-being is the only thing I ought to pursue, then my well-being is

---

[45] For one discussion of the unattractiveness worry, see Hurka 2001: 137–41, 246–9. For questions concerning the sense in which Rashdall can think virtue is the most important good, see Moore 1907–1908: 450–1 and Hurka 2001: 131–3.

[46] They explain Rashdall's claims about motivation, however; a reasonable person would not be motivated to sacrifice: 'in the mind of the philosopher who has discovered [that] ultimate good really consists [in pleasure], the apparent reasonableness of desiring something else must vanish away' (1885: 217). They also explain why Rashdall does not conclude only that one must *believe* that character is good. This belief seems sufficient for motivation, but not for (objective) rationality.

[47] Frankena reads Rashdall's argument as about motivation, but notes that it 'slip[s] into something closer to an egoistic conception of rational action' (1983: 194).

the only thing others ought to pursue; but egoism directs each other person to pursue only his or her own well-being. Rashdall concludes from this argument that 'there can be no rational end of conduct except universal good... [M]y good can only be good at all in so far as it is part of the universal good... [My good] ought to give way when it collides with the greater good of others' (1916: 117–19; also 1916: 131, 1913: 63 n. 2, 1924, i: 79 n.).

Sidgwick combines, perhaps uneasily, two attitudes to common-sense morality—a critical, reforming approach grounded in hedonism and self-evident axioms that lead to utilitarianism, and an approach that takes common-sense morality as itself the ground for utilitarianism. One can see the former approach as deriving from Bentham and the latter as influencing Rashdall. But Bentham and Rashdall can also be contrasted in a complementary respect. For Bentham, the main appeal of utilitarianism rests on the appeal of pleasure. For Rashdall, the appeal rests on the connection between the good and the right. The connection perhaps could not be seen clearly until goods other than pleasure were introduced, but the two appeals can work together in favour of a theory that does not introduce further goods. This may explain the persistence of hedonistic utilitarianism, and the difficulty faced by those who wish to reject it.[48]

Bibliography

Bentham, J. 1830. *The Rationale of Punishment*. London: Heward.
—— 1831. *Parliamentary Candidate's proposed Declaration of Principles*. London.
—— 1838–1843. *Works*, ed. John Bowring. Edinburgh: William Tait, 11 v.
—— 1945. *The Limits of Jurisprudence Defined*, ed. Charles Warren Everett. New York: Columbia University Press.
—— 1970. *Of Laws in General*, ed. H. L. A. Hart. London: Athlone.
—— 1977. *A Comment on the Commentaries and A Fragment on Government*, ed. J. H. Burns and H. L. A. Hart. London: Athlone.
—— 1983a. *Chrestomathia*, ed. M. J. Smith and W. H. Burston. Oxford: Clarendon.
—— 1983b. *Constitutional Code* v. 1, ed. F. Rosen and J. H. Burns. Oxford: Clarendon.
—— 1983c. *Deontology together with A Table of the Springs of Action and Article on Utilitarianism*, ed. Amnon Goldworth. Oxford: Clarendon.
—— 1989. *First Principles Preparatory to a Constitutional Code*, ed. Philip Schofield. Oxford: Clarendon.
—— 1996. *An Introduction to the Principles of Morals and Legislation*, ed. J. H. Burns and H. L. A. Hart. Oxford: Clarendon.
—— 1998. *Legislator of the World: Writings on Codification, Law, and Education*, ed. Philip Schofield and Jonathan Harris. Oxford: Clarendon.
Bright, R. 1991. *Foundations of Utilitarianism*. PhD thesis, Dalhousie University, Philosophy Department.
Broad, C. D. 1930. *Five Types of Ethical Theory*. London: Routledge and Kegan Paul.

[48] Thanks to Roger Crisp, Joyce Jenkins, and Anthony Skelton, for comments on earlier drafts, and to audiences at Manitoba and Western Ontario.

Dinwiddy, J. 1982. 'Bentham on Private Ethics and the Principle of Utility', *Revue Internationale de Philosophie* 36: 278–300.

—— 1989. *Bentham*. Oxford: Oxford University Press.

Ewing, A. C. 1947. *The Definition of Good*. New York: Macmillan.

—— 1953. *Ethics*. New York: Free Press.

Frankena, W. K. 1983. 'Concepts of Rational Action in the History of Ethics', *Social Theory and Practice* 9: 165–97.

Gay, J. 1969. *Concerning the Fundamental Principle of Virtue or Morality*, in D. D. Raphael, *British Moralists*. Oxford: Clarendon, v. i.

Godwin, W. 1971. *Enquiry Concerning Political Justice*, ed. K. Codell Carter. Oxford: Clarendon.

Greene, J. 2008. 'The Secret Joke of Kant's Soul,' in *Moral Psychology*, ed. Walter Sinnott-Armstrong, vol. 3. Cambridge, MA: MIT Press, 35–79.

Harrison, R. 1983. *Bentham*. London: Routledge and Kegan Paul.

Hart, H. L. A. 1982. *Essays on Bentham*. Oxford: Clarendon.

—— 1996. 'Bentham's Principle of Utility and Theory of Penal Law', in Bentham 1996, lxxix–cxii.

Howard-Synder, F. 1994. 'The Heart of Consequentialism', *Philosophical Studies* 76: 107–29.

Huemer, M. 2008. 'Revisionary Intuitionism', *Social Philosophy and Policy* 25: 368–92.

Hurka, T. 2001. *Virtue, Vice, and Value*. Oxford: Oxford University Press.

Laird, J. 1926. *A Study in Moral Theory*. London: George Allen and Unwin.

Lyons, D. 1973. *In the Interests of the Governed*. Oxford: Clarendon.

Matheson, P. E. 1928. *The Life of Hastings Rashdall DD*. London: Oxford University Press.

Mill, J. S. 1969. *Writings on Ethics, Religion, and Society*, ed. J. M. Robson. Toronto: University of Toronto Press. (*Collected Works*, vol. 10.)

—— 1974. *A System of Logic*, ed. J. M. Robson. Toronto: University of Toronto Press. (*Collected Works*, vol. 8.)

Moore, G. E. 1903. *Principia Ethica*. Cambridge: Cambridge University Press.

—— 1907–1908. Review of Rashdall, *The Theory of Good and Evil*, *Hibbert Journal* 6: 446–51.

—— 1965. *Ethics*. New York: Oxford University Press.

Norcross, A. 2006. 'The Scalar Approach to Utilitarianism', in Henry West (ed.), *Blackwell Guide to Mill's Utilitarianism*. Oxford: Blackwell, 217–32.

Nozick, R. 1974. *Anarchy, State, and Utopia*. New York: Basic.

Paley, W. 1969. *The Principles of Moral and Political Philosophy*, in D. D. Raphael, *British Moralists*, vol. 2. Oxford: Clarendon.

Prichard, H. A. 2002. *Moral Writings*, ed. Jim MacAdam. Oxford: Clarendon.

Postema, G. 1998. 'Bentham's Equality-Sensitive Utilitarianism', *Utilitas* 10: 144–58.

—— 2002. 'Introduction' to Postema, *Bentham: Moral, Political and Legal Philosophy*, vol. i. Aldershot: Ashgate, xi–xxvii.

—— 2006a. 'Bentham's Utilitarianism', in Henry West (ed.), *Blackwell Guide to Mill's Utilitarianism*. Oxford: Blackwell, 26–44.

—— 2006b. 'Interests, Universal and Particular: Bentham's Utilitarian Theory of Value', *Utilitas* 18: 109–33.

Raphael, D. D. 2003. *Concepts of Justice*. Oxford: Oxford University Press.

Rashdall, H. 1885. 'Professor Sidgwick's Utilitarianism', *Mind* o.s. 10: 200–26.

—— 1897. 'Professor Sidgwick on the Ethics of Religious Conformity: A Reply', *International Journal of Ethics* 7: 137–68.

——1913. *Ethics*. London: T. C. and E. C. Jack.

——1914. *Is Conscience an Emotion?* Boston and New York: Houghton Mifflin.

——1916. 'Egoism, Personal and National', in *The International Crisis: The Theory of the State*. London: Oxford University Press, 109–37.

——1924. *The Theory of Good and Evil*. 2 vols. London: Oxford University Press. (1st edn. 1907.)

Rosen, F. 1998. 'Individual Sacrifice and the Greatest Happiness: Bentham on Utility and Rights', *Utilitas* 10: 129–43.

Scheffler, S. 1982. *The Rejection of Consequentialism*. Oxford: Clarendon.

Schneewind, J. B. 1977. *Sidgwick's Ethics and Victorian Moral Philosophy*. Oxford: Clarendon.

Shaver, R. 2004. 'The Appeal of Utilitarianism', *Utilitas* 16: 235–50.

——forthcoming. 'Prichard's Arguments Against Ideal Utilitarianism', promised to a volume on impartiality for Oxford University Press, ed. Brian Feltham, Philip Stratton-Lake, and John Cottingham.

Sidgwick, H. 1896. *Outlines of the History of Ethics*. London: Macmillan.

——1981. *The Methods of Ethics*. Indianapolis: Hackett.

Singer, P. 2005. 'Ethics and Intuitions', *Journal of Ethics* 9: 331–52.

Skelton, A. 2011. 'Rashdall's Ideal Utilitarianism', in T. Hurka (ed.), *Underivative Duty: British Moral Philosophy from Sidgwick to Ewing*. Oxford: Oxford University Press, 45–65.

Slote, M. 1985. *Common-sense Morality and Consequentialism*. London: Routledge and Kegan.

Sprigge, T. L. S. 1999. 'The Relation Between Jeremy Bentham's Psychological, and his Ethical, Hedonism', *Utilitas* 11: 296–319.

Unger, P. 1996. *Living High and Letting Die*. New York: Oxford University Press.

CHAPTER 15

···

RATIONALISM

···

MARIA ROSA ANTOGNAZZA

THE use of the term 'rationalism' to label a pigeon-hole into which philosophers are forced inevitably distorts their views. It is even worse when philosophers, so uncomfortably pressed into this narrow space, are then further packaged as 'The Rationalists'. Although there can be little doubt that this pigeon-hole should be dismantled and its prisoners set free, it is the contention of this chapter that the category of 'rationalism' can still serve a useful purpose when employed, not to designate a philosophical system, but as short-hand for a multifaceted tradition which incorporates some fundamental intuitions going back to Plato, Neoplatonism, and their theologized and Christianized Augustinian versions.[1] In other words, one (although not the only) meaningful way to characterize the so-called 'rationalist' tradition is to recognize its debt to some Platonic tenets.

There are in philosophy only a handful of fundamental alternatives, and one of these is what could be broadly called 'Platonism'. Platonism of course is a very rich, dense soup, which has been simmering away for many centuries and can be served up in a wide variety of flavours in combination with other ingredients. Sometimes it is so watered down as to be barely discernable except by the most sophisticated palates. Even then, however, some fundamental ingredients can still be identified as Platonic. This is not to say that the same set of broadly Platonic views was always included. Quite the opposite. Different thinkers took over and reshaped different Platonic and Neoplatonic intuitions while discarding others. One of the most significant of these intuitions consists of conceiving the

---

[1] This interpretation is advanced by Michael Ayers in *Rationalism, Platonism and God* (Ayers 2007b, especially 1–4). See also Ayers 1998, especially 1003–8, 1011–18, and Lennon 1993. Rationalism is commonly described as an epistemological stand which allows for knowledge independent of sense experience, and privileges reason over experience. Jonathan Bennett uses the notion of 'explanatory rationalism' to indicate the rejection of brute facts and the view that 'there is a satisfying answer to every "Why?" question' (Bennett 1996: 61 and Bennett 1984: 29; see also Bennett 2001: vol. 1, ch. 9). Similarly, Michael Della Rocca characterizes rationalism as a position 'powered at each stage by the Principle of Sufficient Reason…, roughly the principle that each fact has an explanation or, equivalently, that there are no brute facts' (Della Rocca 2003: 75).

relationship between God and finite beings as a 'top-down' relationship in which finite beings are ultimately intelligible only in relation to God.[2] From the point of view of the theory of being, this normally means that God and the immutable essences (archetypes, natures) of all things embraced by His mind provide the ultimate ontological grounding of everything.[3] From the point of view of the theory of knowledge, this normally means that finite beings can be understood only when referred to God and the immutable essences in His mind.[4] Although *quoad nos* the way to God might have to start from finite beings (since what we encounter first is what is finite and imperfect), the key claim is that these finite beings and their properties can be explained only in relation to the ontological priority of the perfect or infinite Being in which they are grounded.[5]

The present chapter will pursue this story in the moral philosophy of four early modern thinkers—Descartes, Malebranche, Leibniz, and Spinoza—who in different ways affirm the Platonic intuition of the priority of the perfect or infinite over the limited beings of which we have experience. In making this affirmation, Descartes, Malebranche, and Leibniz share the framework of a substantially traditional conception of God. Spinoza, on the other hand, stands out in that he challenges the Christianized Platonism of the other three while stretching to the extreme some features of Platonism. For this reason, contrary to the customary chronological order, discussion of his thought will provide the last part of the narrative.

Needless to say, these thinkers are part of a fine-grained contemporary debate in which many other authors, from famous to very little known, are also significantly indebted to the Platonic tradition in a variety of ways, including (to mention one obvious example) the Cambridge Platonists. A more historically comprehensive and nuanced study is, however, beyond the scope of this chapter, which will instead focus on some related theoretical issues present in the moral philosophies of these four major thinkers. It is also clear that the ethics of these thinkers is profoundly indebted to other traditions, notably Aristotelian Eudemonism, Stoicism, and Epicureanism. This chapter, however, does not purport to offer a summary of the entire moral philosophies of Descartes, Malebranche, Leibniz, and Spinoza, but only to track a 'rationalist' strand in them, in so far as rationalism can be regarded as a tradition which looks

---

[2] See Adams 2007, especially 91–2. Cf. Ayers 1998: 1011.

[3] A striking exception to this scheme might be thought to be Descartes himself, in so far as his account of the bodily universe, the *res extensa*, seems to introduce a category of substantial beings the defining attribute of which—extension—is not found in God (cf. Adams 2007: 98; Antognazza 2007: 127; Ayers 2007b: 11). Instead of the radical ontological dependence of being from God, Descartes seems to open an early modern way to the ontological independence of the physical universe from God. On the other hand, Descartes is strikingly Platonic in his affirmation of the priority of the perfect / infinite (cf. *Third Meditation*; AT VI 45), as well as in his dualism of mind and body echoing the Platonic view of the rational soul as the true self. More generally, Descartes' relation to Platonism is controversial. To mention two prominent interpreters, according to Kenny 1970, 697, Descartes 'can be called the father of modern Platonism'; according to Gueroult 1984–1985 v. I, 277 'Nothing is more contrary to Cartesianism than the realism of Platonic ideas and the exemplarism of essences'.

[4] Cf. Ayers 2007b, especially 3, 10, 61; Ayers 1998, especially 1004–5, 1011, 1016–18.

[5] Cf. Adams 2007 and Antognazza 2007: 119–26.

back to some basic Platonic intuitions. Conceived in this way, the rationalist tradition in the history of ethics is particularly relevant to contemporary debates on the relation between God and morality, the nature of the good and of moral properties, the Euthyphro dilemma, and ethical voluntarism. By presenting distinctive accounts of the nature of happiness and virtue, the rationalist tradition also leads to reflections of enduring interest on the very aim of morality. Moreover, it advances the discussion on the practicality of reason, its motivational force, its relation to the passions, and the possibility of genuine altruism. Last but not least, it contributes in important ways to moral epistemology.

For all the great differences of their ontologies, Descartes, Malebranche, Spinoza, and Leibniz converge in the Platonic anchoring of the fluctuating testimony of the senses in 'true and immutable natures' which our reason can grasp. The stability and certainty enjoyed by rational knowledge is a function of its ability to track (at least to some significant extent) these true and immutable natures of things.[6] For them as for the Neoplatonic and the Augustinian reinterpretation of the intelligible world, the ontological grounding of the 'forms' or eternal essences of things is the intellect of God. It is therefore only a short step from rational perfection to moral perfection, that is, from the contemplation of the 'forms' to 'the intellectual Love of God' as the pinnacle of ethics. Reason allows us to come as close to God as limited beings can come. To understand the immutable natures is to participate, in some measure, in the mind of God—Malebranche and Spinoza being the most radical in their views of how close this communality with God could be. For Descartes, Malebranche, Spinoza, and Leibniz, ethics is therefore ultimately grounded in a metaphysics in which God plays a fundamental role, both in the theory of being and in the theory of knowledge.[7]

15.1 RENÉ DESCARTES (1596–1650)

The ultimate grounding of ethics in metaphysics is expressed by Descartes in his famous metaphor of the tree of philosophy in the preface to the French translation of the *Principles of Philosophy* (1647):

> the whole of philosophy is like a tree. The roots are metaphysics, the trunk is physics, and the branches emerging from the trunk are all the other sciences, which may be reduced to three principal ones, namely medicine, mechanics and morals. By 'morals' I understand the highest and most perfect moral system, which presupposes a complete knowledge of the other sciences and is the ultimate level of wisdom. (AT IXB 14/CSM I 186)

A 'perfect moral system', conceived as the 'ultimate level of wisdom', is to be the greatest fruit (cf. *Principles*, 'Preface to the French edition'; AT IXB 18) of Descartes' whole

---

[6] Cf. Ayers 2007b: 60.   [7] See Ayers 2007b: 3.

philosophical and scientific enterprise. Following in the footsteps of the ancient conception of philosophy as love of wisdom, the ultimate goal of philosophy for Descartes is the achievement of wisdom and, thereby, of human happiness.[8]

Descartes, however, did not attain the 'complete knowledge of the other sciences' presupposed by the science of Morals. As a consequence, he did not fulfil his vision of a scientific ethics rooted in his new metaphysics and sprouting as a branch from his new physics. His ethics remains the 'imperfect moral code which we may follow provisionally while we do not yet know a better one' (*Principles*, 'Preface to the French edition'; AT IXB 15/CSM I 186–7) outlined in the earlier *Discourse on the Method* (1637) and then developed in his correspondence and in *The Passions of the Soul*.[9] Notwithstanding Descartes' goal of a science of Morals rooted in metaphysics, one might be tempted to conclude that Descartes' actual ethics is based on the rules of positive law and custom, as well as on the inclinations supplied by our bodily passions, rather than on metaphysically grounded values.[10] The 'provisional moral code consisting of just three or four maxims' of Part Three of the *Discourse on the Method* would therefore offer a much more stable accommodation than its advertised status of temporary shelter during the demolition of our alleged certainties might lead one to expect. Its first key plank appears to build Cartesian morality on a voluntaristic and, critics would add, ultimately arbitrary conception of moral rules which seems still to be endorsed by Descartes later on. The first maxim listed in the *Discourse* is 'to obey the laws and customs of my country, holding constantly to the religion in which by God's grace I had been instructed from my childhood' (AT VI 23/CSM I 122). In a letter to Hector-Pierre Chanut of 20 November 1647, Descartes boldly declares that, in his view, 'only sovereigns, or those authorized by them, have the right to concern themselves with regulating the morals of other people' (AT V 86–7/CSMK 326).[11]

This position appears to slot nicely into the voluntaristic framework for which Descartes was castigated by close followers of Platonism (such as Malebranche and Leibniz) on the Euthyphro dilemma. Descartes' view that 'all goodness and truth' depend on God's will places him on the side of those who seize the second horn of the dilemma: what is morally good is morally good because it is commanded by God rather than being

---

[8] Cf. Rutherford 2008 and Verga 1974: 11. This goal points to a centrality of ethics in Descartes' thought well beyond the still common assumption of its marginality in a philosopher taken to be primarily concerned with epistemology and metaphysics. A still illuminating study of Descartes' ethics is Rodis-Lewis 1962. More recent studies of Descartes' ethics include Morgan 1994, Cottingham 1998, Marshall 1998, Williston and Gombay 2003, Brown 2006 (especially chs 7 and 8).

[9] See especially Descartes' correspondence of 1645 with Princess Elisabeth of Boehmia. A draft of the *Passions de l'âme* was completed by 1646. See Gaukroger 1995: xvii.

[10] Cf. for instance Rorty 1992: 386–9.

[11] See also Descartes' moral advice to Princess Elisabeth in his key letter of 15 September 1645 (AT IV 295/CSMK 267): '[O]ne must also examine minutely all the customs of one's place of abode to see how far they should be followed. Though we cannot have certain demonstrations of everything, still we must take sides, and in matters of custom embrace the opinions that seem most probable, so that we may never be irresolute when we need to act. For nothing causes regret and remorse except irresolution.'

commanded by God because it is morally good. In his replies to the sixth set of objections to the *Meditations*, Descartes writes:

> It is self-contradictory to suppose that the will of God was not indifferent from eternity with respect to everything which has happened or will ever happen; for it is impossible to imagine that anything is thought of in the divine intellect as good or true, or worthy of belief or action or omission, prior to the decision of the divine will to make it so. I am not speaking here of temporal priority: I mean that there is not even any priority of order, or nature, or of 'rationally determined reason' as they call it, such that God's idea of the good impelled him to choose one thing rather than another.... Thus the supreme indifference to be found in God is the supreme indication of his omnipotence. But as for man...he finds that the nature of all goodness and truth is already determined by God. (AT VII, 431–2/CSM II 291–2)

Opponents of ethical voluntarism are quick to retort that this position jeopardizes the objective standard of goodness. What is good or evil is here supposed to be determined by the will of the powerful as opposed to expressing eternal truths about the nature of things. In so far as rationalism can be construed as a tradition which looks back to Plato, the category of rationalism seems unsuited to Descartes' ethics, if he is so hopelessly un-Platonic at a crucial juncture of his moral thought.[12] But is this really the case? His stand on the dependence of goodness on God's will is intended to place God beyond any boundaries which might imply any kind of limitation. Platonism in its Neoplatonic variety can actually illuminate what Descartes means in this controversial passage. There is a way in which Descartes' position here is similar to the Neoplatonic conception of the One as beyond being.[13] Its ineffable transcendence is so radical that no category applies to it. It is not bounded by the natures of things because it is beyond them. In Neoplatonism, the world of the forms, of the multiple natures or archetypes of things, is not found in the

---

[12] Cf. Cottingham 2007: 25–7. Interpreters are divided on the issue of the ontological status of eternal truths and immutable natures in Descartes' philosophy. For instance, Gueroult 1984–1985: v. I, 276–7, proposes a strongly non-Platonist interpretation of Descartes: 'a doctrine much like Malebranche's, who holds the essence of created, finite, and contingent things to be uncreated, infinite, and eternal, is, for Descartes, radically unthinkable and even scandalous....Descartes annihilates the concept of a world of intelligible things governing the world of existences'; Descartes' true and immutable natures are just ideas within our mind implanted in us by God. Nolan 1997 and Chappell 1997 also propose a conceptualist interpretation according to which the eternal truths exist only in our minds; mathematical objects are just ideas created by God 'by including them within the minds that are the direct products of his creative action' (Chappell 1997: 125). On the other hand, Kenny 1970: 697 sees Descartes as frankly Platonic on the issue of eternal truths and immutable natures: these are essences distinct from both God's essence and from us: 'for Descartes the geometers' triangle is an eternal creature of God, with its own immutable nature and properties, a real thing lacking only the perfection of actual existence'. Schmaltz 1991: 170 interprets Descartes as taking 'a middle way between Platonic realism and the conceptualism of Gassendi and Locke': immutable essences and the corresponding eternal truths are 'eternal decrees of the divine will that are not really distinct from God himself'; they are 'features neither of our finite minds nor of material substances in our world; rather they are eternal and immutable (weak) attributes of God'. Rozemond 2008: 42 speaks of a moderate Platonism according to which 'eternal truths have a form of being external to human minds as well as to the entire creation, but not external to God'; '*essences* have objective being in God's mind'.

[13] Cf. Ayers 2007b: 62–3.

One but in the first emanation of the One, the *Nous*, traditionally interpreted by Christian thought as the intellect of God. The essences of things are God's eternal thoughts, *ideae in mente Dei*. Although there is no temporal priority, it is clear that in Neoplatonism the One is logically prior. Descartes seems to have thought that this logical priority needed to be stressed in order to account for the absolute perfection and omnipotence of God. Simply to posit in God's intellect 'true and immutable natures' (*Fifth Meditation*; AT VII 64/CSM II 44) co-eternal with God might still imply that there are eternal 'reasons' which logically (if not ontologically) are independent of Him. Of course God constitutes their ontological grounding. Without God there would be no *ideae in mente Dei*, no eternal essences of possible things. Nevertheless, they are what they are and God cannot do anything about it. It is this implication which Descartes seems to have wished to avoid by the introduction of the role of God's will, alongside (as it was commonly accepted) God's intellect, in accounting for the eternal archetypes of things.[14]

It is also not merely a matter of God decreeing what is good and what is evil, as if there were eternal essences of things logically independent of God but in themselves neutral in respect to moral value. Descartes' affirmation of the dependence of things on God is much more radical: they depend on God's will not only for their goodness but also for their truth. That is, there are quite simply no archetypes or immutable natures of things unless God has chosen to think them, and the way in which God chooses to think them is completely undetermined (God's 'supreme indifference' in Descartes' words) because God, as the Neoplatonic One, is beyond any determination. So God did not will that 'the three angles of a triangle should be equal to two right angles because he recognized that it could not be otherwise'. On the contrary, 'it is because he willed that three angles of a triangle should necessarily equal two right angles that this is true and cannot be otherwise' ('Sixth Set of Replies'; AT VII 432/CSM II 291).[15] It is because God chose to think of a triangle in a certain way that the triangle is immutably and eternally that way. Descartes replies to Pierre Gassendi's objections to the 'Fifth Meditation':

> I do not think that the essences of things, and the mathematical truths we can know concerning them, are independent of God. Nevertheless I do think that they are immutable and eternal, since the will and decree of God willed and decreed that they should be so. ('Fifth Set of Replies'; AT VII 380/CSM II 261)[16]

Likewise, good and evil are the expression of eternal truths about the natures of things as contemplated by God's intellect, but the natures of things are eternally

[14] It should be noted that Descartes' position aims also at avoiding a distinction between what God's intellect contemplates and what God wills. This distinction was seen as a possible threat to divine simplicity.

[15] On the dependence of eternal truths (including mathematical truths) from God's will see also the letters of Descartes to Mersenne of 15 April 1630 (AT I 145/CSMK 23), 6 May 1630 (AT I 149–150/CSMK 24–25), and 27 May 1630 (AT I 151–3/CSMK 25); and the letter to Mesland of 2 May 1644 (AT IV, 118–119/CSMK 235).

[16] On the debate between Descartes and Gassendi on the status of eternal truths see Osler 1995. Cf. also Osler 1994.

determined by God's will without any logically antecedent reason determining Him to think of them in a certain way.

This is not the only manner in which Cartesian ethics is deeply rooted in his meta-physics even though it falls short of his desired science of Morals. To Princess Elisabeth, who quite reasonably began to fear that Descartes' account of morality might presup-pose more knowledge than we will ever achieve, Descartes replied by listing 'the truths most useful to us'[17] (AT IV 291/CSMK 265), that is, those truths which are sufficient in guiding our conduct since they 'concern all our actions in general' (AT IV, 294/CSMK 267). These truths bring to light how Cartesian ethics is grounded in a relationship between God and the soul which is the hallmark of a broadly Neoplatonic-Augustinian metaphysics.[18] The first two truths presented to Elisabeth correspond to the two key truths established by Descartes' metaphysics following the *cogito ergo sum*, namely, the existence of a God who is the *Ens perfectissimum*, and the nature of the *res cogitans* as really distinct from the *res extensa*:

> The first and chief of these is that there is a God on whom all things depend, whose perfections are infinite, whose power is immense and whose decrees are infallible. This teaches us to accept calmly all the things which happen to us as expressly sent by God. . . . The second thing we must know is the nature of our soul. We must know that it subsists apart from the body, and is much nobler than the body, and that it is capable of enjoying countless satisfactions not to be found in this life. This prevents us from fearing death, and so detaches our affections from the things of this world that we look upon whatever is in the power of fortune with nothing but scorn. (AT IV, 291–2/CSMK 265–6)

The third truth, concerning the immensity of the universe, corrects our self-importance and avoids the 'vain anxieties and troubles' of those who 'wish to belong to God's council and assist him in the government of the world' (AT IV, 292/CSMK 266). 'After acknowl-edging the goodness of God, the immortality of our souls and the immensity of the uni-verse', the fourth truth is that 'none of us could subsist alone and that each one of us is really one of the many parts of the universe, and more particularly a part of the earth, the state, the society and the family to which we belong by our domicile, our oath of alle-giance and our birth' (AT IV, 293/CSMK 266). Finally, in addition to these general truths, 'many others must be known which concern more particularly each individual action'. The chief of these truths being that 'all our passions represent to us the goods to whose pursuit they impel us as being much greater than they really are; and that the pleasures of the body are never as lasting as those of the soul' (AT IV, 294–5/CSMK 267).

In summary, Descartes' dualism of mind and body implies that the true self is the spiritual and immortal soul. Its happiness is the goal of morality. In turn, 'happiness consists solely in contentment of mind' (to Princess Elisabeth, 18 August 1645; AT IV

---

[17] Descartes to Princess Elisabeth, 15 September 1645.

[18] In her classic study of Descartes' moral philosophy, Geneviève Rodis-Lewis writes: 'la morale remonte...à la source de toute la réflexion philosophique: la relation entre l'âme et Dieu' (Rodis-Lewis 1962: 27).

277/CSMK 262) and 'all our contentment consists simply in our inner awareness of possessing some perfection' (to Princess Elisabeth, 1 September 1645; AT IV 283–4/ CSMK 263). Happiness is a state of satisfaction and pleasure of the mind untroubled by the passions. As Descartes had already written in the youthful *Rules for the Direction of the Mind* (1628), this state is 'the pleasure to be gained from contemplating the truth, which is practically the only happiness in this life that is complete and untroubled by any pain' (AT X 361/CSM I 10). This mental contentment is achieved through the practice of virtue, that is, in doing 'what our reason tells us we should do' (AT IV 284/CSMK 263). In other words, virtue is 'to maintain a firm and constant will to bring about everything we judge to be best, and to use all the power of the intellect in judging well' (AT IV 277/ CSMK 262). Virtue is therefore both an expression of our rational nature and of the freedom of our will. And since 'the will, or freedom of choice…when considered as will in the essential and strict sense [voluntas, sive arbitrii libertas…in se formaliter et praecise spectata]' does not have limits (cf. 'Fourth Meditation'; AT VII 57/CSM II 40), and the will 'tends to pursue or avoid only what our intellect represents as good or bad, we need only to judge well in order to act well' (*Discourse*; AT VI 28/CSM I 125). Virtue is sufficient for happiness because the will to judge correctly about the good (and therefore to act well) is, as it were, in our hands and not in those of fortune. By the time of his correspondence with Princess Elisabeth, the second and the third maxim of the *Discourse*'s provisional moral code—'to be as firm and decisive in my actions as I could' and 'to try always to master myself rather then fortune' (AT VI 24–5/CSM I 123)—are substantiated by the metaphysical certainties established in the *Meditations*, namely that, whatever our fortune, we have the means to be happy because we are immortal, spiritual beings in an immense universe governed by a God of infinite perfection. The fourth maxim of the *Discourse*—to devote his 'whole life to cultivating…reason and advancing…in the knowledge of the truth' (AT VI 27/CSM I 124)—reflects the constantly upheld crucial role of reason in guiding our moral conduct.[19] The voices of Stoicism and Epicureanism, which powerfully resonate in Descartes' ethics, blend here with the echo of Plato's doctrine of the rational soul as our true self temporarily inhabiting a body.

Descartes' doctrine of body, however, is the daughter of mechanism. We are not merely urged to control the passions through reason as the ancients advised. The workings of the body-machine need to be scientifically studied in order to be mastered in a sort of mechanistic version of Socrates' horse training and Aristotelian habituation.[20] Descartes, however, is not as keen as Socrates to leave the body serenely behind.

---

[19] See the summary of how to be happy penned by Descartes for Princess Elisabeth (letter of 4 August 1645) (AT IV 265/CSMK 257): 'It seems to me that each person can make himself content by himself without any external assistance, provided he respects three conditions, which are related to the three rules of morality which I put forward in the *Discourse on the Method*. The first is that he should always try to employ his mind as well as he can to discover what he should and should not do in all the circumstances of life. The second is that he should have a firm and constant resolution to carry out whatever reason recommends without being diverted by his passions or appetites.… The third is that he should bear in mind that while he thus guides himself as far as he can, by reason, all the good things which he does not possess are one and all entirely outside his power.' Cf. Rutherford 2008.

[20] Cf. Cottingham 2007: 36–9.

His metaphysics as well as his moral philosophy are in tension between the affirmation of the priority and independence of the spiritual and immortal self, on the one hand, and the value assigned to its union with the body-machine, on the other hand.[21] Part of the horse-training exercise is aimed at the prolongation of the happy and pleasant union between mind and body which gives life its sweetness (cf. art. 212 of the *Passions of the Soul*; AT XI 488). Passions in so far as they are aimed at the preservation of the body are good; but they need to be controlled so that, while keeping the body healthy, they support the soul's well-being. As Descartes, writing as a physical scientist ('en Physicien' AT XI 326), explains in the *Passions of the Soul* (1649), they originate in the body but affect the soul, moving and disposing it 'to want the things for which they prepare the body' (AT XI 359/CSM I 343). Understanding their physiology is the first step towards properly directing their motivational force.

15.2 NICOLAS MALEBRANCHE (1638–1715)

The Platonic-Augustinian strand present in Descartes, combined with elements which render it ambiguous in various respects,[22] comes fully to the fore in the work of one of Descartes' most original followers, the French Oratorian priest Nicolas Malebranche. To start with, Malebranche rejects Descartes' view that all goodness and truth depend on God's will. On the issue of the status of eternal truths (including moral truths) Malebranche resolutely takes the Platonic side of the Euthyphro dilemma: God wills what is morally good because it is morally good rather than being morally good because it is willed by God. In other words, there are necessary truths expressing, or following from, the natures of things. They are co-eternal with, and contemplated by God's intellect. At the end of his life, in the *Réflexions sur la Prémotion Physique* (1715), Malebranche writes: 'My present design is to prove that God is essentially wise, just and good...; that his wills [*volontez*] are not at all purely arbitrary—that is to say that they are not wise and just precisely because he is All-powerful... but because they are regulated by the eternal Law... a Law which can consist only in the necessary, eternal, immutable relations which are among the attributes and the perfections which God encloses in his necessary[,] eternal essence' (*Prémotion Physique*, XIX; OC 16:101). The frightening scenarios implied by a God resembling 'Princes who glory more in their power than in their nature' (*Prémotion Physique*, XVIII; OC 16:98) are painted by Malebranche in vivid colours:

> If God were merely all-powerful, or if he gloried merely in his omnipotence, without any regard for his other attributes—in a word, without consulting his consubstantial

---

[21] Cf. Rodis-Lewis 1962: 44. Cottingham 2007 draws attention to the tension between the 'contemplative' and the 'controlling' mindsets in Descartes. Recent studies stress the importance of the mind–body unity in Descartes' philosophy. See for instance Brown 2006; Hatfield 2003; Gaukroger 1995 and 2002; Cottingham 1998.

[22] Cf. Cottingham 2007.

Law, his lovable and inviolable Law—how strange his designs would be! How could we be certain that, through his Omnipotence, he would not, on the first day, place all the demons in Heaven, and all the Saints in hell, and that a moment after he would not annihilate all that he had done! (*Prémotion Physique*, XVIII; OC 16:100)[23]

Malebranche's distinctive brand of Platonic Augustinianism, however, is more thoroughgoing than other rejections of the dependence of eternal truths on God's will. The stability of the moral order is guaranteed by its eternal foundation in objective 'relations of perfections' amongst necessary and immutable essences in God's intellect. These essences (and their relations) are necessary and immutable precisely because they are grounded in a 'universal', 'immutable and necessary Reason' (OC 3:129–130; see also OC 9:992). We can have access to this objective moral order because 'we see all things in God' (OC 9:992). This famous Malebranchean claim which, together with his occasionalism, constitutes the hallmark of his philosophical system is already adumbrated in the 'Preface' to the *Recherche de la Vérité*.[24] Following the Augustinian doctrine of divine illumination, Malebranche maintains that the mind 'receives its life, its light, and its entire felicity' (OC 1:9/LO xxxiii) through a union with God. This generic and seemingly commonplace appeal to the centrality of the union of the mind with God is meant by Malebranche in a very specific way, as is made especially clear in the third book of the *Recherche* (discussing the nature of ideas), and in one of the sixteen *Eclaircissements* ('Eclaircissement X') added in 1678 to the *Recherche*. Since 'everyone agrees that we do not perceive objects external to us by themselves' (OC 1:413/LO 217) and 'we can only apprehend the infinite in the infinite itself' (OC 2:372/LO 481), we must conclude that our perception both of the infinite and of an infinite number of external objects is vision in God. That is to say, we see external objects by means of ideas in God, the only Being who can embrace in his intellect an infinity of ideas. Far from being modifications of finite minds, ideas are eternal, immutable, necessary archetypes in God's mind which serve as models to his creation of external things (cf. OC 9:925–6). By seeing them in God we indirectly perceive external things which in themselves, as material objects, would be unintelligible to the spiritual mind. By seeing 'the same eternal truths that God sees', we know 'something of what God thinks, and of the way in which God acts' (*Traité de Morale*, I, I, vi; OC 11:19). According to Malebranche, this is in agreement with Augustine's teaching that we see God through our knowledge of eternal truths.[25] He firmly denies, however, that his doctrine of vision in God implies that we see the divine substance 'in itself or as it really is': 'You see it only in its relation to material creatures, only as it is participable by or representative of them. Consequently it is not strictly

[23] Attention to these passages is drawn by Riley 2000: 236–7. Riley stresses 'Malebranche's Augustine-conveyed Platonism' (2000: 260). See also Riley 2009.

[24] The *Recherche de la Vérité*, first published in 1674–1675, has a complex editorial history. The text translated in LO is that of the last edition in Malebranche's lifetime (1712) as established by Geneviève Rodis-Lewis in OC 1–2.

[25] See Schmaltz 2009 and Nolan 2008. On Malebranche's theory of ideas and vision in God see also Jolley 1990; Nadler 1992; Schmaltz 1996 and 2000.

speaking God whom you see, but only the matter he can produce' (*Entretiens sur la Métaphysique*, II; OC 12:51/JS 21). Nevertheless, through our vision in God of ideas which are 'eternal, immutable, necessary, common to all spiritual beings' (OC 9:933), we have some access also to the 'immutable Order that God consults when he acts—an Order that ought also to regulate the esteem and love of all intelligent beings' (*Traité de Morale*, I, I, vi; OC 11:19).

Our moral life is nothing other than the proper ordering of our love according to the objective 'relations of perfection' amongst beings. The more perfect a being is, the more worthy it is of love. As 'I see, for example, that twice two is four', so I should see 'that my friend is to be valued more than my dog' ('Eclaircissement X'; OC 3:129/LO 613). Following the proper order of the 'relations of perfection' means that only the infinitely and absolutely perfect Being—God—'ought to be loved absolutely and intrinsically' (*Recherche*; OC 1:55/LO 10); any other being ought to be loved only 'in relation to God' (*Conversations Chrétiennes*; OC 4:203). To sin is therefore to stop 'at some particular good' (*Recherche*, 'Eclaircissement I'; OC 3:21/LO 549), that is, to sin is to love a particular good with the absolute and intrinsic love which is due only to God. In the context of Malebranche's occasionalism, according to which God is the only true cause of everything, the question however immediately arises of whether human beings are at all responsible for this disordered and therefore sinful love. Malebranche's answer is an unequivocal 'yes'. Human beings are free to give or suspend consent to a particular good by directing their attention towards some other good. In this way they are free to suspend consent to the temptation of loving a particular good absolutely and intrinsically, that is, they are free to resist the temptation of 'stopping' at a particular good instead of loving it in relation to God. In short, human beings do have freedom and therefore bear moral responsibility for their sins—even if, for Malebranche, the only free acts are acts of will, and freedom is merely freedom of the will.[26]

15.3 GOTTFRIED WILHELM LEIBNIZ (1646–1716)

Leibniz, while adamantly disagreeing with other points of Malebranche's philosophical system, such as his French correspondent's occasionalist account of causality, fully agrees with his views on the Euthyphro dilemma. In an important moral writing of frankly Platonic inspiration, the *Méditation sur la notion commune de la justice* of 1703,[27] Leibniz ponders the vexed question: 'It is agreed that whatever God wills is good and just. But there remains the question whether it is good and just because God wills it or whether God wills it because it is good and just: in other words, whether justice and goodness are

---

[26] Kremer 2000: 191.
[27] The *Méditation* was published for the first time by Georg Mollat in *Rechsphilosophisches aus Leibnizens Ungedruckten Schriften* (Leipzig: Verlag Robolski, 1885).

arbitrary or whether they belong to the necessary and eternal truths about the nature of things, as do numbers and proportions' (PW 45). Leibniz has no doubt: justice and goodness belong to the necessary and eternal truths about the nature of things, just as do the necessary truths of mathematics. Descartes, of course, would have taken umbrage at the suggestion that the alternative horn of the dilemma implies the arbitrariness of justice and goodness. He would have insisted upon their status as eternal and immutable truths despite their dependence (along with immutable mathematical truths) on God's will. Leibniz, Malebranche, and the opponents of ethical voluntarism could reply, however, that Descartes' position still does not guarantee the strict necessity of these truths.[28] Although de facto they are eternally and immutably what they are because of God's eternal decrees and immutable will, they could have been otherwise—and this cannot but imply their contingency and, ultimately, their arbitrariness, since their choice does not depend on reasons but on the will of the supremely powerful. For Descartes' critics, Cartesian ethical voluntarism is no better than that of Hobbes or Pufendorf.

But in defending objective standards of justice, do not the anti-voluntarists compromise God's absolute sovereignty? Are they not reinstating—as Descartes seems to have feared—a Platonic intelligible world of necessary, immutable, and eternal essences which are logically independent of God although, as *ideae in mente Dei*, could not exist without God? In 1706, attacking specifically Pufendorf's account of morality, Leibniz claims that the eternal truths on which the 'essence of the just' depends 'constitute, so to speak, the essence of divinity itself':

> Neither the norm of conduct itself, nor the essence of the just, depends on his [God's] free decision, but rather on eternal truths, objects of the divine intellect, which constitute, so to speak, the essence of divinity itself…Justice, indeed, would not be an essential attribute of God, if he himself established justice and law by his free will. And, indeed, justice follows certain rules of equality and of proportion [which are] no less founded in the immutable nature of things, and in the divine ideas, than are the principles of arithmetic and of geometry. So that no one will maintain that justice and goodness originate in the divine will, without at the same time maintaining that truth originates in it as well: an unheard-of paradox by which Descartes showed how great can be the errors of great men; as if the reason that a triangle has three sides, or that two contrary propositions are incompatible, or that God himself exists, is that God has willed it so. It would follow from this, too, that which some people have imprudently said, that God could with justice condemn an innocent person, since he could make it such that precisely this would constitute justice. (*Monita quaedam ad Samuelis Puffendorfii Principia*; DUTENS IV, III, 280/PW 71–2)

---

[28] Curley 1984 offers a sophisticated discussion of two possible interpretations of Descartes' doctrine of the creation of eternal truths: the 'standard' interpretation according to which this doctrine commits Descartes to the thesis that there are no necessary truths; and the alternative interpretation according to which there are necessary truths, but some or all of them are created. In her illuminating analysis Osler 1995: 153 maintains that 'according to Descartes, the eternal truths are necessary, even though God created them freely and their existence depends entirely on him': once eternal truths have been established through God's unbounded absolute power, they are necessary in relation to the natural order actually chosen by God.

In the context of Leibniz's ontology of logic, in which necessary truths express, or follow from facts about essences and their relations,[29] this passage indicates that eternal truths (such as those on which the nature of justice depends) ultimately express facts about God's essence. The independence of eternal truths from God's will therefore does not imply independence from God—not even logical independence since the most fundamental eternal truths ultimately follow from the nature of God. Leibniz's ontology of logic therefore appears to be stratified in two distinct respects: first in the sense that the most fundamental objects of logic are essences embraced by God's mind, while truths follow from facts about them and their relations;[30] and second, at a deeper level constituted by fundamental, necessary truths which express, or follow from, 'the essence of divinity itself' and on which, in turn, the essences of possible things depend. In sum, the 'essence of the just' cannot be a matter of God's will because it expresses what God is.

Justice takes a central position in Leibniz's moral philosophy: it is the highest virtue, defined from 1677 onward as 'the charity of the wise' (A I, 2, 23).[31] Justice is therefore a kind of love: love or 'goodness toward others which is conformed to wisdom' (*Méditation*; PW 54). Being a virtue, it is a habit: the 'habit of loving conformed to wisdom' (Grua 579/ PW 83). Wisdom is defined in turn as the 'science of happiness'. So wisdom is the way to happiness, and to be wise is to be happy. But what is happiness? As early as 1671–1672 Leibniz links the notions of wisdom, love, and happiness with that of harmony: '*Wisdom* is the science of happiness [scientia felicitatis]. . . . A *good man* is one who loves all human beings. *To love* is to find delight in the happiness of another. To find delight is to feel harmony' (A VI, 2, 485). Happiness is 'a lasting state of pleasure' (Grua 579/PW 83; see also *Nouveaux Essais* Book II, Ch. 21, § 42; A VI, 6, 194/RB 194) or 'delight' which consists in feeling harmony. Harmony, in turn, is the unity in multiplicity of the greatest possible quantity of essence or com-possible beings. In other words, harmony is an expression of perfection or metaphysical goodness, and happiness is nothing other than the perception of perfection. This perception can be achieved in a confused way through the senses ('the confused perception of some perfection constitutes the pleasure of sense'; Grua 579/PW 83), but only rational beings can reach its highest degree, that is, a distinct perception of perfection which can lead to the lasting state of pleasure which constitutes happiness. Happiness, more precisely, is therefore the lasting pleasure of the mind grasping the intelligible order of reality.[32] In maximizing perfection and harmony

---

[29] Adams 1994: 177–8: 'According to Leibniz, the objects of logic exist in the mind of God. Among these objects are mentioned possibilities or possibles, necessary or "eternal" truths, and essences or ideas. They are stratified. The essences are for Leibniz the most fundamental objects of logic. Possibilities depend on essences,. . . and the eternal truths are said to depend on "ideas", by which I believe essences are meant. The essences can be identified with ideas in God's mind, ideas of possible individuals, which constitute the possibility of such individuals, and which are concatenated to constitute the ideas, and the possibility, of possible worlds. And necessary truths express, or follow from, facts about the essences and their relations.'

[30] Cf. Adams 1994: 177–8.

[31] On justice as 'charity of the wise' see especially Riley 1996.

[32] Cf. Rutherford 1995, especially 50–1. On the centrality in Leibniz's ethics of the notion of happiness and on its relation to perfection see also Heinekamp 1969 and 1989, and Blumenfeld 1995.

by the creation of the best of all possible worlds, God also provides the best objective conditions which can lead to the happiness of rational beings.[33] In this way, Leibniz is able to reconcile his view that God aims at the creation of the greatest quantity of essence (conceived, Platonically, in terms of the greatest degree of reality and metaphysical goodness) with his claim that 'the entire universe is made for minds, such that it can contribute to their happiness as much as possible' (K X 10/PW 105).[34] The tension between, on the one hand, metaphysical perfection, and on the other hand, the happiness of rational beings as (apparently competing) aims of creation, is resolved in a system in which the rational apprehension of metaphysical perfection is identified with happiness. At the same time, this rational apprehension increases the perfection of minds and, in doing so, increases the total metaphysical perfection of the world.

There is, however, another tension confronting Leibniz's moral philosophy: on the one hand, no one, in his view, can 'renounce (except merely verbally) being impelled by his own good' (*Mantissa codicis iuris gentium diplomatici*, Hanover 1700; L 424); yet true justice, on the other hand, requires that our love be disinterested, that is, that we love others for their own sake and not as a means to our own good. The challenge faced by Leibniz is how to reconcile the psychological egoism, to which he subscribes as a theory of motivation, with the altruism required by his theory of justice.[35] Leibniz finds a solution in 'the nature of love': 'The true definition of love [is as follows:] When we love... someone, their good is our delight.... Since then justice requires that the good of others is sought for its own sake, [and] since to seek the good of others for its own sake is to love others, it follows that love is of the nature of justice. *Justice* will therefore be the habit of loving others (or of seeking the good of others for its own sake, [or] of taking pleasure in the good of others)' (*Elementa Juris Naturalis*; A VI, 1, 464–5). When we love, we take pleasure in the good of others, and the good of others, which is sought for its own sake, is the immediate cause of our pleasure. As such it is one of those 'things wished for because they are pleasing in themselves, and are consequently good of themselves, even if one should have no regard to consequences; they are ends and not means' (*Sentiment de Mr. Leibniz sur le livre de Mr. l'archevêque de Cambray et sur l'amour de Dieu désintéressé*, 1697; Erdmann 790 / W 565). In true love, the good of others not only coincides with our own good since it is pleasurable to us: it is also our end because it is desired as something pleasing in itself, as opposed to being sought instrumentally as a means to an end.[36] The good of others is nothing else than their perfection and therefore 'to love is to find pleasure in the perfection of another' (Grua 579/PW 83). Since happiness is a lasting state of pleasure which consists in the perception of perfection, loving

[33] Rutherford 1995: 51.

[34] See especially Brown 1988, Blumenfeld 1995, and Rutherford 1995: 46–67.

[35] Brown 1995: 412–13.

[36] See Rutherford 1995: 57 and Brown 2011. Brown's extensive and insightful discussion of Leibniz's notion of disinterested love stresses the importance, for Leibniz's reconciliation of self- and other-regarding motives, of his distinction between desiring something *per se* (that is, as an immediate source of pleasure) and *propter aliud* (that is, for the sake of something else). In disinterested love the good of others is desired *per se* and not for the sake of something else because it is the *immediate* source of our pleasure.

others in a disinterested manner leads to our own happiness. It is in the nature of justice as the 'charity of the wise' to be able to reconcile psychological egoism with altruism.[37]

In the framework of natural law or universal jurisprudence, this conception of justice as the 'charity of the wise' corresponds to the highest degree of justice in the Roman legal tradition. As early as the *Nova Methodus Discendae Docendaeque Jurisprudentiae* of 1667, Leibniz endorsed the three precepts of the Roman jurist Ulpian canonized by the *Digest* of Justinian (cf. *Digest* 1.1.10.1): *neminem laedere* ('harm no one'); *suum cuique tribuere* ('give to everybody his due'); *honeste vivere* ('live honestly') (*Nova Methodus*; A VI, 1, 343–5). These three precepts identify three degrees of justice which remain a constant structure of Leibniz's juridical thought.[38] The lowest degree, expressed by the principle: 'harm no one', corresponds to Grotius' *jus strictum* and to commutative justice. It embraces the minimal requirements of justice. By refraining from harming others we also protect ourselves from giving others reason to harm us. The second degree, expressed by the principle: 'give to everybody his due', corresponds to 'equity' and to distributive justice. The rule of equity, Leibniz explains in the *Méditation*, is the rule 'of our Master' which is, at the same time, the rule of reason: 'what you do not wish to have done to you, or what you do wish to have done to you, do not do to others, or do not deny to others' (PW 56; cf. Luke 6.31; Matthew 7.12). That is to say, 'put yourself in the place of another, and you will have the true point of view for judging what is just or not' (PW 56). Equity, however, still falls short of the highest degree of justice identified by the principle *honeste*—that is, as Leibniz explains in the *Méditation*, 'piously' (PW 60)—*vivere*. To 'live piously' is nothing other than to exercise the 'charity of the wise', namely to imitate God, whose goodness is supreme (cf. PW 57–8). The pinnacle of ethics turns out to be the love of God because to love God is to reach, at the same time, the greatest happiness and the greatest virtue (cf. PW 59). Since happiness is the perception of perfection, and God is the *Ens perfectissimum*, the intellectual apprehension of His perfections will yield the greatest happiness. And since knowing God is loving God, and loving God is 'willing what he wills' (PW 59), 'charity and justice' are the 'inescapable results' (*Dialogue entre Poliandre et Theophile*, c. 1679; A VI, 4, 2220/L 213) of such love. Rational perfection, in the sense of the mind's distinct perception of perfection, is the high road to moral perfection.

15.4 BARUCH SPINOZA (1632–1677)

The love of God, or more precisely, 'the intellectual Love of God' (E Vp33), is also the pinnacle of Spinoza's ethics. But Spinoza's conception of God bends traditional views to the extent that it radically subverts them. In doing so, it also provides a strikingly original

---

[37] Cf. Brown 1995: 413, 426. See also Brown 2011.
[38] See Rutherford 1995: 55–6; Brown 1995: 417–18; Riley's introduction in PW 19–22; Antognazza 2009: 83–4.

metaphysical foundation for a strikingly commonplace seventeenth-century ethical position: namely that passions are disruptive of our well-being, that they therefore need to be controlled, and that reason is the instrument for mastering them.[39] Few thinkers could claim to be as bold as Spinoza in showing that this control comes from understanding. The path to the good life—*beatitudo* ('blessedness') in Spinoza's vocabulary (E V 'Preface')—is rational understanding.

Spinoza's ethical treatise—the *Ethica Ordine Geometrico Demonstrata*, published posthumously in 1677—starts with metaphysics and, more precisely, with God.[40] As Spinoza explains in the Appendix to Part I, ignorance 'of the causes of things' is the source of the common but misguided conception of God:

> from the means [human beings] were accustomed to prepare for themselves, they had to infer that there was a ruler, or a number of rulers of nature, endowed with human freedom, who had taken care of all things for them, and made all things for their use. And since they had never heard anything about the temperament of these rulers, they had to judge it from their own. Hence, they maintained that the Gods direct all things for the use of men in order to bind men to them and be held by men in the highest honor. So it has happened that each of them has thought up from his own temperament different ways of worshipping God, so that God might love them above all the rest, and direct the whole of Nature according to the needs of their blind desire and insatiable greed. Thus this prejudice was changed into superstition, and stuck deep roots in their minds.

The first step on the path toward 'blessedness' is to eradicate these prejudices by understanding what God really is. On the way to this understanding we will discover not only that God is not endowed with a kind of freedom similar to human freedom, but that there is no such thing as human freedom taken in the usual sense.[41] Spinoza's radically non-anthropomorphic conception of God is reached in Part I of the *Ethics*, where God is defined as 'a being absolutely infinite, i.e. a substance consisting of an infinity of attributes, of which each one expresses an eternal and infinite essence' (E Id6). Substance, in turn, is defined as 'what is in itself and is conceived through itself, i.e., that whose concept does not require the concept of another thing, from which it must be formed' (E Id3). 'It pertains to the nature of a substance to exist' (E Ip7). This is because 'a substance cannot be produced by anything else' (E I Dem. of p7), that is, by an external cause, since if this were the case, this substance would involve the

[39] Cf. James 1998, especially 1358–73. See also Kraye 1998.

[40] See *Ethica*, Pars I 'De Deo'. English translation by Edwin Curley in *The Collected Writings of Spinoza*. Vol. 1 (Princeton: Princeton University Press, 1985).

[41] Nadler 2009: § 2.4. Summarizing at the beginning of the Appendix to Part I 'God's nature and properties', Spinoza writes: 'I have explained…that he exists necessarily; that he is unique; that he is and acts from the necessity alone of his nature; that (and how) he is the free cause of all things; that all things are in God and so depend on him that without him they can neither be nor be conceived; and finally, that all things have been predetermined by God, not from freedom of the will or absolute good pleasure, but from God's absolute nature, or infinite power.' On the debate on Spinoza's doctrine of freedom see footnote 43.

knowledge of its cause (cf. E Ia4); therefore it would not be conceived through itself; hence it would not be a substance (cf. E Id3). The only alternative to being produced by something external to itself is to be the cause of itself (*causa sui*). Hence a substance must be the cause of itself, that is, 'its essence necessarily involves existence, or it pertains to its nature to exist' (E Ip7) and its 'nature cannot be conceived except as existing' (E Id1). Therefore, 'God, or a substance consisting of infinite attributes, each of which expresses eternal and infinite essence, necessarily exists' (E Ip11). Moreover, 'except God, no substance can be or be conceived' (E Ip14) since 'if there were any substance except God, it would have to be explained through some attribute of God, and so two substances of the same attribute would exist, which (by P5 [In nature there cannot be two or more substances of the same nature or attribute]) is absurd' (E I Dem. of Ip14). Since 'substance is prior in nature to its affections' (E Ip1), it is clear at this point that 'Whatsoever is, is in God, and nothing can be or be conceived without God' (E Ip15). Spinoza goes on to show that all things follow necessarily from the nature of God: 'from God's supreme power, or infinite nature, infinitely many things in infinitely many modes, i.e., all things, have necessarily flowed, or always follow, by the same necessity and in the same way as from the nature of a triangle it follows, from eternity and to eternity, that its three angles are equal to two right angles' (E Ip17s; see also E Ip29). God is supremely free, not in the sense that he could choose to create some possible things instead of other possible things, but in the sense in which a thing is called free by Spinoza: 'That thing is called free which exists from the necessity of its nature alone, and is determined to act by itself alone' (E Id7). Obviously, on this understanding of freedom, only God is completely free. In the Preface of Part IV, Spinoza distils into a single sentence the essence of his metaphysics: 'That eternal and infinite being we call God, or Nature, acts from the same necessity from which he exists.'

Scholium II to Proposition 40 in Part II summarizes Spinoza's views on cognition (*cognitio*). There are three kinds of cognition. The first one is based on inadequate and confused ideas (cf. E IIp41), that is on notions that, through the senses, represent individual things to our intellect in a mutilated and confused way. This is cognition *ab experientia vaga* ('from random experience'). Another variety of this first kind of cognition derives from signs through which we remember and then imagine things. In both cases we are dealing with a kind of cognition which Spinoza names 'opinion or imagination' and which, being based on inadequate ideas, is the 'only cause of falsity' (E IIp41). When we rely on the senses and imagination we fail to understand things as they really are. We imagine them contingent; we imagine ourselves free; in short we fall prey to the sort of delusions and prejudices described in the Appendix to Part I of the *Ethics*. The second kind of cognition is 'reason', consisting of 'common notions and adequate ideas of the properties of things'. The third and highest kind of cognition is *scientia intuitiva* ('intuitive knowledge'), that is an understanding of the essence of things which proceeds directly from a true understanding of God: 'this kind of knowing proceeds from an adequate idea of the formal essence of certain attributes of God to the adequate knowledge of the essence of things' (E IIp40s). Being both based on adequate—that is, true (cf. E IId4)—ideas, the second and third kind of cognition are 'necessarily true' (E IIp41) and teach us 'to distinguish the true from the false' (E IIp42), namely, they teach us the necessity of everything as modes of the only one substance, God (cf. E IIp44).

These metaphysics and theory of knowledge provide the bedrock of ethics proper and have direct ethical implications. According to Spinoza, adequate understanding has in itself a significant power to control passions.[42] Once we grasp the true nature of things, including the true nature of ourselves, our moral life takes a different course. In the first place, we can now become virtuous, since 'acting absolutely from virtue is nothing else in us but acting...by the guidance of reason' (E IVp24). Moreover, we can now also become free, since to live 'according to the dictate of reason alone' is, in turn, to be 'a free man' (E IV Dem. of p67), that is (following Spinoza's definition of 'a free thing' in E Id7) a man whose action follows from his own nature rather than from external causes.[43] Indeed 'reason demands nothing contrary to nature, it demands that everyone love himself, seek his own advantage, what is really useful to him...and absolutely, that everyone should strive to preserve his own being' (E IVp18s). The essence of any individual thing is in fact a tendency or striving towards self-preservation: 'Each thing, as far as it can by its own power, strives to persevere in its being' (E IIIp6) and 'the striving [*conatus*] by which each thing strives to persevere in its being is nothing but the actual essence of the thing' (E IIIp7). Good and evil is what is useful or harmful to an individual's self-preservation (cf. E IVd1–2).

Once we understand that it is in the nature of any individual thing to strive towards self-preservation, as well as that everything is strictly necessary (E Ip29), we can moderate our passionate reactions to events. The problem with passions is precisely that, when they affect us, we are passive. Our action follows some desire (*cupiditas*) for some external thing which we love, or from some desire to eliminate some external thing which we hate. In both cases we are not free in Spinoza's sense of freedom (cf. E Id7; IV Preface). Controlling passions means going from a state of passivity to a state of activity in which we are the adequate (that is, complete) cause of our action rather than being affected by things external to us. This is of course only partially possible for human beings, who in many cases cannot but be affected by external things (cf. E IVp3). Therefore we cannot completely eliminate the way in which passions affect us but we can minimize it (cf. E Vp20s). Since 'the passions depend on inadequate ideas alone' (E IIIp3) and the mind is necessarily active 'insofar as it has adequate ideas' (E IIIp1), acquiring adequate ideas is *ipso facto* becoming active.

We are affected by *laetitia* (joy) when 'the Mind passes to a greater perfection', and by *tristitia* (sadness) when our mind 'passes to a lesser perfection' (E IIIp11s), and 'the more perfection each thing has, the more it acts and the less it is acted on' (E Vp40). *Laetitia*, *tristitia*, and *cupiditas* (desire)—that is, 'the very essence of man (by Def. Aff. I),

[42] Cf. Garrett 1996: 279.

[43] Cf. Garrett 1996: 286–8. It is debated in the literature whether Spinoza's doctrine of freedom is ultimately incoherent, whether completely different accounts of freedom are given in different contexts, and whether these different accounts can be reconciled. See for instance Bennett 1984: ch. 13 (especially 324–8); James 1996; Sorrell 2008; Kisner 2011.

i.e. (by IIIP7), a striving by which a man strives to persevere in his being' (E IV Dem. of p18)—are the three primary affects (emotions) from which all the others arise (E IIIp11s). Spinoza explains in the last part of the *Ethics* (E V p20s) what 'the power of the Mind over the affects' consists of. His list includes 'the knowledge itself of the affects' and the separation of 'affects from the thought of an external cause, which we imagine confusedly'. It concludes with the observation that 'sickness of the mind and misfortunes take their origin especially from too much Love toward a thing which is liable to many variations and which we can never fully possess. For no one is disturbed or anxious concerning anything unless he loves it, nor do wrongs, suspicions, and enmities arise except from Love for a thing which no one can really fully possess' (E Vp20s).

There can be little doubt that Spinoza's ethics is in key respects deeply indebted, on the one hand, to Hobbes' outlook,[44] and on the other hand, to Stoicism.[45] It is also clear that it runs directly against the Platonic tradition of an objective metaphysical goodness: 'we neither strive for, nor will, neither want, nor desire anything because we judge it to be good; on the contrary, we judge something to be good because we strive for it, will it, want it, and desire it' (E IIIp9s). There is no such thing as objective, metaphysical good and evil corresponding to the natures of things:[46]

> As far as good and evil are concerned, they also indicate nothing positive in things, considered in themselves, nor are they anything other than modes of thinking, or notions we form because we compare things to one another. For one and the same thing can, at the same time, be good, and bad, and also indifferent. (E Preface of Part IV)

Things are just what they are—neither good nor bad in themselves. Likewise 'Perfection and imperfection... are only modes of thinking, i.e. notions we are accustomed to feign because we compare individuals of the same species or genus to one another. This is why I said above (IId6) that by reality and perfection I understand the same thing' (E Preface of Part IV).

There is, however, a complementary perspective from which to observe this. If there is in fact a sense in which Spinoza challenges what Platonism stands for, in another sense the entire thrust of Spinoza's system uses a Platonic/Neoplatonic blueprint for its own subversive outcome.[47] Once God has been posited, everything necessarily follows with no spare, un-chosen, non-existing possible being left. As in Neoplatonism, all possible beings necessarily exist as a result of the ineluctable emanative power of God. It is debatable

[44] Garrett 1996: 267–8. Curley emphasises 'how Spinoza might have arrived at many of his most distinctive doctrines through critical reflection on the Cartesian and Hobbesian systems' (Curley 1988: xii). The relation between Spinoza and Hobbes is the object of numerous studies (see for instance Bertman and Herman de Dijn 1986; Di Vona 1992; Malcolm 2002, especially 46–52).

[45] James 1998: 1374. See also James 1993 and Pereboom 1994. On Spinoza's views of the passions in the context of seventeenth-century philosophy see James 1997.

[46] Curley 1973 explains Spinoza's metaethical theory in terms of a conception of goodness and perfection in which things are judged good or perfect in relation to their approximate or absolute agreement with subjective and variable standards supplied by the general, confused, and arbitrary ideas different people have of the kind of thing in question.

[47] Ayers 2007b: 7 and 78.

whether the identity of God and nature means that God is the whole of nature—that is, both the *natura naturans* (the active aspect of God) and the *natura naturata* (the modes of God which follow 'from the necessity of God's nature' (E Ip29s)), or whether God is, strictly speaking, only the *natura naturans*.[48] But whatever the case, for Spinoza nothing can exist or be conceived apart from God in a much stronger way than orthodox views in which God creates and conserves everything in being. Spinoza's ontology, in which only God qualifies as substance, is *par excellence* the ontology in which the infinite and the absolute is prior to the finite, and the finite is intelligible only in relation to the infinite. Despite dismissing the categories of perfection and imperfection as 'only modes of thinking', Spinoza is in fact radicalizing the Platonic identification of degrees of reality with degrees of perfection by directly identifying reality and perfection (see E IId6).

Likewise, Spinoza's conception of immortality and his idiosyncratic soteriology are in a sense extreme versions of the Neoplatonic return to the One and of the Platonic ascent. One of the reasons why Spinoza is so relevant to contemporary debates is his indication of the identity between the human mind and the human body.[49] On the other hand, Spinoza's metaphysics of mind and body is not easily categorized within present-day physicalist positions. There is an eternal part of the mind which survives (although arguably not in the sense of personal identity) the death of the body: 'the human Mind cannot be absolutely destroyed with the Body, but something of it remains which is eternal' (E Vp23; cf. the final words of E Vp20s introducing Prop. 21–40).[50] Spinoza's key thesis that moral life is aimed at our self-preservation seems also to mean that survival ultimately depends on the enlargement of this eternal part of our mind by increasing the portion of our ideas which are adequate ideas. As in Platonism, we have to turn away from the deceiving testimony of the senses, from *doxa* or opinion based on inadequate ideas, and follow reason. In a way reminiscent of the immortal better part of the Platonic tripartite soul—the rational soul—that portion of the mind which has been able to see from the perspective of the eternal (*sub aeternitatis specie*) will in some form survive death (cf. E Vp29–30). Ideas, in turn, are in the strongest sense all *ideae in mente Dei* ('all ideas are in God' E II Dem. of p36; see also E II Dem. of p5; E Ip15). In so far as we obtain any adequate ideas, we participate in God's own cognition. Immortality is a sort of complete return to God in which the survival of the mind grows in proportion to our mind's adequate ideas. Morality is, basically, to understand that humankind is intelligible only in relation to God in the most radical sense: 'Insofar as our Mind knows itself and the Body from the perspective of the eternal, it necessarily has knowledge of God, and

---

[48] Cf. Nadler 2009: § 2.1.   [49] Cf. Garrett 1996: 270–1, 308; Ayers 1998: 1016.

[50] Spinoza's doctrine of immortality is one of the most baffling aspects of his thought. It has given rise to a variety of interpretations ranging from regarding it as 'rubbish' (Bennett 1984: 374) or, more mildly, as an embarrassing mystical lapse, to a doctrine proposing a kind of immortality that does not imply personal identity, to a robust affirmation of the personal immortality of the soul. According to Wolfson 1934 and Donogan 1973 Spinoza does have a doctrine of personal immortality; according to Nadler 2001 Spinoza denies the immortality of the soul; Garrett 2009: 302 argues that, although there is no personal immortality, human beings can 'achieve a mind the greater part of which is eternal'. Amongst others, see also the interesting discussions of Kneale 1973 and Harris 1975.

knows that it is in God and is conceived through God' (E V p30).[51] The intellectual love of God—reminiscent, once again, of Platonic love, and arising from the intuitive knowledge of the essences of things based on an adequate understanding of the essence God—is the highest virtue (cf. E Vp33 and p36; E IIp40sII; E IIp47; E IVp28).

In stretching the priority of the perfect / infinite to its limit, Spinoza poses the most difficult challenge of all to the classical, Augustine-tinted theism embraced (albeit with debatable orthodoxy) by Descartes, Malebranche, and Leibniz. As Cicero had written in *De Natura Deorum*, and Hume later wrote in the *Dialogues concerning Natural Religion*, no one can reasonably doubt that God exists, but the question is: what is the *nature* of God.[52] God could turn out to be all that there is, namely nature. It is not by chance that Malebranche and Leibniz were haunted by the shadow of Spinoza and devoted so much energy in freeing themselves from it. One of the greatest challenges of those theists who affirm the priority of the perfect / infinite is to avoid Spinozism. Descartes tried to avoid it (*ante litteram*) by affirming what Spinoza (as well as Malebranche and Leibniz) would later on think of as unthinkable, namely that the nature of a triangle could have been different from what it is, and that good and evil depend on God's will.[53]

Bibliography

Abbreviations

A: Leibniz, G. W. *Sämtliche Schriften und Briefe*. ed. by the Academy of Sciences of Berlin. Series I–VIII. Darmstadt, Leipzig, and Berlin, 1923 ff. Cited by series, volume, and page.

AT: Descartes, René. *Oeuvres de Descartes*. 11 vols. ed. by Charles Adam and Paul Tannery. Paris: Léopold Cerf, 1897–1909. Cited by volume and page.

Cicero, *De Natura Deorum*: Cicero, Marcus Tullius. *De Natura Deorum*. 45 B.C. Cambridge, MA: Harvard University Press; London: Heinemann, 1979. In Loeb classical library, 268; Cicero, Marcus Tullius. *Works*. English and Latin, 19.

CSM / CSMK: Descartes, René. *The Philosophical Writings of Descartes*. 3 vols. trans. by John Cottingham, Robert Stoothoff, and Dugald Murdoch (volume 3 including Anthony Kenny; cited as CSMK). Cambridge: Cambridge University Press, 1988. Cited by volume and page.

DUTENS: Leibniz, G. W. *Opera omnia, nunc primum collecta, in classes distributa, praefationibus et indicibus exornata*. 6 vols. ed. L. Dutens. Geneva: De Tournes, 1768. Cited by volume, part, and page.

E: Spinoza, Baruch. *Ethica Ordine Geometrico Demonstrata*. In Benedictus de Spinoza. *Opera*. Vol. 2. ed. by Carl Gebhardt. Heidelberg: C. Winter, 1925. trans. by Edwin Curley in *The Collected Writings of Spinoza*. Vol. 1. Princeton: Princeton University Press, 1985. References to the *Ethics* are by part (I–V), proposition (p), definition (d), scholium (s), and corollary (c).

[51] I have slightly modified Curley's translation.
[52] Cf.Cicero, *De Natura Deorum*, Book II, §§44–46, pp. 164–6 and Hume, *Dialogues*, Part II, pp. 44–5.
[53] I would like to thank Michael Ayers, Roger Crisp, and my colleagues in the philosophy department at King's College London for their helpful feedback. Howard Hotson read several drafts and contributed many perceptive comments.

Erdmann: Leibniz, G. W. *Opera philosophica quae extant Latina Gallica Germanica omnia*. Ed. by J. E. Erdmann. Berlin, 1839–1840.

GP: Leibniz, G. W. *Die Philosophischen Schriften*. ed. by C. I. Gerhardt. 7 vols. Berlin: Weidmannsche Buchhandlung, 1875–1890. Reprint, Hildesheim: Olms, 1960–1961. Cited by volume and page.

Grua: Leibniz, G. W. *Textes inédits d'après les manuscrits de la Bibliothèque Provinciale de Hanovre*. 2 vols. ed. by G. Grua. Paris: Presses Universitaires de France, 1948.

H: Leibniz, G. W. *Theodicy: Essays on the Goodness of God, the Freedom of Man, and the Origin of Evil*. trans. by E. M. Huggard. LaSalle, Ill.: Open Court, 1985.

Hume, *Dialogues*: Hume, David. *Dialogues concerning Natural Religion*. Second edition. London, 1779.

JS: Malebranche, Nicolas. 1997a. *Dialogues on Metaphysics and on Religion*. trans. by N. Jolley and D. Scott. Cambridge: Cambridge University Press.

K: Leibniz, G. W. *Die Werke*. ed. by O. Klopp. 11 vols. Hannover: Klindworth, 1864–1884.

L: Leibniz, G. W. *Philosophical Papers and Letters*. ed. and trans. by L. E. Loemker. 2nd edn. Dordrecht: Reidel, 1969.

LO: Malebranche, Nicolas. *The Search after Truth*. trans. by T. M. Lennon and P. J. Olscamp. Columbus: Ohio State University Press, 1980; Cambridge: Cambridge University Press, 1997. Citations are from the Cambridge edition.

OC: Malebranche, Nicolas. *Oeuvres complètes de Malebranche*. 20 vols. ed. by A. Robinet. Paris: J. Vrin, 1958–1984. Cited by volume and page.

PW: Leibniz, G. W. *The Political Writings of Leibniz*. trans. and ed. with an introduction by Patrick Riley. Cambridge: Cambridge University Press, 1972.

RB: Leibniz, G. W. *New Essays on Human Understanding*. ed. and trans. by Peter Remnant and Jonathan Bennett. Cambridge: Cambridge University Press, 1981.

W: Leibniz, G. W. *Selections*. ed. and trans. Philip P. Wiener. New York: Scribner, 1951.

Other Works Cited

Adams, R. M. 1994. *Leibniz: Determinist, Theist, Idealist*. New York and Oxford: Oxford University Press.

—— 2007. 'The Priority of the Perfect in the Philosophical Theology of the Continental Rationalists', in Ayers 2007a, 91–116.

Antognazza, M. R. 2007. 'Comments on Adams, "The Priority of the Perfect"', in Ayers 2007a, 117–31.

—— 2009. *Leibniz: An Intellectual Biography*. New York and Cambridge: Cambridge University Press.

Ariew, R. and M. Grene (eds) 1995. *Descartes and His Contemporaries*. Chicago: University of Chicago Press.

Ayers, M. 1998. 'Theories of Knowledge and Belief', in D. Garber and M. Ayers 1998, 1003–61.

—— 2007a. *Rationalism, Platonism and God: A Symposium on Early Modern Philosophy*. Proceedings of the British Academy, vol. 149. Oxford: Oxford University Press.

—— (ed.) 2007b. 'Introduction' and 'Spinoza, Platonism and Naturalism', in Ayers 2007a, pp. 1–14 and 53–78.

Bennett, J. 1984. *A Study of Spinoza's Ethics*. Cambridge: Cambridge University Press.

—— 1996. 'Spinoza's metaphysics', in Garrett 1996, 61–88.

—— 2001. *Learning from Six philosophers: Descartes, Spinoza, Leibniz, Locke, Berkeley, Hume*. 2 vols. Oxford: Clarendon Press.

Bertman, M.A. and M. W. Herman de Dijn (eds) 1986. *Spinoza and Hobbes.* [*Studia Spinozana.* 3 (1987)] Alling: Walther & Walther.

Blumenfeld, D. 1995. 'Perfection and Happiness in the Best Possible World', in Jolley 1995, 382–410.

Brown, D. 2006. *Descartes and the Passionate Mind.* Cambridge: Cambridge University Press.

Brown, G. 1988. 'Leibniz's Theodicy and the Confluence of Wordly Goods', *Journal of the History of Philosophy* 26: 571–91.

—— 1995. 'Leibniz's Moral Philosophy', in Jolley 1995, 411–41.

—— 2011. 'Disinterested Love: Understanding Leibniz's Reconciliation of Self and Other-Regarding Motives', *British Journal for the History of Philosophy* 19: 265–303.

Chappell, V. 1997. 'Descartes's Ontology', *Topoi* 16: 111–27.

Cottingham, J. (ed.) 1992. *The Cambridge Companion to Descartes.* New York and Cambridge: Cambridge University Press.

—— 1998. *Philosophy and the Good Life: Reason and the Passions in Greek, Cartesian and Psychoanalytic Ethics.* Cambridge: Cambridge University Press.

—— 2007. 'Plato's Sun and Descartes's Stove: Contemplation and Control in Cartesian Philosophy', in Ayers 2007a, 15–44.

Curley, E. 1973. 'Spinoza's Moral Philosophy', in Grene 1973, 354–76.

—— 1984. 'Descartes and the Creation of the Eternal Truths', *The Philosophical Review* 93: 569–97.

—— 1988. *Behind the Geometrical Method: A Reading of Spinoza's Ethics.* Princeton: Princeton University Press.

Della Rocca, M. 2003. 'A Rationalist Manifesto: Spinoza and the Principle of Sufficient Reason', *Philosophical Topics* 31: 75–93.

Di Vona, P. 1992. *Aspetti di Hobbes in Spinoza.* Naples: Loffredo.

Donogan, A. 1973. 'Spinoza's Proof of Immortality', in Grene 1973, 241–58.

Freeman, E. and M. Mandelbaum (eds) 1975. *Spinoza: Essays In Interpretation.* La Salle, Illinois: Open Court.

Garber, D. and M. Ayers (eds) 1998. *The Cambridge History of Seventeenth-Century Philosophy.* Cambridge: Cambridge University Press.

Garrett, D. 1996. 'Spinoza's Ethical Theory', in D. Garrett (ed.), *The Cambridge Companion to Spinoza.* Cambridge and New York: Cambridge University Press, 267–314.

—— 2009. 'Spinoza on the Essence of the Human Body and the Part of the Mind that is Eternal', in Koistinen 2009, 284–302.

Gaukroger, S. 1995. *Descartes: An Intellectual Biography.* Oxford: Clarendon Press.

—— 2002. *Descartes' System of Natural Philosophy.* Cambridge: Cambridge University Press.

Grene, M. (ed.) 1973. *Spinoza: A Collection of Critical Essays.* Notre Dame, Indiana: University of Notre Dame Press.

Gueroult, M. 1984–1985. *Descartes' Philosophy Interpreted According to the Order of Reasons.* Trans. by Roger Ariew. With the Assistance of Robert Ariew and Alan Donagan. 2 vols. Minneapolis: University of Minnesota Press.

Harris, E. E. 1975. 'Spinoza's Theory of Human Immortality', in Freeman and Mandelbaum 1975, 245–62.

Hatfield, G. 2003. *Descartes and the Meditations.* London: Routledge.

Heinekamp, A. 1969. *Das Problem des Guten bei Leibniz.* Bonn: H. Bouvier u. Co. Verlag.

—— 1989. 'Das Glück als höchstes Gut in Leibniz' Philosophie', in *The Leibniz Renaissance. International Workshop (Firenze 1986).* Florence: Olschki, 99–125.

Hoffman, P., D. Owen, and G. Yaffe 2008. *Contemporary Perspectives on Early Modern Philosophy: Essays in Honor of Vere Chappell.* Peterborough, Ont.: Broadview Press.

Huenemann, C. (ed.) 2008. *Interpreting Spinoza: Critical Essays*. Cambridge: Cambridge University Press.

James, S. 1993. 'Spinoza the Stoic', in Sorrell 1993, 289–316.

—— 1996. 'Power and Difference: Spinoza's Conception of Freedom', *Journal of Political Philosophy* 4: 207–28.

—— 1997. *Passion and Action: The Emotions in Seventeenth-Century Philosophy*. Oxford: Clarendon Press.

—— 1998. 'Reason, the Passions, and the Good Life', in Garber and Ayers 1998, 1358–96.

—— 2009. 'Freedom, Slavery and the Passions', in Koistinen 2009, 223–41.

Jolley, N. 1990. *The Light of the Soul: Theories of Ideas in Leibniz, Malebranche, and Descartes*. Oxford: Clarendon Press; Oxford and New York: Oxford University Press.

—— (ed.) 1995. *The Cambridge Companion to Leibniz*. Cambridge and New York: Cambridge University Press.

Kenny, A. 1970. 'The Cartesian Circle and the Eternal Truths', *Journal of Philosophy* 57: 685–700.

Kisner, M. 2011. *Spinoza on Human Freedom*. Cambridge: Cambridge University Press.

Kneale, M. 1973. 'Eternity and Sempiternity', in Grene 1973, 227–40. Originally published in *Proceedings of the Aristotelian Society* 69 (1969): 223–38.

Koistinen, O. (ed.) 2009. *The Cambridge Companion to Spinoza's Ethics*. Cambridge: Cambridge University Press.

Kraye, J. 1998. 'Conceptions of Moral Philosophy', in Garber and Ayers 1998, 1279–316.

Kremer, E. J. 2000. 'Malebranche on Human Freedom', in Nadler 2000, 190–219.

Lennon, T. M. 1993. *The Battle of the Gods and Giants: The Legacies of Descartes and Gassendi, 1655–1715*. Princeton: Princeton University Press.

Malcolm, N. 2002. 'Hobbes and Spinoza', in *Aspects of Hobbes*. Oxford: Clarendon Press, 27–52.

Marshall, J. 1998. *Descartes's Moral Theory*. Ithaca and London: Cornell University Press.

Mollat, G. 1885. *Rechsphilosophisches aus Leibnizens Ungedruckten Schriften*. Leipzig: Verlag Robolski.

Morgan, V. G. 1994. *Foundations of Cartesian Ethics*. Atlantic Highlands, NJ: Humanities Press.

Nadler, S. 1992. *Malebranche and Ideas*. New York and Oxford: Oxford University Press.

—— (ed) 2000: *The Cambridge Companion to Malebranche*. Cambridge: Cambridge University Press.

—— 2001. *Spinoza's Heresy. Immortality and the Jewish Mind*. Oxford: Clarendon Press.

—— 2009. 'Baruch Spinoza', *The Stanford Encyclopedia of Philosophy* (Winter 2009 edition), E. N. Zalta (ed.), <http://plato.stanford.edu/archives/win2009/entries/spinoza>.

Nolan, L. 1997. 'The Ontological Status of Cartesian Natures', *Pacific Philosophical Quarterly* 78: 169–94.

—— 2008. 'Malebranche's Theory of Ideas and Vision in God', *The Stanford Encyclopedia of Philosophy* (Fall 2008 edition), E. N. Zalta (ed.), <http://plato.stanford.edu/archives/fall2008/entries/malebranche-ideas>.

Osler, M. J. 1994. *Divine Will and the Mechanical Philosophy: Gassendi and Descartes on Contingency and Necessity in the Created World*. Cambridge: Cambridge University Press.

—— 1995. 'Divine Will and Mathematical Truth: Gassendi and Descartes on the Status of the Eternal Truths', in Ariew and Grene 1995, 145–58.

Pereboom, D. 1994. 'Stoic Psychotherapy in Descartes and Spinoza', *Faith and Philosophy* 11: 592–625.

Riley, P. 1996. *Leibniz's Universal Jurisprudence. Justice as the Charity of the Wise*. Cambridge, MA: Harvard University Press.

—— 2000. 'Malebranche's Moral Philosophy', in Nadler 2000, 220–61.

—— 2009. 'Malebranche and "Cartesianized Augustinianism" ', in *A Treatise of Legal Philosophy and General Jurisprudence*. Springer Netherlands, 2009, 463–90.

Rodis-Lewis, G. 1962. *La Morale de Descartes*. Paris: Presses Universitaires de France.

Rorty, A. O. 1992. 'Descartes on Thinking with the Body', in Cottingham 1992, 371–92.

Rozemond, M. 2008. 'Descartes's Ontology of the Eternal Truths', in Hoffman, Owen, and Yaffe 2008, 41–63.

Rutherford, D. 1995. *Leibniz and the Rational Order of Nature*. Cambridge: Cambridge University Press.

—— 2008. 'Descartes' Ethics', *The Stanford Encyclopedia of Philosophy* (Winter 2008 Edition), E. N. Zalta (ed.), <http://plato.stanford.edu/archives/win2008/entries/descartes-ethics>.

Schmaltz, T. M. 1991. 'Platonism and Descartes's View of Immutable Essences', *Archiv für die Geschichte der Philosophie* 73: 129–70.

—— 1996. *Malebranche's Theory of the Soul: A Cartesian Interpretation*. New York: Oxford University Press.

—— 2000. 'Malebranche on Ideas and the Vision in God', in Nadler 2000, 59–86.

—— 2009. 'Nicolas Malebranche'. *The Stanford Encyclopedia of Philosophy* (Winter 2009 Edition), E. N. Zalta (ed.), <http://plato.stanford.edu/archives/win2009/entries/malebranche>.

Sorrell, T. (ed.) 1993. *The Rise of Modern Philosophy*. Oxford: Oxford University Press.

—— 2008. 'Spinoza's unstable politics of freedom', in Huenemann 2008, 147–65.

Verga, L. 1974. *L' etica di Cartesio*. Milan: Celuc.

Williston, B. and A. Gombay (eds) 2003. *Passion and Virtue in Descartes*. Amherst, NY: Humanity Books.

Wolfson, H. A. 1934. *The Philosophy of Spinoza*. 2 vols. Cambridge, MA: Harvard University Press.

CHAPTER 16

....

RATIONAL INTUITIONISM

....

PHILIP STRATTON-LAKE

16.1 INTRODUCTION

THE term 'intuitionism' is applied to many diverse British moral philosophers from the seventeenth century onwards. It may be used to refer to sentimentalists, or 'moral sense' theorists, such as Shaftesbury and Hutcheson, consequentialists, such as Sidgwick and Moore, as well as pluralists such as Clarke, Price, Prichard, and Ross. In this chapter I will be focusing solely on rationalist intuitionists, so will say nothing about Hutcheson and Shaftesbury.

What distinguishes rationalist and sentimentalist intuitionists is their moral episte-mology and their account of how we acquire basic moral concepts, or ideas. For the sen-timentalists, moral judgements refer to or express our sentiments, and the ideas of right and wrong, good and bad, are empirically given, and grasped by feeling. Rationalists do not deny that when we judge that some act is wrong we express feelings of disapproval,[1] but deny that this is all that is going on, and regard such feelings as secondary. We judge, they maintain, that the object of our disapproval has a certain moral property, and dis-approve of it on that ground. Moral properties are real properties of things, or as the early intuitionists would say, part of the nature, or 'reason', of things, there to be discov-ered. Ross summed up this view nicely when he wrote that:

> The moral order expressed in these propositions is just as much part of the funda-mental nature of the universe (and, we may add, of any possible universe in which there were moral agents at all) as is the spatial or numerical structure expressed in the axioms of geometry or arithmetic. (2002 [1930]: 29–30)

---

[1] See e.g. Ross 1939: 255:

> [W]hat we *express* when we call an object good is our attitude towards it, but what we *mean* is something about the object itself and not about our attitude towards it. When we call an object good we are commending it, but to commend it is not to say that we are commending it, but to say that it has a certain characteristic, which we think it would have whether we commended it or not.

See also Ross 1939: 261 and Price 1969 [1758]: 144.

So for the rationalist intuitionists moral judgements are truth-apt claims which, when true, pick out essential moral properties of certain things. Indeed, it was this moral objectivism and essentialism, rather than their epistemological doctrine, or pluralistic normative theory, that early intuitionists, such as Cudworth, Clarke, Balguy, and Price, seemed most concerned to prove.[2]

Although Sidgwick and Moore are rationalists in the specified sense, some people may deny that they are intuitionists, as they are monists about the right—that is, they maintain that there is only one foundational moral principle regarding what we ought to do—and because they allow that the rightness of all actions is capable of 'proof or disproof by an enquiry into the results of such actions' (Moore 1993a [1903]: 35). It is for this reason that Moore himself denied that he was an intuitionist (Moore 1993a [1903]: 35).

But I see no problem with labelling Sidgwick and Moore 'intuitionists', so long as we distinguish different types of intuitionism. Bernard Williams (1995: 182) helpfully distinguished between epistemological and methodological intuitionists. Epistemological intuitionists maintain that basic moral principles or truths are self-evident, and so require no proof. In this sense, both Moore and Sidgwick are intuitionists, as they both maintain that their basic principles are self-evident. Methodological intuitionists, on the other hand, maintain that there is an irreducible plurality of basic moral principles, and that there is no higher-order principle by means of which conflicts between these principles may be resolved. Methodological intuitionists maintain that all attempts to ground the whole of morality in a single principle (egoist, consequentialist, Kantian, etc.) must fail, so most of their arguments are negative, criticizing various monistic theories. This argumentative strategy may seem unsatisfactory to some, but I see no way for pluralists to argue for their view other than by attacking monistic theories.

Methodological intuitionists need not be epistemological intuitionists—although all of the classical intuitionists are—and conversely, not all epistemological intuitionists need be methodological intuitionists.[3] This means that monists, such as Sidgwick and Moore, may quite legitimately be called intuitionists, for their epistemology is clearly intuitionistic.[4]

Another reason for including Sidgwick and Moore is their moral ontology. Both held that moral judgements are truth-apt claims which aim to represent the way things are morally. They also maintained that the way things are morally—i.e. moral properties— is non-natural, although it is unclear what Moore meant by a non-natural property. In this they agree with all other intuitionists.

---

[2] It was with Sidgwick that the emphasis shifted to epistemological issues and whether morality could be grounded in a single, consequentialist principle.

[3] It is also worth noting that not all pluralists are methodological intuitionists, for a rationalized pluralism might have priority rules. Methodological intuitionists form, therefore, a sub-class of pluralist theories. In what follows, however, I shall use the term 'methodological intuitionism' and 'pluralism' interchangeably.

[4] We might also maintain that Moore is a methodological intuitionist in relation to the good, as he held that there is a plurality of intrinsically good things.

16.2 OBJECTIVITY

Although early intuitionists such as Cudworth, Clarke, and Balguy, were methodological and epistemological intuitionists, this is not the aspect of their view that they tended to emphasize. Rather, they seemed more concerned to argue that morality is objective. The impetus for this focus was primarily Hobbes' claim that morality is nothing more than a set of rules agreed on in order that we might live better, and longer, lives. Prior to such an agreement there is, on Hobbes' view, no right or wrong, good or bad, just or unjust acts; everything in its own nature is indifferent, and acquires any moral nature it has by the will and agreement of the community.

Of course, there is a sense in which morality is objective according to Hobbes' theory, as, for him, there are objective moral norms after the original contract, and if one acts contrary to these norms, then one has acted wrongly, irrespective of what one believes, feels, or desires. But this is not the sense of objectivity that the intuitionists sought to defend. Their view was that moral right and wrong, justice and injustice, are objective in the literal sense—that is, these are properties of *objects*—and by this they mean that these are real properties of things, or part of their objective nature. So, for instance, it is part of the objective nature of acts of beneficence, gratitude, fidelity to promises, etc., that they are fit to be done, and their contrary unfit. It is because moral properties are part of the objective nature of certain acts, relations, and things, that we cannot make it the case that acts that are in themselves morally indifferent prior to any act of will or contract, fit to be done after some act of will or contract, any more than we can make colourless objects coloured by an act of will or social contract. Cudworth (1969 [1731]: 107) wrote:

> when things exist, they are what they are, this or that, absolutely or relatively, not by will or arbitrary command, but by the necessity of their own nature.

Even God, Cudworth maintained, could not by an arbitrary decree create an obligation in us to do what he commands:

> no positive commands whatsoever do make any thing morally good and evil, just or unjust, which nature had not made such before. For indifferent things commanded, considered materially in themselves, remain still what they were before in their own nature, that is, indifferent, because (as Aristotle speaks) will cannot change nature. (1969 [1731]: 111)

Samuel Clarke also asserted that moral right and wrong, good and evil, could only stem from the nature of things, not from covenant or will. Contrary to Hobbes' view, Clarke maintained that certain actions are of a nature to be done, and certain relations are of a nature to make certain actions fitting.

> from the different relations of different persons one to another, there necessarily arises a fitness or unfitness of certain manners of behaviour of some persons towards others. (1969 [1706]: 192)

For instance, our relation to God of being his creation is such as to make it fitting for us to worship, honour, and imitate him; the relation that beneficiaries stand to their benefactors is of a nature to make it fitting for them to be grateful; the nature of the relation of promisor to promisee makes it fitting that one do whatever one has promised, and so on.

One might think that it is not these relations that make certain acts fitting, but rather relevant facts about those who stand in that relation. So, for instance, it is not the relation of being created by God that makes it fitting to honour him, but rather the fact that he has created us; and it is not the relation of promisor to promisee that makes it fitting to do what we have promised, but the fact that we have promised to do that act.[5] But this may be just another way of saying that it is particular instances of these relations, rather than the relations themselves, that make certain actions fitting.

Clarke went on to argue that Hobbes' own arguments presuppose that certain things are fitting to be done prior to any contract. Hobbes maintained that for the preservation of mankind men ought to enter into a compact to preserve one another. But, as Clarke rightly points out, if the destruction of mankind is such an evil that it is fit and reasonable that men enter into a compact to avoid it:

> then it was manifestly a thing unfit and unreasonable in itself that men should all destroy one another. And if so, then for the same reason it was also unfit and unreasonable, antecedent to all compacts, that any man should destroy another arbitrarily and without any provocation, or at any time when it was not absolutely and immediately necessary for the preservation of himself. (1969 [1706]: 195)

But this contradicts Hobbes' view that nothing is in itself good or evil, just or unjust, prior to compact and positive law.

Both Cudworth and Clarke go on to maintain that because certain relations and things are, by their nature, such as to make certain acts fitting, and that certain actions are themselves fit to be done, that their fittingness is eternal and immutable. But it is difficult to see how immutability follows from the claim that moral qualities are real qualities in objects. The shape of something is an objective feature of it—that is, a real property of the thing—but it does not follow from this that a thing's shape is immutable and eternal. On the contrary, this, and many other objective properties of things are temporary and changeable. So how can intuitionists such as Cudworth, Clarke, Price, and Balguy jump from the view that certain moral qualities are part of the nature of certain things and relations prior to any compact or act of will, to the view that the moral character of these things cannot change?

Cudworth argues that things that are good cannot be otherwise as this would imply that 'things should be what they are not' (1969 [1731]: 107). But that something that is good might cease to be good in no way entails that it is what it is not, any more than a thing that changes from red to blue over time entails that it is no longer what it is (though of course it is no longer what it was). He states that things are 'white by whiteness, and black by blackness, triangular by triangularity, and round by rotundity' (1969 [1731]: 106), but in claiming that the value of things can change, one is not claiming that something

---

[5] Ross oscillates on this point. Compare, e.g. 2002 [1930]: 17 and 19.

can cease to be good whilst retaining the property of being good, or remain good whilst losing that property.

The intuitionists claimed that the goodness of certain things is part of their essential nature, and if that is true then clearly if those things are good then their goodness will not be contingent. But that moral qualities are part of their essential nature doesn't follow from those qualities being real properties of things, and may be true even if goodness were not a real property of things.[6]

Furthermore, one might plausibly think that certain things are intrinsically good— that is, good solely in virtue of their intrinsic, or internal, nature—though not essentially good. Pleasure might be one such thing. It may be good in virtue of its pleasant nature, and so intrinsically good, but only under certain conditions, e.g. that it is deserved, or not caused by things which are themselves bad. Indeed this seems to be Kant's view about happiness.[7] Certain thick evaluative properties like courage, or generosity, may be good by definition, and so essentially good, but not all goods are thick in this way, and it is hard to defend the view that they are all good by definition.

16.3 RIGHT-MAKING AND REASONS

To get from the idea of moral properties as *objective* features of things to their being *essential* features of certain things one cannot think of these properties as simply added to the other genuine properties of things. One would have to regard them as in some way determined by those other properties such that, as long as an act, disposition, or thing has those other properties, it will have its moral property. This idea of moral properties supervening[8] on other properties is, I think, most clearly laid out by Moore 1993b [1922] and Ross 2002 [1930], but it is also clear that earlier intuitionists endorsed such a view, albeit less clearly than Moore and Ross.

Balguy (1969 [1729]: 404), for instance, seems to have this idea in mind when he says that the fact that I have received a benefit from A *explains why* I ought to be grateful to A. He complicates matters by adding two further thin deontic properties between the benefit and the fact that I ought to be grateful—namely, fittingness and reasonableness. His view seems to be that we ought to be grateful to our benefactors because gratitude is here reasonable, it is reasonable because it is fitting, and it is fitting because they have

---

[6] One might think that God exists necessarily, yet deny that existence is a real property. Similarly one might claim that gratitude, or beneficence, is necessarily good, yet deny that goodness is a real property of things. See Stratton-Lake 2009.

[7] See Stratton-Lake 2000, and Ross 2002: 136–8.

[8] The relevant notion of supervenience is local, not global—that is, the base properties are restricted to (real) properties of the good object (however these are to be defined), not complete ways a world may be. However, at least some relational properties would have to be included in the base properties, as intuitionists clearly thought that relational properties of acts, such as the property an act might have of being the fulfilling of a promise to someone, can determine the moral nature of that act.

benefited us in the past (1969 [1729]: 404–5).[9] I'm not sure that the addition of reasonableness and fittingness really adds to the explanation of why we ought to be grateful to our bene-factors,[10] but that is not really very important. If the fact that I ought to be grateful to A depends solely on the fact that A benefited me in the past (or this plus the fact that my gratitude is fitting and reasonable), then it is plausible to suppose that certain acts of benefiting me[11] are of a nature to make it the case that I ought to show gratitude.

It is a separate question whether something's being of a nature to make gratitude right or fitting implies that gratitude is immutably and eternally fitting, if this is taken to mean universally and always fitting. One might allow that the fact that one has made a promise to Φ is a fact that is of a nature to make it fitting for me to Φ, but think that this disposi-tion to make fitting may be cancelled by other facts, such as the fact that my promise was made under duress, or that it was a promise to do something evil, or that the promisee has freed the promisor from his promise. Alternatively, one might think that the right-making fact is more complex than the intuitionists maintained, such that they include the absence of these cancelling conditions.[12]

Balguy is one of the few intuitionists to talk explicitly of reasons to act, and this is important in relation to the idea of a right-making feature. He maintains not only that we ought to be grateful because we have received some benefit, but also claims that 'every man who receives a benefit, receives along with it a reason for gratitude' (1969 [1729]: 405). So the fact that A benefits me not only explains why (or at least figures in an expla-nation why) I ought to be grateful, but also gives me a reason to be grateful, according to Balguy. The ground of the duty of gratitude is thus a reason in a twofold sense.

This seems to me to be a quite general point about the connection between right-making features and reasons for action. If this is right, then the following principle is true:

If F explains why I ought to Φ, then F will be a reason for me to Φ.

This is important, I believe, in a number of ways, not least because it provides an easy answer to one version of the sceptical question: 'Why be moral?' Standardly we come to

---

[9] 'Between *bounty* and *gratitude* there is a plain congruity of moral *fitness*; and between *bounty* and *ingratitude* a plain incongruity of moral *unfitness.*—Therefore gratitude is *reasonable*, and ingratitude *unreasonable.*—Therefore the one ought to be *observed*, and the other *detested.*' (Balguy 1969 [1729]: 405)

[10] Price (1969 [1758]: 161) makes a similar point on the ground that the terms 'fit', 'reasonable', and 'right' are synonyms. If something's being fit and reasonable is just another way of saying that it is right, then its fitness and reasonableness cannot explain why it is right, or figure in such an explanation.

[11] I say certain acts of benefiting me, as this does not apply to all such acts. If you confer a benefit on me merely by accident, or solely because it is in your interest to do so, then your act will not make it the case that I ought to be grateful to you. This may mean that one has to add more detail to the nature of the act of beneficence, or alternatively one might claim that beneficent acts are of a nature to generate obligations, but this obligation-generating function may be cancelled under certain circumstances. Another option would be to think of the relevant acts in thick evaluative terms—that is, of beneficence as an act of benefiting which is good—such that benefits conferred for ulterior reasons would not count as beneficent acts at all. See Fitzgerald 1998 and Berger 1975.

[12] My own view is close to Jonathan Dancy's—namely that the latter view obscures the different ways in which certain facts may be relevant, and is to be rejected on that ground as oversimplifying. See Dancy 2006: ch. 3.

believe that we ought to Φ by judging that some consideration F makes it the case that we ought to Φ. If the above principle is correct, then once we have come to believe that we ought to Φ in this way, then we cannot have any insurmountable doubts about whether we have any reason to do what we judge we morally ought to do. If you ask me what reason you have to Φ, I will ask you why you think you ought to Φ. You will reply: 'because of F'. I will then say that F is your reason to Φ (at least if I think your explanation of why you ought to Φ is correct). Your belief that F is the reason why you ought to Φ commits you to believing that F is a reason for you to Φ. Of course you might not believe that you ought to Φ, and so you might be asking for a reason to believe that you ought to do this act. But this is not a form of moral scepticism, but rather simple moral debate and discussion.

If the ground of duty—the reason why I ought to do certain acts—is always a reason to do my duty, we may wonder whether duty itself provides a further reason. Although Balguy sometimes seems to suggest that he thinks that obligation, or virtue, is a reason to act, his definition of obligation seems to rule this out. He defines obligation as:

> a state of the mind into which it is brought by the perception of a plain reason for acting, or forbearing to act, arising from the nature, circumstances, or relations of the persons or things. (1969 [1729]: 398)

If this definition is correct, then I cannot judge that my obligation to be grateful is a reason to be grateful without this judgement, or perception, giving rise to another obligation (the state of mind brought into being by my perception of the first obligation as a plain reason to act). But if my being obligated to act is a reason to act, then this further obligation would be a further reason which, when perceived, would generate another obligation, and so on. So his definition of an obligation means that, if obligation itself is a reason to act, then we can never catch up in thought with the reasons it provides.[13]

But although other intuitionists sometimes describe obligation as a state of mind, perhaps we should abandon this definition of an obligation, and agree with other intuitionists that the property of being obligatory is not a state of the mind, but a real property of actions (or of agents). This would *allow* that the fact that I am obligated to be grateful is a reason to be grateful in addition to the reason provided by the fact that I have been benefited in some way. And one might think, as Kant seems committed to maintaining,[14] that this is *the* distinctive moral reason.

Despite the prevalence of this Kantian view, I think it is hard to sustain. Suppose you tell me that I ought to be grateful to Brad, and I ask you to list the reasons to be grateful to him. You reply by listing all the occasions when Brad has helped me in the past, often at considerable cost to himself. Suppose I am persuaded by this. It would be very odd for

---

[13] Price makes a similar point (1969 [1758]: 167).

[14] Kant does not speak of duty or obligation as a reason to act, but only as a motive of (good) action. I think he is committed to its being a reason to act as I take it that rational agents are motivated by what they regard as good reasons for action. So if duty is the moral motive, then it must be regarded as the moral reason by virtuous agents, and it would be very odd if Kant's theory implied that virtuous agents were wrong about this.

me to reply that you have not listed all of the reasons I have to be grateful to Brad, as you have not mentioned the fact that I ought (or am obligated) to be grateful to him.[15] Once we are clear that the ground of duty is reason-providing I would suggest that we will be far less tempted to insist that duty itself is reason-providing, and a fortiori that it is *the* moral reason, as many Kantians think.

16.4 THE SOURCE OF MORAL IDEAS

Cudworth, Price, and Balguy argued that our ideas of right and wrong, just and unjust, good and evil, have their source not in sentiment, or sensibility, as the moral sense theorists maintained, but in the understanding. Sense is, according to Price, a passive faculty that merely receives impressions. 'It lies prostrate under its object, and is only a capacity in the soul of having its own state altered by the influence of particular causes' (1969 [1758]: 136). The understanding, on the other hand, is a discerning and reflective faculty, which as such, is active. Sensibility is concerned solely with particulars—the particular impressions that are forced on it. General ideas arise only from reflection on those impressions, but such reflection is the work of the understanding. Finally, the understanding, but not sensibility, has the power to judge of certain things that they are true or false (1969 [1758]: 136).

The issue of whether our moral ideas have their source in sensibility or the understanding is bound up with the dispute about the objectivity of moral properties—that is, about whether they are real properties of things. Price ascribes to the sentimentalists the view that:

> Moral right and wrong, signify nothing *in the objects themselves* to which they are applied, any more than agreeable and harsh; sweet and bitter; pleasant and painful; but only *certain effects in us*. Our perception of *right*, or moral good, in actions, is that agreeable *emotion*, or feeling, which certain actions produce in us; and of *wrong*, or moral evil, the contrary. They are particular modifications of our minds, or impressions which they are made to receive from the contemplation of certain actions. (1969 [1758]: 133)

As Price understands them, then, the sentimentalists maintain that right and wrong are akin to secondary properties, at least on one interpretation of a secondary quality (which is the one that all of the intuitionists seem to work with).[16] Right and wrong are not real properties in things, and are not identified with powers in things to cause certain

---

[15] It might be claimed that although the fact that I ought to be grateful is not an additional reason to be grateful, it is nonetheless a reason to be grateful (see Schroeder 2009). I have to say that I have some difficulty making sense of this claim, but that is not important for my point here. If it is a reason to be grateful it should figure on an exhaustive list of the reasons to be grateful. My view is that to include it on such a list looks like a category mistake, though I do not quite know how to persuade someone of this if they claim not to see it.

[16] A more plausible interpretation of secondary qualities identifies them with dispositions (in objects) to cause certain mental states in us, rather than with the mental states caused by those dispositions.

positive or negative feelings in us, but are identified with the feelings caused in us, just as colour properties are identified with our colour sensations rather than with the powers in objects to cause those sensations. Thus, Price goes on to say:

> It is, therefore, by this account, improper to say of an action, that it *is right*, in much the same sense that it is improper to say of an object of taste, that it is *sweet*; or of *pain*, that it is *in* fire. (1969 [1758]: 133)

If right and wrong are just feelings of approval or disapproval caused in us by certain properties or objects, then the idea of right and wrong will be given by sense, for these ideas will be merely the effect that the perception of certain things has on sensibility. If, however, right and wrong were real properties of actions, then they could not be apprehended by any empirical sense, for we have no such sensation of right and wrong when we apprehend right or wrong actions. Rather what we see is that these actions are right, or wrong.[17] This seeing still counts as intuition, as it is an immediate apprehension (see the section on self-evidence below), but it is intellectual rather than sensible intuition.[18]

Price tries to persuade us that simple moral ideas have their source in the understanding by first arguing that many non-moral simple ideas originate in the understanding, and thus that the understanding is a source of new simple ideas.[19] The ideas of substance, duration, space, contingency, power, and causation are not given to sensibility. In clear anticipation of ideas later developed by Kant, Price claims that all we perceive through sense are the properties that inhere in certain substances, or the things that exist in space and time, the things and properties that are contingent, the effects of certain powers and causes, but never substance, space, time, contingency, power, and causation themselves. We certainly have ideas of these things (*pace* Hume), but they are not given through sense. And qua simple, they cannot have been constructed from other ideas given through sense. So they must have their source in the understanding.

> If, then, we indeed have such ideas; and if, besides, they have a foundation in truth [by which he means 'in the nature of things'], and are ideas of somewhat really existing corresponding to them, what difficulty can there be in granting they maybe apprehended by that faculty whose object is truth? (Price 1969 [1758]: 139)

That the understanding is the source of knowledge is not controversial, Price asserts. But if the understanding is the source of knowledge, then it must also be the source of new ideas

---

[17] This point applies only in cases where we do not conclude that some act is right or wrong by some form of reasoning.

[18] Cook Wilson (1926: 511 ff.) outlines a very similar view in 'Statement and Inference', and like Price, argues that simple ideas must be apprehended in reality, and cannot be invented, though they are not all apprehended by sense. Although Cook Wilson does not mention moral ideas, here he uses the same examples of simple non-moral ideas that are apprehended by the intellect as Price does, e.g. causality, substance, modality, time, etc.

[19] Following Hutcheson, Price regards a simple idea as one that can only be defined by substitution with synonymous expressions (1969 [1758]: 141). But presumably a concept or idea is indefinable *because* it is simple, so this test doesn't tell us what it is for an idea to be simple. Locke proposes a better account by understanding simplicity in terms of distinct properties, e.g. the idea of the sun is a complex of the ideas of roundness, brightness, heat. See Locke 1977: 188.

(1969 [1758]: 140). Why is this? Well, if we consider two straight lines intersecting at right angles we can know immediately (can see) that the angles either side of the intersecting line are equal. But, Price asks rhetorically, 'is not the idea of *equality* a new simple idea, acquired by the understanding, wholly different from that of the two angles compared, and denoting self evident truth?' (1969 [1758]: 140). His claim seems to be that in coming to see that the two angles are equal, we acquire at the same time the idea of equality, and the same is true of many other ideas. 'Thus the understanding, by employing its attention about different objects, and observing what is or is not *true* of them, acquires the different ideas of, necessity, infinity, contingency, possibility, and impossibility' (1969 [1758]: 138).

Having argued that many of our non-moral simple ideas originate from the understanding, Price goes on to argue that our ideas of right and wrong have the same source.[20] The premise of his argument is that all of our ideas are either simple or complex. All complex ideas are constructions from simple ideas and all simple ideas must 'be ascribed to some power of *immediate* perception in the human mind' (1969 [1758]: 141), i.e. either sensibility or the understanding.[21] The ideas of right and wrong are, he maintains, following most other intuitionists, simple ideas (1969 [1758]: 141), and are thus indefinable. Consequently, they must be immediate perceptions of either sensibility or the understanding.[22]

His argument for the view that they are apprehended by the understanding consists largely in removing obstacles to the acceptance of this conclusion. He claims that one important obstacle was removed by his arguments that we have so many (simple) non-moral ideas which cannot be said to arise from sense (Price, 1969 [1758]: 142). Second, he claims that the view that the understanding is the source of our idea of right and wrong involves no contradiction. All that Hutcheson has shown is that these ideas are simple and indefinable. He has done nothing to show that there is any absurdity in the view that these simple ideas have their source in the understanding (Price 1969 [1758]: 143).

Price's third argument for his thesis is an appeal to common sense. That if we reflect on our own perceptions we will see that the notions of number, diversity, causation, or proportion, signify truth and reality perceived by the understanding, and the same is true of our ideas of right and wrong (1969 [1758]: 144).

---

[20] Although the view that thin moral concepts are simple is not as important for later intuitionists as it was for the arguments of the earlier ones, Ross still repeats Price's argument, which he gets via Cook Wilson, that simple ideas such as 'good' must be acquired by our apprehension of them in the world. Thus, he writes:

> We may, however, not merely ask how the notion could have come into being if it were not the apprehension of a reality. We may claim that we are directly aware that conscientious action, for example, has a value of its own, not identical with or even dependent upon our or anyone else's taking an interest in it. Our reason informs us of this as surely as it informs us of anything, and to distrust reason here is in principle to distrust its power of ever knowing reality'. (2002 [1930]: 82)

[21] Once again, Cook Wilson makes a very similar claim about the reality of the objects of simple ideas (1926: 511–21).

[22] Following Locke, he seems to assume that all simple ideas are necessarily real and correspond to things in themselves. See Locke 1977: 348. See Ross (2002 [1930]: 82).

It is scarcely conceivable that anyone can impartially attend to the nature of his own perceptions, and determine that, when he thinks gratitude and beneficence to be *right*, he perceives nothing *true* of them, and *understands* nothing, but only receives an impression from *sense*. (1969 [1758]: 144–5)

He concedes that certain feelings may attend our apprehension of right and wrong, but these impressions are merely the consequence of our perception of right and wrong. They are not what is perceived.

Finally, if right and wrong were mere sensations or feelings in us, then it would be absurd to suppose that actions can be right or wrong (1969 [1758]: 146). Once again he uses the analogy with a certain understanding of secondary qualities—that is, as modes of consciousness, rather than as (powers) in the objects themselves.

A *coloured body*, if we speak accurately, is the same absurdity as a *square sound*. We need no experiments to prove that heat, cold, colours, tastes, etc, are not real qualities of bodies; because the ideas of matter and of these qualities, are incompatible.—But is there indeed any such incompatibility between *actions* and *right*? Or any such absurdity affirming the one of the other?—Are the ideas of them as different as the idea of a sensation, and its cause?

It is surprising that Price should contrast our idea of right with that of colour, as one would have thought that it is as natural to suppose that things themselves have colours (if not also heat and flavours) as it is to suppose that actions are right or wrong, and if we can be mistaken about whether colours are real properties of objects (given that they appear to us so clearly to be so), then it is surely possible that we are mistaken about whether rightness is a real property of actions. It may have been wiser for Price to be more critical of the empiricists on their account of colours, and other secondary qualities, if he is to pursue this line of argument with regard to rightness.[23]

16.5 EMPIRICAL AND NON-EMPIRICAL IDEAS: NATURAL AND NON-NATURAL CONCEPTS

The early intuitionists maintained that moral ideas are not given through sense, and are thus non-empirical ideas signifying non-empirical properties. It is tempting to assume that the idea of a non-empirical property is the same as what Moore later referred to as a non-natural property. But this would, I think, be a mistake, for it is clear that Price thought of many natural properties, such as causality, impenetrability, and temporal qualities, as non-empirical properties. So we should not equate the notion of a non-empirical idea, or property, with that of a non-natural concept, or property.

Furthermore, for earlier intuitionists like Clarke, Balguy, and Price, it was important for their argument that moral properties are non-empirical properties, that they be

[23] See, for example, McDowell 1985.

simple. For it is because they are simple that they must be apprehended by some faculty of the mind directly, and, they argue, this faculty must be the understanding rather than sense. So the simplicity of these properties is an essential part of the intuitionist argument for their being non-empirical properties.

But although Moore placed a great deal of emphasis on the simplicity of goodness, its simplicity is not needed for his argument that goodness is a non-natural property, for a variety of reasons. First, non-natural properties may be complex,[24] and natural properties may be simple.[25] Second, Moore's argument for the non-naturalness of goodness— the open question argument—need have no recourse to the idea of simplicity. The open question argument runs as follows:

(1) If goodness could be defined naturalistically—that is, wholly in terms of natural properties—then the question of whether something that has those natural properties is good would not be an open question.

(2) The question of whether something that has some natural property is good is always open.

So

(3) Goodness cannot be defined wholly in terms of natural properties.[26]

An open question is a substantive question—that is, it is a question about which there could be serious debate between individuals who understand the terms that figure in the question. A question is closed if it is not open. So, for example, one cannot seriously debate whether someone's brother is male, or whether what is known (in propositional knowledge) is true. (2) seems to be true, as no matter what natural property figures in the definition, it always makes sense to ask whether something that has that property is good. It is always an open question whether something that is pleasant, or which we desire to desire, or which causes the most happiness, is good or right. So given (1) goodness cannot be defined wholly in terms of pleasure, second-order desires, or happiness. This argument does not show that goodness is a simple concept, or property. All it shows is that goodness cannot be defined *in naturalistic terms*, which of course leaves room for it to be defined in non-natural terms. So it is not essential to Moore's argument for the non-naturalness of goodness that goodness is a simple property.

What may have made him *think* this is important is arguments by earlier intuitionists for the non-empirical nature of moral properties. But although these arguments were premised on the simplicity of the idea of good, they were quite different from Moore's argument, and in any case were arguments for something quite different.

That said, the earlier intuitionists did come up with something very much like Moore's open question argument in arguing that goodness is a simple idea. Thus, for instance

[24] As Ewing 1947 thought goodness was.
[25] As Moore thinks colour properties are (1993a [1903]: 62).
[26] For an alternative account of how the open question argument works see Scanlon 1998: 96.

Price writes of definitions of right in terms of divine commands, or of producing good, that if true, they would make it:

> palpably absurd…to ask, whether it is *right* to obey a command, or *wrong* to disobey it; and the propositions, *obeying a command is right*, or *producing happiness is right*, would be most trifling, as expressing no more than that obeying a command, is obeying a command, or producing happiness, is producing happiness. (1969 [1758]: 133)

This line of argument can also be found in Sidgwick (1967 [1874]: 26 n.). But this argument—what Parfit (2011) calls the 'Triviality Objection'—does not show that 'right' or 'good' are simple terms, ideas, or properties. What it shows is that they are not natural properties. The argument works in relation to naturalistic definitions, because the supposed definition turns a substantive moral question (ought I to do what promotes human happiness, or produces the most pleasure, etc.?) into a trivial one (would promoting happiness promote happiness?). But not all definitions of ought do this. Suppose, for the sake of argument, that 'ought to Φ' means 'have most reason to Φ', and suppose that the ought defined here is the 'all things considered' ought. If this definition were true, then the question: 'I have most reason to Φ, but ought I to Φ?' would not be open. But the supposition that this definition is true does not convert a substantive normative question into a trivial one. Saying that I ought to do what I have most reason to do is not making a substantive claim on a par with claiming that I ought to do what will produce the most happiness; for the substantive question remains open about what I have most reason to do. Of course, by substituting the definiendum with the definiens I would make this explicitly a trivial question, but this is true of every true and interesting definition, so it is better if the triviality argument does not work in this way. The crucial point is that by making this substitution I will not have converted a substantive normative question into a trivial one, and since (on the definition we are considering) this was not a substantive normative question before the substitution, the definition doesn't fail this test in the relevant way. So as far as I can see, Price was wrong to think that this is an argument for the view that moral ideas are simple, and hence definable. It is, rather, an argument for the view that normative ideas like good and right are non-natural ideas.[27]

16.6 SELF-EVIDENCE

Price distinguishes between three grounds of knowledge or belief. The first is immediate consciousness or feeling, by which he means the mind's awareness of its own existence and mental states (1969 [1758]: 159). The second is intuition, which includes the 'mind's

---

[27] There are standard objections to any form of the open question argument. See for instance Warnock 1968: 17 and Putnam 1981: 207. It should be noted that although Putnam thought that intuitionists such as Moore did confuse concepts and properties, he agreed with Moore that moral properties are non-natural properties (1981: 211).

survey of its own ideas, and the relations between them, and the notice it takes of what is or is not true and false, consistent and inconsistent, possible and impossible in the nature of things' (1969 [1758]: 159). The third ground of belief he lists is argumentation, or deduction (1969 [1758]: 160). The first is immediate apprehension by sense; the second immediate apprehension by the understanding; and the third truths grasped by arguing *from* what is immediately apprehended.

It is in the second way that we apprehend self-evident truths, general and abstract ideas, 'and anything else we may discover, without making any use of any process of reasoning' (1969 [1758]: 159). It is worth noting that Price, as well as the other intuitionists, does not use the term 'intuition' in the way it is often used in contemporary philosophy—that is, to mean 'strong, pre-theoretical conviction'. It is not contrasted to theoretical views, or those about which we are less certain, but is contrasted to knowledge that is the outcome of argument. It means immediate apprehension of some truth.

Like other epistemic foundationalists, Price insists that all reasoning and knowledge must ultimately rest on self-evident truth grasped by intuition.[28] Price claims that the self-evident truths intuited are 'incapable of proof' (1969 [1758]: 160).[29] Most intuitionists endorse this view, although Ross is, I think, an exception. This is easily missed, for he sometimes states that self-evident moral propositions 'cannot be proved, but…just as certainly need no proof' (2002 [1930]: 30). But elsewhere in *The Right and the Good* he makes only the more restricted claim that such propositions do not *need* any proof,[30] and despite the fact that he sometimes makes the further claim that they *cannot* receive any proof (justification) I do not think this further claim expresses his considered view.[31] Three years before the publication of *The Right and the Good* Ross explicitly states that 'the fact that something can be inferred does not prove that it cannot be seen intuitively' (1927: 121). If he thinks that some proposition can be inferred from (justified by) other propositions and be self-evident, he clearly thinks that its being self-evident does not rule out the possibility of a proof, and he is right to think so, as the fact that some proposition may be known directly in no way implies that it cannot be known in any other way.[32]

But what is it for a proposition, or principle, to be self-evident? Locke says that a self-evident proposition is one that 'carries its own light and evidence with it, and needs no other proof: he that understands the terms, assents to it for its own sake' (1977: 79). Price tells us that a self-evident proposition is immediate, and needs no further proof, and goes on to say that self-evident propositions need only be understood to gain assent (1969 [1758]: 187). These passages suggest that a self-evident proposition is one of which our understanding is sufficient to justify us in believing it.

---

[28] See Sturgeon 2002 for an alternative view.

[29] Although he does allow that such propositions admit of clarification, and that they may be illustrated 'by an advantageous representation of them, or by being viewed in particular lights' (1969 [1758]: 159). Whether it is possible to spell out the distinction between an 'advantageous representation' of such propositions and an argument for them, is something I leave undecided here.

[30] See, for example, 2002 [1930]: 29.

[31] In this I differ from Robert Audi's view (1996: 101–36). See also Audi 1998, 1999, and 2004, 40–79.

[32] See Audi 1996. See Brink 1994 for an alternative view.

This definition does not imply that everyone who understands these principles or truths accepts them as true. Clarke, for instance, allowed that stupidity, corruption, or perverseness may make one doubt them. John Balguy also acknowledges that self-evident moral principles, like many other plain and evident truths, may be, and have been, doubted, 'even by philosophers and men of letters' whom, presumably, he did not regard as stupid or corrupt (1969 [1729]: 406). And Price maintained that all forms of knowledge, including intuitive knowledge, may be evident in different degrees (1969 [1758]: 160). Intuition may be clear and perfect, but may sometimes be faint and obscure. Such variance in degrees of clarity allows that a self-evident proposition may be imperfectly and obscurely grasped, and this may lead to doubts. Similarly, Moore claimed that 'every way in which it is possible to cognise a true proposition, it is also possible to grasp a false one' (1993a [1903]: 36), and Ross notes that self-evident propositions may only be evident to us once we reach a certain moral maturity (2002 [1930]: 29). Given all these ways in which the truth of a self-evident proposition may be missed, it is no surprise that there is no universal assent to them.[33] But the absence of universal assent is quite consistent with self-evidence, as long as one does not regard 'self-evidence' to mean or imply obviousness.[34]

The intuitionists took self-evident moral principles to be basic, or foundational, moral principles and vice versa. All intuitionists agree that a principle of universal beneficence is basic, and self-evident, although some, like Moore, Ross, and possibly Clarke (1969 [1706]: 209) subsumed this principle under the distinct principle of maximizing intrinsic value.

Clarke, Price, and Sidgwick endorsed a principle of equity. Clarke offers different formulations of this principle. Sometimes he describes this duty with reference to how we *desire* others to treat us (see, e.g. 1969 [1706]: 208), and represents this principle as a version of the golden rule. But sometimes he makes no reference to desire in describing this duty, as when he describes it as the requirement that 'we so deal with every Man, as in like circumstances we could reasonably expect he should deal with Us' (1969 [1706]: 207). This is not a point about how we want others to treat us, and so does not seem to be a version of the golden rule. It is rather a point about the universality and impartiality of moral requirements.

Clarke divided his basic duties into three categories: duties owed to God, those owed to our fellow men, and those we owe to ourselves (1969 [1706]: 207, 209, 211), and most intuitionists before Sidgwick included duties to God amongst their basic duties. But it is quite striking that from Sidgwick on there is no reference to any duties to God in the writings of the main intuitionists.

---

[33] A common objection to the view that certain moral propositions are self-evident is the fact that there is disagreement about them. See, for example, MacIntyre 1998: 254. But this disagreement can be explained by the fact that they are supposed to be substantive moral truths, and as such may not be obvious.

[34] Although it should be noted that some intuitionists did claim that self-evident moral truths are obvious. But there is nothing in the idea of a self-evident proposition as we are understanding it that commits one to this view. Indeed, one would have thought that the fact that the intuitionists differed over which principles are basic, and thus self-evident, shows that they are not *obviously* true.

Some intuitionists were more systematic than others. The most systematic were the monistic intuitionists who claimed to derive all our duties from a single basic moral principle. Some pluralists, e.g. Price (1969 [1758]: 185) and Prichard,[35] just offer a sample list of basic duties without claiming that their list is in any way complete. And in between these two extremes there were the more systematic pluralists like Clarke and Ross who argued that we could derive all our duties from a relatively short list of basic duties, but that this list could not be further reduced. Clarke lists four such duties— the duty to honour God, the duty of equity, of universal beneficence, and of self-preservation (1969 [1706]: 212). Ross initially lists seven—the duties of fidelity, gratitude, reparation, beneficence, justice, self-improvement, and non-maleficence (2002 [1930]: 21)—but later reduces this to five by subsuming the principles of beneficence, justice, and self-improvement under the principle of maximizing good (2002 [1930]: 26–7).

Pluralists such as Clarke, Price, Prichard, and Ross, all emphasize the personal nature of morality and the fact that specific relations to particular individuals or groups have a moral importance that cannot be reduced to general beneficence. Examples of such personal duties are gratitude, fidelity to promises, private interest, friendship, 'and all particular attachments and connections' (Price 1969 [1758]: 181). Ross adds the relations of creditor to debtor, of wife to husband, of child to parent, and of fellow countryman to fellow countryman as examples of such morally relevant relations (2002 [1930]: 19). But although Ross' list of basic duties can, arguably, account for the duty of a child to its parent, it is unclear how it can account for the corresponding duty of parents to their children. Parental duties are not the result of any sort of promise to the child, or of reparation, or gratitude. The most plausible ground of parental duties from Ross' list is that of good maximizing, but that is not a personal duty, and so does not explain why parents have a special duty to care for *their* children rather than just for children.

There are some differences between the pluralist intuitionists about which relations are morally basic. For instance, Price regards the duty of veracity as basic, and derived the duty of fidelity from this. For Price, the wrong of breaking a promise consists in the fact that in doing this we knowingly and wilfully make something we said in the past false (1969 [1758]: 182). So, he argues, breaking promises is the same sort of wrong as knowingly and willingly uttering a falsehood. Ross, on the other hand, maintained that the wrong of dishonesty is fundamentally the wrong of breaking an implicit promise to express one's genuine opinion in communication (2002 [1930]: 54).[36]

Price, Prichard, and Ross emphasize that the various basic duties can conflict with each other and that there is no higher-order principle for deciding what to do in particular cases

---

[35] In 'Basis' he gives as examples considerations of self-improvement, friendship, beneficence, and fidelity. In 'Mistake' he adds gratitude to the list (2002b: 12), though there is no assumption that self-improvement, friendship, beneficence, fidelity, and gratitude exhaust the list of fundamental obligation-grounding considerations.

[36] Ross also claims that the duty of honesty may be grounded in that of non-maleficence (2002 [1930]: 54–5). It is not obvious in Ross, but I think that he regards non-maleficence and fidelity as individually sufficient (rather than individually necessary and jointly sufficient) to ground a duty of honesty.

when they conflict. This means that although the universal principles of duty are self-evident, what we ought to do in particular situations will not be self-evident (1969 [1758]: 185). Indeed, Ross goes so far as to state that we can never know what we should do in particular cases, and can only have a probable opinion about such things (2002 [1930]: 30).

Prichard and Ross argued in a more systematic way for pluralism by rejecting the best monistic theories, which they regarded as those which attempt to derive the right from the good—either from the agent's own good, from the intrinsic goodness of our acts, or from the impartial good of the consequences of one's acts. They dismissed the idea that moral obligations can be derived from the agent's own good on the ground that this is irrelevant to what we are obligated to do. That some act will benefit us may get us to want to do it, but cannot get us to believe that we are obligated to do it (Prichard 2002b [1912]: 9; Ross 2002 [1930]: 16). They deny that our obligations stem from the intrinsic goodness of obligatory acts on the ground that the only aspect of an action that could be intrinsically good is its motive, and the motive is never part of what we are obligated to do (Prichard 2002b [1912]: 11; Ross 2002 [1930]: 6). So what we are obligated to do can never be *intrinsically* good. This leaves only the consequentialist view that our obligations are grounded in the goodness of their outcomes.

Both Prichard and Ross reject consequentialism mainly because it fails to take seriously the personal nature of many of our duties. There are, they maintain, plenty of cases in which two acts produce the same amount of good, but our duty is to do only one of them because of some special relation in which we stand to someone. Prichard gives the example of a situation in which a person could help either a stranger, himself, or his father, though the point is made better if we regard a situation where he has to chose only between benefiting his father or the stranger (2002a: 2). Since the good conferred would be equal regardless of who received it, consequentialism must, he argues, say that it does not matter who we benefit. But this view conflicts with a strong conviction that the person should, in such circumstances, benefit his father. If this conviction is sound, then certain personal relations have moral significance that cannot be subsumed under the impartial promotion of the good.[37]

Ross argues in a similar way with regard to the principle of fidelity to promises. In situations where we could benefit two people equally, but we have promised to benefit one, we are sure that it would be impermissible to confer the benefit on anyone other than the promisee. But since the benefit is the same no matter who receives it, consequentialists would have to say that it is permissible to confer this benefit on either person. Since we cannot bring ourselves to accept, or even believe that we ought to accept, that it is permissible in such cases to benefit either person, we must reject any theory that forces us to accept this.

There is a great deal of agreement between Ross and Prichard about the right, and Ross is often content merely to repeat arguments that Prichard makes elsewhere. There is, however, one important difference, albeit one that did not last. Their main difference is in relation to the general nature of principles of right conduct. At the time of writing

---

[37] For an alternative view see Shaver 2011 and Portmore 2003.

'Does Moral philosophy rest on a mistake?' Prichard regarded basic moral principles as stating that we have certain obligations or duties, and understood a conflict of duties as a conflict of, what Ross would call, *actual* obligations or duties—a conflict which is to be decided by deciding which of the conflicting (actual) duties is the most pressing. In such cases then, we always fail to act in accordance with some obligation (the weaker one), even when we act in accordance with the most weighty one.

Ross, however, thought of his moral principles as principles of *prima facie* duty, or rightness, and distinguished prima facie duty from actual duty, duty proper, or actual rightness. An act is prima facie right if it has some feature that tends to make it actually right, and is prima facie wrong if it has some feature that tends to make it actually wrong (Ross 2002 [1930]: 19–20). 'Prima facie' here does *not* mean 'at first sight', but means 'as far as that goes', or 'pro tanto' right. Principles of prima facie duty thus pick out considerations that count in favour of doing certain acts.[38] Whether an act is actually right or wrong depends on all of the prima facie right and wrong features—that is, on *all* of the moral features that count for and against doing it. If the act has, all things considered, a higher degree of prima facie rightness over prima facie wrongness, then it is actually right (obligatory), and conversely if it is more prima facie wrong than right, then it is actually wrong.

Thinking of moral conflicts as conflicts of prima facie duty has the advantage that it does not force us to think that actions that we ought all things considered to do are to a certain degree morally wrong (though less wrong than any other act). For (actual) rightness and wrongness applies only at the 'all things considered' level, or what I call elsewhere, the 'verdictive level'.[39] At this level an act can be either right or wrong, but not both. The idea that there may be something to be said against an act that we ought to do is captured by the claim that it is *prima facie* wrong. But this is not to say that it is, to some degree, actually wrong. Prichard later came to accept Ross' view, as he found it impossible to accept the view that there is some obligatoriness to a wrong act or some wrongness to a right act, although he preferred to describe conflicts in terms of conflicting claims than prima facie duties (Prichard 2002c [1928]: 79).

As we have seen, most intuitionists were pluralists about the right. The most important monists about the right were Sidgwick and Moore. Henry Sidgwick rejected earlier pluralist views on the ground that most of their supposed self-evident principles are either mere tautologies, or are not self-evident at all. For instance, the principle of justice states that we ought to give every man his own. But the only way in which 'his own' may be understood is as 'that which it is right he should have' (1967 [1874]: 375). So this principle states merely that we ought to give every man what he ought to have, and that is uninformative. Other principles that Sidgwick thought were substantive, such as the principle of fidelity to promises or of honesty, were not self-evident. Such principles, he maintained, present themselves as principles that require rational justification (1967 [1874]: 383).

But Sidgwick did not reject all self-evident moral principles. On the contrary he regarded three practical principles as self-evident—rational egoism (according to which

---

[38] For a more detailed account of the notion of a prima facie duty see Stratton-Lake 2000: ch. 5.
[39] See Stratton-Lake 2000: 14.

we ought to aim at our own good on the whole, giving equal weight to distant and near benefits), universal beneficence, and equity. He regarded the last of these as something that *all* moral theories must acknowledge. They will differ with regard to when and why it will be right to treat someone in a certain way, but must accept that the same considerations that make it right for me to treat you in a certain way will make it right for you to treat me in the same way (all other things being equal). We may, then, regard this as a formal principle, rather than a substantive principle telling us *what* we ought to do.

This leaves two substantive practical principles—rational egoism and universal benevolence. It may seem from this that Sidgwick is after all a pluralist, albeit a pluralist with only two basic principles. But his principle of rational egoism is not a moral principle. Only the principle of beneficence is a moral principle. So although he lists two substantive (plus one formal) self-evident principles, he believes that there is only one basic *moral* principle.

G. E. Moore was greatly influenced by Sidgwick, and agreed with him that we ought always to produce as much good as possible. But Moore differed from Sidgwick in several important ways. First, he was pluralistic about the good that is to be promoted. Sidgwick was a hedonist, and so maintained that the only intrinsically good thing is pleasure. But Moore held that although pleasure may figure in many goods, it is not itself of any great intrinsic value, and is certainly not the sole good. Amongst the many diverse goods, Moore held that the admiring contemplation of beauty and pleasures of social intercourse were by far the most important (1993a [1903]: 237).

A further way in which Moore differed from Sidgwick is that in his *Principia* he argued that 'right' *means* 'maximises good' (1993a [1903]: 196). This is quite a surprising thing for Moore to say given that he devoted considerable energy to arguing that 'good' is indefinable in his *Principia Ethica*, and the arguments he uses in support of this view about good apply equally well to right. Nonetheless, in *Principia* Moore regarded his consequentialism as true by definition, though he abandoned this view in his later work (*Ethics*) and claimed that this principle expresses a synthetic truth.

By the 1930s intuitionism fell into disrepute. The moral realism and epistemology that was so central to the intuitionists' views was completely eclipsed by the non-cognitivism of Ayers, Stevenson, and Hare, and interest in normative moral philosophy waned. Intuitionism remained deeply unfashionable until the 1970s and 1980s when confidence grew that some form of moral realism could be defended after all. Many of these neo-realists were naturalist, but with the rise of naturalist moral realism, the intuitionists' anti-naturalistic arguments became relevant again, and the influence of their views can be found in philosophers as diverse as Wiggins (1976), McDowell (1985), Parfit (2011), Scanlon (1998), Audi (2004), Hurka (2001), and Dancy (2006). Furthermore, in normative moral theory the debate between monists and pluralists—which is independent of the intuitionists' epistemological and metaethical views—is as strong as ever. Many current debates about whether the right can be derived from the good, and between impartialist and partialist moral theories, continue to draw on arguments put forward by the intuitionists discussed here, and their influence, significance, and relevance to our understanding of morality now seems secured.

Bibliography

Audi, R. 1996. 'Intuitionism, Pluralism, and the Foundations of Ethics', in W. Sinnott-Armstrong and M. Timmons (eds), *Moral Knowledge?* New York: Oxford University Press, 101–36.

—— 1998. 'Moderate Intuitionism and the Epistemology of Moral Judgment', *Ethical Theory and Moral Practice* 1: 15–44.

—— 1999. 'Self-Evidence', *Philosophical Perspectives* 13: 205–28.

—— 2004. *The Good in the Right: A Theory of Intuition and Intrinsic Value*. Princeton: Princeton University Press.

Balguy, J. 1969 [1729]. *The Foundation of Moral Goodness*, Part II, in D. D. Raphael (ed.), *The British Moralists*. Oxford: Clarendon Press, 404–8.

Berger, F. 1975. 'Gratitude', *Ethics* 85: 298–309.

Brink, D. 1994. 'Common Sense and First Principles in Sidgwick's Methods', *Social Philosophy and Policy* 11: 179–201.

Clarke, S. 1969 [1706]. *Discourse on Natural Religion*, in D. D. Raphael (ed.), *The British Moralists 1650–1800*, vol. 1. Oxford: Clarendon Press, 224–61.

Cook Wilson, J. 1926. *Statement and Inference: With other Philosophical Papers*, ed. A. S. L. Farquarson. Oxford: Clarendon Press.

Cudworth, R. 1969 [1731]. *A Treatise Concerning Eternal Immutable Morality*, in D. D. Raphael (ed.), *The British Moralists 1650–1800*, vol. 1. Oxford: Clarendon Press, 103–34.

Dancy, J. 2006. *Ethics without Principles*. Oxford: Clarendon Press.

Ewing, A. C. 1947. *The Definition of Good*. London: Routledge.

Fitzgerald, P. 1998. 'Gratitude and Justice', *Ethics* 109: 119–53.

Hurka, T. 2001. *Virtue, Vice and Value*. Oxford: Oxford University Press.

Locke, J. 1977. *An Essay Concerning Human Understanding*, edited and abridged by A. D. Woozley. Glasgow: Collins Fount Paperbacks.

McDowell, J. 1985. 'Values and Secondary Qualities', in T. Honderich (ed.), *Morality and Objectivity*. London: Routledge & Kegan Paul, 110–29.

MacIntyre, A. 1998. *A Short History of Ethics: A History of Moral Philosophy from the Homeric Age to the Twentieth Century*. Second edition. London: Routledge.

Moore, G. E. 1993a [1903]. *Principia Ethica*, ed. T. Baldwin. Cambridge: Cambridge University Press.

—— 1993b [1922]. 'The Conception of Intrinsic Value', in *Principia Ethica*, ed. T. Baldwin. Cambridge: Cambridge University Press, 280–98.

Parfit, D. 2011. *On What Matters*. 2 vols. Oxford: Oxford University Press.

Portmore, D. W. 2003. 'Position-Relative Consequentialism, Agent-Centered Options, and Supererogation', *Ethics* 113 (2): 303–32.

Price, R. 1969 [1758]. *A Review of the Principle Questions in Morals*, in D. D. Raphael (ed.), *The British Moralists 1650–1800*, vol. 2. Oxford: Clarendon Press, 131–98.

Prichard, H. A. 2002a. 'What is the Basis of Moral Obligation?', in *Moral Writings*, ed. J. McAdam. Oxford: Clarendon Press, 1–6.

—— 2002b. [1912]. 'Does Moral Philosophy Rest on a Mistake?', in *Moral Writings*, ed. J. McAdam. Oxford: Clarendon Press, 7–20.

—— 2002c [1928]. 'A Conflict of Duties', in *Moral Writings*, ed. J. McAdam. Oxford: Clarendon Press, 77–83.

Putnam, H. 1981. *Reason, Truth and History*. Cambridge: Cambridge University Press.

Ross, W. D. 1927. 'The Basis of Objective Judgements in Ethics', *International Journal of Ethics* 37: 113–27.

—— 1939. *The Foundations of Ethics*. Oxford: Clarendon Press.

—— 2002 [1930]. *The Right and the Good*, ed. P. Stratton-Lake. Oxford: Clarendon Press.

Scanlon, T. M. 1998. *What We Owe to Each Other*. Cambridge, MA: Belnap Press.

Schroeder, M. 2009. 'Buck-passers' negative thesis', *Philosophical Explorations* 12 (3): 341–47.

Shaver, R. 2011. 'The birth of deontology' in T. Hurka (ed.), *Underivative Duty: British Moral Philosophers from Sidgwick to Ewing*. Oxford: Oxford University Press, 126–45.

Sidgwick, H. 1967 [1874]. *The Methods of Ethics*. 7th edn. London: Macmillan.

Stratton-Lake, P. 2000. *Kant Duty and Moral Worth*. London: Routledge.

—— 2009. 'Roger Crisp on Goodness and Reasons', *Mind* 118: 1081–94.

Sturgeon, N. 2002. 'Ethical Intuitionism and Ethical Naturalism', in P. Stratton-Lake (ed.), *Ethical Intuitionism: Re-evaluations*. Oxford: Oxford University Press, 184–211.

Warnock, M. 1968. *Ethics since 1900*. Oxford: Oxford University Press.

Wiggins, D. 1976. 'Truth, Invention, and the Meaning of Life', *Proceedings of the British Academy* 62: 331–78.

Williams, B. 1995. 'What does Intuitionism Imply', in *Making Sense of Humanity and Other Philosophical Papers 1982–1993*. Cambridge: Cambridge University Press, 182–91.

CHAPTER 17

··

MORAL SENSE
AND SENTIMENTALISM

··

JULIA DRIVER

'I am afraid,' replied Elinor, 'that the pleasantness of an employment does
not always evince its propriety.'

'On the contrary, nothing can be a stronger proof of it, Elinor; for if there
had been any real impropriety in what I did, I should have been sensible
of it at the time, for we always know when we are acting wrong, and with
such a conviction I could have had no pleasure.' (Marianne)

from Jane Austen's *Sense and Sensibility*

SENTIMENTALISM is an approach to understanding morality which is, once again, receiving
a good deal of attention in the philosophical literature. Recent books such as Shaun
Nichols' *Sentimental Rules* and Michael Slote's *Moral Sentimentalism* demonstrate that
the approach is one that seems particularly in keeping with our understanding of
human psychology and human nature. Much recent interest has been generated by
findings in empirical moral psychology that seem to support the view that moral judgement engages the emotions (Greene et al. 2001).

Very broadly, sentimentalism is the view that morality is based on sentiment—in
particular, the sentiment of *sympathy*. It was historically articulated in opposition to two
positions: Hobbesian egoism, in which morality is based on self-interest, and Moral
Rationalism, which held that morality is based on reason alone. The Sentimentalists
challenged both views, arguing that there is more to what motivates human beings than
simple self-interest and that reason alone is insufficient to motivate our actions, including our moral actions. It is also important to note at the outset, however, that
Sentimentalists do not reject the use of reason in refining one's moral sentiments, otherwise, they would be making the same mistake Jane Austen's character Marianne makes
in trusting to her immediate emotional responses (Jacobson and D'Arms 2000). Rather,
the *source* of moral approbation itself is not found in reason, but in emotion. Clearly,
then, at least two independent theses need to be distinguished: the motivational thesis

and the authority thesis. These will be discussed further throughout the chapter. The motivational thesis holds that desire, or emotion, is necessary to motivate a person to moral action, and since moral judgements motivate they must at root be desires. This thesis, in various forms, has often been referred to as a form of motivational internalism. The authority thesis, on the other hand, holds that what binds us normatively can be accounted for by distinctively moral sentiments, usually understood in terms of basic desires we have either as individuals or as human beings. It is important to note this distinction. In theory, someone could be a motivational internalist and yet not a sentimentalist about the authority of moral norms. Or, one could hold that the source of normativity lies in desire, and yet hold that actions can be motivated by mere belief as well as basic desire.

17.1 BACKGROUND

In the modern historical context, moral sentimentalism arose out of a reaction to the egoism of Thomas Hobbes' moral philosophy, as well as a reaction against rationalism. The early sentimentalists were also reacting to some of John Locke's work in moral psychology—rejecting some of it, but, at least with Hutcheson and Hume, adopting some features of his views on perception. Hobbes held that human beings were solely or at least largely motivated by self-interest, and that this fact of human nature need not stand in the way of providing an account of obligation. But many philosophers felt that this account did not reflect an accurate view of human nature, nor an accurate view of how moral judgement worked. Without a kind of 'sentiment'—a feeling that gives rise to approval or disapproval based upon the judger's perceptions of the morally significant features of an object of evaluation—we would not be making moral judgements at all.

The philosophers historically most associated with sentimentalism are Anthony Ashley Cooper, the Third Earl of Shaftesbury, Francis Hutcheson, David Hume, and Adam Smith. Of these, Shaftesbury and Hutcheson were clearly moral sense theorists, arguing that there is a distinctive moral sense that allows us to pick up on morally relevant features of the world around us. This view, that we have a moral sense analogous to other senses, very broadly maintains that we perceive moral properties via an 'inner eye' without need for rational mediation, though the moral sense itself involves reflection on one's emotional reactions in determining whether or not one's reactions are appropriate. Some writers view sentimentalism and moral sense theory as synonymous, but this is not the case. The moral sense was postulated as a feature of moral psychology to account for how we acquire reliable moral beliefs, but can be separated from other sentimentalist commitments. Hume is a sentimentalist, but many argue that he rejects the moral sense in the way understood by Shaftesbury and Hutcheson. He agrees with the moral sense theorists regarding many issues, such as how we can become aware of virtue and vice, but disagrees in that he doesn't believe we have a unique, dedicated, faculty of moral perception which detects moral properties (Darwall 1995: 288). Adam Smith, also a sentimentalist, explicitly rejects a moral sense.

The expression 'moral sense' seems to have first been employed by Thomas Burnet (Norton 1995: 32). Moral sense theorists hold the view that human beings possess a capacity to detect moral distinctions directly, rather than simply infer them from basic premises. The capacity is usually compared to an aesthetic sense. We can see whether or not something is beautiful. We do not infer beauty by means of an argument. The view that we have a moral sense on analogy with our other, external, senses is sometimes opposed to the view that moral judgement employs reason at all. But this is not true. Indeed, Shaftesbury would understand the moral sense as crucially involving reflection, which is one reason human beings possess it and animals do not.

Early sentimentalists such as Shaftesbury were concerned to spell out, in more detail, how we, as human beings, thought about moral issues. Shaftesbury was in part concerned with what would be a fatal flaw of the rationalist approach, at least as far as the sentimentalists were concerned. That is the fact that reason does not seem to motivate. My belief that there is food in my refrigerator does not, by itself, motivate me to go to the refrigerator. I must also have the desire for the food in order to be motivated to go to the refrigerator. The belief itself is motivationally inert. Since we are clearly motivated by our moral judgements, this means that something else underlies them, that there is some emotional, desiring, element that gets us to act on what we believe. Again, this is the motivation, or *influence*, thesis. It has often been used to argue that sentimentalism is non-cognitivist.

It is important that this thesis regarding the crucial role desire plays in motivation be kept separate from the *authority*, or *justification*, thesis. The justification thesis holds that the moral sense accounts for the approval or disapproval of ultimate ends to action. It is possible to hold one without the other, though the two are characteristic of sentimentalist approaches. Shaftesbury, for example, did not hold the justification thesis.

The influence thesis in one form or another was accepted by Shaftesbury, Hutcheson, and Hume. It is considered a cornerstone of Hume's position, since Hume famously maintained 'reason' to be the 'slave' of the passions (but see Cohon 2008 for an alternative view). The thesis was attacked by moral rationalists who believed that the truths of morality were discernable through reason. Indeed, some, such as Cudworth, believed that sentiment was far too fickle a basis for morality, and would render the truths of morality mutable and the duty to conform to moral norms subject to whim.

Contemporary moral rationalists continue to attack it, citing the apparent existence of agents who perform virtuous acts but without the requisite feelings. The most plausible version of this objection holds that *evaluative beliefs* do motivate (Shafer-Landau 2003: 123). The plausibility of the Humean claim is laid to the fact that these are not the paradigm sorts of beliefs. The belief that 'triangles are three-sided objects' does not, by itself, motivate. But, the criticism goes, not all beliefs are simply descriptive. Some, like the belief that 'murder is wrong', are evaluative, and it is these beliefs that motivate.

A very naïve sentimentalist approach would hold that we simply trust our emotional reactions completely as given. No sentimentalist holds such a position. Emotional reactions are corrected and refined, given, for example, additional information. Sentimentalist approaches to moral judgement usually employ a 'corrective mechanism' for the moral emotions—this often involves the agent taking a meta-cognitive stance, reflecting on her own mental states and/or the mental states of others in determining whether or not what is being evaluated is a genuine virtue.[1] If the trait is approved of at the critical level of reflection, then one is justified in holding the trait as a virtue.

A striking feature of the early sentimentalist approach to understanding morality is the analogy typically drawn between moral and aesthetic judgement. Moral goodness is a kind of *beauty*; the human being who is properly configured internally will respond appropriately to beauty with approval.

17.2 ANTHONY ASHLEY COOPER, THE THIRD EARL OF SHAFTESBURY (1671–1713)

In his *An Inquiry Concerning Virtue or Merit* Shaftesbury was interested in a kind of moral paradox, or at least a phenomenon that he claimed was puzzling to people at the time, namely, that some atheists are very virtuous people, and some religious exemplars are not. On his view, we have come across individuals who are very enthusiastic about religion, though they:

> have yet wanted even the common affections of humanity, and shown themselves extremely degenerate and corrupt. Others, again, who have paid little regard to religion, and been considered as mere atheists, have yet been observed to practice the rules of morality, and act in many cases with such good meaning and affection towards mankind, as might seem to force an acknolwedgment of their being virtuous. (Shaftesbury 1999: 163)

To resolve this paradox we need to ask ourselves if someone can be virtuous *alone*, without religion. To answer this question, we need an account of virtue itself. It turns out for Shaftesbury that to be a virtuous person one must be performing actions beneficial to the system of which he is a part. How can we detect that someone has virtue? Shaftesbury, as other sentimentalists would, employs an analogy with an aesthetic sense. We have a 'natural' tendency to respond favourably to certain perceptions. This is true in morality as well as aesthetics. Moral beauty, like aesthetic beauty, involves harmony. We immediately recognize good and bad, without intervening considerations,

---

[1] In the psychology literature, 'meta-cognition' is restricted to cognition regarding one's own mental states, 'theory of mind' refers to thoughts on the mental states of others. However, I will be using 'meta-cognition' to refer to both in this chapter.

just as we recognize beauty and deformity immediately. These perceptions of beauty and deformity of character rest on our reflections, or perceptions, of our own mental states and those of others. We can then form a second-order attitude of approval or disapproval to what we are seeing. This was the 'moral sense' for Shaftesbury. When I consider my own motives and either approve or disapprove, I am engaged in a genuine moral judgement. At the core is the emotional reaction to the motive, and thus the sentimentalist commitment. This process involves meta-cogniton, where one understands 'meta-cogniton' very broadly to include affective states regarding other mental states. This is one reason animals, though sensitive creatures, capable of feeling pain and pleasure, do not possess a moral sense. They cannot take the proper perspective of evaluation (see Driver 2011b).

> [I]f a creature be·generous, kind, constant, compassionate; yet if he cannot reflect on what he himself does, or sees others do, so as to take notice of what is worthy or honest and make that notice or conception of worth and honesty to be an object of his affection, he has not the character of being virtuous. For thus, and no otherwise, he is capable of having a sense of right or wrong, a sentiment or judgment of what is done, through just, equal, and good affection, or the contrary. (Shaftesbury 1999: 173)

On Shaftesbury's view animals neither possess virtue nor a moral sense. The capacity to exercise the moral sense is a *requirement* of virtue. Indeed, he seemed to believe that when one engaged in meta-cognitive reflection in a *fully* developed way, one was exhibiting virtue.

It is important to note that Shaftesbury placed a good deal of emphasis on the significance of reason. On Shaftesbury's view, reason is crucial to the proper exercise of the moral sense. Reason is needed to discover the Good. The Good itself, for Shaftesbury, does not in any way depend upon a moral sense. He was a Realist. Thus, while he was a sentimentalist in terms of accepting the need for emotion in motivation and correct moral judgement, he did not believe that moral properties or the truths of morality themselves depended upon the sentiments. Approval of a motive or a trait does not *make* that motive or trait a virtuous one. Michael Gill writes:

> So even if every member of society were to approve of something harmful to humanity, it would still be vicious...Fashion, law, custom, and religion can cause people to develop positive affections toward things harmful to humanity. But the development of such affections will never make such things right. (Gill 2006: 94)

In presenting a realist account of the good, or value, that is accessed via the sentiments supported by reason, Shaftesbury is able to avoid a major problem for sentimentalist accounts of moral truth. This is the *contingency* problem. It is a problem rationalists would use to hammer sentimentalists. Before Hutcheson and Hume, it was used against Hobbes, though Hobbes' contingency problem was not based upon the view that morality rested on sentiment. Rather, Hobbes was perceived as holding the view that normative authority is contingent on features of human nature, particularly, human beings' egoistic tendencies and their fear of death, which, in turn, motivates the giving over of rights to a sovereign who is the source of normative authority. Moral rationalists such as Ralph Cudworth would argue that this is incompatible with 'eternal and immutable' moral truth (Gill 2006: 44). Divine Command theory is afflicted with the same problem as it makes 'right' and 'wrong' literally dependent on the will of God. The will of a Sovereign is no better than the will of God. Likewise, the sentimentalist view that morality depends upon contingent features of human nature, such as our sentiments, will have the same difficulty.

Shaftesbury, however, avoids the problem by embracing moral realism. He shares with the rationalists the view the moral truth is not itself contingent on sentiment. But he parts ways with them as regards how we go about acquiring, picking up on, that truth. In this we need the moral sense that involves approval and disapproval of the features that we are perceiving. One has an immediate negative reaction in witnessing a wilful murder. One's disapproval does not *make* the wilful murder wrong. However, it is a sign that it is wrong. Later sentimentalists, Hutcheson and Hume, are credited with rejecting Shaftesbury's realism.

Stephen Darwall credits Shaftesbury as being an important transitional figure in the development of British moral philosophy (Darwall 1995). This is because Shaftesbury located moral virtue *internally*—that is, the goodness of an agent is to be understood as a matter of his internal psychological states, and not, for example, the fact that his behaviour conforms to religious norms. Indeed, this was a problem that Shaftesbury had with much religiously based ethics—it seemed to misidentify the proper motive of virtue in making it selfish. Virtue, true virtue, on his view, cannot be founded on a fear of damnation. One might exhibit *behaviour* that a virtuous person would exhibit, but it is not true virtue because it lacks the right sort of motivation. Further, the exercise of the meta-cognition, or second-order affective capacity, is an instance of a kind of self-governance in the form of self-regulation of the sentiments.

There are problems with the appropriate exercise of meta-cognition, and Shaftesbury is aware of these. One such problem has to do with identifying one's own motivating states. This ability is something that Kant, for example, was sceptical of. Shaftesbury notes that 'vicious desires' make themselves felt 'indistinctly and confusedly', making identification difficult. Darwall notes that this leads Shaftesbury to argue that in reflecting on our mental states we need as well to engage in self-analysis. This makes the possession of virtue very mentally demanding. My view is that it makes the possession of virtue overly demanding. Later, Hume would distinguish virtue from moral agency. Whatever one thinks of the psychological realism of Shaftesbury's moral psychology, however, it is clear that for him moral authority is found from within the agent, and not via conformance to externally imposed rules.

The significance of proper motivation to virtue is reflected as well in the works of Hutcheson, Hume, and Smith. Hutcheson and Hume would disagree about what *essentially* motivated virtuous action, but would agree on basic sentimentalist commitments, such as the core distinction between reason and passion, and the insufficiency of reason as a source of motivational power.

17.3 FRANCIS HUTCHESON (1694–1746)

Francis Hutcheson was deeply interested in the issue of how it is that we judge persons virtuous, even when they are performing actions and exhibiting qualities that do us, as individual observers of those acts, no good at all. We approve of conduct that exhibits a concern for others, that exhibits benevolence, even when that concern is not directed at us in particular. Like Shaftesbury, Hutcheson believed that human beings possessed a moral sense. It was this sense that allowed us to make moral discriminations. As with Shaftesbury, it was analogous to the aesthetic sense, which allows us to make aesthetic discriminations. It accounts for an alternative form of motivation besides that specified by Hobbes.

Hutcheson believed that we possessed an innate tendency to approve of benevolent traits, as well as to be concerned for the well-being of others. Further, unlike Shaftesbury, he believed we had a moral obligation to promote well-being that was not reducible to self-interest. He did not subscribe to Shaftesbury's view that the sole source of obligation resided in self-interest. If the life of virtue is something that is good for the moral agent, in other words, that can't be the only thing that makes it appropriate for one to act virtuously. We can have reasons to act that are not reducible to our interests.

Of course, what underwrites this feature of our nature is God. God has given us the necessary means to discern good and evil. Indeed, on Hutcheson's view our moral sense is evidence that God is good for having implanted it in us (Hutcheson 1969: 313).

Like Shaftesbury, Hutcheson believed that exercise of the moral sense required reflection. In Hutcheson's case, what the spectator looks for is benevolence in terms of the motivation, or the affection, of the agent performing the action being evaluated. Hutcheson believed that human beings possessed a sense of beauty as part of their nature. This sense determines what we find beautiful—what sort of proportions and features we find pleasing in objects. In addition to this sense is a 'superior' sense, the Moral Sense, 'natural also to men, determining them to be pleased with actions, characters, affections'.

Unlike Shaftesbury, however, Hutcheson believes that moral qualities revealed by the moral sense are like Lockean secondary qualities, such as colour. They are not intrinsic to the 'object' being evaluated (see Winkler 1996). In this case, what is being evaluated is character, virtue, and vice. Virtues and vices are qualities in people that have the power to generate in observers feelings of approbation or disapprobation. Specifically, what we are responding to on Hutcheson's view is the agent's benevolent motive (or lack thereof).

> If we examine all the actions which are counted *amiable* anywhere, and inquire into the grounds upon which they are *approved*, we shall find that in the opinion of the person who approves them, they generally appear as BENEVOLENT, or flowing from *good-will to others*, and a study of their happiness, whether the approver be one of the persons beloved, or profited, or not; so that all those kind affections which incline us to make others happy, and all actions supposed to flow from such affections,

appear *morally good*, if, while they are benevolent towards some persons, they be
not pernicious to others. (Hutcheson 1969: 280)

Hutcheson clearly believes that the moral sense is not infallible—its verdicts can be
distorted by false belief. He discusses this in the context of discussing what makes certain
abilities—such as having a good memory, good judgement, cleverness—admirable.
They are good only in so far as they produce good. He adds: 'A veneration of these qualities any farther than they are employed for the public good is foolish, and flows from our
Moral Sense grounded on false opinion; for if we plainly see them *maliciously* employed,
they make the agent more detestable' (Hutcheson 1969).

Hutcheson is sometimes credited with being an early Utilitarian since he explicitly
recommends a very utilitarian decision procedure in *An Inquiry Concerning Moral Good
and Evil*:

(U)   In comparing the moral qualities of actions, in order to regulate our election
        among various actions proposed, or to find which of them has the greatest
        moral excellency, we are led by our moral sense of virtue to judge thus: that in
        equal degrees of happiness, expected to proceed from the action, the virtue is in
        proportion to the *number* of persons to whom the happiness shall extend (and
        here the *dignity*, or *moral importance* of persons, may compensate numbers);
        and in equal *numbers*, the virtue is in the *quantity* of the happiness or natural
        good; or that the virtue is in a compound ratio of the *quantity* of good, and
        number of enjoyers. (Hutcheson 1969: 283).

However, the focus of moral evaluation for Hutcheson was virtue. It may be that the sort
of theory he had in mind would, by our lights, be a kind of virtue ethics but where the
virtuous decision procedure is utilitarian in form. The right action is the one the virtuous agent *would* perform, virtue is a matter of benevolence, and the benevolent agent
performs actions that conform to the calculations specified in (U).

There are some tensions in Hutcheson's account of the moral sense that Hume would
later use to criticize the account. One tension is that, on the one hand, we have this immediate instinct we employ (the sense) to detect what is morally significant in our environment. Yet, approval requires reflection. Reflection is not immediate. Thus, to employ the
moral sense we are not, in fact, immediately responding to what is morally significant.

Further, Joseph Butler, as well as Hume, would later note that Hutcheson's account of
virtue is too narrow (Butler 1983). The view that virtue is a matter of benevolent motivation fails to model a host of virtues such as honesty and justice. Whether or not a person
exhibits the virtue of honesty has nothing to do with benevolent motivation. The same is
true for justice. In Hume we see the idea that there is an entire set of virtues that fail the
Hutcheson mould—the 'artificial' virtues of chastity, justice, and promise-keeping. The
motives behind these virtues are various, and can include self-interest. In the case of
female chastity, Hume will in fact argue that rendering it a particular vice is necessary so
that it is in a woman's individual self-interest to abide by the norms of chastity—for the
good of the social order.

17.4 DAVID HUME (1711–1776)

Many contemporary sentimentalists trace their inspiration to David Hume. He is widely considered to have written the most systematic account of a sentimentalist morality, setting out his views both in the *Treatise of Human Nature* [THN] and the *Enquiry Concerning the Principles of Morals* [EPM].

Hume famously held that moral distinctions are not derived from reason, and that reason is insufficient to motivate action. Both of these views are features of his sentimentalism. Hume shares with the other sentimentalists the view that egoism is mistaken and that sympathy is a part of human nature. Indeed, it is a *universal* feature of human nature on his account.

17.4.1 Sympathy

In the early sentimentalist tradition, words such as 'sympathy' were often used with a variety of meanings, and some care needs to be taken in disentangling those meanings (Frazier 2010). Sympathy, for Hume, can be regarded in two ways depending on whether one takes the *Treatise* or the *Enquiry* as authoritative on this subject (see also Driver 2011a). In the *Treatise* sympathy is a kind of emotional *contagion*. Emotions such as fear, anger, and excitement can be communicated via sympathy, even though the person responding to another's anger sympathetically does not see the *cause* of the anger. This is evidence that the response is caused by the emotion itself and not the cause of the initial emotional reaction. It explains some of the similarities of behaviour between human beings and animals. Even though animals are not capable of moral judgement on Hume's view, since they cannot adopt the requisite standpoint of the general point of view, they do feel sympathy with each other and even with humans that they interact with. Hume gives the example of dogs hunting in packs: 'Everyone has observ'd how much more dogs are animated when they hunt in a pack, than when they pursue their game apart; and 'tis evident this can proceed from nothing but from sympathy' (THN 2.2.12).

In the *Enquiry*, however, sympathy is more like benevolence. It is not simply the capacity by which we pick up on the emotions of others; it explains why we care about them. It isn't just the capacity to pick up on others' emotions directly; it is the capacity to care about their well-being. He writes, 'no qualities are more entitled to the general good-will and approbation of mankind, than beneficence and humanity, friendship and gratitude, natural affection and public spirit, or whatever proceeds from a tender sympathy with others, and a generous concern for our kind and species' (EPM 2.2). In the *Enquiry* he also speaks of 'social sympathy' giving rise to 'fellow-feeling with human happiness or misery' (EPM 7.29). Further, in the *Enquiry* he maintains that 'the natural sentiment of benevolence' is common to all human beings, and underlies moral judgement (EPM 5.2).

However, even in the *Treatise*, it is clear that he thought the two were at least very intimately connected. Benevolence attends love, but only contingently. Love itself is aroused via sympathy. Thus, given basic facts of human nature on Hume's view, there is a close connection between the two at the very least (THN 2.2.9). In the section on justice Hume argues that the motive behind justice cannot be 'the love of mankind, merely as such', since this love is not present in the minds of all human beings. However, this is not exactly the same as benevolence, either, since Hume could simply be making the point that the sort of benevolence that is universal is particularistic, it is stimulated by either being near someone else whose mental states one is responsive to, or imaginatively engaging with another person's predicament.

Probably the best way to view the overall theory is to hold that there is a distinction between sympathy and benevolence, that is, a conceptual distinction, though the two are causally related. Where sympathy is properly functioning in the human agent, there will be benevolent tendencies—and this is a universal feature of human beings.

17.4.2 Moral Realism

Hume, like Hutcheson, rejected Shaftesbury's variety of realism. When one attributed 'wilful murder' to an action, the description has simply descriptive force without the addition of sympathy; my moral disapproval rests on my sympathy which underlies the condemnation of acts of wilful murder. Thus, when one judges that action to be vicious one is doing more than simply regarding it as an act of wilful murder.

As Barry Stroud notes, Hume does believe that when we hold an action to have the qualities of a wilful murder we also condemn it, and hold it to be a vicious action. However, that

> does not imply that regarding that action as vicious is simply believing that it has those observable [and inferrable] characteristics. He thinks that pronouncing an action to be vicious is something different and that is why he says that the vice entirely escapes *you* as long as you consider only the object thought to be vicious. (Stroud 1977: 178)

Hume did employ analogies between moral perception and other sorts of perception, such as colour perception. In a well-known passage he writes:

> When you pronounce any action or character to be vicious, you mean nothing, but that from the constitution of your nature you have a feeling or sentiment of blame from the contemplation of it. Vice and virtue, therefore, may be compar'd to sounds, colours, heat, and cold, which, according to modern philosophy, are not qualities in objects but perceptions in the mind.

It is clear that Hume rejected the view that moral qualities are intrinsic to actions. However, this does not mean that they are not 'real' qualities. They exist, but *in relation to* human beings with the sentiment of sympathy. This leads to a cognitive view, but one that is a form of relativism. Kenneth Winkler notes that this implication troubled Hume. Hume wrote to Hutcheson about whether or not he should modify the above passage:

> I wish from my Heart, I coud avoid concluding, that since Morality, according to your Opinion as well as mine, is determin'd merely by Sentiment, it regards only human Nature and human Life . . . If Morality were determin'd by Reason, that is the same to all rational Beings: But nothing but Experience can assure us, that the Sentiments are the same. What Experience have we with regard to superior Beings? How can we ascribe to them any Sentiments at all? (Hume, quoted in Winkler 1996 and reprinted in Raphael 1969: 111)

Winkler also points out that one might draw misleading lessons from Hume's use of the comparison. Elsewhere, Hume clearly regards virtues as *in* the person being evaluated. When he defines virtue, it is defined as a 'quality of the mind' that is found pleasing. But the passages comparing virtue to colour make it seem as though virtue is purely relational. My own view, argued for elsewhere, is that Hume believes virtues *are* mental qualities. He has a metaphysics of virtue. But the status of these qualities as virtues or vices depends upon our idealized emotional responses to the traits, refined by reason. The tension that Winker alludes to can be resolved by invoking the distinction between *ontological stance-independence* and *analytical stance-independence*.[2] A property has ontological stance-independence if it exists independently of the observer. Thus, if one views the colour of an object as consisting in the light-reflectance properties of the object, then colour has ontological stance-independence, and one is, in this sense, a realist about colour. However, one can be an ontological realist about colour and yet an analytical anti-realist about colour, since one might also hold that we can't fully *understand* what colour is without reference to our perceptions of it. Thus, a full analysis of colour is not stance-independent.

Virtues may be ontologically real, as dispositions or motives—qualities of the mind in the moral agent—and yet not be amenable to stance-independent analysis since they are qualities of the mind that the spectator finds pleasing from the general point of view. A specific stance is specified in the analysis.

17.4.3 Moral Virtue

Hume's account of moral virtue was similar to Hutcheson's, but also quite dramatically distinct in important respects. Like Hutcheson he believed that we responded favourably to virtue. Hume defines virtue as a quality of the mind that the spectator finds pleasing, from the general point of view. There is a good deal of controversy regarding what Hume had in mind by 'the general point of view'. This was clearly Hume's device for correcting the initial pleasing reaction that a spectator might feel. Often our reactions are distorted by bias and prejudice, and by lack of important information. The general point of view is the point of view that is abstracted away from these distortions.

---

[2] For an analogous distinction in philosophy of mind see Chalmers 2009.

> In order, therefore, to prevent those continual contradictions, and arrive at a more stable judgment of things, we fix on some steady and general points of view; and always, in our thoughts, place ourselves in them, whatever may be our present situation. (THN 3.3.1)

When we observe a motive in someone we may get pleasure or not from that observation. But in taking up our original reaction to the motive, we are in a position, from the general point of view, to approve or disapprove. And that is the genuine moral judgement. One of Hume's examples is the following:

> 'tis evident, that these sentiments, whence-ever they are deriv'd must vary according to the distance or contiguity of the objects; nor can I feel the same lively pleasure from the virtues of a person, who liv'd in *Greece* two thousand years ago, that I feel from the virtues of a familiar friend and acquaintance. Yet I do not say that I esteem the one more than the other. (THN 3.3.1)

This example is one where there is variation in my pleasure responses, as an individual, based on the spatial and temporal proximity of those whose virtue I am considering. I can correct for this variation by adopting the general point of view that indicates to me that both characters are equally admirable.

There is also interpersonal variation, and that variation can be corrected the same way, by appeal to the general point of view. This is crucial, on Hume's view, to successful evaluative communication.

What exactly is the general point of view? Does one consider the point of view of people 'in general'? I have argued elsewhere that this is not the correct interpretation of Hume, at least if we take seriously his view that it is possible for people 'in general' to be mistaken about virtue due to epistemic defects such as lack of full information or religious contamination (Driver 2004).

There were some traits that were 'immediately' agreeable, and those traits did involve the perception of a benevolent motive in the moral agent. In providing a broader definition of virtue, Hume again parted ways with Hutcheson. On Hume's view, virtue is not reducible to a benevolent motive. As we noted earlier, Hutcheson had been criticized for failing to plausibly account for virtues such as justice, which do not seem to require a benevolent motive. Indeed, Hume himself would note that we may feel very badly for someone, and yet note that justice requires a verdict against them.

Hume divides virtue into two broad categories: the natural virtues and the artificial virtues. Natural virtues are qualities of the mind we find immediately agreeable to ourselves or others; the pleasure we get from their survey is not due to any convention or socially constructed activity. An example is benevolence. Some virtues, on the other hand, depend for their pleasing quality on convention of some sort. An example is justice. For Hume, 'justice' is understood very narrowly. Justice is established to regulate property. Human beings, compared to other animals, are lacking in many natural advantages—we lack fur, sharp teeth, physical agility. And yet, like other animals, we have many needs that must be satisfied, needs for food, clothing, and shelter. We gain huge advantages from living in a society which makes satisfying our wants much more efficient. Hume goes as far as to say ''Tis by society alone he [Man] is able to supply his defects' (THN 3.2.2). A system of justice is needed to regulate social interactions surrounding property in a way that promotes this efficiency. As such, individual acts of justice may not strike us as pleasing in themselves. We may recognize the justice of requiring a poor man to pay back a debt to a rich one, while feeling rather badly about it.

However, even in the case of the artificial virtues sympathy is at work. In the case of the artificial virtues, the sympathy is experienced in relation to the systematic good produced by the conventional norms.

17.5 ADAM SMITH (1723–1790)

Smith, like Hume, believed that the basis for morality was sympathy. Smith had been a student of Hutcheson's at Glasgow, and was greatly influenced by Hutcheson. Smith makes several distinctions explicitly that help to expand sentimentalism. He notes that in making some moral judgements, the spectator needs to be able to put himself in the position of the person whose situation or self is being judged.

> As we have no immediate experience of what other men feel, we can form no idea of the manner in which they are affected, but by conceiving what we ourselves should feel in the like situation. Though our brother is upon the rack, as long as we ourselves are at our ease our senses will never inform us of what he suffers.... By the imagination we place ourselves in his situation, we conceive ourselves enduring all the same torments, we enter, as it were, into his body and become in some measure the same person with him; and then form some idea of his sensations. (Smith 2002)

On Smith's view it is this imaginative exercise which is the source of our feelings for others. General fellow-feeling is sympathy (Smith 2002).

The imaginative exercise of sympathy is, in Smith, quite interesting because it can involve either a full or partial putting oneself in the position of another. The most dramatic example of the partial sort is the case of sympathy with the dead. One would have thought that if one put oneself in the situation of a dead person one would feel nothing. Smith, however, seems to ask, how *would you* feel to be deprived of all life's positive experiences?, rather than, how would you feel if you were the person who were dead? The answer to the latter question is 'nothing' and is not so nearly as informative as the first.

It is sympathy that underlies approval. For a person to approve of another person's mental states or feelings, for example, she must sympathize with them. If the agent's sentiment lacks 'propriety', then one will not sympathize with the agent and thus fail to approve. To use Smith's terminology, an action possesses propriety if a spectator (one meeting the appropriate conditions) approves of the sentiment leading to the action; impropriety if that spectator disapproves. In making judgements of propriety we focus on the cause of the action in question, such as the agent's motivational structure, the reasons the agent had for acting as she did. Actions can also be subject to judgements of 'merit' and 'demerit'. A meritorious action is deserving of reward, and one lacking in merit, deserving of punishment (Smith 2002). These distinctions work together in the following way: Consider an action of benevolence, such as Mary providing food to a soup kitchen out of a concern for the well-being of others. In this case she is acting with propriety since the action proceeds from an admirable 'affection' on her part; in addition to the propriety of the act, however, we also notice that the act has what Smith calls a 'beneficent tendency'—it leads, in this case, to the good of others in need of the food. In judging of an action's merit, we not only look at its propriety, but also at what the action tends to produce. Mary's action fully engages our sympathies because it is generated by a good sentiment, and it tends to produce good as well. We recognize that the recipients are called upon to feel gratitude, and we indirectly sympathize with that. The sympathy is indirect since it depends upon a prior approval of the agent's motives. Without that prior approval we would not engage properly with the recipient's gratitude.

Smith moves from describing how people go about making judgements to an account of the best way those judgements are to be made. For a judgement of propriety or merit to be warranted, the spectator making the judgement must be making a judgement that an *impartial* spectator would go along with. It is the responses of the impartial spectator that set the standard for moral judgement. There has been a good deal of discussion of what Smith meant by 'impartial' spectator. Roderick Firth viewed the impartial spectator as an *ideal* observer: 'As an ideal observer . . . it is sufficient that he be capable of reacting in a manner which will determine by definition whether an ethical judgment is true or false' (Firth 1952: 321). The ideal observer possesses qualities that prevent mistakes. The ideal observer is all-knowing with respect to the non-normative facts, he is disinterested, possesses superior imaginative capacities, is dispassionate and consistent. The ideal observer has reactions, then, that are not prone to mistakes.

This account renders moral properties objective in that, in a sense, they are stance-independent in ways discussed in the earlier section on Hume. That x is a moral property is determined by what the ideal observer would approve of. The idea, as it has been further developed in contemporary metaethics, is that moral properties (or concepts) are *response-dependent*. Though, as we noted earlier, moral properties (or concepts) are not *analytically* stance-independent, and this may still be sufficient dependence to make the account susceptible to realist worries—isn't it at least conceptually possible that the well-reasoning, knowledgeable, and properly motivated observer might still get things wrong about what is, objectively, good?

However, response-dependence of the sort suggested by Firth is stance-independent in the ontological sense, the ideal observer's responses providing the truth-makers for moral claims. Both Hume's general point of view and Smith's impartial spectator are mechanisms provided to correct for idiosyncratic responses that can distort judgement. But there has been a good deal of debate on the exact nature of the distortion that needs correction. On the sentimentalist view of basic desires, whatever they are, they are not themselves distorted. Rather, we can fail to recognize or adequately reason about important facts that may alter our views on how best to satisfy basic desires. Matilda wants to be happy. She believes that the best way for her to live a happy life is to try to earn as much money as possible so that she can buy the biggest house and the snazziest car. But suppose that she is just mistaken about those facts. A big house and a nice car will not make her happy. The mistake is in the facts, not in the desire for happiness itself.

If morality is fundamentally about emotion, what does that say about our moral claims? On the ideal observer view we can say that 'Killing an innocent person is wrong' is true, because the ideal observer would disapprove of killing an innocent person. This, again, treats the responses of the ideal observer as truth-makers with respect to moral claims. However, other contemporary writers have taken Humean sentimentalism to be a form of non-cognitivism, in which no moral claims are either true or false—they have no truth value whatsoever. A moral claim, unlike a factual or descriptive one, is an expression of *emotion*. That is how they function. Moral claims merely appear to state objective facts, but this appearance is due to our *projection* of emotion onto the real world (Blackburn 2001).

Blackburn is a writer inspired by sentimentalism to develop a distinctive metaethical view about the nature of moral evaluation. Some contemporary sentimentalists view it as undergirding a distinctive approach to normative ethics as well, as a variety of the 'ethics of care', which can be given a cognitivist underpinning such that some moral claims turn out to be true (along roughly the line suggested by Firth). One writer developing this brand of metaethical sentimentalism is Michael Slote (Slote 2010).

Slote holds that there is an emotive element to moral utterances, but that element is a matter of conversational implication from the moral judgement itself. When Sally holds that 'Murder is wrong' she is conversationally implying that she disapproves of murder, but, on Slote's view, the approval (or disapproval) that *she* feels is not part of the truth conditions for the utterance. In the case of an ideal observer theory, one could still hold that the verdicts of the ideal observer provide the truth conditions, but that the liking implied by the utterer is not itself part of what makes a claim that something is good true. Slote believes we have evidence for this because the 'liking' is detachable from positive moral judgements. If Sally says 'Charity is good', she conversationally implies she likes charity, but that can be detached from the utterance 'Charity is good', thus the utterance that 'Charity is good and I don't really like it very much' is not incoherent; further, the conversational implication can be cancelled; 'Charity is good, but that's not to say I approve of it' is also not incoherent (Slote 2010). This approach seeks to keep the intuition that there is something motivating about moral claims, as well as the view that they have truth values.

One possibility in developing a cognitivist and sentimentalist account of moral claims is to argue for a *substantive* form of constructivism based on sentimentalism. The starting point for such a project is to cite, as the early sentimentalists did, the fact that for human agents (and possibly for the wider category of social agents), capacities such as empathy and sympathy are needed for self-regulation, and it is self-regulation that can be the basis for our normative practices. Self-regulation is to be contrasted with the more familiar constructivist notion—in Kantian constructivism—of self-governance, or self-legislation (Korsgaard 1996). The Humean would hold self-governance to be a form of self-regulation in the form of reason regulating emotional responses. That is, for the Humean constructivist, reason functions in such a way as to regulate emotions, but in line with other emotional commitments, some of which are so basic that they underlie even general agency. In fact, we can return to Hume to get an idea of how this might work. Hume discusses an important category of belief that later commentators would refer to as 'natural' belief (Driver 2008). These beliefs are ones that cannot be discarded or doubted as a practical matter, beliefs such as the belief that the external world at least resembles one's perceptions of it (under normal conditions, etc.). Some normative beliefs are like this as well, normative beliefs having to do with the well-being of others being a *good* thing, for example. In the case of these beliefs, our practical commitment to utilizing them in action is due to sympathy. The ideal sympathizer sets the standard, and through our reflective powers we can have access to at least approximations of the sorts of things such a sympathizer would approve of.

17.6 Psychological Realism

One point of criticism in the contemporary literature is the extent to which Smith's, and to a greater degree, Hume's, views on sympathy are psychologically realistic. In the contemporary literature on the role of sentiment in moral judgement, attention has been paid to the issue of whether or not psychopaths make moral judgements. Psychopaths seem to be a problem for Hume's view that the sentiment of sympathy is universal, since they are people who do not care at all about the well-being of others. Of course, Hume's claim could be understood as pertaining to 'normal' human beings. It is certainly accurate to view psychopathy as a pathology. But some other writers, such as Jeannette Kennett, have noted that there are other forms of what are termed 'empathy deficit disorders' besides psychopathy (Kennett 2002). For example, persons with autism are often characterized as lacking in empathic connections to others. Since they do make moral judgements, Kennett views this as a challenge to Hume's sentiment-based account.

We need to be careful, however, in how we use 'empathy' and 'sympathy'. In the psychology literature a good deal of confusion is generated by very different usages of these terms. I propose to use the terms the following way:

Empathy: the capacity to pick up on the emotions of others and/or to take on the point of view of another

Sympathy: benevolent regard for others

Empathy, as I've characterized it above, is not exactly what Hume had in mind when discussing sympathy in the *Treatise*. There, one picks up on the emotions of others and reflects on them, or adopts them; one doesn't simply note them. Thus, we can distinguish an emotional empathy from a non-emotional empathy. The psychopath is capable of engaging empathically with others in that she can put herself in someone else's position. This may or may not generate any emotional response. But a successful psychopath can probably do this very well. It is what is required for successful deception and lying, for example. One needs to be able to consider a situation from someone else's point of view in order to be able to figure out what that person finds plausible. This is one reason young children are not very good at deception.

Sympathy, as specified above, does involve *some* emotional response. It involves caring about what happens to others. This caring can be *de re* or *de dicto*. When someone cares *de dicto*, she cares about others, but non-particularistically, and non-particularistically in a very specific way. That is, the caring itself may be understood as either disinterested benevolence, that is, as caring about persons in general, or as interested benevolence, caring about a particular person but not caring about particular aspects of that person's well-being that really matter to that person. *De re* caring about a particular person's well-being requires richer detail. It is here that persons with autism may have problems in terms of gathering the right sort of information needed to flesh out that level of detail. But the sort of empathy deficit disorder suffered by persons with autism is quite different from that suffered by psychopaths, and their example does not at all undermine the sentimentalist, or Humean, account of moral agency (see Driver 2011a).

Acting from a *de dicto* desire to do the right thing has sometimes been referred to as 'moral fetishism', as being concerned about the rather abstract demands of morality rather than what actually grounds those demands (Smith 1994). 'Moral fetishism' can be spelled out in different ways (Shoemaker 2007); however, the version that concerns me here is the one that views a failure to appreciate the very basic of moral reasons as a defect that, in effect, cripples moral agency. This seems to some extent unwarranted. It may be that some people, or even many people in some situations—particularly those involving some form of basic normative uncertainty—are only able to act on the *de dicto* desire. There may be serious efficiency costs associated with trying to flesh such desires out. Persons with autism, who may have trouble picking up on how certain activities may bother others, may exemplify this in that dealing with the empathy deficit can involve extremely time-consuming development and adherence to rules and routine. Further, a person without an empathy deficit may be uncertain about what grounds the normative judgement that 'x is wrong'—it might be that x leads to terrible consequences, or that x fails to treat an agent with adequate respect: she just doesn't know *which*. What seems fundamentally important to moral agency is the *de dicto* concern.

Other contemporary writers have argued for sentimentalism, but against the Humean variety based on sympathy. For example, Jesse Prinz is deeply sceptical of any attempts to *base* substantive moral norms on sympathy (Prinz 2011). The major problems he identifies have to do with the variability of sympathy. Early sentimentalists were quite aware of this problem, and thus added corrective mechanisms to the account. In Hume's case, the judgement must be made from the general point of view to have the right kind of authority. Prinz, however, believes that these corrective mechanisms fail.

Shaun Nichols has argued for the empirical support of the Humean view of moral judgement (Nichols 2004). He also holds that the account of moral judgement is incompatible with metaethical realism, or objectivism, of the sort that holds that moral truths are true independent of moral agents. The empirical case is made largely by noting the research in psychology that tests reactions to paradigmatic moral transgressions, such as hitting someone. As Nichols notes, core moral judgements will involve the ability to judge the transgression as distinctively moral as opposed to, for example, merely conventional. Further, a moral transgression does not rely on authority, unlike other norm violations such as violations of etiquette norms. There is a distinctive affective response associated with moral judgements involving transgressions.

17.7 CONCLUSION

Sentimentalism is a view that is actively researched in philosophy and philosophically informed psychology. It was initially developed as a way of understanding morality as based on human nature, and, further, based on the desiring, caring facet of human nature. This basic approach to understanding both the nature of moral judgement and the source of its authority over our actions is compelling, especially in light of how such a view coheres with what we know about human development.

BIBLIOGRAPHY

Baldwin, J. 2004. 'Hume's Knave and the Interests of Justice', *Journal of the History of Philosophy* 42: 277–96.

Blackburn, S. 2001. *Ruling Passions*. New York: Oxford University Press.

Butler, J. 1983. *Five Sermons*, ed. Stephen Darwall. Indianapolis, IN: Hackett Publishing Co.

Chalmers, D. 2009. 'Ontological Anti-Realism', in D. Chalmers, D. Manley, and R. Wasserman (eds), *Metametaphysics: New Essays on the Foundations of Ontology*. New York: Oxford University Press, 77–129.

Cohon, R. 2008. *Hume's Morality*. New York: Oxford University Press.

Cooper, Anthony Ashley (3rd Earl of Shaftesbury). 1999. *An Inquiry Concerning Virtue or Merit*, in L. E. Klein (ed.), *Characteristics of Men, Manners, Opinion, Times*. New York: Cambridge University Press, 163–230.

Cudworth, R. 1969. *A Treatise Concerning Eternal and Immutable Morality*, excerpts in Raphael 1969, 105–19.

Darwall, S. 1995. *The British Moralists and the Internal Ought: 1640–1740*. New York: Cambridge University Press.

Driver, J. 2004. 'Pleasure as the Standard of Virtue in Hume's Moral Philosophy', *Pacific Philosophical Quarterly* 85: 173–94.

—— 2008. 'Imaginative Resistance and Psychological Necessity', *Social Philosophy and Policy* 25: 301–13.

—— 2011a. 'The Secret Chain', *Southern Journal of Philosophy*, Spindel supplement, vol. 29, 234–38.

—— 2011b. 'A Humean Account of the Status and Character of Animals', in T. Beauchamp and R. Frey (eds), *The Oxford Handbook on Ethics and Animals*. New York: Oxford University Press, 144–71.

Firth, R. 1952. 'Ethical Absolutism and the Ideal Observer', *Philosophy and Phenomenological Research* 12 (3): 317–45.

Frazier, M. 2010. *The Enlightenment of Sympathy*. New York: Oxford University Press.

Gill, M. 2006. *The British Moralists on Human Nature and the Birth of Secular Ethics*. New York: Cambridge University Press.

Greene, J. et al. 2001. 'An fMRI Investigation of Emotional Engagement in Moral Judgment', *Science* 293: 2105–8.

Hobbes, T. 1996. *Leviathan*, ed. John Gaskin. New York: Oxford University Press.

Hume, D. 1874. 'Of the Standard of Taste', in *The Philosophical Works of David Hume*, ed. T. H. Green and T. H. Grose, vol. 3.

—— 1998. *An Enquiry Concerning the Principles of Morals*, ed. T. Beauchamp. Oxford: Clarendon Press. [EPM]

—— 2007. *A Treatise of Human Nature*, ed. D. F. Norton and M. Norton. Oxford: Clarendon Press. [THN]

Hutcheson, F. 1969. *An Inquiry Concerning Moral Good and Evil*, excerpts in Raphael 1969.

Jacobson, D. and D'Arms, J. 2000. 'Sentiment and Value', *Ethics* 110: 722–48.

Kennett, J. 2002. 'Autism, Empathy, and Moral Agency', *Philosophical Quarterly* 22: 340–57.

Korsgaard, Christine. 1996. *The Sources of Normativity*. New York: Cambridge University Press.

Nichols, S. 2004. *Sentimental Rules*. New York: Oxford University Press.

Norton, R. E. 1995. *The Beautiful Soul*. Ithaca, NY: Cornell University Press.

Prinz, J. J. 2011. 'Against Empathy', *Southern Journal of Philosophy*, Spindel supplement, vol. 29, 214–33.

Raphael, D. D. (ed.) 1969. *British Moralists: 1650–1800*, Vol. I and II. New York: Oxford University Press.

Shafer-Landau, R. 2003. *Moral Realism: A Defense*. New York: Oxford University Press.

Shoemaker, D. 2007. 'Moral Address, Moral Responsibility, and the Boundaries of the Moral Community', *Ethics* 118: 70–108.

Slote, M. 2007. *The Ethics of Care and Empathy*. New York: Routledge.

—— 2010. *Moral Sentimentalism*. New York: Oxford University Press.

Smith, A. 2002. *A Theory of the Moral Sentiments*, ed. Knud Haakonssen. New York: Cambridge University Press.

Smith, Michael. 1994. *The Moral Problem*. Oxford: Blackwell.

Stroud, B. 1977. *Hume*. New York: Routledge & Kegan Paul.

Wiggins, D. 1987. 'A Sensible Subjectivism', in *Needs, Values, and Truths*. New York: Oxford University Press.

Winkler, K. 1996. 'Hutcheson, Hume on the Color of Virtue', *Hume Studies* 22: 3–22.

CHAPTER 18

BUTLER'S ETHICS[1]

DAVID McNAUGHTON

18.1 INTRODUCTION

IT is often remarked that Butler's primary purpose in his writings was as much practical as theoretical. He wished to bring people to a sense of their duty: what they owed to God and to their fellow humans. Nevertheless, to achieve his practical goals, he was often required to engage in theory. He needed to refute arguments that suggested, for example, that the demands of morality often conflicted with self-interest and that, where they did, reasonable people should ignore the promptings of conscience and pursue their own interests. In refuting such claims, Butler had to go deeply into 'abstruse and difficult' questions, but rarely went further than he needed to for his purposes (P7).[2] In interpreting Butler we should heed this self-imposed limitation. First, he will concede a point to show that his main claims go through even on weaker assumptions than he thinks justified. Second, it is not his aim to produce a complete ethical theory.

Butler's views on ethics are to be found primarily in *Fifteen Sermons* (1726 and 1729), and *A Dissertation of the Nature of Virtue* (1736, as an appendix to his *Analogy*). Since ten years separate the two works, any interpretation should not assume that Butler's views are unchanged.[3]

---

[1] In writing this chapter I have drawn at some points on McNaughton 1996.

[2] There are many editions of Butler's ethical writings so references to Butler's works follow a common convention, where S denotes the *Sermons*; P denotes the Preface to the *Sermons*; D the *Dissertation*; A the *Analogy*. In the case of P and D the following number denotes the number of the paragraph in Bernard's definitive edition. In the case of S, the number of the sermon is followed by the number of the paragraph. In the case of A, references are to Part, chapter, and paragraph.

[3] There are a number of overviews of Butler's moral philosophy. Two good brief ones are Broad 1930 and Arrington 1998. Penelhum 1985 Part One has a rather longer discussion.

18.2 SUPERIORITY AND AUTHORITY

We need to be clear what question Butler is addressing, lest we misunderstand his answer. In the first three Sermons (and the corresponding part of the Preface) Butler asks what 'obligations [we have] to the practice of virtue' (P12), i.e. what reasons we have to live virtuously. His answer is that this is what our nature requires of us. He argues (following ancient moralists, such as the Stoics) that 'virtue consists in following [nature] and vice in deviating from it' (P13).

He rests his case for living virtuously on his celebrated teleological theory of human nature. In the *Sermons* Butler (not unnaturally) takes the existence of a good God for granted. Such a creator will have done nothing in vain; each of our faculties, therefore, must have some proper function that will fit us for life in this world. We can discern that function by reflection on our natures. Such reflection shows that we are made for virtue; when we act virtuously we use our faculties as they are intended to be used; when we act viciously we misuse or abuse them. This teleological note is strongly sounded, so one question is whether his account is of any interest to modern secular moral theory.

He begins his account of our natures by distinguishing between different components of our practical psychology. The most prominent are conscience, self-love, and the particular passions or affections. The particular passions are many and various; what they have in common is that they seek to attain some particular object. Hunger seeks food; compassion, the relief of someone's suffering, and so on. The gratification of any affection gives us pleasure, but gratification of one often impedes the gratification of others. Our overall long-term happiness consists in harmonizing their gratification, so that each affection attains its object within 'its due stint and bound' (S11.9). This harmonizing is the task of self-love. Finally, conscience, or reflection, alerts us to the moral status of our acts and prompts us to do what is right. As we all know, these various sources of motivation can conflict. Our desires and passions are often at odds with our longer-term interest, or our moral obligations, or both. Whether conscience can conflict with self-love, however, is a key question for Butler.

Merely to enumerate the components of our psychology omits its most important feature, namely that our internal principles are ordered hierarchically. They do not have equal claims, for some are superior to others. To say that a principle is superior is to make a normative claim: that it has authority; it has a right to govern. A subordinate principle may be motivationally strong enough to overcome a superior one, but then the agent will not be acting as he ought.

If no principle were superior, whatever we did would be natural, because we would be acting in accordance with some principle in our nature. However, given that these principles are hierarchically ordered, when a superior and an inferior principle conflict, we act unnaturally if we follow the inferior one. Butler illustrates this point by comparing an animal which, attracted by the bait, runs into a snare, with a human agent who indulges some appetite even though he recognizes that it will mean certain ruin (S2.10). The human, but not the animal, is violating his nature, by ignoring the superior principle of self-love. The human can and should recognize that he has good reason not to ruin himself to satisfy an impulse, and that he can be criticized for doing so. Likewise, since conscience is also a superior principle, to ignore its dictates is to act unnaturally; there is a lack of fit between how such an agent acts and how he could and should act which makes him blameworthy. Humans whose capacity for reflection is absent or impaired, such as 'idiots and madmen, as well as children' are held less accountable. They are capable not only of doing harm, but doing it intentionally, but their actions are nevertheless judged, in view of their incapacity, to be 'innocent or less vicious' (D5).

18.3 SUPREMACY OF CONSCIENCE

So much is clear. But various questions about the superior principles remain. Are conscience and self-love the only superior principles, or did (or should) Butler have added benevolence as a third? Are self-love and conscience equally authoritative, or is one supreme? Take the second question first. Butler's official answer is uncompromising.

> [C]onscience or reflection, compared with the rest as they all stand together in the nature of man, plainly bears upon it the marks of authority over all the rest, and claims the absolute direction of them all (P24).[4]

Despite these ringing pronouncements, Nicholas Sturgeon (1976) has famously argued that Butler is committed to theses inconsistent with his claim that conscience is supreme. Indeed, they are inconsistent with the claim that conscience has a voice of its own, independent of self-love.

Here is the problem. The following theses, Sturgeon claims, are central to Butler's theory.

(1) That virtue consists in following nature, vice in deviating from it.
(2) Whenever conscience approves or disapproves of an action, it does so on grounds of the virtue or vice of the action. (Sturgeon 1976: 325)

These two entail what Sturgeon calls the Naturalistic Thesis, that 'conscience bases its approval or disapproval of an action ... on the conformity of the action, or its lack of it, to the nature of the agent' (Sturgeon 1976: 316).[5, 6] To be unnatural, however, an action must violate the verdict of a superior principle. Conscience cannot be that principle, for that would be viciously circular. Conscience cannot deliver its verdict as to whether the act is

---

[4] See also, e.g. S2.8–9.

[5] Sturgeon offers a second argument for attributing the Naturalistic Thesis to Butler, namely that one of his main arguments presupposes its truth. I look at that argument later.

[6] Sturgeon does allow that, in the case of virtuous action, another factor is relevant, namely whether the agent had a virtuous motive. This leads him to a more guarded formulation of Butler's supposed naturalism: the Full Naturalistic Thesis which states that 'conscience never *favours* or *opposes* any action, except on grounds which include its naturalness or unnaturalness' (Sturgeon 1976: 328). But omission of that complicating point does not vitiate my criticism of his interpretation.

right or wrong until it knows if the action is unnatural, but the action could not violate the verdict of conscience until that verdict has been delivered. So conscience must base its verdict on whether the action violates the verdict of some *other* superior principle. That other principle is self-love. So Butler, perhaps unwittingly, is committed to a version of ethical egoism: conscience judges an act to be wrong just if, and because, it conflicts with self-love. But now nothing is left of Butler's repeated claim that conscience is the guide of life. For conscience has nothing to say on its own account, as it were; it simply reports on what self-love favours or opposes.

However, Sturgeon misidentifies the question Butler's account of naturalness is meant to answer. That it is natural to obey conscience is Butler's answer to the question: What reason is there to be virtuous? That question can only arise for someone who already knows what conscience is telling him to do, but wonders whether he is really under an obligation to do it. Butler makes this very clear at S2.13.

> [I]t will often happen there will be a desire of particular objects, in cases where they cannot be obtained without manifest injury to others. Reflection or conscience comes in, and disapproves the pursuit of them in these circumstances; but the desire remains. Which is to be obeyed, appetite or reflection?

That last question (the obligation question) presupposes, as Butler states, that conscience has already supplied a negative answer to the *prior* question: is this action morally right or wrong? If the answer to this prior *deontic* question also appealed to the naturalness of the act, as Sturgeon supposes, then Butler would be open to a charge of circularity. In fact, Butler says little about the *criterion* of right action, i.e. what makes an act right or wrong. Indeed, he is rather dismissive of attempts to provide any general theory.

> The inquiries which have been made by men of leisure, after some general rule, the conformity to, or disagreement from which, should denominate our actions good or evil, are in many respects of great service. Yet let any plain honest man, before he engages in any course of action, ask himself, Is this I am going about right, or is it wrong? ... I do not in the least doubt, but that this question would be answered agreeably to truth and virtue, by almost any fair man in almost any circumstance. (S3.4)

What he does say lends no support to the claim that the rightness or wrongness of an act depends on whether it is natural. The nearest Butler comes to providing a general answer to the criterion question is at D1, where he states that there is a 'universally acknowledged standard' of right action, 'namely, justice, veracity, and regard to common good'. But whether an act is just, truthful, or benevolent, is independent of whether it is natural in Butler's sense. The claim that virtue consists in following nature is not an answer to the question: Which acts are right?, but to the question: Why should I act rightly?[7]

---

[7] Another possible source of confusion is that Butler uses the phrase 'virtue consists in ...' in answering both the obligation question, when it is said to consist in following nature, and in answering the criterion question, when it is said to consist in justice, veracity, and benevolence. But the context makes clear which question Butler is addressing.

I turn now to a crucial passage which Sturgeon cites as evidence that Butler held the Naturalistic Thesis. At the close of Sermon 2, Butler concludes his argument that virtue is natural with a resounding *reductio* argument. What would be the consequence, Butler asks, if no principle of action were superior to any other? Take two actions of very different moral status: e.g. parricide and an act of filial duty.

> If there be no difference between inward principles, but only that of strength; we can make no distinction between these two actions considered as the actions of such a creature; but in our coolest hours must approve or disapprove them equally: than which nothing can be reduced to a greater absurdity. (S 2.17)

Of this passage, Sturgeon writes:

> Butler's crowning conclusion is this: that if no principle of human action has a natural superiority to any other, conscience must approve equally of *any* two actions whatever. And there is a problem, I submit, in seeing why this should be thought to follow. If no principle is superior to any other conscience will be on a par with any passion or appetite; but why should its lack of superiority prevent it, in Butler's view, from distinguishing actions, approving one and disapproving another? (Sturgeon 1976: 322–3)

The only answer, on Sturgeon's view, is that if no principle were superior to any other, no action would be unnatural, and so conscience would have nothing on which to base its approval or disapproval. This explanation presupposes that Butler held the Naturalistic Thesis.

Sturgeon's question is a good one, but we do not have to appeal to the Naturalistic Thesis to answer it. Sturgeon is understandably misled by the fact that we (and Butler) talk of conscience approving or disapproving of an act in two different contexts. Sometimes all we have in mind is what I earlier called the *deontic question*: is this type of act right or wrong? Thus, if I am asked whether or not I disapprove of some activity, fox-hunting, say, my answer will simply reflect whether I think fox-hunting to be morally permissible or forbidden.[8] If, in S2.17, Butler was thinking of disapproval in this sense, then his claim that conscience could not discriminate between parricide and an act of filial duty would be puzzling in the way that Sturgeon claims. Butler holds, however, that when we approve or disapprove of an individual for acting in some way, we use those terms in what we might call their desert-implying sense. At D1, he talks of 'approv[ing] some actions, under the peculiar view of their being virtuous and of good desert; and disapprov[ing] others, as vicious and of ill desert'. As we saw in discussing S2.10, praise and blame are appropriate only if the agent possesses the capacities that make him accountable. Butler is careful, in S2.17, to make it clear that he is thinking of approval and disapproval in the desert-implying sense. He writes: 'we can make no distinction

---

[8]   This seems to be his sense at P19 and S1.8, where Butler tells us that approval and disapproval are the characteristic functions of conscience *before* he has introduced the idea that conscience is a superior principle.

between these two actions *considered as the actions of such a creature*' (my emphasis). That is, if we think of a creature whose inward economy was not hierarchical we could not approve or disapprove of his actions, i.e. praise or blame him, since whatever he did would be equally natural.[9]

To sum up. If *A*-ing is wrong, that will be because *A*-ing is, say, unjust, deceitful, or harmful, not because it is unnatural.[10] However, an agent can only be condemned for *A*-ing if he had the capacity both to recognize that *A*-ing was wrong and to govern his actions by that recognition; in Butler's terms, he must have an authoritative conscience. That it defies his conscience is what makes the agent's *A*-ing unnatural; it isn't, however, what makes it wrong.

Does Butler consistently maintain that conscience is supreme? There are passages where self-love seems to approach, or even surpass, conscience in authority. The most notorious is at S 11.20, which ends

> Let it be allowed, though virtue or moral rectitude does indeed consist in affection to and pursuit of what is right and good as such; yet, that when we sit down in a cool hour, we can neither justify to ourselves this or any other pursuit, till we are convinced that it will be for our happiness, or at least not contrary to it.

Here Butler seems to give self-love a veto. As many commentators contend, this passage should probably be read as a homiletic concession. For it occurs in the course of an argument to show that, however much weight we might accord to the pursuit of our interests, there is no reason to suppose there is any special antipathy between love of self and love of neighbour. To persuade his hearers that he is not loading the dice against self-love, he announces at the outset that 'there shall be all possible concessions made to the favourite passion [i.e. self-love] ... it shall be treated with the utmost tenderness and concern for its interests' (S 11.3). Indeed, the sentence just quoted begins 'Let it be allowed' which I read as merely conceding a point for the sake of argument.

The second such passage occurs when he sums up his account of human nature.

> Reasonable self-love and conscience are the chief or superior principles in the nature of man: because an action may be suitable to this nature, though all other principles be violated; but becomes unsuitable, if either of these are. (S 3.9)

---

[9] This response to Sturgeon, which each of us arrived at independently, can also be found in Akhtar 2006. Akhtar claims that judgements about right and wrong are passive, intrusive, immediate, and do not involve complex reasoning. Judgements as to whether an agent can be held accountable for an act, by contrast, do involve reasoning. While both can be said to be moral judgements, Akhtar claims that only the former are made by conscience. On this last point, I think, the textual evidence is not as clear as he supposes.

[10] As Penelhum wisely remarks, 'Butler's claim that virtue consists in following nature is not intended to help identify what virtue requires, but to help ensure its practice' (1985: 61). This claim is endorsed by Darwall 1995: 255 n. Millar concurs: 'there is no suggestion that conscience works by looking to our nature as the standard of right' (1988: 172). Irwin, however, thinks that the *content* of morality is determined, in part, by what is natural: 'conscience considers what is and is not suitable to my nature as a whole' (2008: 524). In my view, when an agent is virtuous, all the parts of her nature will indeed be functioning as they ought, but that is not what makes her acts morally right.

This passage (along with the one just discussed) was taken by Sidgwick as evidence that Butler treats self-love and conscience as 'independent principles, and so far co-ordinate in authority that it is not "according to nature" that either should be overruled' (Sidgwick 1967a, p. 196).[11] Call this the independent and equal interpretation. On this understanding, there are two viewpoints from which we can assess what to do: those of self-interest and of morality. In the case of conflict, there is no further and authoritative viewpoint to which we can appeal.

Does this passage support Sidgwick's interpretation? True, Butler fails to mention the supremacy of conscience in his final summary of his view, but we need not read too much into this. First, Butler stresses that supremacy elsewhere (e.g. P24–5; S2.8). Second, Butler's main concern, throughout Sermons 2 and 3 has been to show that an agent who acts *on a particular impulse* against the counsels of self-love or of conscience violates his nature. The possibility of a conflict between self-love and conscience has not been raised. Third, in the passage immediately following, Butler denies that there can be such a conflict.

> Conscience and self-love, if we understand our true happiness, always lead us the same way. Duty and interest are perfectly coincident; for the most part in this world, but entirely and in every instance if we take in the future and the whole; this being implied in a good and perfect administration of things. (S 3.9)

To anyone who accepts this claim, the question of whether to follow conscience or self-love cannot arise. So it is scarcely surprising that Butler does not address it here.[12]

Elsewhere, however, Butler recognizes that this question arises for those who doubt his coincidence claim. Indeed, at P26 he raises a difficulty for Shaftesbury,[13] who espouses rational egoism; our only obligation is to promote our own interests. His case for virtue thus rests entirely on the coincidence thesis and so is vulnerable to one who doubts it. Shaftesbury gets into this difficulty, on Butler's view, because he omits the 'natural authority of reflection' or conscience. Suppose we now include that missing element. Someone may object that the doubter still has no reason to obey conscience rather than self-love, for he is now faced with conflicting obligations, which simply cancel out, leaving him with no reason to prefer duty to self-interest.

At this point Butler's argument takes an unexpected turn. We might expect him to appeal directly to the supreme authority of conscience, on which he has just been insisting.

---

[11] See also Sidgwick 1967b: xviii–xix.

[12] These passages seem a slim basis for Sidgwick's claim that the two principles are 'co-ordinate in authority'. Sidgwick found 'with pleasure and surprise' that on re-reading Butler 'with more care' he had a view very similar to Sidgwick's own, namely a belief in the 'Dualism of the Practical Reason' (Sidgwick 1967b: xviii–xix). (I am grateful to Roger Crisp for drawing my attention to these passages in Sidgwick.) This seems a striking instance of our capacity for reading our own views into the authors we admire. Sidgwick took Butler to be his precursor; Darwall, as we shall see, takes him to be a proto-Kantian, and I, as we shall also see, believe that he accepted Rational Intuitionism. Whether we can entirely avoid this pitfall when interpreting other philosophers is doubtful.

[13] Butler draws quite a lot from Shaftesbury's *Inquiry Concerning Virtue or Merit*, including a teleological approach to ethics, and a vigorous defence of the coincidence thesis (Shaftesbury 1999: 163–230).

He does, indeed, argue that our obligation to virtue is the weightier, but the reason he offers concerns the epistemic superiority of conscience.

> But the obligation on the side of interest really does not remain. For the natural authority of the principle of reflection is an obligation the most near and intimate, the most certain and known: whereas the contrary obligation can at the most appear no more than probable; since no man can be *certain* in any circumstances that vice is his interest in the present world, much less can he be certain against another: and thus the certain obligation would entirely supersede and destroy the uncertain one; which yet would have been of real force without the former. (P 26)

We should obey conscience because its verdicts are more certain than those of self-love. This appears to be a new argument for the claim that conscience has the final say—call it the certainty argument. What are we to make of it?

We cannot be sure that an act is in our interest, because it is not certain how things will turn out. But does not the same uncertainty afflict moral action? We may try to fulfil our obligations, but not succeed. Butler's response to this suggestion is to deny that whether an agent acted rightly or wrongly is vulnerable to future contingencies (see D2). It is on the basis of my intentions, and not the outcome, that we judge the morality of my conduct. However, the same distinction can be made with regard to self-love. We can distinguish between what I aimed to do—secure my happiness—and whether or not I succeeded. Butler himself points out in D6 that we can think of self-love in two ways. We can think of it as an affection that seeks gratification in attaining its goal. We *do* desire our own happiness, and are satisfied if we attain that end and frustrated if we do not, even if our conduct was above criticism.[14] We can also think of it, in Butler's terms, as a superior principle: prudence requires that we *should* take reasonable steps to ensure our happiness, and if we do not our conduct is open to criticism even if, contrary to expectations, things turn out well.[15]

In light of this distinction, we can see that Butler's certainty argument is flawed. He is not comparing like with like. If we are comparing *outcomes*, then we cannot be certain that either virtuous or self-interested action will bring about the results we intend. If, however, we are judging *conduct*, then we can be as certain we fulfilled our obligation to be prudent as we can be that we fulfilled our moral obligation. If, as Butler suggests, the competing obligations would cancel each other out, then appeal to certainty cannot settle the conflict in favour of conscience. The certainty argument is thus an aberration;[16] Butler should have stuck with his usual view that conscience is inherently supreme.

[14] Darwall 1995: 280 claims that 'unlike self-love and benevolence, whose objects are *states*, conscience's object is exclusively *conduct* and its regulation'. This claim is inconsistent with the passages I cite here. However, since I later endorse the single standpoint model, I agree with Darwall that, when we do consider whether our conduct was suitably self-interested or benevolent, it is conscience or reflection that delivers the verdict.

[15] At S11.16, Butler draws a similar distinction between benevolence, considered as a natural affection, which gets pleasure when it attains its object, and benevolence as a virtuous principle, where the pleasure comes from the consciousness of endeavouring to do good.

[16] For an interesting alternative account of the certainty argument see Wedgwood 2007: 191–2 and 195–9.

I have argued that Sidgwick's interpretation of the relationship between conscience and self-love is less well supported than what we might dub the independent but unequal interpretation. This retains the view that the standpoints of morality and of self-interest are independent and separately authoritative. In the event of conflict, however, conscience has the final say.

But this is not the only possible interpretation. In D6, Butler argues that prudence is a part of virtue.[17] People are no

> more at liberty, in point of morals, to make themselves miserable without reason, than to make other people so: or dissolutely to neglect their own greater good, for the sake of a present lesser gratification, than they are to neglect the good of others.

Butler's main support for this claim is that we blame people in the same manner for imprudence as for failures in our duty to others (immorality in its modern, narrower, sense).[18] This suggests a different understanding of the relation between conscience and self-love. There are not two standpoints with independent authority but only one. Conscience or reflection urges us to be both prudent and moral, and condemns us for failures in either respect. On this model, reflection or conscience weighs *all* the considerations relevant to how we should act (not just the moral ones) and issues an overall verdict on how we ought to act. This model may offer a pleasing solution to Butler's problem of conflicting obligations (though Butler does not make this point explicitly). For while interest and duty can conflict, or at least be thought to do so, it may be that no virtuous action is *imprudent*. Prudence does not require that we are never willing to sacrifice self-interest, but only that we have 'a *due* concern about our own interest or happiness' and make a '*reasonable* endeavour to secure and promote it' (D6, my emphasis). Considerations of self-interest are only a subset of those that bear upon how we should behave, and reflection will have given them due weight in its final judgement. In following conscience, then, even when it requires me to act in ways that are apparently against my interests, I will have shown due concern for my happiness. I will violate my nature if I risk my own well-being to satisfy some impulse, but not if I am doing what is right.[19]

In the *Sermons* we can find support for both single and dual standpoint interpretations. In favour of the former, Butler repeatedly identifies conscience, but never self-love, with reflection.[20] Furthermore, while Butler says that conscience 'carries its own authority with it' and 'claims authority' (P24; S2.8; S2.14; S3.5) he never makes this claim for self-love.[21] That suggests that conscience is the source of any authority that attaches to considerations of self-interest.[22] In favour of the latter interpretation he frequently

---

[17] I don't believe that he makes this claim explicitly anywhere in the *Sermons*.

[18] We don't, perhaps, blame people as much for imprudence as for vice, but Butler gives plausible reasons why this might be so in the remainder of D6.

[19] This does not mean that an agent might not wonder whether his conscience was paying sufficient concern to his interests.

[20] Throughout the Preface and first three *Sermons* Butler almost always yokes the two together.

[21] I am indebted to O'Brien 1991 for these points.

[22] Darwall also comes to this view, though for rather different reasons.

treats self-love and conscience as distinct principles.[23] However that may be, by the time of the *Dissertation*, Butler seems to have embraced the single standpoint model.

18.4 ASSESSING THE CASE FOR VIRTUE

To what extent does Butler's case for virtue rely on theological assumptions? What force does it have without them? His case is two pronged. First, we should obey conscience, and live virtuously, because that is what our nature requires. Second, we can be assured that duty and interest *never* conflict. Both these claims seem to rest, in part, on claims about God's goodness.

The first claim appears to rest on Butler's theistic teleology. Each aspect of our nature was given to us by God for a purpose. In some cases the purpose is obvious (e.g. hunger and thirst). In others it is not so clear (e.g. resentment). Then we need to ask '"Why or for what end such a passion was given us": and this chiefly in order to shew what are the abuses of it' (S8.1). One clue lies in the direct tendency of any part of our psychology; these are 'signs' (S2.3) or 'indications' (S1.5) that it was given us for that particular purpose.[24] Conscience claims authority to direct our whole lives. Hence we may infer that this is what it was designed to do.[25]

Why is design relevant to how we should live? Darwall objects that, from the mere fact that something was designed to carry out a particular task, no normative conclusions can be drawn. The obvious reply is that here the designer is wholly good, powerful, and knowledgeable, and cares for us. We have been designed for good ends, and ought to achieve them.[26] 'Gratitude, reverence, and prudence' all give us reason to live as we were meant to (O'Brien 1991: 53). That is true even if we do not fully understand how fulfilling our design plan contributes to the overall good.[27]

---

[23] Irwin 2008: 510 notes that Butler sometimes talks of conscience as the generic faculty of reflection, but sometimes, more narrowly, as a specific principle, distinct from self-love.

[24] See O'Brien 1991: 50.

[25] Millar 1988 takes Butler's theistic teleology to be central to his case for supremacy of conscience and goes so far as to claim that we 'can envisage the possibility that we are so made that considerations deriving from "justice, veracity, and regard to the common good" might conceivably be overridden by reasons deriving from the demands of our nature' (p. 175). For objections and a reply see Brinton 1991 and Millar 1992. Penelhum also holds that Butler's theistic teleology is central to his argument (1985: 15).

[26] Wedgwood 2007: 182 considers a possible reply on behalf of Darwall. Since Butler is not a voluntarist, he cannot say that what *makes it the case* that there is overriding reason to lead a virtuous life is that God intended it. Rather, he must take the other horn of the Euthyphro Dilemma, and claim that the fact that God intends us to lead virtuous lives is at best decisive evidence that there is overriding reason for us to be virtuous. So God's design cannot explain why we have overriding reason to be virtuous. Wedgwood rightly points out that Butler's concern is probably not to explain why we have such reason but simply to establish that we do have such reason. Even if Wedgwood is right, that God made us for virtue affects what we have reason to do in two ways. First it reassures us that we are meant to obey conscience. Second, as well as wronging our fellows, vice displays ingratitude and rebelliousness towards our Creator.

[27] As we shall later see, Butler takes seriously this very possibility at D8.

Many commentators agree that if we remove God from the picture Butler's teleological argument for virtue is undermined. Wedgwood denies this.[28] He holds that Butler was arguing *from* teleological facts about our natures *to* God's purposes, rather than the other way round. We need make no theological assumptions in order to understand the function of the eye or the ear. Similarly, Butler presumably thought it obvious that our various mental faculties had various functions. In opposition to Darwall, Wedgwood claims that the notion of teleology involves normativity. A system may malfunction, but there is a *right* and *proper* way for it to operate. Events and capacities are explained teleologically by showing what is good about them. Does that mean we can discover the function of something only on the basis of the relevant normative facts? Wedgwood denies this, claiming that we can investigate the dispositions that seem most fundamental to and characteristic of the system in order to discover its proper end.[29] Conscience claims to be our governor and approves only of actions that accord with virtue, so we may surmise that this is its function, independently of theological considerations. Given Butler's 'assumption that the life that we have overriding reason to lead is the life in which all these elements of our nature are functioning properly ... we have overriding reason to be virtuous' (Wedgwood 2007: 195).

Wedgwood considers an obvious objection. Hasn't the mechanism of natural selection provided a much better explanation of biological phenomena than positing 'a fundamental tendency of living things towards leading the sort of life that it is right and best for them to lead'? Wedgwood's response is that teleology may still be defensible in philosophy of mind, if we suppose that 'the intentional is the normative'. Mental states essentially play certain roles in our mental economy; to lack any disposition to play that role would disqualify something from being a mental state of that kind.

Let us concede, for the sake of argument, that, without assuming a *theistic* teleology, we can think of the characteristic function of reflection or conscience as being to assess and direct conduct. To be functioning properly, however, conscience must not only guide conduct but guide it *correctly*. If reflection does not endorse conduct that is just, honest, and benevolent, then it will not lead us to live virtuously. Butler is confident that the deliverances of an honest conscience are never (or almost never) mistaken. This is not to deny that *we* are often mistaken, but that is because we misuse our conscience; we show partiality to ourselves which takes the form of special pleading, self-deception, or straightforward suppression of conscience's injunctions. But this is a form of dishonesty for which we are responsible and for which we can be blamed

---

[28] As does Brownsey 1995. On his view, when we ask 'what conceivable *role* conscience could play in a life correspondent to human nature' that role must be, given conscience's claims, that it govern our conduct (1995: 83). In Brownsey's view this claim can be supplemented by, but does not depend on, theological considerations.

[29] I doubt Butler holds that we can always discover the function of some part of our psychology without reference to the relevant normative facts. As we saw with resentment, to determine the *proper* use of our various faculties and tendencies we often have to understand for what good purposes they might have been given us.

(S3.4).[30] What underpins, at least in part, Butler's confidence in the inerrancy of conscience seems, once again, to be his theistic teleology. It is tempting to read him as offering a version of Descartes' 'God is not a deceiver' move.[31] God gave us a conscience that claims direction of our lives; it will not mislead us provided we use our faculties aright. Can a secular teleological theory of the mind offer a similar guarantee? Wedgwood suggests it can. An example would be Davidson's claim that we should interpret people so that they turn out not only to believe the truth but also to love the good. But this interpretative constraint is weak. People's desires and aims have to be intelligible. But that only requires that we can see how what they love might *seem* good to them, not that it actually is good. Butler makes a dual claim. We have overriding reason to act as our reflective judgement dictates, *and* that reflection, if honestly undertaken, will always direct us to do what is morally right. A teleological secular philosophy of mind might support the first of these claims, but not the second.[32]

Darwall, as we have seen, denies that facts about God's design yield normative conclusions. But he thinks that Butler has a different argument for the claim that a rationally reflective agent will act as morality requires—an argument that anticipates Kantian constructivism, and does not rely on any teleological assumptions. On this interpretation, Butler asserts both halves of what Darwall calls Kant's reciprocity thesis: 'morality and autonomous agency are mutually entailing' (Darwall 1995: 148). Butler is committed, as we have seen, to the first half of the reciprocity thesis: morality implies autonomy. To be an object of moral assessment, an agent must be capable of reflectively governing her life. Darwall maintains that Butler is also committed to the second half of the thesis: autonomy entails morality. 'Since conscience is the seat of *moral* judgment...this amounts to a claim that the normativity of morality...consists in its being the case that fully exercising the capacity for autonomous agency leads to conclusive motives to be moral' (Darwall 1995: 248).

Why, for Kantian constructivists, does autonomy entails morality? The thought, as I understand it, is that sound practical reasoning must be conducted in accordance with certain *formal* constraints—formal in order to avoid begging any substantive evaluative questions. (In Kant's own case, the maxim of one's action must pass the categorical imperative test.) Only conduct that is morally required or, at least, permissible, will survive this process. What makes this a constructivist, rather than a realist, position? Moral realists hold that moral facts are stance-independent. Moral claims 'are not made true by

[30] Butler does allow, in this passage, that superstition may mislead someone's conscience in a way for which he is not responsible. See also S2.1 where he says that there seems to be 'some small diversity amongst mankind' with respect to the deliverances of conscience. For discussion of the infallibility of conscience see Hebblethwaite 1992. For discussion of the role of self-deceit see Garrett 2011.

[31] This point is mentioned by Darwall 1995: 269.

[32] Indeed, Butler could be seen as making three claims. First, that we ought to act in accordance with the verdict of careful reflection (and not, say, on impulse). Second, that careful reflection will conclude that we should do what seems to us morally right. Third, that, provided we are honest, what seems to us morally right will in fact be so. His confidence in the truth of the second, as well as the third, of these claims may also rest, in part, on his belief in Providence.

virtue of their ratification from within any given actual or hypothetical perspective' (Shafer-Landau 2003: 15). This is what Kantian constructivists deny. Darwall notes that the Kantian version of constructivism has it that 'something's standing as a normative reason ultimately *depends* on its being motivating (treated as a reason) in fully rational deliberation, where the latter is determined by internal, formal features of the deliberative process, not by its responsiveness to independently establishable normative reasons' (Darwall 2006: 299).

Darwall concedes that interpreting Butler as a constructivist, rather than a realist, is at odds with some of what he says, especially with his repeated claim that he accepts the view that there are eternal fitnesses and unfitnesses of things—an allusion to the staunchly realist view of Samuel Clarke.[33] On a realist construal of Butler, the authority of conscience might 'derive from the independent existence of normative practical facts together with the contingent fact that, as God designed us, conscience is our best access to these' (Darwall 1995: 269). But Darwall thinks that to view Butler as a realist would be at odds with one of his most distinctive theses, namely that for a creature who lacked an authoritative conscience there would be no distinction between how she does act and how she should act.[34] If moral facts are really independent of us, then '[j]ust as there would still be objects even if we lacked the means to sense them, so there would be facts about how we should act though we lacked any access to them through conscience' (Darwall 1995: 269).

In fact, however, there is no conflict between the moral realism of Clarke and other intuitionists and Butler's acknowledgement that a creature that lacked a hierarchical motivational structure would lack reason to prefer one course of action to another. The belief that the two are in conflict stems from a misunderstanding of the sense in which, for the realist, reasons to act are independent of the agent. They are, indeed, *stance-independent*, but their existence depends not only on the way things are outwith the agent, but also on how things are with the agent; in particular on her capacities. On an approach like Clarke's, rightness is a relation between an agent, an act, and a circumstance.[35] Reasons to act are reasons *for* a particular agent to perform a particular act in a particular circumstance. Change any of these three, and what the agent has reason to do may change. In that respect, the analogy with the reality of the external world is misleading, since the distribution of objects in space is wholly independent of the capacities, or even the existence, of agents. For S to have reason to A, S must be the kind of agent who is both able to A and also has the capacity to recognize that she should A, and act on that recognition. None of this need push the realist in the direction of constructivism, since facts about the capacities of the agent, the range and nature of the acts open to her, and the circumstances in which she finds herself, are all stance-independent.

---

[33] See e.g. Clarke 1969: 191–206. Irwin 2008: 481–4 thinks that Butler's apparent endorsement of Clarke's rationalism at P12 (and at various points in the *Analogy*) is less than whole-hearted, and that Butler is offering a third way, between Sentimentalists and Rationalists. I am not convinced, but discussion would take us too far afield.

[34] I take it that Darwall is thinking especially of the argument at the end of Sermon 2.

[35] Ross 1939: 52–4 praises Clarke for seeing that rightness is a relation between an act and a circumstance.

The case for viewing Butler as a proto-constructivist looks weak.[36] Moreover, Butler in fact has little to say about *formal* constraints on practical reasoning. All Darwall suggests is that conscience operates properly when it judges coolly and impartially.[37] Not only are these constraints very thin, but also they are not constraints specifically on practical, as opposed to theoretical, reasoning. I conclude that neither Wedgwood nor Darwall has shown that Butler's claim that practical reflection will lead to virtue can be dislodged from its theistic moorings.

How would the coincidence thesis fare in the absence of theistic support? The claim that duty and interest are *perfectly* coincident rests, of course, on there being an afterlife in which a just God will proportion happiness to desert. However, Butler is confident that virtue and happiness will *largely* coincide in this life 'even upon supposition that the prospect of a future life were ever so uncertain' (P28). Butler's confidence is not based on a moralized conception of happiness; he does not assume that possession of the virtues is a constituent part of well-being. Happiness, for Butler, consists in one's appetites and affections enjoying their objects (P37). What pleasures may the virtuous person expect? Many of our passions are directed primarily to social ends. The more we help others, the more pleasure we will get from this source. Further, the closer we get to being *fully* virtuous the more our affections, and not just our conduct, will be shaped by conscience (S3.2 n.). No desire will be excessive or disproportionate; they will harmonize with one another, and so the possibilities of frustration will be minimized.[38] Moreover, the virtuous take pleasure in the exercise of virtue. Given the range of pleasures available to the virtuous, there is no reason, Butler claims, to think that any vicious way of life will offer more. Cupidity, ambition, intemperance, rage, and envy are both miserable in themselves and tend to bring more miseries in their wake. Finally, the vicious stand self-condemned, and the dissatisfaction they feel when they survey their own conduct will compound their unhappiness.

How convincing is this case? Wedgwood describes it as 'pure wishful thinking' (Wedgwood 2007: 203). He thinks Butler exaggerates both the troubles that attach to various vicious ways of life, and the pleasures that supposedly accompany virtue. Is it, for instance, really true, as Butler claims, that 'the temper of compassion and benevolence is itself delightful'? (S3.8). To feel compassion in a suffering world is a source of pain as well as pleasure. Butler also loads the dice, in Wedgwood's view, by focusing on dramatic forms of vice, rather than such unspectacular vices as indifference towards the suffering of those far away. 'It is hard to see how this sort of vice deprives us of many

[36] Butler's assertion, using Pauline terminology, that men are 'by nature a law to themselves' (S2.4) may bring to mind the Kantian doctrine of the autonomy of morality, but it can be construed less grandly as the claim that humans can weigh and assess reasons and can and should act in the light of what they see they have most reason to do.

[37] As we shall see, being impartial for Butler does not imply that we should give equal weight to the interests of all. Rather, we are partial if we give *undue* or *improper* weight to our interests or those about whom we care.

[38] Such perfection is generally beyond us in this life. At best, we can live fully dutiful lives, in which conscience rules, even though particular passions dispute with it for mastery (S3.2 n.).

pleasures, but easy to see how it will spare us the anxiety that more virtuous people will feel' (Wedgwood 2007: 204). In fact Butler does consider those who are willing to submit to nearly all the restraints of morality but wish to 'get over only those which bring more uneasiness and inconvenience than satisfaction'. Butler says that they and 'the men of virtue are *in general* perfectly agreed' (S3.8). He asks only that we are fair-minded in assessing how often duty really will bring more uneasiness than satisfaction.[39] Even so, it is hard to avoid concluding that Butler's confidence stems, in part, from his belief that *this life*, as well as the next, is under providential management.

I conclude that the twin planks of Butler's case for virtue—that we have good reason to live virtuously, and that we shall never be the losers by so doing—are weakened, but not wholly undermined, if we do not share Butler's theological convictions.

18.5 BENEVOLENCE AND VIRTUE

Although his central focus in the first three Sermons concerns what reason we have to be virtuous, Butler also considers, more briefly, what it *is* to be virtuous. In particular he asks whether benevolence is the whole of virtue.[40] His initial answer appears to be a resounding Yes. His opening claim in S12 is that he will show how the commandment to love our neighbour 'comprehends in it all others'. However, Butler progressively qualifies this bold assertion: firstly, in the text of the Sermon; secondly, in a lengthy footnote; finally, in the *Dissertation* where he roundly declares that 'benevolence, and the want of it, singly considered, are in no sort the whole of virtue and vice' (D8). In light of this, should we see Butler as moving away from utilitarianism towards some form of deontological pluralism, or as recognizing the need for a more sophisticated utilitarianism?

Here are some of Butler's qualifications. He identifies the love of our neighbour with benevolence, which is 'an affection to the good and happiness of our fellow creatures' (S12.2). All of our fellows? No, for 'the object is too vast' (S12.3). For practical purposes, the object of our benevolence is those persons who come 'under our immediate notice, acquaintance, and influence' (S12.3). Are we to love our neighbour in the same manner as we love ourselves, or is our love to bear some proportion to the love we bear ourselves, or is it to be equal to the love each of us has for herself? Butler opts for the second of these options, characteristically remarking that what that due proportion is 'can be judged of only from our nature and condition in this world' (S12.13). One thing that is required of us is to make adequate provision for ourselves 'because we are in peculiar manner…intrusted with ourselves' (S12.15).

---

[39] He also concedes that it might be doubtful whether the satisfactions gained from the reputation of justice, honesty, and charity are greater than the satisfaction gained from riches and power.

[40] In these discussions, Butler probably has Hutcheson's early version of utilitarianism in mind (see Hutcheson 2004, Treatise II, Section iii, 116–35). The famous phrase 'greatest happiness for the greatest numbers' is at 125. Note that Butler does not try to offer a complete moral theory, but merely to suggest the constraints that the successful theory must meet.

In both Sermon 12 and the *Dissertation* he also points out that we are required to 'do good to some, preferably to others', either because they are especially entrusted to our care, or because of friendship, or former commitments and obligations. Finally, in a footnote to S12 and in D8, Butler points out that conscience approves of certain kinds of action such as 'fidelity, honour, strict justice', and disapproves of others, such as treachery, falsehood, violence, and meanness, 'abstracted from the consideration of their tendency to the happiness or misery of the world' (S12.31 n.).

What are we to make of this plethora of qualifications and exceptions? First, even if benevolence is the only virtue, it is not, for Butler, the impersonal benevolence endorsed by Bentham. It is false that each is to count for one, and none for more than one. My own interests, and the interests of those to whom I stand in special relationships, are to count for more than the interests of strangers. Second, Butler holds that we rightly approve of or condemn certain kinds of action, without considering the likely consequences. Do these points show that Butler was not a utilitarian? Not necessarily.[41] It is now commonplace to distinguish between a criterion of right action and a decision procedure. That it maximizes happiness may be what makes an action right, but there may be good utilitarian reasons why agents, in deciding what to do, should not undertake utilitarian calculations. Call this a motivationally indirect version of the theory. Butler seems to suggest such a version at S12.27 where he suggests that reason will tell us to pay 'particular regard' to special relationships because 'it is plainly for the good of the world that they should be regarded'. Indeed, in both Sermon 12 and the *Dissertation*, Butler considers, as a speculative possibility, a theological version of what Bernard Williams once mockingly dubbed 'Government House utilitarianism' (Williams 1973: 139). God *might* be a utilitarian, whose only object is the good of His creation, and who therefore endowed us with a conscience that is decidedly non-utilitarian. If He is a utilitarian, He will have given us such a conscience for good utilitarian reasons. 'He foresaw this constitution of our nature would produce more happiness, than forming us with a temper of more general benevolence' (D8). Since this is our constitution, we must steadfastly reject utilitarianism as a decision procedure. '[I]magining the whole of virtue to consist in singly aiming, according to the best of our judgment, at promoting the happiness of mankind' is a source of terrible moral error (D10). Whether this picture of our moral sensibility would amount to a defence of utilitarianism or an abandonment of it, is a moot point.[42]

Fortunately, we do not have to settle this question here. That God might be a utilitarian is something Butler is willing to entertain as a possibility, but in fact it is probably not his considered opinion.[43] Although he is characteristically cautious in speculating about God's purposes, his retributivist views on desert and punishment entail that God, as

---

[41] Louden 1995 lists a number of writers who take these remarks to show that Butler was a deontologist.

[42] I have in mind the debate as to whether morality can be 'self-effacing'. In what sense, if any, would *we* be utilitarians if we were not consciously guiding our actions by utilitarian considerations? For a good discussion of whether Butler might be an indirect utilitarian see Irwin 2008: 516–21.

[43] Louden 1995 disagrees. He argues that Butler's God is a thoroughgoing utilitarian, but he does not consider the issue of retributive punishment.

righteous judge, will not be guided by utilitarian principles in determining everlasting rewards and punishments, but by a just concern to proportion the distribution of goods to merit. If that is correct, then God is no utilitarian.[44]

In view of the importance of benevolence in Butler's account of morality, does he think of it as a third superior principle, subordinate to conscience and to self-love? This is a question that has divided commentators.[45] He never describes it as such. At S11.16, he distinguishes between benevolence as a virtuous principle and as a natural affection. This distinction, which we have already looked at with respect to self-love, concerns what we are pleased or displeased at. If we try to help another but fail, then we shall be pleased with our conduct, but disappointed in the outcome. But that does not show that benevolence has independent authority, since the faculty that issues the verdict on our conduct is conscience. If Butler never says that benevolence is a superior principle, should he have? Those who answer in the affirmative claim that Butler distinguishes between benevolence as a particular affection concerned with the well-being of some *particular* individual on some particular occasion, and its role as a general organizing principle. In this latter role, it has to be 'directed by...reason' in weighing the overall happiness of all affected parties (S12.27). In this respect, it seems to be the impersonal counterpart of calculating self-love, which must harmonize the satisfaction of an individual's affections. I agree that it may require rational *calculation* to determine how to maximize the happiness either of an individual or of a number of persons, but that does not show that benevolence has rational *authority*.[46] For that to be the case, acting against the principle of benevolence would have *itself* to be a violation of our natures, even where the benevolent action was neither prudentially nor morally required. I see no reason to believe that Butler held this view, nor does it seem plausible in itself.[47]

18.6 BENEVOLENCE AND SELF-LOVE

We have seen that Butler was keen to combat popular errors that might offer people an excuse for avoiding the effort to be virtuous. His especial target was a worldly cynicism that denied the reality of disinterested benevolence, claiming either that no one did, or even could, act from a genuine concern for the welfare of others. If that is true, then the preaching of virtue is itself merely self-interested cant, and no one need feel guilty for acting selfishly.

---

[44] Irwin 2008: 521 notes this point.

[45] For a list of those on each side, see McNaughton 1992.

[46] Both self-love and benevolence can be viewed as affections that seek certain outcomes, and so have to engage in the weighing both of likelihood and of value of the consequences of action. But when it comes to judging *conduct* it is hard to see how benevolence could have a voice distinct from that of conscience. If benevolence is the whole of virtue, their verdicts would never differ. And if, as Butler supposes, it is not, then why would a failure to act with impartial benevolence reflect badly on our conduct?

[47] See Frey 1992 and McNaughton 1992. Irwin 2008: 507–9 seems to endorse the view that benevolence is a superior principle.

Among the well-known proponents of such psychological egoism were Hobbes and Mandeville. Butler's direct attacks on Hobbes can be found in two long footnotes in Sermons 1 and 5, where he criticizes Hobbes for defining benevolence as love of power, and pity for someone's misfortune as a fear that a similar calamity might happen to you. Hobbes' accounts can be read in one of two ways. If they are put forward as philosophical analyses of the concepts of benevolence and compassion, then they are clearly inaccurate. Anyone reading them this way would think, Butler observes, that the author had made 'a mistake of one word for another' (S1.6 n.). Understood as empirical claims, they run counter to observable facts and are explanatorily implausible. In this battle, Butler is decisively victorious.

In P35–41 and Sermon 11 Butler aims to show that psychological egoism in general, and psychological hedonism in particular, are not just false but incoherent, and to expose the confusions that have made these views popular. His main arguments against both views draw on his distinction between the particular affections and self-love. The affections are directed towards particular objects or states of affairs; self-love is directed at our happiness which consists in our affections enjoying their objects. Self-love is thus a second-order affection whose goal is that our first-order affections are satisfied. Psychological egoists hold that, though we may disguise it from ourselves, all human action is self-interested, motivated by a desire for our own good or happiness. Translated into Butler's terminology, this amounts to the claim that self-love is our only motivation. But this is incoherent. Self-love achieves its object only if our particular affections achieve their objects; 'take away these affections and you leave self-love absolutely nothing at all to employ itself about' (P37).

This ingenious argument is too quick. The egoist need not deny that we desire particular things and that our happiness consists in achieving them. What he denies is that these desires are disinterested. When we desire anything our ultimate goal, and what motivates us to act, is some good for ourselves. The most popular version of this theory is psychological hedonism, which claims that what motivates us to (say) drink beer, watch cricket, or relieve the distressed, is always the pleasure we shall receive from these activities, and it is this pleasure that is our ultimate goal. Benevolent action is thus self-interested. Our real object in helping others is not their welfare, but our pleasure. Making them happy is but a means to making ourselves happy. Butler also claims that this view is incoherent.

> That all particular appetites and passions are towards *external things themselves*, distinct from the *pleasure arising from them*, is manifested from hence, that there could not be this pleasure, were it not for that prior suitableness between the object and the passion: There could be no enjoyment or delight for one thing more than another, from eating food more than from swallowing a stone, if there were not an affection or appetite to one thing more than another. (S11.6)

How are we to understand this argument? Butler's point is standardly taken to be that my pleasure in A-ing depends on my desiring or caring about A-ing *for its own sake*.[48]

---

[48] That Butler has the contrast between desiring for its own sake and merely as a means in mind is brought out when he writes that 'The principle we call self-love never seeks anything external for the sake of the thing, but only as a means of happiness or good: particular affections rest in the external things themselves.' (S11.5)

If I did not care about cricket itself, I would get no pleasure from watching it. When I help others I may well get pleasure from doing so, but that does not show that my aim was to experience the pleasures of altruism. On the contrary, my pleasure in their well-being depends on my having their happiness as my goal.

This is a famous rebuttal but not, perhaps, as decisive a one as Butler believes.[49] As has often been pointed out, there are obvious exceptions to Butler's claim that we cannot find pleasure in an activity unless we already have a desire to engage in it. Some experiences or activities are intrinsically pleasant, and could be enjoyed in the absence of any prior desire: think of suddenly smelling a delightful scent. Perhaps Butler could evade this objection if we understand differently his notion of a 'prior suitableness between the object and the passion'. He may simply have meant that we can only enjoy those things which we are by nature adapted to enjoy. But this truism is powerless against the hedonist, who can happily agree that we are not adapted to eating stones, and hence find no pleasure in eating them. That hardly refutes the hedonist's claim that we eat our dinner because we find pleasure in alleviating the pangs of hunger, as well as, if we are lucky, in the taste of our food.

The hedonist can make use of the fact that some experiences are intrinsically pleasant to begin to construct a theory in which all intentional action is motivated by a desire for the associated pleasure. We are born, the account runs, with instincts that lead us to explore our environment in various ways in a search for food, warmth, and so on. Our initial behaviour is instinctual, but not intentional; the baby does not seek the breast intentionally. We soon discover, however, that some activities are pleasant, or bring pleasure in their wake, and we then intentionally repeat the activity in order to experience the pleasure again. It is thus always the prospect of further pleasure that motivates the intentional repetition of what was not, initially, intentional action.

However, Butler is surely right in claiming that there are many pleasures whose existence does depend on the satisfaction of a prior desire for something other than pleasure.[50] As well as taking pleasure *in* an experience, such as having a warm bath, we can be pleased that our desires are satisfied. Call the latter desire-dependent pleasures. The benevolent person is pleased that distress is relieved, while a callous person is not. What explains their different reactions? The former desires the relief of distress, whereas the latter is indifferent to it. Thus, in the case of desire-dependent pleasures, Butler's argument seems to go through. One whose goal is to help the needy will indeed feel pleased that he has been able to help, but only because helping, and not being pleased, is his goal. We are pleased because we want to help, rather than helping because we want to be pleased. Thus there can be disinterested benevolence. Has the hedonist any reply to this argument?

[49] Butler's attack on psychological hedonism was often regarded as decisive (e.g. Broad 1930: 54–5) but of late there have been a number of sceptical voices: Sober 1992; Stewart 1992; Phillips 2000. For a partial defence of Butler against Sober see Zellner 1999.
[50] For a good discussion of this point, see Irwin 2008: 499 f.

The hedonist must offer an explanation of why some find helping others pleasant that does not appeal to a desire to help for its own sake. There seems nothing inherently delightful about, say, writing a cheque and mailing it. So how do the benevolent come to associate helping with pleasure? The classic answer is by the principle of psychological association, and the classic example is the miser. There is nothing inherently pleasurable about possessing pieces of metal or paper; we value and desire money only for what it can buy. Because owning money is psychologically associated with the pleasure we gain from buying things, the miser comes eventually to find the mere possession of money itself pleasurable, even though he is not going to use it to buy anything. A similar story might be told about benevolence. Originally we help people either unintentionally, or as a means to some further goal. But often we obtain a hedonic reward—a smile, a word of thanks, a kindness returned. By an associative transfer, we come to find helping itself pleasurable, even when we do not expect to obtain any independent reward. Eventually we are motivated to help others with no further end in view, but the explanation for that lies in the associated pleasure.

The hedonist's story may possibly be true, but is it the most likely explanation of apparently disinterested benevolence? There is a great deal of speculative armchair psychology about the associative mechanism it invokes; the competing explanation offered by Butler seems simpler and more in accord with the phenomenology. So, although Butler's argument does not show hedonism to be incoherent, it may yet be effective, if it offers a better explanation of some of our behaviour than does hedonism.

Even if egoism and hedonism are false, clearly our happiness is of great importance to us, as Butler frequently acknowledges. But isn't benevolence directly opposed to self-love in a way that other particular passions are not? Butler has shown that the exercise of self-love requires us to be motivated by particular affections, and some of these affections, such as ambition and desire for esteem, have some good of our own as their primary end. Between such affections and self-love there seems to be no essential conflict. Benevolence, however, aims at the good of others while self-love aims at my own good; so the more I am motivated by the one the less, it seems, I can be motivated by the other.

Butler's exposition of the mistake behind this line of thought is impressive. It falsely presupposes that the more I promote your interests, the less I am advancing my own. Butler's analysis has shown that happiness consists in my desires being gratified.[51] That is as true of a desire for the happiness of others as it is of any other desire. In so far as I want you to be happy then my happiness depends on, and is bound up with, yours. We must not think of happiness by analogy with property, so that to give happiness to others is necessarily to diminish my own. Benevolence, while distinct from self-love, is no more opposed to it than any other particular passion. Whether self-love endorses or opposes the gratification of any passion depends on whether it happens to threaten my interests.

[51] As I am using the terms, a desire is *satisfied* if the desired state of affairs comes about. But *gratification* requires that the desirer know that her desire has been satisfied.

Impressive though Butler's insight is, it leaves one possible objection unanswered. Even if acting benevolently is not *intrinsically* opposed to my interests might it not conflict more often with my interests than actions from some other motives? To answer this, Butler must appeal to his claim that interest and duty (of which benevolence forms a large part) hardly ever conflict. We have already seen that, in the absence of a theological guarantee, we might be more sceptical of that claim than Butler was.

Finally, Butler argues that an excessive preoccupation with one's own happiness is self-defeating. This is the famous paradox of hedonism, which Sidgwick and others have generalized to other cases.[52] An over-anxious concern for our own welfare breeds the sort of temperament that tells against happiness. His discussion errs at only one point, and that is easily corrected. He equates selfishness with immoderate self-love. But there is another type of person who is also properly regarded as selfish. As Butler points out, while some of our affections, such as ambition or acquisitiveness, have as their primary end some good to ourselves, others, such as compassion or love of one's children, have as their primary end the good of others. Someone in whom the former desires are too strong and the latter too weak is rightly seen as selfish, even if the attempt to satisfy his selfish desires leads him to ignore his real interest. Imprudence and selfishness are not incompatible.[53, 54]

BIBLIOGRAPHY

Akhtar, S. 2006. 'Restoring Butler's Conscience', *British Journal for the History of Philosophy* 14, 581–600.

Arrington, R. 1998. *Western Ethics: An Historical Introduction*. Oxford: Blackwell.

Brinton, A. 1991. '"Following Nature" in Butler's Sermons: Reply to Millar', *Philosophical Quarterly* 41: 325–32.

Broad, C. D. 1930. *Five Types of Ethical Theory*. London: Routledge and Kegan Paul.

Brown, S. (ed.) 1996. *British Philosophy and the Age of Enlightenment*. London: Routledge.

Brownsey, P. 1995. 'Butler's Argument for the Natural Authority of Conscience', *British Journal for the History of Philosophy* 3: 57–87.

Butler, J. 1900. *The Works of Bishop Butler*, ed. J. H. Bernard. London: Macmillan.

Clarke, S. [1728] 1969. *A Discourse Concerning the Unchangeable Obligations of Natural Religion, and the Truth and Certainty of the Christian Revelation*. Extracts in Raphael, 192–225.

Copp, D. 2006. *The Oxford Handbook of Ethical Theory*. Oxford: Oxford University Press.

Cunliffe, C. (ed.) 1992. *Joseph Butler's Moral and Religious Thought: Tercentenary Essays*. Oxford: Clarendon Press.

Darwall, S. 1995. *The British Moralists and the Internal 'Ought'*. Cambridge: Cambridge University Press.

---

[52] Sidgwick 1967b: 48–51. The same point is often extended to consequentialism: she whose sole aim is to maximize the good directly may produce less good than someone who has other motivations.

[53] My understanding of the issues in this section has benefited greatly from Penelhum's discussion (1985: 51–6).

[54] I am grateful to Roger Crisp, Eve Garrard, and Piers Rawling for reading several earlier versions of this chapter and giving me a great deal of very useful advice and feedback.

Darwall, S. 2006. 'Morality and Practical Reason: A Kantian Approach', in Copp, 282–320.

Frey, R. G. 1992. 'Butler on Self-love and Benevolence', in Cunliffe (ed.), 243–68.

Garrett, A. 2011. 'Bishop Butler on Bullshit'. Unpublished.

Hebblethwaite, B. 1992. 'Butler on Conscience and Virtue' in Cunliffe (ed.), 197–208.

Hutcheson, F. [1726] 2004. *An Inquiry into the Original of Our Ideas of Beauty and Virtue in Two Treatises*, ed. Wolfgang Leidhold. Indianapolis: Liberty Fund.

Irwin, T. 2008. *The Development of Ethics, Vol. II*. Oxford: Oxford University Press.

Louden, R. 1995. 'Butler's Divine Utilitarianism', *History of Philosophy Quarterly* 12: 265–80.

McNaughton, D. 1992. 'Butler on Benevolence', in Cunliffe (ed.), 269–92.

—— 1996. 'The British Moralists: Shaftesbury, Butler, Price', in Brown, 203–27.

Millar, A. 1988. 'Following Nature', *Philosophical Quarterly* 38: 165–85.

—— 1992. 'Reply to Brinton', *Philosophical Quarterly* 42: 486–91.

O'Brien, W. 1991. 'Butler and the Authority of Conscience', *History of Philosophy Quarterly* 8: 43–57.

Penelhum, T. 1985. *Butler*. London: Routledge and Kegan Paul.

Phillips, D. 2000. 'Butler and the Nature of Self-interest', *Philosophy and Phenomenological Research* 60: 421–38.

Raphael, D. 1969. *British Moralists 1650–1800 Vol. I*. Oxford: Oxford University Press.

Ross, W. D. 1939. *Foundations of Ethics*. Oxford: Clarendon Press.

Shafer-Landau, R. 2003. *Moral Realism: A Defense*. Oxford: Oxford University Press.

Shaftesbury, Lord [1714] 1999. *Characteristics of Men, Manners, Opinions, Times*. Cambridge: Cambridge University Press.

Sidgwick, H. 1967a. *Outlines of the History of Ethics*. London: Macmillan.

—— 1967b. *The Methods of Ethics*. London: Macmillan.

Sober, E. 1992. 'Hedonism and Butler's Stone', *International Journal of Ethics* 103: 97–103.

Stewart, R. 1992. 'Butler's Argument Against Psychological Hedonism', *Canadian Journal of Philosophy* 22: 211–21.

Sturgeon, N. 1976. 'Nature and Conscience in Butler's Ethics', *Philosophical Review* 85: 316–56.

Wedgwood, R. 2007. 'Butler on Virtue, Self-Interest and Human Nature', in P. Bloomfield (ed.), *Morality and Self-Interest*. New York: Oxford University Press, 177–204.

Williams, B. 1973. *Utilitarianism for and against*. Cambridge: Cambridge University Press.

Zellner, H. M. 1999. 'Passing Butler's Stone', *History of Philosophy Quarterly* 16: 193–202.

CHAPTER 19

HUME'S PLACE IN THE HISTORY OF ETHICS

ANNETTE BAIER

19.1 THE GENERAL CHARACTER OF HUME'S ETHICS

HUME's ethics are found in Books 2 and 3 of his *A Treatise Concerning Human Nature* (1744–1749, hereafter T), in Section 8 of his *Enquiry Concerning Human Understanding* (1745, hereafter EHU), in his *Enquiry Concerning the Principles of Morals* (1751, hereafter EPM), in several essays, such 'Of the Dignity or Meanness of Human Nature', 'Of Polygamy and Divorces', the posthumous 'Of Suicide', and 'Of the Immortality of the Soul', at places in his 'Natural History of Religion' (one of his *Four Dissertations*, 1757), throughout his *History of England* (1754–1762), especially in its appendices, and in the last part of his posthumous *Dialogues on Natural Religion* (1779). Especially in the last three, but also in the *Treatise* and EPM, he continues and extends the work of Hobbes, Spinoza, and Shaftesbury in freeing ethics in the modern era from religion (Mackie 1980: ch. 2). Hobbes wrote scathingly of 'priest-craft', but also said that his 'laws of nature', theorems of peace for 'men in multitudes', could be seen by the theist as commands of God; Spinoza makes intellectual love of God-or-Nature the supreme virtue; and Shaftesbury in his 'Inquiry into Merit' made friendly remarks about the link between moral merit and some belief in a supervisory God, whose existence prevents the universe we live in being seen as a 'distracted' one. But Hume's catalogue of virtues cannot be seen as human traits that are pleasing to an omnipotent God, since he agrees with Shaftesbury that belief in any god whom we must please, to avoid hell, corrupts morality, and so he insists that these traits must be seen as ones *we* have reason to want in each other. We welcome them partly so that there can be peace, not quarrel and war, and partly because such traits as patience, generosity, good humour, and wit, are pleasing both to their possessors and those among whom they live. Hume thought that religious zeal reliably corrupts character, and causes social strife. It tends to 'stupefy the understanding and harden the heart, obscure the fancy and sour the temper'. Hume had read Mandeville (Mandeville 1711; 1714, 1732) perhaps first during his own early breakdown of health, so knew that too much sedentary study could upset one's health, that religious sins in the form of 'private vices', such as greed and vanity, could yield 'public benefits', and knew how 'useful' religious zeal could be to get men to fight. Hume is determined to count as virtue every human trait that we can see to be beneficial, to count as vice only what is clearly harmful. He saw cruelty as the worst vice. And he is not keen to get us to fight, although fighting in self-defence is accepted by him as sometimes necessary.

Hume's ethics are Epicurean in that he assumes that pleasure is good, and every good thing is pleasing. All virtues, for him, are 'agreeable or useful' to their possessor or to others, and the useful is defined as what can be expected to yield future pleasure. To feel approbation is to feel a 'peculiar' species of pleasure, pleasure in character traits, and Hume thinks that ascetic self-denial is displeasing, since not only does it deny harmless pleasures to its possessor, it also sours his temper. When he wrote essays about the Epicurean, the Stoic, the Platonist, and the Sceptic, it is the last that reads like a self-portrait, but his agreement with Epicurus is also considerable. It includes agreement that 'death is nothing to us', so not to be feared. Hume wrote essays, published posthumously, on suicide (defending it) and on the immortality of the soul (rejecting it).

19.2 SYMPATHY AND THE PRINCIPLES GOVERNING OUR APPROBATIONS

In the conclusion of Book 1 of his *Treatise of Human Nature* Hume had said that he would be uneasy to think he approved of one thing, disapproved of another, 'without knowing upon what principles I proceed'. His moral philosophy is part of his theory of human nature, and is a sustained attempt to articulate the principles determining our approvals and disapprovals, to understand how we arrive at them, how we revise them, and what faculties are exercised in them. He believes that, for us to approve of any character trait, we must be capable of sometimes extensive sympathy to see the trait's impact on all those affected by it. (For recognizing the virtues that make a person a good companion, sympathy with only that person's immediate circle will be needed, but usually wider sympathies will come in.) Hume had given a careful account of how we do tend to show sympathy with one another in *Treatise* Book 2, even recognizing the 'presensations'[1] we have of others' feelings, from their expression of them, and their perceived situation, so almost prophesying the recent discovery of our mirror neurons. 'The minds of men are mirrors

---

[1] He takes this term from Shaftesbury, who had spoken of animals' 'pre-sensations' of what their offspring would need, when they build their nests.

to one another', he wrote (T 2.2.5.21, SBN 365[2]). Contemporary simulation theorists, for whom sympathy is important, look back to what Hume and Smith wrote about it (Gordon 1995, 727–42). For Hume, 'sympathy is the chief source of moral distinctions' (T 3.3.6.1, SBN 618). Unlike Hutcheson, he did not invoke a special 'moral sense', since he thought that sympathy, and our dislike of 'continual contradictions' (T.3.3.1.15, SBN 581), could explain how we come to make moral judgements, and ones we expect others to agree with. Morality shows 'the force of many sympathies' (EPM 9.1.11, SBN 276[3]), and sympathy is morality's 'noble source' (T 3.3.6.3, SBN 619). To recognize a character trait as a virtue, we must take up a 'general point of view', and sympathize with all affected parties, in order to be in a position to judge if the trait is to be welcomed by what in EMP Hume calls 'the party of humankind' (EPM 9.1.9; SBN 275). We must look beyond our own viewpoint and that of our 'narrow circle', and ask if, from a more general viewpoint, the trait is desirable. EPM's account of morals differs in some respects from that given in T, but not on the point of view needed to discern virtues (Taylor 2009). Some traits which are found to be virtues from this viewpoint will, however, be ones whose main good effect is on their possessor (prudence and serenity, for example) while others, such as kindness and generosity, benefit other people, and many, such as industry, economy, and honesty, benefit both self and others. Hume believed that when we take up a general point of view, we must expect others who take it up to agree with us about what traits are to be approved. Yet he was also aware, especially in 'A Dialogue', appended to EPM, that there appears to be moral disagreement on such matters as homosexuality, adultery, infanticide, tyrannicide, and suicide, and that different societies have shown differing toleration of these (Mazza 2005: 45–66). Possibly he thought both regulation of sexual expression and permission to kill are always 'artificial', so expected to vary from society to society. Different 'magistrates' will enforce different rules on such matters. (No magistrate, however, is likely to invite tyrannicide.) The 'natural virtues' will be more universally agreed on, though even on such matters as frugality and a taste for luxury, 'A degree of luxury may be ruinous and pernicious in a native of SWITZERLAND, which only fosters the arts, and encourages industry in a FRENCHMAN or ENGLISHMAN. We are not, therefore, to expect, either the same sentiments, or the same laws in BERNE, which prevail in LONDON or PARIS' (EPM, 'A Dialogue, 41. SBN 337). A thoughtful moral judge will take the local conditions into account, so maybe the catalogue of virtues will

---

[2] References to Hume's *Treatise* are to the critical edition, edited by David Fate Norton and Mary J. Norton (Oxford: Oxford University Press, 2007), giving book number, part number, section number, and paragraph number, followed by a page reference to the earlier Oxford edition, 1978, edited by Selby-Bigge and Nidditch (SBN). Thus this reference reads 'Treatise book 2, part 2, section 5, paragraph 21, Selby Bigge Nidditch, page 365'.

[3] References to Hume's *Enquiry Concerning the Principles of Morals* are to the critical edition, edited by Tom Beauchamp (Oxford: Oxford University Press, 1998), giving book number, part number (where applicable), and paragraph number, followed by a page number for the Selby-Bigge Nidditch 1978 edition of Hume's *Enquiries*. When the reference is to one of the three Appendices to EPM, it will be given as App, then Appendix number, paragraph number, and Selby-Bigge Nidditch page number. References to 'A Dialogue' which ends EPM, will be given as EPM, 'A Dialogue', then paragraph number and Selby-Bigge Nidditch page number.

not be universal and eternal. Different traits may be valuable in barbaric conditions from those that are valuable in more civilized conditions. Hume's list makes good sense for a commercial society, indeed for his own society, but he knew that many within it would be offended at the absence of self-denial, humility, and godliness from his catalogue, as some were also offended at the presence on it of wit and charm. Some might indeed be offended that Hume's 'morals' take the form of a list of admired character traits, not a set of commandments. Even today some, such as David Wiggins, fault Hume for the lack, in his ethics, of a core deontological component, ruling out the worst crimes against humanity (Wiggins 2006: lecture 9).

Hume's ethics, like Spinoza's, are firmly grounded in his moral psychology, and in his first work, *A Treatise of Human Nature*, the account of human passions, and of sympathy, in Book 2, is given more space than that of morals, in Book 3 (Ardal Pall 1966). When he finally gets to examine morality, he already has established conclusions about the limited role of reason, about the influence of the association of ideas and impressions, about the force of habit, about the motivating strength of a variety of passions, their need for 'seconding' by other people, about the 'necessity' of our will's decisions, about our near-immediate grasp of what others around us are feeling, and about our capacity for sympathy. The first appearance of virtue in the *Treatise* is in the Book 2 section on virtues and vices as causes of pride and humility. He there notes that those accustomed to the style of the pulpit may be surprised to find pride and virtue thus linked. In Book 3 he finds moral approbation to be a sympathy-dependent species of delight, taken in good character traits, and so also a species of esteem for possessors of them, and so, when self-directed, of pride or self-esteem. The passions that motivate behaviour are what he calls 'direct' ones, such as desire, aversion, fear. But the more complex or 'indirect' passions of pride and love generate desires, aversions, and fears. If we esteem someone for her good character, we may show that esteem by trying to emulate her, but Hume thinks love or esteem can show itself in countless ways, so there is no very direct link between approbation and displaying the approved virtues.

19.3 TRUST AND ITS ENLARGEMENT BY SOCIAL 'ARTIFICES'

Hume recognized an important class of virtues he called 'artificial',[4] which consist in conformity to social 'artifices' or 'conventions', such as those defining private property, its transfer by consent, binding contract, legitimate government, treaty, and marriage. These are all human inventions, schemes of cooperation which increase our security and improve the climate of trust we live in. That there is a role for moral inventors to

---

[4] I here follow the order Hume took in the *Treatise*, of looking at the artificial virtues before the natural. In EPM he looks at benevolence before discussing justice.

design and reform institutions that reduce violence, remedy inconvenience, increase ability, and enlarge the field of appropriate trust, is one of Hume's most important insights. Another is that promises had to be invented, before they could bind. The first reviewers of his *Treatise* found his account of these 'artifices' to be 'Hobbes in new dress', and, like Hobbes, Hume did give self-interest a major role in explaining why we invent them and conform to them, but Hobbes had not recognized that covenants have to be invented, before they can bind, nor spelled out, as clearly as Hume does, the sort of informal agreement there is to accept such social artifices as private property:

> I observe that it will be in my interest to leave another in possession of his goods, *provided* he will act in the same manner with regard to me. He is sensible of a like interest in the regulation of his conduct. When this common sense of interest is mutually express'd, and known to both, it produces a suitable resolution and behaviour. (T.3.2. 2 10, SBN 490)

He gives rowing together in stroke as a simple example of this sort of agreement, and also speaking a common language. His list of beneficial social conventions is left open ended. Magistrates declare and enforce the rules of justice, freedom of the press curbs tyranny in governments, but can be abused, and institutions such as official censors, the law of defamation, courts of appeal, ombudsmen, all take up and extend the work done by the social artifices that Hume analysed. His treatment of how we cope with the evil of violence, however, is implicit only. He assumes that when conventions are breached, the punishment inflicted may involve doing to the rule breaker's 'person' what otherwise would have been criminal assault (EPM 3.1.10, SBN 187), but does not tell us why assault is made criminal, or if it is a natural duty not to assault anyone.

The person Hume calls 'the sensible knave', who pursues his own self-interest directly, so breaks the rules of justice when he thinks he can get away with it, is condemned to keeping his ruling passions secret, and his pride in his clever knavery cannot be seconded by others. He sacrifices 'inward peace of mind, consciousness of integrity' to 'pecuniary advantage', and Hume claims such knaves are 'in the end, the greatest dupes'. He relies on his account of our psychology, and our need to share our self-assessments, for this conclusion to be persuasive. Any knaves who relish secrecy, or who confide only in co-conspirators, may have as much chance of happiness as the honest person. 'The rain it raineth every day, upon the just and unjust fellow. But chiefly on the just because the unjust has the just's umbrella.' Hume's optimistic account of the superior rewards of honesty depends on a uniform need for others' approbation, and on willingness not to mind doing without umbrellas, and other 'luxury and expense'. His essay, 'Of refinement in the arts' was originally called, 'Of luxury', and follows Mandeville in pointing out the benefits to a society of a taste for 'luxury', so his tongue may have been in his cheek in his little sermon against the sensible knave. But he is sincere in thinking the honest person equally sensible, especially when the knave's risk of being found out is taken into account. This would lead to 'a total loss of reputation, and the forfeiture of all future trust and confidence with mankind' (EPM 9.2.24, SBN 283). Few people, however clever and ruthless, can live comfortably with such risk. It is mainly the artificial virtues that the knave lacks, and they all involve schemes to improve a climate of trust, trust that our posses-sions will not be seized by others, trust that promises will be kept, trust that magistrates will be obeyed so law and order will prevail, trust that wives will not expect husbands to provide for other men's children, some degree of trust that treaties be kept. Some trust, such as that between friends, and between child and parent, is natural, but trust of stran-gers usually is mediated by some social artifice, such as contract, or a police force in the background. Hume is one of the few moral philosophers who saw the centrality of trust and distrust to human life, and so to ethics.

Part of what we trust others not to do to us, in a civilized society, is to seize our posses-sions or break contracts. We also trust them not to attack and injure or kill us. Hume neglects discussing this confidence in our personal security, and our belief in the rights that protect it. Yet he knew we could be cruel, and that revenge is instinctive to us, so some social protection of life and limb seems needed. His *History of England* is a string of ghastly assaults on persons, from the hamstringing of Queen Elgiva to the barbarous revenge of Judge Jefferies against the supporters of Monmouth. But the individual rights he recog-nized in his ethics are strangely limited to property and contractual rights, with little atten-tion given to personal rights, such as the right not to be assaulted, raped, tortured, or enslaved. If, on his behalf, we extend his doctrine of artificial virtues, and the prohibitions they involve, to such basic rights, we would face the difficulty that they would, like prop-erty rights, be expected to vary from society to society, and would protect one from cruelty only from civilian members of one's own society, not from police and official punishers, nor from assault from foreigners on foreign soil. Nor does it seem true that unless one's non-cruel behaviour is the rule, there is no point in it. Cruelty is a natural vice, always harm-ful, gentleness a natural virtue, doing good whenever it is shown, yet for Hume any rights there might be thought to be not to be subjected to cruel treatment will come from artifice, from some agreed convention. Perhaps international conventions such as the Geneva con-vention are the best model for how Hume could make room for what Wiggins sees as the inmost core of morality, the prohibition on assault. Hume can be seen as commendably realistic in not pretending that we have effective conventions to protect us from the worst vice. We do bomb civilian targets, we do neglect to feed the starving, and we have regularly inflicted cruel punishments. Hume told Boswell that, as a child, checking his conscience for sins against the prohibitions he had been taught, he skipped murder and theft, 'having no inclination to commit them'. He skipped murder also in his philosophical ethics, where he perhaps over-concentrated on theft. He himself seemed incapable of angry strikes or cruel revenge, but he knew well enough that his own 'good nature' was not the universal rule. Cruelty seems unlike dishonesty in property matters in not depending on any conven-tional rights for the wrong it inflicts: the rights which it infringes seem natural ones.

Conformity to beneficial conventions is atypical, among the Humean virtues, in that it appears to consist mainly in outward behaviour, rather than in any virtuous inner state other than willingness to conform to the convention. Hume in the *Treatise* says he accepts the maxim that moral approbation is given for some natural motive or state of mind, that actions have moral importance mainly for the approved motives leading to them. He then raises a puzzle (not repeated in EPM) about the motive to just acts, and says that neither self-interest, nor public nor private benevolence, can be the natural motive for, say, repaying a secret loan to a vicious miser. The debtor will be the poorer for the repayment, the public will not gain, and the one who does gain, the selfish miser, is not one to whom many feel much sympathy. To say that the only motive is a sense of duty would be to 'reason in a circle'. Hume puts this case as a puzzle, before giving us his account of how it is the long-term 'oblique' interest of all of us, in conditions of moderate scarcity, to invent a social artifice, property as secure rightful possession, so to accept property rules, despite the arbitrary features they will have, varying from society to society, and accept ways of transferring property by consent. In accepting such conventions, we agree not to calculate self-interest, or the now-emerging public interest, on a case by case basis, but to do what is required of us by the rules, even in cases like a secret debt to a vicious miser. He says the 'original motive' to acts of conformity to a newly adopted beneficial convention will be long-term 'oblique' self-interest, including the desire for reputation as cooperative and trustworthy. Then, once the scheme has become established, and found beneficial, 'sympathy with public interest' will lead us to morally approve of willingness to conform to the scheme, and desire for approval, along with pride in one's 'probity and honor', will reinforce enlightened self-interest.

> Thus *self-interest* is the original motive to the *establishment* of justice: But a *sympathy* with *public* interest is the source of the *moral* approbation that attends that virtue. This latter principle of sympathy is too weak to controul our passions, but has sufficient force to influence our taste, and give us the sentiments of approbation and blame. (T 3.2.2.24, SBN 499–450)

Sympathy is always involved as a preliminary to moral approbation or disapprobation. With the natural virtues, approbation more than 'attends' them; it determines their status as virtues. With justice and other artificial virtues, moral approbation comes in only once a convention has created expectations, customary rights, and what Hume somewhat misleadingly terms 'natural obligations', ones which in cases like slavery and polygamous marriage may fail to secure moral endorsement. Hume takes it that we will give moral endorsement to the artifices he analysed, but he also allows that some types of government may merit moral disapprobation, even justify revolution, and he raised questions about the forms of marriage that he was familiar with, which seem to give the husband 'the barbarous title of master and tyrant'.

It is not public benevolence, but sympathy with a common interest, the public interest, which is needed for approbation of conformity to property rules, or the rules of any beneficial social artifice. This special interest comes into being only once the first society-wide cooperative scheme is established, and a plurality of persons is formed into a public, so regard for that interest could not be the approved 'original' motive for conformity to the first artifice, and in any case Hume says regard for it is too weak to motivate, strong enough only to determine what we approve of, not how we behave.[5] While the scheme is getting started, and it still takes somewhat risky exemplary action

---

[5] A somewhat different account is given in the introduction to the Norton and Norton student edition of the *Treatise* (Oxford: Oxford University Press, 2000, 183–189, where it is assumed that self-interest, especially in the form of what Hume terms 'avidity', could only provisionally be a morally approved motive. See also Cohon 2008: Part 2, for an interpretation more like Norton's.

to restrain immediate self-interest to conform to its rules, there will be a common interest in getting the cooperative scheme launched, but not yet, except in prospect, a public interest, since it takes established (and so stable) convention to create that artificial interest. Hume agrees with Mandeville that 'the artifices of politicians and educators' may be needed to get people to respect property rights, and create a sense of pride in their individual 'probity and honor'. He recognizes a natural virtue of equity, one presumably not possessed by the knave, and could have considered it to be at least part of the approved motive for keeping rules which one hopes others are keeping, during the early stages of acceptance of a convention, as well as after it is established, and still later, when magistrates enforce it, or even later still, when the scheme may be reformed, to be more equitable.

19.4 Natural Virtues, Natural Duties, and What They Include and Exclude

The natural virtues are said to differ from justice and other artificial virtues in that 'the good, which results from the former, arises from every single act, and is the object of some natural passion. Whereas a single act of justice, consider'd in itself, may often be contrary to the public good, and tis only the concurrence of mankind, in a general scheme or system of action, which is advantageous' (T 3.3.1.12, SBN 579). Naturally virtuous acts do good act by act. Hume's metaphor in EPM is that they are like stones adding to the height of a freestone wall, whereas justice is like a vault, where any one stone's contribution needs the others to be in place, for it not to 'fall to the ground' (EPM, Appendix 3.5, SBN 305). The natural virtues include benevolence, prudence, courage, due pride, modesty, mercy, gentleness, equity, cheerfulness, kindness, patience, industry, cleanliness, frugality, expressiveness, wit, self-command, presence of mind, quickness of conception, and a 'MANNER a grace, an ease, an I-know-not-what' (EPM 8.14, SBN 267), that 'concealed magic' which, to James Beattie's and James Balfour's outrage, Hume likens to sex appeal. Some of these personal traits are 'abilities' rather than motives, and they need not be voluntary abilities. Hume's first reviewers saw his account of the 'natural virtues' as indebted to Francis Hutcheson, but Hume does not attempt, as did Hutcheson, to reduce all virtue to benevolence, or to any sort of excellence of the will. For Hume benevolence is one virtue, or group of a few virtues, among the sixty-seven which he named. Prudence or concern for our long-term interests is also among the virtues. In EPM Hume speaks of the 'strong interest' each person has in the observance of justice, which for him is a social virtue separate from benevolence, and controlling its displays. Hume said he took his catalogue of virtues more from Cicero than from any Christian moralist, and Hutcheson was, at least nominally, a Christian moralist. Hume's list is controversial in including self-regarding virtues, in demoting the 'monkish virtues' of silence, humility, and self-denial into vices, in omitting any virtue of obedience other than obedience to magistrates, and in taking chastity to be an artificial and very unnatural virtue, demanded of women so their husbands can be sure that the children whom their wives bear are biologically their own, rightful heirs to their property. It is also challenging in querying whether the form of courage encouraged on battlefields, where valour can become indistinguishable from bloodthirstiness, is really to be admired. Hume notes that we admire it in our own troops, but rarely in our enemy's. Another controversial thesis of Hume's is that 'abilities' such as native wit, are not importantly different from virtues shown in what we choose to do. He points out that the undoubted virtue of self-command is not itself in the command of the will. His determinism,[6] as well as his hedonism and his anti-religious stance, makes his ethics distinctive, and controversial.

Hume makes the concept of a virtue, rather than that of obligation or duty, the central one. The artificial virtues give rise to obligations and duties, but natural virtues need not yield any 'ought's to guide behaviour. There are some 'natural duties'. Parental solicitude demands that we care for our children. And beneficence, as a virtue, may imply that we ought to do things for some others, but virtues like serenity and charm do not seem to tell us what actions we ought to perform, since they are among those Hume thinks are not within our will's command. Hume believed that it is 'almost impossible for the mind to change its character... or cure itself of a passionate or splenetic temper' (T 3.3.4.3). Even when approbation shows itself as esteem for the person with good character, or in a wish that we shared that character, it still need not motivate any particular action, such as attempted emulation of the virtuous. And if emulation is attempted, it may fail. ''Tis one thing to know virtue, and another to conform the will to it' (T 3.1.1.22, SBN 465). And the will is not the only part of us which can display the traits Hume sees as virtues.

For a virtue theorist like Hume, morality is not so much a guide to action, as a catalogue of virtues, some, such as patience and serenity, which show as much in quiet inaction as in any motive or any action. Others, like benevolence, will affect action, but the main thing virtues affect is our state of mind. Hume is important in the history of ethics for his challenge to a Christian ethics of self-denial, for his reinstatement of Cicero's *prudentia* among the virtues, and for his refusal to separate out mental abilities, possessed by luck, from 'moral' virtues, displaying how our supposed freedom of will has been used. For Hume every mental trait we admire and would like to have ascribed to ourselves is a moral virtue, part of moral merit.

Philosophers can obviously agree that it is by a special sense or feeling that we recognize virtues, yet disagree in their lists of virtues. For Hume, but not Hutcheson, prudence, charm, and due pride are virtues. Pride is recognition of one's strengths, and pleasure in them. It should always be accompanied not only by modesty, recognition of one's limits, but also by a considerate veiling of one's due pride, lest others be offended. This is rather different from Hutcheson, for whom all virtues are forms of benevolence, good will to

---

[6] In the *Treatise* he had spoken of what he called our 'liberty of spontaneity' present whenever the determining causes of our actions are within our own minds. In his *Enquiry Concerning Human Understanding* he points out that if there is a controlling omnipotent God behind our minds, then responsibility for our actions shifts from us to God. For Hume's views, see Bricke 2007: 201–26.

others. He does not demand Christian humility, but does speak of shame, and the undue love of praise and honour. Hutcheson had replied to Mandeville's charge that virtue is begot by flattery on pride by allowing that we do like to be praised, but feel embarrassed if praised to our faces, and 'choose Secrecy for the Enjoyment of it'. Hume says love of good fame strengthens virtue, and is nothing to be ashamed of. As long as what we are vain about is our good character and reputation, vanity can be 'a bond of union among men'. Just as he sees acceptance of the schemes of cooperation that justice involves as motivated by self-interest, a potentially dangerous and divisive passion turned with good effect on itself, in self-regulation, so he sees our wish to have and be thought to have a good character as another case of a potentially divisive passion, vanity, put to good use, if directed on character. As long as pride in virtue and good reputation is not flaunted, those with pride in their character cannot just endure the company of the similarly proud, but welcome it. Since we need others to 'second' our self-assessments, pride, like other passions, would 'languish' if not 'enjoyed in company'.

Like Hutcheson, Hume sees the moral sentiment to be analogous to our aesthetic sense. In his essay 'Of the standard of taste' he makes the same sort of demands for exten-sive knowledge, sensitivity, and practice in comparison, which are needed for sound moral judgement, to pave the way for judgements of aesthetic merit. Knowing what one likes is never enough for judging merit. Both for judgements about fine characters, and for those about fine works of literature, not only must the judge have the right sort of fine-grained sensitivity, and enough experience, but it will often be necessary that 'much reasoning precede' the final judgement. The treatment of human character as analogous, in the standards of excellence applicable to it, to works of literature, along with Hume's rejection of the 'monkish virtues', can be seen to anticipate Nietzsche's 'transvaluation' of moral values. And the attention Hume gives, in EPM and in his *History*, to the shift from 'barbaric' conditions of life and moral valuation to more 'civilized' conditions, can also be seen to point forward to Nietzsche's 'genealogy' of morals. But nothing in Hume is any sort of equivalent to Kant's *Religion, within the limits of reason alone*. Instead we have, for more intellectual variants of Christianity, and other world religions, Hume's posthumous *Dialogues on Natural Religion*, with their arguments against belief in a pow-erful benevolent creator, leading up to a resounding denunciation of the bad moral effects of religion. In addition to the 'pernicious consequences' for society of religious persecution and religious wars, there is the effect on the individual believer: 'the steady attention to so important an interest as that of eternal salvation is apt to extinguish the benevolent affections, and beget a narrow contracted selfishness' (*Dialogues on Natural Religion*, Part XII). So much for Christian love! Hume had earlier, in his dissertation 'Of the Natural History of Religion', given a scathing treatment of all popular religions, seen as the 'sick men's dreams' of frightened and deranged people, or at best as the 'playsome whimsies of monkeys in human shape'. Hume was too much of a sceptic to call himself an atheist, but he certainly did his best to separate morality from religion, and in partic-ular from the Christian religion, the one he knew best. The doctrine of original sin has no place in his scheme (Gill 2006), but he was by no means starry-eyed about human proclivities.

19.5 Responsibility

Hume takes our characters to be as little of our own choice as our bone structure, and even our choices, which may in youth affect our character development, are determined by our un-chosen ruling passions, directed by our beliefs. Approbation will encourage virtue, 'second' it in those who have it, but its main point is recognition of merit, once it is already there to be recognized. Just as the literary critic does not do much if anything to produce good literature, so the moral judge is in the business of virtue-recognition, not character-formation or reformation. Hume tends to be pessimistic about the chances of much self-induced reformation in adults, but does see social institutions as having some power to reshape the rough timber of humanity, to give better, less socially disruptive directions to forces like self-interest, vanity, ambition, and aggression. He said that only moralists who were 'divines in disguise' need a sharp distinction between character traits like honesty, which may be encouraged by rewards and punishments, and ones like good humour and wit, unlikely to be changed by them. Since his version of moral appraisal is not intended as a prelude to reward or punishment, it need not care much about the extent to which our character is formed by our own choices. And character shows not only in our actions, but also in our reactions. It is a matter of our passions, including motivating passions, as well as our actions.

Hume's version of morality as evaluation of character has little place for moral blame, or for guilt, for the sense that we have done wrong or are personally responsible for some bad outcome. (It may have more room for derision and shame, and expectation of them, when we display vices.) Resentment is an important passion for him, since it is power to make resentment felt which determines who is included in the group of those cooperative schemes that give rise to recognized rights. (He takes this to include all human beings, but no animals.) Behaviour which respects recognized rights can be enforced, but character traits are not the sorts of things that can be enforced. Neither reward and punishment, nor moral approbation and disapprobation, are expected to be effective in changing bad characters into better ones. What can work is change of 'situation', including institutional situation. There is no point in blaming those in barbaric societies for barbaric behaviour, nor for praising those in enlightened societies, with libraries and protection of freedom of the press, for their greater civilization and humanity. Scythians collected the scalps of their slain enemies, and were proud of their collections. Hume and his literati friends collected their good reviews, and each others' handsome books, including those that attacked other authors. There is reason to allocate causal responsibility for good and bad outcomes, so as to try to get repeats of the former, and to prevent repeats of the latter. We may have reason to imprison some people, to protect others from their actions. But this does not mean we must believe them, the imprisoned, to have been able to avoid doing what they did. Hume sees both the criminal's crime, and our likely detestation of him for it, as events that had their determining causes. He hopes our vindictive and hate-inspired actions can be prevented, once an understanding of human nature, and its place in a wider nature, has become cultivated. His own writings aim to increase that saving understanding. He sees it as useful to trace the causal antecedents to any human decision that had important consequences, such as Charles I's decision to issue an impeachment of those who, by their 'Remonstrance', offended him in 1642. This, as Hume sees it, was the precipitating cause of the English civil war, so it is instructive to see what character faults in Charles led him to such a fateful decision. Responsibility can and should be allocated, but that does not mean one should hate the monarch who overstepped his powers, or be unable to shed a tear for his sorry fate. Rarely will responsibility be traced back to only one person; usually it is shared, and it can always be traced yet further back. Tracing causes is important for trying to improve our future, but angry harangues against those who have caused harm does not do any good, either to them or to us, unless they are part of some campaign that will prevent the repetition of such harmful acts.

Hume thought that the study of history could give us some wisdom in this matter, and his *History of England* is a direct continuation of his moral philosophy. Hume was an influential economist and historian as well as a philosopher, and his ethics, especially what is expressed in his later works, is informed by his understanding of these related fields in a way few if any other ethical theorist can match. His friend Adam Smith, of course, has some claims here, but was a historian only of astronomy. Both Smith's moral philosophy and his economic theory were influenced by Hume.

19.6 THE ROLE OF REASON

Hume saw himself to be taking up the 'controversy started of late' between those, like Hutcheson, who believe us to have a 'moral sense' which enables us to tell, fairly directly, which character traits are beautiful, and which ugly, as against rationalists, like Clarke and Cumberland, and later Kant (Guyer 2008: ch. 4) who see morality as the dictates of reason.

In the *Treatise* Hume claimed that the role of reason is to serve the passions, and that morality must depend upon a sentiment, rather than pure reason, or it could never affect our motivation. This influential and much criticized argument, which seems to take morality's main task to be to guide action, is not repeated in EPM. There reason is given the vital task of working out long-term consequences of actions and policies, and so must 'pave the way' for the moral sentiment, whether what it approves is a motive to action, an ability, or a pattern of serene inaction. Even in the *Treatise*, reason was needed to see the need for social artifices, and the extensive sympathy which the moral sentiment required, before approbation or disapprobation is felt, depended on our having come to know the facts about how human happiness is affected by particular ways of behaving, and by particular character traits. Those that 'sour the temper' or 'obscure the fancy' will not be approved, even if the sour temper is well under control, the obscured fancy not motivating anything except dull daydreams. 'Reflections on their tendency to the happiness of mankind' (T 3, 3, 1, 27, SBN 589) presuppose knowledge of those tendencies, so reason had a vital role to play, in the *Treatise*, even if reason alone could not pronounce on virtue. Reason in EPM is still seen as 'cool and inactive', while passions and sentiments are 'warm' and provide not just warm approbation, but also any 'impulse to action'. But for any felt sentiment to count as moral approbation, it is usually necessary that 'much reasoning should precede, that nice distinctions be made, just conclusions drawn, distant comparisons formed, complicated relations examined, and general facts fixed and ascertained' (EPM, 1, 9, SBN173), Although Charles Stevenson was influenced by Hume, Hume's is no emotive theory of ethics, certainly not a 'hooray-boo' theory. He could perhaps be called an expressivist, or a 'sentimentalist'. Hume claims that approbation by a 'moral sentiment' depends on our taking up a special point of view, requiring sympathy with all affected parties, and much reflection and fact-finding, especially when it recognizes artificial virtues, before 'the final sentence' is pronounced by this very special 'sentiment'. When we pronounce it, we must expect others to agree with our findings, just as we do when we reason, and just as Rousseau's citizens have to expect their vote to be echoed by others, when the 'General Will' is determined. Hume is often called a 'non-cognitivist' in ethics, but despite his early anti-rationalist arguments, by the time he wrote his *History of England*, he is willing to say, in Appendix 1, that 'Virtue is nothing but an enlarged and more cultivated reason.' Earlier, in praising King Alfred, he had written that 'good morals and knowledge are almost inseparable in every age, though not in every individual'.

Did Hume recognize anything that could be called practical reason, or instrumental reason (Korsgaard 1997)? He did not use either phrase, and he did call reason in itself 'perfectly inert'. It deals in representations, which can be true or false. Once it is used to 'direct' passions, it informs us of means to our ends, or points out the consequences of satisfying particular passions, and then it does serve a practical purpose, indeed Hume's most famous claim that 'reason is, and ought only to be the slave of the passions, and can never pretend to any other office than to serve and obey them' (T.2.3.3.4, SBN 415). Does this amount to the primacy of practical reason? Scarcely, since one of our passions is the 'love of truth'. Hume in the *Treatise* called reason 'inert' because it deals in ideas, not impressions, and they, by themselves, do not have sufficient 'vivacity' to move the will. When the conclusions of reason are made 'lively' by the passions they serve and direct, they play a vital practical role. It was in the *Treatise* that Hume made the strongest claims about reason's subservient role. By EPM he no longer contrasts vivacious impressions with derivative less vivacious ideas, and there reason is given the vital task of instructing us in 'the pernicious or useful tendency of qualities and actions'. Reason on its own is still 'cool and disengaged', but unless 'warm' impulses to action are informed by what reason tells us about likely consequences, our actions will be hot-headed and impulsive. And for the moral sentiment to pronounce, it is usually necessary that 'much reasoning precede'. It is mainly causal reasoning that 'paves the way' for moral judgements, but sometimes it will be necessary that 'nice distinctions be made, just conclusions drawn, distant comparisons formed, and complicated relations examined', so reason in all its human forms serves the moral sentiment.

One of the most influential passages in Book 3 of the *Treatise* is the little paragraph with which he ends its first section, when he challenges anyone who thinks he can deduce an 'ought' from an 'is' to 'observe and explain' the transition. This follows on from his case for saying that moral distinctions are not perceived by reason. Hume says attention to this transition would subvert all the vulgar systems of morality, and it is most likely that it was the move from 'The Bible forbids it' to 'One ought not to do it' which he wanted more carefully examined. His little 'observation' was promoted by Anthony Flew into 'Hume's Law', forbidding any inference from facts to norms (Flew 1986; MacIntyre 1959: 451–68; Pigden 2011). But as Hume is about to tell us how the obligations of justice arise from the fact that certain conventions have been adopted and established, it is unlikely he meant what he wrote as any sort of general inference barrier. From the fact that one has given a promise, it follows that one ought to keep it. In EPM he says that the fact that we agree in approbation of certain traits as agreeable or useful to self or others makes them virtues, so conclusions about what is virtuous certainly follow from facts about what traits we feel approbation for, once we have taken up the right point of view and cleared our minds of the 'biases of superstition and religion'. As he said in the *Treatise*, 'Here is a matter of fact, but 'tis the object of feeling, not of reason' (T 3.1.1.26, SBN 469). It is a rather complex and conditional fact, but nonetheless a fact, and a discoverable one. He also said in the next section that 'we do not infer a character to be virtuous because it pleases: but in feeling that it pleases after such a particular manner, we in effect feel that it is virtuous' (T 3.1.2.3, SBN 471). The link between feeling the moral sentiment of approbation, felt from the right point of view, and a moral finding, is too close to be called 'inference'. The one is 'in effect' the other. Hume did not repeat his is/ought observation in EPM, where fact-finding usually has to pave the way for the moral sentiment.

Hume sees our nature as continuous with that of other animals, our reason a language-enlarged form of theirs, our passions and capacity for sympathy shared with the higher animals. But animals, although they do like us learn from experience, cannot do the sort of reasoning that must pave the way for the moral sentiment. Hume says that animals have 'little or no sense of vice and virtue', and are incapable of justice. This means they are not parties to cooperative social schemes, so have no obligations. It does not mean that we have no obligations to them—that depends on what practices we see fit to impose on one another. Human vice can show in cruel treatment of animals. The natural virtue of gentleness will show not just in gentle treatment of fellow-persons, but in 'gentle usage' of animals. And because animals show sympathy, and can tell the difference between cruel and kind treatment, they do have some primitive sense of at least some natural virtues (Pitson 2003: 639–55). Hume raises the question of why incest is criminal in human beings but not in animals, and thinks rationalists can give no good reason for this. For him all sexual permissions and prohibitions seem to be 'artificial', and vary from society to society. He notes that animals 'quickly lose sight of the relations of blood', and one would think that would be a fact that rationalists could cite, to justify treating animal incest as innocent, while taking a different attitude to the behaviour of human beings who are aware of relations of blood, and aware of what their own society forbids.

Hume's challenge to the rationalist to show what is wrong, for us but not animals, with incest and murder, is not repeated in EPM, and he himself does little to tell us what is wrong with incest,[7] murder, or manslaughter.

19.7 RIGHTS

Some moral theories put great emphasis on rights. Hume sees all rights as arising from cooperative schemes, so has no place for natural rights, except possibly for the right to express resentment if excluded from the schemes of rights others are adopting, and the rights of children to parental care. There is also a right, in a weak sense, to rebel against tyrannical rulers, and to end one's own life. The law may sometimes protect the latter right, but not the former, since Hume thought it impossible to spell out the precise conditions that justify revolution, and unwise to try.

If women, or others, such as slaves, are treated as chattels, excluded from property and other rights, they are within what we might call (but Hume does not call) their 'moral rights',[8] if they show resentment in whatever way they can. When Hume discusses this important question of who gets included in our schemes of right-recognition, he points out that no one is self-sufficient when it comes to reproduction, and that women have a monopoly of knowledge about who fathered their children, so have formidable bargaining power, should they feel that their deal in marriage, or in other social schemes, is unfair. They can, if they choose, muddy the inheritance lines, prevent men from being sure who their children are. This, in its time, was a fairly revolutionary invitation to women to rebel, and Hume accompanies it with several essays about love and marriage. He is not usually credited with the married women's property act, or with women's liberation, but he did see the power relations between the sexes, and their potential, with stunning clarity. As a young man he had been named, in absentia, as father of an illegitimate child of a young serving woman, Agnes Galbraith, who was punished for her sin by the Chirnside church, by being put in sack cloth and the pillory (Mossner 1980: 81–3). Did she so resent the unequal treatment of men and women that she used her power to mislead about her child's father? Did she inspire Hume to invite more women to do the same? We

---

[7] He suggests in EPM 4.8–9 that the turpitude of incest lies in the allowing of sexual attraction between those growing up in one household, as if this would contaminate childhood and family affection, and turn homes into house parties. The blood relation itself seems not to be the main thing; it is membership of one household. One family: one pair of sexual partners? This is interesting, as Hume's own parents grew up at Ninewells, though not related by blood. His mother's mother, in her second marriage, was third wife to Hume's father's father. In 'A Dialogue' 25 he says love between near relations is 'contrary to reason and public utility' but that natural reason cannot determine just how near is too near, so the law must specify this. Just what kind of exogamy is required by reason is not clear, whether it is inbreeding that is to be avoided, or altering affectionate household relationships.

[8] If Hume implicitly allows any use for this notion, it is for such conventional rights as do get moral approbation. So rights to have promises made to one kept are moral rights, as are rights to property in most societies, but not rights of slave owners to their slaves.

do not know if David Hume was father of that child, and likely he did not either. (Of course it is also possible that Agnes herself did not know.)

This right of the excluded and aggrieved to express resentment might be thought to extend not just to slave rebellions and peasant uprisings but to actions by groups like the Taliban, excluded from international cooperation. Whether Hume would have seen some terrorism as justified is unclear, but he certainly thinks we should not be surprised if the excluded, whoever they are, show resentment by using whatever power they have. This right to be included in cooperative schemes is not the only right Hume implicitly recognizes as natural, or independent of the details of such schemes. The right of children to be cared for by their parents is implied by their obligation of care, which he takes to be self-evident. It is the father's, not the mother's duty he speaks of, but he assumes mothers will fly to the relief of their children, and he recognizes the father's right to some guarantee of paternity, in the form of the mother's chastity, if he is to be expected to show paternal affection and care. Hume's morality of the natural family is quite complex, since the father's natural duty is dependent on his conventional right to chastity in his partner, so he can know which children are those towards whom he has a paternal duty.

Hume believed that magistrates were invented to declare and enforce pre-existent obligations, such as contractual ones, and extend cooperative schemes to large-scale ones such as building harbours, raising armies. His political philosophy is certainly not Hobbes in new dress. Rulers are there mainly to declare and enforce obligations, not create new ones. They may of course conscript people to military service, if the nation has to defend itself, and they may impose taxes. They have the responsibility of ensuring that authority is passed on without bloodshed, when their time is up. Hume saw hereditary monarchy as having at least that advantage, and he praised England's 'mixed monarchy', the rule of monarch in parliament, but his 'perfect commonwealth' is a republic, headed by a 'protector'. When rulers become tyrants, there is a right to rebel, as a last resort. (Hume showed sympathy with the American rebels against colonial oppression, but not with the rebels in England's 'Great Rebellion' against Charles I, a rebellion which he saw to have predictably led to new tyranny under Oliver Cromwell.)

Hume in his posthumous essay on suicide defended the right to end one's life, if it becomes intolerable, but he believed that that there was, in other conditions, a natural wish to postpone death, and that, if there were not, then the preservation of our species would be threatened. He did not foresee the advent of suicidal religious martyrs, who are willing to die along with those they kill, to protest intolerable perceived wrongs. His ethics of killing, as I have emphasized, is not very developed—no right to life is spoken of, but a right to self-defence is indirectly recognized. The wrong of parricide and murder figure at most as examples of a recognized wrong which rationalists may have trouble distinguishing from vegetable death-dealing. (The young oak, which grows up beside and eventually kills its parent.) Gentleness is a virtue, cruelty the worst vice, but the status of willingness to kill painlessly is not made clear. The ethics of killing is not really spelled out by Hume, but then it has not been fully articulated by any great moral philosopher. Hume assumes, I think, that we may kill animals, and kill each other in self-defence, and that magistrates will forbid civilian assault, but he does not take up Grotius' questions about when, and when not, war is excusable. His treatment of those who went to war, in his *History of England*, is the place to look for his detailed treatment of particular wars and particularly atrocious killings, most of them official killings, such as burnings at the stake, hanging, drawing and quartering, and beheading. His hero-king is Alfred, who did go to war against the Danes, but that was a defensive, not an aggressive, war. In his ethics Hume recognizes courage as a virtue, but warns against the forms of it that devastate cities and kill their inhabitants.

19.8 Influence on Later Writers on Ethics

Hume's naturalism, and his claims about morality being based on a knowledge-informed sentiment, expressed in our moral judgements, have had an influence on many subsequent moral philosophers. He clearly influenced Kant, who felt challenged to restate how reason might issue moral imperatives, and he may have had a more positive influence on Nietzsche (Beam 1996: 299–324). In recent times Charles Stevenson, Bernard Williams, John Mackie, Alan Gibbard, and Michael Smith have all looked back to Hume. His anti-rationalist legacy has recently been called one of 'contradiction' (Botros 2006) because he seems to vacillate between saying that morality, if it is to have any influence on behaviour, cannot be founded on reason, and saying that it cannot be founded on 'reason alone'. The latter reading is more plausible, and is the one which has been more influential. But he found the moral sentiment to determine what we judge to be virtuous, more than to directly motivate behaviour. It is, after all, a sentiment, not a desire, and reliably influences our 'taste' rather than our motivation.

Utilitarian moral theorists, like Jeremy Bentham and John Stuart Mill, look back to Hume as one who put emphasis on utility. Hume saw all virtues to be either agreeable or useful to their possessors or to others, but restricted the term 'utility' to long-term good, what serves our interests, and so never, like Bentham, included what gave immediate pleasure in 'utility'. Nor did he see either the need for, or the possibility of, the sort of moral calculus Bentham advocated, to work out what was in the greatest happiness of the greatest number. He did think morality's role was to increase human happiness, but since for him it does this by giving recognition to pleasant and useful character traits, rather than prescribing individual actions, the sort of balancing of good versus bad consequences which a hedonic calculus would enable us to do has to be constrained by taking our moral psychology seriously, and shifting the question from, 'what actions will do most good?' or even 'what action policies will do most good?' to 'what sort of people have we most reason to welcome?'. Only for designing and reforming social institutions do we need people with what he calls 'the legislative spirit', which may require some sort of calculation, and possibly the sacrifice of the interests of some to those of others. Magistrates and legislators may need a calculus, but most people who exhibit the virtues Hume listed will not make this sort of contribution to human happiness. Ordinary people at most help elect those with such extensive powers, and the best they can do is conform to existent laws, protest tyranny and corruption, and, in extreme conditions, when all else has failed, support violent revolution to end tyranny. Hume's fictional perfect character in EPM, Cleanthes, combines public spirit with gentleness and wit. His historical perfect character, King Alfred, enacted wise legislation, read widely and thought deeply (indeed burned the cakes in a fit of abstraction), founded England's first university, fought bravely to defend his country, invented the jury system, and on top of all this was a good father. He combined domestic with public virtue in a way few monarchs, or others, have managed to. He is not reported to have been guided by any hedonic calculus, indeed seems to have been guided by his good sense and his Christian faith. Hume accepts him as a creature of his superstitious times, yet gives him the highest praise of any person whose character he considers.

Utilitarians are not the only calculating moral theorists who look back to Hume for inspiration. Contractarians and game theorists have also taken his version, and acceptance, of a beneficial 'convention' as exemplary moral theory. Yet Hume sees only a restricted set of virtues to depend upon this sort of rational self-interested 'agreement'. Such 'artificial' virtues are important, but so are the 'natural' virtues, and without some of them, such as equity, or being fair-minded, and long-sighted prudence, the 'artificial' ones could not be cultivated. The 'sensible knaves' among us, who steal, break promises, and cheat are 'free-riders' on schemes of cooperation that the rest of us sustain. The terrorists and conmen among us exploit, for their own ends, the climate of trust that the rest of us make possible, by our normal trustworthiness and trust.

Hume's *Treatise* claim that moral approbation is always for some 'natural' motive has made him a hero for those who espouse 'internalism' in ethics (Brown 1988: 69–87; Radcliffe 1996: 383–407). He did think that morality had to be linked with what we naturally desire, and take pleasure in. But he also thought that the moral sentiment, pleasure in virtuous character traits, was quite special in its dependence on a knowledge-informed extensive sympathy that might be difficult to be sure we had achieved, so in a sense is 'external' to natural dispositions favouring ourselves and our nearest and dearest. We can be wrong in labelling something we feel 'moral approbation', and can easily confuse prejudice with that impartial and well-informed sentiment. Some take Hume to have an 'ideal observer' view of moral judgement, like Adam Smith's, but Hume thinks the viewpoints needed for discerning virtues (and different view points may be needed for different virtues) are obtainable by ordinary people, as long as they are able to feel extensive sympathy, and willing to listen to each other's corrections of any biases and blind-spots they may have (Sayre-McCord 1994: 202–28; Cohen 1997: 827–43).

By some interpreters, such as Barry Stroud (Stroud 2000: 16–30) and P. J. Kail (Kail 2007: part 3), Hume is found to have a 'projectionist' theory of virtue, in that it is our feelings of agreed approbation for some character traits that make them virtues, and Simon Blackburn claims Hume as a predecessor for his 'quasi-realism' (Blackburn 1993). Hume did in EPM liken approbation to the action of 'gilding' natural objects with a gilt that gives them a preferred status. But they are quite real psychological features that are selected for this moral 'gilding', and we have good reasons for our approbations, so those, like John Mackie, who incline to an 'error theory' of ethics, cannot very plausibly claim Hume as a predecessor. Hume finds error only in 'rationalist' and religious versions of ethics.

Hume's views on the position of women were ahead of his time, and he has influenced many recent feminists (Jacobson 2000). Some of his remarks about women being the 'weak and pious sex' have been provocative, while others, about women's superior 'grace and delicacy', have seemed rather condescending deference, but his real challenge was in his call to women to realize what power they had, should they choose to exercise it to get a better social deal (EPM 3.2 2, SBN 193), in his analyses of powerful women such as Elizabeth of England, in his relating of the courage of Joan of Arc, of the impassioned intercession of Queen Philippa to save the lives of the brave burghers of Calais.

19.9 HUME AND THE PRESENT

In terms of today's classifications of moral theories, Hume counts as a secularist (Russell 2008), a hedonist, a determinist, a naturalist, an anti-rationalist, a virtue theorist, and a proto-feminist, but he also put great emphasis on the agreements we can make and respect, the social artifices we can invent, to improve our life together. Were he alive today, he would hail the internet as a great enlarger of human ability, and of ability to communicate and share ideas, but might also see some dangers in it, new forms of theft and fraud made possible by it, and new threats posed to privacy and security. In his *History* he emphasized the transformation that the printing press made to human life, bringing both enormous benefit and the possibility of new wrongs, such as libel, and published incitement to violence and rebellion. New threats have arisen since Hume's time, and some of them are threats to our climate of trust. More than one sort of climate change threatens us, at present, and new artifices are needed to help us cope with the new challenges. As it is natural virtues such as thrift and economy which will be needed to combat the physical climate change, so it is natural virtues like steadfastness, courage, patience, willingness to listen to grievances, and the moral imagination to invent new paths to peace, which are called for in the face of international terror campaigns. Some new moral invention may be needed, before we succeed in living at peace with people of other faiths than our own, especially when they have reason to see us as colonialists and exploiters.

Late in life Hume became very pessimistic about how human life was going, especially in England. Had he seen what has recently happened in the way of reconciliation of former enemies in Ireland and South Africa, he would have been heartened. Had he lived to see a black president of the USA, he would have revised some of his footnotes. Had he seen how the US delegation in Bali let themselves be booed into concessions in an international forum on carbon emissions, had he foreseen the United Nations, then he would have wanted to extend his brief treatment of 'laws of nations', to allow new ways in which cooperation can occur between peoples, and in which disapprobation can deter the powerful. He spoke of the international agreement to refrain from the use of poisoned arms. Fuels that poison are now of as much importance as poisoned arms, though nuclear weapons count as an extreme case of the latter. Just as the lack of ways of containing the poison was a good reason for eighteenth-century armies to agree not to use the poisons known to them, so the same reason can stop us from continuing the poisoning we advertently or inadvertently began, and have knowingly continued.

What Hume would say about wars to control oil fields, or terrorist action against such wars, is a purely speculative question. That he would want to rewrite his essays on suicide, and on immortality, given the rise of suicidal terrorist killers confident of paradise, is pretty certain. That he would extend his treatment of laws of nations to include more curbs on aggression than poisoned arms and inhumane treatment of prisoners is also pretty clear. But what he would advocate to pacify aggrieved groups, and divert their indignant energies, is less certain. It would not surprise him that their motivation is partly religious zeal, since he knew the lethal potential of that. In his day, Muslims were as much the victims of Christian zeal as vice versa, so he did not dwell on the special perils of Islam. That they happen to live over oil fields which Christian nations covet could be seen as a continuation of the situation when they controlled the holy sites in Jerusalem, inspiring bloody crusades. He calls the crusades 'the most signal and most durable monument of human folly that has yet appeared in any age or nation' *(History of England,* vol. 1, ch. V, 334). Would he revise that judgement had he foreseen the war in Iraq? (Or, for that matter, the Israel–Palestinian disputes over territory, including territory in Jerusalem.) Many aspects of today's world would amaze him, airplanes, nuclear weapons, telephones, radio, television, the internet. He would not, I think, be amazed at the number of powerful women, as he regarded Elizabeth I of England one of its most competent rulers. What he would say about climate change is anyone's guess. It is easier to guess what he would say about terrorism, and genocide. The Holocaust would not unduly surprise the historian of the treatment of the Jews in York in the time of Richard I, but a militant Israel, oppressing Palestinians, and supported by the United States, might surprise him.

Of course one of the main social developments since Hume's time has been communism. Its curtailment of individual freedom would surely have appalled him; its goal of economic equality was one he could sympathize with. But he had predicted that any regime that tried to prevent morally offensive inequalities of wealth from developing would have to employ 'rigorous inquisition' and 'severe jurisdiction', which would eventually degenerate into tyranny. What he would have said about Soviet Russia and communist China's abolishment of religion, or about the relation of that move to their other tyrannical features, is not easy to say. I think he would be as appalled at capitalist and religious America as at atheist and communist Russia or China. Of today's societies, probably the most attractive to him would be the Scandinavian nations, and Iceland, which combine freedom and democracy with a fairly secular spirit, but he would also want to raise questions about whether the arts and sciences are thriving better there than in more authoritarian or more religious cultures. No nation would come at all close to his version of a perfect commonwealth, but he would expect the best modelled governments to be found in lands where the better spinning wheels and knitting looms are crafted. Industrial innovation along with democracy is found in today's world in many places, not least New Zealand, whose woollen cloth and knitting skills (like Iceland's) are pretty good. No statue of Hume yet graces the Edinburgh of the South, where I write this chapter, but I think he would approve of the life that goes on here, of our multi-party political system, our encouragement of innovation, our high book consumption (shared with Iceland), even of the fact that till recently Dunedin held a yearly continuous reading of Milton's 'Paradise Lost'. (Hume has high praise for Milton.) This would compensate for the fact that there also is a yearly toasting of Robbie Burns, on his birthday, around his statue in the centre of the city, with civically supplied haggis and a 'wee dram'. He would feel at home here, I like to think, and not just because our street names echo those of Edinburgh. (There is even a St David Street, leading, appropriately enough, to the University. I first read him there, guided by David Daiches Raphael, and later by John Passmore.)[9]

BIBLIOGRAPHY

Ardal Pall S. 1966. *Passion and Value in Hume's Treatise*. Edinburgh: Edinburgh University Press.

Beam, C. 1996. 'Hume and Nietzsche: Naturalists, Ethicists, Anti-Christians', *Hume Studies* 22 (2): 299–324.

Blackburn, S. 1993. *Essays in Quasi-Realism*. Oxford: Oxford University Press.

Botros, S. 2006. *Hume, Morality, and Reason: A Legacy of Contradiction*. London, Routledge.

Bricke, J. 2007. 'Hume on Liberty and Necessity' in E. S. Radcliffe (ed.), *A Companion to Hume*. Oxford, Blackwell, 201–16.

Brown, C. 1988. 'Is Hume an Internalist?', *Journal of the History of Philosophy* 26: 69–87.

Cohen, R. 1997. 'The common point of view in Hume's ethics', *Philosophy and Phenomenological Research* 57 (4): 827–50.

—— 2008. *Hume's Morality: Feeling and Fabrication*, Part 2. Oxford: Oxford University Press.

Flew, A. 1986. *David Hume: Philosopher of Moral Science*. Oxford: Blackwell.

Gill, M. 2006. *The British Moralists on Human Nature, and the Birth of Secular Ethics*. Cambridge: Cambridge University Press.

Goldman A. 2006. *Simulating Minds: the Philosophy, Psychology, and Neuroscience of Mindreading*. Oxford: Oxford University Press.

Gordon, R. M. 1995. 'Sympathy, Simulation and the Impartial Spectator', *Ethics* 105: 727–42.

Guyer, P. 2008. *Knowledge, Reason and Taste: Kant's Response to Hume*. Princeton: Princeton University Press.

Hume, D. 1975. *Enquiry Concerning the Human Understanding and Concerning the Principles of Moral*, ed. L. A. Selby-Bigge and P. H. Nidditch. Oxford: Oxford University.

—— 1978. *Treatise of Human Nature*, ed. L. A. Selby-Bigge and P. H. Nidditch. Oxford: Oxford University.

—— 1998. *Enquiry Concerning the Principles of Morals*, ed. T. Beauchamp. Oxford: Oxford University Press.

---

[9] This entry has benefited from good comments on earlier versions from Roger Crisp, Rob Shaver, and Jacqueline Taylor.

Hume, D. 2000. *Treatise of Human Nature*, ed. D. F. Norton and M. J. Norton. Oxford: Oxford University Press.

—— 2007. *Treatise of Human Nature*, ed. D. F. Norton and M. J. Norton. Oxford: Oxford University Press.

Jacobson, A. J. (ed.) 2000. *Feminist Interpretations of Hume*. University Park: Penn State Press.

Kail, P. J. 2007. *Projection and Realism in Hume's Philosophy*. Oxford: Oxford University Press.

Korsgaard, C. 1997. 'The normativity of instrumental reason', in G. Cullity and B. Gaut (eds), *Ethics and Practical Reason*. Oxford: Clarendon Press, 213–54.

MacIntyre, A. 1959. 'Hume on "Is" and "Ought"', *Philosophical Review* 68: 451–68.

Mackie, J. 1980. *Hume's Moral Theory*. London: Routledge & Kegan Paul.

Mandeville, B. 1711. *A Treatise on the Hypochondriack and Hysterick Passions*. London.

—— 1714. *The Fable of the Bees, or Private Vices, Public Benefits*. London.

—— 1732. *An Enquiry into the Origin of Honour, and the Usefulness of Christianity in War*. London.

Mazza, E. 2005. 'Cannibals in "A Dialogue" (in search of a standard of morals)', in E. Mazza and E. Ronchetti (eds), *Instruction and Amusement: Le ragioni dell'illuminismo britannicco*. Padua: Il Poligrafo, 45–66.

Mossner, E. 1980. *The Life of David Hume*. Second edition. Oxford: Oxford University Press.

Pigden, C. (ed.) 2011. *Hume on Is and Ought*. Basingstoke: Palgrave Macmillan.

Pitson, T. 2003. 'Hume on Morals and Animals', *British Journal for the History of Philosophy* 11(4): 639–55.

Radcliffe, E. 1996. 'How does the Humean Sense of Duty Motivate?', *Journal of the History of Philosophy* 34: 383–407.

Russell, P. 2008. *The Riddle of the Treatise: Skepticism, Naturalism, and Irreligion*. Oxford: Oxford University Press.

Sayre-McCord, G. 1994. 'Why Hume's general point of view isn't ideal—and should not be', *Social Philosophy and Policy* 188: 37–58.

Stroud, B. 2000. '"Gilding or staining" the world with "sentiments" and "phantasms"', in R. Read and K. A. Richman (eds), *The New Hume Debate*. London: Routledge.

Taylor J. 2009. 'Hume's Later Moral Philosophy', in D. F. Norton and J. Taylor (eds), *The Cambridge Companion to Ethics*. Second edition. Cambridge: Cambridge University Press, 311–40.

Wiggins, D. 2006. *Ethics: Twelve Lectures on the Philosophy of Morality*. Cambridge, MA: Harvard University Press.

CHAPTER 20

ADAM SMITH[1]

JAMES OTTESON

20.1 INTRODUCTION

ADAM Smith (1723–91) was the author of two books: the 1759 *Theory of Moral Sentiments* (TMS) and the 1776 *Inquiry into the Nature and Causes of the Wealth of Nations* (WN). TMS, Smith's main contribution to ethical thought,[2] went through six editions during his lifetime.[3] The second and sixth editions received the largest revisions. Part VI of TMS, 'Of the Character of Virtue', was an entirely new addition in the sixth and final edition, which appeared a few weeks before Smith died in 1790. The first edition appeared when Smith was thirty-six years old, and edition six when he was sixty-seven; if we count the years he had been delivering the lectures on which TMS was based, that means that he worked on the materials in TMS with some regularity for nearly forty years. I believe the central parts of TMS's argument did not change, however, and hence in what follows I shall focus on those aspects that remain constant, and I shall regard the sixth and final edition of Smith's lifetime as the definitive one.[4]

I shall first give an overview of what I believe Smith's theory is meant to show, and then I shall elaborate on several of the main elements of the theory.

[1] I would like to thank Roger Crisp for invaluable help, suggestions, and encouragement during the writing of this chapter. All errors are mine.
[2] Some scholars believe important ethical claims can be constructed from discussions in some of Smith's other works. See, for example, Schliesser 2006 and 2008.
[3] The most comprehensive biography of Smith is Ross 1995. Still quite useful is Rae 1895.
[4] Whether the changes in the succession of editions of TMS are in fact significant is debated. For discussion, one might begin with the editors' introduction to the Glasgow Edition of TMS. For discussion of the importance of the sixth edition's new Part VI, see Hanley 2009.

20.2 THE BASIC ACCOUNT

Smith argues that moral standards arise on the basis of an interactive process that takes place in and over specific historical locations. Since human beings live in different times and places, the systems of commonly shared moral standards vary in their details; but since human beings also share, in some specific relevant respects, a common human nature, their moral systems also enjoy significant overlap. The element of human nature most crucial for Smith's account is what he calls the *desire for mutual sympathy of sentiments*. Smith's technical usage of 'sympathy' is broader than mere pity: 'Pity and compassion are words appropriated to signify our fellow-feeling with the sorrow of others. Sympathy, though its meaning was, perhaps, originally the same, may now, however, without much impropriety, be made use of to denote our fellow-feeling with any passion whatever' (TMS I.i.1.5).[5] Thus the desire for the mutual sympathy of sentiments is, for Smith, the desire to see our own sentiments, whatever they are, reflected in others: 'nothing pleases us more than to observe in other men a fellow-feeling with all the emotions of our own breast; nor are we ever so much shocked as by the appearance of the contrary' (TMS I.i.2.1).

This desire is the *sine qua non* of Smith's theory. Smith believes it is what drives us into society, what motivates much of our conversation and conduct, what leads us to moderate our sentiments and behaviour so that they more closely accord with what others would expect, and what ultimately gives rise to the habits and rules of moral judgement that come to constitute commonly shared morality. Smith provides many examples—we agonize when we see 'our brother' 'upon the rack' even when we ourselves are not threatened (TMS I.i.1.2), we 'naturally shrink and draw back our own leg' when 'we see a stroke aimed and just ready to fall upon the leg or arm of another', the 'mob, when they are gazing at a dancer on the slack rope, naturally writhe and twist their own bodies, as they see him do' (TMS I.i.1.3), etc.—that he believes show that we not only feel, to varying degrees, the 'sentiments' of others but that we also receive pleasure from realizing or imagining that our sentiments correspond with those of others. This is thus a descriptive claim for Smith, but it serves as the mechanism that generates what we regard as 'moral' sentiments.

Smith seeks in TMS to understand why people make moral judgements, how they make them, and what the mechanisms are that explain (1) why nearly all people develop moral codes and (2) why people's moral codes significantly overlap with the codes of their loved ones and friends. Here are some observations Smith made that animated his investigation. First, nearly all human beings transition during their lifetimes from having no moral code as infants and small children to having complex, sophisticated moral codes as adults. Second, all human communities have prevailing moral codes.

---

[5] I use the Glasgow Edition of the Works and Correspondence of Adam Smith throughout. I also use the now standard notation in referring to TMS and to WN: 'TMS I.i.1.5' means *Theory of Moral Sentiments*, part one, section one, chapter one, paragraph five.

Third, the moral codes of these communities overlap but are not identical. And fourth, some aspects of moral codes change over time, yet other aspects endure. To explain these observations, Smith saw himself as following Newtonian methodology: Study the phenomena, look for regularities, propose mechanisms that can explain the regularities, and test the putative mechanisms against future or larger data. Thus Smith's theory is largely a genealogy of morality. Criticizing morals, as well as encouraging people to abide by the proper moral code, are secondary concerns.[6]

How, then, does Smith propose that individuals develop moral codes? We are born, he thinks, with no morality. A baby knows only its own wants, with no notion of a proper (or improper) thing to ask for, of a proper (or improper) way to ask for it, or of shame or remorse for having asked for something it should not have asked for. The baby attempts to have its wants satisfied simply by alarming its caregiver with howls and cries. According to Smith, it is not until the baby begins playing with other children that it has jolting experiences leading it to realize that it is not the centre of everyone's life. This is the child's introduction into the 'great school of self-command' (TMS III.3.22): the experience of being *judged* by others creates in the child the displeasure associated with not sharing a mutual sympathy of sentiments (MSS). And displeasure it is. A small but telling example: 'A man is mortified when, after having endeavoured to divert the company, he looks round and sees that nobody laughs at his jests but himself. On the contrary, the mirth of the company is highly agreeable to him, and he regards this correspondence of their sentiments with his own as the greatest applause' (TMS I.i.2.1). When one becomes aware that others do not share one's sentiments—that is, that no 'correspondence', 'harmony', 'concord', or 'sympathy' of sentiments obtains—one feels embarrassed, chagrined, isolated. The degree of one's feeling of isolation depends on the particulars of the situation, but it is never pleasant. When the child is spurned by his playmates, it causes the child to cast about for a way to relieve the displeasure. Eventually the child comes to modify his behaviour to more closely match the expectations of his playmates.[7] When he does so, a new pleasure is experienced, that of MSS, and a new and permanent desire for that pleasure has been aroused. From that point on, according to Smith, the child regularly engages in trial-and-error investigation into what behaviours will achieve this sympathy and thus satisfy this desire.

This investigation encourages the individual to discover and then adopt rules of behaviour and judgement that increase the chance of achieving mutual sympathy. By the time the individual becomes an adult, he has adopted, often unconsciously or only implicitly, a wide range of principles of behaviour and judgement. Everyone else is similarly engaging in the same investigation.[8] Our strong desire for mutual sympathy of sentiments can therefore lead to

---

[6] That does not mean he is unconcerned with the task of being a 'moralist', as against the task of being a 'scientist', but he is concerned first and foremost with the scientific aspects. See Den Uyl 2011 and Otteson 2011.

[7] Smith's audience for the lectures on which TMS was based would have been all male, a fact reflected in various references retained in TMS to 'our' sex as opposed to the 'fair' one, etc. For this reason, and not to beg any questions, I retain Smith's use of the masculine pronouns throughout.

[8] See TMS I.i.2.6.

reciprocity and mutual seeking of sympathy, thereby generating, via an invisible-hand mechanism,[9] commonly shared standards of behaviour and judgement and even a shared *system* of morality. It is an *invisible* hand because the agents in question do not intend to create a shared system of morality—they intend only to achieve mutual sympathy here, now, with this person. In so doing, however, they (unintentionally) establish the precedents and behavioural habits that will generate, constitute, and maintain a shared system of expectations and sentiments. Thus when moralists proclaim rules of morality, on Smith's account their proclamations are based on observed regularities in people's behaviours and judgements. In this they are like grammarians who identify the rules of a language. They can, and sometimes do, affect practice at the margins—as, for example, prescriptivist grammarians can marginally affect the way people use their language[10]—but most behaviour we identify as distinctively 'moral', as well as judgements about what is moral and what is immoral, is, Smith argues, the result of 'habit and experience' (TMS III.3.2–3).

Moral judgements are, then, for Smith, generalizations arrived at inductively on the basis of past experience. The experience in this case is of our own approvals and disapprovals of our own and others' conduct, as well as of our observations of others' approvals and disapprovals. Frequently repeated patterns of judgement can come to have the appearance of moral duties or even commandments from on high, while patterns that recur with less frequency will enjoy commensurately less confidence. Smith's account thus declasses moral judgements, not to mention moralists, by locating their origins in the messy empirical world of human experience. The job of the moral philosopher becomes, then, principally that of identifying and systematizing these generalizations, and perhaps assisting us in imagining how they might apply to new circumstances.

That is Smith's basic account. Let me now elaborate briefly on several of its elements. I address by turn 'sympathy', 'propriety' and 'merit', 'mutual sympathy of sentiments', imagination and the 'impartial spectator', moral objectivity, and, finally, utility.

20.3 SYMPATHY

In the nineteenth century, some scholars developed and pressed what came to be known as the 'Adam Smith Problem', which alleged that Smith's two books offered potentially inconsistent accounts of human motivation—TMS basing its on 'sympathy', while WN

---

[9] The phrase 'invisible hand' appears three times in Smith's extant works: first in his essay 'History of Astronomy' (EPS III.2), then once in TMS (IV.i.11), and then again, most famously, in WN (IV.ii.9). Discussion of the significance of this phrase is legion. For a selection from a range of perspectives, see Grampp 2000, Kennedy 2008, Montes 2004, Otteson 2002a, and Rothschild 2001.

[10] Early in his career, Smith wrote a short essay entitled 'Considerations concerning the First Formation of Languages' (reprinted in *Lectures on Rhetoric and Belles Lettres*, 201–26) that he instructed to be appended to the second and subsequent editions of TMS that appeared during his lifetime. For discussion of this essay and its connection to Smith's TMS and other work, see, for example, Dascal 2006, Otteson 2000b, and Phillipson 2000.

based its on self-interest. Though there is more to this problem than many contemporary scholars allow,[11] nevertheless its early versions rested on an important mistake. Smithian 'sympathy' is not a motive to action at all. It is, rather, the 'concord' or 'harmony' between agents' sentiments. It is generated, moreover, not by mere observance of another's sentiments,[12] but, rather, by a delicate comparison of a person's sentiments against what one imagines would be the sentiments generated in either oneself or in an impartial observer in the same situation as the 'person principally concerned' (PPC).

Smith argues that this sympathy 'cannot, in any sense, be regarded as a selfish principle': 'though sympathy is very properly said to arise from an imaginary change of situations with the person principally concerned, ...but I consider what I should suffer if I was really you, and I not only change circumstances with you, but I change persons and characters' (TMS VII.iii.1.4). This is a difficult position for Smith to take, for two reasons. First, even in imagining what would be my reaction in your shoes, I must still rely on only my own past experience to formulate a judgement; Smith's earlier argument that all experience is essentially private (TMS I.i.1.2) entails that I have nothing else on which to draw. The most promising way to take Smith's insistence on the non-selfishness of sympathy is by focusing instead on Smith's claim that we strive, in adopting this imaginary change of situation, for impartiality. We try, that is, to render a judgement based not on what my reaction in fact is to the PPC's situation, but rather on what I imagine my reaction would I be if I were properly impartial. There are natural incentives and thus prudential reasons to adopt, or to strive to adopt, such an impartial perspective, to which we shall return momentarily. But Smith's position is that the sympathy of sentiments we seek is motivated because its achievement produces pleasure. Hence there is no immediate conflict, at least not on this count, between the account of natural human motivation offered in TMS and that offered in WN.

Yet the fact that we seek MSS because it produces pleasure seems to conflict with Smith's claim that it is not a 'selfish' principle. Perhaps the first sentence of TMS provides a way to understand Smith's position. Smith opens TMS with: 'How selfish soever man may be supposed, there are evidently some principles in his nature, which interest him in the fortunes of others, and render their happiness necessary to him, though he derives nothing from it except the pleasure of seeing it' (TMS I.i.1.1). We may be motivated by self-interest, but our interests include the 'fortunes' of (some) others. Thus even if our own pleasure remains our motivation, one source of pleasure to us is seeing others do well—in which case the desire for MSS is not strictly 'selfish'.

Whether or not a sympathy of sentiments is achieved in any given case is dependent, for Smith, on the degree to which we can 'bring home to our own breast the situation of those principally concerned' (TMS II.i.5.3 and *passim*). And this, in turn, is dependent on several factors: our knowledge of the PPC and of the PPC's situation; our willingness

[11] I make this case in Otteson 2000 and 2002a. For other discussions of the 'Adam Smith Problem', see the editors' introduction to TMS, Dickey 1986, Göçmen 2007, and Montes 2004.

[12] This is one distinction between Smith's conception and use of 'sympathy' and Hume's. For discussion, see Broadie 2006.

to imaginatively 'enter into' the PPC's situation; our skill at imaginatively fleshing out another's situation; what our experiences have been with the PPC, with people like the PPC, and with situations like the PPC's; and so on. This means that the process of seeking sympathy of sentiments is complicated and delicate and frequently, despite our mutual desires, fails. Some have argued that Smith's description of the process of passing a moral judgement is indeed too complicated to be an accurate portrayal of what we do.[13] But the process is not obviously more complicated than, for example, driving a car in traffic, and if, as Smith suggests, it involves skills, then, as with driving, practice can lead to better, or at least more routine and less deliberate, performance.

20.4 PROPRIETY AND MERIT

Smith divides the moral judgement into two complementary parts, each of which can operate independently:

> The sentiment or affection of the heart from which any action proceeds, and upon which its whole virtue or vice must ultimately depend, may be considered under two different aspects, or in two different relations; first, in relation to the cause which excites it, or the motive which gives occasion to it; and secondly, in relation to the end which it proposes, or the effect which it tends to produce. (TMS I.i.3.5)

The former Smith calls 'propriety' (and its contrary 'impropriety'), the latter he calls 'merit' (and its contrary 'demerit'). When we pass a moral judgement on a person's actions, we will have one or the other of two aspects of the actions in mind: whether the person's actions were caused by sentiments that were fitting responses to the situation in which the person found himself, and whether the consequences of the actions were beneficial to others. An action prompted by sentiments that are fitting given the circumstances is 'proper'; an action whose consequences benefit, or tend to benefit, those affected by it is 'meritorious'.

To illustrate the process, consider again joke-telling, a favourite example of Smith's.[14] There are rules determining what kind of jokes one may tell in what company, how long one may laugh at a joke, whether one should consider a given joke funny, and so on. These rules are both nuanced and context-dependent: they may depend on the age, sex, religion, or ethnicity of one's audience, how well one knows the members of one's audience, what the setting is, and so on. Who is the source of these rules? Who enforces them? Answer: we are and we do—though often without realizing it. Like the rules of language, the rules of joke-telling are a product of unintentional order, habits based on experience. We enforce them by condemning—in various and sometimes exquisitely subtle ways—infractions of them, and we reinforce them by observing or rewarding them.

---

[13] See Raphael 1975.   [14] See, e.g. TMS I.i.2.1, I.i.2.6, and I.i.3.1.

There may be play in the rules, cases in which a range of kinds of jokes might be appropriate, but typically there are also examples that people would consider clearly beyond the pale. Smith's argument is that the process for determining the propriety of joke-telling is the same as it is in the passing of judgements on other sentiments. One imagines oneself in the other's place, imagines what sentiments one would likely have experienced, compares the two, and thence renders the judgement. Similarly with determining whether a person's anger is proper or not, whether a person's happiness or sadness is proper or not, and so on through all the other passions and sentiments.[15]

The complementary part of the moral judgement, what Smith calls 'merit', depends 'upon the beneficial or hurtful effects which the affection proposes or tends to produce, depends the merit or demerit, the good or ill desert of the action to which it gives occasion' (TMS II.intro.2). So for Smith a complete moral judgement comprises *both* a principled part—whether the relevant sentiments comport with the relevant inductively generated rules—*and* a consequentialist part—whether the effects of the action(s) prompted by the sentiments are beneficial or not. Smith thinks we judge whether the sentiments prompting a person's actions are meritorious by determining whether their intended object—the person who is intended to be benefitted (or harmed) by the action— experiences justified gratitude or resentment. If that person experiences gratitude that is justified, it prompts the observer to reward the agent; if the person experiences resentment that is justified, it prompts the observer to punish the agent. One determines whether the object's gratitude or resentment is justified by again comparing that person's sentiments to what would be one's own sentiments as one imagines oneself in that person's position. Thus Smith's argument that the rendering of moral judgements is effected by imaginatively switching places with the people involved explains the central aspect of both parts of the complete moral judgement. In both cases, one's imagination must take into account all the relevant details of the person principally concerned, of the situation in question, and of the object of the PPC's intentions; then it must imagine what one's own sentiments would be, in light of all those details, if one were in the PPC's position; and then it must do all of the same for the person who, as Smith puts it, is 'acted upon'.[16]

Additionally, Smith thinks we must determine whether we think that the agent's motives were justified or not in acting towards the object the way the agent did: 'Our heart must adopt the principles of the agent, and go along with all the affections which influenced his conduct, before it can entirely sympathize with, and beat time to, the gratitude of the person who has been benefitted by his actions' (TMS II.i.4.1). This means that merit is a 'compounded sentiment', made up partly of our relative sympathy with the sentiments of the agent and partly of our relative sympathy with the sentiments of the person acted upon. Thus there are four possibilities: (1) sympathy with both the agent

[15] Smith believes that this imaginative-switching-of-places explains everything from why a mother flies to her child when she hears its 'moanings' from the 'agony of disease' to how we can 'sympathize even with the dead' to how we can sympathize with the plight of a person who has experienced 'loss of reason'. See TMS I.i.1.11–13.

[16] For discussion of what the Smithian account requires of our imaginations, see Brown 1994 and Griswold 1999 and 2006.

and the object; (2) sympathy with the agent but antipathy with the object; (3) antipathy with the agent but sympathy with the object; and (4) antipathy for both. Smith gives examples of some but not all of the cases. For example, reading about Borgia or Nero, he says, gives us an antipathy for their sentiments and a sympathy with the sentiments of those whom they 'insulted, murdered, or betrayed' (TMS II.i.5.6).

Smith's genealogical account is sophisticated and even prescient, but it is also merely suggestive. Many of the details of the process Smith suggests he leaves out. One wonders, for example, how it can account for what we might call 'moral entrepreneurs', people who break away from prevailing moral sentiments. Moreover, it seems that we tend to be more interested in MSS with *some* people than we are of others, yet Smith's account seems to suggest that all mutual sympathy of sentiments is desired. Smith's account also seems to introduce a 'grue'-type problem in moral judgements: if our habits, conventions, and principles develop on the basis of past experience, we cannot know how, or even whether, they will apply to future moral situations. Finally, Smith's account seems not to allow for the common phenomenon of having desires that are undesirable. Perhaps I desire—in some sense 'naturally'—mutual sympathy of sentiments with you, but I may well also, even simultaneously, judge that desire to be (morally) bad.

20.5 MUTUAL SYMPATHY OF SENTIMENTS AND NEGOTIATION

Smith believes that the level of propriety of most sentiments lies 'in a certain mediocrity', by which he means that the 'pitch' of one's passions must not be too high or too low (TMS I.ii.intro.1). This is the natural result of the negotiation Smith believes goes on between the person feeling the sentiment, who wants others to enter into his sentiment, and the spectators, who are not as inclined to enter into them: they settle on a level somewhere in the middle. As these negotiations are executed over and over again, patterns emerge that become, as it were, the default settings. Level L_1 of passion P_1 is typically deemed appropriate by the relevant observers O_1 in situation S_1; level L_2 of passion P_2 is deemed appropriate by O_2 in situation S_2; and so on. Keeping close to those levels typically results in MSS, while straying too far from them results in a lack of sympathy or even an antipathy unless special circumstances obtain.

Striving for MSS, according to Smith, often includes an element of negotiation. Each of us wants the pleasure associated with mutual sympathy, so we try to get others to sympathize with our own sentiments. One aspect of this negotiation is Smith's suggestion that it develops certain skills in us—including the power of persuasion, as well as the ability to describe our situation in vivid detail—all in an effort to increase the chances that others will sympathize with our sentiments. It also leads us to develop our power of imagination: sometimes achieving MSS requires us to fill out in our imagination many details and to run a complex virtual reality movie, as it were, keeping track of these details and how they will or might interact. The better able we are to do this, the more accurate our imagination, and thus our judgement, can become. According to Smith, to judge accurately, one 'must, first of all, endeavour, as much as he can, to put himself in the situation of the other, and to bring home to himself *every little circumstance* of distress which can possibly occur to the sufferer. He must adopt the whole case of his companion with *all its minutest incidents;* and strive to render as perfect as possible, that imaginary change of situation upon which his sympathy is founded' (TMS I.i.4.6; emphasis supplied). When we fail to achieve MSS, Smith says it is usually due to one of two circumstances: the failure 'arises either from the different degrees of attention, which our different habits of life allow us to give easily to the several parts of those complex objects, or from the different degrees of natural acuteness in the faculty of the mind to which they are addressed' (TMS I.i.4.2). Some become better at wielding this complex skill of imagining and judgement-making than others, which might explain the roles for moralists, preachers, and other public arbiters of public morals.

Although this part of Smith's analysis might not qualify as a proper moral injunction, it does indicate that there are incentives at work leading us in mutually beneficial ways. Given that you desire MSS, and given that your chances of achieving it increase with the delicacy of your imagination and the accuracy of your judgements,[17] you should strive to hone your skills of imagining others' situations. If you do so, you will thereby increase the chances of satisfying your own desire for MSS, while simultaneously—if unintentionally—providing others with the MSS they also desire. Though Smith does not use the phrase 'invisible hand' here, I suggest that this is an invisible-hand argument nonetheless. Language from Smith's WN applies here, *mutatis mutandis:* As each of us strives to satisfy his own desire for MSS, each of us is encouraged to behave in ways that enable others to satisfy their desires for MSS, thereby leading to behaviour that 'is most advantageous to the society' (cf. WN IV.ii.4); thus each of us 'is in this, as in many other cases, led by an invisible hand to promote an end that was no part of his intention' (WN IV.ii.9). Taking the first sentence of TMS seriously might moreover imply another maxim: we should encourage others to develop their imaginations and the delicacy of their observations of others' situations. This way we increase the chances of *their* achieving MSS as well.

20.6 THE IMPARTIAL SPECTATOR

Smith argues that the process of passing judgement on oneself is similar to that of passing judgement on others. In the latter case, 'We either approve or disapprove of the conduct of another man according as we feel that, when we bring his case home to ourselves, we either can or cannot entirely sympathize with the sentiments and motives which

[17] Also required is what Smith calls 'self-command', from which Smith says 'all the other virtues seem to derive their principal lustre' (TMS VI.iii.11).

directed it'; similarly, 'we either approve or disapprove of our own conduct, according as we feel that, when we place ourselves in the situation of another man, and view it, as it were, with his eyes and from his station, we either can or cannot entirely enter into and sympathize with the sentiments and motives which influenced it' (TMS III.1.1). In judging oneself, one must try to divide oneself 'as it were, into two persons': the 'I' as agent or person principally concerned, and the 'I' who is judging the PPC (TMS III.1.6). Smith argues that the habit of judging one's own character in this way is what develops into what is often called one's 'conscience'.

Smith offers two reasons why we may care what an imaginary observer thinks of our conduct. First, the habit of doing so is so deeply ingrained in us already that if we do not heed our consciences we will be unhappy. According to Smith, man desires not only to be praised, but has a further desire 'of being what he himself approves in other men' (TMS III.2.7). This further desire results, I believe,[18] from the continued workings of the desire for MSS. All of us, Smith says, have been frustrated when people disapproved of our conduct because, we believe, they did not fully understand the circumstances involved. An only partial familiarity with another's situation might prejudice the judgement one makes, and all of us have experienced the unpleasantness of being on the wrong end of a prejudiced, uninformed, or misinformed judgement (TMS III.2.31–33). Smith argues that unpleasant experiences like these provide natural incentives to consult, in the relevant situations, not the judgement of actual observers, but instead the judgement of an imaginary, fully informed but disinterested observer.[19] Smith calls this standard an 'impartial spectator'. And here we come to one of Smith's great contributions to moral philosophy: the conception of the impartial spectator that constitutes the standard of morality.[20] Smith believes that this standard comes about naturally and unintentionally as a result of individuals' wanting mutual sympathy of sentiments and of their frequent frustration at others' inability or unwillingness to expend the effort that is sometimes necessary to come to understand another's full situation before passing judgement on his sentiments and actions. When mutual sympathy is not forthcoming from actual, often partial, spectators, we repair to an imagined impartial spectator who would approve of our conduct. Over time the practice of doing so becomes habitual, and the judgements of this imagined impartial spectator's sentiments can become the standards against which we judge our actions.

The Smithian moral psychology becomes worryingly complex here. We seem to toggle back and forth between consulting (a) the actual judgement of actual spectators, (b) the imagined judgement of actual spectators (asking what Socrates or Jesus, for example, would do in my situation), and (c) the imagined judgement of imaginary spectators. What causes us to adopt one standard over another? How are we able to juggle multiple

---

[18] Other scholars have different views about the nature and origin of this desire. See, for example, Griswold 1999: ch. 3.

[19] Note that Smith's impartial spectator is not behind a Rawlsian veil of ignorance: he is disinterested, but he has full knowledge of the person(s) involved and the circumstance(s) of the case in question.

[20] D. D. Raphael 2007 argues that this is Smith's most important and enduring contribution to moral philosophy.

standards, even simultaneously? Smith claims that there are, moreover, 'two different standards' by which we can judge our own conduct: 'The one is the idea of exact propriety and perfection, so far as we are each of us capable of comprehending that idea. The other is that degree of approximation to this idea which is commonly attained in the world, and which the greater part of our friends and companions, of our rivals and competitors, may have actually arrived at' (TMS VI.iii.23). Smith claims that we often use *both* standards when reviewing our own conduct, with the apparently natural default inclining us to take whichever standard is the most flattering to ourselves. Yet Smith claims, cryptically, that we are often 'secretly conscious' (TMS III.4.12 and passim) that we are flattering ourselves in our choice of standards by which to judge our own conduct, when other people—even the supposed embodiment of one of the other standards— would recommend that we use another standard instead. Unless we are compelled by circumstances to adopt a less flattering standard, however, we often do not:

> The opinion which we entertain of our own character depends entirely on our judgements concerning our past conduct. It is so disagreeable to think ill of ourselves, that we often purposely turn away our view from those circumstances which might render that judgement unfavourable. He is a bold surgeon, they say, whose hand does not tremble when he performs an operation upon his own person; and he is often equally bold who does not hesitate to pull off the mysterious veil of self-delusion, which covers from his view the deformities of his own conduct. (TMS III.4.4)

Smith refers to this as our natural 'self-deceit'—a 'fatal weakness of mankind, [which] is the source of half the disorders of human life' (TMS III.4.6). Perhaps he is formulating here an early notion of the fundamental attribution error. Yet Smith's general uninterest in metaphysics and in philosophy of mind prevents him from exploring further what conception of mind this psychology entails.

20.7 Moral Objectivity

What is the normative status of the judgements arrived at in the seemingly material and almost mechanistic way Smith suggests? If this process results in the creation of an 'impartial spectator' standard of morality, are there any reasons besides prudential ones to obey this standard?

In Part III of TMS, Smith asks what sort of moral judgements a person would make, and what sort of moral sentiments he would have, if he grew up entirely alone: 'Were it possible that a human creature could grow up to manhood in some solitary place, without any communication with his own species, he could no more think of his own character, of the propriety or demerit of his own sentiments and conduct, of the beauty or deformity of his own mind, than of the beauty or deformity of his own face' (TMS III.1.3). He might have a sense of what things in his environment conduced to his ends and what did not—whether things 'pleased or hurt him' (TMS III.1.3)—but no sense of propriety or impropriety of his own behaviour. The reason is suggested by Smith's continuation of the thought experiment: 'Bring him into society, and he is immediately provided with the mirror which he wanted before' (TMS III.1.3). What the solitary man lacked while in isolation is experience of the judgement of others, which makes him confront his own behaviour: this is the social 'mirror' to which Smith refers. Once in 'society' with other humans, he experiences their (sometimes negative) judgements, and his formerly latent desire for mutual sympathy of sentiments is triggered, initiating the slow process of developing moral sentiments.

This thought experiment provides two key elements indicating what moral objectivity Smith thinks our moral judgements enjoy: (1) moral judgements are the products of rules that develop and are not eternally fixed or handed down from on high; (2) they originate from and depend upon human 'society' and interaction. Smith repeatedly describes the sentiments of morality as unfolding according to a process of negative and positive feedback dependent upon whether people achieve or fail to achieve MSS. Smith writes of the solitary man:

> Bring him into society, and all his own passions will immediately become the cause of new passions. He will observe that mankind approve of some of them, and are disgusted by others. He will be elevated in the one case, and cast down in the other; his desires and aversions, his joys and sorrows, will now often become the cause of new desires and new aversions, new joys and new sorrows: they will now, therefore, interest him deeply, and often call upon his most attentive consideration. (TMS III.1.3)

Here Smith recapitulates the process through which he believes all humans normally go when they transition from infants with no sense of moral propriety to adults with a complicated and delicate sense of moral propriety. The moment in that process described here—when the solitary man is brought 'into society'—is the moment Smith elsewhere describes as normally occurring to children when they first play with their mates and thus enter 'the great school of self-command' (TMS III.3.22).[21]

The mutual adjustment of sentiments and behaviour that begin upon this first experience of being judged by others leads to the development of habits and conventions of behaviour, and then gradually, Smith thinks, to 'general rules of morality'. 'It is thus that the general rules of morality are formed. They are ultimately founded upon experience of what, in particular instances, our moral faculties, our natural sense of merit and propriety, approve, or disapprove of.... The general rule ... is formed, by finding from experience, that all actions of a certain kind, or circumstanced in a certain manner, are approved or disapproved of' (TMS III.4.8). Note the repeated emphasis on *experience*. Smith's argument is apparently that there is no way to form moral judgements other than by relying on one's experience of what oneself and others approve or disapprove. This generalizing from one's past experience is also what generates the perspective of the

---

[21] Smith summarizes this process in an abbreviated, but arguably clearer, way in a crucial letter to Gilbert Elliot dated 10 October 1759 (*Correspondence*, 48 –57; see especially 54–5).

impartial spectator by which we judge ourselves. When judging our own conduct, we thus engage in a kind of moral triangulation. When we behave in a certain way towards another person, we have not two but three perspectives to consider: 'We must view [our sentiments], neither from our own place nor yet from his [i.e. the object of our actions], but from the place and with the eyes of a third person, who has no particular connexion with either, and who judges with impartiality between us' (TMS III.3.3). In practice, Smith thinks we accomplish this feat of triangulation often unconsciously: 'habit and experience have taught us to do this so easily and so readily, that we are scarce sensible that we do it' (TMS III.3.3). Our moral standards thus arise from 'habit and experience', not from apprehension of first principles, and they are pragmatically oriented towards the actual purposes and experiences people have.

But are they *right?* If the perspective of the imaginary impartial spectator is simply the coalescence of our inductively arrived-at generalizations based on our past contingent experiences of what sentiments and behaviours have met with approval, then is this viewpoint not simply a creature of the particular place and time in which one lives? And how could it provide any normative reason to follow its judgements? Thomas Reid argued that on Hume's view all a judge is supposed to do is observe the facts, and, once he has done so: 'Nothing remains, on his part, but to feel the right or the wrong; and mankind have, very absurdly, called him a *judge;* he ought to be called a *feeler.*'[22] This *reductio* reflects an abiding eighteenth-century worry about basing moral judgements on sentiments. Yet Smith's position would not fall prey to Reid's objection.

For Smith, the rendering of the moral judgement includes a deduction from principles, not a mere 'feeling' of the right or wrong. In the process of passing judgement, what one does, according to Smith, is consult the relevant general rules, ask whether the sentiment or behaviour one is judging comports with those rules, and thereby deduce whether it should be approved. Such a deduction might approximate the following form:

Step 1: Observe that a 'stranger passes by us in the street with all the marks of the deepest affliction' (TMS I.i.3.4).
Step 2: Apply the general rule that, unless there are special circumstances, a person should not behave like that in public.
Step 3: Realize that there are no special circumstances in this case.
Step 4: Therefore disapprove of his behaviour.

The disapproval is caused by our realization that the stranger's behaviour is inconsistent with the general rule. But the rule has no special authority of its own; it is merely our short-hand heuristic representing what an impartial observer would hold in the present case.

Suppose, however, that 'we are immediately told that he [the stranger] has just received the news of the death of his father' (TMS I.1.3.4). Now the deduction changes:

Step 1': Same as Step 1.
Step 2': Same as Step 2.

[22] Reid 1991 [1788]: 305.

Step 3': Realizing that this is a special circumstance, apply a new rule based on the nature of the special circumstance in question: People who recently learned of the death of a close relative are given far more latitude to express their emotions, even publicly.

Step 4': Realize that this stranger's public display falls within the proper scope.

Step 5: Conclude that it is now 'impossible that, in this case, we should not approve of his grief' (TMS I.i.3.4).

Moral standards that arise in the way Smith describes are what John Searle calls 'institutional facts', which 'are portions of the real world, objective facts in the world, that are facts only by human agreement'.[23] They are, using Searle's terminology, *ontologically subjective*, meaning that their existence depends on the beliefs and attitudes of particular agents. On the other hand, they are *epistemically objective*, meaning that it is not simply a matter of any single person's opinion whether they exist or not or what their basic features are. Their existence and nature are rather a matter of objectively ascertainable fact. I call this a 'middle-way' objectivity: not directly dependent on any transcendent sanction, like God or Natural Law, and yet neither arbitrary nor dependent on any person's individual opinion. They are objective facts of our social reality. This objectivity arises because they are the result of the invisible-hand process of local (micro) behaviours creating general (macro) patterns of order. It also arises because the shared standards rely on and develop in consequence of certain features of our common human nature—in particular our desire for MSS. A community's moral standards will, Smith says, vary along less important themes—conventions of dress, forms of greeting and address, and so on[24]—so the complete description of any given community's shared system of morality will be itself unique. Nonetheless, because of our shared humanity certain rules will almost invariably obtain—in particular, what Smith calls the 'rules of justice', to which we return momentarily.

Smith's theory thus provides several reasons why one should follow the moral rules of one's community. First, because doing so gives one the best chance of achieving something that one greatly desires, namely MSS. Second, because that is what others expect of one, and in so far as one cares about their chances of achieving mutual sympathy—and according to the first sentence of TMS, we *do* care about others—one should increase those chances by doing what is expected of one. Smith also believes that a principal constituent of happiness is loving and intimate relations with others: 'the chief part of human happiness arises from the consciousness of being beloved' (TMS I.ii.5.1); 'What so great happiness as to be beloved, and to know that we deserve to be beloved?' (TMS III.1.7). The way we become 'beloved' is by spending time with others whom we love and by behaving in ways that we know will inspire and encourage their love. Acting virtuously, or according to the dictates of the impartial spectator, or according to the general rules of morality we have developed, is, according to Smith, perhaps the 'surest way' to achieving happiness:

> No benevolent man ever lost altogether the fruits of his benevolence. If he does not always gather them from the persons from he ought to have gathered them, he seldom

[23] Searle 1997: 1.   [24] See TMS V.2.1 and V.2.7–8.

fails to gather them, and with a tenfold increase, from other people. Kindness is the parent of kindness; and if to be beloved by our brethren be the great object of our ambition, the surest way of obtaining it is, by our conduct to show that we really love them. (TMS VI.ii.1.19)

Happiness, then, attends upon being beloved, which itself attends both upon close and familiar relationships with others and upon our behaving in ways that we know they would, or should, approve—that is, upon the consciousness of being worthy of being beloved. Another reason, therefore, to follow the dictates of the impartial spectator and the general rules of morality issues from a hypothetical imperative: if you want to be happy, you should for the most part follow the moral standards of your community.[25]

The obvious objection to Smith, however, is that although a behaviour like, say, polygamy is *considered* objectionable in one place and *considered* unobjectionable in another, it does not follow from this that it is *in fact* objectionable or not.[26] Polygamy might be objectionable or not quite independently of what any community believes about it. On Smith's account, however, it is apparently not possible to make any such independent or transcendent judgement, since we lack the standard grounds to do so. One might claim that one finds polygamy distasteful, that one wishes that more people in one's community reacted to it the way oneself does, or that it conflicts with one's religious views or other moral commitments. On Smith's view, however, our moral intuitions and our moral traditions are generated and informed by the same mechanism as are those of people whose intuitions and traditions run differently. Now, the actual consequences of practices like polygamy are empirically ascertainable, and that could anchor an objective moral judgement based on a broadly utilitarian premise.[27] But the judgement would again be hypothetical—something like: given your circumstances and your nature, if you want to be happy, you should do *x*. The Smithian account provides no tools with which to generate categorical moral judgements.[28]

Yet Smith sometimes speaks of the impartial spectator's perspective as though it has a more elevated status—as, for example, when he refers to the impartial spectator as a 'demigod within the breast', 'partly of immortal, yet partly too of mortal extraction' (TMS III.2.32).[29] How does this elevated language square with the earthly origins of Smith's impartial spectator? I suggest that this language pertains to an empirical claim Smith is making: The greater the bearing any given habit, convention, or general moral

---

[25] See Forman-Barzilai 2010.

[26] I take this example from Hocutt 2000. Allan Gibbard provided helpful discussion of this section of the chapter.

[27] See, e.g. TMS II.ii.3.8.

[28] Smith is thus no Kantian, but he does sometimes speak of duty in roughly Kantian ways. For discussion, see Fleischacker 1991, 1996, 1999, and White 2010. The normativity of duty for Smith, however, is positive and arises empirically—from the facts of our circumstances, including our nature, the promises we have made, the relationships we have formed, and so on.

[29] In the first editions of TMS, Smith called the impartial spectator a 'vicegerent upon earth', an 'inmate of the breast, this abstract man, the representative of mankind, and substitute of the Deity' (TMS III.2.31 note r).

rule has on the relevant community's survival, the more frequently will its observance be noted, remarked, and insisted upon by the members of that community, and thus the more strongly should the impartial spectator approve following it and condemn disobeying it. The rigours of reality discipline us, as it were, to seek out and observe good behaviours. As we have seen, this will not, according to Smith, be a conscious process of gradation according to utility; rather, it will come about spontaneously, through trial and error, by repetition and reinforcement. For a handful of rules, their connection to a community's survival is so close and so immediate that the impartial spectator insists upon them. Smith argues there are but three such rules: 'The most sacred laws of justice, therefore, those whose violation seems to call loudest for vengeance and punishment, are [1] the laws which guard the life and person of our neighbour; [2] the next are those which guard his property and possessions; and [3] last of all come those which guard what are called his personal rights, or what is due to him from the promises of others' (TMS II. ii.2.2). The observance of these rules of justice constitute 'the foundation which supports the building' of society, 'the main pillar that upholds the whole edifice' (TMS II.ii.3.4). They are so important to a society's survival that even a 'society among robbers and murders' must respect them with one another (TMS II.ii.3.3). Because of their supreme importance to a society's survival, the impartial spectator's perspective we generate comes to approve of their observance in all circumstances and approve of their punishment in all breaches. I suggest that Smith's occasionally elevated language with respect to the impartial spectator reflects those occasions when the rules endorsed are of crucial importance to a community's survival.

Smith also writes: 'When the general rules which determine the merit and demerit of actions, come thus to be regarded as the laws of an All-powerful Being, who watches over our conduct, and who, in a life to come, will reward the observance, and punish the breach of them; they necessarily acquire a new sacredness from this consideration' (TMS III.5.12). This too is a psychological observation Smith is making, not something he is endorsing or condemning: people are more likely to follow rules of behaviour if they think those rules trace to the will of a divine god. Because of this, Smith argues, some general rules—namely those whose observance are most crucial to the survival of the society—come to be 'justly regarded as the Laws of the Deity' (TMS III.5.1). Note that he does not say they *are* the laws of the deity, only that they are justly *regarded* as such, a position consistent with the explanation of the impartial spectator's perspective given earlier.

Thus when Smith writes that 'It is in this manner that religion enforces the natural sense of duty' (TMS III.5.13), my suggestion is that the dynamic he believes he has discovered explaining the natural—if unintentional or 'spontaneous'—progression from 'desired conduct *x*' to 'God commands *x*' parallels the mechanism involved in our sense that the impartial spectator's perspective is or can be a 'substitute of the Deity'. Because of the importance to society's survival of its observance of, for example, the rules of justice, many societies hit upon the device of propagating a belief in their direct connection to God's will. For similar reasons, many societies have discovered and pursued the device of propagating a belief that the impartial spectator is one's 'guardian angel' (in more modern parlance), or God's 'vicegerent upon earth' (in Smith's language). It turns out, then, that this imagined person's perspective is nothing metaphysical or otherwise mysterious, and, as is typical for Smith, he is able to account for its existence by using the explanatory principles he has already developed.[30]

20.8 Utility

As mentioned earlier, Smith's account does suggest that moral systems can be judged by utility. He did not envision an exact mathematical calculation or a summing of individual utility functions, but he does seem to believe that an objectively testable empirical judgement can be formed about whether a given set of rules conduces to people's well-being.[31] His expectation is that the systems of order produced will tend overall and in the long run to be beneficial rather than harmful. Because each person is always acting to better his own condition, the rules of behaviour and judgement that the community develops tend to be conducive to everyone's benefit. There are many ways that this process can be corrupted, but Smith's argument is addressing long-run tendencies.[32]

The role Smith ascribes to utility in morality is more complicated, however, than this description would suggest. Early in TMS, Smith writes, 'Philosophers have, of late years'—he is thinking of Hume—'considered chiefly the tendency of affections, and have given little attention to the relation which they stand in to the cause which excites them. In common life, however, when we judge of any person's conduct, and of the sentiments which directed it, we constantly consider them under both these aspects' (TMS I.i.3.8). Smith continues, 'The utility of those qualities [viz. the intellectual virtues], it may be thought, is what first recommends them to us; and, no doubt, the consideration of this, when we come to attend to it, gives them a new value. Originally, however, we approve of another man's judgement, not as something useful, but as right, as accurate, as agreeable to truth and reality' (TMS I.i.4.4). These passages contain not one but two levels of explanation for a moral judgement.[33] The first is the deduction from the applicable general moral rule of approval or disapproval, as described earlier. This is the level that Smith here describes as what one does 'originally', and a sentiment's or behaviour's comportment with the relevant rule(s) is what he describes here 'as right, as accurate, as agreeable to truth and reality'.

---

[30] I leave here unresolved the issue of whether Smith believed that this was God's intention, whether indeed he believed in God, what his religious beliefs were, and so on. See Denis 2005, Haakonssen 2006, Minowitz 1993, and Oslington 2011.

[31] Fleischacker interprets Smith quite differently: 'Smith's moral theory is deeply opposed to utilitarianism' (Fleischacker 2004: 47).

[32] Scholars disagree about whether Smith was ultimately an optimist or a pessimist about such 'natural' systems of order. See Alvey 2003, Brubaker 2006, and C. Smith 2006.

[33] Failure to distinguish these two levels leads some commentators to find Smith's position on utility 'puzzling'; cf. Shaver 2006.

The second level of explanation, however, pertains to the origin of the general rules themselves: to the winnowing and culling process by which rules of morality are selected according to whether they conduce to MSS. When Smith writes that the 'idea of the utility of all qualities of this kind, is plainly an after-thought, and not what first recommends them to our approbation' (TMS I.i.4.4), he means that the first level of explanation—the deduction—takes place without any conscious reference to utility. He does not mean to suggest, however, that utility is irrelevant to the entire process; utility's role comes in the second level of explanation. Consider, for example, his discussion of 'the young and the licentious' whom we hear 'ridiculing the most sacred rules of morality, and professing, sometimes from the corruption, but more frequently from the vanity of their hearts, the most abominable maxims of conduct' (TMS II.ii.3.8). We naturally get upset at this, Smith says, and our first thought is to appeal to the young profligates with the 'intrinsic hatefulness and detestableness' of their sentiments; when they balk, however, Smith says 'we generally cast about for other arguments, and the consideration that [next] occurs to us, is the disorder and confusion of society which would result from the universal prevalence of such practices' (TMS II.ii.3.8). Smith continues:

> But though it commonly requires no great discernment to see the destructive tendency of all licentious practices to the welfare of society, it is seldom this consideration which first animates us against them. All men, even the most stupid and unthinking, abhor fraud, perfidy, and injustice, and delight to see them punished. But few men have reflected upon the necessity of justice to the existence of society, how obvious soever that necessity may appear to be. (TMS II.ii.3.9)

Hume had argued that utility forms the chief part of our regard for all virtues, and the sole part for many of them.[34] Here Smith acknowledges that while a brilliant philosopher like Hume is able to reconstruct the chain that links the sentiments we approve to our own, others', or society's utility, many people do not, or even cannot, reconstruct that complicated chain; thus few people have any such notions in mind when they actually pass a moral judgement. Coming to realize the utility of an action can make it appear more beautiful, Smith says; 'This beauty, however, is chiefly perceived by men of reflection and speculation, and is by no means the quality which first recommends such actions to the natural sentiments of the bulk of mankind' (TMS IV.2.11). Instead, mankind thinks of what is 'right', not what conduces to utility.

Utility often does not, then, immediately inform the judgement people make about sentiments or behaviours. Instead it is the sentiment's or behaviour's adherence to the applicable general rule. Similarly, it is initially a sentiment's or behaviour's comportment with the relevant general rule that prompts the moral judgement. Awareness of a sentiment's or behaviour's conduciveness towards utility can amplify or diminish the initial judgement but it does not constitute the judgement. On the other hand, a sentiment or behaviour that leads to an increase in utility tends to reinforce the sentiment or behaviour and may ultimately establish a rule that will inform future judgements.

---

[34] See, e.g. Hume 2006 [1751], especially ch. 5.

When, therefore, Smith writes 'But still I affirm, that it is not the view of this utility or hurtfulness which is either the first or principal source of our approbation and disapprobation' (TMS IV.2.3), he is referring to the first level of moral judgement noted above. The rules applied at this level are themselves based in utility, though we often, perhaps usually, do not realize it.

20.9 CONCLUSION

Smith presents morality as systems of overlapping spontaneous order that arise unintentionally on the basis of continuous interactions, reactions, and responses to feedback. Although the philosopher can discover the relative utility of specific aspects of a community's moral standards—even of the entire system of standards—and thus make recommendations or encouragements to increase utility, Smith agrees with Hume that moral distinctions are not derived from reason; indeed:

> it is altogether absurd and unintelligible to suppose that the first perceptions of right and wrong can be derived from reason, even in those particular cases upon the experience of which the general rules are formed. These first perceptions, as well as all other experiments upon which any general rules are founded, cannot be the object of reason, but of immediate sense and feeling. (TMS VII.iii.2.7)

This makes Smith a moral 'sentimentalist', but not a romantic one, since the interactive process of judgement-sharing and negotiation gives rise to intersubjectively objective standards, embodied in the personage of an 'impartial spectator', which is itself answerable to assessment along utilitarian lines. It gives these standards presumptive and hypothetical authority, deriving from key aspects of putatively universal human nature as it is modulated by people's experiences. And it makes reason's role in morality instrumental, albeit in the service of possibly objectively defensible ends (i.e. utility). In contemporary philosophical taxonomy, Smith's moral theory might thus be norm-expressivist and psychological non-cognitivist,[35] and his ethical naturalism might prefigure some recent accounts that draw on evolutionary insights.[36] Although his substantive account of the virtues shows a lot of similarity to Ciceronian and Stoic descriptions of the virtuous life—especially in the centrality of 'self-command' in Smith's roster of virtues[37]—nevertheless the principal philosophical value of his ethical thought today lies in its surprisingly plausible attempt to provide a developmental, even evolutionary,[38] account of morality that is grounded in empirical facts of human psychology and social institutions.

---

[35] Some aspects of Gibbard 1990 and 2003, for example, bear interesting resemblances to Smith. See also Darwall 2009, which partly draws on Smith.

[36] See, for example, de Waal 2007, Harris 2006, Hocutt 2000, Joyce 2006, Pinker 2002, and Wilson 2004. I note that Charles Darwin also read and approved of parts of Smith's analysis; see Darwin 1981 [1871].

[37] See Vivenza 2001.

[38] See Evensky 2005, Otteson 2002a, and Young 1997, and the collection of essays in Zak 2008.

Bibliography

Alvey, J. E. 2003. *Adam Smith: Optimist or Pessimist? A New Problem Concerning the Teleological Basis of Commercial Society*. Burlington: Ashgate.

Broadie, A. 2006. 'Sympathy and the Impartial Spectator', in K. Haakonssen (ed.), *The Cambridge Companion to Adam Smith*. Cambridge: Cambridge University Press, 158–88.

Brown, V. 1994. *Adam Smith's Discourse: Canonicity, Commerce and Conscience*. London: Routledge.

Brubaker, L. 2006. 'Why Adam Smith Is Neither a Conservative nor a Libertarian', *The Adam Smith Review* 2: 197–202.

Darwall, S. L. 2009. *The Second-Person Standpoint: Morality, Respect, and Accountability*. Cambridge, MA: Harvard University Press.

Darwin, C. 1981 [1871]. *The Descent of Man, and Selection in Relation to Sex*. Princeton: Princeton University Press.

Dascal, M. 2006. 'Adam Smith's Theory of Language', in K. Haakonssen (ed.), in *The Cambridge Companion to Adam Smith*. Cambridge: Cambridge University Press, 79–111.

De Waal, F. 2007. *Chimpanzee Politics: Power and Sex Among Apes*, 25th anniv. ed. Baltimore: Johns Hopkins Press.

Den Uyl, D. J. 2011. 'Das Shaftesbury Problem', *Adam Smith Review* 6: 209–223.

Denis, A. 2005. 'The Invisible Hand of God in Adam Smith', *Research in the History of Economic Thought and Methodology* 23, A: 1–32.

Dickey, L. 1986. 'Historicizing the "Adam Smith Problem": Conceptual, Historiographical, and Textual Issues', *Journal of Modern History* 58: 179–609.

Evensky, J. 2005. *Adam Smith's Moral Philosophy: A Historical and Contemporary Perspective on Markets, Law, Ethics, and Culture*. Cambridge: Cambridge University Press.

Fleischacker, S. 1991. 'Philosophy in Moral Practice: Kant and Adam Smith', *Kant-Studien* 82: 249–69.

—— 1996. 'Values behind the Market: Kant's Response to the *Wealth of Nations*', *History of Political Thought* 17: 379–407.

—— 1999. *A Third Concept of Liberty: Judgment and Freedom in Kant and Adam Smith*. Princeton: Princeton University Press.

—— 2004. *On Adam Smith's 'Wealth of Nations': A Philosophical Companion*. Princeton: Princeton University Press.

Forman-Barzilai, F. 2010. *Adam Smith and the Circles of Sympathy: Cosmopolitanism and Moral Theory*. Cambridge: Cambridge University Press.

Gibbard, A. 1990. *Wise Choices, Apt Feelings*. Cambridge, MA: Harvard University Press.

—— 2003. *Thinking How to Live*. Cambridge, MA: Harvard University Press.

Göçmen, D. 2007. *The Adam Smith Problem: Reconciling Human Nature and Society in 'The Theory of Moral Sentiments' and 'Wealth of Nations'*. London: Taurus Academic Studies.

Grampp, W. D. 2000. 'What Did Adam Smith Mean by the Invisible Hand?', *Journal of Political Economy* 108 (3): 441–65.

Griswold, C. L., Jr. 1999. *Adam Smith and the Virtues of Enlightenment*. Cambridge: Cambridge University Press.

—— 2006. 'Imagination: Morals, Science, and Arts', in K. Haakonsse (ed.), *The Cambridge Companion to Adam Smith*. Cambridge: Cambridge University Press, 22–56.

Haakonssen, K. 2006. 'Introduction: The Coherence of Smith's Thought', in K. Haakonssen (ed.), *The Cambridge Companion to Adam Smith*. Cambridge: Cambridge University Press, 1–21.

Hanley, R. P. 2009. *Adam Smith and the Character of Virtue.* Cambridge: Cambridge University Press.

Harris, J. R. 2006. *No Two Alike: Human Nature and Human Individuality.* New York: W. W. Norton.

Hocutt, M. 2000. *Grounded Ethics: The Empirical Bases of Normative Judgements.* New Brunswick: Transaction Publishers.

Hume, D. 2006 [1751]. *An Enquiry Concerning the Principles of Morals*, ed.T. L. Beauchamp. Oxford: Oxford University Press.

Joyce, R. 2006. *The Evolution of Morality.* Cambridge: MIT Press.

Kennedy, G. 2008. *Adam Smith.* New York: Palgrave Macmillan.

Minowitz, P. 1993. *Profits, Priests, and Princes.* Stanford: Stanford University Press.

Montes, L. 2004. *Adam Smith in Context: A Critical Reassessment of Some Central Components of His Thought.* New York: Palgrave Macmillan.

Oslington, P. (ed.) 2011. *Adam Smith as Theologian.* London: Routledge.

Otteson, J. R. 2000. 'The Recurring "Adam Smith Problem"', *History of Philosophy Quarterly* 17 (1): 51–74.

—— 2002a. *Adam Smith's Marketplace of Life.* Cambridge: Cambridge University Press.

—— 2002b. 'Adam Smith's First Market: The Development of Language', *History of Philosophy Quarterly* 19 (1): 65–86.

—— 2011. 'Response to Douglas J. Den Uyl's "Das Shaftesbury Problem"', *Adam Smith Review* 6: 224–7.

Phillipson, N. 2000. 'Language, Sociability, and History: Some Reflections on the Foundations of Adam Smith's Science of Man', in S. Collini et al. (eds), *Economy, Polity, and Society: British Intellectual History 1750–1950.* Cambridge: Cambridge University Press, 70–84.

Pinker, S. 2002. *The Blank Slate: The Modern Denial of Human Nature.* New York: Penguin.

Rae, J. 1895. *Life of Adam Smith.* London: Macmillan.

Raphael, D. D. 1975. 'The Impartial Spectator', in A. S. Skinner and T. Wilson (eds), *Essays on Adam Smith.* Oxford: Oxford University Press, 83–99.

—— 2007. *The Impartial Spectator: Adam Smith's Moral Philosophy.* Oxford: Oxford University Press.

Reid, T. 1991 [1788]. *Essays on the Powers of Man*, in *British Moralists 1650–1800*, vol. II, ed. D. D. Raphael. Indianapolis: Hackett.

Ross, I. Simpson. 1995. *The Life of Adam Smith.* Oxford: Oxford University Press.

Rothschild, E. 2001. *Economic Sentiments: Adam Smith, Condorcet, and the Enlightenment.* Cambridge, MA: Harvard University Press.

Schliesser, E. 2006. 'Adam Smith's Theoretical Endorsement of Deception', *Adam Smith Review* 2: 209–14.

—— 2008. 'Adam Smith's Philosophical Subtlety', *Adam Smith Review* 4: 231–8.

Searle, J. 1997. *The Construction of Social Reality.* New York: Free Press.

Shaver, R. 2006. 'Virtues, Utility, and Rules', in K. Haakonssen (ed.), *TheCambridge Companion to Adam Smith.* Cambridge: Cambridge University Press, 189–213.

Smith, A. 1976 [1759]. *The Theory of Moral Sentiments*, ed. D. D. Raphael and A. L. Macfie. Oxford: Oxford University Press.

—— 1976 [1776]. *An Inquiry into the Nature and Causes of the Wealth of Nations*, ed. R. H. Campbell and A. S. Skinner. Oxford: Oxford University Press.

—— 1977. *Correspondence of Adam Smith*, ed. E. C. Mossner and I. S. Ross. Oxford: Oxford University Press.

Smith, A. 1983. *Lectures on Rhetoric and Belles Lettres*, ed. J. C. Bryce. Oxford: Oxford University Press.

Smith, C. 2006. *Adam Smith's Political Philosophy: The Invisible Hand and Spontaneous Order*. New York: Routledge.

Vivenza, G. 2001. *Adam Smith and the Classics: The Classical Heritage in Adam Smith's Thought*. Oxford: Oxford University Press.

White, M. D. 2010. 'Adam Smith and Immanuel Kant: On Markets, Duties, and Moral Sentiments', *Forum for Social Economics* 39 (1): 53–60.

Wilson, D. S. 2004. 'The New Fable of the Bees: Multilevel Selection, Adaptive Societies, and the Concept of Self Interest', *Evolutionary Psychology and Economic Theory* 7: 201–20.

Young, J. T. 1997. *Economics as a Moral Science: The Political Economy of Adam Smith*. Cheltenham: Edward Elgar Publishing.

Zak, P. J. (ed.) 2008. *Moral Markets: The Critical Role of Values in the Economy*. Princeton: Princeton University Press.

CHAPTER 21

KANT'S MORAL PHILOSOPHY

ANDREWS REATH

21.1 INTRODUCTION

KANT's moral philosophy is one of the most significant treatments of moral thought in the history of philosophy and one of the leading models for thinking systematically about morality to come out of the western tradition. It is prominent in contemporary moral philosophy in that many contemporary theorists take themselves to be developing Kant's basic ideas, and many philosophers believe that moral theory can be advanced by interpreting Kant's texts and working out the details of his arguments.

Kant develops a morality of universal principle with, he argues, a basis in reason, so that moral principles present requirements on action that are valid for any rational agent (regardless of their desires and ends). He purports to articulate the underlying principles and structure of ordinary moral thought and to confirm that the authority that it claims for itself has a rational basis. Although Kant's moral philosophy can be approached without taking on all of his transcendental idealism, it is an integral component of his critical philosophy. 'Critique', for Kant, is the critical self-examination of reason aimed at establishing the basic powers and limits of human cognition. In the *Critique of Pure Reason*, Kant undertakes both to establish the legitimacy of the *a priori* concepts and principles that structure theoretical cognition and to define the limits of theoretical knowledge. His project in moral philosophy is similar—to establish the authority of the concepts and principles that we use in ordinary moral thought, and the legitimacy of the conceptions of self and agency that it presupposes. As a component of his critical philosophy, his moral philosophy attempts to show that the moral law is the basic norm of pure reason applied to action.

Kant's moral theory is non-consequentialist, and is best characterized as a 'principle-based' approach to moral reasoning. It holds that certain ways of acting can be right or wrong in themselves independently of their consequences. In particular, the underlying principle or 'maxim' of action must meet a condition of universal validity, and that is ascertained by determining whether the maxim can consistently be willed as universal law for agents with autonomy. This condition of universal validity leads both to inviolable limits on individual choice and the pursuit of good and to positive requirements to have certain ends and attitudes towards others. This general principle and the subsidiary requirements to which it leads express respect for the dignity of each person as a rational agent with autonomy. Good action or 'good willing' consists in conformity to principle so understood. Kant's theory is standardly thought of as a form of deontology, but it differs from the deontology of rational intuitionism in important respects. Rational intuitionism takes certain basic principles of obligation to be self-evident upon reflection. Further, it holds that it is a mistake to seek a justification of the authority of a moral claim outside of the specifically moral form of reflection through which an action is apprehended as oblig-atory (e.g. an explanation of its obligatory character in terms of some good or value that is realized through an action). (Cf. Prichard 2002.) Kant's theory supports an explanation of the rightness or wrongness of various ways of acting in value-based terms of respect for persons as rational agents. Furthermore, the basic condition of universal validity itself is justified through its connection with the nature of free agency.

Kant's moral philosophy is developed principally in three major works: the *Ground-work of the Metaphysics of Morals*, the *Critique of Practical Reason*, and *The Metaphysics of Morals*. In addition, Book I of *Religion within the Boundaries of Mere Reason* is an important treatment of Kant's moral psychology and theory of free agency, and aspects of his moral thought are filled out in his shorter writings on politics and history (such as *Idea for a Universal History with a Cosmopolitan Aim, On the Common Saying: That may be Correct in Theory but it is of No Use in Practice, Toward Perpetual Peace*). Further insights into his applied moral thought are provided by his *Lectures on Ethics*—compendia of student lecture notes from the 1770's through the early 1790's. Kant gives us both a foundational theory aimed at establishing the authority of ordinary morality and a normative theory—an account of the content of morality and a framework for moral reasoning and judgement. Though his foundational and normative theories are linked, they can be approached separately since one might accept his basic norma-tive theory independently of the ultimate success of his foundational project. I shall pro-vide first an overview of Kant's foundational theory, and then turn, more briefly, to his normative theory. Since a chapter of this nature cannot discuss, much less resolve, all the issues raised by a theory as complex as Kant's, I limit myself to an outline of his views, pointing to issues that require further discussion where possible.

21.2 KANT'S FOUNDATIONAL PROJECT

It may help to begin by highlighting the problem that drives Kant's foundational project and his attempted resolution in the *Groundwork*. Kant describes that work as 'nothing more than the search for and establishment of the *supreme principle of morality*' (G 4: 392). This project involves, first, stating the fundamental principle that underlies common-sense moral thought, and then establishing its authority in reason by connecting it to the nature of rational agency—a task that he here refers to as 'a pure moral philosophy' or 'metaphysics of morals'. The need for such an endeavour becomes evident as soon as we see what goes into the 'common idea of duty and of moral laws' (G 4: 389). Ordinary moral thought (Kant believes) takes moral requirements to apply with 'absolute necessity' and to apply unconditionally to all rational beings. But requirements can apply with genuine necessity only if they have a basis in reason. Moreover, morality presents us with a set of substantive requirements whose authority does not depend on our actual desires and ends and that take priority over and limit the force of desire-based reasons. It is a set of categorical requirements that are not derived from anything else that we might happen (contingently) to care about or will.[1] But one might ask—as Kant explicitly does in the Second Section of the *Groundwork* (G 4: 419)—how are such categorical practical requirements possible? Are we really required and is it reasonable to give deliberative priority to moral requirements when they conflict with our interest in happiness? Furthermore, if morality presents us with requirements that take priority over desire-based reasons, it presupposes a motivational capacity to act independently of empirically given desires and interests. Do we have such practical and motivational capacities? Once we unpack the ordinary understanding of morality, we encounter the possibility that it presents us with unreasonable demands or is based on illusion. Perhaps there really are no duties or moral requirements as we understand these concepts.

Kant's foundational project is to show that the authority of morality is genuine by connecting the moral law to the nature of free rational volition—or as Kant says, to the 'form of volition as such' (G 4: 444). In more technical terms, Kant tries to establish the authority of the moral law by arguing that it is the 'formal principle' of free volition, and that as rational agents we necessarily take ourselves to have and identify with a capacity for free agency. To explain: for Kant, the 'formal principle' of a domain of cognition or rational activity is the internal constitutive norm that a subject must follow in order to engage in that activity—a principle that defines and makes it possible to engage in that activity. As we might say, it specifies the form of that activity.[2] For that reason it provides an authoritative norm that tacitly guides all instances of and necessarily governs the activity—one that cannot be rejected by any subject engaged in the activity. The *Groundwork* contains an extended argument for the claim that the moral law is the formal principle of free volition. Furthermore, Kant claims that it is a necessary feature of the self-consciousness of a rational agent that one is free: a rational agent necessarily 'acts under the idea of freedom' (G 4: 448). In exercising our wills, we understand ourselves to guide our choices by judgements of what we have good reason to do, and free agency is the capacity to originate action in such judgements—a capacity with which we identify as our 'proper self' (G 4: 457–8). In a word, Kant tries to establish the authority of morality by showing that the

---

[1] Kant thinks that the moral law is a synthetic *a priori* practical proposition: it sets out certain requirements on action, including the requirement to have certain ends and values, without deriving those requirements from any prior volition. Further, these requirements take deliberative priority over empirically given interests.

[2] For discussions of the idea of internal constitutive principles, see Korsgaard 2008: 7–10, and Reath 2010: 41–8.

moral law is the internal or constitutive principle of a necessary self-conception, of a way in which we necessarily understand ourselves and our practical capacities when we act.

One of the more striking features of Kant's theory is his thesis that, while moral requirements apply unconditionally, the moral law is a principle of autonomy. Moral requirements are not imposed on us by any external authority (such as society, the will of God, or even our own psychology), but are based on a principle that the rational will in some sense legislates for itself. Indeed, his thesis is that the unconditional authority of morality is genuine only if the fundamental principle is a principle of autonomy that the will gives to itself. Understanding the moral law as the formal principle of free agency helps explain why this is so. The formal principle of volition would be the internal norm that both describes and makes possible the exercise of that capacity and serves as its regulative standard, and its normative hold on us is based on our self-conception as free agents. In that sense it is a principle that the rational will gives to itself. And the formal principle of volition (assuming that we can make sense of this idea) is uniquely suited to govern volition unconditionally. Thus, only if the moral law is the formal principle of volition that the will gives to itself could moral requirements apply with genuine rational necessity.

This line of thought leads Kant to claim that previous moral philosophy has approached its task through the wrong methodology. Kant's predecessors in the tradition all base moral obligation in what he terms 'material principles of morality'. Roughly, they ground the normative force of morality in some good that human beings are presumed to desire or take pleasure in as a natural feature of our psychology. The Epicureans (among whom Kant would presumably include Hobbes) appeal to our interest in happiness, Hutcheson's moral sense theory (of which Kant regards Hume's as a variant) bases moral judgement in the immediate satisfaction that we take in observing virtuous conduct, the perfectionism of Leibniz and Wolff bases obligation in the pleasure that we take in a perfection realized in oneself or observed in others, and theological conceptions derive it from an interest in agreeing with the will of God. The common error of these accounts is that they are theories of 'heteronomy'. They ground the authority of morality in an object, or conception of good, external to the will in which we may have an interest, but without establishing that that interest is rationally necessary. By making the normative force of morality conditional on an interest that one can lack without obvious irrationality, they make moral requirements hypothetical rather than categorical imperatives. Kant's insight is that only by showing that the moral law is the formal principle of volition—a principle internally connected to rational volition—can one ground the necessity that is part of our common idea of moral requirement. Moral philosophy must begin by establishing the fundamental law of practical reason. If morality is to be based on any notion of the good, it must be one that is internally connected to rational volition.

A complete grasp of Kant's foundational project is complicated by the fact that the *Critique of Practical Reason* approaches these issues in a somewhat different way. However, the basic point remains: the moral law is the formal principle of free agency, and it is part of our self-consciousness as agents that we have the capacity for free agency. In the next section, I shall sketch the main lines of argument of *Groundwork* I and II. I then briefly discuss the argument of *Groundwork* III, the argument of the Analytic of the second *Critique* (in particular Kant's claim that the moral law is given as a 'fact of reason'), and some of the apparent differences between these works.

21.2.1 The Argument of the *Groundwork* I and II

As already noted, the project of the *Groundwork* is to 'search for and establish' the fundamental principle of morality that underlies ordinary moral thought, and the argument has both an analytic and a synthetic component. Sections I and II articulate this principle first through analysis of certain judgements of moral value that are central to common-sense moral thought (Section I), then through a more abstract analysis of practical reason or rational agency (Section II). An analysis of a set of concepts and principles can spell out their content, but does not suffice to show that they are legitimately employed. Thus the analytic portion of the argument tells us roughly what goes into our shared conception of morality (e.g. that duties, if there are any, must be expressed as categorical imperatives) but without establishing its rational authority. That task is left to Section III, which is synthetic and provides what Kant calls a 'deduction' of the moral law. This is not a deductive argument in the modern sense, but an argument aimed at establishing the legitimacy and the authority of the principles of ordinary moral thought (similar to the transcendental deduction of the categories of the understanding in the *Critique of Pure Reason*).

Section I of the Groundwork is a 'transition from common rational to philosophic moral cognition': it moves from certain tenets of ordinary moral thought—from analysis of widely accepted judgements about the value of a good will—to a philosophical statement of its fundamental principle. A good will is a disposition to adhere to moral requirements for their own sake, and Kant opens Section I with the claim that only a good will is good absolutely and without limitation. A good will is the condition of the value of all other goods (including happiness) in the sense that they are truly worth having only when acquired or used in accordance with the principles of a good will. Further, a good will is good in all circumstances in the sense that it is never worth abandoning your good will for some other kind of good (Cf. Hill 2002a: ch. 2, and 2002b: 23–8). The absolute value of the good will thus amounts to a claim about the deliberative priority of moral considerations over other kinds of reasons. By itself this formal feature appears to tell us little about the fundamental principle of morality. But if one maintains one's good will by conforming to any objective practical principles that, in one's judgement, apply to one's circumstances and would apply to anyone in one's situation—and moreover, out of a direct recognition of their authority—then the absolute value of a good will points to the necessity of 'the conformity of actions as such with universal law' (*G* 4: 402).

Kant moves closer to a statement of the fundamental principle by developing the concept of good will in imperfectly rational beings subject to non-rational motives— that is, through the notion of duty. He constructs a set of contrasting examples designed to show that we judge an action to have moral worth—to display a good will and thus be worthy of esteem—only when done from duty. The thesis that an action has moral worth only when done from duty is not intended as a general account of good willing or virtue, but rather is a step in the analysis that identifies the principle on which a good will acts. The examples show that the moral worth of action done from duty lies in its underlying principle—specifically in the fact that the agent is moved by the principle of respect for morality, of conforming to moral principle simply because it is required. Assuming that moral principles are universally valid, the formal principle through which one achieves a good will is then the principle of conforming to universal law as such. Kant thinks that this principle is equivalent to the Universal Law formulation of the Categorical Imperative—to act only from maxims that one can consistently will as universal law (G 4: 402). Commentators disagree whether this move on Kant's part is legitimate.[3] But clearly what Kant is getting at is that one has a good will when one's choice satisfies a standard of universal validity (say, of rational acceptability to any agent) and one takes this standard to be authoritative. Kant thinks that one ascertains whether a choice meets this standard of universal validity by asking whether its underlying principle or maxim can be willed as universal law without inconsistency. To be universally valid, a maxim of action must be a possible law for all rational agents, and one that cannot consistently be willed as universal law does not meet this standard.

Before turning to Section II, we should note that Kant's analysis of good will has introduced the distinctly moral motive that he terms 'respect' for the morality. To be moved by respect is to be moved by one's immediate recognition of the authority of moral principle, and this motivational capacity is presupposed by ordinary moral thought.

Section I may well show that the so-called Formula of Universal Law (FUL) underlies common moral thought, but that does not mean that it has a basis in reason. Accordingly Section II derives a statement of this principle 'from the universal concept of a rational being as such' (G 4: 412)—a project that Kant terms a 'metaphysics of morals'. Indeed, by focusing on different aspects of rational agency, Kant lays out a sequence of alternative formulations of the Categorical Imperative that he takes to be equivalent—'so many formulae of the very same law' (G 4: 436). Practical reason or rational agency is the capacity to derive action from the representation of laws, or principles, and this aspect of rational agency leads to the FUL, which Kant regards as the basic statement of the Categorical Imperative—'act only on that maxim through which you can at the same time will that it become a universal law' (G 4: 421). But when the principle is stated in this very abstract way it is natural to ask why we ought to adhere. To make headway with this issue, Kant works through the different formulae of the Categorical Imperative, introducing the ideas of humanity as end in itself ('treat humanity, in your own person or in that of another, always as an end in itself and never merely as a means'), the autonomy of the moral agent (agents subject to moral requirements must be regarded as giving moral law to themselves), and the realm of ends (a union of rational beings under shared moral

---

[3] Commentators who question this move on Kant's part include Hill 1992: 121–2 and Wood 1999: 47–9, 81–2. For further discussion and defences see Allison 1996: 143–55, Kerstein 2002, Reath 2006: 204–11, and Engstrom 2009, especially 5–10, 118–28.

principles which is possible through free agency). The sequence of formulas completes the 'search for' the fundamental principle by fully articulating this principle and its presuppositions (e.g. about persons). Like Section I, it is part of an analytic enterprise: it simply shows that the moral law may be expressed in these different ways or presupposes these ideas, while leaving its authority open. But the sequence of formulas also advances the 'establishment' of the moral law in two ways. First, it shows that respect for persons as ends, the autonomy of the individual, and the ideal of moral community exemplified by the 'realm of ends' are implicit in the FUL. Since these are attractive ideals that can command our allegiance, it brings this principle 'closer to intuition ... and thereby to feeling' and 'gains access for the moral law' (G 4: 436, 437). Second, the sequence of formulas, especially the move from universal law to autonomy, sets up the argument at the opening of Section III that the Categorical Imperative is the formal principle of free volition. This thesis is one key component of Kant's 'deduction' of the moral law.

There is a kind of needle that Kant must thread here. In order to advance the argument in the first of these ways ('gain access' for the moral law), Kant must show that these more substantive values and ideals (of the person, or of moral community) are implicit in or follow from FUL. At the same time, since FUL is a formal principle—the formal principle of moral requirement—and since Kant takes the formulae to be equivalent, the subsequent formulae must likewise be formal principles or expressions of formal features of the moral law. Unless the subsequent formulae are restatements of FUL that draw out what is implicit in it, the sequence cannot advance the overall argument in the desired ways.

Let us now turn to the main formulations of the Categorical Imperative and the movement of the argument through section II.

Kant holds the FUL can be derived from 'the mere concept of a categorical imperative' or 'practical law' (G 4: 420). Presumably that concept emerges from his analysis of practical reason or rational agency, though there is some ambiguity as to how. One might think that the idea of practical reason, or of the complete determination of action through reason, leads to a distinction between practical principles that apply conditionally on something else that one wills and unconditional principles that serve as ultimate starting points of practical reasoning. Since the latter would be 'practical laws' or categorical imperatives, once that concept is in hand Kant can move to FUL. Alternatively, Kant could be giving an analysis of familiar forms of practical reasoning that shows that we take moral requirements to apply categorically. Again, once the concept of a categorical imperative is in hand, he can move to FUL. Since Kant's conception of rational agency (at G 4: 412) is followed by a discussion of imperatives and the distinction between hypothetical and categorical imperatives, the latter seems to be what he actually does. In the balance of Section II he is interested in what is presupposed by genuine moral requirements, which are taken to be an example of practical laws.

The application of FUL is illustrated through four examples that represent perfect and imperfect duties to self and other. Kant argues that suicide to avoid unhappiness and the deceptive promise cannot be conceived as universal law and are thus impermissible;

they violate perfect duties to self and other. The maxims of neglecting to develop one's natural talents and of indifference to the needs of others cannot be made universal without a contradiction in the will, and this reasoning leads to the imperfect duties of self-development and mutual aid. These examples are not meant to be the basis of a complete normative theory, but rather have the more limited aim of showing that the abstract principle just stated does support some familiar duties and maps onto the distinction between perfect and imperfect duties.

The Formula of Humanity (FH)—that rational nature is to be treated as an end in itself, and never merely as a means—is a principle of respect for persons as rational agents with autonomy. Rational nature or humanity is best understood as the full range of our rational capacities, including the capacity to act for reasons and to set ends, moral personality, and theoretical reason.[4] An end in itself has an absolute worth that is the source of laws governing its proper treatment. Kant stresses that it is not an end to be produced, but an 'independently existing end' (G 4: 437) that sets inviolable limits on action and choice of subjective ends. The Formula of Humanity is illustrated through the same four examples. Suicide to avoid unhappiness and deceptive promising are inconsistent with respecting humanity as an end in itself—the latter because others must be able to 'contain in themselves the end of the very same action' (G 4:430), i.e. rationally endorse our actions, and the victim of deception cannot. In addition, respecting humanity as an end requires that one's actions 'harmonize' or 'positively agree' with humanity as an end, and this leads to the imperfect duties to make one's own perfection and the happiness of others one's ends—what Kant in the *Metaphysics of Morals* calls the 'duties of virtue'. Kant's claim that FUL and FH are equivalent can be partially explained as follows: to respect persons as ends in themselves is to act in ways that one can justify to the person (as rational agent with autonomy)— i.e. to act from principles that others can rationally endorse—and that one does by acting from maxims that are fully universalizable. That is, one respects humanity as an end in itself by limiting one's maxims of action by the condition of universal validity (G 4: 437–8. Cf. Rawls 2000: 190–5, O'Neill 1989: 126–44, and Korsgaard 1996: 126–8).

Although it is not difficult to interpret FUL and FH in ways that align their practical implications, questions about their equivalence persist in light of the fact that the Formula of Humanity appears to introduce a very different set of concepts not found earlier in the argument ('rational nature' or 'humanity' and 'an end in itself'). One might address these questions by noting that like FUL, FH is introduced through an analysis of practical reason, though one that focuses on a different aspect of practical reason—that it is a faculty of ends. This argument has two steps. First, Kant claims that practical laws presuppose an end of absolute value. Practical reason is the capacity to derive actions from laws—a faculty of principles—but it is also a faculty of ends (Cf. *KpV* 5: 58–9).

---

[4] For discussion, see Hill 1992: 38–41, Rawls 2000: 187–90, Korsgaard 1996: 110–14, and Wood 1999: 118–22. Hill and Rawls argue that humanity or rational nature include the full range of our rational capacities, while Korsgaard and Wood focus on remarks where Kant identifies humanity with the capacity to set ends for oneself, including non-moral ends.

Since volition must be directed at some end that it aims to realize, a practical principle must specify an end in order to determine the will (*MdS* 6: 385, 395). So if there are practical laws, there must be an end of absolute value. Here Kant need not mean that the existence of such an end is a further condition that has to be satisfied in order for there to be practical laws. Rather, it is another way to spell out the idea of a practical law. 'End in itself' is the same basic concept as 'practical law', expressed through the lens of practical reason as a faculty of ends, or the need for rational volition to have an end.

The second step of the argument specifies what the end in itself is. An end in itself is a necessary end that limits all subjective or relative ends. But an end can be necessary only if it is internally related to practical reasoning—if it is an end that one has or values simply in so far as one engages in practical reasoning. The obvious candidate for such an end is rational nature: in so far as one engages in practical reasoning, one in some way values that capacity and conformity to its standards. There are different ways of understanding this component of Kant's argument. On one standard reading, it amounts to the claim that a commitment to valuing persons as rational agents is built into the nature of practical reasoning. In so far as one responds to reasons and to what one takes to be of value or sets ends for oneself, one values one's rational capacities, which are capacities essential to one's person. Moreover, one values these capacities on general grounds that commit one to valuing them wherever they are found. That is to say that one is committed to valuing persons as rational agents.[5]

Some commentators have recently proposed a thinner and more formal reading of the claim that rational nature is an end in itself because it enables us to understand FUL and FH to be equivalent in a deep sense—in effect, as intensionally equivalent. One necessary value that one has *qua* reasoner is that of correctly exercising one's reason. This would seem to be the formal aim of reasoning, in that someone who did not have this aim would not be engaged in practical reasoning. Moreover, this formal aim is authoritative for all exercises of practical reasoning. Accordingly the idea that rational nature is an end in itself can be read as the claim that rational nature has its own proper exercise as its formal end. If FUL is the basic norm of practical reason, then one values rational nature as an end in itself by treating this norm as authoritative and by subjecting all practical reasoning to the general condition of universal validity. In order to incorporate the substantive value of respect for persons as rational agents, this reading needs to hold that this value is already implicit in FUL—e.g. because it is the principle of acting only from maxims that can serve as universal law for agents with autonomy. It rules out maxims that if universalized undermine rational autonomy, and requires ends that are needed to support its effective exercise in individuals. In that sense, the proper exercise of practical reason will be guided by principles of respect for rational autonomy. According to this line of thought, the moral standing of persons is not a ground of FUL but one if its implications: persons have value because FUL prescribes principles that respect their rational capacities.[6]

[5] See Korsgaard 1996: ch. 4; Hill 1992: 143–6; and Wood 1999: 124–31.
[6] See Herman 2007: 251–2, Engstrom 2009: 167–78, Reath 2012 and 2013, and Sensen 2009 and 2010.

Following the discussion of humanity as an end in itself, Kant introduces the idea of autonomy through a third version of the Categorical Imperative, stated incompletely as 'the idea of the will of every rational being as a will giving universal law' (G 4: 431). The introduction of autonomy marks a turning point in the argument. Until this point Kant has stressed the deliberative priority of moral requirements and subjection to duty. He now claims that the human will is not just subject to duty, but 'subject to it in such a way that it must be viewed also as giving law to itself and just because of this as subject to the law (of which it can regard itself as author)' (G 4: 431). The basis of the authority of morality is that the fundamental principle of morality is a law that the rational will in some sense legislates for itself—which is to say that it is a principle that originates in the very nature of rational volition (G 4: 432–3, 440). Moral agents thus have autonomy in the sense that they are not bound to any external authority, but only by principles that origi-nate in their own rational will, which 'in accordance with nature's end is a will giving universal law' (G 4: 432).

These claims about autonomy appear to follow from the necessity of moral require-ments. Kant's idea is that the necessity and deliberative priority of morality is genuine only if based in a principle that the rational will in some sense gives to itself, or that originates a priori in the nature of rational volition. Earlier in this chapter we sketched one way to understand this idea—that the moral law is the 'formal principle' or internal constitutive norm of rational volition and is thus uniquely suited to govern volition unconditionally. The arguments of Groundwork II have shown that the moral law is a principle that is based in the nature of rational volition by deriving statements of the Categorical Imperative from an analysis of practical reason or rational agency, and these claims figure in the opening argument of Groundwork III. Conversely, these claims about autonomy imply the failure of heteronomy: foundational theories that base moral-ity in some object external to the will present moral requirements as hypothetical, rather than categorical imperatives, because they make its authority conditional on having an interest in that object. Thus no such foundational account provides adequate grounding for the common idea of moral requirements.

If the moral subject is a kind of autonomous legislator, then persons interact with others possessing the same legislative capacities as themselves and the universal laws that they are presumed to will are to govern a community of such agents. In this way, the idea of autonomy leads to the 'very fruitful concept' of the 'realm of ends', which completes the (by Kant's count) third version of the Categorical Imperative—that one is to act from principles that can serve as law for a realm of ends (G 4: 433, 438ff.). The realm of ends is Kant's ideal of moral community based on universally valid principles and relations of mutual respect. Membership is determined by possession of the basic capacities of reason, which confers the capacity for a good will and a 'share...in the giving of universal law' (G 4: 435). Among other things, it would be a social world in which individuals pursue their own ends within the limits of respect for the rights of others, and in addition are moved by the ends of virtue. The realm of ends is an ideal of social relations based on mutual respect and mutual recognition of persons as agents with autonomy.

21.2.2 *Groundwork* III and the *Critique of Practical Reason*

The analytic enterprise of *Groundwork* II articulates the basic principle of common-sense morality and the conceptions of agency that it presupposes, but does not establish its rational authority for us. For example, it may be a conceptual truth that agents subject to moral requirements have autonomy and thus have certain kinds of rational capacities, but that does not mean that we are such agents. To complete the overall argument for the authority of morality, *Groundwork* III offers a 'deduction' of the moral law. Unfortunately, it is the most obscure section of the work, and we can only sketch the main points, ignoring many complications.[7] Furthermore, the second *Critique* offers a somewhat different approach to the authority of the moral law.

Groundwork III opens with two preliminary analytical arguments (G 4: 446–448). The first claims that the moral law is the basic principle of a free will, the second that a rational being necessarily acts under the idea of freedom and is entitled to regard itself as free. The first argument turns on the idea that while a free will is a capacity to act independently of external influence, it is not for that reason lawless. Its activity must be governed by some principle, and moreover by a principle that the will gives to itself, independently of external influence. But *Groundwork* II has argued that the moral law is based in the nature of rational agency and in that sense is the law that the rational will gives to itself. Since it is the principle that originates in the nature of volition *a priori*, choice guided by this principle is fully self-determined. The force of the argument from freedom to morality is that that the moral law is the principle that confers the capacity for free agency and through which it is exercised, and is thus its formal principle.

The idea of freedom in the second argument can be interpreted as a set of general presuppositions about rational deliberation—for example, that in engaging in deliberation, one presupposes that one can determine oneself by one's own judgement based solely on one's grasp of the reasons, and so on—that is to say, independently of influence external to reason. The necessity of *acting* under the idea of freedom applies these presuppositions to practical deliberation. In deliberating about how to act, one presupposes that one has the capacity to set desire or any potential consideration aside if one sees reason to, to judge what one has most reason to do, and to determine one's choice by this judgement. In short it is a necessary feature of the self-consciousness of a rational agent that one takes oneself to have the capacity to determine choice independently of any influences external to one's reasoning.

If a rational agent necessarily acts under the idea of freedom and the moral law is the basic principle of a free will, then any rational agent is bound by the moral law. But these are still analytical arguments and do not show that we have the relevant rational capacities. Kant needs to establish something about us, and the task that he takes on is to show that we have purely rational capacities that make us members of an 'intelligible world'.

---

[7] More complete discussions of the argument of *Groundwork* III are found in Hill 1992: ch. 6 and 2002b: 93–108, 132–44; Henrich 1998; Korsgaard 1996: ch. 6; Allison 1990: chs 11 and 12; Ameriks 2003: chs 6 and 9; Schönecker 2006; Timmermann 2007: 120–51; and Guyer 2009.

An intelligible world is a world governed by rational norms of thought and action. To be a member of such a world is to be subject to such norms, and to have a capacity for spontaneity, or norm-guided self-determining activity that is independent of sensibility and cannot be understood in terms of naturalistic causal laws. If we have such intelligible capacities, we are warranted in ascribing free agency to ourselves. Our capacity to take an interest in and be moved by respect for moral principles appears to be such a capacity. But to appeal to ordinary moral consciousness at this point (to establish that we are free and thus subject to morality) would be to argue in a circle (G 4: 449–450). Instead Kant appeals to features of theoretical reasoning—that it constructs ideas that go beyond anything given in sensibility, that it marks out the limits of the understanding, and that it generates regulative ideals to guide the employment of the understanding. The capacity for theoretical reason displays a spontaneity and independence of sensibility that makes us 'members of an intelligible world' and thus provides non-moral grounds for ascribing freedom to ourselves (G 4: 450–453).

This line of thought is intended to show that we human beings are members of an intelligible world who necessarily act under the idea of freedom and are warranted in ascribing free agency to ourselves. But we are still sensible creatures with desires and an interest in happiness that can conflict with the demands of morality. The deduction proper (G 4: 453–5) appears to rest on the claim that because we identify with our intelligible self as our proper self (G 4: 457, 461)—perhaps because it is our rational capacities that constitute the self—its law has full and immediate authority in cases of conflict with our sensible interests. To summarize the overall trajectory of the argument: Kant argues for the necessary authority of morality by arguing that the moral law is the formal principle of free agency and that we necessarily act under the idea of freedom and identify with our free rational capacities as our proper self.[8]

A standing problem for Kant's claim that the moral law is the basic principle of free agency is how choice can be free when it is not guided by moral principles—for example, when a choice is guided by a maxim that is desire-based or that is contrary to morality. Clearly Kant should and means to hold that we can freely act on non-moral grounds and are responsible for such choices, and in other works he makes it clear that desires or incentives never cause choice directly, but lead to choice only through an act of spontaneity on the part of an agent.[9] One way to address this concern is to hold that the capacity to act from moral principles is sufficient for free choice, whether or not it is fully exercised. An agent with that capacity who acts on his own judgement acts freely, even when he acts on a desire-based or morally unworthy maxim.

[8] Note how this argument would address the worries about the 'common idea of duty' that appear once it is on the table (cited at the beginning of this chapter). If the Categorical Imperative is the internal norm of a necessary self-conception, it is indeed reasonable to acknowledge its deliberative priority. The fact that this self-conception includes a robust idea of freedom speaks to the concern that ordinary moral thought presupposes an untenable conception of our motivational capacities.

[9] This is the so-called 'Incorporation Thesis', stated at Rel 6: 24, that a free will is never determined by any incentive 'except insofar as the human being has incorporated it into his maxim'. For discussion, see Allison 1990: 5ff., 39ff., and Reath 2006: 12–13, 17–21.

Another approach is to attribute to Kant the view that all rational choice is constitutively aimed at good in the sense that it is based on maxims that are taken by the agent to satisfy a standard of universal validity. According to this conception of rational agency, FUL is the formal principle of free agency in that it tacitly guides all rational choice. The freedom and spontaneity of rational volition is captured by the fact that it is guided normatively rather than causally, and moreover by its own internal norm. How would bad choice fit into this picture? Here one needs to hold that even bad choice understands itself to satisfy a condition of universal validity and is tacitly guided by FUL. Since it is guided by the formal norm of volition, it is free. At the same time the choice is bad because it is defectively or incompletely guided by this norm—for example it is guided by bad reasoning or a misrepresentation of this norm. This conception of choice as constitutively aimed at good is controversial, both philosophically and as an interpretation of Kant. But in holding that all choice is in some way guided by the formal norm of volition, it provides a way to make out the view that even choice on desire-based or morally unworthy maxims is free.[10]

Like the *Groundwork*, the *Critique of Practical Reason* aims to establish the authority of the fundamental principle of common-sense morality, but in the context of Kant's overall critical system.[11] The task of the second *Critique* is 'merely to show that there is pure practical reason' (*KpV* 5: 3)—that is, to show, contrary to empiricism, that reason by itself yields a basic principle of conduct, independently of empirically given aims, and that practical reason is not limited to instrumental and prudential reasoning. This principle is, of course, the moral law.

To show that pure reason is practical, Kant begins with a definition of a 'practical law' as a principle with authority for any rational agent, and he moves analytically from this concept to a statement of the 'fundamental law of pure practical reason', which is recognizable as the moral law (*KpV* 5: 19–32). This argument parallels the argument in the *Groundwork* II from the concept of a categorical imperative to the statement of the FUL, and it contains many points of overlap with the earlier work. For example, Kant argues that the fundamental moral principle must be a formal principle—one whose normative force depends upon its form rather than an interest in its purpose or 'matter'—that moral theories that base the fundamental principle on an external object presented to the will lead to heteronomy and cannot ground true practical laws, and that the fundamental moral principle must be a principle of autonomy that the rational will gives to itself (*KpV* 5: 27, 39–41, 33). Furthermore, the *Critique* argues for the same analytic connection between freedom and morality (*KpV* 5: 28–30).

However, there are at least two important differences between these works. In *Groundwork* III Kant attempts a 'deduction' of the moral law, and as we have seen, one component of this argument is that general features of rationality, including the spontaneity of

[10] This approach is endorsed in different ways by Korsgaard 2009, especially ch. 5; Herman 2007: chs 10 and 11; and Engstrom 2009. Hill argues against such a reading in his 2002a: ch. 8.

[11] For overviews of the second *Critique*, see Reath 1997 and Engstrom 2002. Reath and Timmermann 2010 is a volume of critical essays on the *Critique*.

theoretical reason, give us non-moral grounds for ascribing free agency to ourselves. However in the second *Critique*, Kant says that a 'deduction' of the moral law is neither possible nor necessary, and that its authority is established directly as a 'fact of reason' (*KpV* 5: 31, 42, 46–7). Furthermore, he claims that grounds for ascribing free agency to ourselves are found only in moral consciousness. 'Morality first discloses to us the concept of freedom' and in place of the 'vainly sought deduction of the moral principle', this principle 'serves as the principle of the deduction of an inscrutable faculty which no experience could prove…namely the faculty of freedom' (*KpV* 5: 30, 47). Kant retains the idea that the moral law is the formal principle of free agency, but now holds that the capacity for free agency is grounded in our recognition of the authority of and ability to act from moral principle.

The basic idea that the moral law is given as a fact of reason is stated in the following passage:

> Consciousness of this fundamental law may be called a fact of reason [*Faktum der Vernunft*] because one cannot reason it out from antecedent data of reason, for example, from consciousness of freedom (since this is not antecedently given to us) and because it instead forces itself upon us of itself as a synthetic a priori proposition that is not based on any intuition, either pure or empirical. (*KpV* 5: 31)

This passage holds that the authority of morality is ultimately self-standing and not based on anything outside of reflective moral consciousness, for example on general features of rationality or an independently given notion of freedom. Kant is not abandoning the project of justifying the authority of morality, but rather adopts a different approach. One influential interpretation takes the fact of reason to be our consciousness of the authority of morality in everyday thought, judgement, and feeling.[12] For example, in our common-sense judgements about right action (*KpV* 5: 30, 32), recognition of the distinction between moral reasons and reasons based in happiness (*KpV* 5: 91–3), and in the feeling of respect for morality (*KpV* 5: 72–89) we find that on reflection we do accept the authority of morality and cannot reject it without significant loss. A further 'credential' for the moral law is that moral consciousness reveals our free agency, a capacity with which we identify (*KpV* 5: 48, 86–87). Commentators have pointed out that '*Faktum*' is taken from the Latin '*factum*' and should be understood as a deed or action, and early in the *Critique* Kant writes that the reality of pure practical reason is given 'through the deed' [*durch die Tat*] (*KpV* 5: 3). Thus Kant's claim that the moral law is given as a fact of reason is that its authority is established through what reason does in us—that moral consciousness is our awareness of the activity of pure practical reason in us.[13]

There is scholarly consensus that the fact of reason represents an approach to foundational issues that is different from that of *Groundwork* III. But opinion divides over how

---

[12] See Rawls 2000: 255–60, 268–71.
[13] Here see Engstrom 2002: xli–xliii. For further discussion see Kleingeld 2010: 57–65.

deep these differences are, over their relative merits, and how close either approach comes to succeeding. These are ongoing philosophical issues that cannot be settled in this chapter.[14]

21.3 KANT'S NORMATIVE THEORY

The main sources for Kant's normative theory are the *Groundwork* and the *Metaphysics of Morals*. The *Groundwork* is concerned primarily with foundational issues, but Kant illustrates the application of the Categorical Imperative in both its Universal Law and the Humanity versions through a set of examples. Clearly he takes the Categorical Imperative to be the basis of a deliberative procedure that leads to a set of substantive moral principles. The *Metaphysics of Morals* is intended to give a more complete presentation of his normative theory by applying the fundamental principle to the conditions of human life. Many questions about both the interpretation and the assessment of Kant's normative theory remain unresolved. For example, there is disagreement over how best to understand the Categorical Imperative and whether it provides an adequate guide to moral judgement, and the relation between the Categorical Imperative and the system of principles in the *Metaphysics of Morals* is not entirely transparent. I shall offer only a brief outline of his normative theory, beginning with the Categorical Imperative and focusing on the Universal Law version. Difficult issues of application (how to deal with moral conflict, for example) are beyond the scope of this chapter.

The Categorical Imperative applies a condition of universal validity to an agent's maxim of action. A maxim is an agent's subjective principle of action—the principle on which a subject acts or considers acting in some situation, which captures an agent's sincere understanding of what he intends to do and why he thinks it worth choosing.[15] In Kant's examples, maxims contain an action kind as well as the end and features of the agent's circumstances that are taken to support it. We might think of maxims as representations of the practical reasoning that goes into a potential or actual choice. The focus on maxims indicates that Kant's theory assesses volition or choice in terms of the practical reasoning that underwrites and is taken to support it.

The Formula of Universal Law leads to a deliberative procedure for assessing the universal validity of a proposed maxim of action: one must be able both to adopt the maxim and will that anyone adopt the maxim (will it as universal law) without inconsistency or

---

[14] For general discussions of these issues, see Henrich 1994; Rawls 2000: 253–72; Allison 1990: ch. 13; Ameriks 2003: ch. 10; Sussman 2008; Kleingeld 2010; and Timmermann 2010. Ameriks and Wood (2008: 135) are generally critical of the fact of reason approach, while Henrich, Allison, and Rawls defend it. Rawls, for example, does not think that it is a reversion to dogmatism or intuitionism and holds that the idea that morality is self-authenticating is a genuine advance (2000: 266–8).

[15] Rawls stresses that a maxim must be a lucid and sincere statement of an agent's reasons in order to deal with the problem of 'rigged maxims'—artificial maxims designed to evade the criterion of universal validity. See Rawls 2000: 167–70 and Hill 2002b: 67ff.

irrationality. Here Kant draws a distinction between maxims that cannot be conceived as universal law and maxims that are not rationally willed as universal law given certain necessary interests (G 4: 424). The first kind of failure of universality has come to be called a 'contradiction in conception' and the second a 'contradiction in will' (O'Neill 1989: 96–101). The reasoning associated with the first imposes a condition of universal validity on discretionary choice, while that associated with the second grounds duties to adopt certain obligatory ends that Kant in the *Doctrine of Virtue* terms 'duties of virtue' (*MdS* 6: 383).

Kant's maxim of deceptive promising is a maxim that cannot even be conceived as universal law because it is self-defeating if universalized. If everyone were free to make deceptive promises for reasons of self-interest, the practice of binding oneself through a promise and the background of trust on which it depends would be undermined. In such a world, either the idea of a false promise would be incoherent since the practice of promising would no longer exist, or there would be no point in making a false promise since it would not be believed. Thus one cannot consistently will both the maxim and its universalization. Maxims that involve cheating and free-riding fail of universality in the same way. Deception attempts to manipulate another through his rational agency, and focusing on this feature of deception suggests a general strategy for showing that maxims that involve interference with the freedom of another, threat and coercion, exploitation, and so on cannot be willed as universal without inconsistency. All such maxims aim to interfere with or to control the agency of another for one's own purposes. But as rational agents who act under the idea of freedom, we necessarily conceive of ourselves to have the capacity to act from our own judgements about reasons and have an interest in exercising that capacity. To will as universal law a maxim that involves interference with or control of the agency of others for one's own purposes is to will that the general conditions of rational agency be undermined, and is inconsistent with this necessary interest. Along these lines, one might argue that such maxims cannot be conceived as universal law for agents who act under the idea of freedom. In the *Groundwork*, Kant claims that maxims that cannot be conceived as universal law are contrary to perfect or strict duty. He intends this form of reasoning to identify a set of action types undertaken for certain kinds of reasons that are impermissible, and thus to set limits on the ways in which we may pursue our ends.

Kant's maxim of indifference leads to a contradiction in will when universalized. The maxim is that while one is never to interfere with the freedom or property of another, one is never to assist others in need (unless doing so is to one's advantage) (G 4: 423). Kant notes that there is no inconceivability in this maxim holding universally, but that it would be irrational to will it as universal law. As rational agents with the capacity to set our own ends, we necessarily have an interest in being able to achieve them and in the conditions that support the effective exercise of our agency and end-setting capacities. Given our limited powers and vulnerabilities, a social climate in which people are willing to assist others in need is one of these conditions. Willing the maxim of indifference as universal law conflicts with this necessary interest and thus produces a 'contradiction in one's will'. A similar form of reasoning can be used to show that one has a duty to develop one's natural talents. Rather than identifying ways of acting that are impermissible, this form of reasoning leads to imperfect duties—duties to adopt certain general ends or policies (in addition to one's personal ends and interest in happiness).

To provide a rationale for Kant's distinction between these two kinds of reasoning that explains why they lead to different kinds of duties, one might invoke the different ways in which they draw on the conditions of rational agency. Contradiction in conception identifies as wrong maxims whose universalization undermines the conditions of rational agency. The failure of universalizability here is due to the fact that such maxims directly interfere with or exploit rational agency, and they are appropriately classified as violations of perfect duty. By contrast, contradiction in will rejects maxims that fail to support the effective exercise of rational agency—maxims whose universalization is in conflict with our necessary interest in the effective exercise of our end-setting capacities.[16] This form of reasoning leads to the ends of virtue, which are required for 'positive agreement' with humanity as an end in itself. This line of thought connects FUL and FH by bringing out the fact that maxims that do not satisfy the condition of universal validity are in different ways failures to respect rational nature as an end in itself.

Commentators disagree about the role that Kant intends for the FUL and about its adequacy as a general normative principle. For example, problems arise when it is applied to quite specific or qualified maxims, because most are consistently universalized, including many that are intuitively impermissible. Because of such problems, some philosophers argue for giving primacy to FH, despite Kant's claim that FUL provides the 'strict method' for moral appraisal (*G* 4: 436).[17] FUL certainly does not provide a mechanical procedure for assessing maxims of action. Philosophers who have defended its viability argue that it is best applied to maxims of a fairly high level of generality, to yield general moral principles that require further judgement for application to specific circumstances. Another worry is that since FUL most naturally assesses permissibility, it only leads to positive moral requirements indirectly by showing that certain maxims are impermissible. But one might want a more direct route to positive moral requirements (e.g. of honesty, fidelity, or beneficence). To address this concern one might apply the condition of universal validity directly to certain necessary human interests.[18] For example, applying the condition of universal validity to the necessary interest in the exercise of rational agency leads directly to a set of principles that both protect and support the effective exercise of rational agency.

---

[16] For discussion see O'Neill 1989: 96–7, 133–4; Herman 1993: 125–7, 225–30; and Reath 2006: 211–20.

[17] For discussion of some of these problems, including the problems of 'false negatives' and 'false positives', see Wood 1999: 97–110. He argues that FH leads to a more viable approach to moral reasoning. See Wood 1999: 111–56, 182–91, and Wood 2002: 12–13. For other discussions of the application of FH, see Hill 1992: 38–57 and 2002b: 79–83, O'Neill 1989: 105–25, and Korsgaard 1996: 106–32. Philosophers who have defended FUL include O'Neill 1989: 81–104, Herman 1993, Korsgaard 1996: 77–105, and Engstrom 2009.

[18] Such an approach is developed in Engstrom 2009: 184–240.

The *Metaphysics of Morals* distinguishes the domains of right (*Recht*) and ethics, and accordingly contains two parts—the *Doctrine of Right* and the *Doctrine of Virtue*. Each domain is governed by a fundamental principle that is nominally a version of the Categorical Imperative. All duties are principled constraints on free choice. Right and ethics regulate different domains of freedom—outer and inner freedom—and they do so in different ways.

Right regulates external action in so far as it affects the freedom of others in accordance with the necessary conditions of equal outer freedom. Kant's 'Universal Principle of Right' reads: 'An action is right if it can coexist with everyone's freedom in accordance with a universal law' (*MdS* 6: 230). This principle is a pared down version of the contradiction in conception component of FUL that focuses on actions outwardly described. It imposes a formal constraint on actions taken in pursuit of one's purposes and implies that an action is wrong if it interferes with an action that is consistent with the equal freedom of all. The contours of right are determined by the fact that this principle only regulates outer freedom. Because of this, it cannot require compliance from any particular incentive, nor does it require that agents adopt any particular ends. Further, right creates title to employ coercion to protect equal freedom, since coercion that opposes 'hindrances to freedom' is consistent with the equal freedom of all and therefore right (*MdS* 6: 231). From these points it follows that the 'law-giving' employed by right may be 'external'—that is, the incentives that constrain choice to conditions of right may appeal to self-interest and need not include any thought of duty (*MdS* 6: 218–20). Finally, right creates strict requirements, requiring specific actions and omissions.(*MdS* 6: 388–9). The Universal Principle of Right is the basis of Kant's legal and political theory, including his account of private right (property, contract, and status) and his theory of the state.[19]

Ethics goes beyond right by requiring the adoption of certain ends and introduces the important concept of a duty of virtue.[20] A duty of virtue is a requirement of reason to adopt certain general ends, values, and fundamental attitudes towards persons—in effect a duty to adopt some fundamental maxim (*MdS* 6: 389). The 'supreme principle of the doctrine of virtue' is: 'Act in accord with a maxim of ends that it can be a universal law for everyone to have' (*MdS* 6: 396). One should expect this principle to align with the contradiction in will component of FUL (or the positive dimension of FH). The most general duty of virtue is to adopt the fundamental principle of respecting humanity as an end in itself. Kant also stresses the more specific ends of one's own natural and moral perfection and promoting the happiness of others. Moral perfection involves cultivating the disposition to act from the motive of duty—a fundamental commitment to moral principle and the priority of moral considerations. It includes the disposition to comply

[19] For discussion see Ripstein 2009a and 2009b. He argues that Kant's theory of right is based on a conception of external freedom as independence from the will of another and holds that political institutions are necessary conditions of equal freedom as independence.

[20] For general discussions of the *Doctrine of Virtue* see Wood 2002 and Hill 2010, as well as the essays in Timmons 2002 and Denis 2010.

with duties of justice from the motive of duty. In other words it is a duty of virtue to make 'the right of humanity' one's end—to take on the commitment to honour the juridical rights of others out of respect for morality, thus going beyond what right requires (*MdS* 6: 390, 395).

In various ways, ethics is concerned with the conditions of internal freedom, or self-constraint through principles of pure practical reason (*MdS* 6: 396). Because ends are always adopted through free choice and one can never be constrained by others to adopt an end, duties of virtue are not externally enforceable. Thus the ends of virtue require self-constraint through a conception of duty, and in that respect 'ethical law-giving'— the incentive attached to duties of virtue—is internal (*MdS* 6: 218–20, 380–4). Since duties of virtue are duties to adopt general maxims (maxims of ends) they are of 'wide obligation'. They do not require specific actions and leave agents latitude in how to act on these ends and general principles. But Kant also notes that 'a wide duty is not to be taken as permission to make exceptions to the maxims of action but only as permission to limit one maxim of duty by another . . . by which in fact the field for the practice of virtue is widened' (*MdS* 6: 390). Even though agents have discretion in implementing the ends of virtue, Kant appears to assign them an important role in shaping an agent's overall system of ends.[21]

The *Doctrine of Virtue* develops a classification in which duties to oneself figure prominently. In addition to the imperfect duties of natural and moral self-development, Kant includes perfect duties to oneself. Violations of perfect duty to oneself include suicide, and interestingly lying (since it involves misuse of one's capacity to communicate), avarice (which displays 'slavish subjection of oneself to the goods that contribute to happiness' [*MdS* 6: 434]), and servility (as a basic failure of self-respect). These are perfect duties since they are duties to preserve one's natural and moral capacities, but duties of virtue since they are satisfied by adopting certain basic attitudes towards oneself. Kant also includes duties to develop receptivity to moral norms, to cultivate conscience, and to develop the forms of self-knowledge needed for good willing and virtue (*MdS* 6: 399–403, 441–2. Cf. Hill 2010: 246–9). Perhaps the unifying theme in these duties is the preservation and development of the capacity for inner freedom and self-government.

The duties of virtue to others fall into the categories of duties of love and respect. Kant does not understand love and respect in this context as feelings, but rather as maxims or active practical attitudes towards others (*MdS* 6: 449). Duties of love require active concern for the well-being of others—beneficence and the cultivation of a capacity to share others' feelings that supports beneficence (*MdS* 6: 452–7). One respects others by acknowledging their equal standing—'by limiting our self-esteem by the dignity of humanity in another person' (*MdS* 6: 449). Among other things, respect requires restraining the tendency to affirm one's own worth in defective ways, for example through arrogance ('a demand that others think little of themselves in

---

[21] Barbara Herman has argued that the ends of virtue may be understood as ends of all rational choice by shaping one's conception of happiness from the inside. See Herman 2007: 254–75.

comparison with us' [*MdS* 6: 465]) or mocking the faults of others. Kant's discussion of these particular duties should not be understood as an attempt at an exhaustive list, but rather as an illustration of what is called for by respect for humanity in one-self and others.

BIBLIOGRAPHY

Kant's Works

Citations will use the abbreviations given below, and will be to the Prussian Academy of Sciences edition of Kant's collected works (Berlin: de Gruyter, 1900–).

G   *Groundwork of the Metaphysics of Morals* in *Kant: Practical Philosophy*, tr. and ed. M. J. Gregor. Cambridge/New York: Cambridge University Press, 1996.

Idea   *Idea for a Universal History with a Cosmopolitan Aim* in *Kant: Anthropology, History and Education*, tr. and ed. R. B. Louden and G. Zöller. Cambridge/New York: Cambridge University Press, 2008.

KpV   *Critique of Practical Reason* in *Kant: Practical Philosophy*.

LE   *Lectures on Ethics*, ed. P. Heath and J. B. Schneewind, tr. P. Heath. Cambridge/New York: Cambridge University Press, 1997.

MdS   *The Metaphysics of Morals* in *Kant: Practical Philosophy*.

PP   *Toward Perpetual Peace* in *Kant: Practical Philosophy*.

Rel   *Religion within the Bboundaries of Mere Reason*, tr. and ed. A. Wood and G. di Giovanni. Cambridge/New York: Cambridge University Press, 1998.

TP   *On the Common Saying: That may be Correct in Theory but it is of no use in Practice* in *Kant: Practical Philosophy*.

Secondary Sources

Allison, H. 1990. *Kant's Theory of Freedom*. Cambridge/New York: Cambridge University Press.

—— 1996. *Idealism and Freedom: Essays on Kant's Theoretical and Practical Philosophy*. Cambridge/New York: Cambridge University Press.

Ameriks, K. 2003. *Interpreting Kant's Critiques*. Oxford/New York: Oxford University Press.

Denis, L. (ed.) 2010. *Kant's 'Metaphysics of Morals': A Critical Guide*. Cambridge/New York: Cambridge University Press.

Engstrom, S. 2002. 'Introduction', in Kant, *Critique of Practical Reason*, tr. Werner S. Pluhar. Indianapolis/Cambridge, MA: Hackett Publishing, xi–liv.

—— 2009. *The Form of Practical Knowledge*. Cambridge, MA: Harvard University Press.

Guyer, P. 1995. 'The possibility of the categorical imperative', *Philosophical Review* 104: 353–85. Reprinted in Paul Guyer, *Kant on Freedom, Law, and Happiness*. Cambridge/New York: Cambridge University Press, 2000, 172–206.

—— (ed.) 1998. *Groundwork of the Metaphysics of Morals: Critical Essays*. Lanham, MD: Rowman & Littlefield.

—— 2009. 'Problems with freedom: Kant's argument in *Groundwork* III and its subsequent emendations', in Timmermann (ed.), 2009, 172–202.

Henrich, D. 1994. 'The concept of moral insight and Kant's doctrine of the fact of reason', in D. Henrich, *The Unity of Reason*, ed. and tr. Richard Velkley. Cambridge, MA: Harvard University Press, 55–87.

—— 1998. 'The deduction of the moral law: the reasons for the obscurity of the final section of Kant's *Groundwork of the Metaphysics of Morals*', in Guyer (ed.), 1998, 303–41.

Herman, B. 1993. *The Practice of Moral Judgment*. Cambridge, MA: Harvard University Press.

—— 2007. *Moral Literacy*. Cambridge, MA: Harvard University Press.

Hill, T. E. Jr. 1992. *Dignity and Practical Reason*. Ithaca: Cornell University Press.

—— 2002a. *Human Welfare and Moral Worth*. Oxford/New York: Oxford University Press.

—— 2002b. 'Editor's Introduction' and 'Analysis of arguments', in Kant, *Groundwork for the Metaphysics of Morals*, tr. A. Zweig and ed. T. E. Hill, Jr. Oxford/New York: Oxford University Press, 19–177.

—— 2010. 'Kant's *Tugendlehre* as normative ethics', in Denis (ed.), 2010, 234–55.

Horn, C. and Schönecker, D. (eds) 2006. *Groundwork for the Metaphysics of Morals*. Berlin: Walter de Gruyter.

Kerstein, S. 2002. *Kant's Search for the Supreme Principle of Morality*. Cambridge/New York: Cambridge University Press.

Kleingeld, P. 2010. 'Moral consciousness and the 'fact of reason', in Reath and Timmermann (eds), 2010, 55–72.

Korsgaard, C. M. 1996. *Creating the Kingdom of Ends*. Cambridge/New York: Cambridge University Press.

—— 2008. *The Constitution of Agency*. Oxford/New York: Oxford University Press.

—— 2009. *Self-Constitution*. Oxford/New York: Oxford University Press.

O'Neill, O. 1989. *Constructions of Reason*. Cambridge/New York: Cambridge University Press.

Prichard, H. A. 2002. 'Does moral philosophy rest on a mistake?', in his *Moral Writings*. Oxford/New York: Oxford University Press, 7–20.

Rawls, J. 2000. *Lectures on the History of Moral Philosophy*. Cambridge, MA: Harvard University Press.

Reath, A. 1997. 'Introduction', in Kant, *Critique of Practical Reason*, tr. M. J. Gregor. Cambridge/New York: Cambridge University Press, vii–xxxi.

—— 2006. *Agency and Autonomy in Kant's Moral Theory*. Oxford/New York: Oxford University Press.

—— 2010. 'Formal principles and the form of a law', in Reath and Timmermann (eds), 2010, 31–54.

—— 2012. 'Formal approaches to Kant's formula of humanity', in S. Baiasu and M. Timmons (eds), *Kant on Practical Justification*. Oxford/New York: Oxford University Press.

—— 2013. 'The ground of practical laws', in S. Bacin, A. Ferrarin, C. La Rocca, and M. Ruffing (eds), *Kant and Philosophy in a Cosmopolitan Sense: Proceedings of the XIth International Kant Congress*. Berlin: De Gruyter.

—— and Timmermann, J. (eds) 2010. *Kant's 'Critique of Practical Reason': A Critical Guide*. Cambridge/New York: Cambridge University Press.

Ripstein, A. 2009a. 'Kant on law and justice', in T. E. Hill, Jr. (ed.), *The Blackwell Guide to Kant's Ethics*. Malden, MA: Wiley-Blackwell Publishing, 161–78.

—— 2009b. *Force and Freedom: Kant's Legal and Political Philosophy*. Cambridge, MA: Harvard University Press.

Schönecker, D. 2006. 'How is a categorical imperative possible? Kant's deduction of the categorical imperative', in Horn and Schönecker (eds), 2006, 301–24.

Sensen, O. 2009. 'Kant's conception of human dignity', *Kant-Studien* 100: 309–31.

—— 2010. 'Dignity and the formula of humanity', in Timmermann (ed.), 2010, 102–18.

Sussman, D. 2008. 'From deduction to deed: Kant's grounding of the moral law', *Kantian Review* 13: 52–81.

Timmermann, J. 2007. *Kant's Groundwork of the Metaphysics of Morals: A Commentary.* Cambridge/New York: Cambridge University Press.

—— 2010. 'Reversal or retreat: Kant's deductions of freedom and morality', in Reath and Timmermann (eds), 2010, 73–89.

—— (ed.) 2009. *Kant's 'Groundwork of the Metaphysics of Morals': A Critical Guide.* Cambridge/New York: Cambridge University Press.

Timmons, M. (ed.) 2002. *Kant's Metaphysics of Morals: Interpretive Essays.* Oxford/New York: Oxford University Press.

Wood, A. W. 1999. *Kant's Ethical Thought.* Cambridge/New York: Cambridge University Press.

—— 2002. 'The final form of Kant's practical philosophy', in Timmons (ed.), 2002, 1–21.

—— 2008. *Kantian Ethics.* Cambridge/New York: Cambridge University Press.

CHAPTER 22

....

KANTIAN ETHICS

....

OTFRIED HÖFFE

No other philosopher of Modernity has changed the way we think as radically and enduringly as did Immanuel Kant, the high point and turning point of the European Enlightenment. What he accomplished with his first critique in the area of objective knowledge, he also undertook in the area of objective action, in morals: he provided it with a new basis. The corresponding texts, most influentially the *Groundwork of the Metaphysics of Morals* and the *Critique of Practical Reason*, but also the essay 'On a supposed right to lie from philanthropy', *The Metaphysics of Morals*, and in particular its second part, the 'Doctrine of Virtue', the *Religion within the Boundaries of Mere Reason*, and finally the relevant passages out of the first and third critique—all these texts are characterized by such a high level of originality and keen conceptual argumentation that they have shaped not only philosophical but also non-philosophical ethical debates up to this day.

All ethicists who have taken inspiration from Kant's critical moral philosophy itself or its spirit are called 'Kantian'. Broadly understood, the denomination can also be extended to those ethicists who grappled with and rejected Kant or the Kantian spirit. Because Kant's ethics remains the leading moral theory, almost all ethics after him have been, narrowly or broadly conceived, Kantian. In the following, we will start by recalling the core of Kant's ethics, those important theorems that will provide a criterion for determining the extent to which a given ethics is indeed 'Kantian'.

22.1 A GENERAL OUTLINE OF KANT'S ETHICS

Just as he does in his theoretical philosophy, Kant distinguishes between an empirically conditioned part and a 'pure' one in his practical philosophy, too. In the first case, practical reason, that is the will, receives its aims and ends from without—from drives, needs, and pathological feelings of pleasure and displeasure. Because it is thereby following foreign laws, it is acting *heteronomously*, but in the second case, because it is acting entirely on its own, it is doing so *autonomously*. Kant does not deny that a specific action does indeed require experience, and a power of judgement honed through such experience. It is only with respect to one's final motive, say, when deciding in a difficult situation whether or not to be truthful, that experience has no role to play.

More specifically, Kant rejects ethical empiricism, according to which morals depends upon empirical motives, as well as ethical scepticism, which doubts that true morals exists. The core of his alternative view consists in a five-part argument. At the outset Kant defines the concept of morals as that which is absolutely good. He then applies this concept to the situation in which finite rational beings, namely humans, find themselves: because they have in addition sensuous, that is, non-rational drives, morals must be seen as a duty. Conceptually, morals consists in the metaethical element of the categorical imperative, in conceiving of that absolute 'ought' that can only be attained through morality, that is, acting out of duty, as opposed to (ethical) legality, which is acting merely according to duty. The third core element deals with the standard according to which morality is measured, strict universalization, which, however, does not pertain to individual actions or to arbitrary rules, but rather to subjective principles, called maxims. The next core element concerns the origin of morals; it consists in a will that is good without limitation, an autonomous will. Finally, the fact of reason is that by which Kant seeks to establish the reality of morals.

To this five-part core Kant adds numerous further elements. The first group of such elements are not new, but rather serve as explanations: the notion of a pure moral philosophy, 'completely cleansed of everything that may be only empirical' (*Groundwork*, Preface); that the ground of obligation 'must...be sought...*a priori* simply in concepts of pure reason' (*Groundwork*, Preface); that there are three levels of obligation: technical, pragmatic, and categorical imperatives; and that morality proves its worth only when duty is placed in stark contrast to inclination.

Some elements further enrich Kant's core arguments: pragmatic imperatives can only be taken as suggestions, not as objective laws; morals cannot be reduced to a social morality, but incorporates duties towards oneself in addition to those towards others; both of these types of duties include perfect duties, which do not allow any room for manoeuvre, as well as imperfect ones; and this entails the multifaceted distinction between right and morals; morally speaking, it is only one's worthiness to be happy, not happiness itself, that counts; this real and natural human desire to be happy, moreover, permits of the morally, though not theoretically, valid conclusion that two preconditions, the two postulates of pure practical reason, namely the existence of God and the immortality of the soul, are necessary; human beings are (radically) evil; they should overcome the ethical state of nature, in which 'the good principle...is incessantly attacked by...evil' (*Religion*, Pt. III, Sect. 2), and establish a community in which the laws of virtue are accepted without constraint; finally, humanity alone is the final end of nature.

What is more, Kant's philosophy of right and of the state, as well as his contract theory, belong to his ethical programme, but also his decisive cosmopolitanism, which culminates in a theory of a global order of law and freedom.

22.2 RECEPTIVE KANTIANS

Very quickly, Kant—called the 'wise man from Königsberg' by enthusiasts—inspires fervour in many places. 'Kant is not a light in the world', writes the poet Jean Paul, 'but an entire solar system at once' (Letter on July 13, 1788, in *Die Briefe Jean Pauls*, vol. 1, 258). And Friedrich Hölderlin, who, as is known, influenced his two friends Schelling and Hegel, called Kant the 'Moses of our nation' (Letter on January 1, 1799, in *Hölderlin*, *Sämtliche Werke*, vol. VI, no. 172, 304). This solar system or philosophical Moses engendered in general two types of Kantians who can also be found in the field of ethics: the more receptive 'old Kantians' who take Kant's foundation for ethics as their own guideline and wish to apply it 'to life', and those who creatively disagree, seeking either to 'complete' or 'overcome' Kant, depending upon their estimation of their powers, and who lead in ethics as well to German Idealism.

Only two years after Kant's second critique appeared, J. H. Abicht composed a *New System of a Philosophical Doctrine of Virtue Developed from Human Nature* (1790). Following Kant, he assumes that morality depends upon the will. It follows that only that which is done 'for the sake of freedom' or that which flows 'from freedom' is moral, whereas everything that is done for a reward has 'no moral worth' (§128 ff.).

A few years later A. Metz claims that a most 'beautiful harmony' is to be found between Kant's moral philosophy and that of the Gospel (*A Short and Clear Exposition of the Kantian System*, 1795). And A. B. Bethmann-Bernhardi explains in his *Popular Exposition of the Kantian Teachings on Morality* (1796–1797) that the principles behind Kant's conceptions of 'morality, divinity, immortality' are the only ones that are 'entirely true'.

Other 'old Kantians' are so fully concerned with relaying Kant's thought to schools or the general public that their Kantian ethics are hardly philosophically original at all. These include J. Chr. Zwanziger's *Commentary on Prof. Kant's Critique of Practical Reason* (1794), G. S. A. Mellin's *Marginalia and Index to Kant's Critique of the Power of Knowledge Part 2: Groundwork to the Metaphysics of Morals, Critique of Practical Reason and of the Power of Judgement* (1795) and the moral philosophical sections in the *Explanatory Digest of the Critical Writings of Prof. Kant at His Own Suggestion* (3 vol., 1793 and 1796), which were composed by Kant's Königsberg colleague, J. S. Beck.

22.3 EARLY CREATIVE KANTIANS

As a matter of fact, we can begin the list of philosophically independent Kantian ethics with *Friedrich Schiller* (1759–1805), the lofty poet of freedom. He assumes a prominent place within Kantian ethics, if not in the broader history of thought. Schiller, who at an early age had read his way through the late European Enlightenment, draws near to

Kant relatively late, and even then with almost fearful precaution. The intellectual climate at his time, an all but effusive enthusiasm for Kant, inspired his oft-quoted verses with the title 'Kant and his Commentators': 'How a single rich man can feed so many beggars! When kings build, the carters find work.' ('Wie doch ein einziger Reicher so viele Bettler in Nahrung/Setzt! Wenn die Könige baun, haben die Kärner zu tun.' *Xenien: Nationalausgabe* I, 315).

Schiller did not compose a moral philosophy of his own. His Kantian ethics are found dispersed throughout his philosophical aesthetics: The so-called *Kallias Letters On Charm and Worth* (1793) praise Kant's 'grand idea of self-determination', which is the substance of his entire philosophy: 'Determine yourself by yourself!' Schiller, who here feels indebted to Kant, nevertheless draws away from Kant in the rest of the quotation. He claims that the idea of self-determination 'is reflected back at us by specific elements in nature, which we call *beauty*'. Here, as in other places, Schiller's primary interest comes to light, one which is not only unknown to Kant but which also contradicts his moral philosophy. It is to combine the moral and political idea of self-determination with the primarily aesthetic idea of beauty with the goal of bringing our moral and aesthetic existence into that unity which he calls the beautiful soul. But perhaps there is more Kantian ethics to be found in this unity than one might assume at first sight, and than Schiller himself believed.

The term 'beautiful soul', which was very prevalent in the eighteenth century, goes back to Plato, travels through Neoplatonism from Plotinus to Augustine, and has since then become standard in literature. The term indicates a wholeness and an all-encompassing value, a humanity that has come to rest in itself. Schiller remains true to this basic theme of unity and wholeness, as he perceives that 'those sharp boundaries have all disappeared'. The content of four different expressions should thus be brought together: moral feeling, sentiment, emotions, and the will. When this is the case, the opposition between duty and inclination disappears. The most popular expression of this idea was attempted in the following distich: 'I take pleasure in helping my friends, but alas I do so by inclination, and so it rankles me often that I am not virtuous' ('Gerne dien ich den Freunden, doch tue ich es leider mit Neigung/ Und so wurmt es mir oft, daß ich nicht tugendhaft bin.' *Xenien: Nationalausgabe* I, 357).

According to Schiller, the opposition is overcome when morality is linked to its alleged opponent, practical sensibility, and becomes a moral sensibility or a sensitive morality. In the case of the beautiful soul, morality is no longer wrenched away from an inner resistance. In overcoming such a 'beclouded' morality, one attains to a masterly humanity, to a morality that lives in concord and harmony with sensibility, one with which we are well pleased, and which can therefore be said beautiful. The beautiful soul is driven by a harmonious force that is directed by its inner nature to that which is moral. Those who direct their lives entirely in accordance with it can boast of a free and sovereign morality, and can call themselves the maestros of humanity.

Kant would not disagree. For those who only act against an inner resistance do not do so entirely of their own accord. Only those live out of respect for the moral law who adopt an attitude of respect and then follow their duties with a 'valiant and cheerful' frame of mind, as Kant says in his 'Doctrine of Virtue' (§53). They have 'incorporated' them in such a way that it becomes easy to act out of duty ('Doctrine of Virtue', Introduction, Sect. XIV). Thus, reaching beyond the limits of their diverging terminology, a 'beautiful harmony' is to be found between Schiller and his philosophical mentor Kant, but not entirely. In Schiller's texts the beautiful soul appears as a real possibility, whereas Kant would maintain that fundamental anthropological insight that renders the concept of duty itself necessary: as bodily and needy beings, humans have drives that can go against morality. That is why the moral law can never be a natural law to them, one which they would follow necessarily, but is rather an imperative that admonishes them to follow it. Consequently, the beautiful soul cannot possibly ever be fully attained. It remains an ideal, the idea of perfection so far as it might be found in an individual. Such an example is supplied by the Stoic sage (*Critique of Pure Reason*, Transcendental Dialectic, Bk. II, Ch. III, Sect. 1), who is not to be thought of as a real Stoic, but rather as an individual ideal.

Karl Leonhard Reinhold (1757–1823), who played an important role in the development of post-Kantian philosophy, was more interested in theoretical than practical philosophy. He nevertheless closes his principal systematic work, the *Essay at a New Theory of the Human Faculty of Perception* (1789) with an 'Outline of a theory of the faculty of desire', in which he broaches ethical matters: subjects are absolutely free only inasmuch as they follow 'entirely rational, disinterested drives', and thus determine their actions by means of a pure will.

The first philosopher who does not take Kant's philosophy as an already completed whole, but who instead wants to think it through to the end, is *Johann Gottlieb Fichte* (1762–1814). Fichte's fundamental philosophy, his 'Wissenschaftslehre', claims to be no less than a 'science of science' ('Wissenschaft der Wissenschaft überhaupt') that seeks to provide a basis for 'all possible sciences', and in particular theoretical and practical philosophy. His most influential text, the *Foundations of the Entire Science of Knowledge* (1794), which is strictly speaking only an introduction, is, given its idea of the creative freedom of the absolute 'I', a text on fundamental ethics, though not one that deals exclusively with ethics. For this highest principle is to be the 'absolutely first, entirely unconditioned foundation of all human knowledge' (§1). It is ethical inasmuch as this knowledge for Fichte includes all 'representations that are accompanied by a feeling of necessity' (§ 1.), amongst which he places morals.

In the underlying transcendental subject, which he calls 'I', spontaneity combines with oneness and self-certainty. This concept, however, does not designate an individual, natural person who would supposedly create himself as well as his conceptions of the world, as many have thought from Jean Paul to Bertrand Russell and other analytical philosophers. Such an interpretation would require that we view Fichte's 'subjective idealism' as 'folly'. Fichte actually refers to something universal, a 'transcendental I' that is not empirical, but only accessible through thought.

Two elements of Kant's ethics, autonomy and the primacy of practical reason, are thus inordinately broadened and heightened. The principle of autonomy, which for Kant had been restricted to the realm of the practical, is extended to the theoretical realm, which thereby takes on properties connected to action, thus drastically extending the thematic reach of the primacy of the practical. This presupposes that the transcendental 'I' is defined as an action, specifically as that transcendental act that makes the (knowing and willing) subject possible as subject. The goal of this act lies both in the act of knowing as of willing itself. Fichte offers an elegant metaphor: 'The I is a power within which an eye has been placed'.

In order, on the one hand, to provide knowledge and the will with a shared, foundational principle and, on the other hand, to avoid that this foundation fall into an infinite regress, Fichte does not posit, as did Reinhold, an initial fact (Tat*sache*), a 'fact of consciousness', but instead invokes a transcendental productivity, the free action (Tat*handlung*) of the 'I': 'The I originally and absolutely posits its own being' (§1; whereby 'posits' implies a non-sensuous spontaneity).

Fichte's second principle—'The I originally posits a non-I against itself' (§2)—indicates that the transcendental productivity of the 'I' requires an independent opposing pole, a 'non-I'. It is the element around which freedom can gather, with which it can relate back to itself and become determined. In the case of knowledge, the opposing pole consists of the object, that which is known; in the case of the will it is another's freedom. With Fichte, the Kantian philosophy of freedom becomes fundamentally communicative: 'The unity of I and You is the We of a moral world order'.

Kant restricts autonomy to morality; Fichte raises it to the rank of a universal principle that is also applied to theoretical reason. It could be objected that this universalized self-directed action, this 'self-birthing of the human being', is idealistic and arrogant. In fact, there is a valid point: the order of the given natural world does not arise independently of us. It depends on us discovering connections as we construct concepts and establish laws and then apply them to the knower, that is, ourselves. In that sense there is indeed an act of freedom at the actual beginning. But theoretical and practical knowledge do not arise 'in' freedom, rather 'they arise free': one must accept something that one can also refuse; one must open oneself to truth or morality (the first principle) and also obey them (the second principle). In contrast, the philosopher is not the lawgiver of the human mind, but rather its 'historian'.

Fichte also composed an ethics in the strict sense, a 'Theory of the consciousness of our moral nature generally and of our specific duties in particular' (Part I, Preliminary remark). The theory aims at a system of concrete ethics, but begins with a strong fundamental ethics. The *System of Ethics in accordance with the Principles of the Wissenschaftslehre* (1798) is divided into three main parts. In the first part, he 'deduces' a principle of morality which is very much reminiscent of Kant's categorical imperative. Fichte, however, understands this deduction in a way that is quite foreign to Kant: its task is to define 'the morality of our nature from our reason based upon necessary laws' (1798). The result is as follows: 'The principle of morality is the necessary idea that an intelligent being should define its freedom according to the concept of self-sufficiency, without any exception' (Part I, 'Description of the Principle...').

In the second part, which deals with reality and practicality, the natural drive is said to aim at 'that which is material, simply for the sake of matter itself; at pleasure for the sake of pleasure: it is a pure drive towards absolute independence: freedom for the sake of freedom' (§12). In the third part, 'Morality strictly conceived', we find those two of Kant's ends that are also duties: one's own perfection and another's happiness ('Doctrine of Virtue', Introduction, IV). Indeed, Fichte explains that according to the 'formal condition of morality' one must 'decide, simply for the sake of one's conscience, to do what that conscience requires' (§15, V).

In the context of the doctrine of duty itself, Fichte views self-preservation, which includes fostering one's health and well-being, as a qualified duty. He explains that the final end of all the actions of a morally good person can be summarized in the sentence, 'He wants reason alone to rule in the world of sense' (§22). This implies that one might never 'kill with premeditation' (§23, I); that 'the health, strength and preservation of the body and life of others should be one of our aims' (§23, I); further, that 'I must be absolutely sincere and truthful to everyone' (§23, II); and also the prohibition to damage another's property (§23, VI). In case of conflict, 'life before property' always holds (§24). Fichte's concept of duty comes close to Kant's, as he speaks of a continual good will, one that aims to 'promote' the aims 'of the human race' (*The Characteristics of the Present Age*, 1804). Virtue, he continues, 'consists in loving the good without regard for the fact that it is commanded'.

The second important representative of German Idealism, *Friedrich Wilhelm Joseph Schelling* (1775–1854), takes little interest in ethics. One of the high points of his thinking, *Of Human Freedom* (1809), can nevertheless be counted in a broad sense as a Kantian ethics inasmuch as the will has a significant role to play. Contrary to what a contemporary reader might expect given the title, the text is more concerned with the freedom of God than that of human beings. In a few places he does however engage with Kantian thought, specifically with the dark side of freedom that emerges in the concept of evil. But one important dimension of Kant's legal and political ethics is entirely absent, namely social and political freedom as it is ensured by laws and the state. Schelling does not think in a very Kantian way either. Instead of a critical argumentation, we find theological erudition, and most of all a haughty speculation that aims to 'understand the God outside oneself through the God within oneself'. The text is best understood not as 'investigations', as the German title says, but rather as a 'speculative history'. It tells of how God comes into existence and how the freedom to do evil emerges from God.

The thinking of *Georg Wilhelm Friedrich Hegel* (1770–1831) also includes a broadly Kantian ethics. By and large, Hegel's philosophy is a metaphysics predicated upon Kant's critique of metaphysics, but which forgoes his critical method. Excepting his *Lectures on the History of Philosophy*, Kantian ethics appears in two places: in the *Phenomenology of Spirit* (1807) and in the *Elements of the Philosophy of Right* (1821). In both cases, Kant's ethics is both reinforced and emphatically relativized. Kant's insights remain acceptable as long as one is doing ethics in Kant's sense of the term. But for Hegel such an ethics is merely one moment within a dialectical process. Hegel's relative view of Kant rests, however, on a presupposition that does not do justice to Kant. His broad programme of a moral philosophy and a philosophy of right is reduced to a moral philosophy only, which is in turn further reduced to a theory of morality, which Hegel then sublates into a theory of ethical life (Sittlichkeit), a theory of the institutions of objective spirit. Kant's ethics, with its it's legal and political elements taken away, is defined as a theory of moral subjectivity.

In his certainly most brilliant work, the *Phenomenology of Spirit*, Hegel dynamizes Kant's one-time reform of our way of thinking into a process of many reforms, each of which surpasses the previous ones, though none is so obviously missing as Kant's own. Hegel starts off with human beings' 'natural consciousness', shows their perceptions of the world and themselves to be false, and from this misperception extracts a higher viewpoint of consciousness, which brings us step by step, through ever repeating misperceptions, to an ever better, and finally to the correct, form of consciousness and self-perception. The process as a whole results in a historicized, though not relativized, reason, and reaches a qualitatively final point. At the same time, Hegel initiates a speculative philosophy by means of a 'history of the culture of consciousness'.

'Consciousness' does not here only refer to the theoretical aspect of perception. Like Fichte, and in accordance with idealistic system thinking, Hegel is concerned with the entire range of what is human, including morality, society, religion, and art. These are not simply placed one next to the other, but appear rather in a logical hierarchy that follows from consciousness' experience of itself. Consciousness makes a claim which then turns out to be excessive given what it actually achieves. It thus corrects itself in order to overcome this disparity between what it claimed and what it actually achieved, and thus undergoes a 'reversal of consciousness', which brings about a new form of consciousness. As these self-corrections repeat themselves, consciousness reaches a higher level of development which is only brought to completion when claim and achievement come together in the spirit which is transparent to itself.

In this process, Kantian ethics primarily appears in the chapter on 'Conscience, the beautiful soul, evil and its forgiveness'. In his philosophy of right, Hegel shows how the unspoken principle of justice—the free will—becomes real as persons coexist but do so under one of the conditions of modernity: alienation. This practical dialectic mixes normative principles with a diagnosis of modernity. And in that Hegel diverges from Kant in his concepts of freedom and of law, but also in his dialectic argumentation. He understands freedom as a 'being-with-oneself-in-the-other', and the law as 'the existence of free will'—not as Kant's universally compatible freedom—whereby 'existence (Dasein)' means as much as 'complete reality'.

In the course of its dialectical process, free will attains to ever more substantial forms, by means of which Hegel believes he can overcome Kant's distinction between legality and morality. This path takes us from a simply external free will, 'abstract right' (property, contract, fraud, as well as crime and punishment), through the internal free will that is morality (intention and guilt, intent and well-being, the good and conscience), to the external and internal free will, ethical life (Sittlichkeit). Following the model of the antique city and its theoretician, Aristotle, Hegel understands ethical life as the unity of an individual's moral conceptions with those of the 'ethical powers' of a concrete state, with its laws, customs, and religion. This unity is, however, only attained through yet another dialectical process, which goes through three institutions where communication is successful inasmuch as the rights and duties in them help their subjects to become free. The process begins with the family, an 'unmediated home', and continues with alienation from family, history, and religion in the civil society of work and the economy, leading to a 'mediated home', the state. Because the legitimate form of the state, the state of law, is based upon the nation and only exists in concrete, individual states, Hegel rejects all forms of cosmopolitanism. Instead of validating Kant's far-sighted idea of a global rule of law, he flatly rejects it.

Friedrich Schleiermacher's book *Ethics* (1812) and in particular its concept of virtue is influenced by Kant. This applies both to the critique (reminiscent of Schiller) of the idea that virtue consists in a harmonious relationship 'of every inclination to all others', but also to his positive definition of virtue: 'Virtue as the pure ideal content of an action is disposition. Virtue as reason in time is ability' (*Ethics*, 'The Doctrine of Virtue', Sect. 17). For in this definition we recognize Kant's distinction between intelligible and phenomenal virtue (virtus noumenon/phainomenon). And depending upon how one interprets it, one might also recognize Kant in the phrase that follows, 'Neither can ever be entirely separated' (*Ethics*, 'The Doctrine of Virtue', Sect. 17).

22.4 TWO ANTI-KANTIAN KANTIANS

Arthur Schopenhauer (1788–1860) was a great admirer of Kant, and considered Kant's first critique 'the most important book that was ever written in Europe'. But he is particularly hard on Kant's ethics, especially the systematic account of his ethics of right. He can only attribute the lacking breadth, clarity, and acuity of the 'Doctrine of Right' to Kant's old age (*The World as Will and Representation*, Book 4, §62).

As the title of his own main work already indicates—*The World 'as Will' and Representation* (quotation marks added)—Schopenhauer maintains Kant's primacy of practical reason. In accord with many Kantian ethicists, including those of German Idealism, he attempts to overcome Kant's dualism of nature and freedom, but, unlike the idealists, he does so in a 'material' manner, and from the perspective of a philosophy of life. Schopenhauer extends Kant's transcendental view; he does not see the ground for a human being's ability to experience the world as a whole in the power of thought but rather in the body—which wills to live. Thus, it is not Marx but first Schopenhauer who places philosophy on its head—more exactly on its body—inasmuch as the will visibly objectifies itself according to Schopenhauer. In this way Kant's moral philosophy, which he had strictly isolated from all empirical anthropology, becomes an empirical voluntaristic metaphysics of life.

The underlying philosophy is to be found in two academic prize essays that were later published as *The Two Fundamental Problems of Ethics*. The one deals with 'the freedom of the human will' (and was 'crowned' by the Royal Norwegian Academy of Sciences in January 1839; the other, which was 'not crowned' by the Royal Danish Academy of Sciences, considers the 'basis of morality'. The first text grants Kant something that however results in a new kind of dualism: that the will in itself—for human beings this is one's intelligible character—is free, but concrete individuals are not. Their empirical characters are the lifelong determined appearance of their atemporal intelligible characters. According to Schopenhauer human beings are what they are once and for all, and astonishingly they must bear the metaphysical responsibility for it.

In his discussion of the moral law, Schopenhauer wants to show that Kant's ideas of practical reason and of the categorical imperative are altogether unjustified, wholly fictitious 'a priori bubbles of soap'. In their stead he places empirical incentives, which in the case of morality, are stronger than the basic human incentive, egoism. Influenced by Buddhism, the true foundation of morality consists in active compassion.

This compassion need not be aroused anew every time, but rather, the experience of suffering should lead to a 'purpose that is established once and for all'. Schopenhauer is not content with criticizing Kant and proposing an alternative. In his 'sideworks' and 'supplements', the *Parerga and Paralipomena* (1851), he offers amongst others 'Aphorisms on life wisdom' in which he proves to be a master of philosophical prose. His highest rule is apparently taken from Aristotle: 'The prudent man seeks not pleasure, but an absence of pain'. Schopenhauer's pithy directives do not aim at a happy life, but rather one that avoids harm in an inauspicious world. For example: 'Every restriction is a source of happiness. The more restrained the circle of our past, our influence and our acquaintances, the happier we are: the further this circle extends, the more we feel afflicted or frightened; our worries, wishes and fears grow and multiply in accordance with it.'

In the second generation after idealist philosophy, *Friedrich Nietzsche* (1844–1900) developed an ethics that seems to be even less Kantian. A philologist, writer, and philosopher born in a rectory, according to his own lights an 'artist, shaman and seducer', 'more dynamite than man' (*Ecce Homo*, Part IV: 'Why I am a Destiny', Sect. 1), who ranks among the most read philosophers of all time, does indeed sharply criticize the philosopher from Königsberg. And yet he also holds him in high esteem. Though he considers it a pipe dream to view the moral concepts of virtue, duty, and the good as 'impersonal and universally valid' (*The Antichrist*, § 18), this does not prevent him, for example, from granting Kant 'tremendous courage and wisdom' (*The Birth of Tragedy*, §18).

Above all, Nietzsche maintains Kant's primacy of practical reason. Following Schopenhauer, he interprets it as a philosophy of life and also attempts to overcome Kant's dualism. However, he rejects Schopenhauer's principle of compassion, appealing among others to Kant in his 'contempt for compassion', which he classifies as a slave morality (*On the Genealogy of Morals*, Preface, §5). In its stead he places the principle of the intensification of life, which he terms the 'will to power'. This will can certainly fill one 'with pity'; the (Kantian/) Christian 'thou shalt' must however give way to the Dionysian 'I want'.

The principle of an 'intensification of life' in a free spirit leads to an 'eruption of power and will aimed at self-determination', and more generally to those sovereign individuals who bow neither to their own emotions nor to social standards. They act freely and of their own accord, which reminds us of Kant, though shorn of his morality: the individuals who have escaped from their straightjackets are self-determined and no longer weighed down by a 'bad conscience'. This fear having been lifted, they follow the morality of a heightened life, which links 'mastery over oneself' with a 'mastery over one's circumstances, over nature and any creature of lesser will'. In the end, Nietzsche is only concerned with the sovereign individual, the human being as an aristocrat of the mind.

One of the theses of which Nietzsche is particularly proud—that humanity was not endowed from birth with pure practical reason but instead had to gradually develop it—he actually shares with Kant, perhaps without knowing it. The research project that goes with it, his genealogy of morals, does however go beyond Kant.

22.5 NEO-KANTIANS

The neo-Kantian rallying call 'Back to Kant!' was also headed in philosophical ethics. The movement, which ruled over German-language academic philosophy for half a century from 1870 to 1920, understood philosophy primarily as epistemology and as the foundational discipline underlying the sciences, which were first understood to include mathematics and natural science, then also the social sciences and humanities, and with Ernst Cassirer the world outside of science.

Herman Cohen (1842–1918), the founder and main proponent of Marburg neo-Kantianism, wrote an *Ethics of pure Will* (1904), which promises already in its title a comprehensive new foundation for ethics in a Kantian spirit. In fact, the author confined himself to a legal and political ethics, which he links to a foundation for the humanities and which leads to the idea of an ethical socialism. Cohen wants to tie ethics back to a fact of science, and finds this fact in the humanities, the paradigm being jurisprudence.

The concept of the autonomy of moral individuals is certainly important for people in a concrete way. Cohen emphasizes four aspects: (1) autonomy as giving laws to oneself, understood as 'lawgiving towards the self'; (2) self-determination, that is, an active response to the world; (3) responsibility towards oneself which begins with accountability, and (4) self-preservation, which maintains or re-establishes moral identity under the condition of fallibility.

Another neo-Kantian, Max Wentscher (1862–1942), is so far from Kant as to optimistically believe 'that in the end moral behaviour is actually followed by happiness' (*Pädagogik. Ethische Grundlegung und System* 1926: 374).

The second, south-western German school of neo-Kantians frees ethics again from a 'logic of the humanities' and thus brings it back closer to Kant's own project. Here Kant's double concept of the formal and the material plays an important role. According to Bruno Bauch, 'life only receives value inasmuch as it is dependent upon an absolute, upon ends that rise above life itself' (*Ethik* 1907: 264). This end must in no way be determined by the content of the material act (*Ethik* 1907: 257), and the empirical, material conditions, the individual circumstances, fall away: 'The individual finds in his cultural context the material upon which he is to apply his moral disposition' (*Ethik* 1907: 265).

22.6 CONTEMPORARY KANTIAN ETHICISTS

The most impressive and certainly the most influential Kantian ethics of the last few decades is that of the Harvard philosopher John Rawls (1921–2002). His main work, *A Theory of Justice* (1971), which has been the subject of discussions for a long time now, has become a classic. He succeeds in bringing about such a profound change in ethics and political philosophy that one can speak of a multifaceted paradigm shift.

The paradigm shift first affects the task of philosophical ethics. Whereas English-speaking philosophy was primarily concerned with metaethical questions, Rawls focused directly on a Kantian and systematic topic, justice. Starting out from a basic moral intention, freedom and equality of all citizens, Rawls succeeds in formulating complicated issues in such a way that they simply make sense: the idea of an original position corresponds approximately to the state of nature of the classical theory of the social contract. But it already contains a moral element, the veil of ignorance, which incorporates the fundamental idea of justice, impartiality. Later, in *Political Liberalism* (1993), he adds the idea of an overlapping consensus.

Rawls' second basic change: when the English-speaking world before Rawls had been concerned with ethical questions, it had focused upon utilitarianism; Rawls, however, promoted an alternative basic moral intuition. The utilitarian principle of the 'greatest happiness for the greatest number' is replaced by 'justice as fairness'. The benefits and the burdens of every form of social cooperation should be distributed in such a way that each individual receives the greatest possible advantage. The philosophical role model is now no longer Bentham or Mill but Kant. Utilitarianism has been driven into a defensive position in much of the English-speaking world, and Kant has moved into the foreground.

The third change consists in two further elements which open up ethics to an interdisciplinary debate and force the previously dominant philosophy of language into the background. Rawls borrows the elements from two different styles of thought and kinds of arguments and thus shows how to reconcile methodologically competing trends. In order to rationally decide between utilitarianism and justice as fairness by using a kind of 'moral geometry', Rawls resorts on the one hand to the 'language' of decision and game theories, which currently dominate economics. With their help he tries to bring classical contract theory, and primarily its Kantian version, to a higher level of abstraction in order to reconstruct every single element. The reformulated contract theory derives the fundamental principles of justice from enlightened self-interest. The veil of ignorance is of course a precondition as it ensures that one's own interest coincides with the standpoint of justice.

On the other hand, Rawls proceeds in an almost empirical fashion, seeking to bring the well-considered moral judgements of a society into a coherent whole, which he calls a 'reflective equilibrium'. Rawls assumes an environment that is already normatively determined, which restricts the reach of his contract theory. From a methodological and legitimatory point of view, his is primarily a coherence theory of justice and only secondarily a contractarian one. Whereas a contract theorist would argue ahistorically using decision theory, for Rawls history and one's culture play an important role in the reflective equilibrium.

For this reason *A Theory of Justice* is a kind of hermeneutic of Western democracy and, despite its academic credentials, a personal book. It not only shows which learning processes can be rationally advocated, but also the path that American and Rawls's own learning processes have taken. In the end, *A Theory of Justice* presents itself as a specific society's, and even a specific person's sophisticated—but yet only well-considered—idea of justice. This raises a question that Rawls cannot, but Kant can, answer: What is one to do when Rawls's assumption of a substantial minimal consensus about justice begins to fracture in periods of moral crisis or when cultures clash?

A fourth change: because of his recourse to the language of economics, Rawls runs the risk of making purely formal observations. To avoid this, he not only advances the ideas of well-considered judgements and of the reflective equilibrium but also that of social primary goods, of which everyone should desire as much as possible. These are goods that are produced through cooperation and which are indispensable for people's life plans, and thus are generally valued in a pluralistic society. Furthermore, Rawls also allows for theories with empirical content.

Fifthly, Rawls expects a fair amount of welfare from the American political liberalism, thus following in the tradition of John Stuart Mill and John Dewey, who have helped to bridge the gap between liberalism and socialism, or Marxism, which has prevailed since the nineteenth century. However, this expectation, which proved successful both in political debates and even in politics itself, applies mostly to the USA. There, political and philosophical discussions were primarily influenced by the classical liberalism which Locke inspired, that is, linking rights to freedom and to democratic participation with expectations that market economies will produce wealth. Rawls, on the contrary, adds a substantial welfare state element to liberalism, something that needn't be argued for in such a basic manner in western and northern Europe. The normative core of Rawls's theory of justice consists of two of his famous principles of justice:

> *First Principle:* each person is to have an equal right to the most extensive scheme of equal basic liberties that is possible for all.
>
> *Second Principle:* social and economic inequalities are to be arranged as follows:
>
> (a) they must, conditioned upon the just savings principle, bring the greatest benefit to the least advantaged, and
> (b) they must be attached to offices and positions open to all under conditions of fair equality of opportunity (1971, §46).

Of Rawls's principles of justice, the first is broadly Kantian and the second half of the second principle is uncontroversial and has long been accepted. The same goes for the first half of the second principle, the *difference principle*, inasmuch as it is concerned with the conditions for realizing these basic rights. But many are still sceptical of the further claim that the least advantaged must be benefited as much as possible. A Rawlsian state is more paternalistic than generally accepted ideas of justice would permit.

In the *Lectures on the History of Moral Philosophy* (2000), Rawls demonstrates his profound understanding of modern ethics. His section on Kant confirms what one might already have suspected when reading Rawls' *A Theory of Justice*, namely, that when he appeals to Kant he is mostly thinking of his general foundation of morals, primarily the *Groundwork to the Metaphysics of Morals* and the *Critique of Practical Reason* or even *Religion*. But he neglects the one text which is of systematic importance for a theory of political justice, the 'Doctrine of Right'.

For a long time western Marxism rejected any kind of philosophical ethics. The social theory of the 'Frankfurt Institute for Social Research', which was developed in the 1920s and 1930s and stood within this tradition originating in Hegel and Marx, expanded the ideas of Kant, Hegel, Schopenhauer, and Nietzsche in light of social interests, sometimes of Jewish messianism and of Freud's psychoanalysis. The movement called itself 'Critical Theory' but went also under the name 'Frankfurt School'.

According to one of the protagonists, *Max Horkheimer*, human beings, by using technology and science to dominate nature, must pay for this increase in their power with greater alienation from that over which they exercise this power (*Traditional and Critical Theory* 1937). Rather than underpin unjust social relations, 'critical theory' instead wants to change the world into one that justly responds to the needs and powers of people who are no longer alienated. With this aim it draws attention to hidden forms of oppression and exploitation, explains their origin, and formulates a state in which we are freed either of actual (the modest utopia) or all alienation (the grand utopia).

Though the protagonists, being Jewish, must go into exile, where they take into account the protection of human rights (an advantage of liberal democracies), they nevertheless remain for a long time fixated upon a critique of capitalist economies instead of adding a theory of liberal democracy to this critique. *Jürgen Habermas* (1929–) fundamentally alters this state of affairs. This sociologist, political essayist, and philosopher leads the Critical Theory out of the 'negative limitations' into which Theodor W. Adorno had brought it. He soon expands the Theory into a theory of democracy (*The Structural Transformation of the Public Sphere*, 1962) and softens its sceptical view of the sciences. Influenced by *Karl-Otto Apel* (1922–), he no longer takes the characteristic feature of humanity to be Marx's concept of human nature (Gattungswesen) but rather linguistic communication, which counterbalances the damage done to people by capitalism (*The Theory of Communicative Action*, 2 vols., 1981).

Above all, with recourse to Kant's universalistic ethics, Habermas overcomes the scepticism towards Kant's moral philosophy and with Apel opposes a discourse ethics to it: moral standards can be justified through non-coercive discourse either as its preconditions or as its conclusions (*Moral Consciousness and Communicative Action*, 1983). Only consensus arrived at under ideal conditions counts, not just any naturally arising consensus. These conditions establish an ideal speech situation of non-coercive communication of equal opportunities. Such conditions, however, impose preconditions or structural elements on the discourse. From a legitimatory point of view, these conditions are normative basic principles, which a discourse must meet in order to function as a moral criterion. Discourse ethics thus is in danger of becoming circular: a number of the principles whose moral validity is to be assessed are presupposed by the very enterprise which aims to establish a moral criterion with which to verify the moral validity of all principles. Some of the moral elements for which a criterion is being sought are included, as preconditions and structural characteristics, in the definition of this very criterion.

These elements defining the ideal discourse consist in precisely those fundamental principles which are the primary objects of a philosophical grounding of morality. Explicitly or not, they imply that the discussants' life and limb are inviolable; that one seek consensus consciously and freely, that is, without coercion from any side; that the discussants not lie or deceive one another, etc. The primary task consists not in establishing a discourse under ideal preconditions but rather in finding a criterion for establishing these very preconditions.

As discourse can only function as a moral criterion under certain conditions, which however are no longer the object of the discourse but are presupposed by it, morality must be given a more radical foundation. This must begin, as *Otfried Höffe* (1943–) emphasizes, with a conceptual analysis of morality, of the highest good itself, which can then supply a criterion for morality as a whole. This criterion can then be used to establish the principles of an ideal discourse. Because the protection of life and limb as opposed to violence or truthfulness as opposed to lies and deception represent universalizable principles, they are rightly included in ideal discourse as presuppositions, as prejudices. Hence ideal discourse is no longer the highest moral principle but rather the universalizability of its maxims, that is, the criterion of its ideality.

This new principle entails neither a consensus-seeking process of acting and negotiating persons, nor one that takes place under real or ideal conditions. Instead, it requires a thought experiment through which the conditions of an ideal discourse are first legitimized: the highest criterion does not lie in a real or ideal discourse but rather in this thought experiment, which, moreover, everyone can carry out for themselves. And this ability is in no way secondary for human beings. It characterizes them as moral subjects, who are, despite their intersubjective relations, for the most part individually responsible. It is however up to the moral philosopher, and not moral subjects in general, to offer an understandable description of universalization. The latter nevertheless can—without the help of a philosopher—master the basic task of following maxims that might apply to anyone's situation.

Because they are valid for everyone, maxims can be given an interpersonal basis. Wherein lies, then, the difference from discourse ethics? There are four such differences. (1) From a legitimatory point of view, universalizability is primary and (logically) implies an interpersonal basis. (2) Two levels are important for an ethics of universalizable maxims, moving from what is morally right to what is morally good. (3) The universalizability of principles of the will, maxims, allow duties towards oneself, something discourse ethics usually denies. (On Höffe's systematic account of moral philosophy, which borrows from Kant but also from Aristotle's ethic of a good life, see 2007; see also Höffe 1990, and 2001.) (4) Finally, a systematic account of right, that is, of what we owe each other, must be distinguished from an account of virtue, of that which is meritorious. (For a critical account of right, see Höffe 1990; for its cosmopolitical 'sequel', see Höffe 1999.)

In his book *The Philosophical Discourse of Modernity* (1985) Habermas criticizes the postmodern critique of reason as a half-hearted and inconsistent way to overcome modern philosophies of the subject, and opposes his communicative concept of reason to it. In his 'Contributions to a Discourse Theory of Law and Democracy' (in *Between Facts and Norms* (1992)) he finally abandons Critical Theory's long-held principle of freedom from domination (Herrschaftsfreiheit) and links the concept of right to democracy: democracy is none other than society's influence upon itself through laws. However, instead of providing a philosophical basis for the concept of right—say, as a rational form of social coexistence which culminates in respect for human rights—Habermas considers the latter to be a fact of evolution. Furthermore, he relieves national sovereignty of substantial moral requirements, even though, in order to be legitimate, it must conform to human rights. He thereby does not entirely avoid the danger of reducing political legitimacy to mere procedural legality.

Apel, who strongly influenced Habermas' turn, raises Peirce's theory of truth, consensus achieved by 'endless investigation', to the rank of an *a priori*. This is meant to overcome the 'methodological solipsism', which is supposedly found in Kant, according to which the individual 'I' is the ground of all objective validity. For Apel, the unlimited community of communication (Kommunikationsgemeinschaft), that is, the ideal and universal community of adult individuals free of social constraints, is the foundational, final principle both of knowledge (consensus theory of truth) and also of action (consensus or discourse theory of morality). It can only be denied 'under penalty of a (pragmatic) self-contradiction'.

BIBLIOGRAPHY

1. *A General Outline of Kant's Ethics*

Kant, I.*Gesammelte Schriften*, herausgegeben von der Königlich-Preußischen Akademie der Wissenschaften zu Berlin. Berlin 1902 ff. English translation: *The Cambridge Edition of the Works of Immanuel Kant in Translation*, ed. by H. Allison et al. Cambridge.

2. *Receptive Kantians*

Abicht, J. H. 1790. *Neues System einer philosophischen Tugendlehre aus der Natur der Menschheit entwickelt*. Leipzig.

Beck, J. S. 1793–1796. *Erläuternder Auszug aus den critischen Schriften des Herrn Prof. Kant auf Anrathen desselben*, 3 Bde. Riga.

Bernhardi, A. Bethmann 1796–1797. *Gemeinfassliche Darstellung der Kantischen Lehren*, 2 Bde. Freyberg.

Hölderlin, F. 1962. *Sämtliche Werke. Stuttgarter Hölderlin-Ausgabe. Im Auftrag des Württembergischen Kultministeriums und der Deutschen Akademie in München*, hrsg. v. F. Beissner. Stuttgart.

Mellin, G. S. A. 1902. *Marginalien und Register zu Kants Grundlegung zur Metaphysik der Sitten, Kritik der praktischen Vernunft, Kritik der Urteilskraft*, bearbeitet von L. Goldschmidt. Gotha.

Metz, A. 1796. *Kurze und deutliche Darstellung des Kantischen Systems, nach seinem Hauptzwecke, Gange und innern Werthe.* Bamberg.

Paul, J. 1922–1926. *Die Briefe Jean Pauls*, 4 Bde., herausgegeben von Eduard Berend. München.

Zwanziger, J. C. 1794. *Commentar über Herr Prof. Kants Kritik der praktischen Vernunft.* Leipzig.

3. Early Creative Kantians

Fichte, J. G. 1794. *Grundlage der gesamten Wissenschaftslehre als Handschrift für seine Zuhörer*, in *Gesamtausgabe der Bayerischen Akademie der Wissenschaften. 40 Bände*, herausgegeben von R. Lauth, E. Fuchs, und H. Gliwitzky. Stuttgart-Bad Cannstatt, 1962 ff., Bd. 1.

—— 1798. *Das System der Sittenlehre nach den Prinzipien der Wissenschaftslehre*, in *Gesamtausgabe der Bayerischen Akademie der Wissenschaften. 40 Bände*, herausgegeben von R. Lauth, E. Fuchs und H. Gliwitzky. Stuttgart-Bad Cannstatt, 1962 ff., Bd. 5.

—— 1804. *Grundzüge des Gegenwärtigen Zeitalters*, in *Gesamtausgabe der Bayerischen Akademie der Wissenschaften. 40 Bände*, herausgegeben von R. Lauth, E. Fuchs und H. Gliwitzky. Stuttgart-Bad Cannstatt, 1962 ff., Bd. 8.

Hegel, G. F. W. 1807. *Phänomenologie des Geistes*, in *G. F. W. Hegel, Werke in 20 Bänden. Auf der Grundlage der Werke von 1832 bis 1845*, neu ediert. Red. E. Moldenhauer und K. M. Michel. Frankfurt am Main, 1969–1971, Bd. 3.

—— 1821. *Grundlinien der Philosophie des Rechts*, in *Werke in 20 Bänden. Auf der Grundlage der Werke von 1832 bis 1845*, neu ediert. Red. E. Moldenhauer und K. M. Michel. Frankfurt am Main, 1969–1971, Bd. 7.

Reinhold, K. L. 1789. *Versuch einer neuen Theorie des menschlichen Vostellungsvermoegens.* Prag.

Schelling, F. W. J. 1809. *Philosophische Untersuchungen über das Wesen der menschlichen Freiheit*, in *Schellings Werke nach der Originalausgabe in neuer Anordnung*, herausgegeben von M. Schröter. München, 1927 ff., Bd. 4.

Schiller, F. 1943/ 1962. *Schillers Werke: Nationalausgabe*, begr. von J. Petersen, hrsg. im Auftr. der Nationalen Forschungs- und Gedenkstätten der Klassischen Deutschen Literatur in Weimar und des Schiller-Nationalmuseums in Marbach, Bd.1. *Gedichte in der Reihenfolge ihres Erscheinens: 1776–1799.* Weimar, 1943. Bd. 2 *Philosophische Schriften.* Weimar, 1962.

Schleiermacher, F. 1812–1813. *Ethik*, herausgegeben von H.-J. Birkner. Hamburg, 1990.

4. Two Anti-Kantian Kantians

Nietzsche, F. 1872. *Geburt der Tragödie aus dem Geiste der Musik*, in F. Nietzsche, *Sämtliche Werke. Kritische Studienausgabe in 15 Bänden*, herausgegeben von G. Colli und M. Montinari. New York und München, 1967ff., Bd. 1.

—— 1882. *Zur Genealogie der Moral—eine Streitschrift*, in F. Nietzsche, *Sämtliche Werke. Kritische Studienausgabe in 15 Bänden*, herausgegeben von G. Colli und M. Montinari. New York und München, 1967ff., Bd. 5.

—— 1895. *Der Antichrist*, in F. Nietzsche, *Sämtliche Werke. Kritische Studienausgabe in 15 Bänden*, herausgegeben von G. Colli und M. Montinari. New York und München, 1967ff., Bd. 6.

—— 1908. *Ecce Homo*, in F. Nietzsche, *Sämtliche Werke. Kritische Studienausgabe in 15 Bänden*, herausgegeben von G. Colli und M. Montinari. New York und München, 1967ff., Bd. 6.

Schopenhauer, A. 1841. *Die beiden Grundprobleme der Ethik: Ueber die Freiheit des menschlichen Willens, Ueber das Fundament der Moral*, in A. Schopenhauer, *Sämtliche Werke in 5 Bänden*, herausgegeben von W. von Loehneysen. Frankfurt am Main, 2005.

Schopenhauer, A. 1851. *Parerga und Paralipomena*, 2 Bände, in A. Schopenhauer, *Sämtliche Werke in 5 Bänden*, herausgegeben von W. von Loehneysen. Frankfurt am Main, 2005.

—— 1859. *Die Welt als Wille und Vorstellung*, 2 Bände, in A. Schopenhauer, *Sämtliche Werke in 5 Bänden*, herausgegeben von W. von Loehneysen. Frankfurt am Main, 2005.

5. *Neo-Kantians*

Bauch, B. 1907. *Ethik*. Berlin.
Cohen, H. 1904. *Ethik des reinen Willens*. Berlin.
Wentscher, M. 1926. *Pädagogik. Ethische Grundlegung und System*. Berlin.

6. *Contemporary Kantian Ethicists*

Habermas, J. 1962–1991. *The Structural Transformation of the Public Sphere*, tr. T. Burger and F. Lawrence. Cambridge, MA, 1991 (orig.: *Strukturwandel der Öffentlichkeit. Untersuchungen zu einer Kategorie der bürgerlichen Gesellschaft*. Neuwied, 1962).

—— 1981–1984. *The Theory of Communicative Action*. 2 vols., tr. T. McCarthy. Boston 1984 and 1987 (orig.: *Theorie des kommunikativen Handelns*, 2 Bände. Frankfurt am Main, 1981).

—— 1983–1990. *Moral Consciousness and Communicative Action*, tr. C. Lenhardt and S. W. Nicholsen. Cambridge, MA, 1990 (orig.: *Moralbewußtsein und kommunikatives Handelns*, 2 Bände. Frankfurt am Main, 1983).

—— 1985–1990. *The Philosophical Discourse of Modernity: Twelve Lectures*, tr. F. G. Lawrence. Cambridge, MA, 1990 (orig.: *Der philosophische Diskurs der Moderne*. Frankfurt am Main, 1985).

—— 1992–1996. *Between Facts and Norms: Contributions to a Discourse Theory of Law and Democracy*, tr. W. Rehg. Cambridge, MA, 1996 (orig.: *Faktizität und Geltung. Beiträge zur Diskurstheorie des Rechts und des demokratischen Rechtsstaates*. Frankfurt am Main, 1992).

Höffe, O. 1990–2002. *Categorial Principles of Law*, tr. M Migotti. University Park, PA, 2002 (orig.: *Kategorische Rechtsprinzipien: ein Kontrapunkt der Moderne*, Frankfurt am Main, 1990–1993).

—— 1999–2007. *Democracy in an Age of Globalisation*, tr. D. Haubrich and M. Ludwig. Dordrecht, 2007 (orig.: *Demokratie im Zeitalter der Globalisierung*. München, 1999).

—— 2001–2006. *Kant's Cosmopolitan Theory of Law and Peace*, tr. A. Newton. Cambridge, 2006 (orig.: '*Königliche Völker*'. *Zu Kants kosmopolitischer Rechts- und Friedenstheorie*. Frankfurt am Main, 2001).

—— 2007–2010. *Can Virtue Make Us Happy?: The Art of Living and Morality*, tr. D. McGaughey. Evanston, IL, 2010 (orig: *Lebenskunst und Moral. Oder macht Tugend glücklich?*, München, 2007).

Horkheimer, M. 1970–1990. 'Traditional and Critical Theory', in his *Critical Theory: Selected Essays*, New York, 1990 (orig.: *Traditionelle und kritische Theorie*, Frankfurt am Main, 1970).

Rawls, J. 1971. *A Theory of Justice*. Cambridge, MA.
—— 1993. *Political Liberalism*. Cambridge, MA.
—— 2000. *Lectures on the History of Moral Philosophy*, Cambridge, MA.

CHAPTER 23

....

POST-KANTIANISM

....

RAYMOND GEUSS

THE subject matter of this chapter is a sequence of thinkers who were active between roughly the late 1780s and late 1880s and whose views on ethics are considered to be of continuing interest in the early twenty-first century. These include Jacobi, Schiller, Friedrich Schlegel, Hegel, Kierkegaard, Schopenhauer, and Nietzsche. One may call these people 'post-Kantians' if one wishes, but they do not constitute anything like a school in the strong sense in which for instance the New Academy in the ancient world or the 'Romantics' in the 1790s were a school. The Romantics (the two Schlegel brothers, Novalis, Tieck, and others) were a small group of people all of whom knew each other, who were committed to a number of common ideas, developed their views in discussion with each other, and even occasionally wrote works jointly. The 'post-Kantians' who are the subject of this chapter also did not form a 'school' in a weaker sense: they did not all discover something which they thought was particularly important and distinctive in Kant's philosophy and which they thought it fundamentally important to endorse, develop, revise, or criticize. It was not even the case that each of them independently of the others was inspired by a different distinctive feature of Kant's philosophy. Some, such as Schiller, did see their work as a direct (positive or negative) response to Kant, but others, like Kierkegaard, would more properly be called 'post-Hegelians' in that Hegel and his followers were the main objects of their criticism, and one of them, Nietzsche, was, if anything, a 'post-' (that is, 'anti-') Platonist and anti-Christian, who had no relation to Kant except to the extent to which he was one more instance of a general type of Christian rationalism deriving ultimately from Plato.

The era under discussion begins historically with the French Revolution and the initial public assimilation of the Kantian philosophy, and ends when the Second German Empire succeeded in establishing itself and neo-Kantianism was beginning to consolidate its hold on academic philosophy. The period falls into two almost equal halves, with the caesura being conveniently marked by the traumatic failure of the revolutionary uprisings which took place throughout Europe in 1848–1849.

The best way to understand this period in the history of ethics as a whole is to put aside the common model for studying the history of philosophy which consists in assuming that philosophy is a free-standing, internally structured, and unified continuous conversation, in other words a continuous sequence of responses by one philosopher to what previous philosophers have said. For certain short periods in particular epochs, this might be a useful way of representing what was going on. Locke did read Descartes and can be seen as responding to his views. Hume did read Descartes and Locke and can be understood as responding to them. Kant did read Descartes, Locke, and Hume (among many others) and was trying to 'answer' them. However, this model gives a completely incorrect account of the nineteenth century as a whole, which is *not* a period structured around a single *continuous* conversation. The discussion is broken and discontinuous. Fichte read Kant, Schelling read Kant and Fichte, and Hegel read all three of the aforementioned, but there is a clear rupture after that, in 1849. Political reform and progressive politics had become closely associated with Idealism and particularly with Hegel's optimistic view that reason was in itself historically sufficiently powerful eventually to sweep aside archaic, repressive social structures. This view came to seem completely unfounded when in 1849 'reason' showed itself to be no match for the bayonets of various princes, kings, and emperors, and when 'rational' reform failed, idealism itself was discredited. Between 1850 and 1900, the works of the Idealists, including those of Hegel, were not reprinted, and not widely read or studied. Thus, Nietzsche, who was born in 1844 and whose training in his youth was in any case as a historical philologist, probably never read through and certainly never studied carefully any work by Hegel. In addition, philosophers in the nineteenth century were not merely trying to respond to what other previous philosophers had said, but were also trying to respond to actual historical events. If Kant wanted to 'answer' Hume on causality, Hegel wanted *both* to respond to Kant by criticizing what he took to be some of the philosophical deficiencies he thought he had discovered in Kant's view, *and* to develop a 'philosophy' which would allow him to understand certain real historical events such as the Napoleonic Wars, events on which Kant, who died in 1803, could obviously not have had anything to say at all. External events break into the conversation by virtually forcing certain historically specific topics on to the agenda, but also by producing more intangible changes in the way people felt and thought, what they were able to imagine, and so on.

23.1 IDEALISM

Although, as we saw, the model of philosophy as continuous conversation is a nonstarter for the period between the late 1780s and the late 1880s as a whole, the model does have a certain limited plausibility and usefulness for the first half of this epoch, in that during this period there was a common conversation among the philosophers whose work we still read about a set of shared topics and burning issues. There were three common topics—the self-destruction of rational theology, the French Revolution, and the alienation generated by the new commercial society—and there was a single point of common reference in that everyone in it *did* read Kant, and saw their own task as in some sense that of responding to his work, and read the work of predecessors who were responding to Kant. Part of the unique vitality of philosophy during this period was that it was *both* (incipiently) academic *and* also had a distinct cultural, social, and political reformist agenda. That is, there were some internal, technical issues raised by Kant, and also the great political, social, and economic issues of the day.

23.1.1 Religion and Ethics

To start with the first of the three common topics, philosophers in the eighteenth century saw themselves as confronted with a certain traditional constellation: rational theology—the purported study of the nature of God by reason—Christian religious faith—including faith in supernatural events such as the resurrection of Jesus from the dead—and traditional European ethics were supposed to belong together. Morality was deeply informed in Christian religious faith, and that faith in turn was thought to be, if not exactly supported by, at any rate not incompatible with natural reason. By the end of the eighteenth century this constellation had begun to come under attack: doubts about the ability of reason to discharge its prescribed function of demonstrating the existence of a transcendent, benevolent God of the traditional kind led to fears for the traditional synthesis of ethics and religion.

Friedrich Jacobi, a contemporary of Kant, put the point very powerfully in his *Briefe über die Lehre Spinozas* (written in 1783).[1] Spinoza, he argues, takes the concept of rational inference with appropriate seriousness and *as a consequence* ends up with a completely deterministic metaphysical system of pantheism which leaves no room either for human freedom or for the notion of a personal God. Spinoza, that is, gives a convincing general demonstration of the complete inability of reason to give any rational theology that would accommodate the very possibility of Christianity, and hence also of Christian ethics. Jacobi himself draws the conclusion that one must detach Christian religious faith from Reason altogether, and construe it as based on feeling or intuition. In a highly idiosyncratic, if not perverse, reading of Hume, Jacobi tries to marshal Hume in support of religious faith. After all, Jacobi argues, what Hume claims is that even our certainty that external objects in the world exist is based not on any rational process of inference, but on immediate feeling or habit or faith. Nevertheless, Hume did not think that nothing at all existed in the external world. If this is the case, then why could one not equally appeal to immediate faith in the existence of God? Kant can be seen to take a similar position, asserting that he had 'to destroy knowledge [i.e. the pretensions of rational theology to be a form of knowledge] to make way for faith'.[2]

---

[1] Jacobi 1968; see also Jacobi 1916.   [2] Kant 1956: 28.

23.1.2 The French Revolution

The second major topic was the French Revolution: the fundamental political fact of the contemporary world, and one which had to be understood and assessed (one way or another). The revolution called into question many traditional forms of political authority and the modes of social deference associated with them. Taking this together with the breakdown of traditional natural theology mentioned above, it was perfectly understandable that many contemporaries experienced the vertigo that is often the precursor of philosophical reflection. What form can and will 'the moral life' and ethical reflection take, they wondered, if social life is suddenly supposed to be based not on inherited privilege, unquestioned religious revelation, and historically established status, but rather if *all* claims have to show themselves to be valid in the public forum of reason, and some version of a commitment to the ideals of liberty, equality, and fraternity is accepted? There were, of course, thinkers on *both* sides of the debate about the Revolution, assuming for the sake of simplicity that there were only two sides, but the ones who are nowadays most likely to be remembered (the early Romantics and Idealists including Friedrich Schlegel, Fichte, and Hegel) were all of the opinion that the old feudal order was (rightly) doomed, that the Revolution represented a positive reconfiguration of human life and its possibilities, and that, although the Old Order might resist for a while, it was both unavoidable and desirable that all societies should accommodate themselves politically, socially, and culturally to the undeniable positive features of the Revolution in one way or another; a new form of human life would require new ways of thinking about ethics.

23.1.3 Alienation

Although the first two of the three 'common topics' of discussion are relatively easy to formulate in a sharp way, that is not the case with the third, although, or perhaps because, it is the most important. The central line of thinkers in the late eighteenth and early nineteenth century who have been isolated for discussion thought that there was something problematic or deficient or defective in their own society which prevented their contemporaries from leading a full and happy life and which it was incumbent on them to reflect on and try to help remedy. There was very wide agreement, then, that something was wrong, and also a general sense that the defect had something to do with a loss of social unity or a fragmentation of life. This disharmony or alienation had a number of interlinked aspects: (a) individuals could not see themselves as unified and develop all their powers harmoniously, with the result that they became 'one-sided', (b) individuals were subject to systematically binding, yet irreconcilably conflicting, demands, arising, for instance, from clashes between moral principles, political necessity, and the desire for personal well-being, (c) individuals were unable to 'identify with' and have a positive and affirmative attitude towards themselves, their fellow humans, and their own social and political institutions. This was also virtually universally construed as a specifically contemporary problem. It was not thought to have beset the ancient Greeks (according to Schiller[3] and Hölderlin[4]) or the members of the Universal Church in the middle ages (according to Novalis[5]). This makes it seem natural to supplement traditional forms of ethics with a philosophy of history.

We might in retrospect see the crisis as a result of the advent of what some thinkers were already calling 'commercial society'. There was no consensus on that, but many of the most astute thinkers of the period recognized a need to come to some kind of new understanding of what place was to be assigned to commerce in modern society and its associated virtues (and vices) in modern ethics.

One way of thinking about this is that the basic idealist project was that of establishing 'the truth' in an archaic sense of that term. Thus Hölderlin in one of his letters to his school-friend Hegel, dated 1794, says that when they parted upon leaving school to go out into the world they gave themselves the password 'The Kingdom of God'.[6] By 1796, when Hegel sent to Hölderlin the poem he had dedicated to him, 'Eleusis', his interpretation of this is that it is a covenant: 'to live only [in and for] the free truth, and never, never to make peace with the established order which [attempts to] regulate[s] opinion and sensibility'.[7] 'To live only for the free truth' does not here mean to devote oneself exclusively to the pursuit of theoretical knowledge. If one takes the old scholastic tag, 'veritas est adaequatio rei et intellectus', one might note that 'adaequatio' is symmetrical. Thus the tag can mean either of two things: (a) adaequatio intellectus *ad rem*, which is 'theoretical truth', or (b) adaequatio rei *ad intellectum*, which is a kind of 'practical truth'. Ideally, (full) truth would be a state in which people could fully and correctly know the world around them, including the human world and in particular including their own desires and motivations, and could act in such a way as to express and realize those real desires and aspirations (construing 'aspirations and desires' for the moment as forms of 'intellectus'). To establish 'the truth', then, means to construct a society and establish a form of collective life in which this is realized, and is seen by everyone to be realized. The claim is that in such a society fragmentation and 'alienation' would not exist. Idealist ethics are all directed at the construction, or are informed by a purported anticipation, of such a state of human 'truth' (which the more theologically minded might well have called 'the Kingdom of God').

What this might mean in a slightly more concrete form becomes visible in an anonymous fragment of a manuscript which can be dated to 1796, but which was published only in 1917. This document, which is often referred to as the 'Oldest Fragment of a System of German Idealism', is preserved in Hegel's handwriting, but it is unclear whether he is the author, one of the authors of a collective work, or a mere copyist. The fragment begins at the torn top of the page with the words 'an ethics', which must be the end of a sentence the beginning of which is lost. It then goes on to develop a programme of establishing an organic community in which free humans would cooperate and

[3] Schiller 1967: vol. 5, 570–669.   [4] Hölderlin 2008: 13–175.   [5] Novalis 1961: 3–48.
[6] Hegel 1952: vol. 1, 9.   [7] Hegel 1970: vol. 1, 230–3.

develop their powers without the state. Poetry was to be the normative guide of the new society, and a new religiously tinged popular 'mythology' which was both rational and aesthetically pleasing was to play an important role in unifying people. Social classes were to be reconciled with each other; art, sensation, physics, and reason were to be reunited.

23.2 AWAY FROM KANT

When discussing the nineteenth century, one can, of course, play the game of historical continuity versus discontinuity to great effect: is it best understood as essentially Kantian, that is, as productively developing further certain themes originally introduced by Kant, as essentially anti-Kantian, i.e. as trying to get away from the perceived weaknesses of the Kantian synthesis, or as non-Kantian, i.e. not orienting itself on Kant positively or negatively in any important respect? Most of the existing secondary literature in English on this period takes the first of these tacks, which makes it relatively easy to assimilate the nineteenth century to twentieth-century 'analytic' modes of moral philosophizing, by de-emphasizing the centrality for nineteenth-century thinkers of topics like history, the various forms of social cohesion and alienation—and also, to a lesser extent, of topics like art, culture, real politics, and religious belief—which get short shrift both in Kant and in analytic philosophy. This allows one to construct an apparent continuity between 'modern' forms of ethical thought and similarly ahistorical and asociological canonical texts from earlier periods, such as those by Plato, Aristotle, and Thomas Aquinas. The more philosophically interesting, and also historically accurate, way to see the nineteenth century, however, is as a series of attempts to be radically anti-Kantian and of projects that are simply non-Kantian.

One can see why Kant was thought to have little to contribute to a project like that sketched in the 'Oldest Fragment'. The 'Kant' who figured as a point of orientation at the turn of the nineteenth century was seen as an inherently two-faced figure. He seemed to offer something visibly with his left hand, which he secretly immediately took back with his right. There was the Kant whom Jacobi called 'der Alles-Zermalmer', i.e. 'The Universal Pulveriser', who with his left hand conducted an apparently liberating destruction of all theology and of traditional claims to external authority over the individual. This is the Kant whose pathos of individual autonomy and reason seemed to make him a natural ally of the French revolutionaries, and of their idealist friends. There was however also the Kant of the right hand, who reinstated much of the historical rubbish he seemed to clear away. Thus the Kant of the right hand reintroduced into his system a large number of the propositions of traditional dogmatic theology, such as the existence of God and the immortality of the soul, merely rebranding them as necessary 'postulates of pure practical reason' rather than 'beliefs'. That is, they were claimed to be on the one hand utterly outside the range of human cognition and thus strictly unknowable, but also utterly indispensable as presuppositions to human action, so at best objects of 'faith'.[8] The Kant of the right hand also denied any right of political resistance to tyrannical or oppressive government,[9] was a 'republican' only in a sense which many found etiolated,[10] defended capital punishment on *a priori* grounds,[11] and espoused a number of other reactionary views.

Those who engaged with Kant as an ethical thinker between 1781 and the 1880s agreed on what the essentials of his approach were. Kant, they thought, held that ethics was about a pure absolute 'ought', and that what one 'ought' to do was dictated by reason alone. Ethics had to be insulated from all empirical considerations and the ethical sharply distinguished from the useful, the pleasant, or the aesthetically pleasing, and from anything having to do with the passions and emotions. What one ought to do was called one's 'duty', and the only thing in human life that had unconditional value was doing one's duty for its own sake. One can discover what one's duty is in each instance by applying a simple rule of reason, which is to act in such a way that one could will the principle or 'maxim' of one's action consistently, i.e. without formal contradiction. Since all humans are by nature rational creatures, in following a rule or law which reason itself prescribes, the law of consistent action, I am acting on my own nature and can hence be said to be acting freely. When I am doing my duty for its own sake, and only then, can I be said to be acting freely.

One utterly devastating objection to the whole Kantian project was first formulated by one of Kant's slightly younger colleagues, Herder.[12] Herder notes that there is no discussion at all of the phenomenon of 'language' in the Kantian corpus. Kant writes as if 'reason' were a fully self-transparent human faculty and operates with abstract notions of the 'concept', and of 'judgement', as if the fact that concepts are for us humans finally always embodied in some natural language is of no significance. Herder puts particular emphasis on the fact that any empirical language will be deeply rooted in a specific actually existing form of human social life and thus will have an important historical dimension. Whatever the merits of this Kantian approach for the study of nature, it has none for the study of ethics. No serious study of the ethics of, or for, any real human society can ignore the fact that ethics deals with the actions of humans who structure their world around notions of 'areté', 'fides', 'gratia', sincerity, class-consciousness, or similarly 'thick' and historically specific notions. Oddly enough, this objection, which seems so commonsensical to us in the early twenty-first century and which, if taken seriously, would stop the whole Kantian project from ever even getting started, went largely unnoticed during the first half of the nineteenth century. Perhaps it simply was too far ahead of its time and the entrenched assumptions of rationalism were too unmovable. Hegel to some extent takes over Herder's point about the need to locate ethics in its social and historical context, but for various complex reasons, he does this without explicitly accepting Herder's views on the nature of language. When something like Herder's position about

---

[8] Kant 1967: 140–53.   [9] Kant 1968: vol. 12, 153–64.
[10] Schlegel 1980: vol. 1, 55–73.   [11] Kant 1963: vol. IV, 452–9.
[12] Herder 1799; a theoretically similar, although more obscurely formulated version of the same criticism had already been given in 1784 by Hamann 1957.

the centrality of language to philosophy, and particularly ethics, was formulated next, by Nietzsche, for instance in *Genealogie der Moral*, it seems to be Nietzsche's own independent (re)discovery.

A second objection—perhaps the most common one—to Kant's ethics was that it simply did not perform the task it set itself. It was intended to give people guidance in deciding whether or not something they proposed to do was morally acceptable, but it was 'empty' because it did not really exclude anything; with sufficient ingenuity *any* action could be re-described so as to be made to conform to the dictates of reason. 'All enemies of the Republic should be guillotined'; 'all military men whose honour is challenged should fight a duel'; 'one should lie only in cases of necessity' are all maxims that could be consistently and universally willed, if, as Kant requires, all empirical considerations are excluded. This line is most strongly stated and developed by Hegel, who argues that there must be a notion of substantively rational social institutions and forms of customary life to provide determinate content to Kant's empty formalism.[13]

A third objection addressed the hysterical Kantian concern with policing all the various distinctions he makes, such as that between reason and inclination, and in particular his devotion to the purity of 'duty'. Not only is the exclusive focus on duty implausible in itself, but it also has as one of its effects an unnecessary impoverishment of human life. As Schiller wrote, Kant gives an ethics for the servants in the house, not for the children of the house,[14] and Friedrich Schlegel added tartly that duty was Kant's one-and-all and so he must even have become a great man only out of a sense of duty.[15]

The fourth kind of objection was that Kant's notion of the human subject, ego, or person was at best extraordinarily complex, obscure, and implausible and at worst completely incoherent, as was his view that freedom must consist in acting according to a self-imposed universal law of reason.

The fifth line of objection was to the hidden authoritarianism of Kant. The 'freedom' he preached, it was argued, was in fact pitiless self-subjection to the abstract demands of a highly formalized reason. If every Prussian was said to have a gendarme in his own breast,[16] Kant's intention and partial effect was to keep the consistency-policeman alive, well, and at attention in each of our breasts.

The fourth and the fifth of these objections are both versions of the view that Kant only thought he was post-authoritarian. He really replaced Church and King with a similar authority which he called reason, but retained the same authoritarian structure. The empty formalism and the authoritarian structure complement each other nicely, so that many found it in no way surprising when in the 1930s the Kantian establishment (and the Darwinians), in sharp contrast to the Hegelians and positivists, flocked to the banner of National Socialism with remarkably few reservations. Legislation by reason only counts as self-legislation, and hence freedom, if I am in some way 'essentially' reason. This puts an unbearable weight both on the notion of a single clearly specifiable notion of reason and on my complete identification with such reason. As against Kant's general

[13] Hegel 1970: vol. 7, 252–4.   [14] Schiller 1967: vol. 5, 466.
[15] Schlegel 1980: vol. 1, 189.   [16] Stirner 1972: 55.

view, Friedrich Schlegel claims that freedom must have some element of (potentially disordered and disordering) spontaneity, which Kant, who construes 'spontaneity' as a mere metaphysical or transcendental concept, overlooks and denigrates. Real freedom does not consist only in following a law, even a self-given law, but is instantiated also in such phenomena as whim, idiosyncrasy, fancy.[17] I am fully free only if I can both give myself laws and also decide to violate them. I am not 'really' reason alone, but reason *and* other things too, such as passion, impulse, and so on. If that is true, then why does coercion of passion by reason count as 'freedom' when coercion of reason by passion counts as 'real' coercion? Various good answers might be given to this question, such as empirical observations about the results of allowing one's passion to play itself out in many circumstances, but they will all lie outside the domain of anything Kant can acknowledge.

Kant, then, only appeared to be a post-authoritarian thinker. Actually he replaced King and Church with a sadistic reason and an incoherent 'faith' (in the form of the postulates of pure practical reason). He was of no use whatever in solving the problem of alienation that confronted the idealists and Romantics. His beloved and multitudinous dichotomies (empirical and transcendental, freedom and determinism, means and ends, etc.), and especially his sharp picture of human life as an unrelenting struggle between reason-based pure 'duty' and any form of passion, emotion, or inclination, were an *expression* of the fragmented state of man, not a contribution to a potential solution. What the idealists saw as the historically specific problem of 'alienation' he saw not as a problem, but simply as the human situation, and he preached acceptance of it as an unavoidable necessity. Two decades or so of reflection on the inadequacies of Kant's practical philosophy culminated in Hegel's synthesis: a system based on expanded and substantive notions of freedom and reason as developing inexorably through history and ending in a society of reconciliation. Hegel died in 1832, but he had been an influential teacher, and he left behind a large and institutionally well-placed group of students who carried on his intellectual legacy for a decade and a half.

23.3 POLITICAL RESTAURATION AND PHILOSOPHICAL DISORIENTATION

What, however, is to be done when the public chairs of philosophy are occupied by Hegelians, but Hegel's optimism seems to be refuted by history itself, as it was in 1849? A space opens for philosophical francs-tireurs such as (dismissed) newspaper editors (Marx), failed academics (Schopenhauer), rentier belle-lettristes (Kierkegaard), and professors of classics in early retirement (Nietzsche). Marx, the one of these four who remained most faithful to the original inspiration of the Hegelian project, will be the

---

[17] Schlegel 1980: vol. 2, 9–99.

subject of another chapter in this *Handbook* and so will not be discussed further here. Of the others, all, in one way or another, turned away from politics and the problem of alienation, and became suspicious of claims about the historical effectiveness and normative standing of reason.

23.4 KIERKEGAARD

The Danish philosopher Sören Kierkegaard (1813–1855) can be seen as engaged in a two-step process of trying to restructure 'practical philosophy' away from the concerns of the Idealist period. First, he wishes to shift emphasis away from social and political issues, institutions, practices, habitual forms of behaviour, and social morality to the individual, his relation to his own life, his decisions, and his own identity. The central question of practical philosophy should not be: 'How shall we construct our political and social institutions so as to maximize the possibilities for living a full, happy, rational, non-alienated human life?' but the double-barrelled question: 'How can I be somebody—anybody at all—and, if I am somebody, who am I?' After all, one might think, it makes little sense to investigate what I 'ought' to do if there is no 'me' there in the first place to be subject to potential moral demands, and it is at least arguable that what I ought to do has something to do with who I am. On the other hand, this very question might seem tremendously silly and pointless. Surely, one might argue, questions about my 'identity' are no more than the usual questions about my spatio-temporal location or my properties, including those ascribed to me by others, or my thoughts and beliefs about myself. Kierkegaard does not deny that human beings are creatures who have various properties that can be investigated in the normal empirical way, but he thinks that this misses the point altogether if one is interested in human life and practical agency as seen from the point of view of any given human agent. There is a specific, distinctive, agency-centred sense that can be given to the questions: 'Am I anyone at all?' and 'Who am I?' In this sense it is in principle an open question whether a biologically complete human being is or is not anyone, or, as one might also phrase it, is or is not a self. 'Who am I?' in this context is also properly thought to be a distinctive question, very different in kind from the question '*What* is X?' and one which requires a different mode of investigation and a different kind of answer than *definitio per genus proximum et differentiam specificam*.

Kierkegaard's starting point for asking the question of my identity or my self (of who I am) is Hegel's concept of *Geist*.[18] In the social and moral world the relevant properties I have are ones I *make* myself have. 'Spirit' exists only to the extent to which it is in a process of making itself something; to speak of forms of 'spirit', such as, for instance, 'The Enlightenment' is not to speak of a set of beliefs certain individuals have or factual properties of their society, but of a historical process in which many people in communication with each other act so as to transform themselves and their societies in a certain

---

[18] Hegel 1970: vol. 3, 145, vol. 10, 366–7, vol. 12, 94–105.

way relative to certain ideals and aspirations. One can, as Hegel would put it, isolate a set of characteristic 'beliefs' held by people associated with this transformational process, and this might have some value in some investigative contexts, but to do that without remaining aware of the fact that this is an abstraction which finally makes sense only if related to the full historical process in which it is embedded is to miss the point. So Geist for Hegel has three properties:

(a) it is essentially a social phenomenon, that is a phenomenon involving a group of people who distinguish themselves from each other by saying 'I', but also consider themselves members of a 'we'
(b) it is always essentially historical, in perpetual movement
(c) it is practical: it is self-transformational, a process by which individuals and groups change what they are

To take the example that obsesses Kierkegaard, an archetypical answer to the question 'Who am I?' would be 'I am a Christian'. To be a Christian, however, is not to have certain beliefs, character traits, or simple properties. An inherent part of what it is to be a Christian, if one takes that seriously, is that one is constantly striving for self-improvement in faith and action and never considers oneself to have attained any kind of complete and secure status in either domain. To *be* a Christian means always to be on the path of trying to become a Christian.[19] The similarity with the second of the three characteristics of Hegel's 'spirit' is clear. Similarly, Kierkegaard's account of what it is to be(come) a Christian is not restricted to an account of the acquisition or evaluation of beliefs; there is a practical and transformational aspect to the process. However, Kierkegaard tends to emphasize an aspect of this that is not of great importance for Hegel, namely that trying to become a Christian is a matter of making a choice or a commitment or executing a decision. Kierkegaard is most emphatic that one is not and does not become a Christian simply by being brought up in a traditionally Christian environment, and assimilating the prevailing surrounding beliefs, attitudes, and forms of interaction with others. Christianity is neither a matter of intellectually subscribing to a particular set of theological beliefs, for instance about the existence of a Supreme Being who created the world, nor a matter of participating adequately in a Christian form of *Sittlichkeit*. To be(come) a Christian is not to refrain from lying and murder from a fixed disposition, but to act in certain positive ways that do not include murder and lying *because* these positive ways of acting arise from a specific form of Christian faith, which must be construed as an act of continual choice. The major difference between Hegel's spirit and Kierkegaard's 'self' is that Hegel regarded this temporally extended reflective mechanism as central to human life and history, but for him it was always embedded in a larger context which was one in which human individuals were being formed by, but then themselves informing, larger social institutions. To put it in Kierkegaard's terms, Hegel thinks I can never say who 'I' am in any interesting way except relative to who some 'we' are, where the 'we' in question is held together by some

---

[19] Kierkegaard 2009: 511–14.

shared language and beliefs, reciprocal desire, and some forms of common action (and similarly we cannot say who 'we' are except relative to who each member of the relevant group is: 'I' and 'we' are co-relative terms). Kierkegaard wishes to drop the social context and construe the process of 'becoming somebody' as a strictly individual religio-psychological movement.

23.4.1 Choice

As the account of spirit is the key to Hegel's philosophy, so the analysis of 'choice' is central to Kierkegaard's philosophical work. When Kierkegaard speaks, as he often does, of 'choice' in the emphatic sense he does not mean the simple choices we face in ordinary life, because in such everyday situations we can generally assume that the choice is being made relative to *some* fixed preferences, values, and principles: I know I like risotto, so I will have it for dinner. 'Existential choices', like the decision to try to become a Christian, Kierkegaard claims, have a very different structure, because they are instances not just of trying to decide what to do in a situation in which the terms of reference and values are relatively clear and stable, but of deciding who to be, and that means making a commitment both to a form of life and to a set of values. Given the nature of this commitment one must decide *at the same time* how one proposes to live and act, *and* what final framework one will adopt for evaluating forms of life and what ultimate standards one will use for judging action. One of Kierkegaard's basic claims is that choices like this are forced on us—we can't avoid them—and because they are choices of fundamental standards of normativity, they cannot be said to be 'rational'.

   Kierkegaard claims that one cannot live without having made some commitment to some ultimate standards. One can, of course, *claim* that one has not done so, but that just means that one is duplicitously pretending or is honestly deceived about oneself and one's life, or that one has made a commitment of an idiosyncratic, and necessarily self-frustrating, kind: namely to be committed *not* to make any ultimate commitments. Kierkegaard calls the attempt to live a life devoted systematically to avoiding ultimate commitments 'aesthetic', and devotes an early work, *Either/Or*, to trying to depict literarily why such a life will not be satisfactory or fulfilling for one who lives it.[20] He recognizes the theoretical possibility of a life of complete innocence (or, as he calls it, using Hegelian terminology, 'immediacy'), one *prior to* choice, as it were the idea of a human simply and unreflectively following instinct and social habit. The young girl who is the object of the attentions of the 'seducer' in the final part of *Either* is a kind of pale reflection of this possibility. However, *complete* lack of having-chosen is just an imaginary construct, which no real human, certainly no adult, could fully instantiate. Not even the young girl is completely innocent and unreflective. Anyone who was would not really be a self—a entity about which it would make sense to ask '*who* is that?'—at all.

---

[20] Kierkegaard 1988.

Kierkegaard thinks that one particularly pernicious form of attempting to pretend that one has not chosen is to claim that one is simply following some 'objective' criteria, which as it were impose themselves on all rational creatures by themselves or by virtue of some inherent force of their own, rather than having the relevance to my situation which they have by virtue of being actively adopted and recognized by me. All Kantians perpetrate this pretence when they appeal to objective laws of reason as grounds for their dutiful action.

Existential choice is not a momentary decision that somehow binds me in itself for the whole of my future and thus introduces substantial stability into my life. If the final standards of evaluation I use do not impose themselves, but need to be activated by me, then they retain their relevance only to the extent to which I continue to give them that relevance, and I can do that only if I am always in a state of having-already-chosen (some standards and form of life) and needing-to-(continue-to)-choose some standards. I also can never know I have committed myself 'aright'—it isn't even clear what sense it makes to speak of 'aright' in this context. This is a state of high anxiety, and this explains the persistence and force of the illusion that there are 'objective' standards; if they existed, we could escape the anxiety generated by the constant need for choice and commitment.[21]

If existential commitment has the structure it does, that is, if it is a choice, as it were, of what final standards of 'rationality', relevance, and value to accept, then it would seem that that choice itself cannot on pain of circularity be *presupposed* to *have* to take place according to some pre-given notion of what is rational. It must, thus, be construed as a completely non-rational decision. One consequence of this, Kierkegaard thinks, is that it is not directly communicable, that is, I cannot explain it to anyone else because public communication depends on shared standards or public points of reference, and this decision by its very nature is not one that can be justified or rationalized relative to any such points of reference. A further harsh consequence of this, which Kierkegaard himself actively affirms, is that my non-communicable, non-rational commitment may well require me to do things that are at odds with anything we humans could recognize as 'morality' (such as killing. one's son for no clear reason). The story of Abraham's (aborted) sacrifice of Isaac in the Old Testament is not an archaic remnant of a traditional tale from a pre-civilized age, or part of a divine plan of gradual revelation, a way of teaching human groups in a vivid and unforgettable way that they ought not to sacrifice their children, but is meant for real. Abraham did not become a 'self' by *not* sacrificing Isaac, but by really being willing to do it.[22] The story tells us something about the self-constitution of the human subject at levels prior to that at which our usual ethical systems operate but on which they in the final analysis depend.

Given Kierkegaard's views about the essential location of philosophical reflection in the lived individual human life, it is natural to try to get a purchase on his own views by studying their development in the context of his biography, and this gives much of the existing secondary work about him a slightly non-standard character. It requires considerable steadiness of hand and deftness of touch to keep the more strictly biographical and more 'philosophical' elements of the discussion in appropriate alignment.

---

[21] Kierkegaard 1980.   [22] Kierkegaard 1983.

23.5 Schopenhauer

Arthur Schopenhauer (1788–1860) was a slightly older figure than Kierkegaard, but his work was 'untimely' in that although he had elaborated his position fully by 1818, he began to be read and discussed only in the late 1850s. Schopenhauer shares with Kierkegaard the turn away from society, history, and politics, and from the optimism that was an important part of the Idealist project, to issues that were once the preserve of religious doctrines of individual salvation.

Schopenhauer considers and rejects two types of ethical doctrine: first, eudaimonism, the doctrine that happiness is the goal of human life and that ethics is the doctrine of how best to attain that goal, and second, the rationalist ethics of duty of the type developed most fully by Kant.[23] He has a rather quick way with eudaimonism. Such an ethical view presupposes that it is in principle possible for humans to attain what they want and satisfy their desires reliably and stably, for what can 'happiness' mean if not the satisfaction of desire? However, even a cursory inspection of human desire and its role in human life should suffice to disabuse a reflective person of the idea that happiness is a possible or even coherent human goal. Schopenhauer thinks it is a deeply rooted metaphysical truth about humans that we are essentially creatures of continuously welling desire; even if one does not accept this as a metaphysical proposition one might allow it to stand as a well-supported empirical generalization. As such a creature of desire I am faced with two possible situations. Either my desire is frustrated, in which case I am unhappy, or my desire is satisfied, in which case another desire will simply well up to replace the previous one, and that new one will now need to be satisfied, and so I also will not be happy. In either case, then, unhappiness is the human lot.

Schopenhauer claimed on rather weak grounds to be a follower of Kant in matters of epistemology and metaphysics. Nevertheless, his ethics was consciously and virulently anti-Kantian in inspiration, structure, and content. First of all he completely rejected the basic assumption that ethics is to be a discipline with an 'imperative' character, i.e. one that orders people about and tries to tell them what to do. According to him, Kant does not argue for the existence of any such thing as a 'pure moral ought', 'pure duties', or a 'moral' law, but rather merely presupposes that they exist, and then fumbles around looking for various specious arguments connecting these imaginary entities with one another and with his own religiously and theologically derived prejudices. The whole of Kantian ethics, then, is a huge '*petitio principii*'.[24] Rather than trying to give an account of, or even to issue, 'moral imperatives', Schopenhauer argues, ethics should be an empirical science devoted to explaining and interpreting what actually happens, not the pseudo-subject of studying what people 'ought' to do.

---

[23] Schopenhauer 1986: vol. 3, 642–715.   [24] Schopenhauer 1986: vol. 3, 645–6.

23.5.1 Pity

If one looks at the real motives that bring people to act, one will observe that people are moved by perceptions of 'welfare' and 'woe' ('*Wohl und Wehe*').[25] In some cases the 'welfare' and 'woe' in question is my own, but in some cases I find myself motivated by perception of others' welfare and woe. In the first of these cases we speak of 'egoism', and we attribute moral value to actions that are free of such egotistical motivation. There is, Schopenhauer thinks, still a potential question to answer, namely, how can it come about that I can be motivated by another's welfare and woe? The answer to this is an empirical theory of the ways in which one person can come to 'identify' with another so that I come to participate in the other's welfare and woe. In this process, identification with another's woe has a kind of priority over identification with the other's welfare. Such participation in another's woe is what we call in everyday life 'pity' (Mitleid). Ethics, then, is not about imperative calls to do one's wholly imaginary 'duty', but about the cultivation of pity. This is, as advertized, an empirical theory and would have to stand on its own two feet as such, but Schopenhauer also believes that there is a metaphysical basis for the empirical phenomenon he describes in that he holds that 'metaphysically' it is not at all surprising that I can in fact be motivated by another's welfare and woe: metaphysically the whole distinction between individual persons is an illusion, and we are all nothing but, as it were, figments of the imagination of a single underlying will. I feel your pain because all pain is 'really' (metaphysically) the pain of the one will.

In this world of recurrent desire, pain, and pity there is no room for happiness, social or political improvement, or moral progress, however there is a tiny place for a momentary cessation of pain and a tiny spark of hope for complete release. In the (disinterested) contemplation of art, Schopenhauer believes, the will can be brought to suspend its desires and thus be free of the frustration they bring with them. Such respite can, however, only be at best momentary, a brief interlude before the imperious demands of desire reassert themselves. The only hope for permanent escape from the cycle of frustration and pain is a form of Buddhism, a systematic attempt on the part of the human will to extinguish itself, thus putting an end to all desire, which at the same time means my self-dissolution as the individual that I am.[26]

23.6 NIETZSCHE

One immediately striking feature of the philosophy of Friedrich Nietzsche is the aphoristic character of most of his work in this area. The use of this literary form is not accidental. In 1797 Friedrich Schlegel developed a sophisticated theory of the aphorism, what he called the 'fragment'—a tiny, highly stylized, intricately wrought, separate little

---

[25] Schopenhauer 1986: vol. 3, 715–44.   [26] Schopenhauer 1986: vol. 1.

world 'perfect in itself like a hedgehog' and containing a witty insight[27]—as the appropriate literary form for a spirit who held that because it was equally deadly to have a system and not to have a system, it was necessary to connect the two.[28] The aphorism/ fragment is systematic because it is internally highly structured and gives some kind of significant insight into an important connection in our world; writing the fragment is compatible with not having a system because one fragment can stand next to others which are different internally structured worlds, without it being necessary to specify what relation the various fragments have to each other. Nietzsche himself treats the very idea of having a 'system' with considerable suspicion, if not contempt. To have an ethical system is, to put it slightly paradoxically, a moral and intellectual failing: a sign of weakness—the inability to tolerate the multitudinous variety of human and natural phenomena means that one feels the need to 'reduce' them to manageable form—and of bad taste. 'Ethics' should be, on the one hand, a 'natural history' of the different moralities which one can encounter in history[29]—an empirical study of the way in which different moralities flourish in different environments—and, on the other hand, experimentalist, inventing and trying out new configurations of value.[30] Herodotus, Montaigne, and Herder are better models for ethics (as natural history) than Aquinas or Kant, and Brecht was closer to the experimentalism of Nietzsche than Beckett was. Collections of aphorisms, then, are an especially good way of doing 'ethics'.

Nietzsche's avoidance of the closed literary form of the systematic treatise, then, is connected with his suspicion of the very idea of the philosopher as a person with a fixed unitary doctrine, rather than someone engaged in shifting studies and experiments. This, in turn, is connected with a rejection of traditional views about the self. Either the self is considered to be a naturally given fundamental unity, even if that unity is overlaid with surface conflicts, or it is considered of the highest importance to impose unity on my soul or personality, and the most effective means of doing that is by subjecting myself to the discipline of a single unitary doctrine which gives true insight into the fundamental nature of reality. One could, of course, combine these two non-exclusive views and think that by virtue of correct insight into the underlying essential unity of my soul I could resolve the surface conflicts and thus allow that unity to emerge more clearly. Nietzsche will have no truck at all with views like that. The philosopher is not admirable by virtue of holding fast to a fixed true doctrine which allows him to impose inflexible order on his soul or allows an underlying unity to emerge. The philosopher is the man of many masks, deft at shifting from one to the other, and beneath any mask, there is nothing but another mask, all the way down.[31] These masks are to be adopted, used, and then discarded as required and are not in themselves appropriate objects with which I should identify myself or to which I should have any ultimate commitment. So whereas, as we have seen above, Kierkegaard thinks no one can live without having made a commitment to some ultimate standards, Nietzsche suggests that lacking such a commitment is a sign of admirable strength and flexibility and the characteristic of a genuine philosopher.

---

[27] Schlegel 1980: vol. 1, 214.   [28] Schlegel 1980: vol. 1, 196.   [29] Nietzsche 1980: vol. 5, 105–28.
[30] Nietzsche 1980: vol. 5, 59.   [31] Nietzsche 1980: vol. 5, 57, 233–4.

Equally the philosopher is not a man of indubitable conviction in the truth of a systematic doctrine, but rather someone who may have no final opinions at all.[32] He is best seen as something like an ancient sceptic.[33] The ancient sceptic distinguished himself from the dogmatist. The dogmatist had firm beliefs which he asserted, even if the beliefs in question were, for instance, that no reliable knowledge of the external world was possible. The sceptic in contrast did not affirm or deny any given beliefs, he 'investigated' ('*skepto*' in Greek) them, and while he was investigating, he suspended judgement. It merely turned out that he never had occasion to stop the suspension. It is an open question whether such a position can successfully be maintained in the long run, just as it seems to be an open question whether a human can consist merely of a play of masks with no face beneath them.

23.6.1 Valuation

Among the many hypotheses that Nietzsche investigates during the course of his experiments, there is one which recurs, and which, if it were to turn out to be warranted, would have significant consequences for ethics. Whatever his theoretical views about the need to avoid commitment, we know that in fact one of Nietzsche's own most deeply seated and most abiding character traits was his detestation of 'equality' in all its forms.[34] He eventually found what he took to be an argument for this prejudice.

A human being, Nietzsche observes, is an inherently *valuing* animal.[35] Such 'valuation' need not take the form of articulating a proposition: 'That is good', and is in fact in one way the more powerful the less conscious. If I move closer to the fire I am demonstrating that I value it positively; if I pull my hand back when it is burnt, I am valuing the fire negatively. Human 'health' or flourishing (in a very broad moral and psychological sense) depends directly on being able to carry out the activity of valuing at this basic level, but also increasingly at ever 'higher' levels, including eventually the production of original works of art. Valuation, however, he argues, is an inherently differentiating activity. I can in everyday life say simply that I value some X as if that were some kind of categorical statement, but actually that always means that I prefer X to something else. I like tea means I would prefer to have a cup of tea rather than a cup of coffee, prefer to have tea now rather than not, etc. From this Nietzsche often goes on to argue that valuing requires an internal tension in the soul: I need as it were to feel psychically impelled to want a cup of tea rather than coffee. Such a tension, however, cannot simply stand on its own; it cannot maintain itself without an appropriate social setting, which, given the inherently differential and discriminatory nature of all valuation, must be hierarchical, that is must be based on the (ideally) unquestioned political and social domination of one group over another. Nietzsche also calls this the principle of 'rank-ordering'.[36]

[32] Nietzsche 1980: vol. 5, 233–4.   [33] Nietzsche 1980: vol. 6, 178.
[34] Nietzsche 1980: vol. 5, 60–3.   [35] Nietzsche 1980: vol. 5, 22, 306.
[36] Nietzsche 1980: vol. 5, 154–6.

In rank-ordered society members of one group are considered to be qualitatively superior to members of others. In such a society there is a creative pathos of distance[37] between members of a qualitatively 'superior' order and members of some lower orders. So in a slave-holding society, like ancient Greece, slavery was not an unfortunate necessity so that the masters could be free to engage in politics, but the real significance and function of the slaves was *to be despised* by the masters. The tension thus created and maintained was the origin of all creativity. So if a society is to remain vital, it must be able to cultivate active valuation, particularly positive valuation of itself, but this is possible only if society is anti-egalitarian. So any form of social or political equality will undermine the conditions under which alone society can continue to value itself and thus remain healthy.

Within this general hypothetical framework Nietzsche sketches the outlines of a history of Western morality which emphasizes the highly contingent, not to say quirky, nature of the course it has taken. Rather than being devoted to a straightforward development of immediately comprehensible forms of positive valuation, cultivation of the directly given good, Western morality took a deeply deviant turn.[38] What one would expect is that strength, vitality, and aggression would be recognized as the objects of positive valuation (and thus as 'good'), and what lacked strength and health would count as 'bad', i.e. not-good. At a certain point in history, however, a group of 'slaves', weak agents who were socially oppressed by healthy 'masters', succeeded in turning their own real weakness into a form of imaginary strength. They did this by changing the system of valuation and redefining the moral vocabulary. What the masters called 'good'—the healthy, active, vital—the slaves rejected in their imagination, inventing the new word 'evil' to refer to it. The slaves then went on to give the old word 'good' a new meaning: 'good' was now asserted to mean 'not-evil', i.e. not like what the masters naturally value. This allows the slaves to stylize their own weakness as a virtue ('It is good to be weak because that is to be not-like what the masters like, not-active, not-vital, not-aggressive'). It also gives their life a kind of meaning because it gives them a goal they actually have some chance of aspiring to attaining: the weak have no chance of being 'strong' and active, but it is at least conceivable that they might successfully cultivate the 'ascetic ideal' of turning their aggressive instincts against themselves in order to make themselves even weaker, more debilitated, less active than they were before. Christianity and Buddhism are both forms of the pursuit of this ascetic ideal, as is also the latter philosophical position of Schopenhauer. This 'slave-uprising' in morality, although it has its roots in a way of trying to deal psychologically with the facts of human weakness, secretes around itself a metaphysics (of the 'soul') and an epistemology (about the conditions of the acquisition of true knowledge of the soul) which function to support it. One such support is the way in which the traditional philosopher tried to give himself and his life Unity, Substance, and Gravity by identifying with fixed set of true, rationally held beliefs, and acting consistently on these. Nietzsche, in contrast, wishes to give his

---

[37] Nietzsche 1980: vol. 5, 205–6, 258–60.   [38] Nietzsche 1980: vol. 5, 247–412.

life 'style' which is not based on reason or intended to represent any substantial Objectivity, but is a matter of free constructive choice.[39]

During the past eighty years there have been roughly two general ways of interpreting Nietzsche, which, for the sake of simplicity, one can call the 'German' line, running from Heidegger's lectures in the 1940's, and the 'French' line, one of whose most distinguished early representatives was Giles Deleuze.[40] The 'German' line takes Nietzsche to be a systematic philosopher like his predecessors, Aristotle, Kant, or Hegel, or a person aspiring, but failing to be such a systematic philosopher, or, finally a person who tried to 'overcome' the temptation to be a systematic philosopher, but, in the end, failed. In Heidegger's interpretation, this takes the form of attributing to Nietzsche as his central idea 'the will-to-power', and construing that as a 'metaphysical' idea (although admitting, sometimes, that Nietzsche might have thought it was not a metaphysical idea). Nietzsche then is a kind of latter-day Leibniz, who sees the world as composed of packets of self-aggrandizing will-to-power, and sees each such packet as imposing a point of view, or perspective, or interpretation on the rest of the world as a whole (as part of its project of self-aggrandizement). Nietzsche, then, has an 'ethics' which is some version of the doctrine that one 'ought' —in a quasi-Kantian mode—or 'should'—in a more 'perfectionist' mode—maximize the will-to-power, or that— in a gesture to 'naturalism'—given the nature of the world, no one really has any alternative but actually to maximize their will-to-power, because try as one will, that is what one is really going to be doing anyway. One can then try to ring a variety of changes on these themes.

The other, Deleuzian, way of approaching Nietzsche starts from the notion of a free activity of interpreting or construing or 'reading', more exactly from the idea that there can be an interpretative activity which is not necessarily the activity of a subject. Of course, one can always, if one so chooses, ascribe a 'subject' to any activity, including the activity of interpreting, but that is only itself another instance of the interpretative activity in question. 'The will-to-power' then becomes merely one such hypothetical construal of the world, the usefulness of which Nietzsche investigates in his work.

The major difficulties of the 'German' way of reading Nietzsche are that it makes his work traditionalist and boring, that it is difficult to render it compatible with his repeated and extensive criticisms of 'metaphysics', that it makes his literary style merely eccentric and adventitious, rather than, as he himself saw it, an integral part of his philosophical project, and that on most apparently plausible readings of 'will-to-power' an ethics based on that concept would be humanly deeply unappealing. The major difficulty with the French Nietzsche is the inherent obscurity of the notion of a subjectless interpretative activity, and the fear that countenancing it will lead to cognitive and moral anarchy, nihilism, relativism, and so forth.

The two major productive philosophical appropriations of Nietzsche during the past decades, Alexander Nehamas' *Nietzsche: Life as Literature* (1985) and Bernard Williams' *Truth and Truthfulness* (2002) are both closer to the French than to the German mode of interpretation.

The history of academic philosophy from the early 1890s to 1933 in central Europe is essentially the story of the struggle between successive variants of these Nietzschean

---

[39] Nietzsche 1980: vol. 3, 530–1.   [40] Heidegger 1961; Deleuze 1961.

views, which were extremely strongly represented among the cultural and artistic elite, and one or another form of neo-Kantianism, which was dominant among the professoriate. To the extent to which National Socialism had a coherent ideology at all it was a mixture of Kantian, Darwinian, and Nietzschean elements in more or less equal parts. The events between 1933 and the stabilization of political and economic conditions in Europe in the late 1940s (with the proclamation of the German Federal Republic in May 1949, and of the German Democratic Republic in October 1949) represent a further caesura. The Federal Republic in the 1950s and 1960s saw an intense three-way discussion between Heidegger, a non-orthodox National Socialist who had survived the war and was rehabilitated in 1951, the members of the Left Hegelian 'Frankfurt School' who had returned from emigration in the early 1950s, and a few students of the Viennese-British philosopher Karl Popper, who called themselves 'critical rationalists' and were called by their opponents 'positivists'. The second neo-Kantian revival began in the mid-1970s (after the failure of the student movement of 1968).

A NOTE ON THE SECONDARY LITERATURE

The European nineteenth century has not fared well at the hands of English-language commentators during the past hundred years or so. The best overview is still that given by Alasdair MacIntyre in his *Short History of Ethics* (1966). Karl Löwith's *From Hegel to Nietzsche* (1964) is also extremely useful. There is no reliable philosophical book on Friedrich Schlegel and the early Romantics, but Ernst Behler's *German Romantic Literary Theory* (1993) and *L'absolu littéraire* by Philippe Lacoue-Labarthe and Jean-Luc Nancy (1978) contain much that will be of interest to the philosophical reader. The student interested in Kierkegaard should consult *Kierkegaard* by Alastair Hannay (1982), *Kierkegaard and the limits of the ethical* by Anthony Rudd (1993), and the essays collected in the *Cambridge Companion to Kierkegaard* (ed. Hannay and Marino, 1998). Julian Young has written two useful books on Schopenhauer (1987 and 2005), and Christopher Janaway's *Schopenhauer* (1994) also gives a penetrating philosophical account of Schopenhauer's central ideas. Books on Nietzsche are legion, and there is less consensus on how his work is to be understood than on virtually any other major philosopher since Socrates,[41] so any list of suggestions will of necessity seem partisan. As general introductions I suggest: Henry Staten, *Nietzsche's Voice* (1990), Alexander Nehamas, *Nietzsche: Life as Literature* (1985), Gilles Deleuze, *Nietzsche et la tragédie* (1961), Lawrence Hatab, *Nietzsche's Life Sentence* (2005), and Simon May, *Nietzsche's Ethics and his War on Morality* (1993). On Nietzsche's *Genealogy of Morality* see Christopher Janaway, *Beyond Selflessness* (2007), and Simon May (ed.) *Nietzsche's* Genealogy of Morality: *A Critical Guide* (2014). Two essays by Philippa Foot have been influential: 'Nietzsche: The Revaluation of Values' (1973) and 'Nietzsche's Immoralism' (1993).

---

[41] See, e.g. Aschheim 1992.

Bibliography

Aschheim, S. 1992. *The Nietzsche Legacy in Germany 1890–1990*. Berkeley and Los Angeles: University of California Press.

Behler, E. 1993. *German Romantic Literary Theory*. Cambridge: Cambridge University Press.

Deleuze, G. 1961. *Nietzsche et la philosophie*. Paris: Presses universitaires de France.

Foot, P. 1973. 'Nietzsche: The Revaluation of Values', in R. Solomon (ed.), *Nietzsche: Critical Essays*. Notre Dame: University of Notre Dame Press, 156–96.

——1993. 'Nietzsche's Immoralism', in R. Schacht (ed.), *Nietzsche, Genealogy, Morality*. Berkeley and Los Angeles: University of California Press, 3–15.

Hamann, J. G. 1957. *Metakritik über den Purismum der reinen Vernunft*, in *Sämtliche Werke*, ed. J. Nadler. Vienna: Herder.

Hannay, A. 1982. *Kierkegaard*. London: Routledge.

——and Marino, G. (eds) 1998. *The Cambridge Companion to Kierkegaard*. Cambridge: Cambridge University Press.

Hatab, L. 2005. *Nietzsche Life Sentence*. London: Routledge.

Hegel, G. F. W. 1952. *Briefe*, ed. J. Hoffmeister. Hamburg: Meiner.

——1970. *Werke in zwanzig Bänden*, ed. E. Moldenhauer and K. M. Michel. Frankfurt/M: Suhrkamp.

Heidegger, M. 1961. *Nietzsche*. 2 vols. Pfullingen: Neske.

Herder, J. G. 1799. *Eine Metakritik der Kritik der reinen Vernunft*. 2 vols. Leipzig: Hartknoch.

Hölderlin, F. 2008. *Hyperion, Empedokles*, ed. J. Schmidt and K. Grätz. Frankfurt/M: Deutscher Klassiker Verlag.

Jacobi, F. H. 1916. *Die Hauptschriften zum Pantheismusstreit*, ed. H. Scholz. Berlin: Reuther and Reichard.

——1968. *Werke*, ed. J. P. Köppen and C. J. F. Roth. Darmstadt: Wissenschaftliche Buchgesellschaft.

Janaway, C. 1994. *Schopenhauer*. Oxford: Oxford University Press.

——2007. *Beyond Selflessness*. Oxford: Oxford University Press.

Kant, I. 1956. *Kritik der reinen Vernunft*, ed. R. Schmidt. Hamburg: Meiner.

——1963. *Werke in sechs Bänden*, ed. W. Weischedel. Darmstadt: Wissenschaftliche Buchgesellschaft.

——1967. *Kritik der praktischen Vernunft*, ed. K. Vorländer. Hamburg: Meiner.

——1968. *Theorie-Werkausgabe*, ed. W. Weischedel. 12 vols. Frankfurt/M: Suhrkamp.

Kierkegaard, S. 1980. *The Concept of Anxiety*, ed. R. Thornte. Princeton: Princeton: University Press.

——1983. *Fear and Trembling*, ed. H. V. Hong and E. H. Hong. Princeton: Princeton University Press.

——1988. *Either/Or*, ed. H. V. Hong and E. H. Hong. 2 vols. Princeton: Princeton University Press.

——2009. *Concluding Unscientific Postscript*, ed. A. Hannay. Cambridge: Cambridge University Press.

Lacoue-Labarthe, P. and Nancy, J.-L. 1978. *L'absolu littéraire*. Paris: Seuil.

Löwith, K. 1964. *From Hegel to Nietzsche*. New York: Columbia University Press.

MacIntyre, A. 1966. *A Short History of Ethics*. London: Macmillan.

May, S. 1993. *Nietzsche's Ethics and his War on Morality*. Oxford: Oxford University Press.

——(ed.) 2014. *Nietzsche's Genealogy of Morality: A Critical Guide*. Cambridge: Cambridge University Press.

Nehamas, A. 1985. *Nietzsche: Life as Literature*. Cambridge, MA: Harvard University Press.

Nietzsche, F. 1980. *Kritische Studien-Ausgabe*, ed. G. Colli and M. Montinari. 15 vols. Berlin: De Gruyter.

Novalis [Friedrich von Hardenberg] 1961. *Die Christenheit oder Europa*. Stuttgart: Reclam.

Rudd, A. 1993. *Kierkegaard and the Limits of the Ethical*. Oxford: Oxford University Press.

Schiller, F. 1967. *Sämtliche Werke*, ed. G. Fricke and H. G. Göpfert. 5 vols. Munich: Hanser.

Schlegel, F. 1980. *Werke in zwei Bänden*, ed. W. Hecht. Berlin and Weimer: Aufbau.

Schopenhauer, A. 1986. *Sämtliche Werke*, ed. W. F. von Löhneysen. 5 vols. Frankfurt/M: Suhrkamp.

Staten, H. 1990. *Nietzsche's Voice*. Ithaca, NY: Cornell University Press.

Stirner, M. 1972. *Der Einzige und sein Eigentum*. Stuttgart: Reclam.

Williams, B. 2002. *Truth and Truthfulness*. Princeton: Princeton University Press.

CHAPTER 24

···

HEGEL AND MARX

···

TERRY PINKARD

BOTH Hegel and Marx represent a stream in modern ethical theory that, while having little reverberation in mainstream Anglophone philosophy, has nonetheless exercised a profound effect on European (or, in today's argot, 'continental') ethical thought.[1] Part of the reason for this neglect lies in their having rejected a central part of what counts as 'philosophical ethics'. To see why this is so, we must turn to their thought itself.

24.1 HEGEL

···

24.1.1 The One or the Many Hegels?

Hegel has never been an easy read. To make matters worse, his followers have interpreted him in almost mutually exclusive ways. What are the elements at stake?

Clearly, Hegel is some kind of holist. However, exactly what kind of holist he is sharply divides Hegel scholarship. Since Hegel's own day, the dominant motif for interpretation of his work has been, to put it very roughly, neo-Platonic. On the most expansive neo-Platonic interpretation, the 'whole' is something like the Christian God, and the various stages of the famous Hegelian dialectic are each something like emanations from the Christian God (an emanation which supposedly follows a logic of its own).[2] There is also a small-scale Platonist interpretation that sees Hegel's system as tracing out or mirroring

---

[1] See Raymond Geuss, *Outside Ethics* (Princeton: Princeton University Press, 2005).

[2] Among the better known proponents of this view are: Charles Taylor, *Hegel* (Cambridge and New York: Cambridge University Press, 1975); Frederick C. Beiser, *Hegel* (New York and London: Routledge, 2005); Stephen Houlgate, *Freedom, Truth and History : An Introduction to Hegel's Philosophy* (London: Routledge, 1991); Michael Rosen, *Hegel's Dialectic and Its Criticism* (Cambridge and New York: Cambridge University Press, 1982); Dieter Henrich, *Hegel Im Kontext* (Frankfurt am Main: Suhrkamp, 1971). Taylor, Henrich, and Beiser are much more robustly neo-Platonist, whereas Houlgate is much less so. Rosen takes Hegel's neo-Platonism to be a reductio argument against him.

the conceptual structures already there in reality; this 'conceptual realist' reading also has a neo-Aristotelian version.[3] More recently, there has been a characterization of Hegel not as any kind of Platonist at all but as a kind of neo- or post-Kantian, a kind of Kant who has seen the difficulties in his view and has seen that the only way to maintain the key Kantian commitments about the centrality of apperception is to move in Hegel's direction.[4] Another interpretation which has recently emerged is of Hegel as a kind of inferentialist about meaning, and on this view, he is also almost always taken to be a kind of social pragmatist. (This interpretation has much in common with the post-Kantian interpretation, although the overlaps and differences are too subtle to discuss here).[5]

[3] Robert Stern, *Routledge Philosophy Guidebook to Hegel and the Phenomenology of Spirit* (London and New York: Routledge, 2002); Kenneth R. Westphal, *Hegel's Epistemology: A Philosophical Introduction to the Phenomenology of Spirit* (Indianapolis, IN: Hackett, 2003). Stephen Houlgate is also a 'realist' after a fashion, as is James Kreines. See James Kreines, 'Hegel's Critique of Pure Mechanism and the Philosophical Appeal of the Logic Project', *European Journal of Philosophy* 12 (1) (2004): 38–74; and James Kreines, 'Hegel's Metaphysics: Changing the Debate', *Philosophy Compass* 1 (5) (2006): 466–80. John McDowell reads Hegel as a realist of sorts, but his position is more difficult to characterize. McDowell's language seems to suggest that of a conceptual realist in the Stern/Westphal mode, namely, that in thinking, we are delineating the conceptual structures in reality itself. However, McDowell consistently denies that this is his view. John Henry Mcdowell, *Having the World in View : Essays on Kant, Hegel, and Sellars* (Cambridge, MA: Harvard University Press, 2009).

[4] Robert B. Pippin, *Hegel's Idealism: The Satisfactions of Self-Consciousness* (Cambridge: Cambridge University Press, 1989); Robert B. Pippin, *Idealism as Modernism: Hegelian Variations* (Cambridge: Cambridge University Press, 1997); Robert B. Pippin, *The Persistence of Subjectivity: On the Kantian Aftermath* (Cambridge: Cambridge University Press, 2005); Robert B. Pippin, *Hegel's Practical Philosophy: Rational Agency as Ethical Life* (Cambridge: Cambridge University Press, 2008); Allen Speight, *Hegel, Literature, and the Problem of Agency* (Cambridge and New York: Cambridge University Press, 2001) and Allen Speight, *The Philosophy of Hegel* (Montréal and Ithaca: McGill-Queen's University Press, 2008); Sebastian Rand, 'The Importance and Relevance of Hegel's Philosophy of Nature', *Review of Metaphysics* 61 (2) (2007): 379–400; Terry P. Pinkard, *Hegel's Phenomenology: The Sociality of Reason* (Cambridge: Cambridge University Press, 1994); Terry P. Pinkard, *Hegel : A Biography* (Cambridge: Cambridge University Press, 2000); Terry P. Pinkard, *German Philosophy, 1760–1860: The Legacy of Idealism* (Cambridge: Cambridge University Press, 2002). Tom Rockmore takes Hegel to be a post-Kantian in a more specialized sense as offering a theory of knowledge in Tom Rockmore, *Cognition : An Introduction to Hegel's Phenomenology of Spirit* (Berkeley, Los Angeles, and London: University of California Press, 1997). Another version of a kind of post-Kantian Hegel is to be found in the 'categorical' or 'transcendental' interpretation of Hegel in Klaus E. Brinkmann, *Idealism without Limits: Hegel and the Problem of Objectivity* (New York: Springer, 2010). Brinkmann's book is linked to a similar line of thought presented in Klaus Hartmann and Olaf Müller, *Hegels Logik* (Berlin: De Gruyter, 1999). The more overtly metaphysical-organicist interpretations of Hegel are dissected in Sally Sedgwick, 'The State as Organism: The Metaphysical Basis of Hegel's Philosophy of Right', *Southern Journal of Philosophy* 39 (suppl.) (2001): 171–88.

[5] The interpretations associated with this come from Robert Brandom, *Making It Explicit: Reasoning, Representing, and Discursive Commitment* (Cambridge, MA: Harvard University Press, 1994); Robert Brandom, *Tales of the Mighty Dead: Historical Essays in the Metaphysics of Intentionality* (Cambridge, MA: Harvard University Press, 2002); Robert Brandom, *Between Saying and Doing: Towards an Analytic Pragmatism* (Oxford and New York: Oxford University Press, 2008); Robert Brandom, *Reason in Philosophy: Animating Ideas* (Cambridge, MA: Harvard University Press, 2009); Dean Moyar, *Hegel's Conscience* (New York: Oxford University Press, 2010); and also among the people associated with the post-Kantian interpretation (Robert Pippin, Terry Pinkard). Moyar adheres more to the inferentialist but

Others maintain that although Hegel is some kind of holist, one can safely ignore those big-picture issues and focus instead on his specific arguments for specific theses. They thus disagree with those (of whom there are many) who argue that one can understand Hegel's particular theses only if one understands the entire system.[6] There are also those who see Hegel's holism as anticipating some key Heideggerian issues.[7]

Thus, the nature of Hegel's holism remains thoroughly contentious, and unless one contents oneself with simply reciting Hegel's text, just about anything one says about Hegel will find fierce opposition from within some quarter of Hegel scholarship.

As if the contested interpretations of Hegel's overall system were not enough, there is also the problem of figuring out what counts as his ethics. He only wrote one book—the 1820 *Elements of the Philosophy of Right*—which can be considered a work on ethics. However, his 1807 *Phenomenology of Spirit* had quite a bit of material on ethics in it, and several of his published essays and the unpublished attempts at creating his 'system' prior to the publication of the *Phenomenology* clearly touched on matters of ethics. Not unsurprisingly, there is almost as much disagreement about the nature of the relation among all these different statements as there is about his views in general. There are even

not the social pragmatist view, whereas Paul Redding, *Hegel's Hermeneutics* (Ithaca, NY and London: Cornell University Press, 1996) has a quite original combination of post-Kantian views with a pragmatist stance. John McDowell is a more complex case, since although his views are sometimes associated with the social-pragmatist reading, his own interpretation is more Aristotelian (coloured by Wittgenstein), and it incorporates much of the neo-Kantian elements into his view. By and large, the readings play out along national lines; the neo-realist reading is British, with strong representation from those with links to Cambridge University (Stern and Houlgate; although Westphal teaches in Britain, he is American). The pragmatist and pragmatic-neo-Kantian interpretations are American. The Australian school led by Redding is an original synthesis of both the analytic-pragmatist interpretations and the more 'continental' post-Kantian reading. Tom Rockmore argues that Hegel's project should not be confused with either the pragmatist or inferentialist programmes in Tom Rockmore, *Hegel, Idealism, and Analytic Philosophy* (New Haven: Yale University Press, 2005). A good criticism of Rockmore is to be found in Christopher Yeomans, 'Review of Tom Rockmore, *Hegel, Idealism, and Analytic Philosophy*', *Review of Metaphysics* 60 (3) (2007): 686–7. The most detailed and interesting discussion of the recent analytic appropriations of Hegel is to be found in Paul Redding, *Analytic Philosophy and the Return of Hegelian Thought* (Cambridge: Cambridge University Press, 2007). The most overtly 'realist-neo-Platonist' interpretations are German: Dieter Henrich and David S. Pacini, *Between Kant and Hegel: Lectures on German Idealism* (Cambridge, MA and London: Harvard University Press, 2003); Rolf-Peter Horstmann, *Die Grenzen der Vernunft: Eine Untersuchung zu Zielen und Motiven des Deutschen Idealismus* (Frankfurt a.M.: Anton Hain, 1991); Ludwig Siep, *Der Weg der Phänomenologie des Geistes: Ein einführender Kommentar zu Hegels "Differenzschrift" und zur "Phänomenologie des Geistes"* (Frankfurt am Main: Suhrkamp, 2000). Frederick Beiser belongs to the Anglo-American line of neo-Platonist interpretation, but he takes his lead from the Germans.

[6] Allen W. Wood, *Hegel's Ethical Thought* (Cambridge and New York: Cambridge University Press, 1990); to some extent, Frederick Neuhouser, *Foundations of Hegel's Social Theory: Actualizing Freedom* (Cambridge, MA: Harvard University Press, 2000); Alan Patten, *Hegel's Idea of Freedom* (New York: Oxford University Press, 2002); Michael Quante, *Hegel's Concept of Action*, tr. Dean Moyar (Cambridge and New York: Cambridge University Press, 2004); Robert R. Williams, *Recognition: Fichte and Hegel on the Other* (Albany: State University of New York Press, 1992).

[7] John McCumber, *The Company of Words: Hegel, Language, and Systematic Philosophy* (Evanston, Ill: Northwestern University Press, 1993); John Russon, *Reading Hegel's Phenomenology* (Indianapolis: Indiana University Press, 2004).

disagreements about which texts should even count as expressing his most considered views on ethics and on whether the views expressed in the 1807 *Phenomenology* are the same as (or worse or better than) those expressed in the 1820 *Philosophy of Right*.[8] Thus, any short summary of Hegel's thought is going to appear, from the standpoint of at least some other Hegel scholars somewhere, as dogmatic in tone. With that in mind, I shall take the 1820 *Philosophy of Right* as the basic text, accompanied by the caveat that far more needs to be said in defence of that choice than can be said here.

24.1.2 The Elements of the Philosophy of Right

One way of framing the question to which Hegel's philosophy is supposed to be an answer is in light of the four questions Kant thought animated philosophy: What can we know, what ought we to do, for what can we hope, and, as Kant added, knowing that these all amount to a fourth question—what is man?

Although one might think that this would simply call for yet another metaphysics and another moral philosophy, Hegel seemed to think that it instead showed that any—at least traditional—metaphysical answer was beside the point and that constructing any moral philosophy, at least strictly speaking, would not work. Why did he think that? To answer that, we need to look at three controversial Hegelian ideas: Dialectic, alienation, and actuality (*Wirklichkeit*).

24.1.2.1 *Preliminaries: Kantian and Hegelian Dialectic*

For understanding the dialectic, a simple contrast will help. Like Kant, Hegel also thought that reason, once detached from experience and in search of 'the unconditioned', inevitably generates mutually exclusive positions—antinomies—about its results, and the extent and variety of the antinomies is limited probably only by the ingenuity of individual thinkers to come up with new arguments for one side or the other. Like Kant, he also called the generation of these kinds of conceptual puzzles 'dialectic'.

Kant took the existence of such antinomies to be grounds for concluding that we could in principle know nothing about the world as it existed 'in itself', apart from the (in a very qualified sense) subjective conditions under which we could experience it. Hegel, on the other hand, thought they revealed instead something about us, not that the world in itself is unknowable.[9] Against Kant, Hegel wanted to assert an older, 'Greek'

---

[8] Axel Honneth, for example, has defended a broadly 'Frankfurt School' claim that it was only Hegel's ethical thought around 1803 and not the new turn taken in 1807 that deserves our attention. Axel Honneth, *The Struggle for Recognition : The Moral Grammar of Social Conflicts* (Cambridge, MA: Polity Press, 1995).

[9] When reason is not taken up with seeking the unconditioned but operates at the level of what Hegel called 'the understanding', such conceptual puzzles do not play much of a role at all. Moreover, changes in what we know about the world through the natural sciences make a huge difference as to what can count as the unconditioned. Although this may come as a surprise to those otherwise unacquainted with Hegel, philosophical knowledge for him also crucially involves the natural sciences

conception of the ultimate intelligibility of the world (which was the background to his assertion in the *Philosophy of Right* that the actual was the rational, and the rational was the actual [10]).

Hegel's own dialectical approach also holds, to put it in the most general terms, that such conceptual puzzles can never be solved, but the threat they make to rational intelligibility can nonetheless be tamed. The 'dialectic' moves from a set of conceptual puzzles (or antinomies) in one realm to a different, more determinate context from which those antinomies cease to be as threatening to the very rationality of the system as they had originally seemed to be (Hegel uses the German term, '*Aufhebung*', with its twin meanings of both 'cancelling' and 'preserving', to characterize this kind of move). Hegel's dialectical procedure thus resembles in a highly general way some of the views of the later Wittgenstein, since Hegel holds that moving to a different context dissolves or mitigates the threat these puzzles seemed to offer to our various practices of holding ourselves to determinate norms, but the 'puzzles' themselves are never definitively resolved. (A major caveat: this is admittedly a weaker presentation of Hegel's dialectic. The stronger view would involve looking at Hegel's more robust views on how the different sides of the antinomies imply each other, or how, in Hegel's richer terminology, each is 'the other of itself'.)

Hegel puts this 'dialectical' approach to work in two ways. First, there is his well-known and very robust view that all the conceptual puzzles of traditional philosophy do not constitute merely an arbitrary collection but have a kind of logic to them, such that they can all be related as parts of a whole. His extended argument for that is in books such as his *Science of Logic*.

The second way has to do with the dialectic as experiential and practical. For a human organism to become an agent, she must be brought up such that she acquires a set of social skills and dispositions that function as a 'second nature' to herself. In thus acquiring the ability to move around in a normative social space (which is necessary for an organism to become an agent at all), an agent thus becomes more than the organic animal 'substance' she originally is and becomes in addition a self-conscious 'subject' capable of guiding her actions by norms.[11] (This also has to do with the idea of 'recognition' in Hegel's philosophy.[12]) To be an agent, a 'subject', is thus to inhabit a kind of social,

since, as he himself puts it, 'the *origin* and *formation* of philosophical science has empirical physics as its presupposition and condition'. G. W. F. Hegel, *Enzyklopädie der philosophischen Wissenschaften II*, ed. E. Moldenhauer and K. M. Michel. 20 vols. Theorie-Werkausgabe, 9 (Frankfurt a. M.: Suhrkamp, 1969), §246.

[10] In this light, see the discussion by Robert Stern, 'Hegel's Doppelsatz: A Neutral Reading', *Journal of the History of Philosophy* 44 (2) (2006): 235–66.

[11] Hegel expressed this in the *Phenomenology* by saying that the truth must be comprehended 'not merely as *substance* but also equally as *subject*'. G. W. F. Hegel, 'Phenomenology of Spirit (Translated by Terry Pinkard)', <http://terrypinkard.weebly.com/phenomenology-of-spirit-page.html>, §17.

[12] To have a basic normative status is to have the status conferred on oneself via 'recognition'. This theme of recognition (*Anerkennung*) in Hegel is vast and requires an entirely separate treatment. It forms the core of some of the non-neo-Platonist interpretations of Hegel. A representative sample but not exhaustive would be: Kojève and Queneau, *Introduction to the Reading of Hegel* (New York: Basic Books,

normative status. Hegel's thesis—to state it baldly and in overly general terms—is that a form of life, as a normative social space, makes certain unconditional demands on the agents living within it, and if those demands turn out to be unintelligible, then the agents can no longer inhabit those statuses—they can no longer be the people they are. When that impossibility comes to full self-consciousness, the norms lose their grip on those people and something new emerges from having to deal with that normative loss.[13]

Hegel's paradigm case for such a practical dialectic is presented in the 1807 *Phenomenology* in his discussion of Sophocles' *Antigone*, where Antigone is presented as having three unconditional and incompatible demands placed on her by virtue of being the Greek woman she is. She unconditionally must bury her brother, she unconditionally must obey her uncle Creon's order not to bury her brother, and she unconditionally must not choose for herself which of these duties to obey. Whatever she does is thus deeply wrong, and her plight, for Hegel, manifests a deeper contradiction in ancient Greek life which, by making Greek life ultimately unintelligible to itself, made it ultimately uninhabitable for those Greeks. (It is abundantly clear that much more needs to be said about this. It also does not rule out, as Hegel also makes clear, that the human capacity for denial will enable that form of life to continue for centuries.)

24.1.2.2 *The Realization of Freedom*

In the introduction to the *Philosophy of Right*, Hegel asserted that, for us, his modern audience, the elements of practical normativity had to be drawn out from the social conditions in which freedom could be actualized, that is, made *wirklich*, efficacious in the world.[14] This rested on a more complicated defence of the idea that freedom's status as the 'baseline' of 'right' had to do with the way it had come to be required of us by virtue

---

1969); Pippin, *Hegel's Practical Philosophy: Rational Agency as Ethical Life*; Brandom, *Tales of the Mighty Dead: Historical Essays in the Metaphysics of Intentionality*; Brandom, *Reason in Philosophy: Animating Ideas*; Pinkard, *Hegel's Phenomenology: The Sociality of Reason*; Moyar, *Hegel's Conscience*; Ludwig Siep, *Anerkennung als prinzip der praktischen Philosophie : Untersuchung zu Hegels Jenaer Philosophie des Geistes* (Freiburg [Breisgau]; München: Alber, 1979); Honneth, *The Struggle for Recognition: The Moral Grammar of Social Conflicts*.

[13] One of the major ways of taking the dialectic does not see it as being anything like a Wittgensteinian conception of the intractability of philosophical problems. It is instead supposed to indicate a real movement in things themselves. One of the best statements of that way of understanding the dialectic is to be found in Stephen Houlgate, *Hegel and the Philosophy of Nature* (Albany: State University of New York Press, 1998); and Houlgate, *Freedom, Truth and History : An Introduction to Hegel's Philosophy*.

[14] The term 'actuality' is the term of art for translating Hegel's use of *Wirklichkeit* which in more ordinary German simply means 'reality'. However, Hegel distinguishes reality (*Realität*) from actuality (*Wirklichkeit*). Roughly, that amounts to saying that reality is merely what exists, whereas actuality is what is efficacious. The neo-Platonist interpretation generally sees the distinction as that between what exists and that which is a more full expression of what it is. Hegel notes: 'What is actual is what is efficacious (*was wirklich ist, kann wirken*), its actuality announces itself through that which it brings forth.' G. W. F. Hegel, *Wissenschaft der Logik II*, ed. E. Moldenhauer and K. M. Michel. 20 vols. Theorie-Werkausgabe, 6 (Frankfurt a.M.: Suhrkamp, 1969), 208; A. V. Miller translates the relevant phrase as 'what is actual can act'. G. W. F. Hegel, *Hegel's Science of Logic*, tr. A. V. Miller (London and New York: Allen & Unwin; Humanities Press, 1969), 546.

of the failures of past alternative concepts of a baseline—or what Kant called 'the unconditioned'—for preceding forms of life. That particular argument, he thought, had been carried out in the 1807 *Phenomenology*, and it thus formed the unargued starting point of the 1820 book.

For Hegel, to be free is, first, a way of 'being at one with oneself' (*Beisichsein*), and one is ultimately at one with oneself when one's actions and dispositions are intelligible to oneself—when one's life, as it were, makes sense to oneself. Second, Hegel did not think that freedom had to involve a kind of non-standard conception of causality (as did Kant). Instead, he thought that it involved an agent's 'second nature' (her acquired dispositions and habits) and the ability to make one's own character (as constituted by those dispositions, skills, and so forth) itself an object of action, such that one's own character can be modified over time in light of one's own values.[15] (Clearly much more needs to be said about this, but that at least is the basic view.[16])

With that in mind, an outline of Hegel's ethical system thus goes something like this. We inhabit various statuses in social life, and we can be efficaciously free in those statuses only if, first of all, our social world exhibits a collective and effective commitment to something like the very basic rights of traditional liberal theory. The employment of those rights, however, can itself be actual only if agents are capable of subjecting themselves to universal norms of the domain of morality. Finally, morality itself can be actual only if there is a much more substantive domain to practical life, which Hegel calls ethical life and in which our character is shaped and oriented by more determinate ideas of the ethos of the social world around us about how one is to live a satisfying life within the span of birth, aging and death.

The unconventionality of Hegel's general line of argument is that he is not proposing a new theory of rights, morality, or ethics. Rather, he is arguing that none of the key disputes in moral or ethical theory can ever be solved in the sense that there can be a

---

[15] As Hegel quasi-paradoxically puts it, 'the abstract expression of the Idea of the will is itself the free will that wills the free will'. G. W. F. Hegel, *Grundlinien der Philosophie des Rechts*, ed. E. Moldenhauer and K. M. Michel. 20 vols. Theorie-Werkausgabe, 7 (Frankfurt a.M.: Suhrkamp, 1969), §27. Hegel holds that the ability to subject our own second nature to the deliberative powers we have acquired in acquiring a second nature is itself historically structured.

[16] Whether Hegel is indifferent to the causal conditions of action is part of a lively debate in contemporary Hegel scholarship. Robert Pippin argues that Hegel's account is more in keeping with the expressionist theories of action advanced by Elizabeth Anscombe (see G. E. M. Anscombe, *Intention* (Cambridge, MA: Harvard University Press, 2000)) and Charles Taylor (see Charles Taylor, 'Hegel's Philosophy of Mind', *Human Agency and Language* (Cambridge and New York: Cambridge University Press, 1985), 77–96); Pippin holds not that Hegel denies any causal conditions of action so much as he thinks that a purely 'voluntarist-causalist' account of action is insufficient. See Pippin, *Hegel's Practical Philosophy: Rational Agency as Ethical Life*. The counter-position for the importance of a causal account even for the expressionist view is argued by Christopher Yeomans, *Freedom and Reflection: Hegel and the Logic of Agency* (London: Oxford, 2011). A more common way of reading Hegel's theory of freedom is either to assimilate it to a kind of Kantian 'what I would do under the conditions of proper reflection' (see Patten, *Hegel's Idea of Freedom*) or to see it as a version of 'actions that express my true self' (see, for example, Paul Franco, *Hegel's Philosophy of Freedom* (New Haven, CT: Yale University Press, 1999)).

definitive argument in favour of one side of one of the many antinomies that make their appearance in the history of philosophy. The resolution of the problem is practical in that different practical contexts circumscribe the authority of others and thus manage to take away the threat the conceptual puzzle seems to present to reason. For example, we moderns must, so it seems, think of ourselves as self-originating sources of claims and thus think of ourselves as having general inalienable rights to life, liberty, and property. However, since the conflicts among these rights are obvious, and the basis for the claim to them is itself at issue, it becomes unclear is one can fully inhabit the status of a rights-holder without being alienated from it. The conceptual puzzles about rights—'Are rights relative to social purposes or do they have independent status?', 'Does life trump property?'—cannot be resolved in a philosophical theory. Rather, they are made livable by being circumscribed within another practical context, namely, that of 'morality'. In 'morality', an individual leads a life of holding himself only to norms he can universalize—of, as Hegel puts it, occupying a subjective standpoint that speaks of 'a justice freed from subjective interest and subjective shape and from the contingency of power'.[17] The argument is thus that 'morality' makes the claims of general inalienable rights actual, *wirklich*, effective and not that it solves for all time the issue between, say, Locke and Hobbes. The problems do not go away, but the threat they pose is now not so apparent.

Hegel makes the same kind of move with 'morality' itself. There are its various puzzle cases—utilitarian versus Kantian theories, egoism, perfectionism, etc.—and its various conflicts—Hegel cites at various points what he calls 'lifeboat cases' and what we nowadays would call cases of 'agent regret' and 'moral luck'—and there is the problem of circumscribing the kind of appeal to conscience that is so much part of the moral point of view. All of these threaten a kind of alienation that would make the moral life only barely inhabitable. The puzzles of moral philosophy cannot go away, and, within the terms of 'morality' itself, they cannot be definitively solved. Hegel's point is, again, not that it would be impossible to lead the life of a rights-bearing, moral individual. It is that a purely moral life would be rather empty—a correct life but without definite direction for itself and perhaps without warmth.

This general discussion of Hegel's dialectical approach means that Hegel can have no *a priori* method for arguing about any particular move (say, from 'abstract right' to 'morality').[18] (He does of course think he has a 'logic' that tells him about what kinds of antinomies generally emerge and how they are to be dealt with theoretically.) Thus, the generality of this discussion here has to be unsatisfying for philosophers since it outlines

---

[17] Hegel, *Grundlinien der Philosophie des Rechts*, §94.

[18] In his *Logic*, Hegel notes that some post-Kantians—he means most likely J. F. Fries—take up Kantian ideas without asking 'whether and how they [the ideas] are able to be determinations of the thing-in-itself (following the Kantian mode of expression), or rather to be determinations of what is rational', to which he then immediately adds: 'The objective logic is consequently the genuine critique of those determinations—a critique which considers them not in terms of the abstract form of apriority as opposed to a posteriori, but rather considers them themselves in their particular content.' G. W. F. Hegel, *Wissenschaft der Logik II*, ed. E. Moldenhauer and K. M. Michel. 20 vols. Theorie-Werkausgabe, 5 (Frankfurt a.M.: Suhrkamp, 1969), 62.

only Hegel's general approach and general conclusions, not his particular arguments, which is what he thinks are at stake.

24.1.2.3 *Ethical Life*

We can actually be 'moral individuals' only if there are institutions and practices that provide more determinate orientation for us, which Hegel calls *Sittlichkeit*—'ethical life' (the term of art generally adopted in English for translating Hegel's usage of the German term). Ethical life consists of a set of basic practices and institutions—one might say 'social facts'—that point to various goods which are to serve as orientations for rights-bearing, moral agents when they reflectively attempt to make sense of the course of a life from birth to aging and death. Unlike Kant's postulation of a future state in which virtue would be rewarded, Hegel instead claimed that within some existing practices, there can be a rational expectation that a life lived by an orientation to those goods-as-social-facts would itself be a successful life—a moral and satisfying life which, even if not always a happy life, is meaningful. ('Satisfaction', *Befriedigung*, was Hegel's replacement-concept for Aristotle's conception of *eudaimonia* as the flourishing life.[19])

'Ethical life' thus supposedly circumscribes the authority of 'abstract right' and 'morality'. It does not solve the problems of 'morality'—the conceptual puzzles remain—but it provides a more concrete set of ethical statuses that prevent the moral life from being alienated from what is required of it. It is articulated within three practices: the family, civil society, and what Hegel called 'the state'.

Humans have to deal with each other in terms of facts about infancy, aging, and vulnerability and the psychological dimensions of humans coming to terms with those facts. The family is the most immediate human institution that deals with the ethical goods associated with those facts of human life. In this light, Hegel thinks that, in particular, the biological differences between men and women and the necessity of raising children so as to form their characters in the right way means that in modern times the relation between men and women in the family must be that of ethical equality, and that the differences based in the different organic needs of the sexes and of children must be reflected in the structure of marriage and the family. The social statuses to be found in modern family life must, that is, actualize, make inhabitable the demand for universality found in 'abstract right' and 'morality'.

The obvious problem with Hegel's conception of what is implied by the ethical equality of the sexes is that, by our standards, his conception is not merely sexist but ridiculously so and thus 'for us' uninhabitable. For Hegel, it seemed to be simply a fact that men are made for wielding power and pursuing rigorous intellectual pursuits, whereas women are really only cut out for taking care of men (and children) and that therefore

---

[19] In his lectures on the history of philosophy, Hegel identified *eudaimonia* as 'the energy of the (complete) life willed for its own sake, according to the (complete) virtue existing in and for itself'. G. W. F. Hegel, *Vorlesungen über die Geschichte der Philosophie I*, ed. E. Moldenhauer and K. M. Michel. 20 vols. Theorie-Werkausgabe 19 (Frankfurt a.M.: Suhrkapm), 222. ['Die Energie des um seiner selbst willen seienden (vollkommenen) Lebens, nach der an und für sich seienden (vollkommenen) Tugend.']

something like a nuclear bourgeois family incorporating a clear division of labour between hard-put breadwinners and emotionally nurturing housekeepers is the only way to render family life rational and free. (That Hegel even thought he had to make such an argument is also evidence that the 'facts' he cites were already in dispute in his own time. Hegel's discussion is also another paradigm case about how a status can historically become uninhabitable, even though centuries of humans prior to that time found it perfectly natural.)

On the other hand, his treatment of the family may be seen as asking the right questions—namely, about what is necessary to secure ethical equality between the sexes—without at the same time coming close to what would count as a satisfactory answer. That it would turn out that men and women jointly found it increasingly impossible to fully inhabit those nineteenth-century statuses should not have been surprising to a Hegelian.

The family makes the universality of moral duties more concrete in the way it takes the socially established institution of the family itself to be the 'universal' in terms of which all particular duties and such are to be articulated—parents have special duties to their own children, spouses to each other, etc. However, subordination by individuals to the needs of the family will inevitably come into conflict with the demands made by other families, and the dialectic of clashing duties—for example: should the special obligations of the family trump moral duties or vice versa?—will be irresolvable within the terms strictly of 'morality' or even those of 'family' itself. For Hegel, there can be no overarching strictly 'moral' code that will successfully balance the competing claims of morality and the family without simply begging all the questions at hand. The moral problem of special duties versus universal duties is not to be solved intellectually in moral philosophy. Rather, it is to be dissolved practically in ethical life.

The normative authority of the family needs to be circumscribed by another social grouping, that of civil society. In the ancient world, that circumscription came directly from political society itself. However, in the modern world, a mediating social arrangement between families and political life has come into existence, namely, civil society—*bürgerliche Gesellschaft*—a semi-public, semi-private arrangement in which a world of 'individuals as burghers' cooperate and compete with each other in ways that are neither fully political nor fully private but which are nonetheless supposed to involve civility towards each other. The 'moral' individual has to balance the demands of his or her own family with the demands of morality, but only in civil society does the social space appear in which that balance can be actually struck. The burgher of civil society is thus entitled to seek the protection of his own interests—in Hegel's case, almost always a 'his'—and those of his family (thus overruling what seems to be 'morality's' demand to look after all children and people fully equally), while still being required to demonstrate civility in this way of life as a component of what is required to make civil society itself an actual, efficacious social space and thus to balance fairly his family's claims against others. (Hegel's holism makes it an open question as to what happens to the ethical structure of the family when the 'his' is augmented by a 'her' in civil society, but that is another story.)

As a grouping of individuals and associations within the structure of a market economy, civil society in turn requires for its own maintenance two kinds of self-regulation. There has to be a collection of private associations whose purpose is to look after the interests of their members and uphold the kinds of standards and ethical behaviour appropriate to the association—such that the good burgher knows what it means to be a good lawyer, accountant, craftsman, mechanic, etc., and how that can override what might seem like the impartial claims of morality, as when, for example, somebody favours another simply because 'she is her client', as well as knowing when favouring one's own client must give way to more impartial standards. The practices that are the social glue of civil society are supposed to enable practical judgements, such as 'Any rational agent who was a middle-aged mechanic with an ill child would ...'. In carrying out the requirements of his various statuses in civil society, the individual thus fleshes out for himself the project of being a 'moral' individual.

In addition to that kind of self-regulation, there must also be a quasi-political structure within civil society which Hegel calls the 'state based on need' (*der Notstaat*). The 'state based on need' approximates to the kind of state imagined by traditional social contract and liberal theorists. Its function is to look after the common welfare by establishing and sustaining institutions for keeping public order, making sure that the essentials of common life—clean drinking water, food supply, satisfactory treatment of waste, etc.—are regulated and supervised and that the push and pull of economic competition is kept from tipping too much to one side or another. Its legitimacy arises out of the shared sense that without it, things would go rather badly. Civil society is thus a patchwork of individual interests playing off each other so as to produce a common interest in the way life goes on in the cooperative-competitive arrangements of modern social life.

With its private associations and regulatory agencies, civil society provides the social space for rights-bearing, moral agents in which they can effectively step outside of the more restricted world of their family lives and lead lives approaching actual freedom. That freedom is nonetheless always at the edge of alienation, and it lives by a measure that is not immune from change. Its day to day functioning—as each burgher learns to bend to the will of others while displaying his own *amour propre* to the world—is the stuff of satire and provides the material for the rich nineteenth-century novel.

However, the balance of interests that make up civil society cannot itself be in a normative position to judge how best to strike that balance. As a market society, civil society will have winners and losers (as do all competitive situations). The winners will want to see the balance as properly leaning more in their direction. The losers will wish to see the balance going another way.

One of Hegel's most controversial theses is that the resolution of these types of conflicts cannot itself be adjudicated in any way in keeping with the norms that sustain the legitimacy of 'abstract right', 'morality', 'family', and 'civil society' itself (including 'the state based on need'). Instead, they must be the shared norms of a political life, and the social space in which that takes place is called 'the state'.

For Hegel, the 'state' consists of the institutions and practices that make up the social space in which 'burghers' become 'citizens' and thus become actually free. For there to be such a status as 'citizen', there must be a subjective identification on the part of the individual with the common project of his or her co-citizens, and there must be (from the objective side) these common commitments themselves. The principles appropriate to the 'state' are thus not moral principles, strictly speaking, since what is required of a citizen—that he or she take a special concern for his or her own political community, even at the expense sometimes of members of other communities—is an ethical and not a universal moral demand. The state thus does not abolish universal moral duties; it only circumscribes the principles of morality (and family and civil society) and supposedly provides a context within which the moral life may be actual and not be merely the dream of saints.

Those 'common commitments' take on flesh in terms of the constitution of a particular state (whereas 'morality' leads in the direction of cosmopolitanism), and for the citizens to see themselves as citizens—as co-participants in the common life and not merely as the subjects of a sovereign—they must also see their interests represented in such a political unity. Although that sounds like it would lead Hegel to an endorsement of representative democracy, he in fact does the opposite. Why he does this is a complicated story, but, in a nutshell, for Hegel democracy can only be the direct democracy practised in ancient Athens, and any attempt to make a democratic state out of the modern bureaucratic state would, he thought, only be a recipe for repeating and possibly magnifying the worst excesses of the French Revolution while throwing out the vast gains the Revolution made possible. Thus, he argued instead for a highly bureaucratic state with a representative government consisting, roughly, in an old-fashioned system of estates with a figurehead constitutional monarch at its head. Politics takes place more or less purely at the ministerial level. This bureaucratic state was to be led by proper men with the proper degrees from the proper universities where they have been taught by the proper professors.[20]

Nobody in contemporary times, including Hegel's biggest fans, can read Hegel's laudatory account of the state without experiencing some kind of apprehensive shudder. To be sure, much of the apprehension is alleviated once one understands that Hegel has a much more Aristotelian sense of the polis in mind than he does anything like the horrors that the late nineteenth century called 'the state' or especially with the way those horrors came to actualization in the twentieth century. Nonetheless, although Hegel was no nationalist and looked on the rising German nationalism of his own time with a mixture of revulsion, disdain, and dismissive sarcasm, he still thought that the only way such a representative constitutional state could be sustained was by its being embedded within a nation state. (Hegel's own antipathy to empire was partially rooted in that.)

To hold such a view, he thus also had to argue that the different nation states of Europe at their basis were at one with each other and that the differences among them was at

---

[20] In his rightfully lauded study of the *Philosophy of Right*, Jean-François Kervégan argues that Hegel's version of the bureaucratic state actually has more in common with the kinds of large-scale bureaucratic democracies than Hegel has been given credit. Jean-François Kervégan, *L'effectif et le Rationnel: Hegel et l'esprit objectif* (Paris: J. Vrin, 2007).

best the differences of various relatively non-important national ethos. He thought that this was supported by the social sciences of the day (many of which subscribed to what we now see as clearly racist ideas), and he could thus conclude that citizens brought up and subjected to the ethos of, say, Germany and France would nonetheless be free in that the citizens of each would have characters that rationally compelled them to take certain actions, even though those characters and those actions would at least superficially look somewhat different. What would be therefore rationally compelling in specific national cases would be superficially different from nation to nation. If anything, Hegel simply did not take seriously enough the deeper tensions already at work in his own resolution of the problem of providing an answer to the questions raised by the modern, market-oriented political nation state. The nation state, of course, has turned out to be a much more complicated realization of freedom—it has at times even turned into its very opposite—than Hegel had thought.

Finally, as embedded in a nation state, this modern emphasis on freedom, so Hegel also thought, could thus only be legitimated by an appeal to history. It is, once again, another story altogether, but his general idea was that the normative status of freedom in the modern world had to do with the way it resulted from the specific failures of earlier forms of life in which an agent's will was determined by baseline principles that were ultimately not intelligible. That the baseline for one's will lay in some given fact (for example, that so-and-so was 'the chief' or that God had inscrutably decreed that some but not others belonged to a ruling noble class) had turned out to make no sense. In the famous short-hand Hegel used for his students, history had thus progressed from the state where one was free (the ruler, the pharaoh, the tribal chief) to the state where some were free (the aristocratic males of ancient Greece and Rome) and then finally to the state in which all were free (which had its penultimate consummation in the Rousseauian-Kantian idea that in a rational world, each agent would be both sovereign and subject in the fashioning of moral and ethical ideals). What remained was to make practical and political sense of what was required to actualize the freedom promised by that ideal of the equal freedom of all.

24.1.3 The Final End of the World

What remained of Kant's three questions? First, as we noted, Hegel held that we can indeed know the world as it is 'in itself'. The contradictions involved in thinking of the world 'unconditionally' reveal something about us, not that the world in itself is unknowable. Second, we can know what is unconditionally required of us by attending to what is rational in the ethos of our modern social lives (which involves understanding that what counts as unconditionally required of us is itself historical in nature). Third, we may therefore rationally hope for a satisfying, flourishing life in the here and now by leading an ethical life in terms of the rational orientations within our own actual ethos.

Although nature as a whole aims at nothing, it does produce life, and life has produced self-conscious creatures. Such self-conscious creatures seek to understand what it is that they are about and to what they are committed. In turn, the final end of the world is that of *Geist* (our own mindedness) coming to a full self-consciousness. To use a phrase Charles Taylor made famous, we are self-interpreting animals, and as we finally come to understand ourselves as such self-interpreting animals, we now know that we have been and always will be a problem to ourselves.[21] The dialectic of searching for the unconditioned never stops—or, rather, to use Hegel's own semi-paradoxical image, its only rest lies in its comprehending its own perpetual movement. Thus, the answer to Kant's fourth question is that we are 'minded'—*geistig*—creatures. This self-reflection on the part of natural creatures is the final end of the world at least in the sense that there is no further purpose outside of that end and that purpose is intelligible to itself. (Note that Hegel's thesis is not that the world was designed in any way to achieve that goal.) Moreover, this final end is, in the modern articulation of this view, actual in the here and now, not something which we must postulate as lying in an indeterminate future. (One of the most controversial elements of Hegel's view is whether 'this world as involving self-conscious creatures' constitutes what we are to call the divine. His own school broke apart over that issue, and to this day the issue about Hegel's Christianity or his lack of it remains a potent force in Hegel scholarship.)

On Hegel's view of this final end, neither the moral life nor the political life in any 'state', however well organized, can on its own be fully satisfactory. Life lived solely within the terms set by the 'state' produces its own set of antinomies, and it requires a standpoint outside of itself to provide the context in which to evaluate it. 'Absolute' spirit—the institutions and practices of art, religion, and philosophy—thus circumscribes even the authority of the state. However much Hegel may have underestimated the more sinister possibilities of the nation state, he never thought it was 'absolute', and, like his hero, Aristotle, he thought that the ethical life complemented by contemplation was the most satisfactory life possible. (Whether Hegel's version of contemplation as the highest good is able to avoid all the difficulties of Aristotle's own version of it is another question, just as whether his substitution of satisfaction—successfully accomplishing a set of ethical, rational goals—adequately avoids the difficulties within Aristotle's idea of *eudaimonia*.)

24.2 MARX

Marx claimed to have found Hegel standing on his head (as an idealist) and to have set him back on his feet (as a materialist). Although it has always been a matter of great controversy as to just exactly how much Marx preserved of Hegel, it is clear that Marx thought Hegel's philosophy was, if anything, too contemplative. Marx's famous eleventh Thesis on Feuerbach expressed the point succinctly—'The philosophers have only interpreted the world in various ways; the point, however, is to change it.'

---

[21] Charles Taylor, *Human Agency and Language. Philosophical Papers* (Cambridge and New York: Cambridge University Press, 1985).

No less controversial is the issue of whether Marx had anything like an ethics. Marx clearly did not like capitalism and the 'bourgeois society' in which it expressed itself. However, he also did not think 'bourgeois society' was unjust. Both in the *Communist Manifesto* (co-authored with Friedrich Engels) and in his *Critique of the Gotha Program*, he made it very plain that his misgivings about capitalism did not have to do with any claim about its injustice. Marx either thought that there simply was no abstract concept of justice but only conceptions particular to a given economic and political order, or perhaps that even if there were an abstract conception of justice (such as 'like cases treated alike'), it would be useless in adjudicating competing realizations of that principle in different economic and political orders. Since both in practice worked out to the same thing, he obviously felt no particular need to take a side on that issue. However, in any event he clearly thought that the idea that the worker was not receiving his 'fair share' of goods in society was simply mistaken. In capitalism, the worker gets exactly what he deserves according to the rules which regulate capitalist exchange, and that amounts to virtually nothing.

It is also clear that Marx thought that capitalism is deeply irrational, since, having once unleashed enormous productive forces in its origins, it now necessarily unleashes social forces that will prove to be its own doom—it creates, in Marx's phrase, its own grave-diggers—but that kind of irrationality could not have been the sole source of Marx's distaste for it. After all, many early Romantics saw ancient Greek life as digging its own grave but nonetheless as having greater or equal value to what came after it.

Marx's chief complaint about capitalism is not only that is it irrational, but that it is based on *exploitation* and that it *alienates* the people living under it.[22] In other places, he seems to think, in a quasi-Aristotelian vein, that it prevents both a full flourishing of human life and/or that it prevents an equality of such flourishing.[23] In still other places, he suggests a third complaint: capitalism is a system of *servitude* (namely, to capitalist production) which because of its own necessary dynamic places a burden on workers that can neither be sustained nor rationally defended.[24] Because of his distaste for servitude, some have taken him to be implicitly arguing for an ideal of equality that, although also at home in 'bourgeois' theory, is impossible to realize in capitalist society.[25]

---

[22] Allen W. Wood, *Karl Marx* (second edition, New York and London: Routledge, 2004) argues that issues of justice are derivative from issues about exploitation and surplus value.

[23] Jonathan Wolff, *Why Read Marx Today?* (Oxford: Oxford University Press, 2003) argues that it has to do with more people flourishing under socialism in contrast to the few who do under capitalism.

[24] Allen E. Buchanan, *Marx and Justice: The Radical Critique of Liberalism* (Totowa, NJ: Rowman & Allanheld, 1982). Buchanan thinks that for Marx capitalism disguises its servitude under the banner of free exchange. Nonetheless, Buchanan argues that the ultimate criterion for Marx is one which he never succeeded in delineating fully, namely, that a 'better' society than capitalism would be one in which non-distorted needs are fulfilled. (It is unfulfilled because Marx never gave anything approaching a criterion for distinguishing a non-distorted from a distorted need.)

[25] Gerald Cohen's work as a whole argues for this thesis, although the greater emphasis on equality only comes out in the later works. See G. A. Cohen, *Karl Marx's Theory of History : A Defence* (expanded edition; Princeton: Princeton University Press, 2001); and G. A. Cohen, *Why Not Socialism?* (Princeton, NJ and Oxford: Princeton University Press, 2009).

One of the things that Marx inherited from Hegel is the conviction that we cannot specify the content of at least the important ethical concepts without attending to their realization. But in standing 'Hegel back on his feet', Marx wanted to argue that Hegel got it all wrong in his own views about this. For Marx, Hegel's conception of the realization of the concept, if nothing else, put too much emphasis on the concept and not enough on the realization. Whereas for Hegel, the concept 'gave itself its own actuality' in the sense that the norms of the concept pressed for their own realization—the idea that 'all are free' presses for the kind of institutional reform that took almost 1,800 years to manifest itself—for Marx talking like that in effect simply obfuscated the more basic fact that the concepts themselves are merely the normative articulation of the practices in which they are embedded, and it is those practices to which attention must be paid, not primarily the concepts into which they are articulated. To do otherwise, Marx thought, was to fall into the trap of 'idealism', that is, into the belief that ideas determine the reality of practice and not the other way around.

However, even practices are not themselves bedrock explanatory items. Marx held that the ways in which a society makes itself explicit to itself—what he called the elements of the 'superstructure' of any society—are in fact dependent on and therefore to be explained by the underlying economic structure of the society—roughly, the forces of production (that is, the productive powers and capacities of a society, which includes its level of technological development) and the relations of production (roughly, who owns what in the system of production). A further Marxian thesis is that this economic structure produces classes within itself (where 'class' is defined in terms of its relation to the means of production, that is, in terms of who owns what). On the traditional reading of Marx, the existence of classes and how they formed the consciousness of their members takes explanatory priority over the behaviour of individuals in the classes. (Some of the most creative interpreters of Marx have challenged that very claim in trying to develop Marxist theory in ways that answer to later criticisms of it and to show how Marxist conclusions can be drawn from premises that do not presuppose the primacy of class action over individual action.[26])

In practice, these ways of making explicit the normative proprieties of the economic—and, therefore, class—structure of society inevitably constitute different ideologies, that is, false but attractive ways of presenting the existing social order that serve to underwrite the claims of a class (or the members of a class) to exercise power over others in the name of reason, nature, religion, or whatever serves to bolster that rule. (That is, in general, 'ideologies' attempt to offer an attractive picture of why the interests of one or a few are supposedly the interests of all.) The contrast to 'ideology' is *science*, and thus Marx almost always presented his views as a set of scientific analyses of capital and the economy and not as pieces of philosophy (which, as the analysis or development of concepts, is always going to end up being merely a supple tool for the ideologists of the existing order).

In particular, for Marx, the dominant ideological ideas of the existing bourgeois order were those of 'the individual' and of 'free choice'. The basic norm of bourgeois society is

[26] The most famous and best argued version is Cohen, *Karl Marx's Theory of History: A Defence.*

that 'individuals' as rational, autonomous agents should be allowed to make whatever free choices they wish to make, and neither the state nor any local governing body should interfere with that choice. For Marx, the various philosophical defences of the set of norms connected with those ideals should be analysed not so much in terms of the arguments that, say, Kant or Mill managed to put together to make the ideals coherent or attractive, but in terms of what the norms really mean when they are viewed in their practical employment in the reality of a class society. The ideal of free choice, for example, underwrites the view that free exchange between worker and employer is an ideal to be protected as the only way of securing human dignity. Such an ideal thus disguises or makes practically invisible the facts of exploitation. Someone may be said to exploit another when they use them as a means, when the person (or class) exploited is harmed, and when the person doing the exploiting benefits from it. The very possibility of exploitation rests on the vulnerability of those exploited, and the kind of economic vulnerability which capitalism exploits is by and large a product of capitalism itself. For Marx, the usual set of 'bourgeois' arguments that turn on what 'really' constitutes 'free exchange' are all therefore ways of ideologically covering up the real fact of exploitation which, for example, neo-Kantian theories—which insist on the sacrosanct character of consenting relations between consenting adults—cannot, because of the very terms they use, even have in view.

A huge part of Marx's argument thus rests on the claim that capitalism necessarily exploits the worker and that in doing so, it digs its own grave. Marx's argument for this, in its barest outlines, is something like the following. The explanation of the possibility of the real phenomenon of profit in a capitalist order presupposes that there must be a commodity that creates more value in its use than its costs. This is to be found in the concept of 'labour power'. The capitalist purchases not the worker's labour but his labour power (roughly, the worker's ability to produce commodities). The capitalist owns the means of production (the technology, the raw materials, etc.), and the worker owns only this capacity to labour. From the standpoint of the individual capitalist (whether it be a person or a firm), the labour power of workers is simply one more cost (one more commodity) in the market to be factored into the productive process. In that respect, the worker's labour power is on the same level as, say, the cost of raw materials. The price the capitalist has to pay for such labour power is the amount necessary for the labourer to show up again for work (or, to put it in Marx's terms, the cost of the labourer 'reproducing' himself, i.e. getting just enough food and rest to continue working). Furthermore, it is rational for the capitalist to purchase the worker's labour power only if the worker creates a 'surplus value', that is, works for x hours to produce the commodity and then works for x+n hours for the capitalist in effect without compensation. Now, to compete in the capitalist market, the individual capitalist must purchase labour power at the lowest possible cost to himself or be wiped out by his competitors, and this fact pushes capitalists both to develop new technology—machines that will do the work at a lower cost than it formerly took human beings to do—and to globalize their firms in the search for cheaper labour markets around the world. Eventually, as the whole world has become subject to the demands of capitalism, the workers of the world become increasingly squeezed until they can stand it no more, and then out of desperation and their own self-interest will revolt against the rule of capital and replace it with a socialist, more humane form of social order in which (somehow) the means of production will be subordinated to human need, instead of human need remaining distorted under the capitalist order. In such a system, servitude will have been abolished, lives will not be (as) alienated, and people will flourish (or have equal opportunity to flourish).

Marx would not deny that there are 'moral' questions to be raised within the capitalist order. Perhaps, say, child labour should be condemned or made illegal, or perhaps there should be policy initiatives taken to preserve the health of the environment. However, all such moral questions ultimately run up against the limits of capitalism as a whole, which itself rests on the exploitation of material and people. Moral demands to humanize the system of exploitation will ultimately have to face the barriers set by the very terms of capitalism, such as how far capitalists themselves can move in a more ethical or equitable direction and still be around the next day to do business (that is, will not be taken over or simply put out of business by more ruthless, less 'ethical' competitors).

Marx therefore tended to dismiss all 'bourgeois' philosophies as simply competing ideologies that one and all begged the question of whether 'the individual' was the basic unity of analysis. However, Marx had kinder words for Hegel than for others. Thus, although from Marx's point of view, both Hegel and Mill were 'bourgeois' philosophers, Marx nonetheless cast far more vituperation in Mill's direction, since Marx shared with Hegel the view that we cannot understand our ordinary ethical and political concepts except by understanding them in some more holistic way—in Hegel's case, in terms of a 'form of life' (Gestalt des Lebens) and in Marx's case in terms of the class system that is concomitant with a certain form of economic organization. (Whether this is fair to Mill is another issue.)

A Marxian critique of bourgeois moral theory therefore takes the form of a critique of the ideology behind bourgeois theory. Rather than analyse concepts such as 'obligation', Marx would advise us to look at whose interests—in particular, which class interests—are being served by doctrines of 'rightness' and 'goodness' or on how a focus on certain ideas simply amount to ways of turning people's attention away from the real issues and onto issues of more 'bourgeois' concern (such as worries about self-perfection or the final goods of life that somehow presuppose individualism at their core). For a Marxian (of at least relatively orthodox persuasion), anything like, say, a Rawlsian theory with its ground-level commitment to ideals of 'fairness' will have to be taken as a well-meant but misguided attempt to overcome the contradictions in capitalist society by appeal to the interests of all the parties—misguided because in fact there are basic disputes between workers and capitalists that simply cannot be resolved by an appeal to 'fairness'. It is right for the workers to demand a greater share of the fruits of their labour, it is right for capitalists to refuse to grant that demand (since it will mean their own ruin), and there simply is no 'fair' solution to that basic contradiction. In such a fully contradictory social and economic order, Marx, echoing Hegel at this point, argued that it was the inhabitability of the status of being a 'worker' that would push the old order into the new one.

Fully committed Marxists are, of course, in shorter supply these days than they were previously. What survives of the Marxist critique? Marx's interest in teasing out the role of ideology in social thought remains a staple of political theory even if not much of a theme in mainstream Anglophone political philosophy. His suspicions about the origin of certain key ideas do not play a great role in mainstream normative ethics—one finds little echo of his suspicions that what counts as the 'paradigm case' or the 'settled intuitions' of moral theory themselves are really only symptoms of something deeper, such as class position and social politics. (On the other hand, one might do a quick look at all the thought experiments in contemporary journal articles on normative ethics and ask which ones represent, say, the dilemmas of working-class men and women struggling with sporadic employment as they work at two to three jobs in an environment plagued with drug wars and the like, versus the ones that have to do with upper middle class people failing to show up for engagements for which they have made a promise or with the way personal advancement might conflict with something like friendship or family life. A Marxian hunch would be that many more of one type than the other will surface in those articles, and that this is not accidental.)

Marx's critique of the irrationality of capitalism has also been taken up and incorporated into various 'continental-philosophical' views, which typically incorporate Max Weber's more conservative view that capitalism has locked us into the 'iron cage' of rationalization and economic efficiency, and Heidegger's conception of the way in which such rationalization indicates some kind of end-point for the West in particular and perhaps even humanity in general.

Nonetheless, one thing that does remain *au courant* is Marx's materialism, or what is nowadays called 'naturalism', which, apart from Marx's use of it, is a potent force in contemporary philosophy.

Other features of Marx's theory have not fared so well.[27] The labour theory of value can be upheld only by adding lots of epicycles to it, and the view that there is a sharp cognitive separation between the kind of science he claims to do versus the supposed exercises in mere ideology that philosophers carry out is, to put it mildly, difficult to defend. However, now that Marxism is no longer a state orthodoxy in major parts of the world, Marx may finally take his place alongside Hume, Rousseau, Kant, Hegel, Mill, and other classical ethical and political theorists of the eighteenth and nineteenth century, all of whom continue to inspire new interpretations of their work and continue to suggest new ways of looking at old problems.

BIBLIOGRAPHY

Anscombe, G. E. M. 2000. *Intention*. Second edition. Cambridge, MA: Harvard University Press.
Beiser, F. C. 2005. *Hegel*. First edition, Routledge philosophers. New York and London: Routledge.

[27] The canonical list of all the alleged failures of Marxist theory may be found in Leszek Kolakowski, *Main Currents of Marxism: The Founders, the Golden Age, the Breakdown* (New York and London: W. W. Norton, 2005).

Brandom, R. 1994. *Making it Explicit: Reasoning, Representing, and Discursive Commitment*. Cambridge, MA: Harvard University Press.

—— 2002. *Tales of the Mighty Dead: Historical Essays in the Metaphysics of Intentionality*. Cambridge, MA: Harvard University Press.

—— 2008. *Between Saying and Doing: Towards an Analytic Pragmatism*. Oxford and New York: Oxford University Press.

—— 2009. *Reason in Philosophy: Animating Ideas*. Cambridge, MA: Harvard University Press.

Brinkmann, K. E. 2010. *Idealism without Limits: Hegel and the Problem of Objectivity*. First edition. New York: Springer.

Buchanan, A. E. 1982. *Marx and Justice: the Radical Critique of Liberalism*. Philosophy and Society. Totowa, NJ: Rowman & Allanheld.

Cohen, G. A. 2001. *Karl Marx's Theory of History: a Defence*. Expanded edition. Princeton: Princeton University Press.

—— 2009. *Why not Socialism?* Princeton, NJ and Oxford: Princeton University Press.

Franco, P. 1999. *Hegel's Philosophy of Freedom*. New Haven, CT: Yale University Press.

Geuss, R. 2005. *Outside Ethics*. Princeton: Princeton University Press.

Hartmann, K. and Müller, O. 1999. *Hegels Logik*. Berlin: De Gruyter.

Hegel, G. W. F. 1969a. *Enzyklopädie der philosophischen Wissenschaften II*, ed. E. M. Moldenhauer and K. M. Michel. 20 vols. Theorie-Werkausgabe, 9. Frankfurt a.M: Suhrkamp.

—— 1969b. *Grundlinien der Philosophie des Rechts*, ed. E. Moldenhauer and K. M. Michel. 20 vols. Theorie-Werkausgabe, 7. Frankfurt a.M: Suhrkamp.

—— 1969c. *Hegel's Science of Logic*, tr. A. V. Miller. Muirhead library of philosophy. London and New York: Allen & Unwin; Humanities Press.

—— 1969d. *Vorlesungen über die Geschichte der Philosophie II*, ed. E. Moldenhauer and K. M. Michel. 20 vols. Theorie-Werkausgabe, 19. Frankfurt a.M.: Suhrkamp.

—— 1969e. *Wissenschaft der Logik I*, e. E. Moldenhauer and K. M. Michel. 20 vols. Theorie-Werkausgabe, 5. Frankfurt a.M.: Suhrkamp.

—— 1969f. *Wissenschaft der Logik II*, ed. E. Moldenhauer and K. M. Michel. 20 vols. Theorie-Werkausgabe, 6. Frankfurt a.M.: Suhrkamp.

—— n.d. 'Phenomenology of Spirit (translated by Terry Pinkard)', <http://web.me.com/tit-paul/Site/Phenomenology_of_Spirit_page.html>.

Henrich, D. 1971. *Hegel im Kontext*. Edition Suhrkamp. Frankfurt a.M.: Suhrkamp.

—— and Pacini, D. S. 2003. *Between Kant and Hegel: Lectures on German Idealism*. Cambridge, MA and London: Harvard University Press.

Honneth, A. 1995. *The Struggle for Recognition: the Moral Grammar of Social Conflicts*. Cambridge, MA: Polity Press.

Horstmann, R.-P. 1991. *Die Grenzen der Vernunft: Eine Untersuchung zu Zielen und Motiven des deutschen Idealismus*. Frankfurt a.M.: Anton Hain.

Houlgate, S. 1991. *Freedom, Truth and History: an Introduction to Hegel's Philosophy*. London: Routledge.

—— 1998. *Hegel and the Philosophy of Nature*. SUNY series in Hegelian studies. Albany: State University of New York Press.

Kervégan, J.-F. 2007. *L'effectif et le rationnel: Hegel et l'esprit objectif*. BibliothÁeque d'histoire de la philosophie temps modernes. Paris: J. Vrin.

Kojève, A. and Queneau, R. 1969. *Introduction to the Reading of Hegel*. New York: Basic Books.

Kolakowski, L. 2005. *Main Currents of Marxism: the Founders, the Golden Age, the Breakdown.* New York and London: W. W. Norton.

Kreines, J. 2004. 'Hegel's Critique of Pure Mechanism and the Philosophical Appeal of the Logic Project', *European Journal of Philosophy* 12 (1): 38–74.

—— 2006. 'Hegel's Metaphysics: Changing the Debate', *Philosophy Compass* 1 (5): 466–80.

McCumber, J. 1993. *The Company of Words: Hegel, Language, and Systematic Philosophy.* Northwestern University Studies in Phenomenology and Existential Philosophy. Evanston, Ill: Northwestern University Press.

McDowell, J. H. 2009. *Having the World in View: Essays on Kant, Hegel, and Sellars.* Cambridge, MA: Harvard University Press.

Moyar, D. 2010. *Hegel's Conscience.* New York: Oxford University Press.

Neuhouser, F. 2000. *Foundations of Hegel's Social Theory: Actualizing Freedom.* Cambridge, MA: Harvard University Press.

Patten, A. 2002. *Hegel's Idea of Freedom* (online text). Oxford: Oxford University Press. <http://www.columbia.edu/cgi-bin/cul/resolve?clio7692586%3E>.

Pinkard, T. P. 1994. *Hegel's Phenomenology: the Sociality of Reason.* Cambridge: Cambridge University Press.

—— 2000. *Hegel: a Biography.* Cambridge: Cambridge University Press.

—— 2002. *German Philosophy, 1760–1860: the Legacy of Idealism.* Cambridge: Cambridge University Press.

Pippin, R. B. 1989. *Hegel's Idealism: the Satisfactions of Self-Consciousness.* Cambridge: Cambridge University Press.

—— 1997. *Idealism as Modernism: Hegelian Variations.* Modern European philosophy. Cambridge: Cambridge University Press.

—— 2005. *The Persistence of Subjectivity: on the Kantian Aftermath.* Cambridge: Cambridge University Press.

—— 2008. *Hegel's Practical Philosophy: Rational Agency as Ethical Life.* Cambridge: Cambridge University Press.

Quante, M. 2004. *Hegel's Concept of Action*, tr. D. Moyar. Modern European philosophy. Cambridge and New York: Cambridge University Press.

Rand, S. 2007. 'The Importance and Relevance of Hegel's Philosophy of Nature', *Review of Metaphysics* 61 (2): 379–400.

Redding, P. 1996. *Hegel's Hermeneutics.* Ithaca, NY and London: Cornell University Press.

—— 2007. *Analytic Philosophy and the Return of Hegelian Thought.* Modern European philosophy. Cambridge: Cambridge University Press.

Rockmore, T. 1997. *Cognition: an Introduction to Hegel's Phenomenology of Spirit.* Berkeley, Los Angeles, and London: University of California Press.

—— 2005. *Hegel, Idealism, and Analytic Philosophy.* New Haven: Yale University Press.

Rosen, M. 1982. *Hegel's Dialectic and its Criticism.* Cambridge and New York: Cambridge University Press.

Russon, J. 2004. *Reading Hegel's Phenomenology.* Indianapolis: Indiana University Press.

Sedgwick, S. 2001. 'The State As Organism: The Metaphysical Basis of Hegel's Philosophy of Right', *Southern Journal of Philosophy* 39 (suppl.): 171–88.

Siep, L. 1979. *Anerkennung als Prinzip der praktischen Philosophie: Unters. zu Hegels Jenaer Philosophie d. Geistes.* Reihe Praktische Philosophie; Freiburg [Breisgau]; München: Alber.

—— 2000. *Der Weg der Phänomenologie des Geistes: Ein einführender Kommentar zu Hegels "Differenzschrift" und zur "Phänomenologie des Geistes".* Suhrkamp Taschenbuch Wissenschaft. Frankfurt a.M.: Suhrkamp.

Speight, A. 2001. *Hegel, Literature, and the Problem of Agency*. Modern European philosophy. Cambridge and New York: Cambridge University Press.

—— 2008. *The Philosophy of Hegel*. Continental European philosophy. Montréal and Ithaca: McGill-Queen's University Press.

Stern, R. 2002. *Routledge Philosophy Guidebook to Hegel and the Phenomenology of Spirit*. Routledge Philosophy Guidebooks. London and New York: Routledge.

—— 2006. 'Hegel's Doppelsatz: A Neutral Reading', *Journal of the History of Philosophy* 44 (2): 235–66.

Taylor, C. 1975. *Hegel*. Cambridge and New York: Cambridge University Press.

—— 1985a. 'Hegel's Philosophy of Mind', *Human Agency and Language*. Cambridge and New York: Cambridge University Press, 77–96.

—— 1985b. *Human Agency and Language*. *Philosophical Papers*. Cambridge and New York: Cambridge University Press.

Westphal, K. R. 2003. *Hegel's Epistemology: a Philosophical Introduction to the Phenomenology of Spirit*. Indianapolis, IN: Hackett.

Williams, R. R. 1992. *Recognition: Fichte and Hegel on the Other*. SUNY series in Hegelian studies. Albany: State University of New York Press.

Wolff, J. 2003. *Why Read Marx Today?* Oxford: Oxford University Press.

Wood, Allen W. 1990. *Hegel's Ethical Thought*. Cambridge and New York: Cambridge University Press.

—— 2004. *Karl Marx*. Second edition. Arguments of the Philosophers. New York and London: Routledge.

Yeomans, C. 2007A. 'Review of Tom Rockmore, *Hegel, Idealism, and Analytic Philosophy*', *Review of Metaphysics* 60 (3): 686–87.

—— 2011. *Freedom and Reflection: Hegel and the Logic of Agency*. New York: Oxford University Press.

CHAPTER 25

....

J. S. MILL

....

HENRY R. WEST

JOHN Stuart Mill (1806–1873) was the greatest British philosopher of the nineteenth century. His importance in the history of ethics is that he defended to a wide public the philosophy called 'Utilitarianism' that had been founded two generations earlier by Jeremy Bentham (1748–1832). Utilitarianism is the theory that actions, laws, institutions, and policies should be critically evaluated by whether they tend to produce the greatest happiness. Mill's short book *Utilitarianism* is the most widely read statement of utilitarian ethics in the history of philosophy.

25.1 MILL'S LIFE AND PHILOSOPHY IN GENERAL
....

Mill's reputation as a philosopher was established by his *System of Logic* (1843), which is not only about logic in the narrow sense but includes a radically empiricist philosophy of language, philosophy of science, and general theory of knowledge. Mill's *Principles of Political Economy* (1848) made him the leading economic theorist of his day. His *On Liberty* (1859), defending freedom of thought and expression, and of liberty of actions and lifestyles that do not harm the legitimate interests of others, is a classic text defending those freedoms. His *Subjection of Women* (1869) was a pioneering work of feminist philosophy. He wrote extensively on political topics, including *Considerations on Representative Government* (1861a). His *Collected Works* (1963–1991) running to 33 volumes, includes his *Autobiography* (1873), six volumes of letters, other books, essays, and speeches. His notes on his father's *Analysis of the Phenomena of the Human Mind* (1869), as extensive as the original text, summarize his psychological theories. Two lengthy books are critical of other thinkers: *Auguste Comte and Positivism* (1865b) and *An Examination of the Sir William Hamilton's Philosophy* (1865a). *Three Essays on Religion* (published posthumously in 1874) contain his critical evaluation of religion, religious ethics, and of an ethics appealing to nature. Early essays on ethics, written in 1833, 1835, and 1852, are reprinted in volume X of the *Collected Works*.

Mill never attended school. He was tutored (as Americans say, 'home schooled') by his father, starting to learn Greek at age 3, Latin at age 8, higher mathematics, economic theory, and nearly everything else taught at the universities by age 15, when he studied law with John Austin, a utilitarian law professor. His education was rigorous, with no vacations. He had no time for amusement or play with other children. His father, James Mill (1773–1836), was a disciple and close associate of Jeremy Bentham, the founder of utilitarianism as a programme in philosophy and political action, and instilled in the young Mill the Benthamite philosophy. Mill was to criticize Bentham in some of his writings, but he never gave up the greatest happiness principle.

When Mill was seventeen, his father, who by that time held an important position in the British East India Company, secured a position in the company for his son. John Stuart was to have a career there until the company was nationalized in 1858, by which time he held a position on a level with a Secretary of State. He never visited India but advised the officers in India by correspondence. The working hours were not excessive, and Mill met with his philosophical friends and did extensive editing and writing while carrying out his duties. At age twenty, Mill suffered what he called a 'mental crisis'. It has sometimes been described as a mental breakdown, but that is a false description. Mill carried on all of his activities with vigour, but he felt depressed that even if the utilitarian project were successful in producing the greatest happiness, it would not make *him* happy. As he recovered from it, he drew two lessons. One was that his education had been one-sided. His intellect had been developed but not his emotions. As a correction, he began to read poetry, especially Wordsworth, and began to seek insights from thinkers outside of the utilitarian tradition. The other lesson was what has been called the 'hedonistic paradox': that one can attain the greatest happiness not by seeking it directly but as a by-product of other activities.

In 1830, when Mill was twenty-five, he met Harriet Taylor, an attractive woman of twenty-two, who was married and the mother of two young children. They developed a 'Platonic' relationship, sharing philosophical ideas, especially their shared interest in the liberation of women from subjection in the family and in other institutions. Two years after her husband died in 1849, they were married, but it is likely that their relationship, which had never been sexual before marriage, remained that way until her death in 1858. Mill called her co-author of much of his writings, especially *On Liberty*. To call her co-author is probably an exaggeration, but her influence was great. She suggested topics for him to write on, and she suggested revisions before publication. After early retirement from the East India Company, Mill had more time for writing. He also was eligible to stand for elected office and was elected to Parliament in 1865. In Parliament he supported the most unpopular causes, including suffrage for women, introducing an amendment to a Reform Bill to substitute 'person' for 'man'. The amendment was defeated, but a substantial minority voted with him. Most unpopular was Mill's support for a working-class candidate who was an avowed atheist. Mill was not surprised when he was not re-elected. After Harriet died, Mill spent much of his time near her grave in Avignon. He died in 1873, recognized as the foremost British philosopher of his time.

Mill's ethical theories are in a context of what John Skorupski calls his 'naturalistic' epistemology and metaphysics and his 'political liberalism' (Skorupski 2006: 45ff). As a naturalist, Mill thinks that human beings have no supernatural or other non-natural powers or influences. They belong to the natural order that is studied by science. He is a determinist and finds human freedom only in the ability to carry out our choices and desires, including our desires to modify our existing desires, not in the power to create choices and desires out of nothing. Mill's epistemology entails that the only 'proof' that can be given for the principle of utility must come from something about scientific human psychology, in his day introspective psychology. It is in that context that one can read Chapter IV of *Utilitarianism*.

In *On Liberty* Mill argues that social coercion should not be used against an individual who is doing no illegitimate harm to others, even if harming him or herself. This is a reflection of Mill's liberal confidence that in general individuals can be the best judges of their own welfare: they best know their likes and dislikes and have the keenest motivation to fulfil their own lives. This view is reflected in Mill's theory of morality. Mill does not require that every choice seek to maximize utility with failure to do so a matter deserving moral censure. There is a standard to which individuals should be coerced morally if not legally, but above that standard maximizing utility should be a matter of merit going beyond the call of duty. Mill believes that some 'higher' pleasures require individual choice, and so he has confidence that this liberty is grounded in utilitarianism. Mill's political liberalism includes his concept of individuality. He thinks that social good is a summation of the goods of individuals' welfare.

In the first chapter of *Utilitarianism*, Mill contrasts his own tradition, which he calls the inductive or empirical, with the intuitive or *a priori* school. According to his opponents, we have a natural faculty, or sense or instinct, informing us of right and wrong. According to the inductive school, right and wrong, as well as truth and falsehood, are questions of observation and experience. This contrast reflects Mill's opposition to *a priori* knowledge in his *System of Logic*. There he argued that *all* knowledge, including mathematics and logic, is based ultimately on the evidence of the senses.

Mill held that the contest between morality based on intuition and that based on the 'external' standard of utility is the contest between a progressive morality and a stationary one, of reason and argument against deification of mere opinion and habit. Mill made the same claim against morality based on 'Nature'. He said that the doctrine that the existing order of things is the natural order, and that, being natural, all innovation upon it is criminal, is as vicious in morals as it has been recognized to be in physics. Mill said that the appeal to what is 'natural' is nothing but an appeal to existing prejudice. We can see the background of Mill's feeling on this subject in his liberalism, his feminism, and his ideas on political reform. In advocating freedom to be unconventional in the living of one's life, in advocating equality in marriage and women's freedom to engage in traditional male roles, in proposing universal adult suffrage, in wishing for freedom from religion as well as freedom of religion, Mill was challenging existing attitudes. Thus he believes that utilitarianism, with its 'external' standard of what empirically has best consequences, is a progressive morality in contrast to one of stagnation.

Mill's chief contributions to the history of ethics are twofold. The first was to popularize utilitarianism: to present utilitarianism in a short text, written by a recognized great philosopher, which could be read with apparent understanding by an ordinary person. The second was to persuade academic philosophers to take utilitarianism so seriously that utilitarianism could compete with Aristotle and Kant as one of the three greatest traditions in ethics. Within that tradition, Mill also made important and controversial contributions. Among these, his distinction between pleasures and pains on the basis of 'quality' as well as quantity is one of the most controversial. Another is his attempt to give a 'proof' of the principle of utility. Not so notorious, but very important, is his placing of morality within a hedonistic 'Theory of Life' as only one of its branches, with moral wrongdoing limited to those actions deserving punishment. Still another is his effort to subordinate justice to utility with a theory of rights based on utility. The remainder of this chapter will examine some of these controversies.

25.2 QUALITATIVE HEDONISM

Mill and Bentham were both hedonists. They believed that the only things of value and disvalue as ends of actions were pleasures and pains. And they both gave a 'mental state' analysis of pleasure and pain. One might be pleased or displeased that some external state of affairs existed or that some external event occurred, but the pleasure or displeasure would be in one's mind, in the consciousness of it.

Bentham analysed the measure of pleasures and pains as two-dimensional. A 'lot' of pleasure or pain consisted of a certain intensity per moment and a certain duration. Bentham did not believe that there are no differences in kind between feelings of pleasure and pain from different sources, and he listed many different sources of pleasures and pain. Some are physical, such as the pleasure of 'sense', and some are psychological. I doubt that he thought that the pleasure from 'power' or from 'piety' felt the same as pleasures or that the pains of hunger and a toothache felt the same as pains. But he believed that all differences were commensurable and could be resolved into a quantitative amount of intensity per unit of time and a quantitative length of duration. He is famous for saying 'Quantity of pleasure being equal, pushpin is as good as poetry'. He did not deny that there were instrumental differences between equal quantities of immediate pleasure or pain, but he thought that if they were of equal quantity they were of equal value in the experience of having them.

Mill seeks to analyse 'higher' and 'lower' qualitative differences between pleasures, introducing the notion that these qualitative differences can make a difference in the value of the pleasures. Mill is responding to the criticism of utilitarianism that it is a doctrine worthy of swine. Mill's reply is that if human beings were capable of no pleasures except those of which swine are capable, the rule of life that is good enough for the one would be good enough for the other. But human beings have faculties more elevated than the animal appetites, and when once made conscious of them do not regard anything as happiness that does not include their gratification. The higher faculties that he names are the intellect, the feelings and imagination, and the moral sentiments (1861b: 211; II: 4; references to *Utilitarianism* will include references to chapter in Roman numerals and paragraph in Arabic). He claims that it is quite compatible with the principle of utility to recognize that some kinds of pleasure are more desirable and more valuable than others, not just instrumentally but as immediate pleasurable experiences. Mill explains what he means as follows:

> If I am asked, what I mean by difference of quality in pleasures, or what makes one pleasure more valuable than another, merely as a pleasure, except its being greater in amount, there is but one possible answer. Of two pleasures, if there be one to which all or almost all who have experience of both give a decided preference, irrespective of any feeling of moral obligation to prefer it, that is the more desirable pleasure. If one of the two is, by those who are competently acquainted with both, placed so far above the other that they prefer it, even though knowing it to be attended with a greater amount of discontent, and would not resign it for any quantity of the other pleasure which their nature is capable of, we are justified in ascribing to the preferred enjoyment a superiority in quality, so far outweighing quantity as to render it, in comparison, of small account. (1861b: 211; II: 5)

Mill claims that those who are equally acquainted with, and equally capable of appreciating and enjoying, both the pleasures of animal appetites and those of distinctly human faculties do give a preference to 'the manner of existence which employs their higher faculties' (1861b: 212; II: 6). Few humans would consent to be changed into any lower animal even for the fullest amount of the beast's pleasure, and 'no intelligent human being would consent to be a fool, no instructed person would be an ignoramus, no person of feeling and conscience would be selfish and base, even though they should be persuaded that the fool, the dunce, or the rascal is better satisfied with his lot than they are with theirs' (1861b: 211; II: 6). Mill explains that this is due to a sense of dignity, 'which all human beings possess in one form or other...and which is so essential a part of happiness of those in whom it is strong, that nothing which conflicts with it could be, otherwise than momentarily, an object of desire to them' (1861b: 212; II: 6). He says that those who think that this takes place at a sacrifice of happiness are confusing happiness with contentment. A being with fewer capacities may be more easily contented but is not thereby happier. 'It is better to be a human being dissatisfied than a pig satisfied; better to be Socrates dissatisfied than a fool satisfied. And if the fool, or the pig, is of a different opinion, it is because they only know their own side of the question. The other party to the comparison knows both sides' (1861b: 212; II: 6).

The wording of Mill's presentation of the distinction between pleasures on grounds of quality is so similar to that of Francis Hutcheson (1694–1746) that Mill must have been influenced by Hutcheson's account in *A System of Moral Philosophy* (1755). There Hutcheson distinguishes between pleasures of the same kind, whose values are 'in joint proportion of their intenseness and duration' and pleasures of different kinds, whose value includes that of 'dignity' (1755: 421). Hutcheson says that we have a sense of dignity of some kinds of enjoyment that no intensity or duration of the lower kind can equal, were they also as lasting as we could wish. 'What may make a brute as happy as that low order is capable of being, may be despicable to an order endued with finer perceptive powers, and a nobler sort of desires... The superior orders in this world probably experience all the sensations of the lower orders, and can judge of them. But the inferior do not experience the enjoyments of the superior' (1755: 421). The higher enjoyments that Hutcheson names are social affections, admiration of moral excellence, and pursuits of knowledge. This list compares with Mill's list of the intellect, the feelings and the imagination, and the moral sentiments.

Mill says that the only procedure available for judging which of two pleasures is the most worth having, apart from their moral attributes and their consequences, is the judgement of those who are qualified by experience of both. But he claims that there is no other tribunal for judgements of *quantity* between two pleasures or whether a particular pleasure is worth having at the cost of a particular pain. The test of quality, and the rule for measuring it against quantity, is 'the preference felt by those who, in their opportunities of experience, to which must be added their habits of self-consciousness and self-observation, are best furnished with the means of comparison' (1861b: 214; II: 10). The preference of these competent judges does not *constitute* the value of the experiences. It is evidential. It requires practice in self-observation and can be improved by the insights of others. There may be differences in preferences between presumably competent judges, and their preferences may change over time. Majority opinion does not settle the matter, but it is the best evidence for a general statement about the value of different kinds of pleasures (Crisp 1997: 36–7).

Critics have asserted that Mill's distinction between kinds of pleasures and pains makes a calculus of pleasures and pains impossible. But Wendy Donner has pointed out that Bentham's quantitative dimensions of pleasures and pains are not as simplistic as they appear. 'Quantity' is not a single property. It is a combination of at least intensity and duration. Bentham assumed that these should be given equal weight, but agents of different character and outlook will differ in how to weigh them. How much intensity in a brief period would outweigh less intensity over a long period of time? (2006: 121–2).

When *Utilitarianism* was first published, Mill was immediately charged with deserting hedonism in his distinction between pleasures on the basis of quality: either it is quantity under a different name or it is appeal to a non-hedonistic value. One of the best known of these critics is F. H. Bradley, who claims that qualitative distinctions make it impossible to make a judgement between different pleasures:

> Given a certain small quantity of higher pleasure in collision with a certain large quantity of lower, how do you decide between them? To work the sum you must reduce the data to the same denomination. You must go to quantity or to nothing; you decline to go to quantity, and hence you can not get any result... Higher, then, as we saw above, has no meaning at all, unless we go to something outside pleasure. (1876: 119; see also Schneewind 1976: 46–7; Grote 1870: 45–57; Albee 1902: 251–2; Moore 1903: 77–8)

In these critiques as in so many since then, the basic assumption is made that pleasure is a kind of sensation that feels the same no matter its source; so only the intensity and duration of this one kind of sensation can be grounds for preference. This begs the question against Mill. If Mill is correct that there really are introspectively different feelings that are all varieties of pleasure and not of something else, then it is possible for these to be compared on the basis of their felt differences and for some to be preferable to others. However, the pleasure is not qualitatively superior because it is preferred. It is preferred because it is qualitatively different, and this difference can be found to be more desirable.

Mill is surely correct that there are qualitatively different pleasures and pains. This is more obvious in the case of pains. If we compare two sensations of pain, such as a stomach ache and a toothache, they are not just in different bodily locations. They feel different as pains. If we compare the pain of grief with the pain of shame, they feel different as pains, and both different from a toothache. Why then are they all called pains?

Mill's theory of language accounts for this. With regard to simple sensations, Mill appeals to remembered resemblance to explain the signification of names: 'the words sensation of white signify, that the sensation which I so denominate resembles other sensations which I remember to have had before, and to have called by that name' (1843: 136). Mill does not say that the qualitative resemblance must be identity, so long as it resembles other experiences of that sort more than it resembles my experience of a different sort. In this example, it need not be a sensation of pure white. So long as it resembles other sensations of white more than grey or yellow or some other colour sensation, it counts as a sensation of white.

Supposing that Mill is correct that there exist qualitative differences between pleasures and pains, there remain the questions whether some are more valuable than others apart from quantity, and, if so, whether the superiority in quality is correlated consistently with the use of 'higher' faculties. The first of these questions is difficult to answer for pleasurable and painful experiences are complex, having instrumental as well as intrinsic value or disvalue, and we have second-order attitudes towards our pleasures and pains that may be part of the total experience. This may explain Mill's reference to the sense of dignity that gives superiority to pleasures of the higher faculties. If one is engaging in an activity that one regards as degrading, there is a second-order pain as part of the total experience. If one is engaging in an activity in which one feels pride, there is a second-order pleasure in one's sense of self-respect. This need not be a feeling of moral obligation regarding the pleasure, and it is not introducing dignity as a non-hedonistic value. It is a pain or pleasure felt as part of the experience. Mill's competent judges are to base the judgement of the qualitative superiority of a pleasure on it 'merely as a pleasure', irrespective of any feeling of moral obligation to prefer it and independent of its consequences, but the experience merely as a pleasure may include the complex pleasure of first- and second-order pleasure and pain. Mill could regard the second-order pleasure or pain as what makes the first-order pleasure or pain 'higher' or 'lower'. It is what distinguishes me from animals as much or more than the fact that the pleasure or pain is one involving the distinctively human faculties.

Mill's argument for the superiority of pleasures that involve the higher faculties is not that one would prefer a single experience of a higher pleasure for a greater quantity of a lower on every occasion, for Mill says that 'the test of quality, and the rule for measuring it against quantity' (1861b: 214; II: 10) is the preference of competent judges, implying that at least in some cases quantity may outweigh quality. Mill does not argue that one would choose a higher pleasure on every occasion of choice. The argument rests on a different question: whether one would be willing to *resign* the higher pleasures for any quantity of the lower; whether one prefers a 'manner of existence' that employs the higher faculties or would be willing to sink into a lower 'grade of existence'. This is not a 'lexical' ordering of pleasures case by case, but of grades of existence. And when asked what one would be willing to resign, the question can be reversed. Would one be willing to resign all the pleasures that we share with animals—eating, drinking, sexual gratification, physical exercise, and physical comfort—for any amount of pleasures of the intellect?

Mill also says that a happy life consists of few and transient pains, many and *varied* pleasures. As long as one does not devote oneself to *exclusively* animal appetites, it would seem that Mill should approve a life of sensory as well as of higher enjoyments.

I conclude that Mill was correct in introspectively analysing pleasures and pains as being of qualitatively different kinds; that those regarded as higher include a second-order pleasure without which one with a sense of dignity could not regard one's manner of existence as a happy one, but Mill did not hold, and should not have held, that a single episode of a higher pleasure outweighs any quantity of the lower.

25.3 MILL'S COMPLEX THEORY OF MORALITY

In the twentieth century a distinction was made between 'act-utilitarianism' and 'rule-utilitarianism' (Brandt 1959: ch. 15). Even before this terminology came into use, J. O. Urmson argued for an interpretation of Mill that would be rule-utilitarian (1953). Others have interpreted Mill as an act-utilitarian. One version of act-utilitarianism would be to say that an act is right if the consequences of the particular act in its unique circumstances would be as good as those of any alternative, otherwise wrong. We can call this 'maximizing act-utilitarianism'. In one important passage, Mill could easily be interpreted as such. He gives as the utilitarian creed that 'actions are right in proportion as they tend to promote happiness, wrong as they tend to produce the reverse of happiness' (1861b: 210; II:2). But it is not obvious that by 'actions' Mill is referring to token actions in particular situations rather than types of actions that have varying consequences on different occasions, but with a *tendency* to produce happiness or unhappiness in the majority of cases. In answering the objection that there is not time, prior to action, for calculating the consequences on human happiness, he says that throughout all of human history, mankind have been learning the tendencies of actions, 'and the beliefs that have thus come down are the rules of morality for the multitude, and for the philosopher until he has succeeded in finding better' (1861b: 224; II: 24). This passage looks as if the rules of morality are merely 'rules of thumb', rules summarizing past experience.

A distinction can be made between the criteria for right action and the criteria for making correct decisions. These could differ. It could be that the act-utilitarian formula works for identifying right actions, but attempting always to use act-utilitarian calculation as a decision procedure may not be as good at achieving the act-utilitarian result as by sometimes appealing to a justified rule (Crisp 1998: 113). Mill could be interpreted in this way, as holding a 'strategic' conception of rules as a means of achieving an act-utilitarian result (Berger 1984: ch. 3). In some passages, however, Mill seems to have a stronger conception of *moral* rules. He says: 'It is truly a whimsical supposition that if mankind were agreed in considering utility to be the test of morality, they would remain without any agreement as to what *is* useful, and would *take no measures for having their notions on the subject taught to the young, and enforced by law and opinion*' (1861b: 224; II: 24; later emphasis added). If there are 'measures' taken for teaching the rules, and rules are to be 'enforced', there is a social dimension to the rules that makes them more than rules of thumb for the individual utilitarian agent's choice of action case by case. Mill also would not permit there to be moral 'free riders'. An individual agent is not permitted to benefit from the security of laws and moral rules and not follow them himself. Mill considers, as an example, the murder of someone whose cruel behaviour tends to increase human unhappiness. The individual act of murder has consequences that favour it, but the counter-consideration, on the principle of utility is: 'that unless persons were punished for killing, and taught not to kill; that if it were thought allowable for any one to put to death at pleasure any human being whom he believes that the world would be well rid of, nobody's life would be safe' (1852: 181). If one person may break through the rule on his or her own judgement, 'the same liberty cannot be refused to others' (1852: 182).

This social view of morality and of rules is supported by what Mill says about sanctions in Chapter V of *Utilitarianism*, where he introduces a criterion by which to distinguish moral duty from general expediency: 'We do not call anything wrong, unless we mean to imply that a person ought to be punished in some way or other for doing it; if not by law, by the opinion of his fellow creatures; if not by opinion, by the reproaches of his conscience. This seems the real turning point of the distinction between morality and simple expediency' (1861b: 246; V: 14). Alan Fuchs has used this and other passages to interpret Mill as a rule-utilitarian regarding *morally* correct action, with any act-utilitarian practices outside of morality in other parts of what Mill calls the 'Art of Life' (2006: 144ff). Henry West has argued that even in morality Mill is neither a pure act-utilitarian nor a pure rule-utilitarian (2004: ch. 4). Mill approved a quotation from one of his father's works that in the performance of our duties there are two sets of cases. In one set of cases a direct estimate of the good of the particular act is inevitable; and the agent acts immorally without making it. There are other cases of such ordinary and frequent occurrence that they can be distinguished into classes, such as just, beneficent, brave, and so on, to which belong an appropriate rule (James Mill 1869: 312–3). It should also be noted that these classes are the names of virtues; so their practice is a practice of the virtues.

Mill evidently thinks that there is a convergence between act-utilitarian considerations, rule-utilitarian considerations, and the virtues. The multiplication of happiness is the object of virtue. He points out that telling a lie does that much to weaken the useful character trait of honesty and to weaken the transcendently useful rule of veracity. But even this rule admits of exceptions, and he says that there is 'no ethical creed which does not temper the rigidity of its laws, by giving a certain latitude, under the moral responsibility of the agent, for accommodation to peculiarities of circumstances' (1861b: 225; II: 25).

Mill's conception of morality is thus complicated. Sometimes morality requires following recognized rules. He wants the practice of some of these rules to be developed into habitual character traits, i.e. virtues. Sometimes morality requires act-utilitarian reasoning and action. But even as a criterion for right action, rather than a decision procedure, Mill is not a maximizing act-utilitarian. He does not want every act to be subject to *moral* evaluation, morally right or wrong. Once basic moral standards have been met, he wants individuals to be free to live their lives without worrying about whether they are doing the act having marginally better or worse consequences than all alternatives. There is also room for 'supererogation', actions that are morally meritorious but which go beyond the call of duty. In his book *August Comte and Positivism*, Mill says:

> It is not good that persons should be bound, by other people's opinion, to do everything that they would deserve praise for doing. There is a standard of altruism to which all should be required to come up, and a degree beyond it which is not obligatory, but meritorious. It is incumbent on everyone to restrain the pursuit of his personal objects within the limits consistent with the essential interests of others. But what those limits are, it is the province of ethical science to determine; and to keep all individuals and aggregates of individuals within them, is the proper object of punishment and moral blame. If in addition to fulfilling this obligation, persons make the good of others a direct object of disinterested exertions, postponing or sacrificing to it even innocent indulgences, they deserve gratitude and honour, and are fit subjects of moral praise... but the encouragement should take the form of making self-devotion pleasant, not that of making everything else painful. (1865b: 337–8)

Mill's position is still further complicated by the fact that some rules have correlative rights that are to be respected and that entitle the right holder to make valid claims even if recognition of those claims in a particular case does not maximize utility. This is stated explicitly in a letter to George Grote in 1862, shortly after the publication of *Utilitarianism*. There he says:

> [R]ights and obligations must, as you say, be recognized; and people must, on the one hand, not be required to sacrifice even their own less good to another's greater, where no general rule has given the other the right to the sacrifice; while, when a right *has* been recognized, they must, in most cases, yield to that right even at the sacrifice, in the particular case, of their own greater good to another's less. (1862: 762)

Still a further complication arises from the fact that some types of acts that might have best consequences on rare occasions cannot be done but from motives that are incompatible with overall behaviour having best consequences. There are two reasons for this. First, states of character are confirmed patterns of behaviour that do not have complete flexibility. The habit of honesty, which is useful as a virtue, cannot be maintained while telling lies on all the occasions when a lie would have marginally better consequences; to be able to lie on every occasion when a lie would maximize utility is incompatible with the most useful degree of habitual honesty. Secondly, acts presuppose states of mind that may be in themselves states of enjoyment or of wretchedness. Such mental states are important in a utilitarian calculation, for Mill considers the pleasures of a nobleness of character, of being a person of feeling and conscience rather than selfish and base, among the qualitatively higher pleasures. Furthermore, these states of mind are fruitful in other consequences besides any particular act: 'No person can be a thief or a liar without being much else: and if our moral judgments and feelings with respect to a person convicted of either vice, were grounded upon the pernicious tendency of thieving and lying, they would be partial and incomplete' (1833: 7). There is nothing inconsistent about this. The ultimate principle for Mill is promotion of the greatest happiness. Whether to calculate consequences case by case, or to act in accordance with rules, or to respect rights, or to practise justified virtues, is a matter of choosing the appropriate means for the promotion of greatest happiness.

25.4 MILL'S 'PROOF'

In Chapter IV of *Utilitarianism*, Mill discusses 'Of What Sort of Proof the Principle of Utility is Susceptible'. He says that it is not proof in the ordinary sense, meaning, presumably, that it is not a deductive entailment from premises. It is an argument based on introspective psychology 'capable of convincing the intellect' (1861b: 208; I: 5), and he says that this is the equivalent of proof.

The evidence on which the argument is based is what people desire as ends. The claim in that when properly analysed each person desires his or her own happiness, in so far as it is believed to be attainable, and all other things that are desired as ends in themselves, such as possession of money, or power, or even virtue, are desired as 'parts' of one's happiness. These are not originally desired as ends, but by association with pleasure and avoidance of pain, individuals become such that they cannot be happy without the possession of these.

If all things desired as ends are desired as parts of happiness, then happiness is the kind of thing that is the end of all deliberate actions and, therefore, the end of moral actions, as moral actions are a part of all actions.

Mill recognizes that some actions are done as ends without thought of any pleasure or pain, but he says that these kinds of actions were originally based on desire and are now done from habit. 'Will is the child of desire and passes out of the dominion of its parent only to come under that of habit. That which is the result of habit affords no presumption of being intrinsically good' (1861b: 238; IV: 11).

The interpretation and evaluation of Mill's 'proof' has been the subject of much discussion. Writing in 1965, J. B. Schneewind said that in the last fifteen years there had been more essays dealing with the topic of 'Mill's Proof' than with any other single topic in the history of ethical thought (1965: 31).

One of the challenges was to Mill's analogy between 'desirable' and 'visible'. Mill says that the evidence that something is visible is that it is seen. The evidence that something is desirable as an end is that it is desired as an end. Mill does not mean by 'desirable' *capable* of being desired. The analogy is that both are appeals to evidence—in one case the evidence of the visual sense; in the other case, the evidence of our 'desiring faculty'.

Mill also generalizes from the fact that each person desires his or her own happiness to the conclusion that the general happiness is what is desirable for the aggregate of all persons. This has been criticized as a fallacy of composition, but in correspondence Mill makes clear that he does not regard the general happiness as anything but a summation of the happiness of the individuals making up the aggregate. If happiness is the *kind* of thing that is desirable, the instances of it in the consciousness of different individuals can be added to constitute what is desirable for an aggregate. Not all present-day philosophers accept that this kind of addition is possible, but it is now generally accepted as Mill's position.

Another source of controversy is Mill's statement: 'desiring a thing and finding it pleasant, aversion to it and thinking of it as painful, are . . . two different modes of naming the same psychological fact . . . to desire anything, except in proportion as the idea of it is pleasant, is a physical and metaphysical impossibility' (1861b: 237–8; IV: 10). This statement is puzzling to the twenty-first-century reader, but in context Mill is asking the reader to engage in 'practiced self-consciousness and self-observation' (1861b: 237; IV: 10). If the terms were reducible to one another independent of observation, it is hard to see why he would invite one to attempt what appears to be an empirical confirmation. It has also been pointed out that the term 'metaphysical' means approximately 'psychological' to him (Mandelbaum 1968: 39). Mill also, in his notes on his father's *Analysis of the Phenomena of the Human Mind*, says that desire is more than the idea of pleasure desired. 'In what we call Desire there is, I think, always included a positive stimulation to action' (James Mill 1869: vol. 2, 194, note 37).

Mill's psychology may be mistaken, but there is now a growing consensus that in his 'proof' the author of *A System of Logic* is not committing elementary logical fallacies unworthy of a logician. He is appealing to psychological evidence to move from the facts of pleasure and pain and of desires and aversions to judgements of good and bad as ends of actions.

25.5 MILL'S THEORY OF JUSTICE

Mill thought of *Utilitarianism* as an essay on the foundations of ethics. But the format is primarily an answer to objections to utilitarian ethics. In Chapter II, he answers various objections: that it is a doctrine worthy of swine, that there is no time prior to action to calculate the consequences of actions, that happiness is unattainable, that utilitarianism renders people cold and unsympathizing, that it is a godless doctrine, and so on. He saves a major objection for Chapter V, the objection that justice is a moral consideration independent of utility and often in conflict with it. Mill attempts to rebut this with arguments that justice is an important part of utility. He recognizes that the subjective mental feeling, the 'sentiment', attached to justice and injustice is different from that which commonly attaches to the general promotion of happiness. Also, except in extreme cases, justice is far more imperative in its demands. He admits that the sentiment is not derived from utility, but in the course of the chapter he argues that what is moral in the sentiment does depend upon utility. And he argues that there is a utilitarian basis for distinguishing justice from other moral obligations and for making the requirements of justice more demanding. If justice is something altogether distinct from utility, which the mind can recognize intuitively, why is there so much controversy over what is just in punishment, in wages, and in taxation? If, on the other hand, justice is subordinate to utility, this is explicable. There will be as much difference of opinion about what is just as about what is useful to society.

Before addressing the connection between utility and justice, Mill gives an analysis of the concept of justice (or of injustice): what is its distinguishing quality. He lists six candidates that make something just or unjust: it is unjust to violate the *legal rights* of anyone; to violate a *moral right*, since it is admitted that there may be rights not recognized by law; for persons not to get what they *deserve*; to *break faith* with anyone; to be *partial* in matters in which favour and preference do not properly apply; and to treat people *unequally* without justification. Mill examines the etymology and the history of usage of the word. He says that it has an origin connected with conformity to law, but not attached to all laws but to such laws as *ought* to exist, and that there may be behaviour that is just or unjust where there are no laws that apply. Even here, Mill thinks that the idea of a penal sanction is the generating idea of the notion of justice, but that is true, he says, of all wrongdoing. The distinguishing feature of justice, he claims, is that duties of justice have a correlative *right* in some person or persons. In the preceding survey the term 'justice' appeared generally to involve the idea of a personal right. Whether the injustice consists in depriving persons of possessions, or in breaking faith with them, or treating them worse than they deserve, in each case the supposition involves a right in some person correlative to the moral obligation. 'Justice implies something which it is not only right to do, and wrong not to do, but which some individual person can claim from us as his moral right. No one has a moral right to our generosity or beneficence, because we are not bound to practice those virtues towards any given individual' (1861b: 247; V: 15).

Turning to the feeling, which accompanies the idea of justice, Mill says that two essential ingredients of it are the desire to punish a person who has done harm and the belief that there is some definite individual or individuals to whom harm has been done. He thinks that this desire is derived from two more basic sentiments that either are or resemble instincts: the impulse of self-defence and the feeling of sympathy. 'It is natural to resent, and to repel or retaliate, any harm done or attempted against ourselves, or against those with whom we sympathize' (1861b: 248; V: 20).

Having analysed justice as the class of obligations that have correlative rights, Mill gives an analysis of what it is to have a right: 'When we call anything a person's right, we mean that he has a valid claim on society to protect him in the possession of it, either by the force of law, or by that of education and opinion' (1861b: 250; V: 24). So far Mill has been analysing the concept of justice and of rights independently of the principle of utility. Now he introduces that principle. When asked why society ought to recognize such rights, Mill says that he can give no other reason than general utility. If that does not convey a sufficient feeling of the strength of the obligation, it is because there goes into the feeling the animal element of self-defence as well as the rational element, and because it is an extraordinarily important and impressive kind of utility that is concerned—that of security. Security no human being can possibly do without. On it we depend for all immunity from evil and the whole value of every good beyond the passing moment (1861b: 251; V: 25).

One of the most influential recent alternatives to the utilitarian theory of justice is that presented by John Rawls in *A Theory of Justice* (1971). Rawls contrasts his approach with utilitarianism by saying that the latter adopts for society as a whole the principle of rational choice for one person. Just as it is rational for an individual to undergo a period of pain to achieve greater happiness at some later time in life, he implies that a utilitarian would inflict pain on one individual in order to achieve greater happiness for other individuals. He says, 'Utilitarianism does not take seriously the distinction between persons' (1971: 27). This description may apply to some versions of utilitarianism, but it does not obviously apply to Mill. The goal of utilitarianism is impartial, but the system of rights envisioned by Mill does not assume that people are not self-interested. Rights are protections of the security of self-interested individuals against other self-interested individuals. As quoted earlier from Mill's letter to George Grote, 'when a right *has* been recognized, [people] must, in most cases, yield to that right even at the sacrifice, in the particular case, of their own greater good to another's less' (1862: 762). It does not follow that individual rights can never be overridden for the greater social good, but Mill does take seriously the difference between persons.

So far we have Mill's statement that justice is subordinate to utility in the broadest sense. The alternative is that we just know what justice and injustice is independently of utility. To this Mill points to great controversies about what policies, in punishment, wages, and taxation are just and unjust. If justice is something that the mind can recognize by simple introspection, it is hard to understand why that internal oracle is so ambiguous.

Mill gives examples of conflicting theories regarding the justice of punishment, wages, and taxation. He is putting these theories forward to assert that they are only partial truths. They are considerations that have plausibility, but their conflict shows that none is definitive of justice. They help persuade the reader that utility is more fundamental than intuitions about justice. Principles of justice are not self-evident. They require a foundation, and Mill believes that utility is the foundation of, and the arbiter in case of conflict between, principles of justice.

Mill still recognizes an important distinction between justice and general utility. He thinks that justice that is grounded on utility is the chief part and the most sacred and binding part of morality.

> Justice is a name for certain classes of moral rules, which concern the essentials of human well-being more nearly, and are therefore of more absolute obligation, than any other rules for the guidance of life ...
>
> The moral rules which forbid mankind to hurt one another (in which we must never forget to include wrongful interference with each other's freedom) are more vital to human well-being than any maxims, however important, which only point out the best mode of managing some department of human affairs ... It is their observance which alone preserves peace among human beings: ... a person may possibly not need the benefits of others; but he always needs that they should not do him hurt. (1861b: 255–6; V: 32–3)

Mill summarizes by saying that justice is the appropriate name for certain social utilities that are vastly more important, and therefore more absolute and imperative, than any others are as a class and that, therefore, ought to be, as well as naturally are, guarded by a sentiment 'distinguished from the milder feeling which attaches to the mere idea of promoting human pleasure or convenience, at once by the more definite nature of its commands, and by the sterner character of its sanctions' (1861b: 259; V: 37).

Thus, Mill feels that he has answered the objection that justice is distinct from utility. His claim is that the modes of conduct required by justice can be given a utilitarian justification and, in cases of conflict between competing theories of justice, even require a utilitarian arbitration. And although the sentiment attached to instances of justice is different from that which attaches to utility in general, the very existence of that distinct and stronger sentiment has a utilitarian support.

25.6 Conclusion

Mill popularized utilitarianism and dignified it by a defence from the greatest philosopher in Britain of his time. He also worked out a complex theory that is not subject to many of the criticisms that have been directed against utilitarianism in its more simplistic forms. His theory is not a maximizing act-utilitarian version of utilitarianism. It has a role for authoritative rules, rights, and virtues. In some details of psychology and argument it may be subject to criticism, but it is a plausible theory that must be taken seriously by ethical philosophers.

Bibliography

Albee, E. 1902. *A History of English Utilitarianism*. London: Sonnenschein; New York: Macmillan.

Bentham, J. 1789. *An Introduction to the Principles of Morals and Legislation*, ed. J. H. Burns and H. L. A. Hart. London: University of London, Athlone Press, 1970.

Berger, F. R. 1984. *Happiness, Justice, and Freedom: The Moral and Political Philosophy of John Stuart Mill*. Berkeley and Los Angeles: University of California Press.

Bradley, F. H. 1876. *Ethical Studies*. Second edition. London: Oxford University Press, 1927.

Brandt, R. B. 1959. *Ethical Theory*. Englewood Cliffs, NJ: Prentice-Hall.

Cooper, W. E., Nielsen, K., and Patten, S. C. (eds) 1979. *New Essays on John Stuart Mill and Utilitarianism. Canadian Journal of Philosophy*, supp. vol. 5. Guelph: Canadian Association for Publishing in Philosophy.

Crisp, R. 1997. *Routledge Philosophy Guidebook to Mill on Utilitarianism*. London and New York: Routledge.

—— (ed.) 1998. *J. S. Mill: Utilitarianism*. Oxford: Oxford University Press.

Donner, W. 1991. *The Liberal Self: Mill's Moral and Political Philosophy*. Ithaca: Cornell University Press.

—— 1998. 'Mill's Utilitarianism', in Skorupski (ed.) 1998, 255–92.

—— 2006. 'Mill's Theory of Value', in West (ed.) 2006, 117–38.

—— and Fumerton, R. 2009. *Mill*. Chichester: Wiley-Blackwell.

Dryer, D. P. 1969. 'Mill's Utilitarianism', in Mill 1969, lxiii–cxiii.

Eggleston, B., Miller, D. E., and Weinstein, D. (eds) 2011. *John Stuart Mill and the Art of Life*. Oxford and New York: Oxford University Press.

Fuchs, A. 2006. 'Mill's Theory of Morally Correct Action', in West (ed.) 2006, 129–58.

Grote, J. 1870. *An Examination of the Utilitarian Philosophy*, ed. J. Bickersteth Mayor. Cambridge: Deighton, Bell, and Co.

Hutcheson, F. 1755. *A System of Moral Philosophy*. Reprinted in part in *British Moralists*, ed. L. A. Selby-Bigge. Oxford: Clarendon Press, 1897.

Lyons, D. 1994. *Rights, Welfare, and Mill's Moral Theory*. Oxford: Oxford University Press.

Mandelbaum, M. 1968. 'On Interpreting Mill's *Utilitarianism*', *Journal of the History of Philosophy* 6: 35–46.

Mill, J. 1869. *Analysis of the Phenomena of the Human Mind*. Second edition, ed. John Stuart Mill (first edition 1829). 2 vols. Reprint, New York: Augustus M. Kelley, 1967.

Mill, J. S. 1833. 'Remarks on Bentham's Philosophy', in Mill 1969, 3–18.

—— 1835. 'Sedgwick's Discourse', in Mill 1969, 31–74.

—— 1838. 'Bentham', in Mill 1969, 75–116.

—— 1843 (eighth edition 1871). *A System of Logic: Ratiocinative and Inductive*, in Mill 1963–1991, vols. 7–8.

—— 1848 (sixth edition 1871). *Principles of Political Economy*, in Mill 1963–1991, vols. 2–3.

—— 1852. 'Whewell on Moral Philosophy', in Mill 1969, 165–202.

—— 1859. *On Liberty*, in Mill 1977, 213–310.

—— 1861a. *Considerations on Representative Government*, in Mill 1977, 371–578.

—— 1861b. *Utilitarianism*, in Mill 1969, 203–60.

—— 1862. 'Letter to George Grote, January 10, 1862', in Mill 1972, 762.

—— 1865a (fourth edition 1872). *An Examination of Sir William Hamilton's Philosophy*, in Mill 1963–1991, vol. 9.

—— 1865b. *Auguste Comte and Positivism*, in Mill 1969, 261–368.

—— 1868. 'Letter to Henry Jones, June 13, 1868', in Mill 1972, 1414.

—— 1869. *The Subjection of Women*, in Mill 1984, 259–340.

—— 1873. *Autobiography*, in Mill 1981, 1–290.

—— 1874. *Three Essays on Religion*, in Mill 1969, 369–489.

—— 1963–1991. *Collected Works of John Stuart Mill*, eds. J. M. Robson. 33 vols. Toronto: University of Toronto Press.

—— 1969. *Essays on Ethics, Religion and Society*, ed. J. M. Robson, in Mill 1963–1991, vol. 10.

—— 1972. *The Later Letters of John Stuart Mill 1849–1874*, ed. F. E. Mineka and D. N. Lindley, in Mill 1963–1991, vols. 14–17.

—— 1977. *Essays on Politics and Society*, ed. J. M. Robson, in Mill 1963–1991, vols. 18–19.

—— 1981. *Autobiography and Literary Essays*, in Mill 1963–1991, vol. 1.

—— 1984. *Essays on Equality, Law, and Education*, in Mill 1963–1991, vol. 21.

Miller, D. E. 2010. *J. S. Mill: Social and Political Thought*. Cambridge and Malden, MA: Polity Press.

Moore, G. E. 1903. *Principia Ethica*. London and New York: Cambridge University Press, 1959.

Packe, M.St. John 1954. *The Life of John Stuart Mill*. London: Secker and Warburg.

Rawls, J. 1971. *A Theory of Justice*. Cambridge, MA: Harvard University Press.

Robson, J. M. and Laine, M. (eds) 1976. *James and John Stuart Mill: Papers of the Centenary Conference*. Toronto: University of Toronto Press.

Ryan, A. 1970. *The Philosophy of John Stuart Mill*. London: Macmillan; New York: Pantheon Books; second edition, New York: Macmillan, 1988.

—— 1974. *J. S. Mill*. London and Boston: Routledge and Kegan Paul.

Schneewind, J. B. (ed.) 1965. *Mill's Ethical Writings*. London: Collier-Macmillan; New York: Collier Books.

—— 1976. 'Concerning Some Criticisms of Mill's *Utilitarianism*, 1861–76', in Robson and Laine ksksizss5–54.

Skorupski, J. 1989. *John Stuart Mill*. London and New York: Routledge.

—— (ed.) 1998. *The Cambridge Companion to Mill*. Cambridge: Cambridge University Press.

—— 2006. 'The Place of Utilitarianism in Mill's Philosophy', in West (ed.) 2006, 26–44.

Sumner, L. W. 2006. 'Mill's Theory of Rights', in West (ed.) 2006, 184–98.

Urmson, J. O. 1953. 'The Interpretation of the Philosophy of J. S. Mill', *Philosophical Quarterly* 3: 33–40.

West, H. R. 1976. 'Mill's Qualitative Hedonism', *Philosophy* 51: 101–5.

—— 2001. 'Mill, John Stuart', in *The Encyclopedia of Ethics*, 2nd edn., eds L. C. Becker and C. B. Becker. 3 vols. New York and London: Routledge, 1098–104.

—— 2004. *An Introduction to Mill's Utilitarian Ethics*. Cambridge: Cambridge University Press.

—— (ed.) 2006. *The Blackwell Guide to Mill's Utilitarianism*. Malden, MA, and Oxford: Blackwell Publishing.

—— 2007. *Mill's Utilitarianism: A Reader's Guide*. London and New York: Continuum.

CHAPTER 26

SIDGWICK

BART SCHULTZ

26.1 INTRODUCTION

HENRY Sidgwick (1838–1900), born in Skipton, Yorkshire UK, was a product of Rugby and Trinity College, Cambridge University, where he spent his entire collegiate and professional life, from 1883 as Knightbridge Professor of Moral Philosophy.

A brilliant student, Sidgwick was as an undergraduate elected to the 'Apostles', the highly influential secret Cambridge discussion society; allegiance to this group and the free and open enquiry for which it stood profoundly shaped his philosophical outlook. In the 1860s, which he described as his years of religious 'Storm and Stress' when he lost his Anglican faith, he also developed the ethical arguments on which his future fame would rest and solidified his identity as an academic liberal and reformer, out to expand educational opportunities (especially for women), foster greater academic professionalism (especially in philosophy), and fight for wider academic and religious freedom. He famously resigned his Fellowship in 1869 because he could no longer in good conscience subscribe to the Thirty-Nine Articles of the Church of England as that position required. His pamphlet on the question of such religious oaths, 'The Ethics of Conformity and Subscription', explained that religious authority needed a different basis, one more akin to the authority of science, 'formed and maintained by the unconstrained agreement of individual thinkers, each of whom we believe to be seeking truth with single-mindedness and sincerity, and declaring what he has found with scrupulous veracity, and the greatest attainable exactness and precision' (Sidgwick 1870: 14–15).

Sidgwick's masterpiece, *The Methods of Ethics*, was first published in 1874, and according to the received wisdom it marks the culmination of the classical and non-theological utilitarian tradition—the tradition of Jeremy Bentham and James and John Stuart Mill, which took 'the greatest happiness' as the fundamental normative demand. Sidgwick's account of that position is indeed canonical, but the *Methods* also reflects the model of free enquiry that he had admired in science, and it has consequently often served as a general model for academic ethical theory, providing systematic, historically informed comparisons between utilitarianism and leading alternatives. Although Sidgwick did personally favour the utilitarian view, his arguments were very heavily qualified and nuanced, so much so that he allowed that he had not conclusively defended that position. Both critics and defenders of utilitarianism, e.g. John Rawls and Peter Singer, have been inspired by Sidgwick's work. C. D. Broad went so far as to call the *Methods of Ethics* 'on the whole the best treatise on moral theory that has ever been written...one of the English philosophical classics' (Broad 1930: 143).

Sidgwick was not only a pre-eminent ethical philosopher and historian of ethical philosophy, but also an accomplished epistemologist, classicist, political economist, political theorist, political historian, literary critic, parapsychologist, and educational theorist. With his wife, Elearnor Mildred Sidgwick, née Balfour, he was a founder of both the British Society for Psychical Research (Gauld 1968) and Newnham College, Cambridge, one of the first women's colleges (Tullberg 1998).

26.2 ETHICS AND METHODS

Oscar Browning once related how Sidgwick had confessed to him, upon completing the *Methods*, 'I have long wished and intended to write a work on Ethics. Now it is written. I have adhered to the plan I laid out for myself; its first word was to be "Ethics", its last word "Failure"' (Hayward 1901: xix).

Sidgwick never did come to believe that he had fully justified the ethical or religious views that he personally favoured, and his extraordinary capacity for critical self-examination and self-doubt is perhaps the most lasting source of his philosophical fame, though this would have chagrined him considerably. The scrupulous intellectual honesty of his head did not satisfy the longings of his deeply religious heart—a fact that for some makes him a true Victorian and for others makes him a more profound philosophical sensibility than the earlier utilitarians, both theological and non-theological. And for all the seeming clarity of his writing, interpretive controversies over his views abound, as do philosophical controversies about the views that Sidgwick may or may not have defended. If it seems tolerably clear that he did not allow himself a full philosophical embrace of the views he favoured, it is less clear why he favoured those views and conducted (or limited) his enquiry in the ways that he did.

An early account of *The Methods* by one of Sidgwick's critics, Henry Calderwood, provides a concise overview and a characteristic expression of frustration:

A threefold classification of Ethical theories is given: Egoistic Hedonism, which makes self-love or self-interest the sole test of what is right; Intuitionalism, which makes absolute and self-evident law the standard; and Universal Utilitarianism, which takes as its test the greatest happiness of the greatest number. The author avows himself an Intuitional Utilitarian. Throughout the work Psychological analysis is little employed. The objective method, or that of external observation, is generally preferred. Great favour is shown for an Eclectic mode of dealing with conflicting theories. In consequence, it is often difficult to say towards which side the discussion is tending, while assertions are commonly guarded with 'it seems,' or 'upon the whole,' or similar modifying phrase. A condensed statement is not easily attempted. (Calderwood 1888: 343)

Still, Calderwood does take the work to be 'A vindication of Utilitarianism' and 'a criticism of rival theories, tested by the question of the moral standard adopted', and if he has some difficulty fitting Sidgwick's argument to that description, and largely relies on citations of chapter and verse to explain what Sidgwick is about, he remains persuaded that the many qualifications still move the argument in a particular and less than impartial direction.

Calderwood's dilemmas in making sense of Sidgwick's masterpiece have proved enduring. In recent years, whole rafts of critics have charged that the *Methods* seriously fails as a piece of impartial enquiry. Thus, as T. H. Irwin forcefully put it, speaking for many:

Sidgwick's discussion of methods shows that he is not an impartial Socratic investigator, but relies from the outset on his dogmatic convictions about the truth of utilitarianism and the conflict between egoistic hedonism and utilitarianism. If he had not relied on these dogmatic convictions, he would not have recognized the three methods that he recognizes. These convictions are 'dogmatic', not in the sense of being unexamined or not open to argument, but in so far as they are positive claims accepted in advance of the inquiry and controlling the shape and direction of the inquiry. (Irwin 2007: 89–90)

Indeed, critics have argued both that Sidgwick begged the question against intutionism, missing how it could be improved in its own terms (Donagan 1992), and that he was mired in a hopeless form of it and/or of ethical cognitivism generally (Deigh 2007; Hardin 2009). Also, that he was prejudiced in his treatment of perfectionism, of Aristotle, of Kant, and of the philosophical idealism of his friend T. H. Green, allowing his utilitarian sympathies and a fixation on the determinacy of practical reason to mislead him (Hurka 2001; Brink 2003; Korsgaard 2009; Irwin 1992, 2007, 2009). Although Rawls emulated Sidgwick's comparative approach, he pitted his own theory of justice as fairness against Sidgwick's utilitarianism and his Kantian constructivism against Sidgwick's 'rational intuitionism', claiming that the *Methods* failed to grasp Kant's best insights (Rawls 1971, 1503, 2007; Parfit 2011). Still more sweepingly, historical philosophers of an anti-modernity bent have claimed that the *Methods* reflects the bankruptcy of Enlightenment philosophizing in general (MacIntyre 1990). And to add to the confusion, the *Methods* has struck others, even some of Sidgwick's contemporaries, as marking the culmination of the rational egoist position (Hayward 1901) and of the theological utilitarian tradition, the tradition famously associated with William Paley's *Principles of Moral and Political Philosophy* (1785), which Sidgwick had imbibed as a Cambridge undergraduate. G. E. Moore (Sidgwick's student) and his Bloomsbury followers owed Sidgwick much, but harshly dismissed his defences of hedonism and rational egoism, and mocked his religious longings (Moore 1903; Schultz 2004b).

Some of these controversies concern Sidgwick's notion of a 'method', which is admittedly obscure and can seem too limited, in its threefold classification. In some respects, his approach on this score is quite historically distant; at least, his notion of a 'method of ethics' is not the same as the familiar terms 'ethical principle', 'ethical theory', or even 'ethical decision-procedure', though it is more like an abstract and purified version of the latter. A method is supposedly 'any rational procedure by which we determine what individual human beings "ought"—or what it is "right" for them—to do' (Sidgwick 1874/1907:1), and thus it might reflect an ethical principle or principles as the ultimate ground of one's determination of what one has most reason to do, while allowing that one might ordinarily be reasoning from such principles either directly or indirectly. The idea seems to be to zero in on how moral judgements are determined or reached from principles, or the various and jumbled leading tactics common sense deploys in reaching conclusions about what it is right to do. Thus, one might, with theological utilitarians, hold that the moral order of the universe is utilitarian, with God willing the greatest happiness of the greatest number, while also holding that the appropriate guide for practical reason is enlightened self-interest, since utilitarian calculations are God's business and God has ordered the cosmos to ensure that enlightened self-interest conduces to the greatest happiness. In this case, one's 'method of ethics' would be rational egoism, but the ultimate philosophical justification for this method would appeal to utilitarian principles.

Yet despite this emphasis on the idealized reasoning process between principles and practical conclusions, Sidgwick does seek a defence of the ultimate principles of practical reason. Moreover, given Sidgwick's vast historical knowledge of the history of ethics, it is difficult to see how he could have unthinkingly supposed the *Methods* did justice to all the important 'methods of ethics' and related issues. He obviously thought highly of the general state of civilization in late Victorian England, and he was candid about his menu of methods being derived from the common sense of his time and place, rather than doing justice to the full range of concerns that historically had made up the subject of ethics. As he noted in *Outlines*:

> the subject of Ethics, most comprehensively understood, includes (1) an investigation of the constituents and conditions of the Good or Wellbeing of men considered individually, which chiefly takes the form of an examination into the general nature and particular species of (a) Virtues or (b) Pleasure, and the chief means of realizing these ends; (2) an investigation of the principles and most important details of Duty or the Moral Law (so far as this is distinguished from Virtue); (3) some inquiry into the nature and origin of the Faculty by which duty is recognized and, more generally, into the part taken by Intellect in human action, and its relation to various kinds of Desire and Aversion; (4) some examination of the question of human Free Will. (Sidgwick 1886: 10–11)

In his concise review of the historical contingencies that have brought one or another element of ethics so construed into prominence in one context or another, Sidgwick urges that there is a divide between ancient and modern ethics, with the latter, more jural approach construing ethics as 'concerned primarily with the general rules of Duty or Right Action—sometimes called the Moral Code—viewed as absolutely binding on every man, and properly to be obeyed by him without regard to his personal interests;

the relation of duty to the agent's private happiness being regarded as a matter of second-ary concern from an ethical point of view' (Sidgwick 1886: 6). This construction of the conflict between an ancient, 'attractive' notion of ethics, with the good taking priority, and a modern 'imperative' or jural notion of ethics, with the right taking priority (and the issue of Conscience coming to the fore), remains highly defensible (Larmore 1996). Although Sidgwick's own theory appropriates much from the ancients, in the end it falls decidedly in the modern camp.

Indeed, as Calderwood noted with dismay, Sidgwick sets aside many of these histori-cally important concerns, ancient and modern. He largely dismisses concern with the 'moral faculty' and moral psychology, arguing that, whatever its source, in any given situation, there is something that one ought to do that is right, and this is the proper sphere of ethics. The basic concept of morality is this unique, irreducible, and highly general notion of 'ought' or 'right' that is *sui generis*, and moral approbation is 'insepara-bly bound up with the conviction, implicit or explicit, that the conduct approved is "really" right—that is, that it cannot without error, be disapproved by any other mind' (Sidgwick 1874/1907: 27). That is, Sidgwick defended what today is typically labelled an intuitionistic form of non-reductive moral realism, the view that we really do have genu-ine value-based reasons for taking one course of action rather than another (but see Crisp 2006 on the issue of irreducibly *moral* reasons). And he seemed to take what would now be called an 'internalist' stance on these, at least concerning motivation, allowing the motivational force of such reasons (though not necessarily their overriding motivational force). For Hayward, it was preposterous to think that this 'emphasis on reason' could be found among Sidgwick's 'Hedonistic predecessors', for whom the very term intuitional utilitarian would have been oxymoronic (Hayward 1901).

In fact, and in contrast to Irwin, Schneewind (1977) has argued in detail that the *Methods* is less a brief for utilitarianism than an attempt to consider that position in a dif-ferent and more (albeit not fully) impartial way, by comparing it with such alternatives as rational egoism and the intuitionism characteristic of the 'Cambridge Moralists', particu-larly Mill's arch antagonist William Whewell, and this in the hope that common-sense morality might yield support for some form of religion. Sidgwick, Schneewind stresses, obviously rejected the utilitarian tradition on many counts, including its characteristic (or at least supposed) empiricism, psychological egoism, and associationism. If Sidgwick claimed Bentham and Mill as major influences (especially in helping to liberate him from his orthodox Anglican views), he claimed many others as well, including Clarke and Cumberland, Butler, Kant, Whewell, and, among the ancients, Plato and Aristotle. With Clarke and Whewell, he held that ethics needed to be grounded on fundamental cogni-tive intuitions; with Butler, he held that humans were capable of genuinely disinterested and benevolent action, governed, that is, by both Self-Love and Conscience. Moreover, Sidgwick was far more concerned with 'private ethics', good or right conduct attainable by individual action, than his utilitarian predecessors, in addition to political philosophy and legislation. And for all his doubts, he had far more developed religious sympathies than either Bentham or Mill, and these informed his overall philosophical outlook in ways that are less than immediately apparent from the *Methods* itself.

The *Methods* itself repeatedly affirms that its aim is less practice than knowledge, 'to expound as clearly and as fully as my limits will allow the different methods of Ethics that I find implicit in our common moral reasoning; to point out their mutual relations; and where they seem to conflict, to define the issue as much as possible' (Sidgwick 1874/1907: vi). On Sidgwick's account, the model for this approach is, not Bentham or Mill, but Aristotle, whose *Ethics* gave us 'the Common Sense Morality of Greece, reduced to consistency by careful comparison: given not as something external to him but as what "we"—he and others—think, ascertained by reflection' (Sidgwick 1874/1907: xix).

The influence Kant and Kantianism—and the Cambridge Moralists—exercised on Sidgwick is patent, but the *Methods* also deviated from some stock features of such views, rejecting the issue of free will as largely irrelevant to ethical theory and taking a compatibilist stance. As Schneewind explains, 'the central thought of the *Methods of Ethics* is that morality is the embodiment of the demands reason makes on practice under the conditions of human life' (Schneewind 1977: 303). But Sidgwick rejects the whole apparatus of the Kantian critical philosophy, and 'in refusing to base morality on pure reason alone, moreover, he moves decisively away from Kant, as is shown by his very un-Kantian hedonistic and teleological conclusions' (Schneewind 1977: 419–20).

26.3 PHILOSOPHICAL INTUITIONISM

What, then, is Sidgwick primarily concerned to argue, in his impartial or dogmatic, prejudiced or eclectic, knowledgeable or ignorant, way?

Sidgwick does deploy a hedonistic theory of the good for two out of the three methods with which he is chiefly concerned—namely, egoistic hedonism (or rational egoism) and universal hedonism (or utilitarianism). But to understand his overall argument, it is better to begin with the other method, which is variously called dogmatic or intuitional morality, and which is somewhat ambiguously construed as either common-sense moral duties or the refined versions of these set out in the intuitionisms of Whewell or Calderwood. This is Calderwood's 'absolute and self-evident law', such that conformity to such moral duties as truth-telling, promise-keeping, temperance etc. is, in Sidgwick's words, held to be 'the practically ultimate end of moral actions'. These duties are 'unconditionally prescribed' and discernible with 'really clear and finally valid intuition', though it is the job of the moral theorist to set them out with proper precision and 'to arrange the results as systematically as possible, and by proper definitions and explanations to remove vagueness and prevent conflict' (Sidgwick 1874/1907: 101).

But intuitionism figures in both the second method of ethics, and, in a more philosophical form, in the treatment of all the methods of ethics, particularly in the discussion of fundamental principles. Thus, Sidgwick explains that 'in order to settle the doubts arising from the uncertainties and discrepancies that are found when we compare our judgements on particular cases, reflective persons naturally appeal to general rules or formulae: and it is to such general formulae that Intuitional Moralists commonly attribute ultimate certainty and validity' (Sidgwick 1874/1907: 214). Hence, dogmatic intuitional morality, which, as Irwin lamented, is taken to cover both more deontological views and those non-hedonistic teleological ones taking virtue as simply the thing to be done, whatever the consequences—and this despite Sidgwick's historical claim that the perfectionism of Plato and Aristotle was an 'attractive' theory with the good taking priority over the right, and not a modern 'imperative' theory with a jural notion of right, the moral law, taking priority over the good. Apparently, what Sidgwick's construction of this method suggests, and what his historical views could in fact be taken to confirm, is that he believed the progress of civilized thought had left the 'attractive' versions of non-hedonistic perfectionist or teleological views behind, had left the most important legacy of such views folded into dogmatic intuitionism. This is certainly how he found the position represented in Whewell's *The Elements of Morality*, another work he had imbibed as an undergraduate:

> The Virtues are what we are; the Duties are what we do... Duties, in their general form, coincide with Virtues. Justice is a Virtue; Justice is also a Duty. But they are generally conceived with this difference; that Virtue is more of an unconscious Disposition; Duty implies more of conscious thought. Our Virtues exist and operate without our thinking about them; we perform an act of Duty, *thinking* that we ought to do it. To think an act a Duty, is to think we ought to do it; it is to think it right; to think it conformable to the Supreme Rule of Human Action. (Whewell 1864: 97–8)

Had Sidgwick cited Whewell more often than he did, it would be rather easier to appreciate the Victorian sources of his approach. His account of the difference between 'right' and 'good' concerns, in both its use as a descriptive historical tool and its current application, how judgements of ultimate good do not in themselves involve definite precepts to act or even any indication that there is some relevant action to take or that the good in question is human good. Like Whewell, or for that matter, Parfit (2011) and Larmore (1996), Sidgwick allows that we can have good reasons both to do something and to desire something; he is simply following Whewell more closely when it comes to thinking of such reasons as being differentiated in a certain way, from more active to more passive, that gives the former priority, as the imperatives of duty. He obviously knew that ancient approaches to perfection, excellence, and virtue took a different form. But that was not the form being impressed upon him by his historical contexts, its common sense and leading lights. Another of the Cambridge Moralists, Sidgwick's friend and senior colleague John Grote, addressed this issue in very similar terms (Grote 1870).

Incidentally, Rawls claimed that Sidgwick endorsed a 'full-information' account of the good that 'characterizes a person's future good on the whole as what he would now desire and seek if the consequences of all the various courses of conduct open to him were, at the present point of time, accurately foreseen by him and adequately realized in imagination' (Rawls 1971: 366). But Sidgwick clearly allowed that some desires, however informed, may be rejected as irrational or unreasonable (Schneewind 1977; Parfit 1984, 2011; but see also Crisp 1990).

At any rate, for Sidgwick there is yet another phase of intuitionism that 'while accept-ing the morality of common sense as in the main sound, still attempts to find for it a philosophic basis which it does not itself offer: to get one or more principles more abso-lutely and undeniably true and evident' (Sidgwick 1874/1907: 102). The ascent to philo-sophical intuitionism is evident in the treatment of common-sense or intuitional morality, the relentless critical reflection in Book III of the *Methods* that has the utili-tarian repeatedly demonstrating to the dogmatic intuitionist

> that the principles of Truth, Justice, etc. have only a dependent and subordinate validity: arguing either that the principle is really only affirmed by Common-Sense as a general rule admitting of exceptions and qualifications, as in the case of Truth, and that we require some further principle for systematising these exceptions and qualifications; or that the fundamental notion is vague and needs further determi-nation, as in the case of Justice; and further, that the different rules are liable to conflict with each other, and that we require some higher principle to decide the issue thus raised; and again, that the rules are differently formulated by different persons, and that these differences admit of no Intuitional solution, while they show the vagueness and ambiguity of the common moral notions to which the Intuitionist appeals. (Sidgwick 1874/1907: 421)

Common sense is thus shown to presuppose utilitarianism, or is revealed as requiring something very like it. This is not to deny that there are better candidate intuitions. But these, Sidgwick holds, are at a more abstract and formal level, and in part provide the precise axioms of the utilitarian position needed to straighten out confused common sense. Such axioms allow that the good of one is no more important than the good of another, that future good is as important as present good, that what is right for one must be right for anyone similarly circumstanced, and that it is right to promote the good generally (Skelton 2008).

Importantly, when Sidgwick fleshes out the notion of good to arrive at his construc-tions of egoism and utilitarianism, he maintains that the proposition that pleasurable consciousness is the good is an informative, non-tautological claim and on balance the best interpretation of what is really, ultimately good. Without some such metric as the hedonistic one, how could we weigh one virtue or perfection or excellence or duty against another? Still, he admitted that the hedonistic account of ultimate good was less than self-evident and there were potential alternatives, chiefly excellence or perfection. As Shaver puts it, 'Sidgwick works out what it is reasonable to desire, and so attaches moral to natural properties, by the ordinary gamut of philosopher's strategies—appeals to logical coherence, plausibility, and judgment after reflection' (Shaver 2000: 270). Moreover, some, such as Sumner, have urged that Sidgwick held that 'what pleasures have in common is not something internal to them—their peculiar feeling tone, or whatever—but something about us—the fact that we like them, enjoy them, value them, find them satisfying, seek them, wish to prolong them, and so on' (Sumner 1996: 86). Others, notably Crisp (2006), have countered that Sidgwick's hedonism was more inter-nalistic, and that many of the stock objections to hedonism—e.g. the famous 'Experience Machine' argument—are less than decisive.

Now, Sidgwick's reconciliation of intuitional morality and utilitarianism relies on a fallibilistic form of intuitionist epistemology with four criteria or conditions 'the complete fulfillment of which would establish a significant proposition, apparently self-evident, in the highest degree of certainty attainable' (Sidgwick 1874/1907: 338). The first, 'Cartesian Criterion', insists that the 'terms of the proposition must be clear and precise', and the second requires that the 'self-evidence of the proposition must be ascertained by careful reflection', which is especially important in ethics because 'any strong sentiment, however purely subjective, is apt to transform itself into the semblance of an intuition; and it requires careful contemplation to detect the illusion' (Sidgwick 1874/1907: 339). The third, coherence, has it that the 'propositions accepted as self-evident must be mutually consistent', since it 'is obvious that any collision between two intuitions is a proof that there is error in one or the other, or in both' (Sidgwick 1874/1907: 341). And the fourth, consensus of experts, is also crucial, since 'it is implied in the very notion of Truth that it is essentially the same for all minds, the denial by another of a proposition that I have affirmed has a tendency to impair my confidence in its validity' (Sidgwick 1874/1907: 341–42). In other works, Sidgwick reduced the first two conditions to one, and explained that these conditions only afforded the best means for reducing the risk of error.

Sidgwick's critique and assimilation of common-sense moral rules thus went far beyond the efforts of J. S. Mill and, again, reflected an intuitionistic epistemology that the earlier utilitarians had mostly rejected. And as noted, it has generated much lively controversy, past and present. Calderwood found the whole supposed problematic here, as presented by Mill and Sidgwick, simply baffling: 'each principle of morals applies to a line of activity all its own, and always its own . . . That principles are distinct, and independent because distinct, does not make them contradictory. Moral principles apply to perfectly distinct lines of activity, and do not claim authority other than is implied in their individual meaning' (Calderwood 1888: 61).

A similar line against even the possibility of 'moral dilemmas' has been taken in more recent times by moral rationalists such as Alan Donagan, who defended the quest for determinacy characteristic of Whewell and Calderwood, and slammed Sidgwick for failing to grasp how to work within a rationalistic system to resolve dilemmas or improve the system by refining the specification of the various duties and their spheres (Donagan 1977, 1992).

Sidgwick did not have the pleasure of replying to Donagan, but he did reply to some of Calderwood's criticisms, explaining:

> If I ask myself whether I see clearly and distinctly the self-evidence of any particular maxims of duty, as I see that of the formal principles 'that what is right for me must be right for all persons in precisely similar circumstances' and 'that I ought to prefer the greater good of another to my own lesser good': I have no doubt whatever that I do not. I am conscious of a strong impression, an opinion on which I habitually act without hesitation, that I ought to speak truth, to perform promises, to requite benefits, &c., and also of powerful moral sentiments prompting me to the observance of these rules; but on reflection I can now clearly distinguish such opinions and sentiments from the apparently immediate and certain cognition that

I have of the formal principles above mentioned. But I could not always have made this distinction; and I believe that the majority of moral persons do not make it...How then am I to argue with such persons? It will not settle the matter to tell them that they have observed their own mental processes wrongly, and that more careful introspection will show them the non-intuitive character of what they took for intuitions; especially as in many cases I do not believe that the error is one of misobservation. Still less am I inclined to dispute the 'primitiveness' or 'spontaneousness' or 'originality' of these apparent intuitions. On the contrary, I hold that here, as in other departments of thought, the primitive spontaneous processes of the mind are mixed with error, which is only to be removed gradually by comprehensive reflection upon the results of these processes. Through such a course of reflection I have endeavoured to lead my readers in chaps. 2–10 of Book II of my treatise; in the hope that after they have gone through it they may find their original apprehension of the self-evidence of moral maxims importantly modified (Sidgwick 1876: 565).

After all, if 'systematic reflection on the morality of Common Sense thus exhibits the Utilitarian principle as that to which Common Sense naturally appeals for that further development of its system which this same reflection shows to be necessary, the proof of Utilitarianism seems as complete as can be made' (Sidgwick 1874/1907: 422). And this is why, Sidgwick explained, he did not just move straight to intuitionism in its most philosophical form. One should not trust one's 'own moral faculty alone'.

The complex fallibilistic nature of Sidgwick's philosophical intuitionism and treatment of common sense or dogmatic intuitional morality has never ceased to irritate critics committed to a different understanding of intuitionism, and the debates were given new life when Rawls in A Theory of Justice (1971) seemed to intimate that his method of reflective equilibrium, bringing together or synthesizing a wide range of considered convictions at all levels of generality, was Sidgwickian. A number of anti-Rawlsian critics sought to distance Sidgwick from any such association (Hare 1981; Singer 1974; Skelton 2007), urging that common sense had no serious evidential or probative value in the Methods.

However, exactly what weight Sidgwick accords to common-sense morality as a cognitive tool is not an issue that can be sensibly addressed without appreciating the significance that he attached to the criterion of consensus, such that achieving a consensus of experts was a co-equal test along with clarity and distinctness, etc. Common sense, for Sidgwick, might be confused, but it nonetheless reflects something akin or connected to expert opinion, accumulated over time, and thus must be taken as seriously as any rival and confidence-reducing intuitions. Indeed, both the intuitional moralists and Sidgwick held that common-sense morality was lacking in precision and system, and needed philosophical repair. But the point, on both sides, was that one of the chief presenting features of common-sense maxims of duty was their claim to self-evidence, to being 'absolute and self-evident law', which needed to be addressed in a serious way. As he put it, in describing the importance of what he called 'Social or Oecumenical Verification':

its practical importance, even for more reflective and more logical minds, grows with the growth of knowledge, and the division of intellectual labour which attends it; for as this grows, the proportion of the truths that enter into our systematization, which for any individual have to depend on the *consensus of experts*, continually increases. In fact, in provisionally taking Common Sense as the point of departure for philosophical construction, it was this criterion that we implicitly applied. (Sidgwick 1905: 464)

In Sidgwick's intuitionism, epistemic humility and concern with the community of enquirers make for a sensitive appreciation of common sense or the common moral consciousness, a more developed appreciation of the extraordinariness of the ordinary than one is apt to associate with Cartesian epistemic individualism.

At any rate, if common-sense morality now has rather different presenting features, or even if it was always more diverse and complex, perhaps more confused, than the *Methods* allowed (as it obviously was and is), Sidgwick's efforts retain their value. He never claimed that his division of the subject matter was valid always and forever—to the contrary, he recognized that there were other methods developing force (notably idealism and evolutionism) that would need to be addressed in somewhat different terms (Sidgwick 1902, 1905).

Intriguingly, some more recent defenders of systematic moral rationalism have credited Sidgwick with having had a dramatic, albeit unfortunate, impact on the common moral consciousness. Thus, Donagan has argued that Whewell's *Elements* was the last major work in the older British intuitionist tradition, which Sidgwick effectively destroyed: 'Such was Sidgwick's authority among philosophers inclined towards intuitionism that they received his criticism of the older intuitionist position as decisive. And so, instead of trying to vindicate a view they thought exploded, they set out to construct a new intuitionism that would satisfy Sidgwick's conditions' (Donagan 1977: 21). The results, e.g. the early twentieth-century work of C. D. Broad and W. D. Ross, had it that the:

> solution was to reinterpret as statements of pertinent moral considerations the vague generalities almost nobody will deny. When such a maxim as 'In general, you should not break your word!' is reinterpreted as equivalent to 'For a proposed course of action to involve breaking your word is always a consideration against doing it,' it looks precise as well as uncontroversial. Under this treatment, popular maxims yield a store of moral intuitions. (Donagan 1977: 22)

For Donagan, however, the new intuitionism completely failed to provide guidance where guidance was needed: 'it is fraudulent to describe what the new intuitionists take to be the process of moral deliberation as one of "weighing" or "balancing" considerations'. By 'repudiating anything that might order the various considerations it acknowledges, and accepting as "weighing" or "balancing" any process whatever in which a man, hesitating before alternatives supported by different considerations, without conscious insincerity overcomes his hesitation, the new intuitionism deprives that description of any definite sense. Hence its laxist consequences. (Donagan 1977: 23–4).

To be sure, Donagan worried that Whewell's vision of progress in intuitional morality (which Sidgwick shared) and Sidgwick's consensus of experts condition were difficult to combine with the other elements of intuitionism. But even so, the new and fraudulent intuitionism had much less to offer. Ironically, as will be indicated below, Sidgwick might well have agreed with this assessment. It is also ironic that, although the comparatively recent revival of cognitive intuitionism in ethics has produced much valuable work on Sidgwick, Moore, Broad, Ross, Prichard et al., it often seems to show little awareness of the divide between the intuitionism of Whewell and that of the post-Sidgwick intuition-ists, a divide that Sidgwick himself straddles (Stratton-Lake 2002). To be sure, such efforts as Shaver (2000) and Crisp (2002) have gone far to rehabilitate intuitionism—in general and in Sidgwick—against the tired charges, pervasive in the mid-twentieth cen-tury, that it requires mysterious metaphysical entities or strange psychological faculties, a moral radar or hotline. But even such sympathetic reconstructions, celebrating a 'golden age' of ethical theory from Sidgwick to the 1940s, balk at older Whewellian elements of Sidgwick's arguments (Hurka 2011).

For all that, one can still maintain that, in many respects, Sidgwick's approach in the *Methods* has served as a model for utilitarian analysis ever since, not least in casting utilitarian conclusions as imperatives of impartial moral reason (Brandt 1979; Hooker 2000; Singer 2000). And like so many utilitarians, when it came to substantive ethical theory, Sidgwick allowed the moral standing of non-human animals, interpreted inten-tion as covering all foreseen consequences, rejected retributivist theories of punishment, and held a cosmopolitan (rather than nationalistic) outlook. The problem of determin-ing justice for future generations and optimal population growth (and considerations of average versus total utility) also came from him (Sidgwick 1874/1907: 415–16), and it continues to defeat the best philosophical efforts, even as its significance grows along with the world environmental crisis.

26.4 ESOTERICISM AND EGOISM

Yet on some counts, even Sidgwick's substantive utilitarianism can seem very histori-cally distant. Although usually classed as an 'act utilitarian', it is not always easy to apply the classification of 'act' or 'rule' utilitarianism to him. But he plainly defended an 'indi-rect' form of utilitarianism, even defending the possibility of utilitarianism entailing a self-effacing, even esoteric morality. In a notorious passage that Hayward (1901) long ago singled out, Sidgwick explained that: 'a Utilitarian may reasonably desire, on Utilitarian principles, that some of his conclusions should be rejected by mankind gen-erally; or even that the vulgar should keep aloof from his system as a whole, in so far as the inevitable indefiniteness and complexity of its calculations render it likely to lead to bad results in their hands' (Sidgwick 1874/1907: 490). This obviously flies in the face of the Kantian insistence on the publicity of fundamental moral principles, even if it might reflect a consistent interpretation of the different 'levels' of moral thinking, critical ver-sus everyday. And philosophers have pushed hard on just how indirect an ethical theory can really be, since the demands of duty or virtue seem to require sincere belief (Hurka 2001). Williams notoriously charged that in this Sidgwick was perhaps an elitist

'Government House' utilitarian whose views comported well with colonialist paternalism, and Korsgaard has argued that Sidgwick could not distinguish genuine communication from 'spin' (Williams 1995; Korsgaard 2009). But Parfit (1984) has treated self-effacing theories very seriously, and Schultz (2004b) has explored some of the Sidgwickian contexts in which esoteric morality has carried weight, notably in areas of sexual ethics and with oppressed minorities. Important defences of such indirection and esotericism have also been mounted by Singer and de Lazari-Radek (2010), in work that strikes directly at the heart of the Kantian alternative.

But perhaps the most important issue in Sidgwick studies, and for Sidgwick himself, continues to be what has been called 'the dualism of the practical reason'. On Sidgwick's view, rational egoism, unlike intuitional morality, could not be reconciled with utilitarianism. Famously, the first edition of the *Methods* concluded that rational egoism and utilitarianism end up in a draw or stand-off, and that as a result, there is a 'fundamental contradiction in our apparent intuitions of what is Reasonable in conduct' such that 'the "Cosmos" of Duty is thus really reduced to a Chaos, and the prolonged effort of the human intellect to frame a perfect ideal of rational conduct is seen to have been fore-doomed to inevitable failure' (Sidgwick 1874/1907: 473). Later editions of the work put the point more gently, but it was the same point.

In other works, Sidgwick often departed from the careful axiomatic language of the *Methods*, simply explaining that along with '(a) a fundamental moral conviction that I ought to sacrifice my own happiness, if by so doing I can increase the happiness of others to a greater extent than I diminish my own, I find also (b) a conviction—which it would be paradoxical to call "moral", but which is none the less fundamental—that it would be irrational to sacrifice any portion of my own happiness unless the sacrifice is to be some-how at some time compensated by an equivalent addition to my own happiness' (Sidgwick 1889: 483). Each of these convictions has as much clarity and certainty 'as the process of introspection can give' and finds wide assent 'in the common sense of mankind'.

Sidgwick considered two possible solutions to the problem, a weakening of epistemological standards or a Theistic postulate about the coherent moral government of the universe. First, if 'we find that in our supposed knowledge of the world of nature propositions are commonly taken to be universally true, which seem to rest on no other ground than that we have a strong disposition to accept them, and that they are indispensable to the systematic coherence of our beliefs,—it will be more difficult to reject a similarly supported assumption in ethics, without opening the door to universal scepticism' (Sidgwick 1874/1907: 509). Second, if 'we may assume the existence of such a Being, as God, by the *consensus* of theologians, is conceived to be, it seems that Utilitarians may legitimately infer the existence of Divine sanctions to the code of social duty as constructed on a Utilitarian basis; and such sanctions would, of course, suffice to make it always every one's interest to promote universal happiness to the best of his knowledge' (Sidgwick 1874/1907: 506; Mackie 1982).

Sidgwick's dualism has led some recent commentators to urge that he is better termed a 'dualist' or 'dual-source theorist' or 'two standpoints' theorist than a utilitarian, and Crisp (2002, 2006) has defended such an approach. Skorupski (2001, 2007) has forcefully argued that there is no dualism of the 'pure' practical reason as such, which is agent neutral, but there are many such conflicts in the larger field of less than pure practical reason, not merely a conflict with egoistic reasons, and that Sidgwick's 'rationalist straitjacket' kept him from appreciating all the sources of reasons. Parfit (2011) has importantly argued that Sidgwick, in taking a two-standpoints approach with one set of reasons coming from one's own standpoint and another from taking 'the Point of View of the Universe' (as Sidgwick termed the impartial perspective), failed to see the reach of the personal perspective and how egoistic reasons might nonetheless be weaker than omnipersonal ones. But Smith (2009) has argued in response that Parfit's own position collapses into something like the Sidgwickian one, albeit generating much more than a mere dualism of reasons. The debates in this area, forming a vast literature, remain evergreen and promise to continue as long as ethical philosophy itself.

For his part, Sidgwick in his private writings made it clear that his devotion to free and open enquiry had not yielded satisfactory results, that he sided with the older intuitionism in thinking that ethical theory should produce determinate answers about what one ought to do in any given situation, and that this dualism motivated him to pursue both other philosophical enquiries and parapsychological research, in the hope that he might find evidence to support a Theistic argument. Although he devoted many hours to both, and emerged thinking that a broader account of reason and philosophy might be defensible and that there was good evidence for such paranormal phenomena as telepathy, he was never satisfied with such progress. Neither common sense, nor theology, nor philosophy, nor parapsychology had yielded the certainty that he sought. This broader view of Sidgwick's project has inspired a great deal of original work in recent years (Schultz 2004b; Bucolo, Crisp, and Schultz 2007 and 2011, Gray 2011).

26.5 Beyond Ethics

Although the *Methods* is best understood in the context of Sidgwick's theological concerns, and his sense of the history of ethical and political controversy, it is all too rarely read in that way.

This is a pity not least because a fuller appreciation of Sidgwick's larger philosophical concern with, as he liked to put it, 'the deepest problems of human life' and the historical perspectives he brought to bear on them might help deflect and deflate much cheap criticism. Sidgwick well understood the historical contingencies that have brought one or another element of ethics onto the philosophical stage. Again, he saw a divide between ancient and modern ethics, between attractive and imperative approaches, and his views on this subject continue to attract first-rate philosophical defenders (Larmore 1996; Schneewind 2010). And unlike so many of his contemporaries, including Mill, Comte, Spencer, and Marx, his visions of progress and historical theories of it were cautious and highly guarded, so much so that he came to share many of the late nineteenth-century anxieties about decline and degeneracy.

So worried was Sidgwick that he felt bound to avoid openly contributing to religious scepticism or the decline of the churches. As he explained in some revealing correspondence:

> In fact, the reason why I keep strict silence now for many years with regard to theology is that while I cannot myself discover adequate rational basis for the Christian hope of happy immortality, it seems to me that the general loss of such a hope, from the minds of average human beings as now constituted, would be an evil of which I cannot pretend to measure the extent. I am not prepared to say that the dissolution of the existing social order would follow, but I think the danger of such dissolution would be seriously increased, and that the evil would certainly be very great. (Sidgwick and Sidgwick 1906: 357)

Ultimately, this obsession with a Cosmic invisible hand structuring the moral Universe to render the conflict between intuitional egoism and intuitional utilitarianism nugatory is more Paley's than Bentham's or Mill's. If Whewell had established himself as the dominant philosophical force in the Cambridge curriculum in part by challenging Paley's system, Sidgwick sought, in effect, to appropriate Whewellism in order to turn the clock back and rehabilitate Paley. As Moore noted so long ago, for Sidgwick, rational egoism just had to be tamed, had to be worked or transfigured into the system of duties supported by utilitarianism, rather than allowed the liberty to undermine that system. Self-interest well understood could be quite elevated, and at a far remove from mere selfishness. But it would never be elevated enough.

Sidgwick's conception of the growth of sympathetic understanding, of the capacity for taking the 'Point of View of the Universe', was certainly tied to his wider epistemological and religious interests. At one level, at the point where it might seem there is no possible ground for the choice between the egoistic and the utilitarian act, his position might seem to verge towards that of his very orthodox friend, Charles Gore, who held that:

> the power of sympathy is a power of self-abandonment, or self-effacement, which enables a man to abjure the platform of a rightful superiority, and enter into the conditions of another person's experience, thinking with his thoughts, seeing with his eyes, feeling as he ought to feel, and so raising him, as it were, from within. Of such self-abandoning sympathy the Incarnation of God is the prototype; it is more intelligible to the heart than to the head; but this is exactly what is true of all self-sacrifice and sympathy. (Gore 1891: 111)

Gore was deeply impressed by Sidgwick's faith in following reason; he was more impressed by where Sidgwick went when reason failed him. That Sidgwick plumped so strongly for this side of his dualism, and so longed to vindicate Theism throughout his life—describing his true or deepest self as Theistic—are for some commentators powerful reasons for reading him as a theological utilitarian of sorts, finding more of a role for faith in his enquiries than has generally been recognized (Bucolo 2007). Counterbalancing such readings are the many bits of evidence indicating, as Sidgwick's widow put it, that 'he had not been able to find the truth that he sought' (Schultz 2007: 399).

The intriguing philosophical weirdness of his quest, his embrace of the uncanny, is increasingly sparking insightful commentary (Warner 2006; Gray 2011).

What is very clear, however, is that much of Sidgwick's life and professional work proceeded on admittedly utilitarian assumptions, which he took to be the going considered convictions of advanced civilization, and more clearly so in economics and politics than in ethics. Both his *Principles of Political Economy* (1883) and his *Elements of Politics* (1891/1919) are extremely valuable works for elaborating the utilitarian side of his vision as it applies to political economy and political theory. Both works are in part descriptive and in part normative, and both are open about proclaiming their utilitarian framework with respect to the latter. Although Sidgwick certainly recognized the role that a narrower form of self-interest played in economics and politics, he also recognized that 'economic man' was an abstraction that scarcely did justice to all dimensions of human nature, particularly in its historical development. True, both works took a strong anti-paternalistic intermediate principle as the starting point for analysing economic and political policy, such that:

> what one sane adult is legally compelled to render to others should be merely the negative service of non-interference, except so far as he has voluntarily undertaken to render positive services; provided that we include in the notion of non-interference the obligation of remedying or compensating for mischief intentionally or carelessly caused by his acts—or preventing mischief that would otherwise result from previous acts. This principle for determining the nature and limits of government interference is currently known as 'Individualism'... the requirement that one sane adult, apart from contract or claim to reparation, shall contribute positively by money or services to the support of others I shall call 'socialism'. (Sidgwick 1891/1919: 42)

But in both works this principle is qualified and compromised to such an extraordinary degree, and so worked over by larger utilitarian considerations, that one can be forgiven for wondering if the twentieth-century libertarian F. A. Hayek was right in thinking that Sidgwick paved the way for the more socialistic policies of the 'New Liberalism', Fabianism, and other welfare statist policies of the early twentieth century.

Sidgwick's economic and political thinking, its influence and relationships both to the Cambridge school of Marshall, Pigou, and Keynes and to later libertarian and 'law and economics' approaches, has been the subject of some excellent recent work (Backhouse 2007a; Medema 2004). And much important new work has been devoted to the larger cultural contexts of the political and economic dimensions of Sidgwick's viewpoint, reading it as part of the 'new imperialism' that so marked the late-Victorian era (Schultz 2004b; Bell 2007; Medema 2008). These more encompassing, critical interpretations of Sidgwick's work are vital for understanding in a detailed and historically accurate way how he understood the force and future of the utilitarian views he favoured, and the social institutions needed for their success. If his views were often far too naively Eurocentric, and uncritical of the racist currents of his very racist political context, he at least appreciated the importance of a more internationalist and cosmopolitan outlook and the growth of effective international institutions for ensuring world peace, against the Machiavellianism of national power politics, global or domestic, which he abhorred. 'Ethical socialism', the fostering of humanity's sympathetic and cooperative tendencies, was the road he favoured in all regions.

Indeed, the *Elements*, with its liberal elitist rather than populist democratic perspective, was perhaps most eloquent when calling for the state to encourage a class of teachers who could illustrate the ways in which the individual could find his or her happiness in the performance of social duty, or at any rate be inspired by social duty:

> the only teaching likely to be effective is such as will powerfully affect the emotions of the taught, no less than their intellects; we should, therefore, generally speaking, need teachers who themselves felt, and were believed to feel, sincerely and intensely, the moral and social emotions that it was their business to stimulate; and governmental appointment and payment would hardly seem to be an appropriate method of securing instructors of this type. If a spirit of devotion to a particular society or to humanity at large, and readiness to sacrifice self-interest to duty, are to be persuasively inculcated in adults, the task should, generally speaking, be undertaken by persons who set an example of self-devotion and self-sacrifice, and therefore by volunteers, rather than by paid officers. (Sidgwick 1891/1919: 214–15)

Ultimately, Sidgwick was to the end an educational reformer—or rather, a reformer who always came back to education as the crucial issue for historical progress, in ethics, economics, politics, and other areas. His practical ethics, often only indirectly utilitarian, mostly concerned finding common ground despite foundational ethical differences, and that common ground was the cultivation of humanity:

> Since the most essential function of the mind is to think and know, a man of cultivated mind must be concerned for knowledge: but it is not knowledge merely that gives culture. A man may be learned and yet lack culture: for he may be a pedant, and the characteristic of a pedant is that he has knowledge without culture. So again, a load of facts retained in the memory, or a mass of reasonings got up merely for examination—these are not, they do not give culture. It is the love of knowledge, the ardour of scientific curiosity, driving us continually to absorb new facts and ideas, to make them our own and fit them into the living and growing system of our thought; and the trained faculty of doing this, the alert and supple intelligence exercised and continually developed in doing this—it is in these that culture essentially lies. (Sidgwick 1904: 353)

Given such views about the crucial need to cultivate the more critical, sympathetic, and altruistic capabilities of humanity, Sidgwick, it should be clear, scarcely fits the still too pervasive, confused conception of the utilitarian as someone out to defend the low-minded, narrowly useful, egoistic policies that would undermine, say, a commitment to liberal education and the humanities. Fortunately, however, interest in his philosophy has reached the point where one might hope that that hostile conception of the 'utilitarian' will be finally buried. Indeed, we appear to be well on the way to adding the term 'Sidgwickian' to the philosophical lexicon, along with Millian, Cartesian, Kantian, Marxian, etc. Its uses should be most illuminating.

BIBLIOGRAPHY

Backhouse, R. 2007a. 'Sidgwick, Marshall, and the Cambridge School of Economics', *History of Political Economy* 3: 15–44.

—— 2007b. 'Bart Schultz, Henry Sidgwick: Eye of the Universe. An Intellectual Biography', *Journal of the History of Economic Thought* 29 (3): 396–8.

Bell, D. 2007. *The Idea of Greater Britain: Empire and the Future of World Order, 1860–1900.* Princeton: Princeton University Press.

Brandt, R. B. 1979. *A Theory of the Good and the Right.* Oxford: Clarendon Press.

Brink, D. 2003. *Perfectionism and the Common Good.* Oxford: Clarendon Press.

Broad, C. D. 1930. *Five Types of Ethical Theory.* London: Routledge and Kegan Paul.

Bucolo, P. 2007. 'Theism and Sanctions', , *Proceedings of the World Congress on Henry Sidgwick*, 50–104.

—— Crisp, R., and Schultz, B. (eds). 2007 and 2011. *Proceedings of the World Congress on Henry Sidgwick.* 2 vols. Catania: Universita degli Studi di Catania.

Calderwood, H. 1888. *Handbook of Moral Philosophy.* Fourteenth edition. London: Macmillan.

Crisp, R. 1990. 'Sidgwick and Self-Interest', *Utilitas* 2(2): 267–80.

—— 2002. 'Sidgwick and the Boundaries of Intuitionism', in P. Stratton-Lake (ed.), *Ethical Intuitionism.* Oxford: Oxford University Press, 56–75.

—— 2006. *Reasons and the Good.* Oxford: Clarendon Press.

—— 2007. 'Sidgwick's Hedonism', in P. Bucolo, R. Crisp, and B. Schultz (eds), *Proceedings of the World Congress on Henry Sidgwick*, 104–56.

Deigh, J. 2007. 'Sidgwick's Epistemology', *Utilitas* 19 (4): 435–46.

Donagan, A. 1977. *The Theory of Morality.* Chicago: University of Chicago Press.

—— 1992. 'Sidgwick and Whewellian Intuitionism: Some Enigmas', in B. Schultz (ed.), *Essays on Henry Sidgwick*, 123–42.

Gauld, A. 1968. *The Founders of Psychical Research.* New York: Schocken Books.

Gore, C. 1891. *The Bampton Lectures.* London: John Murray.

Gray, J. 2011. *The Immortality Commission.* London: Allen Lane.

Grote, J. 1870. *An Examination of the Utilitarian Philosophy.* London: Macmillan.

Hardin, R. 2009. *How Do You Know? The Economics of Ordinary Knowledge.* Princeton: Princeton University Press.

Hare, R. M. 1981. *Moral Thinking: Its Levels, Method, and Point.* Oxford: Clarendon Press.

Hayward, F. H. 1901. *The Ethical Philosophy of Sidgwick.* London: Swan Sonnenschein.

Hooker, B. 2000. *Ideal Code, Real World.* Oxford: Clarendon Press.

Hurka, T. 2001. *Virtue, Vice, and Value.* Oxford: Oxford University Press.

—— (ed.) 2011. *Underivative Duty.* Oxford: Oxford University Press.

Irwin, T. H. 1992. 'Eminent Victorians and Greek Ethics: Sidgwick, Green, and Aristotle', in B. Schultz (ed.), *Essays on Henry Sidgwick*, 279–310.

—— 2007. 'A 'Fundamental Misunderstanding', *Utilitas* 19: 78–90.

—— 2009. *The Development of Ethics*, vol. 3. Oxford: Oxford University Press.

Korsgaard, C. 2009. *Self-Constitution.* New York: Oxford University Press.

Larmore, C. 1996. *The Morals of Modernity.* New York: Cambridge University Press.

MacIntyre, A. 1990. *Three Rival Versions of Moral Enquiry.* Notre Dame: University of Notre Dame Press.

Mackie, J. L. 1982. *The Miracle of Theism.* Oxford: Clarendon Press.

Medema, S. G. 2004. 'Sidgwick's Utilitarian Analysis of Law: A Bridge from Bentham to Becker?', *Social Science Research Network* 1, <http://papers.ssrn.com/sol3/papers.cfm?abstract_id=560842>.

—— 2008. ' "Losing My Religion": Sidgwick, Theism, and the Struggle for Utilitarian Ethics in Economic Analysis', *History of Political Economy* 40 (5): 189–211.

Moore, G. E. 1903. *Principia Ethica*. Cambridge: Cambridge University Press.

Parfit, D. 1984. *Reasons and Persons*. Oxford: Oxford University Press.

—— 2011. *On What Matters*. Oxford: Oxford University Press.

Rawls, J. 1971. *A Theory of Justice*. Cambridge, MA: Harvard University Press.

—— 1999. *Collected Papers*, ed. S. Freeman. Cambridge, MA: Harvard University Press.

—— 2007. *Lectures on the History of Political Philosophy*, ed. S. Freeman. Cambridge, MA: Harvard University Press.

Schneewind, J. B. 1977. *Sidgwick's Ethics and Victorian Moral Philosophy*. Oxford: Clarendon Press.

—— 2010. *Essays on the History of Moral Philosophy*. Oxford: Oxford University Press.

Schultz, B. (ed.) 2004a. *Essays on Henry Sidgwick*. New York: Cambridge University Press. First published 1992.

—— 2004b. *Henry Sidgwick, Eye of the Universe*. New York: Cambridge University Press.

—— 2007. 'Why Read Sidgwick Today?', in P. Bucolo, R. Crisp, and B. Schultz (eds), *Proceedings of the World Congress on Henry Sidgwick*, 368–407.

Shaver, R. 1999. *Rational Egoism*. New York: Cambridge University Press.

—— 2000. 'Sidgwick's Minimal Metaethics', *Utilitas* 12: 261–77.

Sidgwick, E. M. and Sidgwick, A. 1906. *Henry Sidgwick, A Memoir*. London: Macmillan.

Sidgwick, Henry 1870. *The Ethics of Conformity and Subscription*. London: Williams and Norgate.

—— 1874/1907. *The Methods of Ethics*. Seventh edition. London: Macmillan.

—— 1876. 'Professor Calderwood on Intuitionism in Morals', *Mind* 1: 563–66.

—— 1883. *The Principles of Political Economy*. London: Macmillan. Reprinted 1887, 1901.

—— 1886. *Outlines of the History of Ethics for English Readers*. London: Macmillan.

—— 1889. 'Some Fundamental Ethical Controversies', *Mind* 56: 473–87.

—— 1891/1919. *The Elements of Politics*. Fourth edition. London: Macmillan.

—— 1902. *Lectures on the Ethics of T. H. Green, H. Spencer, and J. Martineau*, ed. E. E. Constance Jones. London: Macmillan.

—— 1904. *Miscellaneous Essays and Addresses*, ed. E. M. Sidgwick and A. Sidgwick. London: Macmillan.

—— 1905. *Lectures on the Philosophy of Kant and Other Philosophical Lectures and Essays*, ed. J. Ward. London: Macmillan.

—— 2000. *Essays on Ethics and Method*, ed. M. G. Singer. Oxford: Clarendon Press.

Singer, P. 1974. 'Sidgwick and Reflective Equilibrium', *The Monist* 58: 490–517.

—— 2000. *Writings on an Ethical Life*. New York: HarperCollins.

—— and de Lazari-Radek, K. 2010. 'Secrecy in Consequentialism: A Defence of Esoteric Morality', *Ratio* 23 (1): 34–58.

Skelton, A. 2007. 'Schultz's Sidgwick', *Utilitas* 19: 91–103.

—— 2008. 'Sidgwick's Philosophical Intuitions', in *Etica & Politics* 10: 9–18.

Skorupski, J. 2001. 'Three Methods and a Dualism', in R. Harrison (ed.), *Henry Sidgwick*. Oxford: Oxford University Press, 61–81.

—— 2007. 'Sidgwick and the Many-Sidedness of Ethics', in P. Bucolo, R. Crisp, and B. Schultz (eds), *Proceedings of the World Congress on Henry Sidgwick*, 410–43.

Smith, Michael 2009. 'Desires, Values, Reasons, and the Dualism of Practical Reason', in J. Suikkanen and J. Cottingham (eds), *Essays on Derek Parfit's On What Matters*. Oxford: Wiley-Blackwell, 116–43.

Stratton-Lake, P. (ed.) 2002. *Ethical Intuitionism: Re-evaluations*. Oxford: Clarendon Press.

Sumner, L. W. 1996. *Welfare, Ethics & Happiness*. Oxford: Clarendon Press.

Tullberg, R. McWilliams 1998. *Women at Cambridge*. Cambridge: Cambridge University Press.

Warner, M. 2006. *Phantasmagoria*. Oxford: Oxford University Press.

Whewell, W. 1864. *The Elements of Morality, Including Polity*. Fourth edition. Cambridge: Deighton, Bell.

Williams, B. 1995. 'The Point of View of the Universe: Sidgwick and the Ambitions of Ethics', in his *Making Sense of Humanity*. Cambridge: Cambridge University Press, 153–71.

CHAPTER 27

....

BRITISH IDEALIST ETHICS

....

W. J. MANDER

In the late 1870s there emerged on the British philosophical scene a new moral philosophy; one which we might call the idealist ethic of social self-realization. Rapidly catching on it became the dominant mode of moral thought for twenty years, and a major force for twenty more after that. It is a view associated principally with the names of F.H. Bradley and T. H. Green, its pioneers; although it attracted many other thinkers as well, some followers, some more independent.[1]

27.1 F. H. BRADLEY

Bradley's first book *Ethical Studies*, caused a considerable stir and was the work more than any other that really drew attention to the new idealistic mode of thinking—in retrospect Bernard Bosanquet described it as 'epoch-making'.[2] There were several things that made it memorable. One was its distinctive *style*, which is bold, lively, and picturesque. It still makes an exciting read. But what rendered the book truly radical when first published was its use of Hegel. It has often been noted that *Ethical Studies* was in fact the most Hegelian of all Bradley's writings. This is so in two respects. Firstly, there is the Hegelian pedigree of many of its concepts and themes; its central claim that neither individuals nor their ethical duties can be understood except in the context of the wider social whole in which they occur is a clear, and acknowledged, reworking of the Hegelian notions of *Sittlichkeit* and concrete universality. But secondly, the Hegelian influence

---

[1] Key names to note here are J. S. Mackenzie and J. H. Muirhead, who popularized the doctrine through best-selling textbooks, Bernard Bosanquet who focused on its implications for political philosophy, D. G. Ritchie who sought a mode of reconciliation with both Utilitarianism and Darwinian evolution, and James Seth who moved away from the Absolute towards a more personal and theistic species of idealism.

[2] Bosanquet 1924: 58.

extends beyond the book's content to its very structure. It has an explicitly dialectical form in which positions are advanced, criticized, and then modified in an ever-advancing sequence, which is why Bradley insisted that 'the essays must be read in the order in which they stand'.[3] The book is constructed as a continuous argument with the earlier essays preparing the way for those that follow, the later ones amplifying or qualifying those that come before it. Many of its claims are provisional only, asserted at one point only to be modified later on. The debt to Hegel should not be allowed to obscure all others, however, for the book also drew heavily on Aristotle in its emphasis on the development of character and the fundamentally social or political nature of human being.

A recurring difficulty in understanding and assessing Bradley's *Ethical Studies* lies in the fact that much of what he assumes is left unsaid. His aim was to write a book of moral philosophy only, without trespassing into matters of logic, metaphysics, or psychology, but he is handicapped in this ambition by the very fact that he himself did not believe that there were any sharp or final divisions between questions in ethics and deeper questions about the nature of ultimate reality. In consequence we find him constantly touching on more fundamental issues which underlie and explain his meaning, but from which he draws himself back or at which he merely hints. Many of these he went on to deal with in later works, for example, the doctrine of the concrete universal in his *Principles of Logic*, the nature of relations in his *Appearance and Reality*, or the status of psychology in his *Essays on Truth and Reality*; and a full understanding of his position requires a grasp of the rest of his thought; but the reader of *Ethical Studies* alone does not have available that material.

27.1.1 Self-Realization

After an initial discussion about the nature of free will, the substance of the book proper begins with a consideration of the question 'Why should I be moral?', which Bradley rejects as senseless on the grounds that to morally approve of anything is precisely to regard it as valuable in itself, so that were we to seek it for other ulterior reasons our action would not be moral at all. In other words, there can be no categorical imperative, no rule a man may be compelled to recognize regardless of his own personal ends or values. If he asserts scepticism and just does whatever he likes, if he will not acknowledge some particular value, or others which entail it, including that of consistency itself, then argument ceases.

Thus we cannot prove that there is anything good in itself, we can only assume that there is, and ask what it might be. That, of course, is not something to be answered in simply a sentence—it is the topic of the whole book—but there is, thinks Bradley, merit in offering as a place to start from the most general expression possible of our target. In its very broadest terms Bradley suggests we may find the end of all action in *self-realization*.[4] The fundamental issue of ethics is not what we do but what we are. He does not offer to prove the appropriateness of this 'formula',[5] in part because that would require a completed

---

[3] *Ethical Studies*, viii.   [4] *Ethical Studies*, 64.   [5] *Ethical Studies*, 65.

metaphysical system, but also because it is to some extent simply a blank schema, some-thing to be filled in and rendered plausible in the essays that follow. But if not proved, the claim may be explained. Were we able to assert the psychological egoistic doctrine that people aim only at pleasurable states of their own being, it would follow immediately that all action aims at self-realization. Bradley rejects that, but even so he holds on in some sense to the notion that we only aim at what we desire and that thus in a way all actions realize ourselves; in wanting a given state to obtain our very identity becomes bound up with it and thus its realization becomes too a realization of our own self. However, Bradley goes on, what we aim to realize not simply *a state* of the self but rather *the self as a whole*. For the self is more than simply a sum of its parts. What is needed instead is 'some concrete whole that we can realize in our acts, and carry out in our life',[6] something with a persistent overall cohesive pattern and not simply a haphazard series of disconnected individual elements. The good life is not that which jumps from what-ever is best at one moment to whatever is best at another. The good life is rather a life good as a whole, one springing from a unity of vision, a life which manifests a single aim and overall coherence—whatever the vicissitudes of the world around us. It is a life of integrity. We seek to realize ourselves as what he calls an 'infinite whole'.[7] This Bradley understands, not in the mathematical sense of being without end, but in the Hegelian sense of being self-contained; the finite is that which is limited from outside, the infinite that which is limited from within. Understood in this way Bradley's demand that the moral life be infinite has clear parallels with Kant's demand that it be autonomous rather than heteronymous. It must, of course, be asked how, if human beings are finite and inevitably affected from outside, they could ever become an infinite whole of the kind that is suggested here. Bradley's reply is this: 'You cannot be a whole, unless you join a whole'.[8] In other words, only as an integral member of a whole with whom we are fully identified, can we enjoy anything like the autonomy of existence which is recommended here. It is worth stressing that at this stage the notion of 'self-realization' remains an entirely formal one, not any sort of rule for action—an immoral man realizes himself as much as a moral one—and thus 'the question in morals is to find the true whole, realiz-ing which will practically realize the true self'.[9] It is to this question Bradley now turns, considering two standard ethical positions, both of which could be thought of as ways of fleshing out this bare pattern: Hedonism or 'Pleasure for Pleasure's sake', and Kantianism or 'Duty for Duty's sake'.

27.1.2 Hedonism and Kantianism

To begin with Bradley objects that the doctrine of hedonism fails to accord with our ordinary moral beliefs; 'if there be any one thing that well-nigh the whole voice of the world, from all ages, nations, and sorts of men, has agreed to declare is *not* happiness,

6 *Ethical Studies*, 95.   7 *Ethical Studies*, 74.   8 *Ethical Studies*, 79.
9 *Ethical Studies*, 69.

that thing is pleasure, and the search for it'.[10] But it is theoretically flawed too. In his eyes the fundamental problem is its inability to provide us with any solid or realizable goal for our lives. In conceiving of pleasures as mental states isolated from the means by which they are arrived at it fixes on merely subjective and transitory feelings, and reduces the good life to nothing but a series of such 'perishing particulars'.[11] The 'self' realized evaporates into a sequence of instantaneous and heterogeneous 'satisfactions'. The hedonist attempts to give more unity and coherence to his postulated ideal by suggesting we aim at a 'sum' of pleasures, but the pleasures *of a lifetime* cannot be summed until we are dead and past enjoying them. We might seek instead to maximize the pleasures *of the moment*, but if our target is as much pleasure as possible, we must all fail to reach it since no one can experience an infinity of pleasures, while if we aim for as much pleasure as we can get everyone all of the time achieves that, at least by the lights of the hedonist psychology that underlies this theory in the first place.[12] But if these are the problems of egoistic hedonism, it clear that they cannot be overcome by 'modern utilitarianism' which seeks not the pleasure of one but that of all. For if there can be no greatest happiness for an individual, the sum of happiness of many is just as much of a 'wild and impossible fiction'.[13] Nor thinks Bradley is hedonism even practical. John Stuart Mill would have us believe that the rules or morality lay down our gathered knowledge of what produces pleasure, a kind of 'moral Almanac',[14] but it is always possible to imagine cases where following these rules would not produce the greatest happiness. In such cases, if we keep to the rule it is unequal to its professed end, but if we break it then it seems to show itself unnecessary. Bradley's attack on hedonism has become justly famous, and in it his invective reaches great heights.

Turning his attention to hedonism's main rival, Bradley objects that Kantianism is no more able to face the court of common sense than it, for the ethic that urges 'duty for duty's sake' insists that laws are exceptionless, but ordinary morality does not suppose this at all. There can be no absolute universal rules of moral action, for inevitably laws conflict and there is no rule which in some circumstances might not be broken. Nor again is Kantianism without deeper theoretical defect. It's weakness lies, Bradley urges, in the excessively abstract or formal character of its conception. For no act can be the mere carrying out of an abstract principle of duty, and we cannot will without willing something definite, but there is no way of passing from the mere form of duty to any particular duties themselves, or what comes to the same thing, any act whatsoever can be shown to be in accordance with such abstract principles. Bradley was not, of course, the first to make these objections, and he makes explicit debt to Hegel in his critique.[15]

Hedonism was found excessively particular, Kantianism excessively universal. Both errors, argues Bradley, arise out of a false abstraction, in the one case of pleasure itself apart from pleasant acts, and in the other of the general form of duty apart from individual duties themselves. What is needed is a middle path between these two extremes, a

---

[10] *Ethical Studies*, 86–7.   [11] *Ethical Studies*, 96.   [12] *Ethical Studies*, 97–8.
[13] *Ethical Studies*, 103.   [14] *Ethical Studies*, 105.   [15] *Ethical Studies*, 148 n. 1.

combination of the particular and the universal, a reconciliation which can at the same time hold on to their other valid insights. This is precisely what Bradley offers in the next chapter entitled 'My Station and its Duties'.

27.1.3 My Station and Its Duties

Progress is made once we see that previous theories, especially hedonism (but to an extent Kantianism also), operate with a mistaken conception of individuality. They treat individuals as distinct elements that can be added up to form an aggregate. But that is wrong. For humans are social creatures. They do not live alone (like, say, polar bears) but in communities. Moreover this is essential to their being. Although the actual forms of association which we find among people are conventional we can have strong grounds for saying that social life itself is both natural to and constitutive of our being.

This idea is hardly original. Many of the idealists were wont to trace it back to Aristotle, and even Plato. Bradley's immediate source was more contemporary however, and his account owes much to Hegel's conception of the self; indeed the case is advanced in part through extensive quotation from Hegel.[16] A conception at that time still unfamiliar in Britain, Bradley develops it with great vigour and intensity, for he is reacting against the strong individualism of prevailing British philosophy. The key figure here he wishes to take issue with is Mill who asserts the metaphysical autonomy of the individual. For Mill, individuals combine together in societies like collections of atoms in physics, not fusions of substances in chemistry.

The falsity of such individualism (Bradley claims) can be seen in many different ways. Socialization begins with our birth. We are not born a blank state, argues Bradley, but come into the world already bearing the characteristics of our family, our nation or race, and our species. Although the second is in this day more controversial, the first and third must be allowed. Much of the character with which we are born we share with family and species, from whom we inherit it. But what nature starts nurture only confirms, because from the moment it is born the child is educated and socialized by and into its community. Our whole life is a constant education, and it inevitably shapes us profoundly—who but the wisest and most stubborn among us could resist such pressure, asks Bradley? Which of our beliefs and attitudes have we come to by ourselves unaided? Nearly everything we think or feel is a social product. Bradley particularly emphasizes language, for language is far less flexible than we imagine. It shapes our very thoughts and characters, but at the same time carries with it the ideas and sentiments of society. But the social nature of our character does not cease with our education. Once we reach adulthood, we take up a position in life, and, argues Bradley, our identity is largely determined by our station and role in society. A person may be, say, an office worker and a parent and probably most of his or her daily activities can be explained under those two headings. We like to think that we make our place in life, but in truth matters are reversed and it is our place

---

[16] *Ethical Studies*, 185–7.

in life that makes us. As much as by our position in life, our identity is largely determined by our relations to others. 'I am who I am because of everyone,' a recent advertising slogan for a mobile phone company (Orange), could well have been Bradley's own here, for he argues social relations make for personhood. We define who we are, we become who we are, through our interrelations with others.

Where do all these points take us? What Bradley is arguing here is that the mere individual, the unit out of which Mill wished to build society, is a non-existent 'fiction'.[17] The individual apart from the community is an unreal 'abstraction',[18] not even comprehensible except as a member of a society. The idea that society is assembled out of distinct units, Bradley dismisses as a 'fable'.[19] Not even marriage, he says, the seemingly most obvious and simple such social composition, is really like this; the marriage unit shapes its two members as much as the other way round. Society, Bradley is suggesting, is an organic whole in which we are but members; like ants in a colony. On our own apart from the wider whole we are really incomplete beings. The agent must not be abstracted out of this context and considered apart from his social relations, for it is they that constitute his very identity. 'To know what a man is...you must not take him in isolation. He is one of a people, he was born into a family, he lives in a certain society, in a certain state. What he has to do depends on what his place is, what his function is, and all that comes from his station in the organism.'[20]

This essentially metaphysical account of self and society has an ethical dimension too. Fulfilment lies in my station and its duties: 'What [a man] has to do depends on what his place is, what his function is, and all that comes from his station in the organism.'[21] To be moral is to be a good member of one's society, loyally discharging the various responsibilities which membership involves. To some extent this is something which can be demonstrated empirically. For doubtless one of the most satisfying of human joys is that of friendship and community, that of belonging. But more deeply the point is a philosophical one. Because the self we realize is social, so necessarily its happiness is social. A happy father is one whose family is well and content, a happy ruler is one whose subjects are happy, a happy teacher is one whose students are happy, a happy shopkeeper is one whose customers are satisfied. Whatever his private feelings, in his social role, his content or discontent is social in nature. But it is our social self, Bradley argues, that is our true self. Since we are social, it is only within a society that we can properly realize ourselves. Ethics is not about private individuals, not even about the relations between such private individuals, but a matter of the communal life in which we all share, and therefore continuous with political philosophy. This politicizing of moral philosophy, whose other side is precisely a moralizing of political philosophy, is typical of idealist thought but less familiar in modern thinking where the problem of political philosophy tends to be regarded as precisely the puzzle of reconciling to a shared civil existence those defined by private (and potentially conflicting) moral outlooks.[22]

---

[17] *Ethical Studies*, 168.   [18] *Ethical Studies*, 173.   [19] *Ethical Studies*, 174.
[20] *Ethical Studies*, 173.   [21] *Ethical Studies*, 173.
[22] For a recent discussion of British Idealist political thought see Boucher and Vincent 2000.

The goal we sought was a combination of the universal and the particular. The ideal of 'My Station and its Duties', as a unified aim for a whole life rather than just a disparate set of targets and as something pertaining not simply to the individual but to the wider social whole, is certainly 'universal'; yet it is in no way formal or abstract, existing as it does only through the concrete details of the actual duties of any given station. It is thus what Bradley calls a 'concrete universal'.[23] Although the term itself falls out of use in his later writings, the basic notion of a whole which incorporates diversity, 'a perfect unity of homogeneity and specification',[24] remains a very central one throughout his philosophy.

27.1.4 Ideal Morality

Presented as a dialectical solution to hedonism and Kantianism, many have thought that 'My Station and its Duties' was Bradley's final position. Moreover widely reported and anthologized the doctrine has often been taken as crude conservatism ('accepting and keeping to your position in the social hierarchy') or relativism ('our moral duty is set by whatever community or age to which we happen to belong to'). But the material to avoid these errors may be found in the last few pages of the chapter, as Bradley himself lists a series of 'very serious objections'[25] to his theory. We hope to leave our bad selves behind and find our higher truer self in our social station, but a self may become so corrupted or encrusted by bad habits as to be unable to take up its station, and even the best of us can claim the benefits of service only for that period of time in which we are fully engaged in the satisfying work which it gives us. Moreover, even so far as we succeed in placing ourselves in society, we can have no guarantee of self-fulfilment in doing so. For the social whole in which an agent finds himself may demand of him self-sacrifice, or itself 'may be in a confused or rotten condition'.[26] Nor may a man take his morality *simply* from the society in which he lives. For that is something in a state of historical transition, and as a rational creature he cannot give up the capacity to stand outside it, reflect upon it, and work to make it better. Nor finally is quite everything that we are given us by society; there are some aspects of self-development which do not involve others at all. Says Bradley, 'the content of the ideal self does not fall wholly within any community, is in short *not* merely the ideal of a perfect social being'.[27]

In other words, there is more to ethics than just my station and its duties. Just what more that may be emerges as we move on to consider the next stage of the journey, which Bradley designates 'ideal morality'. Evolving out of the previous stage by retaining its genuine advances at the same time as correcting its flaws, the content of the good self to be realized at this level can be placed under three different heads. The first and still most important (in the sense of providing the largest part of our duties) is one's station and its duties, but to this is added a second element which, although still social, covers our aspirations 'beyond what the world expects of us, a will for good beyond what we see to be

---

[23] *Ethical Studies*, 162.   [24] *Ethical Studies*, 188.   [25] *Ethical Studies*, 202.
[26] *Ethical Studies*, 203.   [27] *Ethical Studies*, 205.

realized anywhere.[28] Many people have no moral ideal beyond the station in which they live, but there are others capable of rising to a point of view from which to see a better morality for society. They are, of course, its critics and reformers. The third region concerns duty which, although a recognizable moral imperative, such as the pursuit of beauty or of truth, 'in its essence does not involve direct relation to other men'.[29] Although neither science nor art could ever have arisen without society, and both undoubtedly benefit society, they may be pursued as ends in themselves without appeal to any social organism. It is vital that we notice these two further elements of Bradley's moral system, for they serve to clear him of charges all too often made, that his thought is overly conservative and that he wholly subordinates or even reduces the needs of the individual to those of society. Individuals may, indeed must when necessary, criticize their society, nor are they merely its pawns; they have a life of their own not given to them by their context. But for all that individuals cannot be understood apart from society.

27.2 T. H. GREEN

As influential as Bradley in the spreading of idealist ethics was the figure of T. H. Green. Bradley sought (not always successfully) to avoid metaphysics, but Green makes no such pretention, and his ethics begins with an explicitly metaphysical exercise, in effect a proof of idealism, in which he argues that nature can only be known if consciousness stands 'outside it', free from its limitations and autonomously functioning by itself. Reality he argues is made by relations, but relations are 'the work of the mind'. They are not, to be sure, the work of yours, or mine, or any other finite mind, and therefore Green postulates a higher experience to undertake the task, which sharing in the unalterable character of the relations it grounds he calls the 'Eternal Consciousness'.[30] As the underlying ground of all reality, including our own finite experience in which it gradually realizes itself, it is essentially the same as what Bradley calls the Absolute; the world-mind which manifests itself through us.

Green calls this analysis his 'metaphysics of knowledge' and its significance is seen as we pass from the first to the second book of his *Prolegomena to Ethics* which deals with action. For Green thinks that what holds of knowledge is paralleled by what holds of action; just as naturalism is unable to explain conscious knowledge, it is also unable to explain conscious purposive action. In so far as we are conscious we are free. Green has a distinctive conception of what it is for an action to be free. He opposes any notion of freedom as indeterminism; nothing happens without a reason. The only question is what sort of reason is at work? A free action is one brought about from within rather than imposed from without, and brought about, moreover, through conscious choice

[28] *Ethical Studies*, 220.   [29] *Ethical Studies*, 222.
[30] *Prolegomena*, §67. This argument has attracted controversy from the start. For two contemporary points of view see Nicholson 2006 and Mander 2006.

rather than blind impulse, instinct, or desire. Unmotivated willing of the latter kind would make action but 'an arbitrary freak of some unaccountable power' and nothing to be proud or ashamed of. [31]

But if what we choose is a function of our character and circumstances how can it be free? It all depends, argues Green,[32] on how we understand the terms 'character and circumstance'. If these are understood as mere natural phenomena (such as animal desires, instincts, and surrounding causal contexts), phenomena with the power to bring about behaviour, then this must indeed destroy freedom. But the introduction of consciousness into the picture changes everything, and the threat to freedom vanishes if character and circumstance are understood instead on the idealist model. Desires become 'motives' and the circumstances of action those things only which are taken in by self-consciousness and understood as the possibilities for action.

27.2.1 Self-Satisfaction

Human agency, then, is to be explained in terms of motive rather than desire. Unlike the mere animal pushed behind by some want, desire, or impulse, because they are self-conscious, human beings have the capacity in thought to transcend both the present and the actual and look forward to possible future states, thereby creating for themselves ends which they then endeavour to bring about.

Green goes on to argue that the motive determining an agent's will is always an idealized future state of his own self, a conception of himself as satisfied—whatever it may be that he seeks. For this reason, argues Green, moral action is 'an expression at once of conscious contrast between an actual and possible self, and of an impulse to make that possible self real; or, as it is sometimes put, it is a process of self-realization, i.e. of making a possible self real'.[33] This position is clearly in line with that of Bradley—indeed it is Bradley who more commonly uses the term self-realization'; Green tends to prefer 'self-satisfaction'—and in historical terms their arrival at this common formula represents an important shift in ethical thinking. Instead of asking with the utilitarian, intuitionist, and even Kantian philosophers of the day, 'what ought I to do?', they—and the many idealists that followed them—re-construed ethical enquiry in the mould of an older question, namely, 'what kind of person ought I to be?', in the eudaimonistic tradition of Plato and Aristotle .

The claim that all conscious purposive action seeks self-satisfaction may seem like the most ruthless psychological egoism, and in places Green appears to speak in such a fashion. But on closer reflection we see his view is quite otherwise. Rather the derivation flows from the very definition of conscious action itself. Whatever we want, in wanting it we necessarily want also a state in which our own wanting is satisfied. There is nothing necessarily self-directed in the content of the want. This is important, for only such a derivation can explain the categorical nature of demand; the call to self-realization is

---

[31] *Prolegomena*, §110.   [32] *Prolegomena*, §106.   [33] *Works* III, 224.

universal and exception less. But now the formula begins to look trivial. Whatever we want, it is self-satisfaction, just because we want it. Or to put the same point another way, it is useless to say we should aim at self-realization, for there are many selves we might realize, many of which might far better be left unrealized.

Content is provided, however, if we reflect further about the nature of satisfaction. Presented at first with just a sequence of wants, the self cannot be content with a piece-meal approach, and 'there arises the idea of a satisfaction on the whole'.[34] The generic notion of the good is that 'it satisfies some desire'[35] but, as the idea that we might become 'better' than we are inevitably leads on to the idea that we might become 'the best' we can possibly be, so the generic notion of the good begets that of the true or unconditional good, as 'an end in which the effort of a moral agent can really find rest'.[36] It is that which fulfils the agent's desire for 'an abiding satisfaction of an abiding self';[37] an idea clearly related to Bradley's injunction to be an 'infinite whole'. Nor can satisfaction of the self simply be restricted to the satisfaction of desires; it calls for the realization of capacities. Morality demands that through right action we realize our potential. But any given act realizes our capacity only in part, a fact which itself gives birth to the idea of our com-plete realization. We thus arrive at the conclusion that the ultimate goal must be the complete development of our potentiality, human perfection.

But if, as Green tells us, the moral ideal amounts to the complete realization or perfec-tion of human capacities, it is only natural that we should ask just what this means. Here, however, we meet an obstacle. Since our potential have never yet been perfectly realized, we cannot properly say what that would amount to. Green's moral theory is a species of ideal or perfectionist ethics, but since our moral understanding stands in need of develop-ment just as much as our moral nature itself, a measure of ignorance is he concludes una-voidable. The utilitarian takes us as we are and uses current values to define the ideal, but as we grow so do our ideals and so our conception of the goal must also grow and develop.

27.2.2 Moral Development

Fortunately, even if it may not yet be known in full, the moral ideal may be known in part for we are not left entirely without help. Some of what is needed Green thought we could learn by looking at actual historical moral developments. Ethical codes change over history and, although there is no chance for us to stand outside of time and antici-pate the ideal from which they all fall short, relativism is not our only alternative, for we may yet regard this history as the gradual unfolding of the divine spirit within us. Green believes that 'the history of human character has been one in which the [eternal] con-sciousness has throughout been operative upon wants of animal origin, giving rise through its actions upon them to the specific quality of that history'.[38] Though our poten-tial cannot yet be known, 'To a certain extent it has shown by actual achievement what it

---

[34] *Prolegomena*, §85.   [35] *Prolegomena*, §171.   [36] *Prolegomena*, §171.
[37] *Prolegomena*, §234.   [38] *Prolegomena*, §95.

has in it to become, and by reflection on the so far developed activity we can form at least some negative conclusions in regard to its complete realisation.'[39] A 'subjective' history of the moral feelings of mankind would be hard to write, but these also exist 'objectively' in the norms, practices, and institutions of society,[40] and Green speaks of the 'institutions and useages…the social judgments and aspirations, through which human life has been so far bettered'.[41] We are bound within moral world views that inevitably change over time, but if we understand this as a process of evolution, perspective enough is found for the present to pass judgement on the past. And perhaps a little more: with the insight afforded by where we have got to so far, even if we cannot say what would be 'best', we can see what personal and institutional changes would make life 'better'.

And the relationship is reciprocal. Not only does history give some content to the moral ideal, but the notion of an operating moral ideal is (thinks Green) the only plausible way we have of explaining the actual facts of human moral effort. Thus for Green the idea of the supreme good is not just an ideal, something potential, but also something at work in the world, an idea that 'has been the essential influence in the process by which man has so far bettered himself' and which 'is the condition of character and conduct being morally good'.[42] For where does the idea come from that we might become better than we are, that we might even become perfect, except from the eternal consciousness within us? The better self we already implicitly are.

We find a direct parallel between Green's metaphysical position about knowledge and his moral claims. As current knowledge and the possibility of future knowledge are both explicable only on their being reproductions in us of a vision already realized in the mind of God, likewise actual progress and the possibility of future development is ultimately explicable only as the reproduction of itself of a divine life already living the perfection after which we strive. Through moral progress we bring about the kingdom of heaven.

27.2.3 Intuitionism, Hedonism, and Kantianism

We get some further idea of what Green thought the true good would consist in by considering his criticisms of some alternative theories. Green rejects as false and unnecessary the intuitionist assumption of any special moral sense or faculty. The way in which we discover ethical truth—what *ought* to be—is the same as that in which we discover metaphysical truth—what ultimately *is*—namely, reason (where this is understood in a broad sense to cover the full range of human cognitive powers, not simply the narrow and formal manipulation of concepts). To suppose otherwise that we have some special ability (intuition) to make moral judgements without deriving them deductively or inductively from others is to undermine the unity of knowledge and of the moral agent. It is not some part of our mind or part of ourselves that feels and acts morally. An act of will is an expression of the whole person.[43]

[39] *Prolegomena*, §172.   [40] Tyler 2010: ch. 3.4.   [41] *Prolegomena*, §180.
[42] *Prolegomena*, §173.   [43] *Prolegomena*, §153.

Utilitarianism, the main contemporary rival, fares no better. Green objects that we seek many goals quite other than pleasure and often we seek that which will give us no pleasure at all.[44] Nor can Hedonism explain the imperative we feel, instead of seeking satisfaction in what currently seems most attractive, to become better human beings than we currently are, and to find more worthy desires whose satisfaction might lead to a deeper, more permanent happiness.[45] The standard rejoinder to such points rests, he objects, on a psychological hedonism long ago shown to be false by Butler.[46] The fact that pleasure inevitably accompanies satisfying oneself by achieving some end does not imply that pleasure is the object of desire. To be sure, what is good will give pleasure, but the pleasure comes from the goodness, not vice versa.[47] To a degree Mill understood this, but the changes he introduced to accommodate it (a doctrine of higher pleasure, and doctrine of pleasure with many diverse parts) amount to the 'virtual surrender' of utilitarianism.[48] Moreover, the hedonist ideal conflicts with its psychology. We are pleasure seekers and so ought to maximize pleasure, we are told, but 'A sum of pleasures is not a pleasure.'[49] Echoing Bradley's objection, Green complains that pleasures follow one another in a series and even if they may be added in thought, there is no means in reality of accumulating and enjoying them as a whole.

In his Preface to the 1907 edition of the *Prolegomena* Edward Caird describes Green's position as a modification of Kant. And certainly Green's ethics is in many ways close to that of Kant. Like Kant, Green regards the ethical obligation of self-realization (with all that entails), as flowing from the very nature of conscious action and independent of our desires, as something categorical or applicable to all rational beings. But Green finds problems with Kant too. The problems (to be sure) lie not so much in the system itself as in his statement of it[50] —'though his doctrine is essentially true, his way of putting it' is defective[51]—but they are serious.

He rejects what he sees as Kant's claim that man has a twofold nature and a twofold causality; a moral self and a sensuous self; a self on the one hand intelligible, noumenal, and free and a self on the other hand sensible, phenomenal, and determined. Since all we are acquainted with is the later, complains Green, Kant's doctrine amounts to an admission of utter ignorance about the true self and its manner of connection with the world. In knowing actions as they present themselves to us, we known them as 'they really are not'.[52] Moreover, in ruling out desire as a motive he rules out just what makes actions valuable, as well as rendering them psychologically impossible.[53] For Green, Duty need not be independent of *all* desire, only of natural pre-conscious pre-deliberative desire. In so far as desire is rational and conscious it has a place in ethics. Kant's mistake is to assume there is no alternative between determination by natural desire for pleasure, and determination by abstract conception of the moral law; we often in all consciousness desire things other than pleasure.[54] Green's case against Kant's 'two-worlds' is strong, but of course, he

[44] *Prolegomena*, §159.   [45] *Prolegomena*, §223.   [46] *Prolegomena*, §161.
[47] *Prolegomena*, §171.   [48] *Prolegomena*, §167.   [49] *Prolegomena*, §221.
[50] Irwin 1984: 32.   [51] *Works* II, 124.   [52] *Works* II, 104.
[53] *Works* II, 155.   [54] *Works* II, 140.

faces his own (not so different) difficulties in relating together his two 'worlds' of *cause* and of *motive*. Just as he struggles to explain exactly how the eternal consciousness relates to historical knowledge, a deep puzzle remains as to how this world of 'free' actions relates to the causal world which underlies and indeed expresses it.

As did Bradley, Green complains also that in refusing any appeal to experience, the Kantian idea of duty is but an 'empty abstraction, an idea of nothing in particular to be done'.[55] He focuses solely on the *form* of the motive—to do our duty—without regard to its *content*—whatever object it is that we will. Taken strictly this would lead to the complete 'paralysis of the will'.[56]

In specifying a goal of action—human perfection—Green would seem to be putting forward a variety of teleological ethics. But crucially, like Kant, he stresses the absolute importance of motives. This is vital, not just for freedom, but also for the very value of an action. Ethics is founded on the distinction between the good and bad will;[57] it consists in 'the imposition . . . of rules requiring something to be done irrespectively of any inclination to do it, irrespectively of any desired end',[58] '[T]he one unconditional good is the good will',[59] he allows, for the motive not merely determines the act, it '*is* the act on its inner side'.[60] But if this is an area in which consequentialists are weak, Green objects too that in concentrating wholly on the motive, Kant himself makes the opposite error, of too much ignoring the consequences of action.[61] Ascertaining the right course for action is certainly more than a calculus of possible outcomes, but neither should they be utterly ignored. For as long as we take a full view of the matter, 'There is no real reason to doubt that the good or evil in the motive of an action is exactly measured by the good or evil in its consequences.' Appearance to the contrary—appearance, that is, of good action from bad intentions or vice versa—is but the result of the limited view we take of both motive and consequences.[62] A wider view may show us to more instruments than agents, and the value of what we may do may change with our perspective.

But is this not contradictory?[63] Either goal is everything, or motive is everything. Surely we cannot say both. Green however rejects such a choice. It implies that goal and will are separate, but where the goal itself is human perfection that can never quite be the case; 'when we are giving an account of an agent whose development is governed by an idea of his own perfection, we cannot avoid speaking of one and the same condition of will alternately as means and as end'.[64] Our effort to realize the good is itself also part of the good we try to realize, so that in circular fashion right effort is that aimed at perfection, while perfection is what right effort aims at. The good we seek is precisely to do or be good. But rather than 'an illogical procedure', this is, suggests Green, 'the only procedure suited to the matter in hand'. 'It means that such an ideal, not yet realised but

[55] *Works* II. 154.   [56] *Prolegomena*, §247.   [57] *Prolegomena*, §155.
[58] *Prolegomena*, §193.   [59] *Prolegomena*, §292.   [60] *Prolegomena*, §105.
[61] *Works* II, 154.   [62] *Prolegomena*, §295.
[63] For further discussion of this complex dual relationship see Weinstein 2007 and Simhony 1995.
[64] *Prolegomena*, §195.

operating as a motive, already constitutes in man an inchoate form of that life, that perfect development of himself, of which the completion would be the realised ideal itself.'[65]

27.2.4 The Common Good

The last point which helps Green to define more substantively his moral ideal—providing content to what would otherwise remain a merely formal notion—is perhaps the most import of all. Transforming the seemingly individualistic doctrine of self-satisfaction into something almost directly its opposite, Green argues that while it is indeed true that the moral ideal is one of personal development, it needs to be recognized that people are fundamentally social creatures, and hence that our true personal good properly understood turns out to be a common or social good. 'Finding our own pleasures and pains dependent on the pleasures and pains of others, we form the idea of a satisfaction of self which includes the satisfaction of others, not simply as a means to our own pleasure, but as ends in themselves deserving their own satisfaction,'[66] for 'man cannot contemplate himself as in a better state, or on the way to the best, without contemplating others, not merely as a means to that better state, but as sharing it with him.'[67] As well as, indeed part of, our interests in ourselves we have interests in other persons, such that our own good is really part of something wider than us; 'the idea of an absolute and a common good; a good common to the person conceiving it with others, and good for him and them, whether at any moment it answers their likings or no'.[68]

This doctrine that the true good is a common one (something we designate with capitals as the Common Good) does away with the age-old distinction and conflict between egoism and altruism. It is an idea which 'does not admit of the distinction between good for self and good for others'.[69] To pursue a selfish life is to misunderstand one's own true nature and hence where one's own true happiness lies. It renders the distinction between benevolence and reasonable self-love 'a fiction of philosophers'.[70]

To unpack this idea further we may note three senses in which the common good is 'common'. (a) It is thought (by some relativists) that there are as many different conceptions of the good as there are individuals who seek it, and no way to choose between them. This is not Green's view. He believes that, whatever the differences in what we seem to seek—the result of our varying times, cultures, and temperaments—and whatever the differences in the degree to which we recognize it, at bottom we are all led by a common ideal standard of the good; a common sense of what is needed to bring about ultimate human satisfaction; 'the true good is a good for all men, and good for them all in virtue of the same nature and capacity'.[71] (b) But even if all people have the same ultimate ends, these may be incompatible. If we both want to win, or if we both want great power and influence, we may find ourselves in competition. This is

---

[65] *Prolegomena*, §196.   [66] *Prolegomena*, §201.   [67] *Prolegomena*, §199.
[68] *Prolegomena*, §202.   [69] *Prolegomena*, §235.   [70] *Prolegomena*, §232.
[71] *Prolegomena*, §244.

another thing Green means to deny. The common good 'is common to all men in the proper sense,—in the sense, namely, that there can be no competition for its attainment between man and man'.[72] Distinguishing between the 'good things of the soul' and the 'good things of the body'[73] we see at once that what we seek must be a spiritual good, since material goods will always be scarce or potential sources of conflict. The good (as we noted above) is something to be or do, not something to have. (c) But even if we have the same harmonious goals, these may only run in parallel. There is for example no conflict in knowledge, but we could both be locked in our ivory towers. The strongest sense of common good is that of a single project in which we are all involved. This too Green wishes to endorse. Against this last idea of a unique goal for all members of society, Isaiah Berlin famously argued that there can be no one good but only a plurality of conflicting ones, and many have thought him correct. But it needs to be remembered that this identical task need not prescribe identical role, and may be more like an orchestra. This is how Green would regard that joint venture to which we are all committed, a multi-stranded creation which we could regard either as the perfection of human nature or the realization of God.

But it may be asked what Green thinks entitles him to make this astounding claim. At times Green suggests that it is our desire for a more permanent or stable kind of satisfaction that calls us to pursue a common good. Man pursues his desires, but as Schopenhauer noted, there is a certain futility in seeing to meet a desire which as soon as it is met, as we ourselves continually change, morphs into boredom or the desire for something else. But if thus reflecting on the transitory nature of our pleasures and desires, we ask ourselves 'what can satisfy the self which abides throughout and survives those desires',[74] the thought of ourselves as permanent gives rise to the 'idea of a social good—of a good not private to the man himself, but good for him as a member of a community'.[75] Rather as short strands of wool fibre are spun together into a continuous thread, the ever-changing and, indeed, short-lived self, by interweaving its own with other equally transient contributors, becomes part of something larger that is both constant and enduring—at first perhaps the family line, but spreading out perhaps to the wider school or college tradition, the community, the nation, the religion, or the race. The idea of ourselves as permanent is always the idea of ourselves as social. As private individuals we change all the time. Our appearance, our knowledge, our feelings, our desires, none of them are constant; not least because the world is always changing around us. Only in so far as our self is defined by a wider framework—in so far as we stand as a member of some family, profession, nation, or religion—is there any constancy in us. And of course such wholes may continue after our death, so 'It is this association that neutralises the effect which the anticipation of death must otherwise have on the demand for permanent good'.[76] Our identity is given in part by our interests, but in so far as our interests are identified with those of a wider body to which we belong, their pursuit and thus our own identity continues after our death.

[72] *Prolegomena*, §281.
[73] *Prolegomena*, §243.
[74] *Prolegomena*, §229.
[75] *Prolegomena*, §232.
[76] *Prolegomena*, §231.

But perhaps Green's strongest argument for the common good is one about *psychological development*. We may set down the good as a matter of individual self-development, but it must be recognized that selfhood or personality can only develop in a social setting. Simply in ourselves we are only potential people, and that potentiality is never realized until we live in society, for 'social life is to personality what language is to thought' says Green. 'Language presupposes thought as a capacity, but in us the capacity of thought is only actualised in language. So human society presupposes persons in capacity—subjects capable each of conceiving himself and the bettering of his life as an end to himself—but it is only in the intercourse of men, each recognised by each as an end, not merely a means, and thus as having reciprocal claims, that the capacity is actualised and that we really live as persons'.[77] Less a kind of substance than a species of relation, only in a social context can I become a person.

What Green is arguing here is the fundamentally social nature of the self, the same point that Bradley urged in 'My Station and its Duties'. Green says the self is from the first a self 'existing in manifold relations to nature and other persons' and 'these relations form the reality of the self'.[78] The self in which we are interested 'is not an empty or abstract self' but one affected 'by manifold interests, among which are interests in other people'.[79] The self must be regarded 'as at once individual and universal'.[80] Reciprocality is the key in the relationship between men and the society 'which is at once constituted by them and makes them what they are'.[81]

But alongside all this holistic talk, it is important to note Green's strong insistence that the 'ultimate standard of worth is an ideal of *personal* worth'.[82] For Green, apart from embodiment in individual personalities, larger notions such as 'nation' or 'humanity' are mere abstractions. Likewise the notion of 'spiritual progress' means nothing unless manifested in individual lives.[83] The goal is one that must be realized in *persons*, and no goal could ever be accepted requiring their 'extinction'—even by absorption into something greater.[84] This last point marks a crucial difference between Green and Bradley in that it would seem to rule out any understanding of ultimate reality as so unified a whole that finite minds are simply lost or absorbed into it.

Idealist ethics dominated until the turn of the century but from that point onwards experienced a steady decline until by the 1930s it had all but vanished from the scene. This was due in part to the success of rivals such as H.A. Prichard and W.D. Ross (in Oxford) and G.E. Moore (in Cambridge) who, rather than ground ethics in complex and contentious systems of metaphysics, reasserted a more direct intuitionism, free from such vague and contentious notions as 'the true self', 'the common good', and 'the Absolute'. But external factors also played their part; to an age increasingly focused on scientific and technical advance, more and more detached from religious concerns and sickened by the carnage of the Great War, the once potent attraction of a spiritual, nation-based, and profoundly optimistic ethic evaporated away.

[77] *Prolegomena*, §183.   [78] *Works* II, 146.   [79] *Prolegomena*, §199.
[80] *Works* III, 99.   [81] *Prolegomena*, §110.   [82] *Prolegomena*, §184.
[83] *Prolegomena*, §§184–5.   [84] *Prolegomena*, §189.

BIBLIOGRAPHY

Bosanquet, B. 1924. 'Life and Philosophy', in J. H. Muirhead (ed.), *Contemporary British Philosophy: First Series*. London: George Allen and Unwin, 51–74.

Boucher, D. and Vincent, A. 2000. *British Idealism and Political Theory*. Edinburgh: Edinburgh University Press.

Bradley, F. H. 1876. *Ethical Studies*. Oxford: Clarendon Press. (2nd edn 1927.)

Brink, D. 2003. *Perfectionism and the Common Good*. Oxford: Clarendon Press.

Green, T. H. 1883. *Prolegomena to Ethics*. Oxford: Clarendon Press. (5th edn 1907.)

—— 1885–1888. *Works of T.H.Green*, ed. R. L. Nettleship. 3 vols. London: Longmans.

Irwin, T. 1984. 'Morality and Personality: Kant and Green', in A. W. Wood (ed.), *Self and Nature in Kant's Philosophy*. Ithaca, NY: Cornell University Press, 31–56.

—— 2009. *The Development of Ethics: A Historical and Critical Survey; Volume III*. Oxford: Oxford University Press, chs 84–5.

Mander, W. J. 2000. *Anglo-American Idealism 1865–1927*. Westport, CT: Greenwood Press.

—— 2006. 'In Defence of the Eternal Consciousness', in W. J. Mander and M. Dimova-Cookson (eds), *T. H. Green: Ethics, Metaphysics and Political Philosophy*. Oxford: Oxford University Press, 139–59.

Nicholson, P. P. 2006. 'Green's Eternal Consciousness', in W. J. Mander and M. Dimova-Cookson (eds), *T. H. Green: Ethics, Metaphysics and Political Philosophy*. Oxford: Oxford University Press, 187–206.

Simhony, A. 1995. 'Was T. H.Green a Utilitarian?', *Utilitas* 7: 121–44.

Sprigge, T. L. S. 2006. *The God of Metaphysics*. Oxford: Oxford University Press, ch. 7.

Tyler, C. 2010. *Liberal Socialism of Thomas Hill Green*. Exeter and Charlottesville, VA: Imprint Academic.

Weinstein, D. 2007. *Utilitarianism and the New Liberalism*. Cambridge: Cambridge University Press, ch. 2.

Wempe, B. 2004. *T. H. Green's Theory of Positive Freedom*. Exeter and Charlottesville, VA: Imprint Academic.

CHAPTER 28

....

ETHICS IN THE ANALYTIC TRADITION

....

JOHN DEIGH*

28.1 REVOLUTIONARY IDEAS: MOORE'S *PRINCIPIA*

....

THE revolution in British philosophy that gave birth to the analytic tradition, like many social and intellectual revolutions, has a storied beginning. Its moment was set by the unusually strong influence of continental metaphysics on British philosophy at the end of the nineteenth century. Idealism, having overthrown the long dominant empiricist school in British thought, was the prevailing philosophical school at that time. Its hub was Oxford. Its leading voice was F. H. Bradley, a gifted philosopher and formidable rhetorician. The main doctrines of Bradley's philosophy were monism and rationalist idealism. The universe, Bradley held, was a whole no part of which could be adequately understood independently of its other parts, and its nature was that of a rational soul or spirit. Bradley's absolute idealism continued a programme of thought that T. H. Green had entrenched at Oxford in years prior to Bradley's ascent. Idealism was well represented at Cambridge too, though the university's main exponent, James Ward, rejected Bradley's absolutism.

G. E. Moore and Bertrand Russell were undergraduates at Cambridge during Bradley's ascendancy. They matriculated in the early 1890s.[1] By the time they had finished their exams and begun work on their dissertations, they had come completely under Bradley's spell. Their enthusiasm, however, was short-lived. For Moore, the spell wore off in the

* I am grateful to Jonathan Adler, Roger Crisp, Jonathan Dancy, and Kevin Toh for their helpful comments on an earlier draft of this chapter.
[1] Russell began his studies in 1890; Moore began his in 1892. For an account Moore's student years at Cambridge see Moore 1952a: 12–25.

course of his work on the dissertation that won him a fellowship.[2] And as is common when a youth comes to doubt what he had once greatly admired, Moore's turn against Absolute Idealism was fierce. In a series of publications, beginning with his 1899 article in *Mind*, 'The Nature of Judgment', Moore attacked Absolute Idealism mercilessly (Moore 1899). Russell followed his lead. Their powerful opposition to Bradley's philosophy at the turn of the century precipitated idealism's decline. Realism, the metaphysical view for which they argued, eventually replaced it.[3]

Moore published his two most influential works of this period, 'The Refutation of Idealism' and *Principia Ethica*, in 1903 (Moore 1903a and 1903b). Both are seminal contributions to the analytic movement in British philosophy that he and Russell initiated. Both feature the realist doctrine and the method of decompositional analysis that are the hallmarks of Moore's early philosophy. According to this doctrine, the objects of consciousness are real, and their reality does not depend on any mind's attending to or experiencing them. Idealism in modern philosophy, Moore argued in 'The Refutation of Idealism', springs from arguments that depend on a confusion of the objects of consciousness with the contents of consciousness. Objects of consciousness, Moore held, are either objects of sensation or objects of thought, and the latter are no less real and independent from minds that attend to them than the former. Consciousness of objects of either type, Moore argued, presupposes that those objects are distinct from that consciousness. None is part of the consciousness of which it is an object. None is contained within it. The analysis in this case is the same as the analysis one would give of the relation between a joke and the laughter it produces when someone tells it. The joke is the object of the laughter. Its audience laughs at it. It is thus distinct from the laughter it produces, so it is neither part of nor contained within that laughter. Idealism, because it fails to treat the relation between states of consciousness and their objects as having the same logic, misconstrues it as a relation of a whole to one of its constituent parts. And because of this mistake, Idealism's distinctive arguments for understanding space, time, numbers, material things, and so forth as figments or constructions of thought are all fallacious. Or so Moore argued.

Moore, in his opening attack on Bradley's philosophy in 'The Nature of Judgment', identified objects of thought as concepts (Moore 1899: 177). He took them to correspond to what Bradley called 'universal meanings'. Afterwards he stopped using 'concept' to mean an object of thought and used several different terms, seemingly indiscriminately, instead. These include 'idea', 'notion', 'quality', and 'property'. He used the latter two to mean objects of sensation as well, and in light of this usage, I will, in discussing Moore, use these two terms to mean objects of consciousness generally. I will use 'intellectual object' specifically to mean objects of thought. In any case, whatever term one uses to capture Moore's position, one must understand the objects to which it refers to be real regardless of whether any mind is attending to or experiencing them. For their reality, in Moore's view, does not depend on their being attended to or experienced.

---

[2] This was his second dissertation; his first did not win him a fellowship (Moore 1952a: 20–2).
[3] See Hylton 1990.

In addition, Moore held that these objects neither arise from nor presuppose physical objects. Moore embraced Platonism. Accordingly, he denied that intellectual objects were abstractions from our sensory experiences of the world. Like his idealist opponents, Moore rejected Locke's empiricism as well as Hume's and Mill's. His Platonism is perhaps most evident in his thesis that existence is a quality of some objects but not all. Objects that are subject to change have this quality. They exist over some stretch of time and may undergo change during that stretch. Objects such as numbers, by contrast, being immutable, lack this quality. Though real, they do not, in Moore's sense of the word, exist. The same holds for such intellectual objects as propositions, relations, and value. All are real, immutable, and timeless.

Ethics in the analytic tradition begins with Moore's study, in *Principia Ethica*, of value. Ethics, he maintained, is not just the study of good conduct. It is, rather, 'the general enquiry into what is good' (Moore 1903b: 2). Moore's study of value is an enquiry of this sort, and it radically changed the orientation of the field. The questions it raised and the debates it generated continue to be among the field's major preoccupations. To be sure, debates among philosophers about the nature of goodness go back to Plato. But Moore, with the backing of his arguments against Idealism, introduced into these debates a distinction that no philosopher before him had used or considered. One must keep separate, Moore observed, the question of what is good in the sense of what sort of thing is good from the question of what is good in the sense of what does 'good' mean. To arrive at a correct answer to the former question, Moore argued, one must first correctly answer the latter. Ethics, he held, cannot be a systematic science, a branch of knowledge, unless its students proceed in this way. For ethical knowledge consists in sound ethical judgement, and to make such judgement one must first identify the intellectual object whose apprehension in the act of judging is essential to it. Only then can one determine whether one's ethical judgement is sound. Philosophers before Moore had not done this, for none had sharply distinguished the question of what 'good' means from questions about what sort of thing partakes of the quality the word signifies. After Moore, the question of meaning stood alone and became fundamental.

Moore, in putting forward the question of what 'good' means, took himself to be asking for the definition of the intellectual object that the word 'good' stands for. Answering this question, as Moore understood it, thus requires more than giving a synonym or synonymous expression for the word. The definition that a correct answer consists in is not the kind of definition one finds in a dictionary. The question is not, Moore said, 'a verbal question' (1903b: 6). It is not about English usage. Rather, it is about the nature of the intellectual object that 'good' signifies. As Moore saw the matter, this object is either simple or complex, and if it is complex, then it is composed of parts the interrelation of which constitutes the whole. A definition, if the object is complex, specifies what these parts are and how they are interrelated. If it is simple, on the other hand, one cannot define it. Simple intellectual objects, according to Moore, are indefinable. Being the elements by reference to which all definitions are constructed, they cannot themselves be defined. Good, in his view, is such an object. '[G]ood is good', he declared, 'and that is the end of the matter' (1903b: 6,).

It follows, Moore argued, that no system of ethics whose first principles are supposed to be true by virtue of the meaning of 'good' is sound. It does not represent knowledge. What it represents is ill-founded belief. Moore, for this reason, rejected any system that was founded on a definition of good or a proposition identifying as the word's meaning some property like pleasure, conformity to nature, or being more evolved. Mill's hedonism, the perfectionism of the Stoics, and Herbert Spencer's evolutionary ethics all come in for criticism by Moore as ill-founded theories. All, he maintained, exemplify the same error. They all mistakenly treat good as definable or take the word as having the same meaning as a term for some property that was manifestly a different object of consciousness from good. And because Moore regarded this error as especially evident in naturalist theories of ethics, he called it 'the naturalistic fallacy'.

Few of the philosophers Moore criticized for committing this fallacy expressly set down a definition of good and made it a first principle of their system. Few expressly grounded their theory on a thesis about what the word 'good' means. Nonetheless, Moore took them to have founded their systems on such principles or theses because they plainly took themselves to be advancing ethical knowledge through the presentation of these systems and could take themselves to be doing so only if they saw their systems' fundamental tenets as not just true but warranted. Their taking these tenets to be fundamental meant of course that they took them to be warranted in themselves and not by virtue of their being derivable from some other proposition. And unless a philosopher expressly maintained that the fundamental tenets of his system were self-evident and known by intuition, Moore understood him to be treating 'good' as if it meant the property with which that philosopher equated being good. In other words, Moore understood him to be taking his identification of good with this property as either an analytic truth or as a true equation between what 'good' means and what the term on the other side of the equation means. Accordingly, Moore characterized all such philosophers as holding either that good is definable or that the word has the same meaning as a term for a property that is manifestly a different object of thought from good. In either case, then, they commit the naturalistic fallacy.

Moore thought that one finds this fallacy 'in almost every book on Ethics; and yet', he noted, 'it is not recognized: ...' (1903b: 14). What explains this widespread blindness to the fallacy, he observed, is that the fallacy consists, not in affirming a false principle such as the principle of hedonism, 'pleasure and nothing but pleasure is good', but rather in the principle's being treated as if it were true by virtue of the identity in meaning of the terms 'good' and 'pleasure'. One indication of its being so treated is that it is commonly stated in the abbreviated formulation 'Pleasure is good'. The full formulation of the principle—the correct formulation, according to Moore—does not express a proposition about pleasure's being identical with good. Rather it expresses a proposition according to which goodness is uniquely predicated of pleasure. The proposition answers the question what sort of thing is good, not the question what does 'good' mean. Thus, its truth or falsity does not depend on whether 'good' and 'pleasure' have the same meaning. Since anyone who carefully attended to good and to pleasure would see that each is an object of consciousness distinct from the other, the common use of the abbreviated formulation of the principle must be due to confusion about what proposition this formulation expresses. The confusion is this: The writers who use it mean to be expressing the principle but treat it instead as if it expressed a proposition about pleasure's being identical with good. Consequently, they fail to recognize the fallacy they are committing in using it. The same observation also applies to discussions of competing principles such as the principle of subjectivist ethics, 'The desired and nothing but the desired is good' and the principle of Stoic ethics, 'Conformity to nature and nothing but conformity to nature is good.'

Moore believed that recognition of the naturalistic fallacy would bring clarity to ethics. For one thing, if philosophers recognize the fallacy, they will heed the distinction between the question what sort of thing is good and the question what does the word 'good' mean. As a result, they will debate the merits of different answers to the first question without confusing it with the second. They will, in other words, engage in debate over what sort of things are good without, in effect, attempting, by laying down a definition of good or stipulating the meaning of 'good', to shut off the debate and insulate the answer they favour from being challenged (1903b: 20–1). For another, philosophers will be disposed to see and allow that more than one kind of thing may be good. Confusion of the second question with the first leads to the view that only one sort of thing is good, since the typical assumption behind giving a definition of good or stipulating the meaning of 'good' is that the word, in its intended use, denotes a single property and one's definition or stipulation identifies it. Hence, if philosophers heed the distinction between the two questions, they will recognize that the truth of, say, the proposition that pleasure is good does not preclude some other sort of thing from also being good. They will recognize, that is, that in affirming this proposition, they are predicating goodness of pleasure and such predication is consistent with predicating goodness of other sorts of thing as well.

These points are reflected in what many regard as Moore's most powerful argument for the indefinability of good: his famous *open question argument*. Of any proffered definition of good, Moore argued, one can ask whether the complex property that the definition identifies as the meaning of 'good' is good, and this question will always be open. The same is true of any proposition that equates the meaning of 'good' with the meaning of a term for an ostensibly different property. To ask whether pleasure is good, for instance, is to ask a significant question. Yet if 'good' and 'pleasure' had the same meaning, it would not be. Rather it would be like asking the trivial question, 'Is pleasure pleasant?' As Moore put the point,

> [W]hoever will attentively consider with himself what is actually before his mind when he asks the question 'Is pleasure (or whatever it may be) after all good?' can easily satisfy himself that he is not merely wondering whether pleasure is pleasant. And if he will try this experiment with each suggested definition in succession, he may become expert enough to recognise that in every case he has before his mind a unique object, with regard to the connection of which with any other object, a distinct question may be asked. (1903b: 16)

The failure of philosophers to recognize the indefinability of good has resulted, Moore concluded, in their taking as fundamental principles of ethics either propositions about words and their meanings or propositions about some other property than good or right. In either case, they have failed to ground their systems on ethical principles.[4]

28.2 Moore and Sidgwick

Moore directed this criticism at virtually the whole canon of moral philosophy and all of its contributors. He acknowledged one exception, Henry Sidgwick, whose lectures he had attended at Cambridge.[5] Sidgwick alone among writers of major works in ethics, Moore noted, understood and avoided the naturalistic fallacy. Sidgwick had argued, in the third chapter of his *Methods of Ethics*, for a conception of ethical judgement that Moore found congenial. On this conception, an ethical judgement is a judgement of what it is right to do or what one ought to do in the sense of 'right' and 'ought' that is strictly ethical, and the strictly ethical sense of these words, Sidgwick held, is 'too elementary to admit of any formal definition' (Sidgwick 1907: 32). Moore, in view of such statements, understood Sidgwick to be agreeing with him in holding that the basic notion of ethics is simple and indefinable. Indeed, Moore credited Sidgwick with being alert to the naturalistic fallacy itself, though not, of course, by that name, because Sidgwick had remarked in a footnote that Bentham, in his explanation of the Greatest Happiness Principle, the principle that to act rightly one must do the action that conduces to the happiness of all whose interests are in question, had, by taking 'right' to mean conducive to the general happiness, reduced the principle to something close to a tautology.[6] Sidgwick thus appears to have been an important source of Moore's thesis that 'good' is a simple and indefinable notion and the correlative idea of a fallacy in the very attempt to define good.

Other features of Moore's ethics also show Sidgwick's influence. In particular, Moore adopted Sidgwick's view that the fundamental principles of ethics are self-evident truths. Following Sidgwick, he distinguished between propositions the knowledge of which requires proof from other propositions knowledge of which requires no proof.[7] Propositions

---

[4] See Moore 1903b: 19, where Moore uses Bentham's taking 'right' to mean conducive to general happiness to illustrate this general conclusion.

[5] Moore remembered finding the lectures dull and least beneficial of the lectures he attended in the two years he studied moral sciences prior to working on his first dissertation. By contrast, he reported gaining a great deal from Sidgwick's writings, especially, *Methods of Ethics*. See Moore 1952a: 16–17.

[6] See Sidgwick 1907: 26 n. Sidgwick's criticism of Bentham, however, is not that by taking 'right' to mean conducive to general happiness, Bentham had confused what ethics is the general study of for something else, i.e. that he fallaciously replaced the simple property that is the proper object of ethical study with a different property. It is not, in other words, that Bentham commits what Moore calls 'the naturalistic fallacy'. It is rather that the Greatest Happiness Principle ceases to be a normative principle if 'right' is taken to mean conducive to the general happiness and hence cannot serve as a fundamental principle of ethics.

[7] Indeed, on his conception of knowledge, it was not possible to have inferential knowledge of them.

of the former type are either demonstrably evident or evident in view of the data that supports them. Propositions of the latter type are self-evident. And Moore, like Sidgwick, took the fundamental principles of ethics to be of the latter type (Moore 1903b: 143). The distinction between these two types of proposition, moreover, corresponds to the distinction between inferential and intuitive knowledge. Accordingly, Moore took the fundamental principles to be known intuitively and thus to qualify as intuitions. Moore's ethics, by his own account of it, is a form of intuitionism. In this respect, too, he aligned himself with Sidgwick (1903b: x).

Still, there is a profound difference between them. Indeed, one cannot fully understand how Moore's argument in *Principia* radically changed the orientation of ethics in Anglophone philosophy if one fails to see the chasm between them.[8] While Moore and Sidgwick are both ethical intuitionists, they nonetheless hold basically different conceptions of the discipline. Moore's conception is of a piece with his Platonism. For Moore, the question of the meaning of 'good' is a question about an object of consciousness that exists independently of the mind and that one can study apart from its role in practical thinking.[9] For Sidgwick, by contrast, ethics is the study of practical thinking. Specifically, it is the study of practical reason. Its basic notions are expressed by the words 'right' and 'ought' when these words are used in a strictly ethical sense, and these notions are essential to exercises of practical reason that result in judgements about what it is right to do or what ought to be done. The words 'right' and 'ought', as expressions of these notions, have no meaning apart from those judgements. Sidgwick's conception belongs to the tradition in ethics that had been dominant in British philosophy for two hundred years and that had obvious affinities with the thought of such major continental thinkers as Kant. In contrast to Moore's conception, this traditional conception is not rooted in realism about ethical notions or properties. And with the rise of Realism that accompanied Moore's attack on Idealism, it was displaced and, within the analytic movement, largely discounted for half a century.[10]

On the traditional conception of ethics as the study of practical reason, the discipline consists in investigating questions of right action understood as actions that reason requires or dictates that one do. Sidgwick, for instance, organized his treatment of ethics around the study of its different methods, which he defined as rational procedures for determining what one ought to do or what it is right to do, in the strictly ethical sense of

---

[8] Recent treatments of the relation of Moore to Sidgwick miss or underestimate the gap between them. See e.g. Hurka, 2003 and Irwin, 2010. An exception is Darwall 2003. Scholars may be prone to miss this gap because they accept without question Moore's attributing to Sidgwick recognition of the naturalistic fallacy as well as his expressly aligning himself with Sidgwick's epistemology. That the former is misleading, see n. 6 above. On the differences in their epistemology, see Deigh 2007 and 2010.

[9] Bosanquet, commenting in his report for Trinity College on the dissertation Moore submitted for his fellowship, wrote, 'In sum, the intellectual motive of the Dissertation, as I read it, is to dissociate Truth from the nature of Knowledge, and Good from the nature of the Will, so as to free metaphysics from all risk of confusion with psychology.' Quoted in Hylton 1990: 120.

[10] While the conception had no presence in the analytic tradition during the first half of the twentieth century, it did have a presence elsewhere in Anglophone philosophy, notably, in the work of John Dewey and other thinkers who worked in the tradition of American Pragmatism.

'ought' and 'right' that he identified as the basic notion of ethics. In this sense, 'ought' is used in judgements of the form 'φ ought to be done', where φ is an action whose performance is within the volitional power of the person to whom the judgement is addressed, and any such judgement is essentially a cognition of the rightness or reasonableness of φ-ing. And similarly, for the use of 'right' in its strictly ethical sense. What is more, Sidgwick maintained, the cognition is such that 'in rational beings as such [it] gives an impulse or motive to action' (Sidgwick 1907: 34). Accordingly, he characterized it as a dictate or imperative of reason. Indeed, he sometimes echoed Kant in referring to ethical judgements as categorical imperatives (1907: 35). And while Sidgwick steered clear of Kant's distinction between the phenomenal and noumenal realms and the programme in epistemology it implied, it is clear that he was sympathetic to Kant's project of identifying the fundamental principles by which reason operates and Kant's understanding of these principles as latent in the common-sense or ordinary thought of men and women as rational beings.[11]

Such an understanding of ethical principles is wholly foreign to Moore's conception of ethics. To begin with, Moore's Platonism about the objects of thought precludes any understanding of ethical principles as latent in the moral thought of rational beings. That is, Moore's sharp distinction between the objects of thought and the content of thought flatly opposes the idea that certain ethical notions and principles inhere in our rational powers and are exercised in the judgements in which sound determinations of right action consist. Sound ethical judgement, on Moore's view, consists in directly perceiving what is good and soundly calculating how to bring it about, where to perceive something directly is to perceive it without mediation by any structure or arrangement that the mind imposes on or insinuates into experience. Accordingly, one directly perceives ethical principles. One does not extract them from one's experiences or discover them by examining the processes of ethical judgement and the different rational procedures for determining right action that correspond to those processes.

Secondly, on Moore's conception of ethics, its fundamental principles are not principles about what it is right to do or what one ought to do. Rather they are principles about what is good. For they are the results of ethical enquiry, which, as we earlier noted, Moore defined as 'the general enquiry into what is good' (Moore 1903b: 2). As such, ethics is not concerned exclusively with 'what is good or bad in human conduct' (1903b: 2). It is not to be identified with practical philosophy if by 'practical philosophy' one means a philosophical study wholly focused on human action and practice and their sources in human thought, volition, and feeling (1903b: 2). Hence, Moore abandoned identifying ethical principles with principles of practical reason. Some kinds of thing, Moore held, may be good even if it is beyond the power of human beings to bring such things about or affect them. There may, in other words, be things of a kind that ought to exist for their own sake, even though men and women are incapable of either producing them or

---

[11] 'The aim of Ethics', Sidgwick writes, 'is to systematize and free from error the apparent cognitions that most men have of the rightness or reasonableness of conduct, whether the conduct be considered as right in itself, or as a means to some end commonly conceived as ultimately reasonable' (Sidgwick 1907: 77).

protecting them from damage or destruction. Affirming that such things are good would nonetheless, on Moore's conception, be a finding of ethical enquiry.

For Moore, therefore, good, as an object of knowledge, is no different from other intellectual objects. To judge that something is good is, in his view, no more distinctively practical than judging that something is whole or finite. It is, in other words, no more essential to judging that something is good that one be moved to seek that thing, than it is essential to judging that something is whole or finite that one be moved to seek it. Sidgwick's understanding of ethical judgement as a cognition that 'in rational beings as such gives an impulse or motive to action' is not Moore's. Nor does Moore, unlike Sidgwick, take such judgements or any of their consequences as dictates or imperatives of reason.[12] Indeed, when Moore turns to questions of right action and duty, he treats them as identical to questions about causal relations between actions and good results. 'What I wish first to point out', he declares, 'is that "right" does and can mean nothing but "cause of a good result"' (1903b: 147), and similarly, he continues, 'Our "duty", therefore, can only be defined as that action, which will cause more good to exist in the Universe than any possible alternative' (1903b: 148). Since judging that something is a good result or that more good would exist in the Universe if its future unfolded in one way rather than any other does not yield any impulse or motive to action, judging that a certain action will have that result or lead to the unfolding of the Universe's future in that way yields no such impulse or motive either. Neither has any imperatival force. In short, on Moore's conception of ethics, the study is distinguished as a branch of knowledge from other branches of knowledge by its subject matter alone.[13] Any division of the branches of knowledge into the practical and the positive disciplines, which is crucial to Sidgwick's understanding of ethics (Sidgwick 1907: 1–2), is meaningless for Moore.

28.3 OXFORD REALISM

The dominance of Idealism in British philosophy came to an end in the early years of the twentieth century when it gave way to Realism. Even Oxford experienced this change in prevailing philosophical opinion. The most influential realist at Oxford was John Cook Wilson. His influence was great, though not because he was widely read. Having strong reservations about putting his ideas into print, he published little in philosophy, and what little he published was on minor topics. His influence was transmitted, instead, through his teaching and through conversation and correspondence with his colleagues. His students included H. A. Prichard, H. W. B. Joseph, and W. D. Ross. It is largely through their publications that thinkers beyond Oxford learned about his ideas and that those ideas had an impact in ethics (Passmore 1957: 240–57).

---

[12] On Sidgwick's understanding of ethical judgement as having inherent conative power, see Deigh 1992.
[13] See Moore's comparisons of ethics and casuistry to chemistry and physics at Moore 1903b: 4–5.

Like Moore, Cook Wilson held that objects of thought are real and their reality does not depend on any mind's experiencing or attending to them. He also held, as Moore did, that we have knowledge of such objects by virtue of direct perception. Moore included truth among the objects of thought that are directly perceived, and he characterized its direct perception as an intuition. By 'intuition' Moore meant that the proposition whose truth one directly perceives is 'incapable of proof or disproof' and nothing more (Moore 1903b: ix). He avoided, in particular, questions about the kind of cognition intuition is and about its origins. Cook Wilson went further. He held that knowledge is a distinct mode of thought. As such, he maintained, it is different in kind from belief and opinion. Indeed, according to him, knowledge is the basic mode of thought in contradistinction to which belief and opinion are defined. He used the term 'apprehension', where Moore used the term 'intuition', to capture this mode when it consisted in direct perception of its object. Like Moore, then, Cook Wilson held that such knowledge is not prey to scepticism. In addition, though, he held that scepticism about the external world and attempts to answer such scepticism by showing that at least some of our beliefs about the external world are justified spring from the same error. Both sceptics and their opponents in this familiar dialectic, he argued, misconceive knowledge, for both erroneously take belief to be a mode of thought prior to knowledge and assume that to vindicate claims to knowledge requires showing that beliefs that one regards as knowledge really are knowledge.

These ideas were introduced into ethics by Prichard in his most famous article, 'Does Moral Philosophy Rest on a Mistake?' (Prichard 2002a). He published the article in 1912. He published little else for the next fifteen years. The article's main thesis is that just as modern scepticism about our knowledge of the external world rests on the mistake about the nature of knowledge that Cook Wilson exposed, so ancient scepticism about justice, the scepticism of the Sophists, that Plato sought to overcome in the *Republic* and that moral philosophers ever since have wrestled with rests on a mistake about the basis of duty. In either case, the sceptical argument consists in raising a specious challenge to something by misconstruing what it is. And consequently, in either case, answers that philosophers who seek to defeat this challenge give rest on the same mistake. Thus, Descartes misconstrued knowledge as belief that one could certify by showing that its ideational content passed the test of clarity and distinctness, and Plato misconstrued the basis of our duties as a good one achieved by doing them. Once these misconceptions are recognized and removed, Prichard argued, the sceptical challenges collapse and the answers to them that have long dominated the fields of epistemology and ethics are seen to be irrelevant to the objects of study in those fields.

The argument Prichard pressed against both the Sophists' sceptical challenge and Plato's answer to it is elusive. In part, it is an argument for the independence of the study of duty from that of good. Yet Prichard's treatment of duty, in contrast to Moore's treatment of good, does not depend on analysis for gaining an understanding of duty. Prichard did not consider whether duty or any kindred notion, like obligation or rightness, was definable. Indeed, he did not argue from direct consideration of any of these notions. Rather Prichard's argument proceeds from a critique of various attempts to answer the question what one ought to do, when it is a question about what one's duty is, by citing the beneficial consequences of an action, its intrinsic goodness, or the praiseworthiness of its motives. All such attempts, Prichard argues, fail to yield satisfactory answers because they fail to capture the binding character of the sense of duty one has when one recognizes what one ought to do. The mistake in these answers, according to Prichard, is due to the presupposition that one knows what one's duty is by inference from knowledge one has that an action open to one promotes or realizes certain values. Knowing that an action open to one promotes or realizes certain values does not, however, yield consciousness of one's being morally bound to do that action. At most, it yields a desire to do the action in view of the attractiveness of its end, and such desire is a different mode of consciousness from feeling morally bound to do the action. In feeling morally bound to do an action, one directly perceives the duty one has to do it. Knowledge of duty is, in other words, the apprehension of something self-evident in one's circumstances. Accordingly, the Sophists' sceptical challenge and Plato's attempts to answer it originate in a misunderstanding of the nature of moral knowledge. Or as Prichard put it, the whole subject of ethics as it is commonly expounded by moral philosophers 'consists in the attempt to answer an improper question' (Prichard 2002a: 7).

Prichard's argument is more compelling as an argument for the independence of the study of duty from that of good than it is as an argument against the Sophists' sceptical challenge. Indeed, its enduring significance is due to the cogency of the evidence it presents for seeing the study of duty as independent of that of good. A duty, on Prichard's view, involves any of several different kinds of relation between the bearer of the duty and others or his own nature. Thus, when we are conscious of having a duty, we are conscious of being in a situation that consists in one of these relations. At the same time, the facts that such a situation comprises are different in kind depending on the kind of relation it consists in. Hence, there is no one kind of fact we grasp in apprehending a duty. Sometimes what we grasp is that a prior act of ours, such as a promise we made to another, puts us in a specific relation to that person in virtue of which we have a duty to do what we promised. At other times what we grasp is that we stand in relation to all men and women as individuals with interests like ours in virtue of which we have a duty to refrain from harming the interests of this particular man or woman with whom we are dealing and whom we could harm. And sometimes what we grasp is that we stand in a relation to ourselves such that a deficiency in our capacities reliably to act as we ought gives us a duty to remove the deficiency.

Plainly, in view of the heterogeneity of these relations, we do not, according to Prichard, apprehend our duties by discerning some duty-conferring property that is common to all of them. We do not, in particular, arrive at our knowledge of them by inference from some proposition about all duties. This view sharply contrasts with influential accounts of duty like Moore's. On Moore's account, knowing that one has a duty to do a certain action is a matter of seeing whether doing the action would produce more good than doing some other action open to one in the circumstances. Accordingly, all actions one has a duty to do have some property in common that explains one's having a duty, and therefore knowledge of one's duty in every case results from one's determining which action has that property. One measure of the effectiveness of Prichard's argument was its success in undermining the support that such accounts enjoyed.

Not that Prichard's 1912 article deserves all or even most of the credit for its argument's success at undermining such accounts. A large part of the credit is due to Ross' restatement of the argument in the first two chapters of his book *The Right and the Good* (Ross 1930). Indeed, whether Prichard's argument, as he originally presented it, would have had any lasting significance in the absence of Ross' restatement is a real, albeit unanswerable, question, for the peculiarities of Cook Wilson's programme might well have doomed Prichard's article to obscurity had Ross not reworked its argument as he did. His reworking of the argument consisted in his applying Moore's analytic method to the study of duty and at the same time de-emphasizing the appeals to modes of thought that characterized Prichard's treatment. The de-emphasis entailed removing the Sophist's sceptical challenge to justice from being the target of the argument's critical force and making that target, instead, the consequentialist accounts of duty exemplified by ethical egoism, classical utilitarianism, and, above all, Moore's ethics. Ross, by the time he wrote *The Right and the Good*, had become one of the foremost Aristotle scholars of his generation, and the book's treatment of its subject is, as one might expect, decidedly Aristotelian. It exhibits no interest in scepticism or in attempts to defeat it. The topic is consigned to a footnote (1930: 20–1 n.).[14] The book's purpose, rather, is to expound systemically ethical knowledge as it is found in common-sense thinking about morality. 'The moral convictions of thoughtful and well-educated people', Ross declared, 'are the data of ethics' (1930: 41). Refashioning Prichard's argument as a criticism of consequentialism served this purpose. And the result was an ethical system that attracted and continues to attract broad support.

Ross accepted Moore's dictum that, in ethics, one must settle questions of meaning before taking up substantive ethical matters. The first chapter of his book concerns the meaning of the word 'right' when one applies it to actions.[15] Attention to questions of meaning, Ross maintained, somewhat in the manner of Moore, shows that, whether or not right action is action that produces the most good that one can produce, 'right' as applied to actions does not mean productive of the most good that one can produce. Clarity about what 'right' means when so applied shows, Ross declared, that its meaning is a distinct notion from that of productive of the most good. Consequentialism, even if true, is not true by definition. Thus, Ross observed, Moore erred in *Principia* when he took 'right' to mean cause of a good result.[16] Moore, in fact, as Ross also observed, had long since given up this view. He expressly rejected it in his second book, *Ethics* (Moore 1912), which appeared ten years after *Principia*,[17] and Ross took Moore's rejection of it as

[14] Note that Ross here deals with scepticism by applying Cook Wilson's views on knowledge to ethics.
[15] I am here ignoring Ross' distinction between an act and an action. See Ross 1930: 7. I use the terms 'act' and 'action' interchangeably.
[16] See last paragraph of section 28.2 above.
[17] Indeed, Moore gave up the view that 'right' means cause of a good result soon after the publication of *Principia*. See Moore 1952b: 558, where he cites, as persuading him to give up the view, the objection Russell had made to it in his review of *Principia*.

corroborating the view, which he favoured, that 'right' in its ethical sense expresses 'an irreducible notion' (Ross 1930: 12).[18] Having, then, settled the question of the meaning of 'right', Ross turned in the second chapter of his book, to the question of what sorts of action are right.

The answer he gave followed Prichard's observation, in his 1912 article, that people's duties are different in kind, and the different kinds are 'very different' from each other (Prichard 2002a: 13). Ross proposed a sevenfold division of them, though he also made clear that he was not 'claiming completeness or finality' for this division (Ross 1930: 20). The seven kinds of duty he distinguished are duties of fidelity, reparation, gratitude, justice, beneficence, non-maleficence, and self-improvement. Unlike Prichard, however, Ross distinguished between *prima facie* duties and duties *sans phrase*. He introduced the distinction in light of situations in which an agent faces a moral conflict. These are situations in which one and the same action fulfils a duty of one kind and breaches a duty of another. For instance, if one has made an appointment to meet someone for lunch and, just as one is leaving to meet that person, one hears a cry for help from one's neighbour, who has seriously injured himself, then one faces a situation in which fulfilling the duty of fidelity that one has in virtue of the appointment entails breaching the duty of beneficence that one has in virtue of the aid one could give one's neighbour. Having stated that, as a matter of meaning, only one of the actions available to an agent in the situation he faces can be labelled 'the action it is his duty to do', Ross saw that he could not coherently describe a situation of moral conflict as one in which the agent has more than one duty. Hence, he invented the distinction between *prima facie* duties and duties *sans phrase* to avoid the incoherence. *Prima facie* duties, he explained, are not actual duties. Rather they are best understood as conditional duties, that is, properties of actions in virtue of which actions of that kind would be actual duties if they had no other 'morally significant' property (1930: 19). One's actual duty in a situation of moral conflict, then, is the action that is most incumbent on one in virtue of the greater stringency of one or a combination of the *prima facie* duties one has in that situation. One's actual duty is one's duty *sans phrase*.

This innovation introduced an important change in the account of ethical knowledge that Ross inherited from Prichard.[19] Because Ross took judgements of actual duty to result from one's apprehending what *prima facie* duties one has in the situation one faces and seeing that none conflicts with any others or, in the event of moral conflict, weighing the different *prima facie* duties that do conflict to see which is the more stringent, he could not identify knowledge of duty, as Prichard had done, with the apprehension of an actual duty. The sense of duty—one's being conscious of being morally bound to do an action—is not, on Ross' account, a state of knowledge. Rather, what one apprehends are

---

[18] Ross, for the most part, treated 'right' in this sense as having the same meaning as what we mean when we say of some action that it ought to be done or that it is one's duty to do it. The one difference he noted is that 'right action' sometimes applies to more than one of the actions available to the agent in the situation he faces whereas only one of the actions available to an agent in the situation he faces can be labelled 'action that ought to be done or is one's duty to do'. See Ross 1930: 3.

[19] This is the account Prichard gives in 'Does Moral Philosophy Rest on a Mistake?'. Later, Prichard revised this account in ways that bring it closer to Ross'. See e.g. Prichard 2002c and 2002d.

the *prima facie* duties one has in a situation, that is, certain properties of actions in virtue of which actions of that kind would be actual duties if they had no other 'morally significant' property. On Ross' account, in other words, what is self-evident in a situation are these properties and not one's actual duty. Indeed, Ross held that judgements of actual duty are always to some extent problematic, since one cannot know all of the consequences for good or ill of the actions open to one and therefore cannot know with respect to any of those actions that one has no *prima facie* duty of non-maleficence to forbear doing it or some *prima facie* duty of beneficence to do it whose stringency is greater than any *prima facie* duty one has to forbear doing it.

Further, not only did Ross distinguish the sense of duty from knowledge of duty but he also made the sense of duty an auxiliary to one's judgement of duty. A judgement of duty in itself, Ross held, has no inherent motivational power. To judge that one has a duty, whether *prima facie* or actual, to do an action A is thus distinct from one's feeling morally bound to do A. Feeling so bound, while a common accompaniment of the judgement, according to Ross, is not inherent in it. Unlike Prichard, then, who had identified knowledge of duty with the sense of duty and inferred from the latter's being a distinct mode of consciousness from desire that the former was distinct from knowledge of value, Ross held that what distinguished knowledge of duty, which is to say, knowledge of *prima facie* duty, from knowledge of value is the brute distinction between rightness and goodness as indefinable, non-natural properties. In so drawing the distinction and taking judgements of rightness (i.e. *prima facie* duty) as apprehensions of an intellectual object just as Moore had taken judgements of goodness to be intuitions of an intellectual object, Ross transformed the conception of ethics for which Prichard had argued in his 1912 article into one that agreed with Moore's in its rejection of the traditional conception of ethics as the study of practical reason.[20] Ross, in other words, as a consequence of using Moore's analytic method to rework Prichard's argument, came to conceive ethics, not as an essentially practical discipline, but rather as the study of certain intellectual objects whose reality is independent of any mind's being conscious of them and the knowledge of which is possible through direct perception of these objects.

28.4 METAETHICS

By the 1930s debates in ethics among British philosophers, along with a growing number of American philosophers, came to be dominated by the question of whether ethical terms were definable by terms for natural properties. Ross, for instance, began his second book, *Foundations of Ethics*, with a discussion of the definability of ethical terms (Ross 1939: 5–10). He divided ethical theories into two types, naturalistic theories,

[20] Prichard too came to deny the identification of knowledge of duty with the sense of duty and to hold that judgements of duty had no inherent motivational power. He does not, however, acknowledge this change in his view and thus his reasons for making it are obscure. See Prichard 2002b: 37–8.

according to which all ethical terms are ultimately defined exclusively in terms for natural properties, and non-naturalistic theories, according to which some ethical terms—at least one—are indefinable.[21] Ross attributed this division to Moore, and it plainly owed its inspiration to Moore's thesis that the question of what good means is the first question of ethical enquiry and to Moore's view that all attempts to define good commit the naturalistic fallacy. Nevertheless, it misrepresented how Moore had divided the field, for it excluded one of the chief types of theory against which Moore argued. It excluded what Moore, in *Principia*, had called metaphysical ethics, a type of ethical theory according to which the meaning of every ethical term is definable but not in naturalistic terms. The exclusion is noteworthy. Moore had identified the ethical theories of Idealism as belonging to this type. That Ross, through this division, had effectively wiped such theories from the scene is rather telling evidence of how far Idealism had fallen into disfavour by the end of the 1930s. The dominance of Realism in ethics during this decade was such that its principal doctrines were taken for granted.

The two sides of the debate that Ross' division represents comprise defenders of naturalistic theories, on the one hand, and the followers of Moore and Prichard, on the other. The former were largely represented by such American realists and pragmatists as George Santayana, John Dewey, C. I. Lewis, and R. B. Perry. The latter included C. D. Broad, A. C. Ewing, and Ross's student, E. F. Carritt, as well as Ross. They, along with Moore and Prichard, were alternately known as non-naturalists and intuitionists. While Ross' division did not admit of any further type of theory, Ross did acknowledge a third type that he saw as having 'affinities' with naturalism (Ross 1939: 30). He identified Rudolph Carnap and A. J. Ayer as the chief exponents of theories of this type, and he took such theories to be part of the general programme of logical positivism that Carnap 1935 (see also Carnap 1959) and Ayer 1952 defended. On this programme, assertions are meaningful only if they are either tautologies or imply propositions that are verifiable by the methods of empirical science.[22] Accordingly, since ethical assertions such as *Lynching is wrong* and *Nero was evil* are not tautologies and do not imply propositions that are verifiable by the methods of empirical science, they are, on the theories Carnap and Ayer expounded, meaningless. That ethical assertions are meaningless is, then, the principal negative tenet of their theories. In addition, Carnap and Ayer advanced theses about the expressive function of ethical assertions. These are their theories' principal positive tenets. Specifically, they held that such assertions serve to express feelings and emotions and to arouse in those to whom they are directed similar feelings and emotions (Carnap 1935: 23–4 and Ayer 1952: 107–10; see also Carnap

---

[21] C. D. Broad had earlier, in the concluding chapter of his *Five Types of Ethical Theory* (Broad 1930), proposed the same division, which he applied to the five theories discussed in his book.

[22] To say that tautologies are meaningful is to say that they express propositions. In each case, the proposition expressed is a logical truth. For this reason, Carnap also described tautologies as empty propositions. That is, they lacked content. By the content of a sentence, Carnap meant any and all synthetic propositions that the proposition the sentence expressed entailed. Because tautologies express analytic truths they do not have content in this sense. See Carnap 1935: 56.

1959: 278). In view of these positive tenets, Ayer came to call his account of ethical assertions the emotive theory of ethics (Ayer 1952: 20–1).[23]

Ross, unsurprisingly, had no patience with any doctrine that restricted the class of meaningful assertions to tautologies and assertions verifiable by the methods of empirical science. Nothing one can say supports this restriction, he argued, unless one has already assumed that no proposition can be both synthetic and known *a priori*, and Ross could see no sound basis for such an assumption (Ross 1939: 35). In other words, as far as he could see, Carnap and Ayer were simply begging the question in basing their argument for the meaninglessness of ethical assertions on this assumption. Ross, in consequence, saw no hope for theories of this third type. In coming to this conclusion, however, he misgauged the potential of such theories for success. Their cogency does not, contrary to what he argued, depend on the impossibility of synthetic propositions that one can know *a priori*.

Ross' error was due to his treating the theories as mere appendages of logical positivism. In particular, he failed to see that their positive tenets could on their own support the theories' negative tenet, or one that is equally destructive of ethics as a branch of knowledge, provided that one could make a strong case for the positive ones independently of appealing to the semantic and epistemological doctrines of logical positivism. To be sure, such a case was unavailable to Carnap. His theory of ethics—what he called 'normative ethics' as distinct from certain scientific studies of a culture's mores—is wholly grounded in these doctrines. By contrast, it is in the offing in Ayer's theory, though because Ayer presented his theory as part of his exposition of logical positivism, the possibility of an independent case for an emotive theory was not apparent. It became apparent, however, through a series of articles Charles Stevenson published in *Mind* in the late 1930s (Stevenson 1937, 1938a, and 1938b). Beginning with 'The Emotive Meaning of Ethical Terms', Stevenson developed an account of the semantics of ethical assertions on which their expressive function is the dominant factor in determining their import in rational discourse and consequently entail that such discourse, when it concerns ethical questions, is necessarily indeterminate. Thus, while Stevenson did not draw from this account the conclusion that ethical assertions had no meaning, the thesis of indeterminacy he did draw matched in its implications for normative ethics the negative thesis Carnap and Ayer endorsed. Hence, to naturalists and intuitionists alike, Stevenson's account presented as much of a challenge to their theories as Carnap's and Ayer's. At the same time, the challenge created more of a threat to intuitionism than to naturalism, and as a result, the rise in the influence of the emotive theory over the next decade sent intuitionism into retreat.

It will be useful for understanding the force of the theory's challenge to intuitionism briefly to lay out the history of the theory's emergence in analytic philosophy. To do so requires going back more than thirty years to Russell's abandonment of the form of Realism that he and Moore presupposed in their initial attacks on Idealism. This form of

---

[23] The reference is to statements contained in the introduction to the second edition of Ayer's book. Ayer did not use the expression 'the emotive theory of ethics' in the first edition.

Realism included a thesis about meaning that Russell, in his characteristically pithy style, put as follows, '[I]f a word means something, there must be some thing that it means' (Russell 1959: 49). Russell had relied on this thesis in his attack, in *The Principles of Mathematics*, on Idealism's philosophy of mathematics (Russell 1903). Like Moore, he had held that if two words had different meanings, then whatever each word meant was a distinct thing from what the other meant. Such a view plainly contradicted the monism of Absolute Idealism. Russell, however, gave up the thesis soon after he published *Principles*. 'The theory of descriptions', he wrote in recounting this change in his thinking, 'which I arrived at in 1905 showed that this [thesis] was a mistake and swept away a host of otherwise insoluble problems' (Russell 1959: 49). This celebrated transition in Russell's thought initiated a strand of analytic philosophy that not only rejected the form of Realism he and Moore used against Idealism but eventually came to reject metaphysics generally. Its opposition to metaphysics came to full flower in the works of logical positivism.

It began with Russell's applying the method of analysis at work in his theory of descriptions to show how one can accept Realism about some intellectual objects without affirming the reality of such imaginary or made-up objects as Polyphemus or the tallest man on Pluto (Russell 1905). That is, Russell used this method to show how one can take proper names, like 'Polyphemus', and other expressions, like 'the tallest man on Pluto', which appear to refer to some thing, as meaningful when they occur in such assertions as 'Polyphemus is stupid' and 'The tallest man on Pluto is bald' without having to suppose that they refer to any thing. Accordingly, he held that using this method allows one to make assertions about Polyphemus without having either to affirm his reality or to abandon Realism. And similarly for assertions about the tallest man on Pluto. Using the same method, Russell further showed how Realists can accept mathematics as a branch of knowledge and at the same time avoid affirming the reality of numbers and, indeed, classes.[24] These results were the basis of the programme of treating philosophical questions within mathematical logic that Russell created and that came to define a practice of analytic philosophy distinct from Moore's.

Plainly, once it became evident that one could maintain, as Russell had done, a form of Realism without having to affirm the reality of numbers, the idea of treating values similarly was bound to attract interest and support. Indeed, the very arguments that Moore and other intuitionists put forward for the indefinability in naturalistic terms of moral and aesthetic values invited those who pursued Russell's programme to treat such values as analogous to numbers and therefore to regard them as dispensable as well. The first among Russell's followers to arrive at this conclusion was Ludwig Wittgenstein. Near the close of his *Tractatus Logico-Philosophicus*, Wittgenstein declared that there can be no truths about moral values (Wittgenstein 1961, pars. 6.42 and 6.421). Or as he put it, there can be no ethical propositions.

---

[24] Russell's interest in denying the reality of classes came from his discovery of the paradox about classes that bears his name, and his denying the reality of numbers followed from his denying the reality of classes, given his scheme in *Principles* for defining each natural number as the class of all classes similar to each other in having that number of members.

Wittgenstein, however, did not arrive at this conclusion in the course of expounding a form of Realism. Far from it. His ambition in the *Tractatus* was to use Russell's programme to transform philosophy in a way that removed from the discipline such questions as whether the universe consisted of one thing or many and whether it was essentially mental or included objects whose reality did not depend on any mind's being conscious of them. It was the same ambition that subsequently fuelled Carnap's efforts to eliminate metaphysics and normative ethics from philosophy. Thus, when Carnap, who was profoundly influenced by the *Tractatus*, declared in his *Logical Syntax of Language* that the sentences of normative ethics were 'pseudo-sentences' (Carnap 1959: 278), which is to say, lacking in meaning, he acknowledged his debt to Wittgenstein on this point (1959: 282). And Ayer, no doubt, was echoing Carnap on the same point when he too declared that ethical assertions were meaningless (Ayer 1952: 102–4). The negative tenet of their ethical theories thus directly descends from the programmes of Russell and Wittgenstein.

What Carnap and Ayer added were the positive theses about the expressive function of ethical assertions. Carnap distinguished two general functions of language, representative and expressive (Carnap 1935: 27–8). When people speak, Carnap noted, they act, and all acts express the feelings, moods, attitudes, dispositions to react, and similar states of mind or character of their agents. Hence, language serves an expressive function in being the medium of speech acts. In addition, some speech acts consist in the utterance of a sentence that represents a fact or state of affairs. In such cases the asserted sentences are meaningful. That is, they express propositions and are therefore either true or false. By contrast, sentences that can serve only the expressive function of language cannot be used to assert propositions and hence are neither true nor false. These include sentences of normative ethics as well as those of metaphysics, for sentences of either kind do not imply empirical hypotheses. Nor are they analysable as tautologies. One expresses one's feelings, moods, attitudes, etc., in uttering them, but one does not, with such utterances, represent any fact or state of affairs. The sentences are, in Carnap's words, lyrical rather than factual (1935: 30).

Ayer's account of the expressive function of ethical assertions differs from Carnap's. Ayer attributed the expressive function of language exclusively to certain words and implied that a speaker could not use such words to make assertions of fact. Ayer thus held, in effect, that the sentences a speaker uses to make assertions of fact do not contain words that have an expressive function. That is to say, he implicitly distinguished the sentences that served such a function from those that served the representative function. The former, according to Ayer, are exemplified by the sentences of ethics and aesthetics. 'Good', 'duty', 'beauty', and the other words that are the basic terms of these fields have as their specific linguistic function to express feelings and are, consequently, different in kind from words whose function is to represent facts. This distinction invites further enquiry into the linguistic work of the words that serve the expressive function, and Ayer pursued it. The basic terms of ethics not only serve to evince feelings, he observed, they are also used 'to arouse feelings, and so stimulate action' (Ayer 1952: 108). And elsewhere in the chapter he suggested that such terms are used to express ethical feelings, that the word 'wrong', for instance, in a sentence like 'Your stealing that money was wrong' evinces moral disapproval. He thus began expounding what he later came to call the emotive theory of values and to argue for its superiority, as a philosophical account of values, to subjectivism and intuitionism.

The difference between Carnap's account of the expressive function of ethical assertions and Ayer's is significant. Ayer took his account of this function to be a philosophical theory that rivalled naturalism and intuitionism. Carnap, by contrast, because he took the expressive function of language to be a function that any sentence can serve, held that its study was exclusively the business of science. That is, he did not regard the basic terms of ethics, words like 'good' and 'duty', for instance, as belonging to a class of words that were distinct from other words by virtue of their being used to express feelings. So regarding them would ill-reflect his view that philosophy can be a branch of knowledge only if it complements science by restricting the object of its studies to the logical syntax of scientific language. A scientific language, after all, does not include words whose defining function is to express feelings. In any case, no such class of words, on his view, could be the subject of philosophical study, since he held that the expressive function of words is not determined by the logical syntax of language.[25]

Carnap's view that the expressive function of language is exclusively a subject of scientific study follows from the anti-psychologism about meaning that he inherited from Frege.[26] Accordingly, general propositions that correlate utterances of words with the psychological states of speakers and hearers are to be confirmed or disconfirmed by the methods of science. Because they are not propositions about the logic of the words uttered or the meaning that science confers on them, the methods of philosophy, specifically, those of logical analysis, are of no use in determining their truth or falsity. Ayer's emotive theory, therefore, because Ayer presented it as a contribution to philosophy and not a piece of armchair psychology, is in tension with Frege's anti-psychologism. His thesis that ethical terms belong to a class words that are distinct from other words, specifically those used to state facts, in virtue of their serving an expressive function is a thesis about the logic of such terms, and consequently, the language that Ayer presupposes as the language in which scientific knowledge is expressed must allow for predicates corresponding to such terms. To explain how these predicates are used, Ayer had then to appeal to the psychological states they express—that is, the feelings and emotions they evince. At the same time, given his adherence to the core doctrines of logical positivism, in particular, the doctrine that only tautologies and assertions implying empirical hypotheses have meaning, he had to avoid appealing to psychological states to explain how the predicates that go into forming meaningful sentences are used. For such an appeal would subvert the programme of treating philosophical questions within mathematical logic that is the backbone of logical positivism.

---

[25] Consequently, when Ross criticizes Carnap for proposing that ethical assertions be taken as equivalent to commands, he misunderstands Carnap's point. See Ross 1939: 33.

[26] Carnap was Frege's student at Jenna. For Carnap's statement of anti-psychologism about meaning, see Carnap 1935: 14–15 and 56–57 and Carnap 1959: 42.

And while there is no contradiction in appealing to psychological states to explain the usage of one kind of predicate but not another, there is obviously a question about the coherence of doing so.

Stevenson, because he constructed his emotive theory independently of logical positivism, avoided this problem. Indeed, in sharp contrast to Carnap's and Ayer's negative tenet, he held that ethical assertions were meaningful. His account of their meaning is complex. It follows from a general theory of language that, like Carnap's, attributes two functions to language. Stevenson characterized one as descriptive and the other as dynamic. Assertions serve the former by communicating beliefs. They serve the latter by influencing feelings and attitudes. Accordingly, Stevenson explained the meaning of words by reference to their power to serve these functions. They acquire this power through a history of usage within the language as a result of which their utterance in, say, assertions of simple declarative sentences tend to cause in their audience certain cognitive processes and affective states. Moreover, Stevenson conceived of their power to serve these functions as being like the power of liquor to dull the mind or the power of caffeine to stimulate it. The model he applied, that is, was a causal one according to which a linguistic utterance directed to an audience was a cause of psychological responses in that audience and the meaning of each term that was uttered was its power to produce in audiences in normal conversational circumstances psychological responses of a certain type. To correspond, then, to the distinction between cognitive and affective responses by which he defined the two functions of language, he distinguished two types of meaning, descriptive and emotive. His account of meaning was thus thoroughly psychologistic. Indeed, he expressly described it as an account of 'meaning in the psychological sense' (Stevenson 1944: 42).

On this account, words can have both descriptive and emotive meaning. Hence, to distinguish the terms of science from those of ethics Stevenson held that the predominant meaning that the former had was descriptive and any emotive meaning they had was secondary, and conversely that the predominant meaning the latter had was emotive and any descriptive meaning they had was secondary. Thus the meaning of the word 'ancestor' in the expression 'x is the ancestor of y' is its power to communicate to an audience a belief about y's descending from x. The word may also have, secondarily, an emotive meaning in so far as it tends to arouse in the same audience worshipful attitudes towards whoever or whatever is said to be an ancestor. But it is its descriptive meaning, owing to its greater power, that determines its force in rational discourse. Similarly, the meaning of the word 'good', on Stevenson's view, is predominantly its power to arouse in an audience an attitude of approval towards whatever object is said to be good. It may also have, secondarily, a descriptive meaning in so far as saying that an object is good tends to communicate to the same audience a belief that the speaker approves of the object. But in this case it is its emotive meaning, owing to its greater power, that determines the word's force in rational discourse.

This difference between the force of scientific words in rational discourse and that of ethical words, Stevenson argued, results in a difference between the nature of disputes in science and ethics. All disputes in science are, in principle, resolvable through agreement on the facts that bear on the question in dispute and application to those facts of principles of sound reasoning. This is because such disputes—for instance, a dispute over someone's ancestry—consist in disagreements in belief, and once the disputants come to agree on the relevant facts, sound reasoning alone is sufficient to resolve their initial disagreement. By contrast, some disputes in ethics are not resolvable, not even in principle, through agreement on facts and application of the principles of sound reasoning. This is because disputes in ethics—for instance, a dispute over the goodness of some public policy—consist in disagreements in attitude, and such disagreements may persist even when the disputants agree on all the facts that bear on the question in dispute and reason soundly from them. Of course, such disagreements are in some cases the result of a disagreement in belief since each disputant may take a certain attitude towards an object because he holds certain beliefs about its nature and those beliefs clash with his opponents' beliefs about the object's nature. In these cases, agreement on all the facts that bear on the question can bring a resolution of the disagreement, since agreement on these facts should bring agreement in belief and therefore bring some of the disputants to change their attitude. But because attitudes do not wholly depend on beliefs, there can be cases, Stevenson maintained, in which the disagreement in attitude is irresolvable despite there being agreement on all the facts and no failure to reason soundly from them. Consequently, Stevenson concluded, questions of ethics, unlike those of science, are essentially indeterminate.

Stevenson's conclusion about the indeterminacy of questions of ethics represented as much of a threat to the status of ethics as a branch of knowledge as Carnap's and Ayer's thesis about the meaninglessness of ethical assertions. At the same time, it escaped the objections Ross had made to Carnap's and Ayer's views since it was not premised on any of the controversial doctrines of logical positivism. In addition, because it was not premised on naturalistic definitions of ethical terms, it escaped the objection to naturalism that Moore had made in *Principia* and to which intuitionists typically recurred in defending their theory. For these reasons Stevenson succeeded in establishing emotivism as a type of metaethical theory that stood on its own feet, so to speak, and was distinct from the two major theories, naturalism and intuitionism, opposition between which had largely defined the debates in metaethics of that period.

Moreover, Stevenson, in expounding his theory, effectively presented it as an advance on intuitionism. Indeed, those persuaded by Moore's objection to naturalism were particularly susceptible to being won over by Stevenson's argument. For Stevenson turned Moore's open question argument, the argument that had become most closely identified with Moore's objection to naturalism, against intuitionism itself. Recall that Moore took this argument as a refutation of all attempts to define good. With any such attempt, he argued, the question whether the property or properties said in the attempted definition to be identical with good are good is open. Consequently, the attempt fails. The failure of all such attempts shows, therefore, that good is a simple, non-natural property. Taking this conclusion, that good is a simple, non-natural property, as a hypothesis that explains the failure of all attempts to define the word 'good' in naturalistic terms, Stevenson offered an alternative hypothesis. What explains the failure of all such attempts is that no set of naturalistic terms has the emotive meaning of the word 'good'. To ask whether the properties those terms denote are good is to wonder whether to take an attitude of approval towards things that have those properties, and with respect to any natural object, no matter its properties, one can always wonder whether to take such an attitude towards it. On this explanation, Stevenson observed, one accounts for the force of the open question argument without positing any non-natural properties. One can therefore understand how ethical enquiry is distinct from the enquiries of empirical science without supposing a realm of purely intellectual objects that includes the objects of ethical enquiry.

Of course, the success of Stevenson's use of the open question argument against intuitionism depended on changes in philosophical fashion. Without an emerging interest among Anglo-American philosophers in avoiding the supposition of a realm of purely intellectual objects, it would have received little attention. Moore, after all, had expressly denied that his question about the meaning of 'good' was a request for a verbal definition (Moore 1903b: 6). The kind of definition about which he was asking, he declared, was a definition of the object that the word 'good' denotes, and not of the word itself. Thus the word's having, as a consequence of common usage, an emotive atmosphere was irrelevant to Moore's enquiry. That it denotes some object was for Moore a given, as the remark of Russell's I quoted earlier makes clear. The thrust of the open question argument, then, was to show the simplicity of the object it denoted and that no other simple object—in particular, no simple natural property—was identical with it. Cook Wilson too thought the simplicity of a property guaranteed its reality.[27] He too treated language as a veil through which one directly saw the simple objects that indefinable words denoted. By the time Stevenson published his influential papers, however, consensus among analytic philosophers on these Realist assumptions had eroded. First, the treatment of language as a veil was undermined by Russell's programme for eliminating problematic referring expressions. Then, owing to the influence of Wittgenstein's *Tractatus*, the idea that language was itself the proper object of philosophical investigation began to take hold and spread. This linguistic turn, as it came to be called (Rorty 1967), and the disdain for metaphysical assumptions it brought were well under way in Anglo-American philosophy by the 1940s, and Stevenson's theory was part of this trend. As analytic philosophers completed the turn by the end of the decade, intuitionism found itself falling further and further behind the curve.

28.5 Post-War Ethics: The End of An Era

Stevenson drew his ideas about language from accounts of meaning that were rooted in C. S. Peirce theory of signs. One of them was the account C. K. Ogden and I. A. Richards gave in their influential work *The Meaning of Meaning* (Ogden and Richards 1923). Stevenson's idea of a word's having emotive meaning comes from this work. In particular,

---

[27] John Cook Wilson, *Statement and Inference*, ii, pp. 511–21, as cited in Ross 1930: 82 n.

Stevenson, citing the passage in which Ogden and Richards identify 'good', when it is used to denote the subject matter of ethics, as having 'a purely emotive use' (Ogden and Richards 1923: 125), credited their work with being the source of his own account of the emotive meaning of the word. The work's influence on Stevenson, however, went beyond its observations about the use of 'good' in ethics. He was influenced as well by its general account of the meaning of words. In giving this account, Ogden and Richards followed Peirce in treating such meaning on analogy with the meaning of sunsets or footprints. All are signs. The latter are natural signs. Words, by contrast, are conventional signs. Sunsets, for instance, have meaning for sailors in so far as sailors interpret them as signs of clear skies the next day, and analogously words having meaning for speakers of the language to which they belong by virtue of what these speakers interpret them as signs of when they hear or read them. Further, to place this account of meaning on a scientific basis, Ogden and Richards proposed to take the interpreting of a sign by someone to consist in the interpreter's being caused to have certain thoughts upon encountering the sign. And because 'good' in its use as a term of ethics causes feelings rather than thoughts in an interpreter, its meaning is purely emotive. The causal model Stevenson used to explain meaning thus descends from Ogden and Richards' account.

The model, however, did not fare well among analytic philosophers in the years following World War II, when the linguistic turn was in full force.[28] Given this model, Stevenson had to deny that statements of fact could serve as rational bases for evaluative statements. Statements of fact could cause an interpreter to have attitudes towards some object that the interpreter would naturally express in evaluative statements. But causation is not rationalization, and consequently, Stevenson could not distinguish between evaluations arrived at rationally, in view of certain facts, and evaluations that resulted from persuasive manipulation of feelings through bringing certain facts into view. It is, after all, one thing to conclude that the water in the country one is visiting is bad from being told that it comes from rivers untreated for sewage and another to be persuaded that the water is bad by being told that it came from a well owned by convicted child molesters. A theory of meaning that could not, in effect, account for the difference between sound practical argument and propaganda was evidently defective, and several philosophers seized on this defect in criticizing the theory. Their criticisms set much of the agenda of Anglo-American ethics in the immediate post-war period.

The programmes in ethics to which this criticism gave rise included both those that incorporated Stevenson's thesis about the essential indeterminacy of questions of ethics and those that rejected it. A principal aim of the former was to place the thesis on firmer ground. A principal aim of the latter, by contrast, was to produce accounts of sound practical argument on which, contrary to the thesis, questions of ethics are not necessarily indeterminate. These latter programmes, no less than the former, were undertaken in the spirit of the linguistic turn and accordingly were committed to excluding from the views they produced metaphysical doctrines of the sort that logical positivism had rejected as meaningless. Hence, the accounts of sound practical argument they aimed to

---

[28] See e.g. Grice 1957.

produce, unlike those of intuitionism, did not rest on such assumptions as that there are non-natural properties and that basic ethical knowledge consists in the direct apprehension of them. Rather, the philosophers who pursued these programmes focused on the reasoning by which we reach ethical conclusions and characterized it in a way that preserved its power to yield, when used in arguments whose premises were entirely factual, determinate answers to questions of ethics without presupposing such assumptions. Programmes of both sorts, then, while they were the products of criticism of Stevenson's theory, were equally opposed to intuitionism.

The theories that programmes of the former sort yielded maintained the primacy of the question of meaning that, since Moore, had preoccupied the field. R. M. Hare's theory was the most influential of these (Hare 1952). Hare saw that to place Stevenson's thesis on firmer ground requires a different explanation from Stevenson's of the sharp distinction between descriptive and evaluative language on which the thesis depends. Accordingly, Hare, in drawing this distinction, replaced Stevenson's focus on the effects that words have on their audience with a focus on the tasks that words are used to accomplish. Descriptive words, Hare argued, have a different task from that of evaluative words. Their task is to state facts. The task of evaluative words is to prescribe action. On Hare's prescriptivist theory, the relation between descriptive and evaluative words is mediated by standards of evaluation that are implicit in the use of the latter. These standards provide the descriptive criteria by which one applies evaluative words to persons, actions, objects, and the like. Such criteria vary with different objects of evaluation. We evaluate knives by how easily we can cut things with them; we evaluate carpets by how dense their pile is; and we evaluate water by how potable it is. Hence, a good knife is one that is sharp; a good carpet is one that is plush; and good water is water that is pure. What is common to these evaluations, Hare noted, is their prescriptive implication. Each implies that, with respect to objects of the kind that one is evaluating, objects with the properties by virtue of which one has evaluated them as good are to be chosen when one is selecting objects of that kind. This prescriptive element, therefore, Hare argued, because it is common to all evaluations, is the primary meaning of evaluative terms, whereas the criteria by which an evaluative term is applied, because they vary with the kind of object that one is evaluating, are secondary.

Like Stevenson, then, Hare held that the meaning of ethical terms was not wholly cognitive and that the non-cognitive aspect of their meaning was the primary one. Hare identified this aspect as the prescriptive meaning of ethical terms in place of Stevenson's emotive meaning. Further, Hare took the cognitive aspect of the meaning of ethical terms to be determined by the standards that the use of these terms implies, for these standards provide descriptive criteria for applying the terms. And since we use different standards depending on whether we are evaluating people or their intentions, motives, or actions, the terms' descriptive meaning varies with the standards that are used. Moreover, these different standards, Hare maintained, are not fixed by the nature of the object of evaluation but rather are determined by the evaluators' own tastes and interests in making the evaluation or by the tastes and interests of the relevant community to which he belongs and whose standards he endorses. Consequently, disputes in ethics may be unresolvable, according to Hare, even when the disputants agree on the facts that bear on the question in dispute, for the disputants may not agree on what standards of evaluation to apply in answering the question. In other words, because these standards are not fixed by the nature of the objects of evaluation, no set of facts is ever sufficient to resolve a question of ethics. To the contrary, it is always open to someone to find the very facts that others take as sufficient for evaluating something as good to be insufficient for so evaluating it because the standards for evaluating such things that he endorses are different from the standards that they endorse. Thus, by holding that each person is the final arbiter of what choices he or she prescribes, Hare preserved Stevenson's thesis about the indeterminacy of questions of ethics.

The success of Hare's theory kept non-cognitivist accounts of the meaning of ethical terms at the forefront of Anglo-American ethics for another generation. In time, though, the way Hare distinguished between descriptive and evaluative language so as to provide firmer ground for Stevenson's thesis proved to be the theory's Achilles heel. His way of distinguishing between them, which turned on the different tasks that descriptive and evaluative language are used to accomplish, reflected the greater interest and attention that philosophers at Oxford were giving, in the post-war period, to the different acts people perform in speaking and thus the different uses to which speakers put words. Breaking off from the strand of analytic philosophy that used the formal languages of mathematical logic to study philosophical questions, these philosophers proposed to study the workings of natural language in everyday use for the light they shed on philosophical questions. While initially the practitioners of ordinary language philosophy, as it was called, treated these studies as disclosing aspects of meaning that the use of formal languages to study philosophical questions obscured, many of them later came to see their study of speech acts as a separate study from that of the meaning of words. And as this view took hold, Hare's distinction between prescriptive and descriptive meaning, as distinct aspects of the meaning of ethical terms, became open to a powerful objection that not only brought it into question but brought into question all non-cognitivist accounts of the meaning of ethical terms.[29]

The objection greatly weakened support for theories, like Hare's, that sought to provide firmer ground for Stevenson's thesis about the essential indeterminacy of questions of ethics. The importance of these theories had significantly diminished by the beginning of the 1970s. By contrast, the theories that were the fruit of programmes of the second sort, programmes whose principal aim was to produce accounts of sound practical argument on which, contrary to Stevenson's thesis, questions of ethics are not necessarily indeterminate, became increasingly important in the last half of the twentieth century. The movement that produced them began with the publication, in 1950, of Stephen Toulmin's *An Examination of the Place of Reason in Ethics* (Toulmin 1950). Toulmin's signal contribution in this work was to undermine the thesis on which Moore had founded the analytic tradition in ethics and with which subsequent philosophers

[29] The most powerful statements of this objection are found in Geach 1960 and 1965; Ziff 1961; and Searle 1962. See also Urmson 1968.

working in that tradition were mainly preoccupied. Ethics, when understood as centrally the study of sound practical arguments, Toulmin argued, does not require, as a condition of its contributing to knowledge, that the question of the meaning of 'good' or 'right' be answered prior to examining the questions of what sorts of things are good and what types of act are right. The study of sound practical argument consists in the study of good reasons for action, and one can examine what counts as a good reason for action, Toulmin maintained, without supposing distinct properties that characterize actions that people do for good reasons and that the words 'good' and 'right' denote. At the same time, proceeding without such a supposition does not mean that whether someone has a good reason for action depends on his having some attitude or feeling towards that action. That the water in a country one is visiting is untreated for sewage is a good reason for not drinking it regardless of one's attitudes or feelings towards drinking it.

In undermining Moore's thesis that the first order of business in ethics is to determine the meaning of the word 'good', Toulmin helped to reinstate, in Anglo-American philosophy, the conception of ethics as the study of practical reason that Moore's conception of it had displaced.[30] This was the chief upshot of his making the study of good reasons for action central to ethics. In consequence, disputes over the reality of ethical properties and the status of ethics as a branch of knowledge that had dominated the field slowly receded in importance. What took their place were disputes over the criteria of sound ethical reasoning, whether such reasoning was irreducibly distinct from prudential reasoning, and if so, how. While Toulmin's own account of ethical reasoning in his book did not have the same impact as his arguments for the centrality in ethics of the study of good reasons, others soon produced accounts that supplied the needed substance and punch. In particular, Kurt Baier, who had worked with Toulmin at Oxford, advanced an account in his book *The Moral Point of View* that provided firm, rational grounds for understanding moral reasons as at once irreducibly distinct from prudential reasons and equally good reasons for action (Baier 1958). The apex of this movement was reached in 1971 with the publication of John Rawls' *A Theory of Justice* (Rawls 1971).[31] It fully returned the conception of ethics that had previously reached its most rigorous realization in Sidgwick's *Methods* and then been abandoned by Moore. The ascendancy of Rawls' work thus coincided with the fading away of the orientation to ethics that Moore had fixed on the field at the beginning of the analytic tradition and that had subsequently defined its debates for the next fifty years.

BIBLIOGRAPHY

Ayer, A. J. 1952. *Language, Truth and Logic*. Second edition. Reprint edition. New York: Dover Publications, Inc.

Baier, K. 1958. *The Moral Point of View: A Rational Basis of Ethics*. Ithaca: Cornell University Press.

Broad, C. D. 1930. *Five Types of Ethical Theory*. London: Routledge & Kegan Paul.

---

[30] See n. 10 above.

[31] Rawls expressly acknowledged his debt to Baier's work in relation to his own account of how principles of justice derive from practical reason (Rawls 1971: 130 n.).

Carnap, R. 1935. *Philosophy and Logical Syntax*. London: Kegan Paul, Trench, Trubner & Co.

—— 1959. *The Logical Syntax of Language*, tr. A. Smeaton. Reprint edition. Paterson, NJ: Littlefield, Adams & Company.

Darwall, S. 2003. 'Moore, Normativity, and Intrinsic Value', *Ethics* 113: 469–89.

Deigh, J. 1992. 'Sidgwick on Ethical Judgment', in B. Schultz (ed.), *Essays on Sidgwick*. Cambridge: Cambridge University Press. Reprinted in J. Deigh, *The Sources of Moral Agency: Essays in Moral Psychology and Freudian Theory*. Cambridge: Cambridge University Press, 181–97.

—— 2007. 'Sidgwick's Epistemology', *Utilitas* 19: 435–46.

—— 2010. 'Some Further Thoughts on Sidgwick's Epistemology', *Utilitas* 22: 78–89.

Geach, P. 1960. 'Ascriptivism', *Philosophical Review* 69: 221–5.

—— 1965. 'Assertion', *Philosophical Review* 74: 449–65.

Grice, H. P. 1957. 'Meaning', *Philosophical Review* 66: 377–88.

Hare, R. M. 1952. *The Language of Morals*. Oxford: Clarendon Press.

Hurka, T. 2003. 'Moore in the Middle', *Ethics* 113: 599–628.

Hylton, P. 1990. *Russell, Idealism, and the Emergence of Analytic Philosophy*. Oxford: Clarendon Press.

Irwin, T. 2010. *The Development of Ethics*. Oxford: Oxford University Press.

Moore, G. E. 1899. 'The Nature of Judgment', *Mind* 8: 176–93.

—— 1903a. 'The Refutation of Idealism', *Mind* 12: 433–53.

—— 1903b. *Principia Ethica*. Cambridge: Cambridge University Press.

—— 1912. *Ethics*. Oxford: Oxford University Press.

—— 1952a. 'An Autobiography', in P. Schilpp (ed.), *The Philosophy of G. E. Moore*. 2nd edn. New York: Tudor Publishing, 3–39.

—— 1952b. 'A Reply to My Critics', in P. Schilpp (ed.), *The Philosophy of G. E. Moore*. 2nd edn. New York: Tudor Publishing, 535–677.

Ogden, C. K. and Richards, I. A. 1923. *The Meaning of Meaning: A Study of the Influence of Language upon Thought and of the Science of Symbolism*. New York: Harcourt, Brace, and Company.

Passmore, J. 1957. *A Hundred Years of Philosophy*. London: Duckworth.

Prichard, H. A. 2002a. 'Does Moral Philosophy Rest on a Mistake?', in J. MacAdam (ed.), *Moral Writings*. Oxford: Clarendon Press, 7–20.

—— 2002b. 'Duty and Interest', in J. MacAdam (ed.), *Moral Writings*. Oxford: Clarendon Press, 21–49.

—— 2002c. 'A Conflict of Duty', in J. MacAdam (ed.), *Moral Writings*. Oxford: Clarendon Press, 77–83

—— 2002d. 'Green: Political Obligation', in J. MacAdam (ed.), *Moral Writings*. Oxford: Clarendon Press, 226–52.

Rawls, J. 1971. *A Theory of Justice*. Cambridge, MA: Belknap Press.

Rorty, R. 1967. 'Introduction', in R. Rorty (ed.), *The Linguistic Turn: Recent Essays in Philosophical Method*. Chicago: University of Chicago Press, 1–39.

Ross, W. D. 1930. *The Right and the Good*. Oxford: Clarendon Press.

—— 1939. *Foundations of Ethics*. Oxford: Clarendon Press.

Russell, B. 1903. *The Principles of Mathematics*. Cambridge: Cambridge University Press.

—— 1905. 'On Denoting', *Mind* 14: 479–93.

—— 1959. *My Philosophical Development*. London: George Allen & Unwin, Ltd.

Searle, J. 1962. 'Meaning and Speech Acts', *Philosophical Review* 71: 423–32.

Sidgwick, H. 1907. *Methods of Ethics*. Seventh edition. London: Macmillan and Company.

Stevenson, C. 1937. 'The Emotive Meaning of Ethical Terms', *Mind* 46: 14–31.

—— 1938a. 'Ethical Judgments and Avoidability', *Mind* 47: 45–57.

—— 1938b. 'Persuasive Definitions', *Mind* 47: 331–50.

—— 1944. *Ethics and Language*. New Haven: Yale University Press.

Toulmin, S. 1950. *An Examination of the Place of Reason in Ethics*. Cambridge: Cambridge University Press.

Urmson, J. O. 1968. *The Emotive Theory of Ethics*. New York: Oxford University Press.

Wittgenstein, L. 1961. *Tractatus Logico-Philosophicus*, tr. D. F. Pears and B. F. McGuinness. London: Routlege & Kegan Paul.

Ziff, P. 1961. *Semantic Analysis*. Ithaca: Cornell University Press.

CHAPTER 29

....

FREE WILL

....

DERK PEREBOOM

29.1 INTRODUCTION

....

THE problem of free will and moral responsibility arises from a conflict between two powerful considerations. On the one hand, we human beings typically believe that we are in control of our actions in a particularly weighty sense, very different from how a thermostat controls a furnace's operation, or a computer controls the marking of typographical errors. We express this sense of difference when we attribute moral responsibility to human beings but not to such machines. Traditionally, we suppose that moral responsibility requires us to have some type of free will in producing our actions, and hence we assume that humans, by contrast with the thermostat and the computer, have this sort of free will. At the same time, there are reasons for regarding human beings as relevantly more like mechanical devices than we ordinarily imagine. These reasons stem from various sources: most prominently, from scientific views that consider human beings to be components of nature and therefore governed by natural laws, whether deterministic or statistical, and from theological concerns that require everything that occurs to be causally determined by God. For many contemporary philosophers, the first of these is especially compelling, and as a result, they accept causal determinism or else claims about the universe similarly threatening to moral responsibility.

The history of philosophy records three standard types of reaction to this dilemma. *Compatibilists* maintain that it is possible for us to have the free will required for moral responsibility if determinism is true. Others contend that determinism is not compossible with our having the free will required for moral responsibility—they are *incompatibilists*—but they resist the reasons for determinism and claim that we do possess free will of this kind. They advocate the *libertarian* position. *Hard determinists* are also incompatibilists, but they accept that determinism is true and that we lack the sort of free will required for moral responsibility.

Especially since David Hume's discussion of these issues, the concern about the existence of the sort of free will required for moral responsibility has been extended to whether it is compatible with the *indeterminacy* of actions.[1] This development has challenged the value of the threefold classification just canvassed, despite its persistence in the contemporary debate. In particular, some maintain that the free will required for moral responsibility is not only incompatible with determinism, but with at least some varieties of indeterminism as well. Agent-causal libertarians typically hold that this type of free will is incompatible with the kind of indeterminism according to which only events (or states, or property-instances) are causes. Free-will sceptics typically agree. A sceptic such as Galen Strawson maintains that this kind of free will is incompatible with any variety of indeterminism.[2] I argue that it is incompatible only with the event-causal sort, and not with indeterministic agent-causation, but that agent-causation is empirically implausible.[3] Complications arise on the compatibilist side as well. Hume, and later R. E. Hobart and Alfred Ayer, contend that while the sort of free will required for moral responsibility is compatible with determinism, it is in fact incompatible with indeterminism, at least with indeterminism located at the point at which a decision or an intention is produced.[4] This tradition continues in the work of philosophers such as Ishtiyaque Haji and Alfred Mele.[5] A different sort of compatibilism, according to which this sort of free will is compatible with both determinism and indeterminism, is inspired by some remarks of Hume's, and is developed in detail by P. F. Strawson in his 'Freedom and Resentment'. In this view, the practice of holding people morally responsible has its own internal system of norms, but is not subject to a legitimate external challenge, from, for example, general scientific discoveries about the universe. Whether the universe is deterministic or indeterministic is claimed to be irrelevant to whether our holding agents morally responsible is legitimate, and in this respect Strawson's compatibilism is *insulationist*.

It is important to recognize that the term 'moral responsibility' is used in a number of ways, and that the moral responsibility in several of these senses is uncontroversially compatible with the causal determination of action by factors beyond our control. Yet there is one particular sense of moral responsibility, and a correlative type of free will,

[1] D. Hume, *A Treatise of Human Nature* (1730–1740) (Oxford: Oxford University Press, 1978); *An Enquiry Concerning Human Understanding* (1748) (Oxford: Oxford University Press, 1999). This issue also arose in antiquity, in response to the Epicurean claim that indeterminacy in the motion of atoms might account for free action (Lucretius; Bobzien).

[2] G. Strawson, *Freedom and Belief* (Oxford: Oxford University Press, 1986).

[3] D. Pereboom, 'Determinism Al Dente', *Nous* 29 (1995): 21–45; *Living without Free Will* (Cambridge: Cambridge University Press, 2001).

[4] R. E. Hobart, 'Free Will as Involving Determinism and Inconceivable without It', *Mind* 43 (1934): 1–27; A. J. Ayer, 'Freedom and Necessity', in Ayer, *Philosophical Essays* (London: Macmillan, 1954), 271–84.

[5] I. Haji, *Moral Appraisability* (New York: Oxford University Press, 1998); Alfred Mele, *Free Will and Luck* (Oxford: Oxford University Press, 2006).

that have been at play in the historical debate, and these notions are not uncontroversially compatible with this sort of determinism:

> For an agent to be *morally responsible for an action in the basic-desert entailing sense* is for it to belong to her in such a way that she would deserve to be the recipient of an expression of moral resentment or indignation if she understood that it was morally wrong, and she would deserve to be the recipient of an expression of gratitude or praise if she understood that it was morally exemplary. The desert at issue here is basic in the sense that the agent, to be morally responsible, would deserve to be the recipient of the expression of such an attitude just because she has performed the action, given sensitivity to its moral status; not, for example, by virtue of consequentialist or contractualist considerations.

Moral responsibility in this sense is presupposed by our attitudes of resentment, indignation, gratitude, and moral praise, since having such an attitude essentially involves the supposition that the agent in question basically deserves to be the recipient of its expression. In P. F. Strawson's account, moral responsibility is essentially tied to these reactive attitudes, and hence the basic-desert entailing sense is plausibly the variety that he brings to the fore.[6]

Alternative notions of moral responsibility have not been a focus of the free will debate. For example, an agent could be considered morally responsible just in case it is legitimate to expect her to respond to such questions as: 'Why did you decide to do that?' or 'Do you think it was the right thing to do?' If the reasons given in response to such questions are morally unsatisfactory, we deem it justified to invite the agent to evaluate critically what her actions indicate about her intentions and character, to demand apology, or to request reform. Engaging in such interactions is reasonable in light of how they contribute to our understanding of our moral commitments and to our moral improvement. The moral responsibility invoked here has been called the *moral answerability* or the *fittingness of providing a moral explanation* sense, and it is the variety of moral responsibility that is most thoroughly ingrained in our practice and least controversial.[7] Our capacity to be sensitive to, to act on, and to evaluate behaviour on the basis of moral reasons is essential to our being moral responsible in this way. However, incompatibilists would not regard the control required for moral responsibility in such an answerability sense to be incompatible with determinism. The type of moral responsibility that incompatibilists do claim to generate an incompatibility with determinism is instead characterized by basic desert and the reactive attitudes that presuppose it. From this point on, unless otherwise indicated, I will use the term 'moral responsibility' to refer to this particular variety.

---

[6] P. F. Strawson, 'Freedom and Resentment', *Proceedings of the British Academy* 48 (1962): 1–25.
[7] H. Bok, *Freedom and Responsibility* (Princeton NJ: Princeton University Press, 1998); T. M. Scanlon, *What We Owe to Each Other* (Cambridge, MA: Harvard University Press, 1998).

29.2 Source and Leeway Theories

In recent decades, by contrast with the previous history of the debate, it has been common to claim that agent's moral responsibility for an action is not explained (at least not primarily) by the availability to her of alternative possibilities, for example by the ability to do otherwise than what she has actually done. Rather, responsibility is to be explained by the agent's being the actual source of her action in a specific way. One might thus adopt a *source* as opposed to *leeway* position on the sort of free will required for moral responsibility. Examples of the kind devised by Harry Frankfurt supply the standard challenge to the leeway position.[8] An agent considers performing some action, but an intervener is concerned that she will not come through. So if she were to show some sign that she will not or might not perform the action, the intervener would arrange matters so that she would perform it anyway. Here is one of John Fischer's examples: Jones will decide to kill Smith only if Jones blushes beforehand. Jones' failure to blush (by a certain time) can then function as the prior sign that would occasion the intervention that would cause her to kill Smith. Suppose that Jones acts without the intervention. We might well have the intuition that she is morally responsible for killing Smith, although she could not have done otherwise than to kill Smith, and despite the fact that she could not even have formed an alternative intention. More cautiously, Fischer concludes that if Jones is not morally responsible for her action, it wouldn't be because he couldn't have done otherwise. Jones could have failed to blush, but Fischer contends that such a 'flicker of freedom' is of no use to the libertarian, since it is not *robust* enough to play a part in grounding her moral responsibility.[9]

Frankfurt-style arguments have met with significant opposition,[10] and Frankfurt-defenders have devised cases intended to avoid the concerns raised.[11] If there are indeed successful cases, both compatibilist and incompatibilist versions of the source position

[8] H. G. Frankfurt, 'Alternate Possibilities and Moral Responsibility', *Journal of Philosophy* 66 (1969): 829–39.

[9] J. M. Fischer, *The Metaphysics of Free Will* (Oxford: Blackwell, 1994), 131–54.

[10] R. Kane, *Free Will and Values* (Albany: SUNY Press, 1985); D. Widerker, 'Libertarianism and Frankfurt's Attack on the Principle of Alternative Possibilities', *The Philosophical Review* 104 (1995): 247–61, 'Libertarianism and the Philosophical Significance of Frankfurt Scenarios', *Journal of Philosophy* 103 (2006): 163–87; C. Ginet, 'Freedom, Responsibility, and Agency', *Journal of Ethics* 1 (1997): 85–98; M. McKenna, 'Alternative Possibilities and the Failure of the Counterexample Strategy', *Journal of Social Philosophy* 28 (1997): 71–85; K. Wyma, 'Moral Responsibility and Leeway for Action', *American Philosophical Quarterly* 34 (1997): 57–70; M. Otsuka, 'Incompatibilism and the Avoidability of Blame', *Ethics* 108 (1998): 685–701; C. Franklin, 'Neo-Frankfurtians and Buffer Cases: The New Challenge to the Principle of Alternative Possibilities', *Philosophical Studies* 152 (2011): 189–207; D. Palmer, 'Pereboom on the Frankfurt Cases', *Philosophical Studies* 153 (2011): 261–72; D. Nelkin, *Making Sense of Freedom and Responsibility* (Oxford: Oxford University Press, 2011).

[11] E. Stump, 'Libertarian Freedom and the Principle of Alternative Possibilities', J. Jordan and D. Howard Snyder (eds), *Faith, Freedom, and Rationality* (Lanham, MD: Rowman and Littlefield, 2006), 73–88; A. Mele and D. Robb, 'Rescuing Frankfurt-Style Cases', *Philosophical Review* 107 (1998): 97–112; D. Hunt, 'Moral Responsibility and Unavoidable Action', *Philosophical Studies* 97 (2000): 195–227, 'Moral Responsibility and Buffered Alternatives', *Midwest Studies in Philosophy* 29 (2005): 126–45; D. Pereboom, 'Alternative Possibilities and Causal Histories', *Philosophical Perspectives* 14 (2000), 119–37, *Living without Free Will*; M. McKenna, 'Robustness, Control, and the Demand for Morally Significant Alternatives', in

emerge as options, and each of these types of view has its advocates. According to source incompatibilism, moral responsibility requires that the agent be the source of her action in a way incompatible with her being causally determined to act by factors beyond her control. It might well be that alternative possibilities—not necessarily of the robust sort—are entailed by her being the source of her action in this way. But these alternative possibilities would not have the primary role in explaining an agent's moral responsibility. Rather, they would be a consequence of the factor that did: the agent's being the source of her action in the right way.[12]

For proponents of the leeway position, both compatibilist and incompatibilist, the accessibility of alternative possibilities is crucial for explaining why an agent would be morally responsible. For them, despite the claims of the defenders of Frankfurt examples, the intuition that an agent's moral responsibility for an action requires that she could have done otherwise retains considerable force. This force is aptly captured by what David Widerker calls the *W-defense*. About an agent who breaks a promise, but could not have done otherwise he writes:

> Still, since you, [Harry] Frankfurt, wish to hold him blameworthy for his decision to break his promise, tell me *what, in your opinion, should he have done instead*? Now, you cannot claim that he should not have decided to break the promise, since this was something that was not in his power to do. Hence, I do not see how you can hold Jones blameworthy for his decision to break the promise. (D. Widerker, 'Frankfurt's Attack on Alternative Possibilities', 191).

Michael McKenna expresses the source theorists' main response to the W-Defence. When Widerker asks of an agent, in view of the fact that he had no robust alternative possibility, 'What would you have him do?', it should be admitted that there is no good answer. Yet in opposition to this initially disturbing result, we should instead draw attention to what the agent has actually done, and to the actual causal history by which his action came about.[13]

29.3 COMPATIBILISM

Retaining the legitimacy of our ordinary attitudes towards human actions and at the same time regarding them as causally determined has been so attractive that a large proportion of contemporary philosophers classify themselves as compatibilists. Two prominent routes to compatibilism can be distinguished. The first and more common kind

---

M. McKenna and D. Widerker (eds), *Freedom, Responsibility, and Agency: Essays on the Importance of Alternative Possibilities* (Aldershot UK: Ashgate, 2003), 201–16; D. Widerker, 'Libertarianism and the Philosophical Significance of Frankfurt Scenarios', *Journal of Philosophy* 103 (2006): 163–87; J. M. Fischer, 'The Frankfurt Cases: The Moral of the Stories', *Philosophical Review* 119 (2010): 315–36.

[12] M. Della Rocca, 'Frankfurt, Fischer, and Flickers', *Noûs* 32 (1998): 99–105; D. Pereboom, *Living without Free Will*, 37.

[13] M. McKenna, 'Where Frankfurt and Strawson Meet', *Midwest Studies in Philosophy* 29 (2005): 163–80.

aims to differentiate causal circumstances of actions that exclude moral responsibility from those that do not. The core idea is that moral responsibility requires some type of causal integration between the agent's psychology and her action, while it does not demand the absence of causal determination. This route to compatibilism is typically developed by surveying our intuitions about blameworthiness and praiseworthiness in specific kinds of examples—involving, for instance, coercion, addiction, mental illness, hypnotism, and brainwashing. These reactions are then employed to motivate conditions on causal integration required for moral responsibility. Compatibilisms of this sort have arguably been advanced in antiquity by Aristotle and later and more systematically by the Stoics (although for Aristotle and the Stoics it is not clear that the notion of moral responsibility at stake involves basic desert); [14] in the modern period by Thomas Hobbes, John Locke, G. W. F. Leibniz, and Hume;[15] and in the twentieth century by Moore, Hobart, Ayer, Frankfurt, Dennett, Watson, Fischer and Ravizza, Wallace, Haji, Mele, Nelkin, and at least with respect to praiseworthiness, by Wolf.[16] The second route to compatibilism is the one advocated by P. F. Strawson, which specifies that despite what

[14] Aristotle, *Nicomachean Ethics*, tr. R. Crisp (Cambridge: Cambridge University Press, 2000); cf. T. Irwin, *Aristotle's First Principles* (Oxford: Oxford University Press, 1990); S. Meyer Sauvé, *Aristotle on Moral Responsibility* (Oxford: Oxford University Press, 1993); on the Stoics, B. Inwood, *Ethics and Human Action in Early Stoicism* (Oxford: Oxford University Press, 1985); S. Bobzien, *Determinism and Freedom in Stoic Philosophy* (Oxford: Oxford University Press, 1998); T. Brennan, *The Stoic Life: Emotions, Duties, and Fate* (Oxford: Oxford University Press, 2005); M. Frede, *A Free Will* (Berkeley and Los Angeles: University of California Press, 2011). In *A Free Will*, Michael Frede provides an overview of the treatment of freedom and moral responsibility from Aristotle through Augustine. He argues that a desert-entailing notion of responsibility was not at stake for Aristotle and the Stoics, but became especially prominent with the rise of Christianity, particularly in the theology of Origen.

[15] T. Hobbes, *Of Libertie and Necessity. A treatise, wherein all controversie concerning predestination, election, free-will, grace, merits, reprobation, &c., is fully decided and cleared, in answer to a treatise written by the Bishop of London-Derry, on the same subject*, London, 1654; cf. S. Rickless, 'Will and Motivation', in P. Anstey (ed.), *The Oxford Handbook of British Philosophy in the Seventeenth Century* (Oxford: Oxford University Press, 2013); J. Locke, *An Essay Concerning Human Understanding*, ed. Peter H. Nidditch (Oxford: Oxford University Press, 1975); cf. G. Yaffe, *Liberty Worth the Name: Locke on Free Agency* (Princeton: Princeton University Press, 2000); S. Rickless, 'Locke on the Freedom to Will', *The Locke Newsletter* 31 (2000), 43–67; R. M. Adams, *Leibniz: Determinist, Theist, Idealist* (Oxford, Oxford University Press, 1994); D. Hume, *A Treatise of Human Nature, An Enquiry Concerning Human Understanding*.

[16] G. E. Moore, 'Free Will', in G. E. Moore, *Ethics* (London: Williams and Norgate, 1912). R. E. Hobart, 'Free Will as Involving Determinism and Inconceivable without It', *Mind* 43 (1934): 1–27; A. J. Ayer, 'Freedom and Necessity'; H. G. Frankfurt, 'Freedom of the Will and the Concept of a Person', *Journal of Philosophy* 68 (1971): 5–20; G. Watson, 'Free Agency', *Journal of Philosophy* 72 (1975): 205–20; R. J. Wallace, *Responsibility and the Moral Sentiments* (Cambridge, MA: Harvard University Press, 1994); I. Haji, *Moral Appraisability*; J. M. Fischer, *The Metaphysics of Free Will* (Oxford: Blackwell, 1994); J. M. Fischer and M. Ravizza, *Responsibility and Control: A Theory of Moral Responsibility* (New York: Cambridge University Press, 1998); D. Dennett, *Elbow Room* (Cambridge: MIT Press, 1984); *Freedom Evolves* (New York: Viking, 2003); A. Mele, *Freewill and Luck*; S. Wolf, 'Asymmetrical Freedom', *Journal of Philosophy* 77 (1980), 151–66 *Freedom within Reason* (Oxford: Oxford University Press, 1990); D. Nelkin, 'Responsibility and Rational Abilities: Defending an Asymmetrical View', *Pacific Philosophical Quarterly* 89 (1998): 497–515, *Making Sense of Freedom and Responsibility*; .

incompatibilists suppose, the truth of determinism is irrelevant to whether we have the sort of free will required for moral responsibility. In his view, the basis of moral responsibility is to be found in reactive attitudes such as indignation, moral resentment, guilt, and gratitude. For example, the fact that agents are typically resented for certain kinds of immoral actions is what constitutes their being blameworthy for performing them. In particular, justification for claims of blameworthiness and praiseworthiness ends in the system of human reactive attitudes. Because moral responsibility has this type of basis, the truth or falsity of determinism is immaterial to whether we are justified in holding agents morally responsible.

The Humean tradition, developed with intensity during the first half of the twentieth century by philosophers such as Hobart and Ayer, features a family of causal integrationist conditions. Perhaps most prominently, Hume himself, following Hobbes and Locke, advocates a conditional account of the ability to act otherwise. To be free in the sense at issue, an agent must satisfy the following criterion: 'by liberty, then, we can only mean a power of acting or not acting according to the determinations of the will—that is, *if we choose to remain at rest, we may; if we choose to also move, we also may*'.[17] G. E. Moore advanced a view of this type, arguing that to say that I could have acted otherwise is to claim that I would have acted otherwise *if I had so chosen*. Even if I am causally determined to act as I do, it might still be true that I would have acted otherwise if I had chosen so to act. This position was highly prominent over the subsequent half-century; Ayer, for example, provides a classic statement of this position.

Such conditional analyses of 'could have done otherwise' were challenged by C. D. Broad, C. Campbell, and especially forcefully in the 1960's by Roderick Chisholm and Keith Lehrer by way of the following type of consideration.[18] Suppose Brown does not at some time t jump in the sea to save a drowning child, and we say:

(1) Brown could have jumped into the sea at t.

A proponent of conditional analysis proposes that (1) is equivalent to:

(2) If Brown had chosen to jump into the sea at t, he would have jumped into the sea at t.

(Variants of (2) substitute for 'chosen': 'willed', 'tried', 'set himself', or 'wanted.') Chisholm and Lehrer argue that this sort of analysis is subject to a counterexample of the following form. Suppose that the sea is very cold, and Brown knows it, and as a result it is psychologically impossible for him to choose to jump into the sea. But we might suppose that if he did choose to jump, he would actually jump. Thus here (2) is true, and yet it is strongly intuitive

[17] D. Hume, *An Enquiry Concerning Human Understanding*, §8.

[18] C. D. Broad, 'Determinism, Indeterminism, and Libertarianism', inaugural lecture delivered at Cambridge in 1934; reprinted in C. D. Broad, *Ethics and The History of Philosophy* (London: Routledge, 1952), 195–217; C. A. Campbell, 'Is Free Will a Pseudo-Problem?', *Mind* 60 (1951): 446–65; R. Chisholm, 'Human Freedom and the Self', The Lindley Lecture, Department of Philosophy, University of Kansas, 1964; K. Lehrer, 'Cans without Ifs', *Analysis* 29 (1968): 29–32; P. van Inwagen, *An Essay on Free Will* (Oxford: Oxford University Press, 1983).

that (1) is false—Brown could not have jumped into the sea. The conclusion is that (2) is not a correct analysis of (1). Recent times, however, have seen the development of more sophisticated conditional analyses, for example by Kadri Vihvelin and Michael Fara.[19]

Second, Humeans, in accord with a tradition that traces back to antiquity, specify that *absence of constraint* is an important necessary condition for moral responsibility. In the *Treatise of Human Nature* Hume characterizes *liberty of spontaneity* as 'that which is opposed to violence', arguably intending that an action is performed with liberty of spontaneity just in case the agent is not constrained to act as she does.[20] In Ayer's exposition, when an agent is under constraint, desires that genuinely belong to her do not play the causal role necessary for her action to be free in the sense required for moral responsibility. Against this it is frequently argued that despite initial appearances, absence of constraint is not a necessary condition for moral responsibility. Suppose someone threatens to kill Green unless he kills five other people, and Green proceeds to kill them. Green could nevertheless be morally responsible for this action, even though he was constrained to act as he does. Moreover, one could be morally responsible even if one acts under certain internal sorts of constraint. Kleptomania is often cited as a paradigm of such a condition.[21] Whether kleptomania undermines responsibility depends on certain characteristics of this illness. Perhaps if it merely strongly inclines an agent towards stealing, and he can nevertheless resist the inclination, this condition does not undermine moral responsibility.

A third member of the Humean family is the claim that an agent is morally responsible for an action only if it flows from her 'durable and constant' character.[22] One difficulty for this proposal is that an agent who kills his superior for firing him might then be exempt from moral responsibility if he is at all other times law-abiding and not given to violent behaviour. It would appear that in some cases of this sort, the action will be out of character, but intuitively the agent could still be morally responsible.

Harry Frankfurt sets out another highly influential causal integrationist route to compatibilism.[23] On his proposal, an action is free in the sense required for moral responsibility when the first-order desire that results in action conforms in a certain way to the agent's second-order desires. More precisely,

1. *First-order desires* are identified by statements of the form 'A wants to X' in which the term 'to X' refers to an action.
2. The desire identified by 'A wants to X' is (part of) A's will just in case 'A wants to X' is either the desire by which he is motivated in some action he performs or the

---

[19] K. Vihvelin, 'Freedom, Causation, and Counterfactuals', *Philosophical Studies* 64 (1991): 161–84, 'Free Will Demystified: A Dispositional Account', *Philosophical Topics* 32 (2004): 427–50; M. Fara, 'Masked Abilities and Compatibilism', *Mind* 117 (2008): 843–65; for a critical review of recent conditional analyses, see R. Clarke, 'Dispositions, Abilities to Act, and Free Will: The New Dispositionalism', *Mind* 118 (2009): 323–351.

[20] D. Hume, *A Treatise of Human Nature*, 407; for the discussion of this requirement in antiquity; see M. Frede, *A Free Will*.

[21] A. J. Ayer, 'Freedom and Necessity'.

[22] D. Hume, *A Treatise of Human Nature*, 411.

[23] H. Frankfurt, 'Freedom of the Will and the Concept of a Person'.

desire by which he will or would be motivated when or if he acts. The will consists in *effective desires*, as opposed to, for example, desires that one has that never would result in action.

3. *Second-order desires* are identified by statements of the form 'A wants to X', in which the term 'to X' refers to a first-order desire.

4. A *second-order volition* is a kind of second-order desire, and is identified by a statement of the form 'A wants to want X' when it is used to mean that A wants X to be part of his will, i.e. he wants to will X (and not that A wants merely to want X without willing X).

5. A person *acts freely and of his own free will* just in case he wills X and wants to will X (and, Frankfurt specifies, he wills X *because* he wants to will X—although this clause is typically ignored).

Acting freely and of one's own free will is the type of freedom required for moral responsibility. Suppose that Scarlet kills Mustard, and this is what Scarlet desired to do, and she wanted her desire to kill Mustard to be effective. According to Frankfurt, Scarlet then satisfies the crucial condition for acting freely in the sense required for moral responsibility. Frankfurt can be viewed as attempting to capture the intuition that for an agent to be morally responsible for an action is for it to be really hers, for it genuinely to belong to her. What it is for an action to genuinely belong to an agent is for her to *identify* with it, and the mechanism of identification is a second-order desire for a first-order willing, that is, a second-order volition.

From the development of Stoicism onward, it has often been argued that the feature of human agency that undergirds moral responsibility is the capacity to rationally regulate one's actions.[24] When we take people to be the sorts of beings who are morally responsible, we expect them to govern their behaviour by, for example, choosing on the basis of available reasons, considering good reasons that were previously ignored, and weighing heretofore unappreciated reasons differently. In recent times, John Fischer and Mark Ravizza, Jay Wallace, Susan Wolf, and Dana Nelkin have developed positions in which a capacity to regulate one's behaviour by reasons is the key condition for moral responsibility.[25]

Fischer initially argued that a fairly weak notion of *reasons-responsiveness* is what is crucially required for moral responsibility:

> An agent is *weakly reasons-responsive* when a certain kind K of mechanism, which involves the agent's rational consideration of reasons relevant to the situation, issues in action, and in at least some alternative circumstances in which there are sufficient reasons for her to do otherwise than she actually does, she would be receptive to these reasons and would have chosen and done otherwise by the efficacy of the same deliberative mechanism that actually results in the action. (*The Metaphysics of Free Will*, 166–7)

---

[24] B. Inwood, *Ethics and Human Action in Early Stoicism*; S. Bobzien, *Determinism and Freedom in Stoic Philosophy*; T. Brennan, *The Stoic Life: Emotions, Duties, and Fate*; M. Frede, *A Free Will*.

[25] S. Wolf, *Freedom within Reason*; J. M. Fischer, *The Metaphysics of Free Will*; J. M. Fischer and M. Ravizza, *Responsibility and Control*; R. J. Wallace, *Responsibility and the Moral Sentiments*; D. Nelkin, *Making Sense of Freedom and Responsibility*.

By 'sufficient reason' Fischer means 'justificatorily sufficient reason', that is, a reason that is, all things considered, an agent's strongest or best reason for action. Thus White is morally responsible when she decides to pay her telephone bill, for the usual reasons, next week rather than today, if, in circumstances in which she knew that her telephone would be disconnected if she did not pay today—and she has the ordinary sufficient reasons to want her telephone be functional—she would, by the deliberative mechanism that actually results in her deciding to pay next week, appreciate the different reasons and decide to pay today instead. If her practical reasoning would not differ in varying circumstances in which there are sufficient reasons to do otherwise, she would not be morally responsible.

In response to counterexamples in which the agent is weakly reasons-responsive and yet acts in accord with a pattern of reasons so odd that it seems clear that the agent is not morally responsible, Fischer and Ravizza later required that the mechanism by which the agent acts be receptive to a *pattern* of reasons that is intuitively rational. They call the revised criterion *moderate reasons-responsiveness*. But at the same time, they in effect continued to endorse the original weak version of *reasons-reactivity*, on the ground that agents can be morally responsible when they are receptive to sufficient reasons to do otherwise, but yet do not react to those reasons. In addition, they contend that to be morally responsible, the agent must, through a historical process, *take responsibility* for the springs of her action, and this involves coming to see herself as a rational agent, and as a fair target of the reactive attitudes, in a way that is appropriately based on evidence.[26]

Like Fischer and Ravizza's proposal, Wallace's focuses on our capacity for regulating our behaviour by reasons. First of all, in his view, *holding a person morally responsible* is to be characterized as applying to particular acts, with essential reference to the reactive attitudes of resentment, indignation, and guilt, and to moral obligations that one, as moral judge, accepts. What is required for legitimately holding an agent morally responsible for a particular act is that it would be appropriate to have a reactive attitude of indignation, resentment, or guilt directed towards the agent in that situation, and what would make such an attitude appropriate is the agent's having violated a moral obligation.[27] Wallace distinguishes the conditions of holding someone morally responsible, which apply to a particular act, from the conditions of *accountability*, which apply to agents over an extended period. To regard someone as a morally accountable agent is 'to view the person as the sort of agent whose violation of moral obligations one accepts would render reactive emotions appropriate'.[28] In order for an agent to be legitimately considered morally accountable, she must possess the *powers of reflective self-control*: the power to grasp and apply moral reasons, and the power to control or regulate her behaviour by the light of such reasons.[29]

[26] J. M. Fischer and M. Ravizza, *Responsibility and Control*, 65–82.
[27] R. J. Wallace, *Responsibility and the Moral Sentiments*, 58–93.
[28] R. J. Wallace, *Responsibility and the Moral Sentiments*, 70.
[29] R. J. Wallace, *Responsibility and the Moral Sentiments*, 154–94.

Psychopaths, for example, are not morally accountable because they lack these powers of reflective self-control, as is the case for those who have a strong form of drug addiction.[30] Yet normal agents, even given the truth of causal determinism, do have these powers. It is important for Wallace that an agent may possess the powers for reflective self-control even though a particular circumstance prevents him from applying these powers. In his terminology, the requirement of having these powers is thus to be understood *generally*. In making this point, he aims to pre-empt the incompatibilist criticism that supposing the murderer was causally determined to commit his crime, he did not have the capacity to regulate his behaviour by moral reasons when he acted.[31] Wallace maintains that even if the murderer did not have the capacity to apply the powers in this particular case he could still be morally responsible because he retains the powers in the general sense.

Susan Wolf contends that an agent is morally responsible just in case she could have acted in accordance with Reason—that is, just in case she could have done the right thing for the right reasons.[32] On her conception, this condition results in an asymmetry, on the assumption that an agent can never do otherwise due to causal determinism. For if the agent is causally determined to do the right thing for the right reasons, then a fortiori she can do this, and hence she meets the proposed condition on responsibility. But if she is causally determined to do the wrong thing for the wrong reasons, then it might well be that she could not have done the right thing for the right reasons, whereupon she would not be morally responsible. Recently, Nelkin provides a development of this position in which this asymmetry is further grounded in a parallel asymmetry regarding the 'ought implies can' principle.[33] By this principle, if one does not do what one ought, then one must have been able to do otherwise, but if one does what one ought, this ability is not required. Given plausible connections to praiseworthiness and blameworthiness, the result is that blameworthiness requires the ability to do otherwise, but praiseworthiness does not.

The second type of route to compatibilism is suggested by Hume in a discussion of the effect the thesis of divine determinism does and should have on the moral sentiments.[34] He first argues for a psychological thesis, that the sentiments of approbation and blame cannot be affected by a belief in theological determinism or in any philosophical theory; and subsequently for a normative thesis, that these sentiments should not be affected by a belief in theological determinism or in any philosophical theory. Because the generation of sentiments of approbation and blame in certain circumstances is inevitable and not preventable by us, having these sentiments is compatible with any general metaphysical claim about the nature of reality and should not be controlled or altered by any philosophical theory.[35]

[30] R. J. Wallace, *Responsibility and the Moral Sentiments*, 170–8.
[31] R. J. Wallace, *Responsibility and the Moral Sentiments*, 207–21.
[32] S. Wolf 'Asymmetrical Freedom', *Freedom within Reason*.
[33] D. Nelkin, *Making Sense of Freedom and Responsibility*.
[34] D. Hume, *An Enquiry Concerning Human Understanding*, §8.
[35] See P. Russell, *Freedom and Moral Sentiment* (New York: Oxford University Press, 1995).

P. F. Strawson's position has a similar core, but is developed in more detail.[36] He begins by characterizing two opposing participants in the controversy about determinism and moral responsibility, the 'optimist' and the 'pessimist'. The optimist is a compatibilist of the sort who justifies the practices of moral disapproval and punishment on the basis of their social utility (e.g. Moritz Schlick).[37] The pessimist is an incompatibilist who wants libertarianism to be true. Strawson rejects the incompatibilism and libertarianism of the pessimist, but he also contends, with the pessimist, that the optimist is missing something significant in the account of moral responsibility.

Rather than justifying the practice of holding people morally responsible solely on utilitarian grounds, in Strawson's account it is the reactive attitudes to which people are subject by virtue of participation in interpersonal relationships that play the central role. He proposes that these reactive attitudes provide what is missing in the optimist's theory. In fact, in his view it is the reactive attitudes alone that provide the foundation for our holding people morally responsible. To secure his case for compatibilism, Strawson, like Hume, argues first for a psychological thesis, that the reactive attitudes cannot be affected by a belief in causal determinism, and then for a normative thesis, that they should not be affected by this belief. Thus, what fills the role of what the pessimist correctly judges to be missing in the optimist's account of our moral life—our reactive attitudes—cannot and should not be undermined by a belief in causal determinism.

The reactive attitudes are natural human reactions to the good or ill will of others towards us, as displayed in their attitudes and actions. Strawson's examples include gratitude, moral resentment and indignation, guilt, forgiveness, repentance, and love. These attitudes are essential features of ordinary human interpersonal relationships. Sometimes we can and at times we appropriately do forgo or suspend reactive attitudes. Excuses invite us to view an injury as one in respect of which a particular one of these attitudes is inappropriate even though the agent is more generally a fitting target for reactive attitudes. Exemptions, by contrast, invite us to view the agent as someone in respect of whom these attitudes are inappropriate. In Strawson's conception this involves adopting an objective attitude towards him, which amounts to treating impersonally, as something to be controlled or managed. But none of this shows that a belief in universal determinism would lead to a suspension of reactive attitudes, for

> the human commitment to participation in ordinary interpersonal relationships is…too thoroughgoing and deeply rooted for us to take seriously the thought that a general theoretical conviction might so change our world that, in it, there were no

---

[36] P. F. Strawson, 'Freedom and Resentment'. Compatibilist views inspired by Strawson can be found in G. Watson, 'Responsibility and the Limits of Evil', in F. Schoeman (ed.), *Responsibility, Character, and the Emotions* (Cambridge: Cambridge University Press, 1987), 256–86; N. Arpaly, *Merit, Meaning, and Bondage: An Essay on Free Will* (Princeton, NJ: Princeton University Press, 2006); and M. McKenna, *Conversation and Responsibility* (New York: Oxford University Press, 2012).

[37] M. Schlick, 'When is a Man Responsible', in *Problems of Ethics*, tr. D. Rynin (New York: Prentice-Hall, 1939), 143–56.

longer any such things as interpersonal relationships as we normally understand them; and being involved in interpersonal relationships as we normally understand them precisely is being exposed to the range of reactive attitudes and feelings that is in question. ('Freedom and Resentment', 11)

According to Strawson, both the optimist and the pessimist are wrong in thinking that the reactive attitudes must be justified from outside of the practice of holding people morally responsible in which these attitudes are embedded. This is, in fact, where their deepest mistake lies. The framework of these attitudes 'neither calls for, nor permits, an external "rational" justification'.[38]

A number of criticisms have been raised against Strawson's position. A first is that he is mistaken to hold that the reactive attitudes cannot be affected by the belief that determinism is true. Another is that supposing a belief in determinism did issue in a theoretical or epistemic conflict with the ordinary reactive attitudes, it is not clear that rational appraisal of these attitudes would always favour retention over revision. A third is that it is mistaken to maintain that a challenge to the reactive attitudes based on causal determinism is external to the practice of holding people morally responsible and therefore illegitimate. Rather, exemptions from moral responsibility that are widely regarded as acceptable and are thus internal to the practice will generalize to an incompatibilist condition on moral responsibility. Manipulation arguments against compatibilism, which will be examined in the next section, require that suitably manipulated agents are not responsible, and that relevantly similar cases should receive the same moral assessment, and each of these principles seems internal to the practice of holding agents morally responsible.

29.4 Incompatibilism

Various arguments have been devised to support the incompatibilist's claim that free will and determinism are not compossible. One prominent contention is that the relevant sort of free will is the ability to do otherwise, and this ability is precluded by determinism. For if determinism is true, then facts about the remote past, together with the laws of nature, entail every subsequent fact, including facts about actions. The Consequence Argument, developed by Carl Ginet and Peter van Inwagen, among others, aims to develop this idea with rigour and precision.[39]

---

[38] P. F. Strawson, 'Freedom and Resentment', 70.

[39] C. Ginet, 'Might We Have No Choice', in K. Lehrer (ed.), *Freedom and Determinism* (New York: Random House, 1966), 87–104, *On Action* (Cambridge: Cambridge University Press, 1990); P. van Inwagen, 'The Incompatibility of Free Will and Determinism', *Philosophical Studies* 27 (1975): 185–9, *An Essay on Free Will*; cf. J. Lamb, 'On a Proof of Incompatibilism', *Philosophical Review* 86 (1977): 20–35; T. Warfield, 'Causal Determinism and Human Freedom are Incompatible', *Philosophical Perspectives* 14 (2000): 167–80.

Peter van Inwagen's version of the Consequence Argument begins with a characterization of determinism:

> Determinism = df the non-relational facts of the past (P), indexed to any time, t, in conjunction with a complete description of the laws of nature (L), entails every non-relational fact at any time later than t (F).

To this are added two principles expressing metaphysical truths, the *Principle of the Fixity of the Past*, FP, and the *Principle of the Fixity of the Laws*, FL. FP states that for any agent, the past is fixed for her relative to the present; she is powerless to render false any truth about the past (this needs to be made more precise in view of 'soft' facts about the past, such as the partition of India's occurring more than 60 years prior to your choice to continue reading this chapter). FL asserts that, for any person, the laws of nature are fixed; it's not up to her whether or not they obtain. She is powerless to render false any law of nature.

At this point we can define a 'powerlessness' modal operator 'Np', which can be read as 'p is true, and [the relevant agent] is powerless to render p false'. One can first of all derive true claims of powerlessness by this inference rule:

Rule α: $\Box p \to Np$

where '$\Box$' expresses logical necessity. Applying Rule α, one can conclude that any logically necessary truth is such that any selected agent is powerless to render it false. Next, van Inwagen invokes an inference principle that transfers powerlessness from one fact to another one that is entailed by the first:

Rule β: $N(p \to q), Np \to Nq$

With these resources, the Consequence Argument can now be employed to show that any action performed in a deterministic world is one the agent is powerless to avoid. Let s be the claim that a sample actual action is performed. Then:

1. $\Box(P \cdot L \to s)$ Assume determinism; apply it to s.
2. $\Box(P \to (L \to s))$ 1, and Logic.
3. $N(P \to (L \to s))$ 2, Rule α.
4. $N(P)$ Assume FP.
5. $N(L \to s)$ 3, 4, Rule β.
6. $N(L)$ Assume FL.
7. $N(s)$ 5, 6, Rule β.

This argument tells us that, at the determined world W, the agent is powerless to render s false; in other words, the agent is powerless to avoid the action referred to in s.

The Consequence Argument has been strongly contested. Frequently discussed objections include: David Lewis' proposal that contrary to 6, the agent can act in such a way that, if she were to so act, the laws of nature that do obtain at W would not;[40] Thomas

---

[40] D. Lewis, 'Are We Free to Break the Laws?', *Theoria* 47 (1981): 113–22.

McKay and David Johnson's claim that Rule β is invalid and therefore one cannot infer the powerlessness of the agent to avoid her action from the truth of determinism and her lack of power over the past and the laws;[41] and Michael Slote's concern that the powerlessness invoked in the argument does not uncontroversially transfer across events that involve agency that satisfies compatibilist conditions on moral responsibility.[42]

On a source compatibilist position, the availability of alternative possibilities does not characterize the crucial kind of free will, and it is thus open to such a compatibilist to contend that the Consequence Argument does not challenge her view. But a cousin of the Consequence Argument, the Direct Argument, also set out by van Inwagen, does pose a threat to source compatibilism.[43] The Direct Argument's core principle transfers *non-responsibility* across entailment relations, instead of powerlessness, to force the conclusion that any action is such that its agent is not responsible for it. The more general proposal is that given the assumption of determinism, non-responsibility transfers from the past and the laws to all subsequent events. One important objection to this argument is McKenna's, and it is analogous to Slote's response to the Consequence Argument: non-responsibility does not uncontroversially transfer across contexts in which the compatibilist conditions on moral responsibility are satisfied by agents.[44]

Another prominent type of argument against compatibilism begins with the intuition that if an agent is causally determined to act by, for example, scientists who manipulate her brain, then she is not morally responsible for that action, even if she meets compatibilist conditions on moral responsibility.[45] The subsequent step is that there are no differences between such manipulated agents and their ordinary deterministic counterparts that can justify the claim that the manipulated agents are not morally responsible while the determined agents are.

My multiple-case version of such an argument first of all develops examples of an action that results from an appropriate sort of manipulation, and in which the prominent compatibilist conditions on moral responsibility are satisfied.[46] These examples, taken separately, indicate that it is possible for an agent not to be morally responsible even if the compatibilist conditions are met, and that as a result these conditions are inadequate. But the argument has additional force by virtue of setting out three such

[41] T. McKay and D. Johnson, 'A Reconsideration of an Argument against Compatibilism', *Philosophical Topics* 24 (1996): 113–22; cf. E. Carlson, 'Incompatibilism and the Transfer of Power Necessity', *Noûs* 34 (2000): 277–90.

[42] Michael Slote, 'Selective Necessity and the Free Will Problem', *Journal of Philosophy* 79 (1982): 5–24; cf. J. Bishop, *Natural Agency* (Cambridge: Cambridge University Press, 1989).

[43] P. van Inwagen, *An Essay on Free Will*, 188ff.

[44] M. McKenna, 'Saying Good-Bye to the Direct Argument in the Right Way', *Philosophical Review* 117 (2008): 349–83; for a defence of the direct argument in response to McKenna's criticisms, see S. Shabo, 'The Fate of the Direct Argument and the Case for Incompatibilism', *Philosophical Studies* 150 (2010): 405–24.

[45] R. Taylor, *Metaphysics*. Fourth edition (Englewood Cliffs NJ: Prentice-Hall, 1974); C. Ginet, *On Action*; D. Pereboom, 'Determinism al Dente', *Living without Free Will*; R. Kane, *The Significance of Free Will*; A. Mele, *Free Will and Luck*.

[46] D. Pereboom, *Living without Free Will*, 110–25.

cases, each of which is progressively more like a fourth, in which the action is causally determined in a natural way. The first case involves manipulation that is local and determining, and hence very likely to elicit the non-responsibility intuition. The second is like the first, except it restricts manipulation to the beginning of the agent's life. The third is similar, except the manipulation results from strict community upbringing. The aim is to formulate the cases so that it is not possible to draw a principled line between any two adjacent cases that would explain why the agent would not be morally responsible in the first but would be in the second, largely because all of the prominent compatibilist conditions are satisfied in each. The conclusion is that the best explanation for why the agent is not responsible in the four cases is that he is causally determined by factors beyond his control in each of them, and this result conflicts with the compatibilist's central claim.

29.5 LIBERTARIANISM

Incompatibilism divides into two positions, the libertarian view according to which determinism is false and we have the free will required for moral responsibility, and the hard determinist perspective in which determinism is true and we lack this kind of free will. Libertarianism has from ancient times been a prominent position, and its early defenders include Epicurus and Lucretius, Alexander of Aphrodisias, and certain Patristic Christian theologians, notably Origen.[47] Several of libertarianism's most prominent contemporary features were carefully articulated in the late thirteenth and fourteenth centuries by Franciscans Peter Olivi, John Duns Scotus, and William of Ockham, and then in the sixteenth century by Francisco Suarez. Scotus defends the position that the will is subject to two basic affections, for happiness and for justice, and that the will is free to choose in accordance with either, independently of how the intellect represents the options. While in the spirit of the Platonic tradition Aquinas held that the will is restricted to what the agent's intellect represents as good, Scotus maintained that for each of the two basic affections, the agent is capable of willing what it represents as best, and also of not-willing, or refraining from willing, this option. Thus, in the case of each of these affections the agent has the capacity for alternatives, defined not as the power to will and to positively will otherwise, but as the power to will and to refrain from willing.[48] Suarez's (1597) formulation was highly influential and widely disseminated beginning

---

[47] Lucretius, *De Rerum Natura*, tr. by W. H. D. Rouse (Cambridge, MA: Harvard University Press, 1982); for discussions of Alexander of Aphrodisias and Origen on free will, see M. Frede, *A Free Will*, 95–101; for Alexander of Aphrodisias' text, see R. W. Sharples, *Alexander of Aphrodisias on Fate* (London: Duckworth, 1983); for Origen's, see *De Principiis*, in *Origenes Werke*, ed. P. Koetschau, vol. 5 (Leipzig, 1913).

[48] R. Pasnau, 'Olivi on Human Freedom', in *Pierre De Jean Olivi (1248–1298)* (Paris: Vrin, 1999), 15–25; J. Duns Scotus, *Duns Scotus on the Will and Morality*, ed. and tr. A. Wolter (Washington, DC: The Catholic University of America Press, 1986); M. Adams, 'The Structure of Ockham's Moral Theory', *Franciscan Studies* 24 (1986): 1–35, 'Duns Scotus on the Will as Rational Power', in L. Sileo (ed.), *Via Scoti, Methodologica ad Mentem Joannis Dunds Scoti* (Rome: PAA Edizioni Antonianum, 1995), 839–54.

in the late sixteenth century. In it the essentials of modern libertarianism are in place: following the Franciscans, his view specifies that agents are free in the sense that by virtue of
their will and power they have the ability both to perform and to refrain from performing the action at issue; and following in a long tradition in Christianity beginning with
Origen, he explicitly characterizes of the kind of free will at stake as the sort required for
basic-desert-involving moral responsibility.[49]

More recent times have witnessed the explicit differentiation of two major versions of
libertarianism, the event-causal and the agent-causal types. In event-causal libertarianism, actions are caused solely by way of events, standardly conceived as objects having
properties at times, and some type of indeterminacy in the production of actions by
appropriate events is held to be a decisive requirement for moral responsibility.[50] This
position has an ancestor in the Epicurean view according to which a free decision is an
uncaused swerve in the otherwise downward path of an atom.[51] According to agent-
causal libertarianism, free will of the sort required for moral responsibility is accounted
for by the existence of agents who possess a causal power to make choices without being
determined to do so. In this view, it is essential that the causation involved in an agent's
making a free choice is not reducible to causation among events involving the agent, but
is rather irreducibly an instance of the agent-as-substance causing a choice not by way of
events. The agent, fundamentally as a substance, has the causal power to cause choices
without being determined to do so.

Robert Kane has developed a much-discussed version of event-causal libertarianism.
In his proposal, the paradigm case of an action for which an agent is responsible is one of
moral or prudential struggle, in which there are reasons for and against performing the
action in question.[52] The sequence that produces the action begins with the agent's character and motives, and proceeds through the agent's making an effort of will to act, which
results in the choice for a particular action. The effort of will is a struggle to choose in one
way in a situation in which there are countervailing pressures. In the case of a freely willed
choice, this effort of will is *indeterminate*, and as a result the choice produced by the effort
is *undetermined*. Kane explains this last specification by drawing an analogy between an
effort of will and a quantum event (on one conception).[53] The effort of will is indeterminate in the sense that its causal potential does not become determinate until the choice
occurs. Prior to this pivotal interaction, there are different ways in which this causal
potential can be resolved, and thus when it is resolved, the resulting choice will be undetermined. Significantly, Kane cautions against construing his view in such a way that the
indeterminacy occurs after the effort is made: 'One must think of the effort and the indeterminism as fused; the effort is indeterminate and the indeterminism is a property of the

[49] F .Suarez, *Disputationes Metaphysicae* (1597), Vivès edition, 28 vols. (1856–1861) (Paris), reprinted by
Georg Olms, Hildesheim, 1965; Sydney Penner, 'Suarez on Human Freedom' (unpublished manuscript).
[50] R. Kane, *The Significance of Free Will* (New York: Oxford University Press, 1996); L. W. Ekstrom,
Free Will: A Philosophical Study (Boulder: Westview, 2000); M. Balaguer, *Free Will as an Open Scientific
Problem* (Cambridge, MA: MIT Press, 2009).
[51] Lucretius, *De Rerum Natura*.   [52] R. Kane, *The Significance of Free Will*.
[53] R. Kane, *The Significance of Free Will*, 161.

effort, not something that occurs before or after the effort.' If an agent is morally responsible for a choice, it must either be free in this sense or there must be some such free choice that is (or has a key role in) its sufficient ground, cause, or explanation.[54] Kane embellishes his account by endeavouring to show how the particle analogy for free choice might actually work in the functioning of the brain's neural networks.[55]

Critics of libertarianism have argued that if actions are undetermined, agents cannot be morally responsible for them. A classical presentation of this objection is found in Hume's *Treatise of Human Nature*.[56] In Hume's version, the concern highlighted is that if an action is uncaused, it will not have sufficient connection with the agent for her to be morally responsible for it. This idea might profitably be explicated as follows. For an agent to be morally responsible for a decision, she must exercise a certain type and degree of control in making that decision. In an event-causal libertarian picture, the relevant causal conditions antecedent to a decision—agent-involving events—would leave it open whether this decision will occur, and the agent has no further causal role in determining whether it does. With the causal role of these antecedent conditions already given, it remains open whether the decision occurs, and whether it does is not settled by anything about the agent. So whether the decision occurs or not is in this sense a matter of luck, and, intuitively, the agent lacks the control required for moral responsibility for the decision.

Libertarians agree that an action's resulting from a deterministic sequence of causes that traces back to factors beyond the agent's control would rule out her moral responsibility for it. The deeper point of this objection is that if this sort of causal determination rules out moral responsibility, then it is no remedy simply to provide slack in the causal net by making the causal history of actions indeterministic. Such a move would yield a requirement for moral responsibility—the absence of causal determinism for decision and action—but it would not supply another—sufficiently enhanced control, as Randolph Clarke argues.[57] In particular, it would not provide the capacity for an agent to be the source of her decisions and actions that, according to many incompatibilists, is unavailable in a deterministic framework.

The agent-causal libertarian's solution to this problem is to specify a way in which the agent could have this enhanced control, which involves the power to settle which of the antecedently possible decisions actually occurs. The proposed solution is to reintroduce the agent as a cause, this time not merely as involved in events, but rather fundamentally as a substance.[58] The agent-causal libertarian maintains that we possess a distinctive

---

[54] R. Kane, 'Responsibility, Luck, and Chance: Reflections on Free Will and Indeterminism', *Journal of Philosophy* 96 (1999): 217–40, at 232.

[55] R. Kane, *The Significance of Free Will*, 128–30.

[56] D. Hume, *A Treatise of Human Nature*, 411–12; cf. A. Mele, *Free Will and Luck*.

[57] R. Clarke, 'On the Possibility of Rational Free Action', *Philosophical Studies* 88 (1997): 37–57, *Libertarian Theories of Free Will* (Oxford: Oxford University Press, 2003).

[58] I. Haji and A. Mele deny that the move to agent-causation would avoid the luck objection; Haji, 'Active Control, Agent Causation, and Free Action', *Philosophical Explorations* 7 (2004): 131–48; A. Mele, *Free Will and Luck*.

causal power—a power for an agent, fundamentally as a substance, to cause a decision without being causally determined to do so. This position might well be incipient in the medieval originators of modern libertarianism, but the Humean objection to indeterministic free will occasioned a more precise formulation. Thomas Reid provides an agent causal account in direct response to Hume, and arguably, Kant does as well in his account of transcendental freedom.[59]

One traditional objection to the agent-causal picture is that we have no evidence that we are substances of the requisite sort. Kant expresses two further concerns for the agent-causal view, which in his account calls for our endorsement on practical, but not on evidential grounds. One is that despite our inability to discern an internal incoherence in our conception of transcendental freedom, our having this power might nonetheless not be really or metaphysically possible. In Kant's view, we can discern something to be really possible only through experience, and we do not experience ourselves as agent-causes. The second concern is that agent-causation might not be reconcilable with what we would expect given our best empirical theories. Kant himself believed that the physical world, as part of the world of appearance, is governed by deterministic laws, while the transcendentally free agent-cause would exist not as an appearance, but as a thing in itself. In this agent-causal picture, when an agent makes a free decision, she causes the decision without being causally determined to do so. On the path to action that results from this undetermined decision, alterations in the physical world, for example in her brain or some other part of her body, are produced. But it would seem that we would at this point encounter divergences from the deterministic laws. For the alterations in the physical world that result from the undetermined decision would themselves not be causally determined, and they would thus not be governed by deterministic laws. One might object that it is possible that the physical alterations that result from every free decision just happen to dovetail with what could in principle be predicted on the basis of the deterministic laws, so nothing actually occurs that diverges from these laws. However, this proposal would seem to involve coincidences too wild to be credible. For this reason, it seems that agent-causal libertarianism is not reconcilable with the physical world's being governed by deterministic laws. Kant thought that more needed to be said. In one text he appears to claim that when an agent makes a transcendentally free decision, he, as atemporal noumenal subject, also freely produces everything in the past that causally determines his free

[59] I. Kant, *Critique of Pure Reason* (1781/1787), tr. P. Guyer and A. Wood (Cambridge: Cambridge University Press, 1997), *Critique of Practical Reason* (1788), tr. M. Gregor (Cambridge: Cambridge University Press, 1996); T. Reid, *Essays on the Active Powers of Man* (1788), in *The Works of Thomas Reid, D.D.*, ed. Sir W. Hamilton (Hildesheim: G. Olms Verlagsbuchhandlung, 1983); cf. W. Rowe, *Thomas Reid on Morality and Freedom* (Ithaca, NY: Cornell University Press, 1991); G. Yaffe, *Manifest Activity: Thomas Reid's Theory of Action* (Oxford: Oxford University Press, 2004); R. Chisholm, 'Human Freedom and the Self', *Person and Object* (La Salle: Open Court, 1976); R. Taylor, *Action and Purpose* (Englewood Cliffs, NJ: Prentice-Hall, 1966); T. O'Connor, *Persons and Causes*; R. Clarke, *Libertarian Theories of Free Will*; M. Griffith, 'Why Agent-Caused Actions are Not Lucky', *American Philosophical Quarterly* 47 (2010): 43–56.

actions.[60] But this sort of atemporalist line is at best insignificantly more credible than an overt contradiction.[61]

More recent expositors of the agent-causal view, such as Clarke and Timothy O'Connor, suggest that quantum indeterminacy can help with the reconciliation project.[62] On one interpretation of quantum mechanics, the physical world is not in fact deterministic, but is rather governed by laws that are fundamentally merely probabilistic or statistical. Suppose, as is controversial, that significant quantum indeterminacy percolates up to the level of human action. Then it might seem that agent-causal libertarianism can be reconciled with the claim that the laws of physics govern at least the physical components of human actions. However, it appears that wild coincidences would also arise on this suggestion.[63] Consider the class of possible actions each of which has a physical component whose antecedent probability of occurring is approximately 0.32. It would not violate the statistical laws in the sense of being logically incompatible with them if, for a large number of instances, the physical components in this class were not actually realized close to 32 per cent of the time. Rather, the force of the statistical law is that for a large number of instances it is correct to *expect* physical components in this class to be realized close to 32 per cent of the time. Are free choices on the agent-causal libertarian model compatible with what the statistical law would have us to expect about them? If they were, then for a large enough number of instances the possible actions in our class would almost certainly be freely chosen near to 32 per cent of the time. But if the occurrence of these physical components were settled by the choices of agent-causes, then their actually being chosen close to 32 per cent of the time would also amount to a wild coincidence. The proposal that agent-caused free choices do not diverge from what the statistical laws predict for the physical components of our actions would be so sharply opposed to what we would expect as to make it incredible.

At this point the agent-causal libertarian might suggest that exercises of agent-causal libertarian freedom do result in divergences from what we would expect given our best assessments of the physical laws. Roderick Chisholm proposes such a view.[64] Divergences from the probabilities that we would expect absent agent-causes do in fact occur whenever we act freely, and these divergences are located at the interface between the agent-cause and that part of the physical world that it directly affects, likely to be found in the brain. There are different ways in which agent-caused free choices might diverge from what the laws would predict. One way is by not being subject to laws at all. Another is by

[60] I. Kant, *Critique of Practical Reason*, (Ak) 97–8.

[61] A. Wood, 'Kant's Compatibilism', in *Self and Nature in Kant's Philosophy* (Ithaca NY: Cornell University Press, 1984), 73–101; D. Pereboom, 'Kant on Transcendental Freedom', *Philosophy and Phenomenological Research* 73 (2006): 537–67.

[62] R. Clarke, 'Toward a Credible Agent-Causal Account of Free Will', *Noûs* 27 (1993): 191–203, *Libertarian Theories of Free Will* ; T. O'Connor, *Persons and Causes* (New York: Oxford University Press, 2000); 'Agent-Causal Power', in T. Handfield (ed.), *Dispositions and Causes* (Oxford: Oxford University Press, 2009), 189–214.

[63] D. Pereboom, *Living without Free Will*, 82–5.

[64] R. Chisholm, 'Human Freedom and the Self'.

being subject to different statistical laws, an option on which the agent-cause would be governed by probabilistic laws that are its own due to the fact that they emerge only in the right sorts of agential contexts, and not to those that generally govern the physical events of the universe.[65] A concern for these kinds of claims is that we currently have no evidence that they are true.

A third type of libertarianism is non-causal, and is advocated by Henri Bergson, Carl Ginet, Hugh McCann, and Stewart Goetz.[66] Bergson argues that although action occurs in time, the time of conscious agency does not divide into the kinds of quantities or magnitudes that make objects in space subject to causal natural laws. On Ginet's conception, the key conditions for a basic action's being free are that it has an agent as a subject, it has an actish phenomenological feel, and it is uncaused, or not causally determined. An often-cited objection to this type of libertarianism is that control in action is fundamentally a causal matter, and thus such theories cannot secure the type of control in action required for moral responsibility.[67] This objection is resisted by non-causalists, and such theories continue to be attractive, especially given the problems that arise on causal libertarian theories due to the expectation that the causality of libertarian agency must be reconciled with the causality of the natural world.

29.6 Scepticism about Free Will

Due to the difficulties for both the compatibilist and libertarian positions, some have endorsed that sceptical outlook that we do not have the sort of free will required for moral responsibility. Hard determinists argue that because determinism is true and compatibilism is implausible, we lack free will of this kind. This perspective is defended by Baruch Spinoza, Paul Holbach, Joseph Priestley, Ted Honderich, and Bruce Waller.[68] Critics have expressed a number of concerns about this type of view. They have argued, for example, that hard determinism would threaten our self-conception as deliberative agents, that it would undercut the reactive attitudes essential to good

[65] T. O'Connor, 'Agent-Causal Power'.

[66] H. Bergson, *Essai sur les données immédiates de la conscience* (Paris: F. Alcan, 1889); translated as *Time and Free Will*, tr. F. L. Pogson (London: Allen and Unwin, 1910); C. Ginet, *On Action*, 'Freedom, Responsibility, and Agency', *Journal of Ethics* 1 (1997): 85–98; H. McCann, *The Works of Agency* (Ithaca: Cornell University Press, 1998); S. Goetz, *Freedom, Teleology, and Evil* (London: Continuum, 2008).

[67] T. O'Connor, *Persons and Causes*; R. Clarke, *Libertarian Theories of Free Will*.

[68] B. Spinoza, *Ethics* (1677), in *The Collected Works of Spinoza*, ed. and tr. E. Curley, vol. 1 (Princeton: Princeton University Press, 1985); P. Holbach, *Système de la Nature* (Amsterdam, 1770); J. Priestley, *A Free Discussion of the Doctrines of Materialism and Philosophical Necessity, in a Correspondence between Dr. Price and Dr. Priestley* (1788), Part III reprinted in J. Priestley, *Priestley's Writings on Philosophy, Science, and Politics*, ed. J. Passmore (New York: Collier, 1965), 147–52; T. Honderich, *A Theory of Determinism* (Oxford: Oxford University Press, 1988); B. Waller, *Freedom without Responsibility* (Philadelphia: Temple University Press, 1990).

human interpersonal relationships, and that if hard determinism were true morality itself would be incoherent.

Hard determinists maintain that it is because of the truth of causal determinism that we lack the sort of free will required for moral responsibility.[69] By contrast, many contemporary free will sceptics are agnostic about causal determinism. I argue, for example, that we would not be morally responsible if determinism were true, but also that we would lack moral responsibility if indeterminism was true and the causes of our actions were exclusively events. Such indeterministic causal histories of actions would be as threatening to this sort of free will as deterministic histories are. However, it might be that if we were undetermined agent-causes we would then have this type of free will. But although our being undetermined agent-causes has not been ruled out as a coherent possibility, it is not credible given our best physical theories. Thus I do not claim that our having the sort of free will required for moral responsibility is impossible. Nevertheless, since the only account on which we are likely to have this kind of free will is not credible given our best physical theories, we must take very seriously the prospect that we are in fact not free in the sense required for moral responsibility.

Galen Strawson, also a free-will sceptic, argues that moral responsibility requires a conception of agency that human beings could not satisfy, and its impossibility for us can be established independently of an examination of the truth of determinism.[70] Strawson, then, is a no-free-will-either-way theorist, that is, he maintains that for us moral responsibility is incompatible with both determinism and indeterminism. The specific type of agent-causal libertarianism whose coherence I defend is relevantly similar to what he calls the 'Leibnizian' variety of agent causation. In this conception, the agent's reasons (which consist of beliefs and desires) constitute only one component of the cause of a free decision, since they may incline but do not all by themselves cause the agent to choose. The agent's causation of a choice constitutes the remaining part. But, Strawson contends—as he does against any theory of morally responsible agency—that rational actions must have a full causal explanation in terms of the agent's reasons alone. More precisely, rational actions must have an explanation in terms of reasons the agent has that indicates all of what there was about the agent, mentally speaking, that causally brought it about that she performed the action she did.[71] Otherwise only the 'reasons' part of the action's cause would be rational, and the remaining mental aspects would not be. 'Upon what', he asks, 'are the decisions about actions now supposed to be based, other than upon its reasons?'[72] The decisions cannot be based on further principles of choice or on further reasons, because the same questions can be asked about those. Either the reasons all by themselves cause the decision, in which case the agent-cause has no causal role and the decision is not free, or the agent-cause plays a part that is not rational.

---

[69] See, for example, B. Spinoza, *Ethics*, 440–4, 483–4, 496–7; cf. M. Della Rocca, *Spinoza* (London: Routledge, 2008).

[70] G. Strawson, *Freedom and Belief.*   [71] G. Strawson, *Freedom and Belief,* 52–6.

[72] G. Strawson, *Freedom and Belief,* 53.

Consequently, these agent-caused actions must either be unfree or 'rationally speaking random', and thus rationally deficient.

But one might contest Strawson's argument against agent-causation on the ground that the standard for rationality it assumes is too stringent. Imagine that you are in a situation of conflict between self-interested and moral reasons; one possible decision is morally justified but is not on balance in your self-interest, the other is not morally justified but is in your self-interest. You have the capacity to freely agent-cause either choice, you cause the moral one, and this decision is on balance justified by your reasons overall. Strawson would judge that the agent is unfree because the choice is not fully caused by your reasons, and thus rationally speaking random. Yet in this situation it might be intuitive that the action is in fact sufficiently connected to your reasons to count as rational. The rationality of action would then not require its complete determination by the agent's reasons, but rather only being justified by them.[73]

Saul Smilansky concurs with Strawson's argument that the sort of free will required for moral responsibility is impossible for us, and thus he too is a no-free-will-either-way theorist.[74] He argues, however, that a valuable type of moral self-respect, respect for oneself as the moral agent one has freely made oneself, would be undermined if we did not believe we are free in the sense required for moral responsibility. Having the sort of self-respect at issue requires maintaining or fostering an *illusion* of free will, which Smilansky recommends for this reason, and for others as well, such as justification of criminal punishment.

My own view is that the denial of moral responsibility in the basic-desert sense does not issue in the deleterious moral consequences it is often thought to have.[75] In criminology, for instance, the free-will sceptic might endorse a theory that draws an analogy between the treatment of criminals and the treatment of carriers of dangerous diseases. Ferdinand Schoeman argues that if we have the right to quarantine carriers of serious communicable diseases to protect people, then for the same reason we also have the right to isolate the criminally dangerous.[76] Quarantining a person can be justified when he is not morally responsible for being dangerous to others. If a child is infected with a deadly contagious virus transmitted to her before she was born, quarantine can still be justified. By analogy, even if a violent criminal is not morally responsible for his crimes (say because no one is ever morally responsible), it might well be as legitimate to isolate him as it would be to quarantine a non-responsible carrier of a dangerous communicable disease.

[73] R. Clarke, 'On an Argument for the Impossibility of Moral Responsibility', *Midwest Studies in Philosophy* 29 (2005): 13–24.

[74] S. Smilansky, 'Can a Determinist Help Herself?', in C.H. Manekin and M. Kellner (eds), *Freedom and Moral Responsibility: General and Jewish Perspectives* (College Park: University of Maryland Press, 1997), 85–98, *Free Will and Illusion* (Oxford: Oxford University Press, 2000).

[75] D. Pereboom, *Living without Free Will*, 127–213.

[76] F. D. Schoeman, 'On Incapacitating the Dangerous', *American Philosophical Quarterly* 16 (1979): 27–35.

On scepticism's consequences for interpersonal relationships, P. F. Strawson may be right that if we persistently maintained an objective attitude towards others, our relationships would be undermined.[77] But one might reasonably deny that scepticism about free will and moral responsibility would justify adopting this attitude in particular. Indeed, certain reactive attitudes would in fact be threatened, since some of them, such as moral resentment, indignation, and a variety of guilt would have the false presupposition that the person who is the object of the attitude is morally responsible in the basic-desert entailing sense. But one might relinquish these attitudes while retaining non-reactive emotions such as moral sorrow and regret, which might have similar salutary roles in relationships. In addition, the attitudes that we most clearly want to retain, such as gratitude and love, either would not be threatened in this way, or else have analogues or aspects that would not have false presuppositions. For example, one aspect of gratitude is simply to be thankful to someone for what she has done, and mere thankfulness does not require a presumption of basic desert. Thus it might well be that the surviving emotions would not amount to the objective attitude, and at the same time would be sufficient to sustain good human relationships.[78]

About the view that we lack the sort of free will at issue, Spinoza says: 'this doctrine contributes to the social life insofar as it teaches us to hate no one, to disesteem no one, to mock no one, to be angry at no one'.[79] Often we justify expressions of moral resentment or indignation by contending that their targets are morally responsible in the basic-desert entailing sense for what they have done. If we became convinced that we lack the type of free will required for this sort of moral responsibility, we would regard such justifications as illegitimate. Spinoza is concerned about the damage to which these reactive attitudes give rise, and in his view our coming to believe that we lack the sort of free will that justifies their expression is on balance to our advantage.

BIBLIOGRAPHY

Adams, M. 1986. 'The Structure of Ockham's Moral Theory', *Franciscan Studies* 24: 1–35.
—— 1995. 'Duns Scotus on the Will as Rational Power', *Via Scoti, Methodologica ad Mentem Joannis Dunds Scoti*, ed. L. Sileo. Rome: PAA Edizioni Antonianum, 839–54.
Adams, R. 1994. *Leibniz: Determinist, Theist, Idealist*. Oxford: Oxford University Press.
Aristotle. 2000. *Nicomachean Ethics*, tr. R. Crisp. Cambridge: Cambridge University Press.
Arpaly, N. 2006. *Merit, Meaning, and Bondage: An Essay on Free Will*. Princeton NJ: Princeton University Press.
Augustine. 1993. *On Free Choice of Will*, tr. T. Williams. Indianapolis: Hackett.
Ayer, A. J. 1954. 'Freedom and Necessity', in A. J. Ayer, *Philosophical Essays*. London: Macmillan, 271–84.

---

[77] For a criticism of this claim of Strawson's, see T. Sommers, 'The Objective Attitude', *Philosophical Quarterly* 57 (2007): 321–41.

[78] D. Pereboom, *Living without Free Will*, 199–213.

[79] B. Spinoza, *Ethics*, in *The Collected Works of Spinoza*, vol. 1, 490.

Balaguer, M. 2009. *Free Will as an Open Scientific Problem*. Cambridge, MA: MIT Press.

Bergson, H. 1889/1910. *Essai sur les données immédiates de la conscience*. Paris: F. Alcan, 1889. Translated as *Time and Free Will*, tr. F. L. Pogson. London: Allen and Unwin, 1910.

Bishop, J. 1989. *Natural Agency*. Cambridge: Cambridge University Press.

Bobzien, S. 1998. *Determinism and Freedom in Stoic Philosophy*. Oxford: Oxford University Press.

Bok, H. 1998. *Freedom and Responsibility*. Princeton NJ: Princeton University Press.

Brennan, T. 2005. *The Stoic Life: Emotions, Duties, and Fate*. Oxford: Oxford University Press.

Broad, C. D. 1934/ 1952. 'Determinism, Indeterminism, and Libertarianism', inaugural lecture delivered at Cambridge in 1934; reprinted in C. D. Broad, *Ethics and The History of Philosophy*. London: Routledge, 195–217.

Campbell, C. A. 1951. 'Is Free Will a Pseudo-Problem?', *Mind* 60: 446–65.

Carlson, E. 2000. 'Incompatibilism and the Transfer of Power Necessity', *Noûs* 34: 277–90.

Chisholm, R. 1964. 'Human Freedom and the Self', The Lindley Lecture, Department of Philosophy, University of Kansas.

—— 1976. *Person and Object*. La Salle: Open Court.

Clarke, R. 1993. 'Toward a Credible Agent-Causal Account of Free Will', *Noûs* 27: 191–203.

—— 1997. 'On the Possibility of Rational Free Action', *Philosophical Studies* 88: 37–57.

—— 2000. 'Modest Libertarianism', *Philosophical Perspectives* 14: 21–46.

—— 2003. *Libertarian Theories of Free Will*. Oxford: Oxford University Press.

—— 2005. 'On an Argument for the Impossibility of Moral Responsibility', *Midwest Studies in Philosophy* 29: 13–24.

—— 2009. 'Dispositions, Abilities to Act, and Free Will: The New Dispositionalism', *Mind* 118: 323–51.

Della Rocca, M. 1998. 'Frankfurt, Fischer, and Flickers', *Noûs* 32: 99–105.

—— 2008. *Spinoza*. London, Routledge.

Dennett, D. 1984. *Elbow Room*. Cambridge: MIT Press.

—— 2003. *Freedom Evolves*. New York: Viking.

Ekstrom, L. W. 2000. *Free Will: A Philosophical Study*. Boulder: Westview.

Fara, M. 2008. 'Masked Abilities and Compatibilism', *Mind* 117: 843–65.

Fischer, J. M. 1994. *The Metaphysics of Free Will*. Oxford: Blackwell.

—— 2010. 'The Frankfurt Cases: The Moral of the Stories', *Philosophical Review* 119: 315–36.

—— Kane, R., Pereboom, D., and Vargas, M. 2007. *Four Views on Free Will*. Oxford: Blackwell Publishers.

—— and Ravizza, M. 1998. *Responsibility and Control: A Theory of Moral Responsibility*. New York: Cambridge University Press.

Frankfurt, H. G. 1969. 'Alternate Possibilities and Moral Responsibility', *Journal of Philosophy* 66: 829–39.

—— 1971. 'Freedom of the Will and the Concept of a Person', *Journal of Philosophy* 68: 5–20.

Franklin, C. 2011. 'Neo-Frankfurtians and Buffer Cases: The New Challenge to the Principle of Alternative Possibilities', *Philosophical Studies* 152: 189–207.

Frede, M. 2011. *A Free Will*. Berkeley and Los Angeles: University of California Press.

Ginet, C. 1966. 'Might We Have No Choice', in K. Lehrer (ed.), *Freedom and Determinism*. New York: Random House, 87–104.

—— 1990. *On Action*. Cambridge, Cambridge University Press.

Ginet, C. 1996. 'In Defense of the Principle of Alternative Possibilities: Why I Don't Find Frankfurt's Arguments Convincing', *Philosophical Perspectives* 10: 403–17.

—— 1997. 'Freedom, Responsibility, and Agency', *Journal of Ethics* 1: 85–98.

Goetz, S. 2008. *Freedom, Teleology, and Evil*. London: Continuum.

Griffith, M. 2010. 'Why Agent-Caused Actions are Not Lucky', *American Philosophical Quarterly* 47: 43–56.

Haji, I. 1998. *Moral Appraisability*. New York: Oxford University Press.

—— 2004. 'Active Control, Agent Causation, and Free Action', *Philosophical Explorations* 7: 131–48.

Hobart, R. E. 1934. 'Free Will as Involving Determinism and Inconceivable without It', *Mind* 43: 1–27.

Hobbes, T. 1654. *Of Libertie and Necessity. A treatise, wherein all controversie concerning pre-destination, election, free-will, grace, merits, reprobation, &c., is fully decided and cleared, in answer to a treatise written by the Bishop of London-Derry, on the same subject*. London.

Holbach, P. 1770. *Système de la Nature*. Amsterdam.

Honderich, T. 1988. *A Theory of Determinism*. Oxford: Oxford University Press.

Hume, D. 1978. *A Treatise of Human Nature*. Oxford: Oxford University Press.

—— 1999. *An Enquiry Concerning Human Understanding*. Oxford: Oxford University Press.

Hunt, D. 2000. 'Moral Responsibility and Unavoidable Action', *Philosophical Studies* 97: 195–227.

—— 2005. 'Moral Responsibility and Buffered Alternatives', *Midwest Studies in Philosophy* 29: 126–45.

Inwood, B. 1985. *Ethics and Human Action in Early Stoicism*. Oxford: Oxford University Press.

Irwin, T. 1990. *Aristotle's First Principles*. Oxford: Oxford University Press.

James, W. 1909. 'The Dilemma of Determinism', in *The Will to Believe and Other Essays*. New York, Longman, 145–83.

Kane, R. 1985. *Free Will and Values*. Albany: SUNY Press.

—— 1996. *The Significance of Free Will*. New York: Oxford University Press.

—— 1999. 'Responsibility, Luck, and Chance: Reflections on Free Will and Indeterminism', *Journal of Philosophy* 96: 217–40.

Kant, I. 1996. *Critique of Practical Reason*, tr. M. Gregor. Cambridge: Cambridge University Press.

—— 1997. *Critique of Pure Reason*, tr. P. Guyer and A. Wood. Cambridge: Cambridge University Press.

Lamb, J. 1977. 'On a Proof of Incompatibilism', *Philosophical Review* 86: 20–35.

Lehrer, K. 1968. 'Cans without Ifs', *Analysis* 29: 29–32.

Lewis, D. 1981. 'Are We Free to Break the Laws?', *Theoria* 47: 113–22.

Locke, J. 1975. *An Essay Concerning Human Understanding*, ed. P. H. Nidditch. Oxford: Oxford University Press.

Lucretius. 1982. *De Rerum Natura*, tr. W. H. D. Rouse. Loeb Classical Library. Cambridge, MA: Harvard University Press.

McCann, H. 1998. *The Works of Agency*. Ithaca: Cornell University Press.

McKay, T. and Johnson, D. 1996. 'A Reconsideration of an Argument against Compatibilism', *Philosophical Topics* 24: 113–22.

McKenna, M. 1997. 'Alternative Possibilities and the Failure of the Counterexample Strategy', *Journal of Social Philosophy* 28: 71–85.

—— 2003. 'Robustness, Control, and the Demand for Morally Significant Alternatives', in M. McKenna and D. Widerker (eds), *Freedom, Responsibility, and Agency: Essays on the Importance of Alternative Possibilities*. Aldershot UK: Ashgate, 201–16.

—— 2005. 'Where Frankfurt and Strawson Meet', *Midwest Studies in Philosophy* 29: 163–80.

—— 2008. 'Saying Good-Bye to the Direct Argument in the Right Way', *Philosophical Review* 117: 349–83.

—— 2012. *Conversation and Responsibility*. New York: Oxford University Press.

Mele, A. 1995. *Autonomous Agents*. New York: Oxford University Press.

—— 1999. 'Ultimate Responsibility and Dumb Luck', *Social Philosophy and Policy* 16: 274–93.

—— 2005. 'Libertarianism, Luck, and Control', *Pacific Philosophical Quarterly* 86: 395–421.

—— 2006. *Free Will and Luck*. Oxford: Oxford University Press.

—— and Robb, D. 1998. 'Rescuing Frankfurt-Style Cases', *Philosophical Review* 107: 97–112.

Meyer, S. Sauvé. 1993. *Aristotle on Moral Responsibility*. Oxford: Oxford University Press.

Moore, G. E. 1912. *Ethics*. Oxford: London: Williams and Norgate.

Nelkin, D. 2008. 'Responsibility and Rational Abilities: Defending an Asymmetrical View', *Pacific Philosophical Quartely* 89: 497–515.

—— 2011. *Making Sense of Freedom and Responsibility*. Oxford: Oxford University Press.

O'Connor, T. 2000. *Persons and Causes*. New York: Oxford University Press.

—— 2009. 'Agent-Causal Power', in T. Handfield (ed.), *Dispositions and Causes*. Oxford: Oxford University Press, 189–214.

Origen. 1913. *De Principiis*, in *Origenes Werke*, ed. P. Koetschau. Volume 5. Leipzig.

Otsuka, M. 1998. 'Incompatibilism and the Avoidability of Blame', *Ethics* 108: 685–701.

Palmer, D. 2011. 'Pereboom on the Frankfurt Cases,' *Philosophical Studies* 153 (2011): 261–72.

Pasnau, R. 1999. 'Olivi on Human Freedom', in *Pierre De Jean Olivi (1248–1298)*. Paris: Vrin, 15–25.

Penner, S. 'Suarez on Human Freedom', unpublished manunscript.

Pereboom, D. 1995. 'Determinism *Al Dente*', *Nous* 29: 21–45.

—— 2000. 'Alternative Possibilities and Causal Histories', *Philosophical Perspectives* 14: 119–37.

—— 2001. *Living without Free Will*. Cambridge: Cambridge University Press.

—— 2004. 'Is Our Conception of Agent Causation Incoherent?', *Philosophical Topics* 32: 275–86.

—— 2006. 'Kant on Transcendental Freedom', *Philosophy and Phenomenological Research* 73: 537–67.

Priestley, J. 1788/1965. *A Free Discussion of the Doctrines of Materialism and Philosophical Necessity, in a Correspondence between Dr. Price and Dr. Priestley* (1788). Part III reprinted in J. Priestley, *Priestley's Writings on Philosophy, Science, and Politics*, ed. J. Passmore. New York: Collier, 1965, 147–52.

Reid, T. 1983. Essays on the Active Powers of Man, in *The Works of Thomas Reid, D.D.*, ed. Sir W. Hamilton. Hildesheim: G. Olms Verlagsbuchhandlung.

Rickless, S. 2000. 'Locke on the Freedom to Will', *The Locke Newsletter* 31: 43–67.

—— 2013. 'Will and Motivation', in P. Anstey (ed.), *The Oxford Handbook of British Philosophy in the Seventeenth Century*. Oxford: Oxford University Press.

Rowe, W. 1991. *Thomas Reid on Morality and Freedom*. Ithaca, NY: Cornell University Press.

Russell, P. 1995. *Freedom and Moral Sentiment*. New York: Oxford University Press.

Scanlon, T. M. 1998. *What We Owe to Each Other*. Cambridge MA: Harvard University Press.

Schlick, M. 1939. 'When is a Man Responsible', in *Problems of Ethics*, tr. D. Rynin. New York: Prentice-Hall, 1708 143–56.

Schoeman, F. D. 1979. 'On Incapacitating the Dangerous', *American Philosophical Quarterly* 16: 27–35.

Scotus, J. Duns 1986. *Duns Scotus on the Will and Morality*, ed. and tr. A. Wolter. Washington, DC: The Catholic University of America Press.

Shabo, S. 2010. 'The Fate of the Direct Argument and the Case for Incompatibilism', *Philosophical Studies* 150: 405–24.

Sharples, R. W. 1983. *Alexander of Aphrodisias on Fate*. London: Duckworth.

Slote, M. 1982. 'Selective Necessity and the Free Will Problem', *Journal of Philosophy* 79: 5–24.

Smilansky, S. 1997. 'Can a Determinist Help Herself?', C. H. Manekin and M. Kellner (eds), *Freedom and Moral Responsibility: General and Jewish Perspectives*. College Park: University of Maryland Press, 85–98.

—— 2000. *Free Will and Illusion*. Oxford: Oxford University Press.

Sommers, T. 2007. 'The Objective Attitude', *Philosophical Quarterly* 57: 321–41.

Spinoza, B. 1677 /1985. *Ethics*, in *The Collected Works of Spinoza*, ed. and tr. E. Curley. Vol. 1. Princeton: Princeton University Press.

Strawson, G. 1986. *Freedom and Belief*. Oxford: Oxford University Press.

Strawson, P. F. 1962. 'Freedom and Resentment', *Proceedings of the British Academy* 48: 1–25.

Stump, E. 1996. 'Libertarian Freedom and the Principle of Alternative Possibilities', in J. Jordan and D. Howard Snyder (eds), *Faith, Freedom, and Rationality*. Lanham, MD: Rowman and Littlefield, 73–88.

Suarez, F. 1597/ 1861/ 1965. *Disputationes Metaphysicae*. Vivès edition, 28 vols. (1856–1861). Paris. Reprinted by Georg Olms, Hildesheim, 1965.

Taylor, R. 1966. *Action and Purpose*. Englewood Cliffs NJ: Prentice-Hall.

—— 1974. *Metaphysics*. Fourth edition. Englewood Cliffs, NJ: Prentice-Hall.

van Inwagen, P. 1975. 'The Incompatibility of Free Will and Determinism', *Philosophical Studies* 27: 185–9.

—— 1983. *An Essay on Free Will*. Oxford: Oxford University Press.

Vihvelin, K. 1991. 'Freedom, Causation, and Counterfactuals', *Philosophical Studies* 64: 161–84.

—— 2004. 'Free Will Demystified: A Dispositional Account', *Philosophical Topics* 32: 427–50.

Wallace, R. J. 1994. *Responsibility and the Moral Sentiments*. Cambridge, MA: Harvard University Press.

Waller, B. 1990. *Freedom without Responsibility*. Philadelphia: Temple University Press.

Warfield, T. 2000. 'Causal Determinism and Human Freedom are Incompatible', *Philosophical Perspectives* 14: 167–80.

Watson, G. 1975. 'Free Agency', *Journal of Philosophy* 72: 205–20.

—— 1987. 'Responsibility and the Limits of Evil', in F. Schoeman (ed.), *Responsibility, Character, and the Emotions*. Cambridge: Cambridge University Press, 256–86.

Widerker, D. 1995. 'Libertarianism and Frankfurt's Attack on the Principle of Alternative Possibilities', *The Philosophical Review* 104: 247–61.

—— 2000. 'Frankfurt's Attack on Alternative Possibilities', *Philosophical Perspectives* 14: 181–201.

—— 2006. 'Libertarianism and the Philosophical Significance of Frankfurt Scenarios', *Journal of Philosophy* 103: 163–87.

Wolf, S. 1980. 'Asymmetrical Freedom', *Journal of Philosophy* 77: 151–66.

—— 1990. *Freedom within Reason*. Oxford: Oxford University Press.

Wood, A. 1984. 'Kant's Compatibilism', in *Self and Nature in Kant's Philosophy*. Ithaca NY: Cornell University Press, 73–101.

Wyma, K. D. 1997. 'Moral Responsibility and Leeway for Action', *American Philosophical Quarterly* 34: 57–70.

Yaffe, G. 2000. *Liberty Worth the Name: Locke on Free Agency*. Princeton: Princeton University Press.

—— 2004. *Manifest Activity: Thomas Reid's Theory of Action*. Oxford: Oxford University Press.

....

CHAPTER 30

EMOTION AND
THE EMOTIONS

....

SUSAN SAUVÉ MEYER AND ADRIENNE M. MARTIN

A prominent theme in twentieth- and early twenty-first-century moral philosophy is that a full and accurate picture of the ethical life must include an important role for the emotions. The neglect of the emotions has been a major point of criticism raised against the dominant consequentialist, Kantian, and contractualist theories by virtue ethicists such as G. E. M. Anscombe, Alasdair MacIntyre, Martha Nussbaum, and Michael Stocker. Bernard Williams and Susan Wolf also develop a similar line of criticism as part of their arguments against the supremacy or priority of moral values as conceived by utilitarianism and other 'impartialist' theories.

There are a number of reasons why it might be a mistake for moral philosophy to neglect the emotions. To name just three:

1. It seems obvious that emotions have an important influence on motivation, and that proper cultivation of the emotions is helpful, perhaps essential, to our ability to lead ethical lives.
2. It is also arguable that emotions are objects of moral evaluation, not only because of their influence on action, but in themselves. In other words, it is a plausible thesis that an ethical life involves feeling certain ways in certain circumstances and acting from certain feelings in certain circumstances.
3. Finally, a more contentious thesis, but certainly worth considering, is that some emotions are forms of ethical perception, judgement, or even knowledge.

The bulk of this chapter surveys the ancient ethical tradition that inspires the virtue ethicist's critique, revealing versions of each of these three theses in one guise or another. After briefly considering the medieval transformations of the ancient doctrines, the remainder of the chapter focuses on the third, more contentious thesis, distinguishing several versions of it in the moral philosophies of the seventeenth and eighteenth century and indicating some contemporary exemplars as well.

First, let us clarify what we mean by 'emotions'. While the category of emotion has imprecise and disputed boundaries, paradigm instances include anger, fear, joy, love, and hate. As the notion is invoked today, it includes feelings of affection, animosity, attraction, and revulsion that are distinct from bodily sensations yet are intimately bound up with feelings of pleasure and pain. So understood, it corresponds roughly to the ancient psychological category of the 'passions' *(pathe*; singular *'pathos'*), which Aristotle demarcates as encompassing 'appetite (*epithumia*), anger, fear, daring, spite, delight, liking, hatred, yearning, admiration, pity' (*Nicomachean Ethics* II 5, 1105b21–2).[1] While many theorists in the present day distinguish between desires and emotions, and certain thinkers in the Christian and early modern tradition follow the Stoics in distinguishing between 'passions' and what they take to be nobler sentiments,[2] the ancient category of the *pathe* encompasses all these items, and hence it will be the starting point of this study.

30.1 Emotions in Ancient Moral Philosophy

30.1.1 Plato

While Plato does not use *'pathos'* as a general term for the range of attitudes that Aristotle and later writers demarcate with this term, he clearly recognizes a category with roughly the same boundaries and takes it to be of ethical and epistemological significance. He consistently groups emotions such as fear, anger, and grief together with certain desires, pleasures, and pains. For example, in the *Phaedo*, 'pleasures and desires, pains and fears', are attributed to the soul's involvement with the body.[3] The *Republic* lists 'sexual feelings, anger, desires of every sort, and all the pains and pleasures in the soul that accompany all our actions' as arising from the non-rational part of the soul (606d1–3). Likewise, in the *Timaeus*, love, fear, anger, 'and the like', along with a general attraction to pleasure and aversion to pain, are said to result from the embodiment of an otherwise purely intellectual soul.[4] In the *Laws*, the non-rational principle of human action is described as issuing in 'pleasures and pains, angry feelings, and passionate desires (*erotas*)' (645d6–8), while in *Philebus*, 'anger, fear, lamentation, love, jealousy, malice and the like' (47e1–3), are invoked as 'pains of the soul'.

A persistent theme across these works is that the passions, if improperly cultivated, preclude the achievement of knowledge. While the *Phaedo* and *Timaeus* make this point about theoretical knowledge, our discussion will concern dialogues whose focus is ethical knowledge and the virtues.

---

[1] On the difficulties involved in translating *'pathos'* as 'emotion', see Konstan 2006: ch. 1.
[2] A point stressed by Dixon 2003.
[3] *Phaedo* 83b6–7, 81a–84a; cf. *Theaetetus* 156b, *Republic* 430a.   [4] *Timaeus* 42a–b, 69c–d; cf. 88b.

30.1.1.1 *The Protagoras*

Even in *Protagoras*, a dialogue that does not invoke a distinction between rational and non-rational parts of the human psyche, the passions are identified as potential spoilers of the epistemic quest. Here Socrates denies that a person can knowingly do what is wrong when under the influence of 'anger, pleasure, pain, love, or fear and the like'[5]—a phenomenon described under the general label 'being overcome by pleasure'.[6] The agents in such cases, Socrates argues, are like observers who overestimate the size of physical objects in the foreground (356a–357b); they mistakenly believe that the present pleasure they elect to pursue is greater than the longer-term pleasure they would get from eschewing it. With pleasure the only criterion of goodness allowed in the argument, it follows that the agent mistakenly thinks the action he performs is better than the alternative (357e). The details of the argument are tortuous, and the ethical hedonism on which it depends is anomalous in the rest of Plato's dialogues.[7] Nonetheless, we can identify two assumptions at work in the argument that are relevant to our investigation of the passions.

First of all, the argument is evidently intended to apply to the person acting on emotions such as anger, fear, and love (352b–e), and not just to one being seduced by the prospect of bodily gratification. Second, the argument presupposes that the passions in question involve a judgement or belief of sorts. The person who finds a prospect pleasant thereby supposes (in some sense) that it is worth pursuing; otherwise the passion would not impugn his claim to know that the option is wrong. Whatever the criterion of choiceworthiness at play—be it pleasure or something else—the argument crucially depends on the assumption that the option taken by the agent *appears to him* to have more of it than the alternative.[8] This appearance or 'seeming', integral to the emotion, cannot, on Socrates' account, coexist with the knowledge, or even belief, to the contrary. A person who *knows*, or even believes, that an action is wrong will not be pleased at the prospect of doing so, or pained at the alternative (358c–e); for example, the courageous person, who acts on his knowledge of the good, does so without fear (359c–360d). Versions of this thesis are consistent across Plato's other treatments of the passions.

30.1.1.2 *The Republic*

The psychology of the *Republic* famously distinguishes two non-rational parts of the soul that must be ruled by reason—the so-called 'appetitive' (*epithumetikon*) and 'spirited' (*thumoeides*) parts—but offers no systematic explanation of how the lists of 'passions' canvassed in other works and in Book X relate to those parts.

The appetitive part of the soul is paradigmatically portrayed as the seat of bodily appetites (for food, drink, and sex), as well as desires for an unspecified range of additional

---

[5] *Protagoras* 352b7–8, d8–e2.   [6] *Protagoras* 352e6–353a6, c2, 354e7, 356a1, 357c7, e2.
[7] Scholars disagree over whether Socrates is genuinely espousing hedonism in the dialogue. See Rudebusch 1999: 129 n. 4.
[8] A point well brought out by Moss 2006: 509–10 and 2008: 51.

objectives as varied as gazing at corpses, acquiring gold and silver, and taking part in philosophical discussion. The characteristic feature of appetitive attraction is that its objects are expected pleasures.[9] The characteristic manifestation of the 'spirited' (thumoeides) part of the soul, by contrast, is in anger (thumos), whence its name.[10] Also identified as the seat of shame, disgust, and revulsion (439e–440a) as well as esteem or respect (553c4–5; 572c) and envy (586c), it is the part that 'seethes' at injustice and seeks to resist, ward off, or avenge it.[11]

As these manifestations of the spirited part are paradigmatic cases of emotions, some scholars have proposed that the spirited part is the seat of emotions in the strict sense, while the appetitive part is the seat of non-rational desire.[12] However, fear is presented as an aversion to pain coordinate with the appetitive attraction to pleasure (Republic 413b–d, 430a; cf. Phaedo 83b6–7) and in Republic X grief is criticized as a pleasurable indulgence (605c–606b), to be resisted with the same array of 'spirited' resources— shame, disgust, and anger—that are arrayed against the carnal appetites of Leontius in Book IV.[13] Alternatively, one might suppose that some emotions are appetitive and others spirited.[14] However, the complaint about grief as a pleasure-directed impulse in Republic X is there generalized to apply to anger (the signature activity of the spirited part) and indeed to all the other passions (606d).

It seems likely that Plato is not concerned in the Republic to classify the passions in terms of his tripartite soul. Nonetheless, he does closely associate with the spirited part a particular kind of feeling of great ethical importance. The musical education that channels the vigour of the spirited part in service to social norms trains the young guardians to discriminate and take pleasure in what is fine (kalon) and to recognize and be pained or disgusted at what is shameful (aischron) (401d–402d, 403c). These feelings of pleasure and pain, even if they do not appear on standard lists of emotions, are of central interest in Plato's ethical philosophy. They are the medium by which the soul resists inappropriate impulses (as in the case of Leontius), and in the fully perfected soul, they 'follow reason' completely: one's loves and hates coincide with what reason judges to be fine and shameful.

In such a case, however, these feelings of pleasure and pain are not directed at what a cognitive faculty has independently identified as fine and shameful; rather, the feelings are an essential part of a person's cognitive grasp, and developing conception, of what is fine and shameful. The account of musical education in Book III makes it clear that the training that yields a passionate love for what is kalon cultivates the capacity to

---

[9] Bodily appetites: 436a, 439d, 580e; non-bodily appetites: 439e–440a, 548a, 560c–d; pleasure as the object of appetite: 436a, 439d, 559d. On the way in which appetites are non-rational, see Lorenz 2006.

[10] Republic 436a, 439e; on 'thumos' as a label for anger, see 440a5, c2.

[11] Republic 440c–d; 442b7; cf. Statesman 307e–308a; Timaeus 70b; Laws 731b.

[12] Thus Irwin 1977: 192 and 1995: 213. By contrast Fortenbaugh 2002: 37 locates emotions in all three parts.

[13] Republic X 603e–604a, 605d–e; cf. III 388a, IV 439e–440a. On the 'appetitive' aspect of the emotions in Republic X, see Moss 2008.

[14] A view with considerable popularity, we shall see, in among medieval philosophers.

discriminate fine and shameful behaviour and characters; it yields beliefs about what is fine and good that are a necessary preparation for the knowledge of these matters that the philosopher will eventually develop.[15] A recurring theme throughout the *Republic* is that inappropriate feelings of pleasure, pain, fear, and desire distort our judgements about what is good and worthwhile—hence the requirement that potential guardians be tested for their ability to retain their 'law-inculcated beliefs regarding what is terrible' in the face of pleasures and pains,[16] and the criticism of tragic poets who, by eliciting inappropriate emotions, inculcate the illusion that a certain kind of action is admirable when in fact it is disgraceful.[17] In *Republic*, no less than *Protagoras*, moral knowledge is incompatible with inappropriate feelings of pleasure and pain.

30.1.1.3 *The Philebus*

The *Philebus* concerns the role of pleasure in the good life, and some find here the first definitive mapping out of the category of the emotions.[18] Without giving a general name to the category, Plato singles it out as 'fear, anger, and everything of that sort' (40e) and more expansively as 'anger, fear, lamentation, love, jealousy, malice and the like' (47e1–3). While the emotions are hardly the focus of his discussion, he mentions them as instances of a broader category: pleasure and pains that are 'of the soul' as opposed to 'of the body'. While displaying no interest here in the psychology of virtue, the partition of the soul, or the role of pleasures and pains in ethical knowledge, he does reiterate two points about the emotions that we have noted in other dialogues. First, he invokes them as examples of pains that are mixed with pleasures—repeating the point made in *Republic* X that grief, anger, and the like are pleasant to indulge (*Philebus* 47e; *Republic* X 606d). Second, he cites 'fear, anger, and everything of that sort' as examples of pleasures and pains that can be false (40e)—a difficult doctrine whose interpretation need not concern us here[19] beyond its clear implication that the emotions have cognitive status.

30.1.1.4 *The Laws*

The *Laws*, Plato's last sustained discussion of moral psychology and politics, concurs with the *Republic* on the points that properly channelled feelings of pleasure and pain, while not amounting to moral knowledge (*phronesis*), are a necessary propaideutic to its acquisition (653a–c), and that our feelings of pleasure and pain are intimately related to our ethical judgements: 'when we think we are doing well (*eu prattein*), we are pleased…and when we are pleased we think we are doing well' (657c). Indeed, the 'greatest ignorance' (*amathia*) occurs when our feelings of pleasure and pain are at odds with our rational judgements (689a).[20] As in *Republic*, incorrect feelings are presented as a cognitive, not merely affective, failure.

---

[15] III 401e–402a, 402c; cf. VII 522a, 538c.   [16] 413a–e, 430a–b, cf. 431c.
[17] X 600e–601a, 602c–d, 603b–606b.   [18] Fortenbaugh 2002, 10–11, 34.
[19] For a recent discussion see Harte 2004.
[20] *Pace* Bobonich 2002: 198–99 who takes the *amathia* to be distinct from ignorance.

In contrast with the *Republic*, the *Laws* does not distinguish between spirited and appetitive parts of the non-rational soul.[21] Instead, the part of the soul that must be trained to follow reason is generally characterized as the seat of pleasures and pains and their 'anticipations' (*elpides*) (644c–d)—evidently intended to include emotions such as anger and love (645d), and fear and daring (644d, 647a–c; cf. 632a). A pervasive theme in the dialogue is that while pleasure and pain are natural objects of attraction and aversion for us, our happiness (and the success of social cooperation) requires us to be selective in our pursuit and avoidance of them.[22] While reason is accorded the task of selecting which pains to endure and which pleasures to resist (644d, 636e), two 'anticipations' are singled out as its 'assistants' (645a) in this project of resistance (646e–649c). One is a species of boldness (*tharros*), and gives reason the force to withstand the pull of inappropriate pleasures and pains. The other is shame, a species of fear, which tempers that force in the service of social ideals.[23] It is to be inculcated by the same cultural media that in *Republic* serve to 'gentle' the *thumos* of the young guardians: a life-long curriculum in music, poetry, and dance that will inculcate in the citizens a taste for the ethical life.[24] As in *Republic*, the virtuous citizens in *Laws* will be pleased by fine actions and good characters, and disgusted at and repelled by their opposites (654c–d, 655d–656b).

30.1.2 Aristotle

Aristotle follows Plato in taking virtue to be a matter of the soul's non-rational part following the rational part. Although in a number of contexts he follows Plato's division of non-rational desire into appetite and spirit,[25] he ignores the Platonic distinction when giving his own account of virtue of character—referring to the relevant non-rational part indifferently as the seat of appetite (*epithumia*), desire (*orexis*),[26] or 'affections' (*pathemata*), and consistently using '*pathos*' (passion) as a general term to refer to its activities.[27] His illustrative lists of the *pathe* conspicuously include feelings characteristic of both Platonic non-rational parts (for example, appetite and anger) and conclude with the general characterization of the *pathe* as 'involving pleasure or pain'[28]—thus reflecting the psychology of Plato's *Laws* rather than the *Republic*'s distinction between spirit and appetite.[29]

---

[21] That the psychology of *Laws* is bipartite is generally accepted: Robinson 1970: 124–5, 145; Fortenbaugh 2002: 24, Schöpsdau 1994: 229–30, Sassı 2008, 133–8. That the division in *Laws* does not invoke 'parts' strictly speaking is argued by Bobonich 2002: 260–67; criticized by Lorenz 2006: 26 and Gerson 2003: 150–3.

[22] 636d–e, 732e, 782d–783a.

[23] An interpretation defended in Meyer 2012a.

[24] *Laws* 653c–654d, 664b–d, 672e–673a.

[25] *De Anima* 414b2, 432b5–10; *De Motu Animalium* 700b22; *Rhetoric* 1369a1–4; *Eudemian Ethics* 1223a26–7, 1225b24–26; cf. *Nicomachean Ethics* 1111b10–12.

[26] Although he does not thereby deny that the rational part itself has desires. See Lorenz 2009: 183.

[27] *Nicomachean Ethics* 1102b30, 1105b20; *Eudemian Ethics* II 1, 1220a1–2.

[28] *Nicomachean Ethics* 1105b21–3 (quoted above); *Eudemian Ethics* 1220b12–14, *Rhetoric* 1378a19–21.

[29] Here we agree with Fortenbaugh 2002 and take issue with the widely influential argument by Cooper 1996a that the distinction between spirit and appetite is crucial to understanding the psychology of virtue in Aristotle.

Since it is Aristotle's moral philosophy that is most often invoked by contemporary critics as a theory according a central role to the emotions, it is worthwhile to clarify precisely the role he accords to the *pathe* in virtue of character. A few negative points may be in order here as a corrective to potential misunderstandings of his view. First of all, although Aristotle explains that the virtues are dispositions (*hexeis*) that determine when and how we will experience the *pathe*,[30] he clearly does not think that a virtue of character is simply a correct disposition of the passions.[31] None of the eleven virtues of character that he enumerates in *Nicomachean Ethics* III.6–V and *Eudemian Ethics* III–IV concerns feelings or passions alone—even those that are billed as such in Aristotle's thumbnail sketch of their domain.[32] For example, courage, while initially billed as the virtue concerning fear and confidence, evidently determines not only when a person will experience these feelings, but also how he will act—for example, whether he will stand his ground, put up a fight, or flee;[33] hence Aristotle's frequent refrain that virtue concerns 'passions and actions'.[34] Moreover, he insists, a genuine virtue of character is a disposition of our capacity for choice (*prohairesis*).[35] He explicitly refuses the label 'virtue' to dispositions governing passions alone on the grounds that they do not involve choice.[36]

Nor is it the case, in Aristotle's view, that the virtues of character are individuated by different *pathe*. One might be misled by his remarks in *Nicomachean Ethics* II 5 and *Eudemian Ethics* II 3 into expecting that each virtue of character concerns a distinctive passion or passions—in the way that courage concerns fear and confidence, temperance concerns appetites for bodily pleasures, and mildness concerns anger. It turns out, however, that it is only these three virtues whose domain Aristotle marks out with reference to a distinctive passion. The remaining virtues are demarcated by reference to types of action (e.g. spending money) or objects of pursuit (e.g. honour). All the same, Aristotle insists that even the latter virtues involve appropriate feelings of pleasure and pain. A truly generous person not only gives an appropriate sum of money, but does so with pleasure, just as a truly temperate person is pleased at abstaining from inappropriate indulgence. It is the mark of the virtuous person quite generally 'to be pleased and pained as one should'.[37]

Not just any pleasure experienced when acting appropriately is the sign of a virtuous disposition for Aristotle. For example, the pleasure of exacting (or anticipating) revenge is not evidence of courage.[38] Taking our cue from Aristotle's comments that the generous person will be pained if he 'happens' to have spent money on something that is 'contrary to what is right and fine',[39] we may suppose that the signature pleasure of virtue is pleasure in the fine (*kalon*), and that the correlative pain has the opposite, the shameful (*aischron*),

---

[30] *Nicomachean Ethics* 1105b25–1106a2; cf. *Eudemian Ethics* 1220b8–20.   [31] See Lorenz 2009.

[32] *Nicomachean Ethics* 1107a33–1108a31; *Eudemian Ethics* 1221a15–b3.

[33] Fear and confidence: *Nicomachean Ethics* 1107a33–b1; cf. *Eudemian Ethics* 1221a17–19; fight or flight: *Nicomachean Ethics* 1111a11–b3.

[34] *Nicomachean Ethics* 1104b13–14, 1106b16–1, 1107a4–9, 1109a22–4; cf. *Eudemian Ethics* 1220a31.

[35] *Nicomachean Ethics* 1106a3–4, b36, 1117a5; *Eudemian Ethics* 1227b8, 12228a23–4.

[36] *Nicomachean Ethics* 1108a30–b10, 1128b10–35; *Eudemian Ethics* III 7, especially 1234a23–6.

[37] Giving and abstaining with pleasure: *Nicomachean Ethics* 1120a25–6, b30; 1104b3–5; being pleased and pained as one should: *Nicomachean Ethics* 1104b12, 1105a7; 1121a3–4; *Politics* 1340a15.

[38] 1116b23–1117a9.   [39] *Nicomachean Ethics* 1121a1–4.

as its object. While such pleasure does not have a distinctive name, and thus does not occur as a distinct item on Aristotle's lists of the *pathe*, he regularly uses *philia* or *stergein* (love or liking) to invoke the requisite pleasures and uses 'hate' (*misein*) or 'hatred' (misos) to refer to the corresponding pain[40]—the same language that Plato uses, especially in *Laws*, to describe the pleasures and pains to be cultivated by the moral educator.[41]

The inadvertent wrongdoer who is pained upon realizing what he has done satisfies Aristotle's requirement that truly involuntary action be painful or regretted.[42] Similarly, the pain of the reluctant agent shows that her action is 'mixed'—that is, performed voluntarily but under necessity or constraint (*Nicomachean Ethics* 1110a11–13). While the latter agent might perform an action that is *kalon*, her failure to take pleasure in it shows that she is not responding to it as *kalon*, since whatever a person takes to be *kalon* appears to her as pleasant.[43] Indeed, her pain reveals that she opts for the action as a necessary evil—as do the soldiers who stand their ground in battle from fear of punishment or lack of opportunity to flee (1116a29–b2) or the intemperate person who refrains from self-indulgence under constraint (1104b3–5).[44]

While Plato emphasizes the role of musical education in shaping these pleasures and pains—a point that Aristotle acknowledges (1104b11–13), Aristotle himself stresses the importance of habituation: we become brave by performing brave actions, and temperate by performing temperate actions, and so on.[45] While such practice will not on its own train us to delight in the actions as fine (a job for which Plato's programme of cultural education is better suited), neither will cultural education on its own redirect or eliminate the fears, appetites, and aversions that might incline one in the opposite direction; for this, practice at performing right actions is necessary.[46] Aristotle concedes that some fears may be ineliminable by habituation (1115b7–12). Yet, with the exception of these limiting cases (with which we will see the Stoics are better equipped to deal), Aristotle conceives of virtue of character as a disposition in which (inter alia) the entirety of a person's affective apparatus is directed towards what is *kalon* and away from its opposite.

---

[40] *Nicomachean Ethics* 1172a22–3; 1179b24–5, b30–31; cf. 1179b9. On the connection between liking (*philia*) and taking pleasure (*chairein*) see 1117b28–31; 1175a31–6. By contrast, in the *Rhetoric* 1382a12–13 and *Politics* 1312b32–4 Aristotle denies that hatred (*misos*) is painful—on which see Fortenbaugh 2002: 105–7 and 2008; Leighton 1996: 232 n. 14; Striker 1996: 301 n. 13 and Dow 2011: 53–5.

[41] *Laws* 653b2–c4, 689a5–b2, 908b6–c1; cf. *Laws* 727e3–728a1, *Republic* 401e4–402a4, 403c6–7. Aristotle describes the requisite pleasures and pains in terms evoking the emotional repertoire accorded by Plato to the spirited part of the soul: it reflects what the person admires (*agapan*) or is impressed at (*timan*) or takes seriously (*Nicomachean Ethics* 1120a31–2, 1120b13, 1121b1; cf. 1124a10–12), or what he is disgusted at or objects to (*duscherainein*) (1179b29–30; cf. 1128a8–9, b 1–3). Burnyeat 1980, 79–80 develops this point in detail.

[42] *Nicomachean Ethics* 1110b11–12, 18–22, 1111a20–21—a requirement rooted in Aristotle's conception of force as a paradigm for involuntariness (Meyer 1993, 83–4).

[43] *Nicomachean Ethics* 1104b35–1105a2, cf. 1113a31–2.

[44] Others have interpreted the agent's pain at 1104b6–7 as due to internal conflict (Burnyeat 1980: 77, following Grant 1885 ad loc). However this would make the action a case of *enkrateia* (self-control; see *Nicomachean Ethics* VII), not the intemperance (*akolasia*) that Aristotle explicitly says it is.

[45] *Nicomachean Ethics* 1104a18–b2,1105a17–19, b5–18. On the difference between Aristotelian and Platonic habituation see Sherman 1989: ch. 5.

[46] *Nicomachean Ethics* III.12, 1119a25–7, VII 1148b15–18, 1154a33

Like Plato, Aristotle takes these feelings to have a cognitive dimension.[47] That emotions affect our judgements is his reason for paying attention to the *pathe* in his treatise on *Rhetoric*; in the *Politics*, he echoes Plato's claim that the musical training that cultivates our pleasure in what is fine and our disgust at what is shameful also shapes our ability to discriminate between fine and shameful actions; and in the *Ethics*, he points out that habituation gives us the 'first principles' of ethical reasoning.[48] Thus only the person whose feelings and desires are properly directed will have a correct grasp of the goal to pursue in his actions, and thus only he will have knowledge (*phronesis*) of what he should do.[49] The *akratic*, whose decision to do the right action is opposed by a recalcitrant desire, does not know, in the fullest sense, that what he is doing is wrong, Aristotle explains in *Nicomachean Ethics* VII 3, thus endorsing a version of Socrates' infamous pronouncement in *Protagoras*.[50]

In the Stoics we will find an even more strongly cognitive status assigned to the *pathe*, but first let us consider the Epicureans.

30.1.3 Epicureanism

According to Epicurus, the prime function of philosophy is to cure the human soul of *pathos* (Usener 221; Long and Sedley (LS) 25C). The 'pathos' he has in mind, however, is neither emotion in general (as in Aristotle's use of the term), nor defective emotion (as on the Stoics'), but rather suffering.[51] In keeping with his central doctrines that pleasure is the goal of life, that the most important pleasure is freedom from pain, and that distress of the soul far outweighs bodily pain in determining the quality of one's experience,[52] it is specifically mental distress—painful emotions—that he targets for therapy. Paramount among these, in Epicurean teaching, is fear. The famous 'four-fold remedy' (*tetrapharmakon*) targets for elimination the four principal human fears: fear of death, fear of the gods, fear that happiness is out of our reach, or that unendurable suffering will befall us (KD I–IV). The therapy it directs at these emotions is cognitive—correcting the false beliefs it takes to underlie them (e.g. that there are gods who meddle in human affairs, that death is an unpleasant experience, or that strong bodily pains are long lasting).[53] It is worth noting that these are false empirical beliefs, in contrast to the false normative judgements that (we shall see) are central to Stoic analyses of the *pathe*.[54]

---

[47] A point widely endorsed, although with considerable variety as to the details: Fortenbaugh 2002: 9–12, 94–103 and 2008 *passim*; Sherman 1989: 166–71, 184–5; Nussbaum 1994: 80–1; Cooper 1996b: 246–7; Leighton 1996: 206–17; Striker 1996: 291; Sihvola 1996: 115–21; Konstan 2006: 20–38, 43–5; Dow 2010.

[48] *Rhetoric* 1356a15–17, 1378a19–20; *Politics* 1339b1, 1340a14–17; *Nicomachean Ethics* 1098b3–4.

[49] *Nicomachean Ethics* 1140b11–20; 1142b33, 1144a29–b1, 1144b30–33, 1151a12–15.

[50] The precise nature of the ignorance that Aristotle attributes to the akratic is disputed but need not concern us here. On the state of the dispute see Price 2006.

[51] Thus Long and Sedley 1987: 25C; by contrast Annas renders it 'emotion' (Annas 1992: 195).

[52] On these doctrines see Meyer 2008: 102–15.

[53] On the range of therapeutic methods see Nussbaum 1994: chs 5–7. Cicero *Tusculan Disputations* (=*TD*) III 28–51.

[54] By contrast, Annas 1992: 190 interprets Epicurus as holding that painful and pleasant emotions involve positive and negative evaluations of their objects. The crucial text, however, says only that *our*

Other Epicurean therapies, less well attested in our sources, concern other painful emotions. Among these is anger, understood as typically involving the beliefs that one has been wronged, and that retaliation will be pleasant.[55] While the Epicureans are unanimous in targeting the latter belief for correction, they do not agree on whether anger itself is to be extirpated.[56] As a form of mental distress it would seem, by Epicurean standards, a proper target for elimination, but some forms of anger (those informed by accurate beliefs about the nature and source of the injury—for example, whether the perpetrator acted voluntarily), were considered 'natural and necessary' by many Epicureans, meaning both that they are necessary for achieving happiness, and that they are ineliminable by habituation.[57] Also natural and necessary on their view is sexual desire—when purged of the 'empty opinions' that have disastrous consequences on one's prospects for achieving *ataraxia*—and even grief.[58]

Pleasant emotions, by contrast, play an important role in Epicurean happiness. While those arising in connection with 'vain and empty opinions' are to be extirpated, those involved in, for example, gratitude and friendship loom large in the best human life—not least because of their usefulness in outweighing the unavoidable pains attendant upon natural human experience.[59] No version, however, of the 'pleasure in the *kalon*' emphasized by Plato and Aristotle figures in Epicurean ethics, presumably as a result of their insistence that virtue has purely instrumental value.[60]

30.1.4 The Stoics

While Aristotle is the first to use the term '*pathe*' to designate the emotions, it is only with the Stoics that we find a systematic and explicit theory of the *pathe* and their relation to moral judgement.[61] Their account takes place in the context of a distinction between four different motions in the soul that register the prospect (or presence) of apparent goods and evils:

---

attraction to pleasure and *aversion* to pain amount to a perception that pleasure is good and that pain is bad (Cicero, *On Moral ends* (=*Fin.*) I 30).

[55] Philodemus, *On Anger* 37:52.

[56] On the debate see Annas 1993: 194–200; Fowler 1997: 24–30, Procopé 1998: 186–9, Armstrong 2008: 112–15, Gill 2003 and 2010: 159.

[57] On natural and necessary desires see Annas 1993: 190–4 and Meyer 2008: 108–11.

[58] On these points (anger, sexual desire, grief) our textual evidence is slight (see Lucretius III, IV.1037–1287; Philodemus, *On Anger* and *On Death*) and scholars are divided on how radical a project of extirpating painful passions Epicureanism advocated. See Gill 2006: 158–9. On sexual passion in Epicureanism see Brennan 1996, Tsouna 2007: 44–7, and Armstrong 2008: 94–7.

[59] *Vatican Sayings* 17, 19, 55; *Letter to Menoeceus* 122; DL X 22, 118.

[60] Cicero, *Fin.* I 25, 35.

[61] Andronicus, *On the Passions*; Stobaeus, *Eclogae* 2.7.10–10d (Wachsmuth (=W) 2.88–92; Pomeroy 1999); Cicero *TD* 3.22–5, 4.11–22; *Lives and Opinions of the Philosophers* (=DL) 7.111–116. Other ancient sources on the Stoic doctrine are collected in Long and Sedley (=LS) 1987 §65 and in Graver 2002: 203–214.

- Reaching (*orexis*) in response a prospective apparent good;
- Swelling (*eparsis*) in response to a present apparent good;
- Shrinking away (*ekklisis*) from a prospective apparent evil;
- Contraction (*sustole*) in response to a present apparent evil.

These motions, which we experience as located in the region around the heart,[62] do not exhaust the impulses (*hormai*) of the soul, but are rather kinds of affective response.[63] The soul's 'reaching' (*orexis*) for a walk on the beach is not simply (or even necessarily) an impulse that brings about my perambulation on the sand, but rather a felt yearning for, or an attraction to, that prospect. Similarly, my soul's shrinking away (*ekklisis*) from the expected agony of a scheduled root canal is not an impulse that keeps me away from the dentist's office, but rather a psychological agitation at that prospect. Thus later writers refer to these motions as *perturbationes* and *adfectus* (affect).

The Stoics take these affective responses to be entirely natural,[64] but appropriate (*hathekon*) only when directed at genuine goods and evils. For the Stoics, virtue and its activities are the only goods, while vice and its activities are the only evils. Thus these are the only appropriate objects for affective response.[65] Such natural objects of pursuit as health, financial security, social standing, and the like, are not good (and their contraries not bad); rather both are 'indifferent'.[66] So even though it is often appropriate to select these objects as targets of pursuit ('preferred indifferents') or avoidance ('dispreferred indifferents'), and to take action accordingly, it is inappropriate to respond to them as if they were good or bad—for example, to be upset at the prospect of losing a limb or a loved one, or to yearn for job security or a good night's sleep. The Stoics reserve the term '*pathe*' for these inappropriate affective responses.

To appreciate why it is inappropriate to respond affectively to 'indifferent' objects, even when it is appropriate to pursue them via other kinds of impulse, it is helpful to note that, for the Stoics, genuine goods are worth pursuing independently of circumstances.[67] Thus they are 'worth persisting in' (*emmeneta*)[68] even when circumstances change.

---

[62] Galen, *Doctrines of Hippocrates and Plato* (=*Plac.*) 3.7 (SVF 2.900).

[63] Graver 2007 is a magisterial exposition and defence of this point (also noted by Sandbach 1975: 61). By contrast, Inwood 1985: 144–5, 146–7, 157 takes *orexis* and *ekklisis* to be generic impulses of pursuit and avoidance while only *eparsis* and *sustole* are affective reactions (this appears to be the view of Brennan 1998: 30–2, and Meyer 2008: 161–4. The Stoics, however, identify many 'practical impulses' that are not reachings, swellings, shrinkings, or contractions—Stobaeus, *Eclogae* 2.7.9–9a (W 2.87). Long and Sedley 1987, vol 1, 420 take stretching, swelling, shrinking, etc., to be marks only of excessive impulse; but this conflicts with the Stoic definitions of the *eupatheiai* as reasonable (*eulogon*) versions of these very motions (DL 7.116, Cic. *TD* 4.12–13).

[64] Cic. *TD* 4.12–13; Epictetus, *Discourses* (= *Diss*) 3.3.2 (LS 60F1).

[65] Thus Frede 1986: 107 and Graver 2007: 35–60. By contrast, Inwood 1985: 175 (criticized by Brennan 1998: 56–7) proposes that the Stoic sage will have appropriately 'reserved' affective responses to indifferents. Cooper 2005 (criticized by Kamtekar 2005) concurs.

[66] Virtue is the only good: DL 7.102; Cic. *Fin* 3.11, 21, 26–29; indifferents: DL 7.104–107; Stob. Ecl 2.7.7 / W 2.79–85.

[67] DL 7.102–4; Stobaeus 2.7.50 (W2.75), 2.7.11f (W 2.98); cf. Sextus *Adversus Mathematicos* 11.22–26.

[68] Stob. 2.7.11f (W 2.98)

Indifferent objectives, by contrast, are worth selecting only in certain circumstances (for example, one's health is not worth preserving when a tyrant is conscripting able-bodied men into his army).[69] On this picture, an impulse appropriately directed towards a good objective would be stable—persisting even in the face of variations in the circumstances—while an impulse appropriately directed towards an indifferent would be reserved and flexible—ready to be withdrawn as circumstances (or information about them) change.[70] Now it is a familiar feature of experience, often noted by the Stoics, that affective response lacks this flexibility and responsiveness to new information: the *pathe* are like bodies in free fall, unable to be called back or redirected once launched at their objectives.[71] An angry judge, for example, may continue to desire the execution of a prisoner even after evidence establishing his innocence belatedly comes to light (Seneca, *Ir.* 1.18.3–6). In this inertia and unresponsiveness to circumstances, the psychic movements of reaching, swelling, shrinking, and contracting respond to their objects as if these were genuine goods or evils[72]—without the flexibility and reserve appropriate to the pursuit of contingently worthwhile objectives.[73]

Affective responses are therefore 'excessive', 'too vigorous', and inappropriate when directed at 'indifferent' objectives. '*Pathos*' is the general term the Stoics use for such responses, which they classify into four genera:[74]

- appetite (*epithumia*)—an excessive 'reaching' (*orexis*) of the soul;
- pleasure (*hedone*)—an excessive 'expansion' (*eparsis*) of the soul;
- fear (*phobos*)—an excessive 'shrinking away' (*ekklisis*) of the soul;
- distress (*lupe*)—an excessive 'contraction' (*sustole*) of the soul.

When directed at genuine goods and evils, by contrast, affective responses constitute *eupatheiai* (good feelings—Latin, *constantiae*), which only the sage experiences:[75]

---

[69] DL 7.102–109; Stob. 2.7.7 (W 2.79–85).

[70] Such things are 'worth selecting' (*lepton*), but not 'worth choosing' (*haireton*): Stob. 2.7.50 (W 2.75); 2.7.7 (W2.79), 2.7.7c (W2.82.5); cf. Cic. *Fin.* 4.72. On 'selection' (*ekloge*) see Inwood 1985: 198, 238–40; Brennan 1998: 35–6.

[71] Seneca, *On Anger* 1.7.4; Cic. *TD* 4.41; cf. Galen, *Plac.* 4.2.10–18 (LS 65J); Stob. 2.7.10a (W 2.89–90 / LS 65A8). While scholarly consensus takes this 'runaway' feature to be distinctive of the *pathe* (see Inwood 1985: 165–72; Graver 2007: 35–60; we take the view that it is a general feature of affective response (which is perfectly appropriate in the face of genuine goods and evils.) The appropriately reserved impulse that can be called back whenever reason decides is not an *orexis, eparsis, ekklisis,* or *sustole* (as Inwood 1985: 174–5 allows it can be) but a 'selection' (*ekloge*).

[72] At least as long as they last, which is only as long as the beliefs they involve to are 'fresh' (Cicero *TD* 3.75, 4.14, 4.39; cf. Stob 2.7.10b (W 2.90)). On 'fresh' see Inwood 1985: 147–55; cf. Graver 2002: 117–19; 2007: 40–6.

[73] On the 'reservation' (*hupexairesis*, Latin: *exceptio*) of the Stoic sage (Epictetus, *Diss.* 2.6.9-10; Stob. 2.7.11s (W 2.115 / LS 65W), see Inwood 1985: 112, 119–26, 165–73—with criticisms by Brennan 2000; Sorabji 2000: 219–20; and Cooper 2005: 211 n. 14.

[74] Cicero *TD* 4.12–13, DL 7.110–111, Stob. 2.7.10 (W 2.88–89).

[75] DL 7.116, Cicero, *TD* 4.12–13; Andronicus, *On the Passions* 6 (SVF 3.432). Stobaeus does not use the generic term *eupatheia*, but includes the species identified by Diogenes and Andronicus among the activities of virtue (Eclogae 2.7.5b (W2.58 / LS 60K), 2.7.5k (W 2.73 / LS 60J), 2.7.9a (W 2.87).

- wish (*boulesis*)—a reasonable (*eulogon*) reaching of the soul;
- joy (*chara*)—a reasonable expansion of the soul;
- caution (*eulabeia*)—a reasonable shrinking away of the soul.

Each 'good feeling' is directed at virtue, vice, or an objective intimately related with these.[76] For example, the sage experiences 'joy' in the activities of temperance and is 'cautious' to avoid shameful or impious behaviour.[77] There is no 'good feeling' involving contraction (*sustole*) of the soul because the sage, being stably virtuous, will never have anything bad happen to him.[78]

So defined, the *pathe* are 'pathological' affective responses and there is no question of training them to accord with correct reason, as Aristotle and Plato taught—a doctrine that came to be known as *metriopatheia* among later philosophers. Instead, the Stoics preached *apatheia*: the wise person will be without *pathe*.[79] However, not all of the affective responses that Plato and Aristotle attribute to the virtuous person will count as *pathe* on the Stoic view. In particular, the pleasure in the *kalon* and pain at the *aischron* invoked by Plato and Aristotle as marks of the properly cultivated soul have virtue and vice as their objects, and thus coincide roughly with the Stoic *eupatheiai*. Indeed, the 'caution' of the Stoic sage would seem to amount to the 'hatred' (*misos*) of the *aischron* that Aristotle invokes. One might therefore wonder whether the Stoic doctrine of 'freedom from passion' is any more than a verbal disagreement with Platonic and Aristotelian *metriopatheia*.[80] However, even granting that the Stoic sage is not without *pathos* in Aristotle's sense of the term, there remain two substantial Stoic disagreements with Aristotle and Plato over the emotions.

The first becomes evident if we descend from the generic classification of the *pathe* and *eupatheiai* to the specific. At the generic level it is plausible to claim that the three kinds of *eupatheiai* are appropriate versions of the same affective responses (shrinkings, reachings, swellings) of which the *pathe* are inappropriate versions. But if we turn to the specific

[76] We follow Graver 2007 and Brennan 1998 and 2005 in taking the *eupatheiai* to be restricted to impulses directed at virtue, vice, and closely related objects, rather than as the class of appropriate impulses quite generally (including those directed at indifferents). The latter interpretation, suggested by Cicero's exposition in *TD* 4.12–13, goes back at least as far as Plutarch (*On Moral Virtue* 449a–b) and Lactantias, *Div. Inst.* VI 15 (SVF 3.437)—as noted by Sandbach 1975, 67–8 and Cooper 2005. Other recent proponents include Long and Sedley 1987: vol. 2, 407; Nussbaum 1994: 399–401; and Meyer 2008: 162–5. The major anomaly for such a view is that the Stoics recognize no *eupatheia* consisting in reasonable 'contraction'.

[77] Andronicus, *On the Passions* 6. On the joy of the sage, see Seneca *Epistle* 59.2. Although all the species of 'wish' (*boulesis*) attested here and in DL 7.116—cf. Stob 2.7.5b (W2.58 /LS60K1), 2.7.5c (W 2.69)—are friendly interpersonal attitudes, friendship, for the Stoics, is intimately bound up with virtue (DL 7. 94–7, 124; Stob. 2.7.11c, 11m (W 2.94–5, 2.108); Graver 2007: 173–90; Vogt 2008: 148–60.

[78] On that rationale, one might doubt that the sage needs caution to avoid wrong-doing (see Brennan 1998: 60 n. 29)—hence the attractiveness of an alternative tradition of the *eupatheiai* that posits confidence (*tharros*) as the normatively correct response that replaces fear in the sage (Cic. *TD* 4.66; Stob. 2.7.5b, 5g). See Graver 2007: 213–20.

[79] Cicero, *On Moral Ends* 3.35; DL 7.117.

[80] A criticism common in later antiquity (see Dillon 1983) and articulated more recently by Rist 1969: 26–7 and Sandbach 1975: 63.

kinds of *pathe*—for example anger (as a species of the pathos genus appetite) and fear of failure (*agonia*—a species of the *pathos* genus fear)[81]—we find no appropriate version of these emotions acknowledged by the Stoics. This is because the species of *pathe* are individuated by their objects, and all of these are 'indifferent' on the Stoic valuation. Anger and *agonia* are directed at revenge and defeat, respectively, and neither of these is the appropriate object of affective response on the Stoic view. The Stoic sage, unlike the Aristotelian, will experience none of the species of *pathe* classified into the four Stoic genera. The only objects to which the Stoic sage is attracted, by which he is delighted, and from which is repelled, are virtue, vice, and objectives intimately related to these.

A second substantial disagreement concerns the division of the soul. Aristotle and his followers, like Plato before him, take the *pathe* to issue from a non-rational part of the soul that is distinct from the properly rational part. The Stoics, by contrast, maintain that the *pathe* are simply false judgements by the rational faculty itself.[82] They are judgements, according to the Stoics, because they are impulses (*hormai*), and all impulses consist in the assent (*sunkatathesis*) by the rational faculty to an impression (*phantasia*) that something is 'appropriate' (*kathekon*).[83] The Stoics make it clear that an agent in the throes of *pathos* not only judges the object of his passion to be good (or bad), but judges it 'appropriate' to reach, shrink, swell, or contract in response to it.[84] So conceived, the passions are not simply feelings that we passively experience. They are as voluntary as any action we undertake because we judge it to be appropriate.

To the objection that human experience provides abundant evidence that we become angry, afraid, and so forth without assenting to the appropriateness of these feelings, the Stoics respond by distinguishing the *pathos* strictly speaking from certain involuntary movements of the soul or 'bitings' that might accompany or be caused by the impulsive impression. For example, the initial jolt one experiences upon the impression that one has been wronged, or that one's life is in imminent danger, is to be distinguished from genuine anger or fear. The latter are impulses that 'rush out' only upon being assented to.[85] Compare, for example, the affect involved in feeling upset in spite of one's considered judgement that nothing terrible has happened and the very different affect involved in thinking 'Woe is me!' in the same circumstances.

This doctrine of 'first movements', as it came to be called, would prove to be of considerable interest to early Christian writers, who incorporated it into the doctrine of sin[86]—without, however, endorsing the Stoic denial that the first movements are genuine *pathe*.

[81] Stob 2.7.10b (W 2.91 / LS 65E); DL 112–113.

[82] Stob. 2.7.10 (W 2.88); Seneca, *On Anger* 1.8.3. Galen reports that Posidonius, a later Stoic, dissented from this view (*Plac.* III & IV). See Cooper 1998.

[83] Stob 2.7.9. On impulsive impressions, see Inwood 1985: 54–66; Frede 1986: 106–7; Annas 1992: 91–102; Brennan 2005: 28–9, 86–90.

[84] Stob. 2.90, 7–18, Cic. *TD* 3.25, 3.76, Andronicus *On the Passions*. 1/ LS 65B.

[85] Seneca 2.1.4; Gellius *Noctes Atticae* 19.1; Cic *TD* 3.83. While it has been argued that this doctrine is a development by later Stoic writers (Sorabji 2000: 70–5 and Rist 1969: 41, with a nuanced assessment of earlier scholarship in Inwood 1985: 175–81), Graver 2007: 85–108 makes an effective case for its origins in early Stoicism.

[86] Sorabji 2000: 346–371; Knuuttila 2004: 123–4; Byers 2003.

Indeed, Augustine objects that once it is acknowledged that the sage will experience such 'first movements', it is mere terminological perversity of the Stoics to deny that the sage will experience passions.[87] This would be a fair objection if the main point to the Stoic doctrine of *apatheia* were to deny affective response to the sage. But we have already seen that this is not the case. Rather, at least one central motivation for the doctrine of *apatheia* is the core Stoic thesis that the sage never makes a false judgement. Since the Stoics take certain affective responses to be false normative judgements—about what is good and bad, and about what it is appropriate—it is reasonable for them to single out these responses and deny them to the sage. In reserving the label *pathe* for this class of feelings, they mark them off both from those affective responses that constitute knowledge (the *eupatheiai* of the sage) and from those that fall below the level of judgement (the 'first movements').[88]

30.2 EMOTIONS IN EARLY CHRISTIANITY AND MEDIEVAL PHILOSOPHY

Stoic views of the passions continue to be influential, even if not widely endorsed, into the middle ages. Among Middle Platonists and neo-Platonists in late Antiquity, a version of the sage's *apatheia* (freedom from passion) is accorded to the fully perfected soul that has become assimilated to the divine, while the synthesis of Aristotelian and Platonic doctrine that had come to be known as *metriopatheia* (moderation of the passions) is the goal for the tripartite soul in ordinary life.[89] A similar dichotomy found expression in early Christian writers such as Clement and Origen in Alexandria and Evagrius in the monastic tradition: here *apatheia* is the goal for those who aspired to a higher, ascetic ideal.[90] Nonetheless, both traditions, like Stoicism, allow that those achieving *apatheia* will still have certain feelings—most notably *agape* (love) and hope and the 'spiritual senses' that constitute knowledge of God.[91]

Augustine of Hippo (354–430 CE) inherits both these traditions and articulates an account of the emotions that will prove to be dominant in western Europe until the twelfth century.[92] Transforming the Stoics' fourfold classification of the passions into a classification of affective response quite generally—desire (*cupiditas*), delight (*laetitia*), fear (*metus*), sadness (*tristitia*) (*CD* 14.6)—he interprets all such responses as expressions of love (14.7). In his version of *metriopatheia*, the passions are good and admirable when

---

[87] Augustine, *City of God* (=*CD*) 9.4.

[88] On the *eupatheiai* as knowledge: Cicero, *TD* 4.80; Brennan 2005: 97–110.

[89] See Dillon 1986; Knuuttila 2004: 87–103. In contrast to Aristotle's view that the emotions should have appropriate intensity and objects, *metropatheia* was typically understood by these thinkers as a condition of considerably diminished emotional intensity.

[90] Knuuttila 2004: 113–51; Sorabji 2000: 385–97.

[91] Clement, *Stromata* 6.9; Origen, *Contra Celsum* 1.48.

[92] Augustine, *CD* 9.4–5, 14.1–26. See James 1997: 114–15; Knuuttila 2004: 152–62; King 2010: 169–70. On Augustine's earlier views on the passions, see Colish 1985: 221–5.

they express love of God, but pernicious when informed by love of mundane objects (14.7, 14.9). A good Christian in the present life will experience appropriate passions of all four kinds, but in the world to come will experience only versions of desire, delight, and a kind of 'tranquil fear' reminiscent of the Stoic *eupatheia* 'caution' (14.9; cf. 9.5)—thus returning to the condition of Adam and Eve before their original sin (14.10). It is the fallen condition of humanity that makes sadness and fear appropriate passions in the present life (14.9), and it is in punishment for Adam and Eve's transgression that we are susceptible to the involuntary 'first movements' (14.12, 15, 19). Augustine conceives of these as painful and disturbing feelings—especially of fear, anger, and sexual arousal—that arise in spite of and even in opposition to our will.[93] For Augustine, as for other early Christian appropriators of this Stoic doctrine, the 'first movements' involve (or are) sinful thoughts and the prescribed remedy is thoroughly Stoic: refuse assent, thereby preventing the initial movements from developing into strong and uncontrollable passions.[94]

By the twelfth century, the Augustinian analysis of the passions as forms of love has absorbed the fourfold Stoic classification to yield a more fundamental dichotomy into those passions that are expressions of love, and those that are expressions of hate, with the four Stoic genera (hope now replacing desire) sorted into these two fundamental categories. In a further twist, not found in Augustine, these two categories now tend to be identified, respectively, as 'concupiscible' and 'irascible'—Latin terminology for Plato's appetitive (*epithume-tikon*) and spirited (*thumoeides*) parts of the soul.[95] The source for this Platonic strand in the doctrinal mixture is the widespread practice in late antiquity of dividing the soul first, as Aristotle did, into passion (*pathos*) and reason, and then further dividing the 'passionate' part (quite contrary to Aristotle's own practice) into *epithumia* and *thumos*.[96] This Platonic division of the non-rational part of the soul persists as a tenet of the new Aristotelianism that arises in the mid-twelfth century when the works of Avicenna, Averroes, and Aristotle become available in Latin translation.[97] The central question addressed by theorists of the passions remains, which passions are concupiscible and which are irascible?

Earlier thinkers in the period take the concupiscible passions to be reactions to apparent goods and irascible passions to be responses to apparent evils; thus hope and joy, given their positive valence, belong to the concupiscible faculty, while the negative

---

[93] *CD* 14.15–19; see Sorabji 2000: 400–17.

[94] Knuuttila 2004: 122–3. Sorabji 2000: 346–55; Byers 2003: 442–8.

[95] Isaac of Stella (1100–1169), *Letter to Alcher on the Soul (Patrologia Latina (= PL)* 194:1877b–1879b) §§4–6 and Anonymous, *On the Spirit and the Soul* (PL 180:779–830, §§4, 13, 46), both translated in McGinn 1977, where 'concupiscible' and 'irascible' appetites are rendered 'positive appetites' and 'negative appetites'. By contrast, Augustine invokes a Platonic division of non-rational impulse into *libido* and *ira* at *CD* 14.19, but does not use it to classify the passions; indeed, he classifies *ira* as a kind of *libido* (14.15).

[96] On the later classical tradition see Vander Waerdt 1985. This hybrid division of the soul, along with a rudimentary attempt to sort the passions into 'spirit' and 'appetite', appears in chapters XVI–XXI of Nemesius, *On Human Nature*—a fourth-century CE work widely excerpted by later Christian writers and attributed to Gregory of Nyssa, which was translated into Latin twice in the eleventh and twelfth centuries (Sharples and Van der Eijk 2008: 4). See Knuuttila 2004: 103–10; Brungs 2002: ch. 1 and 2008: 171–7.

[97] On Avicenna's use of the distinction see Knuuttila 2004: 222; Brungs 2002: 33–40.

valence of fear and sorrow locates them in the irascible.[98] While the terminology here is Platonic, the conception of the 'irascible' part would be unrecognizable to Plato. Later thinkers take the defining mark of an irascible passion to be difficulty in achieving (or avoiding) its object. Thus the Franciscan Jean de la Rochelle and, following him, Albert the Great classify hope and anger as irascible appetites, and desire and sorrow as concupiscible—a view that becomes orthodoxy in Scholastic Aristotelianism when it is taken up by Thomas Aquinas in his magisterial taxonomy of the passions (*ST* IaIIa 22–48).[99] While the latter criterion for the 'irascible' more accurately reflects Plato's own conception of the 'thumoeides' part of the soul[100]—its incorporation into an avowedly Aristotelian psychology is a distinctively medieval synthesis.

On the moral and epistemological status of the passions, even if not on their classification, the Scholastic tradition has many points of continuity with its Classical roots. Aquinas explicitly follows Augustine in advocating *metriopatheia* rather than Stoic *apatheia* (IaIIae 24.2). Like Plato and Aristotle, he takes moral virtue to require not the elimination but the proper direction of the passions (59.2–3)—although the theological virtues he invokes involve feelings (most notably love of God) that he declines to classify as passions in the strict sense, since they are activities of the will (intellectual appetite).[101] Even as activities of the sensible appetite, however, the passions have a significant cognitive component, since evaluative judgements by *ratio particularis* are integral to their causation.[102]

30.3 EMOTIONS IN SEVENTEENTH-CENTURY MORAL PHILOSOPHY

30.3.1 Descartes

While Descartes announces that his account of the passions constitutes a break with 'the ancients' (PA 1),[103] there are many points of continuity between his own analysis and those of his predecessors. His main disagreement is with the Scholastics, whose faculty

---

[98] John Blund, *Treatise on the Soul* (1210), and Alexander of Neckham (1157–1217) following Isaac of Stella (1100–1169) and a tradition of thought going back to Jerome and Gregory in the monastic tradition. Brungs 2002: 40–52; Knuuttila 2004: 228–30; King 2010: 172, 175.

[99] On the 'irascible' as difficult or arduous: Jean de la Rochelle (d. 1245), *Summa de anima* 2.107; Albertus Magnus (d. 1280), *de Homine qq.* 66–7; Thomas Aquinas (1124–1274), *Summa Theologiae* Ia 81.2, IaIIae 23.1; Brungs 2002: ch. 1; Gauthier 1951: 321–38.

[100] See Meyer 2012b.

[101] ST IaIIae.22.3 ad 3; 31.3–4. On passions of the will, see Kent 1995: 211–12, James 1997: 60–2, Hirvonen 2002: 162–5, and Dixon 2003: ch. 2.

[102] *Ratio particularis* in Aquinas: *ST* Ia.78.4, 81.3. See King 1999: 126–31; Brungs 2002: 73–83; and Pickavé 2008: 192–5. Aquinas here develops and dissents from Avicenna's attribution to humans of a *vis estimativa;* see Hasse 2000: 127–53.

[103] *Les passions de l'âme* = PA. On the roots of Descartes' position in late Scholastic criticisms of Aquinas, see King 2002: 251.

psychology he rejects, and along with it the distinction between irascible and concupiscible appetites (PA 68) that was central to medieval taxonomies of the passions. There is only one faculty of the soul, which Descartes, like the Stoics, identifies with the mind. The passions, he writes, are perceptions or feelings that (a) we 'relate especially to the soul' (as distinct from feelings of hunger, which we relate to the body, or perceptions of colour or sound, which we relate to external objects) and that (b) are 'caused, maintained and fortified' by movements of the animal spirits in the body (27), the latter affecting the soul via the pineal gland (30–7). Those animal spirits may and typically do also directly affect the body, as when fear readies the body to flee (38), but the 'principal effect' of the passions is to 'incite and dispose their soul to desire those things for which they prepare their body', as fear inclines one to want to flee (40). Whether the soul accepts what the passion incites it to do is a matter for the will to decide (41, 144). Thus an activity analogous to Stoic assent plays a role in the causal trajectory of a passion, according to Descartes, although he follows his medieval predecessors in classifying as a passion the psychic movement that makes the recommendation, while the Stoics would classify it as a preliminary to passion.

Like Aquinas, Descartes also recognizes a class of feelings that arise from the actions of the will—most notably intellectual joy and sadness (91–3, 147–8). Phenomenally similar to the passions, and often arising in conjunction with them, he calls them *émotions*, which he distinguishes from *passions* on the grounds that the soul is active with respect to them rather than passive (i.e. moved by animal spirits). Intellectual joy, for example, is the enjoyment the soul has 'in the good it represents to itself as its own' (91), and can coexist along with the passion of joy, but also with contrary passions—as for example when one enjoys being frightened at the theatre, or indulging in lamentation (147). Of particular importance is the joy that the soul can derive from its own virtue (148)—Descartes' version of the pleasure in the *kalon* that Plato and Aristotle attribute to the virtuous person, and also akin to the Stoic *eupatheia* of joy. The importance Descartes attaches to this *émotion* lies in its power to outweigh in sheer magnitude the disturbances caused by the passions (148)—a version of Epicurus' point about the primacy of mental over bodily pleasures in the fourth remedy (*Principal Doctrines* (KD) IV).

While Descartes' interest in the passions is avowedly that of the natural philosopher rather than a moralist,[104] he does endorse in passing his medieval predecessors' rejection of Stoic *apatheia*. Not all passions are wrong—pity, compassion, and reverence, for example, are all important (PA 187)—although many passions need to be resisted (144).[105] His accounts of individual passions and the strategies he recommends for controlling them show that he also follows his predecessors in taking the passions to be intimately connected to value judgements. The passions 'fortify and perpetuate thoughts in the soul' (74, 160) about whether or not their objects are 'agreeable' (*convenable*) or 'estimable';[106]

---

[104] Adam and Tannery 1957, XI 326, Preface to *PA*; reply to second letter 14 August 1649.

[105] On mastery of passions in Descartes, see Brown 2002: 261–2.

[106] *PA* 48, 55, 57, 79, 149, 160–162; on passions as involving representations: Brown 2002: 264–6 and 2006: chs 3 and 4; James 1997: 89–90; 1998: 934.

and they exaggerate the strength of the reasons for taking the course of action they urge on the will (211). The principal strategy for resistance that Descartes recommends involves the cultivation of what his predecessors called 'magnanimity' and that he prefers to call 'generosity' (161).[107] This is a complex passion that involves value judgements, highly reminiscent of the Stoic Epictetus, to the effect that the only thing of value is choosing well, and hence that only what depends entirely on our will is an appropriate object of concern.[108] In sketching the value judgements suitable for controlling the passions, Descartes sometimes slips from Stoic to Peripatetic doctrine (according to which things other than virtue can have value), or even into Epicurean counsel against the prudence of cultivating 'vain desires' (145). The eclecticism of his theory of value notwithstanding, the salient point is that Descartes takes passions to present and to be responsive to considerations about value.

The robustly cognitive status that Descartes accords to the passions is a point of continuity with the ancient tradition as far back as Plato and Aristotle, and even with the neo-Aristotelianism of Avicenna and the Scholastics. Unlike the ancients, however, and consistent with his stance as a 'natural philosopher' rather than a moralist, Descartes betrays no interest in articulating a position on the relation of the passions to moral knowledge. Other seventeenth-century philosophers are less reticent about the moral epistemology of the passions. Most notable among these is Spinoza, to whom we now turn.

30.3.2 Spinoza

Spinoza embraces the thoroughgoing cognitivism of the Stoic theory of the passions. Like Descartes, he rejects the faculty psychology of the neo-Aristotelians. For Spinoza, the only activities of the soul are ideas, which affirm or deny what is true or false (2p48–49),[109] and 'affection' (*adfectus*, his most general term for emotions) is a kind of idea: 'By affect I understand affectations of the body by which the body's power of acting is increased or diminished, aided or restrained, and at the same time the ideas of these affections' (3d3). In defining the affects first in terms of bodily states and then in terms of ideas, Spinoza does not mean they have two constituent parts or even moments, one bodily and the other mental,[110] for 'a mode of extension and the idea of that mode are one and the same thing, but expressed in two ways' (2p7s). Bodily states as well as our ideas of those states, in his view, are but two parallel modes of a single substance (God, on his monistic metaphysics). The definition also invokes Spinoza's conatus doctrine:

---

[107] On generosity see Brown 2002: 273–5 and 2006: ch. 8. On magnanimity see Gauthier 1951.

[108] PA 145, 152–161, 203; *Letter to Porot* Jan 1641 AT III 279 (quoted in Brown 2002: 259); cf. Epictetus, *Encheiridion* 1.

[109] See also Curley 1975, Della Rocca 2008, and Marshall 2008. In-text references to Spinoza's *Ethics* are, unless otherwise noted by part, proposition (p), definition (d), scholium (s), and corollary (c).

[110] In this regard, Spinoza is to be contrasted with Malebranche, who held that emotions have seven moments, beginning with a judgement, moving through motivation, and ending with a series of sensations (*The Search After Truth*, V.3).

'Everything, in so far as it is in itself, endeavors to persist in its own being' (3p6). Each mode has a 'power of acting', an increase in which contributes towards the mode's perfection, while a decrease is a move away from perfection. Thus, focusing on the mode of ideas, one's affects are representations of changes in our bodily states—that is, representations of either increases or decreases in one's physical power of acting. At the same time, these representations are themselves changes in the active power of the mind.

Spinoza follows the Stoic classification of the emotions, but combines desire and fear into a single category (cupiditas), resulting in a tri-partite taxonomy:

- *laetitia* (translated as both 'joy' and 'pleasure'), a transition to greater power (3da2);
- *tristitia* ('sadness,' 'pain,' or 'unpleasure'), a transition to diminished power (3da3); and
- *cupiditas* ('desire'), conscious striving in accordance with the conatus (3da1).

All other affects—of which there are innumerably many (3p56)—are built out of these three. For example, 'Love is nothing else but pleasure [joy] accompanied by the idea, of an external cause' (3p13s).

An affect in any of these categories can be either active (an activity of the mind) or passive (a passion, 3d3). As a physical mode, an affect is passive to the degree that it is caused by external sources; as a mental mode, it is passive to the degree that it is 'inadequate and confused' (2p41). Since we are here most interested in the affects as potential forms of knowledge, we will focus on the mental mode. Suppose one experiences joy at a personal accomplishment—say, setting a new personal record in a race. As a mode of thought, this affect is a representation of one's increase in physical power as a result of the win—the thought that one is stronger and faster than one was before, perhaps also that one merits admiration on the part of others, and so on. This thought is 'inadequate and confused' because, very roughly, one's body is not the sufficient cause for one's physical increase in power. Other factors, such as the weather and the course conditions, are part of the story as well; however, we are incapable of adequately conceiving of causes external to our bodies, representing all external causes in terms of how they impinge on our bodies. When the runner feels joy at her success, then, she confusedly represents the entire explanation for her increase in physical power in terms of her bodily states, relying on inadequate conceptions of the weather and course conditions as somehow essentially tied to her physical state. This is what Spinoza calls the 'first kind of knowledge' (2p40schol2)—'particular things represented to our intellect fragmentarily, confusedly, and without order through our senses'—and it is 'the only source of falsity' (2p41). Active affects, by contrast, are adequate and unconfused ideas. They represent changes in physical power as they really are, not simply in terms of how they impinge on the body,[III]

[III] An adequate idea, as Radnor puts it, 'is one which, considered in itself, has all the internal signs of a true idea. Since a true idea is one which represents a thing as it really is, an adequate idea is one which, considered in itself, has all the internal signs of an idea which represents a thing as it really is' (Radnor 1971: 352, Spinoza 2def4).

and arise either from reasoning ('the second kind of knowledge') or from intuition (the 'third kind') (2p39, 2p40schol2).[112]

Not to put too fine a point on it, then, passive affects are false beliefs about the causes of one's increases and decreases in physical power, while active affects are a matter of knowing about ourselves, the world, and our place in the world. To know these matters completely, in Spinoza's view, is to have knowledge of God or Nature, which he calls the highest virtue (4p28, 4p36d).[113] This state of knowledge Spinoza calls 'man's highest happiness' or 'blessedness' (4App4). It is not a feeling that accompanies this knowledge, but rather it is the state of having this knowledge, acquired not through sense perception but through reason and intuition. As knowledge of what increases and decreases one's powers of activity, it amounts, in Spinoza's view, to knowledge of the good.[114] Thus a passive affect is a false belief about the good, while an active affect amounts to knowledge of the good.

Among the active affects Spinoza counts courage, the pleasure of striving to preserve oneself purely under the direction of reason, and generosity, the pleasure of striving to unite with and benefit others, again purely under the direction of reason (3p59c). Another important active affect for Spinoza is the pleasure of knowing oneself and the operations of one's affects, in particular knowing about the passive effects and how they operate upon us (5p15). The latter knowledge, itself an active affect, allows us better to control (even if not entirely expunge) the passive affects. Thus, as with the Stoics, we find in Spinoza an account of the emotions according to which most of them are false beliefs that can be controlled and countered by true beliefs about what is good and virtuous.

30.3.3 The Cambridge Platonists

The seventeenth century also sees the rise of a new twist on the ancient tradition that properly cultivated emotions are necessary for moral knowledge. In contrast to the neo-Stoicism of Spinoza, which identifies passions (and their corrected counterparts) with the activity of intellect, the Cambridge Platonists, most prominently Henry More (1614–1687) and Ralph Cudworth (1617–1689), accept a sharp distinction between reason and emotion. Inspired by the Augustinian and Christian reworking of neo-Platonism, they take the emotion of love (when properly directed to worthy objects)—to be the source of a higher knowledge (non-propositional) than is possible through the use of reason alone.[115]

---

[112] On the relation between reasoning and intuition see Brandom 2008.

[113] Virtue more broadly characterized is simply the power of activity (4def8). Also see Kisner 2008.

[114] At 4p8d Spinoza writes 'We call good or bad that which is advantageous, or an obstacle to the preservation of our being; that is, that which increases or diminishes, helps or checks, our power of activity.' However, he also holds that what helps us to satisfy our desires is good, and that we sometimes desire things other than what strengthens our power of activity. There is thus a debate among Spinoza scholars as to whether Spinoza held a desire-satisfaction theory of the good. Kisner 2010 provides an overview of this debate and argues that, for Spinoza, satisfying our desires necessarily increases our power and vice versa, thereby resolving this apparent tension.

[115] James 1998: 1377, 1381–2, 1385–90.

30.4 EMOTIONS IN EIGHTEENTH-CENTURY MORAL PHILOSOPHY

30.4.1 Kant and the Moral Sense Theorists

In the eighteenth century the 'moral sense theorists' hold that it is not by reason but by the operations of a kind of 'sense' that one grasps moral good and evil.[116] Building on Shaftesbury's work while embracing Locke's empirical methods, Francis Hutcheson argues that we have a 'moral sense' that perceives virtue and vice and also approves and disapproves of them. Immanuel Kant, in his so-called 'Prize Essay' (1770), embraces a similar view, and throughout his career he appears to conceive of emotions as pleasurable and painful representations akin to perceptions. Of course, by the time of the *Groundwork for the Metaphysics of Morals* (1785), Kant no longer thinks that moral knowledge is due to the operations of a sense, but instead argues for the purely *a priori* rational apprehension of the moral law. Feelings, especially respect, continue to play an important, perhaps indispensible role in empirical moral motivation, but are not themselves ways of apprehending or knowing moral obligation.[117] For Hutcheson and the moral sense theorists, by contrast, at least some emotions are a source of what is arguably a kind of moral knowledge.

30.4.2 Hutcheson

A sense, Hutcheson argues in *An Essay on the Nature and Conduct of the Passions and Affections*, is a 'Determination of our Minds to receive Ideas independently of our Will, and to have Perceptions of Pleasure and Pain (*Essay* 1.1, 4).[118] In addition to the five physical senses, he claims, we have four senses 'of the mind': an Internal Sense or Sense of Imagination, a Public Sense, a Moral Sense, and a Sense of Honour. Each of these is a 'Power' to receive pleasurable and painful sensations along with 'Images' or apprehensions of a certain class of objects. The three senses most directly relevant to ethics are the Public Sense, by which we feel pleasure and pain at others' well-being and suffering, the Moral Sense, by which we feel pleasure and pain at our own and others' virtue and vice,

---

[116] Hutcheson distinguishes moral good from 'natural good or advantage' (I 2.1.1, p. 117). In-text references to Hutcheson are to *An Inquiry into the Original of our Ideas of Beauty and Virtue* and the *Essay on the Nature and Conduct of the Passions with Illustrations on the Moral Sense*, by Treatise, Section, and Sub-section. Page references are to the Liberty Fund editions.

[117] See Guyer 2010; *pace* Reath 2006. Kant's views on the role of emotion in moral motivation are beyond the scope of the present chapter, but are the subject of a growing literature. See Denis 2000, Sorensen 2002, and Guyer 2010.

[118] In-text references to *An Essay* are by section and article number, with page references to the Liberty Fund edition.

and the Sense of Honour, by which we feel pleasure and pain at others' approval and disapproval of us.

It is in terms of these pleasures and pains that Hutcheson defines the 'Affections' or 'Passions'. These are 'Perceptions of Pleasure or Pain, not directly raised by the Presence or Operation of the Event or Object, but by our Reflection upon, or Apprehension of their present or certainly future Existence' (*Essay* 2.1, 28). To be clear, Hutcheson is not talking about perceiving pleasure and pain, but rather perceptions that are pleasurable or painful; affections and passions are pleasurable and painful mental states caused by and directed towards the anticipation of or reflection upon direct sensations—hence they might be called 'indirect sensations'. He illustrates the distinction with the examples of, first, the pleasure of viewing a beautiful house versus the pleasure of reflecting on the fact that one owns the house and can enjoy the pleasure of viewing it at any time and, second, the pain of an episode of gout versus the pain of anticipating its return (*Essay* 2.1, 28).

Hutcheson adopts the basic taxonomy inherited from the Stoics by way of Cicero, identifying desire, aversion, joy, and sorrow as the four basic affections (*Essay* 3.2, 63). He sometimes reserves 'affection' for desire and aversion, conceived of as unfelt volitional states, and thereby as distinct from joy and sorrow, which are 'only a sort of Sensation' (*Essay* 3.2, 49).[119] However, he generally uses 'affection' in the wider sense that encompasses unfelt volitional states (desire and aversion), non-volitional reflective or indirect sensations (joy and sorrow), and combinations of the two. Among the affections that are or include sensations, Hutcheson singles out a subset of 'confused' and 'violent' affections, which he calls 'passions' in a restricted sense. These are 'occasioned or attended by some violent bodily Motions' and 'prevent all deliberate Reasoning about our Conduct' (*Essay* 2.2, 29–30). Although Hutcheson does not always follow this terminological distinction, the contrast he indicates here between the calm and the violent is important to his moral theory, which instructs us to use reason and the calm affections to subdue and control the violent passions, ultimately giving precedence to calm universal benevolence.

The affections as Hutcheson describes them involve either 'Apprehension' of good or evil (desire and aversion) or 'Reflection' upon the actual or impending presence of good or evil (joy and sorrow, *Essay* 3.2, 63). Here, 'good or evil' is the prospect of causing agreeable or uneasy sensations, which include sensual pleasures, the pleasures of imagination, pleasures due to perception of public happiness, the pleasures of the moral sense, and the pleasures of honour (*Essay* 1.2, 18–19). For our purposes, the important affections are those involved in the moral sense's apprehension of moral virtue and vice. A person is virtuous in so far as she is motivated by benevolence. Partial benevolence is good, but universal benevolence is better—that is, gives rise to stronger and more pleasurable feelings of approval. These feelings of moral approval and disapproval are (arguably) a kind of cognitive apprehension, even if they do not amount to the kind of knowledge we can acquire through scientific and rational study of the world. Our moral

---

[119] A point he urges against Malebranche.

sense is our power to perceive virtue and vice—that is, to receive the pleasurable and painful ideas of benevolent and malevolent motives. While some of these perceptions may be direct sensations, others are surely genuine affections, arising from reflection upon and anticipation of virtue and vice.

In 1955, William Frankena argued that Hutcheson is a 'non-cognitivist', meaning that he 'regards ethical utterances as purely emotive, expressively or dynamically—as expressing and evoking emotions. But [he] insists that the emotion expressed or evoked is a unique moral emotion, not just any pro or con attitude, not even just the feeling of benevolence or sympathy' (Frankena 1955, 366). Now, it is surely anachronistic to attribute any analysis of ethical utterances to Hutcheson, but the suggestion in broader terms is that Hutcheson is some kind of anti-realist about moral virtue and vice, and believes our feelings of approval and disapproval are purely subjective, reflecting nothing that is 'really in' their objects. This widely respected interpretation derives support from the analogy Hutcheson draws between virtue and beauty, and from his repeated remark that beauty is a mind-dependent quality. For example: '[B]y Absolute or Original Beauty, is not understood any Quality suppos'd to be in the Object, which should of itself be beautiful, without relation to any Mind which perceives it: For Beauty, like other Names of sensible Ideas, properly denotes the Perception of some Mind' (*Beauty* 1.17, 14). On such a reading of Hutcheson, moral approbation and disapprobation cannot count as genuine apprehensions of virtue and vice—instead, they are something more like projections.

While it is not our aim here to insist that the anti-realist reading of Hutcheson is definitely mistaken, we do want to point out an alternative interpretation that is also very plausible, and that gives approbation and disapprobation a more genuinely cognitive role. To be sure, Hutcheson does not think of virtue and vice as Lockean primary qualities—as is clear from the analogy with Beauty, and remarks such as 'Approbation cannot be supposed an Image of any thing external' (*Illustrations* 4.1, 288).[120] On the other hand, there are his repeated arguments against his egoist opponents (Hobbes, Mandeville, Locke), that it would be a capricious creator who made us care only about the interests that serve self-love, because then we would fail to be motivated by what is good. Even more to the point, there is his remark, added to the fourth edition of *An Inquiry Concerning the Original of Our Ideas of Virtue of Moral Good*: 'The Perception of the Approver, tho' attended with Pleasure, plainly represents something quite distinct from this Pleasure; even as the Perception of external Forms is attended with Pleasure, and yet represents something distinct from this Pleasure' (note 47).[121]

The best way to reconcile these remarks with the texts that appear to support the projectivist reading is to attribute two anti-Lockean theses to Hutcheson. First, secondary qualities are real and external to the person representing them, even if they are mind-dependent in the sense that they cannot be fully characterized without reference to an experiencing subject. Second, representation need not involve resemblance.[122] The first

---

[120] Also see Radcliffe 1986: 415.   [121] See Norton 1985.
[122] McDowell 1988 argues for these two theses, though not in connection with Hutcheson.

thesis allows that beauty and virtue may not be 'suppos'd to be in the Object…without relation to any Mind which perceives it' while at the same time the pleasurable idea, approbation, represents 'something quite distinct from this Pleasure'; a secondary quality, as the first thesis characterizes it, is distinct from its representation, and yet is not attributable to objects without mentioning minds. And the second thesis makes this realist account of secondary qualities consistent with Hutcheson's insistence that approbation is not an 'image of anything external' (i.e. emphasis on 'image')—representations of secondary qualities do not resemble them; they are not images.

If something like this interpretation is correct, then approbation and disapprobation, as Hutcheson conceives them, are representations of external though mind-dependent qualities—and when they succeed in representing the world the way it really is, they are genuine apprehensions of virtue and vice. Such 'affects' would amount to a kind of moral cognition.

30.4.3 Hume

In Hume we find a more unambiguous non-cognitivism about the passions. He most often uses the term 'emotion' to refer to a bodily disturbance or 'motion', i.e. pleasure or pain, while referring to the class of phenomena we call emotions as 'passions'. The violent passions cause emotions, while the calm passions—often mistaken for reason—'produce little emotion in the mind, and are more known by their effects than by their immediate feeling or sensation' (T2.3.3.9).[123] In Book II of the *Treatise of Human Nature*, 'Of the Passions', Hume develops a theory of the passions and examines the causes and effects of specific passions. He is particularly interested in what he calls the 'indirect' passions—pride, humility, love, hatred—along with the moral passions of approbation and disapprobation.

In contrast with the views we have reviewed to this point, Hume's account of the passions emphasizes that they are non-representational. Hume quite explicitly thinks of representation as a matter of resemblance, and thus believes that the passions do not represent the world in either the robust Stoicist-Spinozistic sense (involving beliefs) or in the weaker Platonic-Aristotelian-Hutchesonian sense (involving cognitive apprehensions). In Hume's terms, all passions are impressions rather than ideas.

In contrast to the impressions of sensation, the passions are impressions had in response to ideas or to other impressions. Hume thus calls them 'impressions of reflexion' (T1.1.2.1). Although non-representational (for the reasons given above) they still have objects.[124] Hume seems to hold that the passions are directed towards the objects they cause us to

---

[123] In-text references to the *Treatise of Human Nature* (T) are by Book, Part, Section, and Paragraph.

[124] That the emotions have intentional objects is now widely accepted, so that even those who believe emotions are bodily states or perceptions of bodily states (the so-called 'James-Lange' theory of the emotions, endorsed by Damasio 1994 and Prinz 2004, among others) feel obligated to provide an account of how such states can be about or directed towards objects. Although some philosophers argue that the intentionality of the emotions entails that they involve beliefs (Kenny 1963, Taylor 1985), there are many different theories of intentionality that avoid this implication (see Prinz 2004, Goldie 2000, Calhoun 2003).

think about, or to which they direct our attention.[125] The indirect passions, on which Hume lavishes his attention, have a complex 'double' intentionality, one object being the cause ('that idea, which excites them') and the other 'that to which they direct their view, when excited' (T2.1.2.4). For example, when I contemplate the idea of a beautiful house, this idea causes a pleasurable impression, which is a reflective impression or passion. This passion could be simply the direct passion, call it something like *aesthetic enjoyment of the house*, which is both caused by and directed towards the house as a beautiful object. Alternatively (or additionally), the pleasurable impression could lead my thoughts, according to the principles of association developed in the first Book, to a related idea: that of the owner, who happens to be me. In this case, the pleasurable impression takes on a new dimension; it is now directed towards me. Now it is pride.[126] In general, the indirect passions involve the mind's movement from one idea to another, and from one impression to another. This 'double impulse', as Hume calls it, also characterizes the moral passions.

The moral passions—or 'sentiments' as Hume tends to call them—are those involved in moral evaluation, and take character (virtue and vice) as their primary object. 'To have the sense of virtue, is nothing but to feel a satisfaction of a particular kind from the contemplation of a character' (T3.1.2.3). While we do morally assess individual motives, passions, and actions, it is only because of a connection we assume or perceive between them and 'stable and durable principles of the mind, which...enter into the personal character' (T3.3.1.4). Virtue and vice are those character traits the contemplation of which causes a particular kind of pleasure or uneasiness. We feel approbation towards both 'artificial virtues' like justice, fidelity, veracity, and integrity, because they are useful and 'natural virtues' like benevolence, humanity, and friendship' (T3.3.1), because they are immediately pleasing.[127]

In contrast with the almost obsessive detail of the sections on pride, humility, love, hatred and their subsidiaries, Hume's account of the moral passions is surprisingly unclear beyond his unequivocal statement of two key points: that our sense of virtue and vice is not derived from self-interest (T3.1.2);[128] and that it is not derived from reason (T3.1.1). On the question of whether the moral passions are direct or indirect, by contrast, Hume is surprisingly reticent. Indeed, in at least one passage he appears to identify the four, core indirect passions with the moral passions.

> Pride and humility, love and hatred are excited, when there is any thing presented to us, that both bears a relation to the object of the passion, and produces a separate

[125] See Cohon 2008, *pace* Baier 1991.

[126] In fact, strictly speaking, Hume thinks there are two pleasurable impressions at work in pride, one 'separate' from the passion and one a part of it. He doesn't spell it out, but it seems the 'separate' pleasure could be either an impression of sensation—if it is caused by looking at the beautiful house—or the impression of reflection, *aesthetic enjoyment of the house*—if it is caused by contemplating the idea of the beautiful house.

[127] In the *Enquiry Concerning the Principles of Morals*, see Part 3, Section 2, on the artificial and natural virtues.

[128] Though the conventional virtues arise because of self-interest, we do not morally approve them because of their contribution to our interests (T3.1.2).

sensation related to the sensation of the passions. Now virtue and vice are attended with these circumstances. They must necessarily be plac'd in either ourselves or others, and excite either pleasure or uneasiness; and therefore must give rise to one of these four passions. (T3.1.2.5)

On a closer look, however, he equates 'virtue and vice' with only the causes of the person-directed indirect passions. Moreover, by 'virtue and vice' here, he seems to mean the things we evaluate as virtuous or vicious, i.e. the character traits 'plac'd' in persons. In other words, Hume identifies the objects towards which moral passions are directed as possible causes of pride, humility, love, and hatred. We thus feel proud or humble when it is pleasurable or painful to think about ourselves as possessors of admirable or despicable traits, and we feel love or hatred when it is pleasurable or painful to think about others as possessors of their admirable or despicable traits. The moral passions, by contrast, are directed not towards people as possessors of traits, but towards the traits themselves.[129]

The moral passions are revealed as distinct from the person-directed indirect passions because they take different, although closely related, objects. The distinctness of the moral passions cannot be only a matter of their objects, however. One might, for example, both admire and feel anxious about a competitor's industriousness (T3.1.2.4). This is possible, Hume argues, because the two passions presuppose different perspectives: specifically moral passions arise when we consider a character 'in general', and abstract specifically from our own interests (T3.1.2.4). In other passages, he adds that these 'peculiar sentiments' arise when we consider the effects a person's character has on the people with whom she interacts (T3.3.1.17), and even upon herself (for example, T3.3.1.30). When it comes to evaluating our own characters, we look both to how we affect others, and how others evaluate us (T3.3.1.26). In general, the moral passions arise when we take a 'common' point of view.

One might worry that this account of the moral passions contradicts Hume's arguments that our moral sense is not derived from reason—for the effects of a person's character on herself and other people are matters of fact discernable by reason. On Hume's view, however, our observations of or thoughts about these facts lack all evaluative tenor until we have a passionate response, even if a very calm one. We respond to these facts by feeling the moral passions, because of the operations of sympathy.[130] These passions are not derived from reason, and so neither is our moral sense. Our moral passions, entirely non-representational impressions, are crucial to moral motivation, but cannot be forms of moral knowledge, in either of the senses we reviewed previously.

---

[129] In contrast with the first book of the *Treatise*, where Hume despaired of analysing personal identity, in the second and third Books he proceeds without these metaphysical worries, suggesting there are many things that pick us out as individual persons, including our character traits (see Baier 1991).

[130] Hume seems to develop two different accounts of the pleasurable and 'uneasy' responses we have when we think about characters and their effects on people. In the *Treatise*, he appeals to the operations of 'sympathy', an empathetic capacity to, we might say, 'catch' other people's feelings. In the *Enquiry Concerning the Principles of Morals*, he occasionally writes of sympathy as if it is an empathetic capacity, but mostly tends to equate it with benevolence and a feeling of 'humanity'—i.e. a desire for other people's happiness and aversion to their misery.

30.5 Emotions in Contemporary Moral Philosophy

In contemporary taxonomies of theories of the emotions, it is standard to distinguish between 'cognitive' and 'non-cognitive' theories. These are, however, terms of art, and their meaning is not often clear. The canonical examples of non-cognitive theories claim inspiration from James and Lange, and hold that emotions are our experiences of bodily changes.[131] Under the label 'cognitive', one usually finds two broad groups of theories. First, there are those holding that emotions are or essentially include beliefs about their objects.[132] Second, there are those holding that emotions are importantly distinct from beliefs, but nevertheless have some of the marks of that part of the mental often described as having a mind-to-world direction of fit: for example, it often makes sense to talk about having reasons for the emotions one feels.[133] As our historical survey has shown, the non-cognitive analysis of the emotions is a relatively recent development among moral philosophers, finding its first unambiguous expression in the eighteenth century. Among contemporary moral philosophers, those who accord an important but non-cognitive role to the emotions generally take their inspiration from Hume. Some couple this understanding of the emotions with a metaethical non-cognitivism about value: emotions project values onto the world; there is no good to be known or perceived, but our emotional responses to the world lead us to interpret things as good or bad (thus Blackburn 1998 and Gibbard 1992). Others adopt a metaethical subjectivism: the good is that which causes approbation, the bad, disapprobation (see Prinz 2004).

Cognitive conceptions of the emotions, by contrast, are revealed in our survey to have a pedigree dating back at least as far as Plato, Aristotle, and the Stoics. While there is insufficient consensus among contemporary interpreters of Plato and Aristotle to make it uncontroversial which of the two varieties of cognitive analysis best classifies their views on the emotions, the Stoics and Spinoza are clearly proponents of the first variety: emotions simply are moral judgements that are true and false in the same way as any other judgements. While such purely 'intellectualist' conceptions of the emotions are rare among contemporary philosophers, a prominent and influential exception is Martha Nussbaum.[134] Explicitly taking her inspiration from the Stoics, Nussbaum (2001) defends a 'cognitive-evaluative' conception of the emotions as appraisals of things and events as good or bad with regard to one's own flourishing, as well as judgements that these appraisals are justified. Unlike the Stoics, Nussbaum believes that many of our ordinary emotions (not just radically reoriented *eupatheiai*) are true beliefs about our good. Another important difference is that Nussbaum argues that emotions do not presuppose reflective self-consciousness or linguistic capacities (2001, ch. 2).

---

[131] See Damasio 1994 and Prinz 2004.   [132] See Kenny 1963 and Taylor 1965.
[133] See Calhoun 2003, Goldie 2000, and Solomon 1984.   [134] See also Solomon 1980, Neu 2000.

The second variety of cognitivism, on which emotions are a form of cognitive apprehension distinct from belief, is popular in contemporary philosophy of mind and moral psychology.[135] Among moral philosophers, John McDowell (1988), who traces his roots to Aristotle, advocates a view very similar to the one we have attributed to Hutcheson, where certain emotions are cognitive apprehensions of real, yet mind-dependent, virtue and vice. Similarly, Michael Stocker (Stocker and Hegeman 1996) strenuously argues against assimilating emotions to beliefs, but maintains that certain emotions are genuine apprehensions of value.

Bibliography

Adam, Ch. and Tannery, P. 1957. *Oeuvres de Descartes*. 12 vols. Paris: Cerf, 1897–1913; reprinted Paris: Vrin 1957.

Annas, J. 1992. *Hellenistic Philosophy of Mind*. Berkeley: University of California Press.

—— 1993. *The Morality of Happiness*. New York: Oxford University Press.

Anscombe, G.E.M. 1958. 'Modern Moral Philosophy', Philosophy 33: 1–19.

Armstrong, D. 2008. "Be Angry and Fear Not': Philodemus versus the Stoics on Natural Bites and Emotions', in J. T. Fitzgerald (ed.), *Passions and Moral Progress in Greco-Roman Thought*. London: Routledge, 79–121.

Baier, A. 1991. *A Progress of Sentiments: Reflections on Hume's Treatise*. Cambridge: Harvard University Press.

Blackburn, S. 1998. *Ruling Passions: A Theory of Practical Reasoning*. Oxford: Oxford University Press.

Bobonich, C. 2002. *Plato's Utopia Recast: His later Ethics and Politics*. Oxford: Oxford University Press.

Brandom, R. 2008. 'Adequacy and the Individuation of Ideas in Spinoza's Ethics', Journal of the History of Philosophy 14: 147–62.

Brennan, T. 1996. 'Epicurus on Sex, Marriage and Children', Classical Philology 91 (4): 346–52.

—— 1998. 'The Old Stoic Theory of the Emotions', in J. Sihvola and T. Engberg-Pederson (eds), *The Emotions in Hellenistic Philosophy*. Dordrecht: Kluwer, 21–70.

—— 2000. 'Reservation in Stoic Ethics', Archiv für Geschichte der Philosophie 82: 149–77.

—— 2005. *The Stoic Life: Emotions, Duties, and Fate*. Oxford: Oxford University Press.

Brown, D. 2002. 'The Rationality of Cartesian Passions', in H. J. Lagerlund and M. Yrjönsuuri, (eds), *Emotions and Choice from Boethius to Descartes*. Dordrecht: Kluwer, 259–78.

—— 2006. *Descartes and the Passionate Mind*. New York: Cambridge University Press.

Brungs, A. 2002. *Metaphysik der Sinnlichkeit: Das System der Passiones Animae bei Thomas von Aquin*. Halle: Hallescher Verlag.

—— 2008. 'Christliche Denker vor dem 13. Jahrhundert: von der Askese zur Liebestheologie', in Landweer and Renz (eds), 163–84.

Burnyeat, M. F. B. 1980. 'Aristotle on Learning to be Good', in A. O. Rorty (ed.) 1980, 69–92.

Byers, S. 2003. 'Augustine and the Cognitive Cause of Stoic "Preliminary Passions"', Journal of the History of Philosophy 41 (4): 433–48.

---

[135] See especially Calhoun 2003 and Goldie 2000. There are also hybrid theories, which conceive of emotions as blending cognitive, motivational, and bodily elements (for example, Greenspan 1988, Schachter and Singer 1962).

Calhoun, C. 2003. 'Cognitive Emotions?', in R. Solomon, (ed.), *What is An Emotion?* Oxford: Oxford University Press, 236–47.

Cates, D. F. 2009. *Aquinas on the Emotions*. Washington DC: Georgetown University Press.

Cohon, R. 2008. 'Hume's Indirect Passions', in E. Radcliffe (ed.), *The Blackwell Companion to Hume*. Oxford: Blackwell Publishing, 159–84.

Colish, M. 1985. *The Stoic Tradition from Antiquity to the Early Middle Ages*, vol. 2: *Stoicism in Christian Latin Thought through the Sixth Century*. Leiden: Brill, 1985.

Cooper, J. M. 1996a. 'Reason, Moral Virtue and Moral Value', in M. Frede and G. Striker (eds), *Rationality in Greek Thought*. Oxford: Clarendon Press, 81–114.

—— 1996b. 'An Aristotelian Theory of the Emotions', in A. O. Rorty (ed.) 1996, 238–57.

—— 1998. 'Posidonius on Emotions', in J. Sihvola and T. Engberg-Pederson (eds), 71–111.

—— 2005. 'The Emotional Life of the Wise', *Southern Journal of Philosophy*, Supplementary Volume 43, 176–218.

Curley, E. 1975. 'Descartes, Spinoza, and the Ethics of Belief', in E. Freeman and M. Mandelbaum (eds), Spinoza: Essays in Interpretation. La Salle, IL: Open Court, 159–89.

Damasio A. 1994. *Descartes' Error: Emotion, Reason, and the Human Brain*. New York: Putnam Publishing.

Della Rocca, M. 2008. 'Rationalism Run Amok: Representation and the Reality of Emotions in Spinoza', in C. Huenemann (ed.), *Interpreting Spinoza: Critical Essays*. Cambridge: Cambridge University Press, 26–52.

Denis, L. 2000. 'Kant's Cold Sage and the Sublimity of Apathy', *Kantian Review* 4: 48–73.

Dillon, J. 1983. '*Metriopatheia and Apatheia*: Some Reflections on a Controversy in Later Greek Ethics', in J. P. Anton and A. Preus (eds), *Essays on Ancient Greek Philosophy*, vol. 2. Buffalo: SUNY Press, 508–17.

—— 1986. '*Aisthêsis Noêtê*: A doctrine of Spiritual senses in Origen and in Plotinus', in A. Caquot et al. (eds), *Hellenica et Judaica: Hommage à Valentin Nikiprowetsky*. Louvain: Peeters, 443–55. Reprinted in J. M. Dillon (ed.) 1990. *The Golden Chain*. Aldershott: Variorum, 443–55.

Dixon, T. 2003. *From Passions to Emotions: The creation of a Secular Psychological Category*. Cambridge: Cambridge University Press.

Dow, J. 2010. 'Feeling Fantastic: Emotions and Appearances in Aristotle', *Oxford Studies in Ancient Philosophy* 37: 143–76.

—— 2011. 'Aristotle's Theory of the Emotions', in M. Pakaluk and G. Pearson (eds), *Moral Psychology and Human Action in Aristotle*. Oxford and New York: Oxford University Press.

Elwes, R. H. M. (tr.) 1901. *The Chief Works of Benedict de Spinoza, translated from the Latin, with an Introduction*. Vol. 2, *De Intellectus Emendatione—Ethica. Select Letters*. Revised edition. London: George Bell and Sons.

Fortenbaugh, W. 2002. *Aristotle on Emotion*. 2nd edn. London: Duckworth.

—— 2008. 'Aristotle and Theophrastus on the Emotions', in J. T. Fitzgerald (ed.), *Passions and Moral Progress in Greco-Roman Thought*. New York: Routledge, 29–47.

Fowler, D. 1997. 'Epicurean Emotions', in S. M. Brand and C. Gill (eds), *The Passions in Roman Thought and Literature*. Cambridge: Cambridge University Press, 16–35.

Frankena W. 1955. 'Hutcheson's Moral Sense Theory', *Journal of the History of Ideas* 16: 356–75.

Frede, M. 1986. 'The Stoic Doctrine of the Affections of the Soul', in M. Schofield and G. Striker (eds), *The Norms of Nature: Studies in Hellenistic Ethics*. Cambridge: Cambridge University Press, 93–110.

Garrett, A. (ed.) 2002. *Frances Hutcheson: Essay on the Nature and Conduct of the Passions with Illustrations on the Moral Sense*. Indianapolis: Liberty Fund.

Gauthier, R. A. 1951. *Magnanimité: l'idéal de la grandeur dans la philosophie païenne et dans la théologie chrétienne*. Paris: Vrin.

Gerson, L. 2003. 'Incontinence in Plato's *Laws*', in L. Brisson and S. Scolnicov (eds), *Plato's Laws: From Theory Into Practice*. Sankt Augustin: Academia Verlag, 149–54.

Gibbard A. 1992. *Wise Choices, Apt Feelings*. Cambridge, MA: Harvard University Press.

—— 2003. *Thinking How to Live*. Cambridge, MA: Harvard University Press.

Gill, C. 2003. 'Reactive and Objective Attitudes: Anger in Vergil's *Aeneid* and Hellenistic Philosophy', in S. M. Brand and G. Most (eds), *Ancient Anger: Perspectives from Homer to Galen*. Cambridge: Cambridge University Press, 208–28.

—— 2010. 'Stoicism and Epicureansim', in P. Goldie (ed.), 143–65.

Goldie P. 2000. *The Emotions: A Philosophical Exploration*. Oxford: Oxford University Press.

—— (ed.) 2010. *The Oxford Handbook of Philosophy of Emotion*. Oxford: Oxford University Press.

Grant, A. 1885. *The Ethics of Aristotle*, illustrated with essays and notes. 4th edn. London: Longmans, Green, and Company.

Graver, M. 2002. *Cicero's Tusculan Disputations 3 and 4*. Chicago: University of Chicago Press.

—— 2007. *Stoicism and Emotion*. Chicago: University of Chicago Press.

Greenspan P. 1988. Emotions and Reasons: *An Inquiry into Emotional Justification*. New York: Routledge, Chapman and Hall.

Guyer, P. 2010. 'Moral Feelings in the Metaphysics of Morals', in L. Denis (ed.), *Kant's Metaphysics of Morals: A Critical Guide*. Cambridge: Cambridge University Press, 130–51.

Harte, V. 2004. 'The *Philebus* on Pleasure: The Good, the Bad, and the False', *Proceedings of the Aristotelian Society* 104: 118–28.

Hasse, D. 2000. *Avicenna's De Anima and the Latin West*. London: Warburg Institute.

Hill, T.E. (ed.) and Zweig, A. (tr.) 2003. Kant: *Groundworkfor the Metaphysics of Morals*. Oxford: Oxford University Press.

Hirvonen, V. 2002. 'A Nominalist Ontology of the Passions', in Lagerlund and Yrjönsuuri (eds), 155–72.

Inwood, B. 1985. *Ethics and Human Action in Early Stoicism*. Oxford: Oxford University Press.

Irwin, T. H. 1977. *Plato's Moral Theory*. Oxford: Oxford University Press.

—— 1995. *Plato's Ethics*. Oxford: Oxford University Press.

James, S. 1997. *Passion and Action: The Emotions in Seventeenth-Century Philosophy*. Oxford: Clarendon Press.

—— 1998. 'Reason, the Passions, and the Good Life', in M. Ayers and D. Garber (eds), *The Cambridge History of Seventeenth-Century Philosophy*. Cambridge: Cambridge University Press, 1358–96.

Kamtekar, R. 2005. 'Good Feelings and Motivation', Comments on Cooper 2005. *Southern Journal of Philosophy*, Supplemental Volume, 219–29.

Kenny, A. 1963. *Action, Emotion and Will*. London: Routledge.

Kent, B. 1995. *Virtues of the Will: The Transformation of Ethics in the Late Thirteenth Century*. Washington DC: The Catholic University of America Press.

King, P. 1999. 'Aquinas on the Passions', in S. MacDonald and E. Stump (eds), *Aquinas' Moral Theory: Essays in Honor of Norman Kretzmann*. Ithaca, NY: Cornell University Press, 101–32.

—— 2002. 'Late Scholastic Theories of the Passions', in Lagerlund and Yrjönsuuri (eds), 229–58.

—— 2010. 'Emotions in Medieval Thought', in P. Goldie (ed.), *The Oxford Handbook to Philosophy of Emotion*. Oxford: Oxford University Press, 167–87.

Kisner, M. J. 2008. 'Spinoza's Virtuous Passions', *The Review of Metaphysics* 61: 759–83.

—— 2010. 'Perfection and Desire: Spinoza on the Good', *Pacific Philosophical Quarterly* 91: 87–117.

Knuuttila, S. 2004. *Emotions in Ancient and Medieval Philosophy*. New York: Clarendon Press.

Konstan, D. 2006. *Emotions of the Ancient Greeks: Studies in Aristotle and Classical Literature*. Toronto: University of Toronto Press.

Lagerlund, H. and Yrjönsuuri, M. (eds) 2002. *Emotions and Choice from Boethius to Descartes*. Dordrecht: Kluwer.

Landweer, H. and Renz, U. (eds) 2008. *Klassische Emotionstheorie*. Berlin: Walter de Gruyter.

Leidhold, W. (ed.) 2004. Frances Hutcheson: *An Inquiry into the Original of our Ideas of Beauty and Virtue*. Indianapolis: Liberty Fund.

Leighton, S. 1996. 'Aristotle and the Emotions', in A. O. Rorty (ed.) 1996, 206–37.

Lennon, T. M. (ed.) and Olscamp, P.J. (tr.) 1980. Malebranche: *The Search After Truth*. Columbus: Ohio State University Press.

Long, A. A. and Sedley, D. N. 1987. *The Hellenistic Philosophers*. 2 vols. Cambridge: Cambridge University Press.

Lorenz, H. 2006. *The Brute Within: Appetitive Desire in Plato and Aristotle*. Oxford: Clarendon Press.

—— 2009. 'Virtue of Character in Aristotle's *Nicomachean Ethics*', *Oxford Studies in Ancient Philosophy* 37: 177–212.

—— 2011. 'Posidonius on the Nature and Treatment of the Emotions', *Oxford Studies in Ancient Philosophy* 40: 189–211.

McDowell, J. 1988. 'Values and Secondary Qualities', in *Mind, Value, and Reality*. Cambridge, MA: Harvard University Press, 131–50.

McGinn, B. 1977. *Three Treatises on Man*. Collegeville, MN: Cistercian Publications.

MacIntyre, A. 1985. *After Virtue*. Second edition. London: Duckworth.

Marshall, E. 2008. 'Spinoza's Cognitive Affects and Their Feel', *British Journal for the History of Philosophy* 16: 1–23.

Meyer, S. S. 1993. *Aristotle on Moral Responsibility: Character and Cause*. Oxford: Basil Blackwell.

—— 2008. *Ancient Ethics*. New York: Routledge.

—— 2012a. 'Pleasure, Pain, and Anticipation in Plato's Laws, Book I', in R. Patterson, V. Karasmanis, and A. Herman (eds), *Presocratics and Plato*. Las Vegas, Zurich, Athens: Parmenides Publishing, 311–328.

—— 2012b. 'Pleasure and Pains in Laws I–II', in R.Patterson, V. Karasmanis and A. Hermann (eds), *Presocratics and Plato: Essays in Honor of Charles Kahn*. Las Vegas: Parmenides Publishing, 349–66.

Moss, J. 2006. 'Pleasure and Illusion in Plato', *Philosophy and Phenomenological Research* 72 (3): 503–35.

—— 2008. 'Appearances and Calculations: Plato's Division of the Soul', *Oxford Studies in Ancient Philosophy* 34: 35–68.

Neu, J. 2000. *A Tear is an Intellectual Thing: the Meaning of Emotions*. Oxford & New York: Oxford University Press.

Norton, D. 1985. 'Hutcheson's Moral Realism', *Journal of the History of Philosophy* 23: 397–418.

Nussbaum, M. C. 1990. *Love's Knowledge:Essays on Philosophy and Literature*. Oxford: Oxford University Press.

—— 1994. *The Therapy of Desire*. Princeton: Princeton University Press.

—— 2001. *Upheavals of Thought:The Intelligence of Emotions*. Cambridge: Cambridge University Press.

Pickavé, M. 2008. 'Thomas von Aquin: Emotionen als Leidenschaften der Seele', in Landweer and Renz (eds), 185–204.

Pomeroy, A. J. 1999. *Arius Didymus: Epitome of Stoic Ethics*, text, translation, and notes. Atlanta: Society of Biblical Literature.

Price, A. 2006. 'Akrasia and Self-Control', in R. Kraut (ed.), *The Blackwell Companion to Aristotle's Nicomachean Ethics*. Oxford: Basil Blackwell, 234–54.

Prinz J. 2004. *Gut Reactions: A Perceptual Theory of Emotion*. New York: Oxford University Press.

Procopé, J. 1998. 'Epicureans on Anger', in Sihvola and Engberg-Pedersen (eds), 171–96.

Radcliffe, E. S. 1986. 'Hutcheson's Perceptual and Moral Subjectivism', *History of Philosophy Quarterly* 3: 407–21.

Radnor, D. 1971. 'Spinoza's Theory of Ideas', *The Philosophical Review* 80: 338–59.

Reath, A. 2006. 'Kant's Theory of Moral Sensibility: Respect for the Moral Law and the Influence of Inclination', in *Agency and Autonomy in Kant's Moral Theory*. Oxford: Oxford University Press, 8–32.

Rist, J. M. 1969. *Stoic Philosophy*. Cambridge: Cambridge University Press.

Robinson, T. 1970. *Plato's Psychology*. Toronto: University of Toronto Press.

Rorty, A. O. (ed.) 1980. *Essays on Aristotle's Ethics*. Berkeley: University of California Press.

—— (ed.) 1996. *Essays on Aristotle's Rhetoric*. Berkeley: University of California Press.

Rudebusch, G. 1999. *Socrates, Pleasure, and Value*. New York: Oxford University Press.

Sandbach, F. 1975. *The Stoics*. London: Chatto and Windus.

Sassi, M. 2008. 'The Self, the Soul, and the Individual in city of the *Laws*', *Oxford Studies in Ancient Philosophy* 35: 125–48.

Schachter, S. and Singer, J. 1962. 'Cognitive, Social, and Physiological Determinants of Emotional State', *Psychological Review* 69: 379–99.

Schöpsdau, K. 1994. *Platon: Nomoi (Gesetzte) I–IV*. Ubersetzung und Kommentar. Göttingen: Vandenhoek und Ruprecht.

Selby-Bigge, L. A. (ed.) 1975a. David Hume: *A Treatise of Human Nature*. 2nd edn., revised by P. H. Nidditch. Oxford: Clarendon Press.

—— 1975b. David Hume: *Enquiry concerning the Principles of Morals*, in L. A. Selby-Bigge (ed.), *Enquiries concerning Human Understanding and concerning the Principles of Morals*. 3rd edn., revised by P. H. Nidditch. Oxford: Clarendon Press.

Sharples, R. W. and Van der Eijk, P. J. 2008. *Nemesius: On the Nature of Man*, translated with introduction and notes. Liverpool: Liverpool University Press.

Sherman, N. 1989. *The Fabric of Character: Aristotle's theory of virtue*, Oxford: Clarendon Press.

Sihvola, J. 1996. 'Emotional Animals: Do Aristotelian Emotions Require Beliefs?', *Apeiron* 29: 105–44.

—— and Engberg-Pedersen, T. (eds) 1998. *The Emotions in Hellenistic Philosophy*. Dordrecht: Kluwer.

Solomon, R. 1980. 'Emotions and Choice', in A. O. Rorty, (ed.), *Explaining Emotions*. Los Angeles: University of California Press, 251–81.

—— 1984. *The Passions: The Myth and Nature of Human Emotions*. New York: Doubleday.

Sorabji, R. 2000. *Emotion and Peace of Mind: From Stoic Agitation to Christian Temptation*. The Gifford Lectures. Oxford: Oxford University Press.

Sorensen, K. 2002. 'Kant's Taxonomy of the Emotions', *Kantian Review* 6: 109–28.

Stocker, M. 1976. 'The Schizophrenia of Modern Ethical Theories', *Journal of Philosophy* 73: 453–66.

—— and Hegeman, E. 1996. *Valuing Emotions*. Cambridge: Cambridge University Press.

Striker, G. 1996. 'Emotions in Context: Aristotle's treatment of the Passions in his Rhetoric and Moral Psychology', in A. O. Rorty (ed.), *Essays on Aristotle's Rhetoric*. Berkeley: University of California Press, 286–302.

Taylor, G. 1985. *Pride, Shame, and Guilt: Emotions of Self-Assessment*. Oxford: Oxford University Press.

Tsouna, V. 2007. *The Ethics of Philodemus*. Oxford: Oxford University Press.

Usener, H. 1887. *Epicurea*. Leipzig: Teubner.

Vander Waerdt, P. 1985. 'Peripatetic Soul Division, Posidonius, and Middle Platonic Moral Psychology', *Greek, Rome, and Byzantine Studies* 26: 373–94.

Vogt, K. M. 2008. *Law, Reason, and the Cosmic City: Political Philosophy in the Early Stoa*. New York: Oxford University Press.

Wachsmuth, C. and Hense, O. (eds) 1884–1912. *Stobaeus, Anthologium*. Berlin, Weidmann. Reprinted 1958, 1974.

Walford, D. and Meerbote, R. (eds) 1992. Kant: *Inquiry into the Distinctness of the Principles of Natural Theology and Ethics*, in *Theoretical Philosophy*, 1755–1770, 243–86. *The Cambridge Edition of the Works of Immanuel Kant*. Cambridge: Cambridge University Press.

Williams, B. A. O. 1973. 'A Critique of Utilitarianism', in J. J. C. Smart and B. A. O. Williams (eds), *Utilitarianism: For and Against*. Cambridge: Cambridge University Press, 77–150.

—— 1981. 'Persons, character, and morality', in *Moral Luck*. Cambridge: Cambridge University Press, 1–19.

Wolf, S. 1982. 'Moral Saints', *Journal of Philosophy* 79: 419–39.

—— 1992. 'Morality and Partiality', *Philosophical Perspectives* 6: 243–59.

CHAPTER 31

....

HAPPINESS, SUFFERING, AND DEATH

....

RICHARD KRAUT

31.1 PESSIMISM ABOUT THE HUMAN CONDITION
....

HUMAN suffering is all too common, happiness too rarely achieved. Why does this regrettable imbalance exist? Is it reasonable to hope that someday, by altering our attitudes, educational practices, and social arrangements, human beings will generally have much better lives? Or is the existence of widespread suffering in some way an ineradicable part of the human condition? Does something in the human psyche make unhappiness difficult to avoid, happiness elusive and uncommon? Should we therefore distrust our instinctual will to live, and regard death as the final release from our troubles, perhaps even the gateway to a better world? Or should we, on the contrary, look upon death as one of the most unfortunate limitations on the human condition—something that should be placed on the agenda of the human race as an item that, like suffering, is to be combated, postponed, perhaps even eliminated?

One might say, in response to these questions, that anyone who takes seriously such bold generalizations about the human condition is merely expressing his personal outlook on life, or perhaps merely his current mood. If someone thinks that the cards are stacked against the possibility of human happiness, that merely shows that he has a grumpy disposition. But to dismiss a general pessimism about the human condition in this way—without examining its grounds and arguing against it—is to fall into an unreflective optimism. We must of course be cautious about accepting gross generalizations about whether human life is good or bad, but we should not refuse to consider them with an open mind.

Camus says: 'Judging whether life is or is not worth living amounts to answering the fundamental question of philosophy'.[1] Even if we disagree because we find other philosophical questions no less fundamental, we should concede at least this much: the question, is life worth living?, has at least the appearance of a problem that deserves philosophical consideration. If it is misconceived, it will be important to show why that is so. If it is not misconceived, what should be our strategy for responding to it, and what verdict should we reach?

Another option that we should keep open, at least initially, is to affirm that human life is precious and worth living even if suffering is inevitably prevalent and happiness necessarily in short supply. After all, some features of human life might have greater value than happiness or disvalue than suffering. We might even take a more radical step, and cultivate an attitude of indifference to our own suffering, in order to focus our attention on something more worthy of our efforts than that. Kant, for example, holds that we should strain every nerve to make ourselves *worthy* of happiness—not to be happy here and now, but deserving of the happiness that we must reasonably hope for in a future life. A moral agent, he insists, must regard both his own happiness and his misfortunes as matters of secondary importance, and focus above all on fulfilling his moral duties— to advance his own perfection, and the happiness of *others*. He would react with horror and indignation to Camus' statement that 'there is but one truly serious philosophical problem, and that is suicide'.[2] For Kant, anyone who seriously contemplates taking his life merely as a way to avoid suffering is already violating his duty to pursue his obligatory ends as best he can, however miserable he may be.[3]

31.2 HOW HAPPY ARE YOU ON A SCALE BETWEEN 1 AND 10?

Profound pessimism about the human condition is part of our cultural heritage. The works of Schopenhauer are filled with expressions of the idea that suffering, so far from being accidental or occasional, is 'the immediate and direct purpose of our life'.[4] Freud says, in *Civilization and its Discontents*: 'One feels inclined to say that the intention that

[1] Camus 1955: 3.
[2] Camus 1955: 1.
[3] See Kant 2002, 4: 393: 'a good will seems to constitute the indispensable condition even of our worthiness to be happy'. Kant discusses the impermissibility of committing suicide out of unhappiness at Kant 2002, 4: 421–2 and 4: 429. In *The Critique of Pure Reason*, he characterizes the moral law as commanding us: 'Do that through which thou becomest worthy to be happy' (1929: B 837). The moral need to postulate a future life in which virtue is rewarded with happiness is discussed in 'The Canon of Pure Reason' of the *Critique of Pure Reason*. A fuller treatment is found in 'The Dialectic of Pure Practical Reason' of the *Critique of Practical Reason*. For his thesis that self-perfection and the happiness of others are our two obligatory ends, see Kant 1991: 385–6.
[4] Schopenhauer 1970: 41.

man should be happy is not included in the plan of "Creation".[5] Philip Larkin writes, in his poem, 'This Be The Verse': 'Man hands on misery to man / It deepens like a coastal shelf / Get out as early as you can / And don't have any kids yourself.'[6] Echoing the chorus of Sophocles' *Oedipus at Colonus*,[7] Heinrich Heine writes, in his poem, 'Morphia': 'Sleep is good / Death is better, but the best is never to have been born.'[8]

Opponents of these pessimistic sentiments have never been lacking. In his defence of utilitarianism, Mill tries to convince us that the most important sources of human suffering would be greatly diminished, perhaps almost entirely eliminated, were we to change our moral thinking and our social institutions. It is entirely feasible, he holds, to make the future happiness of all humankind our long-term goal.[9] A guarded optimism can be found in ancient ethics as well. To take one example: Aristotle believes that although most citizens of Greek cities have little in the way of practical wisdom, and are full of psychological conflict, these deficiencies are not built into their very nature, but arise from bad moral habits, which are in turn the outcome of defective legal systems.[10] Naturally free males who receive a good moral education have excellent prospects for living well—provided they do not become the victims of unforeseeable misfortune.[11] In the final two books of his *Politics* he envisages a political community filled with citizens who live flourishing lives.

It might be thought that the global pessimism found in Sophocles, Heine, Schopenhauer, Freud, and Larkin has been decisively refuted by recent studies conducted by professional psychologists. When people are asked how happy they are with their lives overall, the average level of satisfaction that is reported, on a scale from 1 to 10, ranges from 5.03 in Bulgaria to 8.39 in Switzerland.[12] Most people, in other words, take themselves to be closer to extreme happiness than to extreme unhappiness, and in many countries most citizens report that they are extremely happy with their lives.

We do not know how such pessimists as Schopenhauer would have reacted to these empirical studies, but in any case an important form of pessimism cannot be undermined by these findings. It holds that human nature being what it is, the lives that most people live are bad lives—not even worth living, in fact. Admittedly, many people report themselves to be somewhat or even very happy with their lives, but, according to the pessimist, that is because they fail to see how little in their lives is worth having.

To use Camus' image, these cheery people might be likened to the mythical Sisyphus, condemned to roll a boulder uphill, only to see it fall back again, and to return to this empty and uncompletable task again and again, without end. Sisyphus might be so dull a fellow that he never loses hope that he might someday complete his work, and he might be happy with his life even though his setbacks always undermine his advances. But his is a life in which nothing worthwhile is accomplished, because its sole activity is not only pointless but endlessly beyond his grasp. If the activities undertaken by most human

---

[5] Freud 1961: 23.   [6] Larkin 1988: 180.   [7] *Oedipus at Colonus*, 1223–7.
[8] Heine 1934: 137.   [9] Mill 2001: 12–15.   [10] Aristotle 2000: X.9.
[11] Aristotle 2000: I.10.   [12] Nettle 2005: 51.

beings bear some similarity to the meaninglessness of Sisyphus' endeavours, and something in human nature guarantees that this will always be so, then pessimism is not refuted by the widespread satisfaction people express with their lives. It holds that little or nothing in their lives is worthwhile, though they do not realize it. An opponent of this form of pessimism might reply that to be generally happy with one's life is of great intrinsic value, so much so that by itself it makes someone's life worth living. For our purposes, the important point is that whether or not that assertion is true, it cannot be supported by empirical investigation. It is a philosophical claim, and must be subjected to philosophical scrutiny.

Pessimism about the human condition, when it takes a form worth discussing, has both an evaluative and a psychological component. As an evaluative thesis, it proposes a standard by which human lives are to be assessed. It says that a human life is worth living if and only if it has certain features. Then, its psychological component asserts that something inheres in all or nearly all human beings that will always prevent their lives from having those valuable features. One way to oppose such pessimism would be to affirm a standard for evaluating human lives that is rather easy for many human beings to meet. One such standard is self-reported happiness. But it is implausible to suppose that this is the *only* dimension along which the value of a life is to be assessed. After all, when people report that they are happy with their lives, they do so because there are other things in their lives, besides their belief in their own happiness, that they take to be reasons for being happy. They may, for example, be thinking of their relationship with their spouses and children, or their success at work, or their lively pursuit of other projects. They regard these relationships and activities as some of the good things in their lives. And that leaves room for the pessimist's question: are the things that these people are happy about really good things after all?

31.3 'When We Exist, Death Is Not Present'

Before we go any further with these issues, we should address a question that can be raised about how to understand the notion of a life 'worth living'. According to the most natural way to construe these words, for a life to be worth living is for it to be better for the person living it than no life at all. So, when the chorus in *Oedipus at Colonus* says that the best thing is never to have been born, it can be taken to mean that every life, even the best of them, is so filled with misery that it would have been better to avoid those sufferings by never having been born in the first place. For we unlucky ones who have been thrown into the world (without our consent!), the second best alternative is for life to end as soon as possible.

But we had better make sure that these comparisons—between being unhappily alive and never having been born, or between being unhappily alive and dead—make sense. After all, there seems to be something confused about the notion that we might have been better off had we never been, or that we can improve our situation by dying. It is certainly not the case that, had I never existed, I would have fared far better than I am now faring. A world that lacked me would be one in which the question how well I am faring lacks an answer, because there would be no one about whom this question can be asked. So, I cannot coherently say: in that world, I would have been better off than I am now.

It might be thought that the same incoherence is present in the idea that were someone to die, he would become better off. Undoubtedly, after someone has gone out of existence, there is, from that time forward, no longer a subject whose level of well-being —good on balance, bad on balance, or neutrally poised between good and bad—is there to be assessed. That fact might tempt us to infer that one cannot become better off, or for that matter worse off, by dying.

An argument of this sort led Epicurus and his followers to the conclusion that the fear of death is irrational. 'That most frightful of evils, death, is nothing to us, seeing that when we exist death is not present, and when death is present, we do not exist.'[13] Epicurus is right to this extent: it would be confused to suppose that after someone dies, he is henceforth in a highly disadvantageous condition, because from now on he is no longer alive, which is a very bad thing. If we think it wise to take precautions to avoid death, we had better not do so on *those* grounds.

But Epicurus arrives at a more radical conclusion: he thinks there can be *no* grounds for the common assumption that it is bad to die. If he is right, then even if someone's life is going well and many more good years are in store for him, his death is not to be regretted. One argument he uses for this conclusion is that 'what has been dissolved has no sense-experience, and what has no sense-experience is nothing to us'.[14] The idea is that being dead is nothing one feels (although there may be pain in the process of dying), and the only things we should regret are painful feelings. But *that* premise—that the only regrettable things are painful feelings—is difficult to accept. If I prevent you from hearing news that would have given you much pleasure, and you never know of my interference, I have caused you no pain, but I have made you less well off than you would otherwise be. Similarly, Epicurus should have admitted that if death prevents us from experiencing many pleasures that we would otherwise have had, it is regrettable. More generally, if we can defend the idea that human beings can, in favourable circumstances, live well, then we are justified in assuming that for these people death is a bad thing. That, at any rate, is a reasonable assumption to make about people who have not yet arrived at the full number of years of a healthy and flourishing human life.

Our conclusion, thus far, is that there is nothing incoherent in the very idea that death might be a bad thing. Death will be bad when it prevents someone from achieving what is good.[15] The pessimist need not resist this conclusion, because he is prepared to argue that human life is, at least for the most part, filled with misery and has little worthwhile to offer in compensation. His says: although you may think that your death will be preventing you from having many good things, you are almost certainly mistaken, because

---

[13] *Letter to Menoeceus*, in Inwood and Gerson 1988: 125.
[14] *Principal Doctrines*, in Inwood and Gerson 1988: 26.
[15] See Nagel 1979 for further discussion.

life generally contains a highly unfavourable mixture of bad and good. He need not be guided by the confused thought that when you die you will henceforth fare much better than you had prior to your death.

The deeply pessimistic thought that it would have been better for each of us never to have been born should also be accepted as coherent (whether or not it is true). It should not be taken to mean that never having existed is a better state for someone to be in than existence. Rather, the idea is that it would be best for the foetus to die in the womb before it comes to term, for it then completely avoids a life of suffering, which begins at the moment of birth. (Why else do new-born babies cry?) And if a foetus feels pain in the womb, it would be best for the fertilized egg to miscarry before it reaches that later developmental stage. The best thing for us to do with regard to any children we are thinking of having is not to have them.

31.4 A LIFE WORTH LIVING

The pessimist takes a stand on whether a human life is 'worth living', so we had better pay some attention to that phrase.

It might be tempting, but would be mistaken, to suppose that this question can be answered only by placing the total amount of what is good in human life on one side of a balance, placing the total amount of what is bad on the other, and assessing which side has greater weight. After all, we often make decisions by weighing costs and benefits. We decide not to take certain risks, for example, because the danger of physical injury is great, and the good we might accomplish insufficient to compensate for those harms. In the same way, we might ask whether a life has more good in it than bad, and judge it not worth living when the bad outweighs the good.

But that would overlook the possibility that even when the amount of good is smaller than the amount of bad, in both severity and duration, it might nonetheless be good enough to make a life worth living. Someone might justifiably believe, for example, that the one good thing he enjoys, writing poetry, is no match for all the suffering he must endure: physical pain, the betrayal of friends, unfavourable reviews. On balance, he holds that there are more bad things in his life than good, and that they are more severely bad than the good things are good. Nonetheless, it would be coherent for him to judge that it is better for him to remain alive than to die because the value of writing poetry makes his life good enough to be worth living. We might compare his evaluation of his life with the judgement we can make about a failed literary work that we recommend to a friend: we might tell him that on balance the novel we just finished is a bad one, because its deficiencies outweigh its merits, but that even so it has sufficient merit to be worth reading. Just as a bad book can still be worth reading because of the small goodness that is in it, so a life that is on balance a bad one for the person living it can nonetheless be worth living because the good in it is sufficiently good to make it desirable to go on living. Someone who looks at his life in this way judges that there is good reason for him to die only if the amount of good in it falls below a certain threshold. He denies that death is to be welcomed just in case the total amount of good outweighs the total amount of bad.

At the end of Woody Allen's film, 'Annie Hall', Alvy Singer recalls a joke told by Groucho Marx about a man who complains that the food served at a restaurant is terrible—and then adds that the portions are too small. Alvy comments: 'That's essentially how I feel about life. Full of loneliness and misery and suffering and unhappiness, and it's all over much too quickly.'[16] We might take the point of this joke to be that a common attitude towards life, however comical and even endearing, is nonetheless irrational. People who are miserable because their lives are 'full of loneliness and misery and suffering and unhappiness' should welcome death, but stupidly cling to life. But there is another way to take the joke, whether it is the one intended or not. After all, if the food in a restaurant doesn't even fill you up, that is a second failing, beyond the poor cooking. There is nothing irrational in making both complaints. Similarly, if something good in your life justifies your wanting to go on living, despite its being small in comparison with your suffering, you can coherently complain about your loneliness and misery, and then complain again that the time you have to devote to that one good thing is far too brief.

I will assume in this chapter that Hamlet is wrong when he says that 'there is nothing either good or bad but thinking makes it so'.[17] Statements about what is good or bad, like assertions about what is morally right or wrong, are not made true simply by their being believed by whomever makes them. Accordingly, if someone wants to end his life because he judges that it contains little or nothing of value, his self-assessment may be incorrect. Now, just as it is possible for someone to be mistaken when he judges that his life is *not* good enough to be worth living, so it is possible to go astray when one judges that one's life *is* good enough to be worth living. The one thing in one's life that one takes to be valuable may be worthless, or may be so small a good that, in light of all that is of negative value in this life, it is no longer worth living.

This allows us to distinguish two kinds of pessimism about the human condition. In its extreme form—the form expressed in the poetry of Sophocles and Heine—pessimism holds that no human life rises to the level of a life worth living, because whatever value a life can have is too small to make it worthwhile to go on living. That form of pessimism counsels us not to have children and to quit our lives as soon as possible. A less extreme pessimism holds that most human lives are, for the most part, just barely worth living, because the suffering they contain is almost always greater than any compensating good they encompass. This less severe form of pessimism does not counsel suicide, nor would it discourage people from having children. It nonetheless insists upon a negative evaluation of the human condition: although we should soldier on with our lives and even produce new generations—there is, after all, *something* worth living for—few lives can be expected to rise above that threshold, because something in

---

[16] Allen 1977.   [17] *Hamlet*, II. ii. 249–50.

the human condition normally prevents us from rising well above the level at which our lives are worth living.

Kant rejects even this mitigated pessimism, although he believes that happiness is an inherently elusive goal.[18] His view is that *all* rational agents have lives that are not merely just worth living, but *well* worth living, because they can never lose the power, precious beyond measure, to act in accordance with a good will. Happiness, as he conceives it, belongs to a lower order of value, because it loses its worth whenever it is severed from a good will, whereas the good will retains its worth under all conditions. He speaks of both the good will and happiness as good things (the first unconditionally good, the second conditionally good), but an act undertaken with a good will has the kind of worth that makes it of incomparably greater value than even the greatest happiness could be.[19] He holds that even though it is often difficult to determine whether people are acting with genuine good will,[20] and human beings can have only limited success in helping their fellows achieve happiness, that does not diminish the preciousness of the potential each rational agent always retains to do what is morally right because it is right. We may be as pessimistic as we like about our chances of becoming and remaining happy, and of making others happy, but there is something in human life, overlooked or mistakenly discounted by every form of pessimism, that should be treasured because every other kind of value is of an inferior order.

Although Kant holds that happiness belongs to a lower order of value, his treatment of it is anything but dismissive. He believes that perfect happiness is necessarily sought by every rational agent,[21] and that what we owe to others is to regulate our relations with them with a view to their present and future happiness. Our virtuous actions have as their goal the establishment, within the empirical world, of a universal system of human happiness, one in which each person is as happy as he has made himself worthy to be. Since that is not a goal we ever have the power to fully achieve through our own efforts, our moral principles require us to maintain the reasonable hope that death will not be the end of our existence, but that our efforts to achieve a world that contains not only virtue but the happiness deserved by virtue will be resumed elsewhere, and will be aided by the governance of a supreme moral intelligence.[22]

31.5 WHAT IS HAPPINESS?

Any discussion of the value of happiness must come to terms with the fact that this psychological condition is understood in different ways by different authors. Many of them use 'happiness' and 'pleasure' interchangeably. The classical utilitarians of the eighteenth and nineteenth centuries—Bentham, Mill, and Sidgwick—use both terms to designate

---

[18] Kant 2002, 4: 395, 418–19.   [19] Kant 2002, 4: 393–6.   [20] Kant 2002, 4: 407.
[21] Kant 2002, 4: 415.   [22] Kant 1997: B834–47.

any agreeable state of consciousness, just as they apply 'pain' and 'unhappiness' to any kind of disagreeable feeling. They maintain not only that happiness, so understood, is of some value, but that it encompasses all that is valuable. Whatever is worth having for its own sake must be something that is pleasurable, and its being pleasurable is precisely what makes it worth having.

This hedonistic thesis can accommodate, to some degree, Kant's claim that moral actions have extraordinary value, and are not merely instrumental means to further ends. The consciousness that one is doing the right thing brings with it a special pleasure, and that state of mind, being a pleasure, is worth having for its own sake. Hedonism is of course entirely compatible with the Kantian thesis that it is our duty to regulate our relations with other people with a view to their happiness. But Kant cannot accept the component of hedonism that asserts that pleasure is the very thing that gives anything that is valuable the value it has.

Common English usage, however, often makes a distinction, overlooked or set aside by the utilitarians, between the terms 'happiness' and 'pleasure'. 'Pleasure', according to this common distinction, applies to any state of mind that its subject finds agreeable, whereas 'happiness' is the name of one kind of agreeable feeling, namely the emotion, often easily detected in people's faces and body language, that is a close cousin to the more intense emotions of joy, elation, and ecstasy. These easily recognized emotions, are, like many others (anger, disgust, surprise), typically of short duration. They are immediate and palpable reactions to something unexpected or unfamiliar in our environment. Typically accompanied by some detectable change in the state of one's body, they generally fade away, as they are replaced by less charged modes of consciousness. Of course, such emotions can recur frequently, but on each occasion, their duration is limited.

In academic departments of psychology, 'happiness' is also used to designate the longer-lasting state of mind that experimental subjects report to interviewers when they are asked to report their overall satisfaction with their lives in general.[23] Although what they report may in some cases be a mere belief or judgement with no affective aspect, being a happy person typically consists partly in a palpable though subtle mode of consciousness—a 'feeling tone', it might be called—that colours one's way of interacting with the world. It is something that can vary in intensity. Although a general sense of well-being cannot remain intense over a long period of time, we can, for short periods, become suffused with a sweet sense of well-being, as we bring to mind the blessings that we normally take for granted as background conditions of our lives. We can meaningfully say that one person is happier than another if his conviction that his life is going well is more firm and is more deeply felt.

Kant uses 'glückseligkeit', the term commonly translated 'happiness', in a somewhat different way: it is 'the satisfaction of all inclinations as a sum',[24] or, more fully, 'the

---

[23] For a brief and helpful guide, see Biswas-Diener, Diener, and Tamir 2004.
[24] Kant 2002, 4: 399.

satisfaction of all our desires, extensively, in respect of their manifoldness, intensively, in respect of their degree, and protensively, in respect of their duration'.[25] So understood, happiness is fully achieved only when every one of our desires over the course of a lifetime is completely fulfilled. Presumably Kant is also assuming that the satisfaction of a desire is an element of happiness only if one is aware that it has been satisfied, and takes pleasure in its satisfaction. After all, it is possible to discover, after one has done what one wanted to do, that the 'satisfaction' of one's desire did not provide the pleasure one was expecting, and that one's desire was therefore unfortunate. What Kant has in mind, when he uses 'glückseligkeit', is a state of perfect happiness, and since he thinks of rational beings as beings who set ends for themselves, he naturally assumes that it can be achieved only by the fulfilment of those ends.[26]

Just as 'happiness' can designate different states of mind, there are a variety of conditions that might receive the opposite designation, 'unhappiness'. Disagreeable states of mind are opposite to agreeable states of mind. Sadness is the opposite of happiness and joy. However, if happiness is the state of mind one introspects, when one is asked, 'Taking things overall, how happy are you with your life in general?'[27], then, although there are degrees of happiness, it is not clear that someone who reports himself as being *not* happy (perhaps giving his satisfaction with his life a score of 1, at the bottom of the scale) is in a state that is the *opposite* of happiness. We could arbitrarily decree that those who assign their lives a number between 1 and 4 are unhappy, those who place themselves between 7 and 10 are happy, and those between these poles are neither happy nor unhappy. But happiness, so conceived, has no opposite, as joy is the opposite of sadness, and pleasure of disagreeable pain. The same can be said of Kant's conception of happiness: we are all less than perfectly happy, and people none of whose desires are fulfilled to the slightest degree—if there are any—might be said to be totally lacking in happiness. But the complete absence of a psychological state is not by itself the presence of the opposite state of mind.

Our term 'suffering', when used as an opposite to 'happiness', names both a group of distressed reactions to physical phenomena (intense pain, severe cold, nausea, noise) and a group of disagreeable feelings: sadness, fear, grief, frustration, irritation, boredom, loneliness, anguish, despair, depression, persistent anxiety, guilt, shame, and so on. What ties these states (pain, nausea, boredom, depression, etc.) together is their being perceived as disagreeable. When someone identifies a sensation as painful, but does not mind it, what he experiences should not be counted as a form of suffering. Strictly speaking, then, it is disagreeable consciousness that is opposed to pleasure—not pain.

---

[25] Kant 1997: B834.
[26] For recent philosophical studies of happiness, see Haybron 2008 and Feldman 2010.
[27] Nettle 2005: 33–4.

31.6 THE BEST FORM OF CONSCIOUSNESS: THE SWEET AND THE BITTERSWEET

Having made these distinctions, we might now ask: What kind of conscious experience would it be best for a person to have? A partial answer to that question immediately suggests itself: all other things being equal, the various states of mind that we call 'happiness' are better than those in which we lack happiness or fall into a condition that is the opposite of happiness. Even if Kant is right that happiness has only conditional value—even if it is good only when accompanied by virtue—it is better to be virtuous and happy than virtuous and unhappy. Since happiness can designate several different kinds of consciousness, why not say, then, that the best kind of consciousness for a human being to experience is one in which one has as much happiness of every variety as possible, and no unhappiness of any form? Such an ideally situated person would always be in a pleasurable state, would have many intensely joyful experiences, would always rate his life as deserving the highest possible mark, would constantly feel a deep sense of well-being, and would always find the most intense satisfaction from the fulfilment of every desire. No disagreeable feelings would be felt, no sadness, no disappointment, no frustration.

Having tentatively postulated this as an ideal form of conscious experience, we might wonder whether it is a psychological possibility, but we should also ask whether someone so uniformly and perfectly happy would really be experiencing the best possible form of human consciousness. Never feeling sadness, fear, loneliness, or anxiety, would this person not be missing aspects of human experience that partially constitute a well-lived life? The thought suggests itself, then, that the value of agreeable forms of consciousness and joy are increased by being integrated into a larger whole with less desirable forms of consciousness and sadness. Some combination of the sweet, the bittersweet, and the sour might, in other words, be better than uniform sweetness.

No doubt, short periods of unmitigated joy are to be welcomed, but so too are much more variegated and complex emotional states in which one experiences a sense of both gain and loss. Consider, for example, the complicated feelings that accompany transitional events in which one moves (as we all should) from one stage of life to another—a graduation ceremony, a farewell party, and the like. Their significance and value consists partly in the mixed emotions that accompany them. Similarly, early periods of sadness and loneliness can later be integrated into a larger picture that one constructs about the progress of one's life, and one's later experiences can be enriched by being seen against the background provided by earlier unhappiness. Someone who never experienced any form of unhappiness could never view his life in this way, and that would be a diminution in the richness and depth of his experience. Some of our 'negative' feelings—negative because initially experienced as disagreeable—can stimulate us to critically examine the roles we have unthinkingly assumed. When suffering is not so extreme that it irreparably shatters the ego, it can be woven into the tapestry of one's experience and thus used to construct a valuable second-order good—a good that integrates the experience of suffering with other components of one's life.

These reflections raise problems both for Kant and utilitarians. If the state of mind that Kant describes as perfect happiness is not the best psychological condition for a human being to be in, because it excludes the mélanges of agreeable and disagreeable feeling that partly constitute a well-lived life, then our duty to others cannot be to bring them as close as morality permits to a condition of perfect happiness. The perfect happiness of another world that Kant thinks we should strive to deserve is not an unmitigated good and so is not the best we should hope for. For the same reason, the utilitarian assumption that our ultimate end should be the greatest possible happiness and the least possible unhappiness is thrown into doubt.

31.7 EUDAIMONIA

If the term 'happiness' is understood as part of our purely empirical vocabulary, and describes a certain state of mind without evaluating it, then it should be distinguished from *eudaimonia*, a central term of Greek moral philosophy that translators commonly render as 'happiness'. 'Happiness' refers to something that can be felt, and is attributed to people entirely on the basis of their attitudes towards their lives. If someone is genuinely satisfied, on balance, with the way his life is going, then that settles the matter: he is happy, even if we think he would have a much better life were he to pursue different ends. By contrast, all the Greek philosophers would agree with Aristotle's remark, in the *Nicomachean Ethics*, that being *eudaimon* and living well are the same thing.[28] It makes no sense to ask, 'is it good for someone to be *eudaimon*?' because we have already given a positive evaluation of a person's life in ascribing *eudaimonia* to him. But to describe someone as happy is to report on his attitudes, feelings, and emotions—without yet making a judgement about the value of having those attitudes, feelings, and emotions. We make an evaluative statement when we say that happiness is a good thing, but not when we ascribe happiness to someone. By contrast, when the ancient moral philosophers assert that a certain individual is *eudaimon*, they are congratulating him for living his life well.

We should not infer, however, that the discussions of *eudaimonia* that we find in ancient moral philosophy can make no contribution to our philosophical reflections about human happiness. Our interest in the topic of happiness derives from the reasonable assumption that, whether or not it is the ultimate goal of human life (as the utilitarians hold), it ought to play a significant role in the way we treat others and the plans we make for ourselves. It is a great good, whether or not it is the supreme good.

Furthermore, as we noted earlier (in section 31.2), when people report that they are happy with their lives, they typically do so because they think of themselves as possessing various good things—a good job, a good marriage, and so on. When they reflect on

---

[28] Aristotle 2000: 1098b20–22.

how happy they are, they are in the business of evaluating and not merely describing their lives. Greek moral philosophy consists in a debate among Platonists, Aristotelians, Stoics, and Epicureans about which among the things normally assumed to be good really are such. Their question—what is good?—need not be studied by empirical scientists whose engagement with happiness leaves entirely aside the question of how important a role happiness should play in human life. But a *philosophical* study of happiness must ask, as Kant and the utilitarians asked, what role it should play in a well-lived life. What is it for a life to be well-lived? That is precisely the question asked by ancient moral philosophy, when it struggled with the question: what is *eudaimonia*?

31.8 SCHOPENHAUER'S COMPLAINT: INTERMITTENCY OF THE WILL

If, as I suggested (in section 31.6), suffering can sometimes be shaped into an essential part of a valuable whole, then even the mitigated pessimism we considered earlier (in section 31.4), which holds that for the most part human lives can never be more than barely worth living, is too extreme. The pessimist must do more than point to the prevalence of suffering; he must also show that much that is bad in our lives can be neither eliminated nor redeemed by absorption into a larger whole.

Let us now give the case for pessimism a fuller hearing by surveying the complaints that some philosophers have made about the human situation. First, there is a pervasive restlessness and insatiability of the will. 'The will', Schopenhauer says, 'can just as little through some satisfaction cease to will always afresh, as time can end or begin; for the will there is no permanent fulfillment which completes and forever satisfies its craving.'[29] Whatever good we can achieve is temporary, because nothing affords the will ongoing satisfaction. Our lives, then, are devoted to the anxious pursuit of what we do not yet have; should we achieve our goals, we do not rest content, but anxiously hunger after new goods that we lack. Our projects are not quite Sisyphus-like, because we do sometimes succeed in pushing our boulders to the top of the hill, where they remain. But that hardly matters. When one boulder reaches the top, a new one awaits us at the bottom, and the cycle repeats itself.

Schopenhauer's observation should be compared with the comparison made in Plato's *Gorgias* between the soul of a foolish and unrestrained person and a leaky jar or sieve.[30] The idea is that people who devote themselves to the satisfaction of their physical appetites can never achieve a final state of contentment, because their satisfactions always leak away and leave a craving for more. This is viewed as a characteristic of only some of our desires—those for food, drink, sex, and the like —and so Plato is implying that if one's life is not dominated by these cravings, but pursues other sorts of goals, one can achieve a

---

[29] Schopenhauer 1969: 362.   [30] *Gorgias* 493a–b.

long-lasting satisfaction. That is precisely what Schopenhauer is denying. His thinks that it is the nature of all human willing that it can achieve at best a temporary good.

Schopenhauer may be right that our conscious experience is often marked by attentiveness to the portions of our projects that remain uncompleted, and there is often something at least mildly disagreeable about our sense that obstacles stand in our way, as they do whenever we undertake any task of some difficulty. But this should not lead us to overlook the pleasure we feel when we are engaged in projects whose difficulties we are overcoming. Furthermore, as the Epicureans point out, we can learn how to control the quality of our experience. Directing our attention to the fact that we are not currently in distress, whereas others are, is a source of pleasure.[31] We can always bring to mind the pleasures we have felt in the past, and those we expect in the future.[32]

In any case, we should not assume that the quality of our conscious experience—its pleasantness or unpleasantness—is the only thing of value in our lives. That is what hedonists claim, but their thesis is rejected by those who, following Plato, regard pleasure as only one good among many.[33] Even if the quality of our conscious life is a complex mélange of satisfaction, dissatisfaction, and other complex feelings that are difficult to describe, it is not the felt quality of our lives that alone determines their value.

31.9 PLATO'S COMPLAINT: THE ANALOGY OF THE CAVE

A further complaint that some philosophers make about our situation is the superficiality of humanity. 'When I see the blind and wretched state of man', Pascal writes, 'when I survey the whole universe in its dumbness and man left to himself with no light, as though lost in this corner of the universe, without knowing who put him there, what he has come to do, what will become of him when he dies, incapable of knowing anything, I am moved to terror.'[34] Pascal's complaint is that people are preoccupied with quotidian tasks of little or no significance, and pay no heed to what is ultimately most important. They prefer to preoccupy themselves with excitements and diversions rather than face the deepest questions.[35]

That attitude towards the general run of humanity can be traced back to Plato's *Apology*, where Socrates chastises his fellow citizens for resting content with their craft expertise and paying scant attention to questions about virtue and goodness. The blindness of most people to the greatest goods is vividly evoked by Plato's comparison of

---

[31] Lucretius 1951, 2: 1–61.   [32] Cicero 1927, 5: 95
[33] Plato seems to flirt with hedonism in *Protagoras*, but unequivocally rejects it in *Gorgias, Republic*, and *Philebus*. Hedonism is affirmed by Epicurus and his followers, and reappears in the modern period in Locke, Bentham, Mill, and Sidgwick.
[34] Pascal 1966: 88.   [35] Pascal 1966: 66–72.

humanity to prisoners acquainted solely with a world of shadows.[36] What they take seriously is removed by several orders of magnitude from what is truly valuable, but they have no idea that they live in so constricted a world. Plato's image does not portray the prisoners as people whose conscious experience is suffused with suffering. He leaves it open that they might be entirely content with their lives, since they have no clues about what they are missing. If they were asked, 'taking things overall, how happy are you with your life in general?' they might assign their lives a score of 10. If that is what happiness is, then Plato takes happiness to be of no value by itself. If it makes the prisoners complacent and prevents them from recognizing a fuller world of value, it is an obstacle to, not a component of, well-being.

Plato does not say whether the prisoners have lives that are worth living, but he thinks that the philosophers of his ideal city are obliged to do what they can to serve those who live in the cave. Most of these people will never arrive at a full understanding of what is valuable. But if they are released from their bondage and devote their lives not to gazing at shadows, but to activities performed in full view of the fire that burns inside the cave, they will certainly have lives worth living—otherwise it would not be worthwhile for philosophers to release and guide them. Plato takes it for granted, then, that the superficiality of most human beings can only be partially remedied. He makes that assumption because he takes goodness to be something that can be fully understood and appreciated only by those who undertake a philosophical study of what it is. He is confident, and justifiably so, that philosophy will always remain an undertaking to which a few people devote themselves.

One way to cast doubt on the pessimism of Pascal and Plato would be to propose that an understanding of value and our place in the universe is not nearly so far beyond the grasp of normal human intelligence as they assume. Our good, it might be said, is not difficult to grasp, once people are guided to it by their parents and the larger community. That is the position adopted by several different schools of philosophy—not only hedonists, but Aristotelians and Stoics as well. Aristotle holds that the ultimate good is virtuous activity supplied by adequate resources, whereas the Stoics equate it with virtue alone. Neither school doubts the ability of ordinary people to grasp what this is. What people need, to reach this understanding, is not rocket science—just good teachers, proper habituation, and intelligent management of their emotions.

31.10 PLATO'S FURTHER COMPLAINT: THE INTERNALLY DIVIDED SOUL

Yet another obstacle to the improvement of the human condition, and a cause of considerable unhappiness, is a phenomenon Plato portrayed in the *Phaedrus*. Here he compares the human soul to a charioteer who must control two horses, one cooperative, the

---

[36] *Republic* VII.

other rebellious. Reason has the task of setting the direction of our lives, but it can get nowhere without the support of psychological forces—our emotions and appetites—that must be brought into harmony both with reason and with each other. Plato's image suggests that these horses have tremendous motivational power and that unless they are properly trained, they will pull in different directions, forcing the chariot to move now in this direction, now in that. According to this picture of the human soul, a fully unified personality is a rare and difficult achievement, because the stuff of the soul—our emotions, feelings, appetites, longings—are by their very nature disorderly and divided, and the motivational power of reason—a mere human being, far less powerful than the horses to which it is yoked—is weak. Little wonder, then, that we often feel conflicted about our decisions, and are subject to second and third thoughts about our plans. Many other philosophers portray our psychological lives as scenes of conflict. According to Kant, when self-love and duty coincide, that is sheer good fortune; the motive of duty must often fight with our inclinations. The Freudian conception of the ego and its relations with the super-ego and the id is no more optimistic.

Plato does not insist that psychological unity is unattainable. His idea, rather, is that it would be unrealistic to expect the human condition to improve over time, so that someday—perhaps in hundreds of years—nearly all people will achieve a fully integrated mental life. Curiously, Mill does not explicitly address Plato's complaint—the unruliness of the human soul—when he discusses the obstacles to human happiness in *Utilitarianism*. He optimistically affirms that every human being can be educated to take much pleasure in the happiness of others and in the rich variety of his own mental life.[37] His tacit assumption is that if we realize that pain can often be reduced to a minimum, that life has a great variety of mental pleasures in store for us, and that we can cooperate with each other in the pursuit of the maximum well-being of humanity, there will be no warring passions or appetites within our souls.

31.11 MORAL STANDARDS AND HUMAN RELATIONS

There is not only a war to be won within each human soul, according to Plato; there is also constant warfare between one city and another, and never-ending conflict within cities (*Laws* 625e–627a). For Freud, 'our relations to other men' is the greatest source of our suffering.[38] One would have to be blind to the ordinary transactions of social life not to recognize that human beings often neglect each other when they should not, and—far worse—deliberately harm each other. Kant, as we noted earlier, holds that acting with good will has incomparable value, but he fully realizes that human beings must struggle against powerful incentives that conflict with morality. Being good, he thinks, generally goes against the grain of human nature.

---

[37] Mill 2001: 13–14.   [38] Freud 1961: 24.

Common-sense psychological observations support the thesis that interpersonal relations are fraught with difficulty. From everyone we encounter, we seek at least minimal respect and often approval. From some of them, we also crave appreciation, esteem, and honour. From others, we hope for friendship, devotion, or love. But it is difficult to win these rewards, and to be justifiably confident that we have done so. And since what we have won can easily be lost, we are often anxious about whether we will continue to bask in the warm glow of favourable human relations. It is rare for envy and rivalry to be completely absent from our relations to others. We are adept at masking our true feelings about others, and often it would be wrong to be fully forthcoming about what we think of each other. As La Rochefoucauld observed, 'we are so accustomed to disguise ourselves from others that we end up disguising ourselves from ourselves'.[39] If we are fortunate, we find a small circle of people with whom we enjoy relations of complete trust, honesty, and intimacy. But if the best we can achieve in our social relations is to create a small haven in which we take refuge from the indifference or hostility of the larger community, we are very distant from the kind of social world we rightly wish for.

In addition, it is no easy task for anyone to know what he owes to others—what justice requires of us, and, more generally, whether we are living up to the demands of morality. There is no consensus among philosophers about which normative theory we should adopt, and no consensus among citizens of good will about which laws are needed, or what the most important needs of the political community are. This does not mean that there is no such thing as moral knowledge or that we all lack it. But it would be complacent or arrogant for anyone to be supremely confident that his views on these matters are justified. When we go beyond the simplest matters, we should have at least some uncertainty about what is right and what is good. That too is one of the burdens of the human condition. If human life has greater value than the lives of brutes in part because moral action has intrinsic value, that advantage carries with it some heavy burdens.

31.12 Life's Brevity

Our bodies, Freud notes, are 'doomed to decay and dissolution' and 'cannot even do without pain and anxiety as warning signals'.[40] We are all heading towards death, so even if our lives are filled with value and happiness, they end all too soon. We are told, in Plato's *Symposium*, that all human beings seek the good—not just for now, not for a brief while, not for the duration of human life, but *forever*.[41] That is not something that our embodied mentality can achieve. So, death is an immense loss for anyone who is living well and who would otherwise continue to do so: the time during which we will have lost the opportunity to live well is infinitely greater than the time during which we have lived well. Little wonder, then, that philosophers have often looked for some reason to affirm the immortality of the soul. Some of them do so because they think we can reasonably

---

[39] La Rochefoucauld 2001: Maxim 119, p. 24.   [40] Freud 1961: 24.   [41] *Symposium*, 206a.

hope that life will become much better when it is transformed by death. But it is also reasonable to hold that even if the kind of life with which we are already acquainted—ordinary, embodied existence—could be prolonged indefinitely, that would be an improvement in the human condition, provided that one's life is worth living.

But conquering death is not presently on the cards. Probably the best we can hope for, as we look to the future of humankind, is the alleviation of the misery that goes beyond the suffering inherent in the human situation, and the preservation of conditions in which people have lives that are, at a minimum, worth living. The supposition that a better world than that can be created for humankind is a hopeful speculation, but should not influence any concrete policies we devise for the alleviation of suffering and the promotion of the good of present and future generations.

At the same time, we must reject Larkin's advice: 'Get out as early as you can / And don't have any kids yourself.' Admittedly, our lives are a complex mixture of good and bad; embodied existence, for most people, is unlikely to be better than that. But our survey of the obstacles to living a life worth living lends no support to the conclusion that all of us would have been better off had we never been born.[42]

BIBLIOGRAPHY

Allen, W. 1977. *Annie Hall*. Directed by W. Allen, screenplay by W. Allen and M. Brickman.

Aristotle 2000. *Nicomachean Ethics*, tr. and ed. R. Crisp. Cambridge: Cambridge University Press.

Benatar, D. 2006. *Better Never to Have Been: The Harm of Coming into Existence*. Oxford: Clarendon Press.

Biswas-Diener, R., Diener, E., and Tamir, M. 2004. 'The Psychology of Subjective Well-Being', *Daedalus* 133 (2): 18–25.

Camus, A. 1955. *The Myth of Sisyphus and Other Essays*, tr. J. O'Brien. New York: Random House.

Cicero 1927. *Tusculan Disputations*. Cambridge, MA: Harvard University Press.

Feldman, F. 2010. *What Is This Thing Called Happiness?* Oxford: Oxford University Press.

Freud, S. 1961. *Civilization and its Discontents*, tr. and ed. J. Strachey. New York: W. W. Norton & Co.

Haybron, D. M. 2008. *The Pursuit of Unhappiness: The Elusive Psychology of Well-Being*. Oxford: Oxford University Press.

Heine, H. 1934. 'Morphia', *Heine's Poetry and Prose*. London: J. M. Dent & Sons Ltd.

Inwood, B. and Gerson, L. P. 1988. *Hellenistic Philosophy: Introductory Readings*. Indianapolis: Hackett Publishing Co.

Kant, I. 1929. *Critique of Pure Reason*, tr. N. Kemp Smith. New York: St. Martin's Press.

—— 1991. *The Metaphysics of Morals*. Introduction, Translation, and Notes by M. Gregor. Cambridge: Cambridge University Press

—— 1997. *Critique of Practical Reason*, tr. and ed. Mary Gregor. Cambridge: Cambridge University Press.

—— 2002. *Groundwork for the Metaphysics of Morals*, tr. A. Zweig, ed. T. E. Hill, Jr. and A. Zweig. Oxford: Oxford University Press.

---

[42] The opposite conclusion is defended in Benatar 2006.

La Rochefoucauld 2001. *Maxims*. South Bend, Indiana: St. Augustine's Press.

Larkin, P. 1988. 'This Be the Verse', in A. Thwaite (ed.), *Philip Larkin, Collected Poems*. New York: Farrar, Straus, and Giroux, 180.

Lucretius 1951. *On the Nature of the Universe*. Translated and introduced by R. E. Latham. London: Penguin Books.

Mill, J. S. 2001. *Utilitarianism*. Indianapolis: Hackett Publishing Co.

Nagel, T. 1979. 'Death', in *Mortal Questions*. Cambridge: Cambridge University Press, 1–10.

Nettle, D. 2005. *Happiness: The Science Behind Your Smile*. Oxford: Oxford University Press.

Pascal, B. 1966. *Pensées*. Translated with an Introduction by A. J. Krailsheimer. Harmondsworth, England: Penguin Books.

Plato 1997. *Complete Works*. Edited, with Introduction and Notes by J. M. Cooper. Indianapolis: Hackett Publishing Co.

Schopenhauer, A. 1969. *The World as Will and Representation*. Volume 1. Translated by E. F. J. Payne. New York: Dover Publications.

—— 1970. 'On the Suffering of the World', in *Essays and Aphorisms*, selected and translated by R. J. Hollingdale. Harmondsworth, England: Penguin Books.

CHAPTER 32

AUTONOMY

JOHN CHRISTMAN

WHAT, if any particular thing, gives human beings the moral value they have? Is there any capacity or characteristic that makes human agents valuable in ways that, say, pencils and peat moss are not? Moreover, is there anything about us that grounds the respect that others should show us but that also serves as the *source* of moral obligation for ourselves as well, as thinkers and agents? If such a moral holy grail exists, it would be philosophically earth-shattering to capture it. As several philosophers in the history of western thought have considered these questions, it is individual *autonomy*—the capacity for us to judge things for ourselves rather than simply to take orders from other sources of authority or merely passively enjoy things as they come—that fulfills this regal promise.

Autonomy—*auto-nomos*—means governing (giving the law to) oneself. It originally applied to city-states that were independent and not merely a client or colony of a larger political power. Only later did it apply specifically to individual human beings. It can be contrasted with freedom (in some of the ways that idea is understood), as we will discuss below. It can also be understood in a variety of ways. In general, however, to be autonomous is to be governed in one's actions (or life as a whole) by values, principles, or reflections that are truly one's own, to be one's own person, as opposed to being guided by external, manipulative, or alien forces. It has been proffered by some to express the seat of fundamental moral value in human lives, while for other thinkers it is merely a valuable characteristic (among others) that some or most adult humans enjoy. In all cases, however, it is thought to be an important moral value and one that connects in crucial ways to basic moral obligations as well as social and political principles.

An overview of how the concept of autonomy has functioned in western moral philosophy should include a discussion of contemporary debates about the idea set against a backdrop of historical traditions that do not always place self-government at the centre of moral value.[1] After a selective overview of those historical trends I will consider some

---

[1] A canonical account of the history of philosophy that traces the roads to seeing autonomy at the center of morality can be found in Schneewind 1998; for an alternative sketch of that history, see Taylor 1989.

controversies in the more recent literature on autonomy in moral philosophy, and I will conclude with consideration of how that notion functions in social and political thought as well. However, we begin with ancient philosophy in order to see how autonomy is in many ways a *modern* idea.

32.1 Autonomy's Pre-History

In the current age, we might naturally think that morality concerns making the right *choices*, being guided by the right principles and having the good judgement to apply them correctly in the situations we face. But for ancient Greek and Roman thinkers the specification of the good, moral life—and of value more generally—was not characterized as a life of independent choice valuable for its own sake. For these thinkers, moral value attached to one's character as a whole, one's life trajectory in its broad contours, and to whether that trajectory aimed at the good, not merely to an individual's capacity to make choices.

In the ancient philosophy of the western tradition, morality was expressed by the *virtues*, and virtues attached to persons generally. Virtues marked out traits and dispositions that defined one's character. Of course it is true that practical wisdom (*phronesis*) played an important role in the specification of the virtuous life. Still such practical judgement was not specified by rules or principles; rather practical wisdom involves the judgement of the wise person viewed as a whole. What matters less in this picture is the particular capacity for reflective *choice*, specifically choice based on rules and principles of the sort that much modern ethics emphasizes.

In Plato's *Republic*, for example, the view of justice that emerges is one of internal harmony, both of the individual soul and the city that mirrors it. A just person is one whose soul (or character) is perfectly structured so that its reasoning part governs the functioning of both the affective parts as well as the appetitive, desiring parts. Reason rules, though not as a dictatorial master of one's internal life, but rather as the ordering principle that allows the other parts of the personality to express themselves in the right situations in the right way. A courageous person, for example, would not suppress all emotion—she might need to be moved by anger at times—but would allow herself to be moved by just the right amount of it. The point is to achieve a functional harmony, both internally as an individual and in the ideally just city (Plato 1992).

But note also that Plato (or his spokesperson here Socrates) explains how in the just city a strategy of social pedagogy might be undertaken that he called the 'myth of the metals'. This would involve a 'noble lie'—a bit of specially fashioned social ideology—that would function to foment the belief in citizens that different orders of people would come to think that they are made of different 'metals'—gold, silver, iron—corresponding to different orders of authority and status in the society. By believing that they are made of different material citizens would accept without question the different roles they would be assigned in the perfectly functioning polis, as the metals symbolize different qualities of humans corresponding to these different roles (Plato 1992: Bk. III).

The thing to notice here is that in the design of the perfect society the role of human *choice* in its own right has been entirely sidelined; indeed it is seen as disruptive or dangerous, given that the purpose of the exercise is the design of the perfectly flourishing person or city. Contrast this with the modern notion that only when citizens and individuals are given choice over their lives and societies is there a minimally acceptable social order.

Aristotle shares with Plato an attention to virtue as the central aspect of the moral life. Indeed, Aristotle is seen as the major source for 'virtue ethics', the view of morality that focuses on character and human flourishing in addition to the capacity for choice itself in theorizing about morality. For Aristotle, human beings fit into a larger metaphysical order characterized by interlocking purposes for all elements of that order. This includes humans and their (mental and physical) parts, but it also covers the (non-human) natural world, both on earth and throughout the cosmos. The essence of a thing is, for Aristotle, its function—its *telos*—so that things hold together by virtue of interlocking functions. Human life and morality, then, are described not by a capacity for choosing as something valuable in itself but by the way that life is organized and how it fits into a larger order of connected purposes (Aristotle 2008).

In a related manner, human *freedom* is not a non-derivative moral or social value in ancient thought. As we saw with Plato, Aristotle specifies the ideal human life without giving much of a role for the freedom to make one's own decisions. Living out the ideal functioning for one's life is the central value; whether or not one chooses such a functioning for oneself is not directly relevant. Now it was surely the case that the idea of a free 'man' was an important concept in this setting, as it was for later thinkers; but what this referred to was not every individual (the use of 'man' here is intentional) exercising a capacity for independent choice. Rather that phrase refers to a particular social *status*, that of a free citizen who is not a slave or a 'barbarian'. This is why no reference to women or barbarians (non-Greeks in the case of Athens for example) is made. To be free was to enjoy the status of a citizen with special prerogatives as well as a cluster of duties and a sense of honour that attaches to that office. Choosing for oneself, simply for the sake of being whatever kind of person one valued being, did not fit into the picture.

One philosophical tradition in the ancient world that did seem to put the power of choice at the centre of their conception of the good life was Stoicism. For example, Epictetus famously advised that we should desire only what is 'up to us' and therefore eschew any project or aspiration that would be frustrated by circumstance (Epictetus 2005: 7). In this way we will achieve a mastery of ourselves as well as a perfect harmony with nature and contentment with our condition. This emphasis on self-control and self-mastery appears to echo the idea of self-government at the centre of autonomy, and stoic thinking was influential on both Rousseau and Kant, the modern standard-bearers for autonomy as we will see. However, it is important to see just how this stoic picture falls short of a call for self-government in the modern sense.[2] For the point of suppressing unsatisfiable desires on this picture is to ensure that one's actions and general path

[2] For an overview, see Annas 1993 and Nussbaum 1994. It is actually controversial whether stoic ethics was tied closely with their metaphysics: for discussion see Cooper 1996 and Annas 1993.

through life is in harmony with *nature*. In the background of this view is the belief that nature, as a whole, is ordered by a rational principle (God), so that conformity with the flow of natural events and laws ensures that our lives reflect that perfection. We as individuals have particular natures which fit in with this larger system and so developing the virtues (especially of self-control) was needed to manifest our unique nature.

Several other steps on the road to the modern conception of autonomy might be worth mentioning, such as the development of republican thought in Machiavelli and the development of natural law theory from the classical Roman thinkers through Thomas Aquinas, Hugo Grotius, and beyond. Such views continued to share the idea that nature and the universe form a moral order that, when fully grasped by reason, provides a guide for a flourishing (moral) life and a well-ordered society. What changes radically in this tradition of thought occurs during and just after the Renaissance in Europe, when there emerged a new approach to the science of nature in which natural entities and events are no longer seen as teleologically ordered (that is, organized by virtue of their functions and purposes) but as a series of events linked by efficient causes. On such a view, nature is but a system of cause and effect which, while it can be seen as the work of (the Christian) God, is not something that individual persons can look to in order to find moral insight and principle. Humans must then think for themselves (guided by reason) to determine such principles. That idea, as it applies to moral and social philosophy, arises most forcefully in the work of those theorists who see political obligation as necessarily arising from human agreement rather than from divine right or the natural order of things. The role of human choice in this picture will become, as we will see, the lynchpin in the story that leads to the centralization of individual self-government in the moral sphere.

32.2 THE MODERN EMERGENCE OF THE IDEA OF AUTONOMY

32.2.1 The Social Contract Tradition

In the seventeenth and eighteenth centuries there developed a conception of moral value and political obligation that came to place individual and collective self-government at the centre of things. As we mentioned, the dominant thinking by the early seventeenth century in this tradition was that nature is morally inert and hence moral obligation was viewed as 'artificial' or a construction of human thought and action (though dictated more generally by natural law). This is especially pronounced in the work of Thomas Hobbes, who viewed political societies as human constructions, albeit fully binding ones and in line with (what we can know of) the will of God. The commonwealth, for Hobbes, is a creation of individual human beings agreeing to forego war and conflict among themselves and to grant unqualified power to a single sovereign who will protect them from the ravages of the state of nature (Hobbes 1651/1986).

The key to Hobbes' picture of society is his view of human nature. For Hobbes, humans are motivated by a fundamental desire to survive and advance their own interests: all other purposes, feelings, and virtues are outgrowths of that basic motive. Natural law and natural right, on this view, are simply the rules that describe how all of nature operates, including the imperative that human beings take those actions that will ensure their survival (to 'seek peace') and satisfy their needs. As a result, political power is justified only as a function of the collective will to allow an all-powerful sovereign to reign over all citizens, ensuring their protection from internal strife and external enemies.

Note that 'natural law' here tells us nothing of what is right or wrong in a substantive sense, apart from dictating that we should (continue to) pursue our own rational interests. Virtue is meaningless in a state of nature, for Hobbes, and agreements, obligations, and contracts are equally meaningless when there is no entity in place to enforce their provisions. All 'right' is a function of enforcement guided by those laws of nature. Individual 'choice' grounds obligation but only in the limited sense that such obligation, being required for peaceful existence, is in keeping with the rational order of self-interested beings.

Contrast that picture with that of John Locke, who saw people in the state of nature as guided by 'reason' which operates in ways that do much more to inform us of the substance of moral obligation than Hobbes' version of natural law did. For Locke, reason tells us that it is permissible to pursue our interests but only within the bounds of the natural rights of others. So reason here not only informs us of the content of those rights—the rights to life, liberty, and property—but also supplies us (reasonable 'men') with the *motivation* to adhere to the dictates of those rights (Locke 1690/1963).[3]

For both Hobbes and Locke, obligation and rightful action are described in social, indeed political, terms. In both cases, however, there develops a view of the source of obligation as individual choice (albeit in Hobbes' case as guided by rational self-interest). This marks a point in the history of philosophy where rightfulness and virtue are not defined simply by one's social role or by one's conformity with nature but by one's actions and choices within that natural order. The idea of 'right' (*ius*) has thus shifted from the prior idea of *rightfulness*, or doing what is called for given one's role or place in the universe, to having a *right*, a prerogative whereby one makes decisions and judgements oneself.

What comes to the fore in this work is the idea that social obligations and, by extension political power, gains its authority as a function of human choice. Hence, the connection between moral authority/obligation and the person's capacity to choose for him or herself was placed at the heart of the moral order.[4] That centrality for the notion of self-government becomes even more pronounced in the next phase of the development of social contract thinking.

---

[3] This summary emphasizes the role of reason in Locke in revealing the substance and force of natural rights. It is an interesting challenge to square this line of thought with Locke's thoroughly *empiricist* epistemology, where no innate ideas can give us knowledge of the world.

[4] The reference to both men and women is quite artificial here, as there is much reason to think that these writers did not think their ideas applied without qualification to people (men and women) as such, in particular to people outside of Europe. For discussion of whether the social contract theorists actually meant their views of natural rights to apply to non-males or non-Europeans, see Pateman 1988 and Mills 1997.

32.2.2 Autonomy as Central to Human Dignity: Rousseau and Kant

Another contrast between Locke and Hobbes is worth discussing, since it marks a fork in the road in thinking about individual freedom in the liberal tradition. For Hobbes, being free simply meant facing no external physical barriers in carrying out one's wishes. Freedom was 'negative' in the sense of referring to an *absence*—the absence of constraints on action. For Locke, however, liberty was to be distinguished from 'license' in that to be free was not only to be left unconstrained, it was also to follow the *law*, specifically the natural law and its particular specification of people's natural rights.

This contrast between seeing freedom as being unconstrained and seeing it as conforming one's actions to law signifies a separation in the philosophical tradition we are discussing that becomes clearly visible by the middle of the eighteenth century. David Hume clearly represents the first of these directions, while Jean-Jacques Rousseau and Immanual Kant pursue the second. This separation is between those who view freedom as more or less observable empirically and which functions as a property of external action, and those who see freedom as an internal aspect of the way motives are formed, specifically the capacity to formulate and act on motives that are one's own in some way.

Rousseau stands out as the theorist that puts freedom most squarely at the centre of moral and political principle, seeing it as essential to man's nature as a moral being ('man is born free, though everywhere he is in chains').[5] While Hobbes saw freedom as the absence of external barriers and Locke viewed freedom as acting in accordance with (God-given) natural law, Rousseau introduced the idea that freedom was acting according to a law that one gives to oneself as a moral being. To be 'driven by appetite is slavery', he writes, and being moved by purposes that are simply internalized forms of social pressure was the mark of a corrupt personality (Rousseau 1760/1987). For Rousseau, only life in a properly organized democracy where basic constitutional principles are fashioned by a sovereign that includes the general will of all citizens could allow human beings to flourish as free persons. At this point we have arrived at the understanding of freedom as the self-imposition of law (in accordance with the necessities of life in a society). Freedom is autonomy or self-government.

While Rousseau set the stage, it is Immanuel Kant who placed autonomy at the centre of practical philosophy in general. For Kant, true freedom was not only independence from all physical causes—having a will that can act independently of 'pathological' desires and forces—it also required acting according to a law that one gives to oneself. Autonomy, then, is not only the most fully developed form of freedom, it is also the foundation of moral obligation. For the law one must impose on oneself is a law that is unqualified in its ground and in its application; it is a categorical imperative to act in accordance with universal principles. To be autonomous is to follow the moral law as a

---

[5] It should be noted that in his reflections on morality Rousseau did not limit his reference entirely to the language of freedom; he also had much to say on the nature of virtue (see for example his essay 'On the Virtues Necessary for a Hero').

universal imperative one applies to oneself as a member of a 'kingdom of ends'. Such a 'kingdom' referred not to the actual societies that Rousseau pictured but to a realm populated only by rational autonomous beings worthy of respect (Kant 1785/1983).

The relationship between autonomy, freedom (more generally), and the moral law in Kant's philosophy is complex and the subject of much scholarly debate. (See, e.g. Allison 1990.) What is clear, however, is that Kant viewed the capacity to govern ourselves as both the source of moral obligation as well as the object of moral respect that we all owe to each other. Just as we must value our own capacity to govern ourselves (and value this capacity without qualification), we must respect that capacity in all other beings and therefore treat them as 'ends in themselves', and never as a mere means to our own ends. We have therefore hit upon what we earlier called (with intentional hyperbole) the 'holy grail' of morality—the capacity in ourselves and all human beings that grounds morality and supplies its main focus—the capacity to govern ourselves.

It should be noted that the idea of autonomy as it functions in Kant's philosophy is the capacity to impose *moral* principles on oneself and guide one's actions in accordance with those (universal) principles. This is what is called *moral autonomy*. It can be contrasted with a broader notion, called *personal autonomy*, which refers to the ability to independently form and act upon values, desires, or principles whether or not these should be classified as moral. To be personally autonomous is to be one's own person, to be guided by motives that are not externally imposed or simply blind responses to social pressure. And while there is some reason to think the idea of personal autonomy (as a basic value) can be found in the work of Rousseau, the figure in the history of (western) philosophy that emphasizes this idea most is John Stuart Mill.

Mill's *On Liberty* is a work that defends the claim that society should be arranged so that individuals enjoy the maximal amount of liberty consistent with the prevention of harm to others. Mill provides a variety of arguments for this position, and many of them advance instrumental reasons referring to the good effects that liberty is likely to have, such as promoting truth, allowing people to verify their beliefs in the face of counter-arguments, the production of creativity and genius, and the like. However, Mill also argues that protecting liberty in this way allows 'individuality' to flourish, and in a famous subtitle to Chapter III of *On Liberty*, he describes individuality as 'one of the elements of well-being', indicating that individuality is a component of a good life itself.

How this relates to autonomy depends on how Mill understands 'individuality' as a value. For in some passages, it appears that the kind of individuality Mill has in mind is a kind of social non-conformism, the disposition to buck social trends in order to engage in 'experiments in living' (Mill 1859/1975, ch. III). However, in other passages, it looks like individuality, for Mill, simply means being your own person, for example when he refers to 'the only freedom which deserves the name is that of pursuing our own good in our own way' (ch. I). Here individuality refers to being one's own person whether or not being so involves conforming to social trends or being iconoclastic.

The idea that self-government involves acting according to values that are truly one's own expresses the core of what most contemporary writers on autonomy attempt to capture with the concept, and it is to these discussions that we must presently turn.

This highly selective journey through the history of western philosophy was not meant to show that all thought led to Kant (or Mill) in these ways,[6] or that important thinking about morality and individual self-government ceased after the mid-nineteenth century—far from it. Rather it was structured to mark out important contrasts and similarities in that history. The most profound contrast is between autonomy-based views of practical reason and moral obligation that emerge in the modern period (after the seventeenth century) and ancient conceptions of the virtuous life. For Plato, Aristotle, and the Stoics, the just and virtuous life was not one led according to rules of one's own determination or choice; rather, it was a life lived in harmonious accord with reason and nature.

Considerations of the importance of autonomy have gained prominence in moral and political thinking since the second half of the twentieth century, largely due to the work of John Rawls in political philosophy but also due to the lasting influence of both Kant and Mill (corresponding roughly to the deontological and utilitarian approaches to moral philosophy, respectively). In more recent discussions of the concept of autonomy, however, the connection between that idea and the complexities of moral theory are not always made explicit. Nevertheless, many fundamental issues in recent moral and political philosophy turn in very interesting ways on the details of the idea of self-government.

32.3 CONTEMPORARY DISCUSSIONS OF AUTONOMY

As we mentioned, autonomy is, most generally, the capacity to govern oneself, either in the determination of moral principles or in one's values and actions more generally.[7] An important distinction, however, is between autonomy as it applies to persons, *per se* (or a person's life as a whole), and autonomy as applied to particular decisions or acts. The former is labelled *global* autonomy and the latter *local* autonomy.[8] In any case, it will have to be determined whether autonomy should be seen as a matter of degree (and if so along what dimension(s) it will vary), or as an all-or-nothing quality. What can be called *basic* autonomy can be used to refer to the (all-or-nothing) quality of being autonomous relative to one's most fundamental values and commitments.[9]

Autonomy can also be distinguished from 'freedom', at least from most versions of that idea. Freedom in a negative sense—referring to the absence of constraints on

---

[6] Though some have traced this history in a way that suggests this; see Schneewind 1998.

[7] There are many overviews of the concept of autonomy: see, e.g. Berofsky 1995, Dworkin 1988, Haworth 1986, Feinberg 1989, Lindley 1986, Young 1986, and the essays in Christman 1989, Christman and Anderson 2005, J. S. Taylor 2005, and Mackenzie and Stoljar 2000a.

[8] Diana Meyers refers to essentially the same distinction with the terms 'programmatic' and 'episodic' autonomy. See Meyers, 1989.

[9] See Friedman 2003 and Christman 2009: ch. 6.

action—can be contrasted with autonomy in that the latter refers to the manner in which decisions are formulated rather than the opportunity to successfully carry them out. However, there are many conceptions of freedom and with some understandings of that idea—for example with some versions of 'positive freedom'—the distinction between freedom and autonomy diminishes.[10] However, autonomy clearly refers to the capacity of persons to act on motives, values, or principles that are self-imposed or self-validating in some sense to be worked out by a theory of the concept.

As we noted in our discussion of Kant, autonomy involves imposing a law on oneself in the determination of the action one should pursue—or more generally determining the motive, value, or 'pro-attitude' one should be moved by. This is to be guided by motives that are one's own rather than being imposed by external forces or arising from processes that are alien to one's sense of self. Now Kant himself claimed that one's own desires are, as such, alien in this way, and only imperatives that function independent of all material causality (which include our desires) can guide the autonomous person. Most theorists in the current literature eschew that particular metaphysical picture, preferring to count desires, attitudes, or other psychological states as part of the agent's authentic motivational structure (though the breadth or narrowness of the categories relative to which one can be autonomous varies).[11]

Conceptions of autonomy typically contain conditions that refer, on the one hand, to an agent's general competence—self-control, the absence of debilitating pathologies, weakness of the will, self-deception, compulsions, and so on—and, on the other, to the 'authenticity' of the values and motives that move one to action. The former set of conditions relate to the person's general ability to carry out her plans in social settings and in response to environmental factors.[12] The latter category of requirements, however, have garnered far more discussion, since it is much more difficult to delineate what it means for desires (or the like) to be truly one's own in the relevant sense without postulating problematic metaphysical entities, such as an ideal 'true self' operating inside us all in mysterious ways.[13]

The most influential approach to the 'authenticity' component of autonomy is one which requires that the autonomous agent be able to reflectively identify with the lower

---

[10] For discussion of negative and positive freedom, see Berlin, 1969. Also, some might claim that autonomy can be captured under the broad tripartite schema of freedom introduced by McCallum (see McCallum 1967), where freedom always involves a relation among three variables: A person, X, being free/unfree from Y, to do or be Z. Autonomy, however, refers not to the Y variable but to the nature of the agent (X) and the character of the values, plans, and desires that move her to do Z.

[11] For a discussion of the different elements of one's character and motivational system that autonomy can be understood to apply to, see Double 1992 and Mele 1995. Also, it should be noted that whether the reflection required for autonomy amounts simply to a desire (or motive or pro-attitude) or an exercise of 'reasons' in some sense still divides thinkers in the literature, exemplified for example by Frankfurt and Mele in the first instance and Korsgaard in the second, who is discussed below.

[12] For a sustained discussion of autonomy competence, see Meyers 1989; see also Benson 2005.

[13] For a worry that some accounts of autonomy rely problematically on the postulation of a 'true self' see Friedman 1986. Also Arneson argues that a proper understanding of the requirement of independence for autonomy would show that further 'authenticity' conditions may be otiose (see Arneson 1991).

order motivations that move her to action. This 'hierarchical' conception developed first by Gerald Dworkin (1970) and Harry Frankfurt (1987) claimed, in its original form, that the autonomous person[14] is one who is moved by first-order desires that she identifies with as a result of critical reflection and such identification amounts to second-order desires to be moved by those first-order motives.

One thing to note about this approach is that it attempts to define autonomy simply in terms of the structure of one's reflective motivational system and not the content of that system. Dworkin, for example, stresses *procedural independence* as a condition of autonomy and not *substantive independence* (Dworkin 1988 ch. 1). The latter refers to being actually and currently independent of the authority, power, or control of others in one's decisions. By not requiring substantive independence, however, it is claimed that we can count as autonomous those who have adopted (in a structurally or procedurally adequate manner) values that include strict obedience to some authority or value system.[15] This implies a 'content neutral' account of autonomy.

Several issues have been raised about this approach. First, the notion of 'identification' is ambiguous between simple acknowledgement and endorsement; in the first case, I merely see the motive as (alas) mine, in the way that I might own up to my failings or other facts about myself, but this is clearly too weak a condition since I could own up to addictions and compulsions in this way as well. The second case—identification as wholehearted endorsement—may be too demanding, since it leaves no room for ambivalence or simply coping with circumstance as part of an autonomous existence, something all of us must do in many areas of our lives.[16]

Moreover, the question can be raised about what gives higher-order reflective identification the authority it needs to express the authentic voice of the agent herself. Indeed, why should higher-order *desires* have any more 'agential authority' than initial desires to do this or that might have?[17] In the model's attempt to avoid the Kantian picture in which higher-order reflection speaks for the agent because it is the voice of 'reason' or one's 'true self', theorists have attempted to qualify the idea of critical self-reflection: such reflection must, on the one hand, convey the authority of the agent herself but not require sill higher orders of reflection to establish that authority, which would lead to a regress of conditions.

Frankfurt answered such charges by postulating a core set of basic 'cares' that, on this view, 'resound' throughout the whole of one's belief and desires system (Frankfurt 1992). These deep expressions of care rest upon convictions and desires that it would be 'unthinkable' for us to reject; they are a matter of 'volitional necessity' (Frankfurt 1994). In these ways, according to Frankfurt, we need not postulate further levels of evaluation

---

[14] In these early formulations the account was of 'freedom', not 'autonomy'. However, in the subsequent literature the latter notion has been used when discussing these views.

[15] There is a lively debate in the literature about whether procedural independence will capture all that is valuable in being autonomous (or whether substantive independence is also required). See, e.g. Benson 2005, Oshana 2006, and Stoljar 2000.

[16] Cf. e.g. Oshana 2005.

[17] See e.g. Thalberg 1989, Watson 1975, Bratman 2003, Friedman, 1986.

to secure the authenticity of second-order reflections, for these evaluations (in so far as they express wholehearted care) are simply a reflection of who we *are*, full stop.[18]

Now this view accepts as an inevitable aspect of our moral personality that our most basic commitments are not things that we can simply jettison or alter at will.[19] What is also implied by this model is that autonomy can be enjoyed independently of how we *came to have* the values we do. As long as the internal coherence of our fundamental cares is established, along with the identification with first-order desires that they endorse, how we developed those commitments is irrelevant. This implication has bothered many thinkers who argue that manipulative, coercive, or deceptive processes by which persons come to have the attitudes they have may well undercut their autonomy (Mele 1995, Christman 2009, Fisher and Ravizza 1998). Spurred by such concerns, these thinkers have, in different ways, developed 'historical' accounts of autonomy. On such models, conditions referring to the processes by which the person came to adopt the desire, value, etc., in question are added to other requirements. These conditions can either specify 'objectively' (or externally) the processes of proper desire/value formation—say that such processes need to involve critical reflection on the part of the agent—or the conditions can be specified with reference to the agent's subjective appraisal of these processes. The first route is taken by Mele (Mele 1995) and the second by Christman (Christman 2009) for example.

In many ways this move brings current thinking about autonomy in line with Rousseau's views (though marks a sharp contrast with Kant's). For as we noted, Rousseau was keenly aware of the ways that the psychological dynamics of social interaction can (and often do in modern societies) have the effect of people internalizing the often slavish and corrupt attitudes that are moulded into them by dominant ideologies and social pressure. *Amour propre*, in this sense undercuts freedom, understood as the ability to govern oneself from a position of equal standing and independence (see Rousseau, *Emile*, Bk. II)

Whether or not current historical views mirror Rousseau's concerns exactly, this reference to one's place in a social network and its bearing on individual self-government leads to another important development in recent thinking about autonomy. Theorists have been sensitive to the charge that traditional liberal accounts of the autonomous 'man' have problematically assumed an 'atomistic' account of human existence and values, one that typically mirrors only the experience of (certain sorts of) men in public positions with independent means. However, a conception of autonomy that is more attuned to the experience of women, family members, care-givers, and other occupants of the 'private' sphere (traditionally speaking) is one that would emphasize social *relations* as central to self-government as much as social separation and independence.[20] Others have stressed the social (or 'communal') nature of the self, and claimed that autonomy must be understood as a property of selves so conceived (Christman 2009, Cuypers 2001.)

---

[18] For further discussion, see the essays in Buss and Overton 2002 and Cuypers 2001: 85–130.
[19] For discussion of this claim, see Mele 1995: 146–50, Christman 2001.
[20] See Nedelsky 1989, Oshana 2006, and the essays in Mackenzie and Stoljar 2000a.

It should be noted, however, that relational views of autonomy must take pains to distinguish necessary conditions of the social background against which autonomy can flourish from the claim that to be autonomous is to maintain certain relational positions oneself, for example that one not be in a position of subservience or dependence. In this latter case, the claim essentially is that autonomy demands *substantive independence* and not merely procedural independence as defined above. In so far, then, as autonomy is meant as a content-neutral (or value-neutral) property of persons, demanding substantive independence of this sort is problematic (see Christman 2004, Rössler 2002). Many have claimed, however, that the very possibility that a procedurally independent person who 'chooses' subservience or domination could be called autonomous on some models shows those models to be inadequate (Oshana 2006). This debate recalls the questions we raised about Mill's view of individuality, referring either to a personal ideal with substantive content (non-conformism and independence from others) or to a standard of simply being true to oneself, even if that means conforming to strict standards of obedience.

One final variation in thinking about autonomy (and freedom) which connects it with strains in the history of philosophy in interesting ways is the view that autonomy requires social relations of a very particular sort, namely relations of *recognition* by others of one's normative authority, one's status as an independent agent, or one's identity as a socially located being. For example, Catriona Mackenzie has argued that to be autonomous, in addition to being competent and reflective, one must be recognized as having 'normative authority' over one's central values and commitments by surrounding others. The normative authority that Mackenzie points to is the ability to self-validate one's judgements and reflections in order to make one's desires effective in action. That is, normative authority involves being taken as the validating source (though not necessarily the origin) of one's values and judgements, one's practical identity (MacKenzie 2008). In a similar vein, Joel Anderson and Axel Honneth have developed a view of autonomy that stresses the need for social recognition in order to ensure that agents' vulnerabilities to threats to their self-respect are obviated. They claim that in at least three spheres, certain forms of social recognition relations—ones that establish self-respect, self-trust, and self-esteem—are required for individuals to avoid particular vulnerabilities to which citizens in current contexts are systematically subject, vulnerabilities which their autonomy is meant to protect them against. Such relations of recognition, they claim, are therefore conceptually required for autonomy in a full sense (Anderson and Honneth 2005). Others have adopted similar views, requiring attitudes of self-trust that, they argue, must be recognized by others (Grovier 1993, Benson 2005).

In some ways, these relational approaches to autonomy can be seen to be retrieving elements of pre-modern conceptions of freedom, specifically the republican idea that to be free was to enjoy a particular social status rather than a set of individual capacities. (This can also be seen in the recent work on neo-republican conceptions of freedom: see e.g. Pettit 1997.) However, most thinking about autonomy in the recent literature has developed in ways that are clearly in a more or less constant dialogue with Kant.

Therefore, in order to bring this overview full circle we should close by examining certain trends in thinking about *moral* autonomy that show the debt owed to Kant (or some might say the baggage left from his legacy).

32.3.1 Moral Autonomy Reconsidered

There have been several recent attempts to revitalize the Kantian approach to morality in general and autonomy in particular (e.g. O'Neill 1990, Korsgaard, 1996, Hill 1991). Of specific interest is the work by Christine Korsgaard, in that she builds a model of the sources of normativity that places autonomy at its centre. She emphasizes the special capacity that we all have as agents to raise questions about the desires and motives we happen to have and ask the 'normative question' about whether it is a good idea to follow them. This cannot merely be the expression of another desire or motive, because, as we saw earlier in our discussion of Frankfurt's view, that would merely push the question back to that higher level. The reflection involved, then, must be the exercise of an evaluative capacity that speaks with the authority of our own agency while at the same time settling the issue of whether this or that action should be done. A key component of this process, for Korsgaard, is what she calls our 'practical identity'. All rational agents, she argues, have a practical identity which orients values and structures the self-concept. Different practical identities ground different kinds of normative commitment, in that one might legitimately reason that 'as a father' or 'as a Muslim' I should do this or that. This will often serve as a guide to our behaviour in ways that settle most normative questions for us and do so in a self-governing manner.

However, the most general form of the normative question is one which abstracts even from those identities, she argues. This is our moral identity, which yields universal duties and obligations independent of contingent factors concerning social roles or positions. This practical perspective is that of a member of the 'kingdom of ends' in the Kantian sense, where we ask not only about our particular identities ('is it morally acceptable to *be* a father of the sort I am, after all?') but about all more localized values and motives. As we saw in Kant, this brings down upon us the unqualified commands of the moral law—the Categorical Imperative—but it is a law we construct from the very process of reflection, not one imposed upon us externally. Autonomy, therefore, is the source of all obligations, whether moral or non-moral, since it is the capacity to impose upon ourselves, by virtue of our practical identities, obligations to act (Korsgaard 1996).

Many objections can be raised about this picture (given here in a very general form), but one of the most interesting for our purposes is a recent line of argument developed by Charles Larmore (Larmore 2008). Larmore argues that 'reason' cannot play the role that Kantians like Korsgaard claim for it in providing a justification for moral obligations (or for value commitments in general). This is because reason only functions as a way of finding the truth about things, the truth about what is valuable or obligatory or other truths. Reason, reflection, and deliberation, which for Korsgaard reveal the value of our own humanity, can only come to a conclusion about the value of something if it has value independently of those reflections. Korsgaard's Kantian constructivism is, in the end, empty, as is the conception of autonomy that provides the basis of all moral value for her.

This objection strikes at the heart of certain approaches to autonomy, namely the view that reflective endorsement of our basic commitments *itself* secures the value of those commitments (and desires and personal characteristics). The 'procedural' and 'content neutral' views we discussed all rely on the claim that autonomy has value not because of what autonomous reflection allows us to achieve or discover (which is independently valuable) but because of what such procedures are in themselves. Now Larmore concludes that this shows that autonomy should not be seen as the core source of moral value, but other theorists of autonomy have claimed that such considerations merely show that autonomy is the source of value only in so far as it is defined in relation to substantive values to which it gives us access, such as the value of an independent and self-directed life.

In a related register, many thinkers have questioned the value of autonomy because of just this kind of value specificity. Namely, they claim that autonomy should not be seen as a universal source of human moral value precisely *because* it marks the perspective of only one specific value orientation, one which reflects the experience of some in the population but not others. This picks up on the feminist complaint discussed earlier that autonomy is overly individualistic in its presuppositions and implications. What defenders of procedural, content-neutral accounts of self-government have tried to do, however, is to build accounts which avoid such contentious value claims—so that those who define themselves in emotional terms, in close connection to others, and as defined by social categories such as gender, race, or ethnicity can achieve autonomy just as easily as the rational individualist of traditional theory.[21]

Whether such a project succeeds depends on broad political issues that relate as much to political philosophy as they do to ethics. For such questions depend on principles of social life and political institutions as much as on broader issues of moral value. To bring out this aspect of thinking about autonomy, I will close with a brief discussion of autonomy in political philosophy.

32.4 CONCLUSION: AUTONOMY AS A POLITICAL IDEA

The idea of autonomy figures most centrally in debates over the structure and defensibility of liberal political philosophy. The liberal approach to political justice has its roots in the social contract conception of political legitimacy as well as the natural rights tradition embodied in the work of Locke, Kant, and others, as mentioned earlier.

---

[21] Cf. e.g. I. Young 1998.

The fundamental idea is that states are just only in so far as they are accepted as legitimate by those living under them—hence displaying *collective* self-government—and they work to protect the fundamental rights and liberties of those citizens, a package of rights and liberties that cluster around the capacity for autonomy, or *individual* self-government. However, deep divisions can be found in such theorists concerning exactly what role autonomy should play in the construction and defence of political principles and what specifically is the nature of its value.

Some liberal theorists insist that political institutions must protect the autonomy of citizens because autonomy is an aspect of a life worth living, a characteristic of a free and equal social existence that is valuable in itself. We can call such approaches 'perfection-ist' since they rely on a hypothesis about the universal value of a certain sort of social life. John Stuart Mill is sometimes interpreted in this way, though several contemporary thinkers also embrace this approach.[22]

Others, however, are bothered by a conception of justice that clearly is not embraced by many in the contemporary world, specifically as an ideal of the good life for the individual person. For such thinkers, autonomy can still function as a lynchpin of justice but it must be understood in a proceduralist manner so that the promotion of autonomy is not simply one contentious vision of the good life but the mechanism to allow various individuals and groups to pursue lives that they think of as valuable. (For discussion of the parallels between debates about the concept of autonomy and those in political liberalism, see Christman 2005.) In the case of Rawls, for example, justice is 'political', not 'metaphysical', in that the fundamental ideas and principles comprising just institutions are not put forward as a philosophical or religious ideal that all should adopt but rather as the subject of an overlapping consensus among citizens who hold very different philosophical or religious views. Autonomy, in such a picture, is claimed as a fundamental value but only because it is part of a broader conception of justice which is accepted by such a consensus, as Rawls says, not because the claim that autonomy is a value is 'true' but rather because it is 'reasonable' (in the sense of being affirmed by those who accept permanent pluralism in the social world and agree to the tolerance and reciprocity that such pluralism requires) (Rawls 1993).

Still others view autonomy as a value that is nested in a broader political framework but not specifically the project of political liberalism of the Rawlsian stripe. These writers see the fundamental aspect of justice to be 'democracy' or collective self-government. To justify principles and policies democratically, they claim, we must presuppose the ability of participants in democratic processes to be able to speak for themselves, equally and independently; that is, it must assume (and so promote and protect) the autonomy of those citizens. But note, this is not because they see autonomy—the capacity to speak for oneself, etc.—as a universal, objective value apart from such social settings, but rather because it plays a role in a democratic arrangement that is itself valued for various reasons.[23]

---

[22] See, e.g. Kymlicka 1989, Raz 1986, and Wall 1998.

[23] The theorists I have in mind here include Cohen 1986 and, albeit expressed in a different way, Habermas 1996.

One issue that divides thinkers engaged in these debates, and which will pick up on themes that we have traced throughout this discussion, is whether political liberalism in any of its modern forms is merely a parochial world view that is sometimes imposed by powerful political actors, and which sometimes (according to critics) expresses intolerance towards particular cultures and world views that do not display commitment to individualist values like autonomy. One aspect of this debate surrounds the question of exactly how we are to define the components of autonomy that is postulated as the bearer of basic social value. On the one hand, we can see autonomy as the competent capacity to reflectively endorse or reject all value commitments, implying that all such commitments can be understood as voluntarily chosen or jettisoned. On this view, those who do not see their identities, fundamental value commitments, religious affiliations, or cultural connections as things that are simply 'chosen' or 'rejectable' will not see conceptions of justice based on this notion of autonomy as particularly hospitable to their moral outlook. On the other hand, we might try to define autonomy that requires competent self-reflection but not necessarily the ability to step back from all such commitments and accept or reject them voluntarily (and as an individual). Such a view would be better positioned to accommodate the kinds of non-liberal social self-conceptions that many debates about multiculturalism bring to the fore. But the question left on the table is whether such a conception of value can be fashioned in a way that is defensible in its own right (as a plausible account of self-government) and that does not simply revert back to the perfectionist conception it was meant to replace.[24]

This last challenge echoes many of the notes we have struck in the broader discussion of autonomy in moral philosophy set out here. Questions about whether autonomy-based conceptions of moral obligation, value, the good life, and social justice are universal in their application and justification or merely the product of a specific intellectual and social location in world history remain on the table. Only further work on both the concept of autonomy itself as well as on the myriad questions that connect to it in moral and political philosophy will help allay such concerns.

Bibliography

Allison, H. 1990. *Kant's Theory of Freedom*. Cambridge: Cambridge University Press.
Anderson, J. and Honneth, A. 2005. 'Autonomy, Vulnerability, Recognition, and Justice', in J. Christman and J. Anderson (eds), *Autonomy and the Challenges to Liberalism: New Essays*. Cambridge: Cambridge University Press, 127–49.
Annas, J. 1993. *The Morality of Happiness*, New York and Oxford: Oxford University Press.
Aristotle. 2008. *Nicomachean Ethics*, ed. W. D. Ross. Pomona, CA: Pomona Press.
Arneson, R. 1991. 'Autonomy and Preference Formation', in J. Coleman and A. Buchanan (eds), *In Harm's Way: Essays in Honor of Joel Feinberg*. Cambridge: Cambridge University Press, 42–73.

[24] Many thinkers and debates are being alluded to here. A selective list of such authors would include: Sandel 1982, Kymlicka 1989, Raz 1986, Young 1990, Sen 2006, and Benhabib 2002.

Benhabib, S. 2002. *The Claims of Culture: Equality and Diversity in the Global Era*. Princeton, NJ: Princeton University Press.

Benson, P. 1994. 'Autonomy and Self-Worth', *Journal of Philosophy* 91 (12): 650–68.

—— 2005. 'Taking Ownership: Authority and Voice in Autonomous Agency', in J. Christman and J. Anderson (eds), *Autonomy and the Challenges to Liberalism: New Essays*. Cambridge: Cambridge University Press, 101–26.

Berlin, I. 1969. 'Two Concepts of Liberty', in *Four Essays on Liberty*. Oxford: Oxford University Press, 118–72.

Berofsky, B. 1995. *Liberation from Self*. New York: Cambridge University Press.

Bratman, M. 2003. 'Autonomy and Hierarchy', *Social Philosophy and Policy* 20 (2): 156–76.

Buss, S. and Overton, L. (eds) 2002. *Contours of Agency: Essays on Themes from Harry Frankfurt*. Cambridge, MA: MIT Press.

Christman, J. 2001. 'Liberalism, Autonomy, and Self-Transformation', *Social Theory and Practice* 27 (2): 185–206.

—— 2002. *Social and Political Philosophy: A Contemporary Introduction*. London: Routledge.

—— 2004. 'Relational Autonomy, Liberal Individualism, and the Social Constitution of Selves', *Philosophical Studies* 117: 143–64.

—— 2005. 'Political Autonomy and Liberal Legitimacy', in J. Taylor (ed.), *Personal Autonomy: New Essays on Personal Autonomy and its Role in Contemporary Philosophy*. Cambridge: Cambridge University Press, 277–98.

—— 2009. *The Politics of Persons: Individual Autonomy and Socio-Historical Selves*. Cambridge: Cambridge University Press.

—— (ed.) 1989. *The Inner Citadel: Essays on Individual Autonomy*. New York: Oxford University Press.

—— and Anderson, J. (eds) 2005. *Autonomy and the Challenges to Liberalism: New Essays*. Cambridge: Cambridge University Press

Cohen, J. 1986. 'Autonomy and Democracy: Reflections on Rousseau', *Philosophy and Public Affairs* 15: 275–97.

Cooper, J. M. 1996. 'Eudaimonism, the Appeal to Nature, and 'Moral Duty' in Stoicism', reprinted in J. Cooper, *Reason and Emotion*. Princeton: Princeton University Press, 1997, 427–48.

Cuypers, S. 2001. *Self-Identity and Personal Autonomy: An Analytic Anthropology*. Aldershot, UK: Ashgate.

Double, R. 1992. 'Two Types of Autonomy Accounts', *Canadian Journal of Philosophy* 22 (1): 65–80.

Dworkin, G. 1970. 'Acting Freely', *Nous* 4 (4): 367–83.

—— 1988. *The Theory and Practice of Autonomy*. New York: Cambridge University Press.

Epictetus. 2005. *The Enchiridion and Selections from the Discourses of Epictetus*, tr. G. Long. Digireads Publishing.

Feinberg, J. 1989. 'Autonomy', in J. Christman (ed.), 27–53.

Fischer, J. M. and Ravizza, M. 1998. *Responsibility and Control: A Theory of Moral Responsibility*. New York: Cambridge University Press.

Frankfurt, H. 1987. 'Freedom of the Will and the Concept of a Person', in *The Importance of What We Care About*. Cambridge: Cambridge University Press, 11–25.

—— 1992. 'The Faintest Passion', *Proceedings and Addresses of the Aristotelian Society* 49: 113–45.

—— 1994. 'Autonomy, Necessity and Love', in *Necessity, Volition, and Love*. Cambridge: Cambridge University Press, 129–41.

Friedman, M. 1986. 'Autonomy and the Split-Level Self', *Southern Journal of Philosophy* 24 (1): 19–35.

—— 2003. *Autonomy, Gender, Politics*. Oxford: Oxford University Press.

Gilligan, C. 1982. *In a Different Voice: Psychological Theory and Women's Development*. Cambridge, MA: Harvard University Press.

Grovier, T. 1993. 'Self-Trust, Autonomy, and Self-Esteem', *Hypatia* 8: 99–120.

Habermas, J. 1996. *Between Facts and Norms*. Cambridge, MA: MIT Press.

Haworth, L. 1986. *Autonomy: An Essay in Philosophical Psychology and Ethics*. New Haven: Yale University Press.

Hill, T. 1991. *Autonomy and Self Respect*. New York: Cambridge University Press.

Hobbes, T. 1651/1986. *Leviathan* Harmondsworth, UK: Penguin Books.

Kant, I. 1785/1983. *Grounding for the Metaphysics of Morals*, in *I. Kant Ethical Philosophy*, tr. J. W. Ellington. Indianapolis, IA: Hackett Publishing Co.

Korsgaard, C. M. 1996. *The Sources of Normativity*. New York: Cambridge University Press.

Kymlicka, W. 1989. *Liberalism, Community and Culture*. Oxford: Clarendon.

—— 1995. *Multicultural Citizenship: A Liberal Theory of Minority Rights*. Oxford: Clarendon.

Larmore, C. 2008. *The Autonomy of Morality*. Cambridge: Cambridge University Press.

Lindley, R. 1986. *Autonomy*. Atlantic Highlands, NJ: Humanities Press International.

Locke, J. 1690/1963. *Two Treatises of Government*, ed. P. Laslett. New York: Cambridge University Press.

McCallum, G. 1967. 'Negative and Positive Freedom', *Philosophical Review* 76: 3112–34.

Mackenzie, C. 2008. 'Relational Autonomy, Normative Authority and Perfectionism', *Journal of Social Philosophy* 39 (4): 512–33.

—— and Stoljar, N. (eds) 2000a. *Relational Autonomy: Feminist Perspectives on Autonomy, Agency, and the Social Self*. New York: Oxford University Press.

—— 2000b. 'Introduction: Autonomy Reconfigured', in C. Mackenzie and N. Stoljar 2000a: 3–34.

Mele, A. R. 1995. *Autonomous Agents: From Self-Control to Autonomy*. New York: Oxford University Press.

Meyers, D. T. 1989. *Self, Society, and Personal Choice*. New York: Columbia University Press.

Mill, J. S. 1859/1975. *On Liberty*, ed. D. Spitz. New York: Norton.

Mills, C. 1997. *The Racial Contract*. Ithaca, NY: Cornell University.

Nedelsky, J. 1989. 'Reconcieving Autonomy: Sources, Thoughts, and Possibilities', *Yale Journal of Law and Feminism* 1 (1): 7–36.

Nussbaum, M. 1994. *The Therapy of Desire*. Princeton: Princeton University Press.

O'Neill, O. 1990. *Constructions of Reason: Explorations in Kant's Practical Philosophy*. Cambridge: Cambridge University Press.

Oshana, M. 1998. 'Personal Autonomy and Society', *Journal of Social Philosophy* 29 (1): 81–102.

—— 2005. 'Autonomy and Self Identity', in J. Christman and J. Anderson (eds), 77–100.

—— 2006. *Personal Autonomy in Society*. Hampshire, UK: Ashgate Publishing, Ltd.

Pateman, C. 1988. *The Sexual Contract*. Palo Alto, CA: Stanford University Press.

Pettit, P. 1997. *Republicanism: A Theory of Freedom and Government*. New York: Oxford University Press.

Plato. 1992. *Republic*, ed. G. M. A. Grube and C. D. C. Reeve. New York: Hackett.

Rawls, J. 1971. *A Theory of Justice*. Revised edition 1999, Cambridge, MA: Harvard University Press.

—— 1993. *Political Liberalism*. New York: Columbia University Press.

Raz, J. 1986. *The Morality of Freedom*. Oxford: Clarendon Press.

Rossler, B. 2002. 'Problems with Autonomy', *Hypatia* 17 (4): 143–64.

Rousseau, J.-J. 1760/1987. *On the Social Contract* in *Rousseau: Basic Political Writings*, tr. D. Cress. Indianapolis, IN: Hackett Publishing Co.

—— 1762/1979. *Emile, Or On Education*, tr. A. Bloom. New York, NY: Basic Books.

Sandel, M. J. 1982. *Liberalism and the Limits of Justice*. Cambridge: Cambridge University Press. Second edition 1999.

Schneewind, J. B. 1998. *The Invention of Autonomy*. Cambridge: Cambridge University Press.

Sen, A. 2006. *Identity and Violence*. New York: Norton.

Sher, G. 1997. *Beyond Neutrality: Perfectionism and Politics*. Cambridge: Cambridge University Press.

Stoljar, N. 2000. 'Autonomy and the Feminist Intuition', in J. Mackenzie and J. Stoljar 2000a, 94–111.

Taylor, C. 1985. 'What's Wrong With Negative Liberty?', in *Philosophy and the Human Sciences: Philosophical Papers Vol. 2*. Cambridge: Cambridge University Press, 211–29.

—— 1989. *Sources of the Self: The Making of Modern Identity*. Cambridge, MA: Harvard University Press.

Taylor, J. S. (ed.) 2005. *Personal Autonomy: New Essays on Personal Autonomy and its Role in Moral Philosophy*. Cambridge: Cambridge University Press.

Thalberg, I. 1989. 'Hierarchical Analyses of Unfree Action', reprinted in J. Christman (ed.), 123–36.

Wall, S. 1998. *Liberalism, Perfectionism and Restraint*. New York: Cambridge University Press.

Watson, G. 1975. 'Free Agency', *Journal of Philosophy* 72: 205–20.

Young, I. M. 1990. *Justice and the Politics of Difference*. Princeton, NJ: Princeton University Press.

Young, R. 1986. *Autonomy: Beyond Negative and Positive Liberty*. New York: St. Martin's Press.

CHAPTER 33

EGOISM, PARTIALITY, AND IMPARTIALITY

BRAD HOOKER

PARTIALITY involves assigning more importance to the welfare or will of some individuals or groups than to the welfare or will of others. *Egoism* is an extreme form of partiality, in that it gives overriding importance to just one individual's welfare. There are different kinds of *impartiality*, but the kind of impartiality that juxtaposes with egoism and partiality is impartiality towards the welfare or will of each. The most natural understanding of impartiality with respect to the welfare of each is that any addition to or subtraction from one individual's welfare is given exactly the same importance as is given to the same size addition to or subtraction from any other individual's welfare. The most natural understanding of impartiality with respect to the will of each is that the will, or consent, of each is equally important for justification.

Egoism is often taken to be one of the main enemies of morality. Concern for others' welfare or will is often assumed to be central to morality. Indeed, many philosophers have assumed that the moral point of view just is the impartial point of view, the point of view in which the welfare or will of each is given equal importance. However, some have rejected the assumption that the moral point of view just is the impartial point of view, mainly because they presume it to be incompatible with the idea that partiality is morally permissible or even morally required. Controversies about impartiality and partiality (including the extreme form of partiality, i.e. egoism) will be explored in this chapter.

33.1 PSYCHOLOGICAL EGOISM

Psychological egoism is the view that, apart from cases of weakness of will, each person always tries to do what is most beneficial to himself or herself. The qualification about weakness of will has to be inserted because of the ubiquitous phenomenon of people's judging that what would be best for themselves is (for example) to stop drinking, to resist the gateau, and to go to bed early, and yet giving in to the temptation to keep drinking, to eat the gateau, and to stay at the party until very late.

A common objection to psychological egoism, influentially made by Bishop Butler, is that someone who cared only about his own welfare could not in fact choose what to do. If his own welfare consists in the satisfaction he derives from the fulfilment of his other desires, then he must have some other desires in order to have any welfare (Butler 1726; Feinberg 2008). Indeed, it is hard to imagine that someone who cared about absolutely nothing other than his own welfare could have a rewarding life. But even if it is paradoxical for someone to care nothing about anything other than her own welfare, there is no conceptual bar on someone's caring more about her own welfare than about anything else. Conceptual analysis on its own cannot show psychological egoism is mistaken.

Some thinkers have been tempted in the opposite direction—that is, tempted to think that psychological egoism is true by virtue of definitions. This line of thought starts by defining intention and desire such that every intentional action aims to fulfil the agent's strongest current desires. The line of thought then defines a person's greatest good as the fulfilment of this person's strongest current desires. From the combination of these definitions, this line of thought concludes that every intentional act aims to bring about the agent's greatest good.

The definitions whose combination generates that conclusion are at best controversial. There is a 'wide' or 'formal' or 'functional' sense of 'desire' such that wherever there is intentional action, the agent of that action has desires that the action intends to fulfil. If the intention in some action of mine was to keep a promise I made to you, then in this wide sense of 'desire' I acted on a desire to keep the promise. The desire here is just whatever motivation was necessary for the intentional action. (In this way, 'desire' is defined by its functional role in motivating intentional action.)

Desires in the wide sense of 'desire' can have virtually any content. Their content can be about the agent (e.g. the agent's desire can be that the agent benefits). Or their content can be about people or projects connected with the agent (e.g. the agent's desire that his friends benefit). Or their content can be about people or states of affairs that have no special connection to the agent (e.g. the desire can be that others in general benefit).

Return to the form of psychological egoism that tries to support itself only by definitions of 'desire', 'intentional action', and 'greatest benefit'. This form of psychological egoism has to contend that the agent who acts on a desire *that he himself benefit* and the agent who acts on the desire *that others benefit* are equally trying to bring about their own greatest good. But such a contention is ridiculous.

Another difficulty with this kind of psychological egoism is that it incorporates desires that have no phenomenology at all. That is, the agent might not have her attention directed by them, and she might not feel satisfied when they are fulfilled or feel frustrated when they aren't fulfilled. Suppose that, although the agent keeps her promise to you, in advance she dreaded keeping it and had trouble remembering to keep it, at the time she hated the experience of keeping it, and after the event she looked back on the experience as one to be forgotten as soon as possible. Thus, she might report to others that, though she kept the promise, it wasn't something she desired to do or derived satisfaction from doing. She might well say the same about going to the dentist last week. In such claims, she is using 'desire' in a narrower sense than is used in the claim that every intentional action aims to fulfil a desire of the agent's (Scanlon 1998: 39–41, 44–5, 47–9).

The relevance of distinguishing between these two different senses of 'desire' is that one sense of 'desire' is used in the claim about intentional action, and the other sense is used in the thesis about the agent's greatest good. Perhaps every intentional action does aim to fulfil a desire of the agent's, but this is true only in the 'wide', 'formal', 'functional role' sense of 'desire'. And if the doctrine that an agent's greatest good consists in the fulfilment of his desires is to be at all plausible, 'desire' is here being used in a narrower sense than in the definition of intentional action.

Be that as it may, the idea that an agent's greatest good consists in the fulfilment of his greatest *current* desires is very implausible. Suppose that at 12:00 Sarah's strongest current desire is for a delicious snack. But suppose also that this very powerful desire is also very fleeting. By 12:05, it will extinguish. Suppose further that she knows in advance that if she eats anything between 12:00 and 12:05, she will die at 12:06, thereby frustrating most of the desires she would have subsequently had. Now, does her greatest good consist in the fulfilment of her strongest current desire at 12:00? No! We would be protecting her good if we prevented her from fulfilling that desire. In fact, frustration of a person's current desires is often necessary in order to promote her or his long-term good.

We have seen that attempts to render psychological egoism true by definition rely on implausible ideas. But denying that definitions of intentional action, desire, and greatest good combine to entail that psychological egoism is true is compatible with claiming that nevertheless psychological egoism is true as a matter of empirical fact. So now let us turn to this idea that psychological egoism is true as a matter of empirical fact.

Is it an empirical fact that, apart from cases of weakness of will, everyone always intends to do what is best for herself of himself? What about the soldier who jumps on a grenade in order to keep others from being killed? What about the people on United Airlines Flight 93 who stormed the cockpit in order to prevent the plane from being used as a terrorist weapon? What about people who dive into dangerous waters in order to rescue others?

There *seem* to be a lot of counterexamples to psychological egoism. So someone who defends psychological egoism has a lot of explaining away to do. But, when these cases are paraded out, someone who defends psychological egoism might say: 'We don't know with certainty what was going through the minds of the soldiers who jumped on the grenades, or the passengers on United Airlines Flight 93, or the people who dived into dangerous water in order to rescue others. Perhaps these people were merely trying to prevent themselves from having crippling guilt feelings later. Or perhaps they thought there would be huge rewards for preventing harm to others.'

Often rescuers survive and then are asked what was going through their minds when they started the rescue. Answers vary. But at least sometimes the answer is along the lines of, 'I wasn't trying to prevent guilt feelings or get a reward for myself; instead, I was motivated purely by the recognition that I could save others.' Sometimes people who say such things are lying or self-deceived. But what evidence is there for the hypothesis that people who say such things are *always* lying or self-deceived?

One piece of evidence against the hypothesis that people who report that they sacrificed themselves for the sake of others are *always* lying or self-deceived comes from introspection (Williams 1973: 262; Kavka 1986: 37). Think to yourself whether you would ever be willing to make a sacrifice for the sake of others. Wouldn't you be willing to make at least a small sacrifice (for example, enduring ten minutes of hunger or boredom) for the sake of saving some other innocent person from suffering acute pain for many years?

Another piece of evidence against the hypothesis that people who report that they sacrificed themselves for the sake of others are always lying or self-deceived comes from the theory of evolution. Being disposed to sacrifice oneself for the sake of certain others is favoured by natural selection, where the genes of those with this disposition are more likely to survive than the genes of exactly similar creatures who do not have this disposition. A simple thought experiment illustrates the point. Suppose two groups of swans are alike except that those of one set have a gene impelling them to fight off predators in order to protect their offspring and those of the other set instead have a gene inducing them to flee while their offspring are eaten. The offspring of the more altruistic parents are more likely to survive and to have offspring of their own that survive.

Not just kin altruism but also reciprocal altruism seems likely to be a product of natural selection. This reciprocal altruism consists in a disposition to help others of the same species unless and until they fail to reciprocate (Kavka 1986: 62; Axelrod 1984).

Although we have here seen a number of arguments for the falsity of psychological egoism, we should also consider why so many people have thought the doctrine correct. The answer might be that psychological egoism overstates the truth that very many human beings are largely motivated by self-interest. Gregory Kavka (1986: 67–80) coined the term 'predominant egoism' for the view that, apart from cases of weakness of will, *most* people *regularly* try to do what is most beneficial for themselves.

But Kavka (1986: 67) observed that, in some people, concern for self is not predominant. He also conceded that many or even most people are willing to make repeated sacrifices for family and others to whom they are closely connected. Actually, the high percentage of people who regularly make uncoerced intentional sacrifices for the sake of others must be shocking to anyone who started off thinking that either psychological egoism or something close to it is true.

Suppose that morality and rationality cannot require people to do what they literally cannot do. On that supposition, then if psychological egoism were true, morality and rationality could not require people to do anything other than try to do what is most beneficial to themselves. The most familiar kind of *ethical* egoism holds that what makes an act morally right is that it maximizes the good of the individual. The most familiar kind of *rational* egoism holds that what makes an act rational is that it maximizes the expected good of the individual. These familiar kinds of ethical and rational egoism would not be interesting if psychological egoism were true, since ethical and rational egoism would merely be telling agents to try to do what they cannot help but try to do.

But what agents can try to do is not always what ethical and rational egoism tell them to try to do. So ethical and rational egoism are important doctrines.

33.2 ETHICAL EGOISM

Ethical egoism should be divided into act and rule varieties. Act ethical egoism, which is by far the most prominent kind of ethical egoism, claims that the morally required thing for one to do is always whatever act would produce as least as much benefit for oneself as any available alternative act. Rule ethical egoism holds that rules are to be assessed in terms of whether they are best (on the whole and in the long run) for oneself, and then the morally required acts are whichever ones are required by the rules most beneficial to oneself.

Act ethical egoism cannot sensibly be put forward as a procedure for making every decision. People typically don't have the information necessary for calculating the expected benefits for themselves of all the available alternative acts. Even if they did have the information, they might not have the mathematical skills necessary. Even if they did have the information and mathematical skill necessary for doing the calculations, they might be biased in certain ways likely to distort their calculations; for example, they might be systematically prone to overestimating the size or probability of benefits that are due to come sooner. Moreover, having a calculating mind might get in the way of spontaneous and wholehearted enthusiasms (cf. Adams 1976).

For all these reasons, one is likely to have a better life, in self-interested terms, if conscious calculation is only an occasional activity and if one routinely follows familiar rules along the lines of 'don't injure others except when necessary for self-defence', 'don't steal', 'keep your promises', 'don't lie', 'don't brag', 'express interest in other people', 'don't put all your eggs in one basket', 'don't burn your bridges behind you', 'don't spit into the wind', etc.

Of course some of these are rules for everyday decision-making that other ethical theories endorse. So endorsing these rules for everyday decision-making is hardly what makes act ethical egoism distinctive. What makes act ethical egoism distinctive is its view about what makes acts morally required. Act ethical egoism holds that any act that is morally required is so because the act would produce at least as much benefit for oneself as any available alternative act would.

There are obvious counterexamples to this theory. Consider a case where someone would benefit from killing his political or professional or romantic rival. Such an action would of course be wrong. The same is typically true of his threatening his rival with physical harm, or framing other people, or stealing, or failing to uphold his side of bargains. In each such case, the action would typically be morally wrong even if it would benefit the person who did it.

Much of morality is composed of requirements on the agent designed to protect other people. This is perhaps clearest in requirements that one not kill or injure others except in certain quite restricted contexts (war, self-defence, etc.), that one not threaten to kill or injure others, that one not kidnap others, that one not steal, that one keep one's promises, and that one not lie. The protection of other people is also one of the main purposes of 'special duties' one has towards family and friends. These protections are not so much against oneself as against whatever else might threaten the people concerned. The protection is provided by the special duty to accord these people's welfare somewhat more weight than the welfare of others when one is deciding how to spend one's time, energy, and other resources. Even the duty to come to the rescue of strangers can be seen as having its main point in protecting others from danger.

In the case of all these requirements and duties, compliance may well involve cost to the agent. This is why the 'standing possibility of conflict' between morality and self-interest is a 'truism in all societies' (Hart 1961: 85; see also Mackie 1977: 106). The standing possibility of conflict between morality and self-interest couldn't be a truism if morality simply required that people maximize their own good.

Another objection to act ethical egoism is that it is badly mistaken in holding that what makes killing someone or stealing or breaking a promise wrong is that the act fails to maximize the agent's own good. Well, what is *the deep explanation* of *why* killing someone or stealing or breaking one's promise is morally wrong? The answer is not clear. If it were clear, then presumably which moral theory (e.g. some version of consequentialism, some version of contractualism, some version of deontological pluralism, or some version of virtue ethics) is correct would be clear. Which moral theory is correct isn't clear. However, we do not have to be able to lay a good egg in order to be able to tell a bad one. And we can tell that the account of what makes acts wrong that is offered by act ethical egoism is a bad one.

There are other powerful objections to act ethical egoism. But the ones I have just outlined are the most compelling. So, in order to have room to discuss other theories, I will not say more about act ethical egoism.

Rule ethical egoism holds that what makes acts permissible is that they are permitted by rules whose acceptance by the agent would have consequences that (on the whole and in the long run) would be more beneficial to the agent than would be the acceptance by the agent of any alternative rules. Rule ethical egoism also faces powerful objections.

Rule ethical egoism runs into trouble justifying rules for the protection or benefit of groups who would never be able to punish or reward our behaviour towards them (Kavka 1993). Intuitively, morality does include rules for the protection of future generations, for the protection of the poorest and least powerful people alive today, and for the protection of animals. But rule ethical egoism cannot explain what the justification could be for moral rules that require us to restrain our behaviour in ways that protect such groups or to make other sacrifices for the sake of such groups.

A second objection to rule ethical egoism is that it is potentially too relativistic in its implications. Suppose that Bob, Carol, and Ted are members of the same society and are in most ways alike. Suppose also that the rules whose acceptance by Bob would be most beneficial *to him* are rules A, B, C, and D. The rules whose acceptance by Carol would be most beneficial *to her* are rules C, D, E, and F. The rules whose acceptance by Ted would be most beneficial *to him* are rules E, F, G, and H. So rules that rule ethical egoism tells Bob to follow do not overlap with the rules that it tells Ted to follow. Such a possibility seems to violate the idea that moral rules should be for *shared* acceptance. Of course there is some room for legitimate variation in rules within a society. But rule ethical egoism sets up a test for rules that invites too much variation. With only limited exceptions, the same moral rules should ideally be accepted by everyone within the same society—if not even more broadly.

A final objection to rule ethical egoism is that, even if it did lead to plausible ethical rules, it would misidentify the basis for these rules. Again, it is not clear what *the deep explanation* is of *why* killing someone or stealing or breaking one's promise is morally wrong. However, the deep explanation offered by rule ethical egoism is implausibly egoistic. Even if the correct deep explanation of moral wrongness isn't wholly impartial, surely the correct deep explanation of moral wrongness is at least partly impartial.

33.3 RATIONAL EGOISM

In many ways, *rational* egoism preserves what normative egoists cherish in their theory without getting embroiled in controversies about how relativistic a moral theory can plausibly be and about what the deep explanation of moral wrongness is. Rational egoism claims that an act is *rational* if, only if, and because it has at least as much expected benefit for the agent as any alternative act. Rational egoism is not a theory about what is ethical.

I have already mentioned one possible argument for rational egoism. If psychological egoism were true, then one could not help but try to do what is best for oneself. Suppose what one rationally ought to do must be something one is able to do. If that view is correct and if psychological egoism is true, then one rationally ought to try to do what is best for oneself. However, as we have seen, psychological egoism is not true.

Another possible argument for rational egoism is that rational egoism is self-evidently true. To claim that a proposition is self-evidently true is to claim that understanding the proposition can, by itself, provide compelling grounds for believing it. Thus, justification for believing a self-evident truth need not come from its inferential relations with other propositions (Audi 1993; 1996; 2004). Many philosophers reject the very idea of self-evidence. But even if some propositions are self-evident, is the proposition that rationality requires one always to try to do what is most beneficial to oneself self-evidently true?

What might be self-evident is that a bias towards the present is irrational. In other words, it is irrational to prefer a smaller benefit sooner over a larger benefit later, given that the two are equally certain (Sidgwick 1907: 381). But rational egoism goes far beyond condemning a bias towards the present. Rational egoism insists on an overriding bias towards benefits for oneself—that is, a bias that overrides any other concern or goal, including benefits for others. Rational egoism entails that, in a case where one is deciding between what is most beneficial to oneself and what is beneficial to others, one could not *rationally* decide to pass up what is most beneficial to oneself. However, it is hardly self-evident that making sacrifices for others is never rational. I will return to this when I consider arguments against rational egoism.

A third possible argument in favour of rational egoism begins with the assumption that, as expressed in a passage from Henry Sidgwick, 'the distinction between any one individual and any other is real and fundamental, and that consequently "I" am concerned with the quality of my existence as an individual in a sense, fundamentally important, in which I am not concerned with the quality of the existence of other individuals' (Sidgwick 1889: 484; 1907: 498). This is a perplexing passage, subject to a number of different possible interpretations (Shaver 1999: 84–98). Part of why it is so perplexing is that it points to the metaphysical claim that the distinction between individuals is real and fundamental (a metaphysical claim relevantly denied by T. H. Green 1888; Derek Parfit 1984: pt. 3; and David Brink 1989: 286 –9; 2003: 68 –9) and then suggests that psychological or normative claims follow from that metaphysical claim.

Consider first matters of *psychology*. Even if it is a psychological fact that I care more about the quality of my existence than I do about the quality of anyone else's existence, I might *not* care *infinitely* more. Even if I prefer a benefit for myself over the same size benefit for anyone else, I might not prefer a tiny benefit for myself over an enormous benefit for someone else. But rational egoism requires an unwillingness to give up even a tiny benefit for myself for the sake of anything other than bigger alternative benefits for myself.

Now, does the metaphysical distinction between individuals (if there is one that is as deep and fundamental as common sense assumes) entail a *normative requirement* that each give *infinite* weight to his or her own good? Imagine a situation where you are certain that your giving up just a moment of pleasure would somehow save me from a few decades of intense agony. In this situation, couldn't you *rationally* decide to make that sacrifice? If so, then rationality *permits* some degree of self-sacrifice.

A further question is whether rationality, or the balance of normative reasons, *requires* (as opposed to merely permits) you to make the sacrifice for me in this case. In order to reject rational egoism, we do not need to answer that further question. Rational egoism is mistaken as long as there is a rational *permission* to sacrifice one's own good for the sake of some other things. And that such a rational permission obtains seems overwhelmingly plausible. Hence, after careful attention to the examples where a very small sacrifice for the agent is needed to bring about a huge benefit for someone else, rational egoism seems extremely counter-intuitive.

33.4 PARTIALITY

In the terminology made popular by Derek Parfit (1984: 143) and Thomas Nagel (1986: 152–3), egoism is 'agent-relative' in the special sense that description of what the agent is required to care about and promote must refer to the agent. Rational egoism tells you to care overridingly about *your* good; it tells me to care overridingly about *mine*. But egoism is 'time-neutral'. The description of what the agent is required to care about and promote does not refer to any particular time. In contrast, a maximally agent-relative and time-relative theory would require you to care about and maximize only *your* own *present* good.

Although that degree of partiality towards your own present good is not attractive, some kinds of partiality are. Imagine a father is in a situation where he could use his money to purchase a benefit—e.g. pay for an inoculation—either for his daughter or for a stranger. Suppose he reasonably believes his daughter and the stranger would benefit the same amount from the inoculation. And suppose that, when asked by the stranger for the inoculation, the father offers to flip a coin to decide who gets it. This father lacks a kind of partiality that morality requires (cf. Crisp 2006: 142–3).

The example could have concerned two siblings instead of a parent and child. Or it could have concerned grandparents and grandchildren, or other family connections, or even just mere friends.

Of course there are plenty of contexts in which partiality towards family and friends is not allowed. In any context in which people are distributing resources that do not belong to them, there will typically be criteria for distributing those resources that exclude personal ties. The bank employee is not allowed to lend to one person rather than another simply because the first of these is his cousin; a government official deciding where to spend public money on road repair should not direct workers to her parents' street (see Cottingham 1998: 11). Still, most of us do have some resources of our own (if not money or property, then at least time, energy, and attention) that we could direct towards family and friends or towards strangers. It is when we come to allocating our own resources that some kinds and degrees of partiality are not only morally permissible but also morally required.

How much partiality is required in such contexts? An infinite degree of partiality is not even permitted, much less required. If you could either buy an inoculation for your child against a very minor ailment or an inoculation for a stranger against a very major ailment, and if neither the child nor the stranger could get the inoculation in any other way, then you should benefit the stranger rather than your child.

I have contended that the degree of appropriate partiality towards one's own family and friends is more than none and less than infinite. I think that, if we consider a range of cases in which one is deciding how to allocate one's own resources and we consider the dependence of friendship on partiality, our intuitions will support the conclusion that the appropriate degree of partiality in such contexts is *substantial*. This conclusion is regrettably vague. But to expect a conclusion about degrees of appropriate partiality not to be vague would be unrealistic.

What special relations other than friendship and family mandate partiality? Some are mandated by professional roles or contractual commitments. For example, the lawyer appointed to defend an accused person has a moral as well as legal duty to make the best case available for this person. The doctor and nurse have duties to their patients that they don't have to equally needy strangers. Elected officials and representatives should give extra weight to the good of their own constituents, especially if this is what they promised their constituents. But whether ordinary citizens should be partial towards other members of the same nation, or should instead be impartial as between their co-nationals and members of other nations, is another matter I cannot address here.

Michael Slote points to what he calls 'self/other moral asymmetry' in common-sense morality (Slote 1985: ch. 1; 1992: 13 –16; see also Portmore 2003: 311–14; 2007: 58; and 2011). Self/other asymmetry is the idea that one's act cannot gain in moral value by benefiting oneself but can gain in moral value by benefiting others.

One upshot of this asymmetry is that common-sense morality gives agents the prerogative to impose sacrifices on themselves for the sake of smaller gains for others. If you give up some benefit for yourself so that I get it instead, though the gain for me will be no more than it would have been for you, you are to be commended. Indeed, if you give up a somewhat larger benefit for yourself in order that I get some smaller benefit, you are to be commended. The qualification 'somewhat' is needed because common-sense morality is unhappy with too big a gap between the cost to the agent and the benefit to others. An example might be someone's giving up her life, which otherwise would have continued for decades, for the sake of giving someone else merely a few days (or hours) more of happiness. But perhaps common sense takes such cases to be instances of irrationality, rather than immorality.

Still, even if the gap between costs to agents and benefits to others must stay within limits, common-sense morality does often allow agents to impose costs on themselves for the sake of smaller benefits to others. Apparently, then, common-sense morality does not take partiality towards oneself to be morally *required*.

But how much partiality towards oneself is *permitted*? If given the choice between an extra three years of healthy life for myself or an extra three years of healthy life for someone who has no special connection with me, I am permitted to choose that I benefit. If given the choice between an extra thirteen seconds of life for myself or an extra three decades of healthy life for someone else, I am not permitted the extra thirteen seconds of life for myself. (Assume here that those thirteen seconds are not ones in which I would do something especially significant, like tell my children that I love them, or my cousin that I forgive him.)

One prominent proposal is that morality permits partiality such that one counts benefits to oneself as some reasonable multiple times more important than the same size benefits to others. This kind of partiality is what Samuel Scheffler dubbed 'the agent-centred prerogative' (1982: chs 1–3).

To get off the ground, the proposal will have to take into account the fact that how much partiality one is permitted by morality depends on whose welfare is at stake. For example, how much partiality is permitted when one is choosing between benefits for oneself and the same size benefits for one's children is very different from how much partiality is allowed when one is choosing between benefits for oneself and the same size benefits for strangers. So the agent-centred prerogative needs to specify not just *a degree* of permissible partiality, but many different degrees. To illustrate, we might imagine that the prerogative holds that, in deciding how to spend one's own time, energy, and other resources, one is *allowed* to count benefits to *oneself* as up to

—half as important as the same size benefits to one's child,
—equally as important as same size benefits to one's parent,
—one and a half times as important as the same size benefits to a close friend,
—ten times as important as the same size benefits to a distant friend, and
—a hundred times as important as the same size benefits to a stranger.

The amount of partiality permitted by this prerogative is limited such that I would be wrong to choose a benefit for myself over a benefit 0.51 or more times as large for my child, wrong to choose a benefit for myself over a benefit 1.1 or more times as large for my parent, wrong to choose a benefit for myself over a benefit 1.6 or more times as large for my close friend, wrong to choose a benefit for myself over a benefit 10.1 or more times as large for my distant friend, and wrong to choose a benefit for myself over a benefit 100.1 or more times as large for a stranger.

The multipliers used in this prerogative are *of course* open to challenge. Even more, the amount of precision suggested by such claims seems ridiculous! On the other hand, there is pressure to quantify the strength of the prerogative, i.e. to specify the multipliers. So how can we go about arguing for any particular set of multipliers?

Scheffler (1982: 56–8, 62, 64–5, 67, 79, 92, 113, 125) thinks the agent-centred prerogative reflects the 'natural independence of the personal point of view'. Consider the idea that morality is a compromise between the personal point of view and the impartial point of view (C. D. Broad 1930: 243–4; W. D. Ross 1930: 26, 27; Nagel 1986: 166–75; Wolf 1992: 243–60; Crisp 2006: 131–41). There is much intuitively attractive in this conception. And yet it seems able to give us little help where intuition runs out. If intuition does not specify how strong justified partiality is, the conception of morality as a compromise between the personal point of view and the impartial point of view cannot provide much help. We are told that impartial concerns and partial concerns have independent weight and have to be balanced against one another in particular cases. We might have hoped for more of a foothold for getting on top of this problem than that.

33.5 IMPARTIALITY

Perhaps the foothold we need will come from pure impartiality. Perhaps there is a plausible picture of morality that begins with the idea of impartial justification and then shows how much partiality is permitted to moral agents and how much partiality is required of them.

Before we explore the idea of impartial *justification*, we should juxtapose it with impartial *application* of principles or rules. Impartial application of principles or rules consists in being guided solely by the principles or rules. Principles and rules purport to identify the distinctions relevant to what should be done. Impartial application of rules or principles consists in being guided solely by the distinctions that the rules or principles identify as pivotal.

For example, to impartially apply the simple rule 'never kill a person' is to be guided solely by the distinction between acts of killing a person and other acts. To impartially apply the more complicated rule 'never kill a person except when necessary to defend the innocent' is to be guided by the distinction between acts of killing a person that are not necessary to defend the innocent and other acts.

Failing *completely* to apply a rule across a range of cases is not to have one's judgements or actions be guided by the rule in any of the cases. Let us now focus on the class of cases where there is not a complete failure to apply a rule, but only a failure in some cases. In particular, let us focus on the sub-class of cases where *a rule is applied but not impartially*. Here is my account:

> When a rule is applied across a set of cases, the rule is not applied impartially if and only if both (a) the agent is at least sometimes guided by partiality and (b) this conflicts with being guided by the distinctions identified by the rule as pivotal.

So if the agent applies a rule across a set of cases and the agent is not guided by partiality at all, then the agent applies the rule impartially. Likewise, if the agent applies a rule across a set of cases and, though the agent is guided by partiality, this partiality is not in conflict with the distinctions identified by the rule as pivotal, then the agent applies the rule impartially. Thus my account of failures in impartial application of rules leaves open the possibility of impartial application of a rule that allows or requires partiality.

This implication of my account is important because, as we have seen, some rules and principles require partiality, e.g. towards one's own family or friends or constituents. Obviously, partiality is required by the rule 'when choosing how to distribute your own resources to others, and where the amount that others would benefit from a given unit of your resources would be not hugely different, direct the benefit to your own children rather than to strangers'.

There could be a complete refusal to apply this rule, but there could also be (not a complete refusal to apply it but) a failure to apply it impartially. Suppose that, when choosing how to distribute your own resources to others, and where the amount that others would benefit from a given unit of your resources would be not hugely different, you directed the benefit to your own children rather than to strangers *except when the strangers praised you highly*. If you did this, you would *not* be *completely* refusing to apply the rule but you would be failing to apply it impartially.

Contrast the acclaimed account of *impartial treatment* put forward by Bernard Gert (1998: 132):

> A is impartial in respect R with regard to group G if and only if A's actions in respect R are not influenced at all by which member(s) of G are benefited or harmed by these actions.

Now, many rules require you to act towards others in ways influenced by who is benefited or harmed by your actions. This is true of rules that require you to direct benefits towards those to whom you are related, or towards those with whom you have close friendships, or towards those who are particularly successful at benefiting others, or towards those who especially need benefits. If you rigorously and impartially apply such rules in your dealings with others, are you treating others impartially? Or are you being partial towards family and friends, and towards the deserving, and towards the needy? As Gert's account of impartial treatment implies, you are *not* treating others impartially here, even if you are applying the rule impartially.

If we are convinced by Gert's account that such cases are ones of partial treatment, then I think his distinction between partial and impartial treatment is not especially helpful in thinking about moral and political philosophy. For impartial treatment, according to his account of it, not only is not always a moral requirement but also is sometimes morally forbidden (as Gert and many others have noted).

More helpful to moral and political philosophy than the concept of impartial treatment are the concepts of impartiality in the application of rules and impartiality in justification of behaviour. I have already set out an account of impartiality in the application of rules. But I have not yet tried to indicate why (or rather when) impartiality in the application of rules is good.

First of all, there are many sorts of situation in which trying to decide what to do by following rules would be inappropriate (unless the rule just is 'do not look to rules to fix on what you ought to do in this case'). Since many sorts of situation do not call for rule-governed decision, there is no need for impartial application of rules in such cases.

Second, even in cases where rule-governed decision is appropriate, there are some imaginable rules that are so bad that departure from them is always good. As we have seen, to fail to apply a rule impartially is to diverge from the decision called for by the distinctions that the rule claims are decisive. Where a rule is so bad that departure from it is always good, failure to apply the rule impartially is good (see Feinberg 1973: 106–7).

But let us turn to rules that are, though less than ideal, reasonably good. And imagine that these reasonably good rules are publicly proclaimed. Impartial application of such rules is normally good. Why?

Suppose, as is often the case, that people generally expect, indeed depend upon, the impartial application of the publicly proclaimed rules. If this is the case, then one boon of impartially applying them is that expectations that have been depended upon are not violated.

Now consider the other possibility: that is, suppose people do not expect and depend upon the impartial application of publicly proclaimed rules. Where people do not expect and depend upon the impartial application of publicly proclaimed rules, expectations might militate against the impartial application of these rules. However, where publicly proclaimed rules are not impartially applied, there is at least hypocrisy, if not frustrated expectations. Hypocrisy leads to distrust, and there are many costs that result from distrust.

Having now explained what impartial application of rules is and why it is desirable, I turn to impartial justification. What is impartial justification? One suggestion is that impartial justification is justification from a point of view that takes no one to be intrinsically more important than anyone else. This is the 'point of view of the Universe' (Sidgwick 1907: 382) or the 'view from nowhere' (Nagel 1986: chs 8–10).

The idea that impartial justification is justification from such a point of view strikes many philosophers as absurd (Gert 1998: 132; Williams 1995). While, from the point of view of the Universe or the view from nowhere, *any one individual matters no more than any other*, this might be because, from this point of view, *nothing matters*. If nothing matters from such a point of view, then there is no such thing as justification from such a point of view (Brandt 1954).

That objection rightly points out that impartial justification should not be characterized purely negatively, as in 'no greater concern for any one individual than for any other'. Impartial justification must be characterized in terms of positive concern. But positive concern for what?

The paradigm example of impartial justification of rules is the utilitarian one. For utilitarians, impartial justification of rules begins with assessment of rules in terms of overall welfare, which is calculated impartially. That is, overall welfare is the aggregate of the welfare of different individuals, and the welfare level of an individual is constituted by the net benefit (benefit minus harm) for that individual. Overall utility is calculated impartially in that a benefit or harm to any one individual is counted exactly the same as the same size benefit or harm to anyone else. Utilitarian impartiality is the paradigm example because not only does it ground justification in an agent-neutral value but also this value is itself impartially calculated.

There are other forms of consequentialism that take impartial justification to be grounded wholly or at least partly in a non-utilitarian agent-neutral value. Prominent examples of non-utilitarian agent-neutral values are equality and autonomy. Admittedly, autonomy can be held to be one self-interested good or one component of welfare. Still, if impartial justification is grounded at least in part in the promotion of autonomy beyond autonomy's contribution to welfare, then here we have an example of justification by reference to a non-utilitarian agent-neutral value.

But many forms of agent-neutral value cannot play a foundational role in *impartial* justification. Imagine that someone said that rules are justified solely to the extent that their social acceptance promotes the welfare of the royal family. If the person who says this is not himself or herself a member of the royal family, then the person is *not* saying 'rules are justified solely to the extent that their social acceptance promotes the welfare of *my* family'. So this person's proposal is that rules are justified in terms of an agent-neutral value, namely the welfare of a family that is not particularly connected to this agent. But justifying rules solely in terms of whether they promote the welfare of *one* family is not impartial justification. On the contrary, it is a paradigm case of partiality, though not an agent-relative kind. Indeed, one of the main objections to any proposal to evaluate rules solely in terms of whether they promote the welfare of one family is that such evaluation could not count as impartial justification. Likewise, a proposal to assess rules solely or even just primarily in terms of whether they promote the welfare of the aristocracy would be condemned as unacceptable partiality, even if the person making the proposal were not herself or himself a member of, or otherwise especially connected with, the aristocracy.

A proposal to assess rules solely or even just primarily in terms of benefits for the intellectual elite, for true believers, for the especially productive, or for the worst off would have the same structural feature as partiality towards the royal family or towards the broader aristocracy. Admittedly, there is more fluidity with (i.e. mobility into and out of) some of these groups than there typically is with royal families and aristocracies. This greater fluidity might make proposals to assess rules in terms of benefits solely or primarily for the members of such groups seem less partial than proposals prioritizing benefits to the royal family or the aristocracy. But careful scrutiny reveals that whether or not there is fluidity into and out of a group does not determine whether assessment solely or primarily in terms of benefits to that group is impartial or partial. Assessment solely or primarily in terms of benefits to a subset of everyone is clearly *not* impartial as between members of that subset and everyone else. This is true whether or not the subset is fluid.

We have been considering the implausibility of identifying the concept of impartial assessment with the concept of agent-neutral assessment. Let us now consider paradigm examples of impartial assessment. Suppose we assess possible acts in terms of expected aggregate welfare, impartially calculated, or in terms of moral rules themselves selected for expected aggregate welfare, impartially calculated. Such assessment would be definitely impartial, in that it counts a benefit or loss to any one individual the same as it counts the same size benefit or loss to any other individual. And these kinds of assessment are utilitarian.

Utilitarian assessment is not the only paradigm of impartial assessment. Indeed, utilitarian assessment is not the oldest paradigm of impartiality. The oldest comes in the form of the Golden Rule—do unto others as you would have them do unto you (see Wattles 1996 for a history of this prescription, including discussions of Confucius, Thales, Jesus, and Hillel).

The Golden Rule can be understood as requiring merely that one be impartial in the application of the rules one thinks correct. Jack is to treat Jill as Jack thinks that Jill (and others) should treat him. In other words, if Jack thinks others should follow a certain rule with respect to him, then he should follow that rule with respect to them. But this idea is hardly sufficient to identify a plausible morality. After all, the agent's views about which rules are correct might be wildly wrong.

Often the Golden Rule is thought to require not merely impartiality in the application of rules but impartiality in their selection. When Jack is trying to decide what rule to follow in his treatment of Jill, his own convenience or advantage is far from the only relevant consideration. He is required by the Golden Rule to ask himself whether he would want others to follow this rule in their treatment of him. This requirement forces Jack to look at the situation from Jill's point of view as well as from his own.

Now suppose Jack's decision about what to do has effects not only on Jill but on Jorge as well. Then Jack is required by the Golden Rule to consider his decision from the point of view of Jorge as well as from Jill's and his own points of view. But what if there is no course of action available to Jack that would please both Jill and Jorge? If the Golden Rule forbids him to do anything that he wouldn't want done if he were in someone else's position, then the Golden Rule forbids any act that displeases someone else. Yet, obviously, very often when there is nothing an agent could do that would please every affected party, there are nevertheless lots of things the agent could choose to do that would be morally permissible. And, of course, some of these permissible alternatives might even be morally required.

One way of dealing with the difficulty for the Golden Rule posed by cases where the agent cannot please everyone is to understand the Golden Rule as requiring the agent to imagine living out the lives of each of the affected parties with the preferences that the people in those lives have. The appropriate way for the agent to address this problem might be thought to be simply to weigh up all those preferences against one another in order to determine an on-balance preference about what happens universally across all relevantly similar actual and imaginary cases in which the agent would be living the lives of the other affected parties (Hare 1981). This way of developing the Golden Rule leads to the theory often called preference-satisfaction act-utilitarianism.

But one striking objection to this way of interpreting the Golden Rule is that it implies that the agent must give weight to what might be perverse preferences. As Samuel Clarke (1728) wrote, 'in judging what you would desire that another, if your circumstances were transposed, should do to you, you always consider, not what any unreasonable passion or private interest would prompt you, but what impartial reason would dictate to you to desire' (Wattles 1996: 83). Clarke's suggestion is that the proper operation of the Golden Rule must presuppose, rather than determine, what one's moral will should be or what impartial reason dictates that one prefer (see also Sidgwick 1907: 380).

The other paradigm of impartial justification is contractualist (Richards 1970; Rawls 1971; Gauthier 1986; Kavka 1986; Nagel 1991; Barry 1995; Gensler 1996; Scanlon 1998; Sayre-McCord 2000; Darwall 2006; Parfit 2011). There are important differences between different varieties of contractualism. The most comprehensive discussion of these is in Parfit 2011. Parfit persuasively argues that contractualism is best construed as seeking rules that each can rationally will (i.e. that each has adequate reason to consent) that everyone accept. We can add that each is being treated as an end, and not merely as a means, in that his or her reasonable consent is necessary for the justification of rules.

What is common to utilitarian and contractualist impartiality? Utilitarian impartiality counts everyone as equally important in that benefits and harms to any individual count for the same as the same size benefits and harms to any other. Utilitarian impartiality then aggregates: benefits or costs to the many added together can outweigh benefits or costs to the few. Contractualist impartiality counts each as equally important in that the reasons each has for willing or rejecting rules are weighed against the reasons any other has, in pair-wise comparison (Nagel 1991; Scanlon 1998: 229–40). The reasons one person has for accepting or rejecting a set of rules are *not* to be set against the aggregate of reasons that others have. Each person's reasons can be weighed against only one other person's reasons at a time.

Contractualism's individualism protects the individual not only against another individual but also against a group of individuals. Contractualism is thus usually thought to oppose what is called aggregative reasoning, that is, reasoning that abandons purely pair-wise comparison by letting the good of many outweigh the good of the few. Some writers agree that contractualism is implacably opposed to aggregative reasoning and think this is fine. Others think that contractualism is implacably opposed to aggregative reasoning and that this renders contractualism implausible. Still others argue that there are ways for contractualism to accommodate aggregative concerns (Parfit 2011). This chapter, however, is not the place to take up those debates.

What degree of partiality would be allowed by utilitarian or contractualist impartial justification?

The set of moral rules whose internalization by future generations would maximize expected aggregate welfare would include rules not only allowing but also requiring partiality when one is allocating one's own resources (see Sidgwick 1907: 431–9; Hooker 2000: 136 –41). One of the main reasons that a cost/benefit analysis comes out in favour of *allowing* some degree of partiality towards oneself and one's family and friends when one is allocating one's own resources is that the costs of trying to expunge partiality completely would be too high. One of the main reasons that a cost/benefit analysis comes out in favour of *requiring* some degree of partiality towards friends and family when one is allocating one's own resources is that, in general, each will get better attention and protection if some others have special obligations to them than if no others do. Why wouldn't this attention and protection be motivated by affection rather than duty? Well, it typically would. But moral requirement is needed as a back-up for situations where affection is too weak.

A contractualist impartial foundation for morality can likewise justify allowing and even requiring partiality in everyday moral thought (Barry 1995: chs 8–10, especially 191–4, 217–21). When thinking about what moral code one could reasonably agree to for acceptance by everyone, one would reasonably consider what sort of projects and relationships would be possible under that code, what sort of assurances one could depend upon with that code, and how much room for personal projects would be allowed by it. How much welfare would each have if everyone accepted a code that effectively precluded both friendship and personal projects? The answer is not much, because of the centrality of friendship and personal achievement to flourishing (cf. Ashford 2003 and Hills 2010). If all partiality had to be eliminated, friendship and personal achievement would be hugely reduced if not extinguished, draining away much of what is valuable in human life. Hence, contractualism, like utilitarianism, puts forward an impartial foundational principle for assessing possible moral rules, and this impartial foundational principle selects rules that allow considerable scope for partiality.*

BIBLIOGRAPHY

Adams, R. M. 1976. 'Motive Utilitarianism', *Journal of Philosophy* 73: 467–81.
Ashford, E. 2003. 'The Demandingness of Scanlon's Contractualism', *Ethics* 113: 273–302.

* For helpful comments on parts of this chapter, I am grateful to George Botterill, John Broome, Jonathan Dancy, David Ekstrand, Dominic Gregory, Robert Hopkins, Steven Laurence, Jimmy Lenman, Douglas MacLean, Jamie McKeever, Eric Olson, David Owens, Nate Sharadin, Yonathan Shemmer, John Skorupski, Susan Wolf, Fiona Woollard, and Ralph Wedgwood. For help in revising the whole chapter, I am grateful to Roger Crisp.

Audi, R. 1993. 'Ethical Reflectionism', *The Monist* 76: 296–315.

—— 1996. 'Intuitionism, Pluralism, and the Foundations of Ethics', in W. Sinnott-Armstrong and M. Timmons (eds), *Moral Knowledge?* New York: Oxford University Press, 101–36.

—— 2004. *The Good in the Right*. Princeton: Princeton University Press.

Axelrod, R. 1984. *The Evolution of Cooperation*. New York: Basic Books.

Baier, K. 1958. *The Moral Point of View*. Ithaca: Cornell University Press.

Barry, B. 1995. *Justice as Impartiality*. Oxford: Oxford University Press.

Brandt, R. 1954. 'The Definition of "Ideal Observer" in Ethics', *Philosophy and Phenomenological Research* 15: 407–13.

Brink, D. 1989. *Moral Realism and the Foundations of Ethics*. Cambridge: Cambridge University Press.

—— 2003. *Perfectionism and the Common Good: Themes in the Philosophy of T. H. Green*. Oxford: Oxford University Press.

Broad, C. D. 1930. *Five Types of Ethical Theory*. London: Routledge.

Butler, J. 1726. *Fifteen Sermons Preached at the Rolls Chapel*.

Clarke, S. 1728. *A Discourse of Natural Religion*.

Cottingham, J. 1998. 'The Ethical Credentials of Partiality', *Proceedings of the Aristotelian Society* 98: 1–21.

Crisp, R. 2006. *Reasons and the Good*. Oxford: Oxford University Press.

Darwall, S. 2006. *The Second-Person Standpoint*. Cambridge, MA: Harvard University Press.

Feinberg, J. 1973. *Social Philosophy*. Englewood Cliffs: Prentice-Hall.

—— 2008. 'Psychological Egoism', in J. Feinberg and R. Shafer-Landau (eds), *Reason and Responsibility: Readings in Some Basic Problems of Philosophy*. Thirteenth edition. Belmont, CA: Thomson Publishing, 520–31. Originally published in 1971.

Gauthier, D. 1986. *Morals By Agreement*. Oxford: Oxford University Press.

Gensler, H. J. 1996. *Formal Ethics*. London: Routledge.

Gert, B. 1998. *Morality*. New York: Oxford University Press.

Green, T. H. 1888. *Prolegomena to Ethics*. Oxford: Oxford University Press.

Hare, R. M. 1981. *Moral Thinking*. Oxford: Oxford University Press.

Hart, H. L. A. 1961. *The Concept of Law*. Oxford: Oxford University Press.

Hills, A. 2010. 'Utilitarianism, Contractualism, and Demandingness', *Philosophical Quarterly* 60: 225–42.

Hooker, B. 2000. *Ideal Code, Real World: A Rule-consequentialist Theory of Morality*. Oxford: Oxford University Press.

—— 2010. 'When Is Impartiality Morally Appropriate?', in J. Cottingham and B. Feltham (eds), *Partiality and Impartiality: Morality, Special Relationships, and the Wider World*. Oxford: Oxford University Press, 26–41.

Kavka, G. 1986. *Hobbesian Moral and Political Theory*. Princeton: Princeton University Press.

—— 1993. 'The Problem of Group Egoism', in B. Hooker (ed.), *Rationality, Rules, and Utility*. Boulder, CO: Westview Press, 149–63.

Mackie, J. L. 1977. *Ethics: Inventing Right and Wrong*. Harmondsworth: Penguin.

Nagel, T. 1986. *The View from Nowhere*. New York: Oxford University Press.

—— 1991. *Equality and Partiality*. New York: Oxford University Press.

Parfit, D. 1984. *Reasons and Persons*. Oxford: Oxford University Press.

—— 2011. *On What Matters*. Oxford: Oxford University Press.

Portmore, D. 2003. 'Position-Relative Consequentialism, Agent-Centered Options, and Supererogation', *Ethics* 113: 303–32.

Portmore, D. 2007. 'Consequentializing Moral Theories', *Pacific Philosophical Quarterly* 88: 39–73.

—— 2011. *Commonsense Consequentialism*. New York: Oxford University Press.

Rawls, J. 1971. *A Theory of Justice*. Cambridge, MA: Harvard University Press.

Richards, D. A. J. 1970. *A Theory of Reasons for Action*. Oxford: Oxford University Press.

Ross, W. D. 1930. *The Right and the Good*. Oxford: Oxford University Press.

Sayre-McCord, G. 2000. 'Contractarianism', in H. LaFollette (ed.), *Blackwell Guide to Ethical Theory*. Malden, MA: Blackwell Publishers, 247–67.

Scanlon, T. M. 1998. *What We Owe to Each Other*. Cambridge, MA: Harvard University Press.

Scheffler, S. 1982. *The Rejection of Consequentialism*. Oxford: Oxford University Press.

Shaver, R. 1999. *Rational Egoism*. Cambridge: Cambridge University Press.

Sidgwick, H. 1889. 'Some Fundamental Ethical Controversies', *Mind* 14: 473–87.

—— 1907. *Methods of Ethics*. 7th edn. London: Macmillan.

Slote, M. 1985. *Common-Sense Morality and Consequentialism*. London: Routledge and Kegan Paul.

—— 1992. *From Morality to Virtue*. Oxford: Oxford University Press.

Wattles, J. 1996. *The Golden Rule*. New York: Oxford University Press.

Williams, B. 1973. 'A Critique of Utilitarianism', in J. J. C. Smart and B. Williams, *Utilitarianism: For and Against*. Cambridge: Cambridge University Press, 77–150.

—— 1995. 'The Point of View of the Universe: Sidgwick and the Ambitions of Ethics', in *Making Sense of Humanity and Other Essays*. Cambridge: Cambridge University Press, 153–71.

Wolf, S. 1992. 'Morality and Partiality', *Philosophical Perspectives* 6: 243–59.

CHAPTER 34

CONSCIENCE, GUILT, AND SHAME

JOHN COTTINGHAM

34.1 INTRODUCTION

A great deal of morality is concerned with the public arena: examining what is required for a just and fair society, and trying to map out the nature and extent of our obligations to our fellow citizens and to the wider world. The concepts of conscience, guilt, and shame, by contrast, seem primarily concerned with what might be called the interior dimension of morality: how each of us thinks and feels about our own conduct when we review it, or when we measure it against our sense of what is expected of us, or how we might have done better.

The idea of conscience carries, etymologically, something of this interior flavour. The Latin word *conscientia*—from *con* or *cum* ('with') and *scientia* ('knowledge')—originally meant knowledge shared with another (e.g. a fellow-conspirator); but it came to be used by extension of the private knowledge an individual shares (as it were) with him or herself, and hence the term is employed quite generally to refer to a person's inner mental awareness. Thus we find Descartes in the seventeenth century reported as saying that if we look within ourselves, we will see that we have 'intimate inner awareness' (Lat. *intime conscii sumus*) of the freedom of the will (Descartes 1648). Elsewhere he defines a thought as 'that which is within us in such a way that we are immediately *aware* [Lat. *conscius*] of it' (Descartes 1641). The thoughts of which we are 'conscious' in this sense need not have anything specifically to do with morality, though of course they may. This may partly explain how the term '*conscience*' in modern French does duty for what in English is conveyed by two separate words, 'consciousness' and 'conscience': it can mean either the direct inner awareness each of us supposedly has of our own mental states in general, or, in a more specifically moral sense, one's inner awareness of, for example, guilt at wrongdoing.

The connection between conscience and guilt is enshrined in common phrases like 'he must have a guilty conscience', used when someone is behaving in an embarrassed or furtive manner, or in a way that indicates awareness of wrongdoing. But conscience need not be guilty conscience. A commonplace book of John Marbeck (1581) defines conscience as 'the knowledge, judgement and reason of a man, whereby every man, in himself, and in his own mind, being privy to everything he either hath committed or not committed, does either condemn or acquit himself' (*Oxford English Dictionary*, s. v. 'conscience'). So conscience can be, as we say, a 'clear conscience', when someone's inner reflection leaves him in the happy position of finding nothing wrong with how he has behaved. Consistently with this, John Locke observes in the *Essay concerning Human Understanding* that 'conscience is . . . nothing else but our own . . . judgement of the moral rectitude or pravity of our own actions' (Locke 1689: Bk I, Ch. 3, §8).

Because of its central importance in the moral life, one might suppose that conscience would be a primary concern of philosophers working in ethical theory. Certainly it bulked large in the writings of many moral philosophers in the seventeenth and eighteenth centuries; but it is surprising to find how comparatively little attention is paid to it in modern anglophone philosophy (see however Donagan 1977, Wallace 1978). One possible reason for the relative neglect of the topic may lie in the increasing secularism of our philosophical culture, and the resulting mistrust of anything that smacks of a religious framework for understanding the human moral predicament. Notions like 'the examination of conscience' (found for example in the *Spiritual Exercises* of Ignatius of Loyola, *c*.1525) are associated in many people's minds, whether explicitly or implicitly, with the religious notion of sin, which many modern philosophers would probably say has no place in a rational theory of ethics. Yet while there have certainly been theological writers on ethics who have seemed preoccupied with the burden of human sinfulness, most of us, irrespective of religious allegiance or its lack, will recognize feelings of guilt and/or shame as having from time to time played a key role in our lives. At the very least they seem to have an indispensable role in the phenomenology and psychology of ethics; and arguably they are an integral part of our sense of ourselves as responsible moral agents.

The discussion that follows will first provide a short survey of the concept of conscience as it has evolved in the Western philosophical tradition. Certain questions arising from this about the supposed authority or normativity of conscience will then be examined. The relation between the idea of conscience and the notions of guilt and shame will be dealt with next, which will in turn lead on to the question (broached in the seminal work of Bernard Williams in this area) of whether the concepts of guilt and shame inhabit essentially different ethical landscapes. The chapter will conclude by looking at the contribution made by psychoanalytic thinking to our modern understanding of the phenomena of conscience, guilt, and shame, and by asking why it is that the resulting insights have been so imperfectly assimilated into contemporary anglophone moral philosophy.

34.2 Conscience in the Western Tradition

One of the earliest Western texts to prefigure the idea of conscience is Psalm 51 in the Hebrew Bible (or 50 in the Vulgate and Septuagint numbering), now generally known as the *Miserere*, and dating from several hundred years BC. Reflecting on his past conduct, the author utters a prolonged plea for mercy, linked to a frank acknowledgement of transgression: 'I acknowledge my guilt, and my sin is ever before me'. Traditionally, the composition of the psalm is attributed to King David, after he had been brought by the prophet Nathan to a keen sense of his wrongdoing in seducing Bathsheba and sending her husband to the front line to be killed. According to the story, what had made David feel the pangs of conscience was Nathan's parable about a rich man who was unwilling to draw on his own flocks and herds to feed a visitor, but instead took from a poor man his one ewe lamb, which he dearly loved. David's outrage at such behaviour was then turned in on himself, when Nathan told him 'thou art the man!' (2 Samuel 12: 1–23). The seemingly simple text presupposes an ethical framework of considerable subtlety. Three key points in particular emerge from the story about how the operation of conscience is envisaged. First, it involves a directing inwards by the subject of the kind of disapproval characteristically felt at the untoward behaviour of another. Second, it is linked to remorse and repentance, which is in turn made possible by a deepening both of self-awareness and of empathy: David's previously shallow grasp of the significance of his actions was altered under the imaginative stimulus of being presented with a vivid analogue of his own conduct, which made him start to appreciate how being treated in such a way would feel for the victim. And third, the required response is not simply implanted from the outside by the prophet's condemnation, but is partly elicited from within. Once certain emotional and cognitive barriers are lifted, it is David's own conscience that convicts him.

The complex psycho-ethical framework presupposed here may be found in one form or another in many prophetic writings from the Old Testament, and it continues on through the parables of Jesus of Nazareth (such as that of the Prodigal Son (Luke 15: 11–32)), and into much subsequent Christian moral philosophy. If, by contrast, we turn to the other great source of Western ethics, namely the philosophy of the classical Greek world, we find a rather different picture. Although the workings of guilt and remorse are vividly present in much Greek tragedy (compare Sophocles' *Oedipus Tyrannus*), in the ethical writings of Aristotle there is no developed idea of conscience. Aristotle does discuss *aidos* ('modesty' or 'shame'), but he characterizes it as a 'fear of disrepute'—something that may be useful in restraining the young, but which should be no part of the make-up of a person of confirmed virtue (Aristotle 325 BC: Book IV, Ch. 9). Aristotle's central ethical preoccupations are not with prophetic calls to righteousness or with self-scrutiny and repentance, but rather with mapping out the virtuous life of a successful and flourishing human being. Harmonious moral development, on the

Aristotelian view, involves a happy match between inclination and right conduct, which arises from an individual's having been inducted as a child into a sound ethical culture. Aristotle does not describe this process in detail, but the main idea appears to be that even at a pre-rational level, the young child will be progressively encouraged to take pleasure in behaving virtuously. At this early stage, he or she need have no clear rational grasp of exactly what makes the relevant actions good or bad; she is simply being habituated to act and feel appropriately. But by the time the child comes of age, habits of right behaviour will be supported by an understanding of what it is about the conduct in question that makes it praiseworthy or blameworthy. The outcome of this process is a person of mature ethical virtue: someone who has the right habits of feeling and action, but who also has the capacity to discern what should be done and why—someone who acts, as Aristotle puts it in the *Nicomachean Ethics*, 'knowing what he is doing and choosing it for its own sake', and who has the right feelings 'at the right times on the right grounds towards the right people, for the right motive and in the right way' (Aristotle 325 BC: Bk II, Ch. 6).

The Aristotelian conception of ethical virtue seems to lack that sense of humans as essentially conflicted beings which emerges so vividly in the Judaeo-Christian world view—a world view in which a sense of sin, and its corollary conscience, has a pivotal place. To be sure, Aristotle did give considerable attention to the phenomenon of *akrasia*—the failure through weakness to choose the best option—and this has some affinities to the disordered and conflicted state of which St Paul famously spoke when he said 'Woe is me! The good that I would, that I do not, and the evil that I would not, that I do' (Romans 7: 19). But Aristotle's model is not that of the transgressor tormented by conscience for his or her lapses of will, but rather of someone who desires the good but (under the influence of passion) is subject to cognitive error, mistaking the lesser good for the greater (Bk VII, Ch. 3).

In the letters of Paul and several other places in the New Testament, as well as in some non-Christian writers of roughly the same period (for example the Stoic philosopher Epictetus, though the interpretation of the relevant passage is disputed), we find the first occurrences of an explicit term for the concept of conscience, namely the Greek word *syneidesis*. This is normally translated into Latin as *conscientia*, and appropriately so, since it is made up of exactly the same corresponding elements, coming from *syn* ('with') and *eidesis* ('knowledge'). In a frequently cited passage Paul remarks that the Gentiles, though not possessing the Law, 'do by nature the things contained in the law, and show the work of the law written in their hearts, their conscience (*syneidesis*) also bearing witness' (Romans 2: 15).

A corruption or copyist's misspelling of the New Testament Greek word appears to have led to the curious term 'synderesis', or 'synteresis', found in later patristic writers (starting with St Jerome in the early fifth century). Jerome speaks of synteresis as the 'spark of conscience [*scintilla conscientiae*] not extinguished in Cain when he was driven from paradise' (Jerome 414, at Ch. 1, v. 7). In Thomas Aquinas, synderesis appears as the name for the innate, God-given cognitive disposition or 'rational power', which enables us to know right and wrong: 'Just as there is a natural habit of the human soul through which it knows principles of the speculative sciences ... so too there is in the soul a natural habit of first principles of action, which are the universal principles of the natural law (Aquinas 1256–1259, Qu. 16). The reference to 'habit' may seem reminiscent of Aristotle (whose account of virtue strongly influenced Aquinas elsewhere), but the emphasis here is not on childhood training but on rational knowledge of principles of action, implanted in the soul by God. Aquinas goes on to distinguish this general rational power of 'synderesis' from the more specific exercise of *conscientia*. The latter involves applying principles of practical knowledge to particular cases, so as to evaluate what one should do now, and what one has done in the past: 'in so far as knowledge is applied to an act as directive of it, conscience is said to prod or urge or bind. But, in so far as knowledge is applied to an act by way of examining what has already taken place, conscience is said to accuse or cause remorse, when what has been done is found to be out of harmony with the knowledge according to which it is examined' (Qu. 17, art. 1).

Although the main elements of this account are cognitive, conscience being seen primarily in terms of knowledge or its application, this last quotation shows that Aquinas also acknowledges the emotional components of conscience, such as feelings of remorse. This corresponds to our modern conception of conscience, which combines cognitive and affective elements (if I have a conscience about X, I *know* that I have done wrong, and I *feel* badly about it). The latter element becomes particularly important in the discussions of conscience found in many of the early modern philosophers, especially those whose 'empirical naturalist' programme (to use Stephen Darwall's label) led them to try to explain our moral capacities and judgements in terms of the natural sentiments, drives, and impulses we find within us (see Darwall 1995: Ch. 1).

In the second of his *Fifteen Sermons* (1726), Joseph Butler, one of the most influential writers on conscience, at first appears to be taking an empirical psychologizing approach, talking of various 'natural principles' in man, including that whereby 'man approves or disapproves his heart, temper and actions'. But Butler then makes a crucial distinction between principles that are natural merely in the sense of being prevalent, or commonly occurring, and those which are natural in the sense that they carry an authoritative or (as philosophers now say) a 'normative' force. (For this latter sense of 'natural', compare the traditional philosophical use of phrases like 'natural law' or 'natural light'.) We may have natural dispositions to kindness and compassion, but 'since other passions [such as anger]...which lead us...astray, are themselves in a degree equally natural, and often most prevalent...it is plain the former considered merely as natural...can no more be a law to us than the latter'. But alongside such naturally occurring impulses, there is 'a superior principle of reflection or conscience in every man...which pronounces some actions to be in themselves just, right, good; others to be in themselves evil, wrong, unjust'. The deliverances of conscience, then, are not to be regarded as simply one group among the many competing internal principles which may motivate us, but have a special authoritative status, which enables them, in Butler's phrase, to 'be a law to us'. Butler concludes that 'it is by this faculty [of conscience], *natural* to man, that he is a moral agent...a faculty in kind and in nature supreme over all others, and which *bears its own authority* of being so' (Butler 1726: Sermon II, §8, emphasis supplied). This idea of the authoritative and quasi-legal status of conscience prefigures the conception of Immanuel Kant, later in the eighteenth century, according to which conscience [*Gewissen*] is the 'consciousness of an *internal court* in man, before which his thoughts accuse or excuse one another'. Every human being, Kant goes on to argue in the *Tugendlehre* or *Doctrine of Virtue*, is 'kept in awe an by internal judge', and 'this authority watching over the law in him is not something that he himself voluntarily makes, but something incorporated in his being' (Kant 1797: §13).

The strongly normative conception of conscience which we find, in different ways, in Butler and in Kant corresponds to an idea of conscience that is still widespread; but it raises the philosophical question of what might be the source of such an authoritative faculty, and of whether its supposed existence is compatible with the naturalistic framework for understanding human nature to which many present-day philosophers are drawn. To this cluster of questions we will now turn.

34.3 THE AUTHORITY OF CONSCIENCE

Kant's solution to the problem of the authority of conscience is too complex to unfold in detail here, but in essence it depends on his notion, found in the *Groundwork for the Metaphysic of Morals*, of the rational will as 'self-legislating' or 'giving the law to itself' (*selbstgesetzgebend*) (Kant 1785: Ch. 2). In the *Doctrine of Virtue*, Kant in effect links this conception to the idea of conscience. Within the 'internal forum' of each of us, my acts are brought before the tribunal of reason. But Kant goes on to argue that it is absurd to think of a human being who is accused as one and the same person as the judge; and hence the subject must think of himself as being judged by another, who is 'an ideal person that reason creates for itself' (Kant 1797: §13). This looks like an internal analogue of the religious idea of a supreme authoritative judge; but on the question of whether it has any real external counterpart, Kant explicitly draws back from saying that a human being is 'entitled, through the idea to which his conscience unavoidably guides him, to assume that such a supreme being actually exists'. The idea of a supreme 'scrutinizer of all hearts', Kant insists, is given 'not objectively, but only subjectively'. At this point, however, the sceptical reader of Kant may be inclined to question how much the argument has achieved. For once the actual existence of a supreme external authority is put to one side, it may appear unclear how our rational will or rational choice, taken on its own, can be enough to supply the requisite authority (for a defence of Kant on this issue, see Korsgaard 1996).

For Butler, following a long religious tradition, things are much simpler: the authority of the 'natural' inner voice of conscience derives from its being implanted in us by God. Conscience is our 'natural guide, the guide assigned to us by the Author of our nature' (Butler 1726: III, 5). Yet for all its apparent straightforwardness, this solution is not without its own problems. For if the moral authority of conscience derives from its supposedly divine source, a question may still arise as to the basis of the moral authority attaching to the source itself (a question that has roots in the so-called 'Euthyphro dilemma' first raised by Plato). The mere fact that a supremely powerful being issues commands, or implants them in our hearts, does not in itself seem enough to endow those commands with moral authority; if on the other hand we say we know the commands should be obeyed because we are told so by the authoritative voice of conscience, this simply takes us back to the original question of what endows our moral sense with the requisite normative status. Notwithstanding such worries, many theists have taken it as a primary datum that we do indeed have an authentically authoritative faculty of conscience, and have used this as a premise providing grounds to infer the existence of God. Thus in the latter nineteenth century, Cardinal Newman wrote in his *Grammar of Assent* that 'in this special feeling of Conscience, which follows on the commission of what we call right or wrong, lie the materials for the real apprehension of a Divine Sovereign and Judge' (Newman 1870: Ch. 5).

Two decades earlier, John Stuart Mill, writing from an entirely secular perspective, in his essay *Utilitarianism*, had provided an analysis of conscience that put pressure on this type of argument from conscience. In line with the 'empirical naturalist' movement referred to at the end of section 34.2 above, he defined 'the essence of conscience' as 'a feeling in our own mind; a pain more or less intense, attendant on violation of duty' (Mill 1861: Ch. 3). He adds various qualifications—that the feeling must be 'disinterested', and connected with the 'pure idea of duty'—but the main effect of his account is a deflationary or demystifying one—to reduce the deliverances of conscience to nothing more than a set of psychological events or purely subjective feelings. The feelings, he observed, are typically 'encrusted over with collateral associations', derived from the 'recollections of childhood' and 'all the forms of religious feeling'; and this, he claims, is enough to explain away 'the sort of mystical character which . . . is apt to be attributed to the idea of moral obligation'.

Mill's account purports to be simply a piece of empirical psychology, but it clearly has serious implications for the normativity of conscience. Painful feelings linked to the violation of duty function as what Mill terms 'internal sanctions', and he wished to enlist these in the service of his own utilitarian ethics. But sanctions, as understood by Mill, are no more than causal motivators—means whereby a desired code may be inculcated into the population so as to reinforce allegiance; we are thus in the territory of inducements for compliance, not in the territory of authoritative reasons for action. Mill was sensitive to the objection that if what restrains me from wrongdoing is 'only a feeling in my own mind', one may be tempted to think that 'when the feeling ceases, the obligation ceases'. But he confines his reply to observing that those who believe in a more exalted and objective source of obligation are just as likely to transgress morally as those who think that what restrains them 'is always in the mind itself' (Mill 1861: Ch. 3). Whether or not his account is ultimately satisfying, Mill's interesting observations about how the feelings of conscience are often 'encrusted' with associations formed in childhood anticipate key elements in later psychoanalytic approaches to conscience, to be discussed in section 34.5 below.

34.4 Guilt and Shame

It appears to be part of the concept of conscience that it involves not just the evaluation of one's past conduct, but also, when the evaluation is negative, a characteristic sense of discomfort. When reviewing what we have done yields a satisfactory verdict, then the conscience is 'quiet'; but when, as often, there is much to regret, then we speak of 'the pangs' of conscience, or being 'pricked' by conscience. Just as imprudent eating produces subsequent indigestion, so immoral conduct generates an unquiet conscience.

Precisely what form this takes will no doubt vary, but one very characteristic human reaction is to feel *ashamed* at what one has done. Though shame is a complicated reaction, at the most basic level it seems to involve an awareness that one's faults have been, or may be, exposed to view. Thus in the ancient story of the Fall of Mankind, Adam, after his act of disobedience, becomes aware for the first time of his nakedness, and hides himself. 'Who told you that you were naked?', God asks; and then, in the archetypal stern voice of authority, 'Have you eaten from the tree from which I told you not to eat?' (Genesis 3:11). The association between shame and nakedness does not, as a widely parroted caricature might suggest, depend on any particular Judaic or Judaeo-Christian 'hang-up' about sexuality, but is found in many cultures. Thus even among the ancient Greeks, who were perfectly unembarrassed about exercising naked, the genitals were commonly referred to as *aidoia*, a derivative of *aidos*, 'shame' (cf. Bernard Williams 1993: Ch. 4). Shame is a matter of being 'embarrassed', in the widest sense of that term: being seen by others in a setting where your untoward behaviour is the object of a certain class of 'participant-reactive attitudes'—in this case negative ones such as scorn, contempt, ridicule, reproach, disapproval, blame, and so on (Strawson 1962; cf. Taylor 1985).

This cluster of reactions appears to extend over wider territory than the domain of what we normally call 'morality'; and indeed shame may be, and often is, felt in situations (such as being accidentally locked out of one's house wearing only one's underwear) where moral censure is not in question. Reflecting on this kind of contrast has led some thinkers to subscribe to a distinction between the kinds of standard that hinge on a person's retaining the honour and esteem thought due to them—keeping their dignity, or not 'losing face'—and the standards that focus on guilt and individual responsibility. In line with this, some anthropologists have suggested a classification of cultures into *guilt cultures* and *shame cultures*, where the former type of society places great emphasis on ideas of conscience, personal accountability, and liability to blame and punishment, while the latter emphasizes personal status or standing, as measured in terms of public esteem or its forfeiture. (For such classifications, and problems with them, see Deigh 1996.)

This kind of distinction has sometimes been thought to imply a contrast between an ethically immature 'shame' system in which all the weight is placed on what others think, or find out, about me, and a more sophisticated 'guilt' system in which personal responsibility and inner moral integrity are paramount (Atkins 1960; cf. Dodds 1951). Against this, Bernard Williams has argued in his landmark study *Shame and Necessity* that a study of ancient texts such as the Homeric epics in which shame plays a major role shows that 'even if shame and its motivations always involve in some way...an idea of the gaze of another...for many of its operations the imagined gaze of an imagined other will do' (Williams 1993: 82). Williams makes a persuasive case for supposing that what he calls the 'internalized other' is typically crucial to how shame works. If this is right, then since (as we have seen in connection with Kant's account) conscience and guilt equally appear to involve the idea of an 'internal forum' in which we are judged by an idealized other, it begins to look as if the contrast between shame and guilt systems is not nearly as sharp as is often claimed.

Nevertheless, Williams does manage to retain elements of the contrast between shame and guilt, in a way that furthers his own distinctive agenda in the philosophy of ethics, namely his critique of what he called the 'morality system'—that 'peculiar institution', with its associated idea of a special class of inescapable obligations (Williams 1985: Ch. 10). Williams felt that this institution exerted a kind of tyranny over our thinking about ethics, and that we would be better off without it; and he further argued that reflecting on the different landscape of Greek ethical culture would help us to see how such an escape might be possible. Once we acquit ancient Greek ethics of the charge of being preoccupied with public esteem and the dangers of 'losing face', we start (on Williams' view) to see that their judgements about shame were reaching towards a much richer conception of how ethical evaluation might work, and one that is arguably in better shape than our own. So instead of the presumptuous 'progressivism' which looks back on the ethical outlook of the Classical world as falling short of our modern Western understanding of morality, we might learn from seeing how the mechanisms of shame are displayed as motivating the characters found in (for example) Sophoclean tragedy: '[these] characters are represented...as experiencing a necessity to act in certain ways, a conviction that they must do certain things... The source of the necessity is in the agent, an internalised other whose view the agent can respect... The sense of this necessity lies in the thought that one could not live and look others in the eye if one did certain things.' For agents to have this kind of conception of what must be done does not, on Williams' argument, require them to acknowledge moral imperatives grounded in 'external reasons'. Rather, 'these necessities are internal, grounded in the *êthos,* the projects, the individual nature of the agent' (Williams 1993: 103).

Complex issues are raised in this passage, whose full explication would require us to move farther afield than is possible here—for example into Williams' interest in the 'genealogy of morals', and his associated attraction for aspects of the philosophy of Nietzsche. But what I think one may nevertheless discern in these arguments is a programme for the radical deconstruction of the Christian concept of conscience, with its vision of the authoritative divine voice (or its Kantian analogue) calling each of us to account for the moral quality of our actions. We are offered instead a Nietzschean vision of an ethical world in which values are grounded in no more than the 'individual nature of the agent' and his or her chosen 'projects' (Nietzsche 1887: First Essay; Nietzsche 1886: §203). Whatever one makes of this (and many will feel serious misgivings about the attempt to establish ethics on such an individualistic base), there is one general lesson on which both supporters and critics of Williams may agree, namely that philosophical discussion of concepts such as conscience, guilt, and shame cannot fruitfully be conducted in abstraction from the history of how those concepts developed, or in isolation from the underlying world view in terms of which they were shaped. Williams' own resistance to the 'morality system', as he implicitly makes clear at the close of *Shame and Necessity*, stems from a world view that wholly rejects any absolute moral framework for understanding the human predicament: 'our ethical condition... lies not only beyond Christianity, but beyond its Kantian... legacies... We know that the world was not made for us, or we for the world, that our history tells no purposive story, and that there is no position outside the world or outside history from which we might hope to authenticate our activities' (Williams 1993: 166). The authoritative status of conscience, at any rate as traditionally conceived, does not look likely to survive in such a world; but if Williams' arguments are accepted, it is a world in which agents will still be able to measure themselves against powerful standards they will be ashamed to fall short of, even if those standards depend in the end on no more than the individual projects they have chosen to make their own.

34.5 CONSCIENCE AND THE UNCONSCIOUS

The concepts of the 'internal forum', in Kant, or of the 'internalized other', as deployed by Williams, will for many modern readers have unmistakeable psychoanalytic overtones. Irrespective of these specific resonances, however, any attempt to provide a philosophical introduction to the topics of conscience, guilt, and shame would be seriously incomplete if it failed to include some reference to how the ideas of Sigmund Freud and his successors have influenced our understanding of the concepts in question.

In a lecture expounding his views on the sources of psychological conflict, Freud discusses some of his patients who were in the grip of a persistent delusion that they were being observed; and he describes how such cases gave him the idea that the *separation* of the observing 'agency' from the rest of the ego might be a regular feature of the ego's structure. 'There is scarcely anything', he observes, 'that we so regularly separate from our ego, and so regularly set over against it, as our conscience'. In the typical case, I want to do something that gives me pleasure, but my conscience makes me abandon it; or, if I go ahead, 'my conscience punishes me with distressing reproaches'. This kind of familiar experience, Freud argues, makes it appropriate to talk of an independent agency in the ego, with a separate existence—what he labels the *Über-ich*—the 'Over-I' or (in the Latinized equivalent used in the standard English edition of Freud) the *Superego* (Freud 1933: 485–7 (Lecture 31, para. 6)).

At first sight this might look like a straightforwardly deflationary view of the conscience, of the kind found in Mill (see above): in place of the authoritative voice of God implanted in the soul, there is simply an 'internal sanction', that is to say a painful feeling, produced by childhood conditioning, that motivates me to conform to prevailing rules, and punishes me when I fail to do so. Freud would certainly have rejected any theistic view of the origins of conscience—indeed, he took a generally sceptical view of religious belief, arguing that it was an illusion generated by the infantile need for security in a hostile world (Freud 1929: 260). But there is much more to Freud's view of conscience than a denial of its divine origins. The crucial thing to note is that the Superego, for Freud, exerts its power precisely in virtue of not being directly accessible to consciousness. On the Freudian analysis, then, the operation of conscience is often more complicated than could be explained by a simple internalizing of a moral rule (such as 'thou shalt not steal!'), backed by feelings that inhibit me from stealing and generate remorse should I transgress. What happens alongside this is often something potentially traumatic, a kind of 'dissection of personality', in which the Superego 'seems to have picked out the parents' strictness and severity, their prohibiting and punitive function, whereas their loving care seems not to have been maintained'. The result is a hapless state in which the individual, without fully consciously appreciating what is happening to him, is locked into an aggressive cycle of self-criticism, as he strives to fulfil ever greater demands for perfection.

> [The child's] aggressiveness [towards the heavily controlling parent] is introjected, internalized, sent back whence it came, that is, it is directed towards his own ego. There it is taken over by a portion of the ego, which sets itself over against the rest of the ego as Superego, and which now, in the form of 'conscience' is ready to put into action against the ego the same harsh aggressiveness that the ego would have liked to satisfy upon others. (Freud 1929: 315)

Successors of Freud such as Jacques Lacan, have laid great stress on this characteristic harshness of conscience, and its damaging effects in the psyche. Lacan in a memorable phrase talks of the *gourmandisme* of the Superego: the more cruel the conscience becomes, the more inescapably it commands obedience, and yet the very obedience only serves to generate an ever more stringent and searching inspection of the guilty secrets of the ego. Like a sinister parasite, the more you feed it, the more it wants (Lacan 1986; cf. Rajchman 1991: 58). Such vivid characterizations of psychic conflict may well strike a chord in many people's minds, but they have possibly had the effect of alienating mainstream philosophical writers on ethics, many of whom are suspicious of psychoanalytic ideas, and tend to approach the arena of morality using only the more straightforward vocabulary of reasons for action, practical deliberation, and an agent's ordinary and relatively transparent projects, desires, and beliefs (interesting exceptions include Scheffler 1992; Lear 2000).

One reaction to this apparent stand-off between psychoanalytic and 'mainstream' approaches to ethics would be for moral philosophers to acquiesce in a compartmentalizing of the subject—a phenomenon already increasingly prevalent in many other areas of philosophical enquiry. Analytic ethicists, on this scenario, would continue largely to ignore the work of Freud and his successors, while writers sympathetic to psychoanalytic ideas would gravitate towards those specializing in 'continental' styles of philosophizing.

Such an outcome, however, seems likely to lead to a serious impoverishment of philo-sophical understandings of concepts such as conscience, guilt, and shame, which, as we have already seen, appear very hard to explicate without something like the idea of an internal forum, where the subject experiences some kind of division or conflict (however these notions are eventually to be unravelled). It may therefore be useful to conclude this part of our discussion by asking how, if at all, psychoanalytic insights into the workings of conscience might be integrated into the rest of philosophical ethics.

The starting point for such a reconciling project might be to note that although many of Freud's theories were developed in the context of his treatment of patients with severe psychological disorders, certain lessons may nonetheless be drawn that have a wider application to the ordinary human ethical predicament—a project that is prominent in much of the work of Carl Jung (cf. Jung 1931: 40). The result which both Freud and Jung envisaged as the goal of therapy was an integrated condition in which the split-off parts of the self were reincorporated into consciousness. The precise details of this envisaged process are explained differently in different psychoanalytic theories, but the central idea is that a psychologically healthy person is one who is *maximally self-aware*—who is able to confront the various desires, inclinations, fears, aspirations, and so on that arise within him, but in their true colours, freed from distortions and projections (Jung 1931; cf. Cottingham 1998: Ch. 4). Applying this to the specific case of conscience, and to the ordinary moral conflicts that most of us face, it seems clear that all but the most perfectly virtuous souls will need the support of feelings of guilt and shame to keep them on the right path. Things go awry not because such feelings exist, but when they are invested with an awesome and tyrannical power that distorts the agent's deliberations so that he is incapable of balanced and rational assessment of how he should act, or unable to reflect on his conduct except with paralysing shame or self-hatred. But self-awareness, self-scrutiny, and a preparedness to delve into the sources of our mistakes, seem to be necessary components in the ethical life of any human being who aspires to integrity and responsibility, as well as being preconditions for the kind of genuine remorse and repentance that allows for healing, moral improvement and growth.

This brings us back to our main theme of the origins of conscience, and the source of its authoritative power. It would take an absurdly blithe and blinkered view of the human condition to fail to acknowledge the moral flaws of our species—the violence and cruelty and the aggressiveness and selfishness of which we are capable. And it does not require a very sophisticated anthropology to realize that the survival of civilization depends on these dire tendencies being held in check, both by the 'external sanctions' of law and social pressure, and by the 'internal sanctions' of conscience, guilt, and shame. But where does this internal, or 'internalized' voice come from? Simply to say that the relevant feel-ings were implanted in us as children by our parents is only a very short-term explana-tion, since the question immediately arises as to how the relevant feelings were transmitted to them, when they were children. Freud was quick to grasp this point: 'parents and authorities follow the precepts of their own super-egos in educating children...Thus a child's super-ego is in fact constructed on the model not of its parents' [ego], but of its parents' superego [and thus] it becomes the vehicle for...the judgements of value which have propagated themselves from generation to generation' (Freud 1933: 493). Explaining away conscience in terms of a parental voice is, in itself, no more satisfying than explaining away the idea of God by saying that I received it from my parents, since it simply postpones the question of ultimate genesis. A systematic enquiry into the origins of conscience would raise many fascinating and controversial issues, but given the constraints of space a few brief reflections will have to suffice to bring our discussion to a close.

34.6 CONCLUSION: CONSCIENCE AND CONFLICT

The persistence, down the generations, of feelings of conscience must surely come from roots that are deep in our human nature, namely that we aspire to the good, and yet are often drawn to evil. Given what seems indisputable, namely our inherent *conflictedness* in this respect, conscience can be seen, as it has been seen by many religious writers, as a necessary ally in the pursuit of the good—something, as traditional language has it, that speaks for our 'higher' nature, against the promptings of the lower. Casting conscience in this perhaps somewhat exalted but at any rate beneficial role turns out on reflection to be quite compatible with psychoanalytic insights about its harshness; for the harshness, as we have seen, stems from its being 'separated off' as an alien voice of punishment and control, whereas the idea of moral growth presupposes that this voice can be freed from its tyrannical overtones, once it is properly integrated into a healthy self-image, and seen as directing us to the good where our true fulfilment lies.

The final question this leaves us with is whether such a positive account presupposes, in the end, a theistic underpinning for the notion of conscience. It is a question that is by no means easy to answer. There seems on the face of it to be a perfectly coherent alternative, namely that the operation of conscience (maintained and transmitted down the generations, and no doubt given specific shape by the mores of society in any given epoch) derives ultimately from no more than contingent facts about the way our species happens to have evolved. David Hume in the eighteenth century was perhaps the most eloquent spokesman for such a view, when he proposed that morality is founded ultimately on the natural feelings of benevolence we find within us. Moral virtues, he remarked, have a 'natural beauty and amiableness' which 'recommends them to the esteem of uninstructed mankind and engages their affections'. An integral part of this is the operation of conscience—although, consistently with his sunny vision of human nature, what Hume stresses is not the torments of guilt and shame, but the joys of a quiet conscience— 'inward peace of mind, consciousness of integrity, a satisfactory review of our own conduct' (Hume 1751: Section IX, part 2).

Yet the conflictedness of our nature cannot be ignored, even by someone who takes such a benign view as Hume. Along with the 'particle of the dove' which he maintained was 'kneaded into our frame', he was obliged to acknowledge 'elements of the wolf and serpent' (Hume 1751: Section IX, part 1). The dove, symbol of peace, is of course also the ancient Christian icon of the Holy Spirit (Matthew 3: 16), though one assumes this is not an echo that Hume can consciously have intended to evoke, given his atheism, or at least his resolute scepticism about the 'ultimate springs and principles' of the cosmos (Hume 1748: Section IV, part 1). The image of the wolf, by contrast, calls to mind the tag of the Roman poet Plautus, 'homo homini lupus', recapitulated by Thomas Hobbes, when he observed in the De Cive 'that Man to Man is an arrant Wolfe' (Hobbes 1642, dedicatory letter)—a comment consistent with his famous account in the Leviathan of the natural state of humankind as the 'war of every man against every man' (Hobbes 1651: Ch. 13). Hume's other iconic image, that of the treacherous serpent, unavoidably conjures up the story of the Fall of Man, the archetypal narrative of human guilt and the unquiet conscience. At all events, the combined effect of these juxtaposed images might seem to be to underline the precariousness of the human condition, beset by contradictory impulses; and given this, it seems plain that the kind of guide to action that conscience has traditionally been supposed to provide cannot be underwritten simply by appealing, along Humean lines, to empirical facts about our nature. More is required; but what that 'more' amounts to is a matter of continuing philosophical debate. One thing at least should by now be clear from our discussion of conscience, guilt, and shame, namely that any plausible philosophical account of their role in the good life will need to be able to draw on the resources of a moral psychology rich enough to do justice to the cognitive and affective complexity of our human make-up.

BIBLIOGRAPHY

Aquinas, T. 1256–1259. *Disputed Questions about Truth* [*Quaestiones disputatae de veritate*]. English version, Washington DC: Regneri Publishing, 1954.

Aristotle *c.*325 BC. *Nicomachean Ethics*, tr. T. Irwin. Indianapolis, IN: Hackett, 1985. Also in *The Ethics of Aristotle*, tr. J. Thomson, rev. H. Tredennick. Harmondsworth: Penguin, 1976.

Atkins, A. H. 1960. *Merit and Responsibility: A Study in Greek Values*. Oxford: Clarendon.

Butler, J. 1726. *Fifteen Sermons*. Extracts may be found in J. B. Schneewind (ed.), *Moral Philosophy from Montaigne to Kant*. Cambridge: Cambridge University Press, 1990. Also in D. D. Raphael (ed.), *British Moralists 1650–1800*. Oxford: Clarendon, 1969.

Cottingham, J. 1998. *Philosophy and the Good Life: Reason and the passions in Greek, Cartesian and psychoanalytic Ethics*. Cambridge: Cambridge University Press.

Darwall, S. 1995. *The British moralists and the internal 'ought' 1640–1740*. Cambridge: Cambridge University Press.

Deigh, J. 1996. *The Sources of Moral Agency*. Cambridge: Cambridge University Press.

Descartes, R. 1641. *Meditations: Second Set of Replies to Objections* [*Meditationes: Secundae Reponsiones*] in J. Cottingham, R. Stoothoff, and D. Murdoch, *The Philosophical Writings of Descartes*, Vol. II. Cambridge: Cambridge University Press, 1985.

—— 1648. *Conversation with Burman*, translation in J. Cottingham, R. Stoothoff, D. Murdoch, and A. Kenny, *The Philosophical Writings of Descartes*, vol. III, *The Correspondence*. Cambridge: Cambridge University Press, 1991, 332ff.

Dodds, E. R. 1951. *The Greeks and the Irrational*. Berkeley: University of California Press.

Donagan, A. 1977. *The Theory of Conscience*. Chicago: University of Chicago Press.

Freud, S. 1929. *Civilization and its Discontents* [*Das Unbehagen in der Kultur*], in *The Penguin Freud Library*. London: Penguin Books, 1985, vol. 12.

—— 1933. *New Lectures on Psychoanalysis* [*Neue Folge der Vorlesungen zur Einfürhung in die Psychoanalyse*], in S. Freud, *The Essentials of Psychoanalysis*, ed. A. Freud. London: Penguin, 1986, 484ff. Also in *The Penguin Freud Library*. London: Penguin Books, 1985, vol. 2, 88ff.

Hume, D. 1748. *An Enquiry concerning Human Understanding*, ed. T. L. Beauchamp. Oxford: Oxford University Press, 1999.

—— 1751. An *Enquiry concerning the Principles of Morals*, ed. T. L. Beauchamp. Oxford: Oxford University Press, 1998.

Hobbes, T. 1642. *De Cive*. English version (possibly by Hobbes) published 1651. Both the English and the Latin versions are available in the edition of H. Warrender. Oxford: Clarendon, 1984.

—— 1651. *Leviathan*, ed. R. Tuck. Cambridge: Cambridge University Press, 1996.

Jerome, St, *Commentary on Ezekiel* [*Commentariorum In Ezechielem Prophetam Libri Quatuordecim*], in J. P. Migne (ed.), *Patrologia Latina*. Paris, 1857–1866), vol. 25.

Jung, C. 1931. 'Problems of Modern Psychotherapy' [from *Seelenprobleme der Gegenwart*], in *Modern Man in Search of a Soul: Essays from the 1920s and 1930s*, tr. C. F. Baynes. London: Routledge, 1933, ch. 2.

Kant, I. 1785. *Groundwork for the Metaphysic of Morals* [*Grundlegung zur Metaphysik der Sitten*], tr. and ed. T. E. Hill and A. Zwieg. Oxford: Oxford University Press, 2002.

—— 1797. *The Metaphysics of Morals: Doctrine of Virtue* [*Metaphysik der Sitten: Tugendlehre*], ed. M. Gregor. Cambridge: Cambridge University Press, 1996, Part II.

Korsgaard, C. 1996. *The Sources of Normativity*. Cambridge: Cambridge University Press.

Lacan, J. 1986. *Le Seminaire: Livre VII: L'éthique de la psychanalyse 1959–60*. Paris: Seuil, 1986. English version: *The Ethics of Psychoanalysis*, tr. D. Porter. New York: Norton, 1992.

Lear, J. 2000. *Happiness, Death, and the Remainder of Life*. Cambridge, MA: Harvard University Press.

Locke, J. 1689. *An Essay concerning Human Understanding*, ed. P. Nidditch. Oxford: Clarendon, repr. 1984.

Mill, J. S. 1861. *Utilitarianism*, ed. R. Crisp. Oxford: Oxford University Press, 1998.

Newman, J. H. 1870. *An Essay in Aid of A Grammar of Assent*. London: Burns, Oates & Co. Facsimile reprint, Elibron Classics: Adamant Media Corporation, 2007.

Nietzsche, F. 1886. *Jenseits von Gut und Böse*, tr. W. Kaufmann, *Beyond Good and Evil*. New York: Random House, 1966.

—— 1887. *Zur Genealogie der Moral*, tr. D. Smith, *On the Genealogy of Morals*. Oxford: Oxford University Press, 1996.

Rajchman, J. 1991. *Truth and Eros: Foucault, Lacan, and the question of ethics*. New York: Routledge.

Scheffler, S. 1992. *Human Morality*. New York: Oxford University Press.

Strawson, P. F. 1962. 'Freedom and Resentment', repr. in Strawson, *Freedom and Resentment*. London: Routledge, 2008, ch. 1.

Taylor, G. 1985. *Pride, Shame and Guilt*. Oxford: Clarendon.

Wallace, J. D. 1978. *Virtues and Vices*. Ithaca, NY: Cornell University Press.

Williams, B. 1985. *Ethics and the Limits of Philosophy*. London: Collins.

—— 1993. *Shame and Necessity*. Berkeley: University of California Press.

CHAPTER 35

....

MORAL PSYCHOLOGY
AND VIRTUE

....

NANCY SHERMAN

35.1 INTRODUCTION

RECENT interest in virtue theory has been concurrent with an explosion of study in moral psychology, pursued separately in philosophy and psychology corridors and increasingly, jointly, in robustly interdisciplinary research programmes.[1] But it is worth remembering that ethics, at least as Plato and Aristotle conceived it, was itself always an exercise in moral psychology (and under Aristotle, pursued both as a speculative and empirical discipline). Conceptions of good living and good character are for human beings, constituted as they are by human reason, desire, emotion, and attachments to things and persons outside themselves. The pull of what is divine or cosmic is always there as a strand in understanding what is *perfectly* good, and in some ancient authors, more so than others, but analysis of the human *psyche* or *anima*, its graspings and impulses and ways of being affected by pain and pleasure, its activities of seeing, imagining, judging, and choosing are what is worked up into excellence (or virtue), as well as what constrains.

Perhaps the greatest legacy of that ancient moral psychology is the analysis of emotions. Aristotle articulates a cognitivist account of the emotions, developed in greater depth by the Stoics, embraced by many contemporary philosophers and psychologists as limning the general lines, or at least spirit, of a plausible conception of the emotions.[2] It is one that also sheds light on the critical role of emotions in virtue.

---

[1] For an excellent overview with a helpful bibliography of empirical approaches to moral psychology by both philosophers and psychologists, see John Doris and Stephen Stich 2006. Also see Walter Sinnott-Armstrong's edited series 2007, 2008a, 2008b. Also, Anthony Appiah's overview 2008; Joshua Knobe and Shawn Nichols 2008; John Mihail 2010; Susan Dwyer 2009 among others.

[2] For a sampling of different cogntivist views, see Robert Solomon 1973, 2003, 2004; Martha Nussbaum 2001; Jerome Neu 2000; Michael Stocker 1996; Robert Roberts 1988, 2009; Peter Goldie 2000; Ronald De Sousa 1987; and Patricia Greenspan 1988. For a view that is critical of belief as constitutive of emotion, but that defends 'seeing as' as the central element in a weaker form of cognitivism, see Cheshire Calhoun

Indeed, it would not be amiss to say that the flourishing of interest in ancient virtue ethics has brought with it a reinstatement of emotions in an account of character. No longer an embarrassment or mere 'mists on our mental windscreen',[3] affect and attitude are, by and large, recognized as constitutive parts of virtues, and things for which, as Rosalind Hursthouse would put it, we often, reasonably, get 'ticks of approval'.[4] In Aristotle's terms, 'the right' or 'appropriate' in the practical sphere, what is *hōs dei* or hits the mean, extends to both actions and emotions. This seems to imply not just that emotions ought to be fitting, in the sense of tracking relevant circumstances, but fitting in the sense of being 'right to feel' in those circumstances.[5]

In this chapter, I turn primarily to ancient sources to construct a cognitivist account of emotions and to indicate the sense in which emotions are candidates for the attribution of moral responsibility. Aristotle and the Stoics provide rich resources here, even if the Stoics themselves ultimately deny a place for ordinary emotions in the best moral life (though they do not advocate *apatheia*, as is sometimes charged. What they advocate, rather is *eupatheiai*, enlightened emotions, but more on this soon). Moral therapy, on the Stoic view, is a disciplined practice of loosening oneself from the sticky attachments that characterize ordinary emotional life. The sage, however statistically rare and unlike most mortals, is the paragon of that achievement. Still, despite the extreme normative model, the Stoics are insightful and systematic in their account of how all emotions, ordinary and enlightened, involve cognition, specifically, evaluative judgements that make them plausible candidates for moral assessability. In a selective engagement with the ancients, Kant happily aligns himself with the Stoic disparagement of the emotions while rejecting their cognitivist account. Emotions, according to Kant, are inclinations distinct from the exercise of practical reason. They not only often conflict with reason, but also are not themselves reason constituted. Still, Kant's picture is complex, and in his later moral writings most perspicuously, he urges a place for emotions in the fine and virtuous character. But, as I shall argue, it is far from clear that his account of what emotions are can adequately support the roles he wants them, in the end, to play.

Before turning to these themes, I begin by reviewing considered intuitions about the moral significance of emotions.

35.2 Moral Significance of Emotions

Reflection about the moral significance of emotions in moral life yields three prominent roles for emotions. The first is an *epistemic* role. Emotions are dispositions or sensitivities that help us recognize or track morally salient features of our environments.

1984. For an important probing of the intentionality of emotions in a series of essays over the years, see the first four articles in John Deigh's anthology 2008. For a helpful critique of cognitivist positions, see Elisa Hurley 2005. For views less sympathetic to cognitivism, see Jesse Prinz 2004; Paul Griffiths 1997.

[3] R. S. Peters and C. A. Mace 1961–1962.   [4] Rosalind Hursthouse 1999b.
[5] See D'Arms and Jacobson 2000 on conflations of these two notions.
[6] For early discussions of moral perception, see John McDowell 1979; Iris Murdoch 1970 in her essay,

They are ways of 'discerning the particulars', to use Aristotelian language. They are modes of moral perception.[6] The sympathetic person is probably more likely than the one who is not to notice that the frail woman carrying a heavy bundle could use a helping hand. An empathetic parent may spot a child's sulky mood as sadness at disappointment. Pity may poise one to see the crippled at the traffic light clad in an Army cap and holding out a cup for change as an unlucky victim of war and not as just one more annoyance in a busy day. Of course, the interpretive information that emotions yield may be incomplete or false. The woman may need some help but she views it as an important point of pride that she can manage on her own down the stairs; the child may be faking it as a way to get attention; the cripple may be posing as a vet to garner extra respect. Some, like the skilful beggar or scheming child, may know how to play on emotions. But that is just to say that we can be mistaken in our emotional readings and that they are defeasible. And it is to acknowledge the commonplace point that sensitivity to situations will require varying levels of background knowledge, familiarity, and insight.

In general, emotions are ways of drawing us in that can rivet attention and in turn, demand with urgency our responses in further emotions or actions.[7] They allow for charged, engaged ways of seeing, critical for practical engagement in the world. Of course, what we notice *via* our emotions, and just what moves us slightly or deeply, and with just what specific emotions, is tightly connected to all sorts of factors, some to do with our histories, some with our personal and social commitments as well as biases, some with situational factors that put our minds elsewhere, even when the press of others' need is at our doorsteps. Often our emotional antennae need to be retuned or paired with those of others, though notoriously, group behaviour can bring its own set of pressures and mimicries. Still, the basic capacity to be aware through the emotions of what is in our environment, both what is physically out there and what is on others' minds (and so not be 'mind-blind'[8]) is an indispensable part of social and moral agency. But it is important to note that emotional sensitivity is not just about reading others' minds. It is about reading our own, disclosing to ourselves through recognition of our feelings of anxiety or swellings of shame and pride just what we are thinking about and how.

Kant himself argues for this general epistemic role within his larger account of the cultivation of moral virtue. Moral worth is a matter of acting from the motive of duty, or from principles of pure practical reason. But we act from the motive of duty on appropriate occasions often because of the input of emotional sensitivities. We have natural susceptibilities to feel others' pleasures and pains, Kant says.[9] We need to cultivate these

'The Idea of Moral Perfection'; Martha Nussbaum 1990 and her chapter 'The Discernment of Perception: An Aristotelian Conception of Private and Public Rationality'; Lawrence Blum 1994; Nancy Sherman 1989; Barbara Herman 1993 for a Kantian development of the theme in her lead essay, 'The Practice of Moral Judgement'. For an anthology of moral particularism, see Hooker and Little 2000.

[7] De Sousa 1987.

[8] Simon Baron-Cohen 1999 uses the term 'mind-blindness' in the context of autism and its attendant deficits in reading others' minds.

[9] *Doctrine of Virtue* (DV) 456.

by directing them towards the right objects—for example, visit debtors' prisons and hospitals—in order to learn to recognize circumstances of need and poverty that are potential occasions for beneficence:

> We have an indirect duty to cultivate the sympathetic natural (aesthetic) feelings in us and to use them as so many means to participating from moral principles and from the feeling appropriate to these principles.—Thus, it is our duty: not to avoid places where we shall find the poor who lack the most basic essentials, but rather seek them out; not to shun sick-rooms or debtors' prisons in order to avoid the painful sympathetic feelings that we cannot guard against. For this is still one of the impulses which nature has implanted in us so that we may do what the thought of duty alone would not accomplish. (DV 456–7)

Put otherwise, the thought of duty, the constraint on our wills derived from a conception of ourselves as free and autonomous, is not itself sufficient for making our way in the world of human circumstance and need. Again, this does not rule out bias or selective attention. And emotional investment may itself heighten certain sensitivities in ways that hinder more judicious 'spectating'. But Kant is well aware that emotional sensitivities need to be schooled and regulated by reason. We don't just put on emotions. We try to grow them.

In addition, emotions play an *expressive* role. We are bearers of emotional attitudes[10]— postures and behaviours of mind—conveyed in facial and bodily gestures or tone of voice and eye gaze that reveal, disclose, and sometimes, leak what we feel. As outward faces, they are also masks, literally, *personae*.[11] They can block full disclosure and allow us to pose rather than disclose. Those intimately attuned with us, or good face readers, in general,[12] may be able to detect the inauthentic from the authentic. And some will give us credit for trying, even if our heart isn't fully in it. We get credit, as it were, for knowing that the emotional conveyance matters in many of our personal interactions, and that trying to muster appropriate affect, even when our feelings pull contrary-wise, is part of what fulsome moral engagement requires.

Seneca, in *De Beneficiis*, is instructive about the 'look and feel' of virtue. He takes up the issue of manners (or etiquette), but also emotional bearing and comportment.[13] And he is insistent that virtuous action can be undermined by inappropriate affect and outward expression of emotion. As Seneca comments, 'There are many who make their kindnesses hateful by rough words and superciliousness. Their language and annoyance are such as to leave you regretting your request was ever granted.'[14] We create ingratitude, he continues, when we do favours with a plaintive attitude and when we are 'oppressive' and nagging in

---

[10] On the moral significance of the expression of emotional attitudes, see Peter Strawson's classic, 'Freedom and Resentment' (1993), and Stuart Hampshire in his essay, 'Morality and Convention' (1983).

[11] See Cicero's extensive remarks in *On Duties*, 1.90–143.

[12] See Goffman 1967, especially 'The Nature of Deference and Demeanor' and 'On Face-Work'; Ekman 1972, 2003.

[13] For a discussion of manners and comportment, see Buss 1999 and Stohr 2006. For a fuller discussion of some of these issues in *De Beneficiis*, see Sherman 2005a ('The Look and Feel of Virtue') and Sherman 2005b (*Stoic Warriors*, ch. 2).

[14] *De Beneficiis* (DB), II.4.1 (Cooper and Procopé's translation).

our demands. 'We spoil the effect entirely, not just afterwards, but while we are doing the favour.'[15] Nor are we really beneficent if favours have to be extorted from us: our reluctance is revealed in 'furrowed brows' and 'grudging words'. We should make favours *appear* as if they have been unsolicited, whether or not they have been: 'to give the impression not of having been asked (*ne rogati videamur*) [to perform some action]...we should make an immediate undertaking and prove by our very haste that we were on the point of actions, even before we were approached'.[16] In the same vein, he says, we should do everything to avoid the *appearance* of having had to think whether to do it (*ne deliberasse videamur*).[17]

The emphasis on play-acting (and hence, on a kind of inauthenticity) may rub us the wrong way. Seneca seems to be giving us lessons on how to make it seem to others that we are doing better than we are. And so we learn to pose and pretend, give impressions and cultivate appearances. We play the 'role of the good person' well (*partes boni viri*).[18] But Seneca's point is that faking it can itself be a lesson in *becoming* good. Properly understood, it can be a form of moral practice, a moment of moral progress, a way of being open to nursing, from outside in, more authentic feelings and engagement, in part by recognizing their value and importance in interpersonal exchange. (That that sort of lesson should come from a Stoic is itself intriguing, and evidence of the complex accommodation of emotions in Seneca's account of moral progress.) Seneca is also implying that full disclosure, verbally or in body language, of one's reluctance, ambivalence, or half-heartedness, would compromise the very point of the beneficence.

Even Kant, rigorist as he is on the subject of benevolent lying, is not especially worried about this kind of semblance:

> Men are, one and all, actors—the more so the more civilized they are. They put on a show of affection, respect for others, modesty and disinterest without deceiving anyone, since it is generally understood that they are not sincere about it. And it is a very good thing that this happens in the world. For if men keep on playing these roles, the real virtues whose semblance they have merely been affecting for a long time are gradually aroused and pass into their attitude of will. (*Anthropology from a Pragmatic Point of View* (Anth.) (Gregor's translation), 151)

Kant's point is that the game is transparent: it is wink, wink, nod, nod. No one is manipulated. The feigned smile keeps under wraps less generous feelings, which, interestingly, in this telling, a duty of beneficence demands be kept just there. The cold-hearted misanthropist, even if he is acting from the motive of duty, should not wear his misanthropy on his sleeve.[19] He is to don an emotional mask that supplements his motive of duty and that can help catalyse emotional change.[20]

---

[15] DB I.1.4.   [16] DB II.2.1.   [17] DB II.1.1; italics added.

[18] Italics added, I.2.4. See Epictetus, *Discourses* 2.8.24 for similar emphasis on external bearing, and changing it.

[19] Cf. *Groundwork of the Metaphysic of Morals* (G) (Paton's translation), 398.

[20] See Sherman 1997 on the role of emotions in Kantian virtue. See also Kant's *Lectures on Ethics* (Infield's translation), 197 on the idea that love born from obligation can itself turn into a more genuine love: with time, as Kant puts it, one acquires 'a taste for' such love. I raise questions about just how tenable his view is later in this chapter.

This is not to minimize Kant's familiar charge against sentimentalism—that the gush and flow of certain emotions can fool us into thinking that we are fully morally engaged when we are not. Pity and glistening tears may be a self-absorbed indolence that detracts from a more pragmatic cast of mind. Feelings of remorse, he chides, may be a poor substitute for more substantive forms of moral repair to others or self-reform: 'We consider our list of debts cancelled merely by it (our penitence) and so spare ourselves the redoubled effort toward improvement that reason now requires.'[21] We feast on the *Sturm and Drang* of some emotions, and on the quietude of others, at the cost of more effective moral empowerment.[22] But 'sitting with an emotion' and allowing oneself to feel it in a fulsome way needn't always be like this. Here I am thinking about savouring the feelings of pride in a child's achievements, thinking to oneself: how simply wonderful that child has become. One may luxuriate in the feeling, catch oneself puffed up in a dreamy reverie. Kant's worry is that it's an idle indulgence that pulls one from the world of moral interaction. But quite to the contrary, the feeling can be a powerful resource to enlist in just those moments when the child looks less than perfect. Feeling the pride and being able to easily refresh it (precisely because it was so vivid and held onto, as if for safekeeping) is part of the 'long view' of moral engagement. In this case, it is part of *affective* moral imagination requisite for loving in a fair-minded way.[23]

The third role emotions often serve is *motivational*. Kant will resist just this move, even if he is liberal with respect to the two other roles. To be *morally* motivated, according to Kant, is to act on principle, from the motive of duty, not from sensuous inclination or impulse. Emotion may play a supportive role, as we have said, in discernment of particulars and as aesthetic enhancement of moral action (it is a 'garment that dresses virtue to advantage', as he cautiously puts it, a 'garment to be recommended to virtue' more than the 'cynic's purism' or the 'anchorite's mortification of the flesh'),[24] but moral motivation itself is purely a matter of the grounding of action in principle.

The Aristotelian, in contrast, embraces all three roles for emotions. But precise comparisons are strained here, for virtuous motivation, as Aristotle understands it, is never a matter of sensuous inclination conceptually pried apart from practical reason. Rather,

The past two decades has seen a resurgence of secondary work on Kantian ethics, both with respect to the emotions and more general non-rule based views of interpreting the Categorical Imperative. For other works that take seriously the role of emotions in Kantian ethics, see Marcia Baron 1995 and Paul Guyer 1993. For a general reworking of Kantian notions of the motive of duty, moral deliberation, and impartiality, see Barbara Herman's classic 1993 collection of essays, and especially the lead essay, 'On the Value of Acting from the Motive of Duty', for an easing of the putative conflict between inclination and duty. For important work on interpreting the formulae of the Categorical Imperative, see Christine Korsgaard 1996. For lively articles on Kantian issues ranging from respect to punishment and welfare, see Thomas Hill's several collections of his essays 1993, 2002, 2004. A helpful collection of seminal critical essays on Kant's *Groundwork* is that edited by Paul Guyer 1998. Many of these works owe an important debt to Onora (O'Neill) Nell's pioneering book (1975) on interpreting Kant's Categorical Imperative.

[21] Anth. 255–6; 235–6.
[22] See Michael Tanner's 1977 lively and perceptive remarks on the pleasures of some emotional rides.
[23] For a related point, see Iris Murdoch's (1970) well-known example of a mother who feels hostility to her daughter-in-law and slowly comes to see her in a new light.
[24] Anth. 282.

virtuous action flows from *deliberative* desire (*boulēsis*) and deliberative choice (*prohairesis*), themselves hybrid constructions of reason and desire, and from emotions that are partially constituted by cognitions. Though Aristotle seats intellectual excellence in the rational part of the psyche and character or moral excellence (virtue) in the non-rational part, he is never fully comfortable with the conventional split. The non-rational part, he insists from the start, has to 'share' in reason in some way.[25] Similarly character virtue, on the full account, is inseparable from the exercise of excellent practical reason, or practical wisdom. Practical wisdom is full virtue in its capacity to choose and act finely in particular situations in ways that constitute good living in general.[26] Stable character requires habituated emotional dispositions, but also cognitive flexibility, the ability to determine the appropriate occasions for action, given the demands of competing ends and the ever-new complexities of circumstance.

On this very point, the picture of character traits that emerges in the empirical psychological literature and is embraced by situationist philosophers, like John Doris and Gilbert Harman, does not capture the ancient view of character.[27] The issue is somewhat tangential here, but it is worth making a few remarks given the indictment of virtue ethics that is at stake. On Doris' view, virtues are character traits that show consistency or a kind of global stability in the sense that they are dispositions to perform stereotypical action patterns elicited across a wide range of putatively similar situations. The expectation is that the person who is helpful, and has the trait of helpfulness, would behave consistently, in helpful ways, across a diverse set of circumstances in which help is demanded. But experimental data show that people's character traits are not as useful for determining what people do as are the situations themselves. And disturbingly, small features in a situation that seem of little moral import can be what are most determinative for behaviour. You may be more likely to receive a helping hand from someone if he has just found a dime in a phone slot, or get a change for a dollar if you ask it for outside a bakery that is wafting sweet smells rather than a 'neutral-smelling dry-goods store'.[28]

The results are taken to cast doubt on the role of character in moral theory. As Gilbert Harman puts it boldly, 'Ordinary attributions of character-traits to people may be deeply misguided, and it may even be the case that there is no such thing as character'.[29] And 'if there is no such thing as character, then there is no such thing as character building'.[30] But the notion of character as specified in stereotypical behaviour patterns, elicited without much reflection or, at least justification, is not an Aristotelian view.[31] Nor is the idea that one virtue can be separated from another, such that a situation determinately and in an isolated way calls up one virtue, rather than a fuller complement of several. Rather, Aristotle's view is that situations may bring to bear competing virtues and

---

[25] *Nicomachean Ethics* (NE) I.13 1102b14; IV.12, 1119b1–15. For cautiousness about the practice of carving up the soul, see *De Anima* 432a30.

[26] NE VI.13 and VI. 5.

[27] John Doris and Stephen Stich 2002; Gilbert Harman 2000. See Ross and Nisbett 1991. For important critiques, see Rachana Kamtekar 2004; Anthony Apiah 2008; Daniel Russell 2009.

[28] Appiah 2008: 41.   [29] Harman 2000: 165.   [30] Harman 2000: 177.

[31] Daniel Russell 2009 and Rachana Kamtekar 2004.

certainly, competing ways of specifying a single virtue.[32] A given individual may not be moved to make change because the last time she did she was assaulted, or because she is in a rush to pick up a sick child, or because that is a street corner (however sweet-smelling the waft) where she knows from a friend, you don't take out your wallet and rummage around for money. The reasons are not necessarily unaltruistic or tell against a helping spirit. Rather, they suggest that seeing a situation, and its relevance to overall virtue, is a complex business and does not always involve acceptance of a pre-given picture of what is in this instant most salient.[33]

35.3 ARISTOTELIAN COGNITIVISM AND RESPONSIBILITY FOR EMOTIONS

It is time now to turn to a cognivist analysis of emotions. Aristotle offers the first such extended account in *Rhetoric*, Book II. Though a practical handbook intended for use by the orator to manipulate emotions in the courtroom, the *Rhetoric* fills in some of the missing theoretical elements in the *Nicomachean* about just how emotions are to 'share' in reason.[34] What becomes clear is that emotions are reason-responsive, can listen to and obey reason, in so far as they are themselves cognitively constituted.

Aristotle limns the model—well reviewed at this point in the secondary literature and its broad lines captured in a number of contemporary cognitivist accounts[35]—in the central case of anger. At the core of anger is a thought, imagining, construal, or perception that I have been unjustly injured. The thought is affective—felt, and experienced with pain. In addition, it typically includes a reactive desire for revenge, the anticipation of which brings its own kind of pleasure.[36] The account is of disparate components—cognitions or appraisals, felt sensations or affects, reactive desires or as sometimes dubbed in the psychology literature, 'action tendencies'.[37] And Aristotle is imprecise as to just how the components ultimately combine to become unified.[38] Still, what he insists on is that the central component will be the cognition, an evaluation about something

[32] See Richardson 1994 on the specification of ends of virtue.
[33] Similarly, early habituation of character excellence, traditionally portrayed as a repetition of action types more or less divorced from the education of the intellect, is misguided in the extreme. For more on this see Sherman 1989: ch. 5.
[34] On whether Aristotle's rhetorician can be viewed as relying on mostly popular *endoxa* or psychological theories, see Cooper 1993; Nussbaum 1994: ch. 3; and Striker 1996.
[35] See Amelie Rorty's 1996 anthology on the *Rhetoric*. On contemporary views, Aristotelian in spirit, see the work of Robert Solomon 1973, 2003, 2004; Michael Stocker 1996; and Martha Nussbaum 2001. For accounts of Aristotle's position, see Sherman 1989 and 1997: ch. 2.
[36] *Rhetoric* (Rh.) 1378a30–b1.
[37] See Frijda 1987: 71: '"Action tendency" and "emotion" are one and the same thing.' For a collection of recent work bringing philosophers and psychologists together in dialogue, see Manstead, Frijda, and Fischer (eds) 2004.
[38] On this, see Elisa Hurley PhD (2005).

good or bad that affects me. And it is this evaluation—in the case of anger, that I have been wrongfully injured—towards which affect is intentionally directed.[39]

Though much has been written on Aristotle's cognitivist account, what remains underexplored still, on my view, is the sense in which we might be held morally accountable for our emotions.[40] Aristotle himself is worried about the issue and raises it as a puzzle in the second and third books of the *Nicomachean*. Emotions are *pathē*, states that affect us, that we suffer, and that do not involve choice or agency in the obvious way that virtuous action does: 'We feel anger and fear without choice (*aproairetōs*), but the excellences are choices or involve choice (*proaireseōs*). Further, in respect to the emotions, we are said to be moved (*kineisthai*).'[41] And yet both emotions and actions are expressive of character and both, on Aristotle's view, are candidates for moral assessment. Both can be praiseworthy and blameworthy, both fine and shameful, both determinable according to the mean. This is the force of familiar remarks that 'we stand well or badly with reference to the emotions',[42] and that 'moral excellence…is concerned with emotions and actions, and in these there is excess, defect, and the mean'.

On this important point he makes explicit that the mean is not simply a matter of steering clear of some quantitative minimum or maximum, but is a matter of sizing up and judging various indices of salience.[43]

> Fear and confidence and appetite and anger and pity and in general pleasure and pain may be felt both too much and too little, and in both cases not well; but to feel them at the right times, with reference to the right objects, towards the right people, with the right aim, and in the right way, is what is both intermediate and best, and this is characteristic of excellence. (NE 1106b19–23, replacing 'emotions' for 'passions' and 'mean' for 'intermediate'. See also, 1108a31 ff., 1106b25, 1109b15.)

Still, Aristotle is unclear about the grounds of attribution here. With regard to choice and action, as he says, attribution of moral assessment, praise and blame, is unproblematic. With regard to emotions (*pathē*), ways of being acted upon or passivity, how we are held responsible is less obvious. And yet, as the above passages indicate, he fully endorses the commonplace opinions and practices (the *endoxa*) that we are accountable.[44] Both action and emotion are indicators of virtue or its lack. We expect both to be present when there is virtue. And when we praise and blame individuals for their emotional habits, it is not just that we are esteeming or disesteeming them for what 'belongs' to

[39] Again, this is not always explicit in Aristotle's formulations. Sometimes he says pleasure and pain 'accompany' or 'follow' (*hepesthai tina hēdonēn*) an emotion, or alternatively, that a particular emotion is 'with' (*meta*) pleasure or pain. Rh. 1378a 31 and 1378b1. Aristotle puts the point more clearly in the case of pity: the painful feeling is *directed at—epi—*a perceived evil that befalls another and that could befall us. Rh. 385b12.

[40] A notable early exception is L. A. Kosman 1980. For a review of the literature, see Sherman 1999.

[41] NE II.5 1106a3–5.

[42] NE II.5 1105b26, replacing 'emotions' for 'passions'.

[43] For this point, see Hursthouse 1999a.

[44] For a contemporary statement of this, see Strawson's influential article, 'Freedom and Resentment' (1993).

them and is proprietary, such as beautiful hair or a tall body or a nice house. Aristotle's point is more robust: that we hold them morally accountable.

In a number of places, Aristotle falls back on the view that the ground of responsibility for emotions has to be rooted in some kind of choice, however unlike action emotion is. Angela Smith has usefully collected various strands of this general view under the heading of 'a volitional view of responsibility'—a view which she goes on to argue is problematic in the case of grounding ascription for responsibility for emotional attitudes. Isolating the different strands of the view is helpful for understanding some of Aristotle's own moves. Smith writes:

> What I have called the volitional view of responsibility is actually better understood as a cluster of distinct views which share a common assumption, namely, that choice, decision, or susceptibility to voluntary control is a necessary condition of responsibility (for attitudes as well as actions). According to all of these views, what ultimately makes an attitude attributable to a person for purposes of moral assessment is that it is connected in some way to her choice: she made choices in the past which led to the development of the attitude in question, she made a choice in the present to endorse or 'identify with' it, or she has the ability to modify her attitudes through the choices she makes in the future. (Smith 2005: 238–9)

On the first strand of this cluster view, one takes responsibility for emotions in so far as they are the consequences of past choices. Even if one cannot now change those present states easily, one may have helped to set them in motion by earlier, deliberate choices. I may not be able to undo my racial prejudices, but I may be responsible for having engendered them or nursed them along in the first place. The attitude can be traced back to my past choices. The point is a familiar one Aristotle makes about responsibility for character: 'When you have let a stone go it is too late to recover it; but yet it was in your power to throw it, since the moving principle was in you' (hē gar archē en autōi).[45] Affective attitudes, as with character states more generally, can be set in motion and become habituated, through earlier patterns of voluntary choice and action. Where the origins are fully outside of myself, my responsibility, on this strand of the view, may be mitigated.

Aristotle also makes ample remarks suggesting that what is essential for responsibility for emotional attitudes is that a person can control them through future choices, by setting in place changes and modifications that will effect attitude. On this future choice view, what matters is not the origin of an attitude, but that it can be changed once it is in place. Aristotle's remarks on friendship are suggestive here, at least for showcasing an arena where this kind of change is central. We are born into certain familial friendships and are socialized with certain dispositions. The parents we have must 'suffice', as Aristotle puts it in the Politics.[46] But we choose adult character friends as a way to take more active control of who we are, and who we would like to become. As he puts it, character friends 'take the mould from each other of the characteristics they approve'. 'They

---

[45] NE III.5 1114a17 ff.   [46] Politics 1262b22–3—to agapēton—one must be content with it.

are thought to become better by their activities and by improving each other.'[47] Character friendship is a place to study ourselves,[48] and an arena for ongoing adult character formation. It is a place to effect the kind of emotional change that is part of ongoing character growth. In the past, I have developed a notion of 'emotional agency' that is broadly Aristotelian, and that draws on psychological developmental studies of children as well as psychoanalytic notions of therapeutic change to fill out a picture of emotional experience as agential in key ways.[49]

But I now want to consider another way of reading Aristotle that moves us somewhat away from grounding responsibility in a notion of agency modelled on choice of actions. The view points forward to the Stoics and is developed by them systematically, but Aristotle makes important opening gestures that prepare us for the Stoic project. The germ of the view is in Aristotle's remark that we are responsible for 'how things appear to us' (*tēs phantasias estai pōs autos aitios*).[50] He has in mind not whether we notice the colour of paint in a room, or hear the air conditioner whir on the third floor. For the most part, though not always, these may be matters of selective attention that have little moral significance. Rather, he has in mind the kinds of perceptions that reveal our moral characters and that disclose our deep commitments about how to live well. These are 'the appearances', or construals that 'answer to character'.[51] And in pointing to responsibility here he is embracing, as it were, the possibility that a certain kind of *passivity*, a way of being affected, is the condition of being held accountable. I leave aside here just what the capacity for *phantasia* is or its precise role in Aristotelian psychology and philosophy of action.[52] The point I wish to make is that Aristotle recognizes an alternative, intuitive way to account for the practice of being held responsible for emotions. And this is through what we see, i.e. what the perceptions, appearances, or construals are, including those that partially constitute emotions.

Aristotle returns to the point again when he says that practical wisdom is a matter of discernment of salient particulars: 'the *krisis* (judgment or discernment) rests in *aisthēsis* (perception)'.[53] The remark is all too familiar at this point in our own contemporary moral debate. But part of the force of the point is that how we perceive grounds our responsibility. Once Aristotle develops the conception of emotions in the *Rhetoric* as including principally construals and perceptions, the way is open for him to look to the capacity for discernment, or evaluation, as the basis for ascription of emotional responsibility. Our judgements, how we evaluate things, what we select as relevant, what we notice and fail to notice, i.e., our appraisals, are what we can be called to account for. Obviously, these will not be 'up to us' in the way that some actions can be commanded directly by the mind and result without hesitancy in action. Nor will entrenched attitudes

---

[47]   NE IX.12 1172a11–14.   [48]   NE IX.9 1169b35. See Sherman 1989: ch. 4, 1997: ch. 5.

[49]   See Sherman 1999. I argue there that from the earliest moments of infancy, we set out with some deliberateness to be agents of our emotional lives.

[50]   NE III.5 1114b1.

[51]   NE III.5 1114b2.

[52]   See Nussbaum's account of *phantasia* in her translation and commentary on *De Motu Animalium* (1978).

[53]   NE 1109b22.

shift without serious work at dislodging whole nests of evaluations that contribute to the attitudes and keep them in play. Many of those evaluations will be unconscious, some masked by more 'respectable' stand-ins. But Aristotle's suggestion in turning to the evaluations reflected in attitudes and comportment, is that we can be asked rationally to defend or reject them, in the way we do other significant beliefs or judgements.[54] There is epistemic responsibility.

Of course, what we see is often a matter of what we have been trained to see, or taught to see, or can see, as a result of natural constitution. But Aristotle is wary of any easy exemption from moral accountability.[55] Still, he does not develop in a sustained way an educational programme for reflecting on or revising how things appear to us. Nor does he give us an example of the sort of emotional changes that would result from radical and systematic revisions of the appearances. I short, he does not develop the idea of how we are affected, or appeared to, as itself a kind of agency.

35.4 THE STOICS AND RESPONSIBILITY FOR EMOTIONS

The Stoics engage in just this debate. The philosophy of mind they develop is technically complex and jargon-filled. And there are distinct historical voices and strands in the account, redacted fragments as well as highly rhetorical, popularized, complete texts. Recent secondary literature has been intellectually robust and prolific, making Stoicism accessible to students in a way that it had not been just twenty or thirty years ago.[56] My own focus here is highly circumscribed. It concerns the pivotal idea in Stoic moral practice that accountability for our emotions rests in accountability for our judgements, and that those judgements are amenable to change through discourse and education. In this regard, the Stoics advance Aristotle's notion that with regard to matters of character and the emotions expressive of character, it is reasonable to be asked to defend how things appear to us.

But first some necessary preliminaries.[57] The general Stoic view, put briefly, is that an emotion is a kind of impulse (*hormē*) or motive to react in certain ways that take effect

---

[54] This is key to Angela Smith's alternative model to the volitional account, what she calls 'the rationalist account of responsibility'.

[55] NE III.5 1141b1–25.

[56] For some important new translations of texts and collections of writings, see: Long and Sedley 1987; Inwood and Gerson 2008; Cooper and Procopé's edition of Seneca's *On Anger, On Mercy, On Favours* (1995a, b, and c); Annas and Woolf's edition of Cicero's *On Moral Ends* (2001); Griffin and Atkins edition of Cicero's *On Duties* (1991); Margaret Graver's edition of Cicero's *Tusculan Disputations* (2002); and Hard and Gill's edition of Epictetus' *Discourses* (1995). Tad Brennan 2005 offers the best overall guide to the Stoics, though the account is sometimes a bit distanced from the texts.

[57] For views on the Stoic account of emotions, I am indebted especially to Julia Annas 1992; Tad Brennan 2005; Martha Nussbaum 2001; Richard Sorabji 2000; and Margaret Graver 2002, 2007.

through an agent's assent (*sunkatathesis*) to an evaluative impression or appearance (*phantasia*). The assent highlights the idea that the psyche reacts rather than is just affected.[58] Zeno, the father of ancient Greek Stoicism, illustrates by putting up his hand. Holding his hand out flat is compared to taking in the appearance. Closing his fingers is compared to assent. Assent is an acceptance of an evaluation. However, it is not a conscious moment of choice or something articulable in words or phenomenologically felt.[59] Rather, it is meant to point to the notion that in human emotion as well as perception we are always interpreting and evaluating what we see; we are engaged in conceptualization, evaluation, and implicit judgements about significance.

The evaluations contained in emotions are about goods or bads that relate to our potential actions. The Stoics carve up all ordinary emotions into four basic types: desire (*epithumia*), fear (*phobos*), pleasure (*hedonē*), and pain or distress (*lupē*). Desire is an evaluative judgement that something is attractive or would be good to go after; fear, an evaluation that something is an evil and to be avoided. Both are future directed. Pleasure and distress are evaluations of good and bad in the present (or past).[60] All other emotions are conceived of as sub-types of these generic ones. So, for example, the Stoics, fixing on the revenge motive that is typically part of anger, classify anger as a desire, alongside sexual appetite and love of wealth and honour. Grief is a kind of distress, as is shame.

The Stoic normative view is that these ordinary emotions are systematic misevaluations. They are irrational or false, not in the sense of mis-tracking circumstances or objects relevant to action, but in the sense of misrepresenting them as genuine goods or evils, things to attach to or avoid, in a good life. On their revision, health and disease, poverty and wealth, friendship and its loss, that is, the objects of ordinary emotions, are really indifferents, things that may be 'preferred or dispreferred', 'selected' or 'disselected' in accord with our natures, but not themselves proper constituents of happiness. Happiness is constituted by virtue alone. The sage alone grasps the sufficiency of virtue in a good life, and has successfully recalibrated perceptions accordingly.

The result is not *apatheia*, eradication of all emotion, but *eupatheiai*, cultivated or good emotions, properly directed at virtue and the avoidance of vice. These cultivated 'good' emotions will be enlightened counterparts of ordinary emotions. In place of desire will arise *boulēsis* or rational willing; in place of fear, rational wariness or caution (*eulabeia*); in place of pleasure, rational joy (*chara*). Distress, significantly, has no correlate in the perfectly moral life, for the sage has rid himself of all vice, and so the grounds for rational, moral anguish.[61] Moral progress will be a journey in transforming what we see as goods and bads. It requires systematic re-evaluation of good and evil, and a commitment to deep examination, with the expectation that evaluative changes will, in time, be reflected in changed emotional attitude and bearing. Epictetus sums up the promise

---

[58] Annas 1992: 78; Brennan 2005: 52.   [59] See Annas 1992: 78.

[60] See the account of Arius Didymus (in Stobaeus) 2.88, 9–90, 6, collected in Long and Sedley 1987, 1: 410–11.

[61] Why the sage is not distressed by the evil others do and inflict on innocents should trouble us. See Sherman 2005b: 83–95. On the emotions of the sage, see Cooper 2004.

of the method: 'Where did he get his haughty look, and solemn face?...As yet I lack confidence in what I have learned, and assented to...Let me but gain confidence a little, and then you shall see me with the kind of expression and bearing that I ought to have.'[62]

In Cicero's redaction in the *Tusculan Disputations*, the evaluation consists in two judgements.[63] So he says distress (and specifically, grief) includes the evaluative judgement, or assent to the impression, that an evil has happened, plus the additional evaluative judgement[64] about what it is appropriate to do in light of that prior judgement: 'But when our belief in the seriousness of our misfortune is combined with the further belief that it is right, and an appropriate and proper thing, to be upset by what has happened, then, and not before there comes about that deep emotion which is distress.'[65]

Cicero argues, plausibly, that we can far more readily revise the second judgement, about what it is appropriate to do (e.g. let tears fall, mourn publically, write consolations, etc.) than we can the first, that we have suffered a genuine bad. And he takes this as a significant point of argument against the orthodox Stoics. He writes the *Tusculans* after his own battle with the crippling grief of losing his beloved daughter, Tullia, in childbirth. Engaging in Stoic doctrine is not just an academic pursuit for him at this point. He is desperate for its consolations, and wants to stop not just the flow of tears, but the grief itself. As he writes to his friend Atticus, about a month after Tullia's death and shortly before setting out to write the *Tusculans*:

> It is like you to want me to recover from my grief, but you are my witness that I have not been remiss on my own behalf. Nothing has been written by any author on the alleviation of grief which I did not read in your house. But my sorrow is stronger than any consolation....I write all day long...and I try all I know to bring my face if not my heart back to composure, if I can. While I do this I sometimes feel I am committing a sin, at others that I failed to do it. (*Letters to Atticus* 12.14; Schackleton Bailey's translation)[66]

But stemming the grief itself and not just the tears, on the strict Stoic view of Cleanthes, depends on a deep change of evaluations, on coming to reject the belief that a bad or evil has really happened. And this is not a change Cicero is prepared to make, not now, when he feels the pain so acutely, nor in principle, given the importance of what he cares about: 'I pass over the method of Cleanthes, since that is directed at the wise person who does

---

[62] *Discourses* 2.8.4.

[63] A structure consistent with the ancient account, summarized by Arius Didymus in Stobaeus, Eclogae 2.88.8–89.3.

[64] The second belief, Cicero says, is Zeno's addition of a belief that is 'fresh', *prosphatos*, and as such, it is the belief that gets a response moving. It need not be 'fresh', in the sense of recent, Cicero qualifies, so long as it is fresh, in the sense of 'renewed'. Here, Cicero points to the example of Artemisia, the wife of Mausolous, king of Caria: 'After she made a tomb for her husband, (now famous as the Mausoleum at Halicarnassus), she spent the remainder of life in mourning and in the end died of grief. For her the opinion [evaluation] remained fresh day by day'. TD 3.75 (Graver's 2002 edition).

[65] *Tusculan Disputations* (TD) 3.62 (Graver's 2002 edition). See also 3.24–25.

[66] On Tullia's death, see also Cicero, *Letters to Friends* 248–49 (Shackleton Bailey's translation).

not need consoling. For if you manage to persuade the bereaved person that nothing is bad but shameful conduct, then you have taken away not his grief, but his unwisdom. And this is not the right moment for such a lesson.'[67]

Cicero's fuller point is that there is no right time for removing such 'unwisdom'.[68] But he doesn't make the point in terms of grief here. Instead, he presses the point about rational distress where he thinks it will hit the Stoics hardest. He picks as his example Alcibiades' shame at perceiving himself as failing to live up to his beloved Socrates' example of virtue. This is distress, grief, shame about loss, not of externals, but of one's own of character. It is based on attachment to the one thing the Stoics hold we have reason to be attached to—namely virtue and its supremacy in a good life. If there were a case for justified, defensible distress, this ought to be it:

> For Cleanthes does not take sufficiently into account the possibility that a person might be distressed over the very thing which Cleanthes himself counts as the worst of evils. For we are told that Socrates once persuaded Alcibiades he was unworthy to be called human, and was not better than manual labourer despite his noble birth. Alcibiades then became very upset, begging Socrates with tears to take away his shameful character and give him a virtuous one. What are we to say about this, Cleanthes? Surely you would not claim that the circumstance which occasioned Alcibiades' distress was not really a bad thing? (TD 3.77)

This is an instance, he implies, where a Stoic moral tutor should recognize that distress is well placed, even if the sage himself, a Socrates figure perhaps, no longer suffers from moral failures and the trials of ardent aspiration and emulation. Shame feelings are glaring, painful exposures of falling short that are at once therapeutic and can kindle fervour to change.

This is a point Seneca is all too willing to admit. He writes in his attempt to console his moral tutee, Lucilius upon the death of his friend, Flaccus, that try as he may, he too was unable to fully vanquish his grief when he lost his beloved friend, Serenus.[69] He suffers from the distress of grief, but also the added shame of that grief, that he is not further along in his own moral progress: 'No doctor lives here', he writes in another letter to Lucilius, 'only a sick man'.[70] And with characteristic self-reproach: 'You are mistaken if you think that you will get any assistance from this quarter.' His letters are always, in part, exhortations to himself. The therapy is for doctor as well as patient.[71] And the cure, at all stages of progress, requires the impetus that shame provides.

I have been arguing that ascription for responsibility for emotions is grounded in the fact that emotions are evaluations that we can somehow change. But it is tempting to read the Stoics as setting the conditions for responsibility for emotions not in the evaluative judgement itself, but more narrowly in the moment of assent, as an isolatable act of will.[72] Consider for example Seneca's sequential account of the genesis of full-blown anger in De Ira II.3.1. It begins with a proto-emotion, a 'first feeling', a tremor or rush or

---

[67] TD 3.77. See also IV.63.   [68] He in fact never mentions Tullia's name in this work.
[69] Epistles 63.   [70] Epistles 68.9   [71] See Marcus Wilson 1997: 49 on the general point.
[72] See Brad Inwood 2005: 132–56 for a helpful review of the literature. Also, Albrecht Dihle 1982.

start or startle that is the result of a seductive impression to which assent has not yet been given. Proper anger requires the assent, or approval:

> So the first mental agitation induced by the impression (*speciem*) of wrong done is no more anger than the impression itself. The impulse (*impetus*) that follows, which not only registers but confirms the impression (*non tantum accepit sed adprobavit*), is what counts as anger, the agitation of a mind proceeding by its own deliberate judgment (*voluntate et iudicio*) to exact retribution. (*On Anger* 2.3.4, Cooper and Procopé's translation; *iudicio* translated as 'judgement' and not, as Cooper and Procopé do, 'decision'.)

But as a number of scholars have argued, assent is only one element in an integrated account of mental agency and effort.[73] The whole evaluative process is active and constructive. The mind and reason are not passive receptors, but *hēgemonikon*, ruling. As Julia Annas puts it, commenting on the comparable role of assent in perception: 'By excluding factors other than assent at times, the Stoics are making the point that perception is not a two-stage process: reception of an uninterpreted sensory given *plus* a separable conceptualization of it.'[74] In a similar vein, Tad Brennan argues that Stoic impulse 'is not like an Aristotelian desire: it is not a mere inclination or drive, waiting around for information about the environment to provide it with effective satisfaction.'[75] Seneca himself warns against misconstruing his presentation of stages as isolating only one moment of active mental agency: 'What we have here is a complex process with several constituents—realization, indignation, condemnation, retribution.'[76]

Still, part of the reason for pinpointing the moment of assent, as Seneca does in this passage, is to give clear allowance to the sage to suffer proto-emotions with impunity. Those first stirrings of anger may be no more morally telling than 'the urge to yawn when someone else yawns' or 'blinking when fingers are flicked at the eye'. So long as the mild symptoms of anger have not come about by mistaken assent, the manifestations are not blameworthy in themselves. In a related discussion, Aulus Gellius reports, even the sage might reasonably turn white if he is caught in a shipwreck.[77] If the pallor is just a physiological movement, not generated by full judgement, then he is not guilty of suffering a real emotion. Thus, assent puts a convenient wedge between mere physiological responses and full-blown emotions for which one can be held accountable. But even the impressions that are experienced, prior to the assent, are not just the flow of uninterpreted sensory givens. They involve, as Kant will go on to formulate far more clearly in his epistemology, conceptualization.[78]

The Stoics never suggest that change in the pattern of assents will effect emotional change in any immediate or instant way. They insist that emotions have a life of their

---

[73] See Dihle 1982: 61 and 110.   [74] Annas 1992: 78; see also 87.   [75] Brennan 2005: 87.
[76] *On Anger* 2.1.4.
[77] Gellius, *The Attic Nights of Aulus Gellius*, vol. 3, 19.1. See Graver and Sorabji for a similar account of *propatheia* or proto-emotion in Philo: Graver 2002: 126, Graver 1999, and Sorabji 2000 for the later history of the notion.
[78] Annas 1992: 78.

own and an intensity and excessiveness that defy easy regulation.[79] They 'begin, grow, and run riot'.[80] As a result, emotional therapy requires disciplined work (askēsis), and even the sage will continue to feel the 'bites' and 'scars' of old emotional habits in physiological leaks.[81] But encouraging good epistemic practices of evaluation will be indispensible for the project, such as nurturing a disposition towards 'non-precipitancy' in accepting or rejecting appearances, and cultivating a sense of earnestness, 'non-frivolity', about knowing how 'to refer appearances to right reason'. Similarly, the epistemic virtue of 'uncarelessness' can help guard against the temptation to 'give in to what is merely plausible'.[82] These are intellectual virtues of no small importance for a view of responsibility for emotions based on a capacity to revise appearances.

35.5 THE KANTIAN LEGACY

Kant inherits the Stoic rant against ordinary emotions, but discards the interesting cognitivist moral psychology that undergirds the Stoic account of emotional reform. He echoes Cicero's early (and by Cicero's own light, problematic) translation of *pathos* as *morbus*[83] (disease), in his notion of sensuous inclinations as 'pathological'. They are maladies, as Kant puts it more boldly in *The Anthropology*, agitations and passions in need of spiritual healing by a 'spiritual doctor'.[84] His general position remains throughout his writings that inclinations are alien to our practical rational agency. They are rooted in our sensuous natures, and as such impel from a source other than autonomous practical reason and its laws. The Stoic doctor, who works directly on beliefs and evaluations in order directly to reconstitute emotions, does not seem to be the right doctor for the Kantian patient.

I have argued elsewhere at considerable length that Kant does not get very far in the development of his full account of morality before he introduces cultivated emotions, what he calls 'practical' emotions (e.g. practical love and sympathy) that support the work of duty and put a genial face on virtue.[85] And in some sense, these practical emotions play a parallel role to that of 'good' emotions (*eupatheiai*) in the Stoic scheme (though they are not restricted in the Kantian model to the kind of rarefied levels characteristic of a Stoic sage's moral perfection). But Kantian practical emotions do not share the psychological underpinnings of ancient emotions, 'good' or otherwise. Kant rejects the weaker Aristotelian position that emotions include cognitions and construals, and certainly, the more robust Stoic position that they are constituted in a more

---

[79] As Arius quotes the sources, an emotion is a *hormē pleonazousa*, 'an impulse that is excessive' 'and disobedient to reason'.

[80] *On Anger* 2.4.

[81] TD 3.8.

[82] Diogenes Laertius 7.46–8. For further suggestive remarks, see Epictetus *Discourses* I.7.2–5, 10 and Cicero, *On Duties (De Officiis)* 1.18–19 on this. On Stoic intellectual virtues, see Sherman 2003.

[83] See TD 4.10 and Inwood's insightful discussion (1985: ch. 5).

[84] Anth. 251.   [85] See Sherman 1997. Note the early mention of 'practical love' at G 399.

thoroughgoing way by evaluative judgements. They are not attitudes conceptually connected or internally constituted by judgements that I can be asked to defend or revise if they are found wanting.

This does not prevent Kant from holding that we ought to cultivate these moral emotions, and indeed, ought to cultivate them as part of a complete programme of moral education. In a repudiation of asceticism, Kant insists in the closing pages of the *Doctrine of Virtue* that moral education should be a training that encourages the pleasure that accompanies virtue. Good cheer (*ein frohliches Herz*) recommends virtue more than Pietist melancholia or morose self-punishment. Only with 'cheerfulness', he says, can virtue become 'meritorious and exemplary'.[86] In a similar spirit, he says, 'love of man' is a 'great moral ornament'. To 'associate virtue with the graces...is in itself a duty of virtue'.[87] Development of the emotions supportive of virtue is a derivative duty of moral self-perfection and duties of beneficence to others. It is part of the 'naturalization' of virtues that helps stabilize the work of duty. But aside from sporadic and tentative remarks, Kant has little interest in matching up what he would like moral emotions to do with an account of their structure that can easily support that work.

The point becomes particularly vexing with regard to the practical emotion of respect, so central to Kantian ethics. To feel respect is to submit, affectively, to the force of the moral law in persons. Respect ('moral interest') is a 'feeling' '*self-produced* by a rational concept'.[88] By this Kant means it is not of empirical origin: it could not exist prior to consciousness of the moral law and its principles. It is a response to recognition of those principles, not something that springs up unbidden from our empirical natures as an antecedent moral sensibility or special moral sense. Rather, it is the causal effect, on our sensuous natures, of a rational engagement of a certain kind. By pointing to respect, Kant is showing, as he puts it in the *Second Critique*, what the moral law 'effects...in the mind, so far as it is an incentive'.[89]

Kant goes on there to characterize respect as a feeling so strong that it 'strikes down', all competing inclinations of self-love and self-conceit.[90] The competition is portrayed, at times, in mechanical terms, as a matter of degree of strength of the contenders. But Kant also says that the moral law, through the work of respect, 'humiliates' and 'condemns'[91] the pretensions of self-love. It rebuts the presumptions of laws generated from mere subjective conditions. There is a battle of ideas unleashed.

In so far as there is, Kant seems to be struggling to articulate not just a non-empirical source for moral impulse, but a specific cognitive content that this non-empirically rooted emotion will have. But strictly speaking, on his view, the moral incentive cannot be ideational. On his model, it is put into battle to enter the realm where the competitors are, sensuous inclinations, in order to remove 'the counterweight to the moral law which bears on a will affected by the sensibility'.[92] To raise the strength of one is to lower the

---

[86] DV 485.   [87] DV 473.

[88] G 401 note, my italics. See also 'Incentives of Pure Practical Reason', in *Critique of Practical Reason* (KpV), 74–5. For more on Kant's account of respect, see Sherman 1998 and Reath 1989.

[89] KpV 75. See DV 399.   [90] KpV 76.   [91] KpV 77, 78.   [92] KpV 78.

strength of the other.[93] They have to do battle on their own terms, as feelings do, by degree and strength of pleasure and pain. But as I say, Kant is ambivalent here. He seems to be talking not simply about an incentive with an external rational source. He is suggesting an incentive that itself has taken on the content of that source, that is able to stare down competitors, not because it is tougher or a messenger that comes from the right place with the right authority, but because it embodies presumptions about value and a proper object of focus that self-conceit lacks. This is what it is to humiliate and condemn—it is to judge.

At least this is a way of making sense of what Kant has in mind. Respect is a matter of seeing in self and others 'the example of the law', as Kant himself states at times.[94] It is a matter of 'taking interest', moral or practical interest, by appeal to the right kind of standard. I *see* myself as a lawgiver and acknowledge that fact, as it is conceptually connected with other evaluations, such as that I am not ruled by others' wills, or by the force of my own desires and inclinations, and that other persons, in virtue of their legislative reason, are in similar ways autonomous and not subject to my rule or that of others. Similarly, in seeing a man of talent, Kant says, I see him again as an 'example of the law', in so far as he illustrates the derivative duty to develop talents as all-purpose means to sustain a capacity to adhere to the moral law. Respect is an attending to certain values that is motivational.

But theoretically, in terms of his epistemology, Kant is committed to keeping separate the evaluative work of moral consciousness and the work of an incentive, produced by it, and that can then be taken up by the will as a motivating force.[95] There is no counterpart in his theory to the Stoic notion of emotion which is at once impulse and evaluation, and a part of an integrated cognitive mind.

The tensions re-emerge when we consider the specific forms of practical respect and love catalogued in the *Doctrine of Virtue* and requisite for full virtue. Practical love and its species of beneficence, gratitude, and sympathy, and moral friendship, moral indignation, all are emotions that seem to be different from their pathological counterparts by content, and not just source. We seem to come by them through an education in value, such that they become new ways of seeing, as he himself understands in the case of moral interest (or respect), more generally. The point emerges in the specific case of moral indignation, itself a species of respect. Moral indignation is the anger through which we protest dignitary violations—the kinds of abuses that demean and diminish or dehumanize others. Indignation requires seeing injury in a specific light, in terms of the denial of the humanity autonomous morality requires. Kant insists that we need to leave room for this kind of anger that expresses justice, and neither conflate it with vengeance[96] nor squeeze it out by too 'conciliatory' a spirit:

> Men have a duty to cultivate a *conciliatory spirit* (*placabilitas*). But this must not be confused with *placid toleration* of injuries . . . renunciation of the rigorous means . . . for

---

[93] KpV 81.   [94] KpV 80; G 401 n.
[95] See *Religion Within the Limits of Reason Alone*, 23.   [96] Anth. 270–1.

preventing the recurrence of injuries by other men; for in the latter case a man would be throwing away his right and letting others trample on it, and so would violate his duty to himself. (DV 460)

Kant does not pick out moral indignation by name here, but it is clear enough that it is what he has in mind as the background alternative emotion here. What he is pointing to is an emotion that embraces evaluations about how we ought to regard individuals if we are to take seriously our duties to them and to ourselves. He is talking about a kind of affective spirit that promotes the cause of humanity and is expressed in a concrete and empathic form of respect.

Of course, if Kant were to fully acknowledge that practical emotions do embrace evaluations (and not just be susceptibilities to be moved by reason),[97] he would have to show how we cultivate them from our starting point in sensuous inclinations, such as natural sympathy, and the like. In the *Doctrine of Virtue*, those are the starting points. The picture is not of striking down inclinations of self-love by respect, as it is in the *Second Critique*, and beginning our work with the ground fully cleared, but rather of transforming the aesthetic sensibilities that we have already. But if this is the case, then it makes sense to think of those starting points, those inclinations, as themselves cognitive, or at least as having the potential to be fully cognitive.

And yet it remains a fixed feature of Kant's view that a cognitive view has to be rejected, both with respect to pathological and practical emotions. Emotions are, at bottom, kinds of pleasure and pain that cannot represent information about the world. As Kant says in the *Second Critique*, the feelings of pleasure and pain register quantitative, not qualitative differences. They 'differ from any other only in degree'.[98] The point remains the same in the later *Doctrine of Virtue*, 'moral feeling (like pleasure and pain in general) is something merely subjective, which yields no knowledge [of objects]'.[99]

The point is that Kant does not have available the resources to build an account of the emotions that can adequately capture the idea he finds so appealing, that mature moral emotions reflect consciousness of the moral law.

35.6 CONCLUSION

I have argued that Aristotle and the Stoics provide important cognitivist accounts of the emotions important for an account of virtue. In a highly systematic way, the Stoics develop Aristotle's suggestion that accountability for emotions is grounded in our capacity to revise appearances. On the Stoic view, this is at the heart of character formation. And this itself becomes a robust kind of agency. Kant, in his later works especially, embraces the significant role that concrete forms of practical love and respect will have in the moral life. They are not just 'garments that dress virtue to advantage', that is, adventitious charms and ornaments. They are themselves expressions of accepting the moral

---

[97] DV 399.   [98] KpV 21–4.   [99] DV 399.

law and the requirements it imposes on self and others. The claim is a throwback to ancient virtue, and to the project of being responsible for character, for both action as well as emotion. But once Kant cuts off the emotions from their cognitive moorings, and specifically, from a capacity to evaluate the world, it is far from clear just how emotions, even cultivated ones, can express the demands of the moral law.

BIBLIOGRAPHY

Annas, J. 1992. *Hellenistic Philosophy of Mind*. Berkeley: University of California Press.

Appiah, K. A. 2008. *Experiments in Ethics*. Cambridge, MA: Harvard University Press.

Aristotle 1984. *The Complete Works of Aristotle*. Revised Oxford translation, ed. J. Barnes. Princeton, NJ: Princeton University Press.

Baron, M. 1995. *Kantian Ethics Almost Without Apology*. Ithaca: Cornell University Press.

Baron-Cohen, S. 1999. *Mindblindness*. Cambridge, MA: MIT Press.

Blum, L. 1994. *Moral Perception and Particularity*. Cambridge: Cambridge University Press.

Brennan, T. 2005. *The Stoic Life: Emotions, Duties, and Fate*. Oxford: Oxford University Press.

Buss, S. 1999. 'Appearing Respectful: The Moral Significance of Manners', *Ethics* 109: 795–826.

Calhoun, C. 1984. 'Cognitive Emotions?', in C. Calhoun and R. Solomon (ed.), *What is an Emotion?* Oxford: Oxford University Press, 327–42.

Cicero 1999a. *On Duties*, tr. M. T. Grffin and E. M. Atkins. Cambridge: Cambridge University Press.

—— 1999b. *Letters to Friends*, tr. D. R. Shackleton Bailey. 2 vols. Loeb Classical Library. Cambridge, MA: Harvard University Press.

—— 1999c. *Letters to Atticus*, tr. D. R. Shackleton Bailey. 4 vols. Loeb Classical Library. Cambridge, MA: Harvard University Press.

—— 2001. *On Moral Ends*, ed. J. Annas and tr. by R. Woolf. Cambridge: Cambridge University Press.

—— 2002. *Tusculan Disputations* in *Cicero on the Emotions: Tusculan Disputations 3 and 4*, tr. M. Graver. Chicago: University of Chicago Press.

Cooper, J. M. 1993. 'Rhetoric, Dialectic and the Passions', in *Oxford Studies in Ancient Philosophy*, vol. 11. Oxford: Oxford University Press, 178–84.

—— 2004. *The Emotional Life of the Wise*. Unpublished manuscript.

D'Arms, J. and Jacobson, D. 2000. 'The Moralistic Fallacy: On the "Appropriateness of Emotions"', *Philosophy and Phenomerological Research* 16 (1) 65–90.

Deigh, J. 2008. *Emotions, Values, and the Law*. Oxford: Oxford University Press.

DeSousa, R. 1987. *The Rationality of Emotion*. Cambridge, MA: MIT Press.

Dihle, A. 1982. *The Theory of Will in Classical Antiquity*. Berkeley: University of California Press.

Diogenes Laertius 1952. *Lives of Eminent Philosophers, Vol. 2*, tr. R. D. Hicks. Cambridge, MA: Harvard University Press.

Doris, J. 2002. *Lack of Character: Personality and Moral Behavior*. Cambridge: Cambridge University Press.

—— and Stich, S. 2006. 'Moral Psychology: Empirical Approaches', in E. N. Zalta (ed.), *The Stanford Encyclopedia of Philosophy*, <http://plato.stanford.edu/moral-psych-emp/notes.tml>.

Dwyer, S. 2009. 'Moral Dumbfounding and the Linguistic Analogy: Implications for the Study of Moral Judgment', *Mind & Language* 24: 274–96.

Ekman, P. 1972. *Emotions in the Human Face.* New York: Pergamon Press.

—— 2003. *Emotions Revealed: Recognizing Faces and Feelings to Improve Communication and Emotional Life.* New York: Times Books (Henry Holt).

Epictetus 1995. *The Discourses of Epictetus*, ed. C. Gill, tr. and rev. R. Hard. London: Everyman Paperbacks.

Frijda, N. 1987. *The Emotions: Studies in Emotion and Social Interaction.* Cambridge: Cambridge University Press.

Gellius, A. 1927. *The Attic Nights of Aulus Gellius*, tr. J. C. Rolfe. vols 1–3. Loeb Classical Library. Cambridge, MA: Harvard University Press.

Goffman, E. 1967. *Interaction Ritual: Essays on Face-to-Face Behavior.* New York: Anchor.

Goldie, P. 2000. *The Emotions.* Oxford: Oxford University Press.

Graver, M. 1999. 'Philo of Alexandria and the Origins of the Stoic Propatheia', *Phronesis* 44: 300–25.

—— 2002. *Cicero on the Emotions: Tusculan Disputations 3 and 4*, translation with Commentary. Chicago: University of Chicago Press.

—— 2007. *Stoicism and Emotion.* Chicago: University of Chicago Press.

Greenspan, P. 1988. *Emotions and Reasons.* NY: Routledge.

Griffiths, P. 1997. *What Emotions Really Are.* Chicago: University of Chicago Press.

Guyer, P. 1993. *Kant and the Experience of Freedom: Essays on Aesthetics and Morality.* Cambridge: Cambridge University Press.

—— (ed.) 1998. *Kant's Groundwork of the Metaphysics of Morals: Critical Essays.* Lanham: Rowman & Littlefield.

Hampshire, S. 1983. *Morality and Conflict.* Cambridge, MA: Harvard University Press.

Harman, G. 2000. 'Moral Philosophy Meets Social Psychology: Virtue Ethics and the Fundamental Attribution Error', in his *Explaining Value and Other Essays in Moral Philosophy.* Oxford: Oxford University Press. Also in *Proceedings of the Aristotelian Society* 99 (1999): 315–31.

Herman, B. 1993. *The Practice of Moral Judgment.* Cambridge, MA: Harvard University Press.

Hill, T., Jr. 1993. *Dignity and Practical Reason.* Ithaca: Cornell University Press.

—— 2002. *Human Welfare and Moral Worth: Kantian Perspectives.* Oxford: Oxford University Press.

—— 2004. *Respect, Pluralism, and Justice: Kantian Perspectives.* Oxford: Oxford University Press.

Hooker, B. and Little, M. 2000. *Moral Particularism.* Oxford: Oxford University Press.

Hurley, E. 2005. 'Beyond Emotional Cognitivism: Feelings, Norms, and Folk Psychological Kinds'. PhD. Georgetown University.

Hursthouse, R. 1999a. 'A False Doctrine of the Mean', in N. Sherman (ed.), *Aristotle's Ethics: Critical Essays.* Lanham, MD: Rowman and Littlefield, 105–19.

—— 1999b. *On Virtue Ethics.* Oxford: Oxford University Press.

Inwood, B. 1985. *Ethics and Human Action in Early Stoicism.* Oxford: Oxford University Press.

—— 2005. *Reading Seneca: Stoic Philosophy at Rome.* Oxford: Oxford University Press.

—— and Gerson, L. P. 2008. *The Stoic Reader: Selected Writings and Testimonia.* Indianapolis: Hackett.

Kamtekar, R. 2004. 'Situationism and Virtue Ethics on the Content of Character', *Ethics* 114: 458–91.

Kant, I. 1956. *Critique of Practical Reason*, tr. L. White Beck. Indianapolis: Bobbs Merrill.

Kant, I. 1960. *Religion Within the Limits of Reason Alone*, tr. T. Greene and H. Hudson. New York: Harper and Row.

——1963. *Lectures on Ethics*, tr. L. Infield. Indianapolis: Hackett.

——1964. *Groundwork of the Metaphysic of Morals*, tr. H. J. Paton. New York: Harper Torchbooks.

——1974. *Anthropology from a Pragmatic Point of View*, tr. M. Gregor. The Hague: Martinus Nijhoff.

——1994. *The Doctrine of Virtue, Part II of The Metaphysics of Morals*, tr. M. Gregor. Philadelphia: University of Pennsylvania Press.

Knobe, J. and Nichols, S. (eds) 2008. *Experimental Philosophy*. Oxford: Oxford University Press.

Korsgaard, C. 1996. *Creating the Kingdom of Ends*. Cambridge: Cambridge University Press.

Kosman, L. A. 1980. 'Being Properly Affected: Virtues and Feelings in Aristotle's Essays', in A. O. Rorty (ed.), *Essays on Aristotle's Ethics*. Berkeley: University of California Press, 103–16.

Long, A. A. and Sedley, D.N. 1987. *The Hellenistic Philosophers*. 2 vols. Cambridge: Cambridge University Press.

McDowell, J. 1979. 'Virtue and Reason', *Monist* 62: 331–50.

Manstead, A., Frijda, N., and Fischer, A. (eds) 2004. *Feelings and Emotions*. Cambridge: Cambridge University Press.

Mikhail, J. 2010. *Elements of Moral Cognition*. Cambridge: Cambridge University Press.

Murdoch, I. 1970. *The Sovereignty of Good*. London: Routledge.

Nell (O'Neill), O. 1975. *Acting on Principle: An Essay on Kantian Ethics*. New York: Columbia University Press.

Neu, J. 2000. *A Tear is an Intellectual Thing: The Meaning of Emotion*. Oxford: Oxford University Press.

Nussbaum, M. 1978. *Aristotle's 'De Motu Animalium': Text with translation, commentary, and interpretive essays*. Princeton: Princeton University Press.

——1990. *Love's Knowledge*. Oxford: Oxford University Press.

——1994. *The Therapy of Desire: Theory and Practice in Hellenistic Ethics*. Princeton: Princeton University Press.

——2001. *Upheavals of Thought*. Cambridge: Cambridge University Press.

Oakley, J. 1992. *Morality and the Emotions*. New York: Routledge.

Peters, R. S. and Mace, C. A. 1961–1962. 'Emotions and the Category of Passivity', *Proceedings of the Aristotelian Society* 62: 117–42.

Prinz, J. J. 2004. *Gut Reactions*. Oxford: Oxford University Press.

Reath, A. 1989. 'Kant's Theory of Moral Sensibility: Respect for the Moral Law and the Influence of Inclination', *Kant-Studien* 80: 284–302.

Richardson, H. 1994. *Practical Reasoning about Ends*. Cambridge: Cambridge University Press.

Roberts, R. 1988. 'What an Emotion is: A Sketch', *Philosophical Review* 97 (2): 183–209.

——2009. 'Emotions and the Canons of Evaluation', in P. Goldie (ed.), *Oxford Handbook of Philosophy of Emotions*. Oxford: Oxford University Press, 561–85.

Rorty, A. O. (ed.) 1996. *Essays on Aristotle's Rhetoric*. Berkeley: University of California Press.

Ross, L. and Nisbett, R. E. 1991. *The Person and the Situation*. Philadelphia: Temple University Press.

Russell, D. 2009. *Practical Intelligence and the Virtues*. Oxford: Oxford University Press.

Seneca 1995a. *On Anger* [*De Ira*], in J. M. Cooper and J. F. Procopé (eds), *Moral and Political Essays*. Cambridge: Cambridge University Press.

—— 1995b. *On Favours*. [*De Beneficiis*], in J. M. Cooper and J. F. Procopé (eds), *Moral and Political Essays*. Cambridge: Cambridge University Press.

—— 1995c. *On Mercy* [*De Clementia*], in J. M. Cooper and J. F. Procopé (eds), *Moral and Political Essays*. Cambridge: Cambridge University Press.

Sherman, N. 1989. *The Fabric of Character*. Oxford: Oxford University Press.

—— 1997. *Making a Necessity of Virtue*. Cambridge: Cambridge University Press.

—— 1998. 'Concrete Kantian Respect', *Social Philosophy and Policy* 15 (1): 119–48. Also in E. Frankel Paul, F. Miller, and J. Paul (eds), *Virtue and Vice*. Cambridge: Cambridge University Press, 1998, 110–48.

—— 1999. 'Taking Responsibility for our Emotions', *Social Philosophy and Policy* 16 (2): 294–323. Also in E. Frankel Paul, F. E. Miller, and J. Paul (eds), *Responsibility*. Cambridge: Cambridge University Press, 1999, 294–323.

—— 2003. 'Intellectual Virtue: Emotions, Luck, and the Ancients', in M. DePaul and L. Zagzebski (eds), *Intellectual Virtue: Perspectives from Ethics and Epistemology*. Oxford: Oxford University Press, 34–54.

—— 2005a. 'The Look and Feel of Virtue', C. Gill (ed.), in *Virtue, Norms, and Objectivity*. Oxford: Oxford University Press, 53–82.

—— 2005b. *Stoic Warriors: The Ancient Philosophy Behind the Military Mind*. Oxford: Oxford University Press.

Sinnott-Armstrong, W. 2007. *The Evolution of Morality: Adaptations and Innateness*. Cambridge, MA: MIT Press.

—— 2008a. *Moral Psychology. Vol. 2. The Cognitive Science of Morality: Intuition and Diversity*. Cambridge, MA: MIT Press.

—— 2008b. *Moral Psychology. Vol. 3: The Neuroscience of Morality, Emotion, Brain Disorders, and Development*. Cambridge, MA: MIT Press.

Smith, A. 2005. 'Responsibility for Attitudes: Activity and Passivity in Mental Life', *Ethics* 115: 236–71.

Solomon, R. 1973. 'Emotions and Choice', *The Review of Metaphysics* 27 (1): 20–41.

—— 2003. *Not Passion's Slave: Emotions and Choice*. Oxford: Oxford University Press.

—— 2004. 'On the Passivity of the Passions', in A. S. R. Mansfield (ed.), *Feelings and Emotions: the Amsterdam Symposium, Volume 2001*. Cambridge: Cambridge University Press, 11–29.

Sorabji, R. 2000. *Emotion and Peace of Mind: From Stoic Agitation to Christian Temptation*. Oxford: Oxford University Press.

Stobaeus, J. 1974. *Eclogae Physicae et Ethicae*. Apud Weidmannos.

Stocker, M. 1996. *Valuing Emotions*. Cambridge: Cambridge University Press.

Stohr, K. 2006. 'Manners, Morals, and Practical Wisdom', in T. Chappell (ed.), *Values and Virtues: Aristotelianism in Contemporary Ethics*. Oxford: Oxford University Press, 189–211.

Strawson, P. 1993. 'Freedom and Resentment', in J. M. Fischer and M. Ravizza (eds), *Perspectives on Moral Responsibility*. Ithaca: NY: Cornell University Press, 45–66.

Striker, Gisela. 1996. 'Emotions in Context: Aristotle's Treatment of the Passions in the *Rhetoric* and his Moral Psychology', in A. O. Rorty (ed.) 1996, 286–302.

Tanner, M. 1977. 'Sentimentality', *Proceedings of the Aristotelian Society* 77: 127–47.

Wilson, M. 1997. 'The Subjugation of Grief in Seneca's "Epistles"', in S. Morton Braund and C. Gill (eds), *The Passions in Roman Thought and Literature*. Cambridge: Cambridge University Press, 48–67.

CHAPTER 36

....

JUSTICE, EQUALITY, AND RIGHTS

....

JOHN TASIOULAS

36.1 THE NATURE OF JUSTICE

....

PHILOSOPHERS have advocated many divergent views as to the content of the correct principles of justice. In contemporary philosophy, for example, the live options range from the austere libertarian thesis that the claims of justice are limited to a small class of rights that protect us from coercive interference by others to more radically egalitarian doctrines that mandate the large-scale redistribution of wealth and other goods. But there is a prior, conceptual question: is there an illuminating sense in which these disagreements are aptly described as concerned with *justice*? Alternatively put, is there a *concept* of justice of which these rival accounts can be interpreted as offering different *conceptions*? (Rawls 1971/1999: 5–6). If not, the dispiriting conclusion looms that these disputes are 'verbal' rather than genuine, like a debate about the nature of 'banks' in which one party has in mind financial institutions and the other party the sloping bits of land at the sides of rivers.

One answer is that the concept of justice marks out the entire domain of moral evaluation, or at least the whole of interpersonal morality, excluding only moral concerns relating purely to oneself or to non-persons, such as animals. This expansive reading of justice—as (interpersonal) moral rightness or virtue—has a venerable pedigree. The Greek word for justice, *dikaiosyne*, can mean acting rightly or as one ought (although there is a real question about the extent to which a specific category of the 'moral' comes into focus within ancient Greek ethical thought). This is a meaning 'justice' bears when Plato and Aristotle claim that all of virtue is contained in justice. The wide sense is also found in modern writers such as Hugo Grotius and Adam Smith, and it persists to the present day, hence the title of a recent book: *Justice: What's the Right Thing to Do?* (Sandel 2009).

But were this the only sense of justice in play, we should be hard pressed to explain the overkill involved in labelling as 'injustices' all moral defects with an interpersonal dimension. Nor would it chime with the common belief in the existence of other *moral* considerations—e.g. loyalty, benevolence, mercy—that are distinct from justice and which may even conflict with it in deliberation about what is, all-things-considered, the morally right thing to do. Unsurprisingly, then, justice also bears a more specific sense according to which it is one moral value among others. One important historical source here is Aristotle's classic discussion in Book V of the *Nicomachean Ethics*. In addition to 'universal' justice (understood as the exercise of 'complete virtue' or general moral righteousness in relation to others), Aristotle distinguishes two forms of 'particular' justice (Aristotle 325BC: 1129b26–30, 1130a14). *Distributive justice* is concerned with allocating goods, such as honour among the citizens of the state, in proportion to the respective merits of the claimants. *Corrective justice* governs the restoration of just allocations disrupted by wrong-doing. Aristotle also addresses other specific forms of justice, including justice in exchange. This bottom-up approach to justice advances by means of the open-ended enumeration of its specific forms, allowing for the recognition of yet other forms, such as retributive justice and procedural justice (see Wiggins 2006: ch. 10). But the question of why they are all properly designated forms of *justice* remains. One answer is that they are unified by a concern with maintaining *equality* (*to ison*, a phrase perhaps more accurately translated as *fairness*): 'What is just is equal [or fair], as seems true to everyone even without argument' (Aristotle 325BC: 1131a). But Aristotle is not an egalitarian who takes justice to demand an equal division of goods; instead, it requires a division proportioned to the relative merits of the claimants. This doesn't necessarily mean that the reference to equality is vacuous, since there is a widely held principle of formal justice or practical rationality—'treat like cases alike, treat unlike cases differently'. But everything now shifts to the particular respects in which *justice*, in contrast to other values, assesses cases as relevantly 'like' or 'unlike', and what these assessments demand in terms of treatment (see Lucas 1980: ch. 9).

This suggests an alternative specification of the concept of justice. According to Justinian's *Digest*, 'justice is a constant and unceasing determination to render everyone his due ["ius suum"]' (Justinian 1904: I.I.10). This historically influential formulation, anticipated by Plato and Cicero, is subsequently affirmed by both Augustine and Aquinas and figures in the development of Roman law, which is the chief historical incubator of the idea of an individual right. But the bare idea of giving everyone their due needs further elaboration, since it is open to radically divergent interpretations, including the notably inegalitarian one adopted by Roman law, in which a person's due is predominantly a function of their social status, whether it be adult free male, woman, resident alien, or slave.

One possibility is to interpret people's 'due' as individual entitlements enshrined in positive law or in societal practices and traditions; after all, law is one sense possessed by the term 'ius'. But although conventionalist *conceptions* of justice have often been advanced—for example, by the ancient sophists, Pyrrhonic sceptics, Thomas Hobbes (1651) and Michael Walzer (1983)—it is implausible to build conventionalism into the very *concept* of justice. After all, justice is generally supposed to be a standard in terms of which any legal system or social practice may be held up to critical scrutiny. Another approach follows Aristotle's lead and focuses on the merit or desert of individuals, such as their virtues, accomplishments, efforts, etc. But today at least it is widely thought that justice includes entitlements that lack any obvious basis in merit or desert, such as rights against murder and assault or to certain forms of material provision.[1]

36.2 JUSTICE AS SUBJECTIVE RIGHT

More promising is a third interpretation of the Justinian maxim, according to which one's 'due' or 'ius' is that to which one has a (subjective) *moral right*. Justice, in the specific sense, is not moral rightness in general, i.e. that which it is morally right to do in any given case (which has traditionally been called 'objective right'). It is rather 'subjective right': a matter of obligations owed to, or (moral) powers inhering in, an individual 'subject'. That the two notions are conceptually distinct is shown by the fact we may intelligibly have a subjective right to do what is objectively wrong, e.g. neglect the development of our talents, make unduly harsh criticisms of others, etc. It is vitally important to note that 'objective' and 'subjective' are not being used here in the sense(s) they bear in metaethics: whether or not claims of subjective or objective right are open to an 'objective' vindication, i.e. whether they can be shown to be true or rationally justified, is a further question.

The language of subjective rights does not explicitly figure in the writings of Aristotle or any other classical Greek philosopher, and whether the concept has any grip on their thought is a matter of ongoing debate (see, e.g. Miller 1995). But conceiving of justice as the realm of rights embraces aspects of a merit-focussed view whilst also overcoming some of its limitations. On the one hand, people's merits may be regarded as issuing in demands of justice only in so far as they give rise to rights on their part.[2] On the other hand, justice as rights allows for the existence of rights which are not grounded in the right-holder's merit or desert, including natural or human rights that we possess simply in virtue of our humanity.

That justice as the domain of moral rights has a worthy claim to embody at least the kernel of the *modern* concept of justice is strongly suggested by the fact that Immanuel Kant and John Stuart Mill—central figures in two radically opposed but also enormously influential modern schools of moral philosophy—both subscribe to it. Of course, the idea of justice as rights can be spelt out in significantly different ways. Nevertheless, for

---

[1] For the claim that such non-merit based demands of justice make 'no sense' from the point of view of the Aristotelian tradition, see Fleischacker 2004: 7, 13–15. A key thesis of Fleischacker's book is that it was not until the late eighteenth century that distributive justice was taken to require a distribution of resources that ensured everyone's basic needs are satisfied independently of their merit or desert.

[2] This attempt to encompass merit and desert is not without difficulty, since it is odd to say that the person who deserves to be punished has a right to punishment (although some have said it, e.g. Hegel). This may be because punishment is not primarily justified by the benefit it confers on its recipients. However, it may not be irrelevant that the paradigm cases in which punishment is thought to be justified—murder, assault, theft, etc.—are cases of rights-violations.

both Kant and Mill, justice is crucially to be understood in terms of the prior distinction between perfect and imperfect moral duties. The former, unlike the latter, involve corresponding rights on the part of assignable individuals:

> Justice is a name for certain classes of moral rules, which concern the essentials of human well-being more nearly, and are therefore of more absolute obligation, than any other rules for the guidance of life; and the notion which we have found to be of the essence of the idea of justice, that of a right residing in an individual, implies and testifies to this more binding obligation. (Mill 1861: 5.2).[3]

The conceptualization of justice as the sphere of subjective moral rights is also endorsed by many philosophers who do not fit smoothly into either the deontological or utilitarian camps. Indeed, it was given a powerful impetus in the seventeenth century by the natural lawyers Hugo Grotius and Samuel Pufendorf, and it is subsequently found in the work of John Locke, Adam Smith, Thomas Reid, and others.[4]

Philosophers who conceive of justice in this way have held differing views as to the nature of such rights. Nonetheless, the following features are typical of most ways of conceiving of them. First, moral rights have corresponding duties, so that A's right to X involves a duty on someone else not to interfere with A's enjoying X or even to protect or promote his access to X.[5] Duties apply independently of their bearer's motivation; they possess a special stringency or weight as compared with other considerations; and violations of them, without justification or excuse, validate a cluster of moral responses, such as blame, guilt, and resentment. Second, the possession of the right typically secures to the right-holder something that benefits them—the thing to which he has a right, such as freedom from assault, or the control over that thing conferred by the right, e.g. the ability to sell property he owns. Third, moral rights that do not owe their existence to the law or some social practice are characteristically thought of as grounded in some quality of the right-holder. Philosophers disagree as to the nature of this quality. Some appeal to a prudential notion, such as the right-holder's needs or interests (see, e.g. Raz 1986: ch. 7 and Griffin 2008: ch. 2), and others to a deontological notion, such as 'inviolability' or membership in the moral community (see, e.g. Nagel 2002: ch. 3 and Kamm 2007: Section II). Yet others invoke an underlying metaphysical fact, for example, that the right-holder is created in the image of God or is the object of divine love (see, e.g. Wolterstorff 2008). Fourth, the obligations associated with moral rights have a special, 'directed' character: violations of them are not just moral wrongs, but involve the *wronging* of the individual in whose right the obligation originates. Finally, the duties corresponding to rights are in principle enforceable against their bearers, whether by law or more informal social

---

[3] For Kant's specification of the Doctrine of Right, see Kant 1797: Part II.

[4] For illuminating discussion of these figures, see Schneewind 1998. For criticism of the identification of justice with subjective rights, on the grounds that it is both over-inclusive (e.g. the keeping of promises) and under-inclusive (e.g. forms of fairness that do not involve respecting rights), see Raphael 2001: 107–12.

[5] So, paradigmatic rights are 'claim rights' that involve correlative duties; in a broader sense, 'right' is used also to encompass privileges, powers, and immunities. For a classic discussion, see Hohfeld 1919.

mechanisms, such as public opinion.[6] This enforceability condition is sometimes presented as characterizing not rights in general but, as in Grotius, Pufendorf, and Locke, the sub-class of rights that constitutes the domain of justice in the strict sense that contrasts with 'universal' justice.

This rough characterization clarifies why moral rights are aptly seen as part of the distinctively 'individualistic' component of morality, one that treats the individual as a basic source and object of moral demands. Hence the special challenge that the notions of justice and rights have posed for the utilitarian tradition, with its commitment to a fundamental moral principle that aggregates welfare across different people, since this apparently countenances the sacrifice of some individuals for the benefit of others.[7] The individualistic character of rights morality has also attracted the objection that it involves an impoverished, 'atomistic' picture of human nature, one that severs us from meaningful personal and social bonds and upholds a narrowly 'egoistic' vision of human ends. This is a criticism famously associated with Karl Marx, who complained that '[n]-one of the so-called rights of man goes beyond egoistic man, man as he is in civil society, namely, an individual withdrawn behind his private interests and whims and separated from the community' (Marx 1977: 54; for a critical discussion, see Buchanan 1982). And it has been taken up in recent years by some neo-Aristotelian, conservative, and feminist writers (see, for example, MacIntyre 2007; Glendon 1991; Minow 1990).

Whatever the force of this critique in relation to particular *conceptions* of individual rights, nothing in the *concept* of individual rights itself limits the goods to which people have rights to those capable of being enjoyed independently of others also enjoying them. Nor does the morality of rights imply that the primary site of human flourishing is the private realm, with communal and political activity being valued only as a means for securing the freedom to pursue private ends. Moreover, belief in individual rights is consistent with admitting a variety of other moral considerations, some of them non-individualistic in character, that temper the content of rights, constrain their exercise, or compete with them in reaching all-things-considered judgements (Raz 1986: ch. 8). This last point is unavailable to those philosophers who regard the whole of morality as rights-based; but this is a view incompatible with taking the distinguishing feature of justice to be that it is the domain of rights. Finally, even the popular designation of rights as 'trumps' against the common good needs to be handled with care (Dworkin 1977: xi–xv, 188–91). It makes most sense against the background of an aggregative account of the common good, setting a limit to what may be done to people in the name of maximizing the overall good. But it is questionable on non-aggregative

---

[6] Hence Mill: 'When we call anything a person's right, we mean that he has a valid claim on society to protect him in the possession of it, either by the force of law or by that of education and opinion. If he has what we consider a sufficient claim, on whatever account, to have something guaranteed to him by society, we say that he has a right to it' (1861: 5.24). See also Kant 1797: 231/p. 57.

[7] '*Right*, the substantive *right*, is the child of law: from *real* laws come *real* rights, but from laws of nature, fancied and invented by poets, rhetoricians, and dealers in moral and intellectual poisons come *imaginary* rights, a bastard brood of monsters, "gorgons and chimeras dire"' (Bentham 1987: 46).

(e.g. Aristotelian) accounts that conceive of rights as *components* of the common good (Finnis 1980: 210–18; Raz 1994).

The conceptualization of justice as the domain of subjective rights offers a way of distinguishing justice from other moral values, notably those of charity, mercy, beneficence, and generosity. Charity, for example, enjoins us to minister in various ways to those in need. But even if some of its injunctions rise to the level of obligations, under the aspect of charity the needy have no corresponding right to be benefited in those ways, or at least no right that ought to be (legally) enforceable. Most proponents of the distinction conceive of the 'perfect' duties of justice as permitting less leeway for discretion regarding the manner and occasion of their fulfilment than the 'imperfect' duties of charity. The former are also generally regarded as being more stringent than the latter, so that acts of injustice are, *ceteris paribus*, graver wrongs than failures of charity. And consequently justice is accorded a general priority over charity: for example, one is not normally permitted to alleviate the needs of the poor by using property stolen from the rich. The justice/charity distinction has been drawn along roughly these lines by a number of modern philosophers over a remarkably long period, including Grotius, Pufendorf, Locke, Hume, Smith, Reid, Kant, and Mill.[8]

But there is another, more straightforward, way of distinguishing between justice and charity, one that has been invoked both as part of the idea of justice as subjective rights and independently of it. This places a constraint on *general* duties of justice, those that are not generated by some special relationship, such as promising or parenthood. According to this constraint, the primary general duties of justice—*primary* here meaning those obligations that do not arise from the violation or non-fulfilment of other obligations of justice—are exclusively negative, i.e. they require the duty-bearer to refrain from certain kinds of conduct, e.g. murder, assault, deception, etc. It follows that any general moral reasons for taking positive steps to assist another, even if they are duties, are not imposed by justice. This 'negative' concept of justice can be traced back to the historically influential writings of Cicero (Cicero 1961: I.20–59, III.21–8. For a critical discussion, see Nussbaum 2000a).

The negative duties thesis has been motivated in a variety of ways. For some it reflects the importance of the 'negative' liberty protected by rights or the apparent fact that compliance with negative duties is comparatively less costly. Alternatively, it may be taken to underline the fact that, other things being equal, violations of negative duties are graver wrongs than violations of positive duties. Thus, according to Adam Smith, the lack of beneficence manifested in failing to assist someone in need when one can easily do so renders one *blameable*, but only positive acts that inflict or risk harm—such as murder, assault, and theft—are proper objects of *resentment*, and hence constitute injustices that may be punished (Smith 1790/2009: II.ii.i). Another, essentially Kantian, line of thought

[8] See discussion of these thinkers in Raphael 2001: chs 6, 9, 10, 11, and 12; Fleischacker 2004: 22–7; and Schneewind 1997: 187–91, which is especially instructive on how the Humean distinction between artificial and natural virtues maps onto the distinction between perfect and imperfect duties. For two excellent contemporary discussions of the justice/charity distinction, see Buchanan 1987 and O'Neill 1989.

that has been powerfully deployed by Onora O'Neill turns on the proposition that duties generated by rights must be *claimable*, i.e. it must be in principle possible to identify both the content of these duties and their bearers by employing only moral reasoning. If these rights are fundamental moral rights that we possess simply in virtue of our humanity, then their existence—including the allocation and content of their associated duties—cannot depend on any institutional recognition or determination. Whilst this condition is satisfied by rights imposing negative duties—pure moral reasoning tells us who bears the duties corresponding to these rights (everyone) and what the content of these duties is (e.g. to refrain from torture)—the same is not true of supposed fundamental moral rights to goods. Although contemporary human rights declarations overflow with so-called 'welfare rights', these are not fundamental moral rights or human rights because they require some sort of institutional mechanism to fix the content of their counterpart duties and allocate them to their bearers (O'Neill 1996, 2005).

The negative duties thesis continues to exert a strong influence on some strains of contemporary philosophical thought about justice and rights. Its popularity, especially among libertarians, has led Thomas Pogge to frame his widely discussed argument that global poverty is a massive violation of human rights in terms of a negative duty. This is a duty to refrain from imposing, or profiting from, institutional schemes that foreseeably and avoidably lead to the impairment of people's capacity to meet their basic needs (Pogge 2002). Others, however, have challenged the negative duties condition. Some question the existence of a non-arbitrary division between 'positive' and 'negative' duties. Others grant its existence, but deny the significance with which advocates of the negative duties thesis invest it. For example, they argue that the fulfilment of 'negative' duties can be just as costly as the fulfilment of positive duties or just as important to the preservation of 'negative' liberty. While yet others dispute that such significance as inheres in the distinction—e.g. the asymmetry in the claimability of negative and positive duties—disqualifies positive duties from corresponding to fundamental moral rights or coming within the scope of justice.

36.3 JUSTICE ECLIPSED

There is, then, a dominant strand in modern philosophical thought that has sought to elucidate the concept of justice as one value among others, and the idea of justice as subjective rights has been a lodestar in this quest. However, a marked feature of English-speaking philosophy in the past hundred years or so has been a countervailing tendency to downplay the significance of the boundaries of justice. This tendency is associated with the powerful influence exerted by utilitarianism up until the 1970s and also, strange though it may seem, with the subsequent influence of Rawls' *A Theory of Justice*. The upshot is that something like the older, broader notion of justice, as interpersonal morality in general, upstaged the idea of justice as one moral consideration among others.

Justice is occluded within utilitarianism—despite Mill's heroic efforts to the contrary—because it ultimately derives all moral requirements from an underlying principle of maximizing overall welfare, one readily construed as a principle of beneficence. The conclusion is explicitly drawn by Bentham: '"Justice" is the name given to beneficence, in so far as the exercise of it is regarded as matter of obligation.'[9] Yet it was through a basic *contrast* with values such as beneficence that the tradition from Cicero to Kant sought to articulate the distinctive nature of justice. In virtue of its commitment to a master principle of maximizing aggregate welfare, utilitarianism was criticized by Rawls for not taking seriously 'the distinction between persons', i.e. for being insensitive to the fact that '[e]ach person possesses an inviolability founded on justice that even the welfare of society as a whole cannot override' (Rawls 1971/1999: 27, 3).

Certainly, Rawls' famous two principles of justice are not joint emanations from anything like a principle of beneficence.[10] But his theory deliberately resembles utilitarianism in its highly systematic character and broad scope. It accords centrality to two (lexically ordered) principles and involves a rejection of what Rawls calls 'intuitionism', according to which there is a plurality of basic moral standards. Moreover, Rawls' two principles seemingly encompass most of the range of moral evaluation. This follows from Rawls' broad understanding of the *concept* of justice—'a characteristic set of principles for assigning basic rights and duties and for determining... the proper distribution of the benefits and burdens of social cooperation' (Rawls 1971/1999: 5)—of which his two principles offer a *conception*. This results in the occlusion of justice through inflation—justice is made to embrace so much of the moral field that it is hard to regard it as but one moral value among others.[11] Admittedly, Rawls says justice is only the 'first virtue of social institutions', but he is notably unforthcoming about how it contrasts with values such as charity, beneficence, and so on. Little wonder then that, under this Rawlsian dispensation, leading anti-utilitarian philosophers now write general treatises on morality under the title of 'justice' (see, for example, Sen 2009, which otherwise contains major criticisms of Rawls' theory).

Now, from another perspective, Rawls has been widely criticized for unduly restricting the subject matter of justice to the basic structure of society and therefore failing to register adequately the bearing of assessments of justice on individual acts and choices, personal character, and the wider social ethos (Cohen 2000, 2008; Wiggins 2006; Sen 2009). This 'institutionalism', although it has antecedents in the work of Kant, is in stark contrast to the mainstream philosophical treatment of justice in the writings of philosophers

---

[9] Bentham 1983: I.2, 127, quoted and discussed in Raphael 2001: 126.

[10] The first gives absolute priority to certain basic liberties over all other values. The other principle has two parts: the first enjoins fair equality of opportunity in competition for offices, the second permits socio-economic inequalities only in so far as they maximize the position of the least advantaged members of society (this second part is the 'difference principle'). Both principles, especially the second, and the priority Rawls assigns to the first, are the subjects of a massive secondary literature. For two excellent surveys of Rawls' philosophy, see Freeman 2007 and Pogge 2007.

[11] A related tendency, here, is the proliferations of 'rights' claims in contemporary life, both amongst philosophers and in the political domain.

such as Plato, Aristotle, Locke, and Mill. G. A. Cohen has made this objection the basis of an important critique of Rawls' claim that the difference principle may permit socio-economic inequalities. However, Rawls does not deny that justice also extends to other subject matters, insisting that his theory is concerned with the discrete topic of 'social justice' (Rawls 1971/1999: 7). But even considered only in its application to social ordering, it might still be thought that Rawls relies on an overly broad and undifferentiated understanding of the scope of justice. Indeed, some such claim bears on the two most celebrated critiques of Rawls' theory, launched from opposite ends of the political spectrum.

In *Anarchy, State and Utopia*, Robert Nozick develops a Lockean approach to justice, conceived as essentially the domain of a small number of negative general rights ('side-constraints'). Although Nozick himself does not explicitly pursue this line of thought, it is arguable that on the concept of justice implicit in this libertarian view, the difference principle is not even a candidate principle of justice, if justice is conceived as one segment of interpersonal morality among others. Positive duties to assist the less well-off are duties of beneficence or charity, with the result that they cannot be enforced and are subordinate to duties of justice. The suspicion of a deep conceptual disconnection between Rawls and his critics applies a fortiori to the most significant leftist critique of Rawls—G. A. Cohen's *Rescuing Justice and Equality* (2008). According to Cohen, Rawls' constructivist procedure for arriving at the principles of justice—whereby they are identified as those principles that would be chosen by parties behind a 'veil of ignorance' in order to regulate the basic structure of their society—conflates the principles of *justice* with the rules that should ideally regulate social life. Even optimal social rules compromise justice in the light of practical constraints and other competing values, hence they cannot be identified with the demands of justice itself. Purified of the extraneous elements, Cohen contends that a more strictly egalitarian principle of distributive justice would emerge, one that enjoins rough equality in people's material prospects. Unlike Rawls' difference principle, it would not validate as just the provision of economic incentives to better-off people (Cohen 2008: ch. 7). But Cohen's critique is hampered by the fact that he offers no adequate account of why his egalitarian principle is a principle of *justice*. Instead, he briskly endorses the Justinian maxim whilst also expressing dissatisfaction with it as an account of the concept of justice.[12] This failure is all the more surprising given that it is crucial to Cohen's overall position that justice is only one politically relevant value among others.

---

[12] 'I assume on the reader's part an intuitive understanding of the sort of principle that a principle of justice is: it is the understanding that she employs when she recognizes that the dispute between John Rawls and Robert Nozick is a dispute about justice, and when she recognizes that the principle that we should respect our natural environment is not a principle of justice, absent some pretty special background beliefs. But if, as some of my critics insist, I simply *must* say what I think justice is, in general terms, then I offer, for those who will be content with it, the ancient dictum that justice is giving each person her due' (Cohen 2008: 7). Note that the first sentence simply identifies justice as concerned with *interpersonal* morality, while the second sentence skates over (as Cohen concedes) the tremendous indeterminacy of the 'ancient dictum'.

These recent debates highlight the need for greater clarity as to what it is for a disagreement to be about *justice*. And in this task reflection on how justice has been construed by philosophers in the past may play a significant role, even if only that of providing an instructive counterpoint to the concept of justice that a contemporary philosopher may wish to espouse. In the remainder of this chapter I shall focus on how the history of ethics might be fruitfully brought to bear on two broad contemporary philosophical concerns with equality and rights: the nature and justification of equal human worth (sections 36.4 and 36.5) and human rights (sections 36.6 and 36.7).

36.4 BASIC HUMAN EQUALITY

The thesis that interpersonal morality in general—in other words, justice in the wide sense distinguished in section 36.1—reflects the basic equality of all human beings is close to an uncontested article of faith in contemporary moral philosophy. This basic equality of status—the idea that 'all people are of equal worth and that there are some claims people are entitled to make on one another simply by virtue of their status as persons' (Scheffler 2003: 22)—has been described as the unquestioned egalitarian plateau on which contemporary ethical debates are enacted, the 'deepest moral assumption' of our age.[13] Nor is this egalitarian consensus confined to philosophers: it pervasively informs the moral consciousness of most contemporary societies, finding expression not only in the ringing phrases of the *Universal Declaration of Human Rights* concerning the equal 'inherent dignity' of 'all members of the human family', but also in the widespread rejection of racist, sexist, and other ideologies that are premised on according some categories of human beings inherently inferior moral worth.

Getting a tolerably firm grip on the import of basic human equality, however, is no easy matter, partly because it is the focus of conflicting interpretations within rival traditions of ethical thought. However, we can give some content to the idea by registering the following widely accepted features.

First, the principle of basic human equality asserts the intrinsically (or non-instrumentally) valuable *moral status* of human beings, articulating the most fundamental moral relations in which they stand to each other. It is therefore conceptually distinct from, although it may be used to justify, egalitarian principles of social relations, political status, and economic distribution.[14] Indeed, some of the most historically influential philosophical advocates of basic human equality, such as the Stoics, Locke, and Kant, have judged it

[13] Dworkin 1973: 532, quoted in Pojman 1997: 297.
[14] Hence Locke's statement: 'Though I have said..., *That all Men by Nature are equal*, I cannot be supposed to understand all sorts of *Equality*' (Locke 1988: 54/304). For a clear appreciation of the difference between 'equality as it is invoked in connection with the distribution of certain goods, some of which will almost certainly give higher status or prestige to those who are more favored, and equality as it applies to the respect which is owed to persons irrespective of social position', see Rawls 1971/1999: 447.

to be compatible with patriarchy, the exclusion of most people from political participation, and even (in the case of Locke and most Stoics, for example) some version of the institution of slavery.[15] Whether they were right to do so is a matter for substantive enquiry, not something already determined in grasping that principle's meaning.

Second, this moral status is possessed in *equal* measure by *all* human beings. Hence some human beings cannot possess greater or lesser moral worth of this type than others. This is perfectly compatible with significant inequalities of various other sorts—in moral virtue, intelligence, beauty, strength, etc. And while who counts as a human being for these purposes is contested, any acceptable understanding is incompatible with the exclusion of humans from this status simply in virtue of their race, gender, religious affiliation, or social position.

Third, and more controversially, all non-human animals known to us lack this status, thus generating a categorical difference in our moral relations to our fellow humans as compared with non-humans: we must recognize each of the former as superior in moral worth to any of the latter.

Fourth, basic equality is supposed to provide a basis for, even if it does not already consist in, a series of moral entitlements that humans possess simply in virtue of their status as human beings, and therefore quite independently of their achievements, social standing, or their comparative intellectual or moral virtues. These entitlements are usually glossed as 'natural rights' or 'human rights'.

Fifth, the principle of basic human equality is understood to be in some sense objectively valid, rather than the product of a personal or cultural outlook that is best explained in terms that do not presuppose the correctness of the principle itself.

In light of these features, basic human equality is an ethical idea intermediate between the abstract notion of inherent moral considerability (something that may be possessed by animals, trees, and perhaps even rocks) and specific egalitarian principles of social relations, political participation, or economic distribution. Yet it is also an idea that is radically inconsistent with doctrines that have been vigorously upheld throughout much of human history. Some, like Hobbes, deny that human beings possess any inherent, as opposed to instrumental or market, value: 'The value, or worth, of a man is, as of all other things, his price; that is to say, so much as would be given for the use of his power' (Hobbes 1651: ch. 10, para 16). For many others, such inherent worth as they possess is in no sense equally distributed; thus, Aristotle, in identifying the locus of inherent human worth in our rational capacities, regards some humans as possessing lesser worth than others, in virtue of their diminished rational capacities: women, labourers, 'slaves by nature', non-Greeks.

One response to the Aristotelian position is that it involves blatant 'empirical' errors about the rational capacities of the supposedly inferior types of people. Although cogent

---

[15] The finding that reprehensible practices such as patriarchy and slavery are compatible with basic human equality cannot *merely* be ascribed to the blindness induced by a self-serving conservatism. One line of thought that appears to have exerted influence on the Stoics and their modern followers, including Kant and Adam Smith, involves the following inference: given that contingencies such as wealth, social rank, birth, ethnicity, nationality are irrelevant to the basic moral worth of all human beings, they must also be irrelevant to what is most important in life. See Nussbaum 2000a: 200–1.

so far as it goes, this response overlooks a deeper problem: given that the quality Aristotle fixes on as the locus of human worth (i.e. rational capacities) is exemplified to different degrees in different people, how can it possibly confer *equal* worth? And how does any other property, in which basic human equality might plausibly be grounded, e.g. the capacity to suffer, to exercise self-control, to reach decisions and pursue them, differ in this respect? Indeed, is there not also a possibility that the salient quality will also be exemplified by some non-human animals, perhaps in some cases to a greater degree than it is exemplified by some humans? Call this problem—of securing the second and third features of basic equality, noted above, in a non-arbitrary way—*the problem of the threshold*.

A related problem is that of the principle's *scope*. Does it extend only to human beings who are persons, with certain psychological capacities, such as the capacities for self-consciousness, rational deliberation, the use of language, autonomous agency, and so on? Or do all members of the species *homo sapiens* come within its embrace, even those that have ceased to possess such capacities (e.g. the irreversibly comatose), or that currently lack them but have the potential to acquire them (e.g. most foetuses and newborn infants), or even those that never possessed them and lack the potential to do so? Or is there some other appropriate specification of its scope?

And there is yet another problem. The contemporary moral philosophers who affirm the idea of basic equality are overwhelming secular in outlook; but the idea itself has a long religious pedigree.[16] Can it be severed from its religious origins without sacrificing its coherence and power? In line with his unsettling hypothesis that modern moral thought systematically fails to acknowledge the inescapably religious character of its key, orienting ideas, Nietzsche mocked the pretensions of a non-theistic egalitarianism: ' "Ye higher men",—thus the mob blink—"there are no higher men; we are all equal; man is man; in the presence of God we are all equal!" In the presence of God? But now that God hath died. But in the presence of the mob we do not wish to be equal' (Nietzsche 1997: 418).[17] This line of thought has been taken up, with a rather different animus, not only by theistic philosophers, but also by some non-believers who, unlike Nietzsche, remain wedded to the morality they fear lacks an adequate grounding within a secular world view.

36.5 GROUNDING BASIC EQUALITY

In spite of their consensus on the basic equality of human beings, contemporary philosophers have largely shirked the burden of justifying it. Some proceed on the optimistic assumption that it is a straightforward and metaphysically lightweight thesis. More interestingly, Rawls argued in *Political Liberalism* (1993) that the fundamental ideas of

---

[16] See Malachi 2:10; Psalms 8:3–6; Romans 2 cited in Pojman 1997: 295.
[17] Nietzsche couples this debunking thesis with the positive claim that the idea of basic equality is a grave threat to the health of the human species.

a *political* conception of justice must be detachable from any 'comprehensive doctrine' that purports to reveal the truth about human nature or the foundations of morality. Thus, although Rawls himself affirms basic human equality—finding its locus in the capacity for moral personality (Rawls 1971/1999: 506; Rawls 1993: 19, 79–81)—he does so on the basis that it is implicit in liberal democratic political culture. But given the problems surrounding the idea of basic human equality, doesn't its widespread acceptance in the absence of an *objective* vindication threaten to cast it as the Noble Lie of contemporary moral and political thought, a mirror image of the grounding inegalitarian myth of Plato's utopia? (see Pojman 1997).

Against this backdrop, two recent attempts to reconstruct the arguments in favour of basic human equality advanced by Locke and Kant deserve special attention. In *God, Locke, and Equality* (2002: ch. 3), Jeremy Waldron offers a theistic interpretation of John Locke's idea '*[t]hat All Men by Nature are Equal*' (Locke 1988: 54/304).[18] A preliminary conundrum in interpreting Locke's egalitarianism is his scepticism about objective, rather than merely conventional, demarcations of species in nature—a scepticism he extends to the species *man*. How can the equality of all humans be meaningfully affirmed as an objective moral doctrine in the absence of a suitably robust version of the idea that people of very different kinds nevertheless belong to the same *species*? Waldron's response is that Locke formulates the doctrine in terms of relevant similarities between individuals, rather than natural kinds or species membership. And the relevant point of resemblance is 'corporeal rationality': the power we have to form and employ *general* ideas, one closely bound up with our capacity for language use, in the conditions that confront us as embodied beings.

The doctrine's irreducibly theistic dimension emerges when we ask why 'corporeal rationality' is anything other than an arbitrary stipulation as the threshold for equal status. This is not just a matter of justifying the inferior worth of beings below the threshold, e.g. non-human animals, psychopaths, etc., but also of neutralizing the significance of the tremendous variation in rational capacities among those beings above it. Waldron's central interpretative claim is that, for Locke, any creatures with the capacity for abstract thought can readily establish the existence of a God whose law governs them in this world and the next. In addition, they can relate the idea of such a law to what is known of God's law through revelation. And they can conceive of themselves as persons subject to God's commandments and therefore as responsible for their transgressions: they are all 'the Servants of one Sovereign Master, sent into the World by his order, and about his business' (Locke 1988: 6/271).

Of course, most contemporary egalitarians will recoil both from the Lockean doctrine's assumption of the ready provability of God's existence and the implication that any ethical principle so consequential for politics relies on a theistic foundation. They may instead be drawn to a version of the doctrine that preserves Locke's emphasis on our rational nature but severs its moral significance from any religious commitment.

---

[18] For a denial of the claim that Locke's formulation of the principle does not extend to women, see Waldron 2002: 35–43.

An obvious alternative source is Kant, for whom rational nature is the fundamental objective and unconditional end in itself, a status reflected in one of the formulations of his supreme principle of morality, the Formula of Humanity as End in Itself: 'So act that you use humanity, as much in your own person as in the person of every other, always at the same time as an end and never merely as a means' (Kant 1785: 4/429). As Allen Wood has argued, 'humanity' here is our 'rational capacity to set ends and devise means to them, and our rational self-love, giving us grounds for forming a conception of our happiness and pursuing it' (Wood 2008: 88). This differs from Locke's doctrine, since Kant conceives of 'humanity' primarily as our capacity for prudential reasoning, rather than our capacity for *moral* reasoning, which he calls 'personality'. The latter is the disposition that confers *dignity* on us, whereby we possess a value that cannot be sacrificed for any other good including dignity itself.

But do not humans differ widely both in the rational capacities that constitute their 'humanity' and in the extent to which they successfully exercise them? Here a second major difference from Locke emerges: where the latter invokes God to solve the problem of the threshold, Wood interprets Kant as invoking moral humility. Humility requires that we assess our individual moral status not in relation to that of others but only by reference to the demands of the moral law itself.[19] But it is doubtful that a policy of humility, adopted in response to the epistemic obstacles to interpersonal comparisons of how different people measure up to the moral law, can preclude any objective judgements on the matter (Wood 1999: 135; for criticism see Wolterstorff 2008: 328–9).

One objection to both the Lockean and Kantian arguments targets their restricted scope: for both, basic human equality extends only to beings endowed with the relevant rational capacities.[20] According to the sponsors of this objection, a capacity-based approach is fatally blind to the unique and equal value that attaches to members of the species *Homo sapiens*, including infants and those suffering from dementia, regardless of the valuable capacities they may or may not possess.[21] Considerations of this sort have recently led Nicholas Wolterstorff, drawing extensively on biblical sources, to present a different theistic grounding of basic human equality. This does not claim that God created all humans with an equal amount of some property—typically, an inherent property in virtue of which they resemble God (*imago dei*)—that confers special value on them. Instead, this worth is *bestowed* on human beings by the fact that God loves them

---

[19] 'the *inner* worth of a person, measured solely by comparison to the moral law, may be greater or less according to one's virtue in fulfilling the law one gives oneself,... the worth of a person never varies in comparison to others, since the good and the bad alike possess the dignity of humanity' (Wood 1999, 135).

[20] In this, they follow a tradition that stretches back to the ancient Stoics, Cicero, and Grotius, see Nussbaum 1997.

[21] For an attempt to modify the Kantian doctrine, to include 'persons in the extended sense', including children and adults who have temporarily ceased to be persons in the strict sense, see Wood 2008: 97 and Wood 1999: 143–4. For some objections to this sort of approach, see Wolterstorff 2008: 330–3.

equally and permanently.[22] Since God loves all members of the species *Homo sapiens* equally, and not in proportion to their varying capacities and achievements, the problem of the threshold is overcome (Wolterstorff 2008: 352–361).

In addition to its controversial assumption of the existence of God, this argument seems vulnerable to a *Euthyphro*-type dilemma. Either humans are intelligible objects of God's love in virtue of qualities they possess or else that love is arbitrarily bestowed. If the former, why can't the relevant qualities directly ground basic equality? If the latter, then can such a seemingly arbitrary attachment really be the source of the special moral status of human beings? And even if some unique value accrues to humans through God's love for them, it is doubtful that equal human worth can derive from a relational property of this sort. Is it really akin to the 'special value' bestowed on an otherwise unexceptional person in virtue of being the Queen's friend as Wolterstorff suggests? This would imply that the special worth of human beings ultimately derives from the worth of God, and that respecting that value is in the end a way of honouring God. The sense in which human beings are originary sources of value is thereby severely attenuated. Finally, this approach has difficulties adequately capturing the fourth feature of basic human equality, since the crop of human rights that emerge on Wolterstorff's theory is very meagre as compared to the ample list in the *Universal Declaration* (Wolterstorff 2008: 315). It is questionable that anything like the standard list of human rights can be meaningfully attributed to all members of the species *Homo sapiens* as such.

There is a larger objection, however, that applies to all three accounts of human equality canvassed so far: their incompatibility with a broadly naturalistic metaphysic. This is most obvious in the case of the explicitly theistic construals, but it also applies to the Kantian argument. In part, this is due to the latter's invocation of a doctrine of the noumenal self to underwrite human equality, one that ultimately locates the capacity for rational agency outside the empirical world. The upshot, as Bernard Williams puts it, is 'a kind of secular analogue of the Christian conception of the respect owed to everybody as equally children of God. Though secular, it is equally metaphysical: in neither case is it anything empirical *about* people that constitutes the ground of equal respect' (Williams 2005: 102). Also at issue, from a broadly naturalistic standpoint, is the Kantian argument's reliance on the supposed deliverances of *a priori* practical reason, in contrast with a conception of reason keyed to sentiments furnished by a biologically given and culturally elaborated human nature (see Wiggins 2006: 133).

The question then arises whether the notion of basic human equality can be upheld not only outside a theistic framework, but also in a broadly naturalistic way. One line of response is the utilitarian construal of equality in terms of the Benthamite dictum 'everybody to count for one, nobody for more than one'. But utilitarianism has enormous difficulties not only in underwriting the unique moral worth of human beings (as emerges in utilitarians' objections to 'speciesism' (see Singer 1993: chs 2–3)), but also in providing a suitably robust account of moral rights. Of course, various other naturalistic

---

[22] Wolterstorff 2008: 352–61. For a helpful distinction between essentialist and grace-based arguments for equal human worth in the Judaeo-Christian tradition, see Pojman 1997: 295–6.

alternatives remain open, including David Wiggins' recent intriguing articulation of the idea of human solidarity within a broadly Humean genealogy of morals, one that seeks to preserve the notion of all human beings as originary sources of moral claims, independently of how their interests factor into any overarching aggregative principle (Wiggins 2008). Among other things, sceptics might question whether this approach is capable of securing an objective grounding of basic human equality, especially as against those who are not party to the sentiments to which it appeals.

36.6 NATURAL RIGHTS: THE QUESTION OF ORIGINS

Let us turn now to the question of the historical origin of the idea of subjective natural rights, conceived as subjective rights possessed by human beings simply in virtue of their humanity and discoverable through the use of 'natural' or ordinary human reason (including any religious truths accessible through such reasoning as opposed to revelation). As previously observed, this has become the most influential way of giving substance to the basic equality of human beings (see the fourth thesis about human equality listed in section 36.4, above). There is a widespread consensus that the idea of individual rights first emerged within Western culture: the phrase *ius naturale*, which originally denominated 'objective' right, eventually also acquires the meaning of 'subjective' right. But controversy still persists as to the character and timing of this momentous transformation.

One typical view, forcefully stated by Alasdair MacInytre, locates the turning point after 1400: 'there is no expression in any ancient or medieval language correctly translated by our expression "a right" until near the close of the middle ages; the concept lacks any means of expression in Hebrew, Greek, Latin, or Arabic, classical or medieval, before about 1400, let alone in Old English, or in Japanese even as late as the mid-nineteenth century' (MacIntyre 2007: 69). Of course, users of a language might possess a concept without having a term or phrase that refers to it.[23] Still, the general view that natural rights are innovations of the late medieval or early modern periods is widely shared. For example, in his *Natural Law and Natural Rights*, John Finnis located the 'watershed' somewhere between the thirteenth and seventeenth centuries, between Aquinas (who lacked a doctrine of natural rights) and Suarez (who possessed one) (Finnis 1980: 206–7).[24] Others have offered more specific turning points, associated with particular thinkers. The French

---

[23] e.g. for the claim that the concept of a natural right is implicit in Aristotle's political theory, see Miller 1995. For biblical antecedents, see Wolterstorff 2008.

[24] Finnis has since revised his view, finding the concept of subjective natural rights, including human rights, in Aquinas (and in this regard disagreeing with Tierney), see Finnis 2002: 407–10 and Finnis 1998: 133–8.

scholar Michel Villey influentially identified William of Ockham as the pivotal figure. On this view, Ockham's metaphysical nominalism, which admits the existence only of individual entities, was a springboard for the elaboration of a theory of subjective rights. Nominalism's supposed normative upshot is that a juridical order must be grounded in the will of the individuals subject to it. In this way, according to Villey, it yielded an intellectual basis for a notion of subjective right that had already emerged in common discourse once the demise of the Roman legal order had unleashed a barrage of conflicting assertions of 'right' among various segments of society—emperors, popes, nobles, and ordinary people (Villey 1964; for a criticial discussion, see Tierney 1997: 28–30. For the rival case that Jean Gerson was the primary innovator, see Tuck 1979). Others have traced the origin of natural rights to the early modern period, often linking it to the nascent capitalist economic order and its ideology of 'possessive individualism'. These interpretations accord a key role to the writings of Grotius (Haakonssen 1996), Hobbes (Strauss 1953), or Locke (MacPherson 1964).

However, in one of the most persuasive contributions to this debate, Brian Tierney in *The Idea of Natural Rights* (Tierney 1997) argues that the notion of subjective rights originates in the humanistic jurisprudence of the twelfth century, especially in the writings of the medieval canon lawyers known as the Decretists. As Tierney summarizes his thesis in a subsequent article:

> When the canonists wrote of *ius naturale* as a faculty or power they meant primarily an ability rooted in human reason and free will to discern what was right and to act rightly. But once the old concept of natural right was defined in this subjective way the argument could easily lead to the rightful rules of conduct prescribed by natural law or to the licit claims and powers inhering in individuals that we call natural rights. Soon the canonists did begin to argue in this way and to specify some such rights. The first one, a very radical one, was a right of the destitute poor to the necessities of life, even if this meant appropriating for themselves the surplus property of the rich. (Tierney 2004: 6)

Essential to this development was the revival of legal studies in the West, initially at Bologna, the recovery of the entire corpus of Roman law at the start of the twelfth century, followed by the codification of canon law in Gratian's *Decretum*. The subjective sense of *ius naturale* was a fruit of the canonists' efforts to harmonize the norms of Roman and canon law. All this was played out against the new emphasis on the person—the individual's will, consent, conscience, etc.—that pervaded twelfth-century European culture.

Of course, a doctrine's historical origin does not settle the question of its meaning, and even less that of its soundness. Still, Tierney's genealogy affords a number of valuable insights into both questions. First, as we should expect from their source in the practical concerns of lawyers, natural rights are not inherently bound up with controversial metaphysical commitments. This applies not only to nominalism, but also to the general idea that human beings share a metaphysical essence. For the twelfth-century jurists, like Ockham and Locke after them, it sufficed that humans generally possessed certain empirically discernible common characteristics, such as rationality, self-awareness, and freedom.[25] Moreover, given the emphasis on natural rights as *natural*—i.e. in the sense of being discoverable by the use of the ordinary reasoning capacities of human beings, rather than *positive* rights laid down by human or divine law or social convention—their identification was not reliant on Christian revelation. Second, this account of the origins of natural rights is at odds with both the Marxist picture of them as an egoist's charter and with the claim that they are a modern corruption of the older idea of natural law construed as a doctrine of 'objective' right. Such an antagonism between the self-realization of the individual, on the one hand, and the demands of community and morality, on the other hand, was anathema to the leading medieval writers on subjective rights. Subjective rights, for them, were inextricably bound up with natural law's requirements of justice and charity (Tierney 1997: 76–7). Finally, as the early affirmation of a right to the necessities of life indicates, the idea that 'welfare' rights with 'positive' corresponding duties is a late and aberrant innovation in natural rights thought is deeply questionable.[26]

36.7 FROM NATURAL RIGHTS TO HUMAN RIGHTS

The idea of natural subjective rights later evolved further at the hands of medieval thinkers such as Ockham and Gerson. Subsequent philosophical landmarks include the writings of the Spanish neo-scholastics, especially as they grappled with questions about the universality of natural rights thrown up by the European conquest of America. The idea was further developed in different ways by early modern philosophers such as Grotius and Hobbes. And it took centre stage during the Enlightenment period that stretched from the late seventeenth century to the end of the eighteenth, finding perhaps its most powerful and influential philosophical expression in the writings of Locke and Kant, and inspiring momentous political events such as the American and French Revolutions. There followed a period of stagnation and decline during which the idea of natural rights was assailed by proponents of utilitarianism, positivism, Marxism, and cultural relativism. However, the post-Second World War period has witnessed a tremendous revival of the doctrine, under the name now of 'human rights', use of which can already be traced to the eighteenth century—for example, in the French Declaration of the Rights of Man and of the Citizen (1789).

[25] Tierney 2004: 12. Contrast the view of Johannes Morsink, who sees appeal to a 'human essence' as decisively marking off the contemporary culture of human rights from the natural rights tradition, Morsink 2009: 32.

[26] For this sort of scepticism about 'welfare' rights, see Cranston 1962: 38. For the claim that virtually every major figure in the natural rights tradition recognizes a right of necessity, including Aquinas, Grotius, Locke, Hume, Kant, and Adam Smith, see Fleischacker 2004: chs 1–2.

The Universal Declaration of Human Rights (1948) (UDHR), which was in significant part a response to Nazi atrocities, gave a powerful impetus to this revival. Although
officially only hortatory in status, the UDHR has since been given legal effect by a series
of binding international treaties and customary norms. In addition, many national
constitutions are fashioned to give expression and force to human rights. Alongside
these legal and political instruments, a variety of international, regional, and domestic
institutions have emerged to interpret and apply human rights or to promote their fulfilment. Although the reliable enforcement of human rights worldwide remains a distant
goal, the discourse of human rights has acquired the status of an ethical *lingua franca* in
the contemporary world. Indeed, this has led to a problem of the 'proliferation' of human
rights claims, since there is now a great incentive to couch moral and political claims
in the rhetorically potent language of human rights.

But this potted history invites an important question. To what extent is the contemporary human rights culture really a continuation of the natural rights tradition? Is there
anything like a unitary concept at play here? Or does the transition from talk of 'natural
rights' to 'human rights' mark a significant shift in sense analogous to that which *ius
naturale* underwent when a notion of subjective rights emerged? The orthodox view is
that there is significant twofold commonality of sense in so far as both natural rights and
human rights are (a) moral rights possessed by all human beings simply in virtue of their
humanity, and (b) discoverable by 'natural' or ordinary moral reasoning as opposed to
the artificial reason of law or extra-rational deliverances of revelation. However, in
recent years, and largely influenced by John Rawls' *The Law of Peoples* (1999), a growing
number of philosophers have abandoned one or both of (a) and (b) in favour of what
may be called a 'political' concept of human rights that severs the link with the natural
rights tradition.

Critics of (a) invoke its supposed lack of fit with contemporary human rights practice.[27] Some interpret (a) as committed to trans-historically applicable human rights,
according to which the selfsame schedule of human rights must be attributable to all
human beings throughout human history. In particular, human rights must be ascriba-
ble to people even in a pre-political state of nature. Yet contemporary human rights
practice abounds with rights—to a fair trial, to an adequate standard of living, to citizenship and democratic political participation—that apparently presuppose the existence
or accessibility of broadly modern social conditions and institutions. Hence, the objection goes, (a) is under-inclusive as to rights that come under it (Beitz 2003; 2009: ch. 3).

One common response to this objection is to formulate a small number of highly
abstract rights of genuinely trans-historical scope, e.g. rights to life, liberty, etc., and to

---

[27] Those who reject (a) as a characterization of human rights tend to fall into two categories. Some
regard (a) as stating a necessary, but not a sufficient condition, for something being a human right. They
conceive of human rights as a subset of the general class of universal moral rights, e.g. Rawls 1999 and
Raz 2010. More radical rejections of (a) treat the notion of human rights as *sui generis*, hence one that
does not need to be explicated by reference to a background notion of universal moral rights, or even of
moral rights, e.g. Beitz 2009.

construe many of the more specific rights of the kind found in the Universal Declaration as applications of the abstract rights to the conditions of modernity (Griffin 2008: 38, 48–51).[28] But there is a real question whether the very abstract rights are genuinely universal *rights*, as opposed to universal human interests and, if they are rights, whether their content can be treated as meaningfully uniform across time. Another response is to deny that (a) entails trans-historical universality. Instead, human rights may be treated as rights possessed by all human beings, simply as human beings, within some specified historical period. Nor would this response be ad hoc. Although some natural rights theorists have subscribed to trans-historical universality, many others—perhaps the great majority— have not. This is arguably true not only of the pioneering medieval thinkers,[29] but also of important modern philosophers, such as Kant (see Simmons 2001: 186).

But even if (a) is interpreted as temporally constrained, some advocates of a political conception claim that it is over-inclusive as an account of human rights. There are potentially many (a)-type rights—such as the right not to be personally betrayed—which do not figure in any of the leading human rights instruments. These rights may be winnowed out by introducing an extra, political dimension into the concept of a human right. Human rights, it has been argued, perform distinctive political functions, such as imposing primary obligations on the officials of states, setting a benchmark for political legitimacy, and establishing triggers for international intervention in cases of sufficiently widespread and grave violations. This sets them apart from natural rights as classically conceived.

One key political role advanced by John Rawls is that human rights are defeasible triggers for military intervention, i.e. they are that subset of moral rights whose violation, if sufficiently widespread and grave, would generate a defeasible case for military action against the society perpetrating the violations. But this interpretation issues in an extremely parsimonious list of human rights, one that regards only Articles 3 to 18 of the UDHR as human rights proper, the remaining articles being consigned to the category of 'liberal aspirations'.[30] Such 'aspirations' include rights to non-discrimination on the grounds of sex, race, and religion; rights to freedom of opinion, speech, movement, and political participation, and rights to education, work, and an adequate standard of living. Other proponents of a political conception of human rights seek to remedy this under-inclusiveness through a more expansive account of the kind of intervention that is the distinguishing feature of human rights, one that encompasses forms of intervention (e.g. economic sanctions, public criticism, etc.) short of military action (see Raz 2010). Indeed, Charles Beitz's *The Idea of Human Rights* (2009) interprets human rights

---

[28] For the Lockean and Jeffersonian antecedents of this approach, see Haakonssen 1996: 50.

[29] '[T]he first rights theories were not derived from contemplation of the individual isolated from his fellows—isolé sur son île comme Robinson—but from reflection on the right ordering of human relationships in emerging societies' (Tierney 1997: 70).

[30] According to Rawls, the list of human rights comprises only: '[the] right to life (to the means of subsistence and security); to liberty (to freedom from slavery, serfdom, and forced occupation, and to a sufficient measure of liberty of conscience to ensure freedom of religion and thought); to property (personal property); and to formal equality as expressed by the rules of natural justice (that is, that similar cases be treated similarly)' (Rawls 1999: 65).

as norms whose violation generates a *pro tanto* reason for 'international concern', where intervention is just one manifestation of such concern among others.

The debate sparked by political conceptions of human rights is in its infancy (see Tasioulas 2009 and 2012). Some critics find it perplexing that human rights should be construed as *conceptually* tethered to something like the state or the state system. After all, are not anarchism and unitary world government, advanced on human rights grounds, perfectly *coherent* positions, regardless of how we judge their substantive merits?

The renunciation of claim (b) is an even more radical departure from the natural rights tradition.[31] But it is needed, according to Rawls, to ensure that human rights do not merely reflect parochial Western values.[32] Now, of course, the problem of parochialism in natural rights thought has traditionally been addressed, or pre-empted, precisely by insistence on (b). Different natural rights theorists have, of course, propounded different views of the precise nature of the relevant moral reasoning that grounds natural rights. For Grotius, natural rights are certain precepts that enable self-interested and sociable human beings to live harmoniously together in a social order; for Kant, by contrast, they possess an *a priori* basis independent of substantive judgements about both the nature of human ends and the most efficacious means of achieving them. Despite these differences, for both Grotius and Kant, no appeal to divine will is needed to grasp the existence of these rights.[33] But, for Rawls, this traditional claim to objective justification is itself irredeemably parochial since, as the disagreements among natural rights theorists themselves illustrate, reasonable people disagree radically about the appropriate standards of justification and whether any particular moral argument satisfies them. Accordingly, he conceives of his doctrine of human rights as part of a Law of Peoples grounded in a *public reason* rather than any comprehensive doctrine about God, human nature, or morality governed by ordinary standards of truth and justification:

> [Human rights] do not depend on any particular comprehensive religious doctrine or philosophical doctrine about human nature. The Law of Peoples does not say, for example, that human beings are moral persons and have equal worth in the eyes of God; or that they have certain moral and intellectual powers that entitle them to those rights. To argue in these ways would involve religious or philosophical doctrines that many decent hierarchical peoples might reject as liberal or democratic, or as in some way distinctive of Western political tradition and prejudicial to other cultures. Still, the Law of Peoples does not deny these doctrines. (Rawls 1999: 68)

According to Rawls, we can model the justification of human rights, along with the other principles of the Law of Peoples, in terms of a two-level social contract. At the first level, liberal democratic societies agree to the Law of Peoples, including its truncated list of human rights. At the second level, non-liberal but decent hierarchical

---

[31]   Rawls 1999; Nussbaum 2000b; Cohen 2004.

[32]   For a more radical rejection of (b), one that *embraces* the idea of an ethnocentric justification for human rights, see Rorty 1993.

[33]   Grotius famously wrote that the principles of natural law would remain valid 'though we should even grant, what without the greatest Wickedness cannot be granted, that there is no God, or that he takes no Care of Human affairs'. Grotius 1625: 89.

societies endorse the same principles. The fact that societies of the latter sort can agree to the doctrine of human rights is supposed to exonerate it from the charge of parochialism. But one may wonder whether it does have this effect. After all, the entire process starts from what *liberal* societies can agree to, and in deciding this appeal is made to a form of public reason that takes standards implicit in liberal democratic culture—in particular, the idea of fellow citizens as free and equal and prepared to cooperate on fair terms—simply as *given*. Does it adequately address the worry about parochialism that some hypothetical non-liberal societies can find their own way to embracing principles that owe their status to the fact that they are derived from liberal democratic values to begin with?

Others, persuaded of the need to reject (b), have sought to ground human rights in a more general doctrine of global public reason that does not prioritize liberal democratic values as Rawls does (Nussbaum 2000b; Cohen 2004). Their success or failure will influence whether we come to regard human rights as significantly discontinuous from the natural rights tradition. In this connection, it bears noting that—after an interval of more than half a century since the UDHR—the basis of human rights has moved to the centre of debate in moral and political philosophy. Philosophers engaged in this debate frequently deploy—often quite self-consciously—ideas with a rich historical pedigree. Some have argued that human rights need a theistic grounding (Wolterstorff 2008). More often, they have claimed that a secular foundation is available. In this vein, there has been a powerful revival of an 'Enlightenment' conception of human rights, one that shares with Locke and Kant the belief that equal freedom is in some sense the master idea in the justification of human rights. But these theorists differ amongst themselves as to the proper characterization of freedom, including whether it is best conceived as a component of a good life (e.g. Griffin 2008: ch. 2) or else in purely deontological terms (e.g. Nagel 2002: ch. 3 and Sen 2009: ch. 17). And then there are those who contend that freedom is but one among a plurality of values that ground human rights (Finnis 1980; Nickel 2007; Buchanan 2010: Part I; Tasioulas 2010).

Today, human rights are widely thought to be fundamental requirements of justice that give expression to the basic equality of all human beings. However, controversies as to both the nature and the foundations of such rights continue to persist. Are they essentially moral rights possessed by all human beings simply in virtue of their humanity? Or should we conceive of these rights in terms of some (combination of) political role(s)? Are they to be identified through ordinary, presumably truth-oriented, moral reasoning, or through the workings of an autonomous form of public reason? Central to the resolution of those controversies is the answer to a largely historical question: to what extent may we fruitfully conceive of human rights as essentially natural rights, and consequently regard our engagement with them a continuation of a tradition that extends back to the medieval canonists of the twelfth century?[34]

---

[34] For helpful written comments on earlier drafts which saved me from various errors I am indebted to Charles Beitz, Allen Buchanan, John Finnis, Tony Honore, George Letsas, Amia Srinivasan, and to the editor of this *Handbook*.

Bibliography

Aristotle c. 325BC. *Nicomachean Ethics*, tr. T. Irwin. Indianapolis, IN: Hackett, 1985. Also in *The Ethics of Aristotle*, tr. J. Thomson, rev. H. Tredennick. Harmondsworth: Penguin, 1976.

Beitz, C. 2003. 'What Human Rights Mean', *Daedalus* 132: 36–46.

—— 2009. *The Idea of Human Rights*. Oxford: Oxford University Press.

Bentham, J. 1983. *Deontology*, ed. A. Goldworth. Oxford: Clarendon Press.

—— 1987. 'Anarchical Fallacies', in J. Waldron (ed.), *Nonsense Upon Stilts: Bentham, Burke and Marx on the Rights of Man*. Oxford: Oxford University Press, 46–76.

Buchanan, A. 1982. *Marx and Justice: The Radical Critique of Liberalism*. Rowman & Littlefield.

—— 1987. 'Justice and Charity', *Ethics* 97: 558–75.

—— 2010. *Human Rights, Legitimacy, and the Use of Force*. Oxford: Oxford University Press.

Cicero 1961. *De Officiis* tr. W. Miller. Cambridge: Cambridge University Press.

—— 1971. *De Finibus* tr. H. Rackham. Cambridge: Cambridge University Press.

Cohen, G. A. 2000. *If You're an Egalitarian, How Come You're So Rich?* Cambridge, MA: Harvard University Press.

—— 2008. *Rescuing Justice and Equality*. Oxford: Oxford University Press.

Cohen, J. 2004. 'Minimalism about Human Rights: The Most We Can Hope For?', *Journal of Political Philosophy* 12: 190–213.

Cranston, M. 1962. *Human Rights Today*. London: Ampersand Books.

Dworkin, R. M. 1973. 'The Original Position', *University of Chicago Law Review* 40: 500–33.

Dworkin, R. M. 1977. *Taking Rights Seriously*. London: Duckworth.

—— 2006. *Is Democracy Possible Here?* Princeton: Princeton University Press.

Finnis, J. 1980. *Natural Law and Natural Rights*. Oxford: Oxford University Press.

—— 1998. *Aquinas: Moral, Political, and Legal Theory*. Oxford: Oxford University Press.

—— 2002. 'Aquinas on *ius* and Hart on Rights: A Response to Tierney', *The Review of Politics* 64: 407–10.

Fleischacker, S. 2004. *A Short History of Distributive Justice*. Cambridge, MA: Harvard University Press.

Freeman, S. 2007. *Rawls*. London: Routledge.

Glendon, M. A. 1991. *Rights Talk: The Impoverishment of Political Discourse*. New York: Free Press.

—— 2001. *A World Made New: Eleanor Roosevelt and the Universal Declaration of Human Rights*. New York: Random House.

Griffin, J. 2008. *On Human Rights*. Oxford: Oxford University Press.

Grotius, H. 1625. *The Rights of War and Peace, Book I*, ed. R. Tuck. Indianapolis, IN: Liberty Fund, Inc.

Haakonssen, K. 1991. 'From natural law to the rights of man: a European perspective on American debates', in M. J. Lacey and K. Haakonssen (eds), *A Culture of Rights: The Bill of Rights in Philosophy, Politics, and Law—1791 and 1991*. Cambridge: Cambridge University Press, 19–61.

—— 1996. *Natural Law and Moral Philosophy: From Grotius to the Scottish Enlightenment*. Cambridge: Cambridge University Press.

Hobbes, T. 1651. *Leviathan*, ed. R. Tuck. Cambridge: Cambridge University Press, 1996.

Hohfeld, W. N. 1919. *Fundamental Legal Conceptions*, ed. W. W. Cook. New Haven: Yale University Press.

Justinian, 1904. *The Digest*, tr. Charles Henry Monro vol. I. Cambridge: Cambridge University Press.

Kamm, F. M. 2007. *Intricate Ethics: Rights, Responsibilities, and Permissible Harm*. Oxford: Oxford University Press.

Kant, I. 1785. *Groundwork for the Metaphysic of Morals* [*Grundlegung zur Metaphysik der Sitten*], tr. and ed. T. E. Hill and A Zweig. Oxford: Oxford University Press, 2002.

——1797. *The Metaphysics of Morals* [*Metaphysik der Sitten*], ed. M. Gregor. Cambridge: Cambridge University Press, 1996, Part II.

Locke, J. 1988. *Two Treatises of Government*. Cambridge: Cambridge University Press.

Lucas, J.R. 1980. *On Justice*. Oxford: Oxford University Press.

MacIntyre, A. 2007. *After Virtue: A Study in Moral Theory*. 3rd edn. Notre Dame, IN: University of Notre Dame Press.

MacPherson, C. B. 1964. *The Political Theory of Possessive Individualism: Hobbes to Locke*. Oxford: Oxford University Press.

Martin, R. and Reidy, D. (eds) 2006. *Rawls's Law of Peoples: A Realistic Utopia*. Oxford: Blackwell Publishing.

Marx, K. 1977. 'The Jewish Question', in D. McLellan (ed.), *Karl Marx: Selected Writings*. Oxford: Oxford University Press, 21–53.

Mill, J. S. 1861. *Utilitarianism*, ed. R. Crisp. Oxford: Oxford University Press, 1998.

Miller, F. D., Jr. 1995. *Nature and Rights in Aristotle's Politics*. Oxford: Oxford University Press.

Minow, M. 1990. *Making All the Difference: Inclusion, Exclusion, and American Law*. Ithaca, NY: Cornell University Press.

Morsink, J. 1999. *The Universal Declaration of Human Rights: Origins, Drafting and Intent*. Philadelphia: University of Pennsylvania Press.

——2009. *Inherent Human Rights: Philosophical Roots of the Universal Declaration*. Philadelphia: University of Pennsylvania Press.

Nagel, T. 2002. *Concealment and Exposure and Other Essays*. Oxford: Oxford University Press.

Nickel, J. 2007. *Making Sense of Human Rights*. Second edition. Oxford: Blackwell Publishing.

Nietzsche, F. 1997. *Thus Spake Zarathrustra*, new ed. trans. W. Kaufmann. New York, Random House.

Nozick, R. 1974. *Anarchy, State, and Utopia*. Oxford: Blackwell Publishing.

Nussbaum, M. 1997. 'Kant and Stoic Cosmopolitanism', *Journal of Political Philosophy* 5: 1–25.

——2000a. 'Duties of Justice, Duties of Material Aid: Cicero's Problematic Legacy', *Journal of Political Philosophy* 8: 176–206.

——2000b. *Women and Human Development: The Capabilities Approach*. Oxford: Oxford University Press.

O'Neill, O. 1989. 'The Great Maxims of Justice and Charity', in *Constructions of Reason: Explorations of Kant's Political Philosophy*. Cambridge: Cambridge University Press, 219–324.

——1996. *Towards Justice and Virtue: A Constructive Account of Practical Reasoning*. Cambridge: Cambridge University Press.

——2005. 'The Dark Side of Human Rights', *International Affairs* 81: 427–39.

Pogge, T. 2002. *World Poverty and Human Rights*. Cambridge: Polity Press.

——2007. *John Rawls: His Life and Theory of Justice*. Oxford: Oxford University Press.

Pojman, L. 1997. 'On Equal Human Worth: A Critique of Contemporary Egalitarianism', in L. P. Pojman and R. Westmoreland (eds), *Equality: Selected Readings*. Oxford: Oxford University Press, 282–98.

Raphael, D. D. 2001. *Concepts of Justice*. Oxford: Oxford University Press.

Rawls, J. 1971/1999. *A Theory of Justice*. Revised edition. Oxford: Oxford University Press.

—— 1993. *Political Liberalism*. New York: Columbia University Press.

—— 1999. *The Law of Peoples with 'The Idea of Public Reason Revisited'*. Cambridge, MA: Harvard University Press.

Raz, J. 1986. *The Morality of Freedom*. Oxford: Oxford University Press.

—— 1994. *Ethics in the Domain*. Oxford: Oxford University Press.

—— 2010. 'Human Rights without Foundations', in S. Besson and J. Tasioulas (eds), *The Philosophy of International Law*. Oxford: Oxford University Press, 321–37.

Rorty, R. 1993. 'Human Rights, Rationality and Sentimentality', in S. Shute and S. L. Hurley (eds), *On Human Rights: The Oxford Amnesty Lectures, 1993*. New York: Basic Books, 111–34.

Sandel, M. 2009. *Justice: What's the Right Thing to Do?* London: Allen Lane.

Scheffler, S. 2003. 'What is Egalitarianism?', *Philosophy and Public Affairs* 31: 5–39.

Schneewind, J. 1997. 'The Misfortunes of Virtue', in R. Crisp and M. Slote (eds), *Virtue Ethics*. Oxford: Oxford University Press, 178–200.

—— 1998. *The Invention of Autonomy: A History of Modern Moral Philosophy*. Cambridge: Cambridge University Press.

Sen, A. 2009. *The Idea of Justice*. London: Penguin.

Simmons, A. J. 2001. 'Human Rights and World Citizenship', in *Justification and Legitimacy: Essays on Rights and Obligations*. Cambridge: Cambridge University Press, 179–96.

Singer, P. 1993. *Practical Ethics*. Second edition. Cambridge: Cambridge University Press.

Smith, A. 1790/2009. *The Theory of Moral Sentiments*. London: Penguin Books.

Strauss, L. 1953. *Natural Right and History*. Chicago: University of Chicago Press.

Tasioulas, J. 2009. 'Are Human Rights Essentially Triggers for Intervention?', *Philosophy Compass* 4: 938–50.

—— 2010. 'Taking Rights out of Human Rights', *Ethics* 120: 647–78.

—— 2012. 'On the Nature of Human Rights', in G. Ernst and J.-C. Heilinger (eds), *The Philosophy of Human Rights: Contemporary Controversies*. Berlin: Walter de Gruyter, 17–59.

Tierney, B. 1997. *The Idea of Natural Rights: Studies on Natural Rights, Natural Law, and Church Law 1150–1625*. Grand Rapids, Michigan: William B. Eerdmans Pub. Co.

—— 2004. 'The Idea of Natural Rights: Origins and Persistence', *Northwestern Journal of International Human Rights* 2: 2–12.

Tuck, R. 1979. *Natural Rights Theories: Their Origin and Development*. Cambridge: Cambridge University Press.

Villey, M. 1964. 'La genèse du droit subjectif chez Guillaume d'Occam', *Archives de Philosophie du Droit* 9: 97–127.

Waldron, J. 2002. *God, Locke, and Equality: Christian Foundations in Locke's Political Thought*. Cambridge: Cambridge University Press.

Walzer, M. 1983. *Spheres of Justice*. New York: Basic Books.

Wiggins, D. 2006. *Ethics: Twelve Lectures on the Philosophy of Morality*. London: Penguin.

—— 2008. *Solidarity and the Root of the Ethical*. Lawrence, Kansas: University of Kansas.

Williams, B. 2005. 'The Idea of Equality', in *In the Beginning Was the Deed: Realism and Moralism in Political Argument*. Princeton: Princeton University Press, 97–114.

Wolterstorff, N. 2008. *Justice: Rights and Wrongs*. Princeton: Princeton University Press.

Wood, A. 1999. *Kant's Ethical Thought*. Cambridge: Cambridge University Press.

—— 2008. *Kantian Ethics*. Cambridge: Cambridge University Press.

CHAPTER 37

....

STYLES OF MORAL RELATIVISM: A CRITICAL FAMILY TREE

....

MIRANDA FRICKER

37.1 CUSTOM IS KING—THE SIGNIFICANCE OF MORAL DIVERSITY

....

CASTING an eye back over the history of moral relativist thinking, one can discern a number of different branches to the family tree, each representing a different impetus to relativism, and so producing a different style of moral relativist thought. At root, however, is a broadly subjectivist parent idea, namely that morality is at least in part the upshot of a shared way of life, and shared ways of life tend to vary markedly from culture to culture. Differences of custom have been observed since the beginning of history. A well-known passage from Herodotus, the ancient Greek historian, in which he tells a story about Darius, King of the Persians, gives us an indication of how long human beings have been aware of, and intrigued or disconcerted by, the fact of moral difference:

> When he was king of Persia, he summoned the Greeks who happened to be present at his court, and asked them what they would take to eat the dead bodies of their fathers. They replied that they would not do it for any money in the world. Later, in the presence of the Greeks, and through an interpreter, so that they could understand what was said, he asked some Indians, of the tribe called Callatiae, who do in fact eat their parents' dead bodies, what they would take to burn them. They uttered a cry of horror and forbade him to mention such a dreadful thing. (Herodotus 440BCE; tr. Sélincourt 1988: 219–20)[1]

---

[1] This passage is frequently quoted: see, for instance, Levy 2002: 89; and Baghramian 2004: 21–2.

Why might an awareness of moral diversity prompt the relativist conclusion that morality itself is relative to culture? (Or, in the terms sometimes used, why might an awareness of descriptive relativism prompt an inference to metaethical relativism?) It does so principally on the assumption that in the moral domain the best explanation of diversity is relativity. Accordingly, there is a tendency to read moral relativism off the surface of foreign moral practices. However, this tendency is dangerous, for 'moral practices'—in the straightforward sense of what goes on apparently within the bounds of the morality of a given culture—can be a matter merely of what certain types can get away with, and others have resigned themselves to, rather than what the collective endorses as morally permissible, let alone good. This question of endorsement has been raised in stark form by Mary Midgley in a discussion of the Samurai custom of *tsujigiri*, and Midgley's point is further developed by Michele Moody-Adams (Midgley 1981; Moody-Adams 1997). As the story goes, there was a custom among medieval Japanese Samurai of 'trying out' one's sword before battle, by testing its capability of slicing through a human torso with one blow. This test is said to have been inflicted at random on the hapless passer-by.

On the face of it, this might plausibly be presented as an example of just how radically different foreign or historically distant practices can be within the moral. It is the sort of example that is often used to expose our latent relativist sympathies by prompting the thought, 'What was morally appropriate for a medieval Samurai is radically different from what is morally appropriate for anyone in our culture.' As Moody-Adams argues, however, this is a perfidious line of thought, for it begs the question by assuming that such arbitrary slaughter on the part of a Samurai *was* morally appropriate for him in his time. That is to say, it makes the unwarranted assumption that there were not articulate moral points of view from which the practice might have been challenged—people with social experiences that equipped them with adequate critical tools to protest the practice in its own time.

Moody-Adams expresses agreement with Midgley in this connection, affirming that 'as Midgley suggests, the assumption that there was uniform cultural approval of the practice requires a further, problematic assumption: that endangered passersby would have generally *consented* to be sacrificed to the ritual' (Moody-Adams 1997: 82). While consent may not be quite the issue—after all, I might withhold consent to many a moral practice my better judgement would endorse—still the general point is well taken. The worry about assuming that the existence of a certain bloody practice on the part of Samurai warriors in medieval Japan signals the moral acceptability of that practice in medieval Japan, is that this assumption may amount to little more than a way of siding with the abuser. As Neil Levy puts the point, 'we can appreciate the force of the claim that relativism sides with the strong against the weak. If we conclude that *tsujigiri* is permissible in medieval Japan, we are allowing the rapacious Samurai to dictate what counts as morality for everyone' (Levy 2002: 112). This is well put; indeed we should acknowledge, further, that the Samurai may have had the social power to get away with the abuse in a double sense, not only getting away with it in practice, but also in collective conscience, in so far as there may have been no collective hermeneutical habit of challenging it by naming it as brutal, dishonourable, murderous, or otherwise wrong. In such a situation, Samurai warriors would effectively possess the power to pre-emptively silence dissent, and so to *constitutively construct* their sword-testing killings as morally acceptable in their time—to make the practice *count as* morally acceptable. But this does not mean that it was, even then.

In any case, we should acknowledge that the scenario of such successful constitutive construction is improbable. The Samurai very likely did not have quite that kind of power, for as Midgley suggests, there would not have been sufficiently widespread moral endorsement of the practice, explicit or tacit. Certainly the soon-to-be murdered party would not have endorsed it in any way, or anyone else likely to share his interests, either because they cared about him personally, or because they could see that they were at similar risk, or could imaginatively identify with those at risk. Such elementary exercises of the moral imagination were surely not beyond the folk who cohabited the medieval Samurai 'moral culture'. And there's the rub: what supposed 'moral culture' are we talking about here? Did these roaming, sword-wielding individuals really belong to an integrated and self-contained moral culture that cast their practices as honourable; or should we suspect this to be a fantasy of the relativist imagination? Moody-Adams makes a powerful case against the habit of positing 'moral cultures' conceived in this way as fully integrated and self-contained systems, for such monoliths are incompatible with the fact that the discursive space of morality is essentially contested:

> Even traditional societies generate 'liminal' space (however ritually structured) that creates room for various kinds of cultural criticism. Any effort at transhistorical moral inquiry and reflection implicitly appeals to this liminal 'cultural space' for moral criticism. (Moody-Adams 1997: 85)

Moody-Adams is surely right to suspect that some relativist writers are bewitched by exoticism. If one looks to grubbier examples in the present, such as the organized thuggery of the Sicilian mafia or the Chinese Triads operating in many cities today, there is far less temptation to infer moral equality for something called the 'mafia moral culture' supposedly owned not only by the mafia themselves but also their victims. Real, evolving moral cultures are never disconnected from the dissenting voices of those on the losing end, however muffled some of them might be. This is key to understanding why morality is an essentially critical domain in which many, often conflicting, points of view are fit for articulation. That is why we cannot automatically read deep moral difference off the surface of foreign moral practices.

All this reminds us that one must be very careful about what to infer, if anything, from the observation of surface differences of custom. Accordingly we must be equally careful about attributing such inferences to others. Michel de Montaigne is standardly interpreted as implicitly making just such an inference to relativism; but we shall see that the relativist's pretension to him as a sixteenth-century French ancestor involves a careless leap of genealogy. Montaigne was the first essayist. He coined the term *essai*—literally, an 'attempt'—in order to create a self-effacing rhetorical space in which to express his reflections, always insisting he was merely writing about himself, with no aspiration to authoritative comment on anything outside. Though the essays are unquestionably a self-portrait, the declared aim of mere self-revelation, combined with his stance of beguiling irony, allowed Montaigne to publicize his bold output without serious risk of being judged impious before God. In 'Of Cannibals', he does, as is so often observed, emphasize diversity of moral custom in a way that echoes Herodotus; and the essay apparently strikes many philosopher-readers, with an ear trained to pick up on anything sounding a bit like a metaethical thesis, as an oblique argument for the idea that custom is all there is to morality. Not just descriptive relativism, then, but metaethical relativism too. Neil Levy, for instance, introduces perhaps the most frequently quoted sentence from Montaigne as follows:

> Reflecting on this diversity, many European intellectuals came to precisely the same conclusion as had Herodotus before them. Moral disagreements reflect the differ- ences between local customs, no more and no less. Thus, for example, Michel de Montaigne... reacts to reports of widespread cannibalism by just such a relativism. 'I think there is nothing barbarous and savage in that nation, from what I have been told, except that each man calls barbarism whatever is not his own practice; for indeed it seems we have no other test of truth and reason than the example and pat- tern of the opinions and customs of the country we live in'. (Levy 2002: 91)

Moody-Adams also brings in Montaigne as a relativist:

> 'Each man calls barbarism whatever is not his own practice,' Montaigne claimed, because 'we have no other test of truth and reason than the example and pattern of the opinions and customs of the country we live in'... Montaigne's observation reminds us that relativism about diverse moral practices is not a new development. (Moody-Adams 1997: 13)

Maria Baghramian too reads Montaigne as a relativist, though she is careful to relate the relativism to his deep-seated Pyrrhonian scepticism, introducing him as 'The most notable proponent of both scepticism and relativism in the early modern period', and rightly emphasizing his combination of interest in diversity of customs with tolerance (Baghramian 2004: 51). Steven Lukes, despite a sensitivity to the ambivalence in Montaigne's essay, ultimately characterizes Montaigne as a relativist with inconsistently universalistic tendencies (Lukes 2008: 31–2). With the exception of David Wiggins, who interprets Montaigne in what I believe to be the right spirit—that is, not as a relativist but as a sceptical essayist keen to emphasize the cardinal importance of cultural context when it comes to morals[2]—it seems that in much philosophical discussion Montaigne has been pinned not only as an important influence in relativistic thinking about moral- ity (which indeed he seems to have become), but as himself advancing moral relativism. This last is however very unfortunate, since Montaigne does no such thing.

That such a rigid interpretation would falsify Montaigne's playful text is indicated even by the sentence immediately following the one so often quoted. The indicative

---

[2] 'The philosophical point of paying heed to Montaigne's essay... is for us to study the interpretive power of contextualism as Montaigne practises it, and to perceive the reach of criticism across difference and the reach of agreement over difference' (Wiggins 2006: 349).

sentence in question mockingly qualifies 'the country we live in' with the sardonic rejoinder: 'There we always see the perfect religion, the perfect political system, the perfect and most accomplished way of doing everything' (Montaigne 1958: 109). Montaigne's point in the much-quoted sentence is not that there are no universal or absolute standards for what is morally right. Rather, he is delivering a sceptical jibe at how his fellow countrymen tend to be hopelessly chauvinistic when it comes to making sense of the customs of cultures alien to their own—a disappointment to be understood in the context of his more general sceptical opinion that such epistemic failure characterizes the human condition. Part of the general diagnosis he offers is that we are too often dependent upon unreliable testimony. Indeed the essay opens with this theme, and recounts the story of Pyrrhus, King of Epirus, as he encountered the well-ordered Roman army for the first time:

> King Pyrrhus remarked: 'I do not know what barbarians these are'—for so the Greeks called all foreign nations—'but the ordering of the army before me has nothing barbarous about it.'...We can see from this how chary we must be of subscribing to vulgar opinions; we should judge them by the test of reason and not by common report. (Montaigne 1958: 105)

Naturally, Montaigne's overall purpose becomes clearer as the essay progresses. Indeed the essay ultimately makes it plain that it has nothing to do with advancing the metaethical thesis of relativism, or indeed any metaethical thesis. On the contrary, the essay is primarily a barbed lament directed against the hypocrisy of his own nation, which he finds not only too quick to judge foreign customs, but also culpably disinclined to turn its critical gaze upon itself and confront the horrifying excesses of a France wracked by religious civil war. The ironically fantasized *Other* to contemporary French consciousness in Montaigne's discussion is that recent addition to the European imagination, the intriguing savages of the New World. The practices at home which Montaigne is primarily concerned to bring to the reader's attention (about which he is notably candid, if brief, in contrast to the digressive pace and twinkling irony of much of the essay) are those most grotesque forms of violence perpetrated against the living in the brutal hostilities between Catholic and Huguenot parties. Acknowledging fully the moral abhorrence of cannibalism, he none the less dares to find that when understood in the light of reason it turns out to compare rather favourably with these home-grown abominations:

> I am not so anxious that we should note the horrible savagery of these acts as concerned that, whilst judging their faults so correctly, we should be so blind to our own. I consider it more barbarous to eat a man alive than to eat him dead; to tear by rack and torture a body still full of feeling, to roast it by degrees, and then give it to be trampled and eaten by dogs and swine—a practice which we have not only read about but seen within recent memory, not between ancient enemies, but between neighbours and fellow-citizens and, what is worse, under the cloak of piety and religion—than to roast and eat a man after he is dead. (Montaigne 1958: 113)

To hammer the point home—making it still more abundantly clear, incidentally, that he is entirely open to the making of non-relative moral judgements, whether about the alleged customs of the New World or those of the old, and in the name of reason to boot—he adds: 'We are justified therefore in calling these people barbarians by reference to the laws of reason, but not in comparison with ourselves, who surpass them in every kind of barbarity' (Montaigne 1958: 114). People who live in glass houses...

'Of Cannibals' employs an ironic conceit whereby the author poses as primarily interested in vindicating the alien customs of the New World (amusingly romanticized by Montaigne[3]) when in fact his main interest is in criticizing barbarism at home. Although the essay, as Lukes rightly observes, contains 'relativist-sounding passages' (Lukes 2008: 32), at least to the analytical ear; none of these in fact forms any part of a case for moral relativism. The real point of the essay is neither moral-cultural description, nor metaethical thesis. Its message is above all political, for Montaigne's primary purpose is to get away with making a political point about the horrors of his own distressed country. While the discussion of cannibalism reflects a genuine interest in the significance of moral diversity, it equally serves as a conceit that permits Montaigne to hold up a salutary mirror to a hypocritical French nation. Contrary, then, to a philosophical *idée reçue*, the sage of Gascony was not a relativist.

With Montaigne duly pruned from our family tree of moral relativism (though not, one hopes, thereby removed from philosophical attention), let us retrace our finger back to an ancient progenitor other than Herodotus, with a view to identifying more genuine branches.

37.2 MAN IS THE MEASURE— SUBJECTIVIST ROOTS

Now, Protagoras, 'Man is the measure of all things' as you people say—of white and heavy and light and all that kind of thing without exception. He has the criterion of these things within himself; so when he thinks that they are as he experiences them, he thinks what is true and what really is for him. (Plato 1997: 178b; quoted in Baghramian 2004: 26)

Protagoras is generally taken as the ancient origin for a different style of moral relativism, not this time the style inspired by the observation of moral-cultural differences read off as deep, but one inspired rather by something more purely philosophical: the proposition that properties taken to be objective features of the world are 'really' the product of human sensibility—the work of a 'criterion' within the subject.[4] Various interpretations

---

[3] Quoting Seneca, Montaigne imagines Plato full of admiration for the simple way of life led by the people of the New World: 'How far from such perfection would he find the republic that he imagined: "men fresh from the hands of the gods"' (Montaigne 1958: 110).

[4] See, however, Richard Bett for the view that not only were the Sophists not generally relativists, but that *pace* Plato even Protagoras should probably not be taken as a relativist. Bett emphasizes Sextus' interpretation, which he summarizes: 'Protagoras held that things are really, in themselves, all the various

of the dictum are attributable to Protagoras via Plato, for it expresses a promiscuous subjectivism equally amenable to liaison with sensory experience, knowledge, truth, objects, and justice.[5] The immediate upshot in relation to any of these is that what may seem objective to us is *really* subjective, and perhaps that we are actively misled in this by the innately objectivizing nature of our experiences. Descendants from this kind of sub-jectivism are surely many, no doubt appropriately traced by way of Hobbes' famous assertion:

> But whatsoever is the object of any mans Appetite or Desire; that is it, which he for his part calleth *Good*: And the object of his Hate, and Aversion, *Evill*; And of his Contempt. *Vile* and *Inconsiderable*. For these words of Good, Evill, and Contemptible, are ever used with relation to the person that useth them: There being nothing sim-ply and absolutely so. (Hobbes 1991: 39)

Subsequent subjectivists have tended to be moved by a sense, first, of the contrast between primary and secondary qualities, the latter alone displaying a dependence on human sensibility that calls for the label 'subjective'; combined, second, with a sense that secondary qualities and moral properties are analogous in terms of their metaphysics and epistemology. Most notably, Hume's moral subjectivism was fundamentally inspired by this combination of commitments, as was Mackie's after him;[6] though importantly, Hume was no moral relativist, his emphasis being on the extensive repertoire of humanly universal 'natural virtues', which contrasts with a small number of socially constructed 'artificial virtues' that prove the rule. Mackie did not quite argue for relativism either, though there was surely room for it, given his view of morality as 'invention'. Subjectivism about moral value provides a fertile basis for moral relativism, but there can be no par-thenogenesis. Something further is required.

   This subjectivist tradition in moral philosophy does ultimately bring forth a range of historically significant relativist positions in twentieth-century moral philosophy, though here the tree divides into two branches. We might label these *Moral Historicism*, and *Moral Reasons*. The historicist line finds its prime advocate in Bernard Williams, though it would (as ever) be artificial to represent him as a lone voice in this regard. Notably one might mention Richard Rorty under the moral historicist head, as he often uses 'historicist' to characterize his brand of relativistic pragmatism. Rorty's interest in history is, however, more *a priori* than historical, for his historicism falls out of a general sceptical stance towards all things presented as objective or universal. For this reason I shall discuss his view under the head of *Moral Truth*—a prior branching in our family tree, stemming not from the local subjectivism about value mentioned above, but from a

---

ways they are perceived as being by different people…And this makes Protagoras not a relativist but, as E. R. Dodds long ago pointed out, "an extreme realist" ' (Bett 1989: 167).

   [5] See Baghramian 2004: 1.2.

   [6] 'Take any action allow'd to be vicious…The vice entirely escapes you, as long as you consider the object…It lies in yourself, not in the object…Vice and virtue, therefore, may be compar'd to sounds, colours, heat and cold, which, according to modern philosophy, are not qualities in objects, but perceptions in the mind' (Hume 1975: 468–9). Mackie 1977: ch. 1.

subjectivism with global scope, under which morality is subsumed along with every other domain of human cognition. Rorty makes a double contrast with Williams because, first, Williams' moral relativism is derived from a localized subjectivism specifically about value properties, and second, his interest in history derives from an imaginative engagement with the past (notably that of ancient Greek culture) combined with a historically informed sense of the differences between ancient and modern.[7] Our historicist branch, then, leads us to Williams' moral relativism—the 'relativism of distance'.

37.3 MORAL HISTORICISM

I have introduced Williams in relation to a broadly Humean subjectivism about value, but it is instructive to note that he labels his own view negatively rather than positively, using instead the term 'non-objectivist'. He has good reason, for he aims to distance it from some of the theses associated with the broad label 'subjectivist'. Firstly, the term 'subjectivist' can indicate a semantic thesis about the meaning of moral sentences—that they report, express, or merely evince a moral sentiment—and Williams does not want to commit himself to any such thing (nor did Mackie, who for the same reason preferred to describe his view as a kind of moral 'scepticism'). Secondly, subjectivism is commonly associated with the denial of moral truth and knowledge, but Williams gives a positive account of these things, albeit in non-objectivist terms. That is to say, moral knowledge is knowledge *within* an ethical outlook, and is gained through the correct application of the thick ethical concepts proper to that outlook. (Thick ethical concepts are moral concepts of the kind effectively introduced by Philippa Foot in a defence of the reasoned nature of moral arguments.[8] In Williams' treatment, they are further explained as ethical concepts that are not only 'action-guiding' but also 'world-guided' in that they have sufficiently substantial empirical content to permit robust conditions of application.[9]) Williams' relativism of distance is intriguingly allied with moral cognitivism, and thereby with much of what relativism is normally conceived as threatening to undermine.

What is Williams' view? His early statement, given in 'The Truth in Relativism' and adhered to later in *Ethics and the Limits of Philosophy*, remains the marker, as he never deviated from its basic argument: the truth in relativism is that over a certain kind of historical distance, specified in the idea of a merely 'notional confrontation' between

---

[7] This interest permeates much of Williams' work, but see in particular *Shame and Necessity* (Williams 1993).

[8] See Foot 1958. See also Iris Murdoch: 'if we picture the agent as compelled by obedience to the reality he can see, he will not be saying "This is right", i.e., "I choose to do this", he will be saying "This is A B C D" (normative-descriptive words), and action will follow naturally' (Murdoch 1970: 42).

[9] Williams rejects Hare's prescriptivist account of moral concepts, which presents their descriptive and evaluative aspects as separable components. Instead he favours the view that these aspects are not separable, and in a note credits this idea to Murdoch and Foot (Williams 1985: 218 n. 7).

two moral cultures, moral appraisal becomes inappropriate, because too much of its normal point is missing (Williams 1981 and 1985). Two moral cultures or 'systems' are in notional confrontation when they fail to be in 'real confrontation' (when one is not a 'real option' for a group of people in the other). That is, if a group from one system could not go over to the moral outlook of the other—really living it out in practice, with the associated moral psychology becoming internalized as their own way of life—then the relation between the two moral systems is not one of real confrontation, but merely notional confrontation. In a situation such as this, moral appraisal cannot play its essential role as part of deciding how one should live, and so becomes inappropriate:

> A relativist view of a given type of outlook can be understood as saying that for such outlooks it is only in real confrontations that the language of appraisal—good, bad, right, wrong, and so on—can be applied to them; in notional confrontations, this kind of appraisal is seen as inappropriate, and no judgments are made. (Williams 1985: 161)

Although in the early paper he did not rule out the possibility of synchronic notional confrontations over cultural distance, he makes it explicit in the later discussion in *Ethics and the Limits of Philosophy* and elsewhere that in the modern era there can be no synchronic application of relativism: 'Relativism over merely spatial distance is of no interest or application in the modern world. Today all confrontations between cultures must be real confrontations' (Williams 1985: 163). The only kind of distance that makes for an application of moral relativism, then, is historical distance: 'Many outlooks that human beings have had are not real options for us now. The life of a Bronze Age chief or a medieval samurai are not real options for us: there is no way of living them' (Williams 1985: 161).

The structure of the relativism of distance, then, is preconditional: real confrontation is a precondition of appropriate moral appraisal, so that over notional confrontation moral appraisal is inappropriate, and relativism applies. This structure allows the relativism to be expressed without self-refutation, for it avoids saying anything that would undermine the expression of the relativist thesis itself. By contrast, forms of relativism that infer from a premise of descriptive relativism a conclusion that it is morally wrong to pass moral judgement on other cultures are famously embroiled in self-refutation, for their very assertion of moral relativism is delivered as a non-relative moral claim. Williams levels this charge of self-refutation at the view he invents for the purpose, 'vulgar relativism'; and some such charge is also, famously, the core of Plato's much-discussed attack on Protagoras.[10] What is especially significant about the relativism of distance is its ability to maintain so much of what moral realists hope to preserve from the objectivizing character of ethical experience and argument: moral truth, moral facts, moral knowledge, moral rationality. In Williams' relativism these things are not *as if, quasi,* or otherwise *ersatz,* but authentic. The availability of moral truth is the key. An unembarrassed commitment to the possibility of moral truth became historically available

---

[10] See Williams 1972: 20; and Plato 1997 (*Theaetatus* 170d–171c). For a helpful discussion of the structure of Plato's charge, see Baghramian 2004: 1.3.

owing to that moment in metaphysics which saw the arrival of various forms of deflationism or minimalism about truth, rendering it as a metaphysically undemanding predicate.[11] From then on, moral propositions could be represented as straightforwardly truth-apt without needing to posit any 'queer' action-guiding moral truthmakers, rubbing along as part of the 'fabric of the world', to use Mackie's evocative terms (Mackie 1977: 15).

Putting this together with the comparatively uncontested idea that there can be moral beliefs, it becomes quickly apparent that moral knowledge too is possible, even on Williams' non-objectivism about value—just plug in the preferred conception of warrant, and there you have it. *We* can now know that caning schoolboys is abusive, or that coerced sexual intercourse in marriage is rape; *the Elizabethans* could know that Queen Elizabeth was chaste, or not, as the case may be. This, as I see things, is how Williams' distinctive historicism kicks in. Moral knowledge, on his conception, is fundamentally a kind of knowledge that constructs a collective way of life; and ways of life change through history. This means that the Elizabethans' moral knowledge of their queen is only available to us in so far as 'chaste' is still one of *our* moral concepts. If it is not (and on the whole it isn't) then we could not know *as a piece of moral knowledge* that Elizabeth had the virtue of chastity. It is transformed into an item, rather, of plain historical knowledge about *their* ethical way of life.[12] We might say that when an item of moral knowledge is put out of our reach in this way—Williams, perhaps provocatively, says 'destroyed'— what history and reflection have removed from our lives, for good or ill, is the ethical force of the concept. As I see it, we can still apply the concept 'chaste' all right, imaginatively grasping its past role in disciplining female sexuality and conserving male heredity, or at any rate knowing it used to be a female virtue; but we can no longer do so with its ethical force intact. That is to say, the concept no longer occupies the same place in our affective economy—it is no longer generally apt, for instance, to inspire feelings of shame in the agent, or of moral disapproval in others. (We might, for instance, think it highly unlikely Elizabeth was chaste, but be glad for her, and admire her genius in making the lurid obsession with female virginity work a little to her advantage in a gender-performative cult of the Virgin Queen.)

But where does this leave us in relation to the most compellingly universal moral examples, such as the practice of slavery? In what sense, if any, might we reasonably judge ancient Greek slavery to be unjust or otherwise morally wrong if the ancients— free and enslaved alike—did not conceive it as such? Wiggins asked this sort of question in a way that resonated critically with Williams. He put the issue in terms of a defence of moral cognitivism to the effect that 'there is *nothing else to think* but that slavery is unjust and insupportable' (Wiggins 1991: 70). The challenge to this cognitivism, however, which Wiggins himself raises, is 'how to demonstrate the necessity to *speak* in this connection

[11] See Wiggins 1987; Wright 1992: ch. 5; and the papers (including those by Wright and Williams) in Hooker 1996. For more background on minimalism, see Horwich 1998.

[12] Williams does not quite say this, but I believe it is a corollary of his view. I argue the point more fully in Fricker 2000.

of "injustice"—or even of "slavery"?' (Wiggins 1991: 78). That is, how to argue against the historicist claim that careful historical interpretation will sometimes reveal that even if there is nothing else to think now, there surely *was* something else to think back then, for there is no trans-historical necessity to bring the practice of slavery under these sorts of moral concepts, or perhaps any moral concepts. Wiggins' answer to this envisaged challenge is to say that 'the opponent... would have himself to show the workability of the scheme of moral ideas that dispenses in the face of phenomena such as the slave trade and its historical effects with ideas like "justice", "slavery", "using human beings as means not ends", etc.'. But then, in relation to this answer, it must be acknowledged that Williams did go on to make just such a robust historical case for the view that the Greeks thought of slavery not in such moralized terms at all, but rather conceived it primarily as a practically *necessary* institution, and as a calamitous piece of *bad luck* for those individuals who are born or become enslaved:

> Slavery was taken to be necessary—necessary, that is to say, to sustaining the kind of political, social, and cultural life that free Greeks enjoyed. Most people did not suppose that because slavery was necessary, it was therefore just... The effect of the necessity was, rather, that life proceeded on the basis of slavery and left no space, effectively, for the question of its justice to be raised. (Williams 1993: 124)

Williams' relativist cognitivism staunchly resisted the sort of trans-historical universalism about even such moral fundamentals as slavery that Wiggins' non-relativist (though always contextualist) cognitivism asserts. Although Williams' relativism presents no obstacle to an assertion in the now that Greek slavery was unjust (or brutal, or cruel—there is no dependence here on Williams' view that the concept of injustice is a special case[13]), the point is he regarded it as senseless to insist, beyond this, that the Greeks themselves should have regarded slavery as we do. Any such insistence could only figure as a piece of moralism, deriving either from specific historical ignorance, or else a general narcissistic refusal to acknowledge that there really have been other ways of life different from our own.

Williams' relativism of distance, then, is part of a thoroughgoing historicism governing the existence of ethical value and availability of ethical knowledge for people in their time. The relativist thesis itself (the idea that moral appraisal is inappropriate over notional confrontation) is born of a dislike for the moralism that leads us to engage in moral appraisal over historical distances that do not sustain appraisal's normal point. We could not go over to the Greek moral outlook, for the question of the moral status of slavery *has* arisen for us, and once it has arisen there is no going back; and, further, the answer to the question of the moral status of slavery is obvious, so that *now* there is indeed '*nothing else to think* but that slavery is unjust and insupportable'. An interest in the contingency and hence plurality of moral practices is at the heart of Williams' historicism, but not in the sense we rehearsed at the outset with Herodotus, which is taken

---

[13] He considered the concept of (in)justice to be applicable even over notional confrontation, and so an exceptional case; see Williams 1985: 166.

to suggest we should be so impressed by the astonishing diversity of moral customs that moral consciousness can but retreat into its own cultural shell. The relativism of distance is not a direct upshot of being impressed by moral diversity *per se*, for there is an indefinite amount of synchronic moral diversity across cultures in relation to which this relativism refuses application. The view is rather a reflective acknowledgement that over notional confrontation the practical point and therefore propriety of moral appraisal goes missing, owing to the fact that precisely at that distance, past moral practices become irrelevant to moral deliberation. At root, the relativism of distance is an oblique assertion of the idea—the signature Socratic idea with which *Ethics and the Limits of Philosophy* opens—that the fundamental question is how one should live. Williams' relativism effectively indexes moral appraisal to its primary role in contributing to ongoing practical deliberation; and that is, most fundamentally, why he casts those ways of life to which we could not convert even if we wanted to as inappropriate objects of our moral appraisal.

I have argued elsewhere that the way Williams characterizes the distinction between real and notional confrontations does not draw the line of distance in the place he wants (Fricker 2010). The condition of real confrontation, that we could reconstruct the past outlook and live it for real in the present, is extremely socially and psychologically demanding, so that just about any past outlook lands outside the remit of appropriate moral appraisal—which is not what he intends. But, more than this, the question must also be asked: why should the possibility of moral conversion stand as a condition on appropriate moral appraisal? I have explained Williams' reason as I understand it above; but I do not believe it is justified to confine practices of moral appraisal to the primary purpose of deciding how to live—of deciding, as he often puts it, 'what to do about' the cultural practice in question. Moral appraisal has other functions besides that one, not least the interpretive function of making sense of the past—ironically, a signature Williams concern. My suspicion is that the basic motive for the relativism of distance, namely Williams' anti-moralism in relation to the past, would be better handled directly by specific critical attention to forms of moralism themselves. This would allow him to attack them not for appraising what he must implausibly allege is simply beyond the remit of moral appraisal, but only for the moralism itself—whether it be the moralism of historically insensitive moral interpretation, or of excessive focus on the moral to the exclusion of other forms of value, or again that of blame being inappropriately directed towards individuals from the past.

Let us now leave the *Moral Historicism* branch of our family tree to trace a finger along the branch concerned with *Moral Reasons*. Here we meet Gilbert Harman's conventionalist relativism, which was first advanced contemporarily with Williams' historicist relativism, but which, despite a certain structural similarity, contrasts with it in many crucial respects. Most obviously, while the relativism of distance allowed that synchronic moral appraisal is always appropriate even between cultures with few shared moral concepts and reasons, the relativist position advanced by Harman posits shared reasons as a condition of all appropriate moral appraisal.

37.4 Moral Reasons

Harman's relativism is explicitly motivated by the question of shared reasons for action, or what in his early statement he called 'shared motivational attitudes' (Harman 1982). In that paper he presents his relativism as a hypothesis about the 'logical form' of sentences containing a distinctively moral use of 'ought'. He distinguishes four uses of 'ought'. There is the 'ought' of expectation ('the bus ought to be along in a minute'); the 'ought' of rationality ('the robber ought to have wiped his fingerprints before the getaway'); the 'ought' of general, non-moral regret ('the *tsunami* ought not to have happened'); and then there is the 'ought' of morality ('she ought not to have betrayed him'). Harman labels ought-statements of this last type 'inner judgements'. His hypothesis is that the logical form of moral statements is such that they have as a precondition that the judging and judged parties share 'motivational attitudes', or moral reasons. (Like Williams' relativism of distance, the structure of Harman's relativism is such that it sets a precondition of appropriate moral judgement—a precondition which ushers in relativism wherever it fails—and thus the view avoids problems of self-refutation.) This means that any time there are not the requisite shared motivational attitudes between two parties, no moral judgement can appropriately be made, and relativism applies.

On Harman's view, then, in cases where the would-be judged party does not significantly share motivational attitudes with the judge, she or he is beyond the reach of moral judgement. The key example he uses is that of Hitler: 'the agent judged [Hitler] seems beyond the pale—in other words beyond the motivational reach of the relevant moral considerations' (Harman 1982: 193). According to Harman, all we can express in relation to Hitler involves the 'ought' not of inner judgements but only the unfocussed regret of judgements about states of affairs or situations. We may lament the historical fact of Nazi genocide thus: 'the holocaust ought not to have happened'. In so far as this is a consequence of his view, however, then I would have thought it made more of a counter-example than a positive illustration. For Hitler is a paradigm of the sort of agent whom we can judge morally, and whose deeds make him a proper object of moral criticism and outrage of a focussed, 'inner' variety. The idea that we cannot judge him morally *because of* his evil psychology is absurd. A morality for which evil is beyond its remit is no morality at all; and a metaethic that casts morality in this mould cannot be right.

We could defend a version of Harman's view by pointing out that if there is something to this idea of shared motivational attitudes being a precondition of moral judgement, then it cannot possibly be a question of *individuals* sharing them as judge and judged parties. It must be a question rather of *moral culture* in what I have elsewhere called the 'structural' sense (Fricker 2010: 167 passim)—that is, in the sense of a concept designed to capture the idea that the relevant moral interpretations were suitably available to the judged party, so that he is culpable if he fails either to grasp them or otherwise live up to them. Hitler will have had the usual social exposure to everyday moral precepts against the evils of spreading hatred and perpetrating mass murder, whatever story might be told about him as an individual to explain how he came to think the thoughts and commit the crimes he did. So, on this finessing of Harman's view, it would not be a consequence of it that the very psychology of evil placed the perpetrator 'beyond the pale' of moral appraisal, rendering them immune to moral censure. In so far as Harman holds that it does—and he does, for in the later work he reiterates the example in different but equivalent terms (Harman 1996: 62)—one can only say that his intended condition of shared motivating attitudes is far too strong.

If Harman were to reply by appealing to the narrowly focussed nature of 'inner judgements' owing to their special logical form, then this merely shows up the spurious nature of the terms in which the argument is conducted. The emphasis on the so-called 'logical form' of an allegedly well-defined class of statements called 'moral' ('inner') is a formal fig leaf for a material claim about the preconditions of moral judgement. In fairness to Harman, he is entirely clear that he is presenting a 'hypothesis' that cannot be proved, but still, what remains spurious is the idea that moral statements *have* a distinctive logical form of a kind that could furnish a metaethical thesis. The claim that the logical form of moral statements presupposes shared motivational attitudes is nothing more than the material claim that there is something off key about making moral judgements in respect of people who do not share in one's reasons. I believe that something along these lines is an eminently sensible thought in respect of certain types of moral judgement—certain judgements of blame, for instance[14]—but as a general statement about moral judgements it is royally disputable, and it distinguishes the claim not in the slightest to dress it up as an insight into logical form. In fact, it obfuscates the issue, because it can only mislead people into thinking that the puzzle of the relative or absolute status of morality is to be solved by trying to identify something called the logical form of moral judgements, when what we should be trying to do is explore which sorts of cultural and historical distances can or cannot sustain the various forms of moral appraisal and accountability.

It must be said that in later work Harman mounts the argument far less in terms of logical form, and instead focuses on relativism as an inference to the best explanation from the observation of moral diversity (Harman 1996: section 1.2). His is the classic inference from descriptive relativism to metaethical relativism (the move which, I argued earlier, Montaigne did not make). He then argues by way of a powerful analogy: just as motion is relative to a given spatio-temporal framework, so moral judgements are relative to a moral framework:

> The moral relativist supposes that there are various moral frameworks from which moral issues can be judged and that none of these frameworks is objectively privileged, even though one might be specially salient to a given person: for example, the moral framework relevantly associated with that person's values. (Harman 1996: 41–2)

A moral framework is constituted by 'a set of values (standards, principles, etc.), perhaps on the model of the laws of one or another state' (Harman 1996: 13). One could perhaps

---

[14] I argue in Fricker 2010 that in circumstances in which the agent was not structurally (historically-culturally) in a position to form the requisite moral thought, judgements of blame are inappropriate.

make explicit the continuity with Harman's early statement by adding that these shared moral conventions generate the shared motivational attitudes that stand as preconditional to moral judgement.

This formulation in terms of frameworks could help mitigate my objection to the Hitler example somewhat, in so far as it invites the 'structural' reading: it stops a lone moral maverick or evil-doer counting as exempt from moral judgement, for whatever an individual's moral depravity, one might suppose that the moral conventions of his culture, his *framework*, would still apply to him. It seems, however, that Harman does not intend the structural reading of 'framework', for he goes on to talk about moral frameworks not as social, collective entities but as individual moral outlooks. Distinguishing 'critic relativity' (relativity of the critic's values) from 'agent relativity' (relativity of the agent's values), he revisits the unfortunate Hitler example as follows:

> The critic will not be able to say, for example, 'It was morally wrong of Hitler to have acted in that way', if the critic is a moral relativist who supposes that Hitler did not have a compelling objective reason to refrain from acting as he did. (Harman 1996: 62)

Clearly, Harman intends 'moral framework' as most basically equivalent to 'individual moral outlook', so that it is a contingent question how far a given outlook is shared throughout society. On Harman's conception, Hitler's 'moral framework' stubbornly places him beyond the reach of moral judgement by non-fascists, even the judgement of those whose lives his actions directly affected. But this is patently absurd. The idea that Nazi ideology qualifies as a 'moral framework' is an extreme version of the mistaken assumption that we saw Moody-Adams expose in relation to relativist attitudes to exoticism; namely, the assumption that local bodies of value automatically qualify as complete moral outlooks, all dissenting voices being deemed external. In 1930s Germany a Nazi ideology surely gained the ascendancy; but a moral culture is more than an incumbent ideology, more than what is got away with by the powerful. The moral culture of Germany in the time of Hitler included the cognitive resources of dissent and resistance expressible by its victims, and indeed among its more inchoately dissident insiders too.[15]

There is room for doubt, indeed, about the whole conception of a moral framework understood by way of analogy with spatio-temporal coordinates. I have already emphasized the presence of resources for contestation in any real moral culture. Stephen Darwall emphasized a different point of disanalogy:

> A doesn't simply believe that not helping those in need is wrong in relation to his values, principles, and norms. Rather he *accepts* those values and norms and, in doing so, thinks that going counter to them is wrong *period*... In the motion case, however, A and B have no such relation to their spatio-temporal positions. (Darwall 1998: 186)

---

[15] For a haunting story of quiet resistance see Hans Fallada's novel, *Alone In Berlin* (Fallada 2009).

The basic moral rules and principles that constitute a moral framework—imagined by Harman as a complex background premise to all our moral judgements—are themselves in the fray of moral attitudes and judgements susceptible to critical assessment, endorsement, or rejection. The nature of moral judgement and interpretation is much more holistic than the 'moral coordinates' metaphor allows.

This mismatch between the Neurath's boat of moral culture and the static metaphor of a moral framework is connected with the difficulty, for Harman, of accounting for moral change. What critical impetus makes moral attitudes develop historically? Harman accounts for it in terms of 'moral bargaining'. The idea that morality is an ongoing bargained compromise between people with different degrees of wealth and power is argued for largely on the grounds that it can explain why we regard the obligation not to harm others as a much stronger principle than the obligation to help others, for such a ranking obviously suits the rich and powerful (Harman 1996: 25). A similar line of argument is given in relation to the way our moral attitudes tend to favour the well-being of humans over animals. This mini-genealogy of the development of moral values, however, backfires. The idea that the driving impulse in moral change is that of the bargain—and the competition of interests that it represents—surely does reflect some of the *real politik* of moral life, but it cannot possibly capture the character of moral argument. Moral argument is moral *reasoning*, and although it is true that when moral arguments are made by the down-trodden then their arguments will inter alia be such as to serve their interests, it would not be a moral argument at all if its *grounds* were mere self-interest. The grounds of a moral argument must be some form of justice. Moral argument may involve sticking up for oneself, but it may equally, and in the same terms, be a matter of sticking up for others. The whole idea of a bargain does not belong to moral reasoning. Real moral debate may often be intertwined with bargain-making, but it is not the same thing.

If, however, we allow Harman's reduction of moral argument to bargaining, what are the implications for moral truth? Here Harman takes up a ready-made expressivist or projectivist position, so that moral truth, and its cognates such as moral reason and moral justification, are all dealt with in the familiar *as-if* or *quasi* mode. Indeed he refers to his general strategy of accommodating these concepts as 'quasi-absolutism'. When we speak of moral truths, and no matter what we intend, we are really speaking of something *ersatz*. He uses capitals for the quasi-absolutist (QA) usage:

> For example, in saying that raising animals for food is WRONG, Veronica expresses her approval of moral standards that would prohibit the practice. In saying that raising animals for food is not WRONG, Archie expresses approval of standards that do not prohibit raising animals for food. (Harman 1996: 35)

In making this move, Harman is in company with many moral expressivists, and in line with a notion of 'relative truth' defended for instance by Foot in her non-partisan investigation of the coherence of moral relativism (Foot 2001). For Harman, the local conventions that constitute morality admit of *quasi*-truth, where this is to be understood as true-relative-to-the-subject's-moral-framework. This question of truth refers us to the next branch of our relativist family tree: that of *Moral Truth*. We could picture

Harman's quasi-absolutism on this branch, but I have featured it on the *Moral Reasons* branch because of the more distinctive and more basic motivating role that the idea of shared reasons plays in his view. Furthermore, the relativism I shall discuss in connection with moral truth is fundamentally different from all those whose genealogy I have so far traced. These views have all stemmed from subjectivism specifically about *value*, conceived by way of contrast with an objective physical realm. The relativism I shall discuss under the head of moral truth, however, stems instead from a *global* subjectivism. The attitude to moral truth that it produces is therefore differently oriented from the one we have seen embraced by Harman. It is a globally sceptical attitude to the very idea of truth as we (allegedly) commonly understand it. This places morality on a strange par with non-evaluative factual discourse, and it means that the issues thrown up for morality have a different aspect. The worry that moral judgements might turn out to be less than they're cracked up to be is no longer a matter of their objectivity comparing disappointingly with that of judgements about the physical world; but rather that the psychological demands of maintaining moral conviction turn out to be a special case of a quite general problem about sustaining convictions of any kind in parallel with a commitment to global scepticism about truth. The species of moral relativism we encounter as we look along the branch of Moral Truth is one whose deconstructionist energy connected philosophical relativism directly to the wider postmodernist *zeitgeist* of the 1970s and 1980s. I turn to the pragmatism of Richard Rorty.

37.5 MORAL TRUTH

> I use 'ironist' to name the sort of person who faces up to the contingency of his or her own most central beliefs and desires—someone sufficiently historicist and nominalist to have abandoned the idea that those central beliefs and desires refer back to something beyond the reach of time and chance. Liberal ironists are people who include among these ungroundable desires their own hope that suffering will be diminished, that the humiliation of human beings by other human beings may cease. (Rorty 1990: xv)

Rorty's 'ironism' is an intriguing form of moral relativism because its philosophical motivations are not special to matters of value, and yet morality none the less poses a special problem in his view—or at any rate, a problem for which he proposes a special solution. 'Ironism' is the solution; so what is the problem? The problem is: how to retain moral conviction if one believes morality has turned out to be radically different from what it seemed—not absolute but relative, not a system of beliefs aiming to match an independent objective morality but a contingent social construct or language game. The problem is one of preserving first-order moral conviction in the face of moral scepticism at the reflective level (a general issue that Williams flagged up in terms of the risk of our moral commitments becoming unstable under reflection). It is a globally sourced version, then, of a problem which in its localized form confronts any moral relativist position, and more broadly any error-theoretical account of morality.

Ironism is an error theory in all but name. The term 'error theory' of course comes from Mackie's moral scepticism, though it is a Humean sceptical trope played out in a new key. Hume held a parallel view concerning a range of things about whose existence he was sceptical—the idea of a necessary connection between cause and effect, for instance, or the idea of the self—but interestingly never in relation to moral conviction, which was not debunked but rather explained, indeed vindicated, in Hume's naturalistic approach. The Hume-style sceptical treatment was meted out to morality only by Mackie, whose naturalism was of a very different genus. Mackie diagnosed an objectivist error in moral consciousness; namely, an erroneous commitment to the strong metaphysical objectivity of moral value. The error is conceived—rather as Hume conceived our commitment to the necessary connection between cause and effect, et cetera—as irremediable, because so deep-seated in our psychological habits. Mackie regarded the objectivist presumption as integral to our moral experience and language. Taking the truth-aptitude of moral statements at face value, he is the most pessimistic of cognitivists, picturing the objectivist error as implicit in all such statements, and so finding them uniformly false. The point of the error theory is to reconcile the sceptical metaethics with the continuation of ordinary authoritative moral talk and experience, error and all. But how to go on? (Should we cross our fingers behind our backs whenever we express a moral conviction?)

Mackie's error theory depended on the idea that we cannot help the error, but while Hume before him could plausibly suggest that our minds cannot help but posit a necessary causal connection, or a self, or whatever it might be, it is thoroughly implausible to suggest that the very nature of moral language and experience irrevocably leads our minds to spread intrinsically motivating, metaphysically objective moral values on the world. I believe the proposal is both intellectualist and historically naïve. Intellectualist because it supposes that such a highly specific set of philosophical commitments could be built into our everyday moral talk and experience as such (not to mention such an *unpromising* bunch of commitments—few moral objectivists would own them); and historically naïve because to imagine that moral experience should be unchanging through every moral social setting—religious or secular, ascetic or libertine, traditionalist or relativistic—is to be in denial about the contingency of moral phenomenology. But I shall not develop these points, since our present interest in Mackie is confined to the parallel that his error theory makes with Rorty's ironist strategy. By dividing the moral subject into two personae, that of the 'private ironist' (the sceptical philosopher) and that of the 'public liberal' (the morally engaged agent), he aims to reconcile his pragmatist brand of scepticism with continued engagement in the business of caring morally about other people's suffering:

> The core of my book [*Contingency, Irony, and Solidarity*] is a distinction between private concerns, in the sense of idiosyncratic projects of self-overcoming, and public concerns, those having to do with the suffering of other human beings. (Rorty 1998: 307–8, note 2)

But the threat to authoritative morality is not quite banished, because the two personae of private ironist and public liberal cannot be entirely separated. By Rorty's own account, there is a porous psychological boundary, so that ironists are never 'quite able to take themselves seriously because always aware that the terms in which they describe themselves are subject to change, always aware of the contingency and fragility of their final vocabularies, and thus of their selves' (Rorty 1990: 73–4). Moral seriousness, or what I have been variously calling authority or conviction, is undermined. Given the commitments of the split personality, this must be right. There can be no hermetic seal between morally committed and sceptical stances in one and the same person. The failure to appreciate this instability was Mackie's own error. Rorty is more sanguine, and his conclusion is a shrug of personal resignation to accompany his easy, frank advice: Relax, and learn to live with the tension.

I do not see how we could live with so great a tension for long. It is fortunate, then, that we do not have to, for the tension in question is a chimera. It is generated only by Rorty's continued implicit commitment to the very conception (the 'metaphysical' or 'representationalist' conception) of moral truth that he urges us to jettison. He evidently still regards moral 'seriousness' as requiring some such metaphysical attitude (that is why ironists cannot quite take themselves seriously). Therein lies *his* error. The rhetoric is repeatedly that of the 'Truth cannot be out there' variety,[16] but with the coming of age of deflationist accounts, one can only ask, Whoever would think that it was? Given a metaphysically undemanding conception of truth, and the consequent easy possibility not only of moral truth but moral knowledge too (all available on a subjectivist conception of value), Rorty's scepticism comes to look decidedly quixotic. In short, his principled wish to shake off representationalism regarding the true could have been well served by a disquotational conception; yet he tilted at anything going by the name of truth. He embraced instead a notion of 'conversation', designed to do service for truth and reason duly relieved of the burden of seriousness. He saw a need for this because he assumed that anyone taking truth or reason seriously must be wedded to the representationalist conception he eschewed: ' "Reason," as the term is used in the Platonic and Kantian traditions, is interlocked with the notions of truth as correspondence, of knowledge as discovery of essence, of morality as obedience to principle, all the notions which the pragmatist tried to deconstruct' (Rorty 1982: 172). But Rorty's assumption quickly proved mistaken, inasmuch as alternative serious conceptions of truth and reason emerged in the evolving philosophical literature, a literature which he (ironically for a declared historicist) imagined as stuck in time, essentializing it in terms of the 'Platonic and Kantian traditions'.

Rorty's conception of 'conversation' is meant to do without seriousness because it styles itself as aspiring not to truth but only to 'solidarity'. The aim of all such discourse,

---

[16] 'Truth cannot be out there—cannot exist independently of the human mind—because sentences cannot so exist, or be out there. The world is out there, but descriptions of the world are not. Only descriptions of the world can be true or false. The world on its own—unaided by the describing activities of human beings—cannot' (Rorty 1990: 5).

we are told, and the signature aim of the public liberal, is to ever-expand the circle of those we call 'us'. But even solidarity is aspired to for a *reason*—grounds of justice, for instance, or equality. These are concepts that make an intrinsic claim to objectivity; they are the sort of thing that people argue for, rather than just bargaining with. Further, the objectivity-claiming discourse Rorty was entreating us to ditch was too often the only platform the powerless had to stand on. This point was powerfully made from a feminist perspective by Sabina Lovibond. Identifying Rorty's pragmatism as a species of post-modernism, she posed the challenging rhetorical question: 'How can anyone ask me to say goodbye to "emancipatory metanarratives" when my own emancipation is still such a patchy, hit-or-miss affair?' (Lovibond 1989: 12).

Rorty of course hoped we could continue to use even our grandest emancipatory moral concepts, if with a resigned nudge and a wink, in the name of a self-consciously 'ethno-centric' approach to ethical thinking. But embracing ethnocentrism adds nothing. It is just a device to put all our objectivity-claiming moral concepts in scare quotes, pre-empt-ing accusations of seriousness in seeking solidarity, and so of hypocrisy or self-refutation. The relevant problem with Rorty's moral ironism is indeed not that it is self-refuting (it isn't), but rather that it would be psychologically unsustainable, given the intrinsically objectivity-seeking nature of moral argument. Rorty is aware of this worry, but he bills it as a purely practical challenge, 'the *practical* question of whether the notion of "conversa-tion" *can* substitute for that of "reason"' (Rorty 1982: 172). There is indeed an important practical question (Will we be able to keep up the business of moral conviction?), but there is also a philosophical complaint to be made: Rorty sells truth and reason short, by characterizing them as serious only on a representationalist conception. This reiterates the error I drew attention to earlier. Contrary to Rorty's philosophical pessimism, anti-representationalists do not have to learn to take truth and reason non-seriously, for there are serious yet non-representationalist conceptions available. As before, ironism became not only psychologically unsustainable, but philosophically unmotivated.

We might want to retain something of Rorty's commitment to the contingency of morality, even while we reject his ironism. A sensible historicism implies a degree of moral contingency, and contingency implies pluralism. Moral pluralism calls for strong forms of non-dogmatism and open-mindedness in relation to one's moral views—what Isaiah Berlin described as a willingness to help 'maintain a precarious equilibrium' of competing values (Berlin 1959: 18). Openness to the revision of one's moral ideas must of course be a desideratum for any moral thinker, on whatever metaethical view. But in Berlin's case we greet a strong version of the point, because it is not intended simply as a warning against having too high an opinion of one's own moral point of view. Rather, the point is made as an integral part of his commitment to pluralism about moral outlooks, a pluralism which organized his thinking about the moral and political order. For Berlin, moral pluralism entailed the permanent importance of keeping an open mind in the strong sense of regarding one's set of moral commitments as one among a range of pos-sibilities. Here I believe we can sense a deep connection between Berlin's pluralism and the historicist approach to morality advanced by Williams. They embraced the contin-gencies of morality, and the freedom it implied, in similar spirit.

And so the final branch of our relativist family tree as I have drawn it is that of *Moral Plurality*. Moral pluralism can find non-relativist expression, as it did in Berlin's writing;[17] but it can also be advanced specifically as a form of moral relativism. So it is by David Wong.

37.6 MORAL PLURALITY

If pluralistic relativism is going to work as a fully spelled out metaethical position, it must supply a convincing account of what constrains the plurality of acceptable moralities. David Wong aims to do just that: 'A distinctive feature of my naturalistic account is that it generates significant constraints on what could count as an adequate morality, given its functions and given human nature' (Wong 2006: 44).

His account echoes a brief genealogical story of morality told by the Chinese philosopher Xunzi:

> On Xunzi's genealogy of morality, the ancient sage-kings saw the need to control the inborn tendency of human beings to seek gain, which consists in satisfying desires of the ear and eye. The fact that such desires have no natural limit makes for chaos when combined with scarcity of resources. The sage-kings invented within ritual and moral principles in order to apportion things, to nurture the desires of men, and to supply the means for their satisfaction. (Wong 2006: 38)

As Wong notes, the argument also echoes a story that Plato puts in Protagoras' mouth to the effect that Zeus gave human beings the virtues of reverence and justice, and the bonds of friendship and conciliation, because without these virtues coordinated life in cities would be impossible. Both genealogical stories give narrative form to the fact that certain basic values or virtues are necessary conditions for social coordination and cooperation. More specifically, Wong breaks these down into a number of conditions on any acceptable moral system. It must: regulate intrapersonal psychological features of the agent; regulate interpersonal coordination; incorporate a norm of reciprocity; place constraints relating to balancing self- and other-concern; it must also be justifiable to those 'governed' by the moral norms; and finally it must require that people can handle disagreement constructively, something Wong labels 'accommodation'.

The requirement that any acceptable morality incorporate some intrapersonal function is best thought of in immediate relation to the requirement of interpersonal function. Obviously, someone whose selfish drives are insufficiently moderated cannot be a good social cooperator; and so a morality must impose pressures to shape individual agents' motivations in a manner that facilitates sociability. These two 'functions' of morality

[17] For a more recent exponent of non-relativist pluralism, see Raz 2003. Maria Baghramian has also argued for the advantages of moral pluralism over relativism (see Baghramian 2004: 9.6).

effectively give rise to the requirement of the norm of reciprocity (the proportional return of good for good) as a way of bolstering social cooperation in the face of self-interest:

> Moral norms need to take into account the strength of self-interest in order to accommodate that motivation and to encourage its integration with motivations that more directly lead to acting on behalf of others. Moralities, then, should not merely restrain actions from self-interest or encourage the development of opposing motivations, though they do these things. They should provide outlets for the expression of self-interest that can be consistent with the expression of other-directed motivations. (Wong 2006: 51)

The requirement that morality incorporate some way of balancing self- and other-concern (egoistic and altruistic impulses) is argued for in relation to evidence for the place of altruistic motives in evolutionary theory. Once again, the idea here is to bolster the interpersonal function; that is, to give some scientific support for the claim that any acceptable morality will ensure interpersonal cooperation rather than merely selfish behaviour. This does not add a new condition on morality, but rather lends empirical support to the interpersonal social-cooperative function that is the organizing idea of Wong's universalist constraint.

At this point it is worth raising a potential objection: Is the kind of cooperative social functionality that Wong argues to be a universal condition on acceptable moralities really strong enough? Or, rather, can it be a strong enough requirement without invoking more substantive and local moral ideas? Take women. Was it, or was it not, a socially functional society in Britain that kept women in their place as disenfranchised, legally second-class citizens through the nineteenth century, albeit often with considerable informal forms of domestic power? I do not know the answer to this question. Since the situation was unjust to women, it is tempting to deem it thereby a non-functional, insufficiently cooperative society. But that would probably be false. One's moral complaint is not really that the society failed in terms of *social cooperation*. On the contrary, men and women cooperated plenty, and while society as a whole may not have been optimal from the point of view of human resources, still it functioned all right. It is therefore a useful question to pose in relation to Wong's pluralism whether the condition of social cooperation can constrain morality sufficiently so that his view does not, on closer inspection, come to resemble a much cruder 'their rules are right for them' moral relativism.

Wong, however, has an answer to this worry, for this is where his condition of justification to those governed by the morality comes in. His discussion makes clear that he regards this constraint as requiring that any given moral system must be justifiable to all those subject to its norms, and that includes its down-trodden. To use my example, Wong would say that the nineteenth-century morality that deprived women of the vote was only acceptable in so far as it could have been justified *to them*, and without trading in falsehoods. But now a worry surely arises from the other direction: the condition of justification to the governed is a very strong liberal condition, not plausibly represented as straightforwardly deriving from the condition of social cooperation. This, however, may not be an insurmountable problem, so long as the condition is defended independently as a condition in its own right, without too much tension with the pluralist framework. The condition does indeed fit Wong's purpose in that it permits a plurality of moralities in just the manner intended: a community-based morality, for instance, might be one that could be justified to the least powerful, just as a more individualistic rights-based moral system might be justified to its least powerful members.

The final condition, stemming more directly from the requirement of social cooperation and coordination, is that of 'accommodation'. Moral cultures are sites of internal moral plurality and dissent ('ambivalence'), and this means that a well-functioning society will be able to handle moral disagreement well:

> Given the inevitability of serious disagreement within all kinds of moral traditions that have any degree of complexity, a particular sort of ethical value becomes especially important for the stability and integrity of these traditions and societies. Let me call this value 'accommodation'. To have this value is to be committed to supporting noncoercive and constructive relations with others although they have ethical beliefs that conflict with one's own. (Wong 2006: 64)

Contemplating this condition of accommodation and the likelihood that it will often take the form of constructing moral *agreements* of various kinds (including agreeing to disagree), we might be moved to ask, Is this pluralism really a kind of relativism? The answer is surely Yes. Although it has a substantial universalist core, provided by the two requirements of social cooperation and justification to the governed, still the remainder has a relativist structure: people and their actions are to be judged according to the values of their culture. At this point, the argument made above in relation to the Samurai practice of *tsujigiri* returns, however, to complicate the picture. Even if Wong is right that after the basic moral constraint of social coordination, plus justifiability to the governed, the rest of morality is up for social invention in a manner that relativizes moral judgement, still we should interrogate any easy reference to this thing called 'moral culture'. As I argued in the first section, agreeing with Moody-Adams, there is almost always marginal moral-interpretive space for the expression of dissent and challenge to the moral status quo, and this puts pressure on the pluralist idea that two apparently different moral cultures really are deeply different. Wong, however, need not be on the defensive over this, for he builds into his conception of moral culture that it is a site of ongoing disagreement—indeed this much is guaranteed by the fact of value pluralism, which naturally generates disagreement and a consequent need for accommodation. Accordingly his conception of moral cultures is such that they have an 'open texture', and that 'moralities themselves are uneasy, somewhat indeterminate combinations of values that are not easily held together' (Wong 1995: 396).

A picture such as Wong's makes for an attractive hybrid, capable of reconciling the universalistic dynamic in moral thinking with its relativistic aspects. It may well be that the best future for metaethics in relation to the universalist–relativist tension is to stop trying to press all of morality into one mould or the other, but to look and see more carefully what sorts of relativizations we are inclined to make in our most sensitive moral thinking, so that we might differentiate that which is contingent and relative from that which is humanly necessary and so universal. I suspect that the moral pluralist branch of our family tree, a close cousin of historicism, may prove to be the strongest relativist line.[18]

BIBLIOGRAPHY

Baghramian, M. 2004. *Relativism*. London: Routledge.
Berlin, I. 1959. 'The Pursuit of the Ideal', in *The Crooked Timber of Humanity: Chapters in the History of Ideas*. London: John Murray Publishers Ltd, 1–19.
Bett, R. 1989. 'The Sophists and Relativism', *Phronesis* 34 (2): 139–69.
Darwall, S. 1998. 'Expressivist Relativism?', *Philosophy and Phenomenological Research* 58 (1): 183–8.
Fallada, H. 2009. *Alone in Berlin*, tr. M. Hofmann. London: Penguin. Originally published 1947. *Jeder stirbt für sich allein*.
Foot, P. 1958. 'Moral Arguments', *Mind* 67: 502–13. Extracted in M. Warnock (ed.), 1996. *Women Philosophers*. London: Everyman, 224–37.
——2001. 'Moral Relativism', in P. K. Moser and T. L. Carson (eds), *Moral Relativism: A Reader*. Oxford: Oxford University Press, 185–98. Also in M. Krausz and J. W. Meiland (eds), *Relativism: Cognitive and Moral*. Notre Dame: University of Notre Dame Press, 149–66.
Fricker, M. 2000. 'Confidence and Irony', in E. Harcourt (ed.), *Morality, Reflection and Ideology*. Oxford: Oxford University Press, 87–112.
——2010. 'The Relativism of Blame and Williams's Relativism of Distance', *Proceedings of the Aristotelians Society*, supp. vol. LXXXIV: 151–77.
Harman, G. 1982. 'Moral Relativism Defended', in M. Krausz and J. W. Meiland (eds), *Relativism: Cognitive and Moral*. Notre Dame: University of Notre Dame Press, 186–204. Originally published in *Philosophical Review* 84 (1975): 3–22. Reprinted in G. Harman, *Explaining Value*. Oxford: Oxford University Press, 2000, 3–19.
——1996. 'Moral Relativism', Part I, in G. Harman and J. J. Thomson, *Moral Relativism and Moral Objectivity*. Oxford: Blackwell, 1–64.
Herodotus. 1988. *The Histories*, tr. A. de Sélincourt. London: Penguin Books.
Hobbes, T. 1991. *Leviathan*, ed. R. Tuck. Cambridge: Cambridge University Press.
Hooker, B. (ed.) 1996. *Truth in Ethics*. Oxford: Blackwell.
Horwich, P. 1998. *Truth*. Oxford: Clarendon Press.
Hume, D. 1975. *A Treatise of Human Nature*, Bk III Part I Sect I, ed. L. A. Selby-Bigge, 3rd edn. Oxford: Clarendon Press.
Levy, N. 2002. *Moral Relativism: A Short Introduction*. Oxford: Oneworld.
Lovibond, S. 1989. 'Feminism and Postmodernism', *New Left Review* I/178, Nov/Dec: 5–28.
Lukes, S. 2008. *Moral Relativism*. London: Profile Books.
Mackie, J. L. 1977. *Ethics: Inventing Right and Wrong*. Harmondsworth: Penguin Books.
Midgley, M. 1981. 'On Trying Out One's New Sword', in *Heart and Mind: The Varieties of Moral Experience*. New YorPk: St. Martin's Press.
Montaigne, M. de. 1958. 'Of Cannibals', Bk I, *Essays*, tr. J. M. Cohen. Harmondsworth: Penguin. First French edition published 1580.
Moody-Adams, M. 1997. *Fieldwork in Familiar Places: Morality, Culture, and Philosophy*. Cambridge, MA: Harvard University Press.

[18] I thank Roger Crisp for very helpful comments on an earlier version of this chapter.

Murdoch, I. 1970. 'The Idea of Perfection', in *The Sovereignty of Good*. London: Routledge, 1–45.

Plato. 1997. *Theaetatus*, in *Plato: Complete Works*, ed. J. M. Cooper and D. S. Hutchinson. Cambridge: Hackett Publishing Co.

Raz, J. 2003. *The Practice of Value*. Oxford: Oxford University Press.

Rorty, R. 1982. 'Pragmatism, Relativism, Irrationalism', in *Consequences of Pragmatism (Essays: 1972–1980)*. London: Harvester Wheatsheaf, 160–75.

—— 1990. *Contingency, Irony, and Solidarity*. Cambridge: Cambridge University Press.

—— 1998. 'Habermas, Derrida, and the Functions of Philosophy', in *Truth and Progress: Philosophical Papers, volume 3*. Cambridge: Cambridge University Press, 307–26.

Wiggins, D. 1987. 'Truth as Predicated of Moral Judgements', in *Needs, Values, Truth*. Oxford: Oxford University Press, 139–84.

—— 1991. 'Moral Relativism and Motivating Moral Beliefs', *Proceedings of the Aristotelian Society* 91: 61–85.

—— 2006. *Ethics: Twelve Lectures on the Philosophy of Morality*. London: Penguin Books.

Williams, B. 1972. 'Interlude: Relativism', in *Morality*. Cambridge: Cambridge University Press, 20–5.

—— 1981. 'The Truth in Relativism', in *Moral Luck: Philosophical Papers 1973–1980*. Cambridge: Cambridge University Press, 132–43.

—— 1985. *Ethics and the Limits of Philosophy*. London: Fontana Press.

—— 1993. *Shame and Necessity*. Berkeley: University of California Press.

Wong, D. B. 1995. 'Pluralistic Relativism', *Midwest Studies in Philosophy* 20: 378–99.

—— 2006. *Natural Moralities: A Defense of Pluralistic Relativism*. Oxford: Oxford University Press.

Wright, C. 1992. *Truth and Objectivity*. Cambridge, MA: Harvard University Press.

CHAPTER 38

....

MORAL METAPHYSICS[1]

....

DANIEL STAR

38.1 INTRODUCTION

....

MORAL metaphysics is that part of philosophy concerned with establishing the exact ontological status of ethical facts. There are many possible views concerning the ontological status of such facts—including, of course, the view that there are none. The purpose of the present chapter is to present a short survey of the most important of the positive views about ethical facts, unapologetically written from the perspective of contemporary metaethics. Since the early twentieth century, moral philosophy has seen previously unparalleled efforts to clearly separate out and delineate distinct moral metaphysical theories, and such carefully delineated theories, apart from each being interesting in their own right, also provide us with conceptual tools which we can use when studying the longer history of ethics. This is not at all to devalue efforts that might instead be made to study particular figures or earlier episodes in that history more on their own terms, nor to deny that the present approach risks falling into the trap of anachronism. Suffice to say, a chapter that covered the long history of moral metaphysics on every period's own terms would either be incredibly long, or need be even more patchy than the present chapter is.

Let us start by attempting to be a little more precise about the space of possible views that we are interested in here. I propose that we begin by thinking of the space of possibilities for moral metaphysics as divided, at the highest level, between those theories that claim that there are ethical facts and those that deny that there are any, even in a weak or qualified sense. By starting with the *ethical*, as distinct from the *moral*, we might aim to begin at the most general level of possible normative and evaluative facts. The ethical egoist position that one should only ever pursue one's own good might be

[1] I am very grateful to Roger Crisp, David Bronstein, and Paul Katsafanas for their helpful comments on a draft of this chapter. I would also like to thank Aaron Garrett and Manfred Kuehn for interesting and relevant conversations.

understood to involve the idea that there are normative ethical facts, but no normative moral facts.[2] By beginning our division of categories with facts, we do not mean to exclude quasi-realist theories, which might be construed as asserting that there are ethical facts of a minimal kind (or ethical truths, if you prefer), but no *robust* ethical facts.[3]

An example of a theory that denies that there are any ethical facts at all is A. J. Ayer's emotivism (which has its origins partly in the ideas of David Hume and partly in logical positivism). Ayer 1950 claimed that all ethical claims express non-cognitive emotions, and can therefore not be appropriately described as either true or false. Another example of a theory that denies that there are any ethical facts, but for very different reasons, is J. L. Mackie's error theory (1977).[4] According to this theory, ethical claims are truth-apt, and moral judgements are cognitive, but all such claims and judgements are untrue. Although the subject matter is clearly very different, it can help to illustrate how this error theory is supposed to work to think of sincere utterances of sentences that use the term 'witch' in an attempt to make substantive assertions about particular people (e.g. 'she didn't drown because she is a witch')—such sentences are clearly truth-apt (and are not expressions of non-cognitive states), yet they are all untrue.[5]

When considering those theories that accept that there are ethical facts, we can divide them into two classes: on the one hand, we have theories that take it that ethical judgements are fundamentally cognitive and that they can succeed in representing stance-independent

---

[2] The distinction I am drawing here between ethics, understood as covering all attempts to answer the broad question 'how should I live?' and morality as a narrower subject concerned principally with the question of how we ought to behave towards others (as well as, according to some, duties to oneself that are not based in self-interest) draws on Williams 2003, although I won't be following William's historicizing scepticism when it comes to viewing morality as a 'peculiar institution'. Of course, some philosophers will deny that there is any real distinction to be drawn here, since some think that there are no ethical facts that are not moral facts.

[3] To simplify, I will focus on normative facts, rather than evaluative facts—that is, facts about what one ought to do, what there is reason to do, and the like, rather than facts about what is good, what is better than what, and the like—although a fuller map of possible positions about ethical facts would include various combinations of the normative and the evaluative possibilities. It is typical to be either a realist about both evaluative and normative facts, or an anti-realist about both, but there is room in logical space for a combination of realism about the evaluative and anti-realism about the normative, and a combination of realism about the normative and anti-realism about the evaluative.

[4] The truth here is a little more complicated. Mackie thinks that there are *some* types of value or reason claims which can be straightforwardly true, but they are not *categorical* moral claims (1977: 25–7). For this reason, one might be tempted to describe Mackie's view as being a view according to which there are ethical reasons, but no moral reasons. It is problematic to describe Mackie's view this way, since the categorical/hypothetical distinction doesn't straightforwardly map onto the moral/ethical distinction. It might be a necessary condition of fundamental moral requirements that they be categorical, but this is not a sufficient condition, since it does not distinguish the requirements of morality from the requirements of etiquette (see 'Morality as a System of Hypothetical Imperatives' in Foot 2001: 157–73). One way to see this is to notice that the ethical egoist might well claim that each of us is categorically required to promote his or her own self-interest, but not construe this as a moral claim.

[5] See Joyce 2001 for a contemporary defence of error theory that uses the example of witchcraft to good effect.

facts or state of affairs.[6] Such theories all adhere to a *strong ethical realism*. On the other hand, some theories deserve the name *weak ethical realism* because they claim that there can be true ethical judgements, which are fundamentally cognitive, but that such judgements do not represent facts that are robustly stance-independent.

On the anti-realist side, so called 'quasi-realists' like Simon Blackburn (1993) and Alan Gibbard (2003) aim to demonstrate that talk of ethical facts can be much more palatable, indeed respectable, for non-cognitivists than Ayer would have allowed. It is an important fact about the way metaethics has developed since Ayer and Mackie that meeting the *pretension* of realism, at least, has become a kind of default desideratum—few moral philosophers now wish to claim that there is no point to us speaking of ethical truths at all. Even error theorists typically wish to promote the idea that it is useful to go on behaving *as though* moral claims are true, and view it as helpful to utilize the notion that fictions consist of claims that are 'true in the fiction'.[7]

Not even strong ethical realism takes you all the way to robust *moral* realism, because it leaves room for amoral ethical egoism—we might call the strong ethical realism that rules out amoral egoistic views, *strong moral realism*.[8] Weak ethical realism similarly does not in itself rule out ethical egoism. Furthermore, taking the further step of adopting weak *moral* realism alone does not, to some philosophers' minds, do much to establish that there is the right degree of *objectivity* about moral requirements that is plausibly a necessary condition for moral realism—strong moral realists tend to suspect that objectivity is a problem for *all* forms of weak ethical realism, but weak ethical realists who take themselves to have objectivist theories wish to deny this (e.g. quasi-realists like Blackburn and Gibbard). Still, *lack* of objectivity is uncontroversially a feature of at least some types of weak ethical realism, especially simple subjectivism (the view that ethical truths are simply truths about particular people having particular attitudes) and ethical relativism (here taken to be the view that the truth of ethical judgements depends on the norms of the speaker's community).

This is a very quick sketch of what the landscape of possible positions, at a certain high level of generality, might be thought to look like from the contemporary perspective. I will next discuss four forms of realism we can ascribe to four great historical figures who helped bring us to the point of being able to peer at and think more carefully about the landscape just sketched. Together they provide us with an important

---

[6] By 'fundamentally cognitive' I mean to exclude quasi-realists theories that would have it that although moral judgements are beliefs, they are beliefs that are *constituted* by non-cognitive states. I take the term 'stance-independent' from Russ Shafer-Landau, who himself takes stance-independence to be essential to moral realism, where 'stance-independence' is understood as meaning that 'the moral standards that fix the moral facts are not made true by virtue of their ratification from within any given actual or hypothetical perspective' (2003: 15).

[7] Joyce 2001, for instance, ends his book with two chapters defending fictionalism.

[8] I say 'amoral ethical egoism' because it is crucial not to include ancient views that can be construed as egoistical in a way that does not deny the other-directed demands of justice, etc. (Plato and Aristotle are strong moral realists, even if they are also egoists of a kind, on the interpretation that they believe the deepest reason to be moral consists in the fact that doing so will make one's own life go best.) Reductionism about the moral and eliminativism about the moral are very different options.

set of more determinate versions of moral realism. In brief: Plato provides us with a picture according to which moral facts exist in a non-concrete realm of abstract universal properties, Aristotle provides us with a picture according to which moral facts exist as concrete facts in the world (in a stance-independent fashion), Hume with a picture according to which moral facts have their basis in universal human sentiments, and Kant with a picture according to which moral facts are simply truths of universal reason (which are neither in the world, nor in a non-natural realm).[9] As I discuss the views of each of these thinkers, it will be important to also say a little about how they are related to certain groups of contemporary realists who it seems natural to compare to each of them.

I will emphasize that the revolution in our understanding of metaphysical explanations that occurred between Aristotle and Hume is one that has important consequences for realist views—we no longer think it is plausible that ethical facts play the same kind of explanatory role that Plato and Aristotle took them to play, since even the contemporary non-naturalist will wish to endorse a view that is *consistent* with a *liberal naturalistic* deferral to modern, post-Aristotelian science (with its rejection of formal and final causes) on all issues that we now take it to be the proper province of science to rule.[10] The sections on Aristotle and Kant are longer than the sections on Plato and Hume because secondary complications arise with Aristotle and Kant: with Aristotle, it is possible to separate out a general metaphysical framework for locating the good and the right from an account of human nature; while, with Kant, it is possible to separate out his basic metaethical position from the particular normative consequences of his formulations of the Categorical Imperative (in both cases the types of separation involved are not often considered). Or so I will suggest. In relation to Plato and Hume, I will also be separating out ideas, but the way the required separation occurs is simpler to describe. One might be tempted to view the history to be covered as one where strong forms of moral realism (with Plato and Aristotle) gave way to weak forms of moral realism (with Hume and Kant), under the influence of a post-Newtonian naturalistic conception of reality; however, some of the complications I will discuss suggest that this might be too simplistic a view.

---

[9] These four forms of moral realism parallel four forms of ethical realism. An amoral ethical egoist could be a non-naturalist, naturalist, sentimentalist, or rationalist about the truth of the ethical egoist principle. I will put the issue of the difference between moral and ethical realism to one side.

[10] I take it most of us these days, even committed non-naturalists in metaethics, are committed to a minimal or liberal naturalism. This is not the scientism that would have it that the only things that exist are entities described in the dialects of the hard sciences, but rather the view that any claims about whatever else exists must not contradict the claims of modern science (so, we must not posit Cartesian minds with causal powers, for instance, but we are free to argue that there are mental, mathematical, modal, and ethical properties that lack causal powers; or, alternatively, such properties possessing causal powers, where these are reducible to, or sufficiently dependent on, the causal powers of more fundamental physical properties). See De Caro and Macarthur 2010 for a range of papers on this issue, in relation to normativity (they use the term 'liberal naturalism' for the stance I have in mind).

38.2 PLATONIC REALISM

The natural place to begin our survey is with Plato's 'Theory of Forms'. Although he discusses the forms (*eidē*) in many places, Plato himself nowhere explicitly says he has developed a theory of them; this theory is something scholars have abstracted out from his corpus, especially from the middle and late dialogues. In doing this, the tradition has followed Aristotle's lead, since it is part of the historical account that Aristotle presents in Book 13 of the *Metaphysics* that Plato reacted to Heraclitus' view that the sensible world is a world in flux by locating universal forms in a separate, intelligible realm (1078b12–34). It is generally agreed that it is in the *Phaedo* that Plato first introduces one of the most important parts of this theory when he claims 'if there is anything beautiful besides the Beautiful itself, it is beautiful for no other reason than it shares in that Beautiful' (100c3).[11] He immediately adds, 'and I say so with everything', indicating that the idea being presented is not just of relevance to the topic of beauty (he has also just mentioned the Good), then refers to what he has provided as a type of cause or explanation. It is by no means clear what it is for something to share in or partake of a form, but, at the very least, Plato is here thinking of each form as in some way causally prior to all instantiations of the relevant property in particular things, hence ontologically more fundamental.

In the *Republic*, we see Plato focusing on the ethical forms in particular. After defining justice as 'doing your own thing' (i.e. behaving appropriately given one's position) in Book IV of the Republic (432d–433b), Plato has Socrates admit defeat when it comes to defining Goodness (506d–e). He says that he is instead going to give us a clearer sense for what Goodness is through the use of three analogies. The first of these is the most straightforward: Plato compares the form of the Good to the Sun, summing up the point of his analogy by declaring 'As goodness stands in the intelligible realm to intelligence and the things we know, so in the visible realm the sun stands to sight and the things we see' (508c).[12] He subsequently clarifies this claim by saying that the Good is what make it possible for us to possess any knowledge at all (but should not itself be identified with knowledge) (508e). This form, then, plays a fundamental epistemic role.

In the discussion of the analogy of the Line (an appreciation of which would require discussion of complexities well beyond the scope of this chapter), we are told something crucial about reason, which is that, through the philosopher's method of *dialectic*, reason seeks out knowledge of the Forms themselves, for 'it makes absolutely no use of anything perceptible by the senses: it aims for forms by means of forms alone' (511c).[13] Philosophy provides the route to a higher type of knowledge than is available to us through mere belief or opinion (*doxa*).

Finally, when it comes to the analogy of the Cave, where our position in forming beliefs about the sensible world is likened to the position of prisoners in a cave watching

---

[11] The quotations are from Plato 1997.
[12] All quotations from the *Republic* are from Plato 1993.
[13] I changed 'types' to 'forms' in this quotation from Plato 1993, since this is a more standard translation.

shadows on a wall and taking them to be real, rather than recognizing the more fundamental reality of the intelligible realm outside, Plato tells us that

> the last thing to be seen—and it isn't easy to see either—in the realm of knowledge
> is goodness; and the sight of the character of goodness leads one to deduce that it is
> responsible for everything that is right and fine, whatever the circumstances, and
> that in the visible realm it is the progenitor of light and of the source of light, and in
> the intelligible realm it is the source and provider of truth and knowledge.... the
> sight of it is a prerequisite for intelligent conduct either of one's own private affairs
> or of public business. (517b–c)

Here we have a bringing together of the view that Forms play a fundamental ontological
grounding role (with a special place being given to the form of the Good, in particular)
and the view that they play an epistemic grounding role, in addition to a clarificatory
claim that it is only through such knowledge of the Good that one is able to get things
right in the practical sphere. Knowledge of the Forms is essential to virtue. Even the
more contingent moral judgements of the virtuous are formed on the basis of knowledge of the forms. The philosopher returns to the cave and, once she has allowed her
vision to readjust, she is able to educate and rule society by making judgements about
the shadows on the wall of the cave better than anyone else, on the basis of what she has
learned of the reality outside of the cave (520c–d).

   It is sometimes said that any talk of locating a 'theory of the forms' in Plato, of the kind
just sketched, is unhelpful or worse.[14] It is certainly true that the story just told simplifies
matters to a large extent (even with respect to the *Republic*), and overlooks the way Plato's
metaphysical views developed and changed across his works. A fuller account would
need to remedy these faults. Nonetheless, one good reason to not abandon the notion
that Plato was, at least for a significant period of time, solidly committed to a theory of the
Forms of precisely the kind just summarized is that Aristotle directly attacks this theory,
and assigns it to Plato. In *Metaphysics* 13 Aristotle presents a fragment of an argument
against this theory that has come to be known as the Third Man Argument.[15]

---

   [14] See, for example, Williams 2006: 154.
   [15] The form of the argument alluded to there seems to be *reductio ad absurdum*. The argument can be
reconstructed as follows: (1) assume, for the sake of argument, that Plato is right to think that the only
way to adequately explain why an individual is of a kind (e.g. why all the individual men share the
property of being men) is to conceive of the forms or ideas as universals separate from the objects that
they cause to be the kinds of objects that they are (e.g. the form of man is not a concrete man, but
separate from all individual men, yet all men are men in virtue of that form); (2) next consider: what is
it that the form of man and individual men share, such that the form of man can be the universal in
relation to those individuals? There must, according to (1), be some third entity that explains what the
Form of Man and men have in common, and that makes them both men, of a kind (the form of Man is
not a concrete man, but we have seen that it is a Man, of a kind, i.e. the most perfect, ideal man). Call this
third entity, Man*; (3) now consider that Man* and Man must also have something in common that can
be abstracted from them, so that Man* is able to explain what Man and men have in common. It follows
that there must be a Man** (4) Notice that the step taken in (3) can be taken again, and again, and again,
ad infinitum. (5) It is absurd to think that there exists an infinitely long explanatory chain of this kind, so
(1) must be false (since (2) and (3) seem to follow from it).

Many of the details of the above metaphysical story are not of direct interest to contemporary metaethicists. Modern *non-naturalist* theories certainly seem to have a Platonic element to them, but they don't take it that the Good (or abstract forms of whatever kind) *explains* anything about the existence of objects in the world, or our knowledge of such objects; the modern non-naturalist G. E. Moore (1993: 135–6) might have thought that beautiful sunsets are intrinsically good, but he didn't think the non-natural property of goodness would in any way help explain the constitution or existence of beautiful sunsets. Furthermore, Moore was not concerned with explaining the relation of universals to particulars (whether or not the universals are thought to explain the existence of particulars), although this is often taken to be an essential part of the rationale for Plato's provision of a theory of the forms.

Despite the huge differences here, it is still appropriate to place present-day non-naturalist views under the Platonic heading. Non-naturalists can also vary in another way when it comes to the strength of their ontological commitments. Recently, Derek Parfit (2011b: 486) has described his non-naturalist view as 'non-metaphysical', yet committed to 'irreducibly normative truths'. Parfit wishes to avoid any commitment to a sphere of fundamental moral facts or properties existing in a separate realm or world. Plato, on the other hand, sometimes seems to suggest he really does have such a separate realm in mind, as when he provides his account of recollection (*anamnesis*) in the *Meno*. Nonetheless, I think we can see that one thing that is fundamental to both of these very different theories is a view according to which (1) moral judgements, at their best, *represent* moral facts; and (2) moral facts (at least those of the most fundamental kind) are *not* to be found anywhere in the natural world (or in pure rationality); and (3) ethical facts are what they are independent of any real or hypothetical stance or perspective. By stating (2) as a negative condition (fundamental moral facts are not in the natural world), we can see what survives in Parfit as the essence of Platonism, enabling us to distinguish his position from the positions of the heirs of Aristotelian realism. (2) and (3) will allow us to distinguish Platonist realism from Humean and Kantian realism.

38.3 ARISTOTELIAN REALISM

Aristotle's general metaphysical picture stands in stark contrast to Plato's. Like Plato, Aristotle sees the forms as necessary for understanding particular individuals, but unlike Plato, Aristotle thinks of these forms as being present in the world, rather than outside of it. It might seem natural to start our discussion of Aristotle with the *Nicomachean Ethics* (2000), but a problem when asking after Aristotle's moral metaphysics is that the *Ethics*, while it does provide us with part of a theory of *human* nature, which has at its centre the claim that the end or purpose (*telos*) of human beings is rational, virtuous activity, does not tell us very much about the ontology of either the right or the good, in general.[16] The most natural way of understanding the place Aristotle would have for fundamental facts about the right and good is provided by his general metaphysics, so I will start there.

In the *Physics*, Aristotle tells us that there are four causes (or, we might say, 'becauses') of things that exist in the world: the material cause, the efficient cause, the formal cause, and the final cause. If we take some bronze and cast it into a statue, then the unformed bronze can be thought of as the material cause of the statue, and our casting of the statue, the efficient cause. The shape or pattern of the statue is its formal cause (194b26–30), while the final cause of the statue is its function, e.g. to decorate a place or commemorate a person. Here we find a thesis about objective metaphysical explanations, since the four causes provide what Aristotle takes to be a set of necessary and sufficient conditions for something to exist as an *intelligible* entity; following Shields 2010: 42, we might call this a 'four-causal account of explanatory adequacy'. In general, we need material causes to explain what remains constant when change in an object occurs, efficient causes to explain the role that external influences play in bringing about changes in an object, formal causes to explain how an object can take on new properties, and final causes to explain the ends for which objects take on new properties. However, Aristotle's example of the statue can be misleading when it comes to natural organisms, since, in the case of organisms, the formal and final causes can be thought of as much more closely related, if not identical.

The fact that we are talking about the *intelligible* realm here (i.e. the realm of things open to general explanations) becomes most clear when one turns to Aristotle's discussion of luck in Chapters 4 to 6. On the one hand, Aristotle admits that 'surely many things come to be and exist as a result of luck and chance' (196a10–15).[17] So, if one person owes money to another and the two people just happen to run into each other, the fact that the debt can be collected on this occasion is due to luck and not something that can be explained by the four-causal account (196b30–197a5). We might think the reference to luck or chance does explanatory work on such occasions, but it can do so only in a secondary, qualified way, since the facts involved in such cases will all separately be able to be explained by the four-causal account (to use Aristotle's example, the man coming to collect the debt has coincidental causes, such as, perhaps, his planning to attend the theatre, 197a15–20). Most importantly, 'Luck is contrary to reason. For rational judgement tells us what is always or usually the case, whereas luck is found in events that happen neither always nor usually' (197a18 21). Chance and luck can thus be classified as posterior to mind and nature (198a8–12).

In Aristotle's mature metaphysics, the final cause or function of any substance is what we will take to be most essential to its nature: the material cause will play a very minor role, due to the fact that a substance must have matter to exist, but matter is impossible

[16] Although, importantly, Aristotle does there criticize Plato's account of the good, suggesting that there is no one universal form of the good—we may infer from what Aristotle says in Chapter 6 of Book I that what is good for a human being is different than what is good for a horse, which is different again from what is good for a god.

[17] All relevant quotations are from Aristotle 1995, unless otherwise indicated.

to understand as anything but shapeless and homogenous in isolation from particular formal causes; even forms may be thought to have secondary importance, despite their essential role in specifying functions. In the *Metaphysics*, Aristotle says,

> All things are defined by their function: for in those cases where things are able to perform their function, each truly is an F, e.g. an eye, when it can see. But when something cannot perform its function, it is homonymously F, like a dead eye or one made of stone, just as a wooden saw is no more a saw than one in a picture. (390a10–15)[18]

Efficient causes also take a back seat, since although they tell us the historical origins of a thing, they can't provide the most fundamental part of an explanation as to why that thing is the thing it is, once it exists.

So far I have been discussing matters that are clearly the concerns of theoretical wisdom, rather than practical wisdom. Aristotle tells us in the *Ethics* that theoretical wisdom requires knowledge and understanding of the first principles of the sciences (1141a16–17), and that since it depends only on thinking and observation, it is possible to have it without as much experience as practical wisdom requires—the latter requires a more extensive familiarity with particulars (1141b14–20).[19] We must also discuss the *Ethics* if we are to get clearer about how the general metaphysical account of purposiveness in nature is related to purposiveness in the ethical life of human beings.

Aristotle begins this text with the claim that every skill, enquiry, action, and rational choice appears to seek some end. He then informs us that the end for man is simply the chief good for man (1094a18–23), and very rapidly argues that there must be such a final end, for the sake of which we pursue other ends, otherwise there would be an infinite regression of ends (each being pursued for the sake of the next), which would imply that we desire things in vain. Whatever one thinks of Aristotle's argument here, the important thing to realize is that it goes hand in hand with his later claim that we never deliberate about independent ends (1112b12), but only about means or ends that are constitutive of further ends.[20] Together these claims imply that the only end that is neither a means, nor a constitutive end, is the final end, or good for man.

Aristotle makes two important claims at the beginning of the fourth chapter of Book I: firstly, he claims that all will agree that happiness (*eudaimonia*) is the highest good;

---

[18] The translation is from Shields 2010: 92.

[19] At 1141b22–23, Aristotle adds that there is also a master science of ethics (or political science), and might be taken to be suggesting that one requires knowledge of both the particular and the universal to succeed at this science; in any case, at 1141a20–21 he makes a point of emphasizing that this is an inferior science, for it is a science that is, in a way, less universal than the higher sciences (as there would be a different practical science for each different kind of being). Even children then have access to more important scientific truths than can be found in ethics. This conclusion fits well with Aristotle's insistence (1103b28–30) that the main reason to study ethics is to learn how to become good (and, in the case of politics, help others become good), rather than attain any particular theoretical wisdom (which, in this area can only be rough and ready, anyway, precisely because it is more tied to the particular [1104a1]).

[20] For a seminal discussion of the difference between constitutive ends and means, see Ackrill 1980.

secondly, he claims that people have differing substantive conceptions of happiness (e.g. pleasure, wealth, honour). In the seventh chapter of that book, we find some criteria (rather than just an appeal to what people believe) that we can use to judge that happiness is the good for man and to determine what it is (1097a15–1097b21), followed by a detailed argument concerning the characteristic activity or function of man (*ergon*), which when fulfilled well constitutes happiness (1097b21–1098a21). I take it that the criteria provided in the first of these two sections (of being a complete end, being self-sufficient, and being most choice-worthy) are meant to help us to see both that happiness (whatever it turns out to be) is the good for man, and also that whatever substantive conception of happiness we conclude is correct does, indeed, specify the good for man. In other words, this section both looks backward to what has been said about what everyone accepts (i.e. that happiness is what we are all aiming for), and looks forward to the correct detailed account of happiness that relatively few will accept.[21] Thus, Aristotle hopes to gain general assent for his criteria, before supplying his own substantive account (he has already suggested some reasons for thinking some substantive accounts cannot be right, in Chapter 5).

Turning to the famous *ergon* argument, this can be understood in two mutually exclusive ways: one might read Aristotle as saying that the function of man is activity of the soul in accordance with reason, where this is ethically neutral (so the wicked person can fulfil this function well), then separately claiming that the good for man (as distinct from his function) is activity of the soul in accordance with virtue; or, one might read Aristotle as saying that activity of the soul in accordance with reason just is activity of the soul in accordance with virtue, which just is the good for man.[22] On either interpretation we can say the wicked man (who rationally chooses the bad) is unhappy, but only on the second interpretation is he also unnatural.

I think that paying close attention to what Aristotle has to say about the wicked should incline one to think that the second of these interpretations, which is also the most common interpretation, is correct. Firstly, the wicked man lacks knowledge of the good (1146b22–24). He is in a state of ignorance, yet it is clear that by nature we desire to know (*Metaphysics* I.1). The wicked person's appetites stand in the way of him coming to know the good. Secondly, the wicked person has a soul that is at war with itself (1166b20–25), and one might think that this can hardly be natural. That being said, we should not think the wicked person does not reason at all (that would make him the kind of damaged person that Aristotle terms 'bestial')—only that he does not reason well.

Apart from considerations concerning the wicked, there are considerations that we might think bear on this matter to be derived from Aristotle's more general metaphysics:

[21] This section is sometimes interpreted as looking forwards, but not backwards. Evidence that the first section looks backwards in this way can be found immediately at the beginning of the second section (1097b21–24), where it is admitted that what has just been said will sound platitudinous, for this echoes the claim already made at the beginning of Chapter 4 (that all will agree happiness is what we are aiming for).

[22] As McDowell 1980, for instance, points out.

firstly, the function or end of an organism, its *telos*, is equated with what is *best* for a thing (see, for example, *Physics* 198b5–20); secondly, there is said to be nothing embarrassing about studying animals, for there is something fine in each animal, and each *telos* is worthy of admiration (*De Partibus Animalium* 645a20–30). Only if being virtuous is essential to our *telos* would it be right to think our *telos* is admirable.

If we accept that virtuous activity is not just the end of the good man, but the characteristic activity of man, we will be led to conclude that very few actual people engage in the characteristic activity of human beings, and, in this respect, we seem unlike other animals, or gods, for that matter (who perform their functions much better). The human condition thus appears more tragic than it would on the view that would have it that even the non-virtuous can fulfil the function of a human being well. Nonetheless, that the human condition is somewhat tragic is just what we would expect if we assume (as Aristotle does) that everybody pursues happiness but very few are actually going to be pursuing the correct final end, hence end up being happy. The pessimism such thinking might result in can also be lightened if put together with the relatively optimistic vision of the last chapter of Book X of the *Ethics*, where it is suggested that a better political structure (with stricter laws and a better education system) could improve the lot of human beings by ensuring the wider inculcation of the habits required for virtue. Healthy children always posses the potential for happiness, after all.

If the first interpretation were correct, there would be less conflict between Aristotle's understanding of human nature and our modern scientific conception of the nature of the human animal. As it is, modern minimal naturalism is incompatible with the idea that what it means for us to flourish as biological creatures is to perform a function of rationally choosing and acting in accordance with virtue,[23] since this is incompatible with the view, essential to contemporary biology, that our nature is the product of evolutionary forces centring on *fitness* (i.e. centring on what is required for survival and reproduction of the species, rather than on what is good).[24]

We have seen that Aristotle agrees with Plato that forms play a key role in explaining both the existence and knowledge of things. So now we are in a position to note that there are two things that are crucial to the way that both Plato and Aristotle utilize the notion of a form that have no close parallel in contemporary metaethics: (1) the good and right, whether viewed as outside of the world or inside the world, play no role in *explaining* the existence of material objects; (2) there is no connection to the problem of universals, either for non-naturalist realists like Moore, or for contemporary naturalist realists.

Just as we saw traditional Platonists and contemporary non-naturalists differ when it comes to the possibility of normative facts explaining non-normative facts, traditional Aristotelians and contemporary non-reductive naturalists might be seen to differ on exactly this issue as well. Still, if we focus on Aristotle's understanding of forms being present in the world this does enable us to align him with contemporary naturalist moral

---

[23] Despite the noble efforts of Foot 2001.

[24] One might be tempted to think fitness and the good (can) work hand in hand, but Powell and Buchanan 2011 present very persuasive arguments to the contrary.

realists, especially the so-called Cornell realists (Sturgeon 1984, Boyd 1988, Brink 1989). These philosophers take it that moral properties are natural, but they are inclined to view them as non-reducible to other natural properties.[25] At the furthest extreme from Aristotle, but still close enough to perhaps fit into the present category, we find reductive realist naturalists who, in effect, deny the need for forms altogether (most notably, Jackson 2000). Such reductive realists are thought by some to be committed to a view of moral facts that is too weak to count as realist (Parfit 2011a, 2011b)—at the very least, we might think their naturalist moral realism, unlike that of the Cornell realists, deserves to be classified as a *weak* realism.[26]

38.4 HUMEAN REALISM

One of the most discussed issues in recent Hume scholarship is the question of what Hume's settled metaethical position really is. Although some have contended that Hume is, at least to some extent, an error theorist,[27] the two most popular candidate interpretations are the *subjectivist* interpretation that moral judgements are projections onto the world, the stability of which enables us to make robustly true statements about what a general observer would be disposed to feel is right or wrong in particular contexts; and, alternatively, the *quasi-realist* interpretation that moral judgements are non-cognitive, but that this does not prevent ethics from being objective.[28] I will not attempt to take a side on the issue of whether the first or the second interpretation is correct. It may well be true, as Terence Irwin puts it, that 'the difference between subjectivism and non-cognitivism is probably not obvious to Hume' (2009: 618).[29] In any case, for my purposes it is enough to argue that the first interpretation is plausible, and that *if* it is correct *and* if we grant Hume a crucial assumption of uniformity in human sentiments, the result will be a moral realism that, broadly speaking, grounds ethical truths in the sentiments. This type of realism is interesting, whether or not Hume was clearly committed to it.

In the first of the appendices to the *Enquiry concerning the Principles of Morality*, Hume tells us that 'The hypothesis we embrace is plain. It maintains, that morality is

---

[25] I believe that Sturgeon is less committed to this non-reducibility thesis. It should also be said that these realists do believe moral properties can appropriately figure in causal explanations; however, I take it they still don't believe that such properties or forms help *constitute* physical objects (to take an example of Sturgeon's, the injustice of slavery at some time might (efficiently) cause a rebellion, but I take it that's different than the injustice constituting, even in part, either the slavery or the rebellion).

[26] If so, my original definition of weak realism needs to be modified.

[27] Mackie 1980: 71–5 warily suggests such an interpretation. Jonas Olson argues in an unpublished paper, 'Projectivism and Error in Hume's Ethics', that Hume is an error theorist when it comes to the commitments of ordinary moral thought, or descriptive metaphysics, but not when it comes to his revisionary metaphysics (he contends Hume is a subjectivist in the latter case).

[28] 'Subjectivist' is a common label in this context, but is perhaps a misnomer, since the view thus picked out is a weakly realist view. I say more about this below.

[29] See also Mackie 1980: 70.

determined by sentiment. It defines virtue to be *whatever mental action or quality gives to a spectator the pleasing sentiment of approbation*; and vice the contrary' (App. 1.10).[30] One might worry that in the *Enquiry* this thesis is only stated explicitly in an appendix, but it seems clear that this view is very close to the view defended in the *Treatise*, where, in the midst of a discussion of the 'artificial' virtue of justice (artificial because it is a general, conventional rule that has us extend our sympathy beyond its original orbit), Hume writes, 'every thing, which gives uneasiness in human actions, upon the general survey, is call'd *vice*, and whatever produces satisfaction, in the same manner, is denominated *virtue*' (III.II.2.24). Three questions immediately arise when we consider this clearly very central idea: (1) if judgements of virtue rest on our internal sentiments, why does it seem to us that virtue (and other moral properties) reside in external objects?; (2) how are we to think of the perspective of the 'spectator', or he who would take a 'general survey', such that we might hope that moral standards are as objective as our experience suggests they are?; and (3) how are we to think of the relation of this idea to Hume's famous claim that 'Reason is, and ought only to be the slave of the passions' (II.III.3.4)?

The answer to the first question is supplied by the doctrine that has come to be known as *projectivism*. This doctrine is an attempt to take moral phenomenology extremely seriously—it appears as if the badness of certain behaviour is there for us to behold in the guilty—while holding fast to the view that moral judgements are based in the sentiments. The solution to meeting both these desiderata is to suppose that we project our moral sentiments onto objects external to us in a manner that leads us to think the properties are really in the world. In a typically eloquent sentence, Hume says '[Reason] discovers objects, as they really stand in nature, without addition or dimunition: [Taste] has a productive faculty, and gilding or staining all natural objects with the colours, borrowed from internal sentiment, raises, in a manner, a new creation' (App. 1.21).[31] Some commentators take it that this moral projectivism is simply continuous with Hume's broader metaphysical project, since Hume also takes *causation* to involve the projection of a causal relation onto the external world; in the case of causation, Hume argues (according to a common interpretation) that the projection in question leads to a *mistake* in the way we understand causation, as we take it to be an external metaphysical relation—once this mistake has been recognized we are expected to replace our faulty ordinary notion of causation with the idea that causation just *is* constant conjunction in our experience. If this interpretation of Hume on causation is even roughly right, we

[30] All quotations from *An Enquiry concerning the Principles of Morals* are from Hume 1998, and all quotations from *A Treatise of Human Nature* are from Hume 2000.

[31] One might worry that in this paragraph Hume is contrasting reason and *taste*, rather than reason and moral sentiments. While recognizing that a more careful study would need to pay attention to the differences between taste and sentiment (and passion), there are two reasons we should not be worried about this here: (i) it is clear from the immediately preceding paragraph in *Appendix* 1 that Hume is talking about 'some sentiment, which [the observation of virtue] touches, some internal taste or feeling, or whatever you please to call it, which distinguishes moral good and evil'; and (ii) Hume elsewhere sometimes refers to 'moral taste' (e.g. 'The approbation of moral qualities most certainly is not deriv'd from reason, or any comparison of ideas; but proceeds entirely from a moral taste' *Treatise* 3.3.1.15), which suggests moral taste is simply a particular type of taste.

shouldn't take his moral projectivism to be completely continuous with his broader project, since there seems to be little evidence that Hume is asking us to replace our ordinary ideas of virtue and vice with alternatives to them.

Hume's projectivism provides an explanation for the sense of objectiveness in our moral phenomenology but not any guarantee that there do in fact exist common, objective moral standards. To see how Hume intends to provide us with the grounds for such standards, we must look to the natural passion of *sympathy*. Sympathy is 'a very powerful principle in human nature', which 'produces our sentiments of morals in all the artificial virtues [such as justice]' (3.3.1.10). It is able to do this because, fortunately, we have the ability to 'fix on some *steady* and *general* points of view' (3.3.1.15), and thereby correct our sentiments to overcome our ordinary biases: 'Experience soon teaches us this method of *correcting* our sentiments [that of adopting the general point of view], *or at least, of correcting our language, where the sentiments are more stubborn and inalterable*' (3.3.1.16, italics added in the last quotation).

As Sayre-McCord 1994 convincingly argues, we should not understand Hume here as suggesting that the correct moral judgements will be made from the perspective of an Ideal Observer who knows all facts and feels sympathy with every individual who stands to be effected by various choices; rather, it is by adopting the general point of view that we are able to form generalizations about the effects various virtues and vices will normally have on people, and thus establish or discover fundamental moral standards.[32] The merits of this interpretation might be observed by considering Hume's statement that

> The intercourse of sentiments, therefore, in society and conversation, makes us form some general inalterable standard, by which we may approve or disapprove of characters and manners. And 'tho the *heart* does not always take part with those general notions, or regulate its love and hatred by them, yet are they sufficient for discourse, and serve all our purposes in company. (3.3.3.2)

The alternative, non-cognitivist interpretation of Hume takes off from his account of the difference between the passions and reason. He tells us that 'A passion is an original existence... and contains not any representative quality' (2.3.3.5); reason, on the other hand works with ideas representing the world, and is motivationally inert. Since morality clearly motivates us, it seems to be on the side of the passions, rather than on the side of reason and the ideas. The problem with this non-cognitivist argument alone[33] is that, as we have just seen, some ideas or beliefs can represent the judgements of the general observer, and these deserve to be called moral judgements, if anything does. Still, one might worry that such beliefs, however lofty their status is meant to be, must, like all

---

[32] Cohon 1997 provides a more complicated take on these matters.

[33] I do not have space here to explore the non-cognitivist interpretation any further than this. This interpretation is sometimes based on Hume's claim that it is impossible to derive an 'ought' from an 'is' (III.1.1.27), although it is now recognized that this view does not entail non-cognitivism (see Pigden 2010, where this is emphasized and non-cognitivism is argued to instead follow from No-Ought-From-Is as a matter of inference to the best explanation).

other products of reason, still be slaves to the passions. I think this apparent contradiction can be resolved if one keeps in mind that, as indicated above, Hume believes we are at least *generally* moved by the sentiment of sympathy whenever we take up the general point of view.[34]

I have followed traditional commentators in labelling Hume's sentimentalism 'subjectivist', but this can mislead, to the extent that 'subjectivist realism' sounds like an oxymoron. Hume the 'subjectivist' may, in fact, be viewed as a type of moral realist, as long as we grant an assumption of conformity in the emotions across all the beings who are rightly considered moral creatures. This view comes in two varieties: we might take it that morality is *for* human beings, and no other creatures, in which case enough commonality in *human* sentiments will suffice to make subjectivism count as objective enough for it to be a form of *weak* realism; alternatively, we might think it possible to argue that *any* creature capable of making genuinely moral judgements *must* have a particular core set of sentiments (where the content of this set is enough to ensure convergence on a set of moral truths, under the right conditions). This alternative, which we might think of as more strongly realist, seems much more difficult to defend, but also more attractive—more difficult because it is no easy task to see how such an argument would proceed, but more attractive because the view that morality is *for* human beings seems open to counterexamples (e.g. we would think moral principles would still apply, on both sides, in our relations with highly sophisticated aliens, were we to come into contact with them).[35] A Humean moral metaphysics that attempts to live up to this challenge will contrast most straightforwardly with the Kantian view that it is *reason* (not specific to human beings) that grounds morality, in a way that might seem to many to be an attractive alternative to that Kantian view.

38.5 KANTIAN REALISM

One of the main keys to understanding Kant's ethics is to appreciate the importance, within his ethical framework, of *the* Categorical Imperative. This is a formal principle or law of practical rationality which, according to Kant, can be derived from reflection on the very concept of a categorical imperative, i.e. an imperative that applies to rational

---

[34] Interestingly, Mackie 1980: 71 says he thinks there is some merit to the type of interpretation of Hume I am pressing here, i.e. an interpretation that views moral judgements as partly cognitive and (at least normally) partly non-cognitive (although, more precisely, Mackie focuses on a mixed descriptivist/non-cognitivist theory concerning the meaning of moral terms, rather than on moral judgements).

[35] As for defenders of *quasi-realism*, they typically contend that the quasi-realist does not have a problem with objectivity when it comes to the contingency of the non-cognitive attitudes that they believe constitute moral judgements (see Blackburn 1993), but an argument that any creature capable of making moral judgements must have a certain core set of sentiments might also go a long way to protecting quasi-realists from the suspicion amongst many strong realists that the quasi-realist wishes to rest morality on too contingent a basis.

being regardless of what any of us happen to contingently desire (4:402 and 4:420–421). The Categorical Imperative is formulated in a number of different ways (Kant seems to think these are identical in meaning, although contemporary Kantians grant that they do not appear to be): the two most important formulations are the Formula of Universal Law, 'act only in accordance with that maxim through which you can at the same time will that it become a universal law' (4:421) (a variation on this is the Formula of the Law of Nature, 'act as if the maxim of your action were to become by your will a universal law of nature' [also 4:421]); and the Formula of Humanity as an End in itself, 'So act that you use humanity, whether in your own person or in the person of any other, always at the same time as an end, and never merely as a means' (4:429).[36] The Categorical Imperative can be used to derive fundamental duties (e.g. a duty not to make lying promises) from subjective maxims or general intentions (e.g. a general intention to make lying promises), just like a basic principle of hypothetical practical reasoning (Kant doesn't call this *the* Hypothetical Imperative, but we well might) will enable us to derive particular means from particular ends.

The crucial thing to note for our purposes is that morality, given the centrality to Kant's ethics of the Categorical Imperative, is based in rationality. Our beliefs about our duties do not represent something outside of us, on this picture, but are instead to be derived from fundamental principles of rationality. For this reason, some have thought it best to describe Kant as an *irrealist*—not an anti-realist, since basic moral principles are taken to be *true*, yet also not a realist, since realism is taken to assume that moral beliefs *represent* truths (Skorupski 2010). It is not clear that this is the best way of interpreting Kant's basic metaethics. We might instead say that the fundamental, true moral principles are true principles of practical rationality, and our most fundamental moral judgements are in the business of representing such principles. Kantians will want to defend very particular formulations of the fundamental principles of rationality (taken to also be fundamental principles of morality), and a detailed account of the particular duties that such principles ground, but it is open to philosophers of very different persuasions to attempt to do this in ways that radically depart from much of the substance of Kant's ethics. In particular, consequentialists may wish to claim that the fundamental consequentialist principle is a true principle of rationality.

Before further exploring Kant's ideas, let me first introduce a distinction I wish to put to use. In this section (and just in this section), I will use the term 'moral fact' to pick out moral truths that are non-fundamental, in the sense that they are not equivalent to fundamental moral principles (roughly, fundamental moral principles have the form 'For all agents, an agent is morally required to X if and only if, and because F'; an example of F would be 'X is one of the acts that maximizes expected utility'). Now let me define *moral fact internalism* as the view that what an agent is morally required to do on any particular occasion is always a function of (a) the correct fundamental moral principle(s); (b)

---

[36] All quotations are from Kant 1996. A third formula is the Formula of Autonomy, with its variant, the Formula of the Realm of Ends (4:438–439). I am following Wood 1999 in the naming and individuation of the formulae.

the correct account of value (or, perhaps, a value ranking function); and (c) the content of the mental states of the agent. *Moral fact externalism* is the view that what an agent is morally required to do on a particular occasion is a function of (a) the correct fundamental moral principle(s) and; (b) the correct account of value; and (c) facts that go beyond the content of the mental states of the agent. Describing a view in one of these two ways does not in itself commit one to any view about the ontological status of the facts (in a broader sense) described by fundamental moral principles, nor any view about epistemic access to either such principles or particular moral facts.[37] However, the epistemic issue, which I will not be discussing, does seem related in one way: *moral fact externalism* rules out a completely *a priori* account of moral knowledge, but *moral fact internalism* does not.

The most straightforward way to grasp what is at issue here is to consider the contemporary distinction between two types of consequentialism: actual value consequentialism and expected value consequentialism. To see the difference between these theories, imagine the following is true. A well-trained, epistemically responsible surgeon can operate on either patient A or patient B, where both patients are of the same age, and equally healthy. Suppose also that the patient not operated on will die, due to an unfortunate shortage of surgeons. Now, let's suppose the best evidence that the surgeon possesses points to patient A having a 6 in 10 chance of surviving the operation in a healthy state, and patient B having a 9 in 10 chance of surviving the operation in a healthy state. The surgeon operates on patient B, and, unfortunately B dies (as well as A). Furthermore, *if* the surgeon had operated on patient A, patient A would have survived in a healthy state, despite the subjective probability that the doctor rationally ascribed suggesting otherwise. Expected value consequentialism and actual value consequentialism will disagree about what morality required the doctor to do in this case. The first theory will say the doctor acted rightly, even though two people died as a result (when just one could have died), while the second theory will say the doctor acted wrongly. This example illustrates that the first theory, as it is commonly interpreted, is committed to *moral fact internalism*, while the second is committed to *moral fact externalism*.[38] And this is true,

---

[37] Particularists, who think that there are no true moral principles (yet still cleave to moral facts), can also accept this distinction, but just assume that fundamental moral principles contribute nothing to the relevant functions. An alternative way of defining *moral fact internalism* would be to define it as the view that the fundamental moral principles take as inputs only the content of mental states internal to the agent. This alternative definition would do for most purposes, but would rule particularism out. We can take it that a standard way of explaining why, for the internalist of the kind we are considering, what an agent is morally required to do on any particular occasion is always a function of (a) the correct fundamental moral principle(s); (b) the correct account of value; and (c) the content of the mental states of the agent, is that this is just *because* the correct ethical theory (consisting of fundamental moral principle(s) and a general account of value) specifies that only facts or properties internal to the agent need to be considered (*mutatis mutandis* for the externalist).

[38] Some people think the best way to interpret expected value consequentialism is to view the theory as asking us to consider *objective*, rather than *subjective*, probabilities. On that interpretation, both actual value and expected value consequentialism are committed to *moral fact externalism*, so the difference between the two theories is more interesting, for our purposes, if we put that alternative interpretation to one side.

regardless of the ontological status of the particular version of the consequentialist principle (i.e. the fundamental principle at the heart of each theory).

Although I have used these consequentialist theories as examples here, I do not think this distinction bears any essential relation to consequentialism. Kant is not a consequentialist, but I believe we shed light on his moral metaphysics if we view him as a *moral fact internalist*. Some of Kant's more controversial claims about particular cases, and his general aversion to considering the consequences of our acts, look less strange than they might otherwise appear to many of us when viewed in this light. Perhaps he thought, like the expected value consequentialist, that *actual* consequences don't matter, so far as the morality of right and wrong action is concerned.[39] The moral fact internalist takes it that in order to assess whether someone deserves moral praise, which is to say that they acted rightly, we need only know their internal states, and need know nothing about the external world. This seems to be what Kant was after.[40]

It is sometimes said that for Kant, the consequences of one's acts simply don't matter, in any sense. This can't be quite right, as a careful reading of the following famous passage from the *Groundwork* reveals:

> Even if, by a special disfavor of nature... this will should wholly lack the capacity to carry out its purpose—if with its greatest efforts it should yet achieve nothing and only the good will were left (not, of course, as a mere wish but as the summoning of all means insofar as they are in our control)—then, like a jewel, it would still shine by itself, as something that has its full worth in itself. (4:394)

Here, Kant is very explicit about two things: (1) the good will is in the business of summoning means to bring about ends (and is not concerned with merely wishing that some state of affairs be instantiated); and (2) as long as the good will does all it reasonably can (given what is in its control) to take the means to the right ends, its worth is not dependent on whether or not the ends are actually brought about. Now, the summoning of

---

[39] Note that I am not saying Kant was an expected value consequentialist, only that he shares the moral fact internalist perspective with the expected value consequentialist, and that he may perhaps have some room for expected consequences at certain points in his theory. When Kant says that one must not lie to the murderer at the door, it is natural to read him as saying that one must not do this, whatever the expected consequences. He also claims that, if one lies, and the murderer is turned away and thereby ends up meeting the intended victim, who has left without one's knowledge, then one shares responsibility for the murder (8:427). Here it might be thought that Kant is appealing to *actual* consequences in his argument for why you ought not to lie. However, I take it that these imagined consequences (even if we take them to be imagined as actual) are not intended to be any part of the explanation of the wrongness of lying (on such an occasion); rather, Kant is arguing that one would share responsibility for the murder if it subsequently occurred, simply in virtue of the fact that one would have acted wrongly when lying.

[40] It is *not* part of the moral fact internalist view that the mental states in question need to be perspicuous to the agent, or even accessible to consciousness. This means that my construal of Kant as a moral fact internalist does not clash with his view that, in fact, we can never be certain of the motivation on which a person has acted. It is nevertheless true for Kant that *if* we knew that a person acted on the right moral motive then we would know that they acted rightly (assuming, I would add, for the sake of veracity, that we also knew they collected their evidence about possible future events in an epistemically responsible way).

means requires the ability to act, at least in some limited way, and action requires paying attention to consequences in at least one sense: we must, at the very least, be concerned with reasonably *attempting* to realize a goal.

Suppose a surgeon with a good will is operating on a sick patient and decides to remove an organ (as a means to restoring the patient's health)—she very reasonably decides that this act of removing a particular organ would be the right thing to do. However, after opening up the patient's body, the surgeon discovers haemorrhaging in a different organ. Realizing that the patient is likely to die if she doesn't first deal with the haemorrhaging, the surgeon postpones the original procedure and deals with the haemorrhaging instead. If the caricature of Kant's position that says consequences (in any reasonable sense of the word) simply don't matter were correct, then we would be left without any way of explaining why it is only reasonable for the doctor to change her mind in this situation. So consequences, in some sense, surely do matter.

Now suppose that because of the surgeon's decision to change the nature of the operation in the middle, the patient in fact dies, and that—although there was no way for the surgeon to predict this, and it goes against the surgeon's best, most epistemically conscientious judgement—the patient wouldn't have died if the surgeon had stuck to his original plan. I think the above quotation from Kant makes clear what he would think about the surgeon's decision: it may still demonstrate the kind of good will that is like a shining jewel (assuming the surgeon is acting on a moral motive, rather than attempting to save the patient out of self-interest). So if Kant is concerned with consequences in some sense, in what sense is he concerned with them? It seems just in the sense of *expected* consequences, where these are distinguished from *actual* consequences. What is crucial is that there is a fact of the matter concerning whether this surgeon deserves moral praise, where this fact is *independent* of whether his actions are ultimately effective in the world—that there is such a fact will flow from accepting *moral fact internalism*, rather than from rejecting the relevance of (expected) consequences.

So much for consequences in relation to *means*. We have not said anything about ends yet, and it is our ends, not our means, that are most fundamentally dictated by duty, according to Kant. Here it is clear that Kant thinks the good will is more fully *unconcerned* with the consequences of acts, perhaps even in an *expected* sense. He writes:

> an action from duty has its moral worth *not in the purpose* to be attained by it but in the maxim in accordance with which it is decided upon, and therefore does not depend upon the realization of the object of the action but merely upon the *principle of volition* in accordance with which the action is done without regard for any object of the faculty of desire...the purposes we may have for our actions, and their effects as ends and incentives of the will, can give actions no unconditional and moral worth...In what then can this worth lie...?...it can lie nowhere else *than in the principle of the will* without regard for any object of the faculty of desire. (4:399–400)

One might suspect that Kant failed to adequately distinguish the view that I am calling *moral fact internalism*, according to which *actual* consequences don't matter morally, from the view that consequences don't matter *in any sense*. One might also suspect that this has something to do with Kant over-generalizing from an observation about the so-called 'perfect' duties (not to lie, not to murder etc.), forgetting his own commitment to the existence of 'imperfect' duties as he did so (to perfect oneself, to be charitable etc.). The observation I have in mind here is that, so far as the perfect duties are concerned, he doesn't think consequences matter in the least. This is easier to say about negative duties (duties to refrain from certain acts) than positive duties (duties to perform certain acts). I do not need to pay any attention to varying possible consequences in order to simply make sure I never murder anyone. On the other hand, it makes no sense to say one has a duty to develop one's talents without paying any attention to rationally expected consequences, for the only way one could possibly hope to fulfil a duty to develop one's talents is by paying attention to the evidence regarding which talents it is going to be possible to develop—of course, it might be that, due to the unpredictable interference of the world, one may fail to develop one's talents when one tries to do so as best one can, but that will be through no fault of one's own. Similarly, it makes no sense to expect to be charitable without paying attention at all to the contingent facts about the possible objects of one's charity. And, in fact, Kant allows room for judgement in the application of imperfect duties (in fact, this might be entailed by the definition of an imperfect duty). When discussing charity and the formula of humanity, Kant says 'there is still only a negative and not a positive agreement with *humanity as an end in itself* unless everyone also tries, as far as he can, to further the ends of others'(4:430). Efforts to try to further the ends of others clearly require us to pay attention to rationally expected consequences.

A defender of Kant might at this point object that the crucial thing to focus on is that the determination *that* one has an imperfect duty of charity (whether resulting from an application of the formula of universal law or the formula of humanity) is itself a rational determination that is to be made without paying any attention to consequences. We do not decide that there is a duty of charity by looking at the consequences that would follow from our taking it to be that there is a duty of charity. This is true, but completely beside the point. To see why, we need only note that, on pain of circularity, the consequentialist would surely also be right to claim that the principle of right action at the heart of her theory is not itself one that is to be justified in terms of consequences: one is not meant to judge that the consequentialist principle is correct by judging that it would be better if people followed it than if they did not (in fact, consequentialists will think it is often better for people *not* to attempt to follow the consequentialist principle).

So far I have been ignoring the most crucial *rationale* Kant provides for the ban on thinking about the consequences of one's acts. He declares, 'What has a price can be replaced by something else as its *equivalent*; what on the other hand is raised above all price and therefore admits of no equivalent has a dignity' (4:434). The reason we cannot weigh consequences that will affect different individuals (e.g. the murderer at the door and the friend that the murderer is looking for) is because to do so involves treating people as interchangeable objects that have prices, rather than treating them with the *respect* that is due to rational beings.

So I most certainly do not mean to say that Kantians have nothing more to say about why we should reject consequentialism, either drawing on Kant, or using arguments that go beyond Kant's writings. And I have not argued that Kant is a consequentialist, even of the expected value variety.[41] My main aim has simply been to suggest that the idea that moral truths are, most fundamentally, truths of reason that can be applied to determine whether acts are right or wrong by taking a perspective that is entirely internal to the agent—an idea that in its non-egotistical version we may rightly associate most closely with Kant—is not in any straightforward or obvious way necessarily deontological, as opposed to consequentialist. This may have important consequences for how we understand the relationship of metaethics and normative ethics. Kantians often take it that there is a very tight connection between the correct moral metaphysics and normative ethical theory, but, in so far as we take the most basic Kantian idea to be that moral truths are truths of reason that conform with moral fact internalism, I have suggested that this is an idea that is neutral between consequentialist and non-consequentialist normative principles.

38.6 CONCLUSION

The four types of moral realism just sketched seem to nicely divide up the landscape of possible types of positive moral metaphysics, but I started this piece by distinguishing between moral realism and ethical realism, and strong and weak realism. I'll end by very briefly considering what more might be said about each of these distinctions.

It pays to be careful when discussing anti-realist positions to distinguish between positions that are ethically anti-realist and positions that are merely morally anti-realist. All ethical anti-realists are moral anti-realists, but not all moral anti-realists are ethical anti-realists. The committed amoral ethical egoist will *need* to be a realist of a sort, i.e. a realist (or at least a quasi-realist) about the principle that each person should pursue their own self-interest. She will also face a choice of whether to be a realist about well-being (even if well-being consists in the satisfaction of preferences, say), or a relativist about well-being (it seems very peculiar to think that well-being could consist in the satisfaction of preferences in my case but consist in the experiencing of pleasure in your case, say, but there is at least room in logical space for this view). In relation to both of these types of realism, correlates of the above four options will all apply: the egoist principle and the facts about well-being (assuming the egoist adopts an objective account of well-being) may have a non-natural foundation, an external natural foundation, a foundation in the sentiments, or a foundation in reason. The crucial point here is that, so far

---

[41] Timmerman 2005 argues against consequentialist readings of Kant.

as *metaphysical commitments* are concerned, egoism is in no stronger a position than positive moral views are.[42]

Moral realists need not necessarily adopt the same account of the grounding of self-interest that they adopt when it comes to morality. One can see an example of how this might work in a certain natural interpretation of Kant: morality for Kant is clearly grounded in reason, but self-interest might be grounded in our empirical nature, which has a teleological structure to it that ensures that we seek out our own happiness; in other words, Kant's account of self-interest is, in some respects, Aristotelian.[43] I don't think we would do an injustice to Kant if we were to thus conclude that his ethical realism is a mixed theory.

Prior to Ayer and Mackie, thoroughgoing ethical anti-realism hovered as a threat, but was not positively embraced by philosophers.[44] It is interesting to note that (moral) anti-realists prior to the modern era, especially those we read about in the *Gorgias* and the *Republic*, were not so much concerned to argue that there is no normativity or value to be found anywhere at all (e.g. that all ethical statements are untrue, or not truth-apt, or truth-apt only in a deflationary or minimal sense), but rather that one only ever ought to pursue one's own good, that the powerful get to determine what is right, etc. In other words, if they had been presented with the distinction between ethical realism and moral realism as I have defined them, even the more sceptical or sophistical ancients would most likely have still accepted the first. And the same can probably be said for most thinkers since.

In fact, one of the most interesting continually recurring topics throughout the history of ethics has been the relationship between self-interest and morality, and it is a shame I will not be able to say more about that topic here. A chapter on the history of this topic would need to cover not just Plato, Aristotle, and Kant, but also, at the very least, Joseph Butler, Thomas Hobbes, Friedrich Nietzsche, and Henry Sidgwick. Five positions in this area would be particularly worth considering: (1) the ethical egoism that rejects the demands of morality (found, perhaps, in Nietzsche, and, unhappily, in a strand of Sidgwick's *The Methods of Ethics*); (2) the reconciliationism that takes the demands of morality to be real and independent, but also sees following them as being in each individual's self-interest (Plato and Aristotle); (3) the contractarianism that takes morality to be an institution that is constructed in order to further the self-interest of each individual (Hobbes); (4) the 'dualism of practical reason' thesis we find in Sidgwick that would have it that self-interest and morality are not reconcilable, but that it is always rationally permissible to act in ways that promote one's own self-interest, and also always

---

[42] Although perhaps egoism is in a stronger *epistemic* position (Crisp 2006: 71–96).

[43] This is true in so far as Kant's understanding of prudence fits into a teleological framework for understanding our biology (see Wood 1999: 215–25), but not in so far as Kant wishes to make much of the dangers of self-love.

[44] Nietzsche presents an interesting case that I don't have space to discuss. He may be an exception to my generalization, but probably not, since it is not clear that his anti-realism extends to the whole of ethics, rather than just to morality. I qualify the claim about Mackie in footnote 4 above.

rationally permissible to act morally;[45] and (5) a 'weighing reasons' position that would understand self-interest and morality as sometimes conflicting, and would contend that, on such occasions, the balance of reasons sometimes requires us to follow self-interest and sometimes requires us to follow morality.[46]

A lesson of this chapter with respect to the distinction between weak and strong varieties of realism that I introduced at the beginning is that it is not always easy to classify a philosopher, or a particular form of moral realism, as promoting a sufficiently robust commitment to truth and sufficiently strong degree of objectivity to count as strongly or robustly moral realist. In the case of non-naturalist realism, we saw that one of the most prominent contemporary non-naturalists, although wishing to deny the term realist to any account that would have it that the moral truths are stance-dependent, does not view his realism as in any way weakened by a claim that there is no realm of entities that fundamental moral judgements correspond to. In the case of naturalist realism, I suggested that those contemporary naturalists committed to complete reducibility likewise move away from Aristotle in a way that might also make us worry about the strength of the moral realism we might impute to them. With respect to the view that fundamental truths are truths of reason, it might be thought that the rejection of the idea that fundamental moral beliefs represent external facts presents a barrier to squaring this view with realism (if this is a problem here, which I said that I doubt it really is, it is also a problem for Parfit's version of non-naturalism), and we saw that this leads some to call this view 'irrealist'. With respect to Hume we find the label 'subjectivist' commonly used to describe his sentimentalist metaethical position, a term that suggests Humeans should celebrate what might be construed as the weak nature of that position's realism. However, in relation to both the rationalist and sentimentalist options, I suggested that I do not find it at all obvious that there cannot be versions of these views that fully deserve to be called strong realisms (although I noted that the obstacles in the case of Humeanism are considerable). I imagine that contemporary philosophers will, for the foreseeable future, remain divided on the question of how important, if at all, it is to be a strong realist in ethics. Hopefully, we will eventually become much clearer about just where we would like the truth to lie, and, much more importantly, where it does in fact lie.

---

[45] The position that Sidgwick reluctantly finds himself adopting in *The Methods of Ethics* (1981) might, in the first instance, be best described as the position that reason does not provide us with a way to decide between the dictates of egoistic hedonism and of universal hedonism. Still, I take it that this position is equivalent to the position that it is always rationally permissible to promote one's own self-interest and always rationally permissible to act morally, given Sidgwick's view that reason requires that one follow one of these dictates, rather than act contrary to them or pursue some third end, since these dictates are provided by the only two substantive and fundamental ethical intuitions that survive rational reflection (and given his view that morality coincides with universal hedonism).

[46] For theories concerning the relation of self-interest and morality that might, with certain qualifications, be thought to be examples of this last position, see Parfit (2011a: 130–49) and Crisp (2006: 131–45).

Bibliography

Ackrill, J. L. 1980. 'Aristotle on *Eudaimonia*', in A. Rorty (ed.), *Essays on Aristotle's Ethics*. Berkeley: University of California Press, 15–33.

Aristotle, 1995. *Aristotle: Selections*, ed. and tr. T. Irwin and G. Fine. Indianapolis: Hackett Publishing Company.

—— 2000. *Nicomachean Ethics*, ed. and tr. R. Crisp. Cambridge: Cambridge University Press.

Ayer, A. J. 1950. *Language, Truth and Logic*. New York: Dover Publications.

Blackburn, S. 1993. *Essays in Quasi-Realism*. New York: Oxford University Press.

Boyd, R. 1988. 'How to be a Moral Realist', in G. Sayre-McCord (ed.), *Essays on Moral Realism*. Ithaca, NY: Cornell University Press, 181–228.

Brink, D. 1989. *Moral Realism and the Foundations of Ethics*. Cambridge: Cambridge University Press.

Cohon, R. 1997. 'The Common Point of View in Hume's Ethics', *Philosophy and Phenomenological Research* 57 (4): 827–50.

Crisp, R. 2006. *Reasons and the Good*. Oxford and New York: Oxford University Press.

De Caro, M. and Macarthur, D. 2010. *Naturalism and Normativity*. New York: Columbia University Press.

Foot, P. 2001. *Natural Goodness*. Oxford: Clarendon Press.

Gibbard, A. 2003. *Thinking How to Live*. Cambridge, MA: Harvard University Press.

Hume, D. 1998. *An Enquiry concerning the Principles of Morals*, ed. T. L. Beauchamp. Oxford and New York: Oxford University Press.

—— 2000. *A Treatise of Human Nature*, ed. D. F. Norton and M. J. Norton. Oxford and New York: Oxford University Press.

Irwin, T. 2009. *The Development of Ethics: A Historical and Critical Study, Vol. II*. Oxford and New York: Oxford University Press.

Jackson, F. 2000. *From Metaphysics to Ethics: A Defence of Conceptual Analysis*. Oxford: Oxford University Press.

Joyce, R. 2001. *The Myth of Morality*. Cambridge: Cambridge University Press.

Kant, I. 1996. *Practical Philosophy*, tr. and ed. M. J. Gregor. Cambridge: Cambridge University Press.

McDowell, J. 1980. 'The Role of *Eudaimonia* in Aristotle's Ethics', in A. Rorty (ed.), *Essays on Aristotle's Ethics*. Berkeley: University of California Press, 359–76.

Mackie, J. L. 1977. *Ethics: Inventing Right and Wrong*. Harmondsworth and New York: Penguin Books.

—— 1980. *Hume's Moral Theory*. London: Routledge & Kegan Paul.

Moore, G. E. 1993. *Principia Ethica*. Cambridge: Cambridge University Press.

Parfit, D. 2011a. *On What Matters*, Vol. I. Oxford and New York: Oxford University Press.

—— 2011b. *On What Matters*, Vol. II. Oxford and New York: Oxford University Press.

Pigden, C. R. 2010. 'Snare's Puzzle / Hume's Purpose: Non-cognitivism and What Hume Was Really Up to with No-Ought-From-Is', in C. R. Pigden (ed.), *Hume on Is and Ought*. Basingstoke: Palgrave Macmillan, 169–91.

Plato 1993. *Republic*, tr. R. Waterfield. Oxford and New York: Oxford University Press.

—— 1997. *Complete Works*, ed. J. M. Cooper. Indianapolis: Hackett Publishing Company.

Powell, R. and Buchanan, A. 2011. 'Breaking Evolution's Chains: The Prospect of Deliberate Genetic Modification in Humans', *Journal of Medicine and Philosophy* 36: 6–27.

Sayre-McCord, G. 1994. 'On Why Hume's 'General Point of View' Isn't Ideal—and Shouldn't Be', *Social Philosophy & Policy* 11 (1): 202–28.

Shafer-Landau, R. 2003. *Moral Realism: A Defence*. Oxford: Clarendon Press.

Shields, C. 2010 *Aristotle*. London and New York: Routledge.

Sidgwick, H. 1981. *The Methods of Ethics*, seventh edition. Indianapolis and Cambridge: Hackett.

Skorupski, J. 2010. *The Domain of Reasons*. Oxford and New York: Oxford University Press.

Sturgeon, N. L. 1984. 'Moral Explanations', in D. Copp and D. Zimmerman (eds), *Morality, Reason and Truth*. Totowa, NJ: Rowman and Allanheld, 49–78.

Timmerman, J. 2005. 'Why Kant Could not Have Been a Utilitarian', *Utilitas* 17 (3): 243–64.

Williams, B. 2003. *Ethics and the Limits of Philosophy*. London: Fontana Press.

—— 2006. 'Plato: The Invention of Philosophy', in *The Sense of the Past: Essays in the History of Philosophy*. Princeton and Oxford: Princeton University Press, 148–86.

Wood, Allen W. 1999. *Kant's Ethical Thought*. Cambridge: Cambridge University Press.

CHAPTER 39

CONSTRUCTING PRACTICAL ETHICS

DALE JAMIESON

39.1 INTRODUCTION

IN this chapter my aim is to shed light on contemporary practices by exposing some of their origins. I proceed by presenting a broad history of practical ethics that is somewhat speculative and impressionistic. My most general conclusion is that the diversity of activities collected under the rubric of 'practical ethics' is fed by a wide range of intellectual and cultural sources. Seeing contemporary practices in the light of their historical background will, I hope, contribute to greater methodological self-consciousness and sophistication, and help to clarify the relationships of practical ethics to the discipline of philosophy.

In constructing such a sweeping narrative I will be accused of overstating some themes and understating others. Moreover, one of the costs of pursuing such a capacious project is that almost certainly some mistakes have crept in. Nevertheless, I think the interpretation that I develop is important and worthy of further discussion, and it is in that spirit that I put it forward.

39.2 OUR SUBJECT

Nowadays, we normally divide ethical theory into two major fields, metaethics and normative ethics. Metaethics concerns the meaning and status of moral language. Normative ethics is divided between moral theory, and applied or practical ethics. Moral theory is concerned with what sorts of things are good, which acts are right, and what the relations are between the right and the good. Practical ethics is concerned with the evaluation of particular things as good and bad, and of various acts, practices, or institutions as right or wrong.[1]

Our subject, practical ethics, is taught in colleges and universities around the world, pursued in dedicated research centres, and discussed in specialized journals. It is usually regarded as encompassing such fields as bioethics, environmental ethics, business ethics, engineering ethics, or professional ethics generally. Abortion, euthanasia, poverty, war, and the moral status of non-human animals are among the topics that have received the most attention.[2]

The history and practice of practical ethics is closely connected to philosophy, but the relation of this field to the discipline is somewhat fraught. This may help to explain why practical ethics is often pursued in interdisciplinary institutes, sometimes by philosophers, but often by academics who are more oriented towards religion than philosophy, or have been trained in a profession such as law, medicine, or business. There are other reasons why this is so, some of which will be illuminated by examining the history of the field.

In this chapter my focus is on practical ethics as it is practised in the secular, Anglophone world of philosophy. This does not cover everything in the domain of practical ethics but it covers a lot, including much of what has been most influential.[3]

39.3 A Standard View

One influential view is that practical ethics is as old as philosophy, but that it was obscured for much of the twentieth century by 'the dominance of positivism and empiricism in the philosophy of science, and the vogue for linguistic analysis in epistemology'.[4] For example, Charles Pigden writes that

> Until about 1920 and since about 1970, practical ethics was regarded as a legitimate branch of philosophy. There are now, and there have been in the past, famous philosophers, such as Jeremy Bentham and Peter Singer, who have devoted themselves to practical ethics. (2003: 477–8)

On this view a continuous thread connects contemporary practical ethics with the concerns of the Greeks, Enlightenment thinkers such as Kant, and progressives such as Bentham and Mill. The connection was ruptured sometime in the early twentieth century, and re-established about 1970 under the influence of the Civil Rights Movement, the anti-Vietnam war movement, and the rise of feminism.

[1] Jamieson 2008: chs 2–3.   [2] See Singer 2011 for a good introduction to the field.
[3] My focus is specifically on Great Britain and the United States and I (regrettably) slight the rest of the Anglophone world.
[4] Almond 1998.

There is something to this story.[5] It is easy to find revealing quotations from the offending period that would have been out of place both earlier and later. Consider two well-known examples. In 1956 Peter Laslett declared that political philosophy was dead (1956: vii).[6] Earlier, in 1930, Broad had written that

> We can no more learn to act rightly by appealing to the ethical theory of right action than we can play golf well by appealing to the mathematical theory of the flight of the golf ball. The interest of ethics is thus almost wholly theoretical. (1930: 285)

Broad and Laslett were expressing views that were commonly held at the time, and this makes the 'continuous thread ruptured by positivism and empiricism' account seem plausible. Still, as I suggest in this chapter, the actual intellectual landscape of the offending period was more variegated and complex than this simple story suggests.

It is true that philosophers have always discussed problems of practical urgency (that they do, may be part of why today we count them as philosophers). Consider, for example, Plato's *Crito*, a text that is often used to introduce students to philosophy. The jail-house discussion of the obligation to obey the law, with the imminent execution (or suicide) of Socrates looming in the background, is about as practical and compelling as it gets.

However, it is also true (as I hinted in the previous paragraph) that our application of the terms 'philosopher' and 'philosophy' is somewhat anachronistic. Socrates did not give lectures, mark exams, have tenure, or even work in a university. Nor did he distinguish his activities from doing cosmology or meteorology. For that matter, his concepts probably would not map very neatly onto any of these notions. While the attributions of terms such as 'philosopher' and 'philosophy' become less anachronistic through time (a fact more about time than about our attributions), there are still important and striking differences between the way in which those philosophers from the past who we often treat as our contemporaries thought about what they were doing, and how we think about ourselves and our activities.

Consider, for example, Henry Sidgwick, whose image has been transformed from 'old Sidg', the stuffy Victorian, as Moore and his contemporaries thought of him, to the philosopher's philosopher on whose shoulders Derek Parfit stands.[7] The moral issues that dominated Sidgwick revolved around the requirement that fellows of Cambridge, Oxford, and Durham colleges subscribe to the Thirty-Nine Articles of the Church of England. In effect, one had to affirm the virgin birth of Jesus, his descent into hell, and various metaphysical doctrines about free will and the nature of the trinity in order to

---

[5] Indeed, I myself have contributed to this narrative in Jamieson 1999: 1–7, and Jamieson 2002: ch. 2. However, it should also make us wonder that some philosophers of this period, such as Broad and Carritt (1925), who were not unduly influenced by positivism and empiricism, were also sceptical of practical ethics.

[6] An implied theme of this chapter that warrants further discussion is that practical ethics and political philosophy are more closely related than has often been acknowledged.

[7] Rawls wrote that 'Sidgwick's *Methods* is the first truly academic work in moral theory, modern in both method and spirit' (1980: 554–5). This would not have been said a generation before. See Schneewind 1977 and Schultz 2004 for their important efforts to place Sidgwick in his historical context. See Phillips 2011 for an interpretation and evaluation of the central argument of *Methods*.

work in these universities. Sidgwick lost his faith, and was thereby confronted with the searing question of whether to resign his fellowship.[8] This was the issue that led him back into philosophy (from classics), and deeply influenced his most important work:

> while struggling with the difficulty thence arising…I went through a good deal of the thought that was ultimately systematized in the *Methods of Ethics*.[9]

Schultz tries to put us in Sidgwick's shoes when he writes that

> Conscientious objection to subscription to the Thirty-nine articles of the Church of England was for Sidgwick and his time what conscientious objection to the draft was to the students in the 1960s. (2004: 15)

While the analogy helps convey the importance of the issue to Sidgwick, teaching at Cambridge is not much like being a grunt in Vietnam and resigning a college fellowship is rather different from going to jail. However, what is most difficult for us to imagine is not the importance of this issue to Sidgwick, but what it would mean to do practical ethics in a world in which universities, religious faith, and deference to authority are so tightly bound.[10]

Concerns about anachronism aside, there is something else to say about the simple thought that philosophers have always discussed problems of practical urgency: Yes they have, but they did not always regard themselves as doing philosophy when they did so.

Consider Bertrand Russell, certainly one of the greatest philosophers of the twentieth century and the author of dozens of books on topics that seem central to practical ethics, including *The Practice and Theory of Bolshevism*, *Why I Am Not a Christian*, *Human Society in Ethics and Politics*, *Marriage and Morals*, and *War Crimes in Vietnam*. Not only did Russell generally disavow such books as works of philosophy, he was quite sceptical about whether ethics in any form counted as philosophy. In a book published in 1927, intended to provide the American public with a general introduction to philosophy, he wrote:

> Ethics is traditionally a department of philosophy…I hardly think myself that it ought to be. (1927: 115)

---

[8] Throughout his life Sidgwick was troubled by the fact that while he believed that it was generally good for people to believe in orthodox religion, he himself could not bring himself to do so, thus motivating his concerns about esoteric morality.

[9] As quoted in Schultz 2004: 115. In the Preface to the first edition of *The Methods of Ethics* Sidgwick (1907: vii) says that the book is not 'directly practical', thus leaving open the question of whether he thinks the book is 'indirectly' practical or not practical at all.

[10] There are other important differences between Sidgwick's outlook and that of most of us today that are often papered over by his fans. One concerns different attitudes towards the 'dualism of practical reason'. For most of us it is a philosophical problem, or a fact that we must live with; for Sidgwick, it was a deeply emotional challenge to the meaning of life and the intelligibility of the universe. He was a fallen Victorian in a way that is inaccessible to most of us. Another area in which there are stark differences concerns his attitudes towards race and colonial domination. See Schultz 2004: ch. 7 for discussion.

Of course it can be said that Russell was one of those infected by, and even gleefully transmitting, 'positivism and empiricism in the philosophy of science, and the vogue for linguistic analysis in epistemology'. Still, it would be something of an irony if it turned out that one of the philosophers who wrote most about practical ethics should also have been one who was trying to excise it from the discipline.[11] We need a larger context in order to understand Russell's attitude.

39.4 THE BRITISH ORIGINS OF PRACTICAL ETHICS

There are two important strands in the development of practical ethics in Great Britain. One is associated with the Scottish Enlightenment; the other with the philosophical radicals.

The first use of the term, 'practical ethics' of which I am aware occurs in a tract, 'On the Plantation-Trade', by Charles Davenant, a seventeenth-century English writer on political economy. Davenant characterizes this tract as

> A short view of Practical Ethicks; which, perhaps may be thought needless at present, and rather useful to posterity.[12]

He discusses the virtues and vices of colonial managers, and how various policies affect their development and inculcation.

> The preventing remedy against such distempers is to be had from the precepts of morality, which writers upon all sort of subjects should endeavour to inculcate; for the vices or virtues of a country influence very much in all its business; so that he who would propose methods by which the affairs of a kingdom may be any ways bettered, should, at the same time, consider the predominant passions, the morals, temper, and inclinations of the people.

Davenant is remembered in the history of economics for publishing the first price-quantity table, on the basis of data provided by Gregory King. We know that both Adam Smith and Jeremy Bentham read his work.[13]

David Fordyce, who was Professor of Philosophy at Aberdeen from 1742 until his death in 1751, popularized the term, 'practical ethics'. His *Elements of Moral Philosophy* was first published in 1748 as Part 9 of Robert Dodsley's *The Preceptor: Containing a General Course of Education*, a widely used educational text, and also appeared in the first edition of the *Encyclopedia Brittanica*. In 1754 it was published as a free-standing book that was used as a text throughout Great Britain and colonial America (including

---

[11] For an excellent account of Russell on ethics see Pigden 2003.
[12] This and the following passage are from Davenant 1697/1771/1967: 75ff. Beauchamp 2007 brought the work of Davenant to my attention.
[13] See Endres 1987, and Giunti, undated, note 46, respectively.

Harvard), and also made its way into French and German translations. In Book 3, Section 1, 'Of Practical Ethics, or the Culture of the Mind', Fordyce describes his purposes in the following way:

> This Section then will contain a brief Enumeration of the Arts of acquiring Virtuous Habits, and of eradicating Vitious Ones. (1748/2003: 119)

On his view, we are governed by the 'Original Constitution and Laws of our Nature', but we can guide our judgements and taste by practising the virtues. The proper attitude towards our 'Supreme Parent' can also help us in this task.

> It will greatly conduce to refine the Moral Taste and strengthen the virtuous Temper, to accustom the Mind to the frequent Exercise of Moral Sentiments and Determinations, by reading History, Poetry, particularly of the Picturesque and Dramatic kind, the Study of the fine Arts; by conversing with the most eminent for Goodsense and Virtue; but above all by frequent and repeated Acts of Humanity, Compassion, Friendship, Politeness and Hospitality…It is a great Inducement to the Exercise of Benevolence to view Human Nature in a favourable Light, to observe the Characters and Circumstances of Mankind on the fairest Sides, to put the best Constructions on their Actions they will bear…Above all, the Nature and Consequences of Virtue and Vice, their Consequences being the Law of our Nature and Will of Heaven; the Light in which they appear to our Supreme Parent and Lawgiver, and the Reception they will meet with from him, must be often attended to. (Fordyce 1748/2003: 119, 129–31)

In 1764 Thomas Reid, who was friends with Fordyce in Aberdeen, assumed the Chair of Moral Philosophy in Glasgow and began lecturing on 'practical ethics'.[14] Reid did not publish on these topics during his lifetime, but his extensive notes and papers have since been published.[15] Reid's lectures were strongly influenced by Pufendorf's Protestant natural law theory, which had been introduced to Scotland by Gershom Carmichael, one of Reid's predecessors in the Glasgow chair. Carmichael influenced Francis Hutcheson, another one of Reid's predecessors, and Hutcheson in turn directly influenced Reid.

For Reid, philosophy was divided between the study of matter (natural philosophy) and the study of mind (pneumatology). Pneumatology was divided between the study of the divine mind and the study of the human mind. The study of the human mind was divided between the study of the intellectual powers, the study of the active powers, and politics. The study of the active powers included the theory of morals, and practical ethics which he also sometimes called morals or ethics. Practical ethics was divided into duties to God, duties to ourselves, and duties to others. Duties to others, which were the most extensive part of the lectures, were divided into duties to individuals ('natural jurisprudence') and duties to societies ('law of nations'). Reid believed in a strong state,

---

[14] While they were both living in Aberdeen in 1735, Forsyth wrote to a friend, 'I have none here with whom I can enter into the Depths of Philosophy' (as quoted in Fordyce 1748/2003: xi, note 7), but by 1737 Reid had written him a letter of introduction for his visit to London. For evidence of Fordyce's influence on Reid, see Haakonssen's commentary in Reid 2007.

[15] Reid 2007.

but one that was circumscribed by natural law. Citizens had the right to resist if the state exceeded its authority. In part because he believed that the state had the right to levy taxes on its citizens he was hostile to the American Revolution, though he supported the French revolution until the height of the terror in 1794.

Debates in the theory of morals, according to Reid, are difficult and abstruse, but are important for defending ethics against scepticism. Different theories of morals 'differ not about what is to be accounted Virtuous conduct but why it is so to be accounted'.[16] Practical ethics, on the other hand,

> Is for the most part easy and level to all capacities. There is hardly any moral Duty which when properly explained and delineated, does not recommend itself to the heart of every candid and unbiased Man. (Reid 2007: 110)

Still, the terrain of practical ethics is vast and there is much to learn about the subject. Moreover, the moral faculty is educable, and one purpose of practical ethics is to inculcate virtue.

The idea of professional ethics was implicit in the way that Reid related duties to stations in life, and it became increasingly explicit as the tradition unfolded. Reid specifically discussed the duties of husbands and wives, parents, masters and servants, kings, magistrates, soldiers, and physicians.[17]

Three of the founders of modern medical ethics—John Gregory, Thomas Percival, and Benjamin Rush—were associated with Edinburgh University during the 1760s. Gregory was Reid's cousin, and Rush became the father of medical ethics in the United States.[18]

The Scottish idea of practical ethics was extremely influential in the United States, especially from the early eighteenth century through the end of the Civil War, when the clergy largely controlled higher education. During this period various books were published that were in the spirit of Fordyce and the Scottish philosophers.[19] These books typically had a strong, mostly liberal, Protestant cast (e.g. Haven, like the Scottish philosophers, was opposed to slavery). American colleges at this time were generally undistinguished, and most of this work bleeds rather naturally into the background of American striving and self-improvement. Another legacy of the Scottish tradition was a focus on professional ethics. As early as the 1820s ethics was taught at the United States Military Academy at West Point.[20]

The second strand in the development of British practical ethics comes from the 'philosophical radicals' (and those influenced by them). As we have seen, Pigden specifically mentions Bentham as a famous philosopher who devoted himself to practical ethics.

---

[16] Reid 2007: 112.   [17] e.g. Reid 2007: 238ff. For general discussion see Gallie 1998: 116–18.

[18] Haakonssen 1997.

[19] e.g. Haven 1859. This tradition continued throughout the nineteenth century, even after it ceased to be dominant. See, for example, Hyde 1892. It is startling to see articles from the late nineteenth century appearing in today's prestigious journals that read like slightly secularized Presbyterian sermons (for example, Knight 1894 (Knight was Professor of Moral Philosophy at St Andrews)).

[20] <http://www.antiquephotographics.com/format%20types/stereos/peoplest.htm>. Before the Civil War there was a Department of Ethics and English, chaired by Reverend J. W. French, whose *Practical Ethics* was published in several editions from the late 1850s.

Mill (1985a) states that in the *Introduction to the Principles of Morals and Legislation* Bentham is occupied with 'constructing the outlines of practical ethics and legislation', and in *Utilitarianism* he says that Bentham's failures to understand character 'greatly limit the value of his speculations on questions of *practical ethics*'(1985b). Yet, as far as I have been able to determine, the expression 'practical ethics' occurs only once in Bentham's corpus.[21] In an essay on 'nomenclature and classification', Bentham divides ethics into the 'genicoscopic' ('general matters-regarding'), and 'idioscopic' ('particular matters-regarding'). He says that 'practical' when applied to ethics is a synonym of 'idioscopic'.[22]

In 1826 Sir Richard Phillips published *Golden Rules of Social Philosophy, Or, A New System of Practical Ethics*, effusively dedicated to Simon Bolivar ('foremost among the great and good'[23]). The book is organized around 'golden rules' for various professions including princes, legislators, magistrates, bankers, and priests. Phillips emphasizes the book's practical nature: his sole goal is to be 'useful',[24] and he expresses contempt for philosophers who he views as authority worshipers.[25] One chapter of the book is devoted to vegetarianism.

In the thirty-three volumes of Mill's collected works there are only eight uses of the expression, 'practical ethics', including the two references to Bentham that I have already cited and several notes. However, in *A System of Logic*, Mill does more to explain his conception of practical ethics. He writes:

> It is customary, however, to include under the term moral knowledge, and even (though improperly) under that of moral science, an inquiry the results of which do not express themselves in the indicative, but in the imperative mood, or in periphrases equivalent to it; what is called the knowledge of duties; practical ethics, or morality. (1974: 943)

In a review for the *Edinburgh Magazine* he says that the question of when it is permissible for citizens to exercise their right to revolution is 'perhaps, altogether the knottiest question in practical ethics'.[26]

What we have thus far may seem higgledy piggledy. For the Scots, practical ethics has to do with natural law, virtue, and moral education. For philosophical radicals (and those influenced by them), practical ethics is about particular ethical concerns typically expressed as imperatives.[27] While these are different streams of thought and have different historical reach and influence, I think it is important to see what they may have in common and how they came together in late nineteenth-century British philosophy.

---

[21] Caution is in order since much of what Bentham wrote has not yet been properly edited and made accessible. This heroic task is currently underway at the Bentham Project, University College, London (for more information, visit <http://www.ucl.ac.uk/Bentham-Project>).

[22] Bentham 1983: 203. His discussion here is even more abstruse than it sounds.

[23] Phillips 1826: vi.

[24] Phillips 1826: xv.

[25] Phillips 1826: xiii.

[26] Mill 1977: 77.

[27] As we have seen Mill was an imperativist about moral language, and Bentham was an imperativist about law and perhaps all normative language. Phillips did not present a metaethic, but he had the habit of addressing his reader in the imperative mood.

The most ubiquitous use of the term 'practical' and its cognates in philosophy is to modify 'reason'. Since at least Aristotle it has been part of the lore of the discipline that theoretical reason concerns beliefs while practical reason concerns action. A looming presence for both the Scottish philosophers and the philosophical radicals was Hume, though each had major disagreements with him.[28] While it is controversial to what extent and in what way Hume can be said to have believed in practical reason, he was adamant that the role of morality is to 'influence our passions and actions',[29] and that 'the end of all moral speculations is to teach us our duty'.[30] I believe that this sense of 'practical' in which it concerns action is key for both the Scottish philosophers and the philosophical radicals. Both believe that ethics is about 'oughts' and the job of practical ethics is to help us to see what we ought to do.

By the end of the nineteenth century a rough consensus had emerged. T. H. Green stated the consensus is the following way. There are three main areas of investigation in ethics: '(1) what is free action?; (2) how do we judge what is to be done?; (3) what is to be done?'[31] Practical ethics is in the domain of the third question.

Sidgwick's last book, published in 1898, was entitled *Practical Ethics*. There he discusses such topics as the morality of war ('strife'), luxury, and truth-telling, and returns again to the subject of religious conformity and tests. While he doesn't provide a systematic account of what practical ethics consists in, he does tell us that it 'inhabits the "region of middle axioms"'[32] and concerns 'the practical guidance of men engaged in the business of the world'.[33]

In a book published posthumously, Sidgwick provided a map of the subject matter of philosophy which helps us to locate practical ethics, though in this book he did not use that expression. He began with the familiar distinction between 'theoretical' and 'practical philosophy'. Theoretical philosophy systematizes 'more completely...the partially systematized aggregates of knowledge which we call the sciences'.[34] Practical philosophy deals 'with the principles and methods of rationally determining "what ought to be"'.[35] It includes 'the study of the fundamental principles of Ethics and Politics, and therefore...[is] equivalent to what is commonly spoken of as Moral and Political Philosophy'.[36] He goes on to say that 'Moral or Ethical Philosophy...is primarily concerned with the general principles and methods of moral reasoning, and only with details of conduct so far as the discussion of them affords instructive examples of general principles and method'.[37] It is the business of Ethics on the other hand 'to supply an answer to questions as to details of duty or right conduct'.[38] The attempt to work out a complete system 'would inevitably lead us out of Philosophy into Casuistry: and that whether Casuistry is a good thing or a bad thing, it certainly is not Philosophy'.[39]

---

[28] And, of course, because of his influence on Hume and the Scottish philosophers another looming presence was Bishop Butler.

[29] Hume 2000: Book 3, Part 3, Section 6, Paragraph 6.

[30] Hume 1998: Section 1. It is also worth remembering that Hume wrote on such topics as suicide, and the nature of non-human animals.

[31] As quoted in Thomas 1987: 87.   [32] Sidgwick 1898: 8.   [33] Sidgwick 1898: 18.

[34] Sidgwick 1902: 21.   [35] Sidgwick 1902: 22.   [36] Sidgwick 1902: 37.

[37] Sidgwick 1902: 25.   [38] Sidgwick 1902: 26.   [39] Sidgwick 1902: 25–6.

So, to summarize, practical philosophy includes 'Moral or Ethical Philosophy' as well as 'Ethics', with the former focused on 'principles or methods' and the latter on questions of duty or right conduct. Casuistry, which is not philosophy, attempts to work out a complete system of duty or right conduct. What is left hanging is exactly what, in Sidgwick's view, practical ethics consists in. One possibility is that the term is redundant: practical ethics is just ethics, and Sidgwick calls his book 'practical ethics' in order to remind us that ethics is a branch of practical philosophy. A second possibility is that practical ethics describes a particular region of ethics, perhaps that region governed by 'middle axioms'.[40]

Writing at about the same time G. E. Moore was quite comfortable using the expression 'practical ethics', and was characteristically clear about what he meant by the expression. In *Principia Ethica* he distinguished two questions of ethics that are 'commonly confused... "What ought to be?" and... "What ought we to do?"'.[41] It is the second of these questions, 'What ought we to do?', that is the domain of practical ethics. In a review of Brentano published the same year Moore was just as clear:

> the one supreme rule of Practical Ethics is that we *ought* always *to do* that which will cause the whole state of the Universe to have as much *intrinsic* value as possible.[42]

For Moore practical ethics seemed to be about the entire range of what we ought to do, with no special connection to this question as it might arise in particular contexts or regarding specific problems.[43]

At the beginning of the twentieth century, the expression 'practical ethics' was in fairly common use. It signalled the subject that investigates what we ought to do, with special interest, for most writers, in particular rather than general issues of concern.

39.5 THE CHALLENGE OF CONCEPTUAL ANALYSIS

Almost immediately, the expression, 'practical ethics', fell out of use. Only nine years after *Principia Ethica* and the Brentano review, Moore published another book on ethics, yet the expression does not occur in this later book nor again in any of his published writings. Something had changed. The idea that the fundamental task of philosophy is

---

[40] A third possibility, suggested by Anthony Skelton in correspondence, is that the account given in Sidgwick 1902 is not true to his thought since it was a posthumous work reconstructed from his notes and manuscripts. Generally on Sidgwick's practical ethics see Skelton 2006.

[41] Moore 1993: 163.   [42] Moore 1903: 122.

[43] Unlike Sidgwick, Moore (1993: 56–7) thought that casuistry is 'part of the ideal of ethical science: Ethics cannot be complete without it... For Casuistry is the goal of ethical investigation'. This appears to be a response to Bradley's dismissive remark, 'Our moralists do not like casuistry; but if the current notion that moral philosophy has to tell you what to do is well-founded, then casuistry, so far as I can see, at once follows, or should follow' (1951: 132).

analysis, an idea that Moore pioneered along with Russell, was gaining traction, and Moore's understanding of its implications was beginning to change. Indeed, I believe that it was this understanding of philosophy as analysis that explains Russell's disparaging view of ethics.[44]

The idea of philosophical analysis was already at the centre of *Principia Ethica*. Moore began the book by telling us that he is 'inclined to think that' if 'a resolute attempt' at 'analysis and distinction' were made, 'many of the most glaring difficulties and disagreements in philosophy would disappear'.[45] He then approaches the question of what is good and this leads him to the question of how 'good' is defined. He shrugs off the idea that this is a purely linguistic question, instead saying that '[w]hat I want to discover is the nature of that object or idea'.[46] He draws an analogy between the question of what is good and the question of what is a horse. The way to answer these questions is through dissection:

> We may mean that a certain object, which we all of us know, is composed in a certain manner: that it has four legs, a head, a heart, a liver, etc. etc. all of them arranged in definite relations to one another.[47]

This, he says, is the 'sense that I deny good to be definable... it is not composed of any parts which we can substitute for it in our minds when we are thinking of it'.[48]

Philosophical analysis did not appear out of nowhere. There are many sources and precursors in the British philosophical tradition including Locke's concern with the relation between language and ideas in Book 3 of the *Essay*, the attempts of Berkeley and Hume to analyse our ideas, as well as in the Scottish philosophers' attempts to understand our common-sense commitments. On this topic, as with so many others, competing strands come together in Sidgwick.

Sidgwick's persistent concern with common-sense morality leads him often to something like conceptual analysis. In the Preface to the Sixth Edition of the *Methods of Ethics* he writes:

> In this state of mind I had to read Aristotle again; and a light seemed to dawn upon me as to the meaning and drift of his procedure... What he gave us there was the Common Sense Morality of Greece, reduced to consistency by careful comparison: given not as something external to him but as what 'we'—he and others—think, ascertained by reflection... Might I not imitate this: do the same for *our morality* here and now, in the same manner of impartial reflection on earnest opinion. (1907: xx)

From a certain perspective, *The Methods of Ethics* can be seen as an inconclusive (and, for its author deeply dissatisfying) exercise in proto- or quasi-conceptual analysis. While Sidgwick makes progress in bringing together common-sense morality, his own intuitions, and the different methods of ethics, there is continual fussing over details that

---

[44] What I say in this section chimes with Darwall's excellent 2006. The distinction between philosophical and conceptual analysis is one of several distinctions that should be tracked, but I don't think that much turns on my failure to observe it in what follows.

[45] Moore 1993: 33.   [46] Moore 1993: 58.   [47] Moore 1993: 60.   [48] Moore 1993: 60.

don't quite fall into place, and the project eventually founders on the dualism of practical reason. In the background is a deep question of which Sidgwick is aware but does not directly acknowledge: how can this methodology produce 'oughts' that we should regard as binding? For it is one thing to explicate 'our' morality, and it is another thing to say what we really ought to do. In this area, as in so many others, Sidgwick wants to gather all good things around him, and in *Principia Ethica*, Moore follows him.

Analysis took on different meanings and varying ambitions as the century unfolded. Ambitions peaked in the first two decades of the twentieth century with the work of Russell and Wittgenstein, both of whom regarded philosophical analysis as reality revealing.[49] In the 1920s and 1930s philosophical analysis played a less ambitious, but no less central, role in the work of the logical empiricists. Only science could provide an account of ultimate reality, but philosophical analysis was the instrument for distinguishing scientific sentences from the analytic sentences of logic and mathematics, and both of these from the nonsense of metaphysics and theology. Beginning in the 1930s under the influence of Moore and the later work of Wittgenstein, a modest form of analysis devoted to mapping the contours of our concepts spread from Cambridge, taking on local colour in Oxford and elsewhere. The arc of ambition ends with P. F. Strawson's 1959 book, *Individuals*, which eschews the pretensions of 'revisionary' metaphysics in favour of 'descriptive' metaphysics.

As the view that the proper job of philosophy is analysis gained influence, it became increasingly difficult to see what place practical ethics could have in such an enterprise. On this view, philosophy is descriptive not prescriptive. Philosophy may be able to tell us something about how we conceptualize our ultimate ends, but it is difficult to see how this can be transformed into an account of what we actually ought to do. Once this implication of philosophical analysis is grasped, Sidgwick's attempt to hold theoretical and practical ethics together in a single discipline comes crashing down. As the century wears on, those inspired by Moore, Russell, the logical empiricists, and others increasingly dominate the British philosophical landscape, and practical ethics is driven further to the margins. The dark night of repression, that is the tale well told by the standard history, begins to set in.[50]

39.6 APPLIED ETHICS IN THE UNITED STATES

Philosophy in the United States unfolded in a different way. In the United States the Scottish philosophical impulse was largely subsumed by religiosity, there was no equivalent to the philosophical radicals, and there was no philosopher of Sidgwick's power

---

[49] What I have in mind is Russell's Logical Atomism and Wittgenstein's *Tractatus*.

[50] From this perspective Rashdall 1907 can be seen as the last major work in the nineteenth-century British tradition of practical ethics, especially volume 2, book 3, chapter 5, where he speaks of 'applied moral philosophy' (1907: 458). A fascinating late contribution is Samuels 1935, published in the same series as Moore 1912, but with a quite different intended audience. It is interesting to ask whether the rise of conceptual analysis and the subsequent exile of practical ethics is related to the increasing

systematizing ethics. Philosophical analysis did not arrive as a powerful subversive force in part because there was so little to subvert. These tendencies did eventually wash up on American shores, but they were late and their force was blunted. They also had to compete with indigenous American Pragmatism and other peculiarities of American thought and culture.

One of these peculiarities was the summer schools devoted to the arts and humanities that became very popular throughout the United States in the late nineteenth century.[51] Important for our story is the 'summer school on applied ethics', held in Plymouth, Massachusetts every summer between 1891 and 1895.[52]

The school had three departments: economics, religion, and ethics. Participants were encouraged to attend lectures in all three areas, and lectures were organized so that they did not compete with each other. The eighteen lectures on ethics were devoted to such topics as 'the development of character', 'suicide', 'ethics of the family', 'professional and political ethics', 'ideals of friendship', 'man's relation to nature and the lower animals', punishment and prison reform, ethics and education, and 'the Indian question'. A contemporary account said that

> the success of this initial season certainly justifies the expectation that the school will become a permanent institution...A host of practical questions of ethical import confront our American society with a distinctiveness that compels recognition; and their study in annual summer conferences at Plymouth, in a scientific and impartial spirit, can but serve a useful service.[53]

The school of applied ethics was founded by Felix Adler, who was born in Germany in 1851. His family immigrated to New York when he was six so that his father could become the rabbi of Temple Emanu-El, which remains one of the largest and most influential reform synagogues in the United States. After graduating from Columbia, Adler went to Heidelberg for rabbinical training and to study philosophy. Heidelberg was one of the centres of the Kantian revival, and like many German Jewish intellectuals of the time, Adler was deeply influenced by neo-Kantianism. On his return to New York it soon became clear that he would not succeed his father as rabbi of Temple Emanu-El. In 1902, after some teaching at Cornell, he was awarded a new chair in political and social ethics at Columbia that was funded by a coalition of 'good government' groups. He held this

professionalization of British philosophy, especially in light of the fact that the Scottish forefathers of the field were clergymen as well as philosophers and the philosophical radicals had contempt for existing universities.

[51] The general term for this is the 'Chautauqua movement'.

[52] For a brief account see Wright 1910: 991. There are also accounts that can be retrieved from the archives of the *New York Times*.

[53] Shaw 1892: 164–5. The only British philosopher who lectured at the summer school, as far as I know, was Bernard Bosanquet. Initially this may seem surprising, but Bosenquet was on the German side of British philosophy, addressed political and social questions, and wrote for the broad educated public. He was a replacement for William Wallace, White's Professor of Moral Philosophy at Oxford, who died in a bicycle accident after having accepted the invitation. Wallace was a Scottish philosopher who is best known for his Hegel translations.

chair until his death in 1933, though during that time much of his attention was focused on the Ethical Culture Society which he had founded in 1877.

The Ethical Culture Society and its associated schools have been extremely influential, especially in New York. It has appealed in particular to non-religious Jews who identify with Jewish ethics and culture. Many of them were not comfortable participating in synagogues, but were blocked from other schools and institutions by anti-Semitism. The Ethical Culture Society provided a home for them.

In 1928 Adler was elected President of the Eastern Division of the American Philosophical Association. He promoted 'applied ethics' throughout his career, writing that:

> We need ... a clearer understanding of applied ethics, a better insight into the specific duties of life, a finer and a surer moral tact. (Adler 1908: 131)

In 1910 former president, Theodore Roosevelt, gave an important lecture at Harvard under the title, 'applied ethics'. Roosevelt began by saying that educational institutions must train character as well as intellect, and that 'I regard the study of ethics pursued merely as an intellectual recreation as being about as worthless as any form of mental amusement can be'.[54] He emphasized the importance of efficiency in carrying out morally worthy actions, and praised people he considered to be morally exemplary. They included those who dug the Panama Canal, those who work for environmental conservation, and those who work for world peace (he is clear, however, that world peace requires a well-armed United States).

Interest in applied ethics flourished in the native soil of Pragmatism. Although Adler never gave up his neo-Kantianism, he had much in common with his Columbia colleague, John Dewey, who sent two of his children to the Ethical Culture Society school and occasionally lectured there as well. Adler and the pragmatists viewed philosophy as part of a progressive political and social project, and shared an orientation towards German philosophy. They were more concerned with contingency than necessity, and saw philosophy as continuous with science. Adler wrote:

> Applied ethics is ... dependent ... on empirical science, that is, on an extended and ever increasing knowledge of physiology, psychology, and the environmental conditions that influence human beings. (1918: 257–8)

Previously James had written:

> On the whole, then, we must conclude that no philosophy of ethics is possible in the old—fashioned absolute sense of the term. Everywhere the ethical philosopher must wait on facts. (1891: 349)

While Sidgwick was no stranger to empirical investigation, unlike the pragmatists he thought there was a bright line between philosophy and empirical investigation.[55]

---

[54] Roosevelt 1911: 5.

[55] Sidgwick wrote on economics and politics as well as philosophy but his main area of empirical investigation was parapsychology. Davis 1998 argues that different attitudes towards the relevance of facts is part of what distinguishes Sidgwick's practical ethics from contemporary practice; Skelton 2006 disagrees.

Only three years before James' paper was published, he had remarked in a lecture to the Cambridge Ethical Society that

> I should be disposed to regard this study of facts as lying in the main beyond the province of our Society.[56]

The rise of Pragmatism was associated with important changes in American higher education. After the Civil War, colleges and universities were becoming liberated from their clerical overseers, new institutions were being established, and German philosophy and culture began to dominate.[57] Johns Hopkins University was founded as a modern, national research university on the German model. Located in a border state, it opened on George Washington's birthday (February 22) in America's centennial year (1876), in part in an attempt to help mend regional divisions in the aftermath of the Civil War.[58] In 1884 John Dewey received his PhD from Johns Hopkins University, studying with Charles Sanders Peirce among others.

It is difficult to overestimate how different the pragmatists were in background, training, disposition, and interests from most of their British contemporaries. Gesturing towards Hegel and Darwin as the major intellectual influences on Pragmatism is revealing, but so are some simple facts about background and experience. British philosophers of this period mostly studied classics and taught philosophy in the universities in which they were educated.[59] The pragmatists were men of science, and often had quirky career paths. Charles Sanders Peirce's only academic qualification was an undergraduate degree in chemistry. For thirty-two years he worked (apparently quite ineffectually) for the United States Coastal Survey. William James trained as a physician and then set up the first psychology laboratory in the United States. He was already a distinguished psychologist when he joined the Harvard philosophy department at age 55. His biographer, Ralph Barton Perry, quotes James as saying:

> I drifted into psychology and philosophy from a sort of fatality. I never had any philosophic instruction, the first lecture on psychology I ever heard being the first I ever gave. (1935/1996: 228)

Of these three important early twentieth-century pragmatists, only Dewey had philosophical training, and his interests were almost as strong in psychology as philosophy. Indeed, his now lost doctoral dissertation was on Kant's psychology.

---

[56] Sidgwick 1898: 16. The 1890s are a rich period for investigating the relations between applied ethics, practical ethics, and Pragmatism. The British ethical societies in which Sidgwick participated were inspired at least in part by Adler's Ethical Culture Society (MacKillop 1986). The *International Journal of Ethics* (which later became *Ethics*) was founded in 1890, and in its first issue published articles by Sidgwick, Adler, and Bosanquet, and in its next issue an article by Dewey.

[57] It is interesting to think about shifts in philosophical influence in relation to immigrant flows. In the eighteenth century, Scots were the largest single group immigrating to the United States. By the second half of the nineteenth century, they were replaced by Germans.

[58] Despite these noble sentiments, like many American universities Johns Hopkins had an appalling history of racism and did not admit black undergraduates until after World War II.

[59] Russell is a major exception, but not much can be further from American experience than the life of a bohemian aristocrat in Edwardian England. The clash between how ethics was practised in Britain and the United States during the 1920s is brought out clearly by Carritt 1925.

In the 1930s the wave of philosophical analysis struck the United States with the arrival of some of the best of the younger generation of logical empiricists. Cambridge analysis had already had some impact, but mainly through Russell's work in logic and the foundations of mathematics. Fleeing Nazi persecution, the logical empiricists brought with them their idea of philosophy and philosophical analysis.

The logical empiricists were extremely influential, but it is easy to overestimate how widely their views were shared. Since both Pragmatism and Logical Empiricism are forms of naturalism that have German roots, it is easy to conflate them. Moreover, while American philosophers were quite receptive to the advanced logic and formal methods that the logical empiricists introduced, that did not mean that they agreed with their philosophical views. Some of the logical empiricists (e.g. Carl Hempel, Hans Reichenbach, Rudolf Carnap, Philipp Frank, and Herbert Feigl) were highly visible because of their appointments in major research universities, yet they were often quite isolated.

One key difference between the pragmatists and the logical empiricists concerned the analytic/synthetic distinction. During this period and up through the 1960s, there was widespread agreement that conceptual analysis required a robust analytic/synthetic distinction.[60] If such a distinction cannot be maintained, then it is difficult to see what distinctive subject matter conceptual analysis would have to work on. This was common ground among those who were sceptical about the distinction (e.g. many American philosophers with pragmatist leanings) and those who defended it (e.g, logical empiricists, and British-style conceptual analysts). What was at stake in this fight was the extent to which philosophy was continuous with empirical science, and the extent to which it was an autonomous subject that could be pursued by armchair methods.

Quine's 1951 rejection of the analytic/synthetic distinction is well known, but less well known is that he expressed doubts about the distinction as early as 1933, when as a twenty-five year old recent PhD he visited Carnap in Prague. Throughout the 1940s Quine, Goodman, Tarski, and White discussed the distinction, and all expressed scepticism. This is especially striking since they were generally attracted to Logical Empiricism. I believe that their almost instinctive scepticism about the analytic/synthetic distinction was rooted in their pragmatist heritage.[61] Morton White exposed some of these roots in a paper published in a festschrift for John Dewey, one year before Quine's paper was published. The paper begins:

> John Dewey has spent a good part of his life hunting and shooting at dualisms: body-mind, theory-practice, percept-concept, value-science, learning-doing, sensation-thought, external-internal. They are always fair game and Dewey's prose rattles with fire whenever they come into view. (1950: 316)

White went on to reject the analytic/synthetic distinction, suggesting that Dewey should have rejected it as well, rather than equivocating as he sometimes did.

---

[60] Many philosophers still believe this, but there has been a large, influential body of post-Quinean work attempting to rehabilitate both the analytic/synthetic distinction and conceptual analysis, sometimes by reinterpreting them, sometimes by disentangling them (see Juhl and Loomis 2010, and Russell 2008).

[61] Excepting, presumably, Tarski, but it is worth noting that he was an admirer of Peirce.

It should not be surprising that a philosophy as empiricist, naturalist, and science-oriented as Pragmatism would reject the analytic/synthetic distinction. But Pragmatism is also historicist, which is part of what distinguishes it from other forms of Empiricism such as Logical Empiricism. Historicists, whatever their ontology, have also typically rejected the analytic/synthetic distinction (e.g. the Anglo-Hegelians).[62]

In the 1950s British conceptual analysis began to have significant impact on American philosophy. Moore and Russell spent most of World War II in the United States, Wittgenstein visited shortly after the war, and academic exchanges became increasingly frequent in the years that followed. The British influence became a rivulet in the stream of American philosophy. It was more influential than the French ideas that were beginning to cross the Atlantic at about the same time, but less important than Logical Empiricism or home-grown American styles of philosophizing.

The resistance of Pragmatism was one of the reasons why no form of conceptual analysis ever dominated American philosophy, but there was an even deeper reason. As Hilary Putnam writes,

> American philosophy, not only in the 1940s but well into the 1950s, was decidedly unideological. If there were "movements" at individual departments, they were represented by one or two people. (1997: 157)

The explanation for this probably has most to do with the decentralized nature of academic life and the cultural diversity of the United States during this period, compared to Great Britain, but part of the explanation also probably has to do with the spirit of tolerance and openness that Pragmatism engendered. This led to some strange consequences. Quine was so isolated at Harvard that in the late 1940s he came close to joining Goodman at the University of Pennsylvania so that he would have a sympathetic colleague.[63]

Meanwhile, the applied ethics movement seems to have been largely absorbed into the broad pragmatist mainstream.[64] Dewey's and Tufts', *Ethics*, which appeared in two editions, one in 1908 and another in 1932, was the most widely used ethics textbook in American colleges and universities well into the 1940s. There was a historical part of the book, a theoretical part, and a part that was called, 'the world of action'. The topics in this section included political order, social problems, labour rights, business ethics, and family values. Douglas Sloan analysed the ethics textbooks that were used after Dewey and Tufts fell out of use, and these were his conclusions:

> the actual teaching was probably much broader and more eclectic than a history of main currents of ethical theory might suggest... The prominence given throughout the forties and fifties to normative ethics and practical problems is striking... Along with the attention devoted to theoretical ethics the texts dealt with such topics as "the nature of capitalism and business ethics," "the ethics of physical and mental

---

[62] For discussion and references see Gewirth 1953. Russell 1897: 55–9 also rejected the distinction when he was in his idealist phase.
[63] Isaac 2011.
[64] Even Kaplan's successor as President of the Ethical Culture Society was a Deweyan.

health," "professional ethics," "ethics and the media of communication," morality and race relations," "marriage and the home," "religion and ethics," "education and ethics," and others. (1979: 31)

Flower and Murphy summarized the historical tenor of American philosophy in the following way:

Americans have constantly assumed that philosophy had a practical role in shaping not only the personal structure of the spirit but the character of human institutions. There are no stout defenders of the purity of philosophy, its neutrality, its studied irrelevance to practice…Not till the mid-twentieth century—beyond our period does philosophy in America toy with ideas of purity and impractability. (1977: xviii)

Why then do so many people think that a dark night of repression fell over applied ethics sometime in the early twentieth century and only lifted around 1970? They may mistake the fate of practical ethics in Great Britain with the story of applied ethics in the United States. Moreover, the expanding academic job market of the 1950s and 1960s may have disproportionately benefited epistemology, logic, and philosophy of language at the expense of other fields. What may have declined is not the amount of activity in applied ethics, but its frequency. In addition, while the pragmatist impulse was very much alive, the two leading inheritors of this tradition (Goodman and Quine) ignored moral and political questions in their professional work, and this may have lowered the visibility of the work in applied ethics that continued to be done in the pragmatist tradition.[65] Generally during this period American universities were becoming more bureaucratized, and most disciplines, including philosophy, were becoming more professionalized. As a result, many philosophers were moving towards what they regarded as the centre of the discipline and writing on more specialized and technical subjects, in contrast to American philosophers of the first half of the century who tended to write about anything that appealed, drawing on whatever sources they fancied.[66]

In addition to these factors, World War II provoked broad cultural changes that made post-war America a different country in many ways than its pre-war counterpart. What this meant for philosophy is that the way people wrote books and articles, how they constructed sentences, the vocabularies they deployed, their strategies for setting out problems, the journals they published in, the ways they behaved at philosophical meetings, and even how they dressed and coifed themselves, all changed dramatically. From the vantage point of the 1960s, the pragmatists looked and sounded old, musty, and boring. They fell out of fashion, and it was easy to pretend that they did not exist.

---

[65] White's interests were much broader and even more continuous with the early pragmatists than Goodman's and Quine's, but for whatever reason his influence was not as great. Perhaps his 1970 move to the Institute for Advanced Study in Princeton, which put him out of contact with graduate students, had something to do with it. Rorty revived the tradition of normatively engaged Pragmatism but well after the prevailing narrative had solidified. Moreover, much of Rorty's work was more in the spirit of metapragmatism than of pragmatism, an approach that would have repelled Dewey.

[66] I suspect this change occurred in other disciplines as well.

A final reason is that in this area as in others, the darkest hour was just before dawn. Conceptual analysis was at the height of its influence at the very moment that practical ethics began to explode. Like most young people, the generation that developed practical ethics in the 1970s and 1980s assumed that the world they grew up in was the world that had always been.

When practical ethics came into view again around 1970, both Pragmatism and the American tradition of applied ethics were still in play, even though there was little awareness of this. Rawls' method of reflective equilibrium was right out of the pragmatist playbook,[67] and he became increasingly pragmatist in methodology as the years wore on. The philosophers who formed the Society for Ethical and Legal Philosophy and the Society for Philosophy and Public Affairs and went on to found the journal, *Philosophy and Public Affairs*, were to a great extent motivated by similar politics and concerns that had led to the applied ethics movement of the early part of the century. They were political progressives living in a time of perceived moral crisis, and they were committed to the idea that philosophy must have something to say about the important issues of the day.

These continuities were largely invisible in 1970. The generation that was making the revolution had been trained in conceptual analysis, and in overcoming its limitations, they employed many of the same methods, thus obscuring their relations to earlier moments in American philosophy. Moreover, some of the specific problems that were in the forefront in the 1960s were different from those that had burned so bright for Adler and Dewey earlier in the century, at least in the way in which they were framed. Finally, Americans (even philosophers) tend not to look in the rear-view mirror; and when they look at all, they usually see Germany or Great Britain.

39.7 THE CONTEMPORARY SCENE

The elements that would lead to the rebirth of practical ethics in Great Britain began to assemble in the immediate post-war period. Interest in 'ought questions' began to revive with the work of W. D. Falk (1947) and others, and by the late 1950s a widely used textbook (Nowell-Smith 1954) returned ought questions to roughly the place that they had occupied at the end of the previous century. Philosophers such as J. L. Austin and Philippa Foot showed in detail how prescriptive and descriptive features are deeply entwined in language. The most influential British moral philosopher of the 1950s and 1960s, R. M. Hare, was a supporter of practical ethics, though his interest in the field was not much expressed in print until the field had already returned to prominence.[68] G. E. M. Anscombe had kept the tradition of casuistry alive in British philosophy.

[67] Rawls credits it to Goodman and, according to Catherine Elgin (in correspondence) Goodman said that his greatest contribution to political philosophy was giving this method to Rawls.
[68] Hare 1981 maintained that conceptual analysis could deliver binding 'oughts'. Other philosophers, such as Hall 1952, claimed that facts about what we ought to do are as fundamental as any other facts.

There are currently at least five distinguishable styles of work in practical ethics and it is difficult to associate them with particular nations. I will conclude by briefly surveying these approaches.[69]

The Vertical Approach identifies a practical issue, and then determines what the advocates of particular moral theories (e.g. consequentialist, deontologist, contractarian) would say about it. This approach 'applies' moral theories to practical problems in the way that a scientist might apply a general theory to a particular problem. A difficulty with this approach is that these moral theories are really families of moral theories, and they do not uniquely identify the right action to take in response to a practical problem, at least not without many assumptions and stipulations that can be rejected.

The Horizontal Approach, influenced by Rawls, involves taking some particular moral principles commonly regarded to have wide application, and applying them to a series of practical problems. The theories, the facts that bear on them, and the intuitive moral judgements that we make about them are then put into reflective equilibrium. This approach tends to take principles, facts, and (some would say) intuitive judgements at face-value rather than interrogating each of them individually, trusting reflective equilibrium to isolate the gold from the fool's gold. This method, it is often claimed, is biased towards conservative (i.e. non-revisionist) outcomes.

Analysis and Intuition is an iterative process that begins with a candidate moral principle, analyses its content, proposes (usually hypothetical) counter-examples, reshapes or accepts the principle on the basis of intuitive responses, and then begins again. When it comes to formulating candidate principles and counter-examples, this approach can lead to cloud cuckoo land and can lead us away from the highly contextualized ought questions to which practical ethics is supposed to respond. As the descendent of conceptual analysis, it is often difficult to see how this approach can generate real 'oughts' rather than hypothetical judgements about extremely hypothetical cases. While this approach practises reflective equilibrium, it is narrow reflective equilibrium, usually without much regard for empirical considerations.

Reasoning From Middle-Level Principles is an elaboration of Sidgwick's idea that people often disagree about which general principles are acceptable and what we ought to do in particular cases, yet agree about middle-level principles. Reasoning that begins from these widely shared middle-level principles can sometimes lead to widely shared conclusions about particular cases, without entering the debate about the most general principles.

The Case Approach, which is in the spirit of American applied ethics, presupposes that sound conclusions about practical matters are sensitive to getting the facts right, where this involves being clear not just about the physical and biological facts that might appear immediately relevant, but also the social facts about who holds what views and why. On this approach, which has much in common with legal reasoning, the justification of an action or policy may be extremely specific and context-relative.

---

[69] I say more about these approaches in two unpublished papers: 'The Methods of (Practical) Ethics', and 'The View From Somewhere: The Use of Thought Experiments in Moral Philosophy'.

Practical ethics is today a glorious mess. Not only do these different approaches imply different views about philosophy and suggest different hopes about what it can deliver, but some individual philosophers practise more than one of these styles, sometimes in the same paper. This helps to explain some of the tension between practical ethics and the discipline of philosophy. If people working in this field can't agree about what they are doing, then it is difficult to locate this field on a map of the discipline. This, of course, assumes that the discipline of philosophy is not itself a glorious mess. Whether or not this is so, however, will have to await further investigation.[70]

BIBLIOGRAPHY

Adler, F. 1908. *Life and Destiny*. New York: McClure and Philips.
—— 1918. *An Ethical Philosophy of Life*. New York: D. Appleton and Company.
Almond, B. 1998. 'Applied Ethics', in E. Craig (ed.), *Encyclopedia of Philosophy*. London: Routledge.
Beauchamp, T. 2007. 'History and Theory in "Applied Ethics"', *Kennedy Institute of Ethics Journal* 17 (1): 55–64.
Bentham, J. 1983. In M. J. Smith and W. H. Burston (eds), *Chrestomathia*. Oxford: Clarendon Press.
Bradley, F. H. 1951. *Ethical Studies: Selected Essays with an Introduction by Ralph G. Ross*. Indianapolis: The Liberal Arts Press, Inc.
Broad, C. D. 1930. *Five Types of Ethical Theory*. London: Routledge and Kegan Paul.
Carritt, E. F. 1925. 'Ethics in Philosophical Education', *Journal of Philosophy* 22: 572–7.
Darwall, S. 2006. 'How Should Ethics Relate to (the Rest of) Philosophy? Moore's Legacy', in T. Horgan and M. Timmons (eds), *Metaethics After Moore*. Oxford: Oxford University Press, 17–37.
Davenant, C. 1697/1771/1967. *Two Discourses on the Publick Revenues and Trade of England*. Farnborough: Gregg Press.
Davis, M. 1998. 'Sidgwick's Impractical Ethics', *International Journal of Applied Philosophy* 12: 153–9.
Dewey, J. and Tufts, J. 1932. *Ethics*. Second edition. New York: Holt.
Endres, A. M. 1987. 'The King-Davenant "Law" in Classical Economics', *History of Political Economy* 19(4): 621–38.
Falk, W. D. 1947. '"Ought" and Motivation', *Proceedings of the Aristotelian Society* 48: 492–510.
Flower, E. and Murphey M. 1977. *A History of Philosophy in America*, 2 vols. New York: Putnam.
Fordyce, D. 1748/2003. *The Elements of Moral Philosophy in Three Books with a Brief Account of the Nature, Progress, and Origin of Philosophy*, ed. T. Kennedy. Indianapolis: Liberty Fund, Inc.
French, J. 1865. *Practical Ethics*. Third edition. New York: D. Van Nostrand.

[70] An earlier version of this chapter was presented at the Henry West Colloquium at Macalester College and as a keynote address at the 2011 Rocky Mountain Ethics Congress. In addition to all those who participated in these discussions, I thank Roger Crisp, William Ruddick, and especially Jerome Schneewind and Anthony Skelton, for their comments on an earlier draft.

Gallie, R. 1998. *Thomas Reid: Ethics, Aesthetics, and the Anatomy of the Self.* Dordrecht, Netherlands: Kluwer Academic Publishers.

Gewirth, A. 1953. 'The Distinction Between Analytic and Synthetic Truths', *Journal of Philosophy* 50 (14): 397–425.

Giunti, G. undated. 'Bentham's Economics of Legislation', <http://pisa.academia.edu/MarcoGuidi/Papers/135019/BENTHAMS_ECONOMICS_OF_LEGISLATION>.

Haakonssen, L. 1997. *Medicine and Morals in the Enlightenment: John Gregory, Thomas Percival, and Benjamin Rush*, Clio Medica, vol. 44. Wellcome Institute Series in the History of Medicine. Amsterdam: Editions Rodopi.

Hall, E. 1952. *What is Value?* New York: Humanities Press.

Hare, R. M. 1981. *Moral Thinking: Its Levels, Method, and Point.* Oxford: Oxford University Press.

Haven, J. 1859. *Moral Philosophy, Including Theoretical and Practical Ethics.* Boston: Gould and Lincoln.

Hume, D. 1998. *Enquiry Concerning the Principles of Morals*, ed. T. Beauchamp. New York: Oxford University Press.

——2000. *Treatise of Human Nature*, ed. D. Norton and M. Norton. New York: Oxford University Press.

Hyde, W. 1892. *Practical Ethics.* New York: Henry Holt and Company.

Isaac, J. 2011. 'Missing Links: W. V. Quine, the Making of "Two Dogmas", and the Analytic Roots of Post-Analytic Philosophy', *History of European Ideas* 37 (3): 267–79.

James, W. 1891. 'The Moral Philosopher and the Moral Life', *International Journal of Ethics* 1 (3): 330–54.

Jamieson, D. 1999. 'Singer and the Practical Ethics Movement', in D. Jamieson (ed.), *Singer and his Critics.* Oxford: Basil Blackwell, 1–17.

——2002. *Morality's Progress: Essays on Humans, Other Animals, and the Rest of Nature.* Oxford: Oxford University Press.

——2008. *Ethics and the Environment: An Introduction.* Cambridge: Cambridge University Press.

Juhl, C. and Loomis, E. 2010. *Analyticity.* New York: Routledge.

Knight, W. 1894. 'Practical Ethics', *International Journal of Ethics* 4 (4): 481–92.

Laslett, P. 1956. 'Introduction', in P. Laslett and W. G. Runciman (eds), *Philosophy, Politics and Society.* New York: Barnes and Noble.

MacKillop, I. D. 1986. *The British Ethical Societies.* Cambridge: Cambridge University Press.

Mill, J. S. 1974. *The Collected Works of John Stuart Mill, Volume VIII—A System of Logic Ratiocinative and Inductive, Being a Connected View of the Principles of Evidence and the Methods of Scientific Investigation (Books IV–VI and Appendices)*, ed. J. Robson. Toronto: University of Toronto Press.

——1977. 'Use and Abuse of Political Terms', in J. Robson (ed.), *The Collected Works of John Stuart Mill, Volume XVIII—Essays on Politics and Society Part I.* Toronto: University of Toronto Press.

——1985a. 'Remarks on Bentham's Philosophy', in J. Robson (ed.), *The Collected Works of John Stuart Mill, Volume X—Essays on Ethics, Religion, and Society.* Toronto: University of Toronto Press.

——1985b. 'Bentham', in J. Robson (ed.), *The Collected Works of John Stuart Mill, Volume X—Essays on Ethics, Religion, and Society.* Toronto: University of Toronto Press.

Moore, G. E. 1903. 'Review of *The Origin of The Knowledge of Right and Wrong*, Franz Brentano', *Ethics* 14 (1): 115–23.

—— 1912. *Ethics*. London: Williams and Norgate.

—— 1993. *Principia Ethica, Revised Edition*, ed. T. Baldwin. Cambridge: Cambridge University Press.

Nowell Smith, P. H. 1954. *Ethics*. Hammondsworth: Penguin.

Perry, R. B. 1935/1996. *The Thought and Character of William James*, vol. 1. Nashville: Vanderbilt University Press.

Phillips, D. 2011. *Sidgwickian Ethics*. New York: Oxford University Press.

Phillips, R. 1826. *Golden Rules of Social Philosophy, or, A New System of Practical Ethics*. London: Printed for the author.

Pigden, C. 2003. 'Bertrand Russell: Moral Philosopher or Unphilosophical Moralist?', in N. Griffin (ed.), *The Cambridge Companion to Bertrand Russell*. Cambridge: Cambridge University Press, 475–506.

Putnam, H. 1997. 'A Half Century of Philosophy, Viewed from Within', *Daedalus* 126 (1): 175–208.

Rashdall, H. 1907. *A Theory of Good and Evil*, 2 vols. Oxford: Oxford University Press.

Rawls, J. 1980. 'Kantian Constructivism in Moral Theory', *Journal of Philosophy* 77 (9): 515–72.

Reid, T. 2007. *Thomas Reid on Practical Ethics: Lectures and Papers on Natural Religion, Self-Government, Natural Jurisprudence and the Law of Nations*, ed. K. Haakonssen. University Park PA: Penn State University Press.

Roosevelt, T. 1911. *Applied Ethics: Being one of the William Belden Noble Lectures for 1910*. Cambridge, MA: Harvard University.

Russell, B. 1897. *An Essay on the Foundations of Geometry* Cambridge: Cambridge University Press.

—— 1927. *An Outline of Philosophy*. London: London: George Allen and Unwin.

Russell, G. 2008. *Truth in Virtue of Meaning*. Oxford: Oxford University Press.

Samuel, H. 1935. *Practical Ethics*. London: T. Butterworth.

Schneewind, J. B. 1977. *Sidgwick's Ethics and Victorian Moral Philosophy*. Oxford: Oxford University Press.

Schultz, B. 2004. *Henry Sidgwick: Eye of the universe*. Cambridge: Cambridge University Press.

Shaw, A. 1892. *Review of Reviews: An International Magazine Published Simultaneously in The United States and Great Britain, American Edition*, Volume IV, August 1891–January, 1892. New York: The Review of Reviews.

Sidgwick, H. 1898. *Practical Ethics*. London: Swan Sonnenschein & Co.

—— 1902. *Philosophy, Its Scope and Relations: An Introductory Course of Lectures*, ed. J. Ward. London: Macmillan.

—— 1907. *The Methods of Ethics*. London: Macmillan and Company.

Singer, P. 2011. *Practical Ethics*. 3rd edn. Cambridge: Cambridge University Press.

Skelton, A. 2006. 'Henry Sidgwick's Practical Ethics: A Defense', *Utilitas* 18: 199–217.

Sloan, D. 1979. The Teaching of Ethics in the American Undergraduate Curriculum, 1876–1976. *The Hastings Center Report* 9 (6): 21–41.

Thomas, G. 1987. *The Moral Philosophy of T. H. Green*. Oxford: Oxford University Press.

White, M. 1950. 'The Analytic and the Synthetic: An Untenable Dualism', in S. Hook (ed.), *John Dewey: Philosopher of Science and Freedom*. New York: The Dial Press, 316–30.

Wright, C. 1910. *The New Century Book of Facts: A Handbook of Ready Reference*. Springfield MA: King-Richardson Co.

INDEX

relativism (*cont.*)
  Moral Reasons view 799, 804–9
  Moral Truth view 799, 808–13
  and Nietzsche 501
  and ethical egoism 715–16, 838
  scope and grounding of human
    rights 786–9
  self-refutation 801, 805, 812
  normative moral, *see* tolerance
Republic, the 4, 21 n1, 23–6, 30–41, 135, 140,
    639–42, 692, 822–3, 839
responsibility 126, 184, 475, 479
  and accountability 618–19, 806
  in Aquinas 161
  in Aristotle 52
  in Butler 387, 388 n30
  causal 12, 409
  of children 284, 379
  for emotions 752–5, 758–60, 763–4
  in Epicurus 80
  and free will, *see* free will
  in Homer 6
  in Hume 409–10
  in Mill 536
  and reactive attitudes, *see* reactive attitudes
  in Scotus and Ockham 175
retributivism 304–5, 392–3, 555, 769
rights 103, 281, 284, 436, 452, 473, 477, 695
  conventional or juridical rights 404–5,
    409, 413, 460–1, 472, 771
  and corresponding duties 771–4
  Hegel's discussion 511–13, 515
  institutional protection of 705, 786;
    see also intervention
  Mill's account 536–7, 539–41, 770–1, 850
  natural rights 240, 249, 251, 297, 404,
    413–14, 695–6, 704, 778, 783–9
  relationship with justice 768–76, 785, 789
  subjective rights 770–7, 783–6
  see also human rights
Romantics, the 483, 486, 491, 519
Rorty, Richard 799–800, 809–12
  view on truth and reason 811–12
Ross, W. D. 292, 301, 589, 601
  intuitionism and objectivity 337, 346 n20,
    350–3, 554, 579, 594
  on the meaning of 'right' 592–3
  on naturalism and non-naturalism 594–6

  on *prima facie* duties 16, 303 n31, 354, 554,
    593–4
Rousseau, Jean-Jacques 272, 280–90, 517
  on autonomy and freedom 693, 696–7, 701
  account of human development 281–2,
    286–7
  educational theory 282, 287–8, 290
  moral psychology 280–9
  on natural goodness 286–7
  political philosophy 280, 282, 287–90, 411
Russell, Bertrand 469, 581–2, 596–8, 602
  and conceptual analysis 150, 582, 590,
    853–4, 859
  disparaging view of ethics 846–7, 853

sacrifice 17, 39, 560, 570
  Abraham's sacrifice of Isaac 495, 196
  and egoism 558, 712–13, 715, 717, 719
  and utilitarianism 298–9, 306–8, 415, 536,
    540, 556, 558, 772
scepticism 231, 240, 254, 261, 400, 499, 556,
    558, 565, 590–2
  about free will, *see* free will
  as a practical activity 120–2, 125; see also
    ataraxia
  about status of ethics 112–17, 118–20, 122–7,
    259, 342–3, 466, 796, 799, 810–11, 849;
    see also relativism
  taxonomy of 112–14
scholasticism 149, 175, 200, 203, 223, 232,
    487
  on fundamental and formal morality 188
  Luther's antagonism towards 191
  and moral systematization 184–6
  nature and natural law 179, 190, 207–8,
    218
  and the passions 654–6
  and psychology 80, 654–5
Schopenhauer, Arthur 473–4, 478, 491,
    496–7, 500, 578
  denial of moral imperativeness 496–7
  on happiness, *see* happiness
    (Schopenhauer's account)
science 478, 602, 684, 694
  as area of ethical application, *see* bioethics
  as an end in itself 571
  and free will 610
  Marx's usage 520, 523

Lightning Source UK Ltd.
Milton Keynes UK
UKOW05f1134100915

258403UK00003B/5/P